The History of Ancient Palestine
from the Palaeolithic Period
to Alexander's Conquest

Gösta W. Ahlström

with a contribution by
Gary O. Rollefson

edited by
Diana Edelman

Journal for the Study of the Old Testament
Supplement Series 146

To
The John Simon Guggenheim Memorial Foundation
in gratitude

Copyright © 1993 Sheffield Academic Press

Published by JSOT Press
JSOT Press is an imprint of
Sheffield Academic Press Ltd
343 Fulwood Road
Sheffield S10 3BP
England

Maps and illustrations drawn from the author's originals
by Jeremy Boucher

Typeset by Sheffield Academic Press
and
Printed on acid-free paper in Great Britain
by Biddles Ltd
Guildford

British Library Cataloguing in Publication Data

Ahlström, G.W.
History of Ancient Palestine from the
Palaeolithic Period to Alexander's
Conquest.—(JSOT Supplement Series, ISSN
0309-0787; No. 146)
I. Title II. Series
933

ISBN 1-85075-367-9

CONTENTS

Foreword, by Diana Edelman and Niels Peter Lemche   7
Preface   10
Editor's Preface   12
List of Maps   13
List of Illustrations   14
Abbreviations   15
Introduction   19

Chapter 1
THE LAND   56

Chapter 2
PREHISTORIC TIME (by Gary O. Rollefson)   72

Chapter 3
THE EARLY BRONZE AGE   112

Chapter 4
THE MIDDLE BRONZE AGE   158

Chapter 5
THE LATE BRONZE AGE   217

Chapter 6
THE TWELFTH CENTURY BCE   282

Chapter 7
THE INCREASE IN SETTLEMENTS DURING THE
   13TH–12TH CENTURIES BCE   334

Chapter 8
JUDGES   371

Chapter 9
TRANSJORDAN IN THE 12TH–10TH CENTURIES BCE   391

Chapter 10
THE RISE OF THE TERRITORIAL STATE   421

Chapter 11
PALESTINE UNDER DAVID AND SOLOMON   455

Chapter 12
PALESTINE AFTER SOLOMON   543

Chapter 13
THE OMRIDES   569

Chapter 14
THE ARAMEAN THREAT   607

Chapter 15
TRANSJORDAN IN THE EIGHTH AND SEVENTH CENTURIES   639

Chapter 16
PALESTINE IN THE ASSYRIAN ORBIT   665

Chapter 17
CLIMAX AND FALL   741

Chapter 18
NEW MASTERS   754

Chapter 19
THE END OF THE BABYLONIAN CAMPAIGNS   784

Chapter 20
PALESTINE AFTER THE BABYLONIAN CAMPAIGNS   804

Chapter 21
THE PERSIAN PERIOD   812

Indexes   907

FOREWORD

It is a serious, bittersweet business to help publish a friend's work posthumously. Despite the best intentions, such a service done on behalf of a scholar may do more harm than good to his memory. However, since the present volume had already been accepted for publication by Sheffield Academic Press and was initial stages of preparation, there was little need for concern. Its author had expressed the half-serious, half-joking concern on many occasions that he wanted to see the book in print 'before he died'. An unanticipated delay with its original US publisher caused him much anguish over the 'currency' of his footnote data. He was keenly aware of the amount of information that was published annually in the six years between the completion of the manuscript and its final, projected publication date with Sheffield Academic Press, and he lamented his inability to include it in the volume without producing a 'revised and updated' manuscript. His quip that 'a scholar's work is never done' aptly encapsulates his personal philosophy and endless thirst for knowledge.

It is hardly accidental that Gösta W. Ahlström was the first scholar to prepare such a synthesis of recent trends in Hebrew Bible studies. He represented a combination of many schools and directions of study. To his death, he was a true Scandinavian with a solid background in the old Uppsala School. While he moved beyond the views of this school in many ways, his ability to formulate theories that were simultaneously independent and controversial continued the ways and manners of his former teacher and the master of the Uppsala School, Ivan Engnell. It should not be forgotten that the Scandinavian School was a part of European continental scholarship, regularly engaging in dialogue with the German School and the Anglo-Saxon 'Myth and Ritual School'. By moving to Chicago in 1962—the year Engnell died—Gösta W. Ahlström established a bridgehead of European scholarship among his North American colleagues.

He eventually formed a school of historical studies at the University of Chicago that counterbalanced the predominantly literary approaches that are so common among North American scholars and so often bereft of any historical dimension. When he first arrived, however, his interests were primarily in prophecy, literature and the history of religions. However, his year as Annual Professor at the Albright Institute in Jerusalem in 1969–70 became turning point in his career, opening up to him the world of archaeology and awakening a strong interest in ancient Syro-Palestinian history that continued until his death. G.E. Wright proved to be instrumental in this transformation. After meeting the young Swede at a conference and being impressed by him, he encouraged him to apply for the professorship. While it would be far from the truth to say that Gösta W. Ahlström became the center of North American scholarship, his work and teaching nevertheless served the vital function, both in North America and around the world, of maintaining history as an integral part of biblical studies, and of examining the methods used to evaluate the relevance of textual and artifactual remains before using them in historical reconstruction.

In his later years, Gösta W. Ahlström felt easily at home among scholars and colleagues, most of whom were far younger, but all of whom were devoted to the renewed study of historical Israel. Through his publications and advice, he was often at the forefront of current approaches—and sometimes so far ahead of them that the rest of us did not fully understand his intentions when they first appeared. Many were clarified in subsequent years as the rest of the field caught up to him and began to ask the same questions. Nevertheless, he was always willing to discuss any topic with anyone who shared his interests, whether or not that person shared his approaches or positions, and he never belittled anyone for incompetence or ignorance. He was always ready to hear another opinion, consider its strengths and weaknesses carefully, and change his mind if the facts or arguments seemed to warrant an adjustment. To the day of his death he remained a true scholar, devoted to the pursuit of knowledge and its synthesis.

By helping with the publication of this volume, we hope that it will become a standard reference that illustrates the current trends toward a revision of Israelite history and demonstrates the need to view the history of ancient Israel and Judah within the larger arena of ancient

Syro-Palestinian and ancient Near Eastern history. At the same time, it is our belief that it will provide the scholarly world with an alternative to the plethora of traditionally arranged 'histories of Israel' that are all too easily accessible today and yet no longer in agreement with our present state of research and knowledge.

Niels Peter Lemche
Diana Edelman

Several years ago a former colleague of mine in Near Eastern studies asked why we needed 'one more history'. My answer was that this one had not been written. The question had been put forward to me with the *a priori* understanding that my opus would be a history of Israel, and there are already enough of those in the market. In this I concur. The existing textbooks about the history of Israel and Judah all have their limitations. Their main concern has been a presentation of the peoples of Israel and Judah, and too often they merely accept the views of the biblical writers as reliable reflections of past events and their causal relationships.[1] Throughout my years of teaching Syro-Palestinian history I have felt the need to try to present the history of the peoples of Palestine through the millennia in a form freed from the bias of the biblical writers, which is difficult. I have also felt the need for a more up-to-date presentation of the history than the one written over half a century ago by the late master of Near Eastern historiography, A.T. Olmstead,[2] who also was influenced by the viewpoints of the selective biblical writers when using their information as source material.

To write the history of ancient Palestine from the earliest times to Alexander's conquest of the Near East may be considered a bold undertaking. Having done this, it still seems to be an almost impossible task because of the enormous wealth of material for certain periods and certain areas, and also because of the need to be well acquainted with both the archaeological and the literary remains. Because of the difficulty of following the rapid development in the prehistoric fields, I happily accepted Professor Gary O. Rollefson's generous offer to write the chapter about 'Prehistoric Time'. Unfortunately, I have not

1. For a résumé of these historiographies, see G. Garbini, *History and Ideology in Ancient Israel* (trans. from the Italian edn by J. Bowden; New York, 1988), pp. 1-20.

2. *History of Palestine and Syria* (New York, 1931).

been able to use Dr Helga Weippert's monumental work about the archaeology of Palestine (*Palästina in vorhellenistischer Zeit* [Munich, 1988]). However, future scholars would benefit by supplementing my work with hers. Concerning recent scholarly literature, the 'curtain' went down in December 1986. Thanks to modern technology, however, I have been able in a few instances to refer to some research published after that date.

Several chapters have been read by experts in the field. I would like to thank Professor James B. Pritchard, Dr Gilian R. Bentley, Dr Diana Edelman, Professor Douglas L. Esse and Professor Israel Finkelstein. They have all contributed with valuable comments. I am also indebted to my colleagues in the Department of Near Eastern Languages and Civilizations at the University of Chicago for their support and encouragement. The generous policy of the University of Chicago Divinity School of allowing me sabbatical quarters should also be acknowledged.

The English has been checked and improved by Dr Peter R. Bedford and Mr Charles Blair, and Dr Steven Holloway has been going through the manuscript with the eye of an editor. I am very grateful for their assistance. The expertise of Ms Wendy S. Lee in computerizing my manuscript has been invaluable.

The final writing up of many years of research has been made possible by a generous grant from the John Simon Guggenheim Memorial Foundation. It is with gratitude that I dedicate my book to the Foundation.

Gösta W. Ahlström

Postscript

We would like to express out heartfelt gratitude and admiration to Diana Edelman. Without her tireless and dedicated efforts, this work—which Gösta Ahlström regarded as his most important—could never have come to completion.

Maria Ahlström
Pernille Ahlström
Hans Ahlström

EDITOR'S PREFACE

I was honored by Sheffield Academic Press with the task of correcting the page proofs and preparing indexes for this magnum opus. As Professor Ahlström's former student and his research assistant for a number of years, I was a logical choice, being familiar with the idiosyncracies of his writing and footnote styles as well as the subject matter. Since he can no longer check my corrections, I only hope that I have remained faithful to his original intentions.

It was hoped that the history would be published in 1992, the same year as its author's death, but this has not been humanly possible. Gösta's magnum opus simply is not right for a 'quick read' nor a fast editorial review. Dr J. Webb Mealy, production editor for the history, and Robert Knight, the typesetter, have been instrumental in deciphering the various corrections and overseeing their incorporation into the finished product. Mistakes are inevitable in a book of this size and are perhaps more easily overlooked by someone who is not its author. I would ask the reader to be understanding under the circumstances and to appreciate the sheer amount of detailed information that Professor Ahlström has synthesized for the benefit of all who share his interest in ancient Syro-Palestinian history.

Diana Edelman

LIST OF MAPS

Map
1. The Ancient Near East
2. Ancient Syria-Palestine
3. Mean Annual Rainfall
4. Ancient Routes
5. Epipalaeolithic Sites
6. Neolithic Sites
7. Early Bronze Age Sites
8. Cities of the Amarna Letters
9. Pharaoh Merneptah's Campaign in Palestine
10. Sites Where Philistine or Philistine Style Pottery
       has been Found
11. Cities Mentioned in Joshua's 'Conquest'
12. Settlements in the Hills in the Twelfth Century BCE
13. Saul's Kingdom
14. David's Kingdom
15. Palestine after Shoshenq's Campaign
16. Aram's Expansion under Ben-Hadad
17. The Time of Omri and Ahab
18. Moab under Mesha
19. The Assyrian Empire
20. Palestine after 720 BCE
21. Palestine after 701 BCE
22. Palestine in the Late Seventh Century BCE
23. The Persian Empire
24. Palestine in the Persian Period (Fifth Century BCE)

LIST OF ILLUSTRATIONS

Figure
1. Wâdī Mujib (Ancient Arnon)
2. 'Ain Ghazal Plaster Statues
3. Middle-Bronze Age Vase or Urn from a Burial
   Chamber at Jericho
4. Relief from the Temple of Ramses III Showing Kneeling
   Peleset/Philistine Warrior
5. Relief from Nineveh Showing an Assyrian Siege
6. Jar in the Shape of a Man from the Edomite Sanctuary
   at Qitmit
7. Relief of Darius I from his Tomb at Naqsh-i-Rustam
8. Jewish Coin Showing a Deity Seated on a Winged Wheel
   (c. 400 BCE)

ABBREVIATIONS

AASOR	Annual of the American Schools of Oriental Research
AB	Anchor Bible
AcOr	*Acta orientalia*
ADAJ	Annual of the Department of Antiquities of Jordan
ADPV	Abhandlungen des Deutschen Palästina-Vereins
ÄAT	Ägypten und Altes Testament
AfO	*Archiv für Orientforschung*
AHw	W. von Soden, *Akkadisches Handwörterbuch*
AION	*Annali dell'istituto orientale di Napoli*
AJA	*American Journal of Archaeology*
AJBA	*Australian Journal of Biblical Archaeology*
AJSL	*American Journal of Semitic Languages*
AnBib	Analecta biblica
ANE Suppl.	J.B. Pritchard (ed.), *The Ancient Near East: Supplementary Texts and Pictures Relating to the Old Testament*
ANEP	J.B. Pritchard (ed.), *The Ancient Near East in Pictures*
ANET	J.B. Pritchard (ed.), *Ancient Near Eastern Texts Relating to the Old Testament*
ANVAO	Avhandlinger utgitt av det Norske Videnskaps-Akademi i Oslo
AnOr	Analecta orientalia
AOAT	Alter Orient und Altes Testament
AOS	American Oriental Series
APAW	Abhandlungen der Preussischen Akademie der Wissenschaft
ARAB	D.D. Luckenbill, *Ancient Records of Assyria and Babylonia*
ARM	A. Parrot and G. Dossin (eds.), *Archives royales de Mari*
ArOr	*Archiv orientálni*
ARW	*Archiv für Religionswissenschaft*
ASTI	Annual of the Swedish Theological Institute
ATANT	Abhandlungen zur Theologie des Alten und Neuen Testaments
ATD	Das Alte Testament Deutsch
AUSS	*Andrews University Seminary Studies*
BA	*Biblical Archaeologist*
BAR	British Archaeological Reports, International Series
BARev	*Biblical Archaeology Review*
BASOR	*Bulletin of the American Schools of Oriental Research*
BBB	Bonner biblische Beiträge
Bib	*Biblica*

BJS	Brown Judaic Studies
BJRL	*Bulletin of the John Rylands University Library of Manchester*
BKAT	Biblischer Kommentar: Altes Testament
BN	*Biblische Notizen*
BO	*Bibliotheca orientalis*
BTAVO	Beihefte zum Tübinger Atlas der Vorderen Orients
BWANT	Beiträge zur Wissenschaft vom Alten und Neuen Testament
BZ	*Biblische Zeitschrift*
BZAW	Beiheft zur Zeitschrift für die alttestamentliche Wissenchaft
CAD	*The Assyrian Dictionary of the Oriental Institute of the University of Chicago*
CAH	Cambridge Ancient History
CBQ	*Catholic Biblical Quarterly*
CJT	*Canadian Journal of Theology*
ConBOT	Coniectanea biblica, Old Testament
DBSup	*Dictionnaire de la Bible, Supplément*
DTT	*Dansk teologisk tidsskrift*
EA	El-Amarna tablets cited from J.A. Knudtzon, O. Weber and E. Ebeling, *Die El-Amarna Tafeln* (2 vols.; Vorderasiatische Bibliothek, 2; Leipzig, 1915); A.F. Rainey, *El Amarna Tablets 359–379: Supplement to J.A. Knudtzon, Die El-Amarna Tafeln* (2nd rev. edn; ADAT, 8; Neukirchen, 1970)
EAEHL	M. Avi-Yonah (ed.), *Encyclopedia of Archaeological Excavations in the Holy Land*
EB	Early Bronze
EI	Eretz Israel
FRLANT	Forschungen zur Religion und Literatur des Alten und Neuen Testaments
GHAT	Göttinger Handkommentar zum Alten Testament
HAT	Handbuch zum Alten Testament
HR	*History of Religions*
HSM	Harvard Semitic Monographs
HTR	*Harvard Theological Review*
HUCA	*Hebrew Union College Annual*
ICC	International Critical Commentary
IDB	G.A. Buttrick (ed.), *Interpreter's Dictionary of the Bible*
IEJ	*Israel Exploration Journal*
JANESCU	*Journal of the Ancient Near Eastern Society of Columbia University*
JAOS	*Journal of the American Oriental Society*
JARCE	*Journal of the American Research Center in Egypt*
JBL	*Journal of Biblical Literature*
JCS	*Journal of Cuneiform Studies*
JEA	*Journal of Egyptian Archaeology*
JEOL	*Jaarbericht... ex oriente lux*

JESHO	*Journal of the Economic and Social History of the Orient*
JJS	*Journal of Jewish Studies*
JNES	*Journal of Near Eastern Studies*
JNWSL	*Journal of Northwest Semitic Languages*
JÖAI	*Jahreshefte des österreichischen archäologischen Instituts*
JPOS	*Journal of the Palestine Oriental Society*
JQR	*Jewish Quarterly Review*
JR	*Journal of Religion*
JSOT	*Journal for the Study of the Old Testament*
JSS	*Journal of Semitic Studies*
JSSEA	*Journal of the Society for the Study of Egyptian Antiquities*
JTS	*Journal of Theological Studies*
KAI	H. Donner and W. Röllig, *Kanaanäische und aramäische Inschriften*
KBo	*Keilschrifttexte aus Boghazköi* (Wissenschaftliche Veröffentlichungen der deutschen Orient-Gesellschaft, 30, 36, 68-70, 72; Leipzig, 1916–23; Berlin, 1954–)
KHAT	Kurze Hand-Commentar zum Alten Testament
KS	A. Alt, *Kleine Schriften zur Geschichte des Volkes Israel* (3 vols.; Munich, 1953–59)
LCL	Loeb Classical Library
MANE	Monographs of the Ancient Near East
MAOG	*Mitteilungen der altorientalischen Gesellschaft*
MB	Middle Bronze
MDAIK	*Mitteilungen des deutschen archäologischen Instituts, Abteilung Kairo*
MDOG	*Mitteilungen der deutschen Orient-Gesellschaft*
MIO	*Mitteilungen des Instituts für Orientforschung*
MUSJ	*Mélanges de l'Université St Joseph*
MVÄG	Mitteilungen der vorderasiatisch-ägyptischen Gesellschaft
NRT	*La nouvelle revue théologique*
OBO	Orbis biblicus et orientalis
OIP	Oriental Institute Publications
OLZ	*Orientalische Literaturzeitung*
Or	*Orientalia*
OrAnt	*Oriens antiquus*
OTS	Oudtestamentische Studiën
PEFA	Palestine Exploration Fund, Annual
PEFQS	Palestine Exploration Fund, Quarterly Statement
PEQ	Palestine Exploration Quarterly
PJ	Palästinajahrbuch
PRU	C.F.A. Schaeffer and J. Nougayrol (eds.), *Le palais royal d'Ugarit*
QDAP	Quarterly of the Department of Antiquities of Palestine
RA	*Revue d'assyriologie et d'archéologie orientale*

RAI	Rencontre assyriologique internationale, Comptes rendus
RB	*Revue biblique*
RHR	*Revue de l'histoire des religions*
RivB	*Rivista biblica*
SANT	Studien zum Alten und Neuen Testament
SAOC	Studies in Ancient Oriental Civilization
SBL	Society of Biblical Literature
SBLMS	SBL Monograph Series
SBM	Stuttgarter biblische Monographien
SBT	Studies in Biblical Theology
SEÅ	*Svensk Exegetisk Årsbok*
Sem	*Semitica*
SHANE	Studies in the History of the Ancient Near East
SJOT	*Scandinavian Journal of the Old Testament*
SJT	*Scottish Journal of Theology*
SOTSMS	Society for Old Testament Study Monograph Series
SSEA	Society for the Study of Egyptian Antiquities
ST	*Studia theologica*
StudOr	*Studia orientalia*
TDOT	G.J. Botterweck and H. Ringgren (eds.), *Theological Dictionary of the Old Testament*
THAT	*Theologisches Handwörterbuch zum Alten Testament*
TLZ	*Theologische Literaturzeitung*
TRu	*Theologische Rundschau*
TZ	*Theologische Zeitschrift*
ThWAT	G.J. Botterweck and H. Ringgren (eds.), *Theologisches Wörterbuch zum Alten Testament*
TSSI	J.C.L. Gibson (ed.), *Textbook of Syrian Semitic Inscriptions* (3 vols., Oxford 1971–1982)
UF	*Ugarit-Forschungen*
UUÅ	Uppsala universitets årsskrift
VAB	Vorderasiatische Bibliothek
VT	*Vetus Testamentum*
VTSup	*Vetus Testamentum*, Supplements
WBC	Word Biblical Commentary
WHJP	*World History of the Jewish People*
WO	*Die Welt des Orients*
WMANT	Wissenschaftliche Monographien zum Alten und Neuen Testament
ZA	*Zeitschrift für Assyriologie*
ZÄS	*Zeitschrift für ägyptische Sprache und Altertumskunde*
ZAW	*Zeitschrift für die alttestamentliche Wissenschaft*
ZDPV	*Zeitschrift des deutschen Palästina-Vereins*
ZA	*Zeitschrift für Assyriologie*
ZTK	*Zeitschrift für Theologie und Kirche*

INTRODUCTION

History and Historiography

τάδε γράφω ὡς μοι δοκεῖ ἀληθέα εἶναι
Thus I write, as the truth seems to be to me.
(Hecataeus of Miletus)[1]

This quotation from Hecataeus describes in a nutshell what history-writing looked like in the ancient world. The writer relied upon what was seen, heard and understood, a 'method' also used by Herodotus. However, the modern idea of history did not exist in ancient times, which presents the problem of finding the 'history' of those times. That task will be more involved for us than for the ancients because of the accumulated source material that is available to the modern historian.

Four points have to be made here. We have to discover, if possible, not only (1) what happened, but also (2) how the events were understood by the ancient writers, (3) how these writers wanted it to have happened, that is, the purpose of the writing, and (4) the audience for whom they wrote.[2] Past time is forever gone, but we can reconstruct part of it, depending upon the character of the available sources. Such a reconstruction is the task of historiography, an art that includes a presentation of sources, their interpretation, and, as a last resort, hypotheses that may solve some problems and in a logical way fill the

---

1. Hecataeus was one of the first Greek prose writers (late sixth cent. BCE). For the, quotation, see F. Jacoby, *Die Fragmente der griechischen Historiker*, I (Leiden, 1957), p. 7. For Hecataeus, see, among others, L. Pearson, *Early Ionian Historians* (Oxford, 1939).

2. Emilio Gabba maintains that 'before one attempts to evaluate critically the significance of any work or to use it for historical purposes, one must investigate the readership or audience for which it was intended, the aims of the author, and the means used to convey his thoughts and organise his text' ('Literature', *Sources for Ancient History* [Sources of History; ed. M. Crawford; Cambridge, 1983], p. 75).

gaps in the source material. History is thus not an exact science, because we do not know all the facts.[1]

Writing history—historiography—can be likened to an archaeologist's struggles to restore a beautiful Mycenaean jar. Even if less than 30 percent of it is available in both large and small pieces, much can be learned about its form and decoration. When the form and decorative pattern from these sherds are known or are made known through some of the indicative pieces, the form of the jar can be restored by filling in the gaps with modern clay. The beauty of the vessel can, however, never be fully restored. Logically, one can state what the decoration might have looked like, but one cannot predict whether this particular vessel was in complete harmony with known patterns or whether there were some deviations, (small) surprises, mistakes, or whether the jar was somewhat deformed. As the restorer of the jar can see the work completed but not see all the original details, so the historiographer can reconstruct the history of a certain period and its people, but cannot 'see' all the events and changes of the lost society. The life of those who created history—in most cases, humans with their psychological problems—escapes us to a large extent.[2]

This volume will not be a textbook on historiography,[3] but certain

---

1.   'The whole truth at any stage of inquiry, is an ideal that ought to be abolished from historiography, for it cannot ever be attained'. So D.H. Fischer, *Historians' Fallacies: Toward a Logic of Historical Thought* (New York, 1970), p. 66.

2.   R. Wittram illustrates this problem with the face of a person. This can be described if we have some information about it, but its expressions and its voice are forever gone (*Das Interesse an der Geschichte* [Göttingen, 1958], pp. 15-16).

3.   For introductions to the theories of history and historiography, see, among others, E.H.Carr, *What is History?* (London, 1961); N.F.Cantor and R.I. Schneider, *How to Study History* (New York, 1967); A.A. Moles, *Information Theory and Esthetic Perception* (Urbana, IL, 1966); B. Trigger, *Beyond History: The Methods of Prehistory* (New York, 1968); D.H. Fischer, *Historians' Fallacies: Toward a Logic of Historical Thought* (New York, 1970); K.-G. Farber, *Theorie der Geschichtswissenschaft* (Munich, 1971); J. Deetz, *Men's Imprint from the Past* (Boston, 1971); M.I. Finley, *The Use and Abuse of History* (New York, 1975); *idem*, *Ancient History: Evidence and Models* (New York, 1986); E. Le Roy Ladurie, *The Mind and Method of the Historian* (trans. S. and B. Reynolds; Chicago, 1987). See also F. Braudel, 'Histoire et science sociales: La longue durée', *Annales. Economies, Société, Civilisations* 13 (1958), pp. 725-53; S. Langholm, *Historisk rekonstruksjon og begrunnelse: En innføring i historiestudiet* (Oslo, 1967); G.H. von Wright, *Problems in the Theory of Knowledge* (The Hague, 1972). Concerning Near Eastern historiography, see M. Liverani, 'Memorandum on the Approach to Historiographic

aspects of the latter art have to be mentioned, most importantly, my understanding of the material on which this presentation will be based. It goes without saying that the task of tracing the history of a country from prehistoric times through several millennia is an immense, albeit a fascinating, task. In the case of greater Palestine, it is an almost impossible task because of the different sources and sometimes the lack of reliable source material, no matter at what point in time one ends the investigation. Like most other historians, the Syro-Palestinian historian has two primary kinds of source material for a reconstruction of the past: archaeological and literary. Information can also be derived from the geography and the climate of the country.

According to the usefulness of the material, distinctions must be made between archaeological material and literary sources, as well as between primary and secondary sources. The latter usually refers to textual material. A primary source is written at a time close to the event. It can be a report, a royal annal, a letter or an original story. Secondary material may be a copy of an original, an interpretive text, a rewriting, re-editing, distortion, falsification or the like.

In principle, archaeological material belongs among the primary sources. It can often be used to corroborate and supplement textual material, but it can correct or even contradict it. In this way archaeological remains can give a more realistic understanding of the societies they refer to, their trade and culture, and so forth.[1] However,

Texts', *Or* NS 42 (1973), pp. 178-94; A.K. Grayson, 'Histories and Historians of the Ancient Near East: Assyria and Babylonia', *Or* NS 49 (1980), pp. 140-94; J. Van Seters, *In Search of History* (New Haven, 1983), pp. 55-208. For history as a written medium for the elite, see, for instance, H.A. Hoffner, 'Histories and Historians of the Ancient Near East', *Or* NS 49 (1980), pp. 283-332. Concerning biblical historiography, see N.P. Lemche, 'On the Problem of Studying Israelite History apropos Abraham Malamat's View of Historical Research', *BN* 23 (1984), pp. 94-124. Compare also T.L. Thompson, *The Origin Tradition of Ancient Israel.* I. *The Literary Formation of Genesis and Exodus 1–23* (JSOTSup, 55; Sheffield, 1987), esp. pp. 22-25. As to the Hellenistic-Roman world, see A. Momigliano, *Alien Wisdom: The Limitations of Hellenization* (Cambridge, 1975); *idem, Studies in Historiography* (History and Historiography; New York, 1985); G. Shepers, 'Some Aspects of Source Theory in Greek Historiography', *Ancient Society* 6 (1975), pp. 257-74; repr. in M. Crawford (ed.), *Sources for Ancient History* (Cambridge, 1983).

1. See M.-H. Gates, 'Dialogues between Ancient Near Eastern Texts and the Archaeological Record: Test Cases from Bronze Age Syria', *BASOR* 270 (1988), pp. 63-91.

completely unknown or unmentioned facts may also be revealed by excavations, thus potentially causing established opinions to be revised.[1] Examples are the steel industry of the Baq'ah Valley in Transjordan from the Iron I period,[2] the Judahite temple at Arad in the Negev, and the finds from Kuntillet 'Ajrud referring to Yahweh and his Asherah, to mention only a few.[3]

No country has been 'dug up' so completely that its history can be written based primarily on archaeological remains. It should also be remembered that Palestinian archaeology has been mainly 'tell-minded'. It is only during the last decades that surface surveys have been undertaken in any large measure, but thorough excavations of the countryside are the exception. However, archaeological source material can be seen to be 'mute',[4] and there is no method for exact dating. It does not tell the whole story by itself. A stone is a stone, a wall is a wall. A grave, for instance, does not tell who dug it, and a mudbrick wall does not say anything *per se* about ethnicity. Yet other circumstances, such as the contents of the grave and the objects in the house, can give information about their respective societies.[5] The culture, habits and political affairs of a country can be only partially reconstructed on the basis of archaeological remains. Information about the people's food supply and sometimes about diseases can be derived from excavated objects.[6] Even if objects and tools can to some extent indicate a community's sophistication, they will only provide a partial picture of the level of that sophistication. Thus, other information, such as textual material, is necessary for drawing conclusions that can

1. Compare also the discussion in A.E. Glock, 'Texts and Archaeology at Tell Ta'annek', *Berytus* 31 (1983), pp. 57-66.

2. Consult M.R. Notis, V.C. Pigott, P.E. McGovern, K.H. Liu and C.P. Swann, in *Late Bronze and Early Iron Ages of Central Transjordan: The Baq'ah Valley Project, 1977–81* (ed. P.E. McGovern; University Museum Monographs, 65; Philadelphia, 1986), pp. 272-78.

3. See my 'An Archaeological Picture of Iron Age Religions in Ancient Palestine', *StudOr* 55.3 (1984), pp. 4-5.

4. A. Moles characterizes it as a 'pseudo-language' in *Théorie des Objects* (Paris, 1972) (quoted after C.-A. Moberg, 'Archaeology and Religion: What Do We Know?', *Temenos* 13 [1977], pp. 98-99).

5. See the discussion by S. Piggott, *Ancient Europe from the Beginnings of Agriculture to Classical Antiquity* (Edinburgh, 1965), pp. 4-8.

6. Compare J. Deetz, *Invitation to Archaeology* (Garden City, NY, 1967), pp. 1-7.

be used for historiography. However, because mute sources and texts do not give all the necessary information, there will always be a need for a method that uses reasoning, hypotheses, logic and imagination (in other words, the 'clay' of the historian) in order to construct something from the available material and to fill in the gaps between the sources.

Among the 'mute' sources can be included geographical changes. Some are permanent, some transient. Some are accidental; others are caused by people. Such changes include natural disasters like mudslides or volcanic eruptions, as well as purposeful alterations to the environment, such as the building of roads and canals, terracing, (de)forestation, the killing of game, and pollution.[1] All this is also evidence for history, and as such it needs to be part of the historiographic picture. There are, however, other random factors that are more problematic to come to grips with, such as a toothache making a ruler temporarily unable to make a sound judgment, or an epidemic reducing the population density in certain parts of a country, or terminating a military campaign, as might have been the case when the Assyrian king Sennacherib besieged Jerusalem in 701 BCE.

As mentioned, knowledge about geography and climate must be taken into consideration in historiography, to add to our understanding of problems like demography and changes in population density, and to answer the question of 'why?' for certain events. Once someone has seen Buseira in Jordan, for instance, it is easy to understand why a city was built on that mountain plateau, which is surrounded by a natural 'moat'.[2] Mountains, valleys, rivers, seas and deserts are of utmost importance for understanding settlement problems, and for learning about the population, its livelihood and its cultural achievements. The central hills of Palestine, being sparsely settled, were considered a place of refuge, as Josh. 15.16 indicates. It should be noted that mountains 'are as a rule a world apart from civilizations', a statement that also

---

1. Compare F. Braudel, who divides history into three levels: 'geographical time, social time, and individual time'. The first level deals with 'man in his relationship to the environment, a history in which all change is slow, a history of constant repetition'. The second level is a 'time with slow but perceptible rhythms', and the third level is that of 'history of events' (*The Mediterranean and the Mediterranean World in the Age of Philip II*, I [New York, 1972], pp. 20-21).

2. This is the site where the Edomite royal city of Bozrah was located.

can be used for large forested areas.[1] Trading posts along trade routes would have attracted certain groups of people as well as military powers, for whom trade and political domination were often identical. The same is the case with promontories and other places suitable for sea trade. Lucrative business opportunities at such places would have attracted people and thus made them open to both political and cultural growth. Examples of the latter are the Phoenician city states and the location of cities and harbors built during the Phoenician expansion to the West.[2]

Oral tradition can also play an important role for the historiographer who studies living societies. However, it cannot serve as a tool for dealing with dead cultures, in which it has to some extent become part of the literary source material.[3] Nevertheless, we may suspect that oral tradition was used to fill in the gaps in an ancient writer's presentation. In Greece, for instance, legends describing 'events of the Bronze and Dark Ages are highly suspect'.[4] Because the Greek writers relied mainly on what they saw and on 'reports from reliable witnesses', they would have had no material other than nonverifiable oral traditions when describing archaic periods.[5] Even though Herodotus is called the 'father of history', his method was one based only on interviewing and listening, which was standard for that time. In certain instances his information might have been quite wrong. It is also uncertain to what extent he recounted stories that he may himself have doubted, just to entertain the 'groundlings' in his audience.[6] Still,

---

1. F. Braudel, *The Mediterranean*, p. 34.

2. See F. Braudel, *The Mediterranean*, p. 278.

3. Cf. M.I. Finley, who says that the ancients 'found great voids in the inherited information about the past, or, worse still, quantities of data that included fiction and half-fiction jumbled with fact'. The modern historian often tries to fill the void with source material based to a perhaps indeterminate extent on oral tradition (*Ancient History: Evidence and Models*, p. 16). In his book, *The Use and Abuse of History*, Finley also states that no historical documents existed in Greece before c. 700 BCE (p. 20). Tradition, he says, 'did not merely transmit the past, it created it' (p. 25).

4. I. Morris, *Burial and Ancient Society: The Rise of the Greek City-State* (New Studies in Archaeology; Cambridge, 1987), p. 24.

5. A. Momigliano, 'Greek Historiography', *History and Theory* 17 (1978), p. 5. Compare J.A. Soggin, who states that the Mycenaean-Aegean world was 'ignorant of writing' (*Introduction to the Old Testament: From its Origin to the Closing of the Alexandrian Canon* [Old Testament Library; London, 1976], p. 59).

6. As A. Momigliano points out, 'Herodotus could be treated by turn as the

his importance lies in his being the first writer to collect a vast amount of information,[1] including geographical and historical facts, as well as stories and legends about the past from both reliable and unreliable persons.[2] All this is presented as a history of the world known in his time; thus, his may be called the first 'universal' history.

It seems indisputable that some written sources were based on oral traditions. The problem is how to establish what part of a text is built on a piece of oral tradition. It may turn out that what has been labeled oral tradition in some cases is nothing more than a legend or a saga,[3] in other words, fiction. An example would be the discussion between Jonathan and the conspirator David behind a bush (1 Sam. 20.11-23). How can that 'conversation' ever be established as an empirical fact?

The theory that most of the biblical material has been preserved by oral tradition over hundreds of years is untenable,[4] even though it

father of history and as a liar, because nobody was in a position to check the stories he had told' (*History and Theory* 17 [1978], p. 8).

1. 'His is a kind of universal history; that is, it is the record of all the logical possibilities, political and human, that coexist in the human world' (D. Grene, 'Introduction', in *The History: Herodotus* [trans. David Grene; Chicago, 1987], p. 21). We should note, for instance, that Herotodus had 'at his disposal excellent information about the city of Babylon', according to P. Calmeyer, but the city 'was described to him as the last capital of Assyria' ('Greek Historiography and Achaemenid Reliefs', *Achaemenid History. II. The Greek Sources: Proceedings of the Groningen 1984 Achaemenid History Workshop* [ed. H. Sancisi-Weerdenburg and A. Kuhrt; Leiden, 1987], p. 20). This can be explained by the fact that in a Persian legend about the Three Empires Assyria had replaced the neo-Babylonian empire (P. Calmeyer, *Greek Historiography*, pp. 18-20).

2. In this connection we should note that Herodotus sometimes gives different accounts of one and the same event, as pointed out by J. Licht, 'Biblical Historicism', in *History, Historiography and Interpretation* (ed. H. Tadmor and M. Weinfeld; Jerusalem, 1983), p. 107.

3. The term 'saga' is in this presentation used in the modern sense. It should not be confused with the old Norse term, which could include both historiography and hagiography. A saga was often a chronicle dealing with the wars and feuds between particular clans describing their heroic courage and demands for justice. There were also some 'fornaldar' (prehistoric) sagas. These mainly described adventures in which the heroes fought some 'mythical' figures (trolls, monsters and imaginary animals); see T.A. Anderson, *The Icelandic Family Saga* (Cambridge, 1967).

4. I. Engnell, *Gamla Testamentet*, I (Stockholm, 1945), pp. 42-43; *idem, A Rigid Scrutiny* (Nashville, 1969), pp. 3-34. Compare also E. Nielsen, *Oral Tradition: A Modern Problem in Old Testament Introduction* (SBT, 11; London, 1954); but see

is agreed that some literature must have had an oral prehistory before being fixed in its present written form.[1] Examples of such orally based literature would be cultic laws and psalms, which may have changed over time because of new situations or new needs.[2] In this connection, the role of memorization should also be noted, something that must have been part of priestly education and which would also have played an important role in prophetic circles. The words of a prophetic master were to be remembered, because they were divine words.[3]

A 'source' thus functions as information which can be viewed as an answer to historical questions we pose. Sources are always limited in time and space. As for literary material, we are always faced with the problem of reliability. We always have to ask, With what kind of material are we dealing? Who wrote it? For whom was it written, and for what purpose? Can the text be trusted? Is it biased? Does it pretend to relate a divine promise, or is it written for a special purpose, as are, for instance, a law code, a sales contract, a treaty text, a letter, a genealogy, a king-list, a chronicle, an apology, or a piece glorifying a person, a myth, a story about a folk-hero? Are we dealing with a form of political-religious advocacy or doctrines? with an etiology? with telescoping or a distortion of events? or nothing other than fiction written as a fairytale? Is a particular text built upon another source and therefore, whether intentionally or not, altering it?

In addition a text often includes literary patterns and 'embroideries', which can make its reliability suspect—perhaps it is overemphasizing one aspect and neglecting another. Such can be the case with religious and political literary products. The latter is common among ancient

---

also his 'The Traditio-Historical Study of the Pentateuch since 1945, with Special Emphasis on Scandinavia', in *The Productions of Time: Tradition History in Old Testament Scholarship* (ed. K. Jeppesen and B. Otzen; Sheffield, 1984), pp. 16-19.

1.   M. Noth, *Überlieferungsgeschichte des Pentateuch* (Stuttgart, 1948), pp. 1-2 (ET: *A History of Pentateuchal Traditions* [Englewood Cliffs, NJ, 1972], pp. 1-2). Compare also S. Mowinckel, *Prophecy and Tradition: The Prophetic Books in the Light of the Growth and History of Tradition* (ANVAO, 2, Hist.-filos. Klasse, 3; Oslo, 1946); G.W. Ahlström, 'Oral and Written Transmission: Some Comments', *HTR* 59 (1966), pp. 69-70.

2.   Concerning laws, I. Engnell also thought they were written down early (*A Rigid Scrutiny*, p. 66).

3.   G.W. Ahlström, *HTR* 59 (1966), pp. 73, 76-81.

Near Eastern historical texts, which also use mythological[1] categories for describing unknown periods or the wonders and disasters of the world.[2] For instance, the beginning of history may start with the creation of the cosmos, which is understood as being the result of a divine action. Prehistoric time with its unknown events is often described in mythical categories in order to produce a link between the unknown and the known. Examples of such 'mythological historiography' are the Babylonian cosmology with Marduk's battle against the chaos monster Tiamat, the concept of *tatenen*, 'the primeval hill', which in ancient Egypt was thought of as rising out of the waters at the beginning of time.[3] The creation narratives in Genesis 1–11 are part of the same urge to explain how the cosmos once upon a time came into being and how life developed because of the divine will.[4] The Exodus legend with its motif of a people saved through the splitting of a sea also belongs to the same category of mythological fiction.[5] The same motif has been used in connection with the crossing

1. The term 'myth' is here used about texts in which god(s) or divine actions are mentioned, i.e. things which cannot be historically checked (see G.S. Kirk, *Myth: Its Meaning and Function in Ancient and Other Cultures* [London, 1970]). This is in contrast to P. Ricoeur, who sees myth as 'a narrative of origins, taking place in a primordial time, a time other than that of everyday reality', in 'Myth: Myth and History', *The Encyclopedia of Religion*, X (ed. M. Eliade; New York, 1987), p. 273. This would mean that any saga, sacred or not, dealing with prehistoric periods is a myth.

2. For the role of myth in historiography, see G. Widengren, 'Myth and History in Israelite-Jewish Thought', in *Culture in History: Essays in Honor of Paul Radin* (ed. S. Diamond; New York, 1960), pp. 467-95; J. Fränkel, *Dichtung und Wissenschaft* (Heidelberg, 1954); B. Albrektson, *History and the Gods* (ConBOT, 1; Lund, 1967); M.I. Finley, *The Use and Abuse of History*, pp. 11-33; J.J.M. Roberts, 'Myth *versus* History: Relaying the Comparative Foundations', *CBQ* 38 (1976), pp. 1-13; G.W. Ahlström, *Who were the Israelites?* (Winona Lake, IN, 1986), pp. 45-55. See also E.W. Count, 'Mythos as World View', in *Culture in History* (ed. S. Diamond), pp. 580-627; W.G. Lambert, 'Der Mythos im alten Mesopotamien, sein Werden und Vergehen', *Zeitschrift für Religionsgeschichte* 26 (1974), pp. 1-16; J. Van Seters, *Der Jahwist als Historiker* (Theologische Studien, 134; Zürich, 1987), pp. 55-95.

3. S. Morenz, *Ägyptische Religion* (Die Religionen der Menschheit, 8; Stuttgart, 1960), p. 45.

4. See T.L. Thompson, *The Origin Tradition of Ancient Israel*, pp. 78-79.

5. For the role of the sea, see H.G. May, 'Some Cosmic Connotations of *Mayyim Rabbim*, Many Waters', *JBL* 74 (1955), pp. 9-21; O. Kaiser, *Die mythische*

of the Jordan river and the entry into Canaan (Josh. 3.7–5.1). The entry is depicted as having been accomplished through a divine wonder.[1] That concept is part of the late settlement theology.

This raises the question of what kind of 'history' is expected in the stories about the Exodus and the wanderings in the wilderness, and its sequel, the 'conquest' of Canaan. This text cycle, composed for religious purposes, is an attempt to explain how the people of Yahweh were created. It is also a kind of history; it is religious historiography, the goal of which is not to present empirical facts. Religion can create whatever 'history' it wants or needs. The modern historian is here faced with two problems, and both are legitimate research objects: the actual history of the peoples/nations, and the history of their self-understanding and religion. In this volume I will be concerned with the former; thus, the religious historiography of the Exodus and the wanderings in the wilderness and the resultant ideology of an invasion and a conquest of Canaan will not solve any problems in the history of Palestine.[2] These texts deal with a certain people's self-understanding and not primarily with empirical history.[3] It is part of a religiously directed historiography.[4] Because there are no other literary sources for this period,[5] the archaeology of Palestine will have to become the

Bedeutung des Meeres in Ägypten, Ugarit und Israel (BZAW, 78; Berlin, 1959). Compare also B.F. Batto, 'The Reed Sea: Requiescat in Pace', *JBL* 102 (1983), pp. 27-35.

1.   Crossing the river Jordan does not really require any miracle, because there are some passable fords.

2.   Another famous invasion theory is the 'Dorian invasion', which, according to A.M. Snodgrass, among others, was not a migration from overseas, but more probably migrations within Greece (*The Dark Age of Greece: An Archaeological Survey of the Eleventh to the Eighth Centuries* [Edinburgh, 1971], pp. 311-13).

3.   This is where N.K. Gottwald has misunderstood history, saying that 'Israel *thought* it was different because it *was* different', in 'Two Models for the Origin of Ancient Israel: Social Revolution or Frontier Development', in *The Quest for the Kingdom of God: Studies in Honor of George E. Mendenhall* (ed. H.B. Huffmon, F.A. Spina and A.R.W. Green; Winona Lake, IN, 1983), p. 18. Gottwald has not shown as an empirical fact that Israel was different.

4.   J. Van Seters sees the 'conquest narrative' as a product of the D historian (*In Search of History*, p. 324). He also points out 'how closely Dtr's work has been made to correspond with the literary pattern of military campaigns in the Assyrian royal inscriptions' (p. 331).

5.   G. Garbini emphasizes that there is '*no evidence* to provide a basis for the usual datings (those which can be found in textbooks); they are only chronological

main source for historiography, and it shows a picture quite different than the religiously motivated writings.

The language of religion is mythological in character, but this langu-age was part of historiographical thinking in the ancient Near East.[1] Any event could be described as an act of the divine, which means that the description could be mythological or ideological, rather than factual, and that its details may therefore not be verifiable. This is common in Egyptian royal inscriptions, for example. The battle at Qadesh between the Hittites and the Egyptians may serve as an example. It almost ended in disaster for the Egyptian army, but Ramses II (1279–1212 BCE) describes it as a victory for himself and his 'father Amon', the main god of Thebes.[2] The 'god-king' cannot be a loser. Sometimes a story takes on the character of being unnatural, as for instance, the splitting of the 'Red Sea' in Exodus, or the drowning of all the Canaanites in Judges 5, in which only the commander Sisera managed to escape when the others drowned. (Did he run on water?) In this context the 'sea motif' has become a literary pattern.

Another example of how mythology could be used in expressing both the royal ideology and its connection with creation is found in Psalm 89. The election of David and his enthronement is presented in the liturgical activity as taking place after Yahweh had defeated the chaos powers and then made his creation.[3] Modern standards of historicity were not part of the ancient world's intellectual life.

The examples mentioned above can show the applicability of J. Huizinga's observation that 'every civilization creates its own form of history'.[4] This kind of history can be labeled 'imaginary history',

hypotheses' (*History and Ideology in Ancient Israel*, p. xv).

1. Consult A. Momigliano, who states that the Hebrews showed no 'distinction between a mythical age and an historical age' (*Essays in Ancient and Modern Historiography* [Middletown, CT, 1977], p. 194).

2. See, for instance, R.O. Faulkner, 'The Battle of Kadesh', *MDAIK* 16 (1958), pp. 93-111.

3. See my book, *Psalm 89* (Lund, 1959), pp. 57-104. E. Lipiński has seen David's relationship to Yahweh as that of a covenant between the god and his vassal. Cf. *Le poème royale du Psaume LXXXIX 1-5.20-38* (Cahiers de la Revue Biblique, 6; Paris, 1967), pp. 35-52. This is not to be denied, but the 'Davidic covenant' is a late theological development with respect to the king's religious status.

4. 'A Definition of the Concept of History', *Philosophy and History: Essays Presented to Ernst Cassirer* (ed. R. Killansky and H.J. Paton; New York, 1936), pp. 7-8; compare J. Van Seters, *In Search of History*, pp. 1-2. O. Spengler states

because it is an expression of a people's self-understanding and is in principle not necessarily based on any empirical events. Only when a people has had a certain amount of time to organize itself can it begin to consider the question of common origin.[1] Not enough is known about all the peoples living in the ancient Near East to accept Huizinga's statement as expressing a rule without exception. For instance, nothing is known about the beginning of a concept of history and its development among the Moabites, the Ammonites, Edomites or Aramaeans, to mention only a few. It can only be assumed that they may have had concepts somewhat similar to those common in the Near East of their time. Migrations, trade connections, political vassalage, deportations, intermarriages, and so forth, might have contributed to a common ideological 'language' among the Semitic peoples. Myths could 'travel'. The importance of scribal schools has also to be considered when studying the spread of legends, myths and folk-tales.

Certain Babylonian legends and myths could have become known to Judahites for the first time after they had been deported to Babylonia. Some historical and geographical knowledge about Mesopotamia may have first become known to the people of Judah during the Exile. For instance, the stories about Nimrod (Gen. 10.8) and the Tower of Babel (Gen. 11.1-9) were most probably composed after the Judahites had been exiled and had become familiar with Babylonian phenomena. They would most probably not have been intelligible before the Exile.

The phrase 'Ur of the Chaldeans' (Gen. 11.31, 15.7 and Neh. 9.7) is an anachronism before the ninth century BCE.[2] The Sumerian city of Ur declined in the second millennium but saw a revival under Babylonia's last king, Nabuna'id, in the sixth century BCE.[3] Did some

---

that 'Classical history down to the Persian Wars, and for that matter the structure built up on traditions at much later periods, are the product of an essentially mythological thinking' (*The Decline of the West*. I. *Form and Actuality* [trans. C.F. Atkinson; New York, 1966], p. 10).

1. Consult M. Liverani, 'Le "origini" d'Israele—progetto irrealizzabile di richerche etnogenetica', *RivB* 28 (1980), pp. 9-32.

2. The Akkadian term ^mat^*kaldu* occurs no earlier than the first half of the ninth century BCE; see H.W.F. Saggs, 'Ur of the Chaldees: A Problem of Identification', *Iraq* 22 (1960), pp. 200-207. For the Chaldeans, see J.A. Brinkman, *A Political History of Post-Kassite Babylonia 1158–722 BCE* (AnOr, 43; Rome, 1968).

3. According to J. Van Seters, the phrase 'Ur of the Chaldeans' (or 'Ur Kashdim') 'points directly to the Neo-Babylonian period' ('Confessional

of the exiled people learn about this city after they had been taken to Babylonia? If so, that could lead to the conclusion that the whole Abraham story is not a piece of history but rather is a literary product aimed at a religious and political situation of a much later time than its supposed Bronze Age setting.[1]

All these aspects have to be considered by anyone who presents a historiographic picture of the peoples of the ancient Near East. In addition, an awareness of the scholarly interpretation of the material is necessary, an interpretation that often might be influenced by cultural trends or the modern historiographer's background within such a trend (Romanticism, Positivism, Idealism, Marxism, cyclical theories, confessional background and so on), which is part of the historiographer's 'world-view'.

For most periods of the history of Palestine the archaeological remains are of the utmost importance.[2] Nothing could be written about certain periods if these remains did not exist or were unknown. This is true not only for the preliterary periods, but also for periods that are represented by textual material, as well as periods in which writing was practiced, but from which no textual records have survived. Times that are completely unchronicled by local written records are, for example, the Early Bronze Age and the Iron I Age. There are no texts from the Egyptian or Mesopotamian kingdoms that describe life and the political circumstances in Palestine and Transjordan during the latter period. Egyptian sources talk about the invasion of the so-called Sea Peoples and their march through Palestine. The result of their unsuccessful invasion of Egypt is now known from the archaeology of the settlements of the Philistines on the coast. One Egyptian papyrus, containing the story of Wenamun's journey to Byblos,[3] mentions that the Tjeker had settled at Dor south

Reformulation in the Exilic Period', *VT* 22 [1972], pp. 454-55). Compare also W.M. Clark, 'The Patriarchal Traditions. §2. The Biblical Traditions', *Israelite and Judean History* (ed. J.H. Hayes and J.M. Miller; Philadelphia, 1977), p. 131.

1. See below, Excursus: Abram/Abraham, Chapter 4.

2. This is also emphasized by M. Noth, who has usually been criticized as having a low appreciation of the archaeological evidence. Noth maintains, however, that a history of the culture and politics of the ancient Near East must be built not only on the literary remains but also on a solidly built archaeological reconstruction (*Gebäude*). Cf. 'Der Beitrag der Archäologie zur Geschichte Israels', in *Congress Volume, Oxford 1959* (ed. J.A. Emerton *et al.*; VTSup, 7; Leiden, 1959), p. 264.

3. See J.A. Wilson in *ANET*, pp. 25-29.

of Carmel. In general, it can be said that the Near Eastern powers during this period were at a 'low ebb'. The unstable political situation in the Levant did not encourage or require any great scribal activity in Akkadian, as had been the case during the Bronze Age. Interestingly, however, the Late Bronze II and Iron Ages were times when alphabetic writing developed and when the old Akkadian syllabic cuneiform was replaced in many places by more practical styles of writing, such as the Phoenician alphabet. Groups of people moving to the very sparsely settled hill country of Palestine from different areas were perhaps not those who were trained in the art of writing. Therefore, it cannot be assumed that they wrote anything down about their past history. They were refugees, pioneers or resettled nomads not connected with each other by any ethnic or political bonds. Their problem was to establish themselves and their villages and to make life possible economically. Writing a 'history' about how they arrived at this or that place could not yet have become part of their life. They had no need for that yet. This simply means that, for the period usually labeled Iron Age I, which includes the time of the so-called Judges, there are no extrabiblical literary sources for the history of this country beyond the information about the so-called Sea Peoples.

A most difficult problem facing a modern historian is the treatment of that part of the history of Palestine which includes the peoples of Israel and Judah. The history that can be detected concerning these peoples is fragmented, despite the wealth of literary material, or rather, because of it. As mentioned above, the biblical writers had a completely different goal than that of the modern historian; the problem, therefore, is to discover what real events if any can be found in these writings. From this it follows that the historiography of certain periods for which there are no other sources available than those of the biblical writers will rest on shaky ground because of the subjective presentation and religious *Tendenz* of the material.

Some attention should be given here to the problem of the prehistory of Israel and Judah, especially since A. Malamat has voiced the opinion that such a concept as 'the prehistory of Israel' should be avoided. It would refer to a time when no Israel existed. He prefers instead the term 'protohistory'. Malamat sees the dividing line between 'protohistory' and actual history as being the period when 'the migratory movements of the Israelites had effectively come to an end', that is, when the tribes had 'consolidated what were to be their hereditary holdings'.[1] Malamat's stance merely transforms the biblical historiographic pattern into an empirical event. Archaeology does not support such a reconstruction. An evolution from tribe to nation is a questionable hypothesis.[2] Some tribal names might originally have been territorial names, which would mean that the 'tribe' is a late development.[3] It seems to me, therefore, that the term 'prehistory' is accurate as long as the existence of any socio-political organization called Israel cannot be established. Malamat acknowledges that the 'Bible does not present authentic documents contemporary to events described'; thus, his theory about a 'protohistory' is weakened. He tries to see the Merneptah stele, which mentions the name Israel, as a contemporary source for a 'pan-Israelite league of twelve tribes, or a more limited group'.[4] This is no more than speculation, because the

1. 'The Proto-History of Israel: A Study in Method', in *The Word of the Lord Shall Go Forth* (Festschrift D.N. Freedman; ed. C.L. Meyers and M. O'Connor; Philadelphia, 1983), pp. 303-304.

2. Compare what M.I. Finley says about tribes: 'No dogma is so pervasive about Greek history (or indeed Roman and "Indo-European") as the one that there was a regular evolution from an early "tribal" organization of society, based on kinship groups, to a political, territorial organization' (*Ancient History, Evidence and Models*, p. 90). See also C.H.J. de Geus, *The Tribes of Israel: An Investigation into Some of the Presuppositions of Martin Noth's Amphictyony Hypothesis* (Assen, 1976), pp. 130-50.

3. Thus C.H.J. de Geus, *The Tribes of Israel*, pp. 130-31. See also N.P. Lemche, *Early Israel: Anthropological and Historical Studies on the Israelite Society before the Monarchy* (VTSup, 37; Leiden, 1985), pp. 282-83.

4. A. Malamat, 'Proto-History', *Word of the Lord* (ed. C.L. Meyers and M. O'Connor), p. 305. The theory about a twelve-tribe amphictyony which supposedly constituted earliest Israel has long been abandoned. The attempt to 'resurrect' it in the form of a pan-Israelite league has not been successful. Nobody has been able to demonstrate the empirical fact of such a league. It is thus impossible to maintain, as does D.N. Freedman, that the origin of the Pentateuch was some epic tradition of the 12th cent. BCE, which had 'its cultic locus in the amphictyonic festivals' ('Pentateuch', *IDB*, III, p. 717). Compare also F.M. Cross, who sees 'J and E as variant forms in prose of an older, largely poetic epic cycle of the era of the Judges' (*Canaanite Myth and Hebrew Epic* [Cambridge, MA, 1973], p. 293). For a critique of this theory, see S. Talmon, 'The "Comparative Method" in Biblical Interpretation—Principles and Problems',*Congress Volume, Göttingen 1977* (ed. J.A. Emerton *et al.*; VTSup, 29; Leiden, 1977), pp. 352-56. Consult also C. Conroy, who states that 'epic' ought to be abandoned 'as a genre-term for the JE *Vorlage*' ('Hebrew Epic: Historical Notes and Critical Reflections', *Bib* 61 [1980], pp. 1-30).

Merneptah stele does not clarify anything about the social organization of the people Israel that it mentions as being in Palestine. Malamat's 'protohistory' looks very much like a rewriting of the biblical narratives. As a matter of fact, a 'protohistory' of Israel and Judah would include Adam and Eve, which can be concluded from the genealogies in Genesis 5 and 10; thus, there is no not need to write any such history. The Hebrew Bible has already done it.[1]

It should be emphasized that in dealing with any society in Palestine the problem is that a mere presentation of facts, as they are understood, is not historiography, because it does not include all the facts. It is therefore no more than an incomplete catalogue. From the available facts certain deductions can be made and the picture thereby filled out. Reasons have to be found, if possible, for the events within a community or nation, and other circumstances that would have affected public or private life. When dealing with the ancient Near East, and with Palestine in particular, however, it is very seldom that a picture can be drawn of the common people's life. Almost nothing is known about how the role of religion affected the individual, about military service, sales contacts, freedom, divorce, adoption, serfdom, or to whom one was sold into slavery.[2] Archaeological material can provide some insight into the life of a household or of a village, a city or a fortress, but the individual disappears from the record. This is to be expected, because the common person did not write down an account of events. Therefore, there always will be some blank spots in the historical picture.

Some periods are more or less difficult to deal with because of the paucity of both textual and archaeological material. For parts of Palestine such a period is the Late Bronze Age. For instance, there are many archaeological remains in the valleys and on the coast, but because the LB Age was a time of very few settlements in the central hills,[3] the archaeological picture will be very spotty. However, the

---

1.   Malamat's 'method' is thus no method at all. For a critique of Malamat's theory, see N.P. Lemche, *BN* 23 (1984), pp. 94-123. If Malamat's method were to be used for a reconstruction of the history of the United States of America, one would have to write about almost all of the peoples of the world.

2.   See also Martha Roth, review of J.J. Finkelstein, 'The Ox That Gored', *BO* 40 (1983), p. 399.

3.   See below, Chapter 7.

tablets from Tell el-Amarna contain the correspondence between the Pharaoh and his Syro-Palestinian vassals during the fourteenth century BCE. The tablets, written in Akkadian, talk about a number of city states in the lowlands and the valleys, but only about a very few in the central hills, namely Shechem and Jerusalem, and Pehel (Pella) in the foothills of Jordan close to the Jordan Valley. How much history do these texts relate? A literary analysis shows a formulaic language with common ideas, such as defense for a city-king's actions and his demands on the Pharaoh to protect and help him with his problems with neighboring city-states, robbers and so on. The problem with these letters is not 'to ascertain if a narrated event is "true", but why it has been stated in that particular way and not in another'.[1] In other words, what kind of motives were there for the letters to be written? There is no corroborative material that can be used, nor is there any information about the chain of events or the context that led to the writing beside what the letters mention.[2] Thus, a history cannot really be written from these texts, but the letters are useful for filling in some gaps in the political and demographic picture of this period.

A period completely unknown in Near Eastern texts except from the Hebrew Bible is that of the so-called united monarchy. No kingdom called Israel or Judah, much less an Israelite empire, is anywhere attested in the records of the non-Palestinian countries.[3] This may be due to the fact that the Egyptian and Assyrian powers were at a low ebb in this period; thus they had no interaction with any kingdom in Palestine. A presentation of the history of this period, as of any other

1. M. Liverani, 'Political Lexicon and Political Ideologies in the Amarna Letters', *Berytus* 31 (1982), p. 42.

2. M. Liverani, 'Political Lexicon', p. 44.

3. According to Josephus (*Apion* 1.112-25), the Annals of Tyre were translated into Greek and used by two Hellenistic historians, Menander of Ephesus and Dius. In these Annals Solomon was supposedly mentioned. The reliability of this information may be disputed, but it is not impossible that certain records were kept in Tyre and other Phoenician cities. If so, Solomon could have been mentioned. As to the discussion, see H. Katzenstein, *The History of Tyre* (Jerusalem, 1973), pp. 77-80; J. Van Seters, *In Search of History*, pp. 195-96; G. Garbini, *History and Ideology in Ancient Israel*, pp. 23-24. B.Z. Wachholder believes that the historian Eupolemus (who could be the same as the one mentioned in 1 Macc. 8.17) borrowed his knowledge about Solomon from Menander (*Eupolemus: A Study of Judeo-Greek Literature* [New York, 1974], p. 110).

period in the history of Palestine which lacks external evidence, will therefore be tentative. This is not to deny that there is any reliable information in the biblical texts, but, without the corroboration of external source material, the picture that can be presented from an examination of Judges, Samuel and 1 Kings, the texts that are available, will be no more than a discussion of what could have been possible. However, when this is supplemented with the archaeological remains, the plausibility of a kingdom in the hills has to be acknowledged. This period shows an intensification of building activities, not only of small farmsteads and villages, but also of monumental buildings such as fortresses, of cities with a certain type of fortification and city gates, and of government building projects, such as store cities. The conclusion to be drawn from all this is that such activities were the result of a governmental policy.

As an example of how some history can be extracted from certain propagandistic textual material, the narratives about King Saul and some of his deeds may be mentioned. The main argument for the existence of Saul and his kingdom is the fact that the biblical writers so strongly and so often emphasize that David, the usurper, was the 'chosen one'. The fact that Saul is said to have fallen from divine grace as ruler shows the writer's problem with an 'ideologically' disturbing personality. If Saul had been an insignificant or nonexistent person, this emphasis would not have been necessary. If Saul did not have to be accounted for, the writers would rather have done as in Egypt: erased the memory of an 'unwanted' or 'evil' king. Obviously Saul was of such a stature that he could not be gotten around or ignored. Thus, for instance, the laconic information in 1 Sam. 14.47 about Saul having battled Moab, Ammon, Edom, Beth-Rehob, and the Aramaean king of Zobah, as well as the Philistines, may be true.

Here arises the difficult question about the reliability of the biblical texts as source material and about how they relate to what history really looked like. This leads to the problem of methodology. Because of the diversity of the source material (textual, archaeological, geographical and so on) there is no one method that can be used to deal with the different sources. For instance, literary patterns, myths and sagas do not relate history; thus any method used for such texts cannot reveal the course of historical events, because the texts were not written for such a purpose. As to the historical books of the Bible, including the historical information in the prophetical books, the methods of literary criticism, form criticism and source criticism, each of which supplements the other, as well as redaction criticism, may be used in some instances. However, these are methods that are used to clarify the history of a *text* and its *composition*;[1] this does not *ipso facto* mean that through such methods we reach the historical event.[2]

For instance, a literary analysis of Judges 3–9 shows a composition made up of smaller units, that is, stories about chieftains, tribes, clans and so on in the so-called premonarchic period of Israel.[3] The first step of an analysis would be to see in what literary context this complex has been placed. It turns out to be part of a literary pattern that has decided the place of the smaller units. This is the ancient Near Eastern historiographic pattern of change between 'good' and 'evil'. A good time is followed by an evil time, fortune is followed by misfortune, light is followed by darkness.[4] The next step would be to identify the smaller units and the kind of literary categories to which they belong: the stories about Othniel, Ehud, Shamgar, Deborah and Barak, Gideon, Jerubbaal and Abimelech. These persons represent in the pattern the 'good' leaders of 'all Israel' (as the historiographic phrase has it), except for Abimelech. The other leaders have all followed an 'evil' period. The altar tradition connected with Gideon (Judg. 6.11-17) may reflect a special source or tradition referring to an event that contributed to Gideon's fame. Can it now be determined as the next step from what sources these writings derived? The answer will be no. It simply is not known whether these stories were part of certain older

1. See W. Richter, *Exegese als Literaturwissenschaft: Einwurf einer alttestamentlichen Literaturmethode und Methodologie* (Göttingen, 1971). Richter's book is a good example of how necessary it is to differentiate between history and biblical historiography. For a review of his book, see J.W. Rogerson in *JSS* 20 (1975), pp. 117-22.

2. Tradition history, as advocated by I. Engnell (*Gamla Testamentet*, I), cannot be used because it refers to the prehistory of the text, something that we do not know anything about.

3. For the methods of form criticism and redaction criticism, see K. Koch, *The Growth of the Biblical Tradition* (New York, 1969); N. Habel, *Literary Criticism of the Old Testament* (Philadelphia, 1971).

4. See T.E. Peet, *A Comparative Study of the Literatures of Egypt, Palestine and Mesopotamia* (London, 1931); H.G. Güterbock, 'Die historische Tradition und ihre literarische Gestaltung bei Babyloniern und Hethitern bis 1200', *ZA* 42 (1934), pp. 1-91 (15ff.).

writing(s) available to the narrator or whether they were compositions inspired by certain oral traditions, fictitious or not. Neither form
nor redaction criticism can uncover what the exact history looked like
in these cases,[1] because no material exists that shows the text in an
earlier stage.

The story about the Yeminite[2] Ehud freeing the 'Israelites' from
Moabite oppression (Judg. 3.12-30) can be used as an example of how
'knowledge' about a certain person has been utilized by the narrator.
First of all, it should be noted that this story is quite different from
the preceding one about Othniel, which contains but a few statements.
The Ehud narrative is in contrast a humorous and ironical folkloristic
hero-story, which may have existed first in an oral tradition,[3] which
has been used by the D historian, who included Ehud among the
'saviors' of the people of Yahweh. There was probably a source, a
tradition, about Ehud that the writer made into a well-structured
composition[4] contrasting the man of 'glory', Ehud, with the fat king
of Moab, the oppressor Eglon. The narrative has three scenes with
actions and speeches (vv. 19, 20-23, 24-25), and it ends with the act
of Ehud and his men victoriously battling the Moabites (vv. 26-30).
Certain phrases recur, such as the $p^e s \hat{\imath} l \hat{\imath} m$, 'gods', at Gilgal (vv. 19
and 26). The text also includes a pun on the word $y \bar{a} m \hat{\imath} n$, 'south, right
side'.[5] Like all the other 'judges', Ehud has been seen as a leader over
'all Israel'. He supposedly had been chosen to pay the tribute to
Moab's king, Eglon, who was said to have enslaved the Israelites for
18 years (3.12-14). Having killed the king of Moab, Ehud fled and

---

1. Compare J. Barton, *Reading the Old Testament* (Philadelphia, 1984), p. 52.

2. Ehud was not a Benjaminite. The phrase *ben-hay^{e}mînî* refers to a man from
the 'land of Yemini' mentioned in 1 Sam. 9.4. It was located in southern Ephraim
just north of Bethel. This would mean that he was an Asherite.

3. See E.G. Kraeling, 'Difficulties in the Story of Ehud', *JBL* 54 (1935),
pp. 205-10. C. Grottanelli sees the story as a literary parallel to Roman, Iranian and
Scandinavian narratives which, by means of military and/or cosmic symbolism,
express victory over the forces of destruction ('Un passo del Libro dei Giudici alla
luce della comparazione storico-religiosa: il guidici Ehud e il valore della mano sinis-
tra', *Oriens Antiqui Collectio* 13 [1978], pp. 35-45).

4. See L. Alonso Schökel, 'Erzählkunst im Buche der Richter', *Bib* 42 (1961),
pp. 148-58. He also indicates that the narrator of the story knows that the time he
has given to the story does not agree with reality (p. 155).

5. His right hand was paralyzed: *'iṭṭer yad-y^{e}mînô* (v. 15). For the structure,
see H.N. Rösel, 'Zur Ehud Erzählung', *ZAW* 89 (1977), pp. 270-72.

came to 'Israel' and blew the trumpet in Mt Ephraim so the 'Israelites' joined him and cut off Moab from access to the fords of the Jordan (vv. 26-30).[1] The important literary points in the text are the descriptions of Ehud and the Moabite king Eglon, and how Ehud killed the king who represents the evil power. Ehud had to use his left hand because the right one was paralyzed,[2] and through treachery he killed the Moabite king. The latter is described as being very fat. His name is an ironical pun on the Hebrew *'ēgel*, 'calf'; in other words, Eglon is pictured as a fat young bull, an ideal animal for the holocaust sacrifice. The rest of the 'details' are embroidery.[3] As a result of a closer look at the text the history disappears. Literary-critical observations do not contribute any historicity to the related events. The narrative is probably a hero story about a local chieftain, whom we cannot exactly place in time, but who in the Bible has been assigned to the premonarchic period. It should also be noted that the only Moabite kingdom known from the period before King Saul is the one that is represented by the Balu'a stela from c. 1200 BCE, from the area just south of Wadi Mujib (c. 24 km north of Kerak). What political unit the king of the stela represents is not known. He could have been a nomadic chieftain, to judge from his clothing.[4] It is improbable that any Moabite kingdom in the period before Saul could have reached as far north as the territories of the Jordan river, especially if the Ammonites were expanding westward. The historicity of Eglon and Ehud is not enhanced by any textual, form or redaction criticism. The result of an analysis of the text is that Ehud and Eglon can only be described as the

---

1.   This shows that he was not a Benjaminite. Nothing is said about the participation of Benjamin and other Cisjordanian peoples in the war against Moab, neither is anything said about 'the Israelites' of Transjordan as having joined Ehud.

2.   The Latin translation and the LXX have read *ambidextrous*, 'with restrained hand'. Ehud had made a sword, which is explained as a two-edged dirk a *gōmed*, 'cubit', long. According to G.F. Moore, *gōmed*, which does not occur anywhere else in the OT (*hapax legomenon*), could be the same as Greek *pygmē*, 'dirk' (*Critical and Exegetical Commentary on Judges* [ICC; Edinburgh, 1975 (1895), p. 94]).

3.   For the structure, see W. Richter, *Exegese als Literaturwissenschaft*, pp. 104-105.

4.   See, for instance, the discussion by W.A. Ward and M.F. Martin, 'The Balu'a Stele: A New Transcription with Paleological and Historical Notes', *ADAJ* 8–9 (1964), pp. 5-29.

two main characters in a literary drama.[1] The same conclusion can be drawn concerning the narratives about the other 'judges'.[2]

From the above it is evident that even if the form of a text can be outlined and the different units separated, establishing some repeated phraseology and detecting some intrusions, all that will result is a history of the text and not the certification of actual events. All these different elements have been woven together by the narrator in order to give a total picture in which some events of the past can be seen to have been part of the people's history. Some other events may have been adapted according to the writer's intentions, others may be fictitious, and some may not have been considered at all.

The above is true in most cases. However, literary analysis, as well as redaction criticism, may now and then help to establish the probability of an event. For instance, Judges 4 and 5 both recount the same battle between a Canaanite coalition and certain Israelites, according to the writers. This is not the place to give a complete literary analysis of these texts. However, because Judges 4 is a narrative while Judges 5 is a poem in archaic style that contains other topics than those in Judges 4, the compositions may be seen to stem from different hands. Judges 5 is a victory hymn composed of various motifs, such as a theophany (vv. 4-5) and reminiscences of past, glorious times including the time of Shamgar, Jael and Deborah (vv. 6-7).[3] In common with other Near Eastern victory hymns, the 'Song of Deborah', as it has been called, expresses the idea that deities effect a miraculous wonder for their own people. The goal of the theophany is to lead up to the 'historical' victory.[4] Judges 4 and 5 have been redacted in a sequence, but the content is different, even if they both deal with the same leaders and their forces. What they have in common is that both texts mention Zebulon and Naphtali as fighting the enemies. This could be redactional, but because Judges 4 does not state that any other group

1.   A literary unit has two (sometimes three) main actors. The others are only filling out the picture, like the crowd on a stage; see, for instance, W. Richter, *Exegese als Literaturwissenschaft*, p. 96.

2.   Compare N.P. Lemche, *Early Israel*, p. 383.

3.   This means that the composition was made quite some time after Deborah's death. When she lived is not known.

4.   Consult, for instance, J. Blenkinsopp, 'Ballad Style and Psalm Style in the Song of Deborah: A Discussion', *Bib* 42 (1961), pp. 61-76, esp. pp. 64-65.

of people joined Zebulon and Naphtali, these two 'tribes' must be original in Judges 4. The poem adds some other 'tribes' which, however, do not participate in the battle. Even though no corroborating nonbiblical texts are available, from a methodological point of view we must take into consideration what is known about the political situation in Syria-Palestine in the so-called premonarchic period. Thus, the question must be asked: Can the battle between the 'Canaanites' under Sisera and the 'Israelites' under Baraq (with the prophetic support of Deborah) really have occurred during the period Late Bronze II–Iron I Ages? Realizing that Egypt dominated Palestine into the mid-twelfth century BCE, followed by the power of the Philistines, a battle between two large coalitions in the strategically important Jezreel plain is out of the question. Without going into all the literary problems of Judges 5 (which could occupy a whole book), I can conclude that the battle was a local event that was utilized by the composer of the poem at a later time and thus has been given an 'all-Israelite' cast. From that point of view, Judges 5 is less historical than Judges 4. However, this does not say anything for certain about the date of the two compositions.

The Near Eastern literary phenomenon of a repeated change between an ideal and orderly period to an evil period of chaos is a device often occurring in so-called prophetic texts using such motifs as light and darkness, fortune and misfortune, blessing and curse.[1] This literary device is also heavily used by biblical narrators and prophets. The so-called deuteronomistic history work (i.e. the books of Deuteronomy, Joshua, Judges, Samuel and Kings) has structured its historiography according to this kind of pattern.[2] For instance, the

---

1.   See, for instance, T.E. Peet, *Comparative Study of the Literatures of Egypt, Palestine, and Mesopotamia*, pp. 120-21; H.G. Güterbock, *ZA* 42 (1934), pp. 15ff.; W. Helck, *Die Prophezeiung des Nfr.tj* (Kleine Ägyptische Texte; Wiesbaden, 1970); H. Hunger and S.A. Kaufman, 'A New Akkadian Prophecy Text', *JAOS* 95 (1975), pp. 371-75; S.A. Kaufman, 'Prediction, Prophecy, and Apocalypse in the Light of New Akkadian Texts', *Proceedings of the Sixth World Congress of Jewish Studies*, I (Jerusalem, 1977), pp. 221-28. See also R.D. Biggs, 'The Babylonian Prophecies and the Astrological Tradition in Mesopotamia', *JCS* 37 (1985), pp. 86-90.

2.   Earlier I have maintained that there is a possibility of seeing the D history as having been written by one person (*Who were the Israelites?*, p. 76). This is also the understanding of H.-D. Hoffmann, who sees the D historian as a composer using the pattern of change in presenting his religious history in which the sometimes fictional

period of the so-called Judges (excluding the appended chs. 17–21) is presented as an era during which 'the people of Israel' often abandoned the 'right' religion of Yahweh and were therefore oppressed by enemies until Yahweh heard their laments and 'raised up a judge' to lead them. When he died the people again abandoned Yahweh, and after a time of oppression Yahweh had to give the people another 'judge'. This 'light and dark periods' scheme also occurs as the basis for the evaluation of the kings of Judah.[1] Such a literary pattern cannot be used for a reconstruction of history.[2]

A parallel to this literary pattern of change between 'good' and 'evil' rulers can for instance be found in Babylonian literature, in the so-called Weidner Chronicle. The Chronicle is a piece of religious propaganda, denouncing kings who did not care enough for Marduk and his temple in Babylon.[3] Corresponding to this phenomenon, Ahaz of Judah is presented as an unfaithful 'Yahwist' who therefore is 'evil', but his son Hezekiah is seen as an ideal king. Hezekiah's son Manasseh, as well as Manasseh's successor, Amon (who did not really count because he was murdered after two years), were 'evil'. Josiah is then hailed as being a king as 'good' as Hezekiah and David. This is an example of the one-sidedness of biblical historiography and of how this 'historiography' follows an ideological pattern. It is not really concerned with facts. Historically, King Hezekiah led his nation of Judah to the brink of disaster, but in the eyes of the biblical narrator

cult reforms play a large role (*Reform und Reformen: Untersuchungen zu einen Grundthema der deuteronomistischen Geschichtsschreibung* [ATANT, 66; Zürich, 1980]). This does not mean that the D historian did not use any literary sources. An indication that he used some written sources is the different spellings of some names; consult P. Machinist, 'Assyria and its Image in First Isaiah', *JAOS* 103 (1983), p. 729.

1.   The kings of the northern kingdom, Israel, are all denounced as being 'evil', because in the narrator's view Israel was an apostate kingdom. From this point of view no Israelite king could have done what was 'right in the eyes of Yahweh'.

2.   See my book, *Who were the Israelites?*, pp. 75-76. See also J. Wellhausen, *Die Composition des Hexateuchs und der historischen Bücher der Alten Testaments* (3rd edn; Berlin, 1899; repr. Berlin, 1963), pp. 210-22.

3.   A.K. Grayson, *Assyrian and Babylonian Chronicles* (Texts from Cuneiform Sources, 5; Locust Valley, NY, 1975), pp. 43-45, 145-51; and *idem, Or* NS 49 (1980), p. 180. Grayson dates it to the latter part of the second millennium BCE (*Assyrian and Babylonian Chronicles*, pp. 278-79).

he scored the highest points as a 'righteous' king because he was a good 'disciple' who followed the advice of the prophet Isaiah. For the biblical writer, nothing was more important than to follow the divine words that were expressed by the divine law or through a prophet who was acceptable to and in harmony with the writer's ideology. An example of this ideology is expressed by the demand that the king obey the law, *torah* (Deut. 17.18-20). Among other things this text states that the king must write a copy of the *torah* 'at the dictation of the Levitical priests', and that he must read it every day as long as he lives. What king would have had the time to study the *torah* every day? Administratively this is quite impossible. This text is a clear indication that the composition of the Bible is late and that this statute (which is reminiscent of the rabbinic ideal) was written when no king was on the Davidic throne any longer. The biblical writer has here presented his ideal.

The basis for this kind of literature is religious zeal, which can use literary patterns, make adaptions, corrections, and sometimes fictional writings, as well as include exact events and exclude others, when it suits the authors' purpose. It could be asked, for instance, why the Judahite temple at Arad in the Negev is never mentioned in the Bible, or why the phenomenon of Yahweh having had a consort, Asherah, has been suppressed. She, too, was worshipped in the Solomonic temple, as was Baal. Why did King Manasseh of Judah become the scapegoat for the disasters of Judah that led up to the Exile? This king maintained peace during his 55-year reign and restored the official Judahite religion in the cities that were returned to Judah from Philistine administration. Manasseh restored the orthodox religion of Judah in these cities, which for some time after Hezekiah's reign must have had Philistine officials and priests or Philistine deities in charge of daily life.[1] Because all this did not suit the ideology of the biblical writers, who had a special purpose in mind when writing, Manasseh became a literary scapegoat.

The above indicates something about the principles guiding the OT writers. The material is specially selected and represents the concepts of a group that advocated a certain line of action and a certain way of thinking about the history of the people of Israel and Judah and their

1. See my *Royal Administration and National Religion in Ancient Palestine* (Studies in the History of the Ancient Near East, 1; Leiden, 1982), pp. 75-81.

'untrustworthy' neighbors. It is doubtful that the group propagating deuteronomistic ideas represented the official ideology of pre-exilic society. The prophetical concepts by which the writers seem to have been influenced were not the official line of thinking in the kingdoms of Israel and Judah, as can be seen from the prophetical polemics against the official religions of these two states. It should also be noted that there was only a small group of prophets that was accepted by this group of tradents, namely those whose utterances could be used or were in line with the theological conceptualization of history of the writers and/or the collectors of the material.

The above shows that my approach has been to gather not only literary information, but also to a large extent archaeological material, in order to get as close as possible to the actual events. The approach also includes critical assessment of the biblical material against the political and cultural situation that can be learned from extrabiblical sources.

Empirical history and the religious, biblical concept of history have usually been mixed in scholarly presentations of the origin of Israel. The religious historiography does not *per se* need to build upon any reality, because religion makes its own reality, as mentioned above. Thus, there is a special purpose for this kind of writing. The biblical texts dealing with the origin of Israel in Palestine belong to this kind of historiography, because they proclaim that behind the creation of the people Israel is the divine will. Therefore they do not provide any basic information about the emergence of the people or nation Israel.[1] As to the date, the texts locating Israelites in the eastern Delta cannot be earlier than the seventh century, when the Saitic 26th Dynasty was in power and when the Wadi Tumilat, part of the biblical land of Goshen, began to be heavily settled.[2] It can therefore be maintained

---

1.   Among the more recent publications dealing with this problem is that of J.M. Miller, who has not made the distinction between religious historiography and empirical history; see his 'The Israelite Occupation of Canaan', *Israelite and Judean History* (ed. J.H. Hayes and J.M. Miller; Philadelphia, 1977), p. 213. The same can be said about B. Halpern, *The Emergence of Israel in Canaan* (SBLMS, 29; Chico, CA, 1983). In his most recent history Miller is more cautious and says that 'the main story line of Genesis–Joshua' is to be understood as an 'artificial and theologically influenced literary product' (J.M. Miller and J.H. Hayes, *A History of Ancient Israel and Judah* [Philadelphia, 1986], p. 78).

2.   See Carol Redmount, 'On an Egyptian/Asiatic Frontier: An Archaeological History of the Wadi Tumilat' (PhD dissertation, University of Chicago; Chicago,

that the demographic and thus also the cultural situation in the Delta known to the narrator of the 'sojourn in Egypt' has been adapted to his historiography.

When the inscriptional material from the Late Bronze period is considered, it is quite clear that the biblical writers knew nothing about events in Palestine before the tenth century BCE. There are no traces of the so-called Amarna period (fourteenth century BCE) known from the correspondence between the Pharaoh and the Syro-Palestinian kinglets. There is no recollection whatsoever of the Egyptian dominion over Syria-Palestine during the Late Bronze period. The biblical writers do not know about the many Egyptian military campaigns through Palestine, which often resulted in destroyed cities and the taking of cattle and prisoners of war to Egypt. 'There are, both in Exodus and in Judges, no heroic Pharaohs striding like colossoi across the map of the Near East, no marching armies of conquerors', no tribute paying city states, 'no cities established in Pharaoh's name'.[1] The events recorded in Pharaoh Merneptah's victory stele, mentioning that he had taken Ashkelon, Gezer and Yeno'am and eradicated the people Israel from the earth,[2] are completely unknown, as is the march of the Sea Peoples through the country down to Egypt, which resulted in the settlement of Philistines and Tjeker on the coast south of Carmel. The first Egyptian Pharaoh mentioned by name in the Bible is Shoshenq (biblical Shishak) of the 22nd Dynasty, to whom Jeroboam was to have fled after opposing Solomon (1 Kgs 11.40). This Pharaoh is also the first one that the biblical narrator credits with a march through Palestine, five years after Solomon's death (1 Kgs 14.25-27; 1 Chron. 12.1-12). The biblical information about this campaign is corroborated in Shoshenq's inscription on a pylon of Amun's temple at Karnak (Thebes). The Egyptian account, on the

---

1988). For a postexilic dating of these texts, see M. Bietak, 'Comments on the "Exodus"', *Egypt, Israel, Sinai: Archaeological and Historical Relationships in the Biblical Period* (ed. A.F. Rainey; Tel Aviv, 1987), pp. 163-71; D.B. Redford, 'An Egyptological Perspective on the Exodus Narrative', *Egypt, Israel, Sinai* (ed. A.F. Rainey), pp. 137-61.

1.   D.B. Redford, in *Egypt, Israel, Sinai* (ed. A.F. Rainey), p. 138.

2.   For this text, see G.W. Ahlström and D. Edelman, 'Merneptah's Israel', *JNES* 44 (1985), pp. 59-61; G.W. Ahlström, *Who were the Israelites?*, pp. 37-42; F. Yurco, 'Merneptah's Canaanite Campaign', *JARCE* 23 (1986), pp. 189-215.

other hand, mentions neither Israel, nor Judah nor Jerusalem;[1] thus the biblical text about this Pharaoh's campaign can be seen to supplement the Egyptian information. However, it can be concluded that the biblical historiography dealing with the periods before Shoshenq primarily presents an imaginary history that builds on a few memories of a past time, such as the existence of Saul's kingdom.[2]

The documentary hypothesis for the Pentateuch developed by K.H. Graf and J. Wellhausen (with its sources J, E, P and D) is of no real use for writing the early history of Israel and Judah, which Wellhausen himself understood.[3] No one has been able to demonstrate the independent existence of any of these literary complexes (besides D, which is mainly the book of Deuteronomy).[4] A priestly code, cut in pieces and affixed between several different stories with whatever kind of ideological glue, never existed as an independent literary source. It is quite another thing to state that there are many sacral laws in the Hebrew Bible occurring in different literary compositions. As in all societies, law-giving is an ongoing process. It is thus natural that we find laws in the Hebrew Bible that reflect both a pre-exilic and a postexilic condition.[5]

In this connection, the question of who the writers in the ancient Near East usually were could be asked. The main part of the literature of these Near Eastern societies including those of Palestine was most

1.   See J. Simons, *Handbook for the Study of Egyptian Topographical Lists Relating to Western Asia* (Leiden, 1937), pp. 89-101, 178-86; W. Helck, *Die Beziehungen Ägyptens zu Vorderasien im 3. und 2. Jahrtausend v. Chr.* (2nd edn; Wiesbaden, 1971), pp. 167-69.

2.   Compare N.P. Lemche, *Early Israel*, pp. 414-15. Consult also T.L. Thompson, *Archaeology and the Historical Origins of Israel: The Early Iron Age and the 'United Monarchy'* (forthcoming).

3.   See, for instance, his *Prolegomena zur Geschichte Israels* (Berlin, 1883), p. 9 (ET Berlin, 1981 [1927], p. 9). It is interesting to note that P, according to Wellhausen, presents the whole of Canaan 'as a *tabula rasa*'. The tribes then receive their inheritance by lot (p. 358 [Germ. edn, pp. 357-58]).

4.   See the criticism by J. Pedersen, 'Die Auffassung vom Alten Testament', *ZAW* 49 (1931), pp. 161-81. For a convenient résumé of this problem, see R.N. Whybray, *The Making of the Pentateuch: A Methodological Study* (JSOTSup, 53; Sheffield, 1987), pp. 17-131.

5.   This would mean that the final composition of the Pentateuch is late. It is probably from the time after Ezra. Compare the discussion in R. Rendtorff, *Das überlieferungsgeschichtliche Problem des Pentateuch* (BZAW, 147; Berlin, 1977), pp. 158-73.

probably written by professionals, such as learned scribes and savants, who could be found in the government, the court, schools, temples and wisdom circles, or else by the nonprofessional elite.[1] There were, for instance, business transactions that also required some trained scribes. Most scribes were writing for a special *publicum* or for a special purpose.[2] In a time when not everybody could read or write, the school became 'an ideological molder of minds'.[3] Scribes therefore became important persons not only representing the accumulated wisdom of a society, but also having the ability to advance to important positions in the government, as was the case with the scribe Setau, who became a viceroy under Ramses II.[4]

The question of how and when historiography in the ancient Near East began merits a book of its own. Royal inscriptions from Anatolia, Mesopotamia and Egypt may represent the beginning of ancient Near Eastern historiographic activity. Egyptian and Sumerian inscriptions are the oldest examples. Annals occur in Hatti c. 300 years before the earliest Assyrian ones (from about the thirteenth century BCE).[5] Most royal inscriptions represent the recording and glorification of royal deeds, but no real concept of historiography. Egyptian inscriptions and reliefs, for instance, often report certain happenings and conflicts with neighboring peoples, but this is mostly done in order to show how the might of Egypt prevailed. There is no continuous history. Reports about the kings and their deeds, such as campaigns to Syria-Palestine, display the same style and the same kind of phraseology and literary patterns. They always praise the 'divine' king. This indicates that the students in the scribal schools were trained in 'the use of

1. Compare H.H. Hoffner, *Or* NS 49 (1980), pp. 283-332.

2. In a relief from Nineveh, Assyrian scribes are shown recording the captured people and the loot; see S. Parpola, *The Correspondence of Sargon II. I. Letters from Assyria and the West* (Helsinki, 1987), p. 137.

3. P. Michalowski, 'Charisma and Control: On Continuity and Change in Early Mesopotamian Bureaucratic Systems', *The Organization of Power: Aspects of Bureaucracy in the Ancient Near East* (ed. M. Gibson and R.D. Biggs; SAOC, 46; Chicago, 1987), p. 63.

4. K.A. Kitchen, *Pharaoh Triumphant: The Life and Times of Ramesses II* (Warminster, 1982), pp. 136-38.

5. See K. Bittel, *Hattusha: The Capital of the Hittites* (New York, 1970), pp. 22-23.

common patterns, with little change throughout the ages'.[1] Thus the Egyptian material is not 'much concerned with historical data on a war past the point of the enemy's defeat'.[2] In other words, many of the details are literary stereotypes.

Concerning Babylonia, the 'scribes simply wished to record what had happened in and around their land'. This could be called history 'written for history's sake'. Its character is 'parochial'.[3] There is no national historiography in Babylonia before the neo-Babylonian empire emerged on the stage of history. In Assyria, collections of cuneiform tablets in libraries, such as that of Ashurbanipal, may have inspired research into the past, and the Babylonian Chronicles series could be seen as a result of such research.[4]

If national historiography first started in Babylonia in the eighth century BCE, might not Hebrew historiography be later, considering that Israel and Judah were relatively young nations? I do not want to deny the possibility that some biblical history-writing occurred earlier. Some annalistic writings may have been authored in the courts of Saul, Eshbaal, David and Solomon. A decision on this matter must be based on what could have been probable in such young nations that were located in the hills outside the mainstream of cultural and material exchange, and that developed relatively late as political units. It must have taken a few hundred years of common life before these small nations could have developed some general views about their history, especially if it is remembered that the different groups of people that settled in the hills[5] would have needed a certain amount of time to meld together and feel or develop a nationality, not to say an ethnicity. It is difficult, therefore, to accept the hypothesis that a historiographer, the so-called Yahwist (J),[6] could have written a

1. A.J. Spalinger, *Aspects of the Military Documents of the Ancient Egyptians* (Yale Near Eastern Researches, 9; New Haven, 1982), p. 239.

2. A.J. Spalinger, *Aspects*, p. 118.

3. A.K. Grayson, *Assyrian and Babylonian Chronicles*, p. 11.

4. See J. Van Seters, *In Search of History*, pp. 79-92.

5. For the settlement of different groups in the central hills, see my *Who were the Israelites?*, pp. 12-36. Here we ought to remember that Palestine had never had a homogenous population. Also, the term 'Canaanite' is not an ethnic term. This is discussed below.

6. The letter J stands for the Yahwist, since in the Germanic languages the first letter in the tetragrammaton JHWH is an elongation of the Latin I when used as a

prehistory of the people of Yahweh during the period of the early monarchy,[1] when the people of Judah[2] and Israel had not yet melded together—which they never really did in any case. It seems that they might have been 'forced' into a union under David and Solomon,[3] because after Solomon's death they fought each other until the period of the Omrides in Israel. The most likely type of 'historiography' to have been written during the period of the early monarchy would have been an apologetic for David's usurpation of the throne. The deuteronomistic emphasis on David as the chosen one points in this direction. The information that, after Sheba's uprising against David, the people of Israel was treated as a suppressed people, as a vassal nation, does not show that any intimate bond connected these two groups of people. Therefore, the composition of any historiography before Sheba's rebellion can be questioned. With the textual material available, it is impossible to answer that question. Another time when the peoples of Israel and Judah were closely connected was during the time of the Omrides, when there were intermarriages between the two royal houses and a common foreign policy. Such a period could have inspired the beginning of a 'common' historiography.

However, the Bible's reconstruction of the 'people' of Israel as twelve tribes with their origin in the prehistoric period raises the suspicion that this is part of a politically useful literary attempt to give Israel and Judah a common origin. After the fall of Israel in 722/20 BCE, the southern kingdom Judah could see itself as the remnant of the people of Yahweh.[4] This attitude, which is to be found among some prophets, may have inspired the biblical writers in their reconstruction of the 'divinely guided' history.

The presentation of the history and life of any society in the ancient

consonant. It is used also in English Bibles when the tetragrammaton is translated as Jehovah.

1. L. Rost dates the J work to the period of Solomon ('Sinaibund und Davidsbund', *TLZ* 72 [1947], col. 132). H.H. Schmid, on the other hand, maintains that the theology of the Yahwist is to be seen as a result of the problems of the fall of Judah and the Exile (*Der sogenannte Jahwist* [Zürich, 1976], p. 181).

2. Archaeologically, the Judean mountains were almost devoid of population before c. 1000 BCE.

3. The term 'forced' can be defended from the point of view that when David had nullified the Saulidic dynasty the Israelites had no other choice than to accept David as their king.

4. See my *Who were the Israelites?*, pp. 103-104.

Near East can only be a torso because of the paucity of information. In addition, it must be realized that much of what was written down was carefully selected by the writer in order to promote his viewpoint.[1] The writing may have referred to a king's 'glorious' campaigns, or his rationale for usurping the throne; it may have reflected the concepts of a religious reformer or propagandist; or it could have recounted folk-tales about past times and their heroes, the memory of which was quite blurred or not at all known. In such matters the biblical narrators were not really concerned about historical truth.[2] Their goal was not that of a modern historian—the ideal of 'objectivity' had not yet been invented. In writing their 'historiography' they maintained that their view of the past corresponded to Yahweh's view. Sometimes their historical novels are no more than that: novels. The stories about the so-called premonarchic period starting with creation are not history. They are literary creations.[3] Just as, for instance, Shakespeare wrote about Richard III, a biblical writer could compose a story about Abraham's journeys from Mesopotamia to Egypt or a story about Joseph and his brothers in Egypt. In these cases they have created some interesting pieces of literature, but not necessarily history. This is pure literature serving the purpose of religious ideology, and, in the case of the Abraham and Joseph stories, literature being used as part of a particular historiographic reconstruction.

In this connection it should be noted that 'new moral and political ideas are often presented in the guise of traditional literature or ascribed to revered personages of the distant past'.[4] Literature ascribed to such persons will naturally cause problems for the modern historiographer.

Most important for a history of the greater Palestinian area during the pre-Hellenistic period is the inscriptional material from neighboring countries, especially from Egypt, Anatolia, Assyria and Babylonia.

---

1. A. Momigliano, *Essays in Ancient and Modern Historiography*, pp. 141-42.
2. Of interest is that we do not even have an epic in the Hebrew Bible, as mentioned above.
3. Compare J. Barr, 'Story and History in Biblical Theology', *JR* 56 (1976), p. 5.
4. I.M. Diakonoff, 'A Babylonian Political Pamphlet from about 700 BCE', *Studies in Honor of Benno Landsberger on his Seventy-Fifth Birthday* (ed. H.G. Güterbock and T. Jacobsen; Assyriological Studies, 16; Chicago, 1965), p. 343. For this text, which uses the style of omens in warning the king, see F.M.T. Böhl, 'Die babylonische Fürstenspiegel', *MAOG* 11.3 (1937), pp. 1-51.

The reader may find that on occasion I have relied more on Assyrian and Babylonian inscriptions than on Old Testament texts relating to the same period. This stems from the fact that even if there are exaggerations and propagandistic tendencies in the nonbiblical material as well, the royal inscriptions of Mesopotamia have been engraved by royal scribes, who were employed by the kings in order to report and magnify the importance of their imperial campaigns and other events, such as building activities. These scribes did not invent such happenings as the capture of foreign cities, the flaying of a king, the devastation or incorporation of enemy territories, the deportation of thousands of people together with their gods, treasures, and cattle and so on.[1] It is noteworthy that there is no criticism of Akkadian kings in the Akkadian royal inscriptions. That would have been fatal for the scribe. The Old Testament 'historiographers' were not, however, royal scribes. Even if they had some knowledge about material from the monarchic period, such as the 'Book of the Deeds of Solomon' (1 Kgs 11.41)[2] and the 'Book of the Chronicles of the Kings of Israel/Judah' (1 Kgs 14.19, 29),[3] they probably used it freely. The references to these 'books' are of a nature such that nothing is known about their contents. What is mentioned of Solomon's deeds in 1 Kings is not presented in chronological order and is, therefore, not strictly based on any annals or chronicles to which the narrator had access.[4] Most of the historiographic writings of the Hebrew Bible emerged during a time when no Israelite or Judahite king was in power, so the writers could not be punished or censored for the antiroyal attitude they often displayed. A Judahite writer, on the other hand, denouncing an Israelite king after Jehu's *coup d'état* in 841 BCE, would have been appreciated by the Jerusalemite court.

One thing these scribes had in common was the idea that the gods directed world events. The will of the divine was behind earthly actions. For instance, wars were undertaken at the 'command' of the deities of the land, whether Ishtar, Teshub, Marduk, Amun, Ashur, Yahweh,

---

1. These numbers, however, seem sometimes to have been exaggerated.

2. It is, of course, impossible to find out how much of this chronicle goes back to the *sōpēr*, 'scribe', of the Solomonic court mentioned in 1 Kgs 11.41, nor do we know whether all the deeds of Solomon were included in this chronicle; see also J. Van Seters, *In Search of History*, pp. 301-302.

3. These Chronicles may originally have been collections by royal scribes.

4. See J. Van Seters, *In Search of History*, pp. 301-302.

Ahura Mazda or Chemosh, to name but a few.[1] The god's territory, 'cosmos', that is, his nation, had to be expanded. Those who opposed him belonged to the powers of evil and had therefore to be annihilated.

The intention of this book has not been to write a theological history of Bible lands. There are already too many of these. My goal has been to try to write a history of ancient Palestine in the same way that the history of any other country and all of its people is normally written.[2] Theological evaluations are therefore not to be found in it.[3] The aim has been to look at events as a historiographer, not through the eyes of the biblical narrators who treated the neighboring peoples as a 'disturbing' factor in the lives of Israel and Judah, God's (usually wayward) children. Because of the character of the source material, my task has been a fascinating one. At the same time it has been not only difficult, but sometimes very frustrating. This is in part due to the religious and propagandistic character of the Hebrew Bible; the Bible is not a textbook in history, and it was never intended to be one. Events were seen from a special point of view and those which were not in harmony with this ideological viewpoint may have been 'adapted' or else not considered at all.

What is regarded as history can only emerge from the result of the historiographer's work. The task of establishing what happened in the past is the ideal, but it can be no more than an interpretation; the full

1.   See the material in B. Albrektson, *History and the Gods*; H.A. Hoffner, *Or* NS 49 (1980), pp. 327-28; W.G. Lambert's criticism of Albrektson's thesis misses the point, because Lambert brings into the discussion the notion of monotheism as a distinction between Mesopotamia and Israel as far as ideas about the divine were concerned ('Destiny and Divine Intervention in Babylon and Israel', *OTS* 17 [1972], pp. 65-72). The phenomenon of monotheism, however, is not a historical fact in the Israel and Judah of the pre-exilic period. It is a literary creation imposed on the past by the Old Testament, to urge the point of view of the writers.

2.   About three and a half decades ago a German student asked me what philosophy I used in studying Old Testament history and religion. My answer was: 'None. If I have a philosophy, it is that one cannot use any philosophical system.' After that our ways parted.

3.   A theological conception of history is exemplified by a statement of R. de Vaux: 'Ultimately, however, human will and caprice have to give way to the demands of nature, which God himself uses to carry out his plans' (*The Early History of Israel* [trans. D. Smith; Philadelphia, 1978], p. 3). A philosopher of religion may come to such a conclusion after having investigated a people's religious literature, but a historian can never demonstrate how any divine plan is carried out, simply because one cannot empirically demonstrate what any divine plan looks like.

truth is never going to be revealed.[1] In principle the full truth may be called 'history', but from a scientific viewpoint only part of history can be revealed, as the crushed Mycenaean jar can only be partly restored. The available facts are the potsherds, but their history comes about in the reconstruction.

Periodization

A historical chronology of Palestine and Syria should start with the period from which the first human remains are known. That means that the earliest period, the Paleolithic Age (the Stone Age), could have begun as far back as 1,500,000 or 600,000 years ago, depending upon where the possibilities for human life were found. The earliest known Palestinian remains are from 'Ubeidiya from the so-called Lower Paleolithic period (Lower and Middle Pleistocene pluvial periods).[2] The site is located in the central Jordan Valley about 23 km south of Lake Tiberias near modern Afikim.[3]

The Paleolithic time is usually divided into three subperiods and is followed by the Epipaleolithic period, which in the Levant is also divided into subperiods according to archaeological remains, such as tools and other artifacts. The following chronological chart (pp. 54-55) gives the approximate dates of the different periods dealt with in this book. It should be remembered that a period does not start simultaneously in the different geographical areas. Thus, for instance, Egyptian chronology of the Delta in the Middle Bronze Age cannot be used for Palestine, which had its own development, even if it was influenced by

---

1. The following presentation will therefore include many statements about what could possibly have happened. I have sometimes been criticized for using too many 'coulds', which I would rather do than stating some uncertainty as a fact. The historian's method is that of a detective. Because not àll the facts are known, we have to use logic and draw conclusions from what is known and from what (therefore) is or 'could' be possible.

2. The pluvial periods are: the Lower Pleistocene (c. 600,000–300,000 BCE), the Middle Pleistocene (c. 300,000–50,000 BCE) and the Upper Pleistocene (c. 50,000–30,000 BCE); see the résumé by A. Anati, *Palestine before the Hebrews* (London, 1963), pp. 59-61.

3. For the reports, see L. Picard and U. Baida, *Geological Report on the Lower Pleistocene Deposits of the 'Ubeidiya Excavations* (Jerusalem, 1966); M. Stekelis, *Archaeological Excavations at 'Ubeidiya, 1960–1963* (Jerusalem, 1966); P.V. Tobias, *A Member of the Genus* Homo *from 'Ubeidiya* (Jerusalem, 1966).

Egypt. Or, the beginning of the Persian period (539 BCE) cannot have had any effect on the material culture in Palestine and Syria before some time had elapsed.

Chronological Periods

Lower Paleolithic	ca. 1,500,000–100,000 BCE
Middle Paleolithic	100,000–40,000 BCE
Upper Paleolithic	45/40,000–18,000 BCE
Epipaleolithic	18,000–4500 BCE
Kebaran	10,000–9000 BCE
Natufian	9000–8500 BCE
Prepottery Neolithic A (PPNA)	8500–7300 BCE
Prepottery Neolithic B (PPNB)	7300–6000 BCE
Pottery Neolithic	6000/5500–4500 BCE[1]
Chalcolithic	4500–3500/3200 BCE
Bronze Age	3500/3200–1200/1100 BCE
Early Bronze I (Late EB I = Egyptian Dynasty 0)	3500/3200–3100 BCE[2]
Early Bronze II (Dyn. I–III)	3100–2700/2650 BCE
Early Bronze III (Dyn. IV–VI)	2700–2250 BCE
Early Bronze IV (Intermediate period)	2250–2000/1950 BCE[3]
Middle Bronze I[4] (Old MB IIA)	1950–1800 BCE
Middle Bronze II (Old MB IIB–C)	1800–1550/1540 BCE
Late Bronze I	1550–1400 BCE
Late Bronze II	1400–1200/1100 BCE[5]

1. The period 6000–3750 BCE is called 'Developed Neolithic' by A.M.T. Moore, in 'The First Farmers in the Levant', *The Hilly Flanks and Beyond* (Festschrift R.J. Braidwood; SAOC, 36; Chicago, 1983), pp. 11-42. For the Neolithic and Early Bronze Ages, see also L.E. Stager, 'The Periodization of Palestine from Neolithic through Early Bronze Times', *Chronologies in Old World Archaeology* (ed. R. Ehrich; Chicago, 1989), pp. 85-114; compare H. Weippert, *Palästina in vorhellenistischer Zeit*, pp. 27-32.

2. The beginning of EB I at Bab edh-Dhra' is dated to c. 3500 BCE by G.R. Bentley, in 'Kinship and Social Structure at Early Bronze IA Bab edh-Dhra', Jordan: A Bioarchaeological Analysis of the Mortuary and Dental Data' (PhD dissertation, University of Chicago; Chicago, 1987), pp. 80-87.

3. For the different suggestions about the terminology (Intermediate, EB–MB, or EB IV), and the dates, see below, Chapter 3.

4. This terminology is also used by R. de Vaux, *The Early History of Israel*, p. 833.

5. Because the use of iron was slow in coming, and because there is no real break in pottery tradition around 1200 BCE, one may see the Iron Age as starting at most places later than 1200 BCE.

Iron Age	1200/1100–539 BCE
Iron I	1200–1000 BCE
Iron II	1000–539 BCE[1]
Persian Period	539–332 BCE[2]

1. The Neo-Babylonian period (c. 600–539 BCE) could also be labeled Iron III.
2. This refers to the political dominions of the Persian empire. From the point of view of material culture, this period could as well be characterized as the Greco-Persian era.

Chapter 1

THE LAND

The Name

For about two thousand years the name Palestine has been used internationally for the lands on both sides of the Jordan river, Cisjordan and Transjordan. The name Palestine will here be used for the same territory, namely, to refer to the area from southern Syria (the Beqa' Valley) to Egypt and the Sinai, and from the Mediterranean to the Arabian desert (see Maps 1 and 2). The Greek historian Herodotus (1.105, 3.5) called Cisjordan the Palestinian Syria or sometimes only *Palaestina*. Thus, there is a tradition from at least the fifth century BCE for the use of this name. Clearly Herodotus did not invent the name but used an already common term. It is derived from the Akkadian *palaštu, pilištu*, in Hebrew *p^eleset*, Aramaean *p^elištā'în*, Egyptian *p-r-st*, which refer to the Philistines.[1] Herodotus' use of the term shows that its content had expanded in the Persian period and that it referred to the people of the coastal areas from Gaza to Carmel.[2] Greek merchants called the whole coastal area Syria, which was the territory with which they came into contact. They distinguished, however, between Syria of the Phoenicians (= Syria) and Syria of the Palestinians

---

1. See S. Parpola, *Neo-Assyrian Toponyms* (AOAT, 6; Neukirchen–Vluyn, 1970), p. 272. It is possible that *pilištu* refers to Palestine in general; cf. D.J. Wiseman, 'Two Historical Inscriptions from Nimrud', *Iraq* 13 (1951), pp. 21-26. The name *palaštu* is known from an inscription by Adad-nirari III (end of the nineteenth cent. BCE): D.D. Luckenbill, *ARAB*, I, §734; A.L. Oppenheim, in *ANET*, p. 281. H. Tadmor reads, however, *mat ḫat-te* instead of *KUR pa-laš-tu* ('Note on the Saba'a Stele of Adad-nirari III', *IEJ* 19 [1969], pp. 46-48).

2. Cf. M. Noth, 'Zur Geschichte des Namens Palästina', *ZDPV* 62 (1939), pp. 136-37 (= *Aufätze zur biblischen Landes- und Altertumskunde*, I [ed. H.H. Wolff; Neukirchen–Vluyn, 1971], pp. 302-303).

(= Palestine south of the Carmel range).[1] In the Roman period the understanding of the name Palestine had widened and included also the interior; thus it was natural that Palestine became the official name for their provinces after 135 CE, i.e., at the time when the term Judea officially went out of use.[2] Around 400 CE the western part (Cisjordan) together with western Transjordan was split up into *Palaestina prima* and *secunda*, and the territory south of Idumaea became *Palaestina tertia*. Militarily these provinces were under the command of a so-called *dux Palaestinae*, as the provinces east of Palestine were under a *dux Arabiae*. *Palaestina prima* comprised the territory south of the Carmel range, the Jezreel Valley, the Beth-Shan Valley and Pella down to Raphia in the south and the western part of Transjordan south of Pella to the Dead Sea in the east. North of the line Pella–Carmel was *Palaestina secunda* including northern Transjordan and most of Galilee as far as Lake Huleh. *Palaestina tertia* (*salutaris*) was the territory south of the Arnon, Idumaea, and south of the Raphia area; in other words, it was mainly the territory of the Nabateans.[3] Because the Hebrew Bible was written long before Palestine became an official name for the country, it naturally will not be found in the Old Testament. After the Arab conquest the former Roman-Byzantine provinces of Palestine including Transjordan were called *Urdunn*, Jordan, but for the western part the old name *Filastin*, Palestine, was retained.[4]

Syria is the Greek name for Aram (and the Aramaeans). Thus it

1.   M. Noth, *The Old Testament World* (trans. V. Gruhn; London, 1966), p. 8 (Ger. edn *Die Welt des Alten Testaments* [Berlin, 1953], pp. 4-6); A.F. Rainey, 'The Satrapy "Beyond the River"', *AJBA* 1 (1969), pp. 51-53.

2.   According to A. Alt, the Roman *limes Palaestinae* was created after the war and destruction of Jerusalem in 70 CE, 'Limes Palaestinae', *Palästinajahrbuch* 25 (1930), pp. 43-82. For the borders with Arabia, see G.W. Bowersock, 'Limes Arabicus', *Harvard Studies in Classical Philology* 80 (1976), pp. 219-29; M. Gichon, 'Research on the Limes Palestine: A Stocktaking', in *Roman Frontier Studies*, III (ed. W.S. Hanson and L.J.F. Keppie; BAR, 71.3; Oxford, 1980), pp. 843-64; S.T. Parker, 'Towards a History of the Limes Arabicus', *Roman Frontier Studies*, III (ed. W.S. Hanson and L.J.F. Keppie), pp. 865-67.

3.   See M. Avi-Yonah, *The Holy Land from the Persian to the Arab Conquests (536 BCE to 640 CE): A Historical Geography* (Grand Rapids, MI, 1966), pp. 108-25, and idem, *Map of Roman Palestine* (London, 1940).

4.   Cf. A.-S. Marmardji, *Textes géographiques arabes sur la Palestine* (Paris, 1951), pp. 160-61.

occurs in the Greek translation of the Old Testament, the Septuagint (LXX). The Arabic form is *al-suri, suriya*. Usually Syria has been seen as being a Greek abbreviation for Assyria. It is not known when the Greeks started to use the name Syria.[1] Some medieval writers have, however, derived the name from *Ṣur*, Tyre. This derivation could be old and could thus explain why the gospel of Mark uses the term 'Syrophoenician' about a woman seeking Jesus (7.26).[2]

Another well-known name for Palestine, which is the most common one in the Bible, is Canaan. The earliest known reference to this name, read as LÚ*ki-na-aḫ-num^meš* 'Canaanites', is in a letter from Mari (on the Euphrates) to Iasmah-Adad from the eighteenth century BCE.[3] It is preceded by LÚ*ḫabbatum*, 'robbers', and could therefore indicate that they were all rebellious soldiers.[4] The letter does not give any information about the territory of these Canaanites. Hurrian inscriptions from Nuzi (fifteenth cent. BCE) use *kinaḫḫu* as a reference to the west, and in Egyptian inscriptions from the time of Amenhotep II (fifteenth cent.) we meet the form *ki-n-'-nu*. The statue of king Idrimi of Alalakh[5] mentions *ma-at ki-in-a-nim*, 'the land of Canaan', which could be a reference to the Phoenician coast.[6] From there Idrimi

---

1. Consult E. Honigmann, 'Syria', in *Paulys Realencyclopädie*, 2nd ser., VIII (Stuttgart, 1932), pp. 1549-50.

2. See C. Cannuyer, 'A propos de l'origine du nom de la Syrie', *JNES* 44 (1985), pp. 133-37. It has also been suggested that the name Syria is a Greek rendering via Coptic *ša(i)ri*, supposedly rendering an old Egyptian designation for southern Syria and Palestine, namely *ḥrw*. There are some examples of Egyptian *ḥ* rendered with an *š* in Coptic, J.A. Tvedtnes, 'The Origin of the Name "Syria"', *JNES* 40 (1981), pp. 139-40.

3. G. Dossin, 'Une mention de canaanéens dans une lettre de Mari', *Syria* 50 (1973), p. 282; A.F. Rainey, 'Toponymic Problems', *Tel Aviv* 6 (1979), pp. 158-62.

4. Thus M. Weippert, 'Kanaan', *Reallexikon der Assyriologie*, V (Berlin, 1980), p. 352.

5. Idrimi probably reigned sometime during the first half of the fifteenth cent. BCE. J.M. Sasson dates the inscription to the thirteenth cent. BCE ('On Idrimi and Sarruwa, the Scribe', *Studies on the Civilisation and Culture of Nuzi and the Hurrians in Honor of Ernest R. Lacheman* [ed. M.A. Morrison and D.I. Owen; Winona Lake, IN, 1981], p. 323).

6. S. Smith, *The Statue of Idrimi* (London, 1949), pp. 14-15, and p. 73, line 63-64; cf. E.L. Greenstein and D. Marcus, 'The Akkadian Inscription of Idrimi', *JANESCU* 8 (1976), pp. 59-96.

sailed with boats he had built to Mt Cassius[1] when he started his campaign back to Alalakh. In Ugaritic there occurs the form *kn'ny*, meaning 'the Canaanite'.[2] The etymology of the word is unknown, but with S. Moscati one may assume that *kn'n* was an old Semitic word for the country[3] or part of it. However, there is really no information in the non-biblical texts about what territory it referred to other than a Hittite text that places Canaan between Alalakh and Amurru and follows it with a reference to Sidon and Tyre.[4] In many Egyptian texts Canaan refers to southern Syria and Palestine; the city of Gaza, for instance, is sometimes called the city of Canaan. The connection with the crimson dye works which occurs in the Hurrian *kinaḫḫu* may be a later development.[5] As to the Greek *phoinix*, this was originally used for the crimson and dark purple colors and also for the red-brown date palm;[6] its association with Phoenicia and the Phoenicians is thus secondary.[7] It became a name for the coastland north of Carmel. 'When the Myceneans gained knowledge of the vastly more exclusive dye works on the Syrian coast, they used their own name for the crimson color produced by the Syrian dye-workers.'[8] This same color was called *kinaḫḫu* by the Sidonians, but they do not seem to have called the country by the same name. The crimson and textile industry meant that the people of Canaan, whom we for convenience call

1. This has been identified with modern Jebel el-Aqra' (Sapanu in the Ugaritic texts).

2. A. Herdner, *Corpus des tablettes en cunéiformes alphabétiques* (Paris, 1963), text 91, 7.

3. 'Sulla storia del nome Canaan', *Studia Biblica et Orientalia*, III (AnBib, 12; Rome, 1959), pp. 266-67. See also R. de Vaux, 'Le pays de Canaan', *JAOS* 88 (1968), p. 25, and M. Astour, 'The Origin of the Terms "Canaan", "Phoenician", and "Purple"', *JNES* 24 (1965), pp. 346-47.

4. See A. Goetze, 'Hittite Rituals, Incantations, and Descriptions of Festivals', *ANET*, p. 352.

5. E.A. Speiser, *Oriental and Biblical Studies: Collected Writings of E.A. Speiser* (ed. J.J. Finkelstein and M. Greenberg; Philadelphia, 1967), pp. 324-25.

6. See H.G. Liddell and R. Scott, *A Greek–English Lexicon*, II (new and revised edn; Oxford, 1925–1940), p. 1948.

7. See also C. Vandersleyen, 'L'étymologie de phoïnix, "phénicien"', in *Phoenicia and the East Mediterranean in the First Millennium BCE* (Orientalia Lovaniensia Analecta, 22; Leuven, 1987), pp. 19-22.

8. J. D. Muhly, 'Homer and the Phoenicians', *Berytus* 19 (1970), pp. 33-34.

Canaanites,[1] became well-known in the Iron Age as merchants.[2] In texts from the time of Amenhotep II Canaanites are mentioned among the nobles of *Reṯnu*, another Egyptian name for Palestine.[3] From an inscription of pharaoh Merneptah (1212–1202 BCE), the so-called Israel stela, we learn after an analysis of its literary structure, that the term Canaan was used for the lowlands and the coastal area of Palestine. The central hill country was probably called Israel.[4] This is the earliest occurrence of the name Israel. Another Egyptian term for southern Syria and Palestine is *ḫrw*, Kharu (Akkadian Hurru), and which is common in inscriptions from the Nineteenth Dynasty. From the list of the 101,000 prisoners taken by Amenhotep II, the majority were Hurrians (36,300); only 640 are called Canaanites.[5] This indicates that 'Canaanite' was not an ethnic term and that the largest ethnic group was non-Semitic, assuming that the Egyptian scribe did not include some Semitic groups under the label Hurrian.

In the biblical traditions Canaan is a name for the ancestor of the Canaanites, a son of Ham, Gen. 9.18-19. In 10.15-18 he is the father of Sidon and Heth, and of the Jebusites, Amorites, Girgashites, Hivites, Arkites, Sinites, Arvadites, Zemarites and Hamathites. This is quite unrealistic, as is the information that Canaan should be the brother of Cush, Misraim and Put (Gen. 10.6). The writer here presents the peoples of past times from Anatolia to Nubia as Canaanites or as being related to the Canaanites in order to maintain that the people of Judah are different.[6]

1.   'Canaanite' is thus not an ethnic term.
2.   Compare also Ezek. 16.29; 17.4; Prov. 31.24; and Job 40.30 (Eng. 41.6). Note also that in Isa. 23.11 the 'fortress of Canaan' is a reference to Tyre and the Phoenicians. In Hos. 12.8-9. Canaan is in parallel with Ephraim, and may therefore refer to the northern kingdom; see H.W. Wolff, *Hosea* (BKAT 14.1; Neukirchen–Vluyn, 1961), p. 277.
3.   J.A. Wilson, 'Egyptian Historical Texts', in *ANET*, p. 246; A. Kempinski, *Syrien und Palästina (Kanaan) in der letzten Phase der Mittelbronze IIB-Zeit (1650–1570 v. Chr.)* (Ägypten und Altes Testament, 5; Wiesbaden, 1983), pp. 63-64.
4.   See G.W. Ahlström and D. Edelman, *JNES* 44 (1985), pp. 59-61; G.W. Ahlström, *Who were the Israelites?*, pp. 37-42. For a different understanding of the structure of the poem, see F. Yurco, *JARCE* 23 (1986), pp. 189-215.
5.   See W. Helck, *Beziehungen Ägyptens*, p. 344; J.A. Wilson *ANET*, pp. 246-47.
6.   Because the Hittites (Heth) are included, one may suspect that the writer did not know anything about the Hittite empire, which went out of existence c. 1200 BCE.

The author of Genesis 10 ('The Table of the Nations') also presents an old opinion about the extent of Canaan, when he says that this country went from 'Sidon in the direction of Gerar as far as Gaza, in the direction of Sodom, Gomorrah, and Admah and Zeboiim, as far as Lasha' (10.19). Here again we meet the idea of Canaan as referring to the coastal area going inland south of the central hill country. This should be compared with the borders of Canaan as they are outlined in Num. 34.2-12, which stretch from the territory just north of Byblos down to the Wadi el-'Arish in the south. In the east the border was the river Jordan south of the Sea of Galilee, but northern Transjordan (Golan, Bashan, Hauran) and the Damascus territory, that is, the former Egyptian province of Upe, were included. This almost reflects the territories under Egyptian rule in the Late Bronze period, save Transjordan south of the Sea of Galilee. Num. 13.29 states that the Canaanites 'dwell by the sea, and along the Jordan', but not in the hills. The name Canaan is thus not used in the biblical texts for Transjordan south of the river Yarmuk, that is, most of the modern state of Jordan. From the above it is clear that Canaan was a name for the more densely populated areas of the land, where the cultural and urban centers were located. The central hill country did not really count, because it was very sparsely settled.

Geography

To write the history of ancient Palestine can be nothing other than an attempt to present a probable picture based on such different kinds of source material as archaeological remains (prehistoric or historic) and written material, as well as to indicate how the climate and the physical structure of the country and its natural resources played a certain role in influencing different types of life-style. The cultivated area of Syria-Palestine is fairly narrow, consisting mainly of mountainous regions between the Mediterranean and the Syro-Arabian desert. In the north, at Hamath, this area is c. 350 km wide at the point where it turns southeast following the Euphrates. The mountains of Palestine

Moreover, the Jebusites, Amorites, and so on, are not personified in this text. They are usually mentioned in postexilic texts as being the 'prehistoric' inhabitants of the hill country (Neh. 9.8), and because the Hamathites are included, we may suspect that they represent the peoples of the province Samerina, i.e., the former Israel.

are a continuation of the Lebanon mountains and the Amanus range in northern Syria.[1]

The geographical contrasts are very pronounced within the relatively small area called Palestine.[2] It is c. 320 km from Mt Hermon in the north to Kadesh-Barnea in the south and c. 130 km from Tel Aviv to the desert east of Amman in Jordan. The country is split in the middle by the Jordan Rift, which is a part of the c. 6500 km long Syro-African Rift that starts in Turkey at Antioch. The rift continues with the Beqa' and Orontes Valleys, the Jordan Valley, the Dead Sea, the Araba Valley, the Gulf of Aqaba, the Red Sea, and ends in Lake Malawi in Africa.[3] The length of the rift from the area of Mt Hermon to the Gulf of Aqaba is about 428 km.[4] The rift drops to about 283 m below sea level at the southern end of Lake Tiberias and to c. 390 m below sea level at the Dead Sea. At times there has been intense earthquake activity along this rift. The Jordan Valley, including the Dead Sea and the Araba, was a lake in prehistoric times (c. 100,000–18,000 BCE), the Lisan Lake. It has been thought that the lake dried out about 13,000–11,000 years ago. The southern basin of the Dead Sea was probably refilled c. 10,000–9000 years ago.[5] On both sides of the rift are mountainous regions, which in the east peter out into the Arabian desert and in the west descend into the Sharon plain with its 'Mousterian Red Sand' (excellent for the cultivation of citrus) and the limestone hills of the lowlands (the Shephelah). Between this and the coastal area with its dunes lies an alluvial plain, which became known as the territory of the Philistines. The coast is unbroken south of the

---

1.   For the geological formations, see conveniently D. Baly, *The Geography of the Bible* (2nd edn; New York and London, 1974), pp. 15-16.

2.   Cf. D. Baly, *The Geography of the Bible*, pp. 28-30; E. Orni and E. Efrat, *Geography of Israel* (3rd edn; Jerusalem, 1971), pp. 3-132; Y. Aharoni, *The Land of the Bible* (2nd edn; Philadelphia, 1979), pp. 21-42. Cf. also D.C. Hopkins, *The Highlands of Canaan: Agricultural Life in the Early Iron Age* (The Social World of Biblical Antiquity Series, 3; Sheffield, 1985), pp. 53-75.

3.   See E. Orni and E. Efrat, *Geography of Israel*, pp. 80-105, and the maps beginning on p. 80.

4.   A. Hadidi, 'The Archaeology of Jordan: Achievements and Objectives', *Studies in the History and Archaeology of Jordan*, I (ed. A. Hadidi; Amman, 1982), p. 15.

5.   C. Vita-Finzi, 'The Prehistory and History of the Jordanian Landscape', *Studies in the History and Archaeology of Jordan*, I (ed. A. Hadidi; Amman, 1982), p. 25. Cf. D. Baly, *The Geography of the Bible*, pp. 26-27.

Carmel range, presenting only a few spots for natural harbors, such as at Dor and Joppa. The plain south of the Carmel widens as one goes south. At Caesarea it is c. 10 km wide, at Tel Aviv about 17 km, and at Gaza c. 40 km. This is in sharp contrast to the Lebanese coast, which has few plains. Byblos is an exception. Sand from the Nile has been carried by the undercurrents of the Mediterranean and deposited as far as Byblos, forming a fertile plain which has been enriched by the soil from the highlands carried down by the rains.

There are several rifts in Western Palestine, the largest being the Esdraelon Valley (the Plain of Jezreel), which cuts the mountainous region into two parts, creating easy access from the sea to Transjordan. The highlands north of the valley reach their highest point at Jebel Jarmaq (Har Meron), 1208 m (3963 ft). The territory south of the Esdraelon down to the Judean mountains, that is the northern central highlands, is called *har 'eprāyim*, Mt Ephraim, in the Bible.[1] Most parts of the highlands are composed of limestone and dolomite, with chalk in the foothills. The soil that has resulted from the weathering of the hard (Cenomian) limestone in these regions is the red, porous *terra rossa*, which is good for agriculture, but because of its shallowness can easily be washed away from the slopes during the heavy rains, something the plains benefit from. The highest point in the central highlands is Jebel el-'Asur (Baal Hazor) which reaches a height of 1016 m (3333 ft). Mt Ephraim presents, however, more plains, valleys and meadows, than the mountains of Judah, which makes the former territory more suitable for settlements and agriculture than the Judean mountains. Still, the mountains have naturally been much more sparsely settled through the centuries than the lowlands (the Shephelah) and the coastal areas.

The so-called Wilderness of Judah (*midbār*), also called Yeshimon,[2] is the territory east of a line from Jerusalem–Bethlehem–Tekoa–Arad down to the Dead Sea. It is an arid region with bare slopes and several wadis cutting sharply into the chalky cliffs, which also have a large amount of caves. The territory is very inhospitable, and was mainly uninhabited in ancient times.[3]

Transjordan is divided into three regions by nature: the Jordan

1. Josh. 17.15; 19.50; Judg. 3.27; 1 Sam. 1.1, etc.
2. Yeshimon occurs in Num. 23.28 as being opposite Peor in Moab.
3. D. Baly, *The Geography of the Bible*, p. 36, and fig. 15. See also E. Orni and E. Efrat, *Geography of Israel*, pp. 66-68.

Valley, the highlands and the desert.[1] The river Jordan's sources are close to Mt Hermon and Banias. The river flows through the swampy Huleh Valley (now mostly drained) to the only fresh-water lake in Palestine, Lake Tiberias, and from there down to the Dead Sea. The highlands, which are part of the Arabian plateau, can be divided into five regions, namely, Bashan with the Jolan (Golan, i.e., the Gaulanitis of antiquity), the 'Aijlun-Irbid region (Gilead) between the Wâdī Yarmuk and the Wâdī Zerqa, the plateau of Ammon, the tableland of Moab, and in the south the mountains of Edom. The mountains of 'Ajlun reach a height of 1260 m. The wadis or canyons of Ḥasa (Zered), Mujib (Arnon), Zerqa (Jabbok), and Yarmuk with their rivers (all tributaries of the Jordan river) were obstacles for human contact; thus these were natural borders in ancient times. Wâdī Mujib, for instance, has rocks which are sometimes almost perpendicular and about 500 m (1600 feet) high (see Fig. 1). Most of the mountains consist of limestone and Nubian red sandstone. Edom (from *'dm*, 'red') derived its name from this sandstone. On the Edomite plateau in the south the mountains reach a height of c. 1000 to 1700 m. The highest peak is Jebel Rumm, 1754 m. Edom can be divided into three parts: Paran, which is west and southwest of the Araba, Seir, the mountainous area east of the Araba,[2] and Teman east of Seir.

Most of the territory of Bashan is north of the Yarmuk river, stretching eastwards to the Hauran (Jebel Druze). This is a very fertile region,[3] rich in basalt soils, as well as basalt rocks, which is a sign of volcanic activities. Unlike the rest of Transjordan, Bashan slowly ascends towards the east and the mountains of Hauran. As a result, the rainfall is abundant in the east in contrast to the rest of the country. The 'Ajlun-Irbid district (Gilead) is more wooded than the rest of the country. It is the part of Jordan which more than other areas resembles Mt Ephraim in Cisjordan in landscape, flora and climate.[4] Its highest

---

1. See more specifically E. Orni and E. Efrat, *Geography of Israel*, pp. 106-22. Cf. D. Baly, *The Geography of the Bible*, pp. 31-33. For the geology of Transjordan, see also A. Konikoff, *Transjordan: An Economic Survey* (2nd edn; Jerusalem 1946, pp. 7-9; C. Vita-Finzi, 'The Prehistory and History of the Jordanian Landscape', *Studies in the History and Archaeology of Jordan*, I (ed. A. Hadidi), pp. 23-27.

2. Heb. *śē'ir* means hairy, and refers to the woods of the mountains.

3. Cf. the figure of speech 'the cows of Bashan' in Amos 4.1.

4. E. Orni and E. Efrat, *Geography of Israel*, p. 113.

peak is Umm al-Daraj, 1245 m. The southern border of this area is the Wâdī Zerqa (Jabbok), one of the largest rivers in Transjordan.

South of the Wâdī Zerqa is the territory which in biblical times was inhabited mainly by Ammonites and Moabites. The mountains of Ammon slope gradually into the Madaba plain in the south; thus there is no sharp geographical feature that separates Ammon from Moab. In the north the border of this area is the Wâdī Zerqa. The southern border is Wâdī Hasa (Zered). Moab is split into two parts through the canyon-like Wâdī Mujib (Arnon), south of which is the so-called Moab Plateau. In the south this plateau reaches a height of over 1200 m. The plateau of Moab is thus higher than the Judean Hills, giving it a greater rainfall than the Judean mountains.

West of the Araba and south of the Judean Hills is the Negev, which can be divided into three main areas, the Paran plateau in the south, the hilly Central Negev region with the Wilderness of Zin, and, in the north, the Beer-sheba depression.[1] The Paran region is very dry and barren and because of its cliffs not easy to pass through. The Beer-sheba depression is rich in loess soil. This consists of small grain (0.04–0.02 mm in diameter) quartz and feldspar and some chalk. The soil can be transported by the wind and be blown far away from its origin, which is usually the desert. The loess of the Negev comes from the Sinai, 'where weathering provides a constant supply of dust particles'.[2] This soil is good for agriculture, but during the winter rains can 'coalesce into a hard crust which is impenetrable to seepage of additional rainwater into the subsoil'. This can force the rainwater to collect, causing damaging floods.[3] The western Beer-sheba region has about 500 sq. km of sand dunes, which continue down into the northern Sinai as a sandy desert.

The Sinai peninsula[4] is not part of Palestine, but because of its

1. E. Orni and E. Efrat, *Geography of Israel*, pp. 15-30, D. Baly, *The Geography of the Bible*, pp. 34-36.

2. M. Evenari, L. Shanan and N. Tadmor, *The Negev: The Challenge of a Desert* (Cambridge, MA, 1971), p. 44.

3. E. Orni and E. Efrat, *Geography of Israel*, p. 28. Examples of well-known loess soil areas (even if their consistency is different) are the Gobi desert in northern China and the black soil of Russia.

4. R. Weill, *La Presqu'île du Sinai: Etude de géographie et l'histoire* (Bibliothèque de l'étude des Hautes Etudes; Paris, 1908). Cf. J. Ball, *The Geography and Geology of West-Central Sinai* (Cairo, 1916); E. Orni and E. Efrat, *Geography of Israel*, pp. 123-32.

geographical location between Egypt proper and Palestine it has a place in a history of Palestine. The peninsula is triangular in form and comprises c. 61,000 sq. km. Geologically, Sinai is a part of N. Africa, but is now separated from it by the Suez Canal. The northern part of the peninsula consists of a great massif reaching a height of about 1400–2600 m. It slopes toward the Mediterannean Sea, and in the north consists mainly of plains and sand dunes. The southern part of Sinai (a third of the peninsula) is a country of high mountain massifs and deep wadis. Besides Nubian sandstone, granite, gneiss and diorite occur. Ores of iron, manganese and copper are present, as is turquoise,[1] which was mined by the Egyptians at Serabit el-Khadem as early as the Third Dynasty (27th cent. BCE). Among the highest peaks are Jebel Musa (2285 m), Jebel Catherine (2640 m) and Jebel Serbal (2077 m).

Wâdī el-'Arish, which empties into the Mediterranean about 50 km south of Raphia (at the southern end of the Philistine coast), has been seen as a natural border between Palestine and Egypt. This, for instance, is the case in Assyrian inscriptions, where the wadi is called Nahal Muṣur. In Josh. 15.4 it is called the River of Egypt ('Brook of Egypt'). This wadi is so wide that it creates a basin draining the northern part of the peninsula. However, in the Late Bronze Age, with the Egyptian hegemony over Palestine the border between Egypt and Canaan was the Wâdī Gazzeh (Nahal Besor).[2] The most northern Egyptian border fortress was located at Deir el-Balaḥ, only c. 7 km SW of the wadi.[3]

Climate

Palestine is part of the Mediterranean zone and thus has a subtropical climate, except for the Jordan Valley which is almost tropical. The

1. Cf. J.G. Davey, 'Turquoise in the Sinai Peninsula', *Transactions of the Royal Geological Society of Cornwall* 16 (1928), pp. 16, 42.

2. N. Na'aman identifies Shur 'that is before Egypt' (Gen. 16.7; 25.18; 1 Sam. 15.7) with Tell el-Far'ah (S), and he therefore identifies the Brook of Egypt with Nahal Besor ('The Shihor of Egypt and Shur that is before Egypt', *Tel Aviv* 7 [1980], pp. 100-109). However, the tell is located on the southwestern side of the wadi, which would make it an Egyptian outpost.

3. See T. Dothan, *Excavations at the Cemetery of Deir el-Balaḥ* (Qedem, 10; Jerusalem, 1979); *idem*, 'Deir el-Balaḥ, 1979–80', *IEJ* 31 (1981), pp. 126-31; *idem*, 'Lost Outpost of Ancient Egypt', *National Geographic Magazine* 162 (1982), pp. 739-69.

summer is therefore hot and dry, especially in the lowlands. There are two seasons, the summer season from June to September, and the rainy season from mid-October to mid-April. The transitional period in May is a period when everything is green and the flowers are blooming. The heat and the dryness of the summer make the landscape look dead in many places. The 250 mm isohyetose (isohyet)[1] goes across the Near East from Moab in the south to the Orontes in Syria in the north, where it turns east to Hama, Aleppo and Harran. Thus west and north of this line dry agriculture is possible.

During the rainy season the temperature can sometimes reach the freezing point, and snow may at times occur in the mountains. The rainy season can be divided into two parts; the early rain (*yôreh*) which occurs in late October and/or November is an occasional rain. The season of more steady rain is January and February, when the temperature also reaches its lowest point. In March and April and sometimes also in May one can expect some rainy days. This period is called *malqôš*, the late rain, in the Bible. The whole season is termed *gešāmîm*, from *gšm*, rain, in Hebrew. Because of the geological unevenness of the country, the difference in annual rainfall between two not too distant places can be great (see Map 3). In general, the rainfall decreases from west to east and from north to south. Thus northern Syria and Lebanon can get between 700 to 800 mm per year, Haifa 650 mm, Jerusalem 580 mm, but Jericho and the western Negev c. 200 mm. In Transjordan, Bashan gets between 500–600 mm, the 'Ajlun-Irbid area 400–600 mm, Moab c. 300 mm, Edom 200 to 400 mm in the north and under 200 mm in the south. The Araba receives between 50–100 mm.[2]

Routes

Palestine has often been characterized as a cultural and economic bridge between Egypt on the one hand and Anatolia-Mesopotamia and Arabia on the other. Thus, the main routes of commerce passed through Syria-Palestine, a fact that has made this part of the Near East strategically important. Not only did caravans follow them, but also

1. This is a line drawn between places which have the same amount of average annual rainfall; the word is from the Greek *isos*, 'equal', and *hyetos*, 'rain'.
2. For the statistics, see D. Baly, *The Geography of the Bible*, pp. 54-56, and E. Orni and E. Efrat, *Geography of Israel*, pp. 135-63.

the armies of the different powers, who also built fortresses at strategic points and junctures along these roads. Because of the geologically broken character of the country there was really no choice other than to follow the 'natural' highways. The main routes followed the direction of the coast, the mountain ridges, and, in Transjordan, the fringes of the desert as well (see Map 4).

One of the most important routes was the trunk road along the coast.[1] It started at On in Egypt, passed Zoan and then turned east to Sile, from where it followed the Palestinian coast over Raphia, Gaza, Ashkelon, Ashdod, Joppa, Aphek, and via the Aruna pass to Megiddo. Another branch went over Gath and Ekron to Aphek. From Megiddo two routes went in a northerly direction; one, via Acco and Tyre, followed the Phoenician-Syrian coast. Another went NE through Hazor, where it again split into two branches, one going straight north to Qatna and Aleppo, the other passing to the east of Mt Hermon on its way to Damascus. From there it passed Tadmor in the NE and went to Mari at the Euphrates. From a south-Canaanite point of view, the road could be called 'the way of the land of the Philistines' (Exod. 13.17). In an Egyptian text (Papyrus Anastasi I) from the time of Ramses II (c. 1270), this way is called 'the Way of Horus' (Horus equals Pharaoh), and Sile is therefore characterized as the 'Fortress of the Way of Horus'. The same terminology is found in the story about Sinuhe from the nineteenth cent. BCE. This is thus the road that the Egyptian kings followed when marching with their armies to Syria-Palestine. This is also the route that the Assyro-Babylonian and the Aramaean kings followed when they campaigned in Palestine. Coming from the south to the Carmel range, one could proceed via one of three passes. The pass at the southeast end led to the Jezreel Valley in the vicinity of Ta'anak. The middle pass, Aruna, was the shortest one, but also the most narrow; it led to Megiddo. NW of Aruna was a pass leading to Jokneam via Zephath. From Megiddo another branch of this trade route went through the Jezreel Valley to Beth-shan, then through

---

1.   This route has often been called the *Via Maris*, a name that does not occur in any writings from the Roman period. The phrase is a Latin translation (Vulgate) of the Hebrew *drk hym*, 'the way of the sea', mentioned in Isa. 8.23 (Eng. 9.1). Scholars have assigned the name to the coastal road; see Z. Meshel, 'Was There a "Via Maris"?', *IEJ* 23 (1973), pp. 162-66, and cf. A.F. Rainey, who thinks that the 'Way of the Sea' went from Banias to Tyre ('Toponymic Problems [Cont.]', *Tel Aviv* 8 [1981], pp. 146-47).

Bashan to Ashtaroth where it met the Transjordanian road.

This Transjordanian route connecting Egypt with the north was known as 'the King's Highway' (Num. 20.17; 21.22). The starting point in Egypt was again On, but from there it went directly eastwards, crossing the Sinai peninsula just north of its mountainous part, Paran. At Elat, at the Gulf of Aqaba, the route turned north, transversing the plateau east of the Araba and the Dead Sea through Transjordan, where Rabbat-Ammon was an important station,[1] with junctions at roads to Cisjordan and Dumah in Arabia. Leaving Rabbat-Ammon, the King's Highway went north to Damascus. North of the Ammonite territory this road is called the Bashan road in Num. 21.33 and Deut. 3.1. Another branch of the King's Highway went to the east of the mountains of Transjordan south of Rabbat-Ammon on the fringes of the desert, and was therefore more vulnerable to attacks by bandits than the other branch.

West of the river Jordan there are not too many roads that can go in a north–south direction. Most of them go east–west, connecting the country with the coast. However, a road from Shur in the Negev passed Beer-sheba and went over Hebron to Jerusalem and from there via Bethel to Shechem and Tirza (Tell el-Far‘ah [N]). This road follows the mountain ridge that goes north–south (cf. Judg. 21.19). From Shechem another branch passes Samaria and Dothan up to the Jezreel Valley at Jenin. This road was one of the few links connecting the peoples of the southern central hills with those of Mt Ephraim. The modern road follows very much the same route. In the Jordan Valley there is also a north–south road on both sides of the river.

It is also possible to travel through the mountainous part of the Sinai peninsula to Egypt. An ancient road from Elat went south and into Wadi Feiran in the central mountain massif and continued via Wadi Mukatteb to the Gulf of Suez, where it followed the coastline up to Egypt. From Wadi Feiran another road went east to Dhahab at the coast of the Gulf of Aqaba. Along these roads both Chalcolithic and Nabatean-Byzantine remains have been found. At Dhahab a concentration of copper slag has also been found.[2]

---

1. The railroad built by the Turks followed basically the same route.

2. For these roads, see B. Rothenberg, 'An Archaeological Survey of South Sinai', *PEQ* 102 (1970), pp. 13-18; cf. G.W. Ahlström, 'A Nabatean Inscription from Wadi Mukatteb, Sinai', *Ex Orbe Religionum*, I (Studies in the History of Religions, 21; Leiden, 1972), pp. 323-24.

Natural Resources

Syria-Palestine is not rich in natural resources. This is because the country is mainly mountainous. However, because of this, at most places stone is available for building, and flint, which was mainly used for tools during the prehistoric period, is easily obtainable in the hills. Of minerals, copper ore is present in the Nubian red sandstone of the Araba Valley, for instance, at Punon and Timna,[1] and manganese also exists in the same area. Eusebius mentions that copper mines existed in Lebanon and Syria. We also know of copper ore in the area of Aleppo in northern Syria. Copper and bronze industries seem to have existed in Sidon, Tyre and Sarepta.[2] The Dead Sea yields bitumen and salt, which may have been the reason for some ancient settlements in that area already in prehistoric times.[3] Iron has been found in the Sinai peninsula and in the eastern Araba (Wâdī Feinan), in Galilee SW of Lake Tiberias, and in the mountains of Moab, 'Ajlun, and Carmel.[4] There are some iron deposits in the area of the sources of the river Jordan and north of Mt Hermon as well as in Lebanon, but the richest areas in northern Syria are in the vicinity of Iskanderum (Alexandria) and north of the city of Doliche (both now in modern Turkey).[5] Precious stones are rare in Palestine, but some turquoise has been found in the Negev. As mentioned above, in the southern Sinai turquoise was mined at Serabit el-Khadem by the Egyptians since the

---

1. Cf. the idealized picture given in Deut. 8.9, which mentions that the stones of the land are of iron and from the 'hills you can quarry copper'.

2. See R.J. Forbes, *Studies in Ancient Technology*, IX (Leiden, 1972), pp. 11-12, 65ff.

3. E. Anati, 'Prehistoric Trade and the Puzzle of Jericho', *BASOR* 167 (1962), pp. 25-27. For the bitumen, see also P.C. Hammond, 'The Nabatean Bitumen Industry at the Dead Sea', *BA* 22 (1959), pp. 40-42. See also E. Orni and E. Efrat, *Geography of Israel*, p. 479.

4. For the sources of iron and other metals in Palestine, see J.C. Waldbaum, *From Bronze to Iron* (Studies in Mediterranean Archaeology, 54; Göteborg, 1978), pp. 59-61. See also T. Stech-Wheeler, J.D. Muhly, K.R. Maxwell-Hyslop and R. Maddin, 'Iron at Taanach and Early Iron Metallurgy in the Eastern Mediterranean', *AJA* 85 (1981), p. 265; H. Liebowitz and R. Folk, 'The Dawn of Iron Smelting in Palestine: The Late Bronze Age Smelter at Tel Yin'am, Preliminary Report', *Journal of Field Archaeology* 11 (1984), pp. 265-80.

5. See R.J. Forbes, *Studies in Ancient Technology*, IX, pp. 193-95.

third dynasty. There is a possibility that the mountains of southern Sinai also contain gold, zinc, lead and tin,[1] but the ancients were not aware of this.

---

1. E. Orni and E. Efrat, *Geography of Israel*, p. 365.

Chapter 2

PREHISTORIC TIME
(by Gary O. Rollefson)

The Paleolithic Period[1]

This period is subdivided into the Lower, Middle and Upper Paleolithic, divisions of enormous duration that witnessed usually gradual changes in climate, topography and plant and animal communities with which our human antecedents interacted. The Lower Paleolithic began as early as 1.5 million years ago in the Near East and lasted until c. 100,000 years ago. It was during this time that much of the great geological Rift Valley system was sculpted, running through Syria's Orontes Valley in the north, the Beqaʻ of Lebanon, the Jordan Valley and Wadi Araba, the Red Sea, and extending through eastern Africa into the inland portions of Mozambique. This great geological crack in the surface of the earth is where the earliest known evidence of human[2] occupation of the Near East is found, for it was here that

---

1. It will be obvious in the following section on the Paleolithic that there is a remarkable bias towards the descriptions of events in the Levant and very little information on the Paleolithic of Turkey, Iraq and Iran. In fact, the bias is very real, for comparatively little field research has been conducted in the latter countries, while Syria, Lebanon, Palestine and Jordan have witnessed prolonged and intensive field investigations. Because the area outside of the Levant is known from principally isolated sites scattered over an immense area, little can be said about *patterns* of cultural development. On the other hand, the cultural patterns recognized in the Levant have general applicability for the Near East as a whole, although there are specific differences in terms of detail.

2. The term 'human' can be defined in a number of ways depending on the interest of the user. Often the term is used to refer only to anatomically modern *Homo sapiens sapiens*, while the term 'hominid' is employed for earlier ancestral forms. Philosophically, both terms are acceptable as far as the relationships that 'human' and 'hominids' had with their contemporaneous plant and animal communities. For the sake of simplicity, 'human' is used in this discussion to refer to both

ancient sedimentary deposits accumulated to protect these oldest archaeological sites. Subsequent erosion has undoubtedly destroyed most traces of human activity (as it has outside the Rift Valley system), but relatively recent exposures have revealed some protected remnants of evidence for the presence of Early Man occupation.

The Lower Paleolithic (c. 1500,000–c. 100,000 Years Ago)

The chipped stone tool industry of the Lower Paleolithic in the Near East is given the cultural designation of the Acheulian. Spanning more than a million years, this cultural tradition has been subdivided into the Early Acheulian (1.5–0.5 million years ago), the Middle Acheulian (500,000–250,000 years ago), and the Late Acheulian (250,000–100,000 years ago).

The earliest firmly dated lower Paleolithic site in the region is 'Ubeidiya, located near the southern end of Lake Tiberias.[1] The site was situated along the western shore of a lake that filled much of the contemporaneous Jordan Valley basin, although the actual geological configuration of the vicinity was different from the circumstances of today. The animal remains show a strong African affinity as reflected by the presence of elephant, hippo, crocodile, giraffe, bear, boar, bison, and many species of birds. The stone tools, which are ascribed to the Early Acheulian culture, consisted of crudely fashioned implements including chopping tools, handaxes, picks and flake tools that altogether reflect a very early stage of human cultural development. This reconstruction of primitive achievement is supported by the identification of human fossil remains to *Homo erectus*[2] and confirmed by a Potassium-Argon date of greater than 690,000 years for an overlying basalt formation.[3] Recent examination of the lifespan of certain animal species found in the artifact-bearing deposits has resulted in a 'most reasonable estimate' for the age of 'Ubeidiya at 1.4

modern human beings and ancestral fossil populations.

1.   M. Stekelis, *Excavations at 'Ubeidiya*; M. Stekelis, O. Bar-Yosef and T. Schick, *Archaeological Excavations at 'Ubeidiya, 1964–1966* (Jerusalem, 1969).

2.   P. Tobias, *A Member of the Genus Homo from 'Ubediya*.

3.   E.g. O. Bar-Yosef, 'Archaeological Occurrences in the Middle Pleistocene of Israel', *After the Australopithecines* (ed. K. Butzer and G. Isaacs; The Hague, 1975), pp. 571-604.

million years,[1] representing the earliest emergence of *H. erectus* from his African homeland.

A site of comparable age, perhaps, is known from Abu Khas in Jordan, located on a high terrace remnant above the Decapolis city of Pella a few miles southeast of 'Ubeidiya. No human or animal bones have been found at Abu Khas, but the stone tool industry is of a similar stage of development as that of 'Ubeidiya.[2] Absolute dates are not available for Abu Khas, but the geological formation from which the artifacts originated is as much as 1.2 million years old. Other sites of very early age, perhaps nearer the end of the Early Acheulian, include Evron, a frequently visited site near the Mediterranean coastal city of Nahariya,[3] and Latamne, an open air camp along the banks of the Orontes River in NW Syria.[4] Finally, a series of artifact assemblages from alluvial deposits in far northeast Iran are remarkably crude in appearance, and all of the collections appear to come from deposits of between 0.8–1.0 million years ago, attesting to an expanding colonization of Asia by *H. erectus*. [5]

The general picture of the Early Acheulian groups of *H. erectus* in the Near East is only dimly perceivable in view of the bare handful of sites attributed to this period. About all that can be said is that they appear to have been aggressive hunters of big game and smaller animal species. The quality of craftsmanship displayed in the stone tools is

1. E. Tchernov, 'The Age of 'Ubeidiya Formation (Jordan Valley, Israel) and the Earliest Hominids in the Levant', *Paléoriant* 14/2 (1988), pp. 63-65. Cf. C. Repenning and O. Fefjar (Evidence for Earlier Date of 'Ubeidiya, Israel, Hominid Site', *Nature* 299 [1982], pp. 344-47), who argue for an even earlier date of 1.7–2.6 million years, a conclusion that conflicts with current evolutionary models by suggesting that *H. erectus* evolved in Asia and later colonized Africa, competing with and replacing the African hominid *H. habilis*.

2. L. Villiers, 'Final Report on Paleolithic Sampling at Abu al Khas, North Jordan', *ADAJ* 27 (1983), pp. 27-44.

3. D. Gilead and A. Ronen, 'Acheulian Industries from Evron on the Western Galilee Coastal Plain', *EI* 13 (1977), pp. 56-86.

4. J.D. Clark, 'The Middle Acheulian Site at Latamne, Northern Syria (first paper)', *Quaternaria* 9 (1966), pp. 1-68; *idem*, 'The Middle Acheulian Site at Latamne, Northern Syria (second paper)', *Quaternaria* 10 (1967), pp. 1-47. Despite the ascription of the site to 'the Middle Acheulian' in the title, many prehistorians consider the stone tools to represent an Early Acheulian industry.

5. A. Ariai and C. Thibault, 'Nouvelles précisions à propos de l'outillage paléolithique ancien sur galets du Khorassan (Iran)', *Paléorient* 3 (1977), pp. 101-108.

very rudimentary, particularly when compared to the specimens produced by later inhabitants of the region. Perhaps attention was simply directed to the functional aspects of the tools, not the elegance of the finished product.

The Middle Acheulian period is also poorly known, but, like its ancestral counterpart, the few sites should not be taken to reflect an absolutely sparse population in the region. Instead, it is very likely that the vast majority of both Early and Middle Acheulian sites have been either washed away during periods of extended erosion or that they have been buried deeply beneath sediments that have accumulated over hundreds of thousands of years. They will thus be invisible to the prehistoric archaeologist exploring modern land surfaces for clues to Lower Paleolithic habitation.

Nevertheless, the several known Middle Acheulian sites reveal improvements in the capabilities of the human groups existing at this time. Although no human skeletal remains have been found for this period in the Near East, contemporaneous evidence from elsewhere in Asia, Africa and Europe indicates that the brain size of humans was increasing throughout the period, and this expanded cranial capacity is demonstrated in the tools that were manufactured. Artifacts from the Wadi Uweinid[1] in eastern Jordan, the upper levels at 'Ubeidiya,[2] and the lowermost layers of the cave of Umm Qatafa in the desert mountains south of Jerusalem[3] exhibit a refinement in the production of handaxes and flake tools. Early Acheulian knappers used stone hammers to produce their tools, but the impact of stone on stone left gouged and severely sinuous cutting edges; Middle Acheulian tool makers added a finishing process using 'soft hammers' of bone or antler to produce sharper edges that were straighter in profile, enhancing the efficiency of the tools in butchering and other tasks.

The rare faunal associations with Middle Acheulian sites still manifest a strong African affinity, although the repeated forms of stone tools themselves indicate cultural patterns long divorced from those of the African continent. All of this serves to emphasize the singularity

1. G. Rollefson, 'A Middle Acheulian Surface Site in the Wadi Uweinid, Eastern Jordan', *Paléorient* 10/12 (1984), pp. 127-33.

2. D. Gilead, 'Some Metrical Studies of Acheulian Assemblages in Israel', *EI* 13 (1977), pp. 38-48.

3. R. Neuville, *Le paléolithique et le mesolithique du desert du Judée* (Archives de l'Institut de Paléontologie Humaine, Memoire 24; Paris 1951).

of the inhabitants of Jisr Banat Yacub to the north of Lake Tiberias.[1] Although abundant quantities of good quality flint could have been used by the groups hunting here, the preferred resource for heavy duty tools was locally available basalt, a material difficult to work into shape but very popular with human groups in Africa. Even the shapes of the implements produced by the occupants of Jisr Banat Yacub are duplicated in many African sites, but they are unique for the Near East.

In contrast to the paucity of evidence for the Early and Middle Acheulian periods, Late Acheulian sites in the Near East are abundant and can be found from the relatively lush Mediterranean zone to the now arid steppes and deserts. While it is likely that the population of the area had grown appreciably by c. 250,000 years ago, it is probably more relevant that the increased amount of evidence is traceable to better conditions of preservation and to less loss because of erosion. By the beginning of the Late Acheulian, which witnessed major changes in the techniques to manufacture a wider variety of stone tools, a new human form entered the stage: early 'Archaic *H. sapiens*' emerged as the product of the long evolutionary trends undergone by *H. erectus*, and the stage was set for rapid cultural development.

One reason (but a minor one in several respects) for the larger number of preserved sites in the Late Acheulian is the protection afforded to these deposits in cave sites.[2] Nevertheless, the principal locations adopted for the daily routine by Archaic *H. sapiens* remained in the open, and both early and recent surveys have found many dozens of Late Acheulian sites along major and minor drainage systems[3]

---

1. M. Stekelis, 'The Paleolithic Deposits of Jisr Banat Yaqub', *Bulletin of the Research Council of Israel* 9G (1960), pp. 66-90.

2. Cave sites such as Umm Qatafa and Tabun in Palestine and Yabrud in Syria are well known, and the quality of the preservation of animal bones is much better, providing a clearer picture of the dietary preferences of Archaic *H. sapiens*. Cf. D. Garrod and D. Bate, *The Stone Age of Mount Carmel*, I (Oxford, 1937); A. Rust, *Die Höhlenfunde von Jabrud (Syrien)* (Neumünster, 1950); R. Neuville, *Le paléolithic*. But such sites are clearly special and very much in the minority. Caves may have been used by many Middle Acheulian groups as well, as Umm Qatafa Layer E suggests. But caves undergo their own evolution, and many may have collapsed, covering early uses from the view of prehistorians.

3. D. Gilead, 'Lower and Middle Paleolithic Settlement Patterns in the Levant', *Problems in Prehistory: North Africa and the Levant* (ed. F. Wendorf and A. Marks; Dallas, 1975), pp. 273-82.

and on the broad expanses of the plateaux.[1]

While most of the occupations are small (c. 100 m^2 or less), others reached gigantic proportions[2] demonstrating the lucrative nature of some areas that drew visits of Archaic *H. sapiens* over and over again. One such large site (c. 15 acres in extent) is Fjaje,[3] high on the Shobak plateau astride a natural animal migration corridor. Archaic *H. sapiens* were able to congregate there in larger than normal numbers each spring, in anticipation of 'harvesting' the annual dense concentrations of herd animals moving from the winter lowlands of the deep Wadi Araba to the spring and summer pastures of Jordan's highland steppe.[4]

There are no human skeletal remains attributable to the Late Acheulian, but there are good indications of the improved capabilities of Archaic *H. sapiens* over those of Middle Acheulian humans. Handaxes, which were produced with increasing quality from the Early through the Middle Acheulian, reach a plateau of perfection in the Late Acheulian. Numerous specimens demonstrate a degree of symmetry and delicate refinement that must have exceeded by far the functional requirements for which they were intended; subjectively, one is struck by an evident sense of pride that motivated some individuals in their craft. A suite of methods to produce pre-shaped flake and blade tools (including projectile points), referred to as the 'Levallois techniques', was also greatly improved during this time, producing tools that needed only a minimum of reshaping for use and that entailed little wastage of raw materials in the process.[5] Finally,

1. E.g. A. Brosh and M. Ohel, 'Factors of Habitat Selection of Acheulian Sites at Ramat Yiron, Israel', *Paléorient* 7 (1981), pp. 23-31; J. Besançon *et al.*, 'The Lower and Middle Paleolithic in the Upper Zarqa/Khirbet Samra Area of Northern Jordan: 1982–1983 Survey Results', *ADAJ* 28 (1984), pp. 91-142; L. Copeland and F. Hours, 'Le Paléolithique du Nahr el Kébir', *Quaternaire et Préhistoire du Nahr el Kébir Septentrional* (ed. P. Sanlaville; Paris, 1979), pp. 29-119; B. MacDonald *et al.*, 'The Wâdī el-Ḥasa Survey 1982: A Preliminary Report', *ADAJ* 27 (1983), pp. 311-23.

2. M. Stekelis and D. Gilead, 'Ma'ayan Barukh: A Lower Paleolithic Site in Upper Galilee', *Mitekufat Haeven* 8 (1966).

3. G. Rollefson, 'The Late Acheulian Site at Fjaje, Wadi el-Bustan, Southern Jordan', *Paléorient* 7/1 (1981), pp. 5-21.

4. G. Rollefson, 'Late Pleistocene Environments and Seasonal Hunting Strategies: A Case Study from Fjaje, Near Shobak, Southern Jordan', *Studies in the History and Archaeology of Jordan*, II (ed. A. Hadidi; Amman, 1985), pp. 103-107.

5. J. Tixier *et al.*, *Préhistoire de la Pierre Taillee* (Cercle de Récherche et Etudes

art makes its appearance for the first time in human history in the form of a small, highly stylized human figurine of shaped scoria at Berekhat Ram.[1]

The Middle Paleolithic (c. 100,000–40,000 BCE).

If one is struck by the relatively large numbers of Late Acheulian sites compared to earlier periods, then one must be even more impressed by the mushrooming of Middle Paleolithic sites throughout the Levant. More than 600 sites were found during one three-season campaign in only part of the Wadi el-Ḥasa drainage system in Jordan,[2] for example, and nearly two-thirds of the sites located in the Kerak region were Middle Paleolithic.[3] A similar wealth of Middle Paleolithic sites has been reported from northern Jordan, Syria, and throughout the caves, rockshelters and open country of Lebanon and Palestine.[4]

Climatic conditions appear to have been especially favorable through the first part of the Middle Paleolithic, but during the last third of the period the region underwent increasing aridity, reaching a climax at about 47,000–45,000 years ago.[5] Under these changing environmental conditions, the tempo of physical and cultural evolution proceeded rapidly, and the Near East was the arena of major developments.

Préhistoriques; Valbonne, 1980), esp. pp. 44-55.

1. N. Goren-Inbar, 'A Figurine from the Acheulian Site of Berekhat Ram', *Mitekufat Haeven* 19 (1988), pp. 7-12.

2. B. MacDonald *et al.*, 'The Wâdī el-Ḥasa Survey 1981: A Preliminary Report', *ADAJ* 26 (1982), pp. 117-32; MacDonald *et al.*, *ADAJ* 27 (1983), pp. 311-23.

3. G. Rollefson, 'Chipped Stone Artifacts from the *Limes Arabicus* Surveys', *The Roman Frontier in Central Jordan* (ed. S. Parker; BAR, 340; Oxford, 1987), pp. 759-92.

4. E.g. L. Copeland, 'Chronology and Distribution of the Middle Paleolithic, as Known in 1980, in Lebanon and Syria', *Préhistoire du Levant* (ed. J. Cauvin and P. Sanlaville; Paris, 1981), pp. 239-63; A. Jelinek, 'The Middle Paleolithic of the Levant: Synthesis', *Préhistoire du Levant* (ed. J. Cauvin and P. Sanlaville), pp. 299-302; A. Marks, 'The Middle Paleolithic of the Negev, Israel', *Préhistoire du Levant* (ed. J. Cauvin and P. Sanlaville), pp. 287-98; S. Muhesen *et al.*, 'Prospections préhistoriques dans la region d''Afrin (Syrie)', *Paléorient* 14/2 (1988), pp. 145-53.

5. E.g. G. Clark, 'The Negev Model for Paleoclimatic Change and Human Adaptation in the Levant and its Relevance for the Paleolithic of the Wadi el-Hasa (West-Central Jordan)', *ADAJ* 28 (1984), pp. 225-48.

The absolute and relative chronologies that guide interpretations of the prehistoric past have changed considerably within the past decade, and the new temporal framework has caused us to rearrange our assessment of developments accordingly. The local Archaic *H. sapiens* 'stock' continued its trends towards modern *H. sapiens sapiens*, but populations in Europe, for example, diverged early in the Middle Paleolithic to become the distinctive *H. sapiens neandertalensis*, the Neandertals so maligned in popular accounts of human evolution. Neandertals differed from their counterparts in a number of respects, including skull contour, dentition and general body build.[1] Intentional burials in the Near East, sometimes involving rather elaborate ritual, as for example at Shanidar,[2] were matched by claims of similar levels of symbolism in Europe, suggesting parallel evolution in the two regions.[3]

The presence of Neandertals in the Near East, long considered to represent a logical stage of human evolution between *H. erectus* and modern *H. sapiens*, has taken on different implications. The results of recent examinations of skeletal and lithic evidence from Kebara Cave, near the Mediterranean coast between Haifa and Tel Aviv, and from Qafzeh Cave, on the outskirts of Nazareth, have challenged the view that the Near East Neandertals are involved in any way with the emergence of modern man. New absolute dates indicate that the 'transitional' or 'progressive Neandertal' fossil forms from Qafzeh and Skhul (a rockshelter not far from Haifa) did not appear late in the Middle Paleolithic, but instead had developed from early Archaic *H. sapiens* near the middle of the period, perhaps even earlier. Nevertheless, 'true' Neandertals have been found in the Near East from Palestine to Iraq, but these are seen as migrants who fled the harsh glacial conditions of Europe at c. 70,000 BCE into the more hospitable climes

---

1. On this, see the discussion in E. Trinkhaus, *The Shanidar Neandertals* (New York, 1983).

2. R. Solecki, 'Shanidar IV, a Neandertal Flower Burial in Northern Iraq', *Science* 190 (1975), pp. 880-81.

3. See the discussion in A.M. Tillier *et al.*, 'Les sepultures neanderthaliennes du Proche-Orient: Etat de la question', *Paléorient* 14/2 (1988), pp. 130-36. At Ferrassie in southwest France, for example, a 'family burial plot' and a 'children's cemetery', including 'grave offerings' in the form of flints and/or animal bones, have been discovered.

of SW Asia.[1] While intriguing in its treatment of new evidence, this hypothesis has not yet won universal acceptance.[2]

The Upper Paleolithic (c. 40–45,000–18,000 BCE)
The increasingly arid conditions in the latter half of the Middle Paleolithic undoubtedly spurred both physical and cultural adaptations among the local groups who had to struggle with less abundant resources, leading to the emergence of the Upper Paleolithic industries. A good example of this transitional process comes from the site of Boker Tachtit in the Negev Desert.[3] The lowermost levels contained a typical late Middle Paleolithic industry dominated by Levallois flakes and points. The artifacts in the middle levels showed an increasing reliance on the production of blades, the type of tool 'blank' that is the hallmark of the Upper Paleolithic demonstrated in the uppermost level at Boker Tachtit.

While a number of transitional sites are known from the southern Levant,[4] it is remarkable to notice a sudden decline in the Upper Paleolithic sites compared to the apparent proliferation of the Middle Paleolithic'.[5] Presumably this is an indication of how severely the environment had been degraded, strictly limiting the amount of available resources and therefore the number of people that could be supported across the countryside. A relatively brief period of warmer and wetter conditions prevailed from c. 30,000–25,000 BCE, but the climate turned drier and cooler again,[6] and population levels appear

---

1.   B. Vandermeersch and O. Bar-Yosef, 'Evolution biologique et culturelle des populations du Levant au Paléolithique Moyen. Les données récentes de Kébara et Qafzek', *Paléorient* 14/2 (1988), pp. 115-16.
2.   E.g. G.A. Clark and J.M. Lindly, 'The Biocultural Transition and the Origin of Modern Humans in the Levant and Western Asia', *Paléorient* 14/2 (1988), pp. 159-67.
3.   A. Marks, 'The Middle to Upper Paleolithic Transition in the Levant', *Advances in World Archaeology* 2 (1983), pp. 51-98.
4.   E.g. B. MacDonald *et al.*, *ADAJ* 27 (1983), pp. 311-323.
5.   For example, surveys in the Wadi el-Ḥasa (e.g. B. MacDonald *et al.*, *ADAJ* 27 [1983], pp. 311-23) and in the Kerak area (G. Rollefson, 'Chipped Stone Artifacts from the *Limes Arabicus* Surveys', in *The Roman Frontier in Central Jordan* [ed. S. Parker], pp. 759-92) of Jordan show a decline from c. 60-65% of the sites attributable to the Middle Paleolithic to only c. 10% assigned to the Upper Paleolithic.
6.   G. Clark, *ADAJ* 28 (1984), pp. 225-48.

never to have regained the levels of the early Middle Paleolithic.[1]

Two distinct Upper Paleolithic traditions have been identified in the Levant at this time: the Levantine Aurignacian and the Ahmarian.[2] The former tradition is characterized by long and thick blades and flakes which served as blanks for the manufacture of numerous burins and endscrapers. The Ahmarian, on the other hand, relied on delicate blades, especially a short and slender variety called 'bladelets', often blunted along one edge and frequently naturally or artificially sharpened at the point; characteristically, endscrapers and burins are rare.

Two interpretations are possible for this dichotomy. First, the two traditions are distinct cultural traditions with different 'ancestral' backgrounds. The Ahmarian may have developed in the southern Levant from an transitional Middle–Upper Paleolithic industry while the Levantine Aurignacian was the outcome of local antecedents in Lebanon and Syria. Alternatively, the differences between the Ahmarian and Levantine Aurignacian may not be cultural but functional, so that the Ahmarian group of tools was manufactured for a specific set of tasks while the Levantine Aurignacian was another 'tool kit' to be used on different kinds of resources.[3] The absence of recognized Ahmarian assemblages in the northern part of the Levant (i.e. Lebanon and Syria) suggests that the first interpretation is valid, although more intensive fieldwork in this area is probably necessary to resolve the problem.

Upper Paleolithic settlement patterns reflect a change in strategies of exploiting the depleted environment compared to those adopted by the Middle Paleolithic groups in the region. In the earlier period hunter-gatherer groups established base camps near permanent sources of water and abundant supplies of flint. From these base camps, which were occupied for weeks at a time, some of the men and

1. The relationship of regional population size and the number of sites may be misleading, for in some cases Upper Paleolithic sites of considerable size occurred along the edges of former pluvial lakes; cf. G. Clark, N. Coinman and J. Lindly, 'Paleolithic Site Placement in the Wadi Hasa, Central Jordan', *ADAJ* 30 (1986), pp. 23-40.

2. I. Gilead, 'Upper Paleolithic Tool Assemblages from the Negev and Sinai, *Préhistoire du Levant* (ed. J. Cauvin and P. Sanlaville; Paris, 1981), pp. 331-42; A. Marks, 'The Upper Paleolithic of the Negev', *Préhistoire du Levant* (ed. J. Cauvin and P. Sanlaville), pp. 343-52.

3. I. Gilead, 'The Upper Palaeolithic to Epi-Palaeolithic Transition in the Levant', *Paléorient* 14/2 (1988), pp. 177-82.

women went into the countryside on hunting expeditions or to take advantage of some maturing plant food, setting up temporary camps as the need arose if distances from the base camp were more than could be covered in a day's walk. This 'radial' pattern would be 'consistent with an environment of abundant and predictable resources',[1] which was evidently the case for the earlier Middle Paleolithic, at least.

The diminished resources (not the least of which was water) of the cooler and drier Upper Paleolithic called for a different approach. Except in special circumstances, such as along the shores of Pleistocene Lake Hasa where supplies of water, plants and animals were more secure,[2] conditions were too severe to permit the establishment of base camps, and Upper Paleolithic hunter-gatherers were forced to be highly mobile,[3] moving from opportunity to opportunity as conditions permitted or demanded. Most Upper Paleolithic sites are comparable in size (small) with low artifact density and variability. This contrasts with the Middle Paleolithic situation of large (basecamp) and small (temporary camp) sites with marked differences in artifact numbers and densities (high and low, respectively) and artifact variability (broad variety of tool types in base camps, versus highly specialized 'tool kits' in temporary hunting, quarrying and overnight camps).

The Epipaleolithic Period

Despite the warmer and moister 'climatic optimum' between 30,000–25,000 BCE, the Upper Paleolithic was generally a period of cool and dry conditions, conditions that continued to deteriorate after 18,000 BCE (see Map 5). The increasing scarcity of wild plants and animals, especially the larger game species such as equids and cattle, intensified the pressure on hunter-gatherer groups throughout the Near East. Not surprisingly, these conditions engendered further modifications of the strategies employed to obtain food. In short, virtually every digestible plant and animal resource was hunted and foraged, and comparisons of species diversity in the Epipaleolithic and Upper Paleolithic

1. A. Marks, 'The Middle Paleolithic of the Negev, Israel', *Préhistoire du Levant* (ed. J. Cauvin and P. Sanlaville; Paris, 1981), pp. 287-98.
2. G. Clark *et al.*, *ADAJ* 30 (1986), pp. 23-40.
3. A. Marks, 'The Upper Paleolithic of the Negev', *Préhistoire du Levant* (ed. J. Cauvin and P. Sanlaville), pp. 343-52.

prompted Flannery to characterize the change as the 'Broad Spectrum Revolution'.[1]

The term 'Epipaleolithic'[2] emphasizes the continuity of techniques used to manufacture stone tools seen in the Paleolithic period. This relationship is particularly evident with the Ahmarian tradition of the Upper Paleolithic; the retouched bladelets ('microliths') of the Ahmarian dominated the stone tool inventories of all the Epipaleolithic cultures.

Another aspect of the continuity from Paleolithic antecedents is seen in the increased diversity of regional traditions of tool manufacture within the approximately 10,000 years' duration of the period. Bar-Yosef has identified four contemporaneous 'Kebaran clusters' of typological variability in Palestine, the Negev and Sinai between c. 18,000–12,500 BCE,[3] to which several others have been added for southern[4] and northern[5] Jordan, and others are possible in Lebanon and Syria.[6] Similar levels of diversity can be seen throughout the Levant during the Geometric Kebaran (12,500–10,000 BCE), with particularly distinctive variants in the Negev and Sinai areas.

Perhaps the most intriguing part of the Epipaleolithic is the latest period, dominated by the Natufian culture that lasted from c. 10,000–8500 BCE. Built on the foundations established over the earlier

1. K. Flannery, 'Origins and Ecological Effects of Early Domestication in Iran and the Near East', *Prehistoric Agriculture* (ed. S. Struever; Garden City, NY, 1971), pp. 50-79.

2. The continuity of lithic traditions from the Paleolithic to the Epipaleolithic is understandable, for the environmental changes from the Pleistocene to the Holocene, which occurred during this period, consisted essentially of expansions or contractions of vegetation zones, resulting in increases or decreases of *existing* plant and animal resources during the Epipaleolithic. Major environmental *replacements*, such as those which occurred in the northern latitudes when dense forests covered former tundra zones following glacial retreats, required major cultural adjustments to cope with different animal and plant communities. The term 'Mesolithic' is usually applied to these situations of fundamental changes in human-land relationships.

3. O. Bar-Yosef, 'The Epipaleolithic Complexes of the Southern Levant', *Préhistoire du Levant* (ed. J. Cauvin and P. Sanlaville; Paris, 1981), pp. 389-408.

4. Cf. D. Henry, 'The Epipaleolithic Sequence within the Ras en Naqb–El Quweira Area, Southern Jordan', *Paléorient* 14/2 (1988), pp. 245-56.

5. B. Byrd, 'Late Pleistocene Settlement Diversity in the Azraq Basin', *Paléorient* 14/2 (1988), pp. 257-64.

6. M.-C. Cauvin, 'L'epipaléolithique du Levant', *Préhistoire du Levant* (ed. J. Cauvin and P. Sanlaville; Paris, 1981), pp. 439-41.

Epipaleolithic, the Natufians represented the culmination of the 'Broad Spectrum Revolution' and reflected the consequences of increased attention to gleaning microresources afforded by the environment.[1] Grinding stones appear as early as the late Upper Paleolithic and occur with increasing frequency in Kebaran sites,[2] but it is not clear if these artifacts were used for the processing of nuts, berries and seeds, or if they were used for the preparation of non-food resources such as minerals for pigments. The proliferation of ground stone (especially mortars and pestles) at many Natufian sites is associated with the recovery of seeds of a variety of wild plants,[3] strong testimony for the use of groundstone for food processing.

Although the seeds of most wild grasses are minute in size, they occur in such enormous quantities that they have tremendous potentials for feeding human groups. For example, enough wild wheat could be collected within two or three weeks to feed a family for more than a year.[4] Beyond abundance, seeds (particularly cereal grains) are easily processed and eminently storable, allowing collectors to provide stable supplies through the seasons following the grain harvest. Focusing on stands of wild cereals near permanent sources of water, these resources permitted the establishment of permanent settlements for the first time, and numerous Natufian hamlets have been found in the southern Levant, especially.[5]

1.   Curiously, this intensification appears to have transpired during an amelioration of the climate, when plant and animal communities began to flourish more vigorously once again. Cf. A. Horowitz, *The Quaternary of Israel* (New York, 1979), pp. 246-49.

2.   O. Bar-Yosef, 'Epipaleolithic Complexes', *Préhistoire du Levant* (ed. J. Cauvin and P. Sanlaville), p. 395.

3.   E.g. P. Edwards, 'Natufian Settlement in Wadi Al-Hammeh', *Paléorient* 14/2 (1988), pp. 309-15.

4.   J. Harlan, 'A Wild Wheat Harvest in Turkey', *Archaeology* 20 (1967), pp. 197-201.

5.   Eg. J. Perrot, 'Le gisement Natoufien de Mallaha (Eynan), Israel', *L'anthropologie* 70 (1966), pp. 437-93; P. Edwards, *Paléorient* 14/2 (1988), pp. 309-15; D. Garrod and D. Bate, *The Stone Age of Mount Carmel*, I, pp. 9-19 and 29-41; B. Byrd and G. Rollefson, 'Natufian Occupation in the Wadi el Hasa, Southern Jordan', *ADAJ* 28 (1984), pp. 150, 443; D. Kirkbride, 'Five Seasons at the Pre-Pottery Neolithic village of Beidha in Jordan', *PEQ* 98 (1966), pp. 5-61. Temporary camps of Natufian groups have been found in many locations, including Jericho, and Natufian gazelle hunters have left their traces in the desert regions of the

The social potentials of abundant and storable food and semipermanent or permanent residence were realized by many Natufian groups. In contrast to the generally small camps (c. 25–200 m^2) characteristic of the early Epipaleolithic periods,[1] Natufian settlements consisted of well-made circular semisubterranean dwellings spread over several thousand square meters, housing a total of as many as a hundred people or more in some cases. It is predictable that relationships within larger populations of permanently interacting people would be more complicated than among the two- or three-family hunting and gathering groups of earlier times. Social distinctions among the members of a community begin to appear for the first time, even at relatively small settlements such as El Wad in Mount Carmel.[2] Burial H.15 at Mallaha[3] is intriguing in its details: the head was 'couched' on a stone pillow, while other stones encircled and 'protected' the skull; a number of other stones were placed over the chest and abdomen and over the knees and elbows, 'weighing down' the body in the burial pit. Popularly referred to as the 'chieftain burial', the name suggests a position of inherited authority, but there is no reason to assume that the individual was not simply afforded special attention because of personal, not ascribed, achievement. Indeed, interpretations of the 'status' of the person are equally likely at both extremes of the scale of social regard: the man could have been well-respected, even revered, or he may have been a sociopath who inspired profound dread among the members of the society.

The Natufian period also saw a virtual explosion of symbolic expression.[4] Jewelry is known from several sites, made of animal

Levant. Cf. A. Betts, 'A Natufian Site in the Black Desert, Eastern Jordan', *Paléorient* 8/12 (1982), pp. 79-82.

1. But see M. Muheisen, 'L'epipaléolithique dans le gisement de Kharaneh IV', *Paléorient* 11 (1985), pp. 149-60, for a description of an immense Geometric Kebaran site, a 'minitell' created by innumerable visits to the edge of the steppe in eastern Jordan.

2. D. Garrod and D. Bate, *The Stone Age of Mount Carmel*, I, pp. 14-19; Plate VII. One Kebaran burial from Kharaneh IV included a gazelle horn core on either side of the skull, and, while ritualistic in nature, it does not necessarily indicate a specific social status for the deceased; cf. S. Rolston, 'Two Prehistoric Burials from Kharaneh', *ADAJ* 26 (1982), pp. 221-29.

3. J. Perrot, *L'anthropologie* 70 (1966), pp. 461-65.

4. Much of Natufian art was expressed in animal bone and teeth, and the absence of art in the Upper Paleolithic in the Near East may be due to the loss of organic materials as the result of normal decay processes, especially in the normally

bones and teeth, marine and terrestrial shell, and polished stone.[1] Carved bone sickle (?) hafts bore exquisite naturalistic renditions of animals,[2] and stylized human heads wearing head coverings (?) were carved from calcite and basalt.[3] Geometric designs also adorned basalt grinding stones and siltstone 'wall stones'.[4] All of this symbolism remains obscure in its implications of social 'meaning', but it seems clear that specialists in art and perhaps in ritual could exist for the first time, freed from a full-time pursuit for food and shelter.

The Neolithic Period

Although originally distinguished as a separate stage of cultural evolution on the basis of the appearance of 'polished stone' tools[5] (and thus the 'New Stone Age'), the importance of this period in human development was correctly identified in the economic 'revolution'[6] that transpired between c. 8500–3700 BCE. Earlier periods, from the Paleolithic through the Epipaleolithic, relied totally on the hunting and gathering of wild animals and plants to provide the food necessary to survive in an environment characterized by seasonal and annual variations in the natural abundance of such resources. During the Neolithic, to the contrary, societies increasingly manipulated the plant and animal communities they depended upon, gradually controlling the food supply with the introduction of agriculture and animal husbandry. The transformation was not 'revolutionary' in sense of an immediate replacement of one subsistence economy by another. Instead, the process was very gradual, proceeding in a series of steps that each lasted numerous centuries. The first change involved the supplementing of wild resources by the sowing and harvesting of cereal grains, and eventually agriculture provided the fundamental source of plant foods. The second change principally concerned the

ephemeral settlements that characterized the Upper Paleolithic.
   1.   See D. Garrod and D. Bate, *The Stone Age of Mount Carmel*, I, Plates XII-XV.
   2.   D. Garrod and D. Bate, *The Stone Age of Mount Carmel*, I.
   3.   D. Garrod and D. Bate, *The Stone Age of Mount Carmel*, I, Plate XIII; J. Perrot, *L'anthropologie* 70 (1966), pp. 461-65, Fig. 23 and Photos 11-12.
   4.   P. Edwards, *Paléorient* 14/2 (1988), pp. 311-12.
   5.   E.g. G. Zumoffen, 'L'age de la pierre en Phénicie', *L'Anthropologie* 8 (1897), pp. 270-83.
   6.   V. Childe, *New Light on the Most Ancient East* (4th edn; London, 1952).

acquisition of animal protein: domesticated goats contributed half of the meat supply by the middle of the seventh millennium, although the hunting of gazelle, wild pig and cattle and small carnivores made up the remainder. By the end of the seventh millennium and into the first half of the sixth, pigs, sheep, cattle and dogs had been added to the suite of domesticates. The third change occurred during the last half of the sixth millennium and provided the general 'modern structure' of the subsistence economy by segregating the pastoralism of goats and sheep in the arid steppes and deserts as a separate economic subsystem, leaving agriculture and cattle and pig husbandry as the foundation of settlements in the moister parts of the Levant (see Map 6).[1]

The Neolithic period is subdivided into two major divisions: the Aceramic (or Pre-Pottery) Neolithic and the Ceramic (or Pottery) Neolithic, distinguished, as the names imply, by the absence or presence of pottery as an element of the technological sphere. Each of these divisions is further divided according to certain economic, technological, architectural and ritual characteristics.

The Pre-Pottery Neolithic A (PPNA) (c. 8500–7600 BCE)
The date dividing the late Natufian from the beginning of the PPNA is essentially arbitrary, for the processes leading to the emergence of domestic cereals in the PPNA probably had their inception perhaps as early as the early Natufian.[2] Early PPNA sites differ little from Natufian settlements in terms of size, architectural construction and general methods of stone tool production. Thus Nahal Oren,[3] near the Mediterranean coast south of Haifa, and PPNA Jericho[4] contained circular semisubterranean houses distributed over several thousand square meters, as was also the case for the southern Jordan Valley sites of

1. I. Köhler-Rollefson, 'Resolving the Revolution: Late Neolithic Refinements of Economic Strategies in the Eastern Levant', *Archaeozoologica* 3 (1989), pp. 201-208.

2. E.g. H. Gebel, *Das Akeramische Neolithikum Vorderasiens: Subsistenzformen und Siedlungsweisen* (BTAVO, Reihe B. Geistewissenschaften, 52; Wiesbaden, 1984).

3. M. Stekelis and T. Yizraely, 'Excavations at Nahal Oren', *IEJ* 13 (1963), pp. 1-12; T. Noy *et al.*, 'Recent Excavations at Nahal Oren, Israel', *Proceedings of the Prehistoric Society* 39 (1973), pp. 75-99.

4. K. Kenyon, *Excavations at Jericho*, III (ed. T.A. Holland; London, 1981), e.g. pp. 6, 114, etc.

Netiv Hagdud[1] and Gilgal.[2] Continuity with the earlier Natufian peoples is evidenced in lithic technology and typology, and it is only the introduction of the small PPNA 'Khiamian point' and the loss of the Natufian lunate microlith that really set the two lithic traditions apart.[3]

The most distinctive difference between the late Natufian and PPNA sites is to be found in the seeds that have been preserved as the result of charring the grain during food processing: only wild forms have been found at Natufian sites, while the larger size and the presence of the rachis at PPNA sites indicates the domesticated form of wheat, barley and oats.[4]

Beyond the wild versus domesticated forms of cereals, which is likely to have been the result of accident rather than plan, there is little to suggest differences in the 'quality of life' between the Natufian and PPNA. There is little evidence that agriculture resulted in a great increase in population, for the size and number of PPNA sites is about the same as in the earlier period.

Nor is there any compelling reason to consider that the newly established farming groups accrued large stores of food to tempt hunting and gathering groups to inflict murderous raids. The 'town wall' and tower at PPNA Jericho, for example, inspired Kenyon to envision such a situation, forcing the inhabitants of Jericho to monumental efforts to protect themselves and their 'wealth' from jealous and starving neighbors.[5] But the absence of such defensive features at all of the other known PPNA sites in the Levant begs the question of why Jericho should have been singled out for attack. A different

1. O. Bar-Yosef *et al.*, 'Netiv Hagdud: A "Sultanian" Mound in the Lower Jordan Valley', *Paléorient* 6 (1980), pp. 201-206.

2. T. Noy *et al.*, 'Gilgal, A Pre-Pottery Neolithic Site in the Lower Jordan Valley', *IEJ* 30 (1980), pp. 63-82.

3. A. Ronen and M. Lechevallier, 'The Natufian–Early Neolithic Site Hatula, near Latrun, Israel', *Quartär* 35 (1985), pp. 141-64; M. Lechevallier *et al.*, 'Une occupation khiamienne et sultanienne à Hatoula (Israël)?', *Paléorient* 15/1 (1990), pp. 1-10.

4. So far oats have been found only at Gilgal. See T. Noy *et al.*, *IEJ* 30 (1980), pp. 63-82. The process leading to domesticated cereals is widely held to be unplanned, principally as the result of unwittingly assisting the spread of a genetic mutation affecting the 'rachis', a filament that holds kernels to the stalk. See K. Flannery in *Prehistoric Agriculture* (ed. S. Struever), pp. 50-79, and L. Binford, 'Post-Pleistocene Adaptations', in *New Perspectives in Archaeology* (ed. L. and S. Binford; Chicago, 1986), pp. 313-41.

5. E.g. K. Kenyon, *Digging up Jericho* (London, 1957), pp. 65-67.

interpretation of the Jericho structures points out that the location of Jericho at the mouth of a drainage system from the western mountains placed the village in jeopardy every rainy season;[1] subject to violent if rare flashfloods, the attraction of the spring at Jericho was strong enough for the inhabitants to invest in a massive diversion wall rather than abandon the area for a safer village site.

Prior to the present decade, prehistoric investigations in Iraq were very sporadic, and consequently little was known about the extent of Levantine cultures towards the east. Recently two projects have revealed that early Neolithic villages[2] were also characteristic of northern Iraq, at least, and preliminary analysis of the finds suggests a close cultural tie to the PPNA of the Levant. Nevertheless, the elegant carved bird figurines from Nemrik 9 and the styles reflected in some of the stone tools (especially projectile points) indicate several areas of cultural independence, and it might be argued that the 'close cultural ties' with the PPNA of the Levant may simply be the result of parallel but unconnected paths of cultural development.

The end of the PPNA period is as indistinct as its beginning. Most of the PPNA sites reflect postabandonment erosion that probably removed much of the crucial evidence to explain the demise of the PPNA way of life.[3] Certainly the cultural characteristics of the period that followed are very different from their PPNA counterparts, enough so that an *in situ* transition is questionable. While the onset of the PPNB is documented relatively well, the appearance of these people may have followed the collapse of the PPNA by several centuries.[4]

The Pre-Pottery Neolithic B (PPNB) (c. 7600–6000 BCE)

Although this period was once considered to be a simple and unbroken sequence of cultural development throughout the Levant, recent research has shown that the PPNB was complex and highly charged with regional distinctions. The earliest evidence of a break in stone

1. O. Bar-Yosef, 'The Walls of Jericho: An Alternative Interpretation', *Current Anthropology* 27 (1986), pp. 159-60.
2. E.g. S. Koslowski, 'Nemrik 9': A PPN Site in Northern Iraq', *Préhistoire du Levant* (ed. O. Aurenche *et al.*); T. Watkins *et al.*, 'Qermez Dere and the Early Aceramic Neolithic of N. Iraq', *Paléorient* 15/1 (1990), pp. 19-24.
3. E.g. K. Kenyon, *Archaeology in the Holy Land* (4th edn; New York, 1979), pp. 30-31.
4. K. Kenyon, *Archaeology in the Holy Land*, pp. 30-31.

tool production comes from Mureybet, in northern Syria, with the appearance of double-ended 'naviform'[1] or 'boatshaped' blade cores and the stemmed Byblos projectile point.[2] Radiocarbon samples from these earliest PPNB layers center around 7600 BCE.[3]

The sequence of occupations at Mureybet and at slightly later sites such as Tell Aswad,[4] also in northern Syria, and Cafer Höyük[5] and Çayönü[6] in southeastern Turkey suggest that the PPNB witnessed three phases throughout the Levant, although the phases in different parts of the region were by no means mirror images of each other.[7]

The Early PPNB (7600–7200 BCE)

The appearance of naviform blade cores and Byblos points (and variations on this style) at Mureybet and Cafer Höyük may seem superficial at first glance, but these two elements of tool production were to characterize the entire Levantine region from Anatolia to the Negev for the next 1500 years. Equally important to this break in stone tool manufacture, architecture in the Early PPNB sites in northern Syria and Anatolia adopted rectilinear shapes on the ground surface as opposed to round or curvilinear semisubterranean houses in the PPNA. Cultivated peas and lentils joined the agricultural crops, and it is likely that goats underwent their initial stages of animal husbandry[8] (even if the bones reflected little morphological change from

1. J. Cauvin, 'Les fouilles de Mureybet (1971–1974) et leur signification pour les origines de la sedentarisation au Proche-Orient', *Archaeological Reports from the Tabqa Dam Project, Euphrates Valley, Syria* (ed. D.N. Freedman; AASOR, 44; Cambridge, MA, 1979), pp. 19-48, esp. p. 34.
2. M.-C. Cauvin, 'L'outillage lithique', *Cahiers de l'Euphrate* 1 (1978), p. 76.
3. J. Cauvin, 'Chronologie relative et absolue dan le Néolithique du Levant Nord et d'Anatolie entre 10,000 et 8000 BP', *Chronologies du Proche-Orient* (ed. O. Aurenche *et al.*; BAR, 379; Oxford, 1987).
4. J. Cauvin in *Chronologies du Proche-Orient* (ed. O. Aurenche *at al.*); *idem*, 'Sondage à Tell Assouad', *Annales Archéologiques Arabes Syriennes* 22 (1972), pp. 85-103.
5. J. Cauvin in *Chronologies du Proche-Orient* (ed. O. Aurenche *et al.*).
6. M. Özdogan and A. Özdogan, 'Çayönü: A Conspectus of Recent Work', *Paléorient* 15/1 (1990), pp. 65-74.
7. Cf. G. Rollefson, 'The Late Aceramic Neolithic of the Levant: The View from 'Ain Ghazal', *Paléorient* 15/1 (1990), pp. 135-40.
8. D. Helmer, 'Le développement de la domestication au Proche Orient de 9500 à 7500 B.P.: Les nouvelles données d'El Kowm et de Ras Shamra', *Paléorient* 15/1 (1990), pp. 111-21; and cf. I. Köhler-Rollefson, 'Changes in Goat Exploitation at

wild goats). Hunting continued to play a major role in the economy of the early PPNB, and gazelles were among the most popular game. This constellation of technology and typology, architecture and subsistence economy contrasted sharply with the PPNA, and Cauvin ascribes these developments to the 'North Levant Facies' of the Early PPNB.[1]

While events were proceeding apace in northern Syria and the Taurus region of Anatolia, the picture for Lebanon, Palestine and Jordan remains obscure in this phase. Until recently, the absolute dates from Jericho and Beidha, near Petra in southern Jordan, constituted a long and unbroken chronology from the middle of the eighth millennium until the final century of the seventh millennium. But a recent examination[2] of the radiocarbon dates has caused a major reassessment of the cultural history of the Levant south of Damascus. Dates from the earliest and latest extremes of the Jericho and Beidha PPNB sequences are no longer valid, so there is some question regarding the time and tempo of change from the PPNA to the PPNB in the southern Levant.

At the present time, the only firmly dated evidence for the Early PPNB is the North Levant Facies. Did the southern Levant persist in an (undated) PPNA tradition while the northern region diverged along a different path of cultural evolution? Were the causes of the abandonment of PPNA lifestyles so severe that the southern Levant was simply depopulated of farmers, the region left to small and non-descript hunting and gathering groups who left little evidence of their presence? Or was a comparable change to the PPNB also true for the southern Levant, a change that simply has not been identified in the middle of the eighth millennium at sites already discovered? At the present time these questions remain unresolved,[3] although recent and unpublished research claims that developments equivalent to the North Levant Facies also occurred in the southern region[4] between 7600–7200 BCE.

'Ain Ghazal between the Early and Late Neolithic, *Paléorient* 15/1 (1990), pp. 141-46.

1. G. Rollefson, *Paléorient* 15/1 (1990), pp. 135-40.

2. H. Waterbolk, 'Working with Radiocarbon Dates in SW Asia', *Chronologies du Proche Orient* (ed. O. Aurenche *et al.*), pp. 39-59.

3. G. Rollefson, *Paléorient* 15/1 (1990), pp. 135-40.

4. A. Betts has argued that sites in the Wadi Jilat area of Jordan's eastern deserts (cf. A. Garrard *et al.*, 'Summary of Paleoenvironmental and Prehistoric Investigations in the Azraq Basin', *The Prehistory of Jordan* [ed. A. Garrard and H. Gebel; BAR, 396; Oxford, 1988], pp. 311-37) contain Early PPNB materials, although no dates have come from these layers. O. Bar-Yosef (pers. comm.) and T. Noy (pers. comm.) also note that a number of sites recently exposed from beneath deep sedimentary

The Middle PPNB (7200–6500 BCE)

This might be referred to as the 'Classic PPNB', for this is the phase when many new settlements were established for the first time; by chance, it is these Middle PPNB settlements that have also received the most intensive research, and consequently this period is better known than the other phases of the PPNB. It is also during this period that the PPNB 'culture area' began to lose much of its integrity, when regional directions of cultural development became increasingly distinct.

Before documenting the regional distinctions that emerged in the Middle PPNB, it is necessary to describe those aspects of the time that bound the greater Levant into a recognizable *koine*[1] or 'cultural community'.

The villages of the Middle PPNB were modest in size, ranging from about four to ten acres for the majority of settlements (with populations ranging from roughly 500 to 1000 people per village).[2] The subsistence economy throughout the Levant was relatively homogeneous, based on the farming of cereals and pulses (now including chickpea[3]) and the husbandry of goats. Hunting was still a major source of food and provided about half of the animal protein in the diet;[4] hunting varied from place to place depending on the local availability of animals, but gazelle, cattle, pig and small carnivores constituted the bulk of wild species.

Architecture, with one notable exception (see below), was generally more spacious in the Levant; relatively spacious multi-roomed

deposits in the Jordan Valley appear to conform to the general character of the North Levant Facies of the early PPNB. Similar suggestions of PPNA–PPNB transitions come from recent work in the Petra area of southern Jordan; see H. Gebel, 'Jordanien: Sabra I und die Wadi Systeme um Petra', *AfO* 29-30 (1983–84), pp. 283-84.

   1.   J. Cauvin, personal communication.
   2.   Cf. G. Rollefson and I. Köhler-Rollefson, 'The Collapse of Early Neolithic Settlements in the Southern Levant', in *People and Culture in Change: Proceedings of the Second Symposium on Upper Paleolithic, Mesolithic and Neolithic Populations of Europe and the Mediterranean Basin*, I, II (ed. I. Hershkovitz; BAR, 508 i-ii; Oxford, 1989), pp. 73-89.
   3.   E.g. M. Donaldson in G. Rollefson *et al.*, 'Excavation at the Pre-Pottery Neolithic B (PPNB) Village of 'Ain Ghazal (Jordan), 1983', *MDOG* 117 (1985), pp. 69-116.
   4.   I. Köhler-Rollefson *et al.*, 'The Fauna from Neolithic 'Ain Ghazal', *The Prehistory of Jordan* (ed. A. Garrard and H. Gebel; BAR, 396; Oxford, 1988), pp. 423-30.

rectangular houses were made of stone or mudbrick (where stone was rare) and floored with lime or gypsum plaster (depending on the availability of limestone and fuel). Chipped stone technology relied basically on blades produced from naviform cores, and projectile points were variants on the Early PPNB stemmed Byblos point style. Long distance contact is evidenced by the widespread presence of marine shells (from the Mediterranean and Red Seas), exotic minerals for jewelry manufacture,[1] and varying quantities of Anatolian obsidian (volcanic glass).

Ritual showed strong underlying components of similarity, particularly the practice of subfloor decapitated burials. Small human and animal figurines of fired or sunbaked clay were also widespread across the region. Little geometric objects of clay (cones, spheres, cylinders, and the like) are also found with regularity and suggest a preliterate means of recording economic and ritual rights and obligations.[2]

But despite these underpinnings of cohesion, several large sections of the Levant began to demonstrate independent cultural change, beginning a process of centrifugal disintegration that increased through the rest of the aceramic Neolithic. The North Levant Facies of the Early PPNB split at the beginning of the Middle PPNB; the northern Syrian sites such as Mureybet and neighboring Tell Aswad[3] and Tell Abu Hureira[4] maintained the general character of the Early PPNB. Southeastern Anatolia, on the other hand, developed the Taurus Facies of the PPNB, most clearly reflected in stone tool manufacture. Sites such as Cafer Höyük and Çayönü largely ignored local sources of good quality flint and chert that had served so well in the Early PPNB in favor of obsidian, obtained at some distance (although relatively 'local' compared to the rest of the Levant) and some degree of additional 'expense'. Specific aspects of architectural design and burial

1.   E.g. G. Rollefson, ''Ain Ghazal: An Early Neolithic Community in Highland Jordan, Near Amman', *BASOR* 255 (1984), pp. 3-14.

2.   D. Schmandt-Besserat, 'The Emergence of Recording', *American Anthropologist* 84 (1982), pp. 871-78; *idem*, 'An Ancient Token System: The Precursor to Numerals and Writing', *Archaeology* 39 (1986), pp. 32-39.

3.   J. Cauvin, 'Sondage à Tell Assouad', *Annales Archéologiques Arabes Syriennes* 22 (1972), pp. 85-103.

4.   A. Moore, 'The Excavation at Tell Abu Hureira in Northern Syria: A Preliminary Report', *Proceedings of the Prehistoric Society* 41 (1975), pp. 50-77.

practices[1] add to the increasingly divergent tack undertaken by the settlements in the Taurus Facies.

In southern Syria, Palestine and Jordan, the area emerges from the cloudy dimness of the Early PPNB as a region of cultural innovation. Beidha[2] began its history with conspicuous singularity in terms of its architecture, for the first phase of occupation contains only circular semiterranean houses reminiscent of the PPNA period at Jericho. Later in the Middle PPNB, Beidha dwellings 'conform' to the general rectilinear standards of the PPNB cultural community, but Beidha maintained its uniqueness in the specific arrangement of rooms. Altogether, sites[3] south of a line parallel with the Wadi Mujib area indicate a local variation that deserves a South Levant Facies distinction.

Between the Wadi Mujib in southern Jordan and the Damascus Basin to the north lies an area that might be termed the Central Levant, incorporating such sites as Jericho,[4] Tell Ramad in southern Syria,[5] and 'Ain Ghazal,[6] near Amman. Although sharing many of the PPNB characteristics of the North Levant and South Levant Facies, these sites reflect specific properties that warrant a Central Levant Facies distinction. The 'Jericho point', with its typical long barbs, and the Abu Gosh point, distinguished by the spiral pressure-flake scars on its tang, are recurrent features in the projectile point inventory, and the use of plaster to make vessels ('white ware' or *vaisselles blanches*) antedates the appearance of similar containers in the North Levant Facies by several centuries. The 'plastered skull cult', centered on the plaster reconstruction of facial features on the defleshed skulls of apparently revered ancestors, is documented only in the Central Levant

---

1.   M. Özdögan and A. Özdögan, 'Çayönü: A Conspectus of Recent Work', *Paléorient* 15/1 (1990), pp. 65-74.

2.   D. Kirkbride, *PEQ* 98 (1966), pp. 8-72.

3.   Although a relatively large number of sites have been discovered on recent surveys, few have received any intensive attention. One possible Middle PPNB village of the South Levant Facies is Khirbet Hammam, on the south bank of the Wadi el-Hasa; see G. Rollefson and Z. Kafafi, 'Khirbet Hammām: A PPNB Village in the Wādī el-Hasā, Southern Jordan', *BASOR* 258 (1985), pp. 63-69.

4.   E.g. K. Kenyon, *Archaeology in the Holy Land*, pp. 30-31.

5.   H. de Contenson, 'La région du Damas au Néolithique', *Annales Archéologiques Arabes Syriennes* 35 (1985), pp. 9-29.

6.   G. Rollefson and A. Simmons, 'The Neolithic Settlement at 'Ain Ghazal', *The Prehistory of Jordan* (ed. A. Garrard and H. Gebel; BAR, 396; Oxford, 1988), pp. 393-421.

Facies. Finally, the stunning caches of plaster human statuary of exquisite craftsmanship from 'Ain Ghazal[1] and Jericho[2] are unknown outside the Central Levant Facies.

Although conditions during the first part of the Middle PPNB appear to have been favorable for population growth with the establishment of new sites throughout the Levant, events at the end of the Middle PPNB indicate a major disruption in the environment with severe consequences for settlements that by that time had enjoyed 700 to 1000 years of continuous occupation. Widespread abandonment occurred throughout the Levant, and sites such as Mureybet, Jericho and Beidha collapsed, never to be inhabited again in most cases. The reasons for this calamity remain speculative for the present, although the persistence of habitation at other sites such as 'Ain Ghazal and Tell Abu Hureira indicate that rainfall was still abundant enough to maintain the agricultural base of these settlements. It is possible that the prolonged exploitation in particularly fragile ecological systems had exhausted and damaged the surrounding farmland and wildlife habitats to the point that populations were forced to relocate to areas previously unoccupied.[3]

One of the areas to receive increasing cultural exploitation in the later part of the Middle PPNB was the arid, unfarmable steppes and deserts of the Negev[4] and the eastern portions of Syria and Jordan.[5] In the Wadi Jilat, southwest of Azraq, for example, small semipermanent hamlets were settled by small groups who evidently herded goats,

1. G. Rollefson, 'Neolithic Ritual and Ceremony at 'Ain Ghazal (Jordan)', *Paléorient* 9 (1983), pp. 29-38; K. Tubb, 'Preliminary Report on the 'Ain Ghazal Statues', *MDOG* 117 (1985), pp. 117-34 (see Fig. 2).

2. J. Garstang, 'Jericho: City and Necropolis, Fifth Report', *Annals of Archeology and Anthropology* (Liverpool) 23 (1935), pp. 143-84.

3. G. Rollefson, *Paléorient* 15/1 (1990), pp. 135-40; I. Köhler-Rollefson and G. Rollefson, 'Cultural Degradation of the Environment During the Neolithic (9000–7000 BCE): Faunal Evidence from 'Ain Ghazal, Jordan', *Proceedings of the XIIth INQUA Congress* (in press).

4. E.g. Appendix in O. Bar-Yosef, 'The "Pre-Pottery Neolithic" Period in the Southern Levant', *Préhistoire du Levant* (ed. J. Cauvin and P. Sanlaville; Paris, 1981), pp. 555-69.

5. E.g. A. Betts, 'The Pre-Pottery Neolithic B Period in Eastern Jordan', *Paléorient* 15/1 (1990), pp. 147-53.

hunted, and possibly even planted small patches of cereals in the relatively wetter wadi bottoms near the end of the Middle PPNB.[1]

The Late PPNB (6500–6000 BCE)

The disaster that befell so many Middle PPNB settlements is reflected in a change in settlement patterns during the Late PPNB phase. Some of the new settlements that were established were of modest size and located in semiarid regions such as Mosad Mazal in the Wadi Araba[2] and Yiftahel[3] in the northern Galilee plain. But by far the most dramatic change was seen in the development of 'megasites' in the Late PPNB in the North, Central and South Levant Facies. Sites that continued from the Middle PPNB grew to enormous proportions with 'Ain Ghazal and Tell Abu Hureira reaching more than 30 acres in area. Several new sites quickly mushroomed to equivalent or even larger size, including Khirbet Sheikh 'Ali[4] in northern Galilee, Beisamoun[5] in the northern Jordan Valley, Wadi Shu'eib[6] across the Jordan Valley from Jericho, and Basta[7] in the Petra region of southern Jordan. In addition to Tell Abu Hureira, other Syrian sites experienced considerable growth to between 15 and 20 acres in extent, including Ras Shamra and Ghoraife,[8] although some newly founded

---

1. A. Garrard et al., 'Environment and Subsistence during the Late Pleistocene and Early Colocene in the Azraq Basin', Paléorient 15/1 (1990), pp. 40-49.

2. W. Taute, 'Mosad Mazzal: Ein Siedlungsplatz des präkeramischen Neolithikums südlich des Toten Meeres (Vorbericht)', Beiträge zur Umweltgeschichte des Vorderen Orients (ed. W. Frey and H. Uerpmann; Beihefte zum Tübinger Atlas des Vorderen Orients, Reihe A, Naturwissenschaften, 8; Tübingen, 1981), pp. 236-56.

3. Y. Garfinkel, 'A Neolithic Village from the Seventh Millennium BCE in Lower Galilee, Israel', Journal of Field Archaeology 14 (1987), pp. 199-212.

4. M. Prausnitz, 'The First Agricultural Settlements in Galilee', IEJ 9 (1959), 166-74; idem, 'Tell 'Eli (Kh. Sheikh 'Ali)', IEJ 10 (1960), pp. 119-20.

5. M. Lechevallier, Abou Gosh et Beisamoun (Mémoires et Travaux du Centre de Recherches Préhistoriques Français de Jerusalem, 2; Paris, 1978).

6. G. Rollefson, 'Observations on the Neolithic Village in the Wadi Shu'eib', ADAJ 31 (1987), pp. 521-24; A. Simmons et al., 'Test Excavations at Wadi Shu'eib, A Major Neolithic Settlement in Central Jordan', ADAJ 33 (1989), pp. 27-42.

7. H. Nissen et al., 'Report on the First Two Seasons of Excavations at Basta (1986–1987)', ADAJ 31 (1987), pp. 79-109.

8. G. Rollefson, 'Local and External Relations in the Levantine PPN Period: 'Ain Ghazal (Jordan) as a Regional Centre', Studies in the History and Archaeology

sites such as Bouqras remained in the small or medium category during the period.

Numerous changes in lifestyle occurred in the Late PPNB, although once again the tempos and directions of change were variable in the different facies of the Levant.

Economic developments are best known for the North Levant Facies, where sheep and cattle were added to the domesticates during the Late PPNB at Ras Shamra, Bouqras and Tell Aswad,[1] at least. The situation for the Central Levant remains less clear, although there are hints that cattle may have been domesticated at this time based on small samples of evidence from Abu Gosh and 'Ain Ghazal.[2] Excavations of Late PPNB sites in the South Levant Facies have not published sufficient details yet concerning the status of domesticates for this part of the Levant.

In terms of architectural developments, Late PPNB Basta emphasizes the continued individuality of the South Levant Facies. Large 'block structures' about 8 × 8 m in extent, built of dressed limestone slabs, consist of a sizeable central room (c. 3 × 5 m) surrounded on three sides by smaller 'cells' (c. 1 × 2 m to 2 × 2 m) that may have served as storerooms. Entry to the 'cells' may have been through the roof, but the presence of window-like openings in the free wall of the central room, beginning at 60 cm above the floor, may have been the means of access to the main living quarters.[3] Another large structure (4.5 × 9 m) is very curious: a layer of fine earth covered a stone slab floor that concealed a series of interlinked subfloor 'channels' 20 cm wide and 40 cm deep. Since the exterior walls of the building were not penetrated by the channels, the function they served remains unknown.

For the Central Levant Facies, architecture at Late PPNB Abu Gosh, Beisamoun, and Tell Ramad suggest little departure from Middle PPNB construction designs and techniques. In the North Levant Facies, the Late PPNB dwellings at Bouqras tended to be rather small and

of Jordan, III (ed. A. Hadidi; Amman, 1987), pp. 32-33.

1.   D. Helmer, *Paléorient* 15/1 (1990), pp. 111-21.

2.   I. Köhler-Rollefson in G. Rollefson *et al.*, 'Excavations at the PPNB Village of 'Ain Ghazal (Jordan) 1982', *MDOG* 116 (1984), pp. 139-83; D. Helmer, *Paléorient* 15/1 (1990), pp. 111-21.

3.   H. Nissen *et al.*, *ADAJ* 31 (1987), pp. 79-119.

L-shaped, with a courtyard and hearth situated in the semi-confined space between the two 'legs' of the L; rooms were variable in size, but overall they were generally long and narrow.[1]

Ritual changes were also multidimensional throughout the Levant. Subfloor decapitated burials and the plastered skull cult continued at Beisamoun, Ramad, and evidently at Wadi Su'eib, and small plaster sculptures came from a Late PPNB context at Tell Ramad.[2] A cache of more than 11 plaster human statues, similar in many respects to the Middle PPNB collection, came from early Late PPNB contexts at 'Ain Ghazal.[3]

It was in the South Levant Facies that major changes in ritual developed during the Late PPNB. Although most Middle PPNB burials at Beidha were decapitated and came from subfloor contexts, Late PPNB humans at Basta were invariably (?) buried in abandoned buildings above the floors with the skulls intact with the rest of the skeleton. (Some skeletons occurred without the skull, but this may have been due to post-burial disturbances).[4]

But perhaps the most impressive ritual developments come from a small cave in Nahal Hemar near the southern end of the Dead Sea. In addition to an unprecedented collection of preserved organic remains (including woven fabrics, cordage, netting, and wooden beads and implements), two carved stone masks with red and green pigment were found, one of which still retained hair imprints and residue on the top and may have been bearded as well.[5] Several animal long bones also represented painted and bearded human faces, and six to eight adult skulls bore modelled asphalt in a net pattern on their rear

---

1. P. Akkermans *et al.*, 'Bouqras Revisited: Preliminary Report on a Project in Eastern Syria', *Proceedings of the Prehistoric Society* 49 (1983), pp. 335-72, 338-43.

2. H. de Contenson, *Annales Archéologiques Arabes Syriennes* 35 (1985), pp. 9-29, especially the figures on p. 15; M. Lechevallier, *Abou Gosh et Beisamoun*; A. Simmons *et al.*, *ADAJ* 33 (1989), pp. 27-42.

3. Cf. G. Rollefson, 'Neolithic 'Ain Ghazal: Ritual and Ceremony II', *Paléorient* 12 (1986), pp. 45-52.

4. H. Nissen *et al.*, *ADAJ* 31 (1987), pp. 79-119.

5. A fragment of a similar stone mask was also recovered from Basta; see H. Nissen *et al.*, *ADAJ* 31 (1987), fig. 16. Three other stone masks have come from Palestine, but their original proveniences are unknown.

portions. Altogether, the Nahal Hemar material indicates a domination of males in the ritual area if not in sociopolitical organization.[1]

The tumultuous events that introduced the Late PPNB—the relocation of so much of the population into gigantic settlements after the widespread abandonments of the Middle PPNB—recurred at the end of the period around 6000 BCE. Once again, villages and even towns became deserted, especially in the Central and Southern Levant. The list includes Abu Gosh, Beisamoun, Khirbet Sheikh 'Ali, Mosad Mazal, Munhata and numerous others, and once again the reasons for this catastrophic disruption remain unclear. For a long time it was considered that only a decrease in rainfall could have accounted for the calamity,[2] and there was some supporting palynological evidence to support this view.[3] Recent paleoclimatic evidence has been more equivocal,[4] and a decrease in precipitation (a regional phenomenon) should have caused the abandonment of *all* agricultural settlements, but this was plainly not the case.

Sites in the North Levant Facies continued to thrive, as Ras Shamra, Bouqras, Tell Abu Hureira and others testify; but it might be argued that northern Syria enjoys a different climatic regime than the central and southern Levant, so this need not contradict the climatic deterioration hypothesis. However, while the vast majority of communities in the central and southern areas of the region were deserted by 6000 BCE, several notable exceptions argue strongly against widespread reductions in rainfall. Instead, it seems very likely that factors that caused the relocation of population in the middle of the seventh millennium once again came into play: five centuries of the combined effects of farming and overgrazing had depleted the fertility of soils (indeed, caused the outright loss of much of the soil cover through

1.   O. Bar-Yosef and T. Schick, 'Nahal Hemar Cave: Early Neolithic Organic Remains from the Near East', *National Geographic Research* (in press); O. Bar-Yosef, 'Excavations at Nahal Hemar', *Mitekufat Haeven* 19 (1986), pp. 94-95.

2.   E.g. K. Kenyon, *Digging Up Jericho*, p. 69; J. Perrot, 'La Préhistoire Palestinienne', in *DBSup*, cols. 286-446, 404-405.

3.   A. Horowitz, *The Quaternary of Israel*, p. 228.

4.   E.g. W. Van Zeist, 'Past and Present Environments in the Jordan Valley', *Studies in the History and Archaeology of Jordan II* (ed. A. Hadidi; Amman, 1985), pp. 199-204; B. Luz, 'Paleoclimatic Interpretations of the Last 20,000 Year Record of Deep-Sea Cores Around the Middle East', *Paleoclimates, Paleoenvironments, and Human Communities in the Eastern Mediterranean Region in Later Prehistory* (ed. J. Bintliff and W. Van Zeist; BAR, 133; Oxford, 1982), pp. 41-61.

erosion and wind-deflation), leaving the steep and dissected country-side around the settlements barren and unproductive.[1]

Notably, all of the known Central and South Levant Facies sites that weathered the troubled end of the seventh millennium fall on a rough north–south line that is close to the modern dividing line between the better-watered and arable soils and the arid and unfarmable steppe and deserts of eastern Syria and Jordan. Thus Tell Ramad, Wadi Shu'eib, 'Ain Ghazal and Basta had access not only to cultivable land, but also the meager yet largely untapped plant resoucres in the dry lands to the east, resources that could be exploited through a change in the basic foundations of the subsistence economy.

The Final PPNB and PPNC (6000–?5000 BCE)

The flatter landscape in northern Syria witnessed less damage to the soils in the vicinity of agricultural villages, and as a consequence there was less of a change in cultural patterns at the beginning of the sixth millennium. In fact, the northern Levant may have been experiencing unprecedented population growth, for sites began to be established far out into the eastern steppe, as the small farming villages at El Kowm[2] indicate. (Bouqras itself, settled in the Late PPNB, is even farther to the east, although it is situated near the confluence of the Euphrates and one of its major tributaries, the Wadi Khabour.) Other settlements were founded for the first time at other, more mesic locations, includ-ing Byblos on Lebanon's Mediterranean shore. Except for some minor stylistic changes in some of the stone tools, lithic technology remained essentially the same as it had been at the beginning of the Early PPNB a millennium and a half earlier. In addition to the domesticates of the Late PPNB, pigs joined the list early in the sixth millennium.[3]

In the Final PPNB at Bouqras, structures became huge (c. 9×15 m to 12×12 m). The floor plans generally comprised three 'axial' rooms running the length of the structure, often subdivided in a com-plex arrangement into numerous smaller and larger chambers;[4]

---

1.   G. Rollefson and I. Köhler-Rollefson, 'The Collapse of Early Neolithic Settlements', *People and Culture* (ed. I. Hershkovitz *et al.*).

2.   D. Stordeur, 'El Kowm Caracol et le P.P.N.B', *Le Préhistoire du Levant*, II (ed. O. Aurenche *et al.*; Lyon, 1989).

3.   D. Helmer, *Paléorient* 15/1 (1990), pp. 111-21.

4.   P. Akkermans *et al.*, *Proceedings of the Prehistoric Society* 49 (1983), pp. 335-72, 338-43.

interior features included ovens, low doorways, and 'weaving installations' built into the walls of some rooms. In the sphere of ritual, abandoned buildings became the sites of burials, with individuals placed above floor and with skulls left intact with the rest of the skeleton.

In the North Levant Facies, pottery had made its first appearance at Middle PPNB Tell Aswad[1] (as it also did at 'Ain Ghazal in the Central Levant[2]), but the quantities were very small and perhaps should be considered to reflect experimentation in a new technological medium. At Final PPNB Bouqras, on the other hand (more than 100 km southeast of Tell Aswad), fine ceramic bowls with geometric designs painted in red occurred with regularity, and gypsum plaster white ware was also produced.[3] Elegantly carved stone vessels also come from Bouqras and Tell Abu Hureira. Contemporaneous sites in the Central and South Levant Facies were strictly aceramic (except for white ware), and stone vessels were very rare (at least one example comes from Tell Ramad[4] and another from a disturbed context at 'Ain Ghazal).

It was in the Central and Southern Levant that major changes accompanied the transition to the sixth millennium. At 'Ain Ghazal, Wadi Shu'eib, and Basta[5] (and evidently at Tell Ramad), for the first time since the beginning of the PPNB, naviform cores became rare, and, although blades continued to be used for a large proportion of the tool kit, flakes now outnumbered blades by about two to one. Projectile points that had been relatively long and heavy during the seventh millennium became significantly shorter, narrower and lighter, and the Byblos Point was only a vague memory. Graving tools (burins) changed in configuration, suggesting that these tools were

1. J. Cauvin, *Annales Archéologiques Arabes Syriennes* 22 (1972), pp. 85-103, esp. p. 87.
2. G. Rollefson and A. Simmons, 'The Early Neolithic Village of 'Ain Ghazal, Jordan: Preliminary Report on the 1983 Season', *BASOR* 23 (1985), pp. 35-51, esp. pp. 43-44.
3. P. Akkermans *et al.*, *Proceedings of the Prehistoric Society* 49 (1983), pp. 351-54.
4. See photo on p. 280 in H. de Contenson, 'Tell Ramad: A Village Site of Syria of the 7th and 6th Millennia BC', *Archaeology* 24 (1971), pp. 278-85.
5. Based on preliminary analysis of samples from the 1988 excavation seasons at the first two sites, and on personal communciation from H. Gebel, one of the principle investigators at Basta.

being used for processing of different resources for different purposes. Pigs also became domesticated (as well as dogs),[1] and presumably only the pigs and cattle were pastured in the vicinity of the
site, with the goats (and possibly sheep) taken to the eastern steppe and
desert on a seasonal basis.

Architecture in the Central Levant Facies also underwent major
changes. At 'Ain Ghazal, PPNB buildings with spacious and simply
arranged rooms gave way to smaller 'main' rooms and adjacent cellu-
lar alcoves and storerooms not unlike the smaller structures at
Bouqras. In contrast to the use of massive wooden posts to support the
roofs, the more closely spaced interior walls of houses now served
this function, indicating the results of prolonged deforestation around
the large population centers.[2]

Ritual also experienced a major departure from PPNB canons. In
contrast to decapitated, individual interments in the PPNB and the
associated implications for the skull cult and ancestor veneration,
people were buried with skulls intact, often several in the same pit.
Human figurines virtually disappear (and those that have been found
may be intrusive from earlier PPNB layers), and animal figurines are
also rarer; notably, a figurine of an equid appears for the first time at
'Ain Ghazal, coincident with the first appearance of bones of wild
equids in the archaeological deposits. Taken altogether, the changes in
lithic production, economy, architecture and ritual appear dramatic
enough to warrant a new name for this different cultural ensemble:
the PPNC[3] of the central and southern Levant.

At present PPNC sites are known only at 'Ain Ghazal, Wadi Shu'eib,
and possibly at Tell Ramad and Basta,[4] but certainly the population of
the central and southern Levant was not confined to these few sites.
Claims of a mass migration out of the region at the end of the seventh
millennium[5] are highly unlikely, for there is no perceptible increase

1.   I. Köhler-Rollefson *et al.*, *The Prehistory of Jordan* (ed. A. Garrard and
H. Gebel), pp. 423-30.

2.   G. Rollefson and I. Köhler-Rollefson, 'The Collapse of Early Neolithic
Settlements in the Southern Levant', *People and Culture* (ed. I. Hershkowitz *et al.*).

3.   G. Rollefson, *Paléorient* 15/1 (1990), pp. 135-40.

4.   Published data for the last two sites are insufficient to determine definitely the
cultural affiliation of the latest occupation horizons, but preliminary information at
least suggests a PPNC-like constellation of cultural features.

5.   E.g. J. Mellaart, *The Neolithic of the Near East* (New York, 1975), pp. 67-
68.

in population in the North Levant Facies of the Final PPNB. Instead, the large population clusters of the Late PPNB in the Central and South Levant Facies probably dispersed from their ruined microenvironmental settings, breaking up into smaller hamlet-sized groups that could be supported by one of the numerous smaller springs that occurred throughout the hinterland, unscathed by earlier PPNB exploitation. Because of their likely diminutive size, such small PPNC settlements have probably escaped the attention of archaeological surveys.[1]

The Pottery Neolithic (5500–c. 4500 BCE)

The ceramic Neolithic of the Levant is in a sense the 'Dark Age' of the region's prehistory. The number of sites known is extremely small for these nearly two thousand years, contradicting the dictum of 'archaeological visibility' (i.e. more sites from more recent times will be exposed than sites from older periods). Several factors are probably responsible for this disparity in site recognition, and all probably contribute rather equally to the imbalance for understanding this vague period of cultural development in the Levant.

First, although a few early Pottery Neolithic sites maintained 'megasite' proportions (e.g. 'Ain Ghazal and Wadi Shu'eib), most settlements of the last half of the sixth millennium appear to be small and therefore liable to being missed during archaeological surveys.

Secondly, pottery from the early ceramic Neolithic is generally crude and relatively nondescript except for rare decorated sherds. Sites with such sherd scatters that are located during surveys often become 'lost' in some catch-all category of 'unidentified', or, perhaps worse, are lumped into misleading 'Chalcolithic/Early Bronze' classifications on the basis of the crudeness of the material.

Thirdly, many tell sites that include extensive and deep deposits of later periods (e.g. Bronze Age, Iron Age) are likely to obscure early Pottery Neolithic occupation levels at their bases, and limited excavations are unlikely to unveil substantial Neolithic exposures.

Because of the rarity of sites (especially in Palestine) and the paucity of associated radiocarbon dates[2] for this period, the situation

1. Numerous small PPN sites have been discovered during surveys, but the characteristics that distinguish the PPNB from the PPNC are unlikely to be revealed on the basis of surface collections.

2. Cf. J. Weinstein, 'Radiocarbon Dating in the Southern Levant', *Radiocarbon* 26 (1984), pp. 333-34.

in the central and southern Levant remains unclear. After nearly a millennium of abandonment, Jericho was resettled by a pottery producing population that lived in circular semisubterranean dwellings. This Pottery Neolithic A (PNA) culture is characterized principally by the ceramics: an undecorated coarse ware and a fine, decorated ware, both expressed in a limited variety of vessel shapes. The decorated ware was slipped in either or both cream and red colors and often bore burnished and red painted geometric designs (usually triangles and chevrons).[1] Identical pottery has been found at only a handful of other sites, including Dhra, near the 'tongue' of the east shore of the Dead Sea,[2] at Munhata[3] and at Wadi Shu'eib.[4]

At Sha'ar ha-Golan, Stekelis[5] recovered considerable quantities of potsherds that differed considerably from the PNA fine ware. This Yarmoukian pottery consisted of similar vessel forms, but, instead of the painted red geometric designs, the pottery bore incised herringbone patterns, often in confined bands, with or without red paint. Since Stekelis's investigations, numerous Yarmoukian sites have been discovered, especially in the northern Jordanian highlands[6] in the past decade, and most of them are hamlet-sized agricultural settlements. Only one radiocarbon date is known for a Yarmoukian occupation: 5530 ± 90 BCE at 'Ain Rahub in northern Jordan.[7]

The major problem concerning the Pottery Neolithic of the central and southern Levant is the relationship of the PNA and Yarmoukian cultures with each other and with regions to the north. Both are at least partially contemporaneous with each other, and in general lifeways (agricultural economy, similar chipped stone tools, and so forth) they are broadly comparable, keeping in mind the absolutely small

---

1. K. Kenyon, *Archaeology in the Holy Land*, pp. 43-45, esp. fig. 6.

2. C.M. Bennett, 'Soundings at Dhra, Jordan', *Levant* 12 (1980), pp. 30-39.

3. J. Perrot, 'Les deux premières campagnes des fouilles à Munhatta (1962–1963): Premiers résultats', *Syria* 41 (1964), pp. 323-45, and plates xxi-xxiv.

4. A. Simmons *et al.*, *ADAJ* 33 (1989), pp. 27-42.

5. M. Stekelis, *The Yarmoukian Culture of the Neolithic Period* (Jerusalem, 1972).

6. Z. Kafafi, personal communication. Cf. Z. Kafafi, 'Jebel Abu Thawwab: A Pottery Neolithic Village in North Jordan', *The Prehistory of Jordan* (ed. A. Garrard and H. Gebel; BAR, 396; Oxford, 1988), pp. 451-71.

7. M. Muheisen *et al.*, 'Excavations at 'Ain Rahub, a Final Natufian and Yarmoukian Site near Irbid (1985)', *The Prehistory of Jordan* (ed. A. Garrard and H. Gebel; BAR, 396; Oxford, 1988), pp. 473-502.

amount of information relating to the PNA sites. Kafafi has claimed that the Yarmoukian antedates the appearance of the PNA[1] on the basis of the stratigraphic sequence at Munhatta, where Phase 2B2 with Yarmoukian pottery underlies Phase 2B1 with PNA ceramics. On the other hand, this sequence appears to be reversed at Wadi Shuʻeib.[2] Preliminary analysis of developments at ʻAin Ghazal suggest an *in situ* transition from the aceramic PPNC to early Yarmoukian levels, indicating a local development of ceramic technology in the central Levant.[3] Prehistorians have seen 'foreign' antecedents for the PNA, brought into the central and southern Levant by migrating populations from Syria and Lebanon.[4]

During the PNA/Yarmoukian period the eastern steppes and deserts of Syria and Jordan underwent intensive exploitation by ostensibly nonceramic societies that specialized in gazelle hunting[5] and, presumably, nomadic pastoralists.[6] One intriguing manifestation of the late sixth millennium and later times is the widespread 'burin site'[7] phenomenon, principally found in the arid regions of Jordan: small (usually one acre or less) but dense concentrations of chipped stone artifacts

---

1. Z. Kafafi, 'The Neolithic of Jordan (East Bank)' (PhD dissertation, Freie Universität, Berlin, 1982), pp. 56-57.

2. A. Simmons *et al.*, *ADAJ* 33 (1989), pp. 27-42.

3. G. Rollefson *et al.*, *MDOG* 116 (1984), pp. 139-83. Notably, it appears that the earliest pottery producing levels (where sherds are very rare and all are undecorated) include substantial stone-built rectilinear dwellings indistinguishable from PPNC counterparts. When decorated Yarmoukian pottery first occurs, dwellings change principally in the flooring, where plaster so characteristic of the PPNB and PPNC periods is abandoned. Later Yarmoukian structures at 'Ain Ghazal, partially semisubterranean, incorporated at least one apsoidal room on an otherwise rectangular plan. Final Yarmoukian architecture seems to have comprised only flimsy, temporary circular semisubterranean buildings.

4. E.g. R. de Vaux, 'Palestine During the Neolithic and Chalcolithic Periods'. *CAH*, I and II, Fasc. 47, pp. 3-43 (13); J. Mellaart, *The Neolithic of the Near East*, p. 238.

5. A. Betts, 'The Prehistory of the Basalt Desert, Transjordan: An Analysis' (PhD dissertation, Institute of Archaeology, University of London, 1986); S. Helms and A. Betts, 'The Desert "Kites" of the Badiyat esh-Sham and North Arabia', *Paléorient* 13 (1987), pp. 41-67.

6. I. Köhler-Rollefson, *Archaeozoologica* 3 (1989), pp. 201-208.

7. A. Betts, 'Prehistoric Sites at Qaʻa Mejalla, Eastern Jordan', *Levant* 14 (1982), pp. 1-34.

with burins overwhelmingly dominating the tool inventory.[1] What functions these highly specialized campsites served will remain speculative until excavations produce associated faunal and floral remains.

Knowledge of the ritual aspects of both the PNA and the Yarmoukian cultural traditions is very limited. No burials have been found at any Pottery Neolithic site, for example,[2] and only a handful of human and animal figurines are known for this general period.[3]

It is not known how long the PNA and Yarmoukian traditions lasted, nor if they both ended at roughly the same time. Only two sites have later occupations above Yarmoukian layers: a probable Chalcolithic at Wadi Shuʻeib,[4] and a Wadi Rabah Chalcolithic at Munhatta.[5] At Jericho the PNA series of occupations was succeeded by the locally developed Pottery Neolithic B (PNB), distinguished from its predecessor by the construction of sturdy ground-level dwellings and new pottery vessel forms (especially the 'bow-rim jar') and decorative techniques. For the last aspect, the frequent appearance of banded herringbone incisions on PNB pots led Kenyon to propose a correlation of the PNB with Yarmoukian sites, placing the Yarmoukian sometime later than the Jericho PNA.[6] On the other hand, the Yarmoukian culture may have lasted during the entire Pottery Neolithic sequence at Jericho, influencing PNB potters after the demise of the PNA. As a reasonable guess, it is suggested that the PNA and the Yarmoukian both began at about 5500 BCE; the Yarmoukian may have continued into the fifth millennium, but at 5000 BCE the PNB replaced the PNA in the central and southern Levant. Although the PNB is known from more than 30 sites in Jordan and Palestine,[7] most of the excavations at PNB sites have been on the scale of small test pits, and consequently little is

1. E.g. G. Rollefson and B. Frohlich, 'A PPNB Burin Site on Jabal Uweinid, Eastern Jordan', *ADAJ* 26 (1982), pp. 189-98; G. Rollefson and M. Muheisen, 'Chipped Stone Artifacts from a Specialized Neolithic Camp Near Kharaneh Castle, Eastern Jordan', *ADAJ* 29 (1985), pp. 141-50.

2. K. Kenyon, *Archaeology in the Holy Land*, p. 67.

3. Cf. J. Perrot, *Syria* 41 (1964), pl. IV; Z. Kafafi in *The Prehistory of Jordan* (ed. A. Garrard and H. Gebel), fig. 11.

4. Z. Kafafi, personal communication; cf. Simmons *et al.*, *ADAJ* 33 (1989), pp. 27-42.

5. J. Perrot, *DBSup*, VIII, col. 415.

6. K. Kenyon, *Archaeology in the Holy Land*, pp. 46-48.

7. Cf. Z. Kafafi, 'The Neolithic of Jordan (East Bank)', pp. 65-82, for a general summary.

known about PNB cultural traditions beyond pottery manufacture.

Contemporary developments in the northern Levant are clearer and more detailed for the period of 6000–4500 BCE, although some problems remain for establishing correlations with the central and southern Levant.[1] What clarity there is for local developments is due to several long and continuous sequences of occupations at sites such as Ras Shamra, Byblos and Tell 'Amuq.

The earliest use of pottery in the northern Levant was during the Middle PPNB (as mentioned earlier), but it was not until the Final PPNB that ceramic production was undertaken consistently throughout the area. Unpainted but burnished fine ware ('Dark Face Burnished Ware') was characteristic of the Final PPNB/'Amuq A/*Byblos néolithique ancien (1)* period (6000–5500 BCE).[2] Notably, this widespread technological development proceeded while the central and southern Levant continued aceramic PPNC cultural traditions.

Painted pottery made its first regular appearance in the northern Levant during the 'Amuq B/*Byblos néolithique ancien (2)* period (5500–5000 BCE), although painted decoration occurred only on some 5–10% of the well-made and varied pottery vessels.[3] Incised and burnished decoration continued to dominate in the north, possibly influencing by separate routes the PNA and Yarmoukian developments farther south.

During the Amuq C/*Byblos néolithique moyen* period (5000–4500 BCE) northeastern Syria (especially the Balikh and Khabour tributaries to the Euphrates) came under strong influences from the greater Mesopotamian region as reflected by the local manufacture of imitation Halaf pottery and the construction of typical circular *tholoi* structures.[4] Nevertheless, northwestern and coastal parts of the northern

1. One source of confusion is the different usage of the terms 'Neolithic' and 'Chalcolithic' by scholars working in the northern Levant. Cf. L. Copeland and F. Hours, 'The Halafians, their Predecessors and their Contemporaries in Northern Syria and the Levant: Relative and Absolute Chronologies', *Chronologies du Proche Orient* (ed. O. Aurenche, *et al.*; BAR, 379; Oxford, 1987), pp. 401-25, esp. p. 403.

2. L. Copeland and F. Hours, 'The Halafians', *Chronologies* (ed. O. Aurenche *et al.*), pp. 402, 404-405.

3. L. Copeland and F. Hours, 'The Halafians', *Chronologies* (ed. O. Aurenche *et al.*), p. 405.

4. P. Akkermanns, 'A Late Neolithic and Early Halaf Village at Sabi Abyad, Northern Syria', *Paléorient* 13 (1987), pp. 23-40; cf. L. Copeland and F. Hours, 'The Halafians', *Chronologies* (ed. O. Aurenche *et al.*), pp. 403, 407-10.

Levant maintained relatively independent courses of cultural development (although Halaf pottery was imported in small quantities), and there is no evidence to suggest that the central and southern Levant felt any perturbations from the north and east during the PNB/late Yarmoukian period.

The Chalcolithic Period

The events that transpired during the period 4500–3200 BCE differed significantly between the northern and southern halves of the Levant, and much of the difference appears to be related to the proximity of contemporaneous developments in the Mesopotamian region.

In the southern part of the region (Palestine and Jordan), developments emerge with credible clarity from the hazy mist of the closing centuries of the Pottery Neolithic.[1] The stunning evidence of settlement patterns, ritual, economy, social organization and technology contrast vividly with the paltry information in the southern Levant from c. 5000–4500 BCE, but it remains likely that the flourishing Chalcolithic period was a direct outgrowth of local changes and not the result of immigrating populations or wholesale importation of ideas from the north and east.

There is little reason to doubt that the Chalcolithic period witnessed major population growth, especially during the fourth millennium. Archaeological surveys have reported numerous new sites in the past decade or two,[2] adding to an already large corpus of Chalcolithic settlements known since the 1920s. Large and small sites were distributed across the landscape in a classic hierarchical arrangement that strongly suggests small political territories/chiefdoms (as small as c. 100 m^2, but others many times larger.[3] Within each territory was

1.   Much of the information on the Chalcolithic presented here relies heavily on the excellent summary recently published by T. Levy, 'The Chalcolithic Period', *BA* 49 (1986), pp. 82-108.

2.   E.g. D. Alon and T. Levy, 'Preliminary Note on the Distribution of Chalcolithic Sites on the Wadi Beersheva and Lower Wadi Besor Drainage System', *IEJ* 30 (1980), pp. 140-47; M. Ibrahim, J. Sauer and K. Yassine, 'The East Jordan Valley Survey, 1975', *BASOR* 222 (1976), pp. 41-66; B. MacDonald *et al.*, *ADAJ* 27 (1983), pp. 311-23.

3.   T. Levy, *BA* 49 (1986), pp. 99-100 and figure, p. 88; cf. T. Levy and D. Alon, 'Chalcolithic Settlement Patterns in the Northern Negev Desert', *Current Anthropology* 24 (1983), pp. 105-107.

one principal settlement 20 acres or more in size (up to 50 acres for Teleilat Ghassul, at the northeastern end of the Dead Sea) that coordinated social, economic and ritual matters for a number of smaller supporting villages and hamlets of one to ten acres in size.

Within the regional centers, buildings were arranged in a systematic manner, and although domestic dwellings varied in size (averaging less than 15 m^2 in area), one or more larger structures (up to 50m^2) probably served some public function. At least some of the larger buildings served as religious centers (as the temple at Teleilat Ghassul demonstrates[1]), perhaps operating as ritual foci for the people living in the smaller satellite villages in the territory. The isolated temple complex at En Gedi is not directly associated with any settlement, and it may have served as a pilgrimage location for the people of a vast area.[2]

Ritual was highly organized, and it seems likely that priests served as full-time religious (and political?) specialists. The wall paintings and other decorative materials from several temples/shrines discovered at Ghassul since the late 1920s reflect an elaborate degree of order and symbolism.[3] Levy also notes that for the first time in the southern Levant cemeteries were established as separate precincts outside Chalcolithic settlements,[4] and variation in the quantity and types of associated grave offerings may reflect differences in social status.

Specialization had also become a special feature in some aspects of Chalcolithic economy and technology early in the period. The term 'chalcolithic' refers to the use of copper, and the technological process of smelting ore to produce the metal was one major distinction between the northern and the southern parts of the Levant. Using resources from the Wadi Feinan area of southern Jordan and from the Timna area northwest of Aqaba, metallurgists practiced a stunning sophistication in the production of copper objects. Although copper may have served in some utilitarian tasks, the metal is best known

1. B. Hennessy, 'Teleilat Ghassul: Its Place in the Archaeology of Jordan', *Studies in the History and Archaeology of Jordan*, I (ed. A. Hadidi; Amman, 1982), pp. 55-58.

2. D. Ussishkin, 'The Ghassulian Shrine at En-Gedi', *Tel Aviv* 7 (1980), pp. 1-44.

3. See D. Cameron, *The Ghassulian Wall Paintings* (London, 1981), for a discussion of the preserved and unpreserved frescoes and fragments.

4. T. Levy, *BA* 49 (1986), p. 97.

from ritual contexts as the cache from the Nahal Mishmar cave in the Judean Desert indicates.[1] This hoard contained more than 400 breathtaking copper objects, including 'crowns',[2] standards, scepters, maceheads, vessels and tools. A second cache of copper artifacts from Kfar Monash,[3] near Tel Aviv, was also very rich, and the use of some 800 small copper plates has been the source of some speculation. Nevertheless, it is clear that the metal was reserved for a select group of people, although whether membership of the group was restricted to priests remains unclear.

Specialization was also likely in the realms of ivory carving, flint quarrying and tool manufacture, basalt acquisition and processing, and pottery production;[4] while much of the domestic repertoire of implements, objects and vessels using these materials may have been produced by local 'cottage industries', the splendid array of ritual objects in these media argue for craft specialization. The segregation of the subsistence economy into the agricultural and nomadic pastoral spheres, begun in the early Pottery Neolithic, was an established economic tradition throughout the Chalcolithic.

In the northern half of the Levant, the term 'Chalcolithic' is perhaps a misnomer,[5] for the use of copper is not strongly attested for the period between 4500–3200 BCE except for sporadic native copper ornaments. Possibly this is a reflection on the rarity of copper ores in the northern Levant, and it need not indicate a lack of ability nor even knowledge of the 'value' of the metal. Nevertheless, other aspects of this period show that important developments occurred that paralleled

---

1. P. Bar Adon, 'Expedition C—The Cave of the Treasure', *IEJ* 12 (1962), pp. 215-26.

2. R. Amiran has suggested that the 'crowns' were actually stackable segments of altar stands. See R. Amiran, 'A Suggestion to See the Copper "Crowns" of the Judean Desert Treasure as Drums of Stand-Like Altars', *Palestine in the Bronze and Iron Ages* (ed. J. N. Tubb; London, 1985), pp. 10-14.

3. R. Hestrin and M. Tadmor, who date these to EB I–II ('A Hoard of Tools and Weapons from Kfar Monash', *IEJ* 13 [1963], pp. 265-88). For the concentration of metal industries in the Negev, see T.E. Levy and S. Shalev, 'Prehistoric Metalworking in the Southern Levant: Archaeometallurgical and Social Perspectives', *World Archaeology* 20 (1989), pp. 353-58, and compare also J.D. Muhly, 'Kupfer', *Reallexikon der Assyriologie*, VI.5 (Berlin, 1983), pp. 348-64, esp. p. 353.

4. T. Levy, *BA* 49 (1986), pp. 90-96.

5. As mentioned above, the term 'Chalcolithic' in the northern Levant is used as it is in Mesopotamia: it refers to the presence of painted pottery, not copper production.

much of the events of the southern Levant and, perhaps more importantly, were influenced by the protohistoric period in Iraq.

During the Halaf period in northern Syria and Iraq, for example, Watson noted that a number of sites appear to be centers of pottery production and export. The 'communication patterns' associated with this distribution of ceramics indicates that these principal sites were 'chiefly centers' with the attendant settlement hierarchy,[1] a situation reminiscent of the 'chiefly territories' of the southern Levant. Halafian economic specialists in economy and pottery production also match southern Levantine patterns, although what degree specialization in religion and the production of 'exotic goods' reached remains obscure.

The period from c. 4500–4000 must have witnessed considerable stresses among the populations and 'territories' of the northern Levant, for both Ras Shamra and Byblos show burned late Halafian levels followed by a series of occupation layers with unsophisticated architecture and technological production.[2] The sequence at Ras Shamra resumes a bit later with the appearance of Late Ubaid pottery and a revitalized, florescent cultural pattern that reflects a focus towards local responses to influences from northern and southern Iraq.

---

1. P.J. Watson, 'The Halafian Culture: A Review and Synthesis', *The Hilly Flanks and Beyond* (ed. T. Young, P. Smith and P. Mortensen; SAOC, 36; Chicago, 1982), pp. 231-49, esp. p. 241.

2. J. Mellaart, *The Neolithic of the Near East* (New York, 1975), p. 237.

Chapter 3

THE EARLY BRONZE AGE

The Early Bronze Age I–III

The culture that follows the Chalcolithic Age is usually labeled the
Early Bronze Age, c. 3500–2000/1950 BCE (see Map 7).[1] As in the
case of the preceding period, this is partly a misnomer. Bronze
objects do not play any significant role in the early part of EB. In
many places a transitional period has been detected, which can be seen
in continuity with the preceding Chalcolithic Age and the following
EB I period.[2] This transitional period ha been characterized by

1. It is usually divided into three or four periods: EB I 3150–2950 BCE, EB II
2950–2700 BCE, EB III 2700–2300 BCE, and EB IV 2300–2000/1950 BCE. Cf.
Y. Aharoni, *The Archaeology of the Land of Israel* (Philadelphia, 1982), p. XIX;
G.R. Bentley, 'Kinship and Social Structure', p. 8. R. Amiran ends the EB IV
c. 2250–2200 and calls the following period MB I (2200–2000/1950 BCE); cf. *Ancient
Pottery of the Holy Land from its Beginnings in the Neolithic Period to the End of
the Iron Age* (Jerusalem, 1969), p. 12. As a consequence of the Arad excavations,
W.G. Dever accepts the high chronology for Arad and dates the EB I to 3400–3100
BCE, EB II 3100–2650, EB III 2650–2350 and EB IVA–C (including MB I) to
2350–2000 BCE, in a review of R. Amiran *et al.*, *Early Arad*, *IEJ* 32 (1982), p. 173.
Because the material culture is not exactly the same in the different geographical
areas, and some phenomena occur earlier in one part of the country than in another,
these figures are approximate only. Because EB II and EB III are hard to distinguish,
I often refer to EB II–III. As to EB I, several scholars have divided it into EB IA–C.
The EB IC is perhaps part of EB II, thus D.L. Esse, 'A Chronological Mirage:
Reflections on Early Bronze IC in Palestine', *JNES* 43 (1984), pp. 317-30. As for
the chronology of Egypt, I have usually followed that of K. Baer and E.F. Wente;
see E.F. Wente, 'History of Egypt', *Encyclopaedia Britannica*, VI (15th edn; Chicago,
1974 [1978]), p. 460.

2. A break between the Chalcolithic and EB I periods has been advocated by,
among others, P.W. Lapp ('Palestine in the Early Bronze Age', *Near Eastern
Archaeology in the Twentieth Century* [ed. J.A. Sanders; Garden City, NY, 1970],
pp. 104-105); cf. J.B. Hennessy, *The Foreign Relations of Palestine during the*

K.M. Kenyon as the Proto-Urban period. The carriers of this culture are said, however, to have been foreigners who invaded Palestine and Jordan in the later part of the fourth millennium BCE. They were 'migrant tribesmen' and not representatives of an urban civilization. As evidence for this, Kenyon points to a new burial system. Tombs were cut in the rocks or natural caves were used. These tombs could be called 'graveyards' because they were used for multiple burials. Gifts or offerings were deposited in the graves which may indicate a certain belief in an afterlife. The pottery containing these gifts (such as food and drink) is, fortunately, mostly intact.[1] This hypothesis about a Proto-Urban Period has been criticized by, among others, R. de Vaux, who points out that at certain places villages of 'huts and a few more solid buildings were abruptly followed by fortified cities'. This was the case, for instance, at Megiddo, Beth-Shan, Jericho and Tell el-Far'ah (N). Others were abandoned and never resettled, and some others were abandoned for quite some time, as was Tell en-Nasbeh.[2] This means that we have to allow for different developments at different places. The earliest remains from the 'Proto-Urban Period' have been found in the Jezreel Valley and in the Beth-Shan Valley. This first phase is also represented at Tulul el 'Alayiq, c. 6 km SSW of Jericho and is contemporaneous with the end of the Ghassulian period.[3] The second and third phases have been found in tombs at several places as well as at the base of some tells, such as Tell ed-Duweir, Tell esh-Shuna, Tulul el-'Alayiq, Megiddo, Beth-Shan, Khirbet Kerak, Jericho, Tell el-Far'ah (N), Tell 'Aireni (Tel 'Erani).[4] Thus, the so-called proto-urban pottery is rather to be seen as the earliest pottery of the urban period. The Grey Burnished pottery (Proto-Urban C) of this period is, as a matter of fact, indigenous.[5] It

Early Bronze Age (London, 1967), pp. 17-18.

1. K.M. Kenyon, *Archaeology in the Holy Land*, pp. 66ff.; *idem*, *Excavations at Jericho*, II (London, 1965), pp. 5 and 8-32.

2. R. de Vaux, *The Early History of Israel*, p. 44. Consult also the investigation by P.R. de Miroschedji, *L'époque pré-urbaine en Palestine* (Cahiers de la Revue Biblique, 13; Paris, 1971).

3. To this period belongs the so-called Gezer Crematorium pottery, cf. the discussion by J.A. Callaway in 'The Gezer Crematorium Re-Examined', *PEQ* 94 (1962), pp. 104-17.

4. See P.R. de Miroschedji, *L'époque pré-urbaine en Palestine*, pp. 58-74.

5. Cf. J.B. Hennessy, *The Foreign Relations of Palestine*, p. 49. See also the discussion in R.T. Schaub, who points out that especially in Transjordan this period

is part of what has been called 'The Esdraelon Culture'.[1] Even if some parallels of Proto-Urban band painted red or brown pottery (Proto-Urban B)[2] have been found in the north, the Palestinian tradition has not been found outside Palestine. This fact does not support the theory about foreigners having invaded Palestine and having been the predecessors of those who built the fortified cities of the Early Bronze Age. The foreign features in the material culture that can be detected have not been introduced through a massive invasion, but rather through peaceful contacts, and one may conclude that newcomers to the country were easily assimilated to the population.[3] Transjordan shows an interesting development. There is continuity at some sites from the Chalcolithic period into the Early Bronze Age I. In the Jordan Valley, for instance, there seems to have been a shift in the location of the settlements from the wadis to the top of the foothills along the valley. Of eight EB I sites, two were new.[4] In the Jerash (Gerasa) region, c. twenty EB I sites are known compared with eight during the Chalcolithic period. The increase in sites may have stemmed from an increase in the population, or may indicate that people relocated within the same territory.[5]

In this connection we should note that the pottery from the last phase of Teleilat Ghassul is contemporaneous with the Palestinian Proto-Urban tradition. The holemouth storage jar, for instance, has been found at sites over almost all of Palestine from the Chalcolithic through the MB I periods.[6] With this as a background one may doubt

---

is a period of an indigenous culture ('The origins of the Early Bronze Age Walled Town Culture in Jordan', *Studies in the History and Archaeology of Jordan*, I [ed. A. Hadidi; Amman, 1982], pp. 67-75).

1.   R. Amiran, *Ancient Pottery of the Holy Land*, pp. 47-49.

2.   Sometimes the bands 'show veining, as if from the hairs of the brush' (K.M. Kenyon, *Archaeology in the Holy Land*, pp. 107-108). Cf. R. Amiran, *Ancient Pottery*, pl. 11; Y. Aharoni, *The Archaeology of the Land of Israel*, p. 53, pl. 9:21.

3.   P.R. de Miroschedji, *L'époque pré-urbaine*, pp. 107-18.

4.   M. Ibrahim, J. Sauer and K. Yassine, *BASOR* 222 (1975), pp. 41-45, 51. Tell esh-Shuneh in the northern Jordan Valley continues from the Chalcolithic through the EB III period, as does Beth-Shan.

5.   Cf. R.T. Schaub, in *Studies in the History and Archaeology of Jordan*, I (ed. A. Hadidi), pp. 73-74.

6.   See I. Beit-Arieh, 'Central Southern Sinai in the Early Bronze Age II and its Relationship with Palestine', *Levant* 15 (1983), p. 42. Cf. Y. Aharoni, *The*

that the Ghassulian culture and its people disappeared. Some of them may have moved to other areas, such as the Negev. Trade contacts with Egypt continued and with trade new impulses may have resulted in changes in the material culture. However, an answer to the question of where the Ghassulians went cannot really be given before an analysis of the available skeletal remains has been made and the evidence for biological continuity, or otherwise, has been clarified.

The Early Bronze Age II is characterized by extensive urbanization with agricultural production forming the major subsistence base for the cities. This is the time in which the typical Canaanite sickle blade was in use and became one of the most important agricultural tools through all the phases of the Bronze Age.[1] Both agriculture and trade may have contributed to the emergence of the city state. We do not know all the reasons for the emergence of the phenomenon called the city. There may have been different reasons in different geographical areas. R.M. Adams maintains that the cities may have 'functioned as junction points or nodes in the appropriation and redistribution of agricultural surpluses.[2] He does not see the development of towns with their monumental buildings and palaces as being stimulated by the growth of the farming population and its villages alone. A contributing factor may also have been 'new patterns of thought and social organization crystallizing within the temples' that were built in this period.[3] The 'patterns of thought' are, of course, impossible to out-

Archaeology of the Land of Israel, pp. 51. For post-Ghassulian features, see J. Perrot, 'Excavations at Tell Abu Matar, near Beersheba', *IEJ* 5 (1955), pp. 167-89; M. Dothan, 'Radioactive Examination of Archaeological Material from Israel', *IEJ* 6 (1956), pp. 112-14.

1. This type of sickle blade seems to occur first in the EB I Canaan. The sickle blades of the Chalcolithic period were typologically different, being 'backed and double truncated'. The Canaanite blades had no backing or 'edge retouch', but show some gloss which may come from 'smearing plant silicas on the edge of the tool during cutting' (S.A. Rosen, 'The Canaanite Blade and the Early Bronze Age', *IEJ* 33 [1983], pp. 20, 22, and fig. 3); cf. Y. Aharoni, *The Archaeology of the Land of Israel*, p. 54.

2. 'The Natural History of Urbanism', *Ancient Cities of the Indus* (ed. G.L. Possehl; Durham, NC, 1979), p. 21. See also *idem, Heartland of the Cities: Surveys of Ancient Settlement and Land Use on the Central Flood Plain of the Euphrates* (Chicago and London, 1981), pp. 52-60.

3. R.M. Adams, 'The Origins of Cities', *Scientific American* 1960 (reprint in *Hunters, Farmers, and Civilizations; Old World Archaeology: Readings from*

line, but we may assume that the temples could have functioned as the administration agents for the redistribution of surpluses.[1] By its nature, a city cannot present a viable mode without an administrative government, and we see also during the Early Bronze Age the emergence of chieftainships and city states. Conflicts between neighboring chieftainships or city states, often of an expansionist character, resulted in defenses being organized as well, as the city state could have developed into a territorial state.[2] However, there was certainly no single reason for the emergence of the city and the city state phenomena. Human behavior and human organization are not always identical. However, to continue to hypothesize, it is possible that some clever ruler got the idea that his position was willed by his god and that the land belonged to the deity.[3] Thus, the 'necessary political duties of state leadership are sacralized'.[4] The king himself was soon thought of as belonging to the divine sphere.[5] The organization of the human society and its political system can be seen as reflected in the mythology, which then is considered the 'prototype' for how the society on

Scientific American [ed. C.C. Lamberg-Karlovsky; San Francisco, 1979], p. 174).

1.   The surplus production can be seen as contributing 'to cover social obligations', B. Bender, 'Gather-Hunter to Farmer: A Social Perspective', *World Archaeology* 10 (1978), p. 210.

2.   See the analysis of H.T. Wright, 'Toward an Explanation of the Origin of the State', *Origins of the State: The Anthropology of Political Evolution* (ed. R. Cohen and E.R. Service; Philadelphia, 1978), pp. 49-68.

3.   This led to the use of the god determinative in front of the king's name, as is, for instance, the case with Naram-Sin of Akkad (c. 2250 BCE). The Hurrian king Tish-atal also used the god determinative (G. Wilhelm, *Grundzüge der Geschichte und Kultur der Hurriter* [Darmstadt, 1982], p. 16). In the Ur III period in Mesopotamia the statues of the dead kings received sacrifices (A.L. Oppenheim, *Ancient Mesopotamia: Portrait of a Dead Civilization* [ed. E. Reiner; 2nd edn; Chicago, 1977]), p. 98; R. Kutscher, 'An Offering to the Statue of Šulgi', *RAI* 17 (1970), p. 55; W.W. Hallo, 'Royal Titles from the Mesopotamian Periphery', *Anatolian Studies* 30 [1980], p. 190). For Ugaritic kings being deified after death and receiving sacrifices, see P. Bordreuil and D. Pardee, 'Le rituel funéraire ougaritique RS. 34.126', *Syria* 59 (1982), pp. 121-28.

4.   R. Cohen, 'Introduction', *Origins of the State* (ed. R. Cohen and E.R. Service; Philadelphia, 1978), p. 16. In Egypt, e.g., the king became a god.

5.   J. Bright thinks that kingship was 'not absolute in theory; power was held by the sanction of divine election' (*A History of Israel*, [3rd. edn; Philadelphia, 1981], p. 34). Bright's theory is misleading. Divine election is a religious-political tool boosting the king's position as ruler.

earth should be organized in order to be 'civilized'.[1] We soon find god and king living in isolation from the urban populus,[2] namely on an acropolis encircled by a wall. It was built on the highest spot on the site, as the name indicates: Greek *akros* = top, and *polis* = city. The acropolis with its temple-palace complex became the center of the world of the god, thus lending a cosmological aspect to the city. We may say that temple and palace constituted the 'essence of the state'.[3]

In certain areas this ideology soon led to an elaborate temple-palace complex being built. If there was no high hill which could serve as a place for the temple, as was often the case in Mesopotamia, one built an artificial mound on which the temple was raised. For instance, the temple at Uruk (Erech) was placed on a 'hill' 40 feet high and covering an area of c. 420,000 square feet.[4] The term for palace and temple in Sumerian is É-GAL which means 'big house'.[5] The distinction between temple and palace is a much later idea. Gods and kings lived in big houses. As for Palestine, the ideology may have been the same, but the temples found at, for instance, Megiddo, Ai and Arad (?) cannot be called elaborate. Thus for Palestine the above can only be used as an illustration. The country of Palestine did not invite the creation of such great material cultures as did Mesopotamia on the Tigris and Euphrates and Egypt around the Nile.

With the concept of the temple representing the god's realm, his

---

1. Cf. T. Jacobsen, 'Primitive Democracy in Ancient Mesopotamia', *JNES* 2 (1943), pp. 159-61. For an example of both city and temple as having their prototypes in heaven, see B. Alster, 'Early Patterns in Mesopotamian Literature', *Kramer Anniversary Volume* (ed. B. Eichler; AOAT, 25; Neukirchen–Vluyn, 1976), p. 19.

2. In the Sumerian epic *Enmerkar and the Lord of Aratta* (from c. 2500 BCE), the god and the king are said to dwell in the same building complex and to share the same throne (S.N. Kramer, *Enmerkar and the Lord of Aratta* [Philadelphia, 1952], p. 38 and ll. 534ff.). This is the same idea that is behind 1 Chron. 29.23, which says that Solomon had been chosen to sit on Yahweh's throne. For the text, see also A. Berlin, *Enmerkar and Ensuhkešdanna: A Sumerian Poem* (Occasional Publication of the Babylonian Fund, 2; Philadelphia, 1979).

3. See further my *Royal Administration*, pp. 3-5. Knowing this, we can understand why the 'destruction of a Sumerian temple was the most disastrous calamity that could befall a city and its people' (S.N. Kramer, *The Sumerians: Their History, Culture and Character* [Chicago, 1963], p. 142).

4. Cf. H. Frankfort, *The Birth of Civilization in the Near East* (Bloomington, IN, 1951), pp. 54-55.

5. It appears as loan-word in Akkadian *ekallu*, Hebrew *hêkāl*, and Syriac *haykal*.

kingdom, and the ruler, the king, governing the god's territory, it is understandable that the temples became big landowners and that the ruler became the organizer of the society's laws and economic system, which included trade and trading posts. Thus, with 'the concentration of wealth, early urban centers became both proponents of expansionism and powerful incentives for external attack. Massive fortifications accordingly became one of their dominant architectural forms.'[1] For Palestine, however, in the EB I period most sites seem to have been unwalled. Cities with huge and thick walls are mainly known from the EB II and III periods. The EB I settlement at 'Ai was at first not fortified, but later a city wall, 6 m wide, was built. J.A. Callaway dates this to EB IC[2] (here EB II). Very large and strong walls from the EB II–III periods have been found at Megiddo (str. XVIII), Tell el-Far'ah (N), Beth Yerah (Khirbet Kerak) and Tell el-'Areini. At the latter site the wall measured up to 8 m in thickness. No other period saw such massive walls. Jericho may be a special case. The city wall of EB I follows mainly the line of the wall of the previous period. It was c. 1.4 m thick, but because of erosion, earthquakes, and fires it was rebuilt several times, which meant that it became thicker at certain spots. At one place the wall had been rebuilt 17 times during the period of Early Bronze. Wooden beams were probably put lengthwise and across the bricks of mud in order to bind the material together. This is the explanation for why it was possible for the wall to burn, as seems to have happened.[3] At Jericho, as time went on, a *fosse* (moat) was also built, in order to make the access to the wall more difficult or to protect the town from flooding.

For Transjordan we should note the city of Bab edh-Dhra'. The site (c. 10 acres) is located in a depression leading down from the Jordanian mountains to the southern *ghor* and the Lisan peninsula.[4] The location is well chosen for a settlement that could dominate the

1. R.M. Adams, 'Natural History', *Ancient Cities of the Indus* (ed. G.L. Possehl), p. 21.

2. 'Ai', *EAEHL*, I, pp. 40-41.

3. K.M. Kenyon, 'Excavations at Jericho, 1952', *PEQ* 84 (1952), pp. 64-65, and *idem, Excavations at Jericho*, III, pp. 97, 193-94.

4. A. Mallon, 'Chronique palestinienne: Voyage d'exploration au sud-est de la Mer Morte', *Bib* 5 (1924), pp. 443-51. Cf. P.W. Lapp, 'The Cemetery at Bab edh-Dhra'', *Archaeology* 19 (1966), pp. 104-11. W.F. Albright thought that the site had been a holy place and not a town ('The Archaeological Results of an Expedition to Moab and the Dead Sea', *BASOR* 14 [1924], pp. 5-9).

access to the southern *ghor* and the Arabah. The town was occupied
from EB I through the EB IV periods and shows links with the
Chalcolithic culture.[1] For instance, a chalcolithic cemetery was found
south of the huge EB cemetery located south of the town. The EB
cemetery contained both charnel houses and shaft tombs.[2] Charnel
houses date mainly from the EB II–III periods. Such a huge cemetery
may indicate that generations of people from the town were buried
there. It does not prove that other communities in the vicinity used the
cemetery, even if such could have been the case.[3] The EB IA cemetery
'probably follows an earlier Chalcolithic tradition of burying the dead
within a specific location'. They belonged to the community and
should, therefore, be buried on their own territory. Thus there is a
'bond' between the living and the dead. This is a conclusion that also
can be drawn from the Chalcolithic cemetery.[4]

From an economic point of view, some agriculture was possible in
the vicinity of Bab edh-Dhra',[5] but the extraction of bitumen, sulphur
and salt that was available through the Dead Sea was perhaps the main
industry of the town. Bab edh-Dhra' is an EB I town that indicates
that the whole of Palestine was not necessarily inhabited by nomads
and pastoralists during the EB I period.[6] Jericho and Arad provide
corroborative evidence.

Returning to the problem of urbanization, the construction of cities
included, for instance, houses, workshops, streets, cisterns, silos and
water conduits. All this required a 'central' plan and division of labor;
thus, some kind of organization making decisions for the society must

1. R.T. Schaub and W.E. Rast, 'Preliminary Report of the 1981 Expedition
to the Dead Sea Plain, Jordan', *BASOR* 254 (1984), pp. 35-60. For a map of the
cemetery and its tomb groups, consult W.E. Rast and R.T. Schaub, 'Preliminary
Report of the 1979 Expedition to the Dead Sea Plain Jordan', *BASOR* 240 (1980),
p. 33, fig. 8.

2. See, for instance, P.W. Lapp, 'Bab edh-Dhra' Tomb 76 and Early Bronze I
in Palestine', *BASOR* 189 (1968),pp. 12-41.

3. As to Bab edh-Dhra', its history and socio-economic system, see
G.R. Bentley, 'Kinship and Social Structure'.

4. G.R. Bentley, 'Kinship and Social Structure', p. 38.

5. See D.W. McCreery, 'The Nature and Cultural Implications of Early Bronze
Age Agriculture in the Southern Ghor of Jordan—An Archaeological Reconstruction'
(PhD dissertation, University of Pittsburgh, Ann Arbor, 1980).

6. G.R. Bentley, *Kinship*, p. 3.

have come into existence.[1] Sociologically, the cities created new classes of people, such as rulers, military and administrative personnel including priests, and several different kinds of craftsmen. Many cities became centers for storage of grain and other necessities. Because this created an increase in needs, new land had to be laid under the plow. As a matter of fact, this is the time when the plow and the wheel came into existence in Mesopotamia. This is also the period in which viticulture started. It is known from Sumer and Egypt from c. 3000 BCE.[2] In the Old Testament its antiquity is expressed through the story about 'prehistoric' Noah, who should have been the first to cultivate the vine, Gen. 9.10. For Mesopotamia, wine is mentioned in the Gilgamesh Epic 11.72.[3]

An administrative apparatus requires that records be kept. Thus, it is not astonishing that the Early Bronze Age has been labeled the period of the formation of written documents. Writing occurs in Sumer before 3000 BCE and shortly afterwards also in Egypt. A. Falkenstein advocated that the Egyptian writing had been inspired by Semitic influences and that it was related to the cuneiform of

1. Cf. R. Amiran *et al.*, *Early Arad: The Chalcolithic Settlement and Early Bronze City*. I. *First–Fifth of Excavations, 1962–1966* (Judean Desert Studies; Jerusalem, 1978), p. 114.

2. W.M.F. Petrie, *Social Life in Ancient Egypt* (Boston, 1923); R.J. Forbes, 'Chemical, Culinary, and Cosmetic Arts', *From Early Times to the Fall of Ancient Empires*, I (ed. C. Singer, E.J. Holmyard and A.R. Hall; History of Technology; 3rd edn; Oxford, 1965), p. 282; P. Garelli, *Le proche-orient asiatique des origines aux invasions des peuples de la mer* (Paris, 1969), p. 56; R. Schoene *et al.*, *Bibliographie zur Geschichtes des Weines* (Munich, 1976); G.W. Ahlström, 'Wine Presses and Cup-Marks of the Jenin-Megiddo Survey', *BASOR* 231 (1978), pp. 19-49 (with bibliog.).

3. The great flood that is mentioned in Gen. 6–8 (the Noah story) may be part of a literary tradition that had its origin in Mesopotamia. This part of the Near East experienced many destructive floodings. One that occurred between the Jemdet Nasr and Early Dynastic periods at Shuruppak (c. 2900 BCE) may have been the source of the tradition. The king of Shuruppak is said to have survived the flood in a boat and was then given eternal life. The hero has different names in different versions, such as Ubar-tutu and Ziusudra in Sumerian texts, and Atrahasis and Utanapishtim in Akkadian texts; see W.W. Hallo in W.W. Hallo and W.K. Simpson, *The Ancient Near East: A History* (New York, 1931), pp. 34-42; cf. S.N. Kramer, 'Reflections on Mesopotamian Flood: The Cuneiform Data New and Old', *Expedition* 9 (1967), pp. 12-18. The biblical hero Noah did not achieve eternal life, but instead lived 950 years, poor man (Gen. 9.29).

Sumer.[1] However, the Sumerian cuneiform is not Semitic. Still, the invention of hieroglyphs may have come as a result of contacts with Mesopotamia, because 'both systems are based on the same principles, and combine elements of the same type'.[2] However, inspiration does not mean that one imitated the other. Because the Egyptian hieroglyphs are quite different, the theory about Mesopotamian influences on the script is less probable.

Concerning the cultural contacts, it has been assumed that there was an overland route from Mesopotamia to Egypt, probably passing through Transjordan. H. Frankfort, among others, has advocated that there existed a sea route from Sumer via the Persian Gulf and the Red Sea.[3] Certain renderings of Egyptian ships on rock drawings are 'overwhelmingly similar to Mesopotamian ones'.[4] Mesopotamian cylinder seals with motifs from the Jemdet Nasr period[5] have been found in Egypt, as has the potter's wheel and a Mesopotamian type of brick architecture.[6] The Mesopotamian elements are 'all from Upper Egyptian sites which would well fit with an entry through the Wadi Hammamat'.[7] One reason for the Mesopotamian cultural expansion is that with greater urban centers and an increase in population the material needs grew. One had to get the raw materials where they were available. The concentration of raw materials perhaps contributed to the growth of urban centers. As to copper, it was obtained

1. *Archaische Texte aus Uruk* (Leipzig, 1936), pp. 63-65.

2. J. Vercoutter, 'The Origins of Egypt', *The Near East: The Early Civilizations* (ed. J. Bottéro, E. Cassin and J. Vercoutter; trans. R.F. Tannenbaum; London, 1967), p. 255.

3. *Birth of Civilization*, pp. 110-11.

4. H.J. Kantor, 'Egypt and its Foreign Relations', *Chronologies in Old World Archaeology* (ed. R.W. Ehrich; Chicago and London, 1954), p. 12.

5. So named after a site between Bagdad and Babylon. The period is a late phase of the Uruk period and is the time of fortified cities and monumental buildings and also when writing was invented. Cylinder seals have figures with animal-like heroes. The pottery has black and red painting on large buff jars. The art of sculpture emerges. The Jemdet Nasr period is the time of the Gerzean and Proto-Dynastic periods in Egypt. Cf. G. Roux, *La Mesopotamie* (Paris, 1985), pp. 79-82.

6. Cf. H. Frankfort, 'The Origin of Monumental Architecture in Egypt', *AJSL* 58 (1941), pp. 329-31; H.J. Kantor, 'The Early Relations of Egypt with Asia', *JNES* 1 (1942), pp. 174-76.

7. H.J. Kantor, 'Egypt', *Chronologies in Old World Archaeology* (ed. R.W. Ehrich), p. 13.

not only from southern Iran and the Indus Valley; it was also shipped from Oman.[1] There are also some copper ores on the Bahrain islands.[2] If the Mesopotamians could sail to Oman, they certainly also could make use of the monsoon winds to navigate to Egypt and to the Wadi Hammamat where the precious metal, gold, was available. At Jebel el-Araq opposite Thinis (Tjene), the capital of the First Dynasty, a knife with a carved ivory handle was found. The handle shows Mesopotamian motifs with boats and animals as well as soldiers fighting with each other.[3] The shortest route from the Red Sea to Jebel el-Araq is through the Wadi Hammamat. Even if the Mesopotamian presence in Upper Egypt did not last long, perhaps only a generation, its impact on art, technology and writing may have been part of the stimulus that soon led to the unification of Lower and Upper Egypt and thus to the emergence of the Egyptian empire.[4]

In order to get a correct perspective on EB I as the time of the emergence of cities and city states and the concomitant social and cultural changes, we should certainly take into consideration the role that the Jemdet Nasr culture played in the Near East. Thus, Ruth Amiran's opinion that the phenomena of EB I cannot be said to have developed out of *'purely and exclusively* local conditions'[5] is certainly close to the mark. Even if we do not need to reckon with an invasion of foreigners as builders of the cities and their huge walls, the inspiration might have come from outside Palestine.

Arad in the eastern Negev is one of the Early Bronze Age towns in Palestine which can be mentioned as an example of the transformation of a Chalcolithic site (str. V) with huts and pits into a real city. In the EB I period Arad (str. IV, Dynasty 0) was an unwalled settlement which developed into a fortified city in EB II (str. III–II). The city reached its 'zenith' in stratum II, which shows a 'more advanced townplanning'.[6] The city wall, 1176 m long and 2–2.5 m wide, encircled

1. Cf. J.D. Muhly, 'Kupfer', *Reallexikon der Assyriologie*, VI.5, p. 357.
2. R.J. Forbes, *Studies in Ancient Technology*, IX, p. 12.
3. See S. Lloyd, *The Art of the Ancient Near East* (London, 1961), p. 31.
4. S. Parpola, 'Mesopotamia', *Cappelens Verdenshistorie*. II. *Flodrikene* (ed. E. Bjöl and K. Mykland; Halden and Otava, 1982), p. 156.
5. 'The Beginning of Urbanization in Canaan', *Near Eastern Archaeology in the Twentieth Century* (ed. J.A. Sanders; Garden City, NY, 1970), p. 83.
6. R. Amiran *et al.*, *Early Arad*, p. 25. The earliest date for str. IV would be the second half of EB I, which is the period of the Egyptian kings Narmer and Hor-Aha (see p. 115).

an area of about 22 acres. It had semicircular towers spaced c. 20 m apart. Whether or not this wall was finished in the EB II period is unclear.[1] There are some parallels to these towers from Mesopotamia and Greece.[2] In this dry climate water conservation was always a problem. The people of Arad solved that by digging a cistern in the lowest part of the town. Most of the houses were of the broadroom type and were dug 50 cm down into the ground. Several of them had benches around the walls. Some pits (bins?) and square and round platforms were built close to many of the houses. The purpose of these is not really known, but one could assume that the round platforms were bases for small silos. A structure of two broadroom houses (1831 and 1894) built together has been interpreted as a 'Twin temple'.[3] Close to it was also a circular basin with a depth of one meter. This 'temple' has been compared with the sanctuaries at En-Gedi, Megiddo, and the Sin temple at Khafaje (on the Diyala river NE of Baghdad), as well as with a temple complex at Byblos from c. 2900–2800 BCE.[4] No oven or cooking pots were found in the structure at Arad, which shows that the complex is not an ordinary house. A stela of stone was, however, found. It was incised with two figures with raised arms and with 'an ear of grain instead of a human head'. R. Amiran sees this as a representation of the Sumerian god Dumuzu, the god of vegetation and grain.[5] The pottery from Arad indicates that the city had trade connections with Egypt. There is Egyptian pottery at the site and some Egyptian objects were also found. Palestinian pottery from the Negev area of this time as well as some Egyptian pottery has also been found at several sites in the Sinai.[6] These facts make one realize that there was a trade route from the Arabah going through the wadis on the western side of the Gulf of Aqaba down into

1. For a discussion about this and about the stratigraphy of Arad, cf. W.G. Dever, *IEJ* 32 (1982), pp. 170-75.

2. R. Amiran *et al.*, *Early Arad*, pp. 4-6, 13.

3. R. Amiran *et al.*, *Early Arad*, pp. 38-41, pls. 159-65.

4. See A. Kempinski, 'The Sin Temple at Khafaje and the En-Gedi Temple', *IEJ* 22 (1972), pp. 10-15; I. Dunayevsky and A. Kempinski, 'The Megiddo Temples', *EI* 11 (1973), pp. 12-13.

5. 'Arad', *EAEHL*, I, p. 79.

6. Cf. I. Beit-Arieh, 'Sinai Survey', *IEJ* 29 (1979), pp. 256-57; R. Amiran, I. Beit-Arieh and J. Glass, 'The Interrelationship between Arad and Sites in Southern Sinai in the Early Bronze Age II', *IEJ* 23 (1973), pp. 193-95, 197.

southern Sinai and to Egypt. Because there were no other cities in the Negev one may see Arad as an administrative center for trade in the regions of Negev and Sinai.[1]

Egypt's interest in the Sinai was not only to secure the trade routes but also to mine the copper and turquoise in the mountainous regions of the peninsula. From the time of the Third Dynasty (27th cent. BCE) Egypt extracted turquoise at Serabit el-Khadem near the stone quarries in Wadi Maghara. The first three kings of the Third Dynasty are mentioned in rock inscriptions close to the mines.[2] To be able to work the mines the people of the area had to be controlled and many of them were probably put to work there.

In northwestern Sinai there were some Chalcolithic settlements along the coast between the Suez and Gaza. The number of sites increased in the EB I (Proto-Dynastic) period to over one hundred. The material culture of these sites was South Palestinian. No Egyptian objects were found.

As an indication for contacts with Egypt one should also notice that the name of pharaoh Narmer (?)[3] occurs in a *serekh* on jar fragments which have been found both at Arad and Tel 'Erani (earlier called Tel Gath). These two fragments together with the Narmer palette have usually been taken as proof for the Egyptian military dominance of southern Palestine during the First Dynasty.[4] They may, however, testify to close trade connections with the Egyptian kingdom,[5] as well

1.   R. Amiran, 'The Fall of the Early Bronze Age II City of Arad', *IEJ* 36 (1986), pp. 74-77.

2.   See R. Giveon, *The Impact of Egypt on Canaan* (OBO, 20; Freiburg, 1978), pp. 51-53; *idem*, 'A Second Relief of Sekhemkhet in Sinai', *BASOR* 216 (1974), pp. 17-20; cf. I. Beit-Arieh, 'New Discoveries at Serabit el-Khadim', *BA* 45 (1982), p. 13.

3.   W.A. Ward has maintained that the *serekh* is an Egyptian potter's mark ('The Supposed Asiatic Campaign of Narmer', *Mélanges de l'Université Saint-Joseph* 45 [1969], pp. 205-21).

4.   See, for instance, Y. Yadin, 'The Earliest Record of Egypt's Military Penetration into Asia?' *IEJ* 5 (1955), pp. 1-16; cf. S. Yeivin, 'Early Contacts between Canaan and Egypt', *IEJ* 10 (1960), pp. 193-95; *idem*, 'Further Evidence of Narmer at "Gat"', *Oriens Antiquus* 2 (1963), pp. 205-207.

5.   R. Amiran dismisses the idea that the Egyptian objects in southern Palestine indicate that the Egyptians militarily dominated this area ('An Egyptian Jar Fragment with the Name of Narmer from Arad', *IEJ* 24 [1974], pp. 10-11).

as perhaps testifying to the knowledge of Egyptian writing in southern Palestine during the EB II period. The pottery from Sinai shows the same kind of trade connection, even though the material culture in Sinai is Palestinian and its pottery shows the same kind of repertoire as that of Arad, the Negev and Jordan.[1] In Egypt Palestinian painted pottery, among other objects, has been found in the graves of the kings of the First Dynasty.[2] From all this Helen J. Kantor draws the conclusion that the connections between Egypt and southern Palestine were very close during the First Dynasty, and were 'even closer than those enjoyed by Byblos'.[3] I should add that Egyptian pottery also has turned up in the 'Amuq area in Syria, but nobody has made an Egyptian empire out of that. In southwestern Palestine, Egyptian 'kitchenwares', such as cooking pots, have been found at, for instance, Tel Halif, Tel 'Erani and 'En Besor. These places may have functioned as trading posts or Egyptian colonies[4] rather than as military bases.[5] After the EB III period there are no traces of Egyptian objects in Palestine and neither are there any artifacts from Palestine in Egypt. Because Arad went out of existence when Egyptian presence

1. I. Beit-Arieh, 'New Evidence on Relations between Canaan and Egypt during the Proto-Dynastic Period', *IEJ* 34 (1984), pp. 20-23. The Sinai settlements have been seen by Beit-Arieh as being dependent upon Arad: cf. *idem*, 'Central-Southern Sinai in the Early Bronze Age II and its Relationship with Palestine', *Levant* 15 (1983), p. 47.

2. The so-called Abydos ware, which has been found in Egyptian tombs from the First Dynasty and which once held wine and olive oil, are of Palestinian origin; cf. R. Amiran, *Ancient Pottery of the Holy Land*, p. 59; Y. Aharoni, *The Archaeology of the Land of Israel*, p. 67. Arad may be seen as one of the places from where this kind of pottery came.

3. *Chronologies in Old World Archaeology* (ed. R.W. Ehrich), p. 16.

4. Cf. R. Gophna, 'Egyptian Immigration into Southern Canaan during the First Dynasty?', *Tel Aviv* 3 (1976), pp. 31-37; A. Ben-Tor, 'The Relations between Egypt and the Land of Canaan during the Third Millenium BCE', *JJS* 33 (1982), pp. 9-10. Consult also A. Kempinski, *The Rise of Urban Culture: The Urbanization of Palestine in Early Bronze Age* (Israel Exploration Society Studies, 4; Jerusalem, 1978), p. 17.

5. J. Weinstein maintains that Tel 'Erani ('Areini) 'has the longest stratified sequence of Egyptian pottery of any excavated site' in southern Palestine during the EB period. As well, he maintains that there are no indications for the city having been destroyed by the Egyptians under Narmer. The pottery indicates that the relationship to Egypt was a commercial one ('The Significance of Tell Areini for Egyptian–Palestinian Relations at the Beginning of the Bronze Age', *BASOR* 256 [1984], pp. 65-67).

was no longer felt in Palestine (Second Dynasty) one may conclude that Arad was one of the Egyptian 'colonies' even if it was not populated by Egyptians.[1]

We have no exact information about how the country was governed, but one may assume that the rulers of the larger and well fortified cities also ruled the surrounding areas together with their farming villages.[2] The term 'city states' would therefore be applicable. The territory between the city states may have been open for nomads and pastoralists who during the summers could not find adequate grazing ground for their herds and therefore had to move into the more arable areas. Economically, these people could supply the cities and the villages with livestock. However, they could also represent a threat to the villagers and their fields, a threat that had to be averted by negotiations or military pressure.[3]

The transition from village life to city life took a longer time in Palestine than in the north, at least it is a somewhat later phenomenon. One of the best known sites in the greater Palestinian area is Byblos. The settlement of the period 3500–3200 BCE had rectangular and apsidal houses, and paved streets and/or paths between some of the houses. From c. 3000 BCE there are rectangular houses with several rooms. This period is rich in pottery and cylinder seals of the Jemdet Nasr type. in the following centuries monumental buildings occur such as a well-built city wall and two temples.[4] The city and its wall are, in the

---

1.   R. Amiran sees the Egyptian occupation of Sinai during the Third Dynasty as a blow to Arad's economy and position as a trading center. The loss of the copper trade would then have been one of the main reasons for the collapse of Arad which probably occurred around 2650 BCE (*IEJ* 36 [1986], pp. 774-76). If this date should turn out to be right, Arad would have been abandoned first in the later half of the time of the Third Dynasty.

2.   Cf. I. Beit-Arieh, *Levant* 15 (1983), p. 47.

3.   On interaction between nomads and villages, cf. M.B. Rowton, 'Autonomy and Nomadism in Western Asia', *Or* NS 42 (1973), pp. 247-58; *idem*, 'Enclosed Nomadism', *JESHO* 17 (1974), pp. 1-30; *idem*, 'Economic and Political Factors in Ancient Nomadism', *Nomads and Sedentary Peoples* (ed. J.S. Castillo; XXX International Congress of Human Sciences in Asia and North Africa; Mexico City, 1981), pp. 25-36. Rowton maintains that an economic exploitation of the environment was made through a symbiosis of animal husbandry and agriculture (*Or* NS 42 [1973], p. 249).

4.   See M. Dunand, 'Chronologies des plus anciennes installations de Byblos', *RB* 57 (1950), pp. 583-603; J. Perrot, 'Palestine–Syria–Cilicia', *Courses toward*

Byblian tradition, said to have been built by the god El (Kronos).[1]
The two temples are known as the Oval Temple and the Temple of
Baalat-Gebal.[2] Baalat may be identified with Ashtarte; for the
Egyptians she was Hathor.

Concerning the architecture of the ordinary houses at Byblos of the
EB II period, we know that they were constructed of sandstone and
solidly built. One type had six pillars along the walls, but none of
them were in the corner of the house. The seventh pillar was placed in
between the two rows at the point of one-third of the length of the
ridge-pole which this seventh pillar then supported. This means that
the pillar was placed so that the distance to the long walls was the
same. One may assume that the ridge pole had the form of a tree
trunk so that the pillar was placed at the spot where the trunk most
likely would break if not supported. The pillars rested on stone bases.[3]
Prov. 9.1 refers to this kind of house:

> Wisdom has built her house,
> she has cut out her seven pillars.

Even if this type of house is not part of the Palestinian building tradition, the saying in Proverbs shows that an ancient custom has become
proverbial and reached areas where its content never was practiced.
The point of the proverb is that it would be foolish to forget the seventh pillar, in other words, nothing in the system should be lacking.[4]

Urban Life: Archaeological Considerations of Some Cultural Alternates (ed.
R.J. Braidwood and G.R. Willey; Chicago, 1962), pp. 160-61. Cf. also T.A. Busink,
Der Tempel von Jerusalem von Salomo bis Herodes, I (Leiden, 1970), pp. 430-32.

1. Cf. J. Barr, 'Philo of Byblos and his "Phoenician History"', *BJRL* 57
(1974), p. 27.

2. An Egyptian seal impression mentions the gods of these two temples as the
Lord and Lady of Gubla, which in Phoenician would be Baal and Baalat; cf.
H. Klengel, *Geschichte und Kultur Altsyriens* (Heidelberg, 1967), p. 18.

3. See M. Dunand, 'Rapport préliminaire sur les fouilles de Byblos en 1948',
Bulletin du Musée de Beyrouth 9 (1949–50), pp. 53-64, pls. i-vii; cf. N. Jidejian,
Byblos through the Ages (Beirut, 1948), p. 15; T.A. Busink, *Der Tempel von
Jerusalem*, I, p. 436. This type of house form has been found also at Punic Mersa-
Madakh in Libya; cf. G. Vuillemont, *Fouilles punique à Mersa Madakh Libyca*
(1954), pp. 299-300.

4. Cf. N. Jidejian, *Byblos through the Ages*, p. 15; T.A. Busink, *Der Tempel
von Jerusalem*, I, p. 437, fig. 119. Because stone bases had to be cut out one does
not need to emend ḥsb, 'cut out', of the Hebrew text to nṣb, hiph, 'to erect', as is

Among the earliest indications for Egyptian contacts with Byblos and Lebanon is a cylinder from Thinis in Upper Egypt from c. 3000 BCE which was found in Byblos. Another piece of information about contact with this area is the so-called Palermo stone from the time of Pharaoh Snefru of the Fourth Dynasty (27th cent. BCE).[1] Its inscription is one of the earliest records for Egypt's import of cedars from Lebanon.[2] These were used not only as building material, but the resin of the trees was also used in the rituals of embalming.

Among new cities from the EB II period are, for instance, Hazor and Rosh Hanniqra in the north, Tell Beit Mirsim, Beth-Shemesh, and Tell el-Ḥesi in the south. From pottery and artifacts one can draw the conclusion that the population of Ḥesi was in the process of moving out to the foothills of Judah at the end of the EB III period. Some caves from the Chalcolithic and EB II periods have been found at Tell ed-Duweir. As for Ḥesi, it does not seem to have had too many settlers in the Early Bronze Age.

Tell el-Far'ah (N) is known from the Neolithic (PPNB) and Chalcolithic periods. In EB I the Chalcolithic remains were levelled off and the buildings were constructed on stone foundations with mud-brick walls. The city wall was also built of mudbrick. In some places the wall reached 3.5 m in height. In the EB II period a stone wall and a glacis outside it were added. Since no remains from the EB III period have been found, the city was probably abandoned shortly before or around 2500 BCE, and there is then a gap in population until the nineteenth century BCE.

Another city which went out of existence c. 2350 BCE is Ai. Like Far'ah (N) it had an outer wall 3 m wide and an inner wall that was up to 6 m in width. Two phases of the inner wall belong to EB I and II. Two sanctuaries have been found, one belonging to the EB I–II periods and another from the EB IIIB. The city is thought to have

---

often done. It weakens the point; cf. G.W. Ahlström, 'The House of Wisdom', *SEÅ* 44 (1979), pp. 74-76.

1.   H. Schafer, *Ein Bruchstück altägyptischer Annalen* (Berlin, 1902); K. Sethe, *Urkunden des alten Reiches* (Urkunden, 1; Leipzig, 1933), pp. 236-37; also J.H. Breasted, *Ancient Records of Egypt*, I (Chicago, 1906), p. 66; cf. J.A. Wilson, *ANET*,

p. 227.

2.   The cedar is a majestic tree that can reach a height of c. 30 m and an age of about 1000 years; cf. H.N. and A.L. Moldenke, *Plants of the Bible* (Chronica Botanica; Waltham, MA, 1952), pp. 66-67.

been destroyed in EB II and rebuilt in EB III. This rebuilding J.A. Callaway attributes to Egyptian control of the site, a control that began to erode in the EB IIIB period. Egypt's interest in Ai was probably 'to secure trade and military routes by land between Egypt and Syria'. Thus, Ai may be understood as a parallel to Megiddo.[1]

In the Early Bronze II/III period a new kind of pottery appears in Palestine, and this has been connected with the arrival of northerners settling mainly in northern Palestine.[2] This is the so-called Khirbet Kerak ware which obtains its name from the place where it was first found, namely Kh. Kerak (Canaanite Beth Yerah, i.e., the house of the moon) at the southwestern end of Lake Tiberias and east of the river Jordan.[3] Other cities where a great amount of this pottery has been found are Beth-Shan, Hazor and Shuneh.[4] The EB III city of Beth Yerah (Khirbet Kerak) situated along the southern end of Lake Tiberias was probably one of the largest cities in Palestine. Its city wall was 1.6 km (one mile) in length. In EB II the city had paved streets, and in EB III the houses were built of mudbrick on foundations of basalt. A large granary complex (1200 sq. m) was built in the same period. It consisted of nine silos surrounding a large, rectangular building.[5] This latter building has been seen by some as a sanctuary. The state and its business, in this case agriculture, were integral parts of one and the same social structure.[6] Most of the Khirbet Kerak pottery that has been found in Palestine comes from this place. The pottery is porous and poorly baked, but has a heavy slip that is burned to a high gloss in red and black. Sometimes it has ribbed or incised

1. J.A. Callaway, 'New Perspectives on Early Bronze III in Canaan', *Archaeology in the Levant* (ed. R. Moorey and P. Parr), pp. 54-55.

2. R. Amiran associates these with the destruction of several sites, as Beth Yerah, Megiddo, 'Ai and Yarmut (*IEJ* 36 [1986], pp. 74-76).

3. In ancient time the river flowed west of the town which thus was located on a peninsula.

4. See D.L. Esse, 'Beyond Subsistence: Beth Yerah and Northern Palestine in the Early Bronze Age' (PhD dissertation, University of Chicago, Chicago, 1982), pp. 371-73.

5. B. Mazar, M. Stekelis and M. Avi-Yonah, 'The Excavations at Beth-Yerah (Khirbet el-Kerak) 1944–1946', *IEJ* 2 (1952), pp. 165-73, 218-19.

6. Cf. E. Anati, *Palestine Before the Hebrews*, p. 337; cf. H. Frankfort, *The Birth of Civilization in the Near East*, pp. 52-54. For the ruler controlling the movements of the products of agriculture and craft, cf. H.T. Wright, 'Recent Research on the Origin of the State', *Annual Review of Anthropology* 6 (1977), pp. 380-82.

decorations.[1] This pottery occurs at several places in the 'Amuq Valley in Syria as well as at Ugarit and Hama. In Palestine it has been found mainly in the northern Jordan Valley, at sites in the Jezreel Valley, at Hazor, Rosh Hanniqrah and sporadically in the south, as for instance, at Gezer, Tell ed-Duweir, Tel 'Erani, Jericho, Ai and Aphek. Because of these occurrences one may conclude that this ware arrived in Palestine with some newcomers from the north. The pottery is also the same as that found in eastern Anatolia from around 2800 BCE,[2] and has by some scholars been associated with the Hurrians (the Horites of the Old Testament).[3] This may be true, but we do not have any literary corroborations about the Hurrians. They are attested in Palestine first from the mid-second millennium BCE. It is possible, however, that some newcomers had settled in Khirbet Kerak, which became a great center for storing and distributing grain. Its large granary complex testifies to its importance, and points to associations with the public granary at Yanik Tepe in Anatolia.[4] Beth Yerah is located at the point where two climatic zones meet. One is a transition type of the western Mediterranean zone. Rainfall at Beth Yerah averages c. 400 mm per year, making the site suitable for agriculture. The other zone is the Irano-Turanian of the Jordan Valley with an annual rainfall of 300–200 mm.[5] Beth Yerah became an important center for intraregional trade, located as it was at the trade route from Damascus to the Esdraelon valley.[6] For the Golan and the Galilean territories north of Beth Yerah transhumance most probably continued as the main way of life.

In this connection we should note that during the EB II/III periods there seems to have been a sharp decline in small sites in the Beth Shan Valley. D.L. Esse sees this as a result of 'the increased specialization of large sites, as for instance, Beth Shan, Beth Yerah and Shuneh'. The population of the smaller settlements were absorbed

1.   See R. Amiran, *Ancient Pottery of the Holy Land*, pp. 68-70.

2.   See S. Hood, 'Excavations at Tabara el-Akrad', *Anatolian Studies* 1 (1951), pp. 113-15; R. Amiran, 'Yarik Tepe, Shengavit and the Khirbet Kerak Ware', *Anatolian Studies* 15 (1965), pp. 165-67. For its distribution in Palestine, see R. Gophna, *Tel Aviv* 3 (1976), p. 35. Cf. also I. Todd, 'Anatolia and the Khirbet Kerak Problem', *AOAT* 22 (1973), pp. 181-206.

3.   For the Hurrians, see G. Wilhelm, *Grundzüge*.

4.   R. Amiran, *Anatolian Studies* 15 (1965), p. 167.

5.   E. Orni and E. Efrat, *Geography of Israel*, pp. 164-72.

6.   D.L. Esse, 'Beyond Subsistence', pp. 230-41.

'into the larger urban polities of EB II/III'.[1] This phenomena probably led to an increase in political 'authority' with greater need for taxes and conscription of people for corvée and military service. From this Esse concludes that the steppe population has been relocated.

Another phenomenon is that geometric cylinder seals with impressions found in northern Palestine including the Jezreel and Beth Shan valleys points to a cultural subdivision somewhat different from the rest of Palestine. In southern Palestine 'the seals themselves but not the impressions make up the overwhelming majority of finds'.[2] There are close parallels to these northern Palestinian seals in the Argolid. The contacts may have been made between Tarsus in Cilicia and Hama in Syria,[3] according to A. Ben-Tor.[4] He also maintains that there probably was an independent center of glyptic art in northern Palestine.[5] If we combine the phenomenon of the distribution of seals and seal impressions with the distribution of the Khirbet Kerak ware, we may have a strong support for seeing northern Palestine, including northern Transjordan, as a cultural subregion.[6]

With the Third Dynasty, Egypt again shows its interest in the east. This is the time when the turquoise mines in Sinai began to be exploited, as mentioned above. However, a clear picture of Egypt's relations with Palestine during the time of the Old Kingdom is impossible to obtain. The textual material is very meager, and drawings, seals and pottery do not tell the full story. F. Petrie considered a drawing from Deshasheh as portraying the siege of an 'Asiatic' city (Fifth Dynasty).[7] Some Egyptian texts mention campaigns against the

---

1. 'Beyond Subsistence', pp. 11-12.

2. A. Ben-Tor, *Cylinder Seals of the Third-Millennium Palestine* (ASOR Suppl. Ser., 22; Cambridge, MA, 1978), p. 102.

3. As for the art of Syrian cylinder seals in the third millenium BCE, H. el-Safadi maintains that an independent Syrian art occurred after the Jemdet Nasr period. He dismisses H. Frankfort's theory about this art being labeled as a peripheral Mesopotamian style ('Die Entstehung der syrischen Glyptik und ihre Entwicklung in der Zeit von Zimrilim bis Ammitaqummu', *UF* 6 [1974], pp. 333-52).

4. *Cylinder Seals*, pp. 96-98.

5. *Cylinder Seals*, p. 109.

6. Cf. D.L. Esse, 'Beyond Subsistence', p. 327.

7. F. Petrie, *Deshasheh* (London, 1898), p. 5 and pl. IV. B.J. Kemp maintains that 'when the Egyptians refer to or depict foreign fortresses we should understand nothing less than the fortified cities of Early and Middle Bronze Age Palestine' ('Old Kingdom, Middle Kingdom and Second Intermediate Period c. 2686–1552 BCE',

'sand-dwellers' and the '3mw which usually has been translated 'Asiatics', referring to nomads and other groups of people east of Egypt and in Palestine.[1] For instance, Weni's cenotaph describes military expeditions to the land of the 'sand-dwellers'. Weni was a commoner who under Pepi I (2390–2361 BCE) of the Sixth Dynasty quickly climbed the ladder to success. He was made a priest, commander, the king's 'friend', and later a governor in Upper Egypt. He is said to have marched north, campaigning against the 'sand-dwellers'. He returned victorious after he had destroyed villages, enclosures, vineyards and had cut down fig trees.[2] However, he had to return in order to put down rebellions. He crossed in a ship to a place beyond the 'Nose of the Antelope/Goat' (sometimes translated the 'Gazelle's Head').[3] Where this place was located is not known, and there are thus several suggestions, such as a place in Wadi Tumilat in the Delta[4] Mons Cassius on the coast of the eastern Delta[5] or the Carmel.[6] The text seems to indicate that the mountain range cannot have been in Wadi Tumilat, and it cannot have been in the territory close to Mons Cassius, because there are no vineyards in that area. There is only sand. The only mountain range that Weni could have reached by boat would be the Carmel. If this is right the Egyptians would have devastated villages in the Jezreel plain. We may, therefore, reckon that Weni's army also destroyed Megiddo (stratum XVI?).[7] As the most

Ancient Egypt: A Social History [ed. B.G. Trigger *et al.*; Cambridge, 1983], p. 143).

1.   According to B.J. Kemp, the term '3mu was 'extended to peoples of the eastern desert' (*Ancient Egypt* [ed. B.G. Trigger *et al.*], p. 142 n. 1). T.L. Thompson connects the term with Egyptian '3m, 'boomerang, throwing stick' (*The Historicity of the Patriarchal Narratives: The Quest for the Historical Abraham* [BZAW, 133; New Haven, 1975], pp. 121-22).

2.   For the text, see J.A. Wilson, *ANET*, pp. 227-28, and A. Roccati, *La literature historique sous l'ancient empire égyptien* (Paris, 1982), pp. 187-97 (with bibliog.)

3.   J.A. Wilson thinks this refers to a fallow deer or to a bubalis, i.e., a north African antelope (*ANET*, p. 228 n. 10). K. Baer thinks that the Egyptian sign refers to 'some kind of a goat' (pers. comm.).

4.   H. Goedicke, 'The Alleged Military Campaign in S. Palestine in the Reign of Pepi I (Vth Dynasty)', *Rivista degli Studi Orientali* 38 (1963), pp. 187-97.

5.   W. Helck, *Die Beziehungen*, p. 19.

6.   A. Gardiner, *Egypt of the Pharaohs* (Oxford, 1961), p. 96; cf. Y. Aharoni, *The Land of the Bible*, 2nd edn, pp. 135-37.

7.   The EB III stratum XVI was totally destroyed; cf. K.M. Kenyon, 'Some Notes on the Early and Middle Bronze Age Strata of Megiddo', *EI* 5 (1958), p. 55*.

important city state in the plain Megiddo may have been the center of rebellion against the Egyptians.

Weni's campaigns may indicate that Pepi I tried to establish supremacy over parts of Palestine, even if the Egyptian rule could not be maintained, and that this coincided with the downfall of the Early Bronze Age culture. Under Pepi's son and second successor, Pepi II (2355–2261 BCE),[1] the decline of the Egyptian Old Kingdom begins with the southern provinces becoming more or less autonomous. The time of the Seventh and Eighth dynasties, with sixteen weak kings, prepared the way for what has been called the First Intermediate Period (2213–1991 BCE). In this period the Egyptian kingship was almost powerless, and governors and feudal lords were competing for power in their districts. Textual information about this time also mentions that *'3mw* invaded the Delta. These have usually been seen as Asiatics, which in many instances may be right, but the word does not only mean 'Asiatic', as is clear, for instance, from a scene on a stone block from a temple at Gebelein. The enemies depicted on this stone are a Nubian, an *'3mw* and a Libyan. The latter two are shown with a head-feather that is Libyan; thus, the *'3mw* in this case is a Libyan too.[2]

The downfall of the EB III culture was earlier seen as the result of an Amorite invasion into southern Syria and Palestine; the invasions into the Delta are also explained through the 'Amorite' hypothesis. These Amorites are said to have been nomads whose migrations should have been experienced all over the ancient Near East from Mesopotamia to Egypt.[3] The hypothesis is nothing else than a mistake. The term 'Amorite' is at home in the Hebrew Bible as a designation for the pre-Israelite inhabitants of the Palestinian hills,[4] and has nothing to do with the Akkadian *amurru*, which is a term for the territories west of the Euphrates. All groups of people living west of the Euphrates could therefore be called Amurru, just as the West itself could be called

---

1. Pepi's long reign means that he became king as a little boy. Cf. A. Gardiner, *Egypt of the Pharaohs*, p. 101.

2. The artist could, of course, have made a mistake. See W.A. Ward, *Egypt and the Mediterranean World 2200–1900 BCE* (Beirut, 1971), p. 61.

3. See W.F. Albright, 'Palestine in the Earliest Historical Period', *JPOS* 2 (1922), p. 125; cf. K.M. Kenyon, *Archaeology of the Holy Land*, pp. 119-21, 145-47; Y. Aharoni, *The Land of the Bible*, 2nd edn, pp. 137-39.

4. See, for instance, J.C.L. Gibson, 'Observations on some Important Ethnic Terms in the Pentateuch', *JNES* 20 (1961), pp. 220-24; J. Van Seters, 'The Terms "Amorite" and "Hittite"', *VT* 22 (1972), pp. 64-81.

'amurru'. They may have been urban or nonurban inhabitants of the country; some of them could have been nomadic.[1] It is less probable that a mass invasion of nomads caused the destruction of such cities as Beth-Shan, Megiddo, Ai and Jericho, where destruction layers have been found. At other places there are settlement gaps but no destruction layers, indicating that the cities were abandoned. A few towns, however, were built, as at Beth-Shemesh and Tell Beit Mirsim. There existed several small settlements both in Cisjordan and Transjordan in this period, according to some surveys.[2] The country was thus not depopulated, as has been maintained; instead, there was a shift in population density. The many tombs found in the hill country, and the many new settlements established in this period in the Negev, are indications that the country was not depopulated.

Early Bronze IV

The reasons for the downfall of the EB III culture are not quite known.[3] It is possible that we have to reckon with both political and

1. Cf. M. Liverani, 'The Amorites', *The Peoples of Old Testament* (ed. D.J. Wiseman; Oxford, 1973), pp. 100-33. See also the discussion in K.A. Kamp and N. Yoffe, 'Ethnicity in Ancient Western Asia during the Early Second Millennium BCE: Archaeological Assessments and Ethnoarchaeological Perspectives', *BASOR* 237 (1980), pp. 85-104.

2. Consult S. Richard, 'Toward a Consensus of Opinion on the End of the Early Bronze Age in Palestine-Transjordan', *BASOR* 237 (1980), pp. 5-34; W.G. Dever, 'New Vistas on the EB IV ("MB I") Horizon in Syria-Palestine', *BASOR* 237 (1980), pp. 35-64; cf. J.A. Sauer, 'Transjordan in the Bronze and Iron Ages: A Critique of Glueck's Synthesis', *BASOR* 263 (1986), pp. 3-4.

3. Usually EB III is seen as coming to an end around 2350/2300 BCE. The periodization accepted here is that of E. Oren, who sees the Albright–Glueck–Wright EB IV and MB I periods as EB IVA (ending c. 2000 BCE) and B (which ends c. 1950–1900 BCE). The following period is labeled MB I by Kenyon, Tufnell and Oren ending c. 1800 (= Albright's MB IIA). See K.M. Kenyon, *Amorites and Canaanites* (Oxford, 1966), p. 55; E.D. Oren, *The Northern Cemetery of Beth-Shan* (Philadelphia, 1973), pp. 58-60; *idem*, 'The Early Bronze IV Period in Northern Palestine and its Cultural and Chronological Setting', *BASOR* 210 (1973), pp. 30-32, 35-37; cf. W.G. Dever, 'The EB IV–MB I Horizon in Transjordan and Southern Palestine', *BASOR* 210 (1973), pp. 60-62. P. Gerstenblith follows Oren's system in *The Levant at the Beginning of the Middle Bronze Age* (ASOR Diss. Ser., 5; Winona Lake, IN, 1983), p. 3. P.W. Lapp preferred the term 'Intermediate Bronze Age I and II' (*The Dhar Mirzbaneh Tombs: Three Intermediate Bronze Age Cemeteries in*

socio-economic factors, and at some places with deforestation. A possible change in climate has also to be taken into consideration. All this may have contributed to the decline of the urban culture and an increase in villages and campsites associated with transhumance. Migrations have occurred, but, as mentioned above, it is impossible to accept the theory about a large invasion of nomadic Semites, 'Amorites',[1] from the north who might have conquered the fortified cities of Palestine.[2] Archaeological finds do not support such a

Jordan [New Haven, 1966]). K. Prag prefers the term EB.MB Age ('The Intermediate Early Bronze–Middle Bronze Age: An Interpretation of the Evidence from Transjordan, Syria and Lebanon', *Levant* 6 [1974], pp. 69-70); J.N. Tubb is in favor of Kenyon's MB I term, but prefers to keep 'MB IIA', because it is 'unambiguous' ('The MBIIA Period in Palestine: Its Relationship with Syria and its Origin', *Levant* 15 [1983], p. 49 n. 1). R. Amiran's dates are: EB IV 2350–2250/ 2200, MB I 2250/2200–2000/1950, MB IIA 2000/1950–1730 BCE (*Ancient Pottery of the Holy Land*, p. 12). The most recent contribution is that of I. Finkelstein, who calls the period the Intermediate Bronze Age (IBA) ('Further Observations on the Socio-Demographic Structure of the Intermediate Bronze Age' [forthcoming]).

The following chart may illustrate the differences in terminology:

c. 2300	c. 2000	c. 1950/1900	c. 1800	
Albright	EB IV	MB I	MB IIA	MB IIB
Kenyon	Intermediate	EB-MB	MB I	MB II
Tufnell	EB IB	Caliciform	MB I	MB II
Oren	EB IVA	EB IVB	MB I	MB II
Dever	EB IVA	EB IVB/EB IVC	MB IIA	MB IIB
Prag	—		MB I	—
Gerstenblith	EB IV '(to be divided)'			
Finkelstein	Intermediate Bronze Age			

For a fuller discussion and a more detailed chart, see W.G. Dever, *BASOR* 210 (1973), p. 38, and cf. P. Gerstenblith, *The Levant*, p. 3.

1. Thus, for instance, K.M. Kenyon, *Amorites and Canaanites*, pp. 15-17; *idem*, 'Syria and Palestine c. 2160–1780: The Archaeological Sites', *CAH* I.2 (3rd edn), p. 594, and *idem*, *Archaeology in the Holy Land*, pp. 120-22; cf. W.F. Albright, 'The Historical Framework of Palestinian Archaeology between 2100 and 1600 BCE', *BASOR* 209 (1973), pp. 12-14; R. de Vaux, *The Early History of Israel*, pp. 63-64; J. Bright, *A History of Israel* (3rd edn), pp. 44, 48-49.

2. For a critique of the 'Amorite hypothesis', see, for instance, M. Liverani, 'The Amorites', *Peoples of Old Testament Times* (ed. D.J. Wiseman), pp. 100-33; T.L. Thompson, *Historicity of the Patriarchal Narratives*, pp. 1-195; J. Van Seters, *Abraham in History and Tradition* (New Haven, 1975), pp. 20-26 *et passim*; S. Richard, *BASOR* 237 (1980), pp. 5-34; W.G. Dever, *BASOR* 237 (1980), pp. 35-

theory.[1] Neither can archaeology prove that there were any settlements in the eastern Delta that had been built by 'Amorite' intruders; yet tribes from the Sinai peninsula may have pushed into the eastern Delta at this time, as is mentioned in the Egyptian text, 'The Instruction for King Meri-ka-re'.[2] Such incursions were not uncommon. They occurred especially in times of famine, as well as in periods of weak Egyptian governments; thus, during the weakness of Pepi II's government more Asiatics may have come into the Delta. The same was perhaps the case during the 'First Intermediate Period' (2160–1991 BCE). However, to see these peoples as being part of a wave of 'Amorite' migrations from Syria through Palestine is no more than a guess. They did not cause the collapse of the Old Kingdom. The intrusions of 'Asiatics' is rather a result of the downfall of the Old Kingdom.[3] Another result of this would probably have been that Egypt's trade with the Levant ceased, which also contributed to the decline of the EB culture in Palestine.[4] This explains why the commercial store jar disappears from the archaeological strata of this period.

As mentioned above, one explanation for the downfall of the Early Bronze Age culture is that there was a change to a somewhat drier climate, which might have forced people to move into the pasture

64. M. Noth acknowledged that the term 'Amorite' had been wrongly used (*The History of Israel* [New York, 1960], p. 24). Here we should mention that W.F. Albright saw Abraham and his family as part of the 'Amorite invasion' (*From the Stone Age to Christianity* [3rd edn; Baltimore, 1957], pp. 236-38).

1.   K. Prag reckons with a 'relatively small influx of new people who intermingle with the earlier inhabitants'; by this means the earlier Bronze Age traditions have been preserved (*Levant* 6 [1974], p. 102).

2.   The text is probably a propaganda text from Merikare's chancellery (c. 2075 BCE) known from a copy from the fifteenth cent. BCE; see J.A. Wilson, *ANET*, pp. 414-18. Consult also A. Volten, *Zwei ägyptische politische Schriften: Die Lehre für König Merikare (Pap. Carlsberg VI) und die Lehre des Königs Amenemhet* (Copenhagen, 1945), pp. 50-52; E. Otto, *Ägypten: Der Weg der Pharaonenreiches* (Stuttgart, 1958 [1953]), p. 101; T. Säve-Söderbergh, *Pharaohs and Mortals* (Indianapolis, 1961), p. 65.

3.   See, among others, W.K. Simpson, 'Egypt', *The Ancient Near East: A History* (ed. W.W. Hallo and W.K. Simpson; New York, 1971), p. 234; K. Prag, *Levant* 6 (1974), pp. 103-104; E.F. Wente, 'History of Egypt', *Encyclopaedia Britannica*, p. 468.

4.   Cf. J.N. Tubb, *Levant* 15 (1983), p. 56.

areas of the Near East.[1] Drier conditions, however, would not lure people to the steppe. The result of a hotter climate could often be crop failure and perhaps also famine. These phenomena have contributed to nomadic incursions into agricultural areas, which by nature caused political instability. We may ask, however, whether it is possible to learn about such a change in the period under consideration. According to J. Henninger, the period between c. 5000–2400 BCE was a wet interval, but from c. 2400 BCE the climate became drier.[2] A.D. Crown has maintained that there was a period of aridity in many parts of the Near East during the time span of 2300–2000 BCE. For instance, the 'Nile floods ceased to inundate the peripheries of the flood plain c. 2350–2180 BCE and famine records persist until c. 1950 BCE'.[3] A 'prolonged insufficiency of the floods' can probably be seen as a contributing factor to the weakening of the central government of Pepi II.[4] The nomadic infiltrations during the period of 2300–1900 BCE and the fall of Akkad and the empire of Ur III 'coincide remarkably with a period of increasing aridity marked by salinization and reduced Tigris-Euphrates streamflow'.[5] If this is the picture in Mesopotamia and in the Nile Valley, the climate in southern Syria and in Palestine could have been affected. It is therefore possible that some change in rainfall and temperature could have occurred in this period in Palestine, causing some population groups to search for new lands and to adopt new subsistence systems.[6] This does not exclude the possibility that groups of people from the north could have been attracted

1. K.W. Butzer, 'Der Umweltfaktor in der grossen arabischen Expansion', *Saeculum* 8 (1957), p. 365.

2. *Über Lebensraum und Lebensform der Frühsemiten* (Arbeitsgemeinschaft für Forschung des Landes Nordreihn-Westfalen, 151; Cologne-Opladen, 1968), pp. 25-26; cf. K.W. Butzer, 'Late Glacial and Postglacial Climatic Variations in the Near East', *Erdkunde* 11 (1957), pp. 21-35.

3. 'Toward a Reconstruction of the Climate of Palestine 8000 BCE–0 BCE', *JNES* 31 (1972), p. 322.

4. B. Bell, 'The Dark Ages in Ancient History. I. The First Dark Age in Egypt', *AJA* 75 (1971), p. 8.

5. J. Neumann and S. Parpola, 'Climatic Change and the Eleventh–Tenth-Century Eclipse of Assyria and Babylonia', *JNES* 46 (1987), p. 177.

6. H. Ritter-Kaplan has maintained that a drop in the sea level occurred in the mid-third millennium and that a drought followed in the later part of the same millennium; cf. 'The Impact of Drought on Third Millennium BCE Cultures on the Basis of Excavations in the Tel Aviv-Exhibition Grounds', *ZDPV* 100 (1984), p. 3.

to the woodlands of Palestine in order to avoid the arid areas. Then again, a change in the climate around 1900 BCE[1] made a resettlement of formerly abandoned sites possible and 'prepared' for the emergence of the Middle Bronze Age culture.

Another factor to take into consideration is that the hills may have become somewhat denuded of trees. With urbanization came deforestation. Wood was needed for buildings and for fire. The crust of the bedrock, the *nari*, could hold only a small amount of soil which could be bound by some shrubbery. Before the process of building terraces started in the Iron Age period, the rainy season caused soil to erode into the valleys. Even if we do not have any exact information available about the density of vegetation we could imagine a situation having occurred in which people had to go farther away in order to obtain wood.

An important role in the process of the decline of the Early Bronze Age urban culture may be ascribed to a disintegration of and disturbances in trade. The conflict between Akkad and Ebla over the control of the trade routes and the ensuing war in northeastern Syria devastated certain areas and caused disruptions in trade. Disturbances in trade would result in less goods and raw materials being available. The destruction of several cities and villages would have forced some groups of people to move in order to earn a living at other places; thus, not only were nomads on the move, but groups of urbanites and villagers also migrated both south and east.[2]

Besides trade and commercial activities, agriculture and animal husbandry were parts of the basic economic system of the Bronze Age cities.[3] As a result of a hotter climate and trade disruptions with ensuing shortages, the subsistence system faltered and a process of depopulation of cities may have started. For Palestine this could mean that some agriculturalists with fewer possibilities to exchange their

1. Cf. A. Horowitz, 'Preliminary Palynological Indications as to the Climate of Israel during the Last 6000 Years', *Paléorient* 2 (1974), pp. 407-14.
2. See H. Kühne, *Die Keramik vom Tell Chuera und ihre Beziehungen zu Funden aus Syrien-Palästina, der Turkei un dem Iraq* (Berlin, 1976), pp. 118-19.
3. Cf. W. van Zeist, 'Preliminary Botanical Results of the 1972 Season at Selenkahiye', *Le Temple et le Culte* (Compte rendu de la vingtième recontre assyriologique internationale, Leiden 1972; Leiden, 1975), p. 26; L. Marfoe, 'The Integrative Transformation: Patterns and Sociopolitical Organization in Southern Syria', *BASOR* 234 (1979), p. 15.

products in the cities therefore moved to other places where perhaps only grazing of herds was possible. In this manner, transhumance as well as nomadism increased. Thus, parts of the agricultural population may have become sheep herders.[1] This is then the explanation for why the Negev saw so many settlements in the EB IV period, especially in the Negev Highlands.[2] Palestine was not depopulated, however, and some agricultural societies did still exist.[3] One could rather say that there was a shift in population density and in life style. Trade shows contacts with Syria, and one may assume that some northerners also could have migrated to Palestine and Transjordan.[4]

The disintegration of trade should be seen as part of the sociopolitical picture. With the weakening or lack of a central political authority, not only trade patterns were disturbed but also the balance between settled areas (cities and villages) and between nomadic and pastoralist groups of people. These latter should not be imagined as living in a no-man's-land. Most of the nomads of Palestine and Transjordan were moving around and living in the territories that were under the political and economic jurisdiction of the various city states, which could have imposed some rules on the tribes.[5] In a time of weak political authority, those rules could not be strictly upheld and nomads could, therefore, more freely move around and move into settled areas without being checked. Thus when the Egyptian authority over Palestine was no longer felt, the cities of EB III 'lacked an ability

---

1.   See, for instance, D.L. Johnson, *The Nature of Nomadism: A Comparative Study of Pastoral Migrations in Southwestern Asia and Northern Africa* (Chicago, 1969); cf. J. Jacobs, *The Economy of Cities* (New York, 1969), p. 38.

2.   T.L. Thompson, *The Settlement of Sinai and the Negev in the Bronze Age* (Tübinger Atlas des Vorderen Orients, Beihefte, Reihe 8; Wiesbaden, 1975), pp. 14-15; W.G. Dever, *BASOR* 237 (1980), pp. 56-58. In all, c. 400 sites from this period have been found in the Negev, to which one should add several hundreds of tumuli. See, for instance, R. Cohen and W.G. Dever, 'Preliminary Report of the Third and Final Season of the Central Negev Highlands Project', *BASOR* 243 (1982), pp. 57-77, and cf. I. Finkelstein, 'Further Observations' (forthcoming).

3.   K. Prag, *Levant* 6 (1974), pp. 102-103.

4.   Cf. S. Richard, *BASOR* 237 (1980), pp. 5-34.

5.   Cf. the remarks of F. Hole, who states that the 'stronger the government of the sedentary zone, the greater the likelihood of integration' ('Pastoralism in Western Iran', *Explorations in Ethnoarchaeology* [ed. R.A. Gould; Albuquerque, 1978], p. 134).

to regulate and maintain infiltration and pastoralist symbiosis to normal levels'.[1]

What should be clear is that we cannot draw the conclusion that most of the country was denuded of people and thus open for a mass infiltration of people from the north.[2] The many caves and rock cut tombs[3] that have been found ought to be a reminder of the opposite. The fact is, however, that Palestine had become a country with a life-style that was mainly nonurban. In this it differed from northwestern Syria where the urban culture continued. The kingdom of Ebla can be mentioned as an example.

The excavations at Tell Mardikh have unearthed one of the great royal capitals of third millennium Syria, ancient Ebla. The tell of c. 140 acres is located about 67 km SSW of Aleppo on one of the main trunk roads from the south to Anatolia and Mesopotamia. This may be seen as the reason for the city's steady growth in importance from its founding, in the later part of the fourth millennium, until it reached its zenith in the middle of the following millennium. In Palace G (destroyed c. 2250 BCE), close to 18,000 clay tablets and fragments of tablets written in Sumerian were found.[4] Some of the tablets are

---

1.   K. Prag, 'Ancient and Modern Pastoral Migration in the Levant', *Levant* 17 (1985), p. 85. We can here also draw a parallel with the situation in the central hills of Palestine in the LB II period. For the nomads as also sometimes being bellicose, see pp. 85-86, and N.P. Lemche, *Early Israel*, pp. 130-31, 154.

2.   As rightly emphasized by K. Prag, *Levant* 6 (1974), pp. 69-116; cf. J.N. Tubb, *Levant* 15 (1983), p. 56.

3.   K.M. Kenyon saw the tombs as proof for the arrival of people from the north. The tombs represent 'tribal burial grounds to which the dead were brought from a relatively wide area' (*Archaeology of the Holy Land*, p. 143).

4.   The Sumerian influence is, according to I.J. Gelb, that of Kish ('Ebla and the Kish Civilization', *La lingua di Ebla* [Atti del convegno internationale, Napoli 21–23 aprile 1980; Naples, 1980], pp. 9-73). For the discoveries and their importance, see, among others, P. Matthiae, *Ebla: An Empire Rediscovered* (London, 1980); *idem,* 'The Mature Early Syrian Culture of Ebla and the Development of Early Bronze Age Civilization of Jordan', *Studies in the History and Archaeology of Jordan*, I (ed. A. Hadidi), pp. 77-91; *idem, Preliminary Remarks on the Royal Palace of Ebla* (Syro-Mesopotamian Studies, 2.2; Malibu, 1978); G. Pettinato, *The Archives of Ebla: An Empire Inscribed in Clay* (Garden City, NY, 1981); R.D. Biggs, 'Ebla and Abu Salabikh: The Linguistic and Literary Aspects', *La Lingua di Ebla* (ed. L. Cagni; Naples, 1981), pp. 121-33; L. Viganò, 'Literary Sources for the History of Palestine and Syria: The Ebla Tablets', *BA* 47 (1984), pp. 6-16.

bilingual, Sumerian and a Northwest Semitic dialect preferably called Eblaite. These bilingual texts may be vocabularies and lists of signs for students who sought to learn the art of writing. Most of the texts are, however, economic and administrative texts telling us about goods and precious metals (gold and silver) acquired by the court and showing Ebla's wide-ranging trade connections. A few are of a more political nature, relating, for instance, to a treaty between Assur and Ebla.[1] There are also some incantations, but we do not get any in-depth information about the religion. We learn about both Sumerian and West-Semitic gods. The West-Semitic Dagan seems to have been the head of the pantheon. He is known as 'Lord of the land', or 'Lord of Canaan', as well as being called 'God of the land'. Among other West-Semitic deities are Hadad, Resheph, Kamish (later on known as Kemosh of Moab), Lim, Baal and Malik. We learn very little about the cultic organization, but more about sacrifices because of the many lists of offerings. As for the myths which are known, they 'are translations into Eblaite of Sumerian myths'.[2]

The cosmological aspect of a city and its acropolis being the center of the universe can be illustrated with the city plan of Ebla (EB IV). In the center of the city, on higher ground than the rest, was a walled acropolis with a palace and temple complex. The lower city was built around it in four quarters. Each one of these quarters could be entered through a gate in the outer city wall and each gate was designed with a god's name.[3]

Ebla, which seems to have been at its peak around 2400 BCE, was destroyed by Sargon of Akkad's grandson, Naram-Sin, c. 2300–2250 BCE. It is possible that there was a conflict of interest concerning the control over districts in the Euphrates area, as Ebla's interest in control over the trade routes collided with Naram-Sin's policies. The destruction of Ebla did not mark the end of 'the mature Early Syrian culture of Mardikh IIB1', which continued, and has been labeled 'the late Early Syrian culture of Mardikh IIB2', which ended c. 2000

---

1. Cf. E. Sollberger, 'The So-Called Treaty between Ebla and "Ashur"', *Studi Eblaiti* 3 (1980), pp. 129-55.

2. P. Matthiae, *Ebla: An Empire Rediscovered* (Garden City, NY, 1981), pp. 186-88; cf. L. Viganò, *BA* 47 (1984), pp. 6-8.

3. See P. Matthiae, *Ebla: An Empire Rediscovered*, pp. 42-44; G. Pettinato, *The Archives of Ebla*, p. 44. The population of Ebla has been estimated by Pettinato to have been c. 260,000 inhabitants (p. 134).

BCE.[1] Ebla was destroyed a second time around 1600 BCE.[2]

The rivalry and wars between the different kingdoms of Syria and Mesopotamia, such as Umma, Kish, Lagash, Ur, Uruk, Akkad, Mari and Ebla should be taken into consideration when discussing the political and cultural situation in Syria in the third millennium BCE. In the twentieth century, for instance, the king of Lagash, Eanatum, fought Ur, Uruk, Mari and Kish. Having captured Kish, he called himself 'King of Kish', probably telling the 'world' that the hegemony in Mesopotamia which was traditionally held by Kish was now in his hands.[3] Another king using the same title was Lugalzagesi of Umma. This king, the son of a prophet-priest, had usurped the throne in Umma, the enemy state of Lagash. Lugalzagesi sacked Lagash, conquered Uruk, and also ruled over Ur, Nippur and Larsa. Thus, he created a territorial kingdom larger than a city state. In claiming that he was king over the land 'from the Lower Sea' (the Persian Gulf) to 'the Upper Sea' (the Mediterranean), he used the imperial phraseology known from the later kings of Akkad. It is doubtful whether his holdings went as far as the Mediterranean. The phrase may imply that Lugalzagesi opened up trade with the coastal city-states of Syria. This meant that his trade routes had to pass through Akkad's territory. This was cause for war, and Lugalzagesi was finally defeated by Sargon.[4] During the reign of Naram-Sin, Sargon's grandson, there were some uprisings in Ur, Kish, Nippur, Sippar, Uruk, Magan and Mari, among other places.[5] Under his successor Sharkalisharri, the end of the Sargonidic empire came about. In the east the Gutians (from the Zagros mountains) pressed their way into Mesopotamia,[6] destroying

1. P. Matthiae in *Studies in the History and Archaeology of Jordan*, I (ed. A. Hadidi), pp. 89-90.

2. For the Middle Bronze Age city of Ebla, see P. Matthiae, 'New Discoveries at Ebla: The Excavation of the Western Palace and the Royal Necropolis of the Amorite Period', *BA* 47 (1984), pp. 18-32.

3. See G. Steiner, 'Altorientalische "Reichs"-Vorstellungen im 3. Jahrtausend v. Chr'., *Power and Propaganda* (ed. M. Trolle Larsen; Mesopotamia, 7; Copenhagen, 1979), pp. 125-43.

4. D.O. Edzard, 'The Early Dynastic Period', *The Near East: The Early Civilizations* (ed. J. Bottéro, E. Cassin and J. Vercoutter; London, 1967), pp. 80-84.

5. See H. Hirsch, 'Die Inschriften der Könige von Agade', *AfO* 20 (1963), pp. 25, 74-75.

6. Å. Westenholz, 'The Old Akkadian Empire in Contemporary Opinion', *Power and Propaganda* (ed. M.T. Larsen), pp. 112-13.

Akkad.[1] They managed to rule Upper Mesopotamia for a short time, the so-called Gutian period, c. 2160–2110 BCE.[2]

With this as a background, one has to reckon with the possibility that the destruction of the Ebla kingdom by Naram-Sin, as well as Sargon's campaigns to the Mediterranean and the destruction of Mari, have caused instability in parts of Syria. The state of warfare, as well as uprisings in Mesopotamia, some perhaps due to nomadic incursions caused by a drier climate, must be taken into consideration as having created unstable conditions in parts of Syria. Thus, some groups of people may have tried to withdraw to other areas less affected by the political problems of northern Syria. The greater Palestinian areas would have been outside the reach of the conflicting powers and could have received new settlers arriving from the north. Among these, craftsmen from the devastated urban centers may have migrated south.[3] This may be one explanation for why there are some northern influences in the material culture of Transjordan and Palestine at this time.

Lack of hard facts has resulted in the development of a hypothesis about nomads who invaded the country during times of transition, causing destruction and devastation. According to this theory, a new period should then have begun in the history of the country: the EB IV period, also called the Intermediate Bronze Age. Nomads coming from the north were to have caused the downfall of the EB culture.[4] These 'newcomers' might have burned down the wall of Jericho and settled on the slopes and in the vicinity of the tell, instead of rebuilding the town.[5] Even though K.M. Kenyon linked the well-cut tomb systems at Jericho from this period to 'professional tomb-diggers', she

1. A Sumerian interpretation of the disaster that befell Akkad is expressed in a text that has been labeled 'The Curse of Agade'. Enlil is said to have brought the Gutians down from their mountains as revenge for the sack of Nippur and Enlil's temple Ekur. Thus, the god is the lord of history. For the text, see S.N. Kramer, *From the Tablets of Sumer* (Indian Hills, CO, 1956), pp. 267-71. See also J.S. Cooper, who maintains that the text 'reflects only the fact and not the actual circumstances', thus it is not an accurate report of the event (*The Curse of Agade* [The Johns Hopkins Near Eastern Studies; London, 1983], p. 10).

2. W.W. Hallo, 'Gutium', *Reallexikon der Assyriologie*, III (Berlin, 1957–71), pp. 708-11.

3. See H. Kühne, *Keramik vom Tell Chuera*, pp. 118-19.

4. See, for instance, K.M. Kenyon, *Amorites and Canaanites*, pp. 15-17.

5. K.M. Kenyon, *Archaeology in the Holy Land*, p. 121.

maintains the nomad theory by saying that, even if the tombs were made by professionals, 'nomadic pastoralists' were buried in them.[1] This may be true, but these nomadic pastoralists need not necessarily be seen as invaders. They could have been indigenous people.

Recent investigations concerning the EB III and IV cultures both in Cisjordan and Transjordan have established that the material traditions of EB III continued mainly intact even after the 'disruption' of urban life, a disruption that did not completely put an end to all cities or walled settlements. In general, one may say that there are some new features which show influences from the north, and, besides influences through trade, one cannot dismiss the possibility of smaller groups of people having moved into Palestine and perhaps also having been absorbed by its population.[2] Permanent settlements with or without walls have, as a matter of fact, been found in Transjordan. A village (unwalled) with parallel streets and houses with large courtyards and small rooms was found at Tell Iktanu in the Jordan Valley.[3] Khirbet Iskander in the Wadi Wala in Jordan is another example of a permanent walled settlement in the EB IV period. The most recent excavation at this site has unearthed a fortified settlement with guardrooms in the city gate. In one room were found large storage jars which do not differ radically from those of the earlier period.[4]

Another permanent settlement that continued into this period is Bab edh-Dhra' just east of the Lisan peninsula. It probably ended c. 2200–2100 BCE. Its life span was about one thousand years.[5] Its large cemetery yielded in all c. 20,000 burials. The EB IV population was buried in shaft tombs.[6] The pottery tradition of the EB IV settlement and

1. *Amorites and Canaanites*, p. 17. Over 340 tombs have been found in the vicinity of Jericho from this period. Kenyon has divided them in seven types; the Outsize type, the Square-shaft type, the Bead type, the Composite type, the Dagger type, the Pottery type, and the Multiple burial type. The last one is represented by one example only! (pp. 14ff.). Kenyon has here confused type with content.

2. Cf. K. Prag, *Levant* 17 (1985), p. 81-83.

3. K. Prag, *Levant* 6 (1974), pp. 97-99; *Levant* 17 (1985), p. 82.

4. S. Richard and R.S. Boraas, 'Preliminary Report of the 1981–82 Seasons of the Expedition to Khirbet Iskander and its Vicinity', *BASOR* 254 (1984), pp. 63-87; S. Richard, 'Excavations at Khirbet Iskander, Jordan', *Expedition* 28 (1986), pp. 3-12.

5. R.T. Schaub and W.E. Rast, *BASOR* 254 (1984), pp. 35-60.

6. The charnel houses represent the EB II–III period. As to the cemetery, see R.T. Schaub, 'Patterns of Burial at Bab edh-Dhra'', *The Southeastern Dead Sea*

burials indicates a continuity with the preceding periods.[1] The conclusion one might draw from this is that the population was probably not nomadic. Nomads would rather bury their dead in individual graves dug wherever they passed. They most probably did not 'return' to some fixed localities as soon as somebody had to be buried.[2]

Among settlements recently unearthed is Tell el-Hayyat in the Jordan Valley, c. 3 km SW of Tabaqat Fahl (Pella, coord. 207–206). Here a farming village was found dating from the end of the EB IV to the MB II (c. 1800 BCE).[3] It is possible that this village could be seen as an indication for some change in the annual rainfall and thus for an increase in agricultural activities. From a sociological point of view the site is interesting because the earliest building is a temple. It was rebuilt during four phases. The ground plan for all four phases is that of a long-room with a 'tower' at each side of the entrance. It is thus the same type as the so-called *migdal*-temples (fortress temples) well known from Ebla, Byblos, Ugarit, Megiddo and Shechem.[4] This could indicate that the construction of the temple at Tell el-Hayyat can be seen as an example of a widespread architectural tradition.[5] The

Plain Expedition: An Interim Report of the 1977 Season (ed. W.E. Rast and R.T. Schaub; Cambridge, 1981), pp. 45-68.

1.   W.R. Rast and R.T. Schaub, 'A Preliminary Report of Excavations at Bab edh-Dhra', 1975', *The Southeastern Dead Sea Expedition* (ed. W.E. Rast and R.T. Schaub), p. 2.

2.   G.R. Bentley, 'Kinship and Social Structure', pp. 12-31.

3.   S.E. Falconer, B. Magnes-Gardiner and M. C. Metzger, 'Preliminary Report for the First Season of the Tell el-Hayyat Project', *BASOR* 255 (1984), pp. 49-74.

4.   The temple towers at Megiddo and Shechem were probably built in the early Late Bronze I period; cf. M.D. Fowler, 'A Closer Look at the "Temple of El-Berith" at Shechem', *PEQ* 115 (1983), p. 51. The date of the temple at Shechem has been estimated by R.J. Bull and J.F. Ross to be c. 1650 BCE (L.E. Toombs and G.E. Wright, 'The Fourth Campaign at Tell Balâṭah [Shechem]', *BASOR* 169 [1963], p. 25). The longroom temples at Alalakh and Hazor had no towers at the entrance.

5.   According to M. Ottosson, the EB IV period is the time of *migdal*-temples of the longroom type (*Temples and Cult Places in Palestine* [Boreas, 12; Uppsala, 1980], p. 61). The Tell el-Hayyat temple supports the thesis that the so-called El-Berith temple at Shechem was a temple, something that has been questioned by M.D. Fowler (*PEQ* 115 [1983], pp. 49-53). B. Mazar thinks that the *migdal*-temple type came 'into vogue in Palestine during MB IIc—probably at the beginning of the invasion of foreign elements from the north' ('The Middle Bronze Age in Palestine', *IEJ* 18 [1968], p. 93). The finds from Tell el-Hayyat have disproved Mazar.

temple was erected inside an enclosure, a forecourt, in which there were some standing stones in the later phases. In the EB IV temple there were some benches (partly) along two walls, but in phase III benches were built along the walls. Pottery from the temple includes carinated bowls from the EB IV period.[1] Here we could have an example of religion and society being inseparable. In the ancient Near East the life of the community was rooted in religion. It was the center of life.[2] A new community had taken land, and expressed divine will and ownership by building a temple. Ideologically, the god had taken the land; his 'realm' was being materialized from the start of the settlement. The god had to be there from the very beginning of the village's existence. Without him there would be no blessings, that is, no yield of crops and birth, as well as no progress.

For the greater Palestinian area in general one may say that most of the pottery 'assemblage represents an indigenous, not an intrusive culture'.[3] Some pottery forms occur earlier in Transjordan than in Cisjordan. Several hundred sites are known from the Jordan Valley and from Transjordan located within the 350–300 mm rainfall zone. They were built mostly along the streams or close to springs reflecting an economic system based on pastoralism. These places may have been chosen in consideration of the flocks. As to the Jordan Valley, the material culture is mainly the same on both sides of the river, which is natural because it is the high mountains that separate people.[4] Sites closer to the so-called King's Highway are poorer in objects of imports and in artifacts, which means that the importance of this trade route was not that great during the EB IV period. The Moab plateau (between Wadi Mujib and Wadi Ḥasa), which had no new sites—as far as is known—in the preceding period of the Bronze Age, shows ten

---

1. S.E. Falconer in a paper ('The Development of MB Age Villages in the Jordan Valley: New Perspectives from Tell el-Hayyat') given at the ASOR annual meetings in Atlanta, GA, Nov. 24, 1986; cf. also S.E. Falconer, B. Magnes-Gardiner and M.C. Metzger, *BASOR* 255 (1984), p. 57.

2. Cf. also the discussion in my *Royal Administration*, pp. 1-3.

3. S. Richard, *BASOR* 237 (1980), p. 8. Cf. also W.G. Dever, *BASOR* 210 (1973), p. 57; K. Prag, *Levant* 6 (1974), pp. 69-116, cf. p. 102.

4. Cf. R. Dornemann, *The Archaeology of the Transjordan in the Bronze and Iron Ages* (Milwaukee, 1983), pp. 4-5. This shows that the geographical unit of the Jordan Valley was also a cultural unit. Valleys and rivers served as connecting bonds between populations; cf. F. Braudel, *The Mediterranean and the Mediterranean World in the Age of Philip II*, I, p. 35.

new sites from the EB IV period. For the area north of Wadi Mujib
and south of the Zerqa (Jabbok), which also did not experience any
new settlements during the Bronze Age, 34 new sites have been
reported for the EB IV period. For northern Transjordan, the figure
is four sites for the same period. In the south there are very few sites
compared with, for instance, the Negev with c. 50 new sites of the EB
IV period.[1] T.L. Thompson lists an increase of altogether 390 sites in
the Negev and Sinai during EB IV–MB I. The settlements in the Negev
he sees as 'based on a mixed economy of agriculture and grazing'.[2]
How much agriculture was possible is a matter of dispute. For many
settlements an economy based on transhumance would be probable.[3]
Seasonal dry farming seems, however, to have been possible in the
Negev highlands where most of these settlements were located.[4] As to
northern Palestine, people could have migrated from the Galilee north
to the Beqa' valley and also to southern Lebanon, since objects from
tombs in these areas correspond with objects from Megiddo.[5]

As for Megiddo, K.M. Kenyon concluded that the inhabitants of this
city were more advanced than their contemporaries at other places
and that they had permanent buildings in this period. In spite of this
she does not say that they were urbanized.[6] She acknowledges, however,
that the people of this period could have belonged to the same cult as
those to whom 'the original temple and the twin temples' (from EB
I/II) of the earlier stage were sacred. This could as well be an indication that all the people of this period were not newcomers to the area.
They may have been survivors rebuilding their town.[7] Pottery from
the shaft tombs show close parallels with Byblos and with Qatna in
Syria, which may indicate not only trade, but that some northerners
have settled at the site. The same kind of pottery has also been found

1. Cf. the statistics by K. Prag, *Levant* 6 (1974), p. 75.
2. *The Settlement of Sinai and the Negev in the Bronze Age*, p. 20.
3. See W.G. Dever, *BASOR* 237 (1980), pp. 56-57.
4. I. Finkelstein, 'Further Observations', (forthcoming).
5. K. Prag, *Levant* 6 (1974), p. 76. Most of the settlements are inland Lebanon on the river banks, not on the coast, thus the population was not sea-minded. They were agriculturists (pp. 70-71).
6. K.M. Kenyon, *Amorites and Canaanites*, p. 32.
7. Kenyon says that Megiddo of the EB IV period 'is characteristic of the northern part of the country', and that there would be 'no doubt that the Megiddo Shaft Tomb people were also at Beth-Shan' (*Amorites and Canaanites*, p. 32).

in the area of Affuleh and at el-Ḥuṣn c. 9 km SSE of Irbid in Jordan.[1] Most settlements of EB IV were small in size, with 'little or no evidence for any form of public or communal architecture'.[2] The picture we get of Palestine and Transjordan for this period is, thus, different from that of Syria. Palestine is a country of mainly village societies while Syria remains urbanized in the EB IV period. The excavations at Tell Mardikh (Ebla), Tell Hadidi (Azu)[3] and Tell el-Selenkahiye[4] are examples of the contrast between Syria and Palestine.[5] The material culture is more advanced in Syria, where, for instance, the fast wheel for pottery-making was in use, and where a great number of bronze objects occur. In Palestine, however, hand-made pottery dominated, even if the fast wheel now was appearing, and objects of bronze do not belong in the picture but copper objects do.[6] This makes one wonder if any great migrations from Syria into Palestine really would have taken place. Smaller groups of people have moved, some north, some south and some perhaps east, and with them new pottery forms have become known and imitated. Much of the northern influences in the Palestinian pottery tradition may also be traceable to some trade connections.[7] Among new forms is the so-called caliciform ware ('tea-pots' and goblets) from Syria (Hama J and 'Amuq J, Ras Shamra and Qatna),[8] which has been found in northern Palestine and northern Jordan, and even at Jericho.[9] The red slip EB

---

1.   This would be R. Amiran's pottery family B which is most common in Byblos ('The Pottery of the Middle Bronze Age I in Palestine', *IEJ* 10 [1960], pp. 205-25); cf. Kenyon, *Archaeology in the Holy Land*, pp. 136-39.

2.   P. Gerstenblith, 'A Reassessment of the Beginning of the Middle Bronze Age in Syria-Palestine', *BASOR* 237 (1980), p. 66.

3.   R.H. Dornemann, 'Tell Hadidi: A Millennium of Bronze Age City Occupation', *Archaeological Reports from the Tabqa Dam Project, Euphrates Valley, Syria* (ed. D.N. Freedman; AASOR, 44; Cambridge, MA, 1979), pp. 113-51; *idem*, 'Salvage Excavations at Tell Hadidi in the Euphrates Valley', *BA* 48 (1985), pp. 49-59.

4.   M. van Loon, 'Preliminary Results of the Excavations at Selenkahiye Near Meskene, Syria', *Archaeological Reports* (ed. D.N. Freedman), pp. 97-112.

5.   For Hadidi, see R.H. Dornemann, *BA* 48 (1985), pp. 49-59.

6.   Consult W.G. Dever, *BASOR* 237 (1980), pp. 50-52.

7.   Cf. S. Richard, *BASOR* 237 (1980), p. 22.

8.   See E. Fugmann, *Hama, Fouilles et recherches de la Fondation Carlsberg 1931–1938* (Copenhagen, 1958), pp. 49-51.

9.   E. Oren, *BASOR* 210 (1973), pp. 30-32.

ware continues at such central Jordanian sites as Bab edh-Dhra', Iskander and 'Aro'er,[1] to mention a few, and is thus an example of the indigenous pottery tradition.

Concerning the burials, however, we should notice that the tombs of EB IV Palestine have close parallels both in Syria and Cyprus.[2] Most of them are shaft tombs, and some are multi-chambered in their layout. The latter type is not common south of Megiddo, indicating that multi-chambered tombs were characteristic of northern Palestine and Syria-Lebanon. The Byblos cemeteries and the tombs of northern Palestine are close in typology and artifacts, including metal objects as well as pottery. The caliciform ware and other objects from Ras Shamra, Qatna, Hazor, Megiddo and also Jericho show close resemblances,[3] which means that we have to do with a common Syro-Palestinian culture. To this we should add that caves used as graves, as well as tumuli, occur in some places both in Transjordan and in western Palestine including the Negev.[4] These types are known also from the previous periods, including the Chalcolithic time, and 'remained in use during the MBI period and later', thus one can say that 'the EB/MB population was not totally wiped out'.[5] New customs have been accepted by the indigenous population.

At Jericho EB IV pottery was found above the remains of the EB III city. The houses were also of another type than those of EB III. The settlement 'seems to straggle irregularly down the slopes of the mound', and was unwalled.[6]

From the above we can conclude that northern Palestine is a sub-region that has had close cultural and economic connections with Lebanon and southern Syria, as was the case in the EB period. Remains

1. Cf. E. Olávarri, 'Sondages à 'Arô'er sur l'Arnon', *RB* 72 (1965), p. 82, and *idem*, 'Fouilles à 'Arô'er sur l'Arnon: Les niveaux du Bronze Intermediaire', *RB* 76 (1969), pp. 230-32.

2. P. Dikaois and J. R. Stewart, *Swedish Cyprus Expedition*. IV:1A. *The Stone Age and the Early Bronze Age in Cyprus* (Lund, 1962), pp. 217-19, 276, and fig. 88; cf. E. Oren, *BASOR* 210 (1973), p. 23.

3. E. Oren, *BASOR* 210 (1973), pp. 30-32.

4. For the different types of graves, see K. Prag, *Levant* 6 (1974), pp. 99-102.

5. K. Prag, *Levant* 6 (1974), p. 101.

6. K.M. Kenyon, *Archaeology of the Holy Land*, p. 140.

at Hazor[1] and Megiddo[2] show that we have to reckon with permanent settlements at these two sites.[3] More excavations would, however, be necessary in order to get a more accurate picture of the situation.

In order to achieve an understanding of the intricate problem of population distribution and the material culture of Palestine during the period from c. 2200 to 1900 BCE, W.G. Dever's six 'families' of 'regional assemblages of material culture' may be used as an illustration of how one scholar has looked at the problem.[4] The first assemblage is called the Northern family (N), and it includes the areas in upper Galilee from the border of Lebanon to the Huleh valley. Pottery and bronze objects show close relationships to Syrian prototypes (21st cent.). The second is called the North Central family (NC) and is found in the Jezreel Valley and southern Galilee, and, it includes also the northern Jordan valley and Transjordan to Tell el-Ḥuṣn. Some metal objects are overlapping with the Northern family. Pottery of the Syrian 'caliciform' is found here as well as in family N. Because the pottery is coarse and not consistently wheel-made, this 'family' is chronologically placed in the earlier part of EB IV. The third group is from the Jordan Valley (J) and covers also Transjordan. In the west it reaches up to the western areas of the Judean hills (21st c.). A fourth group is called the Southern Family (S), and is to be found in the territories south of Jerusalem–Tel Aviv, that is, around Hebron and along the southern Shephelah, the central Negev, and into the Sinai peninsula.[5] Here many copper objects have been found. The

1. Y. Yadin, *Hazor: The Rediscovery of a Great Citadel of the Bible* (New York, 1975), p. 120.

2. Cf. K.M. Kenyon, *Amorites and Canaanites*, p. 32; Y. Aharoni, *EAEHL*, III, pp. 840-41.

3. Archaeologically, too little is known about Beth-Shan from this period. There are some caves that probably were cut in this period. The pottery is about the same as that from Megiddo, Jericho and Tell el-Ḥuṣn in Jordan (F. James, *EAEHL*, I, p. 220).

4. 'The Peoples of Palestine in the Middle Bronze I Period', *HTR* 64 (1971), p. 199; cf. *idem*, *BASOR* 237 (1980), pp. 45-49. Dever has been inspired by R. Amiran (*Ancient Pottery of the Holy Land*, pp. 79-83).

5. As an example of the Sinai-Negev societies of this period, see R. Cohen and W.G. Dever, 'Preliminary Report of the Pilot Season of the "Central Negev Highlands Project"', *BASOR* 232 (1978), pp. 29-45, and W.G. Dever, 'Village Planning at Be'er Resisim and Socio-Economic Structure in Early Bronze Age IV Palestine', *EI* 18 (1985), pp. 18*-28*. Dever concludes that Be'er Resisim was a

burial system shows single chamber tombs with round shafts (21st–20th cent.).[1] The Central Hill Family (CH) can be found from Tekoa in the south to north of Jerusalem, including, for instance, Gibeon and caves in Wadi ed-Daliyeh. Some pottery, such as 'the small necked 'bottles', unique to this area in the hills, have parallels in the Jericho tombs. The connection with the Jericho 'family' is closer than with the NC family. A sixth family is Transjordanian (TR). Typologically this 'family' seems to be earlier than those of Western Palestine. The conclusion drawn from the above is that the pottery of EB IV should not be considered 'homogenous'. The 'archaeological history of Palestine exhibits strong regional patterning in the material culture'. Thus, we have to acknowledge the existence of local groups with their own traditions. Because Dever places the different 'families' in a chronological order (roughly TR, N-NC, J-CH, S) with some overlapping, he maintains that Palestine and Transjordan were 'occupied successively by several small, seminomadic groups', who should have had related material traditions with influences from both Syria and Palestine.[2]

As with all other reconstructions, this is built mainly on the remains of the material culture paired with a theory of population movements. As such, the reconstruction is thorough and well argued, but it only partly explains the situation. As with the 'Amorite' hypothesis, which Dever adhered to in 1971 and 1976[3] but now has abandoned, this new synthesis still builds upon the movements of seminomads coming from Syria. The difference is only a difference in nomenclature and a difference in the amount of people invading the country. Instead of 'Amorites', we now learn about seminomadic West-Semites, and instead of a great number of 'Amorites' invading Palestine and Transjordan, we now learn about small groups of invaders. Dever's system consists of chronological reckoning with no other peoples than newcomers. The indigenous population of Palestine is mainly forgotten. Did they all disappear? Dever's family system reckons with central and

"partly-seasonal encampment" for pastoralists' (p. 23*).

1.   For the cemeteries in the southern hills, see W.G. Dever, *BASOR* 237 (1980), pp. 39-42.

2.   *BASOR* 237 (1980), pp. 48-49.

3.   See W.D. Dever, 'The Beginnings of the Middle Bronze Age in Palestine', *Magnalia Dei, the Might Acts of God* (ed. F.M. Cross *et al.*; Garden City, NY, 1976), pp. 3-38.

southern Palestine as being almost depopulated when the newcomers made their impact on the northern parts of the country.[1]

Amurru

The term *amurru*, referred to above, occurs frequently in reconstructions of the history of the ancient Near East of the EB and MB periods. After the fall of the Ur III culture in Mesopotamia, nomads labeled Amurru are said to have overrun most of Mesopotamia and Syria-Palestine. The earliest references we have about these Amurru, 'Amorites', are texts from Mesopotamia mentioning the MAR.TU, which is Sumerian for *amurru*. This refers to a geographical area as well as to a population group. (KUR)MAR.TU^{KI}, for instance, refers to a mountainous area NW of Babylon. Thus, the people called MAR.TU obtained their Sumerian name from a geographical area, the *amurru*-territory. The term is, therefore, not originally an ethnic term. However, it could be used not only as a geographical term but also for different people, as well as for groups of people of different professions.[2]

The MAR.TU occur for the first time in a text from Tell Fara (from c. 2600 BCE) which refers to a farmer.[3] As time goes on, the references to MAR.TU become more frequent, designating both territory and people.[4] Sargon I says in an inscription that he has conquered the land of the Amurru.[5] Sharkalisharri (2217–2193), son of Naram-Sin, mentions that he defeated the MAR.TU at Basar, which by some has been identified with Jebel Bishri north of Tadmor (Palmyra) 37 km west of the Euphrates.[6] A text from Tell Asmar (a generation after the Ur III dynasty's fall) mentions that MAR.TU people live in the city (probably Eshnunna) and some were employed as tax

---

1. For a criticism of Dever's 'construction', see J.N. Tubb, *Levant* 15 (1983), p. 56, and I. Finkelstein, 'Further Observations' (forthcoming).

2. Cf. A. Saarisalo, *New Kirkuk Documents Relating to Slaves* (StudOr, 3; Helsingfors, 1934), pp. 45-47.

3. A. Haldar, *Who were the Amorites?* (Leiden, 1971), p. 4.

4. G. Buccellati, *The Amorites in the Ur III Period* (Naples, 1966); M. Liverani, 'The Amorites', *Peoples of Old Testament Times* (ed. D. J. Wiseman), p. 103.

5. *ANET*, p. 269.

6. G. Buccellati, *The Amorites of the Ur III Period* (Naples, 1966), pp. 236-37; cf. I.J. Gelb, 'The Early History of the West Semitic Peoples', *JCS* 15 (1961), pp. 29-30.

officials.[1] Administrative texts from the Sumerian Drehem (Ur III) mention the MAR.TU as both traders and businessmen. Drehem was an administrative center and was, therefore, perhaps mainly inhabited by administrative officials, even if there also were some belonging to the lower classes.[2] The same may have been the case at Umma and Lagash. The 'Amorites' of these cities were public servants including soldiers. Thus, one could say that in general the Amurru of the Ur III period and after could be found in all levels of the society. They were both urban and nonurban, nomadic and settled.[3] Some of them had, for instance, oxen. This, being a 'slow' animal, would not be very suitable for nomads. In Syria of the third and second millennia, Amurru, 'Amorites', were the people of the land. The name travelled west and included all peoples of the territories west of the Euphrates where most of the population was West Semitic.[4] However, the Akkadian texts show that the Amurru pushed into Mesopotamia during different times; thus, one could say that the name Amurru 'travelled' west, but the people Amurru 'travelled' east.[5] In this connection we should note that the expansion of the 'Amorites' known from Mesopotamian texts refers to the time before the culture of the Early Bronze Age came to an end in Palestine, thus it is not accurate to use the term Amorites for the migration of groups of people to Palestine.[6] One should rather refer to them as being West Semites.[7]

The biblical Amorites have nothing to do with the Amurru of the Ur III period.[8] In the Bible the term 'Amorite' is used for the non-Israelite population of the hill country on both sides of the Jordan river. The Canaanites lived 'by the sea, and along the Jordan'

1.　Cf. I.J. Gelb, 'An Old Babylonian List of Amorites', *JAOS* 88 (1968), p. 43.

2.　See, for instance, G. Buccellati, *The Amorites*, pp. 281-82.

3.　M. Liverani, in *The Peoples of the Old Testament* (ed. D.J. Wiseman), pp. 100-102; cf. R. Albertz, *Persönliche Frömigkeit und officielle Religion* (Stuttgart, 1978), p. 74; K.A. Kamp and N. Yoffe, *BASOR* 237 (1980), p. 90.

4.　The first scholar to see the Amurru as the people of the west was H. Ranke (*Early Babylonian Names* [Philadelphia, 1905], pp. 24-26).

5.　Cf. P. Michalowski, 'The Royal Correspondence of Ur' (PhD dissertation, Yale University, New Haven, 1976), p. 116.

6.　M. Liverani, in *Peoples of Old Testament Times* (ed. D.J. Wiseman), pp. 101-103.

7.　D.O. Edzard, *Die 'Zweite Zwischenzeit' Babyloniens* (Wiesbaden, 1957), p. 30 n. 127.

8.　Cf. R. de Vaux, *The Early History of Israel*, pp. 63-64.

(Num. 13.29). The 'Amorites' are the dispossessed peoples (Exod. 23.23; Deut. 20.17). A legend about the 'Amorites' as giants and pre-Israelite inhabitants of the land occurs in Amos 9.2.[1] In fact, the Old Testament does not see the Israelites and the Judahites as Amorites. For the biblical writers the Amorites were the enemies.[2] Abraham would certainly not have been identified by any biblical writer with the Amorites.

Because the whole area west of the Euphrates from a Mesopotamian point of view was called Amurru, all Semites in this area could be called Amurru. This does not exactly mean that all groups of people included in the term Amurru were Semitic-speaking peoples. Without textual material, the archaeological remains cannot establish linguistic differences. Architecture and pottery forms may be about the same within two ethnic groups with political and economic relations, and a territorial area may also house different ethnic groups.[3] Because of lack of written sources, we do not know from how far back in time West-Semitic dialects were spoken in Syria-Palestine. However, the texts from Ebla make it clear that a West-Semitic language was spoken in northwestern Syria during the mid-third millennium BCE. We should note that Eblaite was written with Sumerian cuneiform signs, which shows that the Semitic alphabet or script had not yet been invented. The spoken language of the Ebla kingdom was west-Semitic, and thus we may assume that this was the case in most of western and southern Syria. It is doubtful whether Palestine and Transjordan were different. Usually these areas functioned as a cultural extension of Syria. From Egyptian reliefs and paintings, as well as 'from words which were absorbed into the Egyptian language' at this time,[4] the conclusion has been drawn that a large part of the population was Semitic.

1.   The use of the term 'Amorites' in the Bible suggests 'an archaizing tendency by the narrators to give an appearance of antiquity to the stories', a tendency that was not uncommon in the 8th–6th centuries BCE (J. Van Seters, *VT* 22 [1972], p. 81).

2.   Cf. R. de Vaux, 'Les hurrites de l'histoire et les horites de la Bible', *RB* 74 (1967), p. 97.

3.   See, e.g., the discussion in K.A. Kamp and N. Yoffe, *BASOR* 237 (1980), p. 94-95.

4.   On this, see M. Avi-Yonah, *A History of the Holy Land* (Jerusalem, 1969), p. 36.

Semites

The original home of the Semites—if such a thing ever can be established—has traditionally been seen as the Arabian desert, or, rather, the fringes of the desert. Time and time again Semitic nomads are alleged to have moved into the fertile areas of the Near East. However, the earliest records available show settlements of Semites living in Mesopotamia tilling the earth.[1] Nomadism can at certain times be a product of 'agriculture that developed along the dry margins of rainfall cultivation'.[2] Thus, we have to acknowledge the fact that people have moved around seeking new places for their living because of political, economic and climatic circumstances. Some of these have chosen or been forced to choose a nomadic life style, others have moved from their villages and settled in some other area more suitable for agriculture and/or transhumance.

This is the place to emphasize that the term Semite does not refer to ethnicity, but rather refers to peoples speaking a Semitic dialect. The word 'Semite' was first used by A.L. Schlözer in 1781,[3] and was based on the 'Table of Nations' in Genesis 10. The term is derived from the Biblical Shem, Noah's eldest son (Gen. 5.32, 6.10), and on his genealogy in Gen. 10.21-31. In 10.6-16, we can, however, find some Semitic peoples being counted as Hamitic, namely Dedan, Sheba, Canaan, the Sidonians and the Amorites. This is most probably due to political relationships and not ethnicity. Ham in the Old Testament is the ancestor of the Egyptians, the Ethiopians, the Cushites and the Philistines, among others. Because Canaan for a long time had been under Egyptian rule, the biblical writer counted the Canaanites as being Hamitic. In this way he was able to advocate that the Canaanites, whom he disliked,

---

1. J. Henninger, *Über Lebensraum und Lebensform*, p. 13; A. Haldar, *Who were the Amorites?*, p. 4; I.M. Diakonoff, 'Earliest Semites in Asia: Agriculture and Animal Husbandry according to Linguistic Data (VIII–IVth Millennia BCE)', *Altorientalische Forschungen* 8 (1981), pp. 23-74. For J.M. Grintz, the 'cradle of the Semites was in the northern Mesopotamia and southern Armenia' ('On The Original Home of the Semites', *JNES* 21 [1962], p. 205). Cf. H. Crawford, who sees the original homes of the Semites in the areas of the Taurus and Zagros mountains and the Jebel Bishri ('Nomads: The Forgotten Factor', *Orientalia Lovaniensia Periodica* 8 [1977], p. 35).

2. W.G. Dever, *BASOR* 237 (1980), p. 57.

3. *Repertorium für biblische und morgenländische Literatur* 8 (1781), p. 161.

were of a different stock than Israelites and Judahites.

Within the family of Semitic languages, two main groups can be distinguished: East-Semitic and West-Semitic. To the first group belong the Akkadian languages, that is, Babylonian and Assyrian. The West-Semitic group is in its turn also divided in two subgroups: Northwest-Semitic (Ugaritic, Phoenician, Canaanite-Hebrew including Moabite, Ammonite and Edomite, and Aramaic-Syriac), and the Southwest-Semitic languages, Arabic and Ethiopic (with its modern dialects Amharic, Tigre and Tigrinja).

As to northern influences during the later part of EB IV and the following MB I (MB IIA), pottery of the Syro-Cilician type has been found concentrated along the trade routes, particularly along 'the coastal route between the northern and southern Levant'.[1] It is quite possible that the Middle Bronze Age culture developed at settlements along this international trade route, which brought them into contact with the network of trade routes from Mesopotamia via Syria to Anatolia. For instance, Byblos and Ugarit have certainly played an important role in this line of communications, transmitting information about technical advances. Material culture is not necessarily bound to ethnicity.[2] Innovations such as new pottery forms and the fast wheel for making pottery, the knowledge of making bronze tools, as well as ideas about a society's organization may have spread along the trade routes with merchants and caravans, not necessarily with mass migrations.[3] From this point of view the MB I material culture is Palestinian. However, this is not to deny that there are some new features which became part of the Palestinian tradition. These features

1.   P. Gerstenblith, *The Levant*, p. 118.

2.   Cf. K.A. Kamp and N. Yoffe, *BASOR* 237 (1980), pp. 85-104. See also K. Prag, who states that 'pottery changes need not necessarily reflect complete population changes' (*Levant* 6 [1974], p. 100). To this we could add that pottery is not always a good time indicator when found in stratified layers, because the same vessels and forms can be used by several generations.

3.   K. Prag maintains that 'relatively small influxes of new people who intermingled with the earlier inhabitants' around 2350 and after can explain the changes that occurred, but most of the EB tradition was still alive (*Levant* 6 [1974], p. 102); cf. P. Gerstenblith, *The Levant*, pp. 118-19, 125.

are northern. For instance, the painted pottery tradition of the emerging MB I period is Levantine in origin and not from inland Syria.[1]

---

1.   Consult J. N. Tubb, *Levant* 18 (1983), pp. 34-35.

Chapter 4

THE MIDDLE BRONZE AGE

Looking at the many theories about the rise of the Middle Bronze Age, one is struck by the phenomenon that the same arguments are used for the change in periodization as we have found in the discussion of the Early Bronze age. For instance, epidemic illnesses and plagues could have contributed to a certain depopulation of densely inhabited areas, and when normalcy occurred again, these regions were resettled. Climate and an intensified trade, as well as migrations caused by sociological or political circumstances, have played a main role in the historical reconstructions. None of them can be disproved, while none of them can be seen as the only reason for the emergence of what has been called the MB Age culture which saw the reurbanization of Palestine. A somewhat more favorable climate may have caused some groups of people to move. As mentioned above, the Levantine trade probably played an important role 'involving both ideas and commodities'.[1] For instance, the well organized trade by Assyrian families and directed by the Assyrian trade center, *kārum*,[2] at Kanish (modern Kültepe in eastern Anatolia) must be considered as contributing to the cultural wealth of the MB period, and trade can mediate cultural influences.[3] The trade was protected by treaties with the rulers of the territories which the trade routes passed through.[4]

1. P. Gerstenblith, *The Levant*, p. 125.
2. W.W. Hallo labelled this the 'board of trade', in W.W. Hallo and W.K. Simpson, *The Ancient Near East*, p. 95.
3. W.F. Leemans, 'The Importance of Trade', *Iraq* 39 (1977), pp. 2-3, and cf. *idem, Foreign Trade in the Old Babylonian Period* (Studia et documenta ad iura orientis antiqui pertinentia, 6; Leiden, 1960), pp. 98-100.
4. M. Trolle Larson, *The Old Assyrian City-State and its Colonies* (Copenhagen Studies in Assyriology, 4; Copenhagen, 1975); *idem, Old Assyrian Caravan Procedures* (Istanbul, Nederlands Historisch-Arkeologisch Instituut in het Nabije Oosten, 22; Leiden, 1967); cf. *idem*, 'Partnership in the Old Assyrian Trade', *Iraq*

Thus, tin and textiles (much of which probably came from Iran) went west, and wood, wine, olive oil, copper and precious metals, such as gold and silver, went east.[1] Well developed copper industries existed, for instance, in the EB IV period both at Byblos and at Ugarit, as well as in the Amuq area. The sources of copper were probably in south-eastern Turkey. Copper from Iran may also have reached the west.[2] Contacts with the trade routes and trading centers like Ugarit and Byblos of the coastal areas of Syria-Palestine have then been channeling not only commodities but also knowledge about new ideas and technologies to the territories south of the Anatolian-Mesopotamian trade routes. New ceramic forms (on the fast wheel)[3] and the technology of making bronze are certainly indications of northern influences.[4] Because it is impossible to maintain that the population of Palestine greatly increased, the theory of mass invasions has to be abandoned. The settled population seems to have been about the same as in the EB II–III periods.[5] Even so, we may have to take into consideration that an increase in population could have occurred in some areas. This could then have created some pressure and thus

39 (1977), pp. 119-45. Consult also W.F. Leemans, *Foreign Trade in the Old Babylonian Period*.

1.   Anatolian connections can be detected in different parts of Syria: 'Metal and jewelry hoards were accumulating in the strongholds' (M. Mellink, 'The Early Bronze Age in Western Anatolia', *The End of the Early Bronze Age in the Aegean* [ed. G. Cadogan; Cincinnati Classical Studies, NS, 6; Leiden, 1986], p. 151).

2.   J.D. Muhly, *Copper and Tin: The Distribution of Mineral Resources and the Nature of the Metals Trade in the Bronze Age* (Transactions of the Connecticut Academy of Arts and Sciences, 43; Hamden, CT, 1973), pp. 206-207, 233-34. Cf. M. Trolle Larson, *The Old Assyrian City-State and its Colonies*, p. 92-93. Cf. R.J. Forbes, *Studies in Ancient Technology*, IX, p. 91. As for Cyprus, A.S. Merrillees cannot find any evidence for copper being mined and exported in the early second millenium BCE ('Settlement, Sanctuary and Cemetery in Bronze Age Cyprus', *Australian Studies in Archeology*, I [ed. J. Birmingham; Sydney, 1974], pp. 51, 63-63).

3.   Cf. W.G. Dever, 'The Beginning of the Middle Bronze Age in Syria-Palestine', *Magnalia Dei* (ed. F.M. Cross *et al.*), p. 7.

4.   Cf. W.F. Albright, *The Excavations of Tell Beit Mirsim I: The Pottery of the First Three Campaigns* (AASOR, 12; New Haven, 1932), pp. 10-11; J.R. Stewart, *Tell el 'Ajjul: The Middle Bronze Age Remains* (ed. H.E. Kassis; Studies in Mediterranean Archaeology, 38; Göteborg, 1974), p. 50.

5.   M. Broshi and R. Gophna, 'Middle Bronze Age II Palestine: Its Settlements and Population', *BASOR* 261 (1986), pp. 73-90.

contributed to new settlements being built and new technologies being adopted.[1]

Egyptian influences during this period is hard to assess. Politically it is the time of the re-emergence of the power of Egypt, the era of the Middle Kingdom.[2] Pharaoh Mentuhotep II (2061–2010 BCE) of the Eleventh Dynasty seems to have been able to unite most of Egypt, fighting both Nubians and Libyans.[3] During the time of the Eleventh Dynasty the mines in Sinai were also reopened.[4] With the accession to the throne of the vizier Amenemhat I (1991–1962 BCE), the founder of the Twelfth Dynasty, Egypt again enters the international stage.[5] The chaotic period of the 'First Intermediate Period' had come to an end, a period that probably is depicted in the 'Admonitions of the Sage', Ipuwer (Leiden papyrus §344). This text may have been composed during the Nineteenth Dynasty, or it could be a copy of a much earlier text.[6] The 'Admonitions' laments that everything in the society is upside-down. Anarchy rules the country. The poor are rich, the rich are poor. At the end, however, there are some positive

1.   For the possibility of peoples from the north migrating into southern Syria and Palestine because of the unstable political circumstances, see the previous chapter (Chapter 3).

2.   See, for instance, the remarks of A. Gardiner, *Egypt of the Pharaohs*, pp. 124-26.

3.   Cf. T. Säve-Söderbergh, *Ägypten und Nubien* (Lund, 1941), p. 58-59. F. Gomaà, *Ägypten während der ersten Zwischenzeit* (BTAVO, Reihe B, 27; Wiesbaden, 1980), pp. 154-55. Mentuhotep was probably not of royal birth; see F. Gomaà, *Ägypten*, p. 142-43.

4.   See W. Helck, *Wirtschaftsgeschichte des alten Ägypten im 3. und 2. Jahrtausend vor Chr.* (Leiden, 1975), pp. 179-80. Cf. W.A. Ward, *Egypt and the Mediterranean World*, p. 59.

5.   Amenemhat was from Upper Egypt and is probably the 'savior' from the south who was said to make an end of the evil and bad times, according to the 'Prophecy of Neferti' by a priest from Bubastis; cf. J.A. Wilson, *ANET*, pp. 444-46. See also W. Helck, *Die Prophezeihung des Nfr.tj*. E. Blumenthal maintains that the text is composed of different sources according to an old literary pattern of lamentations and utterances about chaos and evil times ('Die Prophetzeihung des Neferti', *ZÄS* 109 [1982], pp. 1-27). G. Posener sees the 'Prophecy of Neferti' as a propagandistic text for Amenemhat I, who did not have any legitimate right to the throne (*Littérature et politique dans l'Egypt de la XIIe dyn.* [Paris, 1956], pp. 21-23).

6.   R.O. Faulkner, 'The Admonitions of an Egyptian sage', *The Literature of Ancient Egypt* (ed. W.K. Simpson; New Haven, 1973), p. 210.

utterances emphasizing the duties of the king.[1]

The 'ascendency of the Amorite kingdoms in Mesopotamia and Syria beginning in Ur III (c. 2060–1950 BCE) and accelerating in the First Dynasty of Babylon' has been coupled with 'Amorite' invasions and with 'prosperity brought about by the renewed political and economic interests of the Egyptian Twelfth Dynasty'.[2] If we discount the 'Amorite invasions', the prosperity in Syria-Mesopotamia with its trade to Anatolia is part of the composite picture, but whether the economic and political interests of Egypt were beneficial for the material culture of Palestine is doubtful. Egypt's interest in Palestine was mainly limited to the coastal area and the fertile Jezreel Valley. The central hills were of less importance, because not very much there could be of use for a kingdom that wanted labor resources, raw material and luxury items. The very sparsely populated hills, with their small trees and bushes were not of prime interest, and we may add that the peoples of the hills had not very much contact with the population on the coast or with the cultural areas north of the Jezreel Valley.[3] The geography divides Palestine in such a way that only the coastal area and the Jezreel and Jordan valleys were of military and economic importance for the Egyptians. In order to secure the coastal area and the products of the Jezreel Valley, as well as to protect the trade route to the north, Megiddo became an Egyptian fortress city during the Twelfth Dynasty.[4] The many villages on the coast,[5] those

1. For the text, see *ANET*, pp. 441-44. The 'Admonitions' can be seen as an expression of a common feature in ancient Near Eastern historiography, used also by Old Testament prophets. The theme is that an evil period will be followed by good times, a bad king will be followed by a good king. For this literary style, see H.G. Güterbock, *ZA* 42 (1934), pp. 15-17; F.M.T. (de Liagre) Böhl, *MAOG* 2.3 (1937), pp. 2-4.

2. W.G. Dever in *Magnalia Dei* (ed. F.M. Cross *et al.*), p. 12.

3. This can explain some differences in pottery forms; see D.P. Cole, *Shechem. I. The Middle Bronze IIB Pottery* (ed. J. Ross and E. Campbell; Winona Lake, IN, 1984), pp. 81-97.

4. A. Harif, 'Middle Kingdom Architectural Elements in Middle Bronze Age Megiddo', *ZDPV* 94 (1978), pp. 24-31.

5. For the many settlements of the Middle Bronze I period on the Palestinian coast, see R. Gophna and P. Beck, 'MB II Settlements of the Coastal Plain', *Tel Aviv* 8 (1981), pp. 45-80, and fig. 1. Cf. also M. Kochavi, P. Beck and R. Gophna, 'Aphek-Antipatris, Tēl Polēg, Tēl Zeror and Tēl Burgā: Four Fortified Sites of the Middle Bronze Age IIA in the Sharon Plain', *ZDPV* 95 (1979), pp. 161-65.

which were not purely fishing villages, most probably shipped some of their products in agriculture and crafts to Egypt, but one may doubt that Egyptian wealth spilled over and inspired the material culture of the villages. As for Syria, Byblos was the port of entry into the more advanced culture of the north, and through Byblos Egyptian culture and art spread both north and south.[1] This means that Palestine often was bypassed. Its economic products including wine and cattle were wanted, but it would be hard to assess the Egyptian influence on the material culture of Palestine for this period. Egypt exploited rather than contributed to the rebuilding of the country,[2] even though the exploitation may have had as a result the building of more villages and towns which could sell their products to Egypt. The Twelfth Dynasty does not seem to have incorporated Palestine as a province, as was the case with Nubia, from where Egypt obtained most of its gold.[3] Fortresses were built in order to incorporate and stabilize Nubia as an Egyptian province and to protect trade.[4] This was not as a rule done in Palestine. Such provincial status was not necessary. Besides Megiddo, there were no military garrisons in Palestine during the MB I period. In the north the Egyptian trade went through its satellite state, Byblos,[5] and from there inland to Syria and down to northern Palestine. The most sought-after products and raw materials (cedar, gold and silver) could be obtained via the sea routes from Byblos and other ports in Syria. This is the explanation for why there are almost no Egyptian objects known from MB I contexts in

1.   Cf. J.R. Stewart, *Tell el 'Ajjul*, pp. 27-28; J.M. Weinstein, 'Egyptian Relations with Palestine in the Middle Kingdom', *BASOR* 217 (1975), pp. 15-16.

2.   Cf. Y. Yadin, 'The Nature of Settlements during the Middle Bronze IIA Period in Israel and the Problem of the Aphek Fortifications', *ZDPV* 94 (1978), p. 206.

3.   A. Gardiner, *Egypt of the Pharaohs*, pp. 133-34; cf. T. Säve-Söderbergh, *Ägypten und Nubien*, pp. 80-82; W.A. Ward, 'Egypt and the East Mediterranean in the Early Second Century BCE', *Or* NS 30 (1961), p. 143.

4.   S. Clarke, 'Ancient Egyptian Fortresses', *JEA* 3 (1916), pp. 155-57; A.H. Gardiner, 'An Ancient Egyptian List of the Fortresses of Nubia', *JEA* 3 (1916), pp. 184-85; A.W. Lawrence, 'Ancient Egyptian Fortifications', *JEA* 51 (1965), pp. 69-94.

5.   The princes of Byblos of this period use, for instance, the Egyptian title 'governor'; see D. Lorton, *The Juridical Terminology of International Relations in Egyptian Texts through Dynasty XVIII* (Baltimore, 1974), p. 64.

Palestine. Only at the end of the period do the contacts between Egypt and Palestine increase.[1]

Concerning the resettlement of Palestine, one can notice a return to many of the sites of the EB Age. For the early MB period the settlement pattern shows, besides some forts, urban centers with sattelite villages. In this MB I is distinguished from the EB period when small villages were 'incorporated' by the urban centers, causing many of the villages to cease to exist. In the beginning of the period the settlements were mainly in the coastal area and in the Jezreel Valley,[2] the exception being Shechem,[3] which was not occupied before MB I. Some house remains have been found at Tell el-Far'ah (N).[4] There is thus not much of an increase in settlements in the hills. In the southern part of the Jordan Valley some decline in comparison with the EB III period can be detected.[5] Archaeological material indicates that there were settlements in places like Ras el-'Ain (Aphek), Jericho and Tell el-'Ajjul.[6] In the Shephelah there seem to be some 'evidence of settlement' at Tell ed-Duweir, and the same may be the case at Tell el-Hesi.[7] Sherds from this period have also been found at Bethel (Beitin),[8] in northern Transjordan, at Araq el Emir and in Amman.[9] It is somewhat astonishing that such very suitable agricultural areas as the Huleh basin and the Beqa' Valley were not resettled in the early period of the MB Age. The probable answer is that they had no easy access to the coast or to the areas of the Orontes Valley.[10]

1. See J.M. Weinstein, *BASOR* 217 (1975), pp. 10-12.

2. Consult R. Gophna and P. Beck, *Tel Aviv* 8 (1981), pp. 45-47; P. Gerstenblith, *BASOR* 237 (1980), p. 73.

3. P. Gerstenblith, *The Levant*, p. 118.

4. R. de Vaux, 'Les fouilles de Tell el-Far'ah', *RB* 69 (1962), pp. 236-52.

5. M. Broshi and R. Gophna, *BASOR* 261 (1986), pp. 73-90.

6. Cf. W.G. Dever in *Magnalia Dei* (ed. F.M. Cross *et al.*), p. 7.

7. D.P. Cole, *Shechem*, I, p. 92.

8. The so-called sanctuary at Bethel is, according to W.G. Dever, the remains of a city gate from Middle Bronze II ('Palestine in the Second Millenium BCE: The Archaeological Picture', in J.H. Hayes and J.M. Miller, *Israelite and Judean History*, p. 99.

9. R.H. Dornemann, *The Archaeology of Transjordan*, pp. 15, 18.

10. P. Gerstenblith, *BASOR* 237 (1980), p. 73. Here we may reckon with Laish-Dan and Hazor as exceptions. Hazor could have been resettled at the end of the MB I period. Pottery from c. 2000 BCE has been found at the site, but no structures; cf. Y. Yadin, *Hazor*, pp. 269-70.

The picture that emerges concerning MB I Palestine as well a Transjordan is that many sites were resettled but that most of them were unwalled.[1] Jawa in Jordan and possibly Yavne-Yam south of Joppa as well as Tēl Polēg, Aphek, Tēl Zeror and Tēl Burga on the Palestinian coast south of Natanyah[2] were fortified. Jerusalem has yielded pottery and a city wall from the MB I period.[3] Tell Beit Mirsim and Megiddo are the best known sites from this period whose reconstructed city plans reveal houses built close together. Monumental buildings, however, are missing here as at most places.[4] A few sanctuaries are known, such as that of Tell el-Hayyat in the Jordan Valley. Temple 4040 of stratum XV at Megiddo and the round altar (4017) have been in use, but later there were only some humble buildings in the cult area. Temple 4040 of Strata XIV had been filled in (in str. XIIIB) and the two temples 5192 and 5269 had gone out of use.[5] A pavement (4009) covering the round altar (str. XIII) shows a reorganization of the cult place which later in the MB II period (str. XII) saw an enclosed sacred area inside a palace complex.[6]

With MB I one may say that urbanism is on the rise again, for instance at Dan, were an impressive city gate was found.[7] Some of the sites were fortified in the MB II period, such as Acco, Achzib, Dan, Hazor, Tirzah, Shechem and Jericho. However, the development of a wealthy urban culture with strong city states having monumental buildings and massive fortifications may have been the result of a

---

1. Cf. D.P. Cole, *Shechem*, I, p. 96.
2. R. Gophna, 'Tēl Polēg', *IEJ* 14 (1964), pp. 109-11. For a Middle Bronze II date, see the discussion by Y. Yadin, *ZDPV* 94 (1978), pp. 5-7, and W.G. Dever in *Magnalia Dei* (ed. F.M. Cross *et al.*), p. 26 n. 59.
3. K.M. Kenyon, *Digging up Jerusalem* (London, 1974), p. 78; Y. Shiloh, *Excavations in the City of David*. I. *1978–1982: Interim Report of the First Five Seasons* (Qedem, 19; Jerusalem, 1984), pp. 12, 26.
4. The city walls dated to this period both at Megiddo (str. XIII) and Tell Beit Mirsim (G–F) are most probably to be dated to the Middle Bronze II period: Y. Yadin, *ZDPV* 94 (1978), pp. 2-4; cf. M. Kochavi, P. Beck and R. Gophna, *ZDPV* 95 (1979), pp. 162-63; W.G. Dever in *Magnalia Dei* (ed. F.M. Cross *et al.*), p. 9 and n. 59.
5. G. Loud, *Megiddo II: Seasons of 1935–39, Text* (OIP, 62; Chicago, 1948), p. 84.
6. I. Dunayevsky and A. Kempinski, *ZDPV* 89 (1973), pp. 172-80.
7. A. Biran, 'The Triple-Arched Gate of Laish at Tel Dan', *IEJ* 34 (1984), p. 15.

gradual process reaching its climax at the end of MB II, which was the time when Egypt's power was again in decline. It seems that the contacts between the coastal areas and inland Palestine were disrupted in the beginning of MB II, probably isolating the hill country from the cultural world. This may partly explain the decline in craftsmanship that is discernable in the pottery of the hills.[1] In other words, the development was regional.

During most of the time of the Twelfth Dynasty, Palestine and Transjordan were of secondary military and economic interest.[2] The economically important areas were Syria-Lebanon and the turquoise mines in the Sinai. Palestine as a transit country was of a certain interest because of its agricultural products and cattle.

The first king of the Egyptian Twelfth Dynasty, Amenemhat I (1991–1962), built fortifications in the eastern Delta in order to stop infiltration by Asiatics,[3] the 'sand-dwellers'. For instance, in the Wadi Tumilat he built the 'Wall of the Ruler' for that purpose.[4] The

---

1. D.P. Cole, *Shechem*, I, pp. 81-97. Cf. W.G. Dever in *Magnalia Dei* (ed. F.M. Cross *et al.*), p. 20 and p. 37 n. 124 and 125; also B. Mazar, *IEJ* 18 (1968), pp. 86-88.

2. J.M. Weinstein, *BASOR* 217 (1975), pp. 1-14. Cf. Y. Yadin, *ZDPV* 94 (1978), pp. 22-23.

3. Concerning the Egyptian term *'3mw*, which often is translated 'Asiatics', we should note that it is also used about peoples living close to the mountainous areas along the Red Sea. It is not an ethnic term; cf. W. von Soden, 'Zur Einleitung der semitischen Sprache', *Wiener Zeitschrift für die Kunde des Morgenlandes* 56 (1960), pp. 181-82. A scene on a stone block from a temple at Gebelein shows a king with a club in his hand smiting an enemy. Three others are kneeling in line. The text refers to a Nubian, a *'3mw* and a Libyan. The latter and the *'3mw* both have a head-feather which is Libyan, thus the *'3mw* is most probably not an Asiatic. W.A. Ward thinks, however, that the artist made a mistake (*Egypt and the Mediterranean World*, p. 61). Philologically the term *'3mw* is not related to the Hebrew *'mry*, Amorite, or the Akkadian *amurru*. It may be connected with the Egyptian *'3m*, 'boomerang, throwing stick', which is used in some texts describing enemies; for instance, the Libyans are called 'boomerang throwers'; cf. T.L. Thompson, *Historicity of the Patriarchal Narratives*, pp. 121-22, cf. also B.J. Kemp in *Ancient Egypt: A Social History*, by (ed. B.G. Trigger *et al.*), p. 142 n. 1.

4. According to W. Shea, this wall may have been part of the canal project that Merikare had been instructed to build. It can be seen in a relief showing Seti I (1291–1279 BCE) returning from a campaign in Asia ('A Date for the Recently Discovered Eastern Canal of Egypt', *BASOR* 226 [1977], pp. 37-38).

Egyptians had, probably, no interest in seeing strong fortified cities developing in Palestine and Transjordan which could have become a danger to their hegemony. Some strongholds were built, however, by the Egyptians, such as Megiddo, where one of Senwosret III's officials, Tuthotep, resided.[1] He may have been the Egyptian commissioner in charge of collecting grain, wine and cattle, and perhaps also dancers,[2] for Egypt. Some Egyptian seals from the vizier's office found at Jericho[3] are indications for the existence of an inland trade route through the Jordan Valley.[4] According to the inscription by Khu-Sebek, Senwosret III (1878–1842) also directed a campaign to Palestine reaching the land of *s-k-m-m*, which usually has been identified with Shechem. The inscription mentions that *s-k-m-m* fell 'together with the wretched Retenu'.[5] This is the only Egyptian military expedition through Palestine (Retenu) during the nineteenth century BCE explicitly mentioned in an Egyptian inscription.[6] As such it most probably was not an ordinary mopping up action against raiders. It could be seen as an effort to stop the many raids against the

1.   The base of a statue of Tuthotep was found at Megiddo (G. Loud, *Megiddo*, II, pl. 265), see J.A. Wilson, *ANET*, p. 228; cf. also A. Harif, *ZDPV* 94 (1978), pp. 30-31.

2.   *ANET*, p. 229.

3.   Cf. W. Helck, *Die Beziehungen*, p. 74.

4.   The tomb inscription of the monarch Khnemhotep from Beni-Hassan in Upper Egypt (during the time of Senwosret II, 1897–1878 BCE) mentions that the *'3mw* from the land of *swt* together with their leader have come to Egypt to sell, among other things, galena (i.e. eye-paint). Their goods were loaded on donkeys. W. Helck assumes that *swt* refers to the Moabite territory. However, T.L. Thompson has maintained that eye-paint is not known from Moab before c. 1400 BCE. He sees the land *swt* as referring to the deserts east of the Nile (*Historicity of the Patriarchal Narratives*, pp. 126-27).

5.   J.A. Wilson, *ANET*, p. 230. On this, see also the discussion in K. Lange, *Sesostris: Ein ägyptischer König in Mythos, Geschichte und Kunst* (Munich, 1954), pp. 15-16.

6.   A stela probably dating from the coregency of Amenemhat I and Senwosret I mentions that the general Nesu-mentu had marched against the 'Sand-dwellers' and destroyed their fortified camps or settlements. J.H. Breasted, *Ancient Records of Egypt*, I, §§469-71; cf. W. Helck, who thinks that this expedition went to Transjordan (*Die Beziehungen*, pp. 42, 62). There is, however, no information about where it went.

caravans and to show the flag to the people of Palestine and thus show them who their master was.[1]

Perhaps it was not only raids against the caravan routes that caused the Egyptian army to march up through Palestine. With the resettling of several sites together with economic growth and prosperity, the Palestinian city states could grow strong and thus become a threat to Egyptian interests. Such a development had to be stopped. This may partly explain the destruction of some MB II sites during the eighteenth cent. BCE. It could thus also be the reason why one has found several stelae and statues (often with inscriptions) of Egyptian kings and royal persons, as well as of high officials, in Syria-Palestine from the period of the Twelfth Dynasty (1991–1784).[2] They have been found, for instance, at Beirut, Qatna, Ugarit, the Baalbek area, Gezer, Megiddo, and Gaza.[3] Scarabs, vases of alabaster, and artifacts of silver and gold, such as jewelry, have been found at several Palestinian places. However, Egyptian or Egyptianizing objects are few in the MB I period (less than fifty)[4] but increasing in MB II. This is quite natural because some time must have elapsed before Egyptian power and economic interests were again felt in Palestine. During the time of Senwosret III Palestine is again in the Egyptian orbit of trade. The commercial relations with Syria were more intense.[5] Enkomi in Cyprus and Troy in western Asia Minor also show contacts with Egypt. In Palestine, the cities along the trade routes were more influenced by Egyptian culture in the MB II period than were cities in the hills, where Shechem and Gibeon may be the exceptions. For instance, Egyptian scarabs have been found in MB II tombs at Hazor,[6] Tell el-'Ajjul, Megiddo and Jericho. Jewelry probably inspired by the Egyptians should also be mentioned. At Tell el-'Ajjul on the coast c. 8 miles south of Gaza, 'the most gold work in the coast lands of Western Asia' have been found from

---

1. Cf. G. Posener, 'Syria and Palestine c. 2160–1780 BCE: Relations with Egypt', *CAH*, I.2, pp. 532-34.

2. M. Bietak puts the end of the Twelfth Dynasty at 1802 ('Problems of Middle Bronze Age Chronology: New Evidence from Egypt', *AJA* 88 [1984], p. 473).

3. Cf. W. Helck, *Die Beziehungen*, pp. 68-70.

4. See, for instance, J.R. Stewart, *Tell el 'Ajjul*, pp. 27-28; J.M. Weinstein, *BASOR* 217 (1975), p. 9.

5. J.M. Weinstein, *BASOR* 217 (1975), pp. 11-12.

6. Y. Yadin *et al.*, *Hazor*, I (Jerusalem, 1958), pp. 130, 133-34, pls. 118.24-33, 171.1-8.

the later part of the MB II period.[1] Tombs at Jericho have also revealed furniture made in an Egyptian style.[2] All this points to the 'upper class' culture of Palestine being Egyptian-inspired, and also Palestine and parts of Syria being dominated by Egypt and its economic interests. As the Middle kingdom grew stronger, more Egyptian objects found their way to Palestine, as did Egyptian officials and merchants.

A tale set in the time of Amenemhat I and Senwosret I, namely the 'Story of Sinuhe', gives some information about Palestine and its people as well as about Egyptian officials at certain places in Syria-Palestine.[3] The text may be understood to represent propaganda from the Egyptian court.[4] Both the Sinuhe tale and the 'Instruction of Amenemhet'[5] are literary pieces originally composed after the murder of Amenemhat I. The 'Instruction' may have been written in order 'to justify a fearful repression following Amenemmes I's death', and the Sinuhe story ends with praising a merciful king (Senwosret I).[6] Sinuhe had been participating in Senwosret's Libyan campaign, and there he learned about the death (murder) of pharaoh Amenemhat. Sinuhe must have been involved in the conspiracy, because as soon as he received the news he secretly left Egypt by crossing the wall in the northeast and continued to Gubla (Byblos), and from there to Qedem; that is, he went east. Perhaps he could not stay in Byblos because it was an Egyptian power base. A prince in Upper Retenu (Palestine), Ammi-enshi, persuaded Sinuhe to stay with him and he also gave him his daughter as wife. He became Ammi-enshi's military commander and lived in the country Yaa,[7] which was rich in cattle, figs, vines, honey and olives. As time passed, and after having had a very success-ful life in Yaa, he wanted to return to Egypt. Most important was that,

---

1.　O. Tufnell, 'El-'Ajjul, Tel', *EAEHL*, I, pp. 57-58. Consult also J.R. Stewart, *Tell el 'Ajjul*, pp. 27-44.

2.　Cf. K.M. Kenyon, *Archaeology in the Holy Land*, pp. 174-75, and fig. 51.

3.　Cf. M. Green, 'The Syrian and Lebanese Topographical Data in the Story of Sinuhe', *Chronique d'Egypte* 58 (1983), pp. 38-59.

4.　See, for instance, G. Posener, *Littérature et politique dans l'Egypt*; W.J. Murnane, *Ancient Egyptian Coregencies* (SAOC, 40; Chicago, 1977, pp. 248-50. For date and composition, see also J. Assmann, 'Die Rubren in der Überlieferung der Sinuhe-Erählung', *Fontes atque Pontes* (Ägypten und Altes Testament, 5; ed. M. Görg; Wiesbaden, 1983), pp. 18-41.

5.　See J.A. Wilson, *ANET*, pp. 418-19.

6.　W.J. Murnane, *Ancient Egyptian Coregencies*, p. 250.

7.　The exact location of this is unknown.

like every Egyptian, he wanted to be buried in his homeland. He received a message from Senwosret with an invitation to return and to become a courtier, and so he did. He received a tomb in the royal necropolis. As the text states, he could then live by the grace of the king until his death. This is the main point of the composition.

The Sinuhe story can be characterized as good propagandistic literature which at the same time presents some knowledge about life in Palestine, but it cannot be used as a detailed historical report.[1] Neither can it be used as proof that the population of Retenu (Palestine) had a nomadic life style.[2] Nomads do not cultivate figs, vines and olives, and neither do they have cattle. What we can learn from this Egyptian tale is that the population of Upper Retenu was settled, and that there were some smaller nations or city states battling each other.[3] The author of the tale thus shows that he is acquainted with Palestinian social and cultural circumstances, and we may conclude that the Egyptian court was well informed about the happenings and events in the different principalities of Palestine.

Other Egyptian texts which often have been used as source material for describing social and political development in Syria-Palestine during the period of the Twelfth Dynasty are the so-called Execration Texts from around the end of the Twelfth Dynasty.[4] These are curses written on clay figurines of captives or on jars listing cities and their rulers. The purpose of these texts is not really known. They may have been used in connection with rituals wherein the jars or figurines would have been crushed. The 'magic' of this would have been the annihilation of the sites and peoples listed on them. The purpose with

1. Cf. W. Helck, *Die Beziehungen*, p. 40.

2. J. Bright has misinterpreted the Sinuhe story when he maintains that this story, as well as the stories in Genesis, 'splendidly' illustrate the 'mode of life' of the Amorites (*A History of Israel*, p. 55). The storytellers of Genesis most probably did not know anything about the events of the twentieth century BCE.

3. Sinuhe is said always to have been victorious as Ammeni-enshi's commander in both destroying enemy camps and taking cattle from the enemies.

4. For the date, see the discussion in G. Posener, *Princes et pays d'Asie et de Nubie* (Brussels, 1940), pp. 33, 94; W. Helck, *Die Beziehungen*, pp. 44-45; T.L. Thompson, *The Historicity of the Patriarchal Narratives*, pp. 106-13 (who identifies them as c. 1810–1770 BCE). The date can be supported by the Egyptian writing of the name for Byblos, *k3p*, *k3pny*, which does not occur before the reign of Amenemhet IV (1797–1788).

this ritual would thus be the security of Egypt's commercial and political interests in Palestine.[1]

There are three groups of Execration Texts referring to Syro-Palestinian sites. The earlier group, found at Thebes (the so-called Berlin group) consists of 289 inscribed sherds mentioning 19 territories or cities with their rulers. More than one princely ruler of each place (usually three) is mentioned.[2] Some of the place names have been identified, such as Ashkelon, Jerusalem, Beth-Shan, Rehob, Byblos, 'Arqat and Ullaza. The Transjordanian Shutu are also mentioned.[3]

A younger group from Sakkara (the Brussels group)[4] with curses on small figurines mentions 64 Palestinian places or peoples. Generally, only the name of one ruler is given, but in a few cases there are two. Five places are mentioned without any ruler. The geographical distribution of the names is much larger than in the Berlin group, comprising not only most of Palestine, Transjordan (the Shutu) and the Lebanese coast, but also the people of Cush (listed with two rulers).[5] The information about several rulers of a people in the older text group may be seen as an indication for the existence of some territorial organization, as is the case also in four instances in the younger group.[6]

A third group of texts with curses on bowls (175 pieces) and three figurines has been found at Mirgissa in Nubia. Because the phraseology is close to that of the Berlin texts, they have been dated to about the same period.[7] Also this group of texts is directed against peoples

1. Cf. W. Helck, *Die Beziehungen*, p. 61.

2. K. Sethe, *Die Ächtung feindlicher Fürsten, Völker und Dinge auf altägyptischen Tongefässcherben des Mittleren Reiches* (Abhandlungen der Preussischen Akademie der Wissenschaften, 1926, phil.-hist. Klasse, 5; Berlin, 1926).

3. Cf. Num. 24.17. According to I.M. Diakonoff, *sutu*, 'shepherd tribes', refers to 'western Semites in Mesopotamia', and may be the same as biblical Seth ('Father Adam', *Vorträge gehalten auf der 28. Reucontre Assyriologique Internationale in Wien, 6–10. Juli, 1981* [ed. H. Hirch; AfO, Beiheft 19; Austria, 1982], p. 19).

4. Published by G. Posener, *Princes et pays.* Cf. W. Helck, *Die Beziehungen*, pp. 60-61; T.L. Thompson, *Historicity of the Patriarchal Narratives*, pp. 98-117.

5. W. Helck sees *k-u-š-u* as referring to Midian, (*Die Beziehungen*, p. 58).

6. A. Alt, 'Herren und Herrensitze Palästinas im Anfang des zweiten Jahrtausends v. Chr.', *ZDPV* 64 (1941), pp. 37-38 (= *KS*, III, pp. 69-71).

7. See G. Posener, 'Les textes d'envoûtement de Mirgissa', *Syria* 43 (1966), pp. 277-87; J. Vercoutter, 'Deux mois de fouilles à Mirgissa en Nubie soudanaise',

in Libya, Nubia and Syria-Palestine, as well as against the forces of evil. Thus one may see the Execration Texts as means of 'promoting' the destruction of evil, with which the enemies were reckoned. From this point of view such a text cannot be taken as a proof for Egypt's political expansion only, or as an indication that the purpose of their writing was solely for the protection of the caravan routes. Whatever political or commercial interest Egypt had during these times (and those interests are very much intertwined), the forces that stood in the way of these interests had to be destroyed.[1] It is very doubtful that we can reconstruct from these texts a development of the social and political organizations in southern Syria and in Palestine reflecting a change from a tribal society ruled by tribal chieftains to a settled society with city states with one ruler, as has been maintained.[2] Ritual texts and curses are not the best sources for historiography. What possibly could be concluded from the Execration Texts is that cities not mentioned, such as Qatna, Ugarit, Megiddo and Jericho, were either on friendly terms with Egypt or under Egyptian control. As mentioned above,[3] an Egyptian official, Tuthotep, resided in Megiddo

Bulletin de la Société francaise d'égyptologie 37–38 (1963), pp. 28-30; T.L. Thompson, *Historicity of the Patriarchal Narratives*, pp. 111-12.

1.   In a cemetery under a street west of the Cheops pyramid were found in 1955 two jars with 223 unbroken small figurines and 26 pieces of figurines, all with names written on them. Most of the names refer to Nubians. The figurines could probably represent 'dangerous' people who have been punished with death; see A.M. Abu Bakr and J. Osing, 'Ächtungstexte aus dem Alten Reich', *MDAIK* 29 (1973), pp. 129-30; cf. also J. Osing, 'Ächtungstexte aus dem Alten Reich (II)', *MDAIK* 32 (1976), pp. 132-85.

2.   K. Sethe, *Die Ächtung feindlicher Fürsten*, pp. 43-44; cf. J. Bright, *A History of Israel*, pp. 54-55; Y. Aharoni, *The Land of the Bible*, p. 144. W.F. Albright thought that one could divide Palestine into two main parts: a northern region including Lebanon and southern Syria, and the southern region including mainly the southern hill country. The coastal area would consist of cities each with a single ruler; the southern area would have had a different political structure with tribes being ruled by several chieftains at the same time ('The Egyptian Empire in Asia in the Twenty-First Century BCE', *JPOS* 8 [1928], pp. 250-51). Albright used the Execration Texts as support for his theory about 'barbarious' tribes having entered the country at the end of the third millennium. Among these 'invaders' he placed the Abraham group known from the Old Testament ('Palestine in the Earliest Historical Period', *JPOS* 15 [1935], pp. 217-18). It should be pointed out that the Bible never depicts Abraham as a barbarian.

3.   Cf. p. 166, above.

during the reign of Senwosret III (1878–1842), and one may assume that this was also the case during his successors of the Twelfth Dynasty.[1]

There is some evidence of Egyptian monuments having been smashed at Qatna and Ugarit in the period before pharaoh Neferhotep I of the Thirteenth Dynasty (1751–1740). The friendly relations between Egypt and Byblos that existed during the Twelfth Dynasty were waning in the time before the accession to the throne of Neferhotep I.[2] Furthermore, since the eighteenth-century texts from Mari seem to show that Byblos was independent,[3] one could assume that Egypt's influence in Syria and northern Palestine had sharply decreased. However, for a short time Egypt's power was again felt during the reign of Neferhotep. For instance, monuments show Byblian kings doing homage to the pharaoh. This state of affairs may also be an indication for the Execration Texts belonging to the period before Neferhotep.

If the Execration Texts are poor as a source for the political and social organization of the territories mentioned in them, they are nonetheless of a certain value for the historian of religion because of the theophoric component in the names of the rulers. Thus we learn about the deity names Haddu, Sin, Yam, Malik, Ilu, Lim, Ksr, Ḥammu, Hauron, Baliḫ, Shamshu, Yapa, Abu, Lawi and Aḫu. This shows that, besides West-semitic deities, the worship of Mesopotamian gods had spread into Syria and northern Palestine. Of a special interest is the fact that the *ba'al* name is missing. This may indicate that the apellative *ba'al*, 'lord', had not yet become a name for a special god. Probably Baal is another form of Hadad, who was worshipped among most West-Semitic peoples.[4] The cult of Baal is known from Tanis in

1.   Cf. B. Mazar, *IEJ* 18 (1968), p. 131.

2.   W.A. Ward, *Or* NS 30 (1961), p. 154. It is, however, doubtful whether the statue smashed at Ugarit really belongs to this period.

3.   A. Goetze, 'The Date of the Hittite Raid on Babylon', *BASOR* 127 (1952), p. 26.

4.   K. Koch maintains that Baal emerged as a new type of god during the first half of the second millennium BCE ('Zur Enstehung der Ba'al-Verehrung', *UF* 11 [1979], pp. 465-75). For Baal and Hadad, see also W.G. Lambert, 'Trees, Snakes and Gods in Ancient Syria and Anatolia', *Bulletin of the School of Oriental and African Studies* 48 (1985), pp. 435-45. The fact that Baal is not mentioned in Genesis may be because the narrator(s) of the Genesis stories did not know anything about life in the 18th–16th centuries BCE Palestine. The legends in Genesis are concerned about an idyllic period in which the historical time's religious problems were

Lower Egypt from c. 1730 BCE. Here he was identified with the Egyptian storm god Seth.[1] This means that Baal was a storm god, and that he was introduced in Egypt about a generation before the so-called Hyksos period began.[2] It also means that Baal has been known in Syria-Palestine some generations before the Semites brought him to Egypt. A new and unimportant god would not have had any possibility of being identified with the Egyptian Seth.

The MB Age II in Palestine has often been characterized as the zenith of the country's cultural development in ancient times. The above has shown that, as so often before, the hills have not had the same cultural exchange as the coastal areas, which, as usual, have been more exposed to the dangers of military expeditions. Thus we still have to reckon with a certain instability which also could have been caused partly by the influx of newcomers from the north, as, for instance, Hurrians.[3] Because Palestine is given the name Hurru (Kharu) in later Egyptian texts, we may see the Hurrians and their *maryannu* nobility as having become the upper crust of the society in most city states.[4]

There are indications for destruction at Shechem and Tell Beit Mirsim from the end of the eighteenth cent. BCE, and at the same time Byblos' importance as a center for Egyptian trade was declining.[5] The latter may be a result of the decline in Egypt's power. The reason for the destructions at Tell Beit Mirsim and Shechem is not known. If they are a sign of one and the same historical event, it is impossible to say. Accidents or some local problems could also have occurred. Whatever the reason, at Shechem we know that around 1700 or shortly before the city had a 'massive embankment' (rampart) 'which at its base was some 38 m wide and 15 m high. This embankment

conceived of as not having existed; cf. J. Gray, *The Legacy of Canaan* (VTSup, 5; Leiden, 1957), p. 123.

1. J. Zandee, 'Seth als Sturmgott', *ZÄS* 90 (1963), pp. 144-56; S. Morenz, *Ägyptische Religion*, pp. 250-51.

2. W. Helck, *Die Beziehungen*, p. 100.

3. Cf. B. Mazar, *IEJ* 18 (1968), pp. 90-91.

4. According to I.J. Gelb, the Hurrians would have gained political dominance in Syria from c. 1700 BCE (*Hurrians and Subarians* [Chicago, 1944]).

5. Cf. G. Posener, 'Syra and Palestine', *CAH*, I.2, pp. 532-34, and see also W.F. Albright, 'Further Light on the History of Middle-Bronze Byblos', *BASOR* 179 (1965), pp. 38-43; O. Negbi and S. Moshkowitz, 'The "Foundation Deposits" or "Offering Deposits" of Byblos', *BASOR* 186 (1966), pp. 21-26.

used Wall D as inside footing.'[1] Wall (D) encircling the citadel (?) was c. 3 m wide and was constructed around 1750 BCE. The so-called Migdal Temple (fortress temple)[2] was built on a plateau (originally a fill) inside the wall.[3] It is quite possible that it dates from the same period as the embankment.[4] This type of temple is said to occur also at Megiddo and Hazor.[5] However, the towers of these two temples were built first after the MB II period.[6] Thus the innovation is much later than the presumed foreigners.

As mentioned above, all of Palestine cannot be seen as part of the Egyptian kingdom during the MB I and MB II periods. Egypt's economic interest was mainly Syria, and Palestine was therefore a country that one of necessity had to deal with. It was a transit country from which one could take the little it could produce. We could say that Palestine was an economic appendix to Syria. Therefore, only certain areas of Palestine, such as the coastal areas and the Jezreel and Jordan Valleys—even though the hills cannot be discounted—were of some importance because of the agricultural products and cattle that could be acquired. From this point of view Megiddo would be an important site furnishing Egypt and its troops with the produce of the surrounding area.

During this period there was an intensified commerce between the kingdoms of Anatolia, Mesopotamia and Syria-Palestine. Among the powers in northern Syria which since the nineteenth cent. BCE had been competing for hegemony in the area were the west-Semitic kingdoms of Yamhad and Mari and the Akkadian kingdom of Ashur. Yamhad's capital was Halab (modern Aleppo). Its territory reached to the Euphrates where it bordered on Ashur (Assyria). To the north of Yamhad was the kingdom of Carchemish. In the southeast was the

1. J.D. Seger, 'The Middle Bronze II C Date of the East Gate at Shechem', *Levant* 6 (1974), p. 117.

2. B. Mazar saw this type of temple architecture as an innovation by foreigners (*IEJ* 18 [1968], p. 93). For a criticism, see M.D. Fowler, *PEQ* 115 (1983), pp. 49-51.

3. See L.E. Toombs and G.E. Wright, *BASOR* 169 (1963), pp. 24-25.

4. Cf. I. Finkelstein, 'Excavations at Shiloh 1981–1984: Preliminary Report', *Tel Aviv* 12 (1985), pp. 163-64.

5. For the plans, see M. Ottosson, *Temples and Cult Places*, pp. 61-63, and fig. 8 (on pp. 54-55).

6. Cf. I. Dunayevsky and A. Kempinski, *ZDPV* 89 (1973), p. 182; A. Kempinski, *Syrien und Palästina*, pp. 172-74.

kingdom of Mari with its capital, Mari (modern Tell Hariri), on the middle Euphrates at the intersection of two caravan routes.

The cuneiform tablets that have been unearthed at Tell Hariri are one of the main sources for our knowledge about west-Semitic peoples and socio-political circumstances in the Syro-Mesopotamian area during the nineteenth and eighteenth centuries BCE. We learn about political zenith of the Mari kingdom, as well as about its fall, and the last three kings of the dynasty, Yaggid-Lim, Yahdun-Lim and Zimri-Lim.

The excavations at Tell Hariri started in 1933 and, with an interruption for the second world war, continued until 1956.[1] An enormous palace was found at the site, occupying about 2.5 hectares. Not only did it function as a palace of the royal family, but it also comprised a caravanserai and a bazaar.[2] Around 24,000 tablets with cuneiform script were also found covering the period 1820–1760 BCE.[3] This archive is the largest ever excavated from the Old Babylonian period.

As we know,[4] the Mari kingdom became a dependent of Ebla during the twentieth century, and during the Ur III period (2060–1950) it was under Ur. After the fall of Ur we find three political powers struggling for hegemony in northern Mesopotamia, namely, Mari, Ashur and Babylon, the latter being until now a relatively insignificant political entity. During the end of the nineteenth century and the beginning of the eighteenth, Mari began to feel the rivalry with Assyria. Shamshi-Adad I (1813–1781),[5] who gained the throne and

---

1. See A. Parrot, 'Les fouilles de Mari: Premier campagne (Hiver 1933–34): Rapport préliminaire', *Syria* 16 (1935), pp. 1-28, 117-140; *idem, Syria* 42 (1965), pp. 1-24, 197-225; *Syria* 49 (1972), pp. 281-302; *Syria* 52 (1975), pp. 1-17. C.-F. Jean, 'Six campagnes de fouilles à Mari (1933–1939) II', *NRT* 74 (1952), pp. 624-33; D. Pardee and J.T. Glass, 'Literary Sources for the History of Palestine and Syria: The Mari Archives', *BA* 47 (1984), pp. 88-99.

2. Cf. S. Dalley, *Mari and Karana: Two Old Babylonian Cities* (London, 1984), pp. 12-15.

3. The Mari texts have been published by M. Birot, J. Bottéro, M.L. Burke, C.-F. Jean, J.-R. Kupper and G. Dossin in *Archives royales de Mari* (Paris, 1950–1986).

4. See above, Chapter 3.

5. W.W. Hallo in W.W. Hallo and W.K. Simpson, *The Ancient Near East*, p. 97. Shamshi-Adad's father, Ila-kabkabi, was king of Terqa, c. 50 km. NE of Mari on the Euphrates. Mari had conquered Terqa, and Ila-kabkabi's family had to go into exile (cf. J. Laessøe, *People of Ancient Assyria: Their Inscriptions and*

freed Assyria from the rule of Eshnunna, managed to expand his rule in Mesopotamia as well as in the West. For instance, he set up a victory stela on Mount Lebanon.[1] Mari was conquered by Shamshi-Adad (c. 1795 BCE), and the Assyrian king installed one of his sons, Yasmah-Adad, as vice regent there. Zimri-lim, the last king of Mari, fled to Yarim-Lim of Yamhad. He returned, however, when Shamshi-Adad died. It is possible that he received help from Yarim-Lim, who also had become his father-in-law. Shamshi-Adad put most of northern Mesopotamia under his crown and seems to have been a good administrator. His fame has, however, been resting in the shadow of a somewhat younger contemporary, namely Hammurapi of Babylon, who put an end to Mari's independence around 1760 BCE and who built an 'empire' in Mesopotamia which, however, did not last long.

The Mari archive includes administrative, legal and economic texts, as well as recording the political and cultural circumstances of the territories concerned. We learn that the rulers of Mari had to deal with several groups of people, both settled tribes and nomads, caravaneers and bandits. Among these groups are, for instance, the Haneans; the *ḫabiru*, 'outcasts, bandits'; the Suteans: the *mārū iamina*, 'southerners'; and the *mārū sim'al*, 'northerners'.[2] The Suteans were nomads. Among the Haneans we find some settled in villages and some having a transhumance life-style. Haneans also turn up as soldiers and among the caravaneers.[3] Many texts show diplomatic relations with other nations, such as Crete, Dilmun, Susa, Hattusas, Carchemish,

---

Correspondence [London, 1963], pp. 44-45). N. Weeks thinks that Shamshi-Adad 'was the leader of a military band which sold its services where it could and seized power for itself where it could' ('Old Babylonian Amorites: Nomads or Mercenaries?', *Orientalia Lovaniensia Periodica* 16 [1985], p. 51).

1.   B. Mazar, *IEJ* 18 (1968), p. 78.

2.   In west-Semitic languages these words mean 'right, south', and 'left, north', respectively. We should note that *mārū iamina* and *mārū sim'al* are hybrid forms. The form *marū(m)* is Akkadian, but *iamin(a)* and *sim'al* are west-Semitic. Akkadian forms would be *imnum* and *sumēlum* (M. B. Rowton, 'Dimorphic Structure and the Parasocial Element', *JNES* 36 [1977], pp. 188-89).

3.   Consult V.H. Matthews, *Pastoral Nomadism in the Mari Kingdom (ca. 1830–1760 BCE)* (ASOR Dissertation Series, 3; Cambridge, MA, 1978); cf. J.T. Luke, 'Pastoralism and Politics in the Mari Period' (PhD Dissertation, University of Michigan, 1965).

Emar, Qatna, and, in Palestine,[1] Hazor.[2] There is no mention of Egypt in these texts. This is not so strange, because Egypt's power was on the decline at the end of the Twelfth Dynasty, thus Egypt's influence did not reach as far north as to the Euphrates at this time.

The language of the tablets is Old Babylonian, but it contains many west-Semitic loan-words and names.[3] These texts have therefore had a considerable impact on the studies of the culture and religion of the peoples of Palestine. Philologically there is a connection because around one thousand names in the archives are west-Semitic.[4] This indicates that large segments of the population of the Mari kingdom, including their rulers, were of west-Semitic stock, who in scholarly treatments are usually called Amorites. From a comparative viewpoint, the Mari texts therefore are of great importance, but from the point of view of Palestinian history very little can be learned. The patriarchal stories in the Book of Genesis do not get any support as historical documents from the Mari texts.[5]

Among the peoples and 'tribes' mentioned, the so-called Benjaminites[6] have been seen to have been part of the 'Amorite' invasions into Palestine.[7] According to this view, they moved to

---

1. *ARM*, XII, 747.

2. Cf. A. Malamat, 'Northern Canaan and the Mari Texts', *Near Eastern Archaeology in the 20th Century (Essays in Honor of N. Glueck)* (ed. J.A. Sanders; New York, 1970), p. 168. That Laish is not the Laish/Dan in Palestine, but Layashim between Halab and Ugarit; see J.M. Sasson, 'Zimri-Lim takes the Grand Tour', *BA* 47 (1984), pp. 250-51.

3. Cf. M. Noth, 'Mari und Israel: Ein Personnamestudie', *Geschichte und Altes Testament* (ed. W.F. Albright *et al.*; Festschrift A. Alt; Tübingen, 1953), pp. 127-52; H.B. Huffmon, *Amorite Personal Names in the Mari Texts* (Baltimore, 1965).

4. *ARM*, XIII (Paris, 1964).

5. Cf. J.M. Sasson, who says that the 'attempts to use Mari documentation to confer historicity on the patriarchal narrative have largely failed' ('Mari', *IDBSup*, p. 570).

6. H. Tadmor has shown that the reading would be (DUMU.MEŠ) *mārū iamina* and not *bānū iamina* ('Historical Implications of the Correct Reading of Akkadian dâku', *JNES* 17 [1958], p. 130 n. 12; cf. I.J. Gelb, *JCS* 15 [1961], p. 38).

7. G. Dossin considered the Mari group as related to the biblical Benjaminites (see 'Benjaminites dans le textes de Mari', *Bibliothèque archéologique et historique* 30 [1939] [Mélanges Syriens offert à R. Dussaud II], pp. 981-96; *idem*, 'A propos du nom des Benjaminites dans les archives de Mari', *RA* 52 [1958], pp. 60-62).

Harran, and, following Hurrian population movements, whould have settled in Canaan.[1] This is no more than a hypothesis that tries to explain why the biblical Benjaminites, 'sons of the south', did not live south of Judah, and, therefore, must originally have been immigrants. J.R. Kupper has shown, however, that the Mari 'sons of the south', the Iaminites, moved from the northwest to the southeast and settled in Babylonia.[2] The 'itinerary' is thus the opposite. The term 'sons of the south' should be seen in relation to some other group of people. In the Mari texts they are south of the *mārū sim'al*, 'the sons of the north',[3] and in the Hebrew Bible the Benjaminites are south of the Ephraimites. 'Southerners' is a term that occurs in several countries.

Among the many words with Hebrew cognates one should mention the term *šāpiṭum*, 'governor, ruler, judge', in Hebrew *špṭ*, and cf. Ugaritic *špṭ*, which in these latter two languages also could be used as a synonym for king.[4] At Mari the word refers to an appointed governor, not to a king. However, the root refers to the idea of governing and making decisions. Thus, it is not astonishing that in the Palestinian territories it became a term for petty rulers, such as the biblical 'Judges'.[5]

Concerning the cult, we learn that Dagan was, as in Ebla, one of the most important deities. However, there is no indication of how the

1. Thus W. von Soden, 'Das altbabylonische Briefarchiv von Mari', *WO* 1 (1948), pp. 197-98.

2. *Les nomades en Mésopotamie au temps des rois de Mari* (Paris, 1957), pp. 75-77; cf. T.L. Thompson, *Historicity of the Patriarchal Narratives*, pp. 58-66.

3. It is possible that the mountain range, Jebel Bishri, in Syria was settled by Iaminites, as well as other 'Amorites'; for this position, see e.g. G. Buccellati, *The Amorites*, pp. 236-38.

4. Cf. H. Cazelles, 'Institutions et terminologie en Deutéronomie 16–17', *Congress Volume, Geneva 1965* (VTSup, 15; Leiden, 1966), p. 168; A. Malamat, 'Mari', *BA* 34 (1971), p. 19; A. Marzal, 'The Provincial Governor at Mari: His Title and Appointment', *JNES* 30 (1971), pp. 188-217. For *špṭ* meaning ruler, cf. G.W. Richter, 'Zu den Richtern Israels', *ZAW* 77 (1965), p. 60; M. Stol, 'Akkadisches *šāpiṭum šapaṭum* und westsemitisches *špṭ*', *BO* 29 (1972), pp. 276-77.

5. For the mistaken connection between *dawidûm* and the biblical name David, H. Tadmor believes that B. Landsberger has shown that the phrase *dawidām dāku* is a phonetic variant of *dabdâ dāku*, 'to defeat', and, therefore, *dawidûm* cannot mean general, nor can it be related to the name *dwd*, *dāwîd*. See H. Tadmor, *JNES* 17 (1958), pp. 129-31; cf. G.W. Ahlström, *Psalm 89*, pp. 168-69; J.R. Kupper, *Les nomades*, pp. 58-60.

cult was performed.[1] We cannot dismiss the fact that Mari, being a kingdom in the Euphrates area, very much was influenced by Sumer and Akkad. This is obvious from the names of the many Mesopotamian gods mentioned in the texts, but the many west-Semitic deities who also are mentioned, such as Dagan, Addu (Hadad), Ḫammu ('Am), Ḫanat (Anath), Erah (Yarih), Ḫal ('Al), Hawran (Horon), Ilum (El),[2] Malik,[3] Rašap (Resheph), Amurrum, and Salim, testify to a very strong west-Semitic culture and population, as well as to the cosmopolitan character of the kingdom and its religion. We learn that the royal government directed religious matters and, for instance, could regulate festivals and sacrifices.[4] As for the royal ideology, the ancestors of the royal dynasty received sacrifices, which shows that they were 'divinized'.[5] Besides priests (*kumru*, Hebrew *kmr*) and singers (*kalu*) we find diviners (*bāru*) and prophets (*maḫḫu* and *āpilum*), male as well as female. The latter category is of interest to the historian of religion even though it is not anything surprisingly new. It shows, moreover, that Hebrew prophecy has not been as unique as so often—almost dogmatically—has been maintained. Prophecy seems to have played an active part in the religion and life of the Mari kingdom. The *muḫḫu(m)*, fem. *muḫḫutu(m)* was the ecstatic, frenzied

1.   D.O Edzard, 'Pantheon und Kult in Mari', *XVe Rencontre assyriologique internationale* (La civilisation de Mari; Liège, 1967), pp. 51-53. It is interesting to note that Shamshi-Adad of Assyria ordered his son Yasmah-Adad (when he was viceroy of Mari) to send horses, mules and chariots to be used in connection with the *akītu* festival. They were then to be returned to Mari, in all a trip of about 600 km. The reason for the request is not given, but one could assume that horses and mules were necessary for pulling the carts in the processions from the temple on the *via sacra* to the *akītu* house. A. Falkenstein suggests that a military 'Heershau' (review, parade) was connected with the *akītu* festival ('akiti-Fest und a-k-i-t-i-Festhaus', *Festschrift Johannes Friedrich zum 65. Geburstag am 27 August 1958 gewidmet* [ed. R. von Kienle *et al.*; Heidelberg, 1959], pp. 157).

2.   J.J.M. Roberts, *The Earliest Semitic Pantheon* (Baltimore, 1972), pp. 31-33.

3.   The form Muluk occurs in the name of a city, Ilum-Muluk, in the Terqa territory; see A. Finet, in 'Repertoire analytique', *ARM*, XV, pp. 127, 163.

4.   Cf. A.L. Oppenheim, 'The Archives of the Palace of Mari II', *JNES* 13 (1954), p. 142; A. Finet, 'La place du devin dans la société de Mari', *RAI*, XIV (Paris, 1966), p. 92; V.H. Matthews, 'Government Involvement in the Religion of the Mari Kingdom', *RA* 72 (1978), pp. 151-56. Consult also S. Dalley, *Mari and Karana*, pp. 112-22.

5.   Cf. M. Dietrich and O. Loretz, 'Totenverehrung in Mari (12803) und Ugarit (KTU 1.161)', *UF* 12 (1978), pp. 53-56.

one, and the *āpilu(m)*, fem. *āpiltu(m)* means 'the one who responds'. The prophetic messages could be political as well as ethical in nature. There are, for instance, oracles for the king[1] about success in war, and admonitions to him to protect the needy and the poor, a phenomenon which also occurs in other Mesopotamian texts. Sometimes there are threats and reproofs, oracles about trust in the god, about a good future, as well as about disaster. As a biblical prophet could begin his message with the phrase 'Thus says Yahweh...', so also a Mari prophet could use the same kind of formula, 'Thus says Dagan...'[2]

Excursus: Abram/Abraham

The texts from Mari have often been used in arguments concerning the date and historicity of the biblical patriarchs. The cultural picture of the so-called patriarchal period has been colored very much by

1. We also learn that Queen Shiptu collected prophetic sayings and told them to the king (P. Artzi and A. Malamat, 'The Correspondence of Šibtu, Queen of Mari in *ARM* X', *Or* NS 40 [1971], pp. 75-89); cf. W.H.P. Römer, *Frauenbriefe über Religion, Politik und Privatleben in Mari* (AOAT, 12; Neukirchen–Vluyn, 1971).

2. For the Mari prophecy, see F. Ellermeier, *Prophetie in Mari und Israel* (Theologische und Orientalische Arbeiten, 1; Herzberg am Harz, 1968); cf. W. von Soden, 'Verkündigung des Gotteswillens durch prophetisches Wort in den altbabylonischen Briefen aus Mari', *WO* 4 (1949), pp. 397-403; H. Schult, 'Vier weitere Mari-Briefe "prophetischen" Inhalts', *ZDPV* 82 (1966), pp. 228-32; G. Dossin, 'Sur le prophetisme à Mari', *La divination en Mésopotamie ancienne* (Paris, 1966); A. Malamat, 'Prophetic Revelations in New Documents from Mari and the Bible', *Congress Volume, Geneva, 1965* (VTSup, 15; Leiden, 1966), pp. 207-27; W.L. Moran, 'New Evidence from Mari on the History of Prophecy', *Bib* 50 (1969), pp. 15-56; J.G. Heintz, 'Oracles prophetiques et "guerre sainte" selon les archives royales de Mari et l'Ancient Testament', *Congress Volume, Rome 1968* (VTSup, 17; Leiden, 1969), pp. 112-38; K. Koch, 'Die Briefe "prophetischen" Inhalts aus Mari', *UF* 4 (1972), pp. 53-77; H.B. Huffmon, 'Prophecy in the Mari Letters', *BA* 31 (1968), pp. 10-124; *idem*, 'Prophecy in the Ancient Near East', *IDBSup*, pp. 697-70; G.W. Ahlström, 'Prophecy', *Encyclopaedia Britannica*, XV (15th edn; Chicago, 1974), pp. 62-68; E. Noort, *Untersuchungen zum Gottesbescheid in Mari: Die 'Mari-Prophetie' in der alttestamentlichen Forschung* (AOAT, 22; Neukirchen–Vluyn 1977); J.F. Craghan, 'The Arm X "Prophetic" Texts: Their Media, Style and Structure', *JANESCU* 6 (1974), pp. 39-57; B. Lafont, 'Le roi de Mari et les prophètes du dieu Adad', *RA* 78 (1984), pp. 7-18. For a bibliography, see also J.G. Heintz, 'Prophetic in Mari und Israel', *Bib* 52 (1971), pp. 554-55.

what can be learned from the Mari texts, and concerning family customs and legal practice, from the later Nuzi texts.[1] The shepherds and nomadic tribes of the Mari texts have been seen as the ethnic relatives of the Abram group that would (on this view) have been part of the 'Amorite invasions'. However, these invasions of west-Semitic groups of people would have taken place during the EB IV period, some hundred years earlier than the Mari archives. The date and the historicity of the biblical patriarchs is, however, impossible to demonstrate from the Mari texts, even if such names as Abram, Laban and Ishmael are to be found in the corpus. Names derived from the root *'qb* (as in Hebrew Jacob), as *Ia-qu-ub-ilu*, are known from Upper Mesopotamia in the Old Babylonian period.[2] Besides Mari, the name Abram is known also from Ebla, Ugarit, Egypt[3] and Cyprus.[4] These occurrences show that the name Abram is authentic and not completely uncommon among west-Semites, but they do not establish the historicity of the biblical Abram/Abraham.[5]

The biblical narrative maintains that Abraham and his clan came from Mesopotamia to Canaan. Gen. 11.31 says that Terah took his son

---

1. For discussion, see R. de Vaux, *Early History of Israel*, pp. 257-266; T.L. Thompson, *Historicity of the Patriarchal Narratives*, pp. 52-57, 175-195 (and for the Nuzi material, pp. 197-203). Cf. also J. Van Seters, *Abraham in History and Tradition*, pp. 65-103. As for the literature, consult M. Dietrich, O. Loretz and W. Mayer, *Nuzi Bibliographie* (AOAT Sonderreihe, 11; Neukirchen–Vluyn, 1972).

2. M. Noth, 'Mari und Israel', *Geschichte und Altes Testament* (ed. W.F. Albright *et al.*, pp. 142-44; M. Rutten, 'Un lot de tablettes de Manana', *RA* 54 (1960) p. 149; R. de Vaux, *Early History of Israel*, p. 191.

3. C.H. Gordon, *Ugaritic Textbook* (AnOr, 38; Rome, 1965), Glossary 8, and cf. no. 46; F. Gröndahl, *Die Personennamen der Texte aus Ugarit* (Rome, 1967), p. 182. The name *abrm msrm* ('Abram the Egyptian') occurs in an Ugaritic text (A. Pohl, 'Forschungen und Funde', *Or* NS 25 [1956], p. 417); cf. W. Helck, *Die Beziehungen*, p. 434; G. Posener, 'Une list de noms propres étrangers', *Syria* 18 (1937), pp. 183-85.

4. E. Vogt, 'Ugaritica', *Bib* 37 (1956), p. 387; cf. F. Gröndahl, *Die Personennamen*, p. 182.

5. Cf. T.L. Thompson, *Historicity of the Patriarchal Narratives*, pp. 19-20. As for the name 'Abram', 'the Father is high, exalted', see for instance M. Noth, *Die israelitische Personennamen* (BWANT, 3.10; Stuttgart, 1928), p. 145 n. 1. The form Abraham can be seen as an etiological form referring to the Patriarch as the leader of a great multitude (see the résumé of the scholarly discussion in T.L. Thompson, *Historicity of the Patriarchal Narratives*, pp. 22-36).

Abram with his wife Sarai, his grandson Lot, the son of Haran, with their families and left 'Ur of the Chaldeans' and came to Haran in upper Mesopotamia. This text is of no help in establishing the origin of Abraham's family, nor the time for the move. The phrase 'Ur of the Chaldeans' (*ksdym*) is an anachronism. As far as is known from the textual material, the Chaldeans do not appear on the historical stage before the ninth century BCE. We could assume that the Chaldeans, like other Aramaeans, infiltrated Babylonia around 1100–1000 BCE. The phrase 'Ur of the Chaldeans' cannot have come into use in any Hebrew writing before the ninth century BCE.[1] In Gen. 15.6 Yahweh is said to have brought Abraham from 'Ur of the Chaldeans' to Canaan in order to give him the land. This phrase does not occur again in the Old Testament before Neh. 9.7, thus it may point to a late date for the origin of the Abraham narrative and for the 'promise of the land'.[2] The Abraham tradition in its present form may have been written after the Babylonian Exile, when the right to the land was denied the returnees. This is the time when such a claim would have been made. When one lives in the country, one does not need such divine legitimation. In support for this understanding of the promise of the land and the purpose of the whole Abraham narrative is the fact that the figure of Abraham does not play any role in the D history work, nor for most of the pre-exilic prophets. Had the promise of the land been known to them, there would have been more of an emphasis on it in this textual material.

A parallel problem is the mention of Haran in the Genesis stories. From this place Abraham is said to have left for Palestine, and Jacob is said to have fled to Haran after having cheated his father and

---

1.   Note that the LXX omits Ur and only mentions the land of the Chaldeans. In Akkadian inscriptions from the ninth century, the term *kaldu* refers to the region between the Persian Gulf and the southern area around the Euphrates and Tigris, a swampy region. The last dynasty of Babylon was Chaldean, 626–539 BCE. For the Chaldeans, see J.A. Brinkman, *A Political History of Post-Kassite Babylonia*, pp. 260-65; M. Dietrich, *Die Aramäer Südbabyloniens in der Sargonidenzeit* (AOAT, 7; Neukirchen–Vluyn, 1970).

2.   Cf. K. Galling, *Die Bücher der Chronik, Esra, Nehemia übersetzt und erklärt* (ATD, 12; Göttingen, 1954), p. 239; cf. also F.V. Winnett, 'Re-Examining the Foundations', *JBL* 84 (1965), p. 13; W.M. Clark, 'The Origin and Development of the Land Promise Theme in the Old Testament' (PhD dissertation, Yale University, New Haven, 1964), p. 98; J. Van Seters, *Abraham in History and Tradition*, pp. 249-79.

brother. In this way a group that entered Canaan from Transjordan became associated with Abraham. The city of Harran (in the upper Balikh area) is archaeologically not very well known from the period of the second millenium BCE. Only some pottery sherds and some fragments of inscriptions have been found.[1] The place is, however, known from the Mari archives[2] and from the so-called Cappadocian texts (20th–19th cent. BCE),[3] as well as being mentioned in some Old Babylonian itineraries.[4] With these sources only a fragmentary picture of Harran's history can be written. Only in the time of Adad-nirari I (1307–1275 BCE) is Harran mentioned again. With such a foggy picture of Harran and its history, it would be hard to establish that some clans—nomads or not—have moved from Harran to Palestine during the nineteenth through fourteenth centuries BCE. During the later neo-Assyrian period, Harran was an important center not only religiously with its Sin cult, but also economically. In the neo-Babylonian period Harran was a devastated place which Nabuna'id, the last Babylonian king, restored, as well as its Sin temple. With this in mind one should look at the narratives in Genesis about Abraham moving from Ur to Harran, two centers of the Sin cult which were restored in this late period.[5] Were Judahite prisoners of war used for the restoration works at these places? What seems to be evident is that the Abraham tradition has received its present 'Mesopotamian' form in the sixth century at the earliest. In biblical historiography Abraham has been made the ancestor not only of Israelites and Judahites, but also of the Arabs through his son Ishmael (Gen. 25.12-18), and of the Aramaeans through his grandson Jacob and Jacob's mother Rebecca. Related to these are then the Moabites and the Ammonites through Abraham's nephew Lot, and the Edomites through his 'grandson' Esau (Gen. 25.25;

1. Cf. K. Prag, 'The 1959 Deep Sounding at Haran in Turkey', *Levant* 2 (1970), pp. 63-94.

2. See J. Bottéro and A. Finet, *Répertoire analytique des tomes I–IV des archives royales de Mari* (Paris, 1954), p. 125.

3. G. Bilgic, 'Die Ortsnamen der "kappadokischen" Urkunden', *AfO* 15 (1945–51), pp. 1-3. It was from these texts and the Mari and Nuzi archives that W.F. Albright got the inspiration of calling Abraham a caravaneer ('Abraham the Hebrew', *BASOR* 163 [1961], pp. 36-54).

4. A. Goetze, 'An Old Babylonian Itinerary', *JCS* 7 (1953), pp. 51-72.

5. The close association with Haran and Ur 'can only reflect a time when both cities were at their height, and this exactly fits the Neo-Babylonian period' (J. Van Seters, *Abraham in History and Tradition*, p. 24).

Deut. 2.4-4; cf. Gen. 26.40-43). In this way most of the west-Semitic world and its peoples have been understood as the descendants of Abraham. Such a literary construction is 'hindsight' historiography and cannot be used as the basis for describing the events and population movements of the Middle Bronze Age Syria-Palestine.

In this connection we should note that in the Bible the 'Patriarchs' are never associated with the Jezreel Valley, Galilee or the Jordan Valley. They are, however, associated with some places and peoples that are not known from Palestine of the Bronze Age periods. For instance, Beer-sheba, which figures in Isaac's life, did not exist before the Iron Age. There is a gap from the Chalcolithic to the early Iron Age period. The Negev was not settled in the MB I (MB IIA) period. Concerning Bethel (Luz), W.F. Albright and J.L. Kelso theorized that the city existed in the EB and MB periods.[1] Kelso believed that he found a sanctuary (labeled 'high-place') from MB II in the gateway.[2] Unfortunately, Albright's theory is built on some few sherds only, and Kelso's sanctuary is, according to W.G. Dever, the foundation phase of a MB II city gate.[3]

Another anachronism is the mention of the Philistines. Abraham and Isaac are both said to have had some dealings with the Philistine king, Abimelech, of Gerar (Gen. 20 and 26).[4] The Philistines were not known in Palestine before the beginning of the Iron I A period (c. 1200 BCE). Also the mention of the camel is an anachronism. The camel was not used as the beast of burden in this part of the Near East before the end of the second millennium BCE even if it is

---

1. *The Excavations of Bethel (1934–1960)* (AASOR, 39; Cambridge, MA, 1968), pp. 55-56.

2. 'The Fourth Campaign at Bethel', *BASOR* 164 (1961), pp. 9-15.

3. 'Archaeological Methods and Results: A Review of Two Recent Publications', *Or* NS 40 (1971), pp. 466-67. Dever sees Bethel as no more than 'a camp-site in MB I'. Even so, the story about Jacob sleeping there would not be unrealistic, but his dream about the 'ladder to heaven' would be out of place, because that reflects the existence of a temple (Gen. 28.10-19). Jacob building an altar at Bethel (Gen. 35.1-8) is the narrator's way of legitimizing an old Canaanite cult place.

4. We do not know where Gerar was located. The Philistine pentapolis did not include any city Gerar. Gen. 26.17 mentions the valley of Gerar, *nḥl grr*, which may be a name from the writer's own time. In Roman-Byzantine time the wooded area southwest of Tell ed-Duweir was called *saltus gerariticus* (see M. Avi-Yonah, *The Holy Land*, p. 160 and map 16).

known as having been domesticated earlier.[1]

From the Mari texts Albright drew the conclusion that Abraham was a 'donkey caravaneer'.[2] This theory has not been very well received because it is unrealistic.[3] Albright was inspired by the Mari texts, but the biblical material does not give any support for the theory. To quote B. Mazar, it seems 'that many contemporary scholars have gone too far in their recurring attempts to discover in the Akkadian sources, such as the Mari documents', the Nuzi texts, as well as in material from the Middle Kingdom of Egypt, 'corroboration of the antiquity of the patriarchal accounts'.[4]

Genesis 14 shows clearly the fictional 'historiography' of the Abraham narrative. Here the 'caravaneer' or nomad Abraham is said to have defeated with his 318 men a coalition of four great kingdoms (14.14). The enemies are said to have first defeated the kings of Sodom, Gomorrah, Admah, Zeboiim and Bela (Zoar) in the area of the Dead Sea (14.1-12). The allies were said to have been Amraphel of Shinar, Arioch of Ellasar, Chedorlaomer of Elam and Tidal of Goyim. The name Goyim, which means peoples,[5] shows how unhistoric the story is. We do not need to refer to all the theories that have been formed concerning Hittites, Hurrians, Elamites and some Semites fighting Abraham and his little group. It is enough to state that Elam and Hatti

---

1.   Bones of camels have been found in graves at Mari. This does not prove, however, that the camel was a domesticated animal in Palestine already in the eighteenth cent. BCE. It was probably not domesticated in northern Mesopotamia in the Mari period (see R.W. Bulliet, *The Camel and the Wheel* [Cambridge, MA, 1975]). As to its domestication, see also B. Bentjes, 'Das Kamel im Alten Orient', *Klio* 38 (1960), pp. 23-52; J. Henninger, 'Zum früsemitischen Nomadentum', *Viehwirtschaft und Hirtenkultur: Ethnographische Studien* (ed. L. Foldes; Budapest, 1969), pp. 33-68; X. de Planhol, 'Caractères generaux de la vie montagnarde dans le Proche Orient et dans l'Afrique du Nord', *Annales de Géographie* 384 (1962); C.H.J. de Geus, *The Tribes of Israel*, p. 126; M. Ripinsky, 'Camel Ancestry and Domestication in Egypt and the Sahara', *Archaeology* 36 (1983), pp. 21-27.

2.   *BASOR* 163 (1961), pp. 36-54. He is followed, among others, by F.M. Cross, *Canaanite Myth and Hebrew Epic*, pp. 8-9.

3.   See N.P. Lemche, *Early Israel*, pp. 51-53.

4.   'The Historical Background of the Book of Genesis', *JNES* 28 (1969), p. 76.

5.   It is common to associate this appellation with the Hittite. Concerning the many efforts to identify these kings, see the résumé in T.L. Thompson, *Historicity of the Patriarchal Narratives*, pp. 187-95; cf. J. Van Seters, *Abraham in History and Tradition*, pp. 112-20.

never were part of any coalition fighting a population group in Palestine. The text is the product of a literary activity advocating that the whole country should have been an inheritance; therefore, the legitimation of this would become clear if Abraham had cleansed the country of enemies. The story is apocalyptic in its use of the motif of the four 'world powers' that should be subdued.[1] This motif of kingdoms that succeed each other occurs in the Near East first in the Persian period.[2] In Genesis 14 the motif has been used, but at the same time it is also changed; the kingdoms are united against Abraham and his people.

It is quite clear that the narrator of the Genesis stories did not have accurate knowledge about the prehistory of the Israelites.[3] That was not necessary either, because his purpose was not to write history. The social milieu and customs we meet in these texts, as well as the many peoples the patriarchs had contacts with reflect a much later time. We should also note that the Egyptian influence that was felt in Palestine and Syria during the Middle and Late Bronze periods is nowhere present in the patriarchal traditions. We could say that the patriarchal stories mirror a time when Egypt's rule over Palestine was nonexistent.

The narrator in Genesis had some special intentions. He assumed, for instance, a certain relationship between the west-Semitic peoples, and this relationship had to be explained.[4] In this explanation Abraham

1. Cf. A. Momigliano, 'The Origin of Universal History', *Annali della Scuola Normale Superiore di Pisa* (Classe di Lettere e Filosofia, Sere III, vol. XII, 2; Pisa, 1982), pp. 533-60. H. Gunkel maintained that the mixing of legendary material and heroic deeds is a form of fictitious writing among the Jews of the Persian and Hellenistic periods (*Die Urgeschichte und die Patriarchen [das erste Buch Mosis]* [Göttingen, 1921], pp. 189-91).

2. Cf. D. Flusser, 'The Four Empires in the Fourth Sibyl and the Book of Daniel', *Israel Oriental Studies* 2 (1972), pp. 166-67.

3. The story about Abraham buying land from the Hittites in Hebron (Gen. 23) cannot refer to any event prior to the fall of the Hittite empire c. 1200 BCE, after which groups of Hittite refugees settled in Syria and perhaps also in Palestine.

4. As for the 'nomadic picture' of the patriarchs, H. Gressmann maintained that this is not based upon any historical recollections, but is rather an artful construction by the narrator, who has twined together different traditions. Thus, writing a history of Abraham's wanderings from Mesopotamia to Canaan must be done with the help of the imagination. It may be good literature, but it cannot be history ('Sage und Geschichte in den Patriarchenerzählungen', *ZAW* 30 [1910], pp. 9-10).

has been given a central role. His wanderings are the means through which the kinship of all these peoples could be established. Even if there are some memories about a personality Abram/Abraham[1] which have been used by the biblical narrator, the 'history' of the patriarch is rather shadowy, which is natural because the narrator's purpose was not to write a biography.[2] Abraham represents the ideal of the time of the writer. He is the ideal ancestor of the peoples of Israel and Judah. In a time when Judah and its postexilic community were in distress, the people's prehistory was idealized. The origin of Yahweh's people was put in the period which was seen as being free from religious conflicts of the sort that the people had had throughout their history. From a literary point of view, Abraham represents the 'golden age'.

Hyksos

With the decline of the Egyptian power during the eighteenth century BCE and Egypt's weak position in the Levant, the Palestinian urban centers could expand and strongly fortified cities could be built. The internal weakness of Egypt 'coincided with a period of prosperity and political growth' not only in Palestine but also in Nubia.[3] For Palestine we should remember, however, that the country's geography did not invite the emergence of large political units. The Egyptian authority, therefore, was slowly replaced with several Palestinian authorities, the city states, which now could begin to carry out a more independent policy. With the weakening of the central Egyptian government and its rule in the Levant there followed movements of different groups of peoples which could not be checked by the Egyptians. There was some unrest in Syria during this time with the Hurrians gaining power. Alalakh, for instance, was sacked. The Egyptian border control did not work, and numbers of Asiatics

1. M. Liverani sees Abraham (Abu-Rahāmi) as the eponym for a people *banū rahāmi* mentioned as *rhm* in a stele by Seti I from Beth-Shan (thirteenth cent. BCE). Later this clan would have been incorporated with one of the groups of the Judean mountains ('Un ipotesi sul nome di Abramo', *Henoch* 1 [1979], pp. 9-18).

2. Because R. de Vaux saw the migrations of the patriarchs being 'closely related to the movement of the Amorites', he felt that the traditions about them had 'a firm historical basis' (*The Early History of Israel*, p. 200).

3. B.J. Kemp, 'Old Kingdom, Middle Kingdom and Second Intermediate Period in Egypt', *Cambridge History of Africa*, I (ed. J.D. Clark; Cambridge, 1982), p. 759.

infiltrated not only the Delta but also parts of northern Egypt.[1] In the seventeenth century BCE we find that some Semites had firmly established themselves in the Delta. With this we have come to what has been called the 'Second Intermediate Period' in the history of Egypt (1802–1541 BCE).[2] This is a time when the central administration's control of the country seems to have collapsed. A contributing factor to the collapse of the Egyptian administration may have been the many high floodings of the Nile that occurred during the period 1840–1770 BCE. With repeated disturbances in this sector of the economy the central Egyptian administration may have had its hands full. Even if the Thirteenth Dynasty kings managed to keep Egypt and Nubia under some (shaky) control, as well as keeping Byblos in a state of vassalage,[3] the establishment of rival kingdoms in the Delta signaled increasing internal troubles.[4] One kingdom (the Fourteenth Dynasty)[5] was established at Xois in the central Delta. Asiatic usurpers (possibly mercenary officers) arose at other places[6] and it is possible that the so-called Fourteenth Dynasty was no dynasty at all, but a period when there were several smaller kingdoms in the Delta. The city of Avaris (Tell el-Dabʻa)[7] was taken around 1720, and about four decades later

1.   One cannot draw the conclusion from Egyptian sources that there had been massive invasions of Semites (cf. W.H. Stiebing, 'Hyksos Burials in Palestine: A Review of the Evidence', *JNES* 30 [1971], pp. 110-17).

2.   For the dates, see M. Bietak, *AJA* 88 (1984), pp. 472-73.

3.   This can be supported by a relief showing a prince of Byblos, Yantin, paying homage to Pharaoh Neferhotep I of the Thirteenth Dynasty (P. Montet, 'Notes et documents pour servir à l'histoire des relations entre l'ancienne Egypte et la Syrie', *Kêmi* 1 (1928), pp. 91-93. Cf. W.F. Albright, 'An Indirect Syncronism between Egypt and Mesopotamia, cir. 1730 B.C.', *BASOR* 99, pp. 11-15 [1945]).

4.   See J. von Beckerath, *Untersuchungen zur politischen Geschichte der zweiten Zwischenzeit in Ägypten* (Ägyptologische Forschungen, 23; Glückstadt, 1965), pp. 29-32.

5.   This may have happened around 1720 BCE. According to Manetho, this dynasty would have had 76 kings (cf. A. Gardiner, *Egypt of the Pharaohs*, p. 147).

6.   Cf. J. von Beckerath, *Abriss der Geschichte des alten Ägypten* (Munich, 1971), p. 30.

7.   For Tell el-Dabʻa being identified with Avaris, see L. Habachi, 'Khataʻna-Qantir: Importance', *Annales du service des antiquités de l'Egypte* 52 (1954), pp. 443-59; J. Van Seters, *The Hyksos: A New Investigation* (New Haven, 1966), pp. 127-51; M. Bietak, *Tell el-Dabʻa II* (Österreichische Akademie der Wissenschaften, Denkschriften der Gesamtakademie, 4; Vienna, 1975), pp. 179-220; and *idem*, 'Avaris and Piramesse: Archaeological Exploration in the Eastern

Memphis fell, which meant the end of the Thirteenth Dynasty. Thus, the soil was prepared for the 'Hyksos' takeover. Around 1650 an Asiatic military leader and his group seized power at Avaris. This may have been the result of a peaceful infiltration[1] that ended in a *coup d'état*, or the result of a takeover by a newly arrived military group.[2] This is the beginning of the Hyksos rule first over the Delta and then extending south, making also Thebes a vassal to the ruler at Avaris.[3] The period has usually been labeled after the Hyksos. Also for Palestine the time after the end of the Twelfth Dynasty inaccurately has been named after the Hyksos. Their relationship with the Syro-Palestinian kinglets, however, is not quite clear. The Egyptian trade connections under the Hyksos rulers reached all the way to the Euphrates, but the Hyksos kings do not seem to have ruled over Syria and the whole of Palestine. This may be the explanation for the strong defenses that were built at this time by the Palestinian city states. When the Egyptian power slackened at the end of the Twelfth Dynasty, the rulers of the Palestinian city states became more independent. The Hyksos rulers, who probably were Semites, had enough trouble keeping their positions in Egypt so that no campaigns to Palestine could be carried out. The south Palestinian coast to Gaza can probably be seen as being under Egyptian rule during the Hyksos time. Nahal Besor was perhaps the northern defense line of the Hyksos kingdom. Several fortified sites (Canaanite city states?) have been found along this wadi, among which Tell el-'Ajjul, Tell Abu Hureirah and Tell el-Far'ah (S) were the most important. Because several scarabs have been found at south Palestinian sites,[4] J.M. Weinstein maintains that

Delta', *Proceedings of the British Academy* 65 (1979), pp. 225-90.

1. T. Säve-Söderbergh, 'The Hyksos Rule in Egypt', *JEA* 37 (1951), pp. 53-71.

2. Thus D.B. Redford, who compares this event with Shamshi-Adad retaking the throne of Assyria and Zimri-Lim's return to Mari ('The Hyksos Invasion in History and Tradition', *Or* NS 39 [1970], pp. 16-17).

3. For the problems of chronology, see M. Bietak, *AJA* 88 (1984), pp. 471-85.

4. These are Gezer, Tell eṣ-Ṣafi, Tell ed-Duweir, Tell el-'Ajjul, Tell Nagila, Tell Jemme, Tell Beit Mirsim, Tel Halif, Tell el-Far'ah (S). Scarabs have also been found at Jericho and Amman, as well as at Shiqmona west of Haifa, and Tell el-'Amr in the Esdraelon. The inscription on the Shiqmona scarab ('the son of Re`, Y'qb-Hr is given life'), which was found in an MB II tomb, A. Kempinski sees as referring to a local ruler preceding Y'qb-Hr of the Fifteenth Dynasty. Thus the ancestors of the Fifteenth Dynasty 'were local rulers on the fringes of the sphere of influence of the

the Hyksos power in Palestine was situated 'in the southern and inland regions' of the country. That may explain why these areas were 'thoroughly destroyed' by the early rulers of the Eighteenth Dynasty.[1] The Canaanite influences in the Delta increased during the MB II period. For instance, the material culture in the eastern part of the Delta is of the same origin as the MB II culture of the south-Palestinian coast.[2] The kinglets of southern Palestine may, as a matter of fact, have been vassals or allies to the Hyksos kings at Avaris.[3] The rest of Palestine may have had friendly relations with Egypt but probably was not part of any Egyptian empire. Finds from Baghdad, Knossos on Crete, and from Boghazköi inscribed with the name of the Hyksos king Khyan does not prove anything about an Egyptian empire during this period.[4] Because of the close connections between Egypt and Byblos during the Twelfth and Thirteenth dynasties, M. Bietak sees the establishment of the MB culture in the Delta as having its origin at Byblos. This would then explain why the Hyksos rulers 'showed scant regard for the Egyptian tradition'.[5] This may be natural for the earlier time of the Semitic settlement at Avaris/Tell el-Dab'a (str. G),

---

Middle Kingdom. The home of this dynasty was Palestine'. Kempinski then theorizes with the help of the Bible that Shechem may have been the original center for this dynasty ('Some Observations on the Hyksos [XVth] Dynasty and its Canaanite Origins', *Pharaonic Egypt, the Bible and Christianity* [ed. S. Israelit-Groll; Jerusalem, 1985], p. 133). It is very doubtful whether a Palestinian local ruler would have applied a pharaonic title to himself. In this period Shiqmona did not exist as a city; only the MB II tomb seems to correspond to the period of the Fifteenth Dynasty. R. Giveon maintains that 'Ya'qob-har' cannot be read as Ya'qob-el, as sometimes has been suggested, and sees this Ya'qob-har as identical with the Egyptian *Mr-wsr-R'* ('Ya'qob-har', *Göttinger Miszellen* 44 [1981], pp. 17-20).

1. A. Kempinski, 'The Egyptian Empire in Palestine: A Reassessment', *BASOR* 241 (1981), p. 10.

2. See A.B. Knapp, 'Pots, PIXE, and Data Processing', *BASOR* 266 (1987), p. 25.

3. Cf. A. Kempinski, who also thinks that the kings of the Fifteenth Dynasty were south Palestinians (*Syrien und Palästina*), pp. 210-11.

4. T. Säve-Söderbergh, *JEA* 37 (1951), p. 63; R. de Vaux, *The Early History of Israel*, p. 79; H. Stock, 'Der Hyksos Chian in Boghazköy', *MDOG* 94 (1963), pp. 73-80.

5. So expressed by M. Bietak, *Proceedings of the British Academy* 65 (1979), pp. 272-73.

but not for the last Hyksos stratum (D/2).[1] As time passed the Semitic kings of the Delta by sheer necessity became Egyptianized.[2] In this connection we should note that one of the largest Canaanite sacred precincts has been found at Tell el-Dab'a, with temples and mortuary temples and cemeteries.[3] In regard to its style, the largest of these temples can be compared with the temple in area H at Hazor (str. II), the architectural layout of which is of a Syrian style. The temple at Alalakh, stratum IV, also could be mentioned.

The term *hyksos* derives from Manetho's[4] Greek translation (*hyksos* = *hq3w-š3sw*, 'shepherd kings') for the Egyptian *hq3 h3swt*, which means nothing else than 'rulers of foreign lands', a term which was used already during the Middle Kingdom as a label for Asiatic kings and sheiks. Thus, the term 'Hyksos' really is a title, and does not refer to a people. The Hyksos kings who were adopting Egyptian customs and names did not call themselves Hyksos, 'foreign rulers', which is a later time's characterization. This term does not say anything about the place of origin nor does it refer to ethnicity. However, because they worshiped Canaanite gods, such as Baal (identified with Seth),[5] Ashtarte-Qudshu,[6] Horon and Resheph,[7] they may be under-

1. Cf. M. Bietak, 'Hyksos', *Lexikon der Ägyptologie*, III (Wiesbaden, 1980), col. 99. Bietak thinks that the Asiatic king Salitis (Manetho's Fifteenth Dynasty) or a local Asiatic dynast during the time of the Thirteenth Dynasty started to build this temple precinct (*Proceedings of the British Academy* 65 (1979), pp. 254-55).

2. Cf. A. Gardiner, *Egypt of the Pharaohs*, p. 170; D.B. Redford, *Or* NS 39 (1970), p. 7.

3. M. Bietak, *Proceedings of the British Academy* 65 (1979), pp. 247-63.

4. An Egyptian priest at Heliopolis who lived in the third cent. BCE and wrote his history at the request of Ptolemy II; see W.G. Wadell (ed.), *Manetho* (LCL; Cambridge, MA, 1940); cf. W. Helck, *Untersuchungen zu Manetho und den ägyptischen Königslisten* (Berlin, 1956).

5. The so-called 400 year stela from c. 1320 BCE, celebrating the reign of the god Seth as king, was later used by Ramses II when making Tanis his capital, in order to maintain that Seth had been king at Tanis for 400 years; see P. Montet, 'La stèle de l'an 400 retrouvé', *Kêmi* 4 (1931), pl. XI, and for the text, see J.H. Breasted, *Ancient Records of Egypt*, I, §§538-42; J.A. Wilson, *ANET*, pp. 252-53; J. Van Seters, *The Hyksos*.

6. Anath does not seem to be mentioned in Egyptian texts before the time of Ramses II.

7. Consult R. Stadelmann, *Syrisch-palästinensische Gottheiten in Ägypten* (Leiden, 1967).

stood as having had their origin in Canaan.[1] The Kamose stela reporting the expulsion of the Hyksos and the end of their rule uses the
terms 'Asiatics' and the 'ruler of Retenu'.[2] This clearly identifies the
Hyksos as Palestinians.[3] Because Palestine had a somewhat mixed
population, this may also have been the case among the Asiatics in the
Delta.[4] A study of the names shows, however, that the majority are
West-Semitic.[5] The Palestinian origin of the Hyksos has partly been
supported by archaeological finds, even though the so-called Tell el-
Yehudiyeh ceramics can be questioned as being of Syro-Palestinian
origin.[6] However, pottery and objects from the graves at Tell el-Dab'a,
located c. 33 km south of Tanis in the eastern Delta, are typologically
identical with those found in MB II sites in Palestine and Syria.[7] This
is the case already for the site in the Thirteenth Dynasty.[8] There are
from the same period also some houses with a U- or L-shaped layout,
that is, houses with a courtyard with rooms on two or three sides.

---

1.   Thus already C.F. Burney, *The Book of Judges* (London, 1918), p. lxv. For
the problem of the so-called Hyksos, see, among others, P. Labib, *Die Herrschaft
der Hyksos in Ägypten und ihr Sturtz* (Glückstadt, 1936); T. Säve-Söderbergh, *JEA*
37 (1951), pp. 53-71; J. von Beckerath, *Untersuchungen zur politische Geshichte*;
H.E. Winlock, *Rise and Fall of the Middle Kingdom in Thebes* (New York, 1947);
J. Van Seters, *The Hyksos*, pp. 97-103; D.B. Redford, *Or* NS 39 (1970), pp. 1-51.
2.   L. Habachi, *The Second Stela of Kamose and his Struggle against the
Hyksos Ruler and his Capital* (Abh. des Deutschen Archäologischen Instituts Kairo,
Ägyptologische Reihe, 8; Glückstadt, 1972), pp. 31-33.
3.   T. Säve-Söderbergh, *JEA* 37 (1951), pp. 53-71; J. Van Seters, *The Hyksos*,
pp. 121-26. Cf. R. de Vaux, *The Early History of Israel*, p. 77.
4.   W. Helck, among others, thinks that the Hyksos were Hurrians (*Die
Beziehungen*, p. 102). Chronologically, this is untenable; see M. Bietak, 'Hyksos',
Lexikon der Ägyptologie, III, col. 100; cf. R. de Vaux, *The Early History of Israel*,
p. 78.
5.   J. Van Seters, *The Hyksos*, pp. 181-90; cf. R. de Vaux, *The Early History
of Israel*, pp. 76-77.
6.   This type of pottery has been found in Egypt from the time before the Hyksos
rule, and occurs, for instance, in Nubia, too; cf. T. Säve-Söderbergh, *JEA* 37
(1951), p. 57.
7.   See M. Bietak, *Tell el-Dab'a* (Denkschriften des Gesamtakademie, Bd. 4–5 =
Untersuchungen der Zweigstelle Kairo des österreichischen archäologischen Instituts,
Bde. 1, 3; Vienna 1975); *idem, Proceedings of the British Academy* 65 (1979),
pp. 225-90.
8.   Consult M. Bietak, 'Tell el-Dab'a', *JÖAI* 52 (1978–80) (Grabungen 1975–
77), pp. 1-8.

These can be seen as the forerunners of the Palestinian so-called four-room house type.[1] Thus, one can draw the conclusion that Asiatics had been living there before the city was made the capital of the Hyksos kingdom.

The recent excavations at Tell el-Dab'a seem to indicate that the horse drawn chariot may have been introduced into Egypt by the Hyksos,[2] even though the horse may have been known in Egypt earlier.[3] However, there is no real evidence for chariots being widely used in the army by Hyksos rulers. The time for chariotry in the Egyptian army had not yet come. It is known from Anatolia and northern Syria from the seventeenth century BCE.[4] The Kamose stela referring to the expulsion of the Hyksos ruler mentions, however, chariotry (*htri*, 1. 13).[5] From this one may draw the conclusion that the Hyksos could have used the horse in the army first towards the end of their rule.[6]

1. See, for instance, M. Bietak, *Proceedings of the British Academy*, fig. 2.

2. Cf. M. Bietak, *JÖAI* 52 (1978–80), p. 5.

3. See W. Helck, 'Ein indirekter Beleg für die Benutzung des leichten Streitwagens in Ägypten zu Ende der 13. Dynastie', *JNES* 37 (1978), pp. 337-40. Bietak sees the donkey burials found at tell el-Dab'a as probably having sacral connections. The ass was the sacred animal of Seth, whose cult probably did not exist at Avaris before the Semites settled there (*JÖAI* 52 [1978–80], p. 4). There are also donkey burials at Tell el-'Ajjul and Jericho from the MB II or early LB I period.

4. See, for instance, P.H.J. Houwink ten Cate, 'The History of Warfare according to Hittite Sources: The Annals of Hattusilis I (Part II)', *Anatolica* 11 (1984), pp. 59-60; cf. P.R.S. Moorey, who says that the 'light chariot served a number of roles in the Middle Bronze Age among which service in war was only one and quite possibly the least common' ('The Emergence of the Light Horse-Drawn Chariot in the Near-East c. 2000–1500 BCE', *World Archaeology* 18 [1986], p. 205). Chariotry should not be paralleled with the tanks of modern warfare. The light, speedy chariot was used for patrolling and protecting the army and for creating chaos in the enemies' infantry ranks before the battle, as well as for pursuing fleeing soldiers (M.A. Littauer and J.H. Crouwel, *Wheeled Vehicles and Ridden Animals in the Ancient Near East* [Leiden, 1979], p. 33; P.R.S. Moorey, *World Archaeology* 18 [1986], pp. 203-204). As to the construction of chariots, see H.A. Littauer and J.H. Crouwel, *Wheeled Vehicles*, pp. 344-51. Cf. also C. Zaccagnini, 'Pferde und Streitwagen in Nuzi: Bemerkungen zur Technologie', *Jahresbericht des Instituts für Vorgeschichte der Universität Frankfurt a.M. (1977)* (Munich, 1978), pp. 21-38.

5. L. Habachi, *The Second Stela of Kamose*, p. 36.

6. Cf. T. Säve-Söderbergh, *JEA* 37 (1951), pp. 39-40.

The expulsion of the Hyksos was due to the nationalistic aspiration of the princes of Thebes in Upper Egypt, the Seventeenth Dynasty. The conflict started with a message sent from Pharaoh Apophis in Avaris to his vassal king Seqenen-Re' at Thebes, saying that the noise of the hippopotami at Thebes made it impossible for Apophis to sleep and therefore he demanded that the hippopotamus pool be destroyed.[1] Because the text is broken in the middle of a sentence we do not know the outcome of the incident, but one may assume that the prince of Thebes managed to counteract or counterinsult the king at Avaris— why else would the text have been preserved?[2] Seqenen-Re''s son and successor, Kamose, seized some Hyksos territory and continued to attack the army of Apophis, but was not able to end his rule.[3] Kamose's brother and successor, Ahmose, in his tenth year, succeeded in ending the Hyksos rule. In 1541 BCE he took Avaris after a long siege.[4] Then he pursued the Hyksos into Palestine and after a three-year siege he took and sacked their fortress at the 'Hyksos city', probably at Tell el-'Ajjul.[5] With this, the road to the conquest of Syria-Palestine and the empire of the New kingdom was opened. The long siege of the city tells us how determined the new Egyptian ruler was to completely end Hyksos dominion. It is possible that Ahmose also installed a garrison

1. There is a distance of something like 800 km (500 miles) between Avaris and Thebes!

2. See J.A. Wilson, *ANET*, pp. 231-32.

3. Cf. B. Gunn and A.H. Gardiner, 'New Reading of Egyptian Texts II: The Expulsion of the Hyksos', *JEA* 5 (1918), pp. 36-56; cf. J.A. Wilson, *ANET*, pp. 232-33. See also L. Habachi, *The Second Stela of Kamose*; W. Barta, 'Bemerkungen zum Feldzugsbericht des Königs Kamose', *BO* 32 (1975), pp. 287-90. For the chronology, see J. von Beckerath, *Untersuchungen zur politischen Geschichte*, pp. 218-20.

4. J. von Beckerath, *Abriss der Geschichte des Alten Ägypten*, p. 33.

5. The biblical Sharuhen has usually been identified with Tell el-Far'ah (S); cf. W.F. Albright, 'Progress in Palestinian Archaeology in the Year 1928', *BASOR* 33 (1929), p. 7; R. de Vaux, *The Early History of Israel*, p. 81. See, however, J.R. Stewart, who sees Tell el-'Ajjul as the more probable site for Sharuhen (*Tell el-'Ajjul*); also A. Kempinski, who thinks that the people of Tell el-'Ajjul moved to Gaza, at which place the Egyptians later placed their center of administration for Palestine ('Tell el-'Ajjāl—Beth Aglaym or Sharuhen?', *IEJ* 24 [1974], pp. 145-52). N. Na'aman maintains that the biblical Sharuhen (Josh. 19.6), may be a corrupt form of Shilhim (Josh. 15.32), and therefore has nothing to do with the 'Hyksos city' ('The Inheritance of the Sons of Simeon', *ZDPV* 96 [1980], pp. 147-48).

at Sharuhen.[1] Ahmose's campaign to Fenkhu and Djahi[2] (the Phoenician coast and northern Palestine) indicates his determination to crush the Hyksos and their allies. We do not learn, however, how successful his campaign in the north was.

The hatred towards the Hyksos that can be detected in Egyptian inscriptions must be seen as part of the propaganda of the rulers of the new dynasty that drove out the 'foreign rulers' from Egypt.[3] In later Egyptian historiography the Hittite thrust down through Syria during the fourteenth and thirteenth centuries (Suppiluliuma and Hattusilis III) was interpreted as a Hyksos 'counter attack', and the Hyksos regime was characterized as a disaster for the Egyptian empire,[4] which it probably was not. The opposite may be the truth. The Hyksos rulers promoted the Egyptian culture and chose names with the theophoric component *-re'*.[5] There is no sharp difference in art or in literature. Some of the most appreciated literary works were products of this period, for instance, the *Westcar Papyrus*, with its folktales about the pharaohs of the Old Kingdom, and the *Golenischeff Papyrus*, with the hymn to the Crown.[6] Thus one may conclude that the Hyksos rulers, even if they could be cruel and destructive, tried to promote Egyptian culture.[7] In using the old administrators and the Egyptian administrative apparatus, the Egyptian system continued, and in establishing their rule over most of Egypt they can be said to have contributed to ending the instability of the Second Intermediate Period.

---

1. See the discussion in D.B. Redford, 'A Gate Inscription from Karnak and Egyptian Involvement in Western Asia during the Early 18th Dynasty', *JAOS* 99 (1979), pp. 271-87.

2. J.A. Wilson, *ANET*, p. 234 n. 18.

3. For the Hyksos rulers as being destructive, see the propaganda inscription by Queen Hatshepsut, J.A. Wilson, *ANET*, p. 231. The same theme can be recognized in the Papyrus Sallier I from the time of Pharaoh Merneptah (*ANET*, p. 231). T. Säve-Söderbergh states that 'the later a text the more hostile it is to the Hyksos' (*JEA* 37 [1951], p. 55).

4. D.B. Redford, *Or* NS 39 (1979), pp. 50-51.

5. Cf. J. Vercoutter, 'The Second Intermediate Period and the Hyksos Invasion of Egypt', *The Near East* (ed. J. Bottéro, E. Casson and J. Vercoutter), pp. 400-401; T. Säve-Söderbergh, *JEA* 37 (1951), pp. 64-65.

6. See the remarks of A. Erman, *Die Literatur der Ägypter* (Leipzig, 1923), pp. 35-36.

7. Cf. W.C. Hayes, *The Scepter of Egypt*, I (New York, 1953).

When the vassal king of Thebes broke the treaty with his overlord[1] and started the war of liberation, with his successor driving out the Hyksos ruler, it was not only a change of ruler and a change of the seat of government. It was a change that stopped the process of splitting Egypt into competing kingdoms.

Middle Bronze Culture

The Middle Bronze Age, from a cultural and economic point of view, has been characterized as the high point of the Bronze Age. Economically Palestine should have prospered from the commerce that went through the country from Egypt. This may be part of the picture, but we should also take into consideration that during the period of the Asiatic Hyksos rulers Palestine did not suffer from any wars of a magnitude as devastating as those that followed the expulsion of the Hyksos. Thus material culture could blossom together with an increase in political independence.[2] Monumental buildings and strong fortifications—now also in the central hills[3]—are signs of the latter, and pottery,[4] furniture[5] and jewelry are some of the signs of a wealthier society than Palestine had known in earlier times. As to pottery, the 'potter's wheel is mainly responsible for the technical advances and for the greater refinement of forms'.[6] This can be detected already at the beginning of the MB period. The fine red slip is common in MB I, but is, however, retrograding already in MB II. Among the new forms we can mention the carinated bowl, a pot that

1. B.J. Kemp thinks that the southern part of Egypt was 'too distant' and perhaps not that rich that it would be of prime interest to the Hyksos rulers (*Cambridge History of Africa*, I [ed. J.D. Clark], p. 747).
2. Cf. B.J. Kemp, *The Cambridge History of Africa*, I (ed. J.D. Clark), p. 759.
3. For instance at Shechem, Shiloh, Bethel, Beth-Zur and Hebron; see I. Finkelstein, 'Excavations at Shiloh 1981–1984: Preliminary Report', *Tel Aviv* 12 (1985), p. 165.
4. For an example, see Fig. 3.
5. Because of the dry climate in the Jordan Valley, tombs at Jericho have preserved pieces of furniture and clothing and other organic material. K.M. Kenyon assumes that 'some gases had accumulated in the tomb chambers which had killed the organisms of decay before they had completed their work' (*Archaeology in the Holy Land*, p. 173).
6. R. Amiran, *Ancient Pottery of the Holy Land*, p. 90; cf. also W.G. Dever, 'The Beginning of the Middle Bronze Age in Syria-Palestine', *Magnalia Dei* (ed. F.M. Cross *et al.*), p. 7.

developed in several forms down through the Late Bronze period. Another well-known example of pottery from the MB period is the above mentioned Tell el-Yehudiyeh (Hyksos) ware. It is black or dark brown and decorated with small white dots. This ware was first found in Lower Egypt at el-Yehudiyeh (Leontopolis), hence its name. It has been found mainly on the Syrian coast and in Palestine.[1] At several places in Syria-Palestine Cypriot pottery (black on white, as well as white painted ware) has been found, and the Tell el-Yehudiyeh ware has also been found in Cyprus, testifying to close trade connections with this island and the Levant. As for decorative art, there are two features which are significant for this period, namely the spiral and the 'sun' wheel, occurring, for instance, on pottery and seals. Both have been interpreted as solar symbols.

A phenomenon that is rare for the MB II period in Palestine is a temple just inside the city gate. This occurs at Shechem, if the interpretation of the building is correct. Shechem had two gates: one in the northwestern part of the city wall and the other in the eastern part. At both sides of the NW gate (three piers) were some buildings adjacent to the inside of the wall. The structure on the southern side of the gate may be a temple. As such it would be the earliest known tripartite temple found in Palestine. W.G. Dever assumes that the style is of northern origin and can possibly be traced back to a Mesopotamian prototype from the third millenium BCE. Next to this temple is a building that has been labeled a palace, and just to the south, in field V, is the so-called Fortress temple. This whole area with its architectural features Dever has compared with the 'Agora' phenomenon, which included 'city walls, gate, barracks for the garrison, plaza and shrine, public temple, palace and royal chapel'. This would thus be the earliest example of this kind of complex which is known from earlier times in Syria, Anatolia and northern Mesopotamia.[2] From an ideological point of view, a temple inside a gate would mean that the deity

---

1. B. Williams sees the territories south of Ugarit and Amurru as 'an archaeological unit' ('Archaeology and Historical Problems of the Second Intermediate Period IV' [PhD dissertation, University of Chicago, 1975], p. 1257).

2. W.G. Dever, 'The MBIIC Stratification in the Northwest Gate Area at Shechem', *BASOR* 216 (1974), pp. 31-33, 48. Temples at the side of a gate from the late LB period have also been found at Kition, Cyprus; see V. Karageorghis *et al.*, 'Kition, Cyprus: Excavations in 1976, 1977', *Journal of Field Archaeology* 5 (1978), pp. 105-10.

is there to protect one's coming in and going out.[1]

In discussing temples, two main types of architecture should be mentioned, namely the longroom and the broadroom. One feature that is distinctive for the Palestinian temples is that there are no columns in the 'Longroom' temples of the Bronze Age, as there often were in the broadroom temples. The supposed columns in the 'Fortress Temple' at Shechem are imaginary.[2]

Among the broadroom temples of the MB II period, the structure found at Nahariyah on the coast north of Acco[3] has been seen as serving the rural population.[4] The first structure, a square building c. 6 × 6 m, was given the name *bāmâ*, which, however, is misleading.[5] Just north of it was then built the broadroom temple. Because a bronze figurine of a woman was found, M. Dothan believes that the sanctuary was dedicated to the goddess Asherat-Yam, who is well known from the Ugaritic mythological texts. Whether or not the Nahariyah temple served only some rural peoples cannot be determined. Because a monkey figurine on the neck of a jug was found, in addition to an Egyptian scarab, one could perhaps say that the sanctuary represents the official religion of the coastal area between Tyre and Acco.[6]

Another temple that has been labeled a village sanctuary has been found at Tell Hayyat in the Jordan Valley.[7] As mentioned above, the first building remains are from the EB IV period. The duration of the

---

1.   Cf. Ps. 121.8.

2.   See G.R.H. Wright, *Ancient Building in Syria and Palestine*, II (Handbuch der Orientalistik, 7 Abt. I B; Leiden, 1985), fig. 181.

3.   M. Dothan, 'Excavations at Nahariyah: Preliminary Report (Seasons 1954/55)', *IEJ* 6 (1956), pp. 14-25; I. Ben-Dor, 'A Middle Bronze Age Temple at Nahariya', *QDAP* 14 (1950), pp. 1-41.

4.   G.R.H. Wright, *Ancient Building*, II, fig. 174.

5.   The biblical term *bmh* refers to official sanctuaries that the biblical narrators did not like, favoring king Josiah's reform. The translation 'high-place' is not accurate because the *bamôt* were located on both high and low ground. The idea of illegitimacy is that of the biblical writers. For a discussion of the term, see W.B. Barrick, 'What do we Really Know about "High-Places"?', *SEÅ* 45 (1980), pp. 50-57; *idem*, 'The Word BMH in the Old Testament' (PhD dissertation, University of Chicago, 1977).

6.   The monkey figurine is an Egyptian feature. It has been found also at Gezer, Byblos, Megiddo and Tell el-'Ajjul.

7.   See S. Falconer *et al.*, *BASOR* 255 (1984), pp. 49-74.

temple was from MB I to the end of the MB II period. This temple, which went through four phases, was built in the so-called migdal style (fortress temple style). The sacred precinct had an enclosure wall, and in the yard in front of the entrance there were some standing stones (*maṣṣēbôt?*). The temple room had benches along the walls. Because a temple traditionally was built before any other structure or house, the new MBI temple indicates that new people have settled at the site. The god is therefore the first one to get a 'house'. The newly taken land was now his territory, his realm.

A MB II longroom temple (6.9 × 5.5 m) at Tell Kittan (Tell Musa, c. 12 km north of Beth Shan) in the Jordan Valley should also be mentioned. It was built of mudbrick on stone foundations (str. V). Inside it were benches along the walls. Also at this place was found a row of stelae outside the temple. The middle stela had the form of a nude woman.[1] We could perhaps see these stelae as representing the divine assembly. The temple of the preceding stratum (IV) had probably been destroyed, and the new, larger structure (14.3 × 11.5 m), also of mudbrick, replaced it. The thick walls suggest that this temple was built in the same style as the MB II temples at Shechem (the so-called Fortress Temple), Megiddo (str. VIII), and a one-room temple at Hazor, stratum XVI. In the LB I period the Kittan temple was again rebuilt in a different style with a cella, two small rooms, and a courtyard.[2]

The so-called 'fortress temples' are longroom temples with very thick walls and a tower (*mgdl*) at each side of the entrance. According to B. Mazar, this type of temple building was an innovation in the MB II period by newcomers from the north.[3] That these temples really were used as fortresses is impossible to say. Concerning the Shechem temple, I. Dunayevsky and A. Kempinski doubt that it should be called a *migdal* temple, pointing out that the eastern tower at the entrance was built later (LB).[4] From a military point of view of defense, one

1. E. Eisenberg, 'The Temples at Tell Kittan', *BA* 40 (1977), pp. 77-81.

2. Eisenberg theorizes that this 'may have been due to a change in ritual' (*BA* 40 [1977], p. 80).

3. *IEJ* 18 (1968), p. 93. A. Kempinski sees the 'sudden appearance' of this type in Palestine as dependent on some inner development within the culture of Syria-Palestine, and this may perhaps be an extension of the influence of the kingdom of Halab (Aleppo) (*Syrien und Palästina*, p. 173).

4. 'The Megiddo Temples', *ZDPV* 89 (1973), pp. 182-85; cf. M.D. Fowler, *PEQ* 115 (1983), p. 50.

wonders why such a temple was built inside the city with no real defensive wall around it. As for Shechem, it would have been much more suitable to see the temple along the NW wall south of the gate house as a fortress temple.

The material culture of Palestine south of the Jezreel Valley during the seventeenth and sixteenth centuries is closely related to that of the Delta during the Hyksos period, which is natural if one takes into consideration that Palestine had long held close cultural and commercial ties with Egypt, and that coastal Syria and most of Palestine probably were under Hyksos dominion. With Asiatics ruling Egypt, Canaanite culture got a foothold there. On the other hand, Egyptian objects of art, such as gold jewelry, scarabs and alabaster vases, became common in Palestine. Tell el-'Ajjul, being under Egyptian rule, may be cited as an outstanding example. The so-called Hyksos period also saw certain weapons coming more into use, for instance, the fenestrated axe, which is known from an earlier period at Ugarit, Megiddo and Jericho. It is also known from wall paintings in Egypt from the period of the Middle Kingdom.[1] Other weapons include daggers with a central rib and the composite bow.[2] Parallels to these have been found also in Persia and Caucasia.

This is also the time when huge ramparts (*terre pisée*) were common as part of the fortification systems. They were made by beaten earth overlaid with a sloping glacis. Sometimes a trench or a moat was dug at its foot. The ramparts have been understood as a phenomenon that would make the battering ram impossible to use.[3] Another explanation is that it was effective protection against chariots coming close to the walls.[4] It should not be overlooked that the ramparts could protect and strengthen the wall itself. With a rampart against the wall, it would be very hard for an enemy to undermine the lower

1. See R. Gophna, 'A Middle Bronze Age Tomb with Fenestrated Axe at Ma'abarot', *IEJ* 19 (1969), pp. 174-77.

2. The composite bow is known from mid-third millennium Mesopotamia; cf. R. Miller, E. McEwen and C. Bergman, 'Experimental Approaches to Ancient Near Eastern Archery', *World Archaeology* 18 (1986), pp. 182-89.

3. Y. Yadin, 'Hyksos Fortifications and the Battering-Ram', *BASOR* 137 (1955), pp. 23-32.

4. R. de Vaux, *The Early History of Israel*, p. 70. However, de Vaux contradicts this in saying that chariots were used first in Palestine after the Hyksos had been expelled from Egypt.

courses of the wall or to climb the wall. These ramparts had been seen as an invention by the Hyksos, but they are now known from Anatolia and Syria (Alalakh and Qatna) in the pre-Hyksos period and from Tēl Polēg in the Sharon plain in the MB I period.[1] Ta'anak of the third millennium BCE also had a glacis,[2] as did Jericho and Tell el-Far'ah.[3] From MB II Palestine we can mention Laish (Dan, probably already in the MB I),[4] Hazor, Megiddo, Ta'anak, Jericho, Tell Beit Mirsim, Tell ed-Duweir, Yavne-Yam, Tel Batash (Timna), Tēl Nagilah, Khirbet el-Meshâsh (Tēl Māśōś), Tell Mubarak (Tēl Mevorak), Gezer, Shiloh,[5] and in Transjordan, Amman and probably also Tell Safut.[6] Of these, the one at Hazor is the largest in Palestine. At its widest point it is 90 m wide. It encircled the lower city on the plateau just north of the tell.

The lower city at Hazor was founded sometime in the eighteenth century BCE and, according to R. de Vaux, was the result of the over-population of the upper city.[7] The many buildings, temples, palaces and tombs are indications enough against the mistaken theory that the plateau may have served as a 'camp' for horses and war chariots. Hazor had close contacts with Qatna and Carchemish as well as with Aleppo, and it is possible that the rampart phenomenon was inspired by these contacts.

Hazor's geographical location at one of the main arteries to northern Syria, as well as on the caravan roads to Damascus, Yamhad and

1. P. Parr, 'The Origin of Rampart Fortifications of Middle Bronze Age Palestine and Syria', *ZDPV* 84 (1968), pp. 18-45.

2. P.W. Lapp, 'The 1963 Excavation at Ta'annek', *BASOR* 173 (1964), pp. 10-14.

3. P. Parr, *ZDPV* 84 (1968), pp. 39-41.

4. The rampart of Dan covered an earlier MB city gate of mudbrick; see A. Biran, 'The Discovery of the Middle Bronze Age Gate at Dan', *BA* 44 (1981), pp. 139-44.

5. I. Finkelstein dates the fortifications at Shiloh to no 'earlier than the 17th century' (*Tel Aviv* 12 [1985], p. 160).

6. See R.H. Dornemann, *The Archaeology of the Transjordan*, pp. 18-19. For Shiloh, I. Finkelstein maintains that the MB II city wall with its glacis was a *temenos* wall. He theorizes that Shiloh at this time 'was primarily a sacred *temenos*', with some residential quarters south of the summit. The temple would have been on the summit, but so far no remains of it have been found (*Tel Aviv* 12 [1985], pp. 164-65).

7. *The Early History of Israel*, p. 70.

Mari, shows that northern contacts were natural. Some architectural features, such as temple buildings (the area H MB II–LB temple and the so-called double temple at area F) show northern features.

The contacts with the north and with Mesopotamia are known from the Mari texts. Two texts deal with the trade of tin. One of them mentions, for instance, that 30 minas of tin were being sent to king Ibni-Adad of Hazor and some eight minas were going to Wari-taldu of Laish.[1] We should note that the king of Hazor has an Akkadian name, but the king of Laish seems to be Hurrian, which may make one doubt that Laish refers to a Palestinian city.[2] A recently published letter from Zimri-Lim of Mari to Yarim-Lim of Yamhad refers to trade between these cities and Hazor. The people of Hazor should have detained a caravan from Mari because a cupbearer had stolen silver, gold and other precious stones that another caravan was supposed to deliver to Mari. He was robbed of it, however, at Emar, located c. 85 km east of Yamhad's capital Halab (Aleppo).[3] This letter reveals something of the wealth of Hazor as well as that of other cities along the trunk road from Egypt, such as Megiddo. Another text mentions messengers from Qatna, Karana, Ekallatum, Yamhad, Babylon and Arrapha, together with one from Hazor.[4] In one tablet the man of Hazor, that is the king, is mentioned in connection with caravans carrying mutton, among other things.[5] These references to Hazor may

---

1.   Cf. A. Malamat, 'Syro-Palestinian Destinations in a Mari Tin Inventory', *IEJ* 21 (1971), pp. 30-38. See also A. Malamat, 'Silver, Gold and Precious Stones from Hazor: Trade and Trouble in a New Mari Document', *JJS* 63 (1982), pp. 71-79. See D. Pardee and J.T. Glass, *BA* 47 (1984), p. 93; cf. also J. Strange, *Caphtor/Keftiu: A New Investigation* (Leiden, 1980), pp. 90-91. Wari-taldu is a Hurrian name. J.M. Sasson does not locate this Laish (Layashim) at Tēl Dan, but rather in Syria, about midway between Ugarit and Halab (Aleppo). He also reads Ewri-talma instead of Wari-taldu as the name of the king (*BA* 47 [1984], pp. 246-51).

2.   Ibni-Adad would in West-Semitic be Yabni-Hadad, a name that leads to associations with king Jabin of Hazor mentioned in Judg. 4.7, 23-24; Josh. 11.1; and Ps. 83.10 (Hebrew). Y. Yadin draws the conclusion that Jabin was a 'royal dynastic name of the Kings of Hazor' (*Hazor, The Head of All Those Knigdoms, Joshua 11:10* [London, 1972], p. 5).

3.   See A. Malamat, *JJS* 33 (1982), pp. 71-79.

4.   *ARM*, VI, p. 23. See J.R. Kupper, *ARM*. VI. *Correspondence de Bahdi-Lim*, no. 78.

5.   *ARM*, XII, p. 747; cf. Y. Yadin, *Hazor of Those Kingdoms*, pp. 2-4.

indicate that it was one of the few important city states in northern Palestine during the eighteenth century BCE. Mari did not do business with unimportant towns in Palestine.

In this connection we should note that the earliest Akkadian inscription found in Palestine comes from Hazor. It was unearthed at area C. In a niche in the revetment were three jugs one of which had some inscribed cuneiform signs which read *išme*-DINGIR.LAM. This can be translated as either 'he heard the god' (DINGIR.LAM = *ilam* = the god Adad), or 'Adad heard'.[1]

The art of the MB II culture in the coastal area seems to have been Egyptianized even though in the north there were potential Mesopotamian and Anatolian influences. Inland Palestine and Syria were less influenced by Egypt. For Palestine this is to be expected, because the hill country was sparsely populated. Geographically, Galilee and southern inland Syria have always had closer cultural and economic contacts with the north and with Mesopotamia.[2] This is not to say that northern features are not to be found in the central hills or in southern Palestine. For instance, a metal hoard with northern influences has been found at Shiloh.[3] A house with a central courtyard surrounded with smaller rooms (usually 8 to 9) on all sides, known from the Middle Assyrian period,[4] has been unearthed at Tananir on the slope of Gerizim.[5] The remains of the same type of house has also been found in the Lower City of Hazor from the LB I period.[6] At Tell

---

1. For the inscription, see Y. Yadin *et al.*, *Hazor*, II (Jerusalem, 1960), p. 115-17, and pl. CLXXX. Above the inscription is the sign for GAL, which can mean both 'great, prince' or 'elder'; cf. I.J. Gelb, *Glossary of Old Akkadian*, p. 233.

2. Cf. J. Kaplan, 'Mesopotamian Elements in the Middle Bronze II Culture of Palestine', *JNES* 30 (1971), pp. 293-307.

3. See *Israel Museum Journal* 4 (1985).

4. Cf. C. Preusser, *Die Wohnhäuser in Assur* (Ausgrabungen der Deutschen Orientgesellschaft in Assur, 6; Berlin, 1954). This type of house continues with some variations into the neo-Assyrian period; cf. R. Amiran and I. Dunayevsky, 'The Assyrian Open-Court building and its Palestinian Derivatives', *BASOR* 149 (1958), pp. 25-32. Whether there is a direct influence from Mesopotamia is impossible to establish.

5. See G. Welten, 'Archäologischer Anzeiger', *Jahrbüch des Deutschen Archäologischen Instituts* 47 (1932), p. 314. This building has usually been interpreted as being a temple. Cf. R.G. Boling, 'Bronze Age Buildings at the Shechem High Place; ASOR Excavations at Tananir', *BA* 32 (1969), pp. 82-103.

6. Y. Yadin has seen this as a temple because of its resemblance to the Late

Beit Mirsim (str. D) Albright felt that a house 'of distinctly superior type' could be classified as a Mesopotamian 'Hofhaus',[1] that is, a courtyard house. The layout of the building is, however, not in agreement with the plan of the house with a central courtyard, because the rooms are placed only on one side of the yard.[2] Still, it could perhaps be a variant of the courtyard house. The layout of the city of stratum D at Tell Beit Mirsim (the last MB II level) was 'more cramped and the majority of the houses smaller' than was the case in the preceding city.[3] Concerning Palestinian architecture, we should note that buildings with three rooms around a courtyard have been found at Megiddo and Tell el-'Ajjul, dating from the MB II period.[4] A MB II house with two (and, in a later phase, three) rooms on two sides of the courtyard is reported from Tell Beit Mirsim. According to G.R.H. Wright both can be aligned with the EB L-shaped house type. In its later version it is close to 'the three-room plan so popular at Tell Beit Mirsim in the Iron Age'.[5]

The courtyard house could be a development of an old tradition of circular or semicircular buildings with rooms along the inside walls. Such a type of building has been found at, for instance, Mureybat in

---

Bronze building found at the Amman airport (*Hazor of Those Kingdoms*, pp. 98-100). This Amman building does not seem to be a temple, but is rather a mortuary building (see below).

1. W.F. Albright, *The Excavation of Tell Beit Mirsim II: The Bronze Age* (AASOR, 17; New Haven, 1938), p. 35.

2. The so-called 'Hofhaus' type also occurs in Amman of the Late Bronze period (the so-called Amman Airport temple, or mortuary). Several objects of Egyptian provenience found in the building may indicate that it could be a house of the Egyptian type known from Tell el-Amarna. This house type may have been inspired by the Asiatic culture that made some impact in Egypt during the Hyksos period. For the Amman structure, see J.B. Hennessy, 'Excavation of a Late Bronze Age Temple at Amman', *PEQ* 98 (1966), pp. 155-62; L.G. Herr, 'The Amman Airport Structure and the Geopolitics of Ancient Transjordan', *BA* 46 (1983), pp. 223-29. This type of architecture has great longevity. It is still to be found in the so-called Persian palace at Tell es-Sa'idiyeh in the Jordan Valley. See J.B. Pritchard, *Tell es-Sa'idiyeh: Excavations on the Tell 1964–1966* (University Museum Monograph, 60; Philadelphia, 1985), pp. 60-66, and fig. 185; *idem*, 'Sa'idiyeh, Tell es', *EAEHL*, IV, pp. 990 and 1030.

3. K.M. Kenyon, *Archaeology in the Holy Land*, p. 169.

4. Cf. K. Beebe, 'Ancient Palestinian Dwellings', *BA* 31 (1968), pp. 46-47.

5. *Ancient Buildings*, II, fig. 224.

Syria dating to c. 5500 BCE.[1] At 'Ain el-Qudeirat in the Northern Sinai, EB II settlements have been found which have housing units with large courtyards surrounded with rooms on three sides.[2] We can conclude, therefore, that this type of building should not be connected with any special ethnic group or territory. Instead, it should be understood from a functional point of view. The courtyard is the center around which the different needs of the family are taken care of or performed. Various rooms were connected with the courtyard for practical and economic reasons. Two lines of development seem to have taken place from the early units. One involved the enclosure of rooms for both people and animals—the so-called *Hürdenhaus* ('a walled enclosure or stall') with a direct entrance to the courtyard.[3] The other involved the total surrounding of the courtyard by rooms to create the *Hofhaus*, which also is called a courtyard building.[4]

In discussing the NW Gate at Shechem, I noted that the temple inside the gate, adjacent to the city wall, was a rare feature in Middle Bronze Age Palestine. The gate itself also represents a new type of architecture. It is built as a tower having a direct entry-way with three piers on each side, thus forming two recesses inside the gate. Therefore it has been called the 'Gate house'.[5] This type of city gate has been seen as an adjustment allowing a horse drawn chariot to pass through the gate. In the main this is the type of gate that can be found in Palestine from the Middle Bronze II Age through the Iron Age. Other well-known examples, besides Shechem, are the gates at Hazor,

---

1. See O. Aurenche, *La maison orientale: L'architecture du proche orient ancient des origines au milieu du quatrième millénaire*. I. *Texte* (Bibliothèque Archéologique et Historique, Tome CIX; Paris 1981), p. 188.

2. I. Beit Arieh and R. Gophna, 'The Early Bronze Age II Settlement at 'Ain el-Qudeirat (1980–1981)', *Tel Aviv* 8 (1981), pp. 128-35. Cf. also J. Beit Arieh, 'An Early Bronze Age II Site near Sheikh 'Awad in the Southern Sinai', *Tel Aviv* 8 (1981), p. 81.

3. G.R.H. Wright, *Ancient Building in South Syria and Palestine*, I (Leiden, 1985), p. 133.

4. G.R.H. Wright, *Ancient Building*, I. p. 133. He maintains that during the 2nd millennium, 'as housing advanced beyond the old two-room village house it may be that the courtyard came to play a bigger role as an articulating feature in house design' (pp. 143-44).

5. G.R.H. Wright, *Ancient Building*, I, p. 173. He also characterizes it as a 'Tower Gate (The Migdol Gate)' (*Ancient Building*, II, fig. 96).

Megiddo, Gezer, Yavne-Yam and Beth-Shemesh.

As for gates, Shechem is of especial interest because it has two different gates from the MB II period, the Northwest Gate and the Eastern Gate. The latter, which probably was built around 1650 BCE,[1] had a gate house with only one 'room'. In its second MB II phase, the so-called Orthostat phase, the gate was rebuilt and was given a threshold at the entrance above the outside glacis. Some steps at the other end led down into the city. The two pairs of piers were double orthostats placed with c. 40–60 cm space in between them. Whether these were meant as the 'run' for sliding doors or had some mechanism that lifted the doors up[2] is impossible to say.

The city of Shechem was allegedly violently destroyed by the Egyptians twice in the mid-sixteenth century BCE, c. 1550 and 1540.[3] This was to have happened in connection with the expulsion of the Hyksos. Who caused the destruction is, however, not known. There is no Egyptian documentation about a campaign in central Palestine at this time,[4] although one could have taken place. An inscription from Karnak mentions that Ahmose campaigned in Fenkhu, Djahi and Qedem,[5] and Amenhotep I campaigned in western Asia. It also mentions that Thutmose I passed through Palestine and reached Naharin (Mitanni).[6] This indicates that the pharaohs of the Eighteenth Dynasty were determined to crush all the Hyksos 'pockets' and the vassals or

1.   For the date, consult J.D. Seger, *Levant* 6 (1974), pp. 117-30. See also G.E. Wright, *Shechem* (New York, 1965), pp. 71-76; G.R.H. Wright, *Ancient Building*, II, figs. 97-100.

2.   Cf. Ps. 24.7, 'Lift up your heads, oh Gates!'

3.   G.E. Wright, *Shechem*, pp. 75-76.

4.   J.J. Bimson dates the arrival of the so-called Bichrome ware in Palestine to the fifteenth century. This would mean that the MB period would be a hundred years longer, because Bichrome ware is a typical LB phenomenon in Palestine. This is part of Bimson's argument for the invasion of 'Israelites' in the fifteenth century and their destruction of many cities (*Redating the Exodus and the Conquest* [JSOTSup, 5; Sheffield, 1978]). For a critique of Bimson's theory, see P. Bienkowski, *Jericho in the Late Bronze Age* (Warminster, 1986), pp. 128-30.

5.   Qedem is inland Syria-Palestine and usually it refers to the areas closest to the desert. We do not know how Ahmose came to Fenkhu and Djahi. He may have gone by sea to Byblos and started his campaign from there. If so, he has not been in the central hills of Palestine. There is no information about whether his campaign was successful or not.

6.   See D.B. Redford, *JAOS* 99 (1979), pp. 271-87.

allies of the Hyksos in Syria and Palestine. We could therefore assume that Shechem was one of the cities that were destroyed by the Egyptians during these actions. Another assumption would be that in the chaos that followed the Egyptian raids some Hurrian military contingents took over. The excavator of Shechem points out that in some areas (the Eastern Gate and Fields III and IV) there 'were two violent destructions of the city within the final years of the Middle Bronze Age'.[1] The second one could have been by Pharaoh Amenhotep I, but it could perhaps as well have been done by Hurrians. This was the time when Hurrian influence was being felt more and more in this country. At the end of the sixteenth century, most north Syrian states had become Mitanni vassals. We should note that on a tablet written in Akkadian found at Shechem the name Suwardata occurs,[2] a name that also occurs in some el-Amarna letters[3] as the name of a prince in the Hebron mountains. This shows the non-Semitic influence in Shechem. To this can be added the OT tradition about the Hivvite Hamor, 'father of Shechem', Gen. 34.2.[4] It is, therefore, possible that Shechem was a city state that was taken over by a Hurrian troop at the end of MB II. Hurrian military bands may have used the opportunities that the Egyptian campaigns offered to establish themselves in several of the destroyed cities.

The Hurrians

Among the invaders of Syria during the second millennium BCE were the Hurrians, a non-Semitic people which, as time went by, created one of the most powerful states in the Near East, namely the Mitanni kingdom. The spread of the Hurrians as well as their importance is

1. G.E. Wright, *Shechem*, pp. 74-75.
2. See W.F. Albright, 'A Teacher to a Man of Shechem about 1400 BCE', *BASOR* 86 (1942), pp. 28-31; cf. G.E. Wright, *Shechem*, pp. 208-11.
3. EA 271, 279-84, 290; *ANET*, p. 486.
4. Some LXX manuscripts have the reading Hurrite instead of Hivvite. As a curiosity we should note that F.M.T. Böhl read the inscription found on a broken stela from Shechem as 'the head of the gate' ('Die Sichem-Plakette: Protoalphabetische Schriftzeichen der Mittelbronzezeit vom *tell balata*', *ZDPV* 61 [1938], pp. 21-23). See, however, B. Maisler (Mazar), who not only pointed to the fact that the stela is broken, but that Böhl's reading would be an aramaism in the MB II period! ('Zur Urgeschichte des phönizisch-hebräischen Alphabets', *JPOS* 18 [1938], pp. 283-86); cf. also E. Puech, 'Origin de l'alphabet', *RB* 93 (1986), pp. 185-88.

witnessed by texts from Nuzi, Boghazköi (Boghazkale), Alalakh, Mari, Ras Shamra, Tell el-Amarna, and from Ta'anak in Palestine, among other places. They are known from Anatolia from c. 2400 BCE,[1] and from about 2300 BCE they were settled in the hilly regions of Upper Mesopotamia where they established a kingdom, Urkish.[2] After the Ur III period they were slowly moving westwards, penetrating not only the rest of Upper Mesopotamia, but also northern Syria.[3] Concerning southern Syria and Palestine, Hurrian influences were not really felt during the eighteenth and seventeenth centuries BCE. The texts from Alalakh (level VII) show that around 1700 a third of the population of that city was Hurrian and c. 100 years later the Hurrians were in the majority.[4] The same is true for Ugarit of the fifteenth century. It was only when Ugarit was freed from Hurrian political dominance in the fourteenth century BCE that its literary 'golden age' came about.

The Hurrians, who seem to have operated on a grand scale, having their 'contacts spreading well into Europe', have been related by some scholars to the Finno-Ugrians, a conclusion that has been drawn from their language.[5] I. M. Diakonoff thinks that the original home of the

1. W.F. Albright and T. Lambdin, 'The Evidence of Language', *CAH*, I (fasc. 54, 2nd edn; Cambridge, 1966), pp. 26-36; cf. M.S. Drower, 'Syria: 1550–1400 BCE', *CAH*, II.1, pp. 417-36; P. Walcot, 'The Comparative Study of Ugaritic and Greek, III', *UF* 4 (1972), p. 131.

2. A. Parrot and J. Nougayrol, 'Un document de fondation hurrite', *RA* 42 (1948), pp. 1-20. Cf. I.J. Gelb, 'New Light on Hurrians and Subarians', *Studi Orientalistici im onore di G. Levi della Vida*, I (Rome, 1956), pp. 378-92; G. Wilhelm, *Grundzüge*; see also W.J. van Liere, 'Urkis, centre religieux hurrite', *Les Annales Archéologique de Syrie* 7 (1957), pp. 91-94.

3. There has been a trend among scholars to place the patriarchs of the Bible in the time of the Hurrian infiltration into Palestine, and thus to explain some features in the Genesis as being of Hurrian origin. For a critique of this, see T.L. Thompson, *The Historicity of the Patriarchal Narratives*, pp. 196-297; J. Van Seters, *Abraham in History and Tradition*, pp. 65-98.

4. Cf. J.-R. Kupper, 'Northern Mesopotamia and Syria', *CAH*, II.1, p. 23; H. Klengel, *Geschichte Syriens im 2. Jahrtausend v.u.Z.* I. *Nordsyrien* (Deutsche Akademie der Wissenschaften zu Berlin, Institut für Orientforschung, 46; Berlin, 1965), p. 214.

5. R.A. Crossland, 'Immigrants from the North', *CAH*, I, pp. 1-61. The relationship has, however, not yet been proven; cf. W.F. Albright and T.O. Lambdin, 'The Evidence of Language', *CAH*, I (fasc. 54, 2nd edn), pp. 32-35. As for the Hurrian language, see I.M. Diakonoff, *Hurrisch und Urartäisch* (Münchener Studien zur Sprachwissenschaft, Beiheft 6, NF; Munich, 1971).

Hurrians could have been in Transcaucasia.[1] The secret of bronze technology was probably discovered in Bohemia which had copper ores rich in tin. A 'branch of the Ugro-Finns' who settled in Hungary is thought to have developed the first bronzes.[2] Metal objects as well as pottery types which show connections between central Europe and the ancient Near East during both the period of Troy II (mid-third millennium) and the period of Troy IV have been used as arguments for the relationship. During Troy IV, which coincides with the time of the Assyrian trading colony in Cappadocia (the Kültepe-*kārum* IV-II period, c. 2100–1900 BCE),[3] tin bronze was among the commodities and appeared now for the first time in the Levant. It is thus possible that tin bronzes have spread from Bohemia to the southeast and into Anatolia and the Near East. Some weapons of bronze appear around 2100 BCE in Anatolia, 'together with painted Cappadocian ware'.[4] J. Mellaart has associated this pottery (which was wheel-made) with the Hurrians.[5] There are also axes of a Hungarian type occurring in the Levant during the so-called Kültepe period.[6]

These phenomena do not really establish an ethnic relationship between the Hurrians and the Finno-Ugrian peoples. Originally they may have been living in close proximity. Hence, some common linguistic features, Indo-Iranian words, as well as some Indian deity names (Mitra, Varuna and Indra)[7] also occur in two Hittite–Hurrian

1.   I.M. Diakonoff, *Hurritisch und Urartäisch*, p. 5 n. 1.

2.   J.E. Dayton, 'The Problem of Tin in the Ancient World', *World Archaeology* 3 (1971), p. 62.

3.   See J. Mellaart, 'Anatolian Chronology in the Early Middle Bronze Age', *Anatolian Studies* 7 (1957), pp. 64-74.

4.   J.E. Dayton, *World Archaeology* 3 (1971), p. 60. For some bronze weapons of probable Aegean origin that also have been found and perfected in western Anatolia, see D.B. Stronach, 'The Development and Diffusion of Metal Types in Early Bronze Age Anatolia', *Anatolian Studies* 7 (1957), pp. 89-125.

5.   See the discussion in J. Mellaart, 'Anatolia and the Balkans', *Antiquity* 34 (1960), pp. 270-78.

6.   J.E. Dayton, *World Archaeology* 3 (1971), p. 63.

7.   This earlier led scholars to maintain that Aryans were in the Near East at this time. A. Kammenhuber has demolished this theory (*Die Arier in Vorderen Orient*, [Heidelberg, 1968]); see also I.M. Diakonoff, 'Die Arier im Vorderen Orient: Ende eines Mythos (Zur Methodik der Erforschung verschollener Sprachen)', *Or* NS 41 (1972), pp. 91-120.

treaty texts.[1] However, these names do not tell very much about an Indian influence upon the Hurrian religion. Neither can one draw any conclusion about the origin of the Hurrians from this.[2] Important Hurrian gods were Kumarbi, in Syria identified with Dagan, the storm god Teshup and his consort, the sun goddess Hepat.[3] The problem of the origin of the Hurrians is complex, and as long as we do not have more information it will be enigmatic. However, the Hurrians who in the twenty-third century BCE settled in the hilly regions north of Mesopotamia had most probably no knowledge of any 'relatives' having invented tin bronze in Bohemia.

From a cultural point of view, the Hurrians can be considered as one of the more important peoples of the Near East. Already in the Agade period (c. 2300 BCE) they had acquired the art of writing using the cuneiform for their own language.[4] Hurrian is an agglutinative language related to Urartian and north Caucasian.[5] The name is not an ethnic but a linguistic term. The Hittites called the language *ḫurlili*.[6] Before the term 'Hurrian' was used in Akkadian cuneiform, the people was referred to by Sumerian SU.BIR4, Subartu.[7]

About four thousand tablets in cuneiform have been found at the important Hurrian site of Yorgan Tepe (Nuzi) in the area of Kirkuk in northern Mesopotamia.[8] These are from the mid-sixteenth century and deal with, for instance, legal matters, social and family customs and myths. In learning the Sumero-Akkadian script, some of the Mesopotamian art of literature became part of their own culture; they also transmitted Mesopotamian legends and myths besides their own to

---

1.   E. Laroche, 'Catalogue des textes hittites', *Etudes et Commentaires*, LXXIV (ed. D.O. Edzard; Paris, 1971), texts 51 and 52.

2.   Consult D.O. Edzard and A. Kammenhuber, 'Hurriter, Hurritisch', *Reallexikon der Assyriologie*, IV, pp. 507-14.

3.   See E. Laroche, 'Panthéon national et panthéons locaux chez les Hourrites', *Or* NS 45 (1976), pp. 94-99. Cf. also V. Haas, 'Substratgottheiten des westhurriti- schen Pantheons', *Revue Hittite et Asianique* 36 (1978), pp. 59-69.

4.   A. Kammenhuber, *Die Arier im Vorderen Orient*, p. 61.

5.   See I.M. Diakonoff, *Hurrisch und Urartäisch*, pp. 4, 157-65.

6.   G. Wilhelm, *Grundzüge*, p. 2.

7.   G. Wilhelm, *Grundzüge*, pp. 2, 9. I.J. Gelb maintained that Hurrian and Subarian were different languages (*Hurrians and Subarians*).

8.   C.J. Gadd, 'Tablets from Kirkuk', *RA* 23 (1926), pp. 49-61. For a bibliography, see, among others, T.L. Thompson, *The Historicity of the Patriarchal Narratives*, pp. 196-99.

others in the Syro-Palestinian region. The Gilgamesh epic, for instance, became known to the Hittites through the Hurrians.[1] We could also mention that a bilingual text in Akkado-Hurrian has been found at Ras Shamra (Ugarit).[2]

Even if one cannot say that the light war chariot was introduced by the Hurrians, it most probably was promoted by them. The horse and chariot seem to have been a characteristic part of their war machinery. It is interesting to note that handbooks dealing with raising horses as well as with horse racing have been found among the texts from Nuzi. The term *maryanni*, which is not an Indo-Aryan word, as often has been advocated, refers to commanders of chariots, the nobility, and representatives of the king.[3] They occur in the texts mainly from c. 1500 BCE. In many places, such as in Alalakh, they 'seem to be the leading citizens in all walks of life'[4] and could also include the *ḫazannu*, the 'governor, mayor'. In other words, they constituted the upper classes of the societies. As a social class they were a new phenomenon in the Near East of the Middle Bronze Age period.[5] It is possible that the *maryannu* should be seen as the inspiration and 'the model for the military aristocrats of the New Kingdom Egypt'.[6]

What has been labeled the dark age in the history of the sixteenth century Syria-Mesopotamia was perhaps not that dark. It may be an 'assyriological' interpretation of the fact that there was some change

---

1. E.A. Speiser, 'Hurrians and Hittites', *World History of the Jewish People*, I (ed. E.A. Speiser; London, 1964), pp. 154-55; A. Kammenhuber, *Die Arier im Vorderen Orient*, pp. 119-41.

2. J. Nougayrol and E. Laroche, *Le palais royal d'Ugarit*. III. *Textes Akkadiens des Archives Sud* (Paris, 1955), p. 324.

3. A. Kammenhuber, *Die Arier im Vorderen Orient*, pp. 220-23.

4. D.J. Wiseman, *The Alalakh Tablets* (Occasional Publications of the British Institute of Archaeology at Ankara, 2; London, 1953), p. 11.

5. P.R.S. Moorey, *World Archaeology* 18 (1986), p. 212. M. Heltzer does not see the *maryannu* warriors as a privileged class of aristocrats ('Problems of the Social History of Syria in the late Bronze Age', *La Siria nel Tardo Bronzo*, IV [ed. M. Liverani; Rome, 1969], pp. 310-46). H. Reviv has a more nuanced opinion. He maintains that as time went on the local princes tried to encourage persons of lower rank to join the chariot forces in order to stem the power of the aristocracy ('Some Comment on the Maryannu', *IEJ* 22 [1972], pp. 218-28).

6. B.J. Kemp, 'Imperialism and Empire in New Kingdom Egypt (c. 1575–1087 B.C.)', *Imperialism in the Ancient World* (ed. P.D.A Garnsey and C.R. Whittaker; Cambridge, 1978), p. 49.

in the scribal tradition at the end of the MB II period. This change can be detected through a comparison between the textual material from Alalakh Level VII and that of Alalakh IV. While the texts from Alalakh VII represent the Old Babylonian scribal tradition, the material of Alalakh IV is that of the Hurrian scribal schools.[1] Even though we know that the Hurrians adopted the cuneiform script, they seem to have developed an independent tradition of cuneiform writing.[2] This scribal tradition then spread over the Near East with the migration of the Hurrians.

On their expansion to the west, the Hurrians established some states of their own, in Cilicia, for instance, where they made themselves independent of Hittite rule after the death of Murshili (c. 1595 BCE). Their greatest kingdom, Mitanni or Hanigalbat,[3] was established in Upper Mesopotamia. The date of its emergence is unknown but is

1. See B. Landsberger, 'Assyrische Königsliste und "dunkles Zeitalter"', *JCS* 8 (1954), pp. 31-73. N. Na'aman does not consider there to have been a 'dark age' in Syria during the sixteenth century. He rather sees a change in culture and social systems coming about with the emergence of the Mitanni kingdom ('Syria at the Transition from the Old Babylonian Period to the Middle Babylonian Period', *UF* 6 [1974], pp. 266-67).

2. Alalakh VII is the city of Yarim-Lim. It has been dated to the time of Hammurabi of Babylon because he is mentioned in some tablets. Level VII, which probably was destroyed by Hattusili I of Hatti, is dated by W.F. Albright, among others, to the seventeenth century BCE ('Stratigraphic Confirmation of the Low Mesopotamian Chronology', *BASOR* 144 [1956], pp. 26-30). See also S. Smith, *Alalakh and Chronology* (London, 1940); and D.J. Wiseman, 'Alalakh', *Archaeology and Old Testament Study* (ed. D.W. Thomas; Oxford, 1967), pp. 119-35; J.D. Muhly, 'Near Eastern Chronology and the Date of the Late Cypriot I Period', *The Archaeology of Cyprus* (ed. N. Robertson; Park Ridge, NJ, 1971), pp. 77-78. M.-H.C. Gates dates the end of Level VII to c. 1575 BCE and the beginning of Level IV to c. 1460 BCE ('Alalakh Levels VI and V: A Chronological Reassessment', *Syro-Mesopotamian Studies* 4.2 [1981] [Monographic Journals of the Near East; Malibu, 1981], p. 35). This means that the date for Hammurabi's reign would be in the late eighteenth to the beginning of the seventeenth century BCE. Level V would be the city of king Idrimi.

3. Hanigalbat is the name that occurs in Akkadian texts. This was the name for northern Mesopotamia; cf. G. Wilhelm, *Grundzüge*, p. 34. In one text from the time of the first Dynasty of Babylon we find the term *birit nārim*, 'between the rivers', but it is not used as a proper name (J.J. Finkelstein, 'Mesopotamia', *JNES* 21 [1962], pp. 73-75).

estimated to have occurred sometime in the sixteenth century.[1] It stretched from Lake Van in the north down over Ashur and Arrapha (Kirkuk) east of Tigris and into northwestern Syria, where the coastal city states became its vassals. During the sixteenth century they penetrated southern Syria and Palestine and may also there have become the leading classes in the different cities. It is therefore understandable that most of Syria-Palestine was called Hurru (Kharu) by the Egyptians in the inscriptions of the New Kingdom.[2]

Mitanni seems to have been organized as a political confederacy, but we have to reckon that some Hurrian city states were not part of the confederacy. Qatna on the Orontes may have been one of these, at least during the Mari period.[3] The westernmost limit of Hurrian speaking territories included Halab (Aleppo), Tunip, Ugarit and Qatna. In these cities indigenous *maryannu* seem to have taken over the rulership. Later on they associated themselves with the Mitanni kingdom.[4] Qadesh in the Orontes valley rose to power in the later part of the MB II period at the same time that Hazor in Galilee seems to have declined.[5] Qadesh, which was part of the Egyptian sphere of interest during the beginning of the Eighteenth Dynasty, came under Hittite rule during the fourteenth century. However, in the later part of the second millennium the majority of its population seems to have been Hurrian.

The campaigns of the Egyptian Eighteenth Dynasty in Syria and Palestine after the expulsion of the Hyksos probably arrested the expansion of the Mitanni kingdom. Because of the threat of the Hittite empire, we even find that Mitanni became an ally of Egypt. This may have happened under Thutmoses IV (c. 1400 BCE), who by letters to king Artatama of Mitanni asked to marry one of his daughters.[6] It is in the period before Mitanni and Egypt became allies that one could see groups of the military aristocracy, the *maryannu* warriors, taking

1. Cf. W.W. Hallo in W.W. Hallo and W.K. Simpson, *The Ancient Near East*, pp. 110-11.

2. Sometimes the name Naharina is used by the Egyptians.

3. H. Klengel, *Geschichte Syriens*, I, p. 159; cf. C.H. Virolleaud, 'The Syrian Town of Katna and the Kingdom of Mitanni', *Antiquity* 3 (1929), pp. 312-17.

4. B. Landsberger, *JCS* 8 (1954), p. 59.

5. D.B. Redford, *JAOS* 99 (1979), p. 279, cf. p. 287 n. 151.

6. W.K. Simpson, in W.W. Hallo and W.K. Simpson, *The Ancient Near East*, p. 265.

over in some of the cities of southern Syria and Palestine, as has been proposed for Shechem.[1]

Transjordan

To what extent Transjordan was the focus of political interest in these days is unknown. We may draw the conclusion that it was of secondary importance. Very little is yet to be known about the country's history from literary sources and from archaeological finds. However, Transjordan was not void of inhabitants, as formerly was thought, but unfortunately it has not been as extensively excavated or explored as Cisjordan. We can get a certain picture regarding the population from tombs at Irbid, Amman and Wadi en-Naml (close to Mt Nebo), as well as from finds from sites in the Beq'a Valley[2] and at Sahab.[3] To these we should add settlements in the northern Transjordan,[4] in the Wadi Zerqa, and in the Jordan Valley, such as Pella, Tell el-Hayyat, Tell el-Mazar and Deir 'Alla. Scarabs found at the Amman 'airport temple', and from Pella, Jerash, al Wir, Kufr Sum, Heshbon and Petra, range in date from the seventeenth through the thirteenth centuries BCE.[5] These show a certain Egyptian interest in the transjordanian territory, and that interest has most probably been commercial. As we know, one of the main arteries of trade went through Transjordan connecting Syria-Mesopotamia with Egypt. It is thus to be expected that Syrian pottery occurs in Jordan, as is the case in the Amman tombs.[6] Other Syrian or Syrian-inspired artifacts have also been found. An example, for instance, is a cylinder seal found at Khirbet Faḥil (Pella), showing a standing deity with a bull's head who

---

1. See above.

2. See P. McGovern, 'Explorations in the Umm ad-Dananir Region of the Baq'ah Valley, 1977–1978', *ADAJ* 24 (1980), pp. 55-67; *idem*, 'Baq'ah Valley Project 1980', *BA* 44 (1981), pp. 126-28; P. McGovern *et al.*, *The Late Bronze and Early Iron Ages of Central Transjordan*, pp. 241-42, 272-77.

3. M.M. Ibrahim, 'Archaeological Excavations at Sahab', *ADAJ* 17 (1972), pp. 29-30. Remains from the Chalcolithic and EB II and III periods were also found.

4. S. Mittmann, *Beiträge zur Siedlungs- und Territorialgeschichte des nördlichen Ostjordanlandes* (ADPV; Wiesbaden, 1970), pp. 256-64.

5. W.A. Ward and M.F. Mastin, 'Cylinders and Scarabs from a Late Bronze Temple at 'Amman', *ADAJ* 8-9 (1964), pp. 47-55.

6. See R.H. Dornemann, who mentions, among other vessels, some 'chalice-like vases' resembling Khabur ware (*The Archaeology of Transjordan*, p. 16).

has in front of him an altar and two men. The deity has in his left hand a lotus flower. The style of the seal is that of Middle Bronze Age Syria,[1] but the lotus flower may belong to the Egyptian features that influenced the Levantine art.[2] The richness of the tomb material, as well as the glacis at the Amman citadel, the remains of Safut, and at the caravanserai (from c. 1700 BCE) at Jawa in the desert[3] indicate that the settlement problem of Transjordan must be solved along other lines of thinking than those advocating that the country was almost devoid of people or that it was inhabited by nomads only.[4] The picture that emerges is that the Jordan Valley and the northern parts of Jordan are richer in MB remains[5] than southern Jordan (the later Moabite and Edomite territories). A survey in Wâdī el-Ḥasā (biblical Zered), for instance, produced MB sherds from only one site and some 'doubtful' sherds from another site.[6] It cannot be concluded that the Jordan Valley and the northern half of Transjordan were never depopulated. Nomadism and transhumance also have to be taken into consideration. Archaeologically, one cannot yet establish the relationship between the urban and settled, rural populations on the one hand and the nomadic people on the other hand. More excavations and surveys are necessary for that.[7] Some shift in population may have occurred because of ecological reasons, as well as some newcomers from the north

1. H. Gese, 'Ein Rollsiegel der späteren Mittelbronze aus Pella', *ZDPV* 81 (1965), pp. 166-79.

2. Cf. G. Widengren, *The King and the Tree of Life* (UUÅ, 1951:4; Uppsala, 1951), pp. 27-32. The lotus flower is part of the many royal motifs that can be seen in Egyptian art from the time of the Eighteenth Dynasty; cf. T. Dothan, *Excavations at Deir el-Balah*, pp. 64-70, and figs. 145, 147-53.

3. S. Helms, *Jawa: Lost City of the Black Desert* (Ithaca, NY, 1981), pp. 222-23.

4. Cf. R.H. Dornemann, *The Archaeology of Transjordan*, pp. 15-19. Cf. also J.A. Sauer, *BASOR* 263 (1986), pp. 4-6.

5. Fourteen MB sites in the Jordan Valley east of the river were found in a survey; see M. Ibrahim, J. Sauer and K. Yassine, *BASOR* 222 (1976), pp. 41-66.

6. B. MacDonald, 'The Wâdi el-Ḥasā Survey 1979 and Previous Archaeological Work in Southern Jordan', *BASOR* 245 (1982), p. 38.

7. M.B. Rowton's 'dimorphic society' is a misnomer. He reckons with three types of society, namely (1) urban villages, (2) tribal villages, and (3) tribal nomads (*Or* NS 42 [1973], p. 251). To this we could also add the phenomenon called transhumance. We should acknowledge, however, that Rowton has rightly emphasized the interaction between settled and non-settled peoples.

probably moving into the area.[1] The 'Syrian-inspired' pottery could point to such a phenomenon, but we have also to consider the fact that trade connections are responsible for some of the pottery forms.

---

1.   Cf. B. Mazar, who sees the end of the MB II as a period when 'Canaan became a settling-ground for peoples of varied origin and culture' (*IEJ* 18 [1968], p. 96).

Chapter 5

THE LATE BRONZE AGE

From a political point of view, the expulsion of the Hyksos from Egypt marks the end of the Middle Bronze Age.[1] With the emergence of the Mitanni kingdom as well as with the growing power of the Egyptian Eighteenth Dynasty, a new era began in the history of Syria-Palestine. This period, which is called the Late Bronze Age (c. 1550/40 to c. 1200/1100 BCE),[2] saw not only the destructive results of some Egyptian campaigns of the New Kingdom pharaohs of the Eighteenth and Nineteenth Dynasties, but also the military confrontation between Egypt, Mitanni and the Hittite empire. Whatever independence the Syro-Palestinian city states could have had now came to an end. The termination of the Hyksos rule in Egypt and southern Palestine resulted in Egypt more than ever before becoming aware of the rest of the world. This is shown by the fact that not only are Egyptian objects very common in Syria-Palestine, but the reverse is also true. A great amount of pottery and other objects from Syria, Cyprus (copper) and the Aegean found their way to Egypt. Most of it was probably shipped from the coastal cities of Syria.[3] Byblos may still

1. Interesting to note is that the new period signified a 'decisive break' with a particular Egyptian tradition of building pyramids as tombs for the pharaohs. From the Eighteenth Dynasty on, the tombs were 'hidden' in the mountains, in the 'Valley of the Kings'; cf. E. Hornung, *Tal der Könige: Der Ruhestätte der Pharaonen* (Zürich, 1983); W.K. Simpson in W.W. Hallo and W.K. Simpson, *The Ancient Near East*, p. 261; W.J. Murnane, *The Guide to Ancient Egypt* (New York, 1983), p. 83.

2. This age is usually divided in two periods, Late Bronze I and Late Bronze II, the latter beginning c. 1400 BCE.

3. See F.H. Stubbings, *Mycenaean Pottery from the Levant* (Cambridge, 1951), pp. 56-58; R.S. Merrillees, *The Cypriot Bronze Age Pottery Found in Egypt* (Studies in Mediterranean Archaeology, 18; Lund, 1968); J. Strange, *Caphtor/Keftiu*, pp. 151-52. A common vessel of this time is the Base Ring I juglet, the

have been the main port for Egyptian trade.

On the political stage, Egypt soon met the challenge from Mitanni. This situation, in connection with the military actions against the 'Hyksos states' in Palestine, made Egypt a more aggressive nation than it had been earlier. We may possibly see the same kind of 'missionary' ideology behind these wars as the one that was the basis for the later Neo-Assyrian empire's campaigns. The enemies belonged to the world of chaos and evil and therefore had to be annihilated or subdued. If the Syro-Palestinian kinglets had expected to become independent at this time they were mistaken. More than ever before this part of the Near East came under Egyptian rule. Even if Egypt did not incorporate Palestine as a province, it became a 'dominion' that had to send its products and valuables as tribute to the Egyptian pharaoh. The political status of the princes of Syria-Palestine was thus that of a vassal,[1] but the oath they had to swear bound them to the reigning pharaoh only, not to his successor.[2] The cities outside the former Hyksos domain, that is, those in the western and northern part of the country, were the centers of supply for Egypt. They were therefore only destroyed if the city prince rebelled.[3] This period of Egyptian supremacy over Palestine lasted until around 1200, when upheavals in the eastern Mediterranean resulted in, for instance, the collapse of the Hittite empire and the destruction of Ugarit and Alalakh, and the arrival of the Philistines and Tjeker who settled on the Palestinian coast. The twelfth century BCE is thus the period that saw the beginning of the decline of the Egyptian empire.

From an archaeological point of view, it is possible to see the LB period as both a continuum of the MB Age[4] and as a time of certain

so-called bilbil jug, which because of its shape often has been associated with the trade of opium.

1.   This is acknowledged by the king of Babylon, for instance, who in a letter to pharaoh Akhenaten says that 'Kinaḫḫi is your land and its kings your servants' (EA 8.25).

2.   See W. Helck, *Die Beziehungen*, p. 247.

3.   J.M. Weinstein, 'The Egyptian Empire in the Late Bronze Period: A Reassessment', *BASOR* 241 (1981), p. 7. The destruction of Middle Bronze II Jericho has been seen by J.R. Bartlett as being caused by an earthquake and fire coinciding with a plague (*Jericho* [Guildford, Surrey, 1982], p. 94). The site would then have been abandoned and rebuilt 'probably soon after 1400 BCE' (K.M. Kenyon, *Excavations at Jericho*, III, p. 375).

4.   See, for instance, J. Garstang, 'Jericho: City and Necropolis', *Annals of*

changes both in population settlements and in material culture. The picture is, naturally, varied by geography and established trade connections. Several of the MB II cities survived into the LB I period. These were all cities north of the former Hyksos realm. Some coastal cities were destroyed first in connection with Tuthmosis III's campaign to Megiddo in 1482/81 BCE. The LB Age is, however, a period in which several sites in the highlands of Palestine were abandoned. In the Beqaʿ Valley massive depopulation occurred, and some sites were abandoned already at the end of the MB II period.[1] The survey in the territory of Ephraim shows that many sites seem to have been abandoned. In the MB II period there were 55 sites in Ephraim but for the LB Age only five are known.[2] The picture is about the same in other parts of the central hills.[3] This fact cannot be ascribed to Egyptian campaigns which seldom went into the hills. It may be that contributing factors were 'stresses and strains within the Canaanite socio-political system', which may have caused some peoples to abandon their small unwalled settlements with one result of this possibly being a 'strengthening of the central sites'.[4] Another result would have been an increase in nomadism. Among the few important fortified sites of the LB period are Shechem, Tirzah,[5] Bethel, Urmeh, Abu Zarad,[6] Tel Marjamme (in the LB I period) and possibly Shiloh.[7] The region around Hebron was almost depopulated in the LB II period.[8] In all,

Archaeology and Anthropology (Liverpool) 20 (1933), p. 27. For the insignificant village of Jericho in the Late Bronze I period in contrast to the Middle Bronze II city, see, among others, P. Bienkowski, *Jericho in the Late Bronze Age* (Warminster, 1986), pp. 32-102, 120-25.

1. L. Marfoe, 'A History on Frontier Settlement and Land Use in the Biqaʿ, Lebanon' (PhD dissertation, University of Chicago, 1978), cf. p. 316.

2. I. Finkelstein, *Tel Aviv* 12 (1985), p. 166; cf. I. Finkelstein, *The Archaeology of the Israelite Settlement* (Jerusalem, 1988), pp. 119-204, 340.

3. Cf. R. Gonen, 'Urban Canaan in the Late Bronze Period', *BASOR* 253 (1984), pp. 61-73.

4. I. Finkelstein, *Archaeology of Settlement*, p. 342.

5. Cf. R. de Vaux, 'el-Farʿa, Tell', *EAEHL*, II, p. 400.

6. Bethel seems to have been destroyed in the latter part of Late Bronze II, but it was rebuilt again. See I. Finkelstein, *Archaeology of Settlement*, pp. 72-73, cf. pp. 186-87.

7. No one has been able to find any building remains from the Late Bronze Shiloh. The new excavations found a dump with Late Bronze I pottery (I. Finkelstein, *Tel Aviv* 12 [1985], p. 166).

8. P.C. Hammond, 'Hebron', *RB* 73 (1966), pp. 566-69.

M. Kochavi's survey found only four LB II sites in the Judahite hills.[1] Among the known sites are Jerusalem and Khirbet Rabud.

The situation in the Manasseh region is somewhat different in that there are more LB sites than in Ephraim. In the MB II period there were 116 sites, but for the LB less than 30 sites have been found in Manasseh,[2] with the majority of them in the north, which may be explained by their proximity to the Jezreel Valley and its agricultural settlements. Less than ten sites are known from Galilee of the LB period. In the south there were no sites at all in the Beer-Sheba Valley.[3]

The above presents us with a picture of the hill country as being very sparsely populated during most of the LB Age. This does not mean that the hills were devoid of people. As mentioned above, when the political and economic system of the MB Age fell apart and some sites were abandoned, groups of people could have reverted to nomadism and sheep herding. One indication for this is the large amount of goat and sheep bones that has been found, for instance, at Shiloh. About 90% of all the animal bones are of sheep or goats.[4] Thus, people have lived in the hills, but cities and villages were not built.

The situation seems to be different in Transjordan. Here several cities continued from the MB II period, such as Sahab, Tell Safut, Jalul, Tell el-Ḥuṣn, Pella, Irbid,[5] and Deir 'Alla in the Jordan Valley. To these we should add Tell es-Saʿidiyeh and Tell el-Mazar, as well as Amman, where there were some fortifications in the MB II period, the so-called Amman Temple representing the LB period. In northern Transjordan the amount of settlements increase in the LB II period.[6] Southern Transjordan (the later Moabite and Edomite territories) has been more sparsely populated.[7] What this shows is that the opinion of Nelson Glueck about Transjordan being depopulated in the LB period

1.   M. Kochavi *et al.*, *Judea, Samaria, and the Golan: Archaeological Survey 1967–68* (Jerusalem, 1972), pp. 20, 83 (Hebrew).

2.   A. Zertal (in a lecture at the University of Chicago, 1985).

3.   See I. Finkelstein, *Archaeology of Settlement*, p. 340.

4.   S. Hellwing and M. Sadeh, 'Animal Remains: Preliminary Report', in I. Finkelstein *et al.*, *Tel Aviv* 12 (1985), p. 179.

5.   C.J. Lenzen, private communication. She cannot find that there was a hiatus at Irbid between the MB and LB periods (Letter of Aug. 31, 1987).

6.   S. Mittmann, *Beiträge*, pp. 256-64.

7.   J.A. Sauer, *BASOR* 263 (1986), pp. 6-8. See also below (Chapter 9).

is not in agreement with the facts. Together with the cities, tombs from all over Jordan and surface finds such as pottery show that human life existed. This does not mean that all had to be living in cities or villages. Certain parts of the country were 'inhabited' by nomads.

Concerning the material culture, there is really no break between the MB II and the LB I periods. We can with some right speak of a cultural continuum. For instance, the fortification system was mainly the same, with walls and gates of the same types as those of MB II. However, even if most of the pottery from the end of MB II continues in the LB Age, it is not of the same quality and finesse as earlier. At the same time, new phenomena do occur, such as Mycenaean pottery and the bichrome ware known from Cyprus. The fifteenth century BCE is the time Mycenaean commercial interests increased in Cyprus and the eastern Mediterranean. From c. 1400 BCE, the Mycenaeans seem to have broken the hegemony of the Cretans as traders.[1] After the fall of Knossos in 1380 BCE, Greek settlers went to Cyprus,[2] and with them the Mycenaean culture was introduced on the island. One of their most important cities was Salamis on the southeastern coast. This is the time when Cyprus became an important and wealthy center between the Aegean and Egypt and the Levant. Ports of entry on the Levantine coast were Ugarit, the Phoenician cities and Abū Hawām (within the city limits of modern Haifa),[3] and south of the Carmel,

1. K. Nicolaou, 'The Mycenaeans in the East', in *Studies in the History and Archaeology of Jordan*, I (ed. A. Hadidi; Amman, 1982), pp. 124-25.

2. In the el-Amarna letters as well as in Egypt and Ugaritic texts, Cyprus is called Alashiya; cf. the biblical Elishah, 1 Chron. 1.7. The term *'ereṣ kittîm*, 'the land of the Kittim' (Isa. 23.1), is probably a reference to Cyprus but may originally have referred to the city of Kition (modern Larnaka); cf. H. Wildberger, *Jesaja* (BKAT, 10; Neukirchen, 1978), p. 870.

3. Tell Abū Hawām seems to have been a fishing village before it obtained its port in the fourteenth century BCE. B. Maisler (Mazar) advocated that it became a base for the Egyptian navy during the reign of Seti I ('The Stratification of Tell Abū Huwām on the Bay of Acre', *BASOR* 124 [1951], pp. 21-25). J.M. Weinstein, however, maintains that stratum Va 'does not represent a 19th-Dynasty naval base'. No Egyptian pottery was found. Instead Weinstein sees Acco as a probable candidate. The town is the most prominent one in the area, judging from Ugaritic and Egyptian texts ('Was Tell Abu Hawam a 19th-Dynasty Egyptian Naval Base?', *BASOR* 238 [1980], pp. 43-46). D.L. Saltz has suggested that T. Abū Hawām probably was the port city of Megiddo and the Jezreel plain ('Greek Geometric Pottery in the East' [PhD dissertation, Harvard University, Cambridge, MA, 1978], pp. 147-49).

Dor,[1] Joppa and Ashkelon.[2] Even if most of the Mycenaean pottery reached Syria-Palestine from Cyprus, some have come directly from Greece, from the Peleponese. The latter is the case at Tell Abū Hawām, where a warehouse with a very large collection of Mycenaean III pottery was uncovered.[3] Concerning this pottery, it is in some way an imitation of Cypriote ware but with a decor in an Aegean style. As to the art of Cyprus, one may say that the fourteenth and thirteenth centuries BCE sees the first orientalizing of Greek art.[4]

The bichrome ware, which is of Cypriot origin, derives its name from the two most common colors that occur in the decorations, red and black. The vessels are usually decorated on the shoulders. Among the motifs are parallel stripes with goats, birds and fish. Geometric patterns are common on the so-called chocolate-on-white pottery.[5] As time went on, Cypriot pottery became very common in Palestine,

---

1.   The settlement at Dor started in the Late Bronze II period. The city is mentioned in an Egyptian list from the time of Ramses II, cf. G. Foerster, 'Dor', *EAEHL*, I, p. 334; for the new excavations at Dor, see A. Raban, 'Dor Yam', *IEJ* 32 (1982), pp. 256-59.

2.   Y. Aharoni thinks that the settlements at Raphia and Tell Abū Seleimeh close to the Egyptian border were established by the Egyptians in this period (*Land of the Bible*, p. 152).

3.   F. Asaro and I. Perlman, 'Provenience Study of Mycenaean Pottery Employing Neutron Activation Analysis', *Acts of the International Archaeological Symposium, 'The Mycenaeans in the Eastern Mediterranean', Nicosia 27th March–2nd April 1972* (Nicosia, 1973), pp. 213-24. For the excavations, see R.W. Hamilton, 'Excavations at Tell Abū Hawām', *QDAP* 4 (1935), pp. 1-69; L. Gershuny, 'Stratum V at Tell Abū Hawām', *ZDPV* 97 (1981), pp. 36-44; J. Balensi and M.-D. Herrera, 'Tell Abou Hawam 1983–1984: Rapport préliminaire', *RB* 92 (1985), pp. 82-128.

4.   See V. Karageorghis, *The Ancient Civilization of Cyprus* (New York, 1969), p. 61.

5.   Because bichrome pottery was very common at Tell el 'Ajjul, it has been suggested that one individual potter was responsible for it; cf. W.A. Heurtly, 'A Palestinian Vase Painter of the Sixteenth Century BCE', *QDAP* 8 (1939), pp. 21-37. R. Amiran ascribed it to a school of potters along the coast between Gaza and Ugarit where it is very common (*Ancient Pottery of the Holy Land*, p. 152). Neutron activation analysis has shown that the ware is Cypriot (M. Artzy, F. Asaro and I. Perlman, 'The Origin of the Palestinian Bichrome Ware', *JAOS* 93 [1973], pp. 446-61). See also *idem*, 'Wheel-made Pottery of the M.C. III and L.C. I Periods in Cyprus identified by Neutron Activation Analysis', *Lawrence Berkeley Laboratory, University of California, Berkeley, Reprint* (LBL-29-75; Berkeley, August, 1975).

testifying to an intensified trade between this island and the Levant.

The spread of the bichrome ware in the eastern Mediterranean is of a certain interest. It occurs at Tarsus and Mersin on the coast of eastern Anatolia, at Alalakh, Ugarit and Tell Sukas in northern Syria, and then in Palestine from Hazor down to Tell el-Far'ah (S). There are no sites in Phoenicia and in the central hill country of Palestine where this kind of pottery has been found. The reasons for this are not fully known. As for the hills, it was a territory outside the main trade routes, and in the LB period there were not very many sites. The hills were, as mentioned, less populated during the LB Age than during the preceding period. It is therefore natural that the highlands of Palestine during this period did not have any direct trade connection with Cyprus. Concerning Phoenicia, one factor that has to be taken into consideration is that the Phoenician cities are not very well known archaeologically, because only small sections of them have been excavated owing to the impossibility of digging under the modern buildings. Another reason would be that only certain commodities were shipped to these places. Other Cypriot imports to Palestine, such as the Base-ring ware, White Slip and White Shaved pottery, should also be mentioned. There are, however, differences in frequency between Cyprus and Palestine in these matters. These 'differences seem to indicate the operation of a well-organized, planned, selective trade', and one may suspect that the 'trade was based upon a thorough knowledge of the market to which the products were traded'.[1]

Concerning Transjordan, few foreign vessels were found, for instance, at Irbid in northern Jordan, but sites as Pella, Deir 'Alla in the Jordan Valley, and the so-called temple at Amman's airport have produced a greater amount of imported pottery, such as Cypriote and Mycenaean vessels. Several vessels of stone from Cisjordan, Egypt and Cyprus were also found.[2] At Irbid, however, tombs yielded Transjordanian ware of the LB tradition with some vessels that can be seen as a 'development of the earlier types'.[3] Pottery from Qwelbe (14 km north of Irbid and east of Abila) yielded forms that have parallels

---

1. B.M. Gittlen, 'The Cultural and Chronological Implications of the Cypro-Palestinian Trade during the Late Bronze Age', *BASOR* 241 (1981), p. 55.

2. R. Dornemann, *The Archaeology of the Transjordan*, pp. 20-21; V. Hankey, 'The Late Bronze Age Temple at Amman: I. The Aegean Pottery', *Levant* 6 (1974), pp. 160-78.

3. R.W. Dajani, 'Iron Age Tombs from Irbeid', *ADAJ* 8-9 (1964), p. 101.

at Hazor, Megiddo, Pella, Amman and Tell ed-Duweir.[1] These all may show some contacts between Cisjordan and Transjordan, but they also point to the fact that trade was heavier in the Jordan Valley than on the Irbid plateau and the 'Ajlun highlands.

Dealing with the problems of trade and its lasting results, the pottery, we should also remember that Palestine and Syria exported certain commodities, such as grain, wine and olive oil. These products went both west to the Aegean and south to Egypt.[2] Thus 'Canaanite jars', specially made large jars which carried the exported goods, have been found, for instance, in excavations both in Athens in Greece, and Thebes in Egypt.[3] A wall painting from the time of Amenhotep III gives an illustration of this. It depicts a ship with merchants unloading their goods consisting mainly of large jars with lids. One may not go too wrong in supposing that these were the so-called Canaanite jars.[4]

At the end of the Amarna period (the latter part of the fourteenth cent. BCE), Cypriot pottery was not imported to Egypt, which may have been because Egypt had lost the port of Ugarit and some other port cities on the Syrian coast.[5] These cities had come into the sphere of the Hittite empire. This may be one reason why Cypriote pottery increased in Palestine during the fourteenth century.[6]

As to the political situation, we should note that the campaigns of

1. Z. Kafafi, 'Late Bronze Age Pottery from *Qwelbe* (Jordan)', *ZDPV* 100 (1984), pp. 12-29.

2. Examples of this trade are the shipwrecks found at the coast of southern Anatolia, one at Cape Gelidonya and the other at Ulu Burun near Kaṣ some 60 km west of Cape Gelidonya. The former had a cargo of mainly copper ingots, and the latter carried besides copper ingots, gold and silver objects, a large number of tools, weapons, ivory, Cypriote and Canaanite pottery, such as Palestinian amphoras. The Cape Gelidonya ship has been dated to c. 1200 BCE (G.F. Bass, 'Cape Gelidonya and Bronze Age Trade', *Orient and Occident Essays Presented to Cyrus H. Gordon* [ed. H.H. Hoffner; AOAT, 22; Neukirchen, 1973], pp. 29-38). The Ulu Burun shipwreck could be from the thirteenth century BCE; see G.F. Bass, 'A Bronze Age Shipwreck at Ulu Burun (Kaṣ): 1984 Campaign', *AJA* 90 (1986), pp. 269-96.

3. Concerning pottery suitable for transport, see A. Leonard, 'Considerations of Morphological Variation in the Mycenaean Pottery from the South-Eastern Mediterranean', *BASOR* 241 (1981), pp. 87-101.

4. R. Amiran, *Ancient Pottery of the Holy Land*, pp. 140-41, and pl. 43.

5. See R.S. Merrillees, *The Cypriot Bronze Age Pottery*, p. 202.

6. B.M. Gittlen, 'Studies in the Late Cypriot Pottery Found in Palestine' (PhD dissertation, University of Pennsylvania, 1977; Ann Arbor, 1980), p. 519.

the first kings of the Egyptian Eighteenth Dynasty into Syria and Palestine may have had the character of razzias against what they probably considered to be Hyksos city-states.[1] As mentioned above,[2] there is not very much inscriptional material about Egyptian campaigns in Palestine for the earliest period after the Hyksos expulsion. Amenhotep I's successor, Tuthmosis I, who was married to a sister of Amenhotep I, is known to have campaigned mainly in Syria, fighting Mitanni in Naharin (between the Habur river and the Euphrates)[3] and setting up a stela on the western bank of the Euphrates river.[4] He had marched through Retenu (probably southern Syria) to the Orontes valley and then to the Euphrates.[5] He also took time off for hunting elephants in Niy (Apamea) in the Nuhashshe territory.[6] Since we do not learn anything about Palestine proper, we may draw the conclusion that the Egyptian army sailed to Byblos and from there started the campaign.

Tuthmosis I's successor, Tuthmosis II, is known to have campaigned against the Shasu people. This is a term that recurs in the inscriptions of the Eighteenth and Nineteenth Dynasties and refers to the nomads of southern Syria, Palestine and Transjordan.[7] Usually Tuthmosis II's campaign has been seen as directed against the Shasu of the Negev, Sharuhen thus being one of his strongholds. Because the Shasu were to be found both in the south and in the north, we do not really know where Tuthmosis fought these people.

1. See, for instance, D.B. Redford, *JAOS* 99 (1979), p. 274; J.M. Weinstein, *BASOR* 241 (1981), p. 7.

2. See Chapter 4, The Middle Bronze Age.

3. It is from this time that we first learn about a nation Mitanni. See H. Brunner, 'Mitanni in einem ägyptischen Text vor oder um 1500', *MIO* 4 (1956), pp. 323-27. Naharin means 'the flood land', and is thus a geographical term, not a political one; cf. W. Helck, *Die Beziehungen*, p. 277.

4. J.H. Breasted, *Ancient Records of Egypt*, II (Chicago, 1906), §478.

5. W. Helck, *Die Beziehungen*, p. 116; D.B. Redford, *JAOS* 99 (1979), p. 279.

6. A. Spalinger, 'A New Reference to an Egyptian Campaign of Tuthmose III in Asia', *JNES* 37 (1978), pp. 38-39.

7. See R. Giveon, *Les bédouins Shosu des documents égyptiens* (Leiden, 1971); cf. M. Weippert, 'Semitische Nomaden des zweiten Jahrtausends, über die ṣ3sw der ägyptischen Quellen', *Bib* 55 (1974), p. 273; M. Görg, 'Zur Geschichte der ṣ3sw', *Or* NS 45 (1976), p. 425; *idem*, 'Tuthmosis III und die š3sw-Region', *JNES* 38 (1979), pp. 199-202. In this article Görg places the Shasu that the Egyptians fought at this time in the Beqa' valley.

Shortly after Tuthmosis had died, his wife and sister Hatshepsut took over the reins and declared herself pharaoh even though her stepson Tuthmosis III (c. 1504–1450 BCE) officially became king.[1] The joint rulership lasted for 21 years. Hatshepsut's interest in Palestine was obviously nonexistent. It is only at the end of Tuthmosis III's 22nd year, a year after Hatshepsut had died, that we learn about his first campaign through Palestine as far north as to Megiddo.[2] Under Tuthmosis the Egyptians are said to have undertaken 16 campaigns in Palestine and Syria.[3] The first expedition is known from two inscriptions. One is the Armant stela from Upper Egypt, and the other is an inscription divided into lists on the walls of the Karnak temple.[4] This campaign had as its objective the quelling of the rebellion of the Syro-Palestinian princes. These allied rulers had gathered their troops at Megiddo under the command of the princes of Qadesh[5] and Megiddo, and they had the backing of the Mitanni kingdom. According to Tuthmosis' inscription, about 100 cities participated in the coalition. After having taken Yurza (probably Tell Jemme, 13 km south of Gaza), Tuthmosis proceeded from the Egyptian base at Gaza to Yaham, south of the Carmel range. The distance was 120 km, which took the army c. 12 days. One detachment under the commander Thoth allegedly took Joppa by a ruse.[6] Two hundred soldiers were hidden in baskets and carried into the city like agricultural products. Five hundred soldiers are said to have been carrying the baskets.[7] That should have

1.   D.B. Redford, *History and Chronology of the Eighteenth Dynasty of Egypt* (Toronto, 1967), p. 76. See also E.F. Wente, 'Thutmose III's Accession and the Beginning of the New Kingdom', *JNES* 34 (1975), pp. 265-72.

2.   See J.H. Breasted, *Ancient Records of Egypt*, II, pp. 175-90.

3.   J.A. Wilson, *ANET*, p. 238.

4.   See the literature in Wilson, *ANET*, p. 234-35.

5.   Seeing that Tuthmosis first took Qadesh at the Orontes in his sixth campaign and that he did not march further north than northern Palestine in his first campaign, it has been suggested that Qadesh refers to the Galilean city that also is mentioned by Seti I (cf. J.H. Breasted, *Ancient Records of Egypt* [Leiden, 1937], III, p. 71 n. a; J. Simons, *Handbook for the Study of Egyptian Topographical Lists relating to Western Asia*, pp. 35-36). On the other hand, the kingdom of Mitanni was too distant from the Galilean Qadesh, but much closer to the Qadesh in the Orontes Valley.

6.   The text is dubious as a historical source (D.B. Redford, 'The Ashkelon Relief at Karnak and the Israel Stela', *IEJ* 36 [1986], p. 190).

7.   J.A. Wilson, *ANET*, pp. 22-23.

made any enemy worried, but Thoth said he and his family would leave the Egyptians and join the 'enemy' of Joppa and that the soldiers were his tribute to the ruler. The historicity of this can, of course, not be checked, but some general of Tuthmosis may have been more clever than most, or the scribe had a good imagination.

At Yaham the king had a staff conference with his generals about which way one should go in order to attack the enemy. There were three alternatives. The northern route would be to go through at Djefti (Zephat—modern Khirbet Sitt Leila?)[1] and come out at Yokneam, c. 12 km NW of Megiddo, or one could go south of the mountain range and reach the Jezreel Valley at Ta'anak c. 9 km SE of Megiddo. The third alternative, which was the shortest way, would be to march through the 'Aruna (Wadi 'Ara) pass. This would lead the army almost directly to Megiddo. 'Intelligence' reports were given that the allied troops had taken up their positions at Megiddo. Because of this, and because of the fact that the pass was very narrow and therefore dangerous for an army to traverse, the generals opted for one of the two other alternatives. To go through via the 'Aruna pass meant that the chariotry had to go in single file. A Pharaoh is, however, wiser than anybody else; he had 'divine' wisdom, thus Tuthmosis chose the quickest route, coming out at Megiddo and surprising the enemies, who had not expected this manoeuvre and therefore had positioned their troops on the south side of the Brook of Qina (south of Megiddo). Their chariotry had taken up their positions at Ta'anak. Thus Megiddo was unprotected, which meant that the coalition's strategy failed from the beginning, and they were completely defeated. The city gates of Megiddo were quickly closed, so soldiers and charioteers who fled had to be hauled up over the walls, if there was time. Tuthmosis did not take the city immediately because his troops started looting and collecting booty. It therefore took him several months before the city capitulated.[2] A great amount of booty was taken, as for instance, 924 chariots,

---

1. Cf. Y. Aharoni, *The Land of the Bible*, p. 53.
2. According to J.H. Breasted, the campaign lasted c. six months from the day the army left Egypt to the day Tuthmosis could celebrate the victory at Thebes (*Ancient Records of Egypt*, II, p. 177). The length of the siege of Megiddo is also mentioned in the Barkal Stela from close to the Fourth Cataract; see J.A. Wilson, *ANET*, p. 238.

2041 horses, 1929 cows, 2000 goats, 20,500 sheep, 2503 prisoners,[1]
207,300 sacks of wheat, together with weapons, some furniture with
gold, vessels and clothing of different kinds.[2] Politically, the victory
meant that the defeated princes acknowledged Egyptian supremacy.
Megiddo was destroyed but obviously rebuilt immediately. Stratum
VIII (from the mid-fifteenth cent. through the first half of the fourteenth) represents the most flourishing period of MB and LB Megiddo,
with monumental buildings such as a palace and the rebuilt temple
(building 2048), labeled by some 'the Fortress Temple'.[3] One may
conclude that Tuthmosis saw the need for a strong fortress city at this
strategic location. From having been a Hurrian 'outpost', Megiddo now
became an Egyptian bastion and a center for collecting the produce of
the Jezreel Valley. This may explain why Ta'anak was not rebuilt on a
grand scale after the battle at Megiddo. In concentrating troops and
tax collectors at Megiddo, the Egyptian government did not need to
overextend itself and new centers of resistance would not emerge.

It was in this city, Megiddo stratum VIII, that an Akkadian tablet
was found with a section from the Gilgamesh Epic. This tells us
something about Akkadian literary influences in the ancient Near East.
Even if the city was under the Egyptian rule and Egyptian literary
traditions became known, the Akkadian scribal tradition was still part
of life. The Akkadian script was still the official means of communication between the rulers and their courts, thus students in the scribal
schools had to practice and learn the signs. As everybody knows, epics
and sagas are easier to use as school texts than lexical lists, because of
the fascination with the content. Thus, one should not be astonished
about a passage from the Gilgamesh Epic turning up in a city state in
Palestine.

---

1.   It is from Tuthmosis' list that we meet for the first time the word *maryannu*,
'charioteer, noble patrician', in Egyptian texts (*ANET*, p. 237).

2.   See *ANET*, p. 237-38.

3.   For the complicated stratigraphy of Megiddo, see, for instance, G.M. Shipton,
Notes on the Megiddo of Strata VI–XX (SAOC, 17; Chicago, 1939), p. 50;
Y. Aharoni, 'Megiddo', *EAEHL*, III, pp. 845-46; A.E. Glock, *Berytus* 31 (1983),
pp. 63-64. H. Kassis sees stratum IX as rebuilding of Stratum X, the latter being
assigned to the mid-sixteenth cent. BCE ('The Beginning of the Late Bronze Age at
Megiddo: A Re-Examination of Stratum X', *Berytus* 22 [1973], pp. 5-22). As to the
temple 2048, it may have been built already in stratum X; see the discussion by
I. Dunayevsky and A. Kempinski, *ZDPV* 89 (1973), pp. 180-84.

Being in the Jezreel Valley, Tuthmosis detached part of his army to conquer Galilee and the northern Transjordan. He could return home as the ruler of both Cisjordan and Transjordan. The cities taken are known from the engravings on the pylons of the temple of Amon at Karnak. In these lists, 119 cities are mentioned as captured by the Egyptians. Most of them are located in northern Palestine and Transjordan, that is, 'Upper Retenu'. This probably indicates that southern Palestine did not participate in the rebellion because it was already in Egyptian hands. The geographical grouping of the listed cities makes it clear that among the members of the coalition were also city states in the Beqa' Valley and the territory of Damascus. From the list we may draw the conclusion that the Phoenician cities and the Amurru territory known from the later Amarna texts were not part of the coalition. Even though Qadesh and Megiddo were the leaders of the coalition, the inclusion of Qadesh does not prove that the Egyptians marched to Qadesh and took the city. That would most certainly have been mentioned. This does not mean, however, that Qadesh at the Orontes could not have been part of the coalition.[1] With the support of the new and expanding confederate state of Mitanni, the prince of Qadesh most naturally has sided with the new neighbor, and in the expeditions of Amenhotep I and Tuthmosis I he has seen the danger of the new rulers of Egypt. It is therefore likely that the prince of Qadesh tried to organize the Syrian princes in order to meet the danger from Egypt.[2]

Although we know that the Egyptian army had scribes following their armies, the lists have been engraved later, and some additions may therefore also have occurred. What is more important to understand is that the scribes could have written down every town or village the army passed by but did not consider necessary to capture. From this point of view, names of cities close by to the military route could also have been mentioned not only as being part of the glorification of the Pharaoh's campaign,[3] but also as being part of the territory that

---

1.   D.B. Redford assumes that the prince of Qadesh had formed the Syro-Palestinian coalition against Egypt already during the reign of Queen Hatshepsut (*History and Chronology*, p. 86).

2.   Cf. H. Klengel, *Geschichte Syriens im 2. Jahrtausend v.u.Z.*, III (Berlin, 1970), p. 181.

3.   Thus, J. Simons, *Handbook for the Study of Egyptian Topographical Lists*, p. 36.

now had come under Egyptian rule. In the Annals Tuthmosis states, for instance, that the capture of Megiddo was equal to 'the capturing of a thousand towns'[1] which means that the princes of the coalition would have acknowledged the Pharaoh as their overlord. Thus to capture them all was not necessary. We may be sure that some cities along the road up to Megiddo (e.g. Gezer, Joppa,[2] Aphek and Ta'anak[3]) were taken.[4] Tell Jerishe on the southern bank of the Yarkon river is another fortress city which was destroyed early in the LB I period. In this case we have to reckon with the possibility that this place probably was part of the Hyksos Palestinian line of fortifications, and thus it could have met its destruction at the time of the expulsion of the Asiatic rulers of Egypt.[5]

Among Transjordanian places mentioned in Tuthmosis' list occurs the name *y-'-q-b-r*, Jacob-el,[6] which probably was located in the vicinity of Gadara. The name is also found in a list by Ramses II in Amon's temple at Karnak,[7] but whether it is the same place is impossible to find out.[8] Here we should note that the biblical tradition connects the Jacobites with the Aramaeans of Transjordan (Gen. 29-31).[9]

---

1. J.A. Wilson, *ANET*, p. 237.

2. J. Kaplan, 'The Archaeology and History of Tel Aviv-Jaffa', *BA* 35 (1972), p. 78.

3. According to P.W. Lapp, Ta'anak was destroyed early in the fifteenth cent. BCE ('The 1968 Excavations at Tell Ta'annek', *BASOR* 195 [1969], pp. 24-26).

4. J.M. Weinstein, *BASOR* 241 (1981), p. 11. According to A.E. Glock, Ta'anak does not seem to have been deserted in the mid-fifteenth cent. but there was most probably 'a deterioration of the quality of life' (*Berytus* 31 [1983], p. 66).

5. Cf. N. Avigad, 'Jerishe, Tell', *EAEHL*, II (Jerusalem, 1976), pp. 575-78. A scarab with an inscription from ch. 30 of the 'Book of the Dead' was found at Tell Jerishe (p. 577).

6. J. Simons, *Handbook*, p. 118; cf. W. Helck, *Die Beziehungen*, p. 128.

7. J. Simons, *Handbook*, p. 158.

8. T.L. Thompson thinks it could be the same site (*The Historicity of the Patriarchal Narratives*, p. 49 n. 233). Thompson also believes that we here, however, 'are dealing with place names and not tribal names' (p. 49 n. 229). In the Semitic world, geographical names and names of people could often be the same, for instance, Ephraim, Assur. M. Astour has also pointed out that 'many anthroponymns could serve as toponyms' ('Yahweh in Egyptian Topographical Lists', *Festschrift Elmar Edel 12. Märtz 1979* [ed. M. Görg and E. Puech; Ägypten und Altes Testament, 1; Bamberg, 1979], p. 30 n. 71).

9. Cf. E. Meyer, who also refers to the funeral service for Jacob at Goren-ha-aṭad, also called Abel miṣraim, which 'is across the Jordan' (Gen. 50.7-11) (*Die*

Because of the biblical information about the Jacobites moving from Transjordan into Cisjordan, and because the 'patriarch' Jacob is given a new name, Israel, when he and his clan move from Transjordan and settle in the territory Israel,[1] we may assume that this group came from an area where the name Jacob had been known for quite some time.[2] In moving into the hills of Cisjordan, where the name Israel belonged, the group, as time passed by, naturally became known as Israelites.

Eight years after his first campaign, Tuthmosis conquered Qadesh on the Orontes, which meant that the role of the prince of Qadesh as the leader of the Mitanni-supported coalition in Syria had ended. Qatna was also taken. The goal of this military expedition was to crush Mitanni. After having taken Qatna, Tuthmosis was able to march to the Euphrates three years later. With boats built close to Byblos or Ṣimyra and transported on ox carts, the army crossed the river at Carchemish. The king of Mitanni for some reason did not like to meet the Egyptians. His strategy could be termed 'elastic warfare', in that he withdrew, and Tuthmosis had to return without the expected glory befitting a victor. Before he left the territory he set up a stela on the east bank of the river as well as placing one close to the stela of his grandfather, Tuthmosis I.[3] Instead of victory, he obtained the honor of receiving gifts from the Hittites and the Babylonians, which for Tuthmosis and the rest of the Near Eastern princes meant that Egypt was now recognized as a world power. Hittites and Babylonians tried in this way to protect their interests and to keep the peace until they learned more about the Egyptian strength.

Tuthmosis is mentioned as having carried out 16 campaigns in Syria–Palestine, but some of these will most probably have been

Israeliten und ihre Nachbarstämme [Halle, 1906], pp. 280-81). Regarding the traditions about Jacob and the Aramaeans, see also T.L. Thompson, *The Historicity of the Patriarchal Narratives*, pp. 300-302.

1. Gen. 32.23-30. A repetition of this tradition occurs in Gen. 35.9-10, which links the change in name to Jacob's return from Paddan-Aram to Bethel. For the lateness of this, cf. R. de Vaux, *The Early History of Israel*, p. 172. The tradition in Gen. 35.1-15 is a 'cult adoption' text giving the ideological legitimation for Bethel as an Israelite cult place. As for the divergences in the Jacob tradition in Hos. 12.4-5, N.P. Lemche maintains that 'the Pentateuchal traditions did not have normative significance in Hosea's own time' (*Early Israel*, p. 314).

2. Cf. G.W. Ahlström, *Who were the Israelites?*, pp. 17-18.

3. J.H. Breasted, *Ancient Records of Egypt*, II, pp. 201-202.

inspection tours in order to keep the princes in line. Tuthmosis seems to have been more interested in the produce of the country than in destroying cities. If a city revolted, however, then it would be destroyed. Thus Tuthmosis' policy was perhaps in general more beneficial for the economy of the country.[1]

From the annals of the sixth campaign of Tuthmosis III we learn not only that he, as usual, took some prisoners, but also that among the prisoners were 'children of the princes and their brothers'. They were brought as hostages to Egypt.[2] In this way a future city ruler could be brought up at the Egyptian court and educated in the administrative affairs of the empire.[3] The aim of this was to 'create' a faithful vassal.

Tuthmosis was followed on the throne by his son Amenhotep II (1453-1419 BCE),[4] lauded as an athlete (which usually is said about every king) and an 'admirable' horseman.[5] As crown-prince he may have been at Megiddo and also may have visited Gaza. At the latter place he wrote two letters to the prince of Ta'anak, Talwashur, asking for horses, tribute and men. The prince is also reprimanded for not having shown up at Gaza. The date for these two letters (nos. 5 and 6) would thus be the time after the Hurrian-backed coalition had been defeated at Megiddo by Tuthmosis III.

According to known inscriptions, Amenhotep undertook at least two campaigns to Syria-Palestine as king. During the first one in his seventh year, quelling a rebellion in Takhshi,[6] the king is said to have reached Naharin. He then proceeded to Retenu and the Orontes area, taking prisoners and booty. The prince of Qadesh submitted and it is possible that Ugarit also acknowledged Egyptian supremacy.[7] The

1.　J.M. Weinstein, *BASOR* 241 (1981), p. 15.

2.　J.A. Wilson, *ANET*, pp. 238-39; cf. W. Helck, *Die Beziehungen*, p. 138; D.B. Redford, *History and Chronology*, p. 81.

3.　Cf. B.J. Kemp, *Imperialism in the Ancient World* (ed. P.D.A. Garnsey and C.R. Whittaker; Cambridge, 1978), p. 47. The same policy was used in Nubia; see P.J. Frandsen, 'Egyptian Imperialism', *Power and Propaganda* (ed. M. Trolle Larsen; Mesopotamia, 7; Copenhagen, 1979), p. 175-76.

4.　For the coregency between Tuthmosis and Amenhotep, see W.J. Murnane, *Ancient Egyptian Coregencies*, pp. 44-57.

5.　A. Gardiner, *Egypt of the Pharaohs*, p. 198.

6.　Probably an area north of Damascus.

7.　J.A. Wilson emends the writing *Ikat* to *Ikarit*, i.e., Ugarit (*ANET*, p. 246 n. 18).

Amada stela summarizing his campaign mentions, for instance, that six prisoners, probably princes, were taken to Thebes and killed there, then hung on the city wall. Another was taken to Napata in Nubia for the same kind of display.[1] These seven could have been those who started the rebellion.

Two years after the above-mentioned campaign, Amenhotep was again on the warpath through the Sharon to the Jezreel Valley, establishing the Egyptian supremacy. The campaign was undertaken in November. That was unusual, because military expeditions were not commonly carried out during the rainy season. Either Amenhotep understood how to stop a rebellion by means of a surprise attack,[2] or else he had to avert the greater threat of a Hurrian takeover. The identifiable cities are Aphek, Socoh and Yaham in the Sharon Plain and Anaharath in the eastern Esdraelon (in Josh. 19.19 assigned to Issachar).[3] The prince Qaqa of *qb'smn*, Geba-shumen (in the Jezreel Valley?),[4] was taken prisoner, dethroned and brought to Megiddo, the Egyptian base.[5]

From the fact that Amenhotep's troops intercepted a messenger[6] from the king of Mitanni during his earlier campaign in Palestine, we may also draw the conclusion that this expedition to the Sharon Plain and the Esdraelon Valley was not aimed only at rebellious Palestinian princes. Behind them was probably Mitanni under king Saustatar. Thus, the intercepted letter from Mitanni's king and the stela from the tell at Oreimeh may very well indicate conflicts between Mitanni and Egypt under Saustatar and Amenhotep II.[7] Egypt's supremacy over

1.   J.H. Breasted, *Ancient Records of Egypt*, II, §797, p. 313; J.A. Wilson, *ANET*, p. 248.

2.   Cf. Y. Aharoni, *The Land of the Bible*, p. 168.

3.   Y. Aharoni suggests that Anaharath should be identified with modern Tell el-Mukharkhash, c. 8 km southeast of Mt Tabor (*The Land of the Bible*, p. 168).

4.   This city has been identified with Tell el-'Amr near Sha'ar ha-'Amuqim by A. Malamat ('Campaigns of Amenhotep II and Thutmose IV to Canaan', *Scripta Hierosolymitana* 8 [1961], p. 223).

5.   J.A. Wilson, *ANET*, p. 247; cf. R. de Vaux, *The Early History of Israel*, p. 93. Because a stela with an inscription about a victory over Mitanni has been found at Khirbet el-'Oreimeh (ancient Chinnereth), Y. Aharoni draws the conclusion that Amenhotep fought a Mitanni army in Palestine (*The Land of the Bible*, p. 168).

6.   The messenger had a clay-tablet 'hanging around his neck' (J.A. Wilson, *ANET*, p. 246). The letter was probably for one of the Palestinian princes.

7.   Cf. W. Helck, *Die Beziehungen*, p. 163.

Palestine and parts of Syria was in danger. It is also during the reign of Amenhotep II that northern Syria and the territory at the Euphrates were lost for Egypt. The first campaign does not mention any cities north of Ni[1] as being taken or having submitted. The second campaign had as its goal the retention of Palestine within the Egyptian orbit. The king of Mitanni had gained some control in the north, and the Egyptians were not powerful enough to change the picture.

The list of prisoners taken during the second campaign is interesting in that it gives us information about the population of the country as seen through the eyes of an Egyptian scribe. A total of about 101,812 prisoners were taken.[2] The majority, 36,300, are called Hurrians (33%). The next two largest groups were the Neges, 15,070 (probably the Nuhashshi from Syria), and the Shasu (nomads) counting 15,000. Only 640 were Canaanites, 550 were the *maryannu*. There were 30,652 family members.[3] In all 232 princes, 323 princesses and 270 royal concubines were among the prisoners. 3600 prisoners are called *'apīru*. These will be discussed below.[4]

From this list we can draw the conclusion that the majority of the population of Palestine was called 'Hurrians' by the Egyptians, even if other groups could have been included. It is not necessary to see 'Hurrians' in this text as referring to ethnicity.[5] The whole country had been called Kharu/Hurru by the Egyptians since the Eighteenth Dynasty.[6] The Canaanites mentioned in the Amenhotep list refer not

---

1.   This is a Syrian city in the area of the northern Orontes. A. Gardiner identified it with Apamea, which would be modern Qalaat el-Madiq, c. 40 km NW of Hamath (*Egypt of the Pharaohs*, p. 179); cf. W. Helck, *Die Beziehungen*, p. 140.

2.   E.F. Wente opines that this large amount of 'prisoners' cannot be understood as 'a large-scale introduction of slaves into Egypt', but that it is perhaps to be understood as a census of the population of the country under Egyptian rule ('Egypt, History of', *Encyclopaedia Britannica*, VI [15th edn], p. 473).

3.   See W. Helck, *Die Beziehungen*, p. 344; J.A. Wilson, *ANET*, pp. 246-47; and Y. Aharoni, *The Land of the Bible*, 2nd edn, p. 168.

4.   We ought to note that the term *'3mw* does not occur in these pharaonic lists, which would have been expected if the so-called Amorites had been identical with these *'3mw*, Asiatics, as sometimes has been maintained. See the discussion in Chapter 3.

5.   The term 'Hurrian' has obviously presented a problem for the biblical writer of Deut. 2.12, who sees the Hurrians as the original inhabitants of Seir-Edom. The Egyptian terminology has thus been long lived.

6.   The term was also used by the scribes of Tuthmosis III (*ANET*, p. 235).

to the population of the country but to the merchants, the wealthy citizens of the country. Thus, Palestine was not yet known as Canaan by the Egyptians.

The list is interesting from the point of view that it provides data not only about the geographical spread of the population, Hurrians being the Palestinians, Neges representing Syrians and the Shasu comprising the nomads. It also provides us with information about social and professional groups, such as the *maryannu* (charioteers, nobility), Canaanites (merchants), and the *'apīru*. This latter term has in this list of Amenhotep probably been used for mercenaries hired by the Syro-Palestinian princes. It is not an ethnic term. Semantically this word could be used for the social class of outcasts, refugees, fugitives, rebels and slaves, as well as for mercenaries.[1] Sometimes it could be used for robbers and raiders, Sumerian SA.GAZ, Akkadian *ḫabirū/ḫapirū*, and also as a synonym for *ḫabbatu*, robber. Another use of the term was as a designation for immigrants and foreigners, and as such one can see it as a parallel to Hebrew *gēr*.[2] In the letters from the fourteenth century BCE found at Tell el-Amarna[3] in Egypt, the *'apīru* are often mentioned as hostile groups or political enemies of the Canaanite city states. Thus, the term came to be used as a characterization for people disturbing the social order.[4] From the Egyptian inscriptions and from

---

1. D.J. Wiseman, *The Alalakh Tablets*, texts 180-82. For the discussion about *'apīru*, see T. Säve-Söderbergh, 'The *'prw* as Vintagers in Egypt', *Orientalia Suecana* 1 (1952), pp. 5-14; J. Bottéro, *Le problème des Ḫabiru* (Cahiers de la Societé Asiatique, 12; Paris 1954); M. Greenberg, *The Ḫab/piru* (AOS, 39; New Haven, 1955); R. Borger, 'Das Problem der 'apīru ('Habiru')', *ZDPV* 74 (1958), pp. 121-32; R. de Vaux, 'Le problème des Ḫapiru après quinze années', *JNES* 27 (1968), pp. 221-28; *idem, Early History of Israel*, pp. 105-12; G. Buccellati, '"Apiru and Munnabtutu—The Stateless of the First Cosmopolitan Age', *JNES* 36 (1977), pp. 145-47; M. Liverani, 'Communautés de village et palais royale dans la Syrie du IIème Millénaire', *Journal for the Economic and Social History of the Orient* 18 (1975), pp. 159-64; M. Weippert, 'Abraham der Hebräer?', *Bib* 52 (1971), pp. 412-14; N.P. Lemche, '"Hebrew" as a National Name for Israel', *Studia Theologica* 33 (1979), pp. 1-23; cf. O. Loretz, *Habiru–Hebräer: Eine socio-linguistische Studie über die Herkunft des Gentiliziums 'ibrî vom Appellativum ḫabiru* (BZAW, 160; Berlin, 1984), pp. 56-88.

2. R. Borger, *ZDPV* 74 (1958), pp. 122-23.

3. On the subject of letters from the Syro-Palestinian princes to the Pharaoh mostly asking for military help against neighboring city states, see below.

4. C.H.J. de Geus says the term *'apīru* 'has been extended in the Amarna period to something that it did not cover before' (*The Tribes of Israel*, p. 184).

the Amarna texts it is clear that *'apīru* is not used as an ethnic term.[1]
From these texts we can draw the conclusion that the term has been
used in order to defame some opponents.[2]

The *'apīru* and the nomads (Shasu) are the people that the Egyptians,
according to the inscriptions of the Eighteenth and Nineteenth dynasties, met in Palestine. These are therefore the ancestors of many of the
'tribes' of the central hill country that we later meet in the biblical
narratives about the period of the so-called Judges.

It is probable that a district division of Palestine came into effect
after Tuthmosis' first campaign which lead to the victory at Megiddo.
Because of the grouping of the cities mentioned in Tuthmosis' list,
S. Yeivin suggested that the list was made up according to the administrative districts.[3] This is impossible to prove, but it is probable that
the Pharaoh had placed administrative supervisors, *rābiṣu*, in some
garrison cities besides Gaza, which seems to have been the center of
the Egyptian administration in Palestine.[4] The town is often called 'the

---

1.   Against the theory that *'apīru* should be identical with *'ibri*, Hebrew, see
B. Landsberger, 'Ḥabiru und Lulaḥḥu', *Kleinasiatische Forschungen* 1 (1930),
pp. 330-34. M. Liverani sees these terms as almost identical as to their content, i.e.,
people who have 'transgressed' socially or geographically ('Il fuoruscitismo in Siria
nella Tarda età del Bronzo', *Rivista Storia Italiana* 77 [1965], pp. 315-36).

2.   Cf. M. Weippert, *The Settlement of the Israelite Tribes in Palestine* (SBT,
2nd Ser., 21; London, 1971), pp. 71-73.

3.   'The Third District in Thutmosis III's List of Palestino-Syrian Towns', *JEA*
36 (1950), pp. 51-62; cf. Y. Aharoni, *The Land of the Bible*, p. 147. J.M. Weinstein
maintains that 'a true political, military, and commercial empire under the domination
of Egypt did not come about until after the conquest of Megiddo', i.e., after 1481
BCE (*BASOR* 241 [1981], p. 7). If so, a district division of the Asiatic holdings
would have come first at that time, and therefore the scribe of the Annals would have
been writing sometime after that division was made.

4.   The mention of Gaza by Amenhotep (II ?) in the Taʻanak letter no. 6.12-14 is
usually seen as an indication for this city being the administrative center of the country; cf. W.F. Albright, 'A Prince of Taanach in the Fifteenth Century BCE', *BASOR*
94 (1944), p. 27; R. de Vaux, *The Early History of Israel*, p. 97. That is possible,
but because Megiddo is also mentioned by a certain Akhiyami (according to Albright
he is Amenhotep II [p. 20 n. 44]), one could as well maintain that Megiddo was an
administrative center too. This would be natural for a garrison city. In agreement
with B. Landsberger (*JCS* 8 [1954], p. 59 n. 123) and A. Malamat (*Scripta
Hierosolymitana* 8 [1961], pp. 218-231), it can certainly be said that Amenhotep II
had been at Gaza but the royal documents from Taʻanak (= letters 5 and 6) do not say
anything about Gaza as an administrative center for the whole country.

city which the ruler has seized', referring to Tuthmosis III's capture of the town. The reason why the Asiatic territory was not incorporated as a province, unlike Nubia, may be that Egypt was not militarily strong enough, and therefore needed the support of city princes. This can be supported by the fact that the Egyptians had to carry out so many campaigns in Syria-Palestine during the Eighteenth and Nineteenth dynasties in order to put down rebellions. The conflicts with Mitanni and later the Hittite empire also indicate that Egypt was not able to impose fully its hegemony in Syria.[1] In fact, after Tuthmosis III the Egyptian sphere of dominion slowly receded, and during the reign of Tutankhamon (1334–1325 BCE) the borderline was just north of Byblos and south of Qadesh.[2] It is possible that the campaigns of Tuthmosis III resulted in Egypt seeing the economic advantage of controlling these Asiatic countries and therefore being more inclined to have the princes acknowledge Egyptian supremacy than militarily subduing the city states. By the oath to the pharaoh the princes were made responsible for law and order, but the Egyptian supremacy was established by some garrisons and store cities with their administrative personnel, as well as by placing 'supervisors' at key positions.[3] During the time of Amenhotep III (1386–1349 BCE) the Egyptian military presence was very small, which indicates that the relationship between Egypt and the Asiatic princes functioned without too much friction.[4] This is the background for the many letters about military help that were sent from the princes to the Egyptian court during the Amarna period (fourteenth cent. BCE) when some internal troubles had begun to boil and the princes asked for military help.

One may speculate that Mitanni's power weakened somewhat during the later part of Amenhotep II's reign. The reason for this was the growing strength of the Hittite kingdom under Hattushili II (c. 1405–1385 BCE) and Tudhaliya III (c. 1385–1365). Aleppo, for instance, was taken and destroyed by Tudhaliya. This meant that Mitanni's king

---

1. Cf. B.J. Kemp, 'Imperialism and Empire in New Kingdom Egypt (c. 1575–1087 BCE)', *Imperialism in the Ancient World* (ed. P.D.A. Garnsey and C.R. Whittaker; Cambridge, 1978), pp. 54-55. It is hard to accept R. de Vaux's statement that Tuthmosis had 'broken the power of Mitanni' (*Early History of Israel*, p. 92).

2. See W. Helck, *Die Beziehungen*, p. 165.

3. See, for instance, P.J. Frandsen, 'Egyptian Imperialism', *Power and Propaganda* (ed. M. Trolle Larsen), pp. 174-75.

4. Cf. W. Helck, *Die Beziehungen*, pp. 253-55.

had to be more concerned than earlier about his western border and his sphere of influence in Syria. Under Amenhotep's son and successor, Tuthmosis IV (1419–1386), the relationship between Mitanni and Egypt changed from hostility to a peaceful coexistence, an alliance, in order to stem the Hittite threat. It is possible that the change in political attitude started under Amenhotep II, who reports that members of the nobility from Mitanni, a country that 'knew not Egypt',[1] came loaded with gifts in order to establish friendly relations.[2] It is possible that the initiative to make an alliance came from Tuthmosis IV, whose goal was to keep the peace with Mitanni. He sent some letters to king Artatama of Mitanni asking to marry one of his daughters. The alliance between Mitanni and Egypt lasted until Suppiluliuma of Hatti conquered Mitanni in the latter half of the fourteenth century and established most of Syria within the Hittite sphere of influence.

There are some inscriptions that mention that Tuthmosis IV campaigned in Asia. For instance, an inscription at Karnak as well as some inscriptions from tombs of two of his officials report that he conquered Babylon, Naharin, Qadesh, Tunip, Takshi (also in the Orontes Valley), and the Shasu people. As well, he is said to be 'the conqueror of the land of Kharu' (Palestine),[3] and to have taken prisoners from Gezer (?).[4] He is also said to have been at Sidon, according to one of the Amarna letters,[5] but whether this refers to a friendly or hostile visit is not known. Concerning the reliability of these inscriptions, one may say that it is probable that Tuthmosis had been campaigning in Asia, but the engraved reports are too much in style with those of his forefathers. The scribes may have copied part of the inscriptions of Tuthmosis III and Amenhotep II. We therefore cannot get a clear picture of this pharaoh's Asiatic campaigns. He may also have been the last pharaoh of the Eighteenth Dynasty to campaign in Asia. His son, Amenhotep III (1386–1349) probably thought that he did not need to.[6]

1.   J.H. Breasted, *Ancient Records of Egypt*, II, §804, p. 317.

2.   W. Helck, *Die Beziehungen*, p. 163.

3.   W. Helck, *Urkunden der 18. Dynastie 2140–2162 (Übersetzung)* (Berlin, 1961), p. 150. Cf. J.H. Breasted, *Records of Ancient Egypt*, II, pp. 324-26.

4.   J.A. Breasted, *Records of Ancient Egypt*, II, §821, p. 326.

5.   EA 85, pp. 69-71.

6.   A Victory tablet in Amenhotep's mortuary temple at Thebes shows the king driving over the enemies of both Cush and Syria-Palestine. This may be part of the royal style, and does not really prove that the king had been campaigning in Asia; cf. J.H. Breasted, *Ancient Records of Egypt*, II, p. 343. During his time, the mining at

After all, he received the tribute and the taxes from the Syro-Palestinian princes. Small military forces in different Syro-Palestinian cities seem to have been enough to keep the city states under control.[1]

The Amarna Period

In 1887 about 350 tablets written in cuneiform were discovered at a forgotten place, Tell el-Amarna, c. 300 km south of Cairo. Later finds have increased the amount to c. 400 tablets. The tell is the modern site of Pharaoh Amenhotep IV's (Akhenaten) capital Akhetaten ('the horizon of Aten'). These tablets were part of the royal archive.[2] The language is Akkadian mixed with some Canaanisms, as well as some Hurrian words. This is understandable because the majority of the letters (c. 300) are written by Syro-Palestinian scribes, and among the tablets are also some school texts. Most of the letters are from Syro-Palestinian princes to Pharaoh and his court. A few are from the Pharaoh himself. About 40 letters show Egypt's diplomatic contacts with Babylon, Mitanni, Cyprus and the Hittite king.[3] The letters span the periods of Amenhotep III and his son, Amenhotep IV (1350–1334 BCE), who moved the capital from Thebes and built a new city for his

Serabit el-Khadem continued, according to a stela found there (p. 352).

1. A.R. Schulman, 'Some Observations on the Military Background of the Amarna Period', *JARCE* 3 (1964), pp. 64-65; W. Helck, *Die Beziehungen*, pp. 253-54.

2. See J.A. Knudtzon, *Die el-Amarna Tafeln* (VAB, 2; Leipzig, 1907–15 [repr. Aalen, 1964]); J. de Koning, *Studien over de el-Amarnabrieven en het Oude-Testament inzonderheid uit historisch oogpunt* (Delft, 1940); W. von Soden, 'Zu den Amarnabriefen aus Babylon und Assur', *Or* NS 21 (1952); W.F. Albright, 'The Amarna Letters from Palestine', *CAH*, II.2, pp. 98-116; E.F. Campbell, *The Chronology of the Amarna Letters* (Baltimore, 1964); C. Kühne, *Die Chronologie der internationalen Korrespondenz von El-Amarna* (AOAT, 17; Neukirchen–Vluyn, 1973); E.K. Werner, 'The Amarna Period of Eighteenth Dynasty Egypt: Bibliography Supplement 1979', *American Research Center in Egypt, Newsletter* 114 (1981), pp. 18-34; and *idem*, 'The Amarna Period of the Eighteenth Dynasty Egypt: Bibliography Supplement 1982–1983', *American Research Center in Egypt, Newsletter* 126 (1984), pp. 21-38. Cf. also M. Mode, 'Die Entdeckung von Tell el-Amarna: Der Beitrag von Lepsuis zur Erforschung der Amarna-Zeit', *Das Altertum* 30 (1984), pp. 93-102. Some of the letters from Palestine are translated by W.F. Albright and G.E. Mendenhall in *ANET*, pp. 483-90.

3. Cf. Y.L. Holmes, 'The Messengers of the Amarna Letters', *JAOS* 95 (1975), pp. 376-81; K.A. Kitchen, *Suppiluliuma and the Amarna Pharaohs* (Liverpool, 1962).

god Aten at modern el-Amarna. Aten was a special aspect of the sun-god, Re, namely the sun disk. This god was now presented as the universal god, the creator god, and the only one worthy of worship. This emphasis on Aten and the promotion of his worship created some problems for Amenhotep IV. The empire god, Amun-Re at Thebes, and his priesthood, may have become too powerful; thus, when the king could not really change things in Thebes, he built a new capital which also seems to have been constructed in some haste. With the king and court followed the royal archives.[1] The move may have been caused not only by religious but also political and financial reasons. One has usually seen Akhenaten as an innovator and a heretic. Even if he was an innovator, his inscriptions present him as a king following the old Egyptian tradition, as may be clear, for instance, from his 'Hymn to Aten'.[2] His 'unique monotheism was itself, in part, an abortive offshoot of royal absolutism'.[3]

The Amarna letters have often been used as indications for the Egyptian empire being in decline during the fourteenth century BCE.[4] The reason for this hypothesis is that the princes of Syria-Palestine very often complain about disturbances caused by the *'apīru* or by some hostile city state, and therefore they want the Pharaoh to send help to restore order and peace. Sometimes they ask for no more than 10–50 men.[5] However, many letters are replies to inquiries by the Egyptian king concerning the duties of the vassals, such as tribute, the security of the caravans, delivering of slaves, and the well-being of Egyptian commissioners, and so forth. We get a picture of particular

1. Cf. E.F. Campbell, *The Chronology of the Amarna Letters*, pp. 32-36.
2. J.A. Wilson, *ANET*, pp. 369-71. This hymn 'contains little that had not been said in earlier hymns to the sun-god' (A. Gardiner, *Egypt of the Pharaohs*, p. 227). The parallels that occur in Ps. 104 of the Old Testament may stem from the influence that the Egyptian court literature had on the sages of Palestine over centuries.
3. D. O'Connor, 'New Kingdom and Third Intermediate Period, 1552–664 BCE', B.G. Trigger, B.J. Kemp, D. O'Connor and A.B. Lloyd, *Ancient Egypt: A Social History* (Cambridge, 1983), p. 221. In this case one could say with J.H. Breasted that 'Monotheism is but imperialism in religion' (*The Development of Religion and Thought in Ancient Egypt* [New York, 1912], p. 315).
4. Cf. Y. Aharoni, *The Land of the Bible*, 2nd edn, p. 170; J. Bright, *A History of Israel*, pp. 109-10; J. Strange, *Caphtor/Keftiu*, p. 110.
5. It is not known whether this meant that Pharaoh should send these as a 'body-guard' for the prince, or whether the request meant officers in command of troops. The latter may be the answer.

political problems of the city states, the warfare between them, and the disturbances of the so-called '*apīru*. We cannot derive a reliable picture of the social conditions of Palestine during the Amarna period from these texts, but it is clear that some social unrest and disturbances did occur.[1] It is impossible, however, to find a peasant revolt being referred to in these letters, as has been maintained by some.[2] For instance, the letters from the kings of Hatti, Babylon, Assyria and Mitanni do not mention anything about a peasant revolt or other unstable social conditions. The letters from the Babylonian king Burnaburiash do not even mention any '*apīru* disturbing the transport of goods and people.[3] Instead we learn from EA 7 and 8 that some vassals of Pharaoh had plundered a caravan. EA 7 mentions Biriawaza, who seems to be one of Pharaoh's most faithful vassals.[4] His residence city is not known, but he seems to have ruled over a territory from northern Transjordan in the south to Qatna in the north. Kumidi (Kamid el-Loz) could have been his seat of residence. Among the robbers mentioned in EA 8 was a son of the city prince of Acco, Sharatum (Zurata in EA 85).[5] It is not possible to maintain on the basis of these letters, as M.L. Chaney does, that there was anarchy in Syria-Palestine during this period.[6] Bandits and outcasts have always existed. We do not have any material from the periods before and after the Amarna time, thus we cannot make any judgment by comparison. To piece together the many incidents in the city states and their troubles with neighbors or citizens in order to present a picture

1. Cf. M. Liverani, 'La royauté syrienne de l'âge du bronze récent', *RAI* 19 (1974), pp. 352-55.

2. G.E. Mendenhall, 'The Hebrew Conquest of Palestine', *BA* 25 (1962), pp. 66-87, followed by N.K. Gottwald, *The Tribes of Yahweh: A Sociology of the Religion of Liberated Israel, 1250–1050 BCE* (New York, 1979); J.M. Halligan, 'The Role of the Peasant in the Amarna Period', *Palestine in Transition: The Emergence of Ancient Israel* (ed. D.N. Freedman and D.F. Graf; Sheffield, 1983), pp. 15-24; R.G. Boling, *Judges* (AB, 6A; Garden City, NY, 1975), p. 12.

3. Cf. F.J. Giles, *Ikhnaton: Legend and History* (London, 1970), p. 158.

4. See the discussion by R. Hachmann in *Kamid el-Loz–Kumidi* (ed. D.O. Edzard *et al.*; Saarbrücker Beiträge zur Altertumskunde, 7; Bonn, 1970), pp. 64-76.

5. Cf. Y. Aharoni, *The Land of the Bible*, 2nd edn, p. 172.

6. 'Ancient Palestinian Peasant Movements and the Formation of Premonarchic Israel', *Palestine in Transition* (ed. D.N. Freedman and D.F. Graf; Sheffield, 1983), p. 79.

of Egypt's political decline would be to misunderstand the message of these letters.[1] To write the history of Palestine during the fourteenth century based on these texts is next to impossible. Still, the information we get from this corpus is most valuable because the period is otherwise meagerly attested. One thing seems to be clear, however. These texts do not support the theory that Egypt's power was on the decline. The infighting between the city princes can as well be taken as an indication for the opposite. The rivalry between the princes may even have been amusing to the Pharaoh. As long as they were feuding, Egypt did not need to worry about any loss of territory. Egypt's power was both acknowledged and recognized, and the princes, for their part, appealed to the king of Egypt in matters that would enhance their own position. From the viewpoint of international politics, the letters from the south-Palestinian princes are thus of less importance, concerned as they are about local problems.

It is understandable that people have seen a decline in the Egyptian power at this time and that the letters found at el-Amarna have been seen to support such a theory (see Map 8). The Hittite kingdom in Anatolia was pressing south, threatening both the position of Egypt and Mitanni as superpowers. The threat is echoed in some Amarna letters, especially those dealing with the conflicts between Rib-Adda of Byblos and the kings of Amurru. We know, for instance, that Rib-Adda complains to Pharaoh in a letter, EA 74, that all his people have chosen to join the *'apīru*. From this we may draw the conclusion that the population of Byblos opposed the rule of their prince or his policies. It is also possible that Abdi-Ashirta of Amurru had encouraged the people of the city state Byblos to rebel. Some of the people living in Amurru could have been refugees, *'apīru*, from Byblos whom Abdi-Ashirta may have used both in his army and as a 'fifth column' undermining the resistance of the Byblites.[2] Abdi-Ashirta's son, Aziru, continued his father's policies, and he seems to have been a most powerful ruler in southern Syria.[3] His problem was to keep his

---

1. M. Liverani: 'The problem is not to identify the facts narrated in the letters, but rather the way in which they are narrated, the reasons for which they are narrated' (*Berytus* 31 [1983], p. 42).

2. Cf. M. Liverani, 'Politics of Abdi-Ashirta of Amurru', *MANE* 1.5 (trans. M.L. Jaffe; Malibu, CA, 1979), pp. 16-18.

3. For Abdi-Ashirta's death, see W.L. Moran, 'The Death of "Abdi-Asirta"', *EI* 9 (1969), pp. 94-99.

territory as an Egyptian vassal state while he at the same time tried to keep friendly diplomatic connections with the Hittites. He well understood that his future would most probably be decided by the northern power rather than by Egypt. Having been called to Egypt several times,[1] he finally went.[2] One of the reasons why he delayed his departure to Egypt could have been that he feared that the Hittite king, Suppiluliuma, would conquer Amurru. The Hittites had taken Qatna and Nuhashshe (EA 164.20-21), and they were thus very close to Amurru. Also, Qadesh had become a vassal to the Hittites and Aziru had allied himself with its king, Aitakama. This was, of course, considered dangerous by the Egyptians, who therefore prompted the Pharaoh to order Aziru to the Egyptian court with the threat to kill both him and his family if he did not obey (EA 162). This shows that Akhenaten did not completely ignore the city states and the problems they could make for him. At the Egyptian court Aziru defended himself by claiming to be the defender of Egypt's interests in Syria, and he returned home as a faithful vassal. He continued, however, his double dealing, and when Tutankhamon died Aziru became a Hittite vassal by signing a treaty with king Suppiluliuma.[3]

Abdi-Ashirta and later his son Aziru[4] always assured the Egyptian court of their faithfulness, but at the same time they could not be indifferent to the danger the Hittites represented. The kingdom of Amurru was located in the mountainous area to the northeast and north of Byblos and west of the Orontes, thus it was very close to the Hittites. The prince of Amurru, Abdi-Ashirta, was a sworn enemy of Rib-Adda of Byblos. Abdi-Ashirta tried with some luck to expand his territory, threatening the cities on the coast. He seems, for instance, to have taken Ṣumur (EA 71 and 84), but later he lost it again to

---

1. See, for instance, EA 162.

2. EA 169.

3. H. Freydank, 'Eine hethitische Fassung des Vertrags zwischen dem Hethiterkönig Suppiluliuma und Aziru von Amurru', *MIO* 7 (1959-60), pp. 356–81. See also H. Klengel, 'Aziru von Amurru und seine Rolle in der Geschichte der Amarnazeit', *MIO* 10 (1964), pp. 57-83; K.A. Kitchen, *Suppiluliuma and the Amarna Pharaohs*, pp. 17-19. For the chronological problems of Aziru's regime, see R. Krauss, *Das Ende der Amarnazeit* (Hildesheimer Ägyptologische Beiträge, 7; Hildesheim, 1978), pp. 59-62.

4. A Hittite inscription gives Aziru the title king: *KBo* X.2aff.

Rib-Adda (EA 102-104).[1] We cannot label his kingdom a city state because it reached from the coast north of Irqata into the mountains of Lebanon and to the Orontes Valley. Its territory has thus been larger than that of Shechem, which reached from the Jezreel Valley down to the vicinity of Gezer and Aijalon and the city state of Jerusalem.

The city of Sumur may have been an old Amurru town. Whether the city had been the capital of the kingdom of Amurru or not is not clear. The country did not have an urban center as its capital. M. Liverani suggests, therefore, that Abdi-Ashirta may have resided in both Sumur and Tunip, and perhaps in some other cities too.[2] This can perhaps be explained by the fact that Amurru was largely a country of pastoralists and farmers. Another problem is that we do not know why the kings of this country had preserved the name Amurru. It is possible, however, that Amurru had been the name of the Hyksos vassal kingdom. This may explain why Sumur also was the district capital of the Beqa' Valley and Upper Galilee. This district may also have comprised the Phoenician cities.[3]

The name Sumur occurs in the Old Testament in the name of the Zemarites, children of Canaan,[4] together with the peoples of Hamath and Arvad. The reference to 'the land that remains', Josh. 13.4, that should be conquered, mentions also the land of 'the Sidonians unto Aphek, to the border of the Amorites'.[5] The term Amorite refers here to the kingdom of Amurru north of Canaan and Phoenicia, a kingdom that had not been forgotten by the tradition. The northern border of Canaan was thus for the biblical writer located between Byblos and Sumur.[6]

The territory of Lab'ayu of Shechem may have been large, probably the largest in Palestine proper, but being in the hills it cannot have had too many settlements. From archaeological surveys we also know that this territory had, besides the cities Shechem, Dothan, Tirzah and

1. Cf. K.A. Kitchen, *Suppiluliuma and the Amarna Pharaohs*, pp. 41-42.
2. 'Social Implications in the Politics of Abdi-Ashirta of Amurru', *MANE* 1.5, p. 15.
3. EA 155.66; cf. M. Noth, *Die Ursprünge des alten Israel im Lichte neuer Quellen* (Cologne, 1961), p. 27.
4. Gen. 10.18; 1 Chron. 1.16.
5. This is the Aphek east of Byblos.
6. Y. Aharoni locates the border point on the coast of Ras Shaqqah, c. 30 km north of Byblos (*The Land of the Bible*, 2nd edn, p. 73).

Bethel, very few sites in the LB period. In the district of Mt Ephraim one has found only five sites, and in the Benjamin territory two or possibly three.[1] In Manasseh were found less than thirty LB sites. Most of them are in the northern areas.[2] In the light of the above, Lab'ayu's need for territorial expansions would be understandable. He needed more land for agriculture. He had alliances with Milkilu of Gezer and with his father-in-law, Tagu,[3] probably from the area somewhere southwest of the Carmel.[4] Later Lab'ayu, however, became an enemy to Milkilu, as to most of the surrounding city states. He had taken Gath-padalla in the Sharon and also Gath-rimmon (EA 250), both probably part of Gezer's territory.

Lab'ayu is often accused of having aided the *'apīru*. In one letter, EA 254, he denies that he knows about his son's association with the *'apīru*. Also the king of Hazor[5] is said to have helped the *'apīru* (EA 148), and several letters seem to indicate that most of Palestine is *'apīru* territory. In the letters EA 287 and 289 Abdi-Hepa of Jerusalem, one of Lab'ayu's adversaries, even complains about the prince of Shechem having given his territory over to the *'apīru*.[6] Shuwardata[7] also accuses Lab'ayu for having taken some of his cities (EA 280.30-32). Later, after Lab'ayu's death, his sons are also accused of doing the same. One may assume that Lab'ayu had hired mercenaries, here called *'apīru*, for his wars of expansion.[8] Lab'ayu also tried to advance into the Jezreel valley, a territory that would have been economically

1. I. Finkelstein, *Archaeology of Settlement*, pp. 185-87.

2. A. Zertal, 'The Israelite Settlement in the Hill Country of Manasseh' (PhD dissertation, Tel Aviv, 1986) (Hebrew).

3. EA 249 and 263-64.

4. R. de Vaux, *The Early History of Israel*, p. 103.

5. Hazor's ruler is the only one of the princes of Palestine who is called king (*šarru*) (EA 148.41), and who also labels himself 'king' (EA 227.3). His name was Abdi-Tishri (EA 228.3).

6. *ANET*, pp. 488-89.

7. It is not known where Shuwardata reigned. E.F. Campbell places him 'south of Jerusalem and east of Lachish' (*The Chronology*, p. 110). W. Helck sees him as the prince of Hebron (*Die Beziehungen*, p. 185). Because of the information given in EA 290 (Abdi-Hepa accusing Shuwardata and Milkilu of getting soldiers from Keilah, Ginti, i.e. Gath, and Gezer), Y. Aharoni sees Shuwardata as the prince of Gath (*The Land of the Bible*, 2nd edn, p. 174).

8. Cf. H. Reviv, 'The Government of Shechem in the el-Amarna period and the Days of Abimelech', *IEJ* 16 (1966), p. 253.

beneficial for his mountain kingdom. He seems to have had some success taking, for instance, Shunem and Burkana south of modern Jenin (EA 250). He also laid siege to Megiddo (EA 244). Having extended his territory into the Sharon plain and now also into the Jezreel Valley, he collided with the economic interests of Pharaoh, who ordered him to go to Egypt. The prince of Megiddo, Biridiya, finally captured him and placed him in the custody of Zurata of Acco. This prince obviously loved money more than keeping an eye on a hostile prisoner, so he obtained a ransom and let Lab'ayu go free. The idea was originally that Lab'ayu should be sent by ship to Egypt (EA 245). Close to Gina (modern Jenin), he was, however, murdered (cf. EA 250.16-18). Biridiya of Megiddo never had time to intercede.

There is some information about Shechem's kingdom in the time after Lab'ayu's death. Two of his sons seem to have ruled the territory, and one of them, Mut-Ba'lu, became king of Peḥel (Pella) in Transjordan. One of the letters of Abdi-Hepa mentions that Lab'ayu's sons were in an alliance with Milkilu of Gezer (EA 287).[1] From this we can draw the conclusion that the Shechem kingdom still reached down to the Gezer territory.

One of the letters mentioning Hazor is of a special interest because Hazor's king, Abdi-Tishri, is the only Palestinian kinglet who labels himself king, *šàr* ^{URU}*ḫa-zu-ri*^{KI}, 'king of Hazor' (EA 227.3). He also stresses for Pharaoh the fact that he protects the cities of the Egyptian king, *šarri beli-ia*, 'the king, my lord'. The prince of Ashtartu (Ashtaroth), Ayyab, accuses 'the man of Hazor' of having taken three of his cities (EA 256.17-20).[2] The impression one gets from the Amarna material is that Hazor is a powerful and aggressive north-Palestinian state. This may explain why the princes of both Tyre and Ashtaroth accuse the king of Hazor of having joined the *'apīru*. Abdi-Tirshi could perhaps be compared with Lab'ayu. It is impossible to get any details about the political situation in northern Palestine during this period. North of Hazor was the territory that Biriawaza ruled over, but there is no information about his relations with Hazor nor the possible conflicts of interest in northern Transjordan between these two states. We do not even know if these two princes were contemporaries. The excavations at Hazor have shown that the city most

---

1.   *ANET*, p. 488.

2.   For the term 'man' as referring to the king, see W. von Soden, *Herrscher im alten Orient* (Berlin, 1954), p. 38.

probably was destroyed in the fourteenth century. Can this have been done by some enemies of Hazor, such as Biriawaza and/or some groups of *'apīru*? Y. Yadin connects the destruction of stratum XIV with Seti I.[1] It could just as well have been done during the Amarna period.

The el-Amarna texts also give some information about the behavior of the Egyptian troops in occupied territories. For instance, the prince of Jerusalem, Abdi-Hepa, complains not only about Milkilu and Tagu having taken Rubutu (?), then asking the king to request that the cities of Lachish, Ashkelon and Gezer supply the Egyptians stationed in the Shephelah, but he also complains about the Nubian troops stationed in Jerusalem and its territory who had burglarized his palace and almost killed Abdi-Hepa himself (EA 287). The Jerusalem prince says that he did not come to power thanks to his father or mother, but rather the 'arm of the mighty king brought me into the house of my father' (EA 286.9-13, and cf. 287.26-28).[2] This phrase should not be taken as proof for Abdi-Hepa not being of royal birth. It is rather a way to acknowledge the vassalship which also is expressed in letter EA 287.60-63: Pharaoh is said to have chosen to 'set his name forever in the land of Jerusalem'.[3]

Other Palestinian city states mentioned in these letters are Lachish, Aijalon, Jarmuth, Ashkelon, Gaza, Achshaph, Beth-Shan, and in Transjordan, Peḥel (Pella), Busruna, Kenath, Ashtaroth, and Upe (the Damascus territory). All of these are more or less involved in intrigues and problems with enemies, marauding bands and mercenary soldiers.[4] We cannot get a clear picture of what the term *'apīru* refers to in every case, but one thing seems to be clear, they are not all newcomers to the country.[5] Therefore it would be wrong to equate them

1. *Hazor of Those Kingdoms*, p. 200.

2. J.A. Wilson, *ANET*, p. 487, cf. p. 488. See also M. Weippert, '*lu*AD.DA.A.NI in den Briefen des Abduheba von Jerusalem an den Pharaoh', *UF* 6 (1974), pp. 415-19; cf. W.L. Moran, 'The Syrian Scribe of the Jerusalem Amarna Letters', *Unity and Diversity* (ed. H. Goedicke and J.J.M. Roberts; Baltimore, 1975), pp. 154-55.

3. The deuteronomic phrase about Yahweh having chosen the place Jerusalem, Deut. 12.11 *et al.*, is thus an expression of a very old treaty tradition.

4. For instance, the king of Ashtaroth, Ayyab, is mentioned in connection with restoring some cities east of Lake Tiberias (the land of Gari) to the king of Pella, Mutba'lu (EA 256; *ANET*, p. 486; cf. W. Helck, *Die Beziehungen*, p. 184).

5. Cf. O. Loretz, *Habiru–Hebräer*, p. 33.

with a 'wave of Semites just beginning to penetrate the lands of the Fertile Crescent, a movement which culminated in the arrival of the Hebrews and Arameans', as Y. Aharoni maintains.[1] We have no reliable information that these *'apīru* represented any tribal societies. Neither do the letters from el-Amarna mention any such settled societies in the hills or in the lowlands. Granted that the situation could very much have changed through the upheavals around 1200 BCE with the influx of new peoples both from the north and the south, the east and perhaps also from the west, some realignment of tribes and/or the formation of new tribes may have occurred, although it should be noted that certain city states such as Shechem and Jerusalem still remained in existence.

As to the Egyptian administrative organization, W. Helck has advocated that Syria-Palestine was divided by the Egyptians into three districts with the administrative centers at Gaza, Kumidi and Ṣumur.[2] The top official in these places is called *rābiṣu*. However, because several men are given this title, one may conclude that either a development in the district division has occurred or the *rabiṣu* title was also used for supervisors of subdistricts. For instance, a certain Shuta is mentioned in some letters, such as EA 288.19 and 234.23. He probably resided in Beth-Shan, a city that did not have an indigenous prince.[3] Interesting to note is that Egypt had not structurally 'integrated' economically the city states into the Egyptian economic system.[4] The small vassal states had their own economic system, and it seems to have been the problem of the princes to satisfy Egyptian demands.

The importance of the Amarna letters has been somewhat exaggerated. They give us a good insight into the political games of a certain

---

1. *The Land of the Bible*, p. 176.
2. *Die Beziehungen*, pp. 246-48.
3. Thus R. Hachmann, 'Die ägyptische Verwaltung in Syrien während der Amarnazeit', *ZDPV* 98 (1982), p. 45. N. Na'aman has opposed Helck's division and thinks that Palestine and Phoenicia were one district, and Syria with Galilee (Hazor's kingdom) and the Bashan another ('Economic Aspects of the Egyptian Occupation of Canaan', *IEJ* 31 [1981], pp. 182-83).
4. P.J. Frandsen, 'Egyptian Imperialism', *Power and Propaganda* (ed. M. Trolle Larsen), p. 177. E.D. Oren maintains, however, that as time went on the concept emerged in Egypt that Palestine was 'the crown property of the Pharaohs' ('Governor's Residences in Canaan under the New Kingdom: A Case Study of Egyptian Administration', *JSSEA* 14 [1984], pp. 37-56).

period, but they do not give us too much insight into the historical development of the country. We learn, however, something about the Egyptian administration, with its 'department' that could be called 'the Bureau for the Correspondence of Pharaoh', with its two branches, one directing the princes and the other directing the governors sent out into the country.[1] Military garrisons were stationed at Gaza, Joppa, Beth-Shan, Ullaza and Ṣumur. As has been shown above, we also learn about the infighting between the princes, but Palestine does not seem to have been too much of a problem for the Egyptians. They knew the situation and also had their officials and soldiers in the country. Not only military but also cultic personnel were visible in the country. For instance, the cities Yenoam (Yanuammu), Nuges and Herenkheru in Upper Retenu (probably in the Galilee) had been given to Amon's temple at Karnak by Tuthmosis III.[2] As property of the Karnak temple, these cities most probably had some Egyptian priests taking care of the interests of the Karnak priesthood. Because there had not been any change in Palestine's position as a 'dominion', these three cities or a temple in them may officially have been the property of the Karnak temple throughout the Eighteenth Dynasty. We can also get an understanding of how these city princes and their scribes in some cases could have misunderstood the intent of the pharaonic letters. Thus, when Pharaoh tells them to protect the city state and the position they have received from him, the princes may have seen this as an indication that Egypt also should militarily protect them against their antagonists. Also, the ideology behind the term 'life' could have been misunderstood because the Akkadian *balāṭu*, 'life', could have the meaning 'victuals'. Thus, a word with an abstract meaning for the Egyptians might be understood by the Canaanites as referring to something concrete.[3] Some complaints and reprimands occurring in the letters may therefore stem from some such misunderstanding.

From the Amarna texts we can draw the conclusion that the Hurrian component of the population is to be recognized all over the country. Many of the rulers of Canaan have non-Semitic names, mostly Hurrian,

---

1.   P.J. Frandsen, 'Egyptian Imperialism', *Power and Propaganda* (ed. M. Trolle Larsen), p. 175. For the districts and the governors, see W. Helck, *Die Beziehungen*, pp. 246-55.

2.   See J.A. Wilson, *ANET*, p. 237 n. 42.

3.   For this and other examples, see M. Liverani, 'Political Lexicon and Political Ideologies in the Amarna Letters', *Berytus* 31 (1983), pp. 41-56.

such as Biriawaza, Namiawaza (in Upe), Shuwardata (prince of Hebron?), Zurata (Acco), Inda-ruta (Achsaph), (the composite) Abdi-Hepa (Jerusalem), and Puwure (one of Abdi-Hepa's officers) and so forth. These names may indicate that the Hurrians had become the upper classes of the urban societies in Palestine. How this happened is unclear, thus we have to reckon with both infiltration and military takeover.

Returning to the question of Egypt's imperial power, we can see that even if the Amarna period cannot be classified as a real decline of the imperial power,[1] the Egyptian policies seem to have avoided coming to grips with the threat represented by the Hittite kingdom's expansion into Syria. Egypt had not lost its power in Palestine and southern Syria, but neither had Egypt collected its strength in order to arrest the growing influence in Syria by the Hittites.[2] Because Abdi-Ashirta and his son Aziru grew in power on the Phoenician coast and in spite of their repeated allegiance to Egypt, their policies promoted Hittite interests by submitting most of Phoenicia and southern Syria to Hittite rule.

There is some information in the Amarna letters about tribute and shipments being sent to Egypt or being robbed in transit. Most of the tribute probably was collected by the Egyptian officials. When payment is interrupted it is mentioned in the correspondence. Lab'ayu of Shechem stresses the fact that because he has not withdrawn tribute he must be considered a faithful vassal. Everything else is slander (254.10ff.).[3] From EA 287.53 we get a glimpse of how heavy the tribute could be. In this letter Abdi-Hepa of Jerusalem writes that he has sent 5000 shekels of silver, several captives and eight porters to

1.   See J.M. Weinstein, *BASOR* 241 (1981), pp. 15-17. Weinstein also points to the fact that at the mines at Serabit el-Khadem 'none of the pharaohs from Amenhotep IV/Akhenaten to Haremhab (i.e. from 1350–1239 BCE) is mentioned' in the 'sequence of royal names' from the beginning of the Eighteenth Dynasty to the later part of the New Kingdom (p. 16). That indicates that there were some problems and that therefore the mining could have been temporarily discontinued during the Amarna period.

2.   A.R. Schulman maintains that there is evidence for an Egyptian campaign to Syria during Akhenaton's time. This campaign would have been led by the general Haremhab, the later pharaoh ('The Berlin Trauerrelief [No. 12411] and some Officials of Tut'ankhamun and Ay', *JARCE* 4 [1965], pp. 55-68; and *idem*, 'Ankhesenamun, Nofretity, and the Amka Affair', *JARCE* 15 [1978], pp. 45-46).

3.   *ANET*, p. 486.

carry the goods, but they were all captured in the plain of Aijalon.[1] Rib-Adda of Byblos, for instance, was at one time ordered to send among other things bronze and copper (EA 69.25ff.).

Among the items paid as tribute to the Egyptians were metals such as silver, copper and bronze, besides slaves, cattle, woods, and the agricultural products of the country.[2] Grain, for instance, was one of the most important and common ones (EA 224). It is not necessary to think that all of it was shipped to Egypt. Most of it could have been used by the Egyptian garrisons in Canaan. An Egyptian granary is known to have existed at Joppa (EA 294.18-24). Registration of grain is also known from Tell ed-Duweir from the time of Nineteenth and Twentieth Dynasties.[3] Other products mentioned as tribute are olive oil and wine (EA 55, 161, 287 and 327). For instance, in Tuthmosis III's 29th year, 95,000 liters of wine were imported from Palestine.[4] To this we should add that cattle also were sent to Egypt, and that the Egyptian campaigns met Egypt's need for slaves.[5] Royal estates seem to have existed in Palestine, and the local population may have been used for the corvée.[6] Such duties are mentioned, for instance, in a letter of Biridiya of Megiddo, EA 365.8-29.

In discussing the Egyptian rule over Palestine, we should also take into consideration the importance not only of military personnel, but also of cultic officials, even if there was not always a sharp delineation between them. Priesthood could be part of the royal administration in the countries of the Near East.[7] We have, for instance, Egyptian temples at Beth-Shan and Ashkelon.[8] The latter was dedicated to

1. *ANET*, p. 488.
2. N. Na'aman, 'Economic Aspects of the Egyptian Occupation of Canaan', *IEJ* 31 (1981), pp. 172-77.
3. J. Černy in O. Tufnell *et al.*, *Lachish*, IV (London, 1958), p. 133.
4. W. Helck, *Urkunden der 18. Dynastie*, IV (Leipzig, 1958), 707.25, 718.9; cf. J.H. Breasted, *Ancient Records of Egypt*, II, §§491, 509, 518. For the trade in olive oil, see A. Leonard, *BASOR* 241 (1981), p. 96.
5. Cf. *ANET*, p. 240.
6. W. Helck, *Urkunden der 18. Dynastie*, IV, 667.11.
7. Cf. my book, *Royal Administration*.
8. G. Loud, *The Megiddo Ivories* (Chicago, 1939), pp. 12-13. See also A. Alt, 'Ägyptische Tempel in Palästina und die Landnahme der Philister', *ZDPV* 67 (1944), pp. 1-20 (= *KS*, I, 1953, pp. 216-30); R. Giveon, *The Impact of Egypt on Canaan*, pp. 22-27.

Ptah.[1] An Egyptian temple in Canaan is known from the reign of Ramses III (1182–1151 BCE) and may have been located in Gaza,[2] which was the administrative capital of Canaan. Perhaps we also can posit a temple at Joppa which had become an Egyptian store city. The stratum VII temple at Beth-Shan has been dated to the Amarna period.[3] In the LB II period this temple was dedicated to Mekal, who was identified by the Egyptians with Seth.[4] In identifying Egyptian gods with the local ones, the Egyptians could claim that their gods were universal and that, with the Canaanite gods being 'Egyptianized', they could not support any rebellion.[5] This may be one way of looking at the problem, but why then were not all the Cannanite gods identified with Egyptian deities? The answer to this question can be twofold. First, we do not know the religious situation in the whole country. Second, the deities of Palestine were, as the princes of the country, vassals to the Egyptian divine state, that is, to Egypt, its god(s) and its pharaoh.

It is impossible to find out how many temples in Syria-Palestine should be seen as Egyptian. We should consider the possibility that existing temples in the cities where Egyptian military and administrative personnel were stationed could have been used by the Egyptians. This may be the case in Beth-Shan. Its temple (stratum VII) is not built in any Egyptian tradition, even though some parallels have been found at Tell el-Amarna.[6] One could perhaps talk about a Canaanite layout with some Egyptian influences. However, the architecture of the Amarna buildings could have been inspired by a Semitic tradition

---

1.   A female singer at this temple had a Canaanite name (W.F. Albright, *Archaeology and the Religion of Israel* [2nd edn; Baltimore, 1946], p. 127). In the Memphite theological system of the Old Kingdom, Ptah was the creator god. His word created the cosmos. Thus, the Egyptian *logos* theology is much older than that of the Semites.

2.   Thus R. de Vaux, *The Early History of Israel*, p. 98.

3.   Y. Aharoni, *The Archaeology of the Land of Israel*, p. 121.

4.   See H.O. Thompson, *Mekal, the God of Beth-Shan* (Leiden, 1970), pp. 128-30.

5.   B.J. Kemp, 'Imperialism and Empire in New Kingdom Egypt (c. 1575–1087 BCE)', *Imperialism in the Ancient World* (ed. P.D.A. Garnsey and C.R. Whittaker), p. 12.

6.   There were 'certain Egyptian design elements', but the temple had a 'locally inspired layout' (B.J. Kemp in *Imperialism in the Ancient World* [ed. P.D.A. Garnsey and C.R. Whittaker], p. 52).

known since the Hyksos period.[1] Even if several Egyptian objects were found in the temple, the Canaanite heritage is also apparent. A stela depicting 'Ashtoreth of the Two Horns' was also found in this temple.[2] Stelae from the reigns of Seti I and Ramses II do not mention any local gods.

Beth-Shan of the Amarna period (Level VII) was much larger than the preceding level. It is not clear whether the town of the Amarna epoch was built during the reign of Amenhotep III or his son Akhenaten.[3] Foundation deposits with cartouches of these two kings were found in the temple, as well as a scarab of Hatshepsut and also one of Amenhotep III and Akhenaten.[4] Besides fortifications and temples, there was also found an underground silo which could take 9270 gallons of grain (c. 35,000 l.)[5] Among the interesting finds from this city is a seal with a picture of an ass, and a scarab with a crocodile, both found in the courtyard of temple VII. There was also an amulet showing a hippopotamus found at the same place.[6] A bronze figurine of the Hurrian god Teshub was also found.[7]

The question whether Beth-Shan was an Egyptian garrison city before the reign of Seti I has been a matter of discussion. The city of the Amarna age saw an Egyptian *rābiṣu*, Shuta,[8] who may have resided in the town. If so, he may as well have had some troops there too.[9] This hypothesis can draw support from the fact that a city prince

---

1. Cf. R. Giveon, *The Impact of Egypt on Canaan*, p. 25. The temple of Level VI is considered by T.A. Busink to be a rebuilding of temple VII in the indigenous tradition of Canaan (*Der Tempel von Jerusalem*, I, p. 420).

2. A. Rowe, *The Four Canaanite Temples of Beth-Shan*, II.1 (Philadelphia, 1940), pls. XXXV.5 and XLIXA.1; cf. p. 81.

3. The date of the different strata is disputed. I have here referred to A. Rowe, *The Four Canaanite Temples*. It is, however, possible that Level VII is that of Seti I; cf. F.W. James, *The Iron Age at Beth-Shan* (Philadelphia, 1966), pp. 1-3. Y. Yadin and S. Geva consider stratum VI as the city of Ramses III. Its destruction marked the end of the Egyptian rule (*Investigations at Beth-Shan: The Early Iron Age Strata* [Qedem, 23; Jerusalem, 1986], p. 89). For the stratigraphy, cf. also H.O. Thompson, *Mekal, the God of Beth Shan*, p. 12.

4. A. Rowe, *The Four Canaanite Temples*, p. 9.

5. Cf. A. Kempinski, 'Beth-Shan', *EAEHL*, I, p. 214.

6. See, for instance, H.O. Thompson, *Mekal*, pp. 137-39.

7. A. Rowe, *The Four Canaanite Temples*, pl. 50A.4.

8. Shuta is given this title in EA 288.19.

9. Y. Aharoni sees Beth-Shan as an Egyptian garrison city (*The Land of the Bible*, 2nd edn, p. 173).

of Beth-Shan is not mentioned in the Amarna letters.

A simple layout in Canaanite style characterizes the Hathor temple at Timna in the Arabah valley (c. 25 km north of Elath), where the Egyptians worked the copper mines during the Nineteenth and Twentieth Dynasties.[1] This temple is an almost square sanctuary, its northwestern wall being the cliff. Even if the temple has been seen as dedicated to Hathor, because a stela with her face has been found there, this temple would have been used by the workers who were indigenous people. This opinion is supported by the pottery, which is mainly of the 'Midianite' type.[2]

As mentioned above, the Egyptians could also dedicate existing temples or cities to their gods. We know that Tuthmosis III gave some cities over to Amon and his temple at Karnak.[3] This was most probably done for economic reasons, and perhaps also in order to appease the god and the priesthood at Karnak. Their support was not to be ignored. Papyrus Harris I mentions that during the reign of Ramses III nine Syro-Palestinian temples belonged to Amon of Karnak.[4] From a history of religion point of view we should note that the Egyptians did not try to force their religion upon the peoples of Syria-Palestine. There is no evidence for such a policy,[5] neither does it seem to have been necessary. The Syro-Palestinian princes and their gods were the vassals of the rulers of Egypt, that is, the pharaohs and their gods.

Even though Egypt dominated the political and religious scenes, architecture and cult objects also show some northern influences. In central and southern Palestine, deity figurines, for instance, have features that show Egyptian influence. This influence came directly from Egypt, as well as being mediated by the Phoenicians, especially via Byblos. What usually has been called Canaanite art is thus very much

1. The mines were abandoned sometime during the twelfth or eleventh centuries BCE, thus the terms 'Solomon's mines' and 'Solomon's pillars' (i.e. the rock formations) should also be abandoned.

2. See B. Rothenberg, *Timna: Valley of Biblical Copper Mines* (London, 1972), pp. 63-207. A stone fragment with a badly damaged cartouche found at Timna has been seen by K.A. Kitchen as referring to a Tuthmosis, and therefore one could perhaps conclude that mining has occurred there before Seti I. However, Kitchen also mentions that the stone could have been brought there from another place ('A Pre-Ramesside Cartouche at Timna', *Or* NS 45 [1976], pp. 262-64).

3. W. Helck, *Die Beziehungen*, p. 253.

4. W. Helck, *Die Beziehungen*, pp. 252-53.

5. W. Helck, *Die Beziehungen*, pp. 444-45.

Egypto-Phoenician inspired.[1] This is very much the case in the coastal area where, in the LB period, however, we also find contacts with Cyprus and the Aegean. In the north, in Galilee, there are by nature more Syrian influences, and the same may be true for certain parts of Transjordan. There is no uniform style. The temples consist most often of a cella sometimes having a niche or a raised platform for the deity statue. We can discern two main types of temple buildings, the longroom and the broadroom, and sometimes it may be almost square, as is the case at Abū Hawām, stratum V, Hazor, area C, and Beth-Shan, stratum VII. Sometimes there are benches around the walls. The style of the temples is less influenced by the Egyptian monumental building tradition, as mentioned above.[2] Instead we find some northern features. Examples of the different styles are, for instance, the above mentioned temples at Megiddo, Shechem, Beth-Shan and Timnah, the temples at Hazor in Galilee, the so-called Fosse Temple at Tell ed-Duweir in the Shephelah, the LB II longroom temple at Tel Mevorakh on the coast c. 9 km south of Tell Dor, and the little temple at Abū Hawām (stratum V).[3] We should also note that some cult installations in the city gates could occur, such as was the case in the last Canaanite stratum of Hazor, area K, where some stelae 'similar to those of the Stelae Temple of Area C and the cult installation near the temple in Area A'[4] were found.

Hazor was one of the largest cities in ancient Palestine. The excavations of LB Hazor have revealed three strata. Four sanctuary precincts from the LB Age were found. On the tell, Area A, was a longroom temple from the MB II period,[5] which in the LB I period received an orthostat entrance. Y. Yadin considers this temple to have been the

---

1. See the discussion in my *An Archaeological Picture of Iron Age Religions in Ancient Palestine* (Studia Orientalia, 55.3; Helsinki, 1984), pp. 1-31. Cf. also H. Leibowitz, who sees the Canaanite art as being Egyptianized ('Late Bronze II Ivory Work in Palestine: Evidence of a Cultural Highpoint', *BASOR* 265 [1987], pp. 3-34).

2. Cf. E. Stern, *Excavations at Tel Mevorakh (1973–1976)*, II (Qedem, 18; Jerusalem, 1984), pp. 32-33.

3. For the different types of temples, consult M. Ottosson, *Temples and Cult Places*, and cf. E. Stern, *Excavations at Tel Mevorakh*, II, pp. 28-36.

4. Y. Yadin, *Hazor of Those Kingdoms*, p. 63; see Yadin *et al.*, *Hazor III–IV: An Account of the Third and Fourth Seasons of Excavations, 1957–1958* (Jerusalem, 1961), pl. CXLII.2.

5. A parallel to this temple building is the stratum VIII temple at Megiddo.

royal temple.[1] In Area F on the plateau the 'Double Temple' of MB II was followed by a holy precinct with some small buildings and a huge open air altar weighing c. 5 tons, with two depressions and some cupmarks. Parallels to this altar have been found at Alalakh in Syria.

A small temple was found in the western rampart, Area C, in some ways resembling the MB temple at Kamid el-Loz.[2] The Hazor temple consisted of one room with benches around its sides, but it also had a niche in the western wall.[3] The finds in the niche have given this temple a certain place in the history of the religion of this country. In the second and last level of this temple there was a slightly bent row of ten basalt stelae in the niche, and close to the left end was also a statue of a seated man with the moon crescent on his chest, holding a cup in his right hand. One of the stelae was engraved with two arms stretched upwards with the crescent and the full moon above them. From the later Punic period we know of stelae with upstretched arms as symbols for the goddess Tanit, the consort of the moon deity Baal-Hamman. Her sacred animal was the snake.[4] Close to the temple in the workshop area were also found some cult masks and a gold-plated standard showing a serpent and the moon crescent. From all this one can draw the conclusion that the temple was dedicated to a moon god and his consort.[5] The stelae surrounding the seated deity can be seen as an illustration of a Canaanite divine assembly.[6] Thus, one may say

---

1. *Hazor of Those Kinghdoms.*

2. See G.R.H. Wright, *Ancient Building in South Syria and Palestine*, II, fig. 137.

3. From an architectural point of view this temple resembles the temple at Timnah in the Arabah Valley. Both are almost square room temples.

4. Cf. Y. Yadin, 'Symbols of Deities at Zinjirli, Carthage, and Hazor', *Near Eastern Archaeology in the Twentieth Century* (Festschrift Nelson Glueck; ed. J.A. Sanders; New York, 1970), p. 221.

5. Y. Yadin, *Hazor of Those Kingdoms*, pp. 71-74.

6. It is possible that this temple can give some clue to the interpretation of the Later Judahite temple at Arad in the Negev. See G.W. Ahlström, 'Heaven on Earth—At Hazor and Arad', *Religious Syncretism in Antiquity* (ed. B.A. Pearson; Missoula, MT, 1975), pp. 67-83. W.F. Albright preferred to see this kind of stela as a memorial for the dead ('The High Place in Ancient Palestine', *Congress Volume, Strasbourg 1956* (ed. J.A. Emerton *et al.*; VTSup, 4; Leiden, 1957), pp. 242-58. K. Galling considers the temple to be a funerary chapel ('Erwägungen zur Stelenheiligtum von Hazor', *ZDPV* 75 [1959], p. 7).

that this little temple was a concrete illustration of the temple as ideologically 'heaven on earth'.

A more 'monumental' temple with clear northern features was found in Area H at Hazor (in the northern part of the enclosure). This is the most elaborate temple ever found in Palestine. The objects found in this temple are of great importance for the understanding of the Canaanite religion in this area. Because of the orthostats lining the walls of the last two phases, it has been labeled the 'Orthostat Temple'. A parallel to this type of temple has been found at Alalakh in Syria.[1] This Hazor temple had four phases. The first was built in the MB II period and consisted of a broad room, the cella, with a niche in the northern wall. The entrance porch was as wide as the temple and was divided into three parts. The orientation of the temple was north-to-south in contrast to the Area C temple which was east-to-west with the niche in the west. The temple of Area H was rebuilt in LB I and in front of it was placed a fenced court having an entrance porch with a room inside it. In the center of the court was a platform 3.5×2 m and c. 0.30 m high. One may perhaps not go too wrong in suggesting that this could have been the place for holocaust sacrifices.[2] Among the finds from this phase of the temple are two fragments of clay liver models both with Akkadian inscriptions. The liver was one of the tools that the Babylonian diviner, *bārû*, often used.[3] The inscriptions mention submission and rebellion in the country and that Ishtar (?) will eat the land. Nergal is also mentioned, but the text at this point is unclear. It ends with the phrase 'the gods of the city will come back'.[4] These fragments are unique in Palestine.[5] They may testify to the existence of well-educated scribes at Hazor, as well as to northern and

1. L. Woolley, *Alalakh: An Account of the Excavations at Tell Atchana in the Hatay, 1937–1949* (Oxford, 1955), pp. 84-85.

2. Y. Yadin sees it either as a *bāmâ* or as an altar (*Hazor of Those Kingdoms*, p. 81). As mentioned before, the word *bāmâ* refers, however, to a sanctuary and not to an altar.

3. For the divination technique developing into a profession of learned scribes, cf. A.L. Oppenheim, 'The Position of the Intellectual in Mesopotamian Society', *Daedalus* 104 (1975), pp. 37-46. For divination and prophecy, cf. G.W. Ahlström, 'Prophecy', *Encyclopaedia Britannica*, XV, pp. 62-68.

4. See B. Landsberger and H. Tadmor, 'Fragments of Clay Liver Models from Hazor', *IEJ* 14 (1964), pp. 201-18; cf. Y. Yadin, *Hazor of Those Kingdoms*, pp. 82-83.

5. Cf. the clay liver model from Megiddo stratum VIII (*ANEP*, fig. 595).

Mesopotamian influences on the religion of Hazor. Another find showing the mixture of cultural influences is a plaque made of a bronze sheet depicting a man, probably a high official, wrapped in a Syrian cloak with his right hand lifted in greeting. The face is shown in profile with the eyes of an Egyptian design. The figure bears a skullcap, which may originally have been a Hittite phenomenon.[1] The plaque can be compared with a seal in the Ashmolean Museum (no. 905) and a seal impression from Alalakh stratum VII in the Louvre (no. 906).[2] To its art form, this plaque from Hazor can be seen as an example of the Syro-Palestinian style known from the Second Intermediate Period.[3]

The rebuilt version of this temple in the LB II period was alotted the same dimensions as the temple cella (13.3 × 8 m), but the entrance porch was now divided into four rooms, and south of it was added another broad room inside which were two pillars. Thus, the temple was a tripartite temple of a type never seen before or after in Palestine.[4] Two lion orthostats guarding the entrance were also found, one of them buried in a pit. A rebuilding of the temple seems to have occurred in the thirteenth century. The only architectural change that occurred was that the middle room was enlarged.

Among the finds from this temple are a basalt altar with a sun emblem (a circle with a cross) engraved on one side, a basin also of basalt, two libation tables, a carinated basalt krater in Mycenaean style, a basalt altar or 'offertory-table', a statue of a seated deity (?) and one statue of a standing deity with the sun emblem on his chest (it is the same emblem as that on the incense altar). A base in the form of a bull was also found. Two other bull figurines can be mentioned. One is in

1.   Consult O. Negbi, *Canaanite Gods in Metal*, pp. 43-44. For Canaanite high officials depicted in Egyptian wall paintings, see *ANEP*, figs. 46-47.

2.   See D. Collon, *The Seal Impressions from Tell Atchana/Alalakh* (AOAT, 27; Neukirchen–Vluyn, 1975), pp. 187-88, and pl. XXXI.14., and for north Syrian seals and their art in general, cf. D. Collon, *The Alalakh Cylinder Seals* (BAR, 132; Oxford, 1982).

3.   See P. Beck, 'The Bronze Plaque from Hazor', *IEJ* 33 (1983), pp. 78-80.

4.   Y. Yadin maintained that this temple 'is similar in concept to the Solomonic Temple' (*Hazor of Those Kingdoms*, pp. 86-87; *idem*, 'Hazor', *Archaeology and Old Testament Study* [ed. D.W. Thomas; Oxford, 1967], p. 251). This is, however, not the case. The Solomonic temple could be called tripartite, which would be the only point of contact between the two. However, the Jerusalem temple was a longroom temple with a porch and a long room divided into two parts.

the form of a Zebu bull, *bos indicus*, the other is a representative of the Mycenaean style.[1] These two thus show the northern and western cultural influences. Because of the bull figurines and the statue of the standing god and his bull base, Yadin has drawn the conclusion that the deity of the temple must have been the Syrian 'Hadad the storm-god'.[2] (He could have been called Baal at Hazor.) This is probable, but because of the fact that the sun disc is found not only on the chest of the standing deity statue but also on the basalt incense altar that was found in the cella, one should not dismiss the possibility that the god of this temple was either the sun-god or perhaps the main god of the Canaanite pantheon, El, whose sacred animal was the bull. However, as the main god and as a heavenly god, El could also have had solar characteristics.[3] But why should only one god have been worshipped in this temple?

The Hazor temples should be seen as indicating what kind of cult and cultic paraphernalia the peoples of Galilee were accustomed to. The destruction of this city did not eliminate religious beliefs and actual rituals. Thus we may take this into consideration when dealing with the later period in which the peoples of this territory became Israelites due to the expansion of the Davidic kingdom.

From what we have seen at Hazor and noticed at other places, for instance at Megiddo and Tell ed-Duweir, when temples were destroyed they were rebuilt on the same spot. This reflects the recognition of a site's holiness. It was the place where the divine was at home. Therefore the realm of the god(s) had to be rebuilt on the same place.

A temple at Tell ed-Duweir is of a certain interest because it was located outside the city proper in a depression just NW of the tell.[4] This depression has been understood as being part of an original moat,

1. See Y. Yadin *et al.*, *Hazor*, III, pls. CCCXXIV-CCCXXXII; Y. Yadin, *Hazor of Those Kingdoms*, pp. 92-94 and pls. XVI-XXI.

2. *Hazor of Those Kingdoms*, p. 95.

3. R. Dussaud, 'La mythologie Phénicienne d'après les tablettes de Ras Shamra', *RHR* 104 (1931), p. 358. El of Ugarit is depicted sitting on his throne and above him is the winged sun disc (*ANEP*, fig. 493).

4. Because of its location in a 'fosse', M. Ottosson draws the conclusion that the city did not have any 'outer fortifications during the Amarna Age and slightly later' (*Temples and Cult Places*, pp. 78-79). This has been confirmed by the most recent excavations by D. Ussishkin ('Excavations at Tel Lachish—1973–1977: Preliminary Report', *Tel Aviv* 5 [1978], pp. 91-92).

fosse,[1] but it is questionable whether a moat ever surrounded the tell. At least there was no moat in the LB period. It was not necessary because the slopes of the tell are very steep and high on three sides. Only *south* of the tell would one have needed a moat. The city seems to have been unwalled in the later part of the LB period.[2] Perhaps the depression, which is very shallow, is natural, or there could have been a quarry there at an earlier time. The depression had been used as a fill in which was found some burned material. Three consecutive temples were built at this place.[3] The first measured 10×5 m with a small room on the western side and an anteroom in the north which did not have any door leading into the temple cella. In the second phase, the temple was enlarged to c. 10×10 m. Another room was added to the temple in the south at the back of the cella. This may be the temple of the Amarna period.[4] In the final stage there were two rooms back of the cella.[5] Benches were found along three sides of the cella in the two last phases. As to the great amount of pottery that was found here, most was of local manufacture. Other finds were seals, scarabs, ivory, glass, bones, and a ewer with a damaged inscription. Outside the temple was found, for instance, a bronze statuette probably depicting the god Resheph.[6] Architecturally, the 'Fosse Temple' should be seen as an example of an indigenous type of building, but it was rebuilt in such a way that it became unique in Palestine.[7] Besides

1. O. Tufnell, C.H. Inge and L. Harding, *Lachish, II (Tell ed-Duweir): The Fosse Temple* (London, 1940), p. 35.

2. Cf. D. Ussishkin, *Tel Aviv* 5 (1978), pp. 91-92.

3. O. Tufnell, *Lachish*, II, pp. 19-24. The chronology suggested is, for structure I: 1600–1450 BCE; structure II: 1450–1370/50 BCE; structure III: 1370/50–1225/1200 BCE (O. Tufnell *et al.*, *Lachisch IV* [London, 1958], pp. 64-66).

4. Cf. D. Ussishkin, *Tel Aviv* 5 (1978), p. 91.

5. See O. Tufnell, *Lachish*, II, pls. LXVI-LXVIII; cf. M. Ottosson, *Temples and Cult Places*, figs. 15-18; Y. Aharoni, *The Archaeology of the Land of Israel*, p. 131, fig. 36.

6. Tufnell, *Lachish*, II, p. 66.

7. M. Ottosson has maintained that the Fosse Temple was no temple at all. He compares it with el-Amarna houses and concludes that it was 'influenced by Egyptian building practice'. He thinks the structure was a 'potter's workshop' (*Temples and Cult Places*, pp. 89-91). I am not convinced about the Amarna influence in this case. From the beginning the structure was a Canaanite longroom building. Later rebuildings made it a three-room building with an anteroom. The locality in the depression may have influenced the builders more than any Amarna archetype. As for the finds from inside the buildings, excavators certainly did not find too many cult objects, but what

the great amounts of pottery (both local and Mycenaean) a clay figurine with a cap (Resheph?) was found in Temple III and in the debris
outside the temple was found a fragment of a ewer with an inscription
in old Canaanite, *mtnšy...ty'lt*, which could be read 'a gift, a lamb...
to my (Lady) Elat'.[1]

Another structure seen as a palace or a temple from about the same
period, Level VI, was found on the summit of the tell. It is a rectangular building and has, as do the temples of strata VII–V at Beth-
Shan, two supporting pillars (octagonal) in the middle of the room. In
the west there seems to have been an entrance room, antechamber, and
in the eastern wall some steps led up to another room which could
have been the holy of holies. It is poorly preserved, but the plan of the
temple seems to show a tripartite structure.[2] This temple, like the
Beth-Shan temples, cannot be characterized as Egyptian in its layout,
but we can in this case, as in many other instances, perhaps acknowledge that the Egyptian supremacy over Palestine influenced people to
imitate their art.[3] One may say that the layout of the temples is
Canaanite, but artifacts and interior decorations may have been
expressions of Egyptian influences in Palestine.[4] Some finds from this
temple may illustrate this phenomenon. There are graffiti with faces
drawn in an Egyptianizing style. One shows 'a standing god(?)' lifting

has some deity figurine to do in a workshop? It would most probably have left the
shop after it was made. The rich amount of pottery does not in itself speak for
identifying the structure as a potter's workshop (see G.R.H. Wright, *Ancient
Building in South Syria and Palestine*, I, pp. 315-16). We should also note that no
Egyptian objects of Level VI has been found in the Fosse Temple (D. Ussishkin
et al., 'The Excavations at Tel Lachish, 1978–1983', *Tel Aviv* 10 [1983], p. 169).

1. J.L. Starkey dates the ewer to the mid-point of the reign of Ramses II
(*Lachish*, II *[Tell ed Duweir]: The Fosse Temple* [ed. O. Tufnell, L.H. Inge and
L. Harding; London, 1940], p. 47. For the texts and the reconstructions of it, see
T.H. Gaster, 'The Archaic Inscriptions', *Lachish*, II, pp. 49-54. Gaster sees the
script as historically representing an 'intermediate stage between the Sinaitic and the
earliest known Phoenician forms' (p. 49). F.M. Cross reads, 'Mattan. A tribute to
my Lady Elath' ('The Evolution of the Proto-Canaanite Alphabet', *BASOR* 134
[1954], pp. 19-21).

2. D. Ussishkin, *Tel Aviv* 5 (1978), pp. 10-25.

3. Cf. M. Ottosson, *Temples and Cult Places*, pp. 50-51; E. Stern, *Excavations
at Tel Mevorakh*, p. 33.

4. This is the case with the octagonal columns (D. Ussishkin, *Tel Aviv* 5
[1978], p. 25).

a lance with both hands.[1] There were fragments of 'alabaster and Egyptian-type faience vessels', pieces of gold foil, a scarab, and a plaque of very thin gold sheeting showing a naked woman/goddess standing on a horse. Her hairdo is the wig of the Egyptian goddess Hathor. Her headgear or crown is in the Egyptian style showing two 'ostrich feathers...flanked by two pairs of cow horns, all set into a pair of ram's horns'. She has a large lotus flower in each hand.[2] This is a common representation of the goddess Qudshu/Ashtarte,[3] one known not only from Canaan, but also occurring in some depictions from Egypt, sometimes associated with the gods Resheph and Min.[4]

A pottery fragment of a rim with red paint and with three letters in the Canaanite script was found in the main hall of the temple. The inscription was probably longer because it is broken off after the third letter. The reconstruction of the letters is debatable,[5] but can be read *gdy*, 'my God'.[6]

The LB Age Tell el-Far'ah (N) is not very well known from archaeology. The city plans seem to have been poor. A large building with a central room (or courtyard) surrounded by several small rooms was found. This has been labeled 'the governor's house'. Another house with two rows of pillars in the main room and a backroom (holy of holies) with steps leading up to it has been understood as being a temple. It had a small anteroom resembling that of the Fosse Temple. Architecturally it also resembled the so-called four-room house, and may be the forerunner of it,[7] the only difference being that the broadroom in the back is on a higher level. A house is a house, and thus a house for a god could also be the same as an

---

1.   D. Ussishkin, *Tel Aviv* 5 (1978), pl. 7.1.

2.   C. Clamer, 'A Gold Plaque from Tel Lachish', *Tel Aviv* 7 (1980), pp. 154-55.

3.   A piriform gold plaque showing a goddess with the Hathor wig and standing on a lion was found at Minet el-Beida. In her hands she holds an animal (gazelle?). On each side of her is a snake. See O. Negbi, *Canaanite Gods in Metal*, no. 1701.

4.   R. Stadelmann, *Syrisch-palästinensische Gottheiten in Ägypten*, pp. 11-123.

5.   See the discussion by D. Ussishkin, who refers to some suggestions by F.M. Cross and J. Naveh ('Excavations at Tel Lachish—1973–1977', *Tel Aviv* 5 [1978], p. 20).

6.   G.W. Ahlström, 'Was Gad the God of Tell ed-Duweir?', *PEQ* 115 (1983), pp. 47-48.

7.   G.R.H. Wright, *Ancient Building in South Syria and Palestine*, I, pp. 236-37, and see vol. II, fig. 148.

ordinary house in architectural form.[1] The el-Far'ah sanctuary was
built on the same spot where the subterranean MB II temple (in three
phases) was located. This may be one indication for seeing the structure as a temple.[2] Among the finds was a figurine of silver and bronze.[3]

A LB temple with three phases that in some way resembles the
Fosse[4] structure was found at Tel Mevorakh (Tell Mubarak) south of
Dor. The temple's interior is no more than 10 × 5 m, with benches
around the northern and western walls and a raised platform in the
NW corner. Floor and walls were coated with thick plaster of lime.[5]
This was the only building excavated on this small mound, and not
many more could have been built there. Possibly houses for the priests
existed outside the excavated area. The mound was not the site of any
city. Thus one would ask what purpose the sanctuary had. E. Stern
thinks that this temple and the Fosse Temple should be labeled 'road
sanctuaries', because they were probably used by travellers. In this
category he also includes the temple at Deir 'Alla in the Jordan Valley.[6]
Because the temple at Tel Mevorakh was located at the junction of two
important trade routes, one could as well call it a crossroad sanctuary.
It was important at a crossroad, when changing route and entering
new territory, to worship the deity and ask for give assistance.

The above mentioned LB II temple at Deir 'Alla was located in a
town without any protective city wall.[7] This has given rise to the
hypothesis that this temple, like the structures at Amman's airport and
the one on the slopes of Mt Gerizim, would be a shrine for tribal
leagues of seminomads.[8] However, since we do not know anything

1. An example of this is the Iron II temple at Arad in the Negev.
2. A. Chambon thinks it possible that the building was used for occasional cultic
activities (*Tell el-Far'ah*, I [Paris, 1984], pp. 20-21).
3. See R. de Vaux, 'Les fouilles de Tell El-Fara'h près Naplouse: Sixième
campagne, rapport préliminaire', *RB* 64 (1957), pp. 574-75; *idem*, 'Far'ah, Tell el-',
EAEHL, II, p. 400.
4. It also resembles the later temple at Tell Qasîle; see A. Mazar, *Tell Qasile*, I
(Qedem, 12; Jerusalem, 1980).
5. The excavator thinks that the walls were therefore 'adorned with frescos', as
is the case in Mycenae (E. Stern, *Excavations at Tel Mevorakh*, p. 4).
6. E. Stern, *Excavations at Tel Mevorakh*, p. 36.
7. H.J. Franken, 'Excavations at Deir 'Alla: Season 1964', *VT* 14 (1964),
pp. 419, 422; cf. H.J. Franken, 'Deir 'Alla', *EAEHL*, I, p. 322.
8. E.F. Campbell and G.E. Wright, 'Tribal League Shrines in Amman and
Shechem', *BA* 32 (1969), pp. 104-16.

about tribal leagues, their organization, cult or territorial rights, this hypothesis does not solve any problems. One may see the temple as a cultic center for the peoples of the area, settled or nonsettled. Knowing that several small settlements came into existence around 1200 BCE both in Transjordan and in the hills of Cisjordan, there will certainly also have been sanctuaries built in some of them. A place does not need a fortified wall because a temple is built on the site.

The temple has been characterized as a 'sanctuary complex' built on an artificial mound.[1] The temple and related small buildings yielded some cult stands, votive objects, a lioness statue, three inscribed clay tablets,[2] and pottery models of temples, plus a faience vase with the name of the Egyptian queen Tewosret, one of the wives of Seti II. She was later coregent with king Ramses/Merneptah-Siptah and took the throne when he died or was dethroned.[3] These two represent the end of the Nineteenth Dynasty.

Deir 'Alla (coord. 208-178) is generally identified with biblical Succoth and is located just north of where the Wadi Zerqa (Jabbok) enters the Jordan Valley. The site was destroyed by an earthquake in the first half of the twelfth century BCE.

Among buildings characterized as temples are also two square structures with several small rooms surrounding a larger center room or courtyard having a pillar in the middle as support for the roof.[4] One was found at the Amman Airport and the other on the slopes of Mt Gerizim (Tananir) outside Shechem.[5] There are no real indications

1. H.J. Franken, *VT* 14 (1964), pp. 417-22.

2. H.J. Franken, 'The Stratigraphic Context of the Clay Tablets Found at Deir 'Alla', *PEQ* 96 (1964), pp. 73-78, and *idem*, 'Clay Tablets from Deir 'Alla, Jordan', *VT* 14 (1964), pp. 377-79. For the different theories about the language of these clay tablets (as Minoan Linear A or B, Etruscan, Philistine, Phoenician, south Arabic), see M. Weippert, who maintains that we here most probably have some northwest-Semitic writing ('Archäologischer Jahresbericht', *ZDPV* 82 [1966], pp. 299-310).

3. K.A. Kitchen, *Pharaoh Triumphant*, p. 216. See also J. von Beckerath, *Abriss der Geschichte des alten Ägypten*, p. 44.

4. W.F. Albright saw the Gerizim structure as a patrician house (*The Archaeology of Palestine*, p. 92). Both buildings are, in fact, built in a style that resembles Mesopotamian houses.

5. G. Welten saw the building at Tananir as a temple with an altar in the center room (*Jahrbuch des Deutschen Archäologischen Instituts* 47 [1932], pp. 313-14). The more recent investigation found that the 'altar' had been removed (R.G. Boling, *BA* 32 [1969], pp. 82-103).

for these being temples. The building at Amman Airport was found in 1955 but was excavated first in 1966. Together with Cypriote pottery, a great amount of Mycenaean pottery was found. The latter was most probably of local imitation.[1] There were also gold pieces in the form of jewelry, hundreds of beads, seals, 13 scarabs, an Egyptian so-called *khepes* sword,[2] and pieces of ivory and bone. It is most interesting, however, that, besides animal and bird bones, one also found in ash layers a large amount of human bones (c. 1000 fragments) in the building. That made the excavator draw the conclusion that the bones were those of children, and thus the structure was a temple associated with some fire cult and child sacrifice.[3] However, about 95% of the bones were of adults,[4] which means that the theory about child sacrifices has to be given up. As an indication of the function of this building we should take into consideration the square pile of rocks (4 × 4 m) located 6 m north of the building. Many of these rocks show traces of burning. It could therefore be the place for cremation, and the building would then be a mortuary.[5] The pottery found in the building, of which much is Myc. IIIC, is common at burials: for example, as bowls, jars and lamps. Rituals of lamentation were also part of the burial ceremonies, thus it is in order that a Kassite seal was found mentioning Amat-Banitu, the daughter of Marduk, and Sarpanitu's handmaid Sappitu, who can be called a specialist in Babylonian lamentations.[6] Can we then assume that northerners have settled in the area of

---

1. Cf. V. Hankey, *Levant* 6 (1974), pp. 130-59.

2. W.A. Ward and M.F. Martin, 'Cylinders and Scarabs from a Late Bronze Temple at Amman', *ADAJ* 8-9 (1964), pp. 47-55. The scarabs are from the Hyksos and the Eighteenth Dynasty's periods, but the local pottery is from the thirteenth century (L.G. Herr, *BA* 46 [1983], pp. 227-28).

3. J.B. Hennessy, 'Excavations of a Late Bronze Age Temple at Amman', *PEQ* 98 (1966), pp. 155-62. For the architecture, see G.R.H. Wright, 'The Bronze Age Temple at Amman', *ZAW* 78 (1966), pp. 351-57.

4. L.G. Herr, 'The Amman Airport Excavations, 1976', *ADAJ* 21 (1976), pp. 109-11.

5. L.G. Herr, *BA* 46 (1983), pp. 223-29. J.B. Hennessy now associates the building with human sacrifices ('Thirteenth Century BCE Temple of Human Sacrifice at Amman', *Studia Phoenicia: Travaux du groupe de contact interuniversitaire d'études phéniciennes et puniques. III. Phoenicia and its Neighbors* [ed. E. Gubel and E. Lipiński; Louvain, 1985], pp. 85-104).

6. R. Tournay, 'Un cylinder babylonien découvert en Transjordanie', *RB* 74 (1967), pp. 248-54; cf. M. Ottosson, *Temples and Cult Places*, pp. 103-104.

Ammon? This would be a probable solution from the fact that crema-
tion has been practiced and that it took place outside the communities.
Cremation was not a Semitic custom,[1] and it may therefore point to
the fact that in the LB II period people from the north migrated to
Transjordan. The control of this territory was important both for the
Hittites and the Egyptians because of the strategic and commercial
importance of the trade route from Egypt through Transjordan to
Syria.[2]

With the movement south of the Egyptian–Hittite border of interest,
southern Syria and Transjordan came into the Hittite sphere and non-
Semitic settlers from the north may also have moved south as a
result.[3] We can probably reckon with Hittite immigrants having
arrived in Syria and the areas of greater Palestine during the thirteenth
century BCE.[4]

A unique row of ten stelae originally from the MB II period (strata
XIX–XVIII) standing in a north–south line were found at Gezer. In
front of them was also a square stone with a square depression (basin

---

1.   For cremation in Anatolia, see A. Kempinski, 'Hittites in the Bible', *BARev*
5 (1979), pp. 20-45. Cremation has been practiced, for instance, by 'Northerners' at
Carchemish (A.F. Olmstead, *History of Palestine and Syria*, p. 260). We find it also
at Tell Nasriye (P.J. Riis, *Hama: Fouilles et Recherches 1931–1938*, II.3
[Copenhagen, 1948], p. 27). Riis found urns of the Mycenaean and Cypriote types
with inscriptions in Hittite. He therefore thinks that the burials can be associated with
the 'Sea Peoples' (pp. 201-202). From Greece cremation is known from the twelfth
century BCE (see D. Kurtz and J. Boardman, *Greek Burial Customs* [Ithaca, 1971],
pp. 26-37). The phenomenon is also known from Sahab in Jordan (E. Bloch-Smith,
private communication). Cremation in Palestine seems to have occurred in Jerusalem
(pre-Israelite time); cf. R.A.S. Macalister and J.G. Duncan, *Excavations on the Hill
of Ophel* (Annual of the Palestine Exploration Fund, 4; London, 1926), pp. 12-14,
35-36. For evidence from Tell Beit Mirsim, see W.F. Albright, *The Excavation of
Tell Beit Mirsim II*, pp. 75-76.

2.   L.G. Herr, *BA* 46 (1983), pp. 223-29.

3.   The men of Jabesh-Gilead who cremated the bodies of Saul and his sons after
the battle on Gilboa (1 Sam. 31.11-13) cannot have been Semites. The cremation
phenomenon shows that they had customs different from the peoples of the mountains of Israel in Cisjordan. Note also that Jephthah is said to be the son of a foreign
woman, labeled *zônâ*, harlot, in Judg. 11.1.

4.   See the discussion in A. Kempinski, *BARev* 5 (1979), pp. 20-45, especially
p. 41.

or socket?). Macalister thought of these as being part of a cult place.[1] In the more recent excavations the place was redug but the real purpose of the stelae still eludes us. It is also doubtful whether the place was in use during the LB period. There were no cultic structures close to the stelae. One suggestion is that they could represent some union of different settlements, and that a treaty ritual was performed at the place. One burned bone was found at the place, which has been taken as an indication for a sacrifice in connection with a covenant ritual.[2]

Very little is known about Palestine in the latter part of the fourteenth century. In Egypt Akhenaten[3] was followed by his son (?) Semenekhkare (1336–1334) and his brother Tuthankhaten (1334–1325).[4] The latter abandoned Amarna after two years and moved the capital to Memphis, which meant that the reforms of his father came to an end.[5] The city of Akhetaten may have had some people staying for a short time, but its role as a political and religious center was forever finished.[6] It is significant that the king now also changed his name to Tuthankhamon. He seems to have restored the Amon cult at Thebes and he was also buried there. His reign was short and his deeds are not well known, but his fame surpasses almost that of any other pharaoh. This is due to the fact that his tomb was found intact, thus

1. Thus, for instance, Y. Aharoni, *The Archaeology of the Land of Israel*, p. 110.

2. See, for instance, C.F. Graesser, who makes a comparison with the stones of Gilgal mentioned in Josh. 4 ('Standing Stones in Ancient Palestine', *BA* 35 [1972], pp. 34-64). See also A.M. Furshpan in W.G. Dever *et al.*, 'Further Excavations at Gezer, 1967–1971', *BA* 34 (1971), pp. 120-22.

3. There are some indications that Queen Nefertiti could have been Akhenaten's coregent; see, among others, J. Samson, *Amarna, City of Akhenaten and Nefertiti: Nefertiti as Pharaoh* (Warminster, 1978).

4. For these two as being the sons of Akhenaten, see E.F. Wente, 'Egypt, History of', *Encyclopaedia Britannica*, VI (15th edn), pp. 474-75. For the chronological problems and the problems of coregencies, see W.J. Murnane, who argues that Semenekhkare moved to Thebes in his second year (*Ancient Egyptian Coregencies*, p. 234).

5. J. von Beckerath maintains that the young Tuthankhaten was forced to abandon Amarna and to change his name. The power behind the young king would thus have been the Amun priesthood at Thebes; and Ay would be their man to re-establish the Amun cult (*Tanis und Theben: Historische Grundlagen der Ramessidenzeit* [Ägyptologische Forschungen, 16; Glückstadt, 1951], pp. 22-23).

6. D.B. Redford, *History and Chronology*, p. 158.

giving us insight into the splendor of Egyptian royal burials.

Around 1400 BCE the Hittite kingdom under Hattusilis II re-enters the stage. One of the most successful kings of this Near Eastern power was Suppiluliuma (c. 1361–1319 BCE),[1] who ascended the throne after having murdered Tudhaliya II. Having restored order in Anatolia during a 20-year long period of battles, Suppiluliuma turned to the 'Hurri lands', Syria.[2] As we have seen from the Amarna letters, Egypt lost the territory north of Byblos to the Hittites under Suppilulima. Having taken Aleppo and made a treaty with king Niqmadu II of Ugarit,[3] Suppiluliuma marched against Mukish, Nuhashshe, Ni, Qatna and Qadesh, all of which were defeated. In a second campaign Carchemish was taken and the Mitanni power broken.[4] The king of Mitanni, Tushratta, was murdered. It was at this time that Aziru of Amurru changed allegiance and became a Hittite vassal.[5] As for Mitanni, its glory was now gone. Tushratta's son, Mattiwaza, became a Hittite vassal.

The political picture of the Near East was almost dramatically changed shortly after Tuthankhamon's death. His widow—her name is not given—sent a letter to the Hittite king requesting one of his sons as a husband who would thus be the future king of Egypt. Suppiluliuma did not believe this at first, but after having learned through one of his messengers that the queen did not have any male offspring, he sent his son Zannanza. The prince never reached Egypt. He was murdered on

---

1. Suppiluliuma should have died five years after Tuthankhamun, who died around 1325; cf. H.J. Houwink ten Cate, review of K.A. Kitchen, *Suppiluliuma and the Amarna Pharaohs*, *BO* 20 (1963), p. 276. K.A. Kitchen reckons with a reign of 41 years maximum for Suppiluliuma. Because there is no fixed date known from Hittite sources, Kitchen builds his chronology upon the Amarna material, as well as upon the theory about a coregency between Amenhotep III and his son Akhenaten, which should have lasted for eight to twelve years (*Suppiluliuma*, pp. 22-24). W.J. Murnane sees a coregency as possible, but its length is unclear (*Ancient Egyptian Coregencies*, pp. 231-33).

2. K.A. Kitchen, *Suppliluliuma*, p. 3, cf. p. 51. See also H.G. Güterbock, 'The Deeds of Suppiluliuma as told by his son Mursili II', *JCS* 10 (1956), pp. 41-68, 75-98.

3. As a vassal of Egypt, Nigmada had married an Egyptian princess; cf. A.F. Rainey, 'The Kingdom of Ugarit', *BA* 28 (1965), pp. 110-11.

4. A. Goetze, *ANET*, p. 319.

5. Cf. H. Freydank, *MIO* 7 (1959–60), pp. 356-81.

his way.[1] Obviously some Egyptian high official did not like the plan of the queen. An alliance with Egypt would not have been out of the question because that would have suited Suppiluliuma's goal of preserving Syria for the Hittites against the pressure and expansion of the Assyrians under Ashur-uballit I (1356–1321 BCE). In breaking the power of the Mitanni kingdom the interests of the Hittites collided with those of Assyria. The Assyrians, who earlier had been vassals to Mitanni, conquered Mitanni under Adad-nirari I (1307–1275) and thus ended the Hittite supremacy there.

When Suppiluliuma learned about the murder of his son, he sent troops into the Egyptian held territory of Amqi,[2] the Beqa' Valley west of the Damascus area. Prisoners brought back from this raid had been smitten by a plague, and through them the plague spread in Anatolia. It killed both Suppiluliuma and his son and successor, Arnuwandas II.[3] We do not know how devastating this plague was, because there is a gap in our knowledge about Syria for this period. However, his successor Mursilis II seems to have managed to control most of Syria during the later decades of the fourteenth century BCE.

Tuthankhamon's successor, Ay,[4] who had the title 'the god's father', probably took the throne with the support of the army. He died in old age after four years' reign, and, having no children, he was followed by the general Haremhab (1321–1293 BCE),[5] who moved the capital to Memphis, which must have been felt as a setback by the Amun priests. This king continued the restitution of the old political order and religion. Atonism was persecuted and Ay's tomb, for instance, was sacked.[6] Haremhab seems to have undertaken some campaigns in Syria, battling the Hittites. This must have taken place during his time as a general of Tuthankhamon or Ay.[7] However, he does not seem to have been

1. A. Goetze, *ANET*, p. 395.

2. R. Hachmann, in *Kamid el-Loz—Kumidi* (ed. D.O. Edzard *et al.*), pp. 84-88.

3. H.G. Güterbock, *JCS* 10 (1956), pp. 94-96 (frag. 28). Cf. W.J. Murnane, *The Road to Kadesh: A Historical Interpretation of the Battle Reliefs of King Sety I at Karnak* (SAOC, 42; Chicago, 1985), p. 35.

4. There is no clear information about a coregency between Tuthankhamon and Ay; see W.J. Murnane, *Ancient Egyptian Coregencies*, p. 181.

5. Four of the so-called Amarna kings were completely ignored by Haremhab, who officially counted Amenhotep III as his predecessor; cf. W.C. Hayes, 'Egypt to the End of the Twentieth Dynasty', *CAH*, I, ch. 4 (rev. edn), p. 18.

6. A.R. Schulman, *JARCE* 3 (1964), p. 68.

7. Cf. A.R. Shulman, *JARCE* 4 (1965), pp. 55-57; *ANET* pp. 250-51.

successful. A bowl with an inscription on the rim mentions that he (in the sixteenth year) went on a campaign from Byblos to Carchemish.[1] Like Ay, Haremhab did not have any son to succeed him. He was followed by his vizier, an army commander, Paramesses, who like Ramses I reigned only a few years (1293–1291), and with whom the Nineteenth Dynasty began. With his son and successor, Seti I (1291–1279) Egypt began reasserting its power in Syria-Palestine. Seti carried out some campaigns in Asia and secured for Egypt the territory up to Qadesh in the north. Amurru thus became an Egyptian vassal again.[2] The Karnak reliefs mention that in his first year he campaigned against the Shasu in Palestine from Raphia to a city of Canaan, but which one is not clear.[3] The reliefs and a stela from Beth-Shan also mention his campaign to the Jordan Valley, where rebellions had broken out.[4] The rulers of Hamath and Pella seem to have been threatening the Egyptian garrison at Beth-Shan. Seti sent different divisions against the rebellious towns and the uproar was quickly quelled. He also sent a division which captured Yenoam close to the Lake of Tiberias.[5] Seti then continued to Acco and Tyre and Lebanon, where the princes submitted to him. At the latter place he also set up a stela.[6] Also important are two stelae[7] from Beth-Shan (Level VI),[8] one of them mentioning that the 'apīru of Mt Yarmuta were causing trouble.[9] Seti sent troops to the hill country of Djahi, and in a few days they returned with prisoners. This would mean that Seti was at

1.   See D.B. Redford, 'New Light on the Asiatic Campaign of Horemheb', *BASOR* 211 (1973), pp. 36-38, 45.

2.   *ANET*, p. 254.

3.   R.O. Faulkner suggested that it was Gaza ('The Wars of Sethos I', *JEA* 33 [1947], pp. 35-36); cf. W. Helck, *Die Beziehungen*, p. 196.

4.   *ANET*, pp. 253-54.

5.   Cf. the illustration in S. Ahituv, *Canaanite Toponyms in Ancient Egyptian Documents* (Leiden, 1984), p. 26, and pl. V.

6.   J. Leclant (*apud* M. Chebab), 'Découverts de monuments égyptiens ou égyptisants hors de la vallée du Nil, 1955–1960', *Or* NS 30 (1961), p. 394.

7.   *ANET*, pp. 253 and 255.

8.   As to the stratigraphy of Beth-Shan, consult H.O. Thompson, *Mekal, the God of Beth-Shan*, pp. 11-12, and n. 27; F.W. James, *The Iron Age at Beth-Shan*, pp. 149-54.

9.   Mt Yarmuta has been identified by Y. Aharoni with Jarmuth-Remeth (Josh. 19.21), NW of Beth-Shan (*The Land of the Bible*, 2nd edn, p. 179). R. de Vaux sees it as Kokab el-Hawa south of Beth-Shan (*The Early History of Israel*, pp. 113-14).

Beth-Shan at this point in time.[1] His strategy in quelling the uprisings was to send out detachments, 'flying columns', to conquer the different areas while marching through the country.[2] Other cities taken in the northern Palestine and in Lebanon were Hazor,[3] and Beth-Anath in the Galilee, Kumidi in the Beqa' Valley, and Acco, Uzu, Tyre and Ullaza on the coast.[4] A later campaign led him to Amurru and Qadesh, where he defeated the Hittites. After the battle he set up a victory stela at Qadesh.[5] This victory means that Seti managed to regain some territory that had been lost to the Hittites. It was during this campaign that Bentesina of Amurru broke his oath to the Hittite king, Muwatallis, and became an Egyptian vassal. There seems to have been a peace treaty between Muwatallis and Egypt,[6] which could have been made at this time, but the Hittite king must have understood that Egypt had come too close and that war was unavoidable.

The confrontation came under Seti's successor and son, Ramses II (1279–1212 BCE). During most of his long reign of 67 years, Ramses tried to re-establish and maintain Egyptian rule over the southern half of Syria. According to an inscription carved on a cliff at Nahr el-Kalb between Byblos and Beirut, Ramses undertook an expedition along the Phoenician coast in his fourth regnal year, 1276.[7] The aim was perhaps to show the flag and secure allies and bases for a decisive battle against the Hittites. This occurred the following year, and again the battleground was at Qadesh.[8] The battle is well known not only from inscriptions, but also from scenes on the temple walls at Karnak and at other temples in Egypt and in Nubia. The texts are known as the 'Poem' and the 'Bulletin'.[9] Ramses boasts about having defeated the

1. Cf. A. Alt, 'Zur Geshichte von Beth-Sean 1500–1000 v. Chr.', *PJ* 22 (1926), pp. 108-20 (*KS*, I, pp. 246-55); W. Helck, *Die Beziehungen*, pp. 190-91.

2. K.A. Kitchen, *The Third Intermediate Period in Egypt (1100–650 B.C.)* (Warminster, 1973), p. 444.

3. The destruction of Hazor's lower city (str. 1B) has been ascribed to Seti I by Y. Yadin (*Hazor of Those Kingdoms*, p. 108).

4. As to the inscriptions, see *ANET*, pp. 253-55.

5. For this as well as the intricate questions of chronology, see W.J. Murnane, *The Road to Kadesh*, pp. 53-144.

6. *ANET*, p. 200.

7. *ANET*, p. 255.

8. *ANEP*, no. 336.

9. See A.J. Spalinger, 'Notes on the Reliefs of the Battle of Kadesh', *Perspectives on the Battle of Kadesh* (ed. H. Goedicke; Baltimore, 1985), pp. 1-42,

Hittites. He himself did it, or rather he and 'his father Amon'.[1]
Historically the truth seems, however, to be somewhat different.

Both Muwatallis and Ramses had raised large armies. The Egyptian
army consisted of four divisions, each named after an Egyptian god,
as was also the case with Seti's army. The first division under Ramses
was named Amun, then came the divisions of Re, Ptah and Sutekh.
They marched north separately, which meant that the Sutekh division
arrived on the battlefield by the time the battle was over. The
Egyptian intelligence had probably been ill-informed about the position of the Hittites; thus, Ramses seems to have marched into a trap.
The Hittite king had sent two nomads, Shasu, in the direction of Ramses'
first battalion in order to have them 'captured' by the Egyptians.
These pretended that they would submit to Ramses and told him that
the Hittite king and his allies were in the territory of Aleppo.[2] Ramses
continued and had passed Qadesh when suddenly the Hittite chariotry
made an attack on the Egyptian second division, that of Re. Ramses
and the Amun division were thus cut off. The second division fled and
the Hittites pursued the first one, which to its surprise found Hittites
behind them instead of Egyptians. This created panic among the
Egyptians and most soldiers fled. The Hittites started also to loot the
Egyptian camp. Ramses was seemingly lost, but was saved in the
critical moment by the arrival of a crops of 'cadets' (*nearin*), who had
just arrived at the battle scene after having finished their 'inspection
tour' of the coast, 'the land of Amurru'.[3] The Egyptian third division
also arrived about the same time. Muwatallis, who for some reason
had not yet used his infantry, retreated and moved his chariotry over
to the other side of the river Orontes. The next day saw some fighting,

and in the same volume, S. Morschauser, 'Observations on the Speeches of Ramses
II in the Literary Records of the Battle of Kadesh', pp. 123-24. See further
R.O. Faulkner, *MDAIK* 16 (1958). For inscriptions and papyri of the reign of
Ramses II, see J.D. Schmidt, *Ramesses II. A Chronological Structure for his Reign*
(The Johns Hopkins Near Eastern Studies; Baltimore, 1973), pp. 22-97. Cf. also
J. Van Seters, *In Search of History*, pp. 153-54.

1.   Ramses claims to have fought alone against 2500 chariots. The ideological
basis for this kind of 'historiography' is that the king is an incarnation of the divine.
The king-god has defeated the forces of evil.

2.   W. Helck, *Die Beziehungen*, p. 199.

3.   *ANET*, p. 256.

but an armistice was declared and the two kings began to count their losses.[1]

It is difficult to get a reliable picture of the events of this battle from the records of Ramses II. If we look at the results of the war, we learn that Qadesh was again lost and came under Hittite dominion. The same goes for Amurru, which Ramses tried to win back in a campaign in his eighth year. The result of this is not very well known, but it is doubtful that Amurru ever again became an Egyptian vassal state. The Hittites invaded the Damascus territory after the Qadesh event, which shows that their supremacy over Syria was unquestioned for the moment. One may say that the battle at Qadesh was in itself probably a draw militarily, but politically the result was clearly in favor of the Hittites. Because of this, the authority of the Egyptians was questioned by some local princes, and this forced Ramses to undertake more campaigns in Syria-Palestine, such as the above-mentioned campaign in his eighth year, when he tried to win back Amurru and went as far as Tripolis.[2] It is possible that it was in the same campaign that he took Beth-Anath in Galilee.[3] A stela from Qarnaim in Bashan has been connected to a campaign of Ramses II.[4]

Ramses is also said to have campaigned in Transjordan in his eighth year. According to K.A. Kitchen, one division marched through the Negev into Edomite territory and northward, while Ramses himself led another division through the central hills passing Jericho and then south into the Moabite territory. This has been inferred from the readings of *mw-í-b*, Moab,[5] and *t-b-n-í* and *b(w)-t-r-t* in a topographical list from Ramses II's court of the temple at Luxor.[6] If *t-b-n-í* is

1. For this and other campaigns of Ramses II, see also K.A. Kitchen, *Pharaoh Triumphant*, pp. 50-70.

2. Cf. J.D. Schmidt, *Ramesses II*, p. 174.

3. *ANET*, p. 256.

4. R. Giveon, 'Two Egyptian Documents concerning Bashan from the Time of Ramses II', *Rivista degli Studi Orientali* 40 (1965), pp. 197-202.

5. J. Simons, *Handbook*, p. 155, list XXII d. 10.

6. K.E. Kitchen, 'Some New Light on the Asiatic Wars of Ramesses II', *JEA* 50 (1964), pp. 47-70, see pp. 50 and 53; cf. W. Helck, 'Die Bedrohung Palästinas durch einwandernde Gruppen am Ende der 18. und am Anfang der 19. Dynastie', *VT* 18 (1968), p. 478. The name *t-p-n* that occurs in a list of Tuthmosis III may refer to a place in Galilee. This name is spelled *t3-p-n* in an Amenhotep III list referring to cities from Alalakh to Dothan, which means that no Moabite city was mentioned; cf. E. Edel, *Die Ortsnamenlisten aus dem Totentempel Amenhophis III* (BBB, 25;

the Old Testament Dibon (modern Dhībân), as has been suggested, then Ramses was there, and then also Dibon existed as a city in the LB age, which, however, the excavations of Tell Dhībân have not been able to show. The town seems to have been destroyed in the latter part of the Early Bronze Age, becoming resettled first during the Iron II period. Some Iron Age I pottery was, however, found at the place.[1] This can perhaps be explained by the fact that a survey has shown the existence of several small unwalled villages from the early Iron I period in Moab.[2] The city of *b(w)-t-r-t* Kitchen identifies with Roman Raba-batora of the *Tabula Peutingeriana* (modern er-Rabbah) c. 23 km north of Wadi Mujib (biblical Arnon). Ramses II also went to Beth-Shan, where he set up a stela of basalt which dates a Palestinian campaign to year 18. It gives a distinctive picture of the king dressed for battle.[3] The text, however, is stereotyped and conventional, with little precise information. It mentions the Semites of Retenu who, having been defeated, sent messengers who submitted to the Pharaoh in his palace.[4] The reliefs in the Hypostyle Hall of the temple at Amarah West (in Sudan) also show some scenes of Ramses' campaigns in Syria-Palestine; cities both in the south and on the coast (e.g. Dor) are mentioned.[5]

There are some other traces of Ramses II's presence or importance

Bonn, 1966), p. 24. We are thus dealing with two different cities. M. Weippert sees *t-p-n* as located in S. Syria ('The Israelite "Conquest" and the Evidence from Transjordan', *Symposia* [ed. F.M. Cross; Cambridge, MA, 1977], p. 27 n. 44); cf. S. Ahituv, *Canaanite Toponym*, p. 189.

1. F.W. Winnett and W.L. Reed, *The Excavations at Dibon (Dhībân) in Moab* (AASOR, 36-37; Cambridge, MA, 1964), pp. 13, 51. See the discussion in A.D. Tushingham, *The Excavations at Dibon (Dhībân) in Moab* (AASOR, 40; Cambridge, MA, 1972), pp. 4-25, and the review by J.A. Sauer, *ADAJ* 20 (1975), p. 104.

2. See J.M. Miller, *Archaeological Survey of the Kerak Plateau* (Asor Archaeological Reports, 1; Atlanta, 1991), p. 309; cf. J.R. Kautz, 'Tracking the Ancient Moabites', *BA* 44 (1981), pp. 27-35.

3. A. Rowe, *The Topography and History of Beth Shan*, I (Philadelphia, 1930), pp. 33-36, and pl. 46; cf. J.D. Schmidt, *Ramesses II*, p. 178.

4. J. Černy, 'Stela of Ramses II from Beisan', *EI* 5 (1958), p. 77*, 11.6-10. Note the royal ideology that is expressed in the text saying that the pharaoh is the 'husband to the widow and the protector of the orphan: he is an intervener for the needy, valiant shepherd in sustaining mankind' (11. 14-15).

5. H.W. Fairman, 'Preliminary Report on the Excavations at Amarah West, Anglo-Egyptian Sudan, 1938–39', *JEA* 25 (1939), pp. 139-41.

in Palestine. Excavations in old Jaffa have revealed a gateway (stratum V) in the eastern part of the 'Hyksos' citadel. The gate is 4 m wide, and the road leading to the citadel measured 18 m. On each side of the road were mudbrick walls. On the stone jambs of the gate are the names of Ramses II. J. Kaplan sees this gateway as an example of Egyptian architecture and he believes that it may have been built when Ramses returned to Egypt after the battle at Qadesh.[1]

In Ramses' twenty-first year, Ramses and Muwatallis' brother and successor, Hattusilis III, concluded a treaty.[2] It was an alliance between equals with stipulations about both common defense and offense.[3] This treaty seems to have lasted as long as the Hittite empire existed, that is, to about 1200 BCE, which can be deduced from the fact that pharaoh Merneptah (1212–1202 BCE) sent grain to the Hittites during a famine.[4] One of the reasons for the making of this treaty may have been that the Hittites had to have their rear secure in order to be able to arrest the threat that the Assyrians represented after the power of the Mitanni kingdom had been broken. With the Assyrian annexation of Mitanni, Hatti lost its buffer state. The expansion of Assyria under Ashur-uballit I (1356–1321 BCE) signalled the decline of the Hittite empire. Adad-nirari I (1307–1275) finally conquered Mitanni, thus ending the Hittite supremacy in Syria. The expansion continued under Shalmanesar I (1274–1245) and Tukulti-Ninurta I (1244–1208 BCE). The latter also sacked Babylon and took its city god, Marduk, prisoner. In the legends of the ancient Near East, Tukulti-Ninurta went down as the great empire builder. In Gen. 10.8-9 he is called Nimrod and characterized as 'the first potentate on earth', a great hunter.[5]

From the many inscriptions and reliefs of Ramses II's reign, one could draw the conclusion that Palestine was not too stable, and that the Egyptian rule often was questioned. Because the second decade of Ramses' reign is an almost 'dark' period and the pharaoh comes into the inscriptional 'limelight' again in his twenty-first year when the treaty with Hattushilis was signed, J.D. Schmidt assumes that Ramses was faced with internal problems in Egypt and that a rebellion could have

1. *BA* 35 (1972), pp. 79-81.

2. See J.D. Schmidt, *Ramesses II*, pp. 178-79.

3. For the text, see J.H. Breasted, *Ancient Records of Egypt*, III (Chicago, 1906), pars. 415-44; cf. J.A. Wilson, *ANET*, pp. 256-58.

4. J.H. Breasted, *Ancient Records*, III, par. 580.

5. Cf. E.A. Speiser, 'In Search of Nimrod', *EI* 5 (1958), pp. 32*-36*.

been boiling. This would also have been the reason why he employed mercenaries, such as the Sherden from 'the midst of the sea', in his army.[1]

The 'Shasu' who are mentioned in several Egyptian inscriptions from the LB Age[2] cannot be seen as an ethnic group.[3] The word means 'to wander around'. Shasu is thus an Egyptian term for the nomads of Palestine, Transjordan and southern Syria. The Akkadian term for nomads, *sutu*, which occurs in a few Amarna letters such as EA 297 written by the prince of Gezer, Yapahu, refers, therefore, to the same Shasu.[4] Other Amarna letters mentioning the *sutu* are from southern Syria. There is also one from the king of Assyria.[5] Thus it is natural that instead of the Egyptian term, the Akkadian word for nomads has been used by these scribes, and one suspects that the scribe of Gezer's prince was a little more educated in Akkadian than other Palestinian scribes. The Sutu are mainly known from Akkadian texts as Syrian nomads, and they seem to have been assimilated with the Arameans.[6] The Shasu should be distinguished from the *'apīru*, which is clear from the list of prisoners of war taken by Amenhotep II, as well as from Amarna letters 195 and 318.[7] The *'apīru* are never characterized as nomads. Both the Shasu and the *'apīru* are to be understood as terms for a certain lifestyle or social status. Concerning the Shasu, they occur in the list of Tuthmosis III as living in the Beqa' Valley.[8] Shasu are also mentioned in connection with Seti I's return

1. J.D. Schmidt, *Ramesses II*, pp. 179-80.

2. Tuthmosis II is said to have fought the Shasu, but there is no information about where the battle took place. However, one inscription mentions a campaign in Syria (J.H. Breasted, *Ancient Records of Egypt*, II, par. 124, p. 51, and cf. par. 85, p. 35).

3. *Contra* R. de Vaux, *The Early History of Israel*, p. 111.

4. W. Helck, *Die Beziehungen*, p. 275.

5. These are EA 16.38, 40 (from Ashuruballit of Assyria), 122.34 (from Rib-Adda of Byblos), 169.25 (by a son of Aziru of Amurru), 195.29 (from Namiawaza in the Upe territory), and 318.13 (from Dagantakala in S. Syria). Namiawaza and Dagantakala used both the *sutu* and the *'apīru* as soldiers.

6. For the Sutu, see R. Zadok, 'Suteans and other West Semites during the Latter Half of the Second Millennium BCE', *Orientalia Lovaniensia Periodica* 16 (1985), pp. 59-70.

7. Cf. W. Helck, *Die Beziehungen*, p. 275; O. Loretz, *Habiru–Hebräer*, p. 53 n. 259.

8. M. Görg, 'Tuthmosis III und die *š3sw*-Region', *JNES* 38 (1979), pp. 199-

from his campaign in 'Upper Retenu', which is northern Palestine.[1]
From Papyrus Anastasi I (from the time of Ramses II)[2] they are
known in the Ṣimyra region on the coast,[3] as well as being found as
marauding bands in the Megiddo area.[4] Seeing the Shasu as the
nomads of Palestine,[5] we have to reckon with the fact that many of
them have settled in the central hill country in the period around and
after 1200 BCE, which was a period when several new settlements
were built.[6] Thus, these Shasu, together with everybody else who
lived in the hills, later became what is known as Israelites.[7]

202; cf. M. Astour, 'Yahweh in Egyptian Topographical Lists', *Festschrift Elmar Edel* (ed. M. Görg and E. Push), pp. 17-33.

1. *ANET*, p. 254.

2. For the text, see A. Erman, *The Literature of the Ancient Egyptians* (trans. A.M. Blackman; London, 1927), pp. 214-34.

3. W. Helck, *Die Beziehungen*, p. 315.

4. Anastasi I, 23.6 f, *ANET*, pp. 476-78. Cf. W.A. Ward and M.F. Martin, *ADAJ* 8-9 (1964), p. 15; W. Helck, *VT* 18 (1968), pp. 477-78. See also the investigation by R. Giveon, *Les bédouins Shosu*.

5. The phrases *š3sw yhw'* and *š3sw s'rr*, i.e. the territories of Yahu and S'rr, which occur in Egyptian lists of the New Kingdom, have often been seen as referring to Se'ir, i.e. Edom, and thus the deity name Yahweh would also have been at home in Edom. The latter may be true. However, the Egyptian *s'rr* is philologically not identical with Hebrew *sē'îr* (where did the second *r* go?). The territory of *s'rr* was most probably in Syria because it is mentioned in connection with other peoples in the Beqa' and Orontes Valleys. The *yhw'* territory of the Shasu is then also to be sought in the same area (see M. Astour, 'Yahweh in Egyptian Topographical Lists', *Festschrift Elmar Edel* [ed. M. Görg and E. Push], pp. 17-33). The name Yahu is thus a toponym here, but it should be kept in mind that 'anthroponymns could serve as toponymns' in the ancient Near East (Astour, p. 30 n. 71). Furthermore, the name of a deity, a nation and a city could be the same, the most famous example being that of Ashur.

6. Cf. I. Finkelstein, *Archaeology of Settlement*, p. 345.

7. Cf. M. Weippert, who maintains that the Egyptians met the Shasu in the non-agricultural areas of Syria-Palestine and that the Israelites may have emerged from the Shasu people (*Bib* 55 [1974], pp. 274, 280). See also A.F. Rainey, review of J.J. Bimson, *Redating the Exodus and the Conquest, IEJ* 30 (1980), p. 251. L.E. Stager has objected to identifying the Shasu of the Merneptah stela with peoples of Israel, because the Shasu of the Egyptian reliefs are dressed differently than the Canaanites ('Merneptah, Israel, and Sea Peoples: New Light on an Old Relief', *EI* 18 [1985], p. 60*). Stager has not seen that the reason why Merneptah did not identify the Shasu with the people of Israel is because the Shasu were the nomads, but the Israelites were settled people. The Shasu that later settled in the hills became known

Hori's Description of Palestine

An Egyptian text, Papyrus Anastasi I, is a rare source for our knowledge about the geography of Palestine, its roads, and its peoples. The text is a letter from one Egyptian scribe, Hori, to another, Amenemopet, and is dated to the latter part of the thirteenth century BCE.[1] The letter is somewhat ironic, telling Amenemopet that he, for instance, did not know how to calculate the needs of the army he was with, which had been sent in order to quell a rebellion in Phoenicia (?). Hori then goes on to describe the geography of Phoenicia and Palestine, its roads, cities, forests and people. The most northern city on the coast he mentions is Ṣumur. We can follow him through the countries of Amurru and Phoenicia, as well as Galilee, Upe (the Damascus territory), and Gari in Transjordan east of the Lake of Tiberias. From Transjordan he describes the crossing of the Jordan river and the way via Rehob to Beth-Shan and Megiddo. Then he describes a wooded valley and how dangerous it is because of its many nomads. In this area he had heard about (and perhaps also met) the chieftain, Qazardi, of the people in Asher, *í-s-r (í-s-rw)*, whom a bear had scared up into a balsam tree. After this Hori describes his amorous adventure with a beauty of Joppa, which resulted in his losing almost everything—blanket, bow, knife, quiver and horses—as well as his chariot, which was smashed. From the Egyptian supplies at Joppa he could, however, get replacements for the stolen things. At the end the scribe also asks whether Amenemopet knows certain places in the south of Palestine and the distance to Gaza.

The mention of Qazardi and the people of Asher is without doubt a reference to an indigenous Canaanite group of people.[2] Later on during the emergence of the Israelite monarchy, this group, like most other groups in Palestine, became nominally Israelite. The genealogy in Gen. 30.12-13 is a clear indication that the people of Asher were

as Israelites because they settled in the territory of Israel (cf. G.W. Ahlström, *Who were the Israelites?*, pp. 37-43).

   1.   See A. Erman, *The Literature of the Ancient Egyptians*, pp. 214-34; J.A. Wilson, *ANET*, pp. 475-79.

   2.   This is the meaning of Judg. 1.32 saying: 'So the Asherites lived among the Canaanite inhabitants of the country'. Cf. W. Helck, *Die Beziehungen*, p. 280 n. 24.

latecomers into the Israelite nation and society. The name is also derived from the Canaanite *'sr*, 'be happy'.[1] The people of Asher are also known from an inscription of Seti I at the temple of Redeshiyeh,[2] as well as from an inscription in the temple of Ramses II at Abydos.[3]

The territory of the Asherites is probably to be located south of Megiddo, because the scribe seems to have met the chieftain Qazardi after he had left Megiddo but before he had reached Joppa. This is then in agreement with the biblical traditions which place some Asherites in the western foothills of the central highlands (Judg. 1.35; Gen. 46.17). Some clans have obviously settled in the territories of Ephraim and Benjamin and therefore they later on have been included in the genealogies of Joseph and his sons, as is the case with Beriah (1 Chron. 8.12), who in 1 Chron. 7.30 is an Asherite and the grandfather of Birzaith, a name that has been identified with modern Khirbet Bir Zeit north of Bethel (Beitin).[4] This supports the theory that some people have moved from the west into the central highlands[5] (as was also the case in the MB I period). As time passes they become known as clans of Ephraim and Benjamin because they live in those territories, but the memory of their origin has not been forgotten. The name Asher is thus at home in Canaan. With the emergence of the monarchy under David, the Asherites of western Galilee and its territory also became part of the new political constellation called Israel. Like so many other peoples of this country, the Asherites could then be nominally called Israelites. This is the explanation for why Asher in the biblical genealogy is said to be a son of Jacob's concubine Zilpah (Gen. 30.12). The same is the case with Dan, Gad and Naphtali, the two latter being reckoned as the sons of Jacob's other concubine Bilhah (Gen. 30.3-8). The territories of these peoples were not part of the territory of premonarchic Israel.[6]

From archaeology, the period of the Amarna Age and the following

1. Cf. W.F. Albright, 'Northwest-Semitic Names in a List of Egyptian Slaves from the Eighteenth Dynasty BCE', *JAOS* 74 (1954), pp. 229-31.

2. J. Simons, *Handbook*, p. 147, list 17.4.

3. J. Simons, *Handbook*, p. 162, list 25.8.

4. Y. Aharoni, *The Land of the Bible*, 2nd edn, p. 244; cf. S. Herrmann, *A History of Israel in Old Testament Times* (trans. J. Bowden; Philadelphia, 1975), p. 93; D. Edelman, 'The "Ashurites" of Eshbaal's State (2 Sam. 2.9)', *PEQ* 117 (1985), pp. 85-91.

5. See my book, *Who were the Israelites?*, pp. 25-36.

6. See the discussion in my book, *Who were the Israelites?*, pp. 37-43.

century is meagerly attested in the central hill country. As has been mentioned above, there were very few sites in the hills during this period, thus most of its population were sheep-herders. As for settlements, Dothan in northern Manasseh attests remains from the LB period on the tell, and there is also a tomb which has been in use from the beginning of LB II through the Iron I period with pottery that shows that there was no real break between the LB and Iron I ages.[1] Tappuah (modern Tell Sheikh Abu Zarad), c. 14 km south of Shechem, controlling the road to the coastal area, as well as the road to Shechem, may have been in existence during the LB I and LB II period, if we can draw an inference from the sherds that have been found there.[2] In contrast to MB II, the highlands of the LB Age were 'demilitarized'.[3] Shiloh may be taken as an example. In the MB II period there were strong fortifications protecting the city, but from the LB period only a few sherds have turned up. Important in this connection is the phenomenon that, of the bones that have been found at Shiloh from the LB period, only 6.6% are of cattle, while sheep and goat bones amount to 92.2%.[4] This would explain why there were no remains of a LB city at Shiloh. Sheep-herders did not build cities. I. Finkelstein hypothesizes that one should reckon with the existence of a cult place during the LB period. This would have served 'pilgrims' who would have come from 'the only large centres that continued to flourish in the region at this time—Shechem and Bethel'.[5] Unfortunately, there is no information to support this hypothesis.

Concerning the Late Bronze Age it is frequently maintained that there is no evidence for the establishment of new settlements. The picture rather shows abandonment and destruction of fortified cities; some of them were rebuilt by the Egyptians. The Amarna texts, however, do not support the idea of large portions of the country as having been abandoned. Instead we learn about small kingdoms and

1. See J.P. Free, 'The Seventh Season at Dothan', *BASOR* 160 (1960), pp. 6-15.

2. Cf. E. Jenni, 'Historisch-topographische Untersuchungen zur Grenze zwischen Ephraim und Manasse', *ZDPV* 74 (1958), pp. 35-40; E.F. Campbell, 'Two Amarna Notes: The Shechem City-State and Amarna Administrative Terminology', *Magnalia Dei* (ed. F.M. Cross *et al.*; Garden City, NY, 1976), p. 44.

3. I. Finkelstein, *Tel Aviv* 12 (1985), pp. 166-67.

4. S. Hellwing and M. Sadeh, 'Animal Remains: Preliminary Report', in I. Finkelstein *et al.*, *Tel Aviv* 12 (1985), p. 179.

5. I. Finkelstein, *Tel Aviv* 12 (1985), p. 167.

city states and their political rivalry. We should also note that the Egyptians built strongholds and fortresses along the coast from northern Sinai[1] up to Aphek, besides keeping the garrison cities they had held since the time of the Eighteenth Dynasty well fortified.[2] On the northern part of the coast some new settlements and harbors were also built in the LB II period, testifying to an increased traffic and trade with the Mycenaeans and with Cyprus.[3] On the coast and in the Shephelah some small and unwalled villages were being established during the fourteenth and thirteenth centuries.[4] This did not really change the picture of urbanization—Canaan was never really urbanized. But we can still see a trend in peoples moving into the land or migrating within the country. The resettling of the highlands also started in the later part of LB II. This can be seen, for instance, in the northern part of the Manasseh territory.[5]

1. E. Oren, 'Egyptian Forts along the "Ways of Horus" in North Sinai', *7th Archaeological Congress in Israel, Jerusalem 1980* (Jerusalem, 1980), p. 25.

2. For Egyptian activities in Palestine in the later part of the LB period, see J.M. Weinstein, *BASOR* 241 (1981), pp. 1-28.

3. The new excavations at Tell Abū Hawām seem to indicate that the place was built in the fifteenth century, if not earlier; see J. Balensi, 'Revising Tell Abu Hawam', *BASOR* 257 (1985), pp. 65-74.

4. See R. Gonen, *BASOR* 253 (1984), pp. 61-73.

5. A. Zertal, *Arruboth, Hepher and the Third Solomonic District* (Tel Aviv, 1984), pp. 42-48.

Chapter 6

THE TWELFTH CENTURY BCE

Ramses II reigned so long that he survived twelve of his sons, to be succeeded by his thirteenth son, Merneptah (1212–1202 BCE), a man already in his sixties when he became king. After the treaty with the Hittites, Egypt had peace in the east and Ramses could turn his attention to internal affairs and building activities. However, the threat from the Libyans was always present. In order to strengthen Egypt's defense in the west, Ramses built several fortresses along the western border and along the Mediterranean coast in Libya as far west as modern el-'Alamein.[1] The garrisons at these places could then easily check the movements of the Libyans. When Merneptah began his reign, the Libyans began to threaten Egypt again. He started to reorganize the army in order to meet the threat. At the same time he was faced with a rebellion in Palestine. The invasion of the Libyans led by the Rebu prince Mereye occurred in Merneptah's fifth year. Other Libyan tribes involved were the Meshwesh, the Temeh and the Tehenu. They were probably joined by peoples coming from the north.[2] The battle against the Libyans was, according to the Merneptah inscriptions,[3] a resounding defeat for the invaders. Among the trophies were the penises of the uncircumcised slain, and the hands of those who were circumcised, representing in all over 9000 fallen soldiers.[4] The battle is commemorated also on a stela from Merneptah's

---

1. J.H. Breasted, *Ancient Records of Egypt*, III, par. 580, 586; cf. K.A. Kitchen, *Pharaoh Triumphant*, pp. 77-78 (el-'Alamein is well-known as marking a turning point in the military fortunes of the second World War).

2. Cf. H.S.K. Bakry, 'The Discovery of a Temple of Merneptah at On', *Aegyptus* 53 (1973), pp. 3-21. An inscription on a column from this temple mentions the Libyans, the Shekelsh, and 'every foreign land'.

3. For Merneptah's war inscriptions as being distinct in style from the 'official diary', see A.J. Spalinger, *Aspects of the Military Documents of Ancient Egypt*, p. 212.

4. See J.H. Breasted, *Ancient Records of Egypt*, III, par. 588, pp. 248-50.

mortuary temple at Thebes, the so-called Israel Stela, now in the Cairo Museum.[1] The name derives from the coda at the end of the text in which the name Israel occurs for the first time in a nonbiblical text.[2] According to this text, Merneptah campaigned in Palestine, but this must then have occurred before he battled the Libyans and their allies. This theory is supported by the Amada stela, dated to Merneptah's fifth year,[3] in which the pharaoh is characterized as the 'Reducer of Gezer'.[4] Thus a campaign in Palestine had been undertaken before the Libyans attacked.[5] The Palestinian campaign could therefore probably

---

1.   For the text, see conveniently *ANET*, pp. 376-78. See also E. Hornung, 'Die Israelstele des Merenptah', *Fontes atque Pontes: Ein Festgabe für Hellmut Brunner* (ed. M. Görg; Ägypten und Altes Testament, 5; Wiesbaden, 1983), pp. 224-33. As to its literary structure, see, in the same collection, G. Fecht, 'Die Israelstele, Gestalt und Aussage' (*Fontes atque Pontes*, pp. 106-38). A.J. Spalinger characterizes the text of this stela as 'an enconium for Merneptah, wherein the king's *nhtw* are recorded' together with speeches by both gods and humans (*Aspects of the Military Documents*, pp. 208-209).

2.   For a literary survey of the different opinions about this text, see H. Engel, 'Die Siegesstele des Merenptah', *Bib* 60 (1979), pp. 373-99.

3.   Because the inscription has been damaged, the text is usually read as giving the information 'the fourth year' (E.F. Wente, private communication).

4.   See A. Abd-el-Hamid Youssef, 'Merneptah's Four Year Text', *Annales du Service des Antiquités de l'Egypte* 58 (1964), pp. 273-80, esp. p. 275; R.O. Faulkner, 'Egypt: From the Inception of the Nineteenth Dynasty to the Death of Ramses III', *CAH*, XI.2 (3rd edn), p. 234. A portable sundial with Merneptah's name has been found at Gezer (E.J. Pilcher, 'Portable Sundial from Gezer', *PEFQS* [1923], pp. 85-89). The recent excavations at Gezer have associated the destruction of Gezer XV with the campaign by Merneptah. Stratum XV was destroyed by fire; see W.G. Dever and D.P. Cole, 'Gezer: The 1968–70 Seasons, Field II', *Gezer*, II (ed. W.G. Dever, H.D. Lance and G.E. Wright; Jerusalem, 1974), p. 50. A bowl inscription tentatively dated to Merneptah's reign is known from Tell ed-Duweir; see J. Černy in O. Tufnell *et al.*, *Lachish IV*, p. 133.

5.   J. von Beckerath, 'Merenptah', *Lexikon der Ägyptologie*, IV (Wiesbaden, 1980), col. 72. The spring of Nephtoah mentioned in the list about the borders of Judah (Josh. 15.9; 18.15), has by some been connected with Merneptah, because Papyrus Anastasi III mentions the wells of Merneptah 'which is [on] the mountain range' (J.A. Wilson, *ANET*, p. 258). F. Buhl locates it at Lifta, c. 5 km north of Jerusalem's Old City (*Geographie des Alten Palästina* [Freiburg, 1896], p. 101); cf. Y. Aharoni, *The Land of the Bible*, 2nd edn, p. 184. Cf. H.Y. Priebutsch, 'Jerusalem und die Brunnenstrasse Merneptahs', *ZDPV* 91 (1975), pp. 21-22. The wells of Merneptah may, however, refer to some springs and fortifications closer to the 'Way of Horus', i.e., the trunk road along the coast.

have occurred already in the third year.[1]

The historicity of this campaign has often been doubted. However, Merneptah's Palestinian campaign is alluded to also in his great Karnak inscription. F. Yurco has discovered that the battle described 'on the outer wall of the Cour de la Cachette' originally belongs to Merneptah and not to Ramses II, as has been commonly advocated. Merneptah's battle scenes 'were carved onto the clean surface which bore no earlier scenes'.[2] It is interesting to note that the city of Ashkelon occurs in both documents. Thus the siege of Ashkelon that is attributed to Ramses II was really that of Merneptah. In fact, Ashkelon is never mentioned in any of the war inscriptions by Ramses II. There is thus a correspondence between the battle scenes at Karnak and the Merneptah stela. From these facts Yurco concludes that the mentioning of Israel in the text of the stela 'is founded upon an actual historical event'.[3] We should note that the text of the 'Israel Stela' has an interesting ring structure,[4] which is informative about geographical matters.

The princes are prostrate and say 'peace',	A
Not one raises his head among the Nine Bows.	
Desolation is for Tehenu; Hatti is pacified;	B
Plundered is Canaan with every evil	C
Carried off is Ashkelon,	D
Seized upon is Gezer,	D.1
Yeno'am is made as that which does not exist	D.2
Israel is laid waste, his seed is not;	C.1
Kharu has become a widow because of Egypt[5]	B.1
All lands together are pacified;	A.1
Everyone who was restless has been bound	
by the king of Upper and Lower Egypt.	
Ba-en-re Meri-Amon; the Son of Re.	
Mer-ne-Ptah Hotep-hir-Maat, given life	
like Re every day.[6]	

1.   J.H. Breasted, *Ancient Records of Egypt*, III, par. 605.

2.   F. Yurco, 'Merneptah's Palestinian Campaign', *The Society for the Study of Egyptian Antiquities Journal* 8 (1982), p. 70.

3.   F. Yurco, *The Society for the Study of Egyptian Antiquities Journal* 8 (1982).

4.   G.W. Ahlström and D. Edelman, 'Merneptah's Israel', *JNES* 44 (1985), pp. 59-61; see also my book, *Who were the Israelites?*, p. 39.

5.   The preposition *n* would here have the meaning 'because of' (E.F. Wente, in conversation).

6.   See J.A. Wilson, *ANET*, p. 378.

Structurally, the poem yields the following pairs of parallels: the introduction and the ending mention the Nine Bows including Libya and all Lands being at peace; then, Hatti and Kharu (i.e. Syria and Palestine), Canaan and Israel (i.e. Palestine), and Ashkelon, Gezer, and Yeno'am (i.e. three city states) are mentioned. Thus, the poem starts with the outer ring, the larger territory, represented by the Nine Bows including Hatti and Kharu. It continues with a smaller geographic unit within Hatti-Kharu, namely Palestine, here represented by the names of the subdivisions Canaan and Israel. Within this territorial unit the text mentions the smallest geographical units, namely the three city states Ashkelon, Gezer and Yeno'am. There is good reason for dividing Palestine into two parts (see Map 9). The Egyptian scribe obviously had a good knowledge of the geography and people of Palestine. 'Canaan' refers to the cultural and urban areas,[1] but the name Israel—which in the poem has the determinative for people and which must be older than the time of Merneptah—refers to the wooded highlands where almost no cities of military importance existed. It was a sparsely settled territory, populated mainly by some farmers and nomads. Because 'Israel' does not refer to a foreign land, the determinative for a nation, a foreign country, could not be used. In such a case the determinative for people, therefore, can refer to their territory.[2] Thus the name Israel can also refer to the people living in the territory. From this we may draw the conclusion that the term 'Israelite' cannot be used about people living outside the central hill country.[3] Anybody moving up to the hills and settling there,

1. Cf. Num. 13.29; Josh. 5.1; Isa. 23.11.

2. The 'people-determinative' does not *per se* refer to nomads. Neither does it necessarily refer to a people with a tribal structure, as has been suggested by J.M. Miller and J.H. Hayes, *A History of Ancient Israel and Judah*, p. 68. We should note that the Egyptian scribes were not always consistent when using the determinatives (K. Baer, private communication). For instance, when the Israel stela for the first time mentions Rebu (Libyans), the determinative is composed of the signs for throw stick, foreign land and people. The next time Rebu is mentioned we only find the signs for throw stick and foreign land. Another example is that the sign for city, *niwt*, can also be used for townsfolk. (I am indebted to my colleague E.F. Wente for this information.)

3. The settlements from the early Iron I period in Jordan, especially on the Madaba plain, can therefore not be labeled Israelite, as is done by R.G. Boling. Boling understands the settlement in Transjordan as the 'first success' of a Yahwist reformation. It was a conquest, 'the victory of a new conviction' (*The Early Biblical*

urbanite, villager or nomad, could, therefore, be known as an Israelite.[1] This makes it impossible to use the name Israel on the Merneptah stela as an argument for the biblical Israel's having experienced the Exodus and having settled in Canaan.[2] In fact, the biblical Israel is an outgrowth of the different groups of people that were living in the hills or which had settled there.[3] Later they became part of Saul's kingdom. Only with the monarchy did the name Israel come to refer to a political unit. If one or a few of these groups had ever been in Egypt, it is impossible to know with certainty, but because of the biblical tradition's emphasis on a sojourn in Egypt, one must reckon with the possibility that some Semites who had left Egypt had settled in the hills of Palestine. It was not uncommon for Semites to infiltrate Egypt as well as to leave it. The biblical narrative is, however, a reconstruction with a theological tendency, explaining why this people was Yahweh's people, and why it should have a claim on the country. To conclude that the Merneptah inscription that it is referring to the Israelites of the Exodus story is mere conjecture. It is completely impossible mehodologically to use the Merneptah stela to fix the date of the 'conquest' of Canaan,[4] as Y. Aharoni has done.[5]

The Israelites of the Merneptah stela were indigenous Canaanites fighting the Egyptian army. The battle scenes from the temple at

Community in Transjordan [The Social World of Biblical Antiquity Series; Sheffield, 1988], p. 63).

1.   Hittite texts from the time of Suppiluliuma I mention that people from Asia Minor had moved to the 'land of Egypt', i.e., southern Syria and Palestine; see O. Gurney, *The Hittites* (Baltimore, 1954), p. 60. Some of these may have settled in the central hills, also.

2.   Merneptah has often been identified as the pharaoh of the biblical narrative about the Exodus. From this stela and from other inscriptions about Merneptah's reign, such an identification is completely impossible to make. The same may be said about his father, Ramses II, who also has been connected with guesses about the Exodus. In fact, no pharaoh ever drove into any sea and disappeared in it.

3.   See below.

4.   For a 'Mosaic' tradition that does not know about any 'conquest', see my article, 'Another Moses Tradition', *JNES* 39 (1980), pp. 65-69.

5.   *The Land of the Bible*, 2nd edn, p. 184. *Contra* Aharoni, see, for instance, M. Weippert, who maintains that the Conquest story in the Book of Joshua 'is unrealistic and reflects the ideas of a later period' ('The Israelite "Conquest" and the Evidence from Transjordan', *Symposia* [ed. F.M. Cross], pp. 32-33).

Karnak show them dressed like other Canaanites.[1] Where the battle occurred is not known. Earlier I suggested that it could have been fought somewhere close to the western hills, because the battle scenes from Karnak seem to show that the people of Israel also had chariots and that the territory of the battle was not hilly.[2] Merneptah's strategy was probably the same as that of Seti I and earlier pharaohs of the New Kingdom, namely, dividing the army and sending out detachments to fight at different places at the same time. It is thus possible that Merneptah first had the two south-Palestinian cities besieged while another part of his army was sent north to Yeno'am. After the city states had been taken, the two Egyptian armies attacked Israel from two directions, north and south, or else conducted a 'mopping-up' operation in the territories between Gezer and Yeno'am, which included parts of the hill country.[3]

Merneptah's Palestinian campaign resulted in Egypt's presence still being felt in Asia. However, the empire's domain had crumbled, and after Merneptah's death the Egyptian hold over Palestine began to slacken. Southern Syria and Transjordan[4] were probably no longer under Egyptian control. In the north kingdoms and empires crumbled and went out of existence. There is some information in Akkadian texts about famine, plagues, and incursions of nomads into the Mesopotamian agricultural areas. This happened in a time of political weakness in Assyria and Babylonia.[5] Thus, population movements and large scale migrations became the order of the day. More than ever

1. F. Yurco (in a communication to L.E. Stager) in *Eretz Israel* 18 (1985), p. 60*.

2. G.W. Ahlström, 'Giloh: A Judahite or Canaanite Settlement?', *IEJ* 34 (1984), pp. 170-71.

3. F. Yurco, private communication.

4. In an Egyptian letter labeled 'The Report of a Frontier Official' (Papyrus Anastasi VI) are mentioned some Asiatic nomadic tribes, Shasu, who were allowed to pass the fortress Merneptah-Hotephirmaat in Tjeku and to proceed to the pools at Per-Atum (Pithom?) so that they could 'keep alive' (see *ANET*, p. 259). Tjeku (or Teku) is a place in the eastern part of Wadi Tumilat in the Delta. The letter is probably from the time of Merneptah. M. Weippert, among others, sees these nomads as the Shasu from Seir (Edom) ('Israelite Conquest', *Symposia* [ed. F.M. Cross], p. 27 n. 45). However, the nomads, the Shasu, were found in Transjordan, Palestine and southern Syria; it is not known from where those mentioned in the papyrus came.

5. See J.A. Brinkman, *A Political History of Post-Kassite Babylonia*, pp. 280-81, 389.

before foreigners entered the picture, and after some time new nations emerged.[1] This is the time when the Aramaeans (the nomads) of Syria were spreading north, east and south, not only into Assyria and Babylonia, but also into Transjordan and northern Palestine;[2] indeed, several Aramaean nations came into being. Hittite peoples moved into northern Syria, which resulted in the creation of neo-Hittite kingdoms.[3] It was also the time of the beginning of a resettlement and a recultivation of the central hills of Palestine and parts of Transjordan, which led to the emergence of new nations, such as Israel, Ammon, Moab and Edom.

Sea Peoples

From what has been said above, this was a period when the countries of the eastern Mediterranean were going through a time of upheaval resulting in a change of political as well as economic constellations. The great powers of the north did not exist any longer; the Hittite empire had disappeared, the Mesopotamian countries were politically at a low ebb, and the economic trade centers of Ugarit and Alalakh were destroyed. Only Egypt was still a power to reckon with. However, its sphere of dominion was reduced, and under pharaoh Ramses III Egypt was put on the defensive by attackers coming from the north, called the 'Sea Peoples' in Egyptian texts.

This is an Egyptian expression for the enemies from the north and from 'the islands in the midst of the sea'.[4] It is a collective term comprising all the different groups of people from the eastern Mediterranean who tried to invade Egypt. They are people with 'ships of war in the midst of the sea'. This is, for instance, how Ramses II characterizes the Sherden, pirates of the sea, whom he had taken prisoner and used as soldiers in his army in the battle at Qadesh.[5] The

---

1. Cf. R.D. Barnett, 'The Sea Peoples', *CAH*, XI.2, pp. 370-71.

2. See below.

3. Hittite texts from the time of Suppiluliuma I (fourteenth cent. BCE) mention that already at this time people from Asia Minor had moved to 'the land of Egypt', probably meaning Retenu/Palestine (see O. Gurney, *The Hittites*, p. 61).

4. The Egyptian term for islands usually refers to the coasts as well as to the islands of the eastern Mediterranean, as does the Hebrew term.

5. J.H. Breasted, *Ancient Records of Egypt*, III, par. 491; A. Erman, *The Ancient Egyptians* (New York, 1966), p. 261.

Sherden in two Amarna letters are also mentioned as mercenaries stationed in Byblos (EA 122 and 123).[1] The king of Alashiya complains to Pharaoh that the people of Lukka (in Anatolia) have raided some of his towns (EA 38). The end of the Late Bronze Age thus has seen some sea piracy; this may have increased during the thirteenth century. This is the reason for the mention of 'Northerners coming from all lands',[2] 'in the middle of the sea', or 'from the islands', phrases that occur several times in Egyptian inscriptions.[3] It has become a literary sterotype, and it may therefore be questionable as a piece of historical information.

It is to be noted, however, that the term 'Sea Peoples' also includes groups of people that were not seaborne. For instance, the Medinet Habu reliefs picture some of them as coming with women and children, with their belongings in carts pulled by oxen. They were clearly people on the move looking for new places where they could settle.[4]

Unfortunately, the period around and after 1200 BCE is poorly documented for most of the Near East. This stems from the fact that the upheavals of this time had as one of their results the abandonment of an internationally accepted system of writing. The Akkadian cuneiform language had been the *lingua franca* of the Near Eastern empires and their vassals. This means that learned scribes and schools had existed in the different courts and major trading centers. With the fall of the Hittite kingdom and the destruction of several Syro-Palestinian cities and trade centers, such as Alalakh, Carchemish, Ugarit, Qatna, Hazor, Sidon, Abu Hawam *et al.*, some scribal schools disappeared, and, as a consequence, international acceptance of the cuneiform writing tradition came to an end.[5] Babylonia was out of the power struggle after Tukulti-Ninurta I (1244–1208) had defeated it and taken the statue of Marduk as prisoner to Assyria. The situation in Assyria

1. Cf. W.C. Hayes, 'Egypt to the End of the Twentieth Dynasty', *CAH*, II.1, p. 366.

2. From the so-called Great Karnak Inscription; see J.N. Breasted, *Ancient Records*, III, par. 574.

3. See J. Vercoutter, *L'Egypte et le monde égéen préhéllenique* (Institut Francais d'Archéologie Orientale, Bibliothèque d'Etude, XXII; Cairo, 1956), pp. 125-58, 375. This phraseology may also express the religious idea of the enemies as representatives of the chaos powers who were always ready to destroy the nation.

4. N.K. Sandars, *The Sea Peoples* (London, 1978), p. 123 fig. 77.

5. Cf. J.D. Hawkins, 'The Neo-Hittite States in Syria and Anatolia', *CAH*, III.1, p. 372.

was, however, critical. Tukulti-Ninurta could only hold his newly-won position for a few years, and he also had to face a revolt by the nobility led by his son Ashur-nasir-apli. It ended with the king's death.[1] Assyria also had to come to grips with the migrations of groups of people from Anatolia and invading Aramaeans from Syria. Thus, any correspondence with a superpower in Mesopotamia was not necessary.[2] A new time began, in fact, with several smaller states and principalities emerging. Archaeologically this period has been labeled the Iron Age, a somewhat misleading characterization because the use of iron was very slow in coming. This new age was in its initial stages not only characterized by migrations and new settlements, which can be seen both in Cisjordan and Transjordan, but also by new, alphabetic types of writing, such as the Phoenicio-Canaanite alphabet, the Deir 'Alla script, and in Syria the neo-Hittite (also called Hieroglyphic Hittite) script.[3] A contributing factor to the popularity of alphabetic scripts may have been that the Akkadian syllabic cuneiform was too laborious to learn and to write. Business transactions and delivery of goods could be speeded up by recording them in an alphabetic script. Also, perhaps, one did not need to be, or to hire, a specially trained scribe to do business on a large scale, something these 'merchants' must surely have appreciated.

Before proceeding we should ask what the causes for these changes and political upheavals could have been. Because of poor documentation, we learn only that the Mycenaean civilization in Greece[4] and the Hittite empire were swept away. Several cities and city states in Syria and Palestine, mainly in the coastal area, were destroyed or else just ceased to exist. The latter is the case with Amurru. The territories inland, southern Syria and the Jordan Valley, however, were less

1. J.A. Brinkman, 'Notes on Mesopotamian History in the Thirteenth Century BCE', *BO* 27 (1970), p. 311.

2. H. Tadmor, 'The Decline of Empires in Western Asia c. 1200 BCE', *Symposia* (ed. F.M. Cross; Cambridge, MA, 1979), pp. 1-2.

3. The West Semitic alphabet can be called monosyllabic, i.e., every consonant is followed by an unmarked vowel. The Greeks were the first to indicate the vowels with letters; see I.J. Gelb, *A Study of Writing* (Chicago, 1952, rev. edn, 1963), pp. 196-97.

4. According to A. Bartoněk, the Sea Peoples can probably be understood as being part of the later Mycenaean population ('The Place of the Dorians in the Late Helladic World', *Bronze Age Migrations in the Aegean* [ed. R.A. Crossland and A. Birchall; Park Ridge, NJ, 1974], pp. 305-11).

exposed to the disasters of the time. In Palestine several cities and city states did not succumb to any 'Sea Peoples' invasion, for example, the Egyptian garrison cities Beth-Shan and Megiddo.[1] Tell ed-Duweir was not destroyed; cartouches of Ramses III have been found from this period on the site (Level VI), as has a so-called Proto-Canaanite inscription on a bowl fragment.[2] Among the finds was also a clay coffin,[3] which may indicate that an Egyptian detachment was placed at the site. Shechem, according to the biblical tradition in Judg. 9.22-49, was destroyed after the turbulent period by indigenous people under its king Abimelech.

The situation in the eastern Mediterranean was that different groups of people were on the move, causing others to be uprooted, which also increased piracy. Because the bureaucracies of the old states were crumbling in the Aegean, many returned to farming, while others took their boats and swords in order to seek new places and fortunes. This may explain the 'large Mycenaean influx' in Cyprus during the twelfth century BCE.[4] Trade was disturbed; thus the economic system did not function as well as before. Another reason for the troubles of the time and the migrations may have been the occurrence of a drought in the Balkans together with a drier period in the Near East. This may have resulted in food shortages, a reduction in livestock, and probably also famine.[5] The consequences of this would be a collapse of the economic system followed by chaos and migrations.[6] Thus, this

1.   Y. Yadin dates the destruction of Megiddo stratum VIIA to the period of Ramses III and Ramses VI ('Megiddo of the Kings of Israel', *BA* 33 [1970], p. 95).

2.   D. Ussishkin *et al.*, *Tel Aviv* 10 (1983), pp. 123, 155-56, 168-70. Ussishkin thinks that the city was destroyed sometime during the reign of Ramses III (p. 169); cf. O. Tufnell *et al.*, *Lachish*, II, pp. 22-24, *Lachish*, III (London, 1953), pp. 51-52, and *Lachish*, IV (London, 1958), pp. 36-37.

3.   O. Tufnell, *Lachish*, IV, pl. 46, and see T. Dothan, *The Philistines and their Material Culture* (Jerusalem, 1982), pp. 276-79.

4.   N.K. Sandars, *The Sea Peoples*, p. 183.

5.   J. Neumann and S. Parpola, *JNES* 46 (1987), pp. 161-82.

6.   R. Carpenter, *Discontinuity in Greek Civilization* (London, 1966). See also R.A. Bryson, H.H. Lamb and D.L. Douley, 'Drought and Decline of Mycene', *Antiquity* 48 (1974), pp. 46-50; H.E. Wright, 'Climatic Change in Mycenaean Greece', *Antiquity* 42 (1968), pp. 123-27; W.H. Stiebing, 'The End of the Mycenaean Age', *BA* 43 (1980), pp. 7-17. As to the discussion about the reasons for the raids of the Sea Peoples, see also A. Strobel, *Der spätbronzezeitlichen Seevölkersturm* (BZAW, 145; Berlin, 1976), pp. 159-61; N.K. Sandars, *The Sea Peoples*, pp. 29-79.

was a time that forced a number of groups of people to seek new areas in which to settle. Many went by boat along the Anatolian coast and tried to settle wherever possible, for instance, in Cilicia. Among Greeks moving east one could perhaps reckon with some of the Ahhiyawa. These often have been identified with the Ekwesh of the Egyptian inscriptions as being part of the Sea Peoples.[1]

In Anatolia also a severe famine threatened life at the end of the thirteenth century. This is documented in both Egyptian and Ugaritic sources. In fact, a food shortage seems to have been the order of the day in Anatolia already by the mid-thirteenth century BCE. This we learn from a letter (KUB 21.38) from Puduhepa to Ramses II, in which the Queen mentions that there is no grain in her country.[2] From Canaan comes a letter about grain that could have been shipped out from Joppa. This letter was found in the excavations of the Egyptian fortress at Aphek in the Sharon plain. Its sender was the 'prefect of Ugarit', Takuḫlinu, who earlier had been an official at the Hittite court. The letter is addressed to Ḥaya, probably the governor of Canaan.[3] Takuḫlinu mentions that some 250 *kor* of wheat had been sent.[4] Egypt may thus for quite some time have helped the Hittites with food. We know, for instance, that Pharaoh Merneptah exported grain to Hatti.[5] Ugarit was a Hittite vassal state and had therefore to support the land of the overlord. For instance, at the request of the Hittite king a ship from Ugarit was sent with grain to Cilicia.[6]

1.   H.G. Güterbock sees no 'evidence for the existence of a country Ahhiyawa in Asia Minor'. All the evidence points to overseas, most probably mainland Greece ('The Hittite and Aegean World: Part I. The Ahhiyawa Problem Reconsidered', *AJA* 87 [1983], p. 138; *idem*, 'Hittites and Akhaeans: A New Look', *Proceedings of the American Philosophical Society* 128 [1984], pp. 114-21).

2.   See W. Helck, 'Urhi-Tesup in Ägypten', *JCS* 17 (1963), pp. 87-97. Puduhepa asks that the princess's dowry (cattle, sheep and deportees) should be delivered as soon as possible.

3.   D.I. Owen, 'An Akkadian Letter from Ugarit at Tel Aphek', *Tel Aviv* 8 (1981), pp. 1-17. See also I. Singer, 'Takuḫlinu and Ḥaya: Two Governors in the Ugarit Letter from Tel Aphek', *Tel Aviv* 10 (1983), pp. 3-25.

4.   I. Singer estimates this at c. 15 tons (*Tel Aviv* 10 [1983], p. 5).

5.   J.H. Breasted, *Ancient Records of Egypt*, III, par. 580; cf. G.A. Wainwright, 'Merneptah's Aid to the Hittites', *JEA* 46 (1960), pp. 24-28.

6.   *Ugaritica*, V (ed. J. Nougayral *et al.*; Paris, 1968), texts 33 and 171; M. Astour, 'New Evidence on the Last Days of Ugarit', *AJA* 69 (1965), pp. 53-58. The amount of grain could have been c. 500 tons, according to I. Singer (*Tel Aviv*

Another letter mentions one hundred ships to be sent with grain from Ugarit.[1] It is possible that this was the occasion when the Ugaritic king, Ammurapi, wrote the king of Alashiya about enemy ships attacking his territory and that his own ships had been sent to Lukka while his troops were 'stationed in the land of Hatti',[2] most probably in order to help the Hittites in their defense. This would then have been a most opportune time for some enemies, 'Sea Peoples', to attack and destroy Ugarit.[3] The king of Alashiya wrote and asked where the troops and chariots of Ugarit were stationed. In his answer Ammurapi says that his troops were fighting in Hatti and that the sea raiders had landed and burned some of his towns. This letter never reached the king of Alashiya because it was found in the excavations of a kiln.[4] This would indicate that, even if there really was an earthquake, Ugarit and its dependent towns and villages were destroyed by invaders.[5]

In the Hittite kingdom several rebellions occurred during the last half of the twelfth century BCE which contributed to its breakup at the end of the century. One may assume that both external and internal factors played a decisive role in this process, for instance a disintegration of the feudal system causing rebellions.[6] Among known enemies of the Hittites at this time were the Urumi and the Apeshlai, the Paleo-Balkanic Mushki,[7] and the Kashka people from northern Anatolia

10 [1983], p. 5) and c. 450 tons, according to M. Astour (*AJA* 69 [1965], p. 255).

1.   H. Klengel, '"Hungerjahre" in Hatti', *Altorientalische Forschungen* 1 (1974), pp. 171-73.

2.   J. Nougayrol, *Ugaritica*, V, text 24; cf. *PRU* II.12 and V.60-62.

3.   The excavator of Ras Shamra-Ugarit, C.F. Schaeffer, has maintained that Ugarit was destroyed by an earthquake (see *Ugaritica*, V, pp. 760-68).

4.   Cf. N.K. Sandars, *The Sea Peoples*, pp. 142-44.

5.   See M. Astour, *AJA* 69 (1965), pp. 253-58; cf. H. Klengel, *Geschichte Syriens im 2. Jahrtausend v.u.Z.*, II (Berlin, 1969), pp. 398-400, and vol. III, p. 242.

6.   E. von Schuler, *Die Kaskäer* (Unterschungen zur Assyriologie und Vorderasiatischen Archäologie, 3; Berlin, 1965), pp. 61-66; cf. K. Bittel, *Hattusa*, *BA* 43 (1980), pp. 18-19. For a general picture of the disturbances in the eastern Mediterranean, see R.A. Crossland and A. Birchall, *Bronze Age Migrations in the Aegean: Archaeological and Linguistic Problems in Greek Prehistory* (Park Ridge, NJ, 1974).

7.   These are the Moskhoi of the Greek texts and the Meshech of the Bible. The Paleo-Balkanic Phrygians who were earlier thought of as being part of the Sea Peoples were not, and they were not among the enemies of the Hittite kingdom who destroyed that empire. They seem to have come to Anatolia after the Hittite empire's

(Pontus). The latter could even have been the direct cause of the collapse of the Hatti kingdom.[1] The Hittite king, Suppiluliuma II, who was not trusted by his people, was campaigning in Cilicia, fighting some invaders who cut him off from his vassals in Syria and thus also cut the lines of trade and food supplies.[2] In this situation the Kashka people may have attacked Hattusha, the capital of the Hittites, and destroyed it. It is possible that an earlier invasion of Cyprus by Sea Peoples caused the state of Alashiya to break its alliance with the Hittites. During the last decade of the thirteenth century the Hittites several times invaded Alashiya.[3] At this time, however, a war on two fronts was too much for the Hittite king. Hatti may have become easy prey for the Kashka and the Mushki. Whoever destroyed Hattusha, the destruction of the Hittite capital was the final blow to the kingdom.

The Hittite documents do not mention the Sea Peoples except for the *sikalayu* from Lukka.[4] There are no indications of Sea Peoples having penetrated into central Anatolia. The above-mentioned letters[5] from king Ammurapi of Ugarit show that a seaborne enemy attacked the coast of northern Syria. Because Alashiya revolted and joined forces with the enemies of Hatti we may conclude that the coast of southern Anatolia was raided or was invaded by some groups of Sea Peoples. Tarsus and Miletus, for instance, were destroyed at this time. Pottery finds tend to indicate that a group of Sea Peoples possibly related to the Philistines settled for a while in Cilicia. Later they could have moved south in connection with the Sea People's attempt to invade Egypt under the reign of Ramses III (1182–1151 BCE). This Pharaoh

---

fall. The Urumi are unknown; the Mushki are probably also Paleo-Balkanic people with respect to their origins, and proto-Armenians, according to I.M. Diakonoff and V.P. Nerozmak, *Phrygians* (Delmar, NY, 1985), pp. viii-x.

1. K. Bittel, 'Einar von Schuler: Die Kaškaër—Ein Beitrag zur Ethnographie des alten Kleinasien', *Acta Praehistorica* 5 (1974–75), p. 420. Cf. N.K. Sandars, *The Sea Peoples*, p. 197.

2. For the situation, see I. Singer, 'The Battle of Nihriya and the End of the Hittite Empire', *ZA* 75 (1985), pp. 100-23.

3. See H.G. Güterbock, 'The Hittite Conquest of Cyprus Reconsidered', *JNES* 26 (1967), pp. 73-81.

4. This term would mean 'those who live on ships', and would be identical with the Shekelesh; see G.A. Lehmann, 'Die SIKALAJU—Ein Neues Zeugnis zu den "Seevölker"—Heerfahrten in späten 13. Jh.v.Chr. (RS 34.129)', *UF* 11 (1979), pp. 471-76.

5. J. Nougrayrol, *Ugaritica*, V, text 24; cf. *PRU* II.12, and V.60-62.

was the son of the founder of the Twentieth Dynasty, Setnakht, who ruled for only two years. Ramses is remembered as the one who halted the Sea People's assault on the countries of the Near East, which may be an Egyptian literary exaggeration. As a matter of fact, they no longer made any concerted efforts—if there ever has been one—to change the political map of the Near East. They simply dispersed, and some settled in Palestine. This could mean that the assault on Egypt was not as massive as the texts and reliefs would have us believe. The irony of the history of the Sea Peoples and their efforts to invade Egypt is not only that their strength diminished, but also that after the death of Ramses III the power of Egypt rapidly declined.[1] Thirty years after Ramses III Egypt had lost all its Asiatic dominions.

It is in the inscriptions of Merneptah that the Sea Peoples first occur as a forceful enemy and as a threat to the Egyptians. A great coalition tried to invade Egypt both from land and sea in the eighth year of Ramses III, according to the Papyrus Harris and the reliefs of the Great Temple at Medinet Habu.[2] The Libyans invaded Egypt in the fifth year of Ramses' reign but were repulsed.[3] The attack in Ramses' eighth year was made by a great coalition of Northerners. The Medinet Habu texts mention six different peoples; other records mention eight or more. The six of the temple inscription are the Purasti/Peleset (Philistines), the Danuna, the Shardanu (Sherden), the Shekelesh (Sicels), the Zakkala (Tjeker) and the Weshesh. From where all these people originally came is not yet known, but most of them seem to have connections with Anatolia and the Aegean.[4] The Danuna are

---

1. The fact that a harem intrigue against Ramses' life occurred, led by queen Tiye and supported by some higher officials among the military and priesthood, may indicate that the last years of this pharaoh were turbulent; see J.H. Breasted, *Ancient Records of Egypt*, IV (Chicago, 1906), pp. 208-21; A. de Buck, 'The Judicial Papyrus of Turin', *JEA* 23 (1937), pp. 152-64.

2. W.F. Edgerton and J.A. Wilson, *Historical Records of Ramses III* (SAOC, 12; Chicago, 1936), pp. 74-76, 87-89. For the Harris Papyrus report, see J.A. Wilson, *ANET*, pp. 262-63.

3. According to Ramses' inscription of the year five, Sea Peoples joined the Libyans. This is questionable. A. Spalinger has maintained that the scribe added these to the campaign against the Libyans. Thus part of the battle in the year 8 is also reported here; see *Aspects of Military Documents of the Ancient Egyptians*, p. 214.

4. Consult A. Strobel, *Der spätbronzezeitliche Seevölkersturm*, pp. 101-75; G.A. Wainwright, 'Some Sea Peoples', *JEA* 47 (1961), pp. 71-90; N.K. Sandars, *The Sea Peoples*, pp. 157-66; R.D. Barnett, 'The Sea Peoples', *CAH*, II.2; cf.

usually identified with the Danuniyim of the Phoenician texts and the Danaoi of the Greek texts. They are commonly seen as the inhabitants of Cilicia, and can probably be identified with Achaeans who settled there.[1] The Shardanu are usually seen as being Sardinians, but some may have emigrated to Sardinia after the battle with the Egyptians; however, some of them may have continued as pirates for a time.[2] The Zakkala (Tjeker) are the people that later settled on the Palestinian coast south of Carmel, with Dor as their capital city. The Shekelesh (Sicels) from Anatolia may have moved around and finally some of them at least may have ended up on Sicily; from them the island would thus have gotten its name.[3] About the Weshesh nothing is known. They are often connected, however, with western Anatolia, as are the Tursha (Teresh, Greek *Tyrsenoi*), who are mentioned in an inscription from Deir el-Medineh.[4] Both in this, and in the Medinet· Habu inscriptions, the Purasti/Peleset are mentioned. This is the first time that this people, the Philistines of the Bible, occur in any historical source.[5]

The Egyptian reports mention that Ramses III fought the invaders both by land and by sea. He would have organized his defense in Djahi, which is another term for Palestine. Ramses is said to have defeated the coalition, and then, in a sea battle, probably at the mouth of one of the branches of the Nile,[6] to have soundly defeated the

W. Helck, *Die Beziehungen*, pp. 224-33; R. de Vaux, *The Early History of Israel*, pp. 501-16.

1. Thus R.D. Barnett, 'The Sea Peoples', *CAH*, II.2, pp. 363-66.

2. A Phoenician inscription from Nora, Sardinia, mentions the island as Shardan (ninth cent. BCE); see R. Dussaud, 'Les inscriptions phéniciennes du tombeau d'Ahiram, roi de Byblos', *Syria* 5 (1924), pp. 147-49; G. Bunnens, *L'expansion phéniciennes en Méditerranée: Essai d'interpretations fondé sur une analyse des traditions littéraires* (Brussels, 1979). For the different readings of the inscription, see B. Peckham, 'The Nora Inscription', *Or* NS 41 (1972), pp. 457-68.

3. E.F. Wente doubts that the reliefs at Medinet Habu depict the Shekelesh. Because there is a lacuna in the inscription that hardly can have room for Shekelesh, he thinks that the Shasu would be a more probable reading (see 'Shekelesh or Shasu?', *JNES* 22 [1963], pp. 167-72); cf. N.K. Sandars, *The Sea Peoples*, p. 112.

4. Cf. N.K. Sandars, *The Sea Peoples*, pp. 158, 163.

5. They are mentioned in Gen. 10, but since this book, like the rest of the Hebrew Bible, was not written before the first millennium BCE, Gen. 10 cannot have priority as being the oldest source.

6. H.H. Nelson, 'The Naval Battle Pictured at Medinet Habu', *JNES* 2 (1943), p. 45.

enemies. The war against the Sea Peoples is vividly depicted on the walls of the Great Temple at Medinet Habu, which show not only tumultuous battles, but also the weapons and helmets, kilts, and so on, of the different warriors, and their ships and chariots. In the middle of it all we also find pictures of women and children with carts pulled by oxen of the *bos indicus* family, also called the Zebu.[1] This clearly shows that they were migrating groups of people in search of new land. The Zebu bull was in this period a common phenomenon in Anatolia and Syria.[2]

Ramses boasts that he annihilated the enemies, in other words, the royal ideology of total destruction of the enemies was at work. However, at the same time the pharaoh declares that he has settled the prisoners in a number of strongholds and that he has assigned clothing and food to them. In other words, the establishing of peaceful conditions starts with defeat. The royal proclamation, as stated in the Papyrus Harris, is worth quoting:

> I extended all the frontiers of Egypt and overthrew those who attacked them from their lands. I slew the Denyen in their islands, while the Tjeker and the Philistines were made ashes. The Sherden and the Weshesh of the Sea were made nonexistent, captured all together and brought in captivity to Egypt like the sands of the shore. I settled them in strongholds, bound in my name.[3] Their military classes were as numerous as hundred-thousands. I assigned portions for them all with clothing and provisions from the treasuries and granaries every year.[4]

This is a typical example of the Near Eastern victory reports. The victory meant total destruction for enemies. If not it was no victory.

1. Y. Yadin, *The Art of Warfare in Biblical Lands* (New York, 1963), pp. 250, 336-38; R. Hestrin, *The Philistines and the Other Sea Peoples* (Muse'on Yisrael, Catal. no. 68; Jerusalem, 1970), fig. 1; N.K. Sandars, *The Sea Peoples*, fig. 77.

2. Cf. P.S. Ronzevalle, 'Le boeuf bossu en Syrie', *MUSJ* 4 (1910), pls. VIII-IX, and X.13-14.

3. This is illustrated in one relief that shows how prisoners were branded on the right shoulder; see H.H. Nelson, *Medinet Habu—1924-1928*. I. *The Epigraphic Survey of the Great Temple of Medinet Habu* (Oriental Institute Communications, 5; Chicago, 1929), p. 34 fig. 25.

4. J.A. Wilson, *ANET*, p. 262. H. Goedicke sees three political events mingled in Ramses III's reports about the Sea Peoples: 'first, the repelling of invaders; second, the submission of people who previously were not under his rule; and third, the quelling of people who had previously been accepted as vassals' (*The Report of Wenamun* [Baltimore, 1975], p. 177).

The idea is that the enemies represented the chaos powers and thus had to be completely defeated.[1] Yet life goes on and the subdued people are being taken care of. Note that in this text the Tjeker and the Philistines are said to have been made into ashes. In reality they were not; they later settled along the Palestinian coast. However, as a result of the defeat of the Sea Peoples' coalition, they never became a serious threat to Egypt and the rest of the Near East again.

One may wonder, however, how reliable Ramses' inscriptions are as historical documents. Perhaps he stands out as a greater ruler than he really was, because in his funerary temple at Medinet Habu he copied lists (from the Ramesseum) of countries conquered by Ramses II.[2] For instance, the scenes of his campaigns in Hatti and Amurru may be 'borrowed' glories. He claims to have taken and destroyed, for instance, Tunip in Hatti (Syria) and the 'city of Amurru', probably Qadesh.[3] One may on good grounds doubt that Ramses ever went that far north. These cities were destroyed by 'Sea Peoples' already before Ramses 'battled' them.[4]

As to the land battle with the 'Sea Peoples', Ramses claims to have organized his defense in Djahi, that is, Palestine; the exact location is not given. The Medinet Habu text mentions that the enemy had defeated Hatti, Kode (in Cilicia and northern Syria), Carchemish, Arzawa (a territory close to Cilicia) and Alashiya, and then set up camp in Amor (probably Amurru). The text then states that they marched against Egypt[5] and that those who reached the frontier, as well as those who came by sea, were killed. Ramses set out 'for Djahi,, like unto Montu,[6] to crush every foreign country that violates his frontier'.[7] This cannot mean anything else than the land battle occurred close to the Egyptian border somewhere in southern Palestine. The territory between Tell Jemme on the Wadi Ghazzeh (Nahal Besor) and Wadi el-Arish would then be the most probable battle ground. In

1.   This ideology and literary style is also well known from the Hebrew Bible.

2.   A. Gardiner, *Egypt of the Pharaohs*, p. 288, W. Helck, *Die Beziehungen*, p. 233.

3.   Cf. E. Drioton and J. Vandier, *L'Egypte* (4th edn; Paris, 1962), p. 438.

4.   Cf. W. Helck, *Die Beziehungen*, p. 233.

5.   Cf. G.A. Lehmann, who says that the battle could not have taken place in the Elutheros valley in Amurru ('Der Untergang des hethitischen Grossreiches und die neuen Text aus Ugarit', *UF* 2 [1970], pp. 70-71).

6.   Ramses here compares himself with the Egyptian god of war.

7.   J.A. Wilson, *ANET*, pp. 262-63.

this territory there were, for instance, two Egyptian strongholds, namely Deir el-Balaḥ on the coast and Tell el-Far'ah (S), which could have served as part of the northern defense line for the Egyptians.[1]

Ramses claims to have fought the Libyans and the Meshwesh again a few years later, according to the so-called Poem of the Libyan War of Year 11.[2] They had managed to settle in the western Delta and plundered some cities, among them Memphis. Ramses says that he defeated them and slew many, but that he branded some of their leaders and settled them and thousands of Libyans and Sherden in strongholds and forts, to which he gave his name.[3] This was an old custom practiced by several of the preceding pharaohs. The western territories of Egypt were always threatened by the Libyans. With Libyan tribes being settled in several of the towns and fortresses and with Libyans as mercenaries in the army, the Delta became infested with non-Egyptians. Many of these Libyans made a career in the Egyptian army and administration.[4] It is no wonder then that a Libyan later took over the reins in Egypt and founded the Twenty-Second Dynasty. This was Shoshenq (biblical Shishak[5]), the grandson of a chieftain of the Meshwesh.

The result of the battle against the Sea Peoples was that the coalition never again came alive. The Near East was entering a period of recuperation and reorganization. What happened to all of the survivors of the battles is poorly documented. For the history of Palestine we have, however, some information from the Bible about the Peleset/Philistines as the inhabitants of the southern part of the coastal area; see Josh. 13.3. The Tjeker are known from the 'Report of Wenamun' as having

---

1.   A letter from a commander, Sumitti, to the king of Ugarit (RS 20.33), mentions that Ugaritic troops were stationed in the areas of Amurru, and that the Egyptian king was marching north. This letter has been put in connection with Ramses III's land battle against the Sea Peoples, which then would mean that Ugarit had not yet been destroyed; see, for instance, A. Strobel, *Der spätbronzezeitliche Seevölkersturm,* pp. 69-72. H. Klengel maintains on good grounds, however, that the letter best suits the reign of Ramses II (*Geshichte Syriens*, II, pp. 213-14); cf. M. Liverani, *Storia di Ugarit* (Rome, 1962), pp. 77-78; G.A. Lehmann, *UF* 2 (1970), p. 69.

2.   W.F. Edgerton and J.A. Wilson, *Historical Records of Ramses III*, pp. 87-94. A. Spalinger does not see the structure of this text as being more poetic than other reports of Ramses' wars (*Aspects of the Military Documents*, p. 218).

3.   J.H. Breasted, *Ancient Records of Egypt*, IV, par. 405; J.A. Wilson, *ANET*, p. 262; K.A. Kitchen, *The Third Intermediate Period*, p. 245.

4.   Cf. A. Strobel, *Die spätbronzezeitliche Seevölkersturm*, p. 95.

5.   1 Kgs 14.25-28; 2 Chron. 12.2-10.

settled on the coast south of the Carmel with Dor as their main city.[1] In these two cases it is possible to entertain the idea that these peoples could have been settled in these areas by the Egyptians, as Libyans were settled in the Delta. Palestine was still an Egyptian dominion. Thus, one could assume that other groups of defeated Sea Peoples could have been settled in other garrison cities in Palestine, such as Megiddo and Beth-Shan. Level VI at Beth Shan is the city of the reign of Ramses III. The temple of Level VII was rebuilt in VI with only small changes; the layout was mainly the same. Anthropoid coffins from Level VI testify that Beth-Shan was still an Egyptian garrison city.[2] Scarabs of Ramses III have been found, for instance, at Ain Shemesh, Tell ed-Duweir, and Tell el-Fara'ah (S). There is also a fragment of a vase with Ramses' name from Gezer.[3] Egyptian temples also existed in the country,[4] as, for instance, at Gaza. Ramses, besides territory and estates in Egypt, gave nine cities to the god Amon at Thebes, thus increasing the wealth of the temple and its priesthood. Some cities were also given to Re of Heliopolis and to Ptah of Memphis. Ramses also assigned prisoners from Palestine and Nubia together with cattle to these temples.[5] In this way the temple aristocracy got cheap labor. The great increase in property[6] and cattle, grain, silver, gold, ships, and so forth meant that the power of the priesthood greatly increased at the expense of the pharaohs. This power continued after Ramses' death, contributing to the weakness of the pharaohs of the Twentieth Dynasty and thus to the fall of the empire.

The Tjekker

The Tjeker, who are mentioned in the inscriptions of Ramses III as being in league with the Peleset, Shekelesh, Denyen and Weshesh,[7]

1. *ANET*, pp. 25-29.

2. J. von Beckerath, *Tanis und Theben*, pp. 56-58.

3. F.W. James, *The Iron Age at Beth Shan*, p. 177.

4. Cf. A. Alt, 'Ägyptische Tempel in Palästina und die Landnahme der Philister', *KS*, I, pp. 216-30.

5. *ANET*, p. 261; W. Helck, *Die Beziehungen*, pp. 444-45.

6. J.H. Breasted estimates that about 722,533 acres belonged to the temples, or c. 15% of the land (*Ancient Records of Egypt*, IV, p. 98).

7. Their origin is debated, as is the case with most Sea Peoples. They have tentatively been identified with the Teukroi, who reputedly left Troy and founded the city of Salamis in Cyprus. This is perhaps no more than a legend. Cf., among

were settled on the Palestinian coast south of Carmel after having been repulsed by the Egyptians. This is documented in the Papyrus Harris[1] and in the Golenischeff papyrus in a narrative about the journey of an Egyptian official, Wen-Amun, from Amun's temple at Karnak. Wen-Amun had been sent on a mission to Gebal (Byblos) in order to get, among other things, cedar wood for Amun's barge called *Amun Userhet*.[2] It is claimed he sailed from Egypt in 1075 BCE. Even if the text is not a reliable source, it seems to reflect the situation in Palestine around or shortly after 1100 BCE and conveys a poorer impression than usual of Egypt's glory and power.[3]

Wen-Amun sailed into Dor, and seems to have been met with more respect by its ruler, Beder,[4] at least in the beginning, than he was shown in Tyre by its ruler, prince Zakar-Baal. The narrative indicates that the city of Dor was in Tjeker territory, which probably reached from the Carmel down to the Yarkon river. Other places that were under Tjeker rule indicate Tel Zeror 21 km south of Dor (coord. 147-203)[5] and Tel Mevorakh.[6]

others, A. Strobel, *Der spätbronzezeitliche Seevölkersturm*, pp. 48-54; R. de Vaux, *The Early History of Israel*, pp. 502-503; R.D. Barnett, 'The Sea Peoples', *CAH*, II.2 (3rd edn), pp. 359-79.

1. See J.A. Wilson, *ANET*, p. 262.

2. For a pictorial reconstruction, see B. Landström, *Ships of the Pharaohs: 4000 Years of Egyptian Shipbuilding* (Garden City, NY, 1970), pp. 120-21, figs. 370-71.

3. J.A. Wilson, *ANET*, pp. 25-29; A. Gardiner, *Egypt of the Pharaohs*, pp. 306-13. See also J.H. Breasted, *Ancient Records of Egypt*, IV, pp. 274-87, pars. 557-91; cf. H. Goedicke, who, among others, thinks that the tale is a copy of a lost original (*The Report of Wenamun*, pp. 6-7).

4. H. Goedicke thinks this individual is identical with Bedan in 1 Chron. 7.17 (*The Report of Wenamun*, pp. 28-29). This is impossible because this Bedan was a Gileadite. One may assume that Beder's behavior was due to the fact that Wen-Amun had been robbed of gold and silver at Dor.

5. Strata XII–XI at Tel Zeror have been collapsed into one stratum by the excavator, the first Iron I stratum. Its time would be from the mid-twelfth to the early eleventh cent. BCE (K. Ohata, *Tel Zeror*, III [Tokyo, 1970], pp. 3, 13). There are some unique pottery lamps with 'closed nozzles', and other pottery that is to be associated with the 'Philistine' style of ceramics, according to T. Dothan (*The Philistines*, p. 70). She also thinks that it possibly was Israelites that built str. XI (p. 69), but on the following page she assigns str. XI–X to the Sea Peoples!

6. This is about the same territory as that of Solomon's fourth district (1 Kgs 4.11); cf. W.F. Albright, 'The Administrative Divisions of Israel and Judah', *JPOS*

The city of Dor (Khirbet el-Burj, close to eṭ-Ṭanṭūra) was located on the rocky coast, which offered some lagoons and bays, making it very suitable for a port. The nautical history of Dor precedes the Tjeker, but there is no literary documentation of its importance before Wen-Amun's visit. However, it is mentioned in a topographical list by Ramses II from Amara, which simply mentions some coastal cities;[1] that is the only previous reference. The most recent excavations at Dor, however, have revealed some quay walls and pottery from the late thirteenth or early twelfth centuries BCE. These finds are of the utmost importance for a discussion of the origin of some of the peoples of the coastal area. It has turned out that these quay walls with their ashlars are of the same type as those found at Kition, Cyprus, at Palaeokastro Maa on the west coast of Cyprus, and at Minet el-Beida and Ras Ibn Hani in the territory of Ugarit.[2] The quay platforms at Kition not only resemble those at Dor, but they are also from the same period. Furthermore, a Bronze Age harbor with stone quays has also been found on Crete at the Minoan Malia.[3] Thus, 'the architectural and engineering concepts' found at Dor are part of a larger picture which can be found 'in similar, earlier structures around the Mediterranean'.[4] Since these concepts were not party to any Canaanite architectural schooling, we can conclude that the planners and architects

5 (1925), pp. 29-32; G.W. Ahlström, *Royal Administratio*, pp. 45 n. 12; N. Na'aman, *Borders and Districts in Biblical Historiography* (Jerusalem Bible Studies, 4; Jerusalem, 1986), pp. 184-86.

1.   Y. Aharoni, *The Land of the Bible* (2nd edn), p. 50. For the history of Dor, see G. Dahl, *The Materials for the History of Dor* (New Haven, 1915); G. Foerster, 'Dor', *EAEHL*, I, pp. 334-35; cf. S. Wachsmann and K. Raveh, 'A Concise Nautical History of Dor/Tantura', *The International Journal of Nautical Archaeology and Underwater Exploration* 13 (1984), pp. 223-41.

2.   See A. Raban, 'The Ancient Harbours of Israel in Biblical Times', *Harbour Archaeology: Proceedings of the First International Workshop on Ancient Mediterranean Harbours Caesarea Maritima 24–28.6.83* (BAR, 257; Oxford, 1985), pp. 23-27. As regards Ras Ibn Hani, this town was destroyed about the same time as Ugarit, but was subsequently rebuilt. Some texts have also been found at this place, which suggests that more could be found at other tells in the vicinity of Ras Shamra; cf. P.C. Craigie, *Ugarit and the Old Testament* (Grand Rapids, MI, 1983), p. 100.

3.   H. van Effenterre, *Le palais de Mallia et la cité Minoénne* (Incunabula Graeca, 76; Rome, 1980), pp. 75-77.

4.   A. Raban, 'The Harbor of the Sea Peoples at Dor', *BA* 50 (1987), p. 126.

of the harbor at Dor were newcomers to the country. The theory that the Tjeker were indigenous Semites in Palestine[1] can therefore be laid to rest. The Medinet Habu reliefs show the Tjeker wearing feathered headgear,[2] which was not characteristic of any indigenous Canaanite warriors.

Because the earliest remains of the harbor at Dor can be dated to the late thirteenth century BCE, it can be surmised that a group of Sea Peoples reached the Palestinian coast and settled at Dor before the attempt to invade Egypt occurred. If so, the phrase stating that the Peleset and the Tjeker were 'cut off from their land',[3] could refer to this prebattle activity.

Politically and economically these newcomers to the coastal area of Palestine could have been associated with the Sidonians. If so they would have regulated the trade both at sea and on land,[4] and with trade follows technical innovation. It is in this light that we may see the reference in 1 Sam. 13.19-21 mentioning that the peoples of the hills, the Israelites, had to go down to the Philistine areas in order to get their tools sharpened. The 'modern' technology of the day had not yet become part of the life of the people of the hills.

The political organization of Dor under Egyptian rule is not known. However, following A. Alt, we could maintain that, where 'the division of the land into city states had been most fully developed' by the Egyptians, it still continued after their rule had come to an end.[5] Thus, the city state of Dor and its surroundings were governed by the Tjeker first under the tutelage of the Egyptian administration, and then, when Egypt's power was declining, more and more independently, as was the case with the Philistine cities. Dor's independence, however, did not last long. Its end came with the expansion of the

---

1. Thus H. Goedicke, *The Report of Wenamun*, p. 28.

2. W.F. Edgerton and J.A. Wilson, *Historical Records of Ramses III*, p. 45 (text to pl. 43).

3. Consult W.F. Edgerton and J.A. Wilson, *Historical Records of Ramses III*, p. 130.

4. Cf. B. Mazar, 'The Philistines and the Rise of the Israelite and Tyrian Kingdoms', *The Israel Academy of Sciences and Humanities: Proceedings*, I (no. 7; Jerusalem, 1964).

5. 'The Settlement of the Israelites in Palestine', *Essays on Old Testament History and Religion* (Garden City, NY, 1967), p. 207.

Israelite monarchy (probably under David). 1 Kgs 4.11 mentions Dor as one of Solomon's district capitals.[1]

To return to the journey of Wen-Amun, he was robbed of his gold and silver at Dor. This was the money with which he was to pay for the cedars. Wen-Amun asked the prince of Dor to catch the thief and recover the money, but Beder declined to do so because the theft was not within his jurisdiction: it had occurred on an Egyptian ship. After nine days Wen-Amun sailed for Byblos followed and watched by several of Beder's ships. Byblos' prince, Zakar-Baal, seems to have been cool towards Wen-Amun. This has been seen as an indication that Byblos was no longer politically dependent upon Egypt. If Zakar-Baal was hostile to Egypt he could easily have rejected Wen-Amun's request for timber, but the problem is more complex than that. The Phoenician cities of Arvad, Sidon and Byblos had been forced to pay tribute to Tiglath-Pileser I of Assyria (1115–1077 BCE), which means that Zakar-Baal's position was more delicate than has formerly been assumed. Here was a problem of diplomacy. The Egyptian emissary could easily have been dismissed because he did not have proper credentials and no gifts from the pharaoh. Officially he was not an envoy of pharaoh Ramses XI (1098–1070 BCE), who, even if he was a puppet king, should have given credentials to an Egyptian messenger. As a matter of fact, pharaoh is not even mentioned in the text. Egypt was at this time divided into two spheres of interest. The high-priest of Amun, Herihor, ruled in Thebes over the south and Nubia. Smendes (Nisubanebded) ruled in the north at Tanis in the Delta. None of these had the title of king at this time,[2] therefore none of them could be recognized in Byblos as the lord of Egypt. This was Wen-Amun's problem. Zakar-Baal, if he wanted, could turn down any request that did not come from the king. He sent Wen-Amun day by day an order to get out of the harbor. This went on for 29 days.

Becoming desperate, Wen-Amun asked for a ship to take him back to Egypt. At this point the 'divine will' put an end to Wen-Amun's

1. According to Judg. 1.27, Manasseh could not 'drive out the inhabitants of Dor and its outlying villages'. The list of 31 kings (including a king of Dor) defeated by Joshua (from Lebanon to Edom) in Josh. 12.8-24 is part of the historical, tendentious reconstruction whose goal was to declare that the whole country was given to the Israelites by Yahweh.

2. Smendes became the founder of the Twenty-First Dynasty in 1070 BCE.

long wait. At a sacrifice, one of Zakar-Baal's young officials, a page (?), was seized by the god and divined, giving the order to bring the emissary and the god-image with him to the king.[1] The prophecy established that the god Amun had indeed ordered the expedition of Wen-Amun. Thus the credentials were in order.[2] Zakar-Baal followed the prophetic voice and received Wen-Amun. After some discussion and after receiving the money requested from Egypt (Smendes), the prince consented to deliver the timber but tried to delay Wen-Amun's departure until the winter season was over.[3] The story ends with Wen-Amun being driven to Cyprus because of a storm. As a piece of literature providing some interesting and probably true insights into eleventh-century courts and their political intrigues, the Wen-Amun story is unique,[4] but it is doubtful whether the tale in all its details can be used as a source for history. The story is rather to be seen as a romantic novella.[5] It may indicate, however, that the sea trade along the Levantine coast had resumed again after the 'Sea Peoples' had been repulsed from Egypt.[6]

A piece of information with special historical significance occurring in this narrative is the mention of 500 rolls of papyri that Smendes is supposed to have sent Zakar-Baal as part of the payment for the lumber.[7] We also learn that Zakar-Baal on one occasion brought forth some scrolls from the archives in order to show Wen-Amun the previous transactions according to the records. This shows that in Byblos one did not write on clay tablets, and no such tablets have been found there.[8] Here we probably have the earliest information about the

1.   The incident shows that ecstatic prophecy was acknowledged in Phoenicia.

2.   This is the literary goal of the tale. What really happened is unknown, but for the writer Egypt and its god Amun had again won a 'battle'.

3.   Cf. H. Goedicke, *The Report of Wenamun*, p. 105.

4.   Cf. A. Gardiner, *Egypt of the Pharaohs*, p. 306.

5.   G. Lefèbvre, *Romans et contes égyptiens* (Paris, 1949), pp. 204-20.

6.   Cf. H. Goedicke, who says that the 'sole mention of Sidon at this point as a representative maritime power is significant', and that *W-r-k-t-r* (l. 22) may be the ruler of Sidon (*The Report of Wenamun*, pp. 70-71).

7.   The papyrus plant (*cyperus papyrus*) was at home in Egypt, especially thriving in the Delta. The Greeks connected the word with Byblos, which shows from where they got the papyrus material. This is the origin of the word Bible, Greek *byblios*, *biblios*, diminutive *biblion*, pl. *biblia*, 'book, books'.

8.   Cf. K.A. Kitchen, *Ancient Orient and Old Testament* (London, 1966), p. 137.

Phoenician script, which may have been inspired by the Egyptians.[1] Knowing that the writing material was papyrus, it justifies the assumption that in Byblos pen and ink had been used for quite some time.

The Philistines

It has often been maintained that the Philistines were allowed to settle on the Palestinian coast with the permission of the Egyptian government, as was the case with the Libyans and Sherden, who were settled in strongholds in the Delta. In this way the Egyptian government saw to it that the defeated peoples were incorporated in their 'cosmological' order. One ought to remember that Palestine was under Egyptian rule, and that the southern coast from Gaza to el-Arish was probably reckoned as Egyptian territory since the time of the Hyksos. There are no indications that the Philistines conquered the areas of the southern coast. As defeated enemies were placed in strongholds in Egypt, the Philistines and the Tjeker, as well as other Sea Peoples, may have been quartered in garrisons at well-fortified places in Palestine. Thus, it cannot be ruled out that some group(s) of Sea Peoples could have been placed in the garrisons at Megiddo[2] and Beth-Shan.[3]

Caution should be used in applying the destruction layers at Ashdod and Ashkelon, which have been associated with the Sea Peoples' advance, to the Philistines. A.S. Rainey has concluded from the levels at these two sites that there was a 'definite span between the beginning

---

1.   For the enigmatic script on two bronze tablets found at Byblos, see M. Dunand, *Byblia grammata: Documents et recherches sur le developement de l'écriture en Phénicie* (Beyrouth, 1945), pp. 78, 136-37; cf. I.J. Gelb, *A Study of Writing*, p. 158.

2.   Cf. A. Strobel, *Die spätbronzezeitliche Seevölkersturm*, p. 88.

3.   It is a mistake to assume that Beth-Shan was occupied by the Philistines, as T. Dothan maintains. She builds her opinion on 1 Sam. 31.8-13, mentioning that the Philistines displayed the bodies of Saul and his sons on the city wall of Beth-Shan after the battle at Gilboa (*Excavations at the Cemetery of Deir el-Balah*, p. 102). The biblical text does not say anything about a Philistine occupation of the city of Beth-Shan. Probably the Philistines were allied to the people of Beth-Shan, which would be natural, considering that both parties had been Egyptian mercenary groups. Another thing to note in this connection is that Beth-Shan is lacking in typical Philistine pottery.

of the 12th century' and the settlement of the Philistines.[1] From what has been demonstrated above, Ashkelon was destroyed by Merneptah; thus it is possible that the Philistines rebuilt the ruined Ashkelon.[2]

The origin of the Philistines has troubled scholars for a long time. As mentioned above, they are counted as one group of Sea Peoples, Northerners, mentioned in the texts about the invasion of Egypt under Ramses III's rule. They are reckoned among the group of people that came by land. In Palestine they were not maritime people, which may be concluded from the fact that they did not build any important harbors on the Palestinian coast.[3] One port city built by the Philistines was at Tell Qasîle. Because the town was located a few kilometers from the sea on the northern bank of the river Yarkon, its port or quay (which has not been found) was probably not suitable for large seagoing ships.[4] Tell Qasîle may have replaced the LB anchorage at Tell Jerishe (identification uncertain)[5] on the southern bank of the river. This was destroyed around 1200 BCE.[6] Ashkelon, which was on the seaboard, had long had a port, and Ashdod's harbor was located at modern Tel Mor (7 km NW of Ashdod on the coast),[7] a site known

1. In Y. Aharoni, *The Land of the Bible*, 2nd edn, p. 268.

2. A. Mazar attributes the rebuilding of Ashdod, str. XII, to the 'second phase of the Philistine culture', which also 'included the development of the local Bichrome Philistine pottery style'. He dates this phase to the time after Ramses VI (*Excavations at Tell Qasile. II. The Philistine Sanctuary: Various Finds, the Pottery, Conclusions, Appendixes* [Qedem, 20; Jerusalem, 1985], p. 120).

3. Cf. N.K. Sandars, *The Sea Peoples*, p. 201.

4. According to A. Mazar, there was no quay, and none was necessary. The boats (no longer than c. 20 m) could unload on the bank (private communication).

5. Gath Rimmon (Josh. 19.45; 21.24), or *knt* (Gath), mentioned in Tuthmosis III's list of Canaanite cities have been suggested; cf. N. Avigad, 'Jerishe', *EAEHL*, II, p. 575. A better suggestion would be 'Me-jarkon and Rakkon with the territory facing Joppa', as the text of Josh. 19.46 says. The phrase *mê hayyarkôn* means 'the waters of the Yarkon', and *hā-raqqôn* would then be a place name near the river; so e.g. F.-M. Abel, who identifies it with modern Tell er-Reqqeit (*Géographie de la Palestine*, I [Paris, 1967], p. 472).

6. E.L. Sukenik, 'Jerishe', *QDAP* 4 (1935), pp. 208-209; N. Avigad, *EAEHL*, II, pp. 575-78. Avigad suggests that the town was destroyed either by the Israelites or the Philistines. He is followed by T. Dothan, *The Philistines*, p. 69. The Israelites are out of the question, as is to be concluded from my book, *Who were the Israelites?* The Philistines may have caused the destruction on their way down to Egypt.

7. J.F. Brug has some problem with seeing Tel Mor as the harbor of the Philistines, if they 'were indeed sea people', because the place 'continued to be a

from the late sixteenth century BCE. Thus the Philistines as displaced Aegeans, having to adapt themselves to the customs and to the terrain of the land, may have done what could be done in a territory not suitable for sea trade.

An interesting passage occurs in the Egyptian text about the preparations for the battle against the Sea Peoples. It says that the 'Peleset are in suspense hidden in their towns'.[1] This should be put together with the information on a stela from Ramses III's twelfth year, in which he says that he 'overthrew the Tjek[er], the land[2] of the Pele[set], the Denyen, the [W]eshesh, and the Shekelesh'.[3] From this we may draw the conclusion that the Peleset/Philistines, from wherever they came, must have settled or been encamped somewhere for some period of time before joining those who marched to Egypt.[4] Were they Northerners who had advanced into Palestine before the other groups and camped there? or did the Egyptian scribe/engraver know that they had been living at some other place which he in his 'generosity' refers to as having been overthrown by the mighty pharaoh who had defeated the 'whole world'?[5] In this kind of laudatory text details of geography are of lesser importance. The purpose of the text is not geographical accuracy, but the praise of Pharaoh and Egypt's 'supreme' power.[6]

Canaanite town for two generations' (*A Literary and Archaeological Study of the Philistines* (BAR, 265; Oxford, 1985), p. 90. It should be noted, however, that we do not have any information about the Canaanites being displaced or 'eradicated' from this part of the earth. The Philistines ruled over the Canaanites.

1. W.F. Edgerton and J.A. Wilson, *Historical Records of Ramses III*, p. 35. The Egyptian sign *dmí*, 'quay', is also used for town and city (R.O. Faulkner, *A Concise Dictionary of Middle Egyptian* [Oxford, 1962], p. 313).

2. It is not clear from the text whether the term *t3*, 'land', refers to the Peleset alone or includes also the Denyen, Weshesh and Shekelesh. It could refer to all four categories (J. Johnson, private communication).

3. W.F. Edgerton and J.A. Wilson, *Historical Records of Ramses III*, pp. 130-31.

4. The term *t3*, 'earth, ground, land', does not necessarily mean that they were settled, *contra* J.F. Brug, *A Literary and Archaeological Study of the Philistines*, p. 19.

5. Because the reports and reliefs are made some time after the battle, one is informed that both the Philistines and the Tjeker had been assigned their respective territories on the Palestinian coast. The word *t3*, 'land', could therefore refer to this fact.

6. Cf. H.H. Nelson, *Medinet Habu—1924–28* (Chicago, 1929), p. 16.

There is, however, one piece of information in the reliefs that may point to the fact that the invasion of the so-called Sea Peoples was not only a military event. As mentioned before, we can see in the reliefs that there are groups of people coming with women and children and carts drawn by oxen.[1] This can only reflect a more or less peaceful migration protected by the men. They are pictured with the so-called feathered headdress ('crown') worn also by the Philistines, which probably is of Aegean origin.[2] The Philistines were not alone in using this headgear as we know from the Medinet Habu reliefs; the Denyen and the Tjeker also wore the same kind of headdress.[3] A portrayal of a Peleset/Philistine warrior on the northern colonnade of the temple at Medinet Habu (see Fig. 4) shows a captured, kneeling warrior without the 'feathered' headdress. He is wearing a kind of cap or turban on his head instead.[4] The humpbacked oxen (*Bos indicus*) pulling the carts were at this time common in northern Syria and in Anatolia.[5] From

1. H.H. Nelson, *The Epigraphic Survey: Medinet Habu*. II. *Later Historical Records of Ramses III* (Chicago, 1932), II, Pl. 118c.
2. The pictographic 'Phaistos disc' from Crete (sixteenth cent.) depicts a warrior with this kind of headdress (A. Evans, *The Palace of Minos*, I [London, 1921], fig. 482; cf. pp. 647-49); C. Davaras sees the headdress as not being 'unminoisch'; ('Zur Herkunft des Diskos von Phaistos', *Kadmos* 6 [1967], p. 105); cf. R.D. Barnett, *CAH*, II (3rd edn), pp. 359-78. A warrior with the same feathered 'crown' is depicted on a vase from Cyprus (Enkomi), thirteenth cent. BCE; cf. also a game box from Enkomi (E. Sjöqvist, *Problems of the Late Cypriot Bronze Age* [Stockholm, 1940], figs. 10, 19). There is also a seal from Enkomi showing a warrior with a shield and a 'feathered' headdress; see P. Dikaios, *Enkomi Excavations 1948–1958*, IIIa (Mainz a.R., 1969), pls. 138.5 and 187.19; cf. J.F. Brug, *A Literary and Archaeological Study of the Philistines*, p. 146 figs. 21.b, c.
3. It is not possible to say whether the 'headdress' was a special hairdo or head wear consisting of feathers or folded material; see N.K. Sandars, *The Sea Peoples*, pp. 134-37. For the headdress and the different bands around them, see E. Oren, *The Northern Cemetery of Beth Shan*, pp. 136-39.
4. See N.K. Sandars, *The Sea Peoples*, p. 165 fig. 113. The same cap or turban is worn by one of the prisoners from Ramses III's 'northern war'; cf. H.H. Nelson, *Medinet Habu Reports*. I. *The Epigraphic Survey 1928–31* (Chicago, 1931), p. 34, fig. 21; N.K. Sandars, *The Sea Peoples*, p. 136 fig. 93.
5. See F.E. Zeuner, *A History of Domesticated Animals* (London, 1963), pp. 236-40; P.R.S. Moorey, 'A Bronze Statuette of a Bull', *Levant* 3 (1971), pp. 90-91; H. Bossert, *Altanatolien* (Berlin, 1942), Nr. 778; H.G. Güterbock, *Siegel aus Boghazköy* (AfO, Beiheft 7; Osnabrück, 1967), Tafel 1.1.

an Egyptian point of view, these groups have been seen as a threatening horde of foreigners. Thus one may ask the question whether or not two originally independent events were joined together by the Egyptians as a military attack.

After Ramses had successfully stopped the invasion(s) he placed some of the groups in border areas of the kingdom under the leadership and protection of their own chieftains to govern the provinces as Egyptian representatives, with all the attendant obligations, including military service in the Egyptian army. Their rulers thus became Egyptian 'governors' and commanders.[1] From this point of view the Philistines and the Tjeker did not have to conquer the coastal areas assigned to them.[2] The result was that the Egyptian government got some caretakers to look after the 'provinces', while the newly arrived Northerners got a new homeland. For Egypt this policy only worked for a short time. Its government was too weak to uphold its authority. Soon the Philistines, as well as the whole of Palestine, were freed from Egyptian rule and new political constellations emerged.

Politically the Philistines organized their territory into five city-states known as the Philistine *pentapolis*. These cities were Ashkelon, Ashdod, Ekron, Gath (Tell eṣ-Ṣafi?, coord. 135-123)[3] and Gaza (Josh. 13.3). Ekron has been seen as a new settlement founded by the

1.   J. von Beckerath, *Tanis und Theben*, pp. 58-59. This can be interpreted as being a sign of weakness concerning the Egyptian government. As time passed by, the Philistines became the real rulers of Palestine—for a short time. J. von Beckerath has compared Ramses III's solution with that of the declining Roman empire, when Germanic tribes were given certain border territories to 'govern' and 'protect' in the interests of the Romans. The chieftains of these provinces soon took over the rule, and this marked the end of the Roman empire (*Tanis und Theben*, p. 59).

2.   They could, however, have destroyed some towns and villages on their way down to Egypt.

3.   Many suggestions have been made for the location of Gath. K. Elliger identified Gath with modern Tell eṣ-Ṣafi at the western end of the Valley of Elah (Wadi es-Sanṭ) ('Der Heimat des Propheten Micha', *ZDPV* 57 [1934], pp. 148-52). This identification is accepted by most scholars; cf. the discussion by A.S. Rainey, 'The Identification of Biblical Gath', *EI* 12 (1975), pp. 63-76; Y. Aharoni, *The Land of the Bible*, 2nd edn, pp. 271-72. However, according to 1 Sam. 30.1, the king of Gath, Achish, gave the town of Ziklag in the Negev to David as his city of residence. Ziklag would then be within the territory of Gath. This means that either Gath must be placed farther south, or that Achish was the first among Philistine princes, or that the biblical writer's knowledge about Philistine administration and geography was not very good.

Philistines, because it is not mentioned in any pre-Philistine sources.[1] However, if Ekron is to be located at Khirbet el-Muqanna' (Tel Miqne, coord. 136-131),[2] the recent excavations give a different picture. The site has yielded remains from the Chalcolithic through the Iron II Ages.[3] The Philistines built and rebuilt cities on the southern coast from Tell Qasîle in the north to Tell Jemme, Qubur el-Walaida (10 km south of Gaza),[4] and Tell el-Far'ah in the south and Tell esh-Shari'a (coord. 119-088, Ziklag?)[5] in the southeast. Ashdod, for instance, was rebuilt according to a new city plan different from that of the preceding stratum XIII.[6] Ashdod's port at modern Tel Mor was unfortified.[7] Among the new settlements were Tel Batash (Timnah?)[8] and the 'port city' at Tell Qasîle (coord. 168-131) on the northern bank of the river Yarkon in the northern outskirts of Tel Aviv. This port shows the maritime interests of the settlers. According to A. Mazar, the people of Qasîle arrived from the south, bringing with them the Bichrome Philistine pottery tradition.[9] One may doubt, however, that all the inhabitants of Qasîle were Philistines. Some indigenous people may also have settled in the town or have been employed by the Philistines. Tell Qasîle on the coast and Aphek, c. 20 km east of Qasîle, were the two northernmost points of Philistia proper. Whether 'Izbet Sartah (3 km east of Aphek) should be mentioned in this connection is a matter of controversy. It will be discussed in connection with the Iron Age I settlement of the central hills. As for Jaffa

---

1. Thus T. Dothan, *The Philistines*, p. 17.

2. See J. Naveh, 'Khirbat al-Muqanna'–Ekron: An Archaeological Survey', *IEJ* 8 (1958), pp. 87-100, 165-70.

3. It was a fortified town in MB II, and obviously had a city wall in LB I and II. Mycenaean IIIC.1b pottery was found in the LB II phase; see T. Dothan and S. Gitin, 'Tel Miqne', *IEJ* 35 (1985), pp. 67-71. Note that Timnah is listed in the Bible as a town belonging to the 'tribe' of Dan (Josh. 19.43).

4. See R. Cohen in 'Notes and News', *IEJ* 28 (1978), pp. 194-95.

5. E.D. Oren has tentatively identified Tell esh-Shari'a (Tel Sera') with biblical Ziklag ('Ziklag—A Biblical City on the Edge of the Negev', *BA* 45 [1982], pp. 155-66).

6. Cf. T. Dothan, *The Philistines*, pp. 36-42.

7. M. Dothan, 'Tel Mor and Ashdod', *IEJ* 23 (1973), pp. 1-17; T. Dothan, *The Philistines*, p. 43.

8. G.L. Kelm and A. Mazar, 'Three Seasons of Excavations at Tel Batash—Biblical Timnah', *BASOR* 248 (1982), pp. 1-36.

9. *Excavations at Tell Qasile*, II, p. 122.

(Joppa), the prosperous Late Bronze Age city was followed by a poor settlement, as far as archaeology has been able to show; very little Philistine ware has been found there.[1] This would mean that Jaffa had lost its importance and its port had perhaps been replaced by that of Tell Qasîle.

The ruler of each city state was, according to the Hebrew Bible,[2] a *seren*, a word that has been understood as a synonym for pre-Greek *tyrannos*, 'chief, ruler',[3] which, however, is problematic.[4] For a Hebrew this term was the same as king, which can be seen in connection with the stories of David's loyalty to the Philistines. The ruler of Gath, Achish, is called king in 1 Sam. 21.11 and 27.2. It is not known whether the position of *seren* was hereditary or not. It may perhaps have been parallel to the Greek *basileus*, which became the title for a ruler in post-Mycenaean times.[5] In later times, the inscriptions of the Assyrian kings indicate that the ruler's position was hereditary, which says no more than that the Philistine societies had adapted to the life of the Near East.[6]

Other rulers from the early period are not mentioned, nor do we learn anything about their administrative or social organizations. From a later period, the Prism of Sennacherib[7] mentions that the population of Ekron was divided into three main categories: (1) the *šakanakkē*, the military chiefs, (2) the *rubē*, the nobility, and (3) the *nišē*, the people, who could also be called the *mārē ali*, 'the sons of the city, citizens'. It is not clear whether this really represents a

---

1.   H. Kaplan and J. Kaplan, 'Jaffa', *EAEHL*, II, pp. 532-41.

2.   1 Sam. 5.8; 6.4, 16.

3.   C. Rabin considers this as being a loan-word from Lydian ('Hittite Words in Hebrew', *Or* NS 32 [1963], pp. 113-39); cf. W. Helck, 'Ein sprachliches Indiz für die Herkunft der Philister', *BN* 21 (1983), p. 31.

4.   See F. Bork, 'Philistäische Namen und Vokabeln', *AfO* 13 (1939–41), p. 228.

5.   C.G. Starr, *The Origins of Greek Civilizations* (New York, 1961), pp. 326-28. According to Starr, the Mycenaean kings, *wanakes*, 'tried to model their bureaucratic economies on the Oriental prototype', i.e., 'divine' kingship (p. 326). The position of *basileus* seems to have been hereditary, while that of the *tyrannos* was not (p. 328).

6.   Cf. T. Dothan, *The Philistines*, pp. 18-19.

7.   D.D. Luckenbill, *The Annals of Sennacherib* (OIP, 2; Chicago, 1924), II.73, III.8. A.L. Oppenheim considers this a social stratification of the society (*ANET*, p. 287 n. 3); cf. *idem*, *Ancient Mesopotamia*, p. 359 n. 44.

Philistine organization of the society or whether it is only the Assyrian understanding of what kind of people they had to deal with.

The main textual source of information about the Philistines is the Hebrew Bible. Here we meet a tradition stating that the Philistines came from Caphtor, in Gen. 10.12, Deut. 2.23, Jer. 47.3-4 and Amos 9.7. Genesis 10 is the so-called Table of Nations, the purpose of which was to use genealogies to the inhabitants of the world in the time after the flood with Noah, the primeval father of humankind. In v. 6 Egypt (Misraim) and Canaan are made the sons of Ham, and one of Egypt's sons is Caphtor, 'from whom the Philistines came'. The Hebrew writer has here lumped together the Hamitic people of Egypt with the Semitic people of Canaan. The Philistines are made to be related to Canaan and Egypt. This has been done because Canaan had once been part of the Egyptian empire and its cultural sphere and because the Philistines had been Egyptian mercenaries, later on succeeding the Egyptians as oppressors.[1] Other peoples have been given the same kind of association because of their relationship to Egypt, namely Lud, Anam, Lehab, Naphtuh, Pathros, Cusluh and Caphtor.[2] These are the sons of Misraim.[3] The Ludim could be the Lydians, who served as mercenaries in the Egyptian army in the seventh century BCE. This would indicate that the text was not created earlier than the seventh century BCE.[4]

Deuteronomy 2.23 seems to identify the Philistines with the Caphtorim who drove out the inhabitants of Gaza, referring to some unverifiable tradition. The prophet Jeremiah says that Yahweh will destroy the Philistines, 'the remnant of the isle of Caphtor' (47.4). Amos 9.7 states that Yahweh brought the Philistines from Caphtor. Jeremiah associates the Philistines and Caphtorites with an island in the Mediterranean. If we then combine this with the information in Ezek. 25.16 that Yahweh's hand will be against the Philistines and the Cerethites (Cretans), and that he will 'wipe out the remnant of the coastland', then the conclusion must be that the Philistines, according to the prophets Jeremiah and Ezekiel, originally were peoples of some

1. Cf. E.A. Speiser, who maintained that 'the classification is geographical' (*Genesis* [Garden City, NY, 3rd edn, 1981], p. 69).

2. The Lehabs are the Libyans and Naphtuh and Pathros are Egyptian peoples. The Cushluh have hot been identified; cf. J. Strange, *Caphtor/Keftiu*, p. 36.

3. Cf. 1 Chron. 1.11-12.

4. Cf. J. Strange, *Caphtor/Keftiu*, pp. 35-37.

sea country.[1] Jeremiah's information is more specific in that he states
that they came from an island called Caphtor. Ezekiel, however,
associates the Philistines with people from Crete, an association that is
also made by most scholars, because Caphtor seems to refer to Crete
in certain nonbiblical texts.[2]

Because the Bible does not specify to what island Caphtor refers, its
location is still debated. The name is known from Assyrian texts of the
Mari period as *kaptara* (Crete),[3] and *kaptaru* (the 'Caphtorite'),[4] in
Ugaritic as *kpt*, and in Egyptian as *kftíw*. The latter is common in
Egyptian inscriptions of the Late Bronze Age, but disappears around
1350 BCE, when there was a discontinuation of the contacts between
Egypt and Crete, because Crete's political and economic rule ended at
this time. Sir Arthur Evans' excavations at Knossos, Crete, probably
inspired most scholars to see Keftiu as referring to Crete.[5] There are,
however, some other suggestions, such as Cyprus and the Cilician-
Syrian coast.[6] J. Vercoutter, however, points to the fact that the
Egyptians considered Keftiu to represent a large 'zone de civilisation'
on a par with those of Hatti, Mitanni and Mesopotamia. This idea is
best explained by seeing Keftiu as a reference to the Minoan

1. Cf. Zeph. 2.4-7.
2. J.D.S. Pendelbury, 'Egypt and the Aegean in the Late Bronze Age', *JEA* 16
(1930), pp. 75-92. J.F. Brug, for instance, acknowledges that 'Caphtor appears to
be Crete in Egyptian and Akkadian usage', but that the name in the Old Testament
may have a broader meaning 'referring to the Mediterranean islands and coasts in
general' (*A Literary and Archaeological Study of the Philistines*, p. 48).
3. *ARM*, XVI.1, p. 19.
4. *CAD*, *s.v.* This could refer to Crete; cf. C.F.-A. Schaeffer, 'Reprise de
recherches archéologiques à Ras Shamra-Ugarit', *Syria* 28 (1951), pp. 1-21. In the
economic texts from Mari there occur both *alašu*, Alashiya/Cyprus, and *kaptara*,
Crete; thus Caphtor cannot refer to Cyprus. See G. Dossin, 'Les archives
économiques du palais de Mari', *Syria* 20 (1939), pp. 111-12.
5. See the investigation by J. Vercoutter (*L'Egypte et le monde égéen*).
6. See the discussion by J. Strange, *Caphtor/Keftiu*, pp. 113-84. A. Furumark
saw the Philistines as coming from Cilicia because he found 'Philistine' pottery there
('The Settlement at Ialysos and Aegean History, c. 1550–1400 BCE', *Opuscula
Archaeologica*, VI [Skrifter utgivna av Svenska Institutet i Rom, 15; Lund, 1950],
pp. 203-71). This does not necessarily mean that the Philistines must originate from
Cilicia. They could have stopped there for a time before continuing south.
G.A. Wainwright thinks the Philistines had been settled in western Cilicia (*JEA* 47
[1961], pp. 78-79).

civilization.[1] The phrase '*kftiw* and the isles in the midst of the sea' does not associate Keftiu with Anatolia.[2] Keftiu represents a country north and west of Egypt. That means that if it is not in Anatolia it must be in the Aegean.[3] Both Keftiu and the isles 'belong to the same geographical entity', that is, the Aegean.[4] This interpretation is supported by a topographical list on the base of a statue from the funerary temple of Amenhotep III mentioning some Cretan and Peloponnesian cities.[5] Besides Mycenae we find Amnisos, Phaistos, Kydonia, Diqa' (Mt Dikte in eastern Crete?),[6] Methana,[7] Nauplia, Kythera, Ilios (?),[8] Knossos, Lyktos, Kefitu and Tinay.[9] Almost all of these places were Aegean ports except Knossos, the harbor of which was Amnisos. Whether Keftiu was a port or a territory cannot be decided. However, the occurrence of Keftiu in this inscription clearly places it in the Aegean.[10] Another conclusion that may be drawn from this list is that there existed a well-developed trade system between the Aegean and Egypt in the fourteenth century BCE.[11] It is possible that

1.   J. Vercoulter, *L'Egypte*, pp. 118-19.

2.   J. Pendelbury, *JEA* 16 (1930), pp. 75-92.

3.   J. Strange, who believes that Caphtor/Keftiu is Cyprus, acknowledges, however, that it could be a reference to Crete (*Caphtor/Keftiu*, pp. 50, 125-26).

4.   R.S. Merrillees, 'Aegean Bronze Age Relations with Egypt', *AJA* 76 (1972), p. 289.

5.   E. Edel, *Die Ortsnamenlisten*, pp. 33-59; K.A. Kitchen, 'Theban Topographical Lists, Old and New', *Or* NS 34 (1965), pp. 1-9.

6.   Thus M. Astour, 'Aegean Place-Names in an Egyptian Inscription', *AJA* 70 (1966), pp. 313-14.

7.   A city in Argolis, as were Nauplia and Mycenae; see H. Goedicke, 'Ägäische Namen in ägyptischen Inschriften', *Wiener Zeitschrift für die Kunde des Morgenlandes* 62 (1969), pp. 7-10. J. Strange follows Edel and reads 'Messania', which was located in the territory of Pylos (*Caphtor/Keftiu*, pp. 21-22).

8.   H. Goedicke points out that Ilios is only an appelative for Troy, and not a place name, and that Troy is too far away from all the other places mentioned in the text. He suggests Aulis in Boeotia (*Wiener Zeitschrift für die Kunde des Morgenlandes* 62 [1969], pp. 9-10).

9.   E. Edel, *Die Ortsnamenlisten*, pp. 33-59. As to the identification of the different names, see also J. Strange, *Caphtor/Keftiu*, pp. 21-23 (with references).

10.   Cf. M. Astour, review of J. Strange, *Caphtor/Keftiu*, *JAOS* 102 (1982), p. 395.

11.   The Mycenaeans would at this time also have been the rulers of Knossos and Crete, according to E. Edel (*Die Ortsnamenlisten*, p. 59).

these contacts started already after the Hyksos were expelled from Egypt, that is, after 1541 BCE.

For the location of Keftiu we should note that in Egyptian texts *kftíw* refers to the north or, in texts with only two directions, the west. In an annalistic text of Tuthmosis III, *kftíw*-ships and *kpn*-ships ('Byblos-ships') are mentioned as being in all the harbors of Egypt loaded with precious things and timber.[1] This refers to Egyptian-made ships sailing to Keftiu and Byblos.[2] In antiquity ships usually sailed along the coasts, not out on the open sea if it could be avoided. The route to and from Keftiu went via Byblos, then probably to Cyprus and further on along the Anatolian coast.[3] This is the reason why one has been able to find pottery resembling the so-called Philistine ware in, for instance, Cappadocia.[4]

The conclusion that can be drawn from the above is that Caphtor/ Keftiu refers to Crete. Still, we do not know whether the Hebrew tradition about the Philistines coming from Caphtor (Amos 9.7) really meant that the Philistines originally were Cretans, or only that they were seen as associated with people who came from Crete and the Aegean.[5] The term had possibly lost its specific meaning so many

1. T. Säve-Söderbergh, *The Navy of the Eighteenth Dynasty* (UUÅ, 1946.6; Uppsala, 1946), pp. 48-50.
2. See T. Säve-Söderbergh, *The Navy*, pp. 47-50. A modern parallel to this would be the term 'America boat' that was used in my childhood in Göteborg (Gothenburg), Sweden. It referred to the Swedish liners sailing to America.
3. T. Säve-Söderbergh, *The Navy*, p. 49 n. 2.
4. A. Furumark, 'Settlement at Ialysos', *Opuscula Archaeologica*, VI, pp. 239-41; cf. G.A. Wainwright, *JEA* 47 (1961), pp. 71-90. For a critique of the so-called Cappadocian theory, see A. Strobel, *Der spätbronzezeitliche Seevölkersturm*, pp. 102-16.
5. One theory is that the Philistines/Peleset would be the same as the Pelasgians, i.e., the pre-Greek population of Thessaly and Epirus. For instance, a wall in Athens was called both the Pelasgic wall and the Pelastic wall; thus the Pelastians could be the same as the Pulasti/Peleset, i.e., Philistines (G. Georgiev, 'Sur l'origine et langue des Pelasges, des Philistins, des Danéens et des Achéens', *Jahrbuch für kleinasiatische Forschung* 1 [1950–51], pp. 136-41). J.P. Brown maintains that the Greek legends about Mopsos of Colophon in Anatolia invading Phoenicia 'have a genuine historical reminiscence of the movements of Sea Peoples'. He also sees the Greek legendary connection between Mopsos and Ashkelon as 'a further indication that the identity Pelasgoi = Philistines is correct' ('Kothar, Kinyras, and Kythereia', *JSS* 10 [1965], pp. 211-12). J. Muhly does not see the Sea Peoples as originally Aegeans. According to Muhly, the Myc. IIIC.1b pottery developed locally in Cyprus

hundreds of years after the Philistines had settled in Palestine. For instance, for the Jews Caphtor had become associated with Cappadocia. This is the translation that the LXX gives for the name Caphtor in Deut. 2.23 and Amos 9.7. The term has thus been expanded and its meaning could therefore have shifted.

This is as far as we can go in trying to determine Philistine origins. Because the literary information we have is circumstantial, the discussion will continue and new theories may see the light of day. As supporting evidence for the western origin of Philistine pottery, both style and decoration have played an important role. That is, an Aegean background for the pottery of the Philistine territory has been detected.[1] It shows strong resemblance to the Mycenaean IIIC pottery of Cyprus, as well as to the LHIIIC pottery of Greece.[2] It is 'locally made ware painted in black and red usually on white-slipped background'.[3] Among the decorative motives we can mention fish, birds, checkerboards, spirals, geometric designs, concentric circles, and the like. Some of the motives can be traced back to the earliest part of the Late Bronze Age and its bichrome tradition.[4] The form and shape are mainly Levantine, as is the clay. The difference between the paint of the Mycenaean and Philistine pottery is that the former is more lustrous and is in general monochrome, while Philistine pottery is bichrome with a matte finish.[5] However, there is another side of the

('The Role of the Sea Peoples in Cyprus during the LCIII Period', *Cyprus at the Close of the Late Bronze Age* [ed. V. Karageorghis and J.D. Muhly; Nicosia, 1984], pp. 39-55). Given that Mycaenean traditions are to be found both in Cyprus and in Palestine, Muhly's opinion does not carry too much weight.

1.   H. Thiersch is the first one to associate this kind of pottery with the Philistines ('Die neueren Ausgrabungen in Palästina', *Archäologischer Anzeiger* 23 [1908], pp. 378-84). Objecting to the nomenclature is W.A. Heurtley ('The Relationship between "Philistine" and Mycenaean Pottery', *QDAP* 5 [1936], pp. 90-110).

2.   For Mycenaean pottery and its use, for instance as oil containers, see A. Leonard Jr, *BASOR* 241 (1981), pp. 87-101.

3.   T. Dothan, *The Philistines*, p. 94. For N.K. Sandars, Philistine pottery 'is a hybrid' (*The Sea Peoples*, p. 166).

4.   See for instance, R. Amiran, *Ancient Pottery of the Holy Land*, pp. 266-68.

5.   Cf. also N.K. Sandars, *The Sea Peoples*, pp. 166-67. For a résumé of the discussion about the pottery, as well as its form and its chronological implications, see A. Strobel, *Der spätbronzezeitliche Seevölkersturm*, pp. 220-40; J.F. Brug, *A Literary and Archaeological Study of the Philistines*, pp. 53-57.

problem, namely the form of the vessels. R. Amiran has maintained that the forms of the so-called Philistine pottery in general represent a continuation of the indigenous Canaanite tradition of the LB period.[1] Through an analysis of the pottery forms from the tombs at Tell el-Far'ah(S),[2] T.L. McClellan[3] came to the conclusion that the Philistine ware, which was rare at the site, did not arrive in Palestine at the same time as the Philistines themselves, nor 'was "Philistine" pottery used everywhere the Philistines settled'. He sees the beginning of 'Philistine' pottery occurring around 1140 BCE or shortly thereafter. 'Philistine' ware never became '*the* pottery of the Philistines', nor did it achieve 'great popularity' among them.[4] In conclusion, 'Philistine' pottery is not that of the incoming Philistines themselves.[5] It belongs to a later phase of the Philistine culture locally developed in Palestine. The date for the beginning of this period would be the mid-twelfth century BCE.[6] But what pottery did they use before that time? T. Dothan believes that one wave of Sea Peoples had arrived in Syria-Palestine before the battle of Ramses III's eighth year. Their pottery was that of the Mycenaean IIIC.1b type.[7] What seems to be clear from

1.   *Ancient Pottery of the Holy Land*, p. 295.

2.   The tombs of 'the Philistine lords', as F. Petrie called them (*Beth-Pelet*, I [London, 1930], p. 7).

3.   'Chronology of the "Philistine" Burials at Tell el-Far'ah (South)', *Journal of Field Archaeology* 6 (1979), pp. 57-73. McClellan emphasizes that the tombs at Tell el-Far'ah are important not only in connection with 'the material culture of the Philistines, but in their bearing on ceramic chronology for Greece and Palestine' (p. 58). For a discussion about the tombs, see J.C. Waldbaum, who attributes them to two 'related groups of foreigners' of Aegean extraction ('Philistine Tombs at Tell Fara and their Aegean Prototypes', *AJA* 70 [1966], pp. 331-40), and W.H. Stiebing, who sees Cypriote bilobate tombs being introduced in Palestine already at the end of the MB II period ('Another Look at the Origins of the Philistine Tombs at Tell el-Far'ah [S]', *AJA* 74 [1970], pp. 139-43). The Philistines may have adopted this type of tomb when they arrived in Palestine.

4.   T.L. McClellan, *Journal of Field Archaeology* 16 (1979), pp. 72-73; cf. J.F. Brug, *A Literary and Archaeological Study of the Philistines*, pp. 115-16.

5.   Cf. R. de Vaux, *The Early History of Israel*, p. 507; also A. Mazar, who maintains that 'the Philistine black and red pottery postdates Ramses III and perhaps even his immediate successors' ('The Emergence of the Philistine Culture', *IEJ* 35 [1985], p. 95).

6.   See A. Mazar, *Excavations at Tell Qasile*, II, p. 120.

7.   *The Philistines*, pp. 294-95; A. Mazar, *IEJ* 35 (1985), pp. 95-96; *Excavations at Tell Qasile*, II, pp. 119-20; L.E. Stager, *EI* 18 (1985), p. 62*.

this is that the peoples settling on the Palestinian coast were related to those who had settled in Cyprus, both using Aegean pottery.[1] This can be seen at Ashdod stratum XIII, which precedes the period of 'Philistine' pottery.[2] Later these settlers, like many others in southern Palestine, produced the so-called Philistine pottery,[3] which can be seen as an 'amalgamation between traditions brought by the Philistine new-comers and traditions retained' by the local population.[4] If we look at the distribution of this ware, we find that it occurs mainly in southern Palestine, from Tell Qasîle and Bethel in the north to Tel Māśōś and Tell ez-Zuweyid (on the coast) in the south. There is nothing from the central hills between Bethel and the Jezreel Valley. North of the central hills, 'Philistine' pottery has been found at Beth-Shan (a few sherds), Megiddo, Tel Zeror, Dor, Tell Qiri, Tell Keisan, Hazor and Dan. Some crude ware of this type has also been found in the Jordan Valley,[5] at Deir 'Alla, for instance.[6] Some sherds have also been reported from Tulul edh-Dhahab (Mahanaim) in Jordan.[7] This may show that 'Philistine' pottery is an indigenous art form of the south which through some trade connection spread also to some northern and Transjordanian sites. One reason why the hills between Bethel and the Jezreel Valley did not yield any of this ware is that this territory

---

1.   J.D. Muhly denies the Aegean connection ('The Role of the Sea Peoples in Cyprus during the LCIII Period', *Cyprus at the Close of the Late Bronze Age* [ed. V. Karageorghis and J.D. Muhly], pp. 39-55). See, however, F. Schachermeyer, *Die Levant im Zeitalter der Wanderungen* (Die Ägäische Frühzeit, 5; Vienna, 1982), pp. 244-49; T. Dothan points out that the terra-cotta figurines of women, among them the figurine in the form of a chair, the so-called Ashdoda figurine, have Mycenaean parallels (*The Philistines*, pp. 234-49). For an anthropomorphic figurine or vessel 'with breast-spouts' found at Tell Qasîle having Mycenaean parallels, see A. Mazar, *Excavations at Tell Qasile*, I, pp. 78-81, and fig. 18.

2.   Stratum XIII represents the city built after the destruction in the latter part of the thirteenth century, the earliest period of Iron I. The few 'Philistine' sherds that have been found there may be due to intrusion. Stratum XII is the first 'well-built Philistine' level (M. Dothan, *Ashdod II–III* ['Atiqot, 9; Jerusalem, 1971], p. 25). Cf. J.F. Brug, *A Literary and Archaeological Study of the Philistines*, p. 67.

3.   M. Dothan, *Ashdod*, II–III, pp. 15-16; T. Dothan, *The Philistines*, pp. 217-18.

4.   A. Mazar, *IEJ* 35 (1985), p. 107.

5.   J.M. Sauer, *BASOR* 263 (1986), p. 12.

6.   H.J. Franken, *VT* 14 (1964), pp. 417-22.

7.   R.L. Gordon, 'Telul edh-Dhahab, Jordan—Not Gold but Iron', *AJA* 86 (1982), p. 266.

was largely unsettled and that the people who began to build their villages there in the twelfth and eleventh centuries used the forms they had known from before. It would take some time before reasons arose for trade between the Philistines and the peoples of the highlands.

The eleventh century is also the time when the Aegean-inspired 'Philistine' pottery fades away and the traditions from Late Bronze age Canaan increase. As an example we can mention that the 'Philistine' pottery from Beth-Shan, where very little was found, represents a 'debased version typical of the last phase of Philistine pottery (the eleventh century BCE)'.[1] The picture is about the same at Afula and Megiddo. The pottery from Beth-Shan thus cannot be taken as proof for a Philistine garrison there, nor does the text in 1 Sam. 31.12 indicate this, as has often been advocated.[2] In fact, the text does not say anything about Beth-Shan's political or ethnic status. The only conclusion one might draw is that the Philistines in the battle against Saul and his army were allied with the city state of Beth-Shan.[3] Thus the Israelite army could have been 'squeezed between two shields'.

From the above we may conclude that the presence of 'Philistine' pottery does not really tell us where the Philistines lived. This ceramic tradition became popular for a short period of time, the Iron Age IB period, and it also spread inland to the mountains of Judah, as well as reaching some of the northern cities (see Map 10). By the end of the eleventh century, however, this kind of pottery-making tradition came to an end.

Earlier it was thought that the anthropoid clay coffins that have been found at a few places in southern Palestine, such as Tell el-Far'ah (S) and Tell ed-Duweir, and at Beth-Shan in the Jordan Valley, all were testimonies of Philistine garrisons. A more nuanced view is

1. T. Dothan, *The Philistines*, p. 82.
2. T. Dothan, *The Philistines*, p. 57; cf. J.F. Brug, *A Literary and Archaeological Study of the Philistines*, p. 99.
3. Beth-Shan's political status after the collapse of the Egyptian rule over Palestine is not documented. Judg. 1.27 mentions Beth-Shan, Ta'anak, Dor, Ibleam and Megiddo, all of which probably were city states that were not 'conquered'. There is no textual evidence indicating that these city states had been under Philistine rule, but one may assume that they all were united in their wish to stop Israel's expansion under Saul. For the Philistines as allies of Beth Shan in Saul's final battle, see T. Koizumi, 'On the Battle of Gilboa', *Annual of the Japanese Institute* 2 (1976), p. 73; D. Edelman, 'The Rise of the Israelite State under Saul' (PhD dissertation, University of Chicago, 1986), p. 296.

justified, however, since this kind of coffin is known also from Nubia, Egypt (especially in the Delta), and Jordan, as well as from the cemetery of the Egyptian settlement at Deir el-Balaḥ on the coast SW of Gaza, which was Egyptian territory. Furthermore, no so-called Philistine pottery is associated with the coffins from Nubia and Egypt nor with the sarcophagi from Beth-Shan.[1] These coffins represent without doubt an Egyptian burial tradition.[2] Concerning the problem of the origin of the Philistines, it is important to note that no coffins of this type are known from Crete, the Aegean or Anatolia. Thus, if the Philistines originally came from one of these areas they must have forgotten their burial customs when they settled in Palestine. In other words, these coffins are not to be taken as proof of Philistine burials. We should note that many of the Palestinian clay coffins are from the Late Bronze period, and the pottery associated with them (in the tombs) includes 'abundant pottery vessels of local Canaanite styles of the thirteenth century BCE'.[3] In other words, these coffins are from the period before the Philistines had arrived in Palestine. For instance, the cemetery at Deir el-Balaḥ yielded burials from the late fourteenth to the twelfth centuries.[4] The conclusion one can draw, therefore, is that this type of burial is Egyptian. However, mercenaries in the Egyptian army could also have been buried in this kind of clay coffin. As long as a skeletal analysis has not been undertaken we will not be able to establish the fact.[5]

The fragments of sarcophagi found at Beth-Shan are estimated to come from about 50 coffins. Only two could be almost completely

1. E. Oren, *The Northern Cemetery at Beth Shan*, p. 139. Among the Sea Peoples having the 'feathered' headdress, only the Denyen can be associated with the coffin burials according to Oren (p. 138).

2. L. Kuchman, 'Egyptian Clay Anthropoid Coffins', *Serapis* 4 (1977–78), pp. 11-22.

3. I. Perlman, F. Asaro and T. Dothan, 'Provenance of the Deir el-Balaḥ Coffins', *IEJ* 23 (1973), pp. 147-51.

4. T. Dothan, *Excavations at the Cemetery of Deir el-Balaḥ*, pp. 3, 103.

5. There has not been any thorough skeletal analysis of the bones from any of these places. However, one could note that D. Ferembach's investigation about the physical anthropology of the Philistines concludes that they probably were of Aegean origin (*apud* B. Arensburg, 'The People in the Land of Israel from the Epipaleolithic to Present Times: A Study Based on their Skeletal Remains' [PhD dissertation, Tel Aviv University, Tel Aviv, 1973], p. 76).

restored. The coffins had movable lids showing the face,[1] the arms and hands of the deceased. The arms are positioned in such a way that they go from the head behind the ears and down under the chin, creating together with the headband a frame for the face. Above the headband one lid had a decoration of lines that may depict the Sea Peoples' 'feathered' headdress.[2]

The clay coffins are usually divided into two groups according to their lids: the naturalistic and the grotesque type. However, after the finds from the Egyptian garrison city at Deir el-Balaḥ, c. 13 km southwest of Gaza, another grouping of coffins from the 'pre-Philistine' period can be made: (A) the mummy-shaped type that delineates the head and shoulders, and (B) the cylindrical type that lacks this delineation.[3] The coffins from Deir el-Balaḥ are Egyptian inspired and could be called mummy-like in form. The Sea Peoples and others who were used as mercenaries in Palestine by the Egyptians were apparently buried according to Egyptian customs. Anthropoid and mummy-like clay coffins are in fact part of a burial custom that goes back to the Twelfth Dynasty (Middle Kingdom). But it was not a tradition for the common people. Only during the New Kingdom did the custom first become in some way 'democratized'. The Palestinian clay coffins were certainly not used for the burial of the society's top officials, but neither were they for the poor. They were most probably made for Egyptian officials, which could include foreigners in Egyptian service, such as Nubians, Canaanites,[4] Peleset, Tjeker and Denyen. As pharaonic officials they may have been highly Egyptianized, but their bodies were not mummified, which was usually the case with Egyptians in high positions.

1.   In a few cases the facial features show Aegean influences resembling the features of the so-called Agamemnon mask; see R. Higgins, *Minoan and Mycenaean Art* (London, 1967), fig. 190. This would be the case for the lid from tomb 66 at Beth-Shan; see T. Dothan, *The Philistines*, pls. 16–18; E. Oren, *The Northern Cemetery*, fig. 62.2.

2.   See, for instance, E. Oren, *The Northern Cemetery*, figs. 62.2, 80; T. Dothan, *The Philistines*, pls. 16–18, and fig. 11.

3.   T. Dothan, *Excavations at the Cemetery of Deir el-Balaḥ*, pp. 99-100.

4.   One cannot dismiss the possibility that some 'adventurous' Canaanite young men also used the opportunity of making a career in the Egyptian administration and its army. As to Nubians having been used in the Egyptian army in Palestine, it is known that Abdi-Hepa of Jerusalem complained to the Pharaoh about their behavior (EA 287).

Anthropoid clay coffins from the thirteenth century BCE have been found at Beth-Shan, Deir el-Balaḥ, Tell ed-Duweir and Tell el-Far'ah (S). Two coffins were found in the so-called Fosse at Tell ed-Duweir (tomb 570).[1] The faces on the lids are in the simple naturalistic style. The pottery associated with them is Palestinian. One of the coffins had an Egyptian inscription and depictions of the goddesses Nephtys and Isis, but there was no name of the deceased. The inscription is not made by a trained scribe, and the text does not seem to make sense.[2] From this we may draw the conclusion that the deceased could be an Egyptian official, but that the place did not have any well-trained scribes. Thus somebody may have copied a phrase common at burials, or somebody simply imitated a few hieroglyphs.[3] From the fact that an Egyptian official was stationed at Tell ed-Duweir one cannot draw the conclusion that there was an Egyptian garrison. As we know from the Tell el-Amarna letters, there were always some Egyptian officials posted in the capitals of the city states, and this was most probably also the case at Tell ed-Duweir until its destruction in the twelfth century BCE.[4]

When the Philistines and other Sea Peoples settled in Palestine, they may have followed the customs of the former officials and mercenaries, since their leaders were now officially representatives of the Egyptian government. Among these customs was the tradition of burial in anthropoid clay coffins. We may ask, however, why these clay coffins have not been found at all the places where the Philistines lived, for instance, in the cities of their pentapolis. The answer may be that those employed in special garrison cities or fortresses followed the custom of the military elite. This custom, however, was not that of the common person in the cities. The conclusion from the above would be that it is incorrect to see these Palestinian coffins as necessarily those of the Philistines. They were not part of the Philistine burial custom, 'as the proportionately greater number of Philistine

---

1. C. H. Inge, 'Excavations at Tell ed-Duweir', *PEQ* 70 (1938), pp. 246-47, and pl. XXII; O. Tufnell *et al.*, *Lachish*, III, p. 219, pl. 126; cf. T. Dothan, *The Philistines*, p. 276.

2. O. Tufnell *et al.*, *Lachish*, IV, pl. 46.

3. Cf. D. Diringer, 'Inscriptions. B. Pseudo-Egyptian Hieroglyphs', *Lachish*, IV (ed. O. Tufnell *et al.*; London, 1958), pp. 131-32.

4. It is fruitless to speculate about who destroyed the city of Level VI, which is the last LB town. The most recent excavations indicate that the town was destroyed during the reign of Ramses III (D. Ussishkin, *Tel Aviv* 10 [1983], pp. 168-69).

tombs containing plain burials attest'.[1] The custom of using anthropoid clay coffins disappeared in Palestine c. 1000 BCE, but clay coffins or pieces of such coffins have been found in Jordan at Sahab (tenth–ninth cent. BCE),[2] Dhiban (eighth cent.), and Amman (seventh cent.).[3]

The above has shown that pottery and clay coffins cannot be used as indicators of how extensive Philistine power in Palestine was in the period before the emergence of the Israelite monarchy. The biblical sources give the impression that the Philistines ruled most of the country including the hills and that they had garrisons at several places. One garrison, for instance, was placed in Bethlehem.[4] Another was located on 'the hill of God' (1 Sam. 10.5), which probably is a reference to Gibeon. The power of the Philistines as lords of Palestine is understandable, since they intially ruled the territory on behalf of the Egyptians, as did the Tjeker at Dor. As such they also had to protect Egyptian interests in such city states as Beth-Shan and Megiddo, which does not mean that Philistines must have moved into these cities. Having been allied with the Tjeker, it is understandable that there are no reported conflicts between these two groups of Sea Peoples after they had settled in Palestine. The Philistine 'oppression' over Palestine is thus a continuation of Egyptian rule.

After the death of Ramses III, Egypt soon lost its superiority over the country, even though some poor attempts to maintain Egyptian rule occurred down to the time of Ramses VI (1141–1134 BCE). Beth-Shan was most likely an Egyptian base through the time of Ramses VI.[5] A base of a bronze statue with a cartouche of this pharaoh has been found at Megiddo.[6]

1.   T. Dothan, *The Philistines*, p. 268.

2.   W.F. Albright, 'An Anthropoid Clay Coffin from Sahab in Transjordan', *AJA* 36 (1932), esp. pp. 295-97. Clay coffins of the so-called bathtub class have been found at Mount Nebo in Jordan (seventh cent. BCE) and Megiddo str. III–II; cf. S. Saller, 'Iron Age Tombs at Nebo, Jordan', *Liber Annuus* 16 (1965–66), pp. 289-90; also O. Tufnell, 'Notes and Comparisons', *Four Tomb Groups from Jordan* (ed. G.L. Harding; PEFA, 6; Manchester, 1953), pp. 67-68. These, however, are of an Assyrian type.

3.   K.N. Yassine, 'Anthropoid Coffins from Raghdan Royal Palace Tomb in Amman', *ADAJ* 20 (1975), pp. 57-68.

4.   1 Sam. 10.5; 13.3-5; 14.21-22; 23.1-5; 2 Sam. 23.14; 1 Chron. 11.16-18.

5.   See W.A. Ward, 'The Egyptian Inscriptions of Level VI', *The Iron Age at Beth-Shan* (ed. F.W. James; Philadelphia, 1966), pp. 172-79.

6.   G. Loud, *Megiddo*, II, pp. 135-37, figs. 373-74.

The picture is the same for the Sinai peninsula. The last known Egyptian inscriptions from Sinai are also from the reign of Ramses VI.[1] Knowing this, it is difficult to find any room for a battle between 'Canaanites and Israelites' in the Valley of Jezreel in the twelfth century,[2] as has been suggested by several scholars on the basis of Judges 4 and 5.[3] Some skirmishes between smaller chiefdoms or city states certainly occurred during most of the Egyptian period. The Amarna letters attest to this. However, a larger battle between a coalition of Canaanites and the peoples of the highlands is unrealistic to assume. Both Judg. 4.6, 10 and 5.18 indicate, in fact, that it was only the people of Zebulon and Naphtali that fought Sisera and his army. Thus the war was only of local importance.[4]

The later history of the Philistines will be discussed in connection with the conflicts between them and Israelites and Judahites, as well as in connection with the power struggle between Egypt, the Syro-Palestinian states and Assyria. Here a few comments on Philistine religion and language should be made. The fact is that nothing really is known about their religion and their language.[5] If it were, we would be able to trace their origin with somewhat greater confidence than has been done as of yet.

We do not have any corpus of Philistine texts that could help in establishing who the Philistines were. Thus we do not know what language they spoke when settling in Palestine and before they had made the Canaanite-Hebrew language of the country their own. There are,

---

1. A. Gardiner and T.E. Peet, *The Inscriptions of Sinai* (ed. J. Černy; London, 1952), §§290-93.

2. Cf. G. Schmitt, *Du sollst keinen Frieden schliessen mit den Bewohnern des Landes: Die Wieisungen gegen die Kanaanäer in Israels Geschichte und Geschichtsschreibing* (BWANT, 91; Stuttgart, 1970), p. 73 n. 77.

3. Cf. K. Budde, who dates Judg. 5 to c. 1100 BCE, indicating that the battle must have taken place somewhat earlier (*Geschichte der althebräischen Literatur* [Leipzig, 1906], p. 7). R.G. Boling assumes that the 'Song of Deborah' is from the third quarter of the twelfth century BCE (*Judges*, pp. 23, 116-18).

4. See, for instance, W. Richter, *Traditionsgeschichtliche Untersuchungen zum Richterbuch* (BBB, 18; Bonn, 1963), pp. 92, 98; cf. G.W. Ahlström, 'Judges 5.20f. and History', *JNES* 36 (1977), pp. 287-88, and *idem, Who were the Israelites?*, pp. 80-81. Again we may note that the biblical writer is ignorant of what role the Egyptian hegemony over Palestine could have played.

5. Cf. O. Eissfeldt, *Philister und Phönizier* (Der Alte Orient, 34.3; Leipzig, 1936), pp. 33-36.

besides *seren*, a few words in the Hebrew Bible, such as *qôbaʿ*, 'hat, helmet', *pilegeš*, 'concubine', Greek *pallax*,[1] *ʾargaz*, 'box, chest', and *ḥermeš*, 'sickle'[2] occurring in connection with the Philistines. Usually these have been understood as either Greek or Anatolian.[3] In any case they are not West-Semitic.[4] The same may be said for a few personal names, such as Achish (king of Gath), Maoch (father of Achish, 1 Sam. 27.2; Maacah in 1 Kgs 2.39) and Goliath. Of these the name Achish has often been understood as the same as Greek *Agkhisaes*, (Anchises, father of Aeneas), in the LXX translation spelled *Agkhous*.[5] Two fragments of a bowl from Qubur el-Walaydah (10 km south of Gaza) are inscribed with characters of the Old Canaanite script, which also occurs on an ostracon from ʿIzbet Ṣarṭah. Two Semitic names are readable, *šimī-paʿal* and *ʾiyya-ʾel* (*ʿayya-ʾel*), and if F.M. Cross's dating of the script to c. 1200 BCE is right, we would have here a pre-Philistine text.[6] However, the text could also have been written after the Philistine settlement had been built. If so, the ostracon only shows that a Semitic population was still there.

It has usually been assumed that the people who rebuilt Deir ʿAlla after the earthquake were Philistines. This conclusion has been drawn from the pottery. As mentioned above, the crude 'Philistine' pottery from Deir ʿAlla is certainly not an indication for what kind of people

1.   F. Bork, *AfO* 13 (1939–41), p. 228. Cf. also C. Rabin, 'On the Origin of the Hebrew Word *Pileges*', *JNES* 25 (1974), pp. 353-64.

2.   The term *hrph* that occurs in connection with warriors from Gath (2 Sam. 21.15-22) is identified by F. Willesen with Greek *harpē*, 'scimitar, sickle' ('The Philistine Corps of the Scimitar from Gath', *JSS* 3 [1958], pp. 327-35). C.E. L'Heureux, however, derives the term from Ugaritic and Hebrew *rpʾ*, and sees the phrase as referring to Philistine warriors, the 'votaries of Rapha' ('The *yĕlîdê hārāpāʾ*—A Cultic Association of Warriors', *BASOR* 221 [1976], pp. 83-84).

3.   Cf. T. Dothan, *The Philistines*, pp. 22-23. J.F. Brug is skeptical about this (*A Literal and Archaeological Study*, pp. 196-200). G. Bonafante, among others, sees here a connection with Illyria ('Who were the Philistines?', *AJA* 50 [1946], pp. 251-62).

4.   Another word, *qrdm*, 'axe', is of unknown origin.

5.   This name occurs as Ikausu (king of Ekron) in inscriptions by Esarhaddon and Ashurbanipal (*ANET*, pp. 291, 294). J.F. Brug thinks that the original form of the name was *ʾakush* (*A Literary and Archaeological Study*, p. 199). This would then be close to the name Ekwesh, which was one group of Sea Peoples. According to F. Bork, the original spelling would be *ekawus* (*AfO* 13 [1939–41], p. 228).

6.   'Newly Found Inscriptions in Old Canaanite and Early Phoenician Scripts', *BASOR* 238 (1980), pp. 1-3.

settled there.[1] Only three pieces out of 454 'have decorative designs similar to distinct Philistine motifs'.[2]

The three small tablets found in the Late Bronze Age sanctuary at Deir 'Alla[3] in the Jordan Valley have been connected by some with the Sea Peoples.[4] At the time that this stratum was destroyed in an earthquake during the reign of Queen Tewosret (1193–1185 BCE) the Philistines would not have been the settlers. Perhaps some other Sea Peoples or some group entering the Jordan Valley from the north settled at Deir 'Alla[5] and built up the metal industry there.[6] The same people may have settled at Tell es-Sa'idiyeh just to the north of Deir 'Alla. Another possibility is that the tablets are indications of trade and therefore do not say anything about the language at Deir 'Alla.

The only textual information about Philistine religion that we possess comes from the Old Testament. As all other ancient peoples, the Philistines had priests and diviners (1 Sam. 6.2; Isa. 2.6). At Gaza and Ashdod they worshiped the god Dagon (Judg. 16.21-23; 1 Sam. 5.2). He is also mentioned in 1 Chron. 10.10 in connection with Saul's death. This god, known as Dagan in the Euphrates area at least from

---

1. Cf. R. de Vaux, *The Early History of Israel*, p. 515.

2. J.F. Brug, *A Literary and Archaeological Study*, p. 102.

3. See H.J. Franken, *VT* 14 (1964), pp. 377-79, 417-22; and 'A Note on How the Deir 'Alla Tablets were Written', *VT* 15 (1965), pp. 150-52; cf. H.J. Franken, *PEQ* 96 (1964), pp. 773-79.

4. Z. Mayani sees the text as Illyrian ('Un apport à la discussion du texte Deir 'Alla', *VT* 24 [1974], pp. 318-23). H.J. Franken saw some 'affinities with the Phoenician Byblos script of Ahiram'. He also maintained that there were 'Semitic elements' in the script (*VT* 15 [1965], p. 379). A. van den Branden suggested that the script of the tablets was Arabic, showing south Semitic resemblances ('Essai de deciffrement des inscriptions de Deir 'Alla', *VT* 15 [1965], pp. 129-50). However, no consensus has as yet emerged. G.E. Wright saw some resemblances between these tablets and the Cypro-Minoan texts that have been found both at Ras Shamra and on Cyprus ('Fresh Evidence for the Philistine Story', *BA* 29 [1966], p. 73). There are, however, only a few signs that could possibly resemble certain Cypro-Minoan signs. We do not have any exact parallels to the Deir 'Alla script; therefore, an identification is impossible.

5. H.J. Franken maintains that the Iron I cooking pot from Deir 'Alla did not develop from the LB II type ('Palestine in the Time of the Nineteenth Dynasty. [b]. Archaeological Evidence', *CAH*, II.2, p. 336).

6. For furnaces at Deir 'Alla, see H.J. Franken, *Excavations at Deir 'Alla*, I (Leiden, 1969), pp. 34-38. Cf. R. de Vaux, *The Early History of Israel*, pp. 515-16.

the time of Sargon of Agade,[1] and from the archives of Ebla and of Ugarit,[2] was also worshiped by the Hurrians[3] and by different groups of people in Palestine, as is clear from a place name like Beth-Dagon, which refers to two different places in Josh. 15.41 and 19.27. One of the princes in southern Palestine during the Amarna period had the name Dagan-takala (EA 317, 318). These references may show that Dagan for some time before the arrival of the Philistines had been worshiped in Palestine. It may seem 'strange' that the Old Testament so often associates Dagon with the Philistines,[4] as if he were 'imported' with them. It should be emphasized, however, that it is in no way strange for newcomers to 'adopt' the religious system of the country they have chosen or been forced to live in. It is a modern idea that wherever you go you can worship your god. In the ancient Near East the gods did not have any power outside their territories or nations.[5] If a kingdom expanded, the god's power also expanded. A god without land was of no use. The gods were the owners of the land. Therefore, in moving to a new country one had to worship its gods in order to have any success, that is, blessing. One way of continuing to worship one's own god was to identify it with one of the deities of the new land. This is how Baal of Canaan became Seth in Egypt, or Hathor of Egypt became Ashtarte in Byblos, or Yahweh of Se'ir, Paran and Teman became El in Canaan and El Elyon in Jerusalem. The name Dagon as the name of a god worshiped by the Philistines does not, therefore, say too much about their religion, nor more than that Dagon as a weather and fertility god must have been important in this part of Palestine.

An ostracon found at Tell Qasîle (surface find) has the inscription 'gold from Ophir to Beth Horon'.[6] This can be interpreted as gold for

---

1. See D.O. Edzard, 'Mesopotamia', *Wörterbuch der Mythologie*, I (Stuttgart, 1965), pp. 49-50.

2. M.H. Pope and W. Röllig, 'Dagān', *Wörterbuch der Mythologie*, I, pp. 276-78.

3. A Mari text has the reading 'Dagan *ša ḫur-ri*' ('Dagan of the Hurrians'); see I.J. Gelb, *Hurrians and Subarians*, p. 62; cf. M.-L. and H. Erlenmeyer, 'Einige syrische Ziegel mit ägäischen Bildelementen', *AfO* 21 (1966), p. 34.

4. Thus J.F. Brug, *A Literary and Archaeological Study*, p. 182.

5. This is why the Syrian commander Na'aman brought back two loads of dirt to Syria. Yahweh had to be worshiped on his own soil (2 Kgs 5.17).

6. B. Maisler (Mazar), 'The Excavations at Tell Qasîle; Preliminary Report', *IEJ* 1 (1951), p. 210.

the temple of the god Horon[1] or for the city Beth-Horon. Paleographically the ostracon is dated to sometime before 800 BCE.[2] Thus it is uncertain if the ostracon has anything to do with the Philistine-Canaanite culture of Tell Qasîle. It could just as well be an indication for the religion of Qasîle or Beth-Horon during the period of the Israelite monarchy.

Another god mentioned in the Bible as Philistine is Baal-Zebub of Ekron, to whom king Ahaziah of Israel sent messengers in order to find out whether he would recover from an illness (2 Kgs 1.2). This means that the god Baal-Zebub must also have been very popular in certain circles outside Philistine territory. We do not learn any more about this god. Usually his name has been emended to Baal-Zebul, 'prince Baal',[3] but that seems unnecessary. Already the LXX and Josephus read 'Lord of the Flies, which most probably should be retained. The name may be a Semiticized form of a deity name behind which there were some old ideas and rituals which still continued as before. There is some biblical information about strange religious customs in Philistia, for instance, the role of mice. When the Philistines returned the Ark of Yahweh to its homeland it was accompanied by offerings of 'five golden tumors and five golden mice' (1 Sam. 6.4). This may indicate a Philistine origin in the Aegean cultural sphere, where the god Apollon Smintheus belonged.[4] He had, for instance, a cult center in Hamaxitos in southwestern Troas. The epithet *sminthos*, 'field-mouse', tells us about the symbolic animal for this deity.

---

1.   For this god, known from Ugarit, Canaan and Egypt, see P. Montet and P. Bucher, 'Un dieu canaanéen à Tanis: Houron de Ramses', *RB* 44 (1935), pp. 161-63; M. Dahood, 'Le antiche divinita semitiche', *Ancient Semitic Studies* (ed. S. Moscati; Studi Semitici, 1; Rome, 1958), pp. 82-83; R. Stadelmann, *Syrisch-palästinensische Gottheiten*, pp. 76-78. Horon was identified with the sphinx at Gizeh (probably by Asiatics), because his name was close to the Egyptian *hwrw*, 'sphinx'. He also received a royal chapel in Tanis; see W. Helck, *Die Beziehungen*, pp. 454-55.

2.   See the discussion in A. Mazar, *Excavations at Tell Qasile*, II, pp. 129-30. Mazar thinks it possible to connect the name Horon of the ostracon with the temple of Philistine Qasîle (p. 130). The possibility is there, but it cannot be established as a fact.

3.   T. Gaster, 'Baal-zebub', *IDB*, I, *s.v.*; J. Gray, *I & II Kings* (Philadelphia, 1976), p. 463.

4.   See also the discussion in my study, *An Archaeological Picture of Iron Age Religions in Ancient Palestine*, pp. 7-8.

J. Oestrup has maintained that Baal-Zebub could be a god of flies and mice,[1] thus an oracle from such a god in a country full of flies and mice would be powerful.

The so-called 'Ashdoda' figurine painted in the Mycenaean tradition[2] has been interpreted as representing a goddess, probably a mother goddess.[3] If so, it could be a Philistine goddess identified with Canaanite Ashtarte. Because the lower part of the body is formed like the seat of a chair or a table, it might have functioned to receive offerings or it could have been a replica of the sanctuary's statue in the form of a throne.[4] Other female figurines that should also be mentioned include those mounted on rims of bowls or kraters. They are known from Tell Eṭun, Tell Jemme, Azor and Beth-Shan. These figurines have their arms raised and their hands resting on their heads, and have been seen as representing mourners. This type is also known from the Mycenaean world, but has no forerunners in Palestine.[5]

Other finds pertaining to the cult are zoomorphic cult masks, cult stands, of which one had a duck's head, bowls, and the so-called kernoi.[6] Many of these vessels show that Philistine material culture was very much influenced not only by Mycenaean and Cypriote traditions but also by Egyptian and local Canaanite traditions. This is quite

---

1. 'Smintheus', *Orientalische Studien Th. Nöldeke zum 70. Geburtstag gewidmet*, II (Giessen, 1906), pp. 865-70. Isa. 65.3-4; 66.17 (cf. 2.20-21), refers to the cultic use of mice among the peoples of Judah. It may be possible that a Philistine custom had spread from the hills. Especially since the cities of Judah were transferred to the Philistines by Sennacherib during his campaign in 701 BCE (*ARAB*, II, par. 240), Philistine religious customs would have become part of the religious life of the Judahites.

2. See R. Hachlili, 'Figurines and Kernoi', *Ashdod II–III* (ed. M. Dothan; 'Atiqot, 9; Jerusalem, 1979), pp. 128-35, fig. 91.1; T. Dothan, *The Philistines*, pp. 234-37, fig. 9 and pl. 19.2.

3. Even if this is not an exact replica of a Mycenaean figurine, A. Mazar maintains that it shows that the Aegean tradition at Ashdod was very strong as compared to, for instance, Tell Qasîle and other places (*Excavations at Tell Qasile*, I, p. 119).

4. See the discussion in M. Dothan, *Ashdod II–III*, pp. 20-21; and T. Dothan, *The Philistines*, pp. 234-37. For Mycenaean parallels, see G.E. Mylonas, 'Seated and Multiple Mycenaean Figurines in the National Museum of Athens', *The Aegean and the Near East: Studies Presented to Hetty Goldman* (New York, 1965), pp. 110-21.

5. T. Dothan, *The Philistines*, pp. 237-49.

6. The function of the kernoi is not known, but they could perhaps have served some libation purposes.

clear from the cult objects found at Tell Qasîle. This latter place, however, was situated at the outskirts of classical Philistine territory, and it is perhaps more an example of cultural syncretism than of typical Philistine traditions.

Three consecutive temples were built on the same spot at Tell Qasîle, strata XII–X, with two adjacent shrines in strata XI–X. The latter is a phenomenon not known from other places in Palestine. Parallels to this have been found in the Mycenaean world as well as in Cyprus.[1] In the first two strata the cella was almost square, and this was also the case in stratum X, when the temple was extended with a room behind the cella and with an entrance room.[2] This type of plan has been called 'megaroid' by J. Schäfer and belongs originally in the Mycenaean world. However, the oblong 'rechteckige' temple room he sees as an indigenous Canaanite tradition that belongs to the LB period.[3] Instead of a niche in the wall of the cella, as is common in many Bronze Age temples, the Tell Qasîle temples had a raised platform. There were also benches along the walls. The Fosse Temple III at Tell ed-Duweir also had a platform and benches inside the cella, as well as a room (or two) behind the platform. However, the temples are not exactly identical, and architecturally, one could maintain that they both are rare in Palestine. There are resemblances in some details with the Mycenaean world, and a temple at Kition, Cyprus has also been taken into consideration.[4] Here, however emerges the uncertainty over the extent to which Cyprus had been affected by Levantine influences.[5]

The excavations at Khirbet el-Muqanna' (Tel Miqne, identified with

---

1. A. Mazar, *Excavations at Tell Qasile*, II, p. 131.

2. For the plans, see A. Mazar, *Excavations at Tell Qasile*, I, p. 63, fig. 15.I, J; and M. Ottosson, *Temple and Cult Places in Palestine*, p. 77 fig. 14.

3. 'Bemerkungen zum Verhältnis mykenischer Kultbauten zu Tempelbauten in Kanaan', *Archäologischer Anzeiger* (1983), pp. 552, 556.

4. V. Karageorghis, *Kition, Mycenaean and Phoenician Discoveries in Cyprus* (London, 1976), pp. 55-94.

5. Agreements in ashlar masonry and some pottery between Ugarit and Cyprus (Enkomi and Kition) has led to the theory that some people fled to Cyprus after the destruction of Ugarit; see the discussion in N.K. Sandars, *The Sea Peoples*, pp. 151-55. Other Ugaritans may have built Ras Ibn Hani where the same ashlar masonry has been found, thus making it older than Israelite masonry; see G. Hult, *Bronze Age Ashlar Masonry in the Eastern Mediterranean, Cyprus, Ugarit, and Neighbouring Regions* (Studies in Mediterranean Archaeology, 66; Göteborg, 1983), pp. 28, 71.

Philistine Ekron) has yielded a large amount of Mycenaean IIIC.1b pottery, a square kiln, an 'Ashdoda' figurine, and other objects of Aegean provenience. In a corner of a large building (palace or temple?) was found a small, rectangular boxlike mudbrick structure c. 1 m high. Its two free sides had benches at their bases. In the courtyard of this building was a round hearth, which is a rare phenomenon in Palestine. It was, however, common in Cyprus and the Aegean in so-called megaron buildings. Close to the hearth some chicken bones were found, something unique for Palestine of this period.[1]

A brick temple at Ashdod is known from a later period, namely the eighth century BCE. The main hall was L-shaped with two adjacent temple rooms in the NW. In the south end of the cella was a brick altar, and close to it were found several figurines of humans and animals, as well as pottery vessels, among them some *kernoi*. One figurine was in the shape of a woman playing the harp or lyre.[2] Figures of musicians in 'windows' also occur on some cult-stands.[3] Thus we have here some indication of the role of music in the cult. But this is not a phenomenon that can be associated with the Philistines uniquely. Music played an important role in the other religions of the ancient Near East.[4]

1. T. Dothan in S. Gitin and T. Dothan, 'The Rise and Fall of Ekron of the Philistines', *BA* 50 (1987), p. 205.

2. M. Dothan, 'Ashdod: Preliminary Report on the Excavations 1962/63', *IEJ* 14 (1964), pp. 85-86; *idem, Ashdod II–III*, pp. 136-38; R. Hachlili in *Ashdod II–III* (ed. M. Dothan), pp. 128-30. L.R. Fisher and F.B. Knutson have seen the lyre as associated with cult prostitution ('An Enthronement Ritual at Ugarit', *JNES* 28 [1969], pp. 165-66). See also the illustrations in U. Winter, *Frau und Göttin* (OBO, 53; Freiburg, 1983).

3. See M. Dothan, 'The Musicians of Ashdod', *BA* 40 (1977), pp. 38-39.

4. Consult P. Calmeyer, 'Federkranze und Musik', *Actes de la XVIIe Recontre Assyriologique 1969* (Paris, 1970), pp. 184-95; H. Hickmann, *Le metier de musicien au temps des pharaons* (Cahiers d'Histoire Egyptienne, VI.5/6; 2nd edn; Cairo, 1954); D. Walstan, 'Music from Ancient Ugarit', *RA* 68 (1974), pp. 125-28; A.D. Kilmer, 'The Cult Song with Music from Ancient Ugarit: Another Interpretation', *RA* 68 (1974), pp. 69-82; U.S. Leupold, 'Worship Music in Ancient Israel', *Canadian Journal of Theology* 15 (1969), pp. 176-86; H. Seidl, 'Horn und Trompete im alten Israel unter Berücksichtigung der "Kriegsrolle" von Qumran', *Wissenschaftliche Zeitschrift der Karl Marx-Universität, Leipzig* (1956–57), pp. 589-99. According to L. Manniche, the musicians were 'blind' or blindfolded when performing for the king, who was a god, because they were 'mediators transferring the essence of food to the king' ('Symbolic Blindness', *Chronique d'Egypte* Tome LIII, 105 [1978], pp. 19-20).

It is hoped that the above has shown that the history, life and culture of the Philistines are only partially known. The evidence we have is too limited, and the gaps confronting the historian are comparable with the gaps to be filled in when restoring an ancient Philistine jar.

Chapter 7

THE INCREASE IN SETTLEMENTS DURING THE THIRTEENTH AND
TWELFTH CENTURIES BCE

Palestine and its population problems must always be seen in the light of the international stage. The collapse of the Hittite empire and other states created political and economic instability in the eastern Mediterranean around the twelfth century BCE. It terminated the Mycenaean 'monopoly' of the sea trade, as well as terminating the big powers' control of the overland trade routes. As we know, many urban economic centers were destroyed during this period, and with them their culture.[1] The result was that such a 'frontier' country as Palestine with its sparsely populated hilly regions no longer benefitted from the international economic system and the kind of stability that the political and international market could provide for communities in marginal areas. This means that the populations on the fringes of the economic trade system (which was an urban phenomenon) had to secure their own economic system, which could mean a change in life-style. Here we may find one of the reasons for the growth of settlements in the Palestinian hills during the twelfth and eleventh centuries BCE. When normalcy returned again, new nations are found to have emerged, such as the Aramaean, Ammonite, Moabite and Israelite monarchies. This may be explained by the fact that when the agricultural communities grew, the need for outside commercial contacts and trade also grew. This created a need for administrative[2] and economic-

1. As mentioned before, trade can transfer not only commodities but also cultural influences; see W.F. Lehmans, 'The Importance of Trade', *Iraq* 39 (1977), pp. 1-10. See also C. Renfrew, 'Systems Collapse as Social Transformation: Catastrophe and Anastrophe in Early State Societies', in *Transformations: Mathematical Approaches to Culture Change* (ed. C. Renfrew and K.L. Cooke; New York, 1979), pp. 481-506.

2. This included scribal activities. Against this background we may look at the

political systems. In the eyes of the majority of people, the natural form for organized agricultural and industrial life had returned: the state.

Before we turn to the new political constellations in Palestine, the complicated picture of population and material culture has to be presented. As has been mentioned before,[1] there are no literary materials describing this period. The texts of the Hebrew Bible dealing with the period preceding the emergence of the kingdom of Israel were not intended to present the history of the population of Palestine; it was an ideological-theological advocacy that steered the biblical writers. These writers did not know the settlement patterns and religious ideals of the twelfth century BCE.[2] Thus the only possible path we can take is to see what picture emerges from an analysis of the archaeological material.

The period following the upheavals in the eastern Mediterranean countries is commonly called the Iron Age period, which ended in the mid-sixth century BCE. It is divided into Iron Age I (1200–1000 BCE) and Iron Age II.[3] This characterization is misleading, however, because of the simple fact that iron did not come into use that early as a metal for tools. The minimal number of iron tools found in Palestine from the twelfth century could be explained by the lack of tin for making bronze, but also by the fact that trade was disturbed. From the Late Bronze II period, only one iron smelting installation is known in Palestine, namely at Tel Yin'am in SE Galilee (coord. 198-235). Iron ore has also been found in its surroundings. It is possible that iron was worked at Kamid-el-Loz already in the fifteenth century BCE. Thus, there was neither a Hittite nor a Philistine monopoly

different types of writing that developed in this period.

1. See Introduction, pp. 33-34.

2. Cf. M. Liverani, review of R. de Vaux, *Histoire ancienne d'Israël*, I-II, *Oriens Antiquus* 15 (1976), p. 154.

3. The two periods have also been subdivided: Iron IA (c. 1200–1150); Iron IB (1150–1000), which is the period of the Philistine pottery; Iron IIA (1000–900), IIB (900–800), and Iron IIC (800–540). The following period has been given the label Iron III by some, but it is usually called the Persian period. Moreover, some Israeli scholars use the terms 'Canaanite' for the Bronze Age and 'Israelite' for the Iron Age, thus arbitrarily dating the beginning of the Israelite material culture to c. 1200 BCE. Would the Merneptah inscription's 'Israel' then be part of the Canaanite period?

on working with this metal.[1] The technology was widespread and, because we know that iron was worked in the north earlier than in Palestine,[2] one may assume that the installation at Tel Yin'am has been worked by people who learned the technique by northerners, or that they themselves may have been immigrants from the north.

Only a few tools and weapons of iron, such as daggers, arrowheads and knives, have been found in Syria-Palestine from around 1200 BCE. In Palestine c. twenty pieces have been found from the twelfth century, none of them in the hills. From the eleventh century BCE excavators have found close to 80 pieces, of which 18 were found in the hills ('Ai, Khirbet Raddana, Tell el-Fûl, and Beth-Zur).[3] In the tenth century, there were more tools of iron than of bronze, but still iron did not replace bronze.[4] The 'Iron Age' in Palestine has thus been understood as starting about a century too early.[5] The arbitrariness of the date becomes clear when it is realized that what is called the Iron Age is mainly a continuation of the Late Bronze Age. The problem is, however, to know what exactly the material culture of the Late Bronze Age looked like in the different parts of Palestine. The hill country, where very few settlements existed, will be of particular interest because of the many new settlements that were built in the period before the emergence of the kingdom of Saul.

1. See H. Liebowitz and R. Folk, 'The Dawn of Iron Smelting in Palestine: The Late Bronze Age Smelter at Tel Yin'am, Preliminary Report', *Journal of Field Archaeology* 11 (1984), pp. 265-80. There is no indication as of yet that the iron mines in the 'Ajlun in Transjordan had been worked at this early period. For iron finds from Transjordan in the area of Khirbet Dananir in the northwestern Baq'ah valley, see C.V. Pigott, P.E. McGovern and M.R. Notts, 'The Earliest Steel from Transjordan', *Masca Journal* 2 (1982), pp. 35-39.

2. See the discussion in T. Stech-Wheeler, J.D. Muhly, K.R. Maxwell-Hyslop and R. Maddin, 'Iron at Taanach and Early Metallurgy in the Eastern Mediterranean', *AJA* 85 (1981), pp. 263-68.

3. Cf. K.M. Kenyon, *Archaeology in the Holy Land*, pp. 225-26. For a detailed investigation, see J.C. Waldbaum, *From Bronze to Iron*, pp. 24-26; *idem*, 'The First Archaeological Appearance of Iron and the Transition to the Iron Age', *The Coming of the Age of Iron* (ed. T.A. Wertime and J.D. Muhly; New Haven, 1980), pp. 84-85.

4. J.C. Waldbaum, *The Coming of the Age of Iron*, pp. 86-87.

5. The Iron Age in Cyprus is usually understood to have started around 1050 BCE, and it is hard to believe that the production of iron tools should have flourished earlier in Palestine.

New phenomena that occurred in different areas of Palestine during the early part of the Iron Age have been used as arguments or proofs for a new people ('Israelites') having settled in the country, as well as forming part of the argumentation for the beginning of a new period. These arguments have been based upon a few iron objects, on some pottery forms, such as the so-called collared-rim store jar, on terraces, pillared houses and four-room houses. All these phenomena do not really signify a radical break with earlier traditions and they cannot, therefore, be seen as inaugurating a new era. Neither can they be seen as products of a special ethnic group,[1] because they seem to have been used by different groups of people.

Cisterns with lime plaster are known from the Early Bronze Age, for instance, at Byblos, Abu Matar, and at Bab edh-Dhra' and Jawa in Jordan.[2] Hazor and Ta'anak of the Late Bronze Age should also be mentioned in this connection.[3] Agricultural terraces were not inventions by the new settlers of the hills.[4] Because not all villagers had been farmers before they settled in the hills, terracing may have been slow in coming into use in certain parts of the hill country; these settlers must have occupied the hills for some time first before soil erosion became a concern.[5]

1. Concerning the pottery, R. Amiran has maintained that it is very much in the same tradition as that of the LB II period (*Ancient Pottery of the Holy Land*, p. 191). Y. Aharoni has also emphasized that the material culture of Palestine of the Iron I period is to be seen as a continuation of the LB II period. He thought that the Israelites did not have any material culture of their own but 'borrowed everything from the previous inhabitants'. In spite of this, Aharoni maintains that the Israelite occupation was of a 'unique nature' (*The Land of the Bible*, 2nd edn, pp. 240-41). Here one could ask: When there were no previous inhabitants where one settled, from whom did one borrow the culture?

2. R. Miller, 'Water Use in Syria and Palestine from the Neolithic to the Bronze Age', *World Archaeology* 11 (1980), pp. 335-41.

3. Y. Yadin, *Hazor*, I, p. 123; P.W. Lapp, *BASOR* 195 (1969), p. 33.

4. Cf. G.W. Ahlström, 'Where did the Israelites Live?', *JNES* 41 (1982), pp. 183-84; L.E. Stager, 'The Archaeology of the East Slope of Jerusalem and the Terrace of Kidron', *JNES* 41 (1982), p. 116. For the use and construction of terraces, see N.N. Lewis, 'Lebanon: The Mountain and its Terraces', *The Geographical Review* 43 (1953), pp. 1-14; Z. Ron, 'Agricultural Terraces in the Judean Mountains', *IEJ* 16 (1966), pp. 111-22; S. Gibson and G. Edelstein, 'Investigating Jerusalem's Rural Landscape', *Levant* 17 (1985), pp. 139-55, esp. pp. 143-44.

5. J.E. Spencer and G.A. Hale, 'The Origin, Nature and Distribution of Agricultural Terracing', *Pacific Viewpoint* 2 (1961), pp. 26-27. Cf. also

The rarity of iron tools has already been mentioned; thus the argument about the coming of iron as signifying a new era cannot be applied to the beginning of the twelfth century BCE. Iron did not play any role in cultivating new areas in Palestine and Transjordan during the twelfth century.

It has often been maintained that new forms in pottery, such as new rims and other features, should be seen as indications for ethnicity. One has thus not reckoned with the possibility of artistic developments within one and the same society.[1] The argument most often used in recent times in connection with pottery is that the so-called collared-rim storage jar should be seen as an Israelite invention. This jar was probably used for collecting water and grain. It was thought as non-existent in Canaan before c. 1200 BCE.[2] However, this vessel has been unearthed at several sites not built by any newcomers, such as Megiddo str. VIIB,[3] Tell Keisan[4] and the LB cemetery at Tel Zeror.[5] Other places are 'Afula, Tel Mevorak, Tell Qasîle, Aphek and 'Izbet Sartah, besides several places in the central hills, such as Giloh, Bethel, 'Ai, Raddana and Tell el-Fûl.[6] It has also been found at some sites in Jordan, such as Khirbet el-Hajjar, Tell Deir 'Alla, Tell el-

D.C. Hopkins, *The Highlands of Canaan*, pp. 180-82.

1.   Cf. my book, *Who were the Israelites?*, pp. 27, 35-36, and also I. Finkelstein, *Archaeology of Settlement*, pp. 276-78. See also D.C. Hopkins, who says that those 'who would attribute certain changes in the pottery culture of the early Iron Age Highlands to the ethnic entity 'Israel' are caught in the double bind of a restrictive and untenable view of social change and a circular argument' (*The Highlands of Canaan*, p. 149).

2.   See, for instance, Y. Aharoni, 'New Aspects of the Israelite Occupation in the North', *Near Eastern Archaeology in the Twentieth Century* (ed. J.A. Sanders, Garden City, NY, 1970), p. 265.

3.   Y. Yadin, 'The Transition from a Semi-Nomadic to a Sedentary Society in the Twelfth Century B.C.E.', *Symposia* (ed. F.M. Cross), p. 64; P. Beck and M. Kochavi, 'A Dated Assemblage of the Late 13th Century BCE from the Egyptian Residency at Aphek', *Tel Aviv* 12 (1985), p. 34.

4.   J. Balensi, 'Tell Keisan, témoin original de l'apparition du "Mycénien IIICla" au Proche-Orient', *RB* 88 (1981), p. 399.

5.   K. Ohata, *Tel Zeror*, III, p. 71.

6.   Consult M.M. Ibrahim, 'The Collared Rim Jar of the Early Iron Age', *Archaeology in the Levant: Essays for Kathleen M. Kenyon* (ed. R. Moorey and P. Parr; Warminster, 1978), pp. 116-26; I. Finkelstein, *'Izbet Sartah: An Early Iron Age Site near Rosh Ha'ayin, Israel* (BAR, 299; Oxford, 1986), pp. 77-84.

Mazar and Sahab.[1] Knowing this, it is hard to accept this vessel as being an 'Israelite' invention.[2] P. Beck and M. Kochavi also see 'its incipient stage' as occurring in the thirteenth century, in other words, before the 'Israelite' settlement of the hills had started. The antecedents of this type of jar seems to be the 'MB IIB–C pithoi'.[3]

The argument from architecture, namely that a new form of house should have had an ethnic association, is no argument, because it had been used by different societies. For instance, a pillared house from the fourteenth century BCE (LB II) has been found at Tel Baṭash (Timnah?), 8 km south of Gezer (coord. 141.6-132.5).[4] The four-room house type, which may be a development of the pillared house form, has been found, for instance, not only at some places in the central hills,[5] but also at Tell Keisan, Megiddo (str. VIB),[6] and at 'Afula[7] in the western Galilee, at Medeyineh in Transjordan,[8] at Tel

---

1. M.M. Ibrahim, in *Archaeology in the Levant* (ed. R. Morey and P. Parr), pp. 116-26, esp. p. 122. Consult also M. Weippert, *The Settlement of the Israelite Tribes*, pp. 134-35; and *idem*, a review of S. Yeivin, *The Israelite Conquest of Canaan*, *BibOr* 31 (1974), p. 298; H.J. Franken, 'The Problem of Identification in Biblical Archaeology', *PEQ* 108 (1976), p. 8; W. Rast, *Taanach*, I, p. 9.

2. Thus also A. Mazar, 'Giloh: An Early Israelite Settlement Site near Jerusalem', *IEJ* 31 (1981), p. 30.

3. I. Finkelstein, *Archaeology of Settlement*, pp. 283-84. It is interesting to note that according to Finkelstein some of the rims of these jars had seal impressions (pp. 279-80). This is a sign of organized business or state administration, and is not a characteristic feature of a nomadic society, even if it had just settled.

4. G.L. Kelm and A. Mazar, 'Three Seasons of Excavations at Tel Batash— Biblical Timnah', *BASOR* 248 (1982), p. 9-13, and fig. 9. Also of potential relevance is the so-called 'Twelfth Century House' at Ta'anak; see P.W. Lapp, *BASOR* 195 (1969), pp. 34-37, and fig. 24.

5. The so-called LB temple at Tell el-Far'ah (N), building 490, has now been reinterpreted as being a four-room house by A. Chambon (*Tell el-Far'ah: L'âge du fer* [Editions Recherche sur les Civilisations, Memoire no. 31; Paris, 1984], plan 1 and fig. 1).

6. The pottery of Megiddo VI is in the Canaanite tradition (W. Rast, *Taanach*, I, p. 35; I. Finkelstein, *Archaeology of Settlement*. Finkelstein also mentions that collared-rim jars were not manufactured after the eleventh century BCE (p. 281).

7. M. Dothan, ''Afula', *EAEHL*, I, p. 35.

8. M. Olávarri, *ADAJ* 22 (1978–79), p. 138. Cf. also J.R. Kautz, who maintains that this house form found in Transjordan cannot be associated with a special ethnic group (*BA* 44 [1981], p. 33).

Māśōś in the Negev,[1] and in Philistine strata at Tell esh-Shariʻa (Tel Sera)[2] and at Tell Qasîle.[3] Only wishful thinking can make this layout an Israelite invention. This type of house developed out of a Bronze Age tradition consisting of a building with a courtyard surrounded by rooms on one or several sides.[4] Instead of associating it with a certain ethnic group, as has been done,[5] one rather should understand this type of house from a functional point of view. It served both the families and their domesticated animals.

Several of the new settlements have been labeled enclosures or 'courtyard sites' because of their layout: the houses or rooms are built in an oval circle creating a large 'courtyard'. These have been found in different geographical areas of Palestine, such as Galilee, the Judean

1. See G.W. Ahlström, 'The Early Iron Age Settlers at *Ḥirbet el-Mśāś* (Tẹl Māśōś)', *ZDPV* 100 (1984), pp. 35-52. A. Mazar, who earlier advocated that the pillared house was a forerunner of the 'Israelite' four-room house, now sees this type as being 'inspired by a Canaanite architectural tradition'; see 'The Israelite Settlement in Canaan in the Light of Archaeological Excavations', in *Biblical Archaeology Today: Proceedings of the International Congress on Biblical Archaeology, Jerusalem, April 1984* (ed. J. Amitai; Jerusalem, 1985), pp. 66-68.

2. E.D. Oren, *BA* 45 (1982), pp. 155-66.

3. For an analysis of this house type and its purposes, see F. Braemer, *L'architecture domestique du Levant à l'âge du fer* (Protohistoire du Levant: Editions recherches sur les civilisations, 8; Paris, 1982).

4. G.W. Ahlström, *ZDPV* 100 (1984), pp. 35-52; cf. L.E. Stager, 'The Archaeology of the Family in Ancient Israel', *BASOR* 260 (1985), p. 17; R.B. Coote and K.W. Whitelam, *The Emergence of Early Israel in Historical Perspective* (The Social World of Biblical Antiquity Series, 5; Sheffield, 1987), pp. 125-26. Log-built houses with rooms on three sides of a central courtyard have been found at the Wasserburg, Federsee, Buchau in southern Germany (tenth-ninth centuries BCE); see S. Pigott, *Ancient Europe from the Beginnings of Agriculture to Classical Antiquity* (Edinburgh, 1965), p. 149 fig. 83.

5. Y. Shiloh sees this house type as an invention by the incoming Israelites ('The Four-Room House: Its Situation and Function in the Israelite City', *IEJ* 20 [1970], pp. 180-90). A. Kempinski and V. Fritz advocated that the four-room house was modeled after the Israelite nomadic tent ('Excavations at Tel Masos [Khirbet el Meshâsh]: Preliminary Report of the Third Season, 1975', *Tel Aviv* 4 [1977], p. 147). Cf. I. Finkelstein, who sees the buildings of the Negev Highlands having the shape of 'tent encampment in the first stage' of the villagers' sedentarization (*'Izbet Ṣarṭah*, p. 117). This possibility cannot be excluded, but there is no way we can learn anything about the structures and layouts of the nomadic tents or huts from the LB–Iron I periods.

Desert and the Negev.[1] Such enclosures may have been built because of geographical, sociological and protective considerations. This type of enclosure cannot be related to an ethnic group[2] uniquely, nor can it be seen *per se* as a sign of nomads having established settlements. It may rather be understood as being part of the culture of settlements in areas close to the desert; thus it was natural for nomads to use it in their process of sedentarization.[3]

Other phenomena seen as indications for new settlements built by Israelite newcomers are pits and poorly built huts. For instance, according to Y. Yadin, the first Iron Age I settlement (str. XII) on the tell of Hazor 'clearly represent[s] a settlement of seminomadic people'. It cannot be called a city. There were 'foundations of huts or tents, cooking and similar installations, and storage pits'.[4] The tell was 'literally strewn with these pits'.[5] According to Yadin, this stratum represents 'the first seminomadic Israelite settlement'.[6] Here Yadin has jumped to a conclusion. There is nothing in the remains of these huts or in these pits that tells us anything about the settlers' ethnicity. One could just as well argue that those who lived at Hazor after the great city had been destroyed were survivors who only had adequate tools for building poor shelters, huts or buildings. These aspects are seldom dealt with by modern historians, but the surviving population of the destroyed cities and of the devastated villages could have tried to rebuild their homes—or perhaps did not move very far when establishing new settlements.

1.   See, for instance, M. Kochavi, 'Excavations at Tel Esdar', *'Atiqot* 5 (1969), pp. 14-48, and *idem*, 'Tel Esdar', *EAEHL*, IV, p. 1169; Z. Herzog, *Beer-Sheba*. II. *The Early Iron Age Settlement* (Tel Aviv, 1984), pp. 15-28, 51; cf. A. Kempinski, D. Zichmoni, E. Gilboa and N. Rosel, 'Excavations at Tel Masos 1972, 1974, 1975', *EI* 15 (1981), p. 177 fig. 12; I. Finkelstein, *'Izbet Ṣarṭah*, pp. 106-107 and fig. 26.

2.   Thus I. Finkelstein, who sees these sites as being built by pastoralists (*'Izbet Ṣarṭah*, p. 117).

3.   For the antecedents of this type of settlement, see I. Beit-Arieh, 'A Pattern of Settlement in Southern Sinai and Southern Canaan in the Third Millennium BCE', *BASOR* 243 (1981), p. 51. For living quarters around a central courtyard at Tell Mureybit from c. 5500 BCE, see O. Aurenche, *La maison orientale*, p. 188.

4.   Silos and storage pits could very well be characteristics for rural people, especially when organizing a new settlement, whatever their ethnicity.

5.   Y. Yadin, *Hazor of Those Kingdoms*, p. 129.

6.   *Hazor of Those Kingdoms*, p. 113.

This may be the case in northern Galilee, where Y. Aharoni found 'a chain' of small unwalled villages from the early period of the Iron Age.[1] Some were on hilltops, some on the slopes, and others in the valleys. The distances between the villages were about one and a half to three kilometers. 'This is a typical picture of families and clans at the beginning of the settling process'. Aharoni associated these settlements with an invasion of Israelite tribes.[2] This is more an assumption than a fact. Other peoples could just as easily have settled in this area, such as indigenous Galileans or migrating Aramaeans. Phoenician influence has been detected in some Galilean pottery, such as the pithoi of the Upper Galilee. These pithoi are not in the same tradition as those of the central highlands.[3] Nevertheless, the cooking pot with an 'erect "tongued" rim' found alongside the pithoi indicates that the material culture of these villages belonged to the pottery tradition of the greater Palestinian area. This cooking pot, which has been found in Upper Galilee villages, is common throughout Palestine in the twelfth and eleventh centuries. It has been found not only in Galilee and in the central hills, but also in the coastal area, for instance at Tell Qasîle, Gezer, Ashdod, and north of Carmel at Tell Keisan, among other places.[4] The latter was a Phoenician city located in the Acco plain (coord. 164-253).[5] As we know, Ashdod was not taken by the Israelites in the Iron I period, and neither was Gezer. This latter city came under Israelite rule first under Solomon, who got the ruined city Gezer from the Pharaoh when marrying his daughter (1 Kgs. 9.16-17). The rest of the pottery from Galilee seems to be derived from the Palestinian Late Bronze tradition, which would point to the fact that most of the settlers were indigenous.

Studying the history of the greater Palestinian area during Iron Age I, three lines of thinking have dominated scholarly investigations. One is that of Albrecht Alt and Martin Noth, who maintained that the biblical narrative about the conquest of Canaan under Joshua was not a reliable account of what had happened. Instead there had been a

---

1.   *The Settlement of the Israelite Tribes in Upper Galilee* (Jerusalem, 1957), pp. 17-19 (Hebrew).

2.   *The Land of the Bible* (2nd edn), pp. 194-95.

3.   I. Finkelstein, *Archaeology of Settlement*, pp. 108-110.

4.   See I. Finkelstein, *'Izbet Ṣarṭah*, p. 65.

5.   For the excavations, see J. Briend and J.B. Humbert, *Tell Keisan (1971–1976): Une cité phénicienne en Galilée* (Paris, 1980).

gradual infiltration of foreigners, that is, nomads, called Israelites, who became associated with each other through the 'bonds' of an amphictyony.[1] The god of that amphictyony would have been Yahweh, a non-Canaanite deity, who would have been worshipped at a special cult center. This peaceful process later became a militant one, because the increase in the population among the newcomers resulted in conflicts with the Canaanites. Because they were not able to eliminate all the Canaanites, religious and cultural problems became the order of the day.[2]

Another school of thought is that of W.F. Albright and his students, sometimes called the Baltimore school. This school, which has had a great following among American and Israeli scholars, is more in agreement with the Old Testament tradition about a violent conquest led by Joshua. However, the fact that such cities as Ai, Gibeon, and Jericho in Cisjordan and Heshbon in Transjordan did not exist in the thirteenth century BCE (see Map 11) makes the conquest model unacceptable. The amphictyonic hypothesis was once widely accepted, but, because of heavy criticism, the amphicityonic component has now been replaced with a 'tribal league' by the younger representatives of this approach.[3] Scholars of this line of thought have thus tried to harmonize the archaeological results, such as destruction layers from thirteenth century Palestine, with the biblical narratives about the Israelite settlement. In other words, the biblical presentation of history (which does not give any fixed date) was in general

1. For the nonexistence of an Israelite amphictyony, see E. Auerbach, *Wüste und Gelobtes Land*, I (Berlin, 1936), p. 72; G. Fohrer, 'Altes Testament— "Amphiktyonie" und "Bund"', *TLZ* 91 (1966), pp. 810-16, 893-904; H.M. Orlinsky, 'The Tribal System of Israel and Related Groups in the Period of the Judges', *Oriens Antiquus* 1 (1962), pp. 11-20; and especially C.H.J. de Geus, who has clearly seen, *contra* Noth, that Israel's origin cannot be solved through the hypothesis of an amphictyony (*The Tribes of Israel*).

2. See A. Alt, 'Die Landnahme der Israeliten', *KS*, I, pp. 89-125; 'Erwägungen über die Landnahme der Israeliten in Palästina', *Palästinajahrbuch* 35 (1939), pp. 8-63 (= *KS*, I, pp. 126-75). M. Noth is the architect of the cultic amphictyony, which, it is claimed, developed into a political league and then was replaced by the monarchy; see his *Das System der Zwölfstämme Israel* (BWANT, 4.1; Darmstadt, 1966 [Stuttgart, 1930]); *Geschichte Israels* (Göttingen, 1950 [5th edn, 1963; ET *The History of Israel*]).

3. The difference between an amphictyony and a tribal league has not been spelled out, and neither has anyone been able to demonstrate the existence of a tribal league.

supported.[1] Both of the above-mentioned 'schools' have in common the basic hypothesis that a new group of nomadic people called Israelites had immigrated.

A third theory was launched by G. Mendenhall in 1962. Utilizing anthropological and sociological research for his reconstruction, he showed the weak points in the two other models. Mendenhall advocated that the new settlers of the central highlands were not nomads but indigenous Canaanite peasants who had revolted against the Canaanite city states and the Canaanite societies in general and had withdrawn to the hills. They preferred to build their own societies. Mendenhall connected this phenomenon with a religious movement. The settlers became Yahweh covenanters creating a theocracy under Yahweh.[2] Why they would call themselves Israelites is not discussed by Mendenhall. The name Israel indicates that the main god of early Israel was the Canaanite El, not Yahweh, arguing against Mendenhall's proposed Yahwistic theocracy.

The same basic idea underlies N.K. Gottwald's concepts concerning the beginning of Israel. Gottwald, however, builds much more than Mendenhall upon the idea of a peasant revolt as the beginning of an increased settlement and a retribalization of the peoples of the hills. It is claimed that this resulted in the creation of a segmented, egalitarian society.[3] Gottwald accepts Mendenhall's theory about a theocratic

1.   W.F. Albright, *The Archaeology of Palestine and the Bible* (New York, 1932); *idem*, 'Archaeology and the Date of the Hebrew Conquest of Palestine', *BASOR* 58 (1935), pp. 10-18; *idem*, 'The Israelite Conquest of Palestine in the Light of Archaeology', *BASOR* 74 (1939), pp. 11-23; *idem*, *The Biblical Period from Abraham to Ezra* (New York, 1963); *idem*, *Yahweh and the Gods of Canaan* (Garden City, NY, 1968). Representatives of this approach are, among others, J. Bright, *A History of Israel*; R.G. Boling, *Judges*, and *idem*, *Joshua* (AB, 6; with an Introduction by G.E. Wright; Garden City, NY, 1982).

2.   G.E. Mendenhall, 'The Hebrew Conquest of Palestine', *BA* 25 (1962), pp. 66-87. F.M. Cross believes that the history of Israel began 'when Yahwism emerged from its mythopoetic environment' (*Canaanite Myth and Hebrew Epic*, p. 135). Against this, see C.H.J. de Geus, who maintains that no nation has originated 'from a religious movement' (*The Tribes of Israel*, p. 186 n. 260).

3.   To use the phrase 'segmented society' for the twelfth-century settlements in the hills, as is done by F. Crüsemann and N.K. Gottwald, is impossible, because we do not know what kind of structural segments those villages had. See F. Crüsemann, *Der Widerstand gegen das Königtum: Die antiköniglichen Texte des Alten Testamentes und der Kampf um den frühen israelitischen Staat* (WMANT, 49; Neukirchen, 1978), pp. 201-208; N.K. Gottwald, *The Tribes of Yahweh*, pp. 322-

association of tribes under Yahweh, but with a different twist. He advocates that a group of slaves under the leadership of Moses fled from Egypt and settled in Canaan, and somewhere in the desert they made a covenant with Yahweh. In Canaan the other settlers accepted this god as theirs through a treaty (Josh. 24), and thus Yahweh became the god of a new society of revolutionary covenanters, the Israelites. In this way Gottwald has tried to answer the question why the Canaanite revolutionaries could be called Israelites. They had El as their god at first, but at Shechem they adopted Yahweh.[1] Gottwald works hard to try to show that the Israelites were different from the Canaanites, obviously forgetting his own theory that the majority of them originally were Canaanites. He even states that 'Israel *thought* it was different because it *was* different'.[2]

The hypothesis about a peasant revolt being the reason for the new settlements of the hills has been impossible to prove.[3] This hypothesis has been built upon the Amarna letters and upon an assumption of social unrest and political instability caused by Egyptian military campaigns and the invasion of 'Sea Peoples'. The latter events may have contributed to a withdrawal from the cultural and agricultural areas in the coastal areas and the Jezreel Valley. Many people may have withdrawn to the hills in order to escape the wars and the destruction of their lands. This assumption can be supported by the fact that the material culture of the highland settlements of the twelfth and eleventh centuries BCE is primarily the same as in other parts of the country. However, the hypothesis about a withdrawal cannot completely explain the 'explosion' of new settlements in the hills during the twelfth and eleventh centuries.

As for the Amarna letters, there is no real information about the peasants having revolted against the princes of some city states which

33; cf. C. Schäfer-Lichtenberger, *Stadt und Eidgenossenschaft im Alten Testament* (BZAW, 156; Berlin, 1983), pp. 333-68. For a critique, see N.P. Lemche, *Early Israel*, pp. 209-31.

1. N.K. Gottwald, *The Tribes of Yahweh*. See, for instance, pp. 564-66. R.G. Boling has accepted the thesis about the 'revolutionary covenanters' (*Joshua*).

2. 'Two Models for the Origins of Ancient Israel', *The Quest for the Kingdom of God* (ed. H.B. Huffmon, F.A. Spina and A.R.W. Green), p. 18.

3. For a critique of this theory, see A.H. Hauser, 'Israel's Conquest of Palestine: A Peasant Revolt?', *JSOT* 7 (1978), pp. 2-19, and the thorough criticism of both Mendenhall and Gottwald by N.P. Lemche (*Early Israel*). See also G.W. Ahlström, *Who were the Israelites?*, pp. 5-9.

can be used as an argument for a peasant revolt in Palestine 100–200 years later. As mentioned above, the sociopolitical problems of fourteenth-century Palestine were not really caused by any large peasant revolt, but rather by fighting between the different city states which was often caused by their policy of territorial expansion.[1] In such a situation trade may have been disturbed; bandits and robbers may have increased their activities, and some military leaders (*maryannu*) may have had greater opportunities for independent action.[2] This may have caused rural unrest. When the control of the country no longer was in the hands of a strong central government, not only may settled people have moved, but also nomads may have sought new areas for grazing, and, because of disturbances in the subsistence system, they may have started dry farming, which would lead to a settled form of life. In summary, there may have been several reasons prompting people to move to the very sparsely inhabited hills.

The many villages and farms that have been discovered in the Negev Highlands may have been part of a process of sedentarization by sheep and goat pastoralists during the early Iron Age.[3] This settlement growth may be traceable to a change in economic life. The nomads could have been benefitting from the economic prosperity of the southern coast and the products of the copper mines at Timna.

1. See my book, *Who were the Israelites?*, pp. 18-19.
2. According to EA 292.28-29, Ba'lu-šipti of Gezer states that there was 'hostility in the mountains' against him. Any ruler could meet hostility both among the mountain peoples and by others. This letter cannot be taken as proof that peasants revolted. We could perhaps rather say, with F. Braudel (*The Mediterranean and the Mediterranean World in the Age of Philip II*, vol. I, pp. 34-35), that the hostility between the ruler of Gezer and the mountain people was an expression of the common enmity between the urban and nonurban population; cf. also L. Marfoe, *BASOR* 234 (1979), pp. 32-33. We could also assume that the mountain people had had a hard time accepting Gezer's rule or expansionist attempts. M.L. Chaney concedes that a peasant revolt leading to the settlement of the hills may be 'plausible' but cannot be proved ('Ancient Palestinian Peasant Movements', *Palestine in Transition* [ed. D.N. Freedman and D.F. Graf], p. 82).
3. For the sites, see E.K. Vogel, 'Negev Survey of Nelson Glueck', *EI* 12 (1975), pp. 1*-17*; for the problems of sedentarization, cf. I. Finkelstein, 'The Iron Age "Fortresses" of the Negev Highlands: Sedentarization of the Nomads', *Tel Aviv* 11 (1984), pp. 189-209.

According to I. Finkelstein, Tel Māśōś in the Negev was a result of this nomadic prosperity.[1]

The many attempts that have been made to make nomadic (or seminomadic[2]) invaders into invincible conquerors of heavily fortified cities or mighty armies are less successful than the biblical presentation, which ascribes the victory to Yahweh. In the view of the biblical writer, Canaan was taken by force, according to the will of Yahweh. This view is in harmony with ancient Near Eastern historiography, in which the gods fought the battles. Therefore, to harmonize the biblical narrative about the conquest with the actual happenings will be impossible.[3] All the events are not known.[4] There are, however, certain biblical statements, as well as some nonbiblical facts, which can be used as a framework for a reconstruction of what could have occurred.

The biblical narrative about the Conquest ends with some statements of 'disappointments'. Judg. 1.27-35 states that Manasseh, Ephraim, Zebulon, Asher and Naphtali could not 'drive out' the inhabitants of the Canaanite cities of the plains and valleys. This should be compared with Josh. 17.11-18, a passage which says that the 'Canaanites managed to hold their own in the country' and that the people of Ephraim and Manasseh would be confined to the wooded mountain area. Thus, even the biblical 'historiographer' has acknowledged that

1. *Tel Aviv* 11 (1984), p. 200. See also J. Finkelstein, 'The Arabian Trade and the Socio-Political Situation in the Negev in the 12–11th Centuries BCE', *JNES* 47 (1988), pp. 241-52.

2. The difference is seldom spelled out. Sometimes seminomadism is confused with transhumance, and it is understood by many as an evolutionary stage between 'pure' nomadism and a settled culture.

3. Long ago E. Meyer stated that there were no really reliable sources for an Israelite conquest ('Kritik der Berichte über die Eroberung Palæstinas', *ZAW* 1 [1881], p. 145). See also S. Mowinckel, *Tetrateuch–Pentateuch–Hexateuch: Die Berichte über die Landnahme in den drei altisraelitischen Geschichtswerken* (BZAW, 90; Berlin, 1964), p. 60.

4. The biblical traditions about the history of Palestine in the thirteenth and twelfth centuries BCE seem to show no historical knowledge about the political scene. For instance, the biblical writers do not know anything about Egypt's rule over the country, nor about the garrison cities and Egyptian temples. No Egyptian campaign is mentioned. Merneptah's destruction of Israel is not known. No Egyptian Pharaoh is mentioned by name before Shoshenq (biblical Shishaq) marched through Palestine in the fifth year of Rehoboam's reign (1 Kgs 14.25). All this may indicate that annalistic writings did not occur before the emergence of the monarchy.

there was no conquest to some degree. In fact, there is no mention in the Hebrew Bible about a conquest of the central highlands.[1] The literary tradition has been modelled in a time when the Davidic–Solomonic kingdom was a past experience. The biblical texts show that the destruction of the Canaanite city states had nothing to do with the settlement process of the central hills. At the same time they indicate that the history of Israel started in the hill country.

The archaeological remains do not fully support any of the scholarly models mentioned above. It should be emphasized that in no instance has archaeology been able to prove that a city was destroyed by incoming Israelites. As mentioned above, the end of the Canaanite city states was not caused by invading, nomadic Israelites.[2] The destruction levels from the thirteenth and twelfth centuries BCE may be ascribed to Egyptian campaigns by Ramses II, Merneptah (who, by the way, fought a Palestinian group of people called Israel)[3] and Ramses III, or to the migrations of Sea Peoples. Already during the end of Ramses II's long reign control of the Egyptian holdings in Asia was slipping,

1.   Note, for instance, that there are no destruction levels from the thirteenth and twelfth centuries BCE at Tell Balaṭa (Shechem). Instead the excavators found a 'continued use and repair of the Late Bronze Age fortifications in the 12th century' (G.E. Wright, *Shechem*, p. 78). From this we can conclude that the kingdom of Shechem known from the el-Amarna letters continued down into the Iron I period.

2.   Tell Beit Mirsim is an example of how doubtful this hypothesis is. The site shows 'an indigenous Canaanite cultural sequence', even if it was destroyed in the twelfth century (R. Greenberg, 'New Light on the Early Iron Age at Tell Beit Mirsim', *BASOR* 265 [1987], p. 55). Greenberg thinks that TBM 'served as a temporary haven… for a small Canaanite population fleeing the disintegration of the central Canaanite towns'. Pottery from str. B2 resembles that of Tell ed-Duweir (Lachish VI) (p. 78). Another example is Hazor. The excavator associated the destruction of str. XIII with the invading Israelites because of Josh. 11.10-13 (Y. Yadin, *Hazor of Those Kingdoms*, pp. 9-10, 131-32). This text mentions that Joshua burnt the city of Hazor. Two other passages, however, state that king Jabin of Hazor sent his army under Sisera to fight the Israelites (Judg. 4 and 1 Sam. 12.9). The latter texts do not report that Hazor was burnt by the Israelites. Josh. 11 is part of the literary 'conquest' construction naming the allies of Hazor as the Hivites, the Perizzites and the Jebusites, who all were nonexistent peoples in the time of the postexilic composer. It is doubtful that Josh. 11 has anything to do with the Israelites. Hazor plays the same literary role as 'Ai and Jericho in the 'conquest' story. The D-historian has found some very good material for his story in these old traditions.

3.   See G.W. Ahlström and D. Edelman, *JNES* 44 (1985), pp. 59-61.

and after the death of Ramses III (1151 BCE) Egyptian rule sharply declined. The last pharaoh to claim authority over Palestine before 1000 BCE was Ramses VI (1141–1134 BCE), who was also the last pharaoh to exploit the turquoise mines in the Sinai. In addition, warfare between Canaanite city states, as well as plagues and accidents, such as fires, could have caused some of the destructions.[1]

Archaeological work, however, has demonstrated a sharp increase in small unwalled settlements in the central Palestinian hills during the twelfth and eleventh centuries (see Map 12). This process may have started already during the thirteenth century. The same early date seems to apply to settlement in the Madaba plain, on the Moab plateau in Jordan,[2] and in parts of northern Jordan.[3] This increase in settlements may support A. Alt's theory about a peaceful infiltration, but it does not give any clear evidence that the villages were built by a new ethnic group of people. The process of 'infiltration' was rather due to movements within the country and was not caused only by nonindigenous immigrant peoples. This assumption can be supported by the archaeological remains from these new villages, which show that the material culture of the new villages was mainly Canaanite.[4] G.E. Mendenhall's hypothesis about a withdrawal to the hills is thus to be taken seriously. People may have moved up from the coastal areas, the lowlands, and valleys to the wooded regions in the mountains in

1. For objections to the theory that invading Israelites caused the destruction of Canaanite cities, see M. Noth, 'Der Beitrag der Archäologie zur Geschichte Israels', *Congress Volume, Oxford 1959* (ed. J.A. Emerton *at al.*), pp. 262-82; J.B. Pritchard, 'Culture and History', *The Bible in Modern Scholarship* (ed. J.P. Hyatt; Nashville, 1965), pp. 319-20; *idem*, 'Arkeologiens plats i studiet av Gamla Testamentet', *SEÅ* 30 (1965), pp. 10-20; M. Weippert, *Die Landnahme der israelitischen Stämme in der neueren wissenschaftlichen Diskussion* (FRLANT, 92; Göttingen, 1967), pp. 124-26 (= *The Settlement*, pp. 128-30); R. de Vaux, 'On Right and Wrong Uses of Archaeology', *Near Eastern Archaeology in the Twentieth Century* (ed. J.A. Sanders; Garden City, NY, 1970), pp. 64-80.

2. About 30 sites with Iron I pottery were found in the vicinity of Ḥisbân; cf. R. Ibach, 'Archaeological Survey of the Ḥesbân Region', *AUSS* 14 (1976), p. 125. For Moab, see J.M. Miller, 'Archaeological Survey of Central Moab: 1978', *BASOR* 234 (1979), pp. 43-52. It seems that the increase in settlements on the Moab plateau started in the LB II period.

3. S. Mittmann, *Beiträge zur Siedlungs- und Territorialgeschichte des nördlichen Ostjordanlandes*. Consult also the statistics in J.A. Sauer, *BASOR* 263 (1986), pp. 1-26.

4. Cf. my book, *Who were the Israelites?*, pp. 25-36.

order to escape the problems of war and devastation, taxes and corvée. An investigation of the burial systems supports such a theory.[1] As mentioned before, during the Late Bronze period the central hills had only a few settlements. The population of the highlands may have been mainly sheepherders. Knowing that the wooded highlands had always been a place of refuge,[2] it is likely that peoples moved to these areas from the north, the south, and the (south) east.[3] In other words, both indigenous people and foreigners probably settled in the hills.[4] The settlers probably also included some nomadic clans (the Shasu of the Egyptian texts). With the collapse of the sociopolitical system during the upheavals at the end of the Late Bronze period, including the fall of the Egyptian empire with its control over Palestine and the trade routes, several nomadic clans changed their lifestyle and settled in the hills.[5] Whether a change in the climate or a disaster like a plague could have played a role is impossible to determine.[6] As far as can be said, the population increase arose not only out of a withdrawal from the urban and agricultural areas in the lowlands; nomads, bandits, refugees and immigrants from the north must also be taken into consideration. That the new settlers of the highlands were mainly Semites can, however, be concluded from the names of the new villages as we know them from the Old Testament. Most of these names are West Semitic.

Through two surveys there is now clear evidence that the central highlands were settled again during the Iron I period. In the Manasseh

1.   E. Bloch-Smith (private communication).
2.   Cf. L. Marfoe, *BASOR* 234 (1979), p. 23; B. Mazar, 'The Early Israelite Settlement in the Hill Country', *BASOR* 241 (1981), pp. 78-79.
3.   Cf. G.W. Ahlström, 'Another Moses Tradition', *JNES* 39 (1980), pp. 65-69.
4.   For a discussion about the settlement problems, see, among others, J.M. Sasson, 'On Choosing Models for Recreating Israelite Pre-Monarchic History', *JSOT* 21 (1981), pp. 3-24. Cf. also N. P. Lemche, *Early Israel*, pp. 1-65, 411-35.
5.   Cf. I. Finkelstein, *The Archaeology of the Israelite Settlement*, pp. 244-45.
6.   A palynological investigation by A. Horowitz indicates that there was a decrease in the pollen spectra after c. 2300 BCE as well as after c. 1100 BCE in northern Palestine (*The Quarternary of Israel*, p. 214). The 'lows' were around 2250 BCE and 950 BCE. His investigation did not really concern the central hills north of Jerusalem, but the territories north and west of the highlands and the Jordan valley. Even so, it would be probable that some decrease in the pollen spectra also occurred in the central hills. Thus deforestation may partly have been a natural phenomenon and not completely traceable to human activities.

survey A. Zertal found 96 sites dated to the Iron I period—if his dating is right. This should be compared with 35 in EB IV, 3 or 4 in MB I (MBIIA), 116 in MB II, but less than 30 (perhaps only c. 20 sites) during the Late Bronze period. For instance, in surveying the areas around the Dothan Valley, A. Zertal found 14 MB II settlements, but only five sites datable to the Late Bronze Age. For the Iron I period 11 sites were found, and in the Iron II period the number of sites increased to 18.

According to A. Zertal, the increase in settlements during the Iron I period seems to have started in the northeastern part of the Manasseh territory, gradually moving west and southwest.[1] The pottery is not quite new. It is part of the Canaanite tradition,[2] but with some distinctive features, such as punched decorations like holes on the handles or small depressions on the rims. No such pottery was, however, found in western Manasseh.[3] Parallels to these pottery decorations have not been found outside Cisjordan, as far as is known, but they occur for instance, at Ta'anak, Afula, Megiddo[4] and Bethel.[5] At these sites, as well as at Dothan, the pottery tradition is that of the Late Bronze II period.[6] The conclusion would then be that the settlements were built by indigenous people who for some reason moved up to the hills. Among the new settlers we have to reckon with some indigenous nomads, too.

A recent survey of the Ephraim territory shows the same kind of development from the MB II to the Iron II periods. For the MB II

1. *Arubboth, Hepher and the Third Solomonic District.* For the sites, see the maps on pp. 153-55.

2. Thus I. Finkelstein, *Archaeology of Settlement*, ch. II, pp. 80-91.

3. A. Zertal, *Arruboth*, pp. 164, 168, figs. 10, 12. According to I. Finkelstein this kind of ware has also been found at 'Afula, and in the hills at 'Izbet Ṣarṭah, Shiloh, Giloh, Ebal, Tell en-Nasbe, Tell el-Fûl and Tell el-Far'ah (*Archaeology of Settlement*, ch. 7, pp. 285-86).

4. I. Finkelstein, *Archaeology of Settlement*, p. 286.

5. W.F. Albright and J.A. Kelso, *The Excavation of Bethel (1934–1960)*, pl. 40:1-2.

6. A tomb at Dothan with a great amount of pottery and other objects does not show any break between LB II and Iron I in the pottery tradition. There were Cypriote milk bowls, wishbone handles, stirrup jars and pyxides, and a large number of weapons; see J.P. Free, *BASOR* 160 (1960), pp. 6-15. For a 'multiple handled' crater with four figures between the handles leaning and 'holding' the rims with outstretched arms, see D. Ussishkin, 'Dothan', *EAEHL*, I, fig. on p. 339.

period 60 sites were registered, but only five (possibly six) during the Late Bronze Age. In the Iron I period the number of sites increased to 115,[1] and for Iron II one found 190 sites. Most of the Iron I settlements were small in size and unwalled. I. Finkelstein sees these settlements to have been built mainly by nomads. The latter he sees as descendants of the 'dropouts' from the abandoned sites of the MB II period, who would have become pastoralists. Because he sees the villages of the early twelfth century BCE as reflecting 'the initial stages of sedentarization' of places which later came under the Israelite government, he labels the settlers 'Israelites', but this applies also the coast and the Jezreel.[2] This means that Finkelstein understands them as being indigenous to the country.[3] This latter conclusion is to be accepted,[4] but to see all the settlements as having been built by nomads is to exclude the complexities of reality. The differences in the layout of the villages may speak for both different needs in different geographical locations, as well as different local traditions. As mentioned above, people may have moved to the hills from different directions. The same considerations should be applied to the new Transjordanian settlements, which also could have been built both by nomads and people migrating both from within the country and from the north, to mention the most likely alternatives.[5] For the central hills in Cisjordan we could even assume that some of the surviving villagers of the

1.   Cf. M. Kochavi *et al.*, *Judea, Samaria, and the Golan.*
2.   Does this mean that we can call the MB II population of the hill country Israelites?
3.   I. Finkelstein, *Archaeology of Settlement*, pp. 338-48. What seems confusing in Finkelstein's writing is that he tries to make a difference between Canaanites and Israelites. Were not his nomads Canaanite nomads? Here we should remember that the term Canaan refers to a geographical territory which in general has been used for Palestine. In the LB period Canaan did not refer to the central hills; see G.W. Ahlström, *Who were the Israelites?*, pp. 37-43.
4.   For the new settlements as being built mainly by indigenous people, cf. G.W. Ahlström, *JNES* 39 (1980), pp. 65-69; *idem*, *Who were the Israelites?*, pp. 26-36; N.P. Lemche, *Early Israel*, pp. 416-32; R.B. Coote and K.W. Whitelam, *The Emergence of Early Israel*, pp. 117-38.
5.   For the settlement picture of Transjordan in the LB and Iron I periods, see, for instance, J.A. Sauer, *BASOR* 263 (1986), pp. 6-14; J.M. Miller, *BASOR* 234 (1979), pp. 43-52; *idem*, 'Recent Archaeological Developments Relevant to Ancient Moab', *Studies in the History and Archaeology of Jordan*, I (ed. A. Hadidi; Amman, 1982), pp. 169-73; J.R. Kautz, *BA* 44 (1981), pp. 27-35. See also below, Chapter 9.

people Israel who were defeated by pharaoh Merneptah's army[1] may have participated in resettling the hills. Theoretically 'Izbet Ṣarṭah and neighboring sites could have been such settlements.

'Izbet Ṣarṭah, located in the hills c. 3 km east of Aphek, has been understood by its excavators to have been Israelite, that is, non-Canaanite.[2] There are five other unexcavated sites from the same period in the vicinity of 'Izbet Ṣarṭah located in a north–southerly direction. We may assume that all six sites were built in the Iron I period and that the subsistence system was the same. The earliest stratum (III) at 'Izbet Ṣarṭah has been dated to the end of the thirteenth century or the beginning of the twelfth; thus it is earlier than those in the eastern part of the hill country.[3] That could mean that these settlers were not part of the same wave of settlers as those in the east. If 'Izbet Ṣarṭah was built by survivors after Merneptah's campaign, it would explain why this was one of the few new settlements that was fortified. Another hypothesis is that the settlers were rural people from the lowlands around Aphek or from the Shephelah.[4] The settlers may have specialized in cereal cultivation and perhaps some horticulture. As for the material culture, a four-room house was found and several pits for storage. The 'local' pottery is clearly in the LB tradition, including such items as Canaanite store jars, cooking pots and bowls. Sherds of pilgrim's flasks with parallels

1. We should note that Merneptah's 'Israel stela' does not mention any nomads, i.e. Shasu, as being defeated.

2. M. Kochavi and I. Finkelstein, "Izbet Ṣarṭah', *IEJ* 28 (1978), pp. 267-68; I. Finkelstein, *'Izbet Ṣarṭah*, p. 202. M. Kochavi believes it to be the ancient site of Eben-Ezer ('An Ostracon of the Period of the Judges from 'Izbet Ṣarṭah', *Tel Aviv* 4 [1977], p. 3). The identity of the site is not yet possible to establish. 1 Sam. 7.12 only states that Samuel erected a stela between Mizpah and *hn*, 'the tooth', and called it Eben-ezer.

3. See I. Finkelstein, who advocates that the settlement started first after the Egyptian-held Aphek had been destroyed. A letter from Ugarit that was found in the 'governor's' building would indicate that the destruction of the town occurred after the mid-thirteenth century (*'Izbet Ṣarṭah*, pp. 198-211). For this letter, see D. Owen, *Tel Aviv* 8 (1981), pp. 1-17; also I. Singer, who dates the letter to c. 1230 BCE (*Tel Aviv* 10 [1983], pp. 3-25).

4. Because archaeology has been mainly 'tell-minded' and no thorough surveys have been undertaken in the territories between the ancient coastal sites, we do not have any reliable knowledge about the rural population and the 'daughter villages'. Thus it is impossible to compare the highland villages with the (Canaanite) villages of the coastal area.

at Beth-Shan (str. VI) and Ashdod were also found.[1] Three collar-rim jars together with some fragments of the same vessels and a Late Mycenaean IIIB stirrup jar were found in the earliest stratum (Str. III).[2] This stratum is seen as being one of the earliest settlements of the 'Israelite nomads'.[3] If so, these settlers rapidly lost their cultural identity and quickly became part of the culture of western Palestine. As to the collared-rim jars, Finkelstein states that they were completely lacking 'at contemporary sites' in the hills.[4] 'Izbet Ṣarṭah can only be labeled Israelite if one sees the central highlands as the territory of Israel.[5] Thus, everybody settling there became an Israelite, a term that for this early period cannot be given any ethnic meaning.

An interesting phenomenon is the finding of a few (five) fragments of pig bones at this site, as is the case at some other Iron Age sites. Those from 'Izbet Ṣarṭah are not stratigraphically certain.[6] The rare occurrences of pig bones in these settlements cannot be explained by any biblical interdiction against the pig.[7] If one assumes, as does

---

1.   For the pottery, see I. Finkelstein, *'Izbet Ṣarṭah*, pp. 38-94. Here we should note that Finkelstein states that 'differences in pottery should not be explained away as simply ethnic in nature' (*The Archaeology of Israelite Settlement*, p. 275).

2.   See V. Hankey, 'A Sherd in the Simple Style of Late Mycenaean IIIB', *'Izbet Ṣarṭah* (ed. I. Finkelstein; BAR, 299; Oxford, 1986), pp. 99-102.

3.   I. Finkelstein, *'Izbet Ṣarṭah*, pp. 198-212. Cf. A. Mazar, *IEJ* 31 (1981), p. 35. The theory that these settlers could have come from the lowlands is unacceptable to Finkelstein because he cannot find that the cities there had any 'daughter' villages. He argues that the settlement is 'totally unlike' those in the coastal plain (p. 205). Archaeologically, the rural settlements of the plains are not known; therefore, a comparison cannot be made.

4.   *Archaeology of Settlement*, p. 320.

5.   Finkelstein believes that 'the rulers of Canaanite-Egyptian Aphek' would not have 'tolerated a concentrated alien population... in such a sensitive location' controlling the 'highway running through the strategic Aphek pass' (*'Izbet Ṣarṭah*, p. 207). This does not square with Finkelstein's theory that the settlers were indigenous to the land.

6.   See S. Hellwing and Y. Adjeman, 'Animal Bones', *'Izbet Ṣarṭah* (ed. I. Finkelstein; BAR, 299; Oxford, 1986), pp. 142-51.

7.   Astragali have also been found in Iron Age strata at Tell el-'Umeiri (c. 10 km S. of Amman) in Jordan, according to L.E. Geraty (in a presentation at the Midwest Annual meetings of the ASOR, AOS and SBL in Berrien Springs, Michigan, February 9, 1986). Tell el-'Umeiri has been (tentatively) identified with Abel-keramim in Judg. 11.33 by D. B. Redford ('A Bronze Age Itinerary in Transjordan', *JSSEA* 12 [1982], pp. 55-74).

I. Finkelstein, that these settlers came from the fringes of the country, they would not have heard about any Mosaic command against eating pigs.[1] I should also add that the wooded hill country was not very suitable for raising pigs.

Using Finkelstein's categorization, it would be inaccurate to call the settlers of 'Izbet Ṣarṭah Israelites because the settlement was abandoned around 1000 BCE. It is uncertain whether the people went to some other place in the highlands and became Israelite subjects, or whether they settled in the coastal area, which would mean that they could have become Philistine subjects. Their identity escapes us. All one can say is that they most probably were indigenous to Canaan.

Among the finds from 'Izbet Ṣarṭah is an ostracon the script of which has been thought to have some implications for the history of the Canaanite alphabet. The ostracon is dated to the twelfth or eleventh century BCE and does not seem to have been inscribed by a person skilled in the art of writing.[2] One suggestion is that the ostracon was written by someone just learning to write, perhaps, or a school boy.[3] A school at 'Izbet Ṣarṭah seems, however, to be an unrealistic assumption. Schools should rather be sought at business or administrative centers. Some scholars have maintained that here we have an example of Old Hebrew writing.[4] That may be if with this term one understands

---

1. In certain cultures of the ancient Near East the pig was a sacred animal; cf. H.O. Thompson, *Mekal*, pp. 140-42; J.C. Moyer, 'Hittite and Israelite Cult Practices: A Selected Comparison', *Scripture in Context*, II (ed. W.W. Hallo, J.C. Moyer and L.G. Perdue; Winona Lake, IN, 1983), pp. 19-38. See also G. Botterweck, '*chazir*', *TDOT*, IV, pp. 291-300.

2. Cf. F.M. Cross, *BASOR* 238 (1980), p. 8.

3. A. Lemaire, *Les écoles et la formation de la Bible dans l'ancien Israël* (Fribourg, 1981), pp. 7-10.

4. See M. Kochavi, who mentions that the ostracon was found in a silo (605), the date of which is uncertain (*Tel Aviv* 4 [1977], pp. 1-13); cf. A. Demsky, 'A Proto-Canaanite Abecedary Dating from the Period of the Judges and its Implications for the History of the Alphabet', *Tel Aviv* 4 (1977), pp. 14-27. See also A. Demsky, 'The 'Izbet Ṣarṭah Ostracon Ten Years Later', *'Izbet Ṣarṭah* (ed. I. Finkelstein; BAR, 299; Oxford, 1986), pp. 186-97. J. Naveh labels the script as 'proto-Canaanite' ('Some Considerations on the Ostracon from 'Izbet Ṣarṭah', *IEJ* 28 [1978], p. 33). The term proto-Canaanite is misleading. Logically it would refer to a script before there was a Canaanite one. F.M. Cross has also objected to labelling the script Hebrew (*BASOR* 238 [1980], p. 13).

nothing else than Canaanite script.[1] The personal names in the text are Canaaneo-Phoenician, according to A. Dotan.[2] What became Hebrew is an adoption of the Canaanite-Phoenician script and belongs to the period of the Monarchy. Logically, it is impossible to presume an 'Israelite' script before there was an organized Israelite community.

The tendency to see all new settlements in the hills, as well as in the Negev, as being built by 'invading' Israelites or Judahites can be exemplified by a few other examples. At Giloh, about 6 km SW of Jerusalem's Old City, A. Mazar found the remains of a walled settlement that probably was built around 1200 BCE and which he maintained was established by invading Israelites of the Judah tribe.[3] Mazar has based his conclusion on the biblical texts and not on the archaeological material found on the site. As has been mentioned above, there were almost no inhabitants during the LB period in the geographical territory called Judah. Jerusalem and Khirbet Rabud were in existence. Bethlehem could perhaps have existed as a Jebusite suburban town. Hebron is not yet known archaeologically from this period. The question who the new settlers at Giloh were must be answered through an analysis of the material remains of the site and not by glancing at the Bible's narrative concerning a time about which the biblical writers had very little knowledge.

If the settlers of Giloh were newly arrived nomadic Judahites, one would have expected their material culture to be of a somewhat different style and form than what was common in most of Canaan at this time. However, as I have mentioned earlier, both architecture and pottery are in the Canaanite tradition.[4] Even Mazar cannot find any 'original pottery making tradition' at this settlement.[5] Thus, his theory about people of the 'tribe of Judah' having settled at this place is not built on any logical deduction drawn from the archaeological material. It would be more logical to conclude that Giloh was built as an outpost of Jebusite Jerusalem. The closeness to that city would speak

1.   Unfortunately, there is no comparative material available that could help in determining a date.

2.   Still, Dotan labels the script Hebrew ('New Light on the 'Izbet Ṣarṭah Ostracon', *Tel Aviv* 8 [1981], pp. 170-71).

3.   *IEJ* 31 (1981), pp. 1-36; *idem*, 'Three Israelite Sites in the Hills of Judah and Ephraim', *BA* 45 (1982), pp. 167-78.

4.   *IEJ* 34 (1984), pp. 170-72.

5.   *BA* 45 (1982), p. 170.

for such a theory. We should not assume that the city state of Jerusalem comprised only the territory within the walls of the city. Every city needed some upland and had perhaps some fortified outposts at several places.[1] In the case of Giloh, which was the only fortified new settlement in the Judean hills,[2] the most plausible theory is that it was built on Jebusite territory.[3] It is reasonable to assume that the Jebusite kingdom had to protect its territory. The reason why the site was abandoned later in the Iron I period may have been that one could not find any water sources in its vicinity.[4] No cisterns were found at the site.

A new settlement from this period was also found in the vicinity of Hebron at Tell Jedur. The material culture does not bear any indications that a new ethnic group settled there. On the contrary, most of the finds represent the LB II tradition. Pottery of the Cypriote and Aegean types was also found, as was a bowl in the so-called Midianite style.[5]

The same picture occurs at Tel Ṣippor (Tell et-Tuyur) about 3 km NW of modern Kiryat Gat. Three strata were found. Stratum III represents the LB II period. Some pottery was Cypriote and Mycenaean. So-called Philistine ware was found mainly in stratum II. From the finds[6] it can be concluded that the site was a Canaanite-Philistine settlement, and there seems to be a 'cultural continuity' between strata II and I. This place was abandoned towards the end of the eleventh century,[7] as was 'Izbet Ṣarṭah. When the state of Israel emerged, these two settlements had ceased to exist.

The same phenomenon is also known from Tel Māśōś (Khirbet el-Meshâsh) in the Beer-Sheba valley in the Negev. This site, located

---

1. D.V. Edelman sees, for instance, Tell el-Fûl and Nob as Jebusite outposts ('Rise of the Israelite State', p. 102).

2. According to I. Finkelstein, most 'Israelite' sites were not fortified (*Archaeology of Settlement*, pp. 360-61).

3. See also my book, *Who were the Israelites?*, pp. 28-30.

4. G.W. Ahlström, *IEJ* 34 (1984), p. 172.

5. See S. Ben-Arieh, 'Tell Jedur', *EI* 15 (1981), pp. 115-28 (Hebrew), and p. 81*; V. Hankey, 'The Aegean Pottery of Khirbet Judur', *EI* 15 (1981), pp. 32*-38*.

6. One of the finds was a statuette of a seated man (god?) in the Egyptian style; see A. Biran, 'Tel Ṣippor', *EAEHL*, IV, pp. 1112-13.

7. A. Biran and O. Negbi, 'The Stratigraphical Sequence at Tel Ṣippor', *IEJ* 16 (1966), pp. 160-73; cf. Biran, 'Tel Ṣippor', *EAEHL*, IV, pp. 1112-13.

about 12 km east of Beer-Sheba, was settled at the end of the thirteenth century and abandoned c. 1000 BCE.[1] It is uncertain whether clashes between the new political constellations, the Philistine pentapolis and the Davidic kingdom, could be the reason for the disappearance of these settlements.

Tel Māśōś has been associated with a wave of settlements built in the Negev during the Iron I period. Others include Tell Esdar c. 5 km south of Tel Māśōś, Tel 'Ira about 3 km NE of Tel Māśōś, Tell Arad, Ramat Matred, Tel Malhata (Tell el-Milḥ), Meṣad Hatira, and Beer-Sheba, to mention a few. Many of these are enclosed sites that form an oval.[2] Their material culture is in the Canaanite tradition with, for instance, some Midianite or Philistine pottery. At Tell Arad, for example, the pottery of the thirteenth–twelfth centuries is in the Canaanite tradition. The pillared houses at Tell Esdar (eleventh cent. BCE) were built in an oval line, creating what could be called a large courtyard settlement.[3] According to the biblical tradition the eastern Negev was inhabited by Edomite clans, which is shown by such phrases as 'the Negev of Jerahmeel', 'the Negev of the Kenites' (1 Sam. 27.10), and 'the Negev of Caleb' (1 Sam. 30.14). Therefore, it is likely that most of these Negev settlements were built by Edomites. Tel Māśōś and Tell Esdar would probably have been within the territory of 'the Negev of Jerahmeel' and Arad within the Kenite Negev.[4] More to the west, in the Nahal Gerar region, were several small, unwalled settlements from the LB II period. They can be seen as the 'daughter villages' of Tell esh-Shari'a and Tell Abu Hureireh (Tel Haror, c. 12 km west of esh-Shari'a, coord. 112-087). The pottery indicates that there was no real break in the tradition, except for Philistine pottery that first develops in the Iron I period.[5]

The site of Tel Māśōś is the largest one in the Negev, and its layout

---

1. For the excavations, see V. Fritz and A. Kempinski, *Ergebnisse der Ausgrabungen auf der Hirbet el-Mšāš (Tel Māśōś) 1972–1974* (Wiesbaden, 1983).
2. Cf. Z. Herzog, 'Enclosed Settlements in the Negeb and the Wilderness of Beer-Sheba', *BASOR* 250 (1983), pp. 41-49.
3. M. Kochavi, 'Tel Isdar', *IEJ* 24 (1974), pp. 111-12; cf. *idem*, 'Tel Isdar', *RB* 72 (1965), pp. 560-61.
4. Cf. N. Na'aman, *ZDPV* 96 (1980), pp. 136-43, and fig. 1.
5. See E. Oren, M. Morrison and I. Gilead, 'Land of Gerar Expedition', *Preliminary Reports of ASOR-Sponsored Excavations 1980–84* (ed. W.E. Rast; BASOR Supplement, 24; Cambridge, MA, 1986).

is also different than those of the other early settlements.[1] It was an unwalled town with some houses built close together but not forming a 'courtyard' settlement. There are both tripartite and quadripartite structures. A building with an annex (314 and 350) has been seen as a government house or a 'Hofhaus' in the Egypto-Canaanite tradition.[2] Its pottery shows contact with both the Midianites and the Phoenicians.[3] The conclusion one can draw from these finds is that the town was a commercial center in the trade between the coast and the Araba and its copper mines at Timna.[4] These mines were under the control of the Egyptians during the time of Seti I (1291–1279 BCE) and possibly through the reign of Ramses III (1182–1151 BCE).[5]

Tel Māśōś and its surroundings may have developed into a chief-dom[6] or a small kingdom[7] monopolizing the trade in the Negev.[8] It is

1. The excavators identified Tel Māśōś with biblical Hormah; see Y. Aharoni, 'Tel Māśōś: Historical Considerations', *Tel Aviv* 2 (1975), pp. 114-18; A. Kempinski, 'Masos, Tel', *EAEHL*, III, p. 816-19. M. Kochavi suggested that Tel Māśōś would be the *'îr 'ᵃmālēq* mentioned in 1 Sam. 15.5 ('Rescue in the Biblical Negev', *BARev* 6 [1980], p. 237); cf. Z. Herzog, *Beer-Sheba*, II, p. 702; A.F. Rainey, *Beer-Sheba*, II (ed. Z. Herzog; Tel Aviv, 1984), p. 101.

2. V. Fritz, 'Die Kulturhistorische Bedeutung der Frühheisenzeitlichen Siedlung auf der Hirbet el-Mšāš und das Problem der Landnahme', *ZDPV* 96 (1980), p. 126; A. Kempinski, *Tel Aviv* 4 (1977), p. 146.

3. V. Fritz, *ZDPV* 96 (1980), p. 151.

4. Cf. Y. Aharoni, 'Nothing Early and Nothing Late: Re-Writing Israel's Conquest', *BA* 39 (1976), p. 66; *idem*, *Archaeology of the Holy Land*, p. 166; A. Kempinski and V. Fritz, *Tel Aviv* 4 (1977), p. 150.

5. See B. Rothenberg, *Were These King Solomon's Mines?* (New York, 1972), pp. 180-83.

6. Thus F.S. Frick, 'Religion and Socio-Political Structure in Early Israel: An Ethno-Archaeological Approach', *SBLSP* (Missoula, MT, 1979), pp. 242-44; I. Finkelstein, *JNES* 47 (1988), pp. 241-52. N.P. Lemche thinks that one could as well see Tel Māśōś as the seat of 'the provincial governor' (*Early Israel*, p. 219). That is possible, but it raises a question that Lemche has not answered: province of what?

7. D. Edelman sees Tel Māśōś as the capital of southern Geshur ('Tel Masos, Geshur, and David', *JNES* 47 [1988], pp. 253-58).

8. Because we do not know the structure of the Tel Māśōś political unit, I am reluctant to call it a kingdom. We do not know anything about its 'hierarchy', and the buildings in this part of the Negev do not show the complexity of a monarchic administration. For these problems, see H.T. Wright and G. Johnson, who see a state as an administration controlling a territory with its small and large settlements and administrative centers, having three or more levels of a 'decision-making hier-archy', something that can be seen in the small villages with their small houses to the

possible that Tell Esdar, for instance, was part of this political unit.[1] As an economic center under the rule of the Egyptians and later, perhaps, the Philistines, it is natural that both Egyptian and Philistine objects were found there alongside objects of local origin. As already pointed out, the material culture and buildings clearly indicate that the people of Tel Māśōś were indigenous to the country.[2] When the Egyptian rule over Palestine had ended it is likely that the inhabitants of Tel Māśōś tried to continue on their own, but that they soon had to face the power of the Philistines reaching down into the Negev, as well as a new power in the north, which took over most of the territory south of the Judean mountains, the kingdom of David. From an economic viewpoint the Judean hills were not very inviting with their few settlements. The re-establishing of the lucrative trade in the south, which David probably had been disturbing during his Philistine years, must have been one of his expansionistic policies.[3]

Most of the settlements that were established in the central hills during the twelfth century BCE were built away from the main thoroughfares. This may be because the settlements were agricultural and therefore were not built on arable land but on the tops of the hills.[4] It is thus natural that excavators have found very few sites in the Judean hills from this period. Among the settlements that emerged in the central highlands during the twelfth–eleventh centuries BCE are 'Ai, Khirbet Raddana (near Ramallah), Tell el-Fûl,[5] Michmas, the so-called Bull Site, Shiloh (?), and Mizpah (Tell en-Naṣbeh). At the latter

---

larger centers with their monumental buildings ('Population, Exchange, and Early State Formation in Southwestern Iran', *American Anthropologist* 77 [1975], pp. 267-89).

1.   F.S. Frick, *The Formation of the State in Ancient Israel* (The Social World of Biblical Antiquity Series, 4; Sheffield, 1985), p. 162.

2.   G.W. Ahlström, *ZDPV* 100 (1984), pp. 35-52.

3.   Cf. the discussion by D. Edelman, *JNES* 47 (1988), pp. 253-58.

4.   See Z. Ron, *IEJ* 16 (1966), pp. 120-21; cf. also D.C. Hopkins, *The Highlands of Canaan*, pp. 161-62.

5.   For Tell el-Fûl's nonidentity with Saul's Gibeah, see J.M. Miller, Geba/ Gibeah of Benjamin', *VT* 25 (1975), pp. 145-66. The 'pre-fortress' remains (1200–1150 BCE) do not indicate any military activity at the site. The so-called Fortresses (I and II) are 'post-Philistine' according to J.A. Graham (*The Third Campaign at Tell el-Fûl: The Excavations of 1964* [ed. D.N. Freedman; AASOR, 45; Cambridge, MA, 1981], pp. 6-17, 23-27). The fortress theory is very shaky because very few building remains have been found.

site there were some LB II remains, but the town was built in the eleventh century BCE. Three Iron I buildings were found outside the city wall.[1] A fortified city just north of Jerusalem points in the direction of a new, emerging political unit having to defend itself against the Jebusite kingdom to the south and against the new political federation of the Gibeonite cities to the west. The only candidate for the building of Tell en-Naṣbeh (Mizpah) would then be the political unit led by Samuel.[2] For Benjamin's territory, one must say that it was sparsely settled during the Iron I period.

Among the Gibeonite cities, Tell el-Jib has yielded burial remains from both the MB II and Late Bronze ages. A city wall is believed to be from the Iron I age.[3] The other Gibeonite cities, Beeroth, Chephirah and Kiriath-Jearim, are not archaeologically well-known.[4] The Gibeonites may have migrated to the central hills, as did so many other groups of people during the early Iron Age. In the Bible they are of Edomite-Hurrian (or Hivite) stock (Josh. 9.7), probably mixed with some Aramaeans. The 'father of Gibeon', Jeiel (1 Chron. 8.29), had a wife named Maacah, which could be an Aramaean name. The same Jeiel is the ancestor of king Saul in 1 Chron. 9.35.

As for other sites, we should remember that 'Ai shows an occupation gap from the end of EB III to Iron I.[5] There was thus nothing for any invaders of the thirteenth century BCE to destroy. The settlement

---

1. C.C. McCown and J.C. Wampler, *Tell en-Naṣbeh*, I–II (Berkeley, 1947), p. 207. Tell en-Naṣbeh probably did not have any strong fortification wall before Iron I; see Y. Shiloh, 'Elements in the Development of Town Planning in the Israelite City', *IEJ* 28 (1978), pp. 38-40; cf. T.L. McClellan, 'Town Planning at *Tell en-Naṣbeh*, *ZDPV* 100 (1984), p. 57.

2. Cf. 1 Sam. 7.15-17, which mentions that the Ephraimite ruler Samuel went once a year on a circuit to Mizpah, Bethel and Gilgal, and then returned to his residence city of Ramah. This is then the territory Samuel ruled over; cf. G.W. Ahlström, *Who were the Israelites?*, pp. 79-80.

3. J.B. Pritchard, 'Gibeon's History in the Light of Excavation' (ed. J.A. Emerton *et al.*; VTSup, 7; Leiden, 1960), pp. 1-12.

4. For Kiriath-Jearim, see the discussion of F.T. Cooke ('The Site of Kirjath-Jearim' [AASOR, 5; Philadelphia, 1924–25], pp. 105-20); R. de Vaux and A.M. Steve, *Fouilles à Qaryet el-'Enab Abou Gosh, Palestine* (Paris, 1950); G. Dollfus and M. Lechevallier, 'Les deux premiers campagnes de fouilles à Abû Gosh (1967–68)', *Syria* 46 (1969), pp. 277-92.

5. J.A. Callaway dates the beginning of the settlement to c. 1220 BCE ('Excavating Ai [et-Tell]: 1964–1972', *BA* 39 [1976], p. 29).

was built instead by newcomers to the area, as was Raddana. 'Ai was an agrarian settlement with pier-constructed houses, cisterns and cobbled streets. Its people also practiced sheep and goat herding. Bones of these animals have been found in most of the houses at 'Ai. A large number of silos were built between the houses later followed by stone granaries built above ground. J.A. Callaway maintains that the people of 'Ai came 'from a background of agricultural life' and knew how to build terraces. Because of a different manner in building streets and granaries, Callaway suggests that a new group of people not too experienced in village life moved into the areas of 'Ai and Raddana around 1150–1125 BCE. Nevertheless, the pottery is in the Canaanite tradition.[1] The settlement at 'Ai went out of existence in the mid-eleventh century BCE. The reason is not known, but competition for land to be cultivated, as well as the emergence of new political constellations, such the spheres of influence of Samuel and Saul, could have been part of the problem. For economic reasons, a political organization could have terminated life at some small sites,[2] or else the people could have moved to other places better suited for agriculture.

The small agricultural settlement at Khirbet Raddana was probably built at the end of the thirteenth century. It went out of existence around 1050 BCE. With the above-mentioned new people, a second phase of the Iron I Age at Raddana would have started. Raddana is thus an example of the different kinds of 'expertise' these early Iron Age settlers had. Its destruction may also be an example of socio-political disturbances in the hills. There was only one large building at Raddana, but in the later phase (Iron I B?) smaller houses were clustered around a courtyard.[3] This may have been for the purpose of protection and defense.[4] Raddana has yielded some fragments of metal and 'pieces of tuyeres' which may indicate that a metal industry had been in existence there.[5] If we connect this with the unique fragment of a large bowl which was found in one of the rooms and with the handle bearing three engraved letters in early Canaanite script,[6] we

1. See J.A. Callaway, *BA* 39 (1976), pp. 18-30.
2. Cf. F.S. Frick, *The Formation of the State*, p. 124.
3. J.A. Callaway, 'Khirbet Raddana', *RB* 81 (1974), p. 92.
4. F. Braemer, *L'architecture domestique*, p. 22.
5. F.S. Frick, *The Formation of the State*, p. 125.
6. F.M. Cross and D.N. Freedman date the engraving to c. 1200 BCE and read the letters as *'hl* (see 'An Inscribed Jar Handle from Raddana', *BASOR* 201 [1971],

most probably cannot label the settlers at Raddana nomads. The bowl fragment shows the remains of nine handles. On the inside of the rim were two spouts in the form of a bull's head connected with a channel inside the rim.[1] The only parallels known thus far are a vase from Inandik in central Anatolia and a jar from Eskiyapar in the same area. The former also had a channel in the rim, and connected with it were a few bull's heads. The same is the case with the jar from Eskiyapar, which had four bull's heads 'functioning as great spouts pouring into the jar'.[2] The Raddana bowl may have had a few more bull's heads on the opposite side of the vessel. The function of these vessels is not known. They perhaps were used for some religious ceremony, because an incense burner was also found. However, the Raddana fragment was found in an ordinary house,[3] which may indicate that it either came there through trade or that the inhabitants had taken it with them from another place. In both cases the fragment could show some northern connections.

Another and perhaps a more probable indication for northerners having moved into the central highlands is a bull figurine of bronze found in the Manasseh territory on a hill close to the Dothan Valley, 4 km east of the village Qabaṭiya (coord. 180.7-201.6, northeast of the Marj Sanur Valley). Here a soldier found a bull figurine and subsequent investigation detected an elliptical enclosure (23 by 21 m) considered to be a cult place.[4] The bull statuette is the largest one ever found so far in Palestine. Its length is 17.5 cm and its height 12.4 cm. Artistically the figurine is unique for Palestine because it represents the Indian hump-backed Zebu bull, *bos indicus*. Only one more example has been found, in Galilee, in the Late Bronze temple (Area H) at Hazor.[5] This bull is known from Mesopotamia, Syria and Anatolia

pp. 9-19). Y. Aharoni dates the script to c. 1300 BCE and reads *'hr* ('Khirbet Raddana and its Inscription', *IEJ* 21 [1971], pp. 130-35). The handle could have come there through trade. It is not a sure proof for either newcomers or indigenous people.

1. See J.A. Callaway and R.E. Cooley, 'A Salvage Excavation at Raddana in Bireh', *BASOR* 201 (1971), pp. 9-19.

2. M.J. Mellink, 'Archaeology in Asia Minor', *AJA* 72 (1968), pp. 129-30.

3. This large building could have served as both the administrative and religious center of this little community.

4. See A. Mazar, 'The "Bull Site"—An Iron Age Open Cult Place', *BASOR* 247 (1982), pp. 27-42.

5. Y. Yadin *et al.*, *Hazor*, III–IV, pl. CCCXLI; also Y. Yadin, *Hazor of Those Kingdoms*, pl. XX:b.

starting in the fourth millennium BCE.[1] Figurines of *bos indicus* have been found, for instance, in Syria and Lebanon.[2] Seals have been found in Anatolia with representations of the Zebu bull. One seal shows such a bull pulling the chariot of the weather god.[3] A seal of the Hittite king Muwatallis (c. 1310–1275 BCE) also shows a Zebu bull.[4] To these examples can be added the reliefs of the battles with the Sea Peoples at the Medinet Habu temple in Egypt. One scene shows that some groups came with their families, children and belongings in carts that were pulled by hump-backed oxen. This indicates peoples coming from territories north of Palestine.[5]

The Zebu bull figurine from Manasseh is probably manufactured according to a Northern tradition. This conclusion is based upon the position of the legs of the bull. As P.R.S. Moorey points out, following Assyrian artistic conventions, the legs show a simultaneous movement which is 'characteristic of Assyrian art'.[6] We should note that this is also the case with the Hazor figurine.

As an object in a non-Palestinian tradition, it is hard to accept A. Mazar's suggestion that the Zebu bull from the hill in Manasseh could have been 'produced by the local Israelite craftsman inspired by Canaanite tradition'. He thinks that the figurine represents 'the West-Semitic storm-god, Hadad (Ba'al)'.[7] However, several male deities in the Semitic world could be associated with the bull figure; thus almost any god could be considered, such as El, Hadad, Baal, and even Yahweh.[8] The last alternative is less probable, however. If the settlers of this place came from the north, Yahweh would not be a likely candidate.

According to Mazar, the figurine had come to the 'Israelites through

1. F.E. Zeuner, *A History of Domesticated Animals*.

2. S. Ronzevalle, *MUSJ* 4 (1910), pls. VIII-IX, and X:13-14; P.R.S. Moorey, *Levant* 3 (1971), pp. 90-91; for an example from Ugarit, see *ANE Suppl.*, p. 352 fig. 828.

3. H. Bossert, *Altanatolien*, Nr. 778.

4. H.G. Güterbock, *Siegel aus Bogazköy*, II; Tafel 65:1. For other seals from about the same period, see Güterbock's Nr. 80 and 81 (his no. 81 is the same as Bossert's no. 719).

5. M.H. Nelson, *The Epigraphic Survey, Medinet Habu*, pl. 32.

6. *Levant* 3 (1971), p. 91.

7. *BASOR* 247 (1982), p. 32.

8. Cf. M.D. Coogan, 'Of Cult and Cultures: Reflections on the Interpretation of Archaeological Evidence', *PEQ* 119 (1987), pp. 1-8.

trade with the Canaanite population of the valleys'.[1] Unfortunately, a link in the chain of deductions is missing because Mazar has not yet established that the people of this place represented a group of incoming 'Israelites' who were supposed to have come from the south or southeast. We simply do not know who made the bull figurine. The facts that it was found in the territory of Manasseh, as well as its northern provenience, may indicate that not only the figurine but also the people worshipping at this place came from the north.[2] They have had their god with them 'blessing' their migration. The people of the 'Bull Site' therefore provide one indication for migrations from the north to the hills of Palestine in this period.

Because archaeology has mainly been concerned with excavating ancient cities, there is inadequate data for a comparison between the material culture of the hill country and the Jezreel Valley. However, some recent investigations show that the Late Bronze tradition in the Jezreel, Beth Shan and the northern Jordan valleys continued well into the twelfth and eleventh centuries BCE.[3] These were territories that became part of the political unit Israel first after Saul. While it would be natural to compare the new settlements in the central highlands with settlements in these valleys, identity in the material culture should not be expected when the settlers in the hills were 'pioneers' starting a new life. They may have been refugees from other territories, urban and nonurban people from the lowlands and the coastal areas, people practicing transhumance or nomads. They would not have had all the tools or all the technological specialization available in the cultural areas, and pastoralists and nomads would have had to learn a different way of life. Bearing these factors in mind,

1. *BASOR* 247 (1982), p. 32.
2. R. Wenning and E. Zenger see the site as an Israelite clan sanctuary of the threshing floor type. They maintain that the 'Bull site' cannot be a Canaanite cult place, because it cannot be associated with the Canaanite city culture ('Ein bauerliches Baal-Heiligtum im samarischen Gebirge aus der Zeit der Anfänge Israels: Erwägungen zu dem von A. Mazar zwischen Dotan und Tirza entdecten "Bull Site"', *ZDPV* 102 [1986], pp. 75-86). It is right that the material from the 'Bull Site' cannot be compared with the culture of the Canaanite cities. It was no town; not even a village has been found at the site. If possible, the site should be compared with another 'farmer's site', the material culture of which would clearly be Canaanite.
3. See, for instance, Z. Gal, 'An Early Iron Age Site near Tel Menorah in the Beth Shan Valley', *Tel Aviv* 6 (1979), pp. 138-45; I. Finkelstein, *Archaeology of Settlement*, pp. 94-97.

there would be differences in the material culture of the new settlements in the hills and the urban and nonurban areas of Canaan.

One of the controversial finds from this period is a large rectangular structure found on the northeastern slope of Mt Ebal.[1] It has a ramp and on three sides a lower ledge. The excavator, A. Zertal, has interpreted the structure as an altar. An elliptical wall enclosed the area around it. His suggestion that this would be the altar Joshua built[2] is a typical example of how the Bible has been used for interpretation when the archaeological material does not provide any clue about function. However, Zertal also thinks the structure has 'Mesopotamian roots'.[3] A closer look shows the base of a building with two interior rooms. They were filled with stones, ashes, and bones of sheep, goats, bulls and fallow deer.[4] The pottery dates to the late thirteenth and early twelfth centuries, with such examples as a collared-rim jar and handles with 'reed-hole decorations' like the punched ware found in the Manasseh survey. The presence of a collared-rim jar in the structure does not seem to support the altar theory. On the contrary, from the poor remains the site would seem rather to have been an enclosed (but not fully developed?) settlement.[5]

According to two of the important towns in the central highlands, the Hebrew Bible, were Bethel and Shiloh. Both have been made into cultic centers for the incoming 'Israelites' as part of the literary and religious reconstruction of the biblical narrators. Bethel was probably destroyed sometime after 1240 BCE and was followed by a poor Iron I settlement.[6] A house with a layout resembling the four-room type was in the LB phase,[7] and punched or punctured handles and rims have

1. Thus it could not be seen from Shechem or from Gerizim.
2. See A. Zertal, 'Has Joshua's Altar been Found on Mt. Ebal?', *BARev* 11 (1985), pp. 26-43.
3. *BARev* 11 (1985), p. 39.
4. N. Na'aman hypothesizes that we are dealing with the remains of the Migdal-Shechem and Mt Zalmon in Judg. 9.46-49 ('Midgdal-Shechem and the "House of El-berith"', *Zion* 51 [1986], pp. 257-80 [Hebrew]).
5. A. Kempinski sees the structure as a watchtower ('Joshua's Altar: An Iron Age I Watch-Tower', *BARev* 12 [1986], pp. 42-49).
6. J.L. Kelso, 'The Third Campaign at Bethel', *BASOR* 151 (1958), pp. 3-8; J.L. Kelso, *et al.*, *Excavations of Bethel*, pp. 28-35.
7. J.L. Kelso *et al.*, *Excavations of Bethel*, pl. 3. Cf. K.N. Yassine, 'Domestic Architecture in the Second Millenium in Palestine' (PhD dissertation, University of Chicago, 1974), pl. XII:2.

been found in Iron I levels.[1] Bethel, like other towns, could have developed into a religious center for surrounding villages.

As for Shiloh, there has not been any consensus whether there was a town or not in the Late Bronze period. The Danish excavations found some MB II remains, but even though some LB finds were excavated, the situation for the Late Bronze Age was not really clearly demonstrated.[2] Supposedly there was a settlement of the LB II period built on the summit above the ruined MB II town. Pottery remains may support such an opinion.[3]

The most recent excavations at Shiloh concentrated on the edges of the tell. No area on the summit was dug because of erosion and the existence of ruins of a medieval village. It is likely that early remains were reused by later settlers.[4] In the areas on the edges of the tell no remains of Late Bronze buildings were found. Instead, there was debris including many animal bones and much pottery.[5] It is unfortunate that this new excavation did not extend its probes onto higher ground, which would have contributed to a fuller picture of the history of Shiloh.

Whatever there was of a settlement or buildings at Shiloh during the Late Bronze Age, the site seems to have been rebuilt in the Iron I period with some pillared buildings constructed with their backs against the MB II wall. Inside were some collared-rim jars. Several silos were found, some of them dug into the LB debris. There is nothing in particular in the material culture that could be labeled 'foreign'.

Among specific finds there are remains of 'cult stands' (?), one with a decoration of what has been understood as a horse.[6] Such a cult stand (if the interpretation is right) would not support the idea that

---

1. J.L. Kelso *et al.*, *Excavations of Bethel*, pl. 40.

2. H. Kjær, 'The Excavation of Shiloh', *JPOS* 10 (1930), pp. 87-174; M.L. Buhl and S. Holm-Nielsen, *Shiloh: The Danish Excavations at Tell Sailun, Palestine, in 1926, 1929, 1932 and 1963* (Copenhagen, 1969).

3. M.L. Buhl and S. Holm-Nielsen, *Shiloh*, pp. 13-62 and pls. 6, 9-10 and 14. The town wall AA, which was dated to the LB period by M.L. Buhl (*Shiloh*, p. 60), is seen by I. Finkelstein to date to the Byzantine period (*Tel Aviv* 12 [1985], p. 165).

4. See I. Finkelstein *et al.*, *Tel Aviv* 12 (1985), pp. 123-80.

5. Finkelstein concludes that the LB material was dumped in the Iron I layer (*Tel Aviv* 12 [1985], p. 166).

6. I. Finkelstein *et al.*, *Tel Aviv* 12 (1985), pl. 19:1, 4.

nomads had settled at Shiloh. Horses were not part of a nomad's life at that time. However, the many sheep and goat bones that have been found at the site would tend to indicate that nomads and pastoralists lived at this place or in its vicinity. They amount to about 75 per cent of all the bones found at Shiloh of the Iron I period.[1] Cattle played a secondary role in the economy of Shiloh during this time. All this could indicate that the majority of the settlers at Shiloh practiced both agriculture and sheep herding.

Because of the limited excavations, the layout of Iron I Shiloh is elusive. Finkelstein assumes, however, that the Tabernacle of the Bible was located on the summit where the Ark of the Covenant was said to have been housed. In fact, he thinks Shiloh was a cult center from the MB II period (with a temple) through the LB and Iron I periods.[2] Archaeologically, this cannot be maintained, especially when the summit failed to yield any finds supporting such a theory and cannot now be investigated. Finkelstein also sees the highland settlers of Iron I to be indigenous nomads and pastoralists. In this case it would be impossible to interpret the finds in light of the biblical reconstruction about the Wanderings in the Wilderness, the Sinai covenant, and the building of the Tabernacle. These nomads would not have had any experience of that kind of literary 'tribal march' through the Wilderness with its religious events.[3]

The biblical narrative about the priest ruler Eli of Shiloh may, as a matter of fact, give us a hint about the fact that Shiloh was a Canaanite town serving as an important cult place for the people in its vicinity. These people may have been recognized as Israelites because they lived in a territory that had become known as Israel. This is the

1.   See S. Hellwing and M. Sadeh in *Tel Aviv* 12 (1985), pp. 177-79.

2.   *Tel Aviv* 12 (1985), pp. 168-69. In his *Archaeology of Settlement*, Finkelstein characterizes Shiloh as 'the first interregional cult in Israel' (p. 231). It is natural that where there was a town there was also a cult place. However, Finkelstein would see Shiloh as a center for 'pilgrims' coming either from Shechem or from Bethel, or from the vicinity. He has not found any cult places in the other new settlements in this territory (*Tel Aviv* 12 [1985], p. 167). It should be remembered that harvest was always done in connection with rituals so that threshing floors and wine vats would serve as temporary cult places for communities; see G.W. Ahlström, *Royal Administration*, p. 25.

3.   For the Ark of Yahweh most probably not ever having been placed at Shiloh, see my article, 'The Travels of the Ark: A Religio-Political Composition', *JNES* 43 (1984), pp. 141-49.

reason why Shiloh, its temple,[1] and its ruler Eli are mentioned in the
Bible. According to 1 Sam. 4.18, Eli 'judged', that is, ruled, Israel
during a generation (40 years). The name Eli could associate the
priest with a god 'Alu (or *'ly*),[2] indicating that Yahweh was not yet
the god of the whole country. That was a later development. The
narrator of 1 Sam. 3.1 says, moreover, that 'the word of Yahweh was
rare in those days'. It was thus known that Shiloh was not in line with
later Yahwistic development.

Finally, the burial systems of the LB and Iron I periods have to be
considered in a discussion of movements of culture and people.
Unfortunately, it has been impossible to get a complete picture of this
phenomenon, because very little has been done in this respect. An
investigation by E. Bloch-Smith shows, however, that some burial
types of the lowlands and the coastal area of the LB II period also
occur in the hills of the Iron Age period. Both acrosolia (for single
burials) and bench tombs (for multiple burials) spread from the coast
up to the hills. The caveat is that in the areas north of the Judean
mountains there are almost no tombs from the Iron I period. How the
dead were disposed of there is thus not known, but cremation,[3] or
burial in pits and caves that have not yet been found, are likely
possibilities. The results of this investigation support the withdrawal
hypothesis. The hills were settled not only by nomads, but also by
people from the west and perhaps also from the north.

The archaeological remains of the central highlands have yielded an
intriguing picture of the country's population and history during the
latter part of the thirteenth century BCE through the twelfth–eleventh
centuries. We are now in a better position than before to reconstruct
that history. The cyclical periods of increase in and abandonment of
settlements can be illustrated with what is now known about the Late
Bronze and Iron I periods in the central highlands of Palestine. The
twelfth–eleventh centuries BCE saw a steady increase in population
resulting from a shift of indigenous people coupled with the immigration of other groups of people to the country. Even if there was

---

1.   If there were a temple at the site, which is probable because a governmental
administration needed one, it could have been built by a predecessor to Eli.

2.   See below, Chapter 8.

3.   E. Bloch-Smith (private communication). According to R. Gonen, pit burials
spread during the LB period from the coastal area into the valleys of Jezreel and
Jordan but not into the hills (private communication).

among them a group coming from Egypt they would have blended quickly with the others. Their importance for the culture and religion of the land is a much later phenomenon inspired by the tragedies of history.

Chapter 8

'JUDGES'

The twelfth–eleventh centuries in Palestine have usually been labeled
either the period of the Judges, following biblical historiography, or
the premonarchic period. Both terms are somewhat misleading. The
persons called 'judges' were not really judges in the modern sense of
the word, and neither did they rule over all of Palestine. The term
'premonarchic' would mean that there were no kings or princes in the
territories called Israel and Judah. The Hebrew *šōpēṭ*, which is
translated judge, is a participle of the verb *špṭ*, which means 'to rule,
to govern' and 'to rule' includes the functions of decision making and
the dispensing of judgments. A ruler is the 'supreme court'. In the
west-Semitic world the root *špṭ* was often used for rulers and
administrators. The Ugaritic god Baal is called *ṭpṭ*, 'judge', and *mlk*,
'king', KTU 1.4 IV 43-44 (UT 51.IV.43-44). Informative in this
connection also is 2 Sam. 15.4, which mentions that David's son
Abshalom wished that he were 'judge' in the country instead of his
father. For the king as judge, see 1 Kgs 7.7, and compare, for
instance, Prov. 8.16. The people requesting Samuel to appoint a king
'to judge' them[1] clearly speaks for the title 'judge' as being a synonym
for 'king', emphasizing the king's function as ruler and judge.[2]
'Prince' and 'judge' are terms also used about Moses in Exod. 2.14.
To this should be added the information in Judg. 2.16, 18-19, which

---

1.   1 Sam. 8.5, 20. Cf. 2 Kgs 15.5; Isa. 40.20; Amos 2.3. Cf. A. Stellini,
'Samuel, Propheta (1 Sam 3, 20) et Iudex (1 Sam 7, 16) in Israel', *These ad Lauram*,
CXIII (Rome, 1957), p. 56; R. Vuilleumir-Bressard, *La tradition cultuelle d'Israël
dans la prophetie d'Amos et d'Osée* (Cahiers Théologique, 45; Neuchâtel, 1960),
pp. 63-65; W. Richter, *ZAW* 77 (1965), p. 60; A.D.H. Mayes, *Israel in the Period
of the Judges* (SBT 2nd Ser., 29; London: SCM Press, 1974).
2.   See K.-Hj. Fahlgren, *ṣĕdāḳā: nahestehende und entgegengesätzte Begriffe im
Alten Testament* (Uppsala, 1932), pp. 120-22.

mentions that the 'judges' were both military and religious leaders.[1] As a military leader the 'judge' could be seen as an *śar*, 'ruler, chieftain, leader'.[2]

Another term used in the Bible for rulers is *mōšēl*, from the root *mšl*, 'to make decisions, have power, to rule'.[3] This is a term used in connection with Gideon, who, according to Judg. 8.22-23, is offered the chance to rule [*mšl*] the people. This offer is extended to his son and grandson, reflecting the presumption that a *mōšēl* would build a dynasty. Gideon's answer that only Yahweh should rule the people shows the narrator's own ideology. Yahweh's people should be a theocracy ruled by Yahweh, and not by a human being.[4] In Judg. 8.18-19 Gideon actually acknowledges his royal birth. Even if the biblical narrator did not like to give Gideon the title 'king', the modern historian cannot draw any other conclusion than that he in reality was a prince or a king.[5]

Realizing the above, the 'judges' (rulers) of the Old Testament[6] have to be seen in the same light as all other Canaanite princes and petty kings.[7] They were princes (*śārîm*), rulers, chieftains over

1. In the Mari texts, *šāpiṭum* occurs as a title for a provincial governor; see A. Marzal, *JNES* 30 (1971), pp. 186-217. For the Semitic root *špṭ*, see further H.W. Hertzberg, 'Die Entwicklung des Begriffes MŠPṬ im Alten Testament', *ZAW* 40 (1922), pp. 256-87; W. Richter, *ZAW* 77 (1965), pp. 58-71; G.W. Ahlström, *Aspects of Syncretism in Israelite Religion*, p. 19; M. Stol, *BO* 29 (1972), pp. 276-77; K.W. Whitelam, *The Just King* (JSOTSup, 12; Sheffield, 1979), pp. 46-69. Via Phoenician and Punic, the word *šōpeṭ* was taken over by Latin as *sufes*, which is known as a title for the two governors of Carthage; cf. J. Teixidor, 'Les functions de *rab* et de *suffète* en Phénicie', *Sem* 29 (1979), pp. 9-17.

2. Cf. C.H.J. de Geus, *The Tribes of Israel*, pp. 204-206.

3. For *māšal b^e*, 'rule over', see 2 Sam. 23.3; Pss. 19.14; 105.21; Isa. 3.4, 12; 19.4; Jer. 22.30; Mic. 5.1; Hab. 1.14; cf. the discussion in G.W. Ahlström, *Joel and the Temple Cult of Jerusalem* (VTSup, 21; Leiden, 1971), pp. 20-21. Cf. also A.S. Herbert, 'The Parable (*māšāl*) in the Old Testament', *SJT* 7 (1954), pp. 180-81.

4. Cf. G.W. Ahlström, *Aspects of Syncretism in Israelite Religion*, pp. 14-16.

5. The story about Gideon and Abimelech has been understood by A. Neher as the blueprint for kingship (*L'essence du prophétisme* [Paris, 1955], p. 199).

6. In the so called appendices to the Book of Judges, namely chs. 17–21, no judges at all are mentioned. R.G. Boling, accepting the historiography of the biblical writer, maintains that in the mid-eleventh century BCE the judges 'were probably quite ineffective and increasingly corrupt' (*Judges*, p. 23). This is no more than a guess.

7. M. Weinfeld maintains that it is the D historian who has designated the

certain territories and clans, societies that were more or less well organized.[1] There is thus no real difference in character between these 'judges' and the later kings. One could perhaps rather say that there was a difference in degree. From the view presented above, the phrase 'premonarchic period' is misleading. What we find in the biblical texts are petty rulers established over limited areas in the central hill country and in Transjordan who have been remembered and, in the later narrator's historiographic reconstruction, have been made leaders of 'all Israel'. This pan-Israelite ideology[2] is the result of the Davidic–Solomonic kingdom's short rule over Palestine. In making the 'judges' rulers of 'all Israel' the narrator also 'created' a nation Israel long before it ever existed. This kind of historiography also required a chronology; thus, the 'judges', or 'saviours', as some of them are called, are said to have followed each other.[3] With this understanding of the 'judges' it is clear that the theory about 'major' and 'minor' judges is unrealistic.[4] It is a modern ideological invention built on Max Weber's theory that only charismatic leaders were real 'judges'.[5] This idea is inspired by the biblical concept that the 'judges' received the spirit of Yahweh, *rûaḥ Yahweh*, which would have made them fit for leadership. Ideologically this is right, and at the same time it is one more indication that the 'judges' were princes or rulers. According to the Old Testament concept, the king received the spirit of Yahweh when he was enthroned. This is expressed in terms of Yahweh's hand always being with the king (Ps. 89.22), or that the king's birth as the son of Yahweh (Ps. 2.7). In other words, he belongs to the divine sphere. His intelligence or his abilities do not count when such words are spoken. Thus, the 'spirit of Yahweh' having come

'saviours' of the post-Joshua period as 'judges' ('The Period of the Conquest and of the Judges as Seen by the Earlier and the Later Sources', *VT* 17 [1967], p. 111).

1. Cf. C.H.J. de Geus, *The Tribes of Israel*, pp. 204-206.

2. For this, see K. Galling, *Die Erwählungstraditionen Israels* (BZAW, 38; Giessen, 1928), pp. 68-70.

3. Cf. R. de Vaux, *The Early History of Israel*, p. 693.

4. The minor judges are listed in Judg. 10.1-5 and 12.7-15. From a literary point of view it is noteworthy that these judges are mentioned in the same stereotyped form as the kings in the succession formulas of the Books of Kings; cf. W. Richter, *ZAW* 77 (1965), pp. 40-42, 47-49. Concerning the deuteronomistic identification of 'judges' with 'saviors', see p. 61.

5. *Gesammelte Aufsätze zur Religionssoziologie.* III. *Das Antike Judentum* (Tübingen, 1921), pp. 92-94.

upon a man is a technical term for rulership. The 'spirit of Yahweh' is the *charisma*, gift of grace, favor, that in principle belongs to the ruler. The position of leadership is seen ideologically as a gift from the deity, even if the people have chosen the man. From this point of view one can, therefore, talk about judges, as well as kings, as charismatic leaders. The distinction that usually has been made between 'charismatic' judgeship and dynastic kingship is an ideological simplification of a historical phenomenon. Leadership is always more or less institutional as an individual tries to keep this power within his family. Hints of this institutional nature also occur in connection with the so-called minor judges, when their many sons are mentioned. Ibzan of Bethlehem in Zebulon[1] had 30 sons and 30 daughters. The latter ones he married off to people outside his territory of jurisdiction, and he brought in women 'from outside' for his sons (Judg. 12.8-9). This may refer to political affiliations.[2] Jair of Gilead had 30 sons riding around on donkeys. They possessed 30 towns (Judg. 10.4), which were called after Jair's name. This is evidence that Jair was a territorial ruler in Gilead. Abdon of Pirathon, 'in the hill country of the Amaleqites', had 40 sons and 30 grandsons riding around on donkeys (Judg. 12.14).[3] Usually one did not ride the donkeys; they were the beasts of burden, that is, the trucks of those days. Only royalty rode them, so that they would not get their feet dirty.[4] We have no information that any of these sons succeeded their father, but that kind of history is not the aim of the narrator. Thus, we cannot dismiss the possibility that rulership in this time could have been hereditary in

1. This cannot be Bethlehem south of Jerusalem, because it was probably part of the Jebusite kingdom until the Philistines put a garrison in the city (2 Sam. 23.15-16). Cf. my article, 'Was David a Jebusite Subject?', *ZAW* 92 (1980), pp. 285-87.

2. Cf. R. de Vaux, *The Early History of Israel*, p. 756.

3. The explanation for this riding around the territory would be that the 'sons' were administrators; cf. the Hebrew term *bn hmlk*, 'king's son', which often could refer to a royal official, who as well could have been the son of a king. For this phrase as referring to an administrative position, see N. Avigad, 'Baruch the Scribe and Jerahmeel the King's Son', *IEJ* 28 (1978), pp. 52-56; cf. also A.F. Rainey, 'The Prince and the Pauper', *UF* 7 (1975), pp. 427-32; A. Lemaire, 'Note sur le titre BN HMLK dans l'ancien Israël', *Sem* 29 (1979), pp. 59-65.

4. Cf. H. Gressmann, *Der Messias* (Göttingen, 1929), p. 269. Judg. 5.10 ('you who mount white she-asses, you who throne on judgment') may refer to nobility or rulers; cf. Prov. 20.8. Note that the donkey was also the animal ridden in sacred processions.

some cases. The stories about Jerubbaal and his son Abimelech point in that direction too,[1] even if Abimelech was not the appointed heir, but seized power in a bloody coup, killing all his brothers save one (Judg. 9.1-6).

The history in the Book of Judges is presented through a literary pattern of change which is determined by the writer's dogmatic opinion about right and wrong cult.[2] This pattern has, as maintained earlier,[3] seven main points.

1. A right Yahwistic leader and cult. After the leader, 'judge', has died,
2. the people worship the Canaanite gods, abandoning Yahweh.
3. The people are punished by Yahweh, who subjects them to their neighbors.
4. After a time the people cry to Yahweh for help, and
5. he answers them by raising up a 'judge/savior'.
6. The 'judge/savior' delivers the people from the oppressors, establishes the right cult, and there is peace for 40 years.
7. The 'judge/savior' dies and the cycle starts anew.

It is self-evident that such a literary pattern does not have as its highest priority the description of actual events. Thus, it cannot be used for writing history. This stylistic pattern is part of an old Near Eastern literary tradition describing the past in terms of periods of order and chaos (*Heil und Unheil*).[4] In the Book of Judges this pattern of change between good and evil periods has been used for a religious

---

1. R. de Vaux, among others, has maintained that the rule of Gideon and Abimelech parallels that of Labayu of Shechem (*The Early History of Israel*, pp. 772, 800-801).

2. This is outlined in Judg. 2.6-23.

3. See my book, *Who were the Israelites?*, p. 75.

4. This change between good and evil times can also be found in prophetic texts; see, for instance, A.K. Grayson and W.G. Lambert, 'Akkadian Prophecies', *JCS* 18 (1964), pp. 7-30; W. Helck, *Die Propheziehung des Nfr.tj*; R.D. Biggs, 'More Babylonian Prophecies', *Iraq* 29 (1967), pp. 117-32; H. Hunger and S.A. Kaufman, *JAOS* 95 (1975), pp. 371-75. As to the *Unheilszeit–Heilszeit* theme in Akkadian texts, see S.A. Kaufman, 'Prediction, Prophecy and Apocalypse in the Light of Neo-Akkadian Texts', *Proceedings of the Sixth World Congress of Jewish Studies*, I, pp. 221-28. For the stylistic pattern of change in the Book of Judges, see W. Richter, *Die Bearbeitungen des 'Retterbuches' in der deuteronomistischen Epoche* (BBB, 21; Bonn, 1964), pp. 75-77.

purpose, explaining the unlucky times with a dogma about the people having abandoned Yahweh. The 'history' we find in the Book of Judges, therefore, is as an ideological reconstruction and as such is a product of the later pure-Yahwistic circles.[1] Thus, the goal of the book is not to present history but to advocate a religious ideal. The events described all serve that purpose, which means that we get only occasional glimpses of actual events concerning various groups of people on both sides of the Jordan. We should note that the activities mainly concern the northern part of the hill country. Transjordan also comes into focus, but southern Palestine, the territory of Judah and the Negev, is mentioned only in connection with the Kenizite Othniel, a 'judge' or 'savior' of obscure origin (Judg. 3.9-12).[2] We may possibly draw the conclusion that more organized political powers, such as Ammonites and Philistines, as well as other groups of peoples, for instance, the Amaleqites, tried to expand into the hills and this caused conflicts. For instance, one of the 'judges', Abdon from Pirathon, was most probably an Amaleqite who lived in Pirathon in Ephraim, 'in the hill country of the Amaleqites' (Judg. 12.15). Because the biblical writer has construed the peoples of the hills as a nation Israel before such a nation emerged, he has explained these incursions as oppression caused by the 'apostasy' of the people. That is a theological interpretation and not history.

From a compositional point of view, chs. 17–21 of the Book of

1. Concerning the composition of the Book of Judges, see among others, A.D.H. Mayes, 'The Period of the Judges and the Rise of the Monarchy', *Israelite and Judaean History* (ed. J.H. Hayes and J.M. Miller; Philadelphia, 1977), pp. 285-93; D.W. Gooding, 'The Composition of the Book of Judges', *EI* 16 (1982), pp. 70*-79*; H. Weippert, 'Das deuteronomische Geschichtswerk', *TRu* 50 (1985), pp. 213-49. Cf. also W. Richter, *Traditionsgeschichtliche Untersuchungen zum Richterbuch* (BBB, 18; Bonn, 1966). In the so-called appendixes to the Book of Judges (chs. 17–21) this pattern has not been used.

2. Othniel is said to have defeated the Aramaean king Cushan-Rishathaim, 'king of Aram Naharaim', Judg. 3.8-10, except that this phrase 'king of Aram Naharaim' shows the writer's poor knowledge of history. The term refers to a territory and not a nation. For the problem of Aramaeans and the Aramaean kingdoms, see Chapter 9. Because Othniel also is the name of a clan of the Kenizites (Josh. 15.16-17; Judg. 1.12-13), one may doubt the existence of the 'judge' Othniel. Cf. M. Noth, who maintained that Othniel and the events connected with him were a creation of the D historian and that there was no connection with events of the time of the judges (*Überlieferungsgeschichtliche Studien*, I (Halle, 1943), pp. 50-51). See also N.P. Lemche, 'The Judges—Once More', *BN* 20 (1983), p. 52.

Judges usually have been characterized as appendices or an epilogue to the book, because the deuteronomistic pattern of change is not found there.[1] The purpose of the stories found in these chapters, however, is to describe the pre-Saulidic period when there was no well-organized national unity embracing all the peoples of the hills. Thus, Israelite law and order as known from a latter time did not yet exist, or, as the Bible expresses it, 'in those days there was no king in Israel, and every man did what was right in his own eyes' (Judg. 17.6; 21.25; cf. 18.1; 19.1).[2] Chapters 17–21 are thus a meaningful part of the deuteronomistic history and not an addition. This material should be seen as leading to the stories about Eli and Samuel and, finally, Saul, who in his turn is the literary introitus to the Davidic kingdom, the climax of the deuteronomistic composition.

The rulers of the pre-Saulidic period that are mentioned in the Bible can be seen as indications for the existence of different political units in Trans- and Cisjordan. Othniel of the clan of Kenaz has already been mentioned. The Yaminite Ehud (3.12-30) is said to have killed Moab's king Eglon by cunning. A coalition between Moab, Ammon and the Amaleqites supposedly defeated the Israelites, after which Eglon is said to have oppressed Israel for 18 years. Ehud and his men then defeated Moab—note that the Ammonites and the Amaleqites are no longer in the picture. The 'Israelites' are then said to have occupied Moab. What historical event—if any—lies behind this narrative is not known. There is no information about Moab being occupied before the time of David.[3] Thus, the narrator may have exaggerated some

---

1.   H. Gressmann characterizes this part as 'lose Erzählungen' (*Die Anfänge Israels* [Die Schriften des Alten Testaments, 1.2; Göttingen, 1914], p. 15).

2.   Whatever criticism one may have had against the institution of kingship, this phrase shows that kingship was in the writer's eyes the only natural way in which a nation could be organized. F. Keil was thus right in maintaining that according to this phrase right and justice could not be administered (*Biblischer Commentar über die prophetischen Geschichtsbücher des Alten Testaments* [Biblischer Commentar über das Alte Testament, 2.1; Leipzig, 1863], p. 355 [ET and repr. Grand Rapids, MI, 1984, p. 463]). R.G. Boling interprets this phrase as Israel 'having repudiated Yahweh's kingship in the premonarchic period' (*Judges*, p. 293).

3.   N.P. Lemche argues that the story about Ehud in 3.12-30 does not give any historically accurate information about Moab and Israel, but it has been 'assimilated into Israelite tradition', or that it might 'just as easily derive from the period of the monarchy, although the oral tradition has assigned it to the period of the Judges' (*Early Israel*, p. 383).

incident of hostilities between some Israelites and Moabites in the pre-Saulidic era, the purpose being to place the subjugation of Moab as far back in time as possible.

From the information about the place of $p^e s \hat{\imath} l \hat{\imath} m$ ('idols') at Gilgal where Ehud received an oracle, $d^e bar\ {}^{\prime e} l \bar{o} h \hat{\imath} m$, we learn that the Benjaminites served several gods in the form of idols. The standard deuteronomistic pattern, in which the Israelites were oppressed because of their worship of other gods than Yahweh, has here been forgotten.

The mention of Shamgar, son of Anath, in 3.31 is a literary intrusion[1] disturbing the story about Ehud. He is mentioned before Ehud's death (4.1). Shamgar is seen as an important man of the past (Judg. 5.6), but the narrator perhaps knew no more about him than that he fought the Philistines.[2] As such he qualified as an 'Israelite' ruler in the northern part of Palestine. His name may be Luwian or Neo-Hittite,[3] and the apposition 'ben Anath' may characterize him as a Canaanite of royal birth.[4]

Two clan leaders are known only by their names, their length of rule and their seat of government, where they also were buried. They are Tola, 'son of Puah, son of Dodo', who is called a man of Issachar but who lived at Shamir in *har* Ephraim,[5] where he was also

---

1. See, for instance, W. Richter, *Die Bearbeitungen des 'Retterbuches'*, pp. 65, 92-94; W. Hertzberg, *Die Bücher Joshua, Richter, Ruth übersetzt und erklärt* (ATD, 9; Göttingen, 1953), p. 168.

2. Cf. A. van Selms, who points out that there is no motivation for an oppression given in the text, and that Shamgar has no tribal connection. None of his cities are mentioned, which shows that Shamgar is 'out of place' ('Judge Shamgar', *VT* 14 [1964], pp. 294-309).

3. It is seen as a Hittite name by, among others, M. Noth, *Die israelitischen Personennamen*, p. xix. F.C. Fensham considers it to be Hurrian ('Shamgar ben Anath', *JNES* 20 [1961], pp. 197-98); cf. R. de Vaux, *The Early History of Israel*, pp. 822-23. E. Danelius sees the name Shamgar as being the 'counterpart' of Gershom ('Shamgar ben 'Anath', *JNES* 22 [1963], pp. 191-93).

4. R. de Vaux maintains that 'ben Anath' very well may refer to the goddess Anath (*The Early History of Israel*, pp. 822-23); cf. my *Who were the Israelites?*, p. 77. Others have suggested that 'ben Anath' would refer to a city, Beth-Anath (M. Noth, *Die israelitischen Personennamen*, p. 123 n. 1; W.F. Albright, *From Stone Age to Christianity*, p. 283).

5. For *har* Ephraim as a term for the central hill country, i.e., between the Esdraelon valley and the mountains of Judah, see Y. Aharoni, *The Land of the Bible* (2nd edn), pp. 28-29. See also N. Na'aman, *Borders and Districts in Biblical Historiography*, pp. 145-47.

buried.[1] He is said to have ruled for 23 years (Judg. 10.1-2). The other is Elon of Zebulon who was a 'judge' for ten years. He was buried at Aijalon of Zebulon (Judg. 12.11-12).

Judges 4 and 5 relate a battle between peoples of the northern parts of the country. The scene is the Jezreel Valley between Tabor[2] at Ta'anak, 'opposite the springs of Megiddo'[3] (Judg. 5.19). The combatants were a Canaanite coalition under Sisera and the peoples of Zebulon and Naphtali under Baraq, son of Abinoam.[4] Both chapters agree that it was only people from Naphtali and Zebulon that risked their lives on the battlefield (4.6 and 5.18). The possibility cannot be dismissed, however, that the poem in Judges 5 has mixed two events and that the mention of Zebulon and Naphtali may be secondary in this poem. The battle seems to have been mainly between the peoples of the hills south of the Jezreel Valley and the Canaanites. Whatever the truth is here, it is a mistake to use the poem of Judges 5 to argue for the existence of a ten-tribe amphictyony or a tribal confederation in the pre-Saulidic time. Some 'tribes' may have banded together temporarily to arrest the danger of being subdued by some city kings, but the text does not prove the existence of a confederation. It merely recalls an *ad hoc* event. The poem celebrates a victory of the past, not a contemporary event, and a poet's celebrations are usually not reliable historical sources. Judg. 5.6 commemorates a famous battle of

1.   The location of Shamir is unknown. It could be a name for Samaria. According to R. Zadok, Tola is probably 'an innovation of the editor' ('Notes on the Prosopography of the Old Testament', *BN* 42 [1988], pp. 44-45).

2.   Baraq is said to have marched up to Mount Tabor with 10,000 men, probably for a cult ceremony before the battle started. One may doubt that this mountain was a Yahweh cult place at that time. Its god may have been a Baal deity. For the name Tabor, see, among others, J. Lewy, who connects it with Akkadian *ti-ba-ra*, 'metal worker', an epithet for Tammuz ('Tabor, Tibar, Atabyros', *HUCA* 23 [1950–51], pp. 357-86); O. Eissfeldt, 'Der Gott Tabor', *ARW* 31 (1934), pp. 14-41. D.W. Thomas sees the name as from the root *nbr*, 'be raised, elevated' (*VT* 1 [1951], pp. 229-30). For Deborah's inclusion among the judges by the deuteronomistic editor, see W. Richter, *Traditionsgeschichtliche Untersuchungen zum Richterbuch*, pp. 37-39; R. de Vaux, *The Early History of Israel*, pp. 762-63.

3.   The Hebrew *'al mē* followed by a toponym refers to a water source, a spring (cf. Num. 20.13, 24; Josh. 15.7; 16.1; also E. Täubler, *Biblische Studien: Die Epoche der Richter* [Tübingen, 1958], pp. 157-59).

4.   The name Abinoam, 'my father is the pleasant one', indicates that Baraq's father was an adherent of the Baal cult, because *nō'am*, 'pleasant, beautiful', was an epithet of the fertility god.

the past and some of its personalities, 'in the days of Shamgar, ben Anath, and in the days of Jael'.[1] It is unknown exactly when this was, but because Shagmar, who fought the Philistines, is mentioned as a man of the past, the date of the battle may be sometime around 1100 BCE.[2] Nevertheless this does not date the text. Because Meggido and Ta'anak are mentioned and both cities seem to have been destroyed at the same time (Meggido str. VIIA around 1130 BCE,[3] and Ta'anak c. 1125 BCE the latter with a population gap down to about 1000 BCE[4]), the battle has usually been dated to the period before the destruction of these cities.[5] This is a poor argument. It certainly did not matter very much for the poet whether the cities were destroyed or not. Their names may have been used for geographical localization only. However, because 5.19 mentions that Sisera's army did not carry away any 'silver spoils', one may see Ta'anak as a rich, functioning city.[6] As to the time, we should also emphasize that all the groups of people mentioned in Judges 5 have had some connection with each other at a later time. Because they belonged to the same nation, the author has had the problem of why all the ancestors of his nation did not participate in the battle.[7] Being concerned with the glorification of his

1. Cf. my article in *JNES* 36 (1977), pp. 287-88.

2. In Judg. 4.2 and 7 Sisera is mentioned as the commander of Jabin, 'king of Hazor'. However, if Hazor was destroyed at the end of the LB II period (we do not know by whom), and the first walled city of the Iron Age is that of Solomon, then the text either refers to a time before Hazor was destroyed and before the Philistines had settled on the coast, or the poet did not know too much about the events and has, therefore, mixed his 'sources'. He only used some old traditions for making a poem. B. Mazar has suggested that the destruction of Hazor occurred after the battle described in Judg. 4 ('Beth She'arim, Gaba, and Harosheth', *HUCA* 24 [1952–53], pp. 80-84).

3. Y. Yadin, 'Megiddo', *EAEHL*, III, p. 850.

4. Thus P.W. Lapp, 'Ta'anach by the Waters of Megiddo', *BA* 30 (1967), p. 8, and 'The 1966 Excavations at Tell Ta'annek', *BASOR* 185 (1967), pp. 2-3.

5. W.F. Albright put the date to c. 1150 BCE (*Yahweh and the Gods of Canaan*, p. 13).

6. Compare G.F. Moore, *Judges*, pp. 134-35. A.F. Rainey maintains that the battle was not at Ta'anak but close to Tabor ('The Military Camp Ground at Ta'anak by the Waters of Meggido', *EI* 15 [1981], pp. 61*-66*). Note, however, that Tabor is not mentioned in Judg. 5.

7. To use this text in an argument for the existence of a ten-tribe amphictyony is thus impossible. It is also clear that this text does not know the later 12-tribe system, as it is found in, for instance, Gen. 49. An indication for the artificiality of the

people and not with history, he therefore had to blame some 'tribes' for not having participated in the battle. This clearly shows that the text is much later than the battle it describes and also much later than 1150–1100 BCE.[1] Judges 5 can thus not be used as an argument for the existence of a tribal confederation of Israelites around 1100 BCE. There is no reliable historical source on which one could build such a theory.

A special literary feature of note in the so-called Song of Deborah is its use of a mythological motif. As I have maintained before,[2] the role of the sea and the chaos waters have been used several times by the biblical historiographers vand authors in describing Yahweh's wonderful help to his people. Historiography often can be portrayed in mythological categories, for instance, the Exodus crossing of the sea, the sea of 'destruction' (*yam sûp*), and the crossing of the Jordan in Joshua 3. In Judges 5 the heavenly bodies (deities) fought the battle and the river Kishon flooded the area so everyone drowned[3] except for Sisera, who is said to have been able to run away (on water?). The poet has here used the author's right to compose as his pleasure or intentions steered him. His aim was to anchor the event in the will of Yahweh, and so he employed mythology.[4] This means that the actual events of the battle play a secondary role, if any. Judges 4, on the other hand, does not have this mythological embroidery. The picture is more realistic and thus closer to the truth. Instead, it contains the common Near Eastern motif of the annihilation of the enemies: they 'all fell by the sword, no one man was left' (4.16). Again Sisera is the sole survivor. If he were not, there would be no story.

12-tribe system is that Machir and Gilead who are mentioned in Judg. 5 are not part of the 'ideal' twelve tribes. It is also interesting to note that Issachar is mentioned in Judg. 5.15. This would make the Song of Deborah a product of the Iron II period, because Issachar was not settled in Iron I, according to a survey by N. Zori (*Nahalat Yissakhar* [Jerusalem, 1977] [Hebrew], pp. 88-90). Cf. also G.W. Ahlström, *JNES* 36 (1977), pp. 287-89.

1. Cf. A.D.H. Mayes, 'The Historical Context of the Battle against Sisera', *VT* 19 (1969), p. 359. A. Alt, 'Megiddo im Übergang vom kanaanäischen zum israelitischen Zeitalter', *ZAW* 62 (1944), pp. 67-68 (= *KS*, I, pp. 256-58); G.W. Ahlström, *JNES* 36 (1977) p. 287-88.

2. *JNES* 36 (1977), pp. 287-88, and *Who were the Israelites?*, pp. 45-55.

3. From Judg. 5.20-21, the conclusion has been drawn that the battle occurred on a rainy day.

4. Whenever the will of god or his actions are referred to, we are in the sphere of mythology that modern scholars call theology.

With Judges 6–8 the scene moves south to the central hill country. Gideon, son of Joash, of the clan of Abiezer in the territory of Manasseh, is a ruler who never is called a *šōpēt*.[1] In the biblical tradition he has been identified with Jerubbaal.[2] His seat of residence was Ophrah, a place of uncertain identification.[3] He is reported to have fought the Midianites in the territory of Issachar, a non-Israelite territory,[4] and he is also said to have pursued them into Transjordan, taking vengeance upon Succoth and Penuel for not having supported him.[5] This does not mean that Gideon ruled over any Transjordanian territory.[6] As a ruler, *mōšēl*, Gideon may have inherited his position as a chieftain over his own clan of Abiezer and then extended his rule over Manasseh.[7] His 'allies' against the Midianites and the Amaleqites

1.   Judg. 6.11-32 is a narrative written from the perspective of a later time. In v. 16 Ehyeh occurs as the name for Yahweh; cf. Exod. 3.14.

2.   One of the first to see that Gideon and Jerubbaal were two different persons was E. Meyer, *Die Israeliten und ihre Nachbarstämme*, p. 482. Cf. B. Lindars, 'Gideon and Kingship', *JTS* NS 16 (1965), pp. 315-26. Lindars sees a conflict between Canaanites and Israelites in Judg. 6.25-27, pp. 324-26. For the two names referring to one and the same person, see J.A. Emerton, 'Gideon and Jerubbaal', *JTS* 27 (1976), pp. 289-312. Emerton points out that the Baal altar Gideon destroyed belonged to his father Joash (p. 294). A conflict between Canaanites and Israelites is thus impossible to extract from this passage, especially when we take into consideration that most Israelites were indigenous people in Canaan.

3.   A. Alt identified Ophrah with modern eṭ-Ṭayibeh located between Beth-Shan and Tabor ('Erwägungen über die Landnahme der Israeliten in Palästina', *KS*, I, p. 160); cf. F.M. Abel, *Géographie de la Palestine*, II (Paris, 1938), p. 402. Y. Aharoni prefers the site of modern Affuleh (*The Land of the Bible*, 2nd edn, p. 263). However, the Manasseh territory was south of the Jezreel Valley. H. Donner identifies Ophrah with modern Tell Ṣōfar, 4 km. NW of Tel Balaṭa (*Geschichte des Volkes Israel* [Göttingen, 1984], p. 171 n. 9).

4.   Cf. 1 Chron. 12.38-40 (39-41), and E.J. Payne, 'The Midianite Arch in Joshua and Judges', *Midian, Moab, and Edom: The History and Archaeology of Late Bronze and Iron Age Jordan and North-West Arabia* (ed. J.F.A. Sawyer and D.J.A. Clines; JSOTSup, 24; Sheffield, 1983), pp. 166-67. See also E.A. Knauf, 'Midianites and Ishmaelites', *Midian, Moab, and Edom* (ed. J.F.A. Sawyer and D.J.A. Clines), p. 151; *idem*, *Ismael* (Wiesbaden, 1985); also my *Who were the Israelites?*, pp. 91-92, 95.

5.   This may be a tradition of Abiezerite origin having no connection with other tribes, cf. K.H. Hecke, *Juda und Israel, Untersuchungen zur Geschichte Israels in vor- und frühstaatlicher Zeit* (Forschung zur Bibel, 52; Würzburg, 1985), pp. 130-31.

6.   Cf. R. de Vaux, *The Early History of Israel*, p. 788.

7.   In Judg. 8.18 Gideon is characterized as the son of a king; cf. E. Auerbach,

were the peoples of Asher, Zebulon and Naphtali (Judg. 6.33-34). From this one may assume that he tried to extended his rule into the Jezreel valley, but it does not follow that he succeeded. There is no textual support for such an assumption.[1] His rule over Manasseh may have included the former city state Shechem or parts of its territory. He is said to have had many (70) sons, which indicates a sizeable harem,[2] and one of his concubines lived at Shechem, if Judg. 8.30-31. really refers to Gideon. This would be the only connection to Shechem we find in the texts. From this it would be hard to establish as a fact that Gideon ruled Shechem. Abimelech's negotiations with the Shechemites indicates, however, not only that the 'king' was dead, but that Shechem had been ruled by a non-Shechemite (Judg. 9.1-6). We may then have a parallel to the rule of the non-Shechemite Labayu of the Amarna period.

The idol, ephod, that Gideon had made, and which he put up in Ophrah, may be an indication that he made Ophrah the capital of his kingdom, 'and all Israel played the harlot after it there' (Judg. 8.27). As we know, it was a royal prerogative to build sanctuaries and make deity statues.[3] The sentence about all Israel worshipping this idol also

---

Wüste und Gelobtes Land, I, pp. 120-21; H. Haag, 'Gideon-Jerubbaal-Abimelek', *ZAW* 79 (1967), pp. 305-14; J.A. Emerton, *JTS* 27 (1976), p. 297. Gideon's refusal to accept kingship is, according to G. von Rad, a later time's theological objection to any kingship other than that of Yahweh (*Theologie des Alten Testaments* [5th edn; Munich, 1966], p. 74). The information about Gideon turning down the offer of kingship may be the writer's way of avoiding the title 'king' for a period in which there should not have been any king—except for Abimelech, who did not qualify as a 'judge'. Ideologically, he has been seen as an 'evil' king, and thus contrasted to his father; cf. F. Crüsemann, *Die Widerstand gegen das Königtum*, p. 42.

1. B. Otzen believes that Gideon tried to unite the peoples of several areas, as did Saul, but that he was not successful (*Israeliterne i Palaestina* [Copenhagen, 1977], p. 128). In Judg. 7.23 there is another reference to the peoples of Zebulon, Naphtali and Asher, which is hard to harmonize with 6.35. A.D.H. Mayes, among others, sees Gideon's war against the Midianites as 'a local action initiated by Gideon leading a band of his own Abiezerites, in which Ephraimites became involved at a later stage' ('Period of the Judges', *Israelite and Judean History* [ed. J.H. Hayes and J.M. Miller], p. 315).

2. This phenomenon, together with the seventy sons and the cult installation at Ophrah, has been seen as a royal feature by G. Wallis ('Die Anfänge des Königtums in Israel', *Wissenschaftliche Zeitschrift der Martin-Luther Universität* 12 [1963], pp. 239-47).

3. G.W. Ahlström, 'Der Prophet Nathan und der Tempelbau', *VT* 11 (1961), p. 126; A.S. Kapelrud, 'Temple Building, a Task for Gods and Kings', *Or* NS 32

shows the cult place at Ophrah to be more than a local shrine.[1] Another conclusion is that people of this period knew nothing of the Yahwism of the author and the later time's proscription of idols.

We have no information regarding the length of Gideon's (or Jerubbaal's) rule. S. Mowinckel has concluded that Gideon ruled around 1050 BCE because 'camel beduins' are mentioned in connection with Gideon's wars,[2] and they may not have appeared in Cisjordan before c. 1100 BCE. Such a date would not be contradicted by the results of the excavations at Tell Balaṭa (ancient Shechem), which show that stratum XI has both LB II and Iron I remains.[3] A date between 1100 and 1060 BCE would thus be probable for the period of Gideon and Abimelech.[4]

Whether Gideon and Jerubbaal are one and the same person, as the Hebrew text advocates, or are two different persons, may be debated. As mentioned above, E. Meyer earlier maintained that they were different persons because ch. 8 uses the name Gideon but ch. 9 Jerubbaal.[5] In the narrative about Gideon's deeds he is nowhere associated with Shechem. Thus, it is likely that the biblical narrator did not really know Gideon's home town and that he was identified with Jerubbaal quite early.[6] To the Gideon-Jerubbaal cycle was appended the story

(1963), pp. 56-62; R. de Vaux, 'Jérusalem et les prophètes', *RB* 73 (1966), pp. 485, 489.

1. Cf. S. Mowinckel, *Israels opphav og eldste historie* (Oslo, 1967), p. 168. Cf. also G.W. Ahlström, *Aspects of Syncretism*, p. 22. The fact that the 'Gideon-Abimelech cycle contains no word of the Ark' (E. Nielsen, *Shechem* [Copenhagen, 1955], p. 320) and does not say anything about the importance of Shiloh shows the artificiality of the deuteronomistic presentation of the Israelite religion.

2. *Israels opphav*, p. 162. The introduction of the camel during the thirteenth and twelfth centuries meant a 'beduinization', according to X. de Planhol (*Annales de Géographie* 384 [1962]).

3. See E.F. Campbell, J.F. Ross and L.E. Toombs, 'The Eighth Campaign at Balaṭa (Shechem)', *BASOR* 204 (1971), p. 15; L.E. Toombs, 'Shechem: Problems of the Early Israelite Era', *Symposia Celebrating the Seventy-Fifth Anniversary of the Foundation of the American Schools of Oriental Research (1900–1975)* (ed. F.M. Cross; Cambridge, MA, 1979), p. 78. D. Edelman estimates that the destruction of Shechem occurred around 1075 BCE ('Rise of the Israelite State', p. 190).

4. R.T. O'Callaghan dates Gideon to around 1070 BCE (*Aram Naharaim* [AnOr, 26; Rome, 1948], p. 121 n. 3).

5. *Die Israeliten und ihre Nachbarstämme*, pp. 481-82. Cf. A.D.H. Mayes, 'The Period of the Judges', *Israelite and Judean History* (ed. J.H. Hayes and J.M. Miller), pp. 316-17.

6. Cf. M. Noth, *The History of Israel*, p. 152 n. 1.

about king Abimelech who came to power over Shechem and surrounding territories through a bloody *coup d'état* (Judg. 9.1-6). H. Donner makes the point that Judges 9 is a piece that does not suit the hero-like character of the 'Judges' and is, therefore, most likely built on historical reminiscences.[1] This would mean that there still had been kingship at Shechem before Abimelech's takeover. It is clear from the text that the dynastic principle was in effect. Abimelech, whose mother was a Shechemite woman, was not the appointed heir. In order to reach the throne he conspired with the elders of Shechem, and, after having been offered the kingship, he hired some mercenaries and killed all his half-brothers but one, thus securing his power. He resided at Arumah c. 8 km southeast of Shechem, probably modern Khirbet el-'Orma[2] (Judg. 9.41). It is unknown whether he first had chosen Shechem and—as Saul later did—chose a new capital.[3] The extent of Abimelech's kingdom is also unknown. He seems to have built up a territorial state in the central hills,[4] and perhaps his rule can be compared with that of Labayu and with the rise of Amurru· under Abdi-Ashirta and his son Aziru, as they are known from the Amarna archives. Conquests or treaties were often the means of expansion and state building, and the result was 'nationality'.[5] Other examples include the kingdoms of Saul and David, as well as the kingdom of Moab under Mesha (ninth cent. BCE).[6]

1. *Geschichte des Volkes Israel*, p. 170. Literarily, the history of Abimelech 'steht mit denen aus der Tyrannen-und Lyderzeit bei Herodot auf einer Linie' (E. Meyer, *Die Israeliten und ihre Nächbarstamme*, p. 481). V. Fritz is skeptical of the historicity of Judg. 9 ('Abimelech und Sichem in Jdc IX', *VT* 32 [1982], pp. 129-44). He has been criticized by H. Rösel, who refers to 2 Sam. 11.21 for support ('Überlegungen zu Abimelech und Sichem in Jdc IX', *VT* 33 [1983], pp. 500-52).

2. Cf. F.M. Abel, *Géographie*, II, p. 251.

3. M. Noth suspects that the move may have been caused by some hostility between Abimelech and the people of Shechem (*The History of Israel*, p. 153).

4. Abimelech's siege of Tebeṣ (modern Ṭubaṣ) is another indication for this: Judg. 9.50-55.

5. Cf. H. Donner, *Geschichte des Volkes Israel*, p. 172. It should be remembered that 'nationality' could not play role before a nation had been created. There was no Israelite nation in the time period before Abimelech. We do not know under what name Abimelech's nation was known, but, being located in the territory of Israel, Abimelech may have chosen 'Israel' as its name. This may be the reason why Abimelech is mentioned in the Book of Judges.

6. Cf. also the Zakkur inscription, B.4ff. (J.C.L. Gibson, *Textbook of Syrian Semitic Inscriptions*, II [Oxford, 1975], p. 11).

According to the text, a conflict between the citizens of Shechem and Abimelech grew to such an extent that Abimelech finally besieged the town and destroyed it. When the people of Migdal-Shechem heard about this they took refuge in the temple of El-Berith.[1] Abimelech marched to the mountain of Zalmon and burned the temple of El-Berith, killing 'about a thousand men and women' (Judg. 9.42-49). This shows that Migdal-Shechem could not be part of the city of Shechem. Located on mount Zalmon, it must have been another settlement.[2] Strategically, it would be natural to have a fortress tower (with a sanctuary) located for instance in the pass leading into Shechem from the NW. Two places with the name Shechem also seem to have been known to the Egyptians of the Twelfth Dynasty. The Khu-Sebek stele (dated to the reign of Senwosret III, 1878–1842 BCE) informs us that *s-k-m-m* together with Retenu (Palestine) had been captured.[3] The same form of the name occurs in the Execration Texts, and has been

---

1.   Tell Balaṭa is not so large that the people in the western part of the city would not have been able to see what happened at, for instance, the East gate. E.F. Campbell and J.F. Ross conjecture that Shechem was destroyed in two stages, first the eastern part of the city, which was on a lower level, and then the acropolis (identified with the Beth-Millo) and the temple and Migdal-Shechem, i.e., the western part of the city. They also claim, however, that there is no destruction level from Iron I 'inside the cella of the temple [!]' ('The Excavation of Shechem and the Biblical Tradition', *BA* 26 [1963], p. 17).

2.   See the discussion by J. Simons, who suggests Jebel el-Kebir NE of Tell Balaṭa ('Topographical and Archaeological Elements in the Story of Abimelech', *OTS* 2 [1943], pp. 50-58). F.M. de Liagre Böhl placed the Migdal-Shechem at modern Tell Ṣöfar (*Palestina in het Licht der jongste opgravingen en onderzoekingen* [Amsterdam, 1931]); cf. J.A. Soggin, 'Bemerkungen zur alttestamentlichen Topographie Sichems mit besonderem Bezug auf Jdc 9', *ZDPV* 83 (1967), pp. 183-98. W.L. Reed thinks that it must be 'a hill near Shechem' ('Zalmon', *IDB*, IV, p. 933). A better candidate seems to be Kumeh on the slopes of Ebal, c. 3 km NW of Balaṭa, as the crow flies (E.F. Campbell, 'Judges 9 and Biblical Archaeology', *The Word of the Lord Shall Go Forth [Festschrift D.N. Freedman]* [Philadelphia, 1983], p. 269). E. Nielsen has suggested that Mt Ebal is to be identified with Zalmon (*Shechem*, pp. 166-67). However, Ebal is nowhere else called Zalmon. The location of Migdal-Shechem was certainly not in the city of Shechem, but it is not yet known.

3.   J.A. Wilson, *ANET*, p. 230; K. Sethe, *Ägyptische Lesestücke* (2nd edn; Leipzig, 1928), pp. 82-83. One gets the impression that Shechem is the most important and geographically central place in Palestine.

understood as a dual form by F.M.T. de Liagre Böhl[1] and S.H. Horn.[2] Thus, there seem to have been two places with the name Shechem, and this could have been the case also during the eleventh century BCE.[3] The temple of El-Berith at Migdal-Shechem is therefore most probably not to be identified with the temple (originally built in the MB II period) that was found in the western part of the city during the excavations in the fifties, as has been suggested by the excavators.[4] The text mentions that after Shechem had been taken and the people slaughtered, Abimelech tore the city down and 'sowed it with salt' (Judg. 9.45).[5] When the inhabitants of Migdal-Shechem heard about these deeds they fled to the temple at Migdal-Shechem. The text clearly indicates that Migdal-Shechem is not to be identified with the city of Shechem.

Having sacked Shechem, Abimelech besieged Tebeṣ, usually identified with Ṭubaṣ c. 15 km NE of Shechem.[6] Here Abimelech met his death, and 'when the men of Israel saw this', they went home (Judg. 9.55). His reign was thus cut short. According to Judg. 9.22 Abimelech was *śar*, 'prince', over Israel for three years at the same time as he was king over Shechem. This would indicate that there probably was a political unit Israel. At this time this unit was associated with Shechem through a treaty.[7] This political unit Israel is then distinct from the geographical territory Israel mentioned in the Merneptah stele.[8] It

1. *Palestina in het Licht*, pp. 65-67.

2. 'Shechem, History and Excavations of a Palestinian City', *JEOL* 18 (1964), p. 283. Cf. J.A. Soggin, *ZDPV* 83 (1967), p. 197.

3. Thus also C.F. Burney, *The Book of Judges*, p. 286.

4. L.E. Toombs and G.E. Wright, 'The Third Campaign at Balatah (Shechem)', *BASOR* 161 (1961), pp. 11-16; also R.J. Bull and J.F. Ross in L.E. Toombs and G.E. Wright, *BASOR* 169 (1963), pp. 5-32; G.E. Wright, *Shechem*, pp. 124-26; E.F. Campbell and J.F. Ross, *BA* 26 (1963), pp. 18-26. E. Nielsen, not knowing the excavation results, maintained that Beth-Millo was the acropolis of Shechem and that it was identical with Migdal-Shechem (*Shechem*, p. 167); M.D. Fowler doubts that the *migdāl* was a temple (*PEQ* 115 [1983], pp. 49-53).

5. This means that life would not be possible there any more (C.F. Burney, *The Book of Judges*, p. 285); cf. S. Gevirtz, 'Jericho and Shechem: A Religio-Literary Aspect of City Destruction', *VT* 13 (1963), pp. 52-62.

6. Because no Iron I remains have been found at Ṭubaṣ, Y. Aharoni suggests that the name is 'a corrupted spelling of Tirzah' (*The Land of the Bible*, 2nd edn, p. 265).

7. Cf. H. Reviv, *IEJ* 16 (1966), pp. 252-57.

8. See the discussion in G.W. Ahlström and D. Edelman, *JNES* 44 (1985),

may have taken its name from the territory, but it did not necessarily include the whole of that territory. As mentioned above, Abimelech may be seen as a predecessor to Saul.[1] His military power may have been less than that of Saul, thus he did not succeed or was not given time to succeed in uniting the peoples of the Highlands, as Saul did. Like Saul he also met a tragic death.

The most legendary character of the so-called judges is the Danite folk hero Samson,[2] who is said to have fought the Philistines single-handedly in different ways. He was a hero with great interest in pretty girls, and because of his love for the Philistine Delilah he was finally taken prisoner. Through his enormous strength he is said to have destroyed the Dagon temple, thereby killing 3000 Philistines (Judg. 13–16). It is clear that Samson was not one who delivered Israel from oppression. He was never a leader of an army. Even if he could have been a clan leader, his heroic deeds have been magnified by the legend and have lost all credibility as sources for history.[3]

Among the important persons remembered by the deuteronomistic historian is the Ephraimite Micayahu (Micah, Judg. 17–18). He has not been ranked as judge, however, but is depicted as a wealthy farmer.[4] A closer look at the information given by the narrator shows that Micah must have been an important ruler in the territory of Ephraim. He was the owner of a *bêt 'elōhîm*, a temple, and made a cast idol for it from money his mother had allocated (17.3).[5] He also had installed one of his sons as priest. To own a temple and to appoint

pp. 59-61; G.W. Ahlström, *Who were the Israelites?*, pp. 37-39.

1.　Cf. E. Nielsen, *Shechem*, pp. 168-69. D. Edelman sees Eli as the immediate successor to Abimelech as *śar* over the political unit Israel moving the seat of rulership to Shiloh ('Rise of the Israelite State', pp. 192-93). Cf. R. Brinker, who mentions that the Samaritan Chronicle sees Eli of the line of Ithamar as originally coming from Shechem (*The Influence of Sanctuaries in Early Israel* [London, 1946], pp. 166-67).

2.　The name is derived from Hebrew *šemeš*, 'sun'.

3.　Samson has often been compared with Gilgamesh, Enkidu or Herakles. R. Mayer-Opificius sees Samson as a hero of the type of 'sechs- oder achtlockigen Helden', known from the period of Sargon II ('Simson, der Sechslockige Held?', *UF* 14 [1982], pp. 149-51).

4.　E. Täubler calls him a rich landowner (*Biblische Studien*, pp. 50-51).

5.　Micah's mother is depicted as the *gebîrâ*, the king's mother, who had her own wealth and administration; cf. G.W. Ahlström, *Aspects of Syncretism*, p. 25 n. 2. The text also indicates what religion looked like in this period before Saul.

priests were a ruler's prerogatives.[1] Micah is thus a ruler, a *śar*, somewhere in the hill country of Ephraim.[2] This opinion can be supported with the information about Micah pursuing the Danites who had robbed him of his idol and taken his new priest, a 'Levite', with them when they migrated north (Judg. 18.21-31).[3] A farmer, even if he were wealthy, could not have raised an army of such strength that it could fight a people on the move. The text originally claimed Yahwistic legitimacy for the temple at Dan,[4] but has been used against the Danite priesthood by the D-historian (Judg. 18.31).[5] Thus, its purpose is different from that of the preceding stories, and because Micah was not a deliverer, but instead a ruler fighting one of the 'tribes', he could not fit into the system and be characterized as a judge. One may rather say that he is a 'demoted' judge.

These are the rulers of the hills that the Book of Judges lists for the pre-Saulidic era. There may have been many more. For instance, a certain Bedan is mentioned in 1 Sam. 12.11 together with Jerubbaal, Jephthah and Samuel.[6] These four are said to have rescued the people from their enemies. Clearly we have here a tradition other than the one the D-historian used for his presentation of the 'judges'. This is supported by the fact that 1 Samuel 12 is unaware of any conquest of

---

1. Cf. David, who also appointed some of his sons as priests (2 Sam. 8.8). To label Micah a 'cultic opportunist', as R.G. Boling does (*Judges*, p. 255), is unclear and confusing. What is a 'cultic opportunist'?

2. J. Morgenstern sees Micah as a local chief ('The Ark, the Ephod, and the Tent of Meeting', *HUCA* 18 [1944], p. 4). R. van der Hart identifies Micah's temple with Shiloh ('The Camp of Dan and the Camp of Yahweh', *VT* 25 [1975], p. 721-28).

3. Judg. 18.3 says that the Danites 'recognized the voice of the young Levite'; how they could when they were foreigners to the territory?

4. Cf. E. Meyer, *Die Israeliten und ihre Nachbarstämme*, pp. 483-84.

5. See my *Aspects of Syncretism*, pp. 26-27. Judg. 18.30 shows that the text has been composed after 720 BCE.

6. The Masoretic tradition is unanimous in reading Bedan so there is no reason to emend Bedan to Baraq, as often has been done; cf. H.W. Hertzberg, *I & II Samuel: A Commentary* (trans. J.S. Bowden; London, 1964), p. 95. The Book of Judges does not give a complete list of all the rulers. T.N.D. Mettinger also objects to the emendation Baraq (*King and Messiah* [ConBOT, 8; Lund, 1976], p. 82). Of certain interest is the fact that neither Baraq nor Deborah are said to have saved Israel. This may be one of the reasons why they are not mentioned in 1 Sam. 12.11.

Canaan by Joshua. The conclusion that ch. 12 is predeuteronomistic is, therefore, a logical one.[1]

From the Book of 1 Samuel we learn about two more men who ruled parts of the central hill country in the time before Saul, namely, the priest-rulers Eli and Samuel. They are not given the title of judge, but are characterized as leaders of 'Israel'. The priest Eli of Shiloh, for instance, is said to have judged, that is, ruled, Israel for a generation (40 years, 1 Sam. 4.18). He is seen as the leader preceding Samuel. His political role is not outlined by the narrator. He is introduced as the priest who taught his disciple Samuel and who then fell out of favor. The disciple took over after having been 'converted' to Yahwism by the narrator. 1 Sam. 3.1 states that 'the word of Yahweh was rare in those days', in other words, the type of religion that the biblical writer would like to have seen did not yet exist and Yahweh was not yet the god of the whole country. The name Eli also points to the fact that the priest was in reality a worshiper and priest of the god *'ly*.[2] This would imply that Shiloh from of old was a Canaanite cult place frequented by some peoples who called themselves Israelites (cf. Josh. 2.2; 22.9 and Judg. 21.12 mentioning Shiloh, 'which is in the land of Canaan'). Shiloh's role as the home of the sanctuary of the Ark is a secondary tradition created as a *hieros logos* to connect the Ark with Shiloh.[3] Still, Shiloh may have been an important religious and political center in the hills and so has been ranked as a successor to Shechem by the biblical writer. It is, of course, also possible that Eli managed to increase his realm of power after Abimelech's death.[4] In the west the Philistines, intruders on the Palestinian stage, threatened the peoples of the central highlands and their growing societies and soon put an end to Shiloh and the rule of its priest dynasty (1 Samuel 4).

1. Cf. N. Lohfink, 'Die Bundesurkunde des Königs Josias', *Bib* 44 (1963), p. 464 n. 2. See also G.W. Ahlström, 'Another Moses Tradition', *JNES* 39 (1980), p. 67.

2. For this god, see, e.g., H.S. Nyberg, *Studien zum Hoseabuche* (UUÅ, 1935.6; Uppsala, 1935), pp. 58-60; M. Pope, 'Baal-Hadad', *Wörterbuch der Mythologie*, I, p. 255; M. Dahood, *Psalms*, I (AB, 16; Garden City, NY, 1966), p. 117.

3. See L. Rost, *Die Überlieferung von der Thronnachfolge Davids* (BWANT, 42; Stuttgart, 1926), pp. 4-47. Cf. G.W. Ahlström, 'The Travels of the Ark: A Religio-Political Composition', *JNES* 43 (1984), pp. 141-49.

4. Cf. D. Edelman, 'Rise of the Israelite State', pp. 107-108.

Chapter 9

TRANSJORDAN IN THE TWELFTH–TENTH CENTURIES BCE

The Arameans

The name Aram, *arammi*, originally denoted a nomad and had nothing to do with language. I.M. Diakonoff says that in 'the sense which it now has in scholarly usage, the term 'Aramaeans' is probably comparatively late. Their general self-denomination at the nomadic stage of their history was probably *'a'lamî* (in Akkadian written *Aḫlami*). Diakonoff translates *Aḫlami* as 'those belonging to one *'A'lamu'* or as 'One-who-knows-the-guiding-signs'—evidently the epithet of yet another ancestor-eponym'.[1] This means that *Aram* and *Aḫlamu* were two terms for one and the same category of people.[2] Since the name Aram was not originally a territorial name, but a description of nomadic lifestyle, the earliest history of the Aramaeans cannot be known. As nomads they inhabited the areas between the cultivated parts of the land and the fringes of the deserts. Over time some of them settled for different reasons, such as food shortage or famine. These phenomena could have forced them to find new pastures,[3] which could have led to closer contacts with the cultural richness. Another factor influencing settlement could have been that less successful members of the clan dropped out of 'the pastoral sector, taking their families into the sedentary agricultural sector and seeking employment there'.[4] It should not be assumed that in the earliest stages of their history the Aramaeans were desert dwellers. Neither should

---

1. 'Father Adam', *28. Rencontre Assyriologique Internationale* (ed. H. Hirsch), pp. 19-20.
2. See, for instance, the discussion in J.A. Brinkman, *Political History*, pp. 267-69.
3. J.A. Brinkman, *A Political History*, p. 281 n. 1825.
4. This is known as the 'Failure and Fall-away' model. See P.C. Salzman, 'Introduction', in *When Nomads Settle: Processes of Sedentarization as Adaption and Response* (ed. P.C. Salzman; Brooklyn, 1980), p. 12.

they be seen as 'a wave of Semites emerging from the desert in the late second millennium' occupying most of Syria and northern Transjordan, as H.W.F. Saggs maintains.[1]

Another term for nomads which we know from Mesopotamia is *sutu, suti'u*, which stands for West Semitic 'shepherd tribes'. According to Diakonoff, this term is the same as Amorite *s^{e}ti'u*, and can be related to the biblical Seth and his descendants. Thus, *sutu* would be an equivalent to Amorites.[2] The Suteans are known, for example, from the Mari texts as bands roaming around and robbing in the areas of Qatna and Tadmar (Tadmor, in the Greco-Roman periods called Palmyra). In a letter from el-Amarna (fourteenth cent. BCE, EA 195), the prince of Damascus, Biriawaza, writes to Pharaoh: 'See, I go before the royal archers, together with my troops and my chariots, and together with my brothers, and together with my *'apīru* (SA.GAZ), and together with my Sutu'.[3]

It is, of course, possible that the term *sutu* could have originated as a territorial name whose inhabitants became known as Suteans. The Egyptian Execration Texts mention rulers of both Upper and Lower *swtw* which would be located somewhere in Syria-Palestine.[4] W. Helck identifies the Upper *sutu* with Moab,[5] but since the rulers of Upper and Lower *sutu* are mentioned just before the ruler of *'(a)r-q-tum*, which is identified with Irqata north of Tripolis, the *sutu* of the Execration Texts would perhaps rather make reference to some Syrian territory.

The Aḫlamu are mentioned in Assyrian inscriptions from the fourteenth century BCE as well as in some Amarna letters (EA 200.8, 10). During the reign of Shalmaneser I (1274–1245) the Aḫlamu occur as allies of Hanigalbat (Mitanni). In his campaigns against the Aḫlamu, Shalmaneser destroyed most of their cities,[6] which shows that 'Aḫlamu' must no longer refer to nomads alone.

In the literary material the name Aram occurs in texts from the Ur

---

1. *The Might that was Assyria* (London, 1984), p. 50.
2. 'Father Adam', *28. Rencontre Assyriologique Internationale* (ed. H. Hirsh), pp. 19-20.
3. For Biriawaza, see R. Hachmann, *ZDPV* 98 (1982), pp. 18-19.
4. G. Posener, *Princes et pays d'Asie et de Nubie*, pp. 89-90. Cf. R.T. O'Callaghan, *Aram Naharaim*, pp. 93-94.
5. *Die Beziehungen*, p. 59.
6. D.D. Luckenbill, *ARAB*, I, pp. 39-41.

III period and in a text from Naram-Sin's time, where it refers to a place or a (small) nation in Upper Mesopotamia. Other occurrences are found in the Mari and Alalakh material.[1] Aram also occurs in an Ugaritic text (UT 321 III, 22) (*bn 'armi*).[2] An Egyptian text, Papyrus Anastasi III, has an early reference to a place or territory named Aram. The text has a border list in which the term *p3'armu*, 'town of Aram', occurs as a name of a settlement in the land of Aram. This may be a reference to the territory of Damascus.[3] It is noteworthy in this connection that 'Aramaeans' are not mentioned in the Amarna letters from the time of Amenhotep III, but the 'Aḫlamu' are.[4]

The earliest references to Aramaeans and Aramaean states in Assyrian inscriptions are from the time of Tiglath-Pileser I (1115–1077 BCE). The Aramaeans had expanded to the east in the twelfth century, and had become a threat to the trade routes of Assyria.[5] Tiglath-Pileser mentions that in 1111 BCE he went into the *mudbara*, the 'desert', the country of the Aḫlamu and the Aramaeans and the Suḫu, and burned their towns. The location probably would have been in the area of Jebel Bishri.[6] These people are said to have had towns. Pressure from the Arameans, who also suffered from a famine,[7] was being felt, and Tiglath-Pileser crossed the Euphrates river 28 times to campaign in the west. Among the areas and places mentioned in his inscriptions are neo-Hittite Carchemish, Tadmar (Tadmor), the mountains of

1. See D.J. Wiseman, *The Alalakh Tablets*, Index, p. 128.

2. See the discussion in R. de Vaux, *The Early History of Israel*, pp. 203-204.

3. W. Helck, *Die Beziehungen*, p. 252. E. Edel considers this the oldest reliable reference to the Aramaeans (*Ortsnamenlisten*, p. 28 n. 34).

4. E. Edel, *Ortsnamenlisten*, p. 28; cf. J.A. Knudtzon, *Die el-Amarna-Tafeln* (Anmerkungen und Register bearbeitet von Otto Weber und Erich Ebeling), II (Leipzig, 1915 [Aalen, 1964]), p. 1294.

5. Cf. D.J. Wiseman, 'Assyria and Babylonia', *CAH*, II, p. 460; J.A. Brinkman, *A Political History*, p. 278.

6. D.D. Luckenbill, *ARAB*, I, p. 83. For Jebel Bishri, see conveniently G. Buccellati, *The Amorites of the Ur III Period*, pp. 236-37. The Suhu on the Euphrates have usually been identified with biblical Suah. In the genealogies, Suah is the son of Abraham with his wife Keturah (Gen. 25.2-3; 1 Chron. 1.32-33). Keturah is the legendary ancestral mother of several Arab tribes as well as of Aramaeans; in other words, she is the mother of nomads. As to the land Suḫi, see N. Háklár, 'Die Stellung Suhis in der Geschichte einer Zwischenbilanz', *OrAnt* 22 (1983), pp. 25-36.

7. J.A. Brinkman, *A Political History*, pp. 129-30.

Lebanon, Amurru and Suhu.[1] This not only shows a need to protect Assyrian interests in the homeland as well as its trade routes, but also reflects Tiglath-Pileser's expansionist politics. He also campaigned, for instance, in Babylonia.[2] However, in the end Tiglath-Pileser's conquests were to no avail and he had to concentrate on protecting Assyria proper because the Aramaeans had succeeded in penetrating the land. Their pressure continued after the death of Tiglath-Pileser, and Aramaeans became firmly rooted in the Assyrian kingdom.[3]

Because in Assyrian texts the Aramaeans seem to have spread out from the Jebel (mount) Bishri area, where the Amorites were also found, it has been concluded that the Aramaeans were the descendants of the Amorites.[4] J.A. Brinkman, for instance, has maintained that one might see the Aramaeans of Babylonia as 'remote descendants of earlier Amorites or at least a group speaking a related West Semitic language'.[5] Because there is no writing in Aramaic from Babylonia before the sixth century BCE, however, he acknowledges that his proposal is no more than a hypothesis. I should add that our knowledge about the Arameans before c. 900 BCE comes mainly from Assyrian texts and some biblical references.[6] From these texts it can only be concluded that the Aramaeans were indigenous to Syria.

In the period under review, Syria was divided into smaller political units. One important reason for this is the geography of the country which did not encourage the build up of larger political units. The mountainous areas such as the Lebanon and the Antilebanon kept peoples separated. The areas on the fringes of the desert, that is,

1. D.D. Luckenbill, *ARAB*, I, texts 287, 292, pp. 94-95.

2. See J.A. Brinkman, *A Political History*, pp. 274-75; *idem*, 'Notes on the Arameans and Chaldeans in Southern Babylonia in the Early Seventh Century BCE', *Or* 46 (1977), pp. 304-25.

3. See J.A. Brinkman, *A Political History*, pp. 277-78. For the conflicts between Tiglath-Pileser and his successors with the Aramaeans, see also H.W.F. Saggs, *The Might that was Assyria*, p. 50.

4. See the discussion in R. de Vaux, *The Early History of Israel*, pp. 205-206.

5. *A Political History*, pp. 282-83. In this connection Brinkman refers to 'the frequent occurrence of the *ia*-prefix and the *-an(um)* suffix in personal names of southeastern Aramaean sheiks', which also occur in old Amorite names.

6. M. Noth saw the Amorites as 'proto-Aramaeans' (*Die israelitische Personennamen*, pp. 43-45). Cf. R. de Vaux, 'Les patriarches hébreux et les découvertes modernes', *RB* 55 (1948), pp. 345-46. Linguistically, *amurru* and *'arammu* are not related (cf. D.O. Edzard, 'Mari und Aramäer?', *ZA* 56 [1964], pp. 142-49).

within the 400–200 mm isohyets, were more suitable for pastoralists and nomads with their particular lifestyle. It is also possible that the Assyrian campaigns in the twelfth and eleventh centuries contributed to the smaller size of individual polities. When, however, Hadadezer of Zobah and Rehob managed to create a more substantial kingdom in Syria, which, including the territory of its vassals, reached to the Euphrates (according to 2 Sam. 10.16), he was able to do so because the power of the Assyrian kingdom was at a low ebb at this time. Egypt's political power in southern Syria had ended around 1200 BCE.

As with the Israelite kingdom, so the Aramaean kingdom of Zobah and Rehob emerged at a time of political vacuum in the ancient Near East. A clash between the expanding Aramaean and Israelite kingdoms was inevitable.[1]

Before continuing, the fate of the kingdom of Amurru should be considered. It is uncertain when it ceased to exist or when it was dissolved. The last mention of Amurru is on the battle scenes of Ramses III at Medinet Habu, where he is shown campaigning in Syria, Amurru and Hatti. These scenes usually have been understood to be copies of the battle scenes of Ramses II. However there is corroboration with scenes from the temple of Mut at Karnak. R. de Vaux has accordingly concluded that Ramses III may have been campaigning in Syria too.[2] Ramses is said to have defeated some Sea Peoples in

---

1. In northern Syria the picture is different. Here the neo-Hittite state of Carchemish was the dominating power for a while. The Assyrians saw Carchemish as the beginning of the Hatti land, *mat ḫatti*, the traditional name for Syria since the time of the Hittite and Egyptian empires. East of Carchemish in the area of the Balih valley, the Aramaean state Bit-Adini (Beth-Eden in Amos 1.5) emerged c. 1000 BCE. Its capital was Til Barsip. For the problem of Bit-Adini as an Aramaean state or a neo-Hittite state controlled by Aramaeans, cf. D. Ussishkin, 'Was Bit-Adini a Neo-hittite or Aramean State?', *Or* NS 40 (1971), pp. 431-37. On the neo-Hittite states, see J.D. Hawkins, 'The Neo-Hittite States in Syria and Anatolia', *CAH*, III.1 (2nd edn, 1982), pp. 372-441. Other Aramaean kingdoms in the Mesopotamian area were Bit-Bahiani in the region of Guzana (Tell Halaf) on the Upper Habur (cf. 2 Kgs 17.6), and Bit-Halupe on the Lower Habur; cf. R.T. O'Callaghan, *Aram Naharaim*, p. 103; M.F. Unger, *Israel and the Aramaeans of Damascus* (London, 1957), p. 42; H. Klengel, *Geschichte und Kultur Altsyriens*, pp. 175-81. In the west the name Yaḫanu appears as a term for the Arpad territory that is known as Bit-Agusi in later Assyrian sources. North of Yaḫanu (Arpad) was Bit Gabbar or Samal (Zinjirli).

2. *The Early History of Israel*, p. 493.

Djahi,[1] but this does not prove that he was ever in Syria. Since Djahi sometimes denotes Syria-Palestine in general, the location of the battle is uncertain. As mentioned above,[2] the land battle against the Sea Peoples most probably was fought close to the Egyptian border. Ramses III's victory did not stop[3] the threat of the Sea Peoples, and he soon had to defend Egypt proper. He was successful, but shortly after his death Egypt's power over Palestine came to an end. It is logical to conclude that it was at this time that Amurru ceased to exist as a state, probably owing to the political disturbances usually connected with the period of the so-called Sea Peoples.

In the territories of Amurru the kingdom of Aram Zobah and Beth Rehob soon emerges, which M.F. Unger sees as the successor to the Amurru kingdom.[4] The origin of this kingdom is not known. The only available information comes from 2 Sam. 8.3, which mentions that a certain Hadadezer ben Rehob joined Beth Rehob and Zobah.[5] The emergence of Aram-Zobah-Beth Rehob could be compared with the emergence and expansion of Israel under Saul and David. Smaller principalities and territories were joined together.[6] Hadadezer also managed to take the Assyrian colonies Pitru and Mutkinu in Syria from Ashur-rabi II (1012–972). Other cities Hadadezer ruled included Berothai, Chun and Tubikh (in Akkadian *Tubiḫi*), of which Berothai

---

1. J.A. Wilson, 'Egyptian Historical Texts', *ANET*, pp. 262-63.

2. See above, Chapter 6 (12th cent.).

3. Wilson, *ANET*, p. 262 n. 21.

4. *Israel and the Arameans of Damascus*, p. 42. It should be noted that Y. Aharoni advocated that Hazor in the Galilee was the capital of the Kingdom of Amurru (*The Land of the Bible*, 2nd edn, pp. 206, 208, 216). He based his suggestion on information in Josh. 11.10 ('Hazor formerly was the head of all those kingdoms') with Josh. 13.4-5 ('the border of the Amorite; and the land of the Gebalite'). In this latter passage the term 'Amorite' is a term for Canaanites, not a term referring to a northern neighbor of the Phoenicians. In the Old Testament it refers to the non-Israelite people of Canaan and not to a nation; on this subject cf. J.C.L. Gibson, *JNES* 20 (1961), pp. 217-66; J. Van Seters, *VT* 22 (1972), pp. 64-81.

5. Zobah is mentioned in Assyrian texts from the eighth–seventh centuries as Ṣubatu, Ṣubutu; cf. J. Lewy, 'Ḥamat-Ṣôbâ and Ṣubat-ḥamâtu', *HUCA* 18 (1944), p. 447 n. 100.

6. On this, see the discussion in G.W. Ahlström, *Who were the Israelites?*, pp. 35-37.

and Tubikh (MT Betah) are mentioned in 2 Sam. 8.8.[1] Hadadezer seems to have expanded his rule to areas of the Euphrates, to judge from 2 Sam. 10.15-19, which mentions that he had several vassals in this area. The Hebrew text gives these rulers the title king (v. 19), which may be correct, but it could as well be the writer's word for sheiks.[2]

The location of Beth-Rehob has been seen on the basis of Judg. 18.28 to lie in the area of Laish-Dan. Thus, F.M. Abel placed it at Banias (Panias), just northeast of Dan, at the source of the river Jordan.[3] M.F. Unger, among others, placed it in the Beqa' valley north of Dan.[4] S. Mittmann, however, locates Beth Rehob at *tell el-mu'allaqa*, close to Khirbet er-Rahub, c. 10 km NNE of Irbid in northern Jordan. Rehob would then have included most of the territory of 'Ajlun up to Wâdī Yarmuk in the north, and perhaps also part of the area north of Yarmuk (Golan).[5] However, it would be more natural to see the southern part of the Golan heights to belong to the small Aramaean kingdom of Geshur. The Yarmuk valley would be a natural division between the peoples of the mountains of the Golan and the northern Transjordan.

It should be noted that more than one place had the name Rehob, which means 'open space, market/place'. It occurs as the name of a city close to Sidon (allotted to Asher, Josh. 19.28). Another Rehob is mentioned in Josh. 19.30, located in the Aphek area (also said to be within Asher's territory). Thus, while Khirbet er-Rahub in Jordan may have preserved an old name,[6] it is doubtful whether this site would be

1. R.T. O'Callaghan, *Aram Naharaim*, p. 105. Pitru and Mutkinu were located in the vicinity of Carchemish.
2. Cf. G. Buccellati, *Cities and Nations of Ancient Syria* (Studi Semitici, 16; Rome, 1967), p. 89 n. 42.
3. *Géographie de la Palestine*, II, p. 279.
4. *Israel and the Aramaeans*, p. 42.
5. *Beiträge*, pp. 225-27. H. Winckler had already advocated that Beth Rehob was located in Transjordan east of Jerash (Gerasa) (*Geschichte Israels*, I (Leipzig, 1895), pp. 141-43.
6. The Egyptian Execration Texts mention both a place '*a-r-ḥ-b-u* and '*a-r-ḥ-u-b-u-m* (W. Helck, *Die Beziehungen*, pp. 47 and 53). Whether or not these refer to the same place is not known. M. Görg thinks that these refer to a Rehob in the Beth-Shan Valley (*Untersuchungen zur hieroglyphischen Ortsnamen* [Bonner Orientalische Studien, 29; Bonn, 1974], pp. 164-77). M. Noth (*The Old Testament World*, p. 81) identifies this site as Beth-Rehob.

identical with the Rehob of Judg. 18.28 and 2 Samuel 10. The information about Rehob's location in the area of Laish-Dan is supported by 2 Sam. 10.6, 8. The Aramaeans are mentioned here in a north–south order: Aram-Beth Rehob and Aram Zobah in the north followed by the king of the Aramaean Maacah and the men of Tob in the south. 2 Samuel 10 could indicate that Maacah and Tob were Hadadezer's southern vassals. If the narratives in 2 Samuel 8 and 10 are reliable, Hadadezer must have emerged as the real power in Syria. Through his Aramaean allies he could control the trade route from Aqaba to Damascus north of Ammon. It would have been natural for the Ammonites to ask such a ruler for help against David.[1]

The above review of the emerging Aramaean kingdoms in southern Syria and northern Palestine leads to the suspicion that many Aramaean clans in search of new pastures also penetrated northern Transjordan at the end of the Late Bronze II period and the beginning of the Iron I Age. S. Mittmann, for instance, maintains that almost all new settlements in northern Jordan from around 1200 BCE were built by Aramaeans.[2] Geographically, this is quite natural because the 'most important route through east Jordan is the one that runs along the edge of the plateau linking northwest Arabia and the Aqaba Gulf on the one hand with southern Syria on the other'.[3] Therefore, P. Parr is correct to maintain that throughout history Jordan 'must have been influenced by, and had an influence on, the cultures of the countries

---

1.   A. Malamat suggests that Aram Zobah and Aram-Beth Rehob were joined in a 'Personalunion' under Hadadezer ('The Aramaeans', *Peoples of Old Testament Times* [ed. D.J. Wiseman; Oxford, 1973], p. 141); *idem*, 'Aspects of Foreign Policies of David and Solomon', *JNES* 22 (1963), pp. 1-17; cf. G. Buccellati, *Cities and Nations of Ancient Syria*, pp. 143-44. This is possible, but there is no way of confirming the thesis. In 2 Sam. 8.3, 12 Hadadezer is called 'son of Rehob', which very well may refer to the land from where he came; cf. W.F. Albright, *BASOR* 163 (1961), p. 47. B. Mazar considers Tob, Geshur and Maacah to have been non-Aramaean kingdoms during the time of Saul and David ('Geshur and Maacah', *JBL* 80 [1961], pp. 27-28). This is not supported by 1 Chron. 19.6, which has the reading 'Aram Maacah'. According to Mazar, however, this text could be corrupt (p. 27).

2.   *Beiträge*, p. 228 n. 52.

3.   P. Parr, 'Contacts between North West Arabia and Jordan in the Late Bronze and Iron Ages', *Studies in the History of Jordan*, I (ed. A. Hadidi; Amman, 1982), p. 127.

immediately to its north and south'.[1] Aramaean settlements and influence would have thus quickly disseminated into the northern Transjordan.

The Hebrew textual material names three Aramaean kingdoms: Maacah, Geshur and Tob. Whether the latter can be called a kingdom is doubtful; perhaps it was an Aramaean principality with some leader, such as Jephthah, perhaps called *r'ōš* (head) and *qāṣîn* (ruler, 'sheik', Judg. 11.8). The borders of these three Aramaean territories are not specified in the texts. Maacah was the northernmost of them, located south of Mt Hermon and covering the areas east of the Jordan river and probably also northern Galilee in the pre-Davidic period. This may be concluded from the city name Abel Beth-Maacah in 2 Sam. 20.15.[2]

The kingdom of Geshur was located south of Maacah and east of Lake Tiberias.[3] Its territory covered most of the modern Jolan (Golan). It has even been proposed that Geshur is the same as the *kšw* of the Sinuhe story.[4] Geshur became an ally to David during his time as king of the territory Judah in Hebron. The alliance was probably directed against Saul's son and successor, Eshbaal. The treaty was sealed by

1. 'Contacts', *Studies in the History of Jordan*, I (ed. A. Hadidi), p. 127.
2. This city has been identified with modern Tell Abil el-Qamh located west of Tel Dan; cf. J. Simons, *The Geographical and Topographical Texts of the Old Testament* (Leiden, 1959), pars. 19, 788. Cf. also M. Noth, *Aufsätze zur Biblischen Landes und Altertumskunde*, I (Neukirchen–Vluyn, 1971), p. 457. According to the biblical tradition, Maacah was a son of Abraham's brother Nahor, the ancestor of the Aramaeans of the Habur area (Gen. 22.24).
3. The emendation Geshurites instead of the Masoretic Text's Ashurites in 2 Sam. 2.9 (following the Peshitta and the Vulgate) is unwarranted; see G.W. Ahlström, *Who were the Israelites?*, pp. 88-90.
4. See M. Green, *Chronique d'Egypte* 58 (1983), pp. 45-46. If this identification is right, *kšw* could be the same as Kushan, which occurs in the name Cushan-Rishataim, king of Aram Naharaim (Judg. 3.8). W.F. Albright identified this king with a certain Qusana-ruma mentioned in Papyrus Harris I, p. 75, ll. 2-5, from the time of Ramses III and referring to a region in Syria (*Archaeology and the Religion of Israel*, p. 205 n. 49). A. Malamat would like to identify Cushan-Rishataim with an Aramaean prince, Irsu, who would have risen to power in Egypt ending the Nineteenth Dynasty ('Cushan-Rishataim and the Decline of the Near East around 1200 BCE', *JNES* 13 [1954], pp. 231-42). However, the identity of Irsu is very uncertain and the phrase Aram-Naharaim in Judg. 3.8 shows that the biblical narrator did not know very much about the history of this early period. Aram-Naharaim was never a name for a kingdom in Syria.

David's marriage to a daughter of Geshur's king, Talmai (2 Sam. 3.3). She later became the mother of Absalom.

The principality of Tob ('good') is to be sought south of Geshur. Usually it has been located in northern Jordan, so the Wadi Yarmuk would have been its northern border. The name Tob may have survived in the name eṭ-Ṭayibe which is the name of both a wâdī and village (coord. 216-218) but the modern site name cannot be used to prove the location of the land of Tob. It would be possible, however, to see this village to have lain within the southern border area of Tob. The village of et-Tayibe has also been proposed as the site for the place *tby* occurring in a list of Tuthmoses III, as well as the site for Gubbu (read Dubu) in the Amarna letter EA 205.3.[1] M. Noth saw Tob to lie in the Eastern area of the 'Ajlun,[2] and R. de Vaux located it 'north or northwest of Jabbok'.[3] According to S. Mittmann's survey, the Aramaeans settled between the 'Ajlun and the Yarmuk.[4] It is thus possible that the land of Tob should be sought somewhere in the 'Ajlun area. Jephthah could not have been too far away when he was summoned to lead the Gileadites against the Ammonites. He seems to have been roaming around as a *ḥabiru* chieftain, and he may have been well known as such by the people of Gilead.[5] Tob was most probably not the name of a city,[6] but of a smaller kingdom or principality in Transjordan. Together with Maacah and Geshur, Tob can be seen as a satellite controlled by Hadadezer.[7]

The pattern of settlements and population in southern Syria and

1.   Thus, F.M. Abel, *Géographie de la Palestine*, I, p. 250; Y. Aharoni, *The Land of the Bible*, p. 103 (2nd edn, p.115).

2.   *Aufsätze*, p. 456-57. Cf. B. Mazar, 'The Aramean Empire in its Relation with Israel', *BA* 25 (1962), p. 102.

3.   *The Early History of Israel*, p. 820.

4.   *Beiträge*, pp. 226-27. Mittman also maintains that it was Aramaeans who settled at Tell er-Ramit (Ramoth-Gilead?) at the end of Iron I (p. 227).

5.   The text of Judg. 10.17-18 gives the impression that the Ammonites and the Gileadites were ready to do battle, but the latter had not yet agreed upon a commander. This may be a literary fiction, but it still shows the narrator's knowledge about Tob and Gilead being neighboring territories.

6.   On this, see R.G. Boling, who sees Tob as 'a Syrian town later... subject to Maacah' (*Judges*, p. 197); cf. P.K. McCarter, *II Samuel* (AB, 9; Garden City, NY, 1984), p. 272.

7.   Cf. B. Mazar, who, however, does not see Maacah and Tob as Aramaean states at this time (*BA* 25 [1962], p. 102).

Transjordan has not been easy to outline because of the poor source material. Several recent surveys undertaken in Transjordan have shown that this part of the ancient Near East was more populated through the periods of the Bronze Age and into the early Iron Age than formerly believed.[1] There does not seem to have been a population gap[2] lasting for several centuries preceding the Iron Age, as Glueck maintained. For instance, the Baq'ah Valley survey seems to show a 'continuity of fully settled population in the Umm ad-Dananir region'.[3] Naturally, there were differences in settlement density for geographic and climatic reasons. Between the Jabbok (Zerqa) river in the south and Yarmuk river in the north, Jordan is no more than about 40 km wide from the Jordan river to the desert in the east. Because two thirds of this area is mountainous and forested (the 'Ajlun mountains), it is not very suitable for settlements dependent on agriculture.[4] Still, S. Mittmann's survey has found several settlements in this area.

The least populated areas were the territories south and southwest of Irbid. The number of settlements, however, is not large. Nineteen sites produced pottery sherds from the LB II period. These were sites that continued into the Early Iron I. The great increase in settlements occurred here, as in Cisjordan, during the Iron I period. Mittmann lists 78 sites from this time and 53 from the Iron II period.[5] On both

1. Thus N. Glueck, *Explorations in Eastern Palestine*, III (AASOR, 18–19; New Haven, 1939, pp. 250-66. S. Mittmann, *Beiträge*; M. Ibrahim, J. Sauer and K. Yassine, *BASOR* 222 (1976), pp. 41-66; B. MacDonald, *BASOR* 245 (1982), pp. 35-52; J.M. Miller, *BASOR* 234 (1979), pp. 43-52; *idem*, 'Archaeological Survey of the Wadi Mujib: Glueck's Sites Revisited', *ADAJ* 23 (1979), pp. 79-92. Cf. also R.H. Dornemann, *The Archaeology of Transjordan in the Bronze and Iron Ages* (Milwaukee, 1983). The Execration texts also confirm the presence of settlement in the Bronze Age; cf. G. Posener, *Princes et pays d'Asie et de Nubie*; A. Alt, 'Herren und Herrensitze Palästinas im Anfang des zweiten Jahrtausends v. Chr.', *KS*, III (Munich, 1959), pp. 57-71.

2. This has also been maintained by M. Noth, 'Das Land Gilead als Siedlungs-gebiet Israelitischer Sippen', *PJ* 37 (1941), pp. 50ff. (= *Aufsätze*, I [1971], pp. 391-433).

3. P. McGovern, *BA* 44 (1981), p. 128, and *idem*, 'Baqah Valley Project, 1981', *BA* 45 (1982), pp. 122-24.

4. See, for instance, S. Mittmann, *Beiträge*, p. 208; cf. D. Baly, *The Geography of the Bible* (2nd edn), p. 92.

5. *Beiträge*, pp. 256-64.

sides of the Jordan valley we find a great population increase after c. 1200 BCE. This cannot be explained by an invasion of Israelites coming from Egypt. The increase may be seen not only as a sign that peoples sought refuge in these wooded areas during the period of the migrations of the so called Sea Peoples, but also as an indication that some nomads had settled. Families and individuals may have moved into these areas from all directions.[1]

Mittmann attributes the population increase in northern Jordan to the fact that Aramaeans had settled not only in the Jolan (Golan) but also south of the Wâdī Yarmuk, possibly down to Jerash (Gerasa).[2] These movements of Aramaeans and other Semites into the hills of Palestine and Jordan may explain a rupture in the pottery sequence at some places in Transjordan. The transition from Late Bronze II to the Iron I period is here characterized by the absence of both Mycenaean and imported Cypriote pottery. The few examples of Mycenaean styled pots that have been found are probably local imitations.[3] This phenomenon may be explained, at least partly, by disturbances in trade during the unstable political circumstances in the eastern Mediterranean at this time.

During the early Iron age, peoples from the Jordan valley and perhaps also from Cisjordan moved east into the wadis and perhaps also up to the mountains of northern Transjordan. The territorial area of Gilead (which later was used as a name for an ancestor) was not completely settled by Aramaeans. It has usually been located south of the Jabbok (Zerqa) river with its eastern border probably being Wâdī er-Rumemin.[4] To outline the original territory of Gilead is, however, impossible, because the term has been used very vaguely in the Old Testament material.[5]

From the information in Judges 12, one can conclude that some

---

1. Cf. G.W. Ahlström, 'Another Moses Tradition', *JNES* 39 (1980), pp. 65-67; idem, *Who were the Israelites?*, pp. 26-28.

2. *Beiträge*, p. 228.

3. See R.H. Dornemann, *The Archaeology of the Transjordan*, p. 167.

4. Cf. S. Herrmann, *A History of Israel in Old Testament Times* (2nd edn), p. 102. See also R. de Vaux, *The Early History of Israel*, pp. 571-72.

5. Note that in 1 Chron. 5.14, for example, Gilead is made into a clan in Gad's territory. As to the history and territory of Gilead, see among others M. Ottosson, *Gilead: Tradition and History* (ConBOT, 3; Lund, 1969), with lit.; M. Wüst, *Untersuchungen zu den siedlungsgeographischen Texten des Alten Testaments*. I. *Ostjordanland* (BTAVO, Reihe B, Nr. 9; Wiesbaden, 1975), pp. 110-15.

Ephraimites (labeled as runaways) had moved to Gilead (v. 4), and there was thus an Ephraimite claim in that territory. Jephthah does not seem to have acknowledged this claim, which resulted in war between the Gileadites, under Jephthah, and the Ephraimites. The diplomatic dispute—via messengers—between Jephthah and the king of Ammon probably refers to an old conflict between the Gileadites and the Ammonites, while apparently mirroring some tradition about an Ammonite incursion into Moabite territory. The tableland north of the Arnon (Wadi Mujib) had been Moabite territory in an earlier period, as the Mesha inscription also advocates,[1] a text that is older than the books of Joshua, Judges and Num. 21.22-35 (the 'conquest' of Sihon's land).[2] The biblical narrator has used the conflict between the Ammonites and the Gileadites under Jephthah to legitimate the Israelite claim to this part of Transjordan. Jephthah's 'speech' is part of a later time's historiographic thinking. Since it is not really directed at the Ammonites but at the Moabites, standing as a résumé of the 'flight' from Egypt, it not only belongs to the late period of biblical historiography, that is, the postexilic time, but it also indicates that the narrator either did not know or did not care about history.[3]

1. See *KAI*, text 181; W.F. Albright in *ANET*, pp. 320.

2. For the relationship between Num. 21 and Judg. 11, see W. Richter, 'Die Überlieferungen um Jephtah, RI 10, 7-12, 6', *Bib* 47 (1966), pp. 485-556. For the late date of Jephthah's speech as a literary product, see also S. Mittmann, *ZDPV* 85 (1969), p. 71; R. de Vaux, *Early History of Israel*, p. 389; J. Van Seters, 'Once Again—The Conquest of Sihon's Kingdom', *JBL* 99 (1980), pp. 117-18. Van Seters maintains that Num. 21.21-35 is dependent on the story in Judg. 11 mentioning the 'settling in the land (v. 26) subsequent to the conquest of the region', which is precisely what Jephthah says in his message to the king of Ammon. See also S. Herrmann, who says that the story about the defeat of Og of Bashan and Sihon of Heshbon 'is not only a simplified account of historical events, but an irresponsibly abbreviated schematization of the territories east of the Jordan and of their allocation' (*A History of Israel* [2nd edn], p. 101). The most recent excavations at Tell Ḥesbân have shown no LBII city existed at the site. There was obviously some settlement in the early Iron age, but a large and fortified city is known first in the ninth century BCE (L. Geraty, private communication).

3. J.A. Soggin thinks this text gives no more 'than generalized historical, geographical and topographical features', and as such it is a text without much of 'a historical basis' (*A History of Israel* [trans. J. Bowden; London, 1984], p. 182). The figure of the 300 years during which Israelites are supposed to have lived in Heshbon, Jazer and the towns and villages 'on the banks of the Jordan' (Judg. 11.26) clearly shows the perspective of the later author. Cf. J. Van Seters, who says

His aim, it seems clear, was not historical but polemical.

It is doubtful that Jephthah thought of himself as an Israelite. As is clear from Judg. 11.8, the territory of Israel did not include Gilead, and during his lifetime there was as yet no nation of Israel. The same two points apply to the 'judge', ruler, the Gileadite Jair (Judg. 10.3-5). These two men may accordingly be viewed as independent rulers in Transjordan. In the biblical narrator's pan-Israelite historiography they have both, like many others, been made 'Israelites'.[1]

The tradition in 1 Sam. 31.11ff. supports the assumption that the Gileadites were not yet under any Israelite cultural influence. The text states that the people of Jabesh-Gilead cremated the bodies of Saul and his sons. Cremation was not a custom of the Semites of western Palestine. Therefore, even if most were of West Semitic stock, the Gileadites had become influenced by some other culture that had come from the north in an earlier period. Cremation was not uncommon among the Hittites and some Indo-European peoples, as well as the Kassites in Babylonia. Since most of the northern Transjordan must have been of vital interest for the Hittite empire in its struggle with Egypt for domination of the Syro-Palestinian countries in the thirteenth century BCE, Hittite influences could have reached down into Gilead and into areas further inland.[2] Cremation (in jars) is also

that 'the device of narrating negotiations between the two warring parties in 11.12-28 allows Dtr to once again recapitulate the sacred history of the exodus and conquest and to fully integrate the exploits of Jephthah into his history' (*In Search of History*, p. 345).

1.   Barzillai, the Gileadite, who has a non-Hebrew name (from *barzel*, 'iron', Hittite [*barzillu*] and Akkadian [*parzillu*]) was probably the Gileadite ruler and vassal to David. Together with Shobi, the son of Nahash from Rabbath Ammon and Machir from Lodebar, this Barzillai furnished David and his men with food and mattresses and the like when David fled to Mahanaim (2 Sam. 17.27). In 2 Sam. 19.31-39, David is said to have asked Barzillai to follow him to Jerusalem and to stay at the royal court. Barzillai turns it down because of old age, but sends his son Chimham instead. For Barzillai as a foreigner who was not suitable for the priesthood, cf. J.F.A. Sawyer, 'The Meaning of *barzel* in the Biblical Expressions "Chariots of Iron", "Yoke of Iron", etc.', *Midian, Moab and Edom: The History and Archaeology of Late Bronze and Iron Age Jordan and North-West Arabia* (ed. J.F.A. Sawyer and D.J.A. Clines; JSOTSup, 24; Sheffield, 1983), p. 129.

2.   L.G. Herr sees the so-called temple found at Amman's airport as a 'mortuary' building or sanctuary, and also as a sign for Transjordan having been under Hittite control during the fourteenth century BCE (*BA* 46 [1983], pp. 223-29).

known in Palestine at Phoenician 'Atlith and Achzib and Philistine Azor (eleventh cent.) and Tell el-Far'ah South (tenth cent.).[1]

The kingdom of Ammon, which seems to have been well established before the nation Israel emerged with Saul, was expanding in the Iron I period, as evidenced by Jephthah's battle. The Ammonites' reported threat against Jabesh-Gilead in 1 Samuel 11 may show that they had expanded north of the 'Ajlun up to Wâdī Yabis, which would suggest that the Ammonite kingdom covered a much larger territory than that around the capital Rabbah (Rabbat-Ammon).[2] The conflict between Saul and the Ammonites represents a conflict between two expanding nations.[3] It is quite possible that the Ammonite kingdom's goal was to stop the movement of Cisjordanian peoples into Transjordan.[4]

Ammon

The name Ammon is from the same stem as Hebrew *'m*, 'kinsman, uncle, group of people', and Akkadian *ammu(m)*, *ḫammu(m)*, 'people' (probably a West-Semitic loan word in Akkadian). In the Mari documents personal names with the theophoric component *ammu* occur. In Ugaritic guild lists the term *bn 'myn* (*'am-mu-ya-na*) can be found.[5]

Cremation has also been practiced at Sahab southeast of Amman (private communication, E. Bloch-Smith).

1. See T. Dothan, *The Philistines and their Material Culture*, p. 57; cf. L.G. Herr, *BA* 46 (1983), pp. 233-35.

2. S. Mittmann, *Beiträge*, p. 229.

3. For the Ammonite claims on Gilead, cf. also Judg. 21.8-10.

4. Judg. 10.9 also provides information about attempted Ammonite expansion into Cisjordan, while Josh. 18.24 refers to a town named Kephar-Ammoni, 'the Ammonite town', located in the territory of Benjamin. When this town was built is not known. In recognizing, however, that the aim of the book of Joshua is 'to bring together the episodes of the settlement on the one hand and the religious and legal consequences of this settlement', it is likely that the composition of the book of Joshua is 'intended to fulfill the needs of a time which is already far removed from that of the settlement' (S. Herrmann, *A History of Israel* [2nd edn], p. 88). This would mean that the town of Kephar-Ammoni could have been built by Ammonites during the Exile.

5. G.M. Landes sees this as an indication that Ammonites were in northern Syria already around 1400 BCE ('The Material Civilization of the Ammonites', *BA* 24 [1961], pp. 64-86).

The ending *-on* is a diminutive ending; thus if *'am* is uncle, *'ammon* is 'the little uncle'.[1] In the Old Testament the phrase *bᵉnê 'ammôn* is the most common expression for both the people of Ammon and for the nation.[2] This has its counterpart in the Assyrian *ba-an am-ma-na* (or *kur ba-an-am-ma-na-aya*).[3] The more common Assyrian phrase for Ammon is, however, *(kur) bit am-ma-na*.[4]

For the origin of the nation Ammon there are no literary sources. From the biblical material we learn that Ammon—like the kingdom of Moab—had come into existence long before the nation Israel (Judg. 3.13; 10.7; 11.12-28). Archaeological remains from Amman and its vicinity, such as Late Bronze Age sherds and tombs in Amman and the so-called Amman Airport temple,[5] indicated that the country was not devoid of population.[6]

The Ammonite kingdom's expansionistic policy during the time of Jephthah and of Saul makes it possible to assume that the kingdom of

1. J.J. Stamm, 'Zum Ursprung des Namens der Ammoniter', *ArOr* 17 (1949), pp. 379-82; D.I. Block, *'Bny 'mwn*: The Sons of Ammon', *AUSS* 22 (1984), pp. 197-212.

2. Cf. D.I. Block, *AUSS* 22 (1984), pp. 202-204.

3. For the different spellings, see S. Parpola, *Neo-Assyrian Toponyms*, pp. 16, 76. H. Donner has maintained that the writing *'ba-an* versucht den stat. cstr. plural *bny* keilschriftlich wiederzugeben' ('Neue Quellen zur Geschichte des States Moab in der zweiten Hälfte des 8. Jahrh v. Chr.', *MIO* 5 [1957], p. 161).

4. See S. Parpola, *Neo-Assyrian Toponyms*, p. 76.

5. For a résumé of the archaeological remains, see R.H. Dornemann, *The Archaeology of the Transjordan*, pp. 20-22, 25-27. For the tombs, see G.L. Harding, 'The Tomb of Adoni Nur in Amman', *PEFA* 6 (1953), pp. 48-65. For the occupational history of Amman, see A. Hadidi, 'The Excavation of the Roman Forum at Amman (Philadelphia), 1964–1967', *ADAJ* 19 (1974) pp. 85-86. For the 'temple' found at the Amman Airport, see J. B. Hennessy, *PEQ* 98 (1966), pp. 155-62; cf. V. Hankey, *Levant* 6 (1974), pp. 131-78. See also the discussion in V. Fritz, 'Erwägungen zu dem spätbronzelzeitlichen Quadratau bei Amman', *ZDPV* 87 (1971), pp. 140-52. G.R.H. Wright sees this building as an amphictyonic temple for the nomads of the area (*ZAW* 78 [1966], pp. 351-53); so do E.F. Campbell and G.E. Wright (*BA* 32 [1969], pp. 104-16). This proposal is merely a guess. Before there can be a discussion of any league or amphictyonic sanctuary, the existence of such a league has to be documented.

6. From the Pella area T. Potts reports that pottery of the Early Iron I Age (area III) is very close to the LBII types and 'may even bridge the transition' (T. Potts in A.W. McNicoll and J.B. Hennessy, 'The 1981 Season of Pella of the Decapolis', *BASOR* 249 [1983], p. 51).

Ammon came into existence sometime after the 'Sea Peoples' period and perhaps in connection with, or after, the Aramaean incursions into northern Transjordan.[1] This is precisely the time when Egyptian domination over the greater Palestinian area had come to an end. It is therefore quite natural that independent principalities arose in Eastern Palestine (as Edom, Moab, Ammon, Gilead, Tob and Geshur) that more or less succeeded in keeping their independence and attempted to increase their territory and power.

The territory of the new nation Ammon may have included an area stretching from the desert east and southeast of Amman to Naur SW of Amman. From Amman the border line may have gone north to where the Wadi er-Rumemin enters the Jabbok river (Zerqa). For geographical reasons it is likely that the settlers in the wadis leading down into the Jordan valley had more agricultural and commercial contacts with the peoples in the valley flow of the Jordan river than they had with the population of the mountains. The story about Saul's war with Ammon shows that the Ammonite kingdom had expanded up through northern Gilead to the Wâdī Yabis.[2] More territorial information is given in the text which deals with Jephthah's conflict with the Ammonites (Judg. 11). The text states that Jephthah marched from Aroer to Minnith (passing 20 towns) and from there to Abel-Keramim (11.33). None of these three places can be located with certainty. They were probably in the territory south of the Jabbok. Aroer has been assumed to be identical with modern Khirbet el-Beder

---

1. R.G. Boling advocates that there was a 'Yahweh revolution' in Transjordan and that the emergence of the nation Ammon can be seen as a result of 'Israel's surprising success at dismantling the older Amorite kingdoms' (*Joshua*, p. 345, and the discussion there). Israel's military success in Transjordan is more a literary fiction than a historical fact. There were no Israelite armies in Transjordan before the time of King Saul.

2. B. Oded sees the border going from Mephaat in the southeast over Heshbon and Jazer to Mahanaim in the north, that is, up to the Jabbok. He builds his construction upon Josh. 13.25, where Gad is said to have been given (by Moses) Gilead and half the country of the Ammonites, as well as most of northern Transjordan. He also considers information supplied by Deut. 3.12, and Josh. 12.2; 13.31 (*Israelite Transjordan during the Period of the Monarchy*, pp. 148-58 [Hebrew], English summary, pp. x-xi). The lists of allotments in Joshua are part of the fictional history this book presents and not source material for historical reconstructions; cf. S. Herrmann, *A History of Israel* (2nd edn), pp. 88-89.

(coord. 238.5-156. 6) c. 5 km north of Amman and should not be confused with the Aroer at the Arnon. Abel-Keramim could then be Kom Yajuz, located about 3.5 km north of Kh. el-Beder.[1]

One way the extent of the classical Ammonite territory has been delimited is by the identification of the nineteen towers found between the Wadi es-Sir west of Amman and the city of Naur as part of a defensive system built by the Ammonites in the Iron I or early Iron II period.[2] However, there is no firm indication that these towers were built in the early periods of the Ammonite kingdom. While H. Gese found some remains of an early Iron Age building in a very ruined condition at Qasr et-Tabaqe (coord. 148.1-228.8), it is not clear that the building was a fortress. Iron Age I and II pottery has been found at some of the other sites,[3] but almost all of them yielded Roman sherds from both inside and outside the towers. In addition, the architecture of some of the towers[4] is uncharacteristic of the Iron Age. These two considertations together tend to indicate that there was no defensive line of fortresses in Ammon in the Iron I period. Recent investigations of a few of these towers have confirmed this suspicion.[5] The tower at Kh. al-Hajjar probably dates to the seventh–sixth century BCE, with subsequent use in the Roman–Byzantine periods.

We have no firm knowledge of the Ammonite language in this period. The incident in Judg. 12.6, in which the Ephraimites were

---

1. Thus S. Mittmann, *Beiträge*, p. 236 n. 85. The Aroer of Judg. 11 could then be the same as the Aroer mentioned in Josh. 13.25, located close to Rabbath-Ammon (*'al pᵉnê rabbâ*).

2. See, among others, H. Gese, 'Ammonitische Grenzfestungen zwischen *wadi eṣ-ṣir* und *na'ur*', *ZDPV* 74 (1958), pp. 55-64; R. Hentschke, 'Ammonitische Grenzfestungen südwestlich von *'amman*', *ZDPV* 76 (1960), pp. 103-23; K. von Rabenau, 'Ammonitische Verteidigungsanlagen zwischen Hirbet el-Bišara und el-Yādūde', *ZDPV* 94 (1978), pp. 46-55. A. Malamat proposes that the twenty cities Jephthah passed by or took in Judg. 11.33 are to be equated with the 19 border fortresses (*The World History of the Jewish Peoples* [First Series, III; London, 1971], p. 157).

3. Cf. R. Hentschke, *ZDPV* 76 (1960), pp. 104-106.

4. For the plans, see R. Hentschke, *ZDPV* 76 (1960), pp. 111-21.

5. H.O. Thompson, 'The Ammonite Remains at Khirbet al-Hajjar', *BASOR* 227 (1977), pp. 27-34; cf. *idem*, 'Rujm al-Malfuf South', *ADAJ* 18 (1973), pp. 47-50. See also R.S. Boraas, 'A Preliminary Sounding at Rujm el-Malfuf, 1969', *ADAJ* 16 (1971), pp. 31-46.

unable to pronounce the *šin* in *šibbōlet*, may indicate the existence of dialectical differences between Cis- and Transjordan. Sibilants are often pronounced differently in different geographical areas. Many Assyrian scribes also had difficulties with sibilants and often mixed them. From the biblical textual material it can merely be concluded that people on both sides of the Jordan as well as Gileadites and Ammonites spoke related languages.[1] The Ammonite language can probably be seen as a Canaanite dialect and as such 'a close relative' to the Phoenician, Moabite, Judahite and Israelite dialects.[2]

Moab[3]

I have already mentioned that the territory north of the Wadi Mujib up to the area of Naur was contested by both Ammonites and Moabites. In later times, after David's occupation of Transjordan, the nations of Israel and Judah also tried to control this region. The area is called the Mishor (= the Plain) in the Bible. The classical territory of Moab has been seen to lie between the Wâdī Mujib in the north and the Wâdī Hasā in the south. The plateau of this area, which reaches up to about 1065 m at Jebel Shihan in the north and to over 1200 m in the south at several locations, is fairly level and is well suited for agriculture.[4]

According to biblical traditions, Transjordan was divided by Moses between Reuben, Gad and Manasseh (Num. 21.21-35; 32; Deut. 2.26–3.22; Josh. 13.8-32). Some scholars think that the texts reflect the events of a later time.[5] The Mesha inscription states that the people of

---

1. The Hebrew *šibbōlet* means 'ear of grain'; cf. E.A. Speiser, 'The Shibboleth Incident (Judges 12.6)', *BASOR* 85 (1942), pp. 10-13; P. Swiggers, 'The Word *šibbōlet* in Judges XII.6', *JSS* 26 (1981), pp. 205-207. G. Mendenhall believes that this dialectical difference shows the existence of a 'proto-Aramaic' language in Transjordan (*BA* 25 [1962], p. 85). However, such a term is meaningless. 'Proto' could mean any language in such a case.

2. K. Jackson, *The Ammonite Language of the Iron Age* (HSM, 27; Chico, CA, 1983), p. 108. According to F. Israel, the Ammonite language belongs to the 'Canaanite' family ('The Language of the Ammonites', *Orientalia Lovaniensia Periodica* 10 [1979], pp. 143-59).

3. The LXX to Gen. 19.37 explains the name as meaning 'from my father'.

4. As to the geography, see E. Orni and E. Efrat, *Geography of Israel* (3rd edn; Jerusalem, 1971), pp. 110-12; Y. Aharoni, *The Land of the Bible* (2nd edn), pp. 39-40.

5. Cf. O. Eissfeldt, 'Palestine in the Time of the Nineteenth Dynasty', *CAH*,

Gad had lived in this territory since 'time immemorial' (*m'lm*, Mesha l. 10). Thus, they may well have been an indigenous people who later became both Moabite and Israelite subjects as their fortunes changed. It is impossible to discover the original homelands of all the peoples of Transjordan. It is likely that many of them came from the north. Num. 24.17 mentions Moab in conjunction with 'the sons of Seth', which may point to an old tradition about an association between Moabites and the Syrian Sutu. Thus, they could have been a wave of nomads who migrated to Transjordan in the Bronze Age. Recent archaeological surveys have found evidence of settlements on the Moabite plateau in the Middle and Late Bronze periods. The population increased in the Late Bronze Age, although no walled towns have been found as of yet.[1]

The earliest mention of Moab (*mw-í-b*) is found in a temple list of Ramses II at Luxor. The same list contains a city *t-b-n-í* which has been identified with Dibon.[2] To this we should add the Balu'a stele,

II.2, p. 329; cf. J. Van Seters, *In Search of History*, pp. 334-35; A.G. Auld sees the language of the book of Joshua to reflect both Pentateuchal and Chronistic material (*Joshua, Moses and the Land* [Edinburgh, 1980], pp. 93-95), while M. Ottosson considers the book of Joshua to advocate the D program ('Joshuaboken en deuteronomistisk propagandaskrift', *Religion och Bibel* 40 [1981], pp. 3-13). Josh. 22, for instance, may indicate that the Reubenites, Gadites and the half-Manasseh were not really considered to be Israelite, if the text reflects an old tradition. If it is a late text, it is of no value for the history of premonarchic times. In 22.10-11. these peoples are said to have built a great altar at the circles of stones at the Jordan river located 'in the land of Canaan', that is, in foreign territory. When the people of Israel heard about this they made war against these Transjordanians (v. 12) for breaking the command for the existence of a single cult place (vv. 13-16). This text may have dealt with a later event in which Transjordanian groups were denied cultic communion with Judah. In order to give the law the character of being authoritative, it has been put back into the 'invasion' period. It has been legitimized by association with the divine will. Cf. C. Steuernagel, who maintained that Joshua 22 was in its language and style very much influenced by P (*Deuteronomium und Josua* [GHAT, 1.3; Göttingen, 1900], pp. 235-37).

1. See, for instance, J.M. Miller, *BASOR* 234 (1979), pp. 43-52; J.R. Kautz, *BA* 44 (1981), pp. 27-35.

2. For the temple list of Ramses, see K.A. Kitchen, *JEA* 50 (1964), pp. 47-50, 50; cf. W. Helck, *VT* 18 (1968), p. 478. Archaeologically, Dibon does not seem to have existed in the LBII period, but since the whole area of the tell has not been excavated, one should not dismiss the possibility that a settlement could have been located there in the LB period. For the excavations, see F.V. Winnett and

which indicates the existence of a kingdom in central Moab during the thirteenth–twelfth centuries BCE.[1] Other textual references to Moab do not occur for this period. M. Weippert maintains that 'the reasons for the silence in the texts' concerning the geographical areas between Pella and Wâdî el-Ḥasā cannot 'be found in the history of settlement'. He thinks the silence is due to the existence of a political border between the Egyptian empire and its (Egyptian) district of Upe. The territory between Pella and Wâdî el-Ḥasā (Zered) would have belonged to Upe,[2] whereas the Egyptian texts are from Egypt, and not from Upe.

The archaeological picture of Early Iron Age Moab—as well as of Jordan in general—is not yet clear enough for a historical résumé. Compared with the northern areas of Jordan the classical Moabite territory is less known. However, there is some evidence for Iron I period settlements also in this area.[3] At Khirbet Medeiyine South (Mudaiyina, coord. 233-074), for instance, both Iron I sherds and the remains of a four-room house were found.[4] The remains of what was probably a pillared house possibly designed as a courtyard surrounded by rooms on one or several sides has been found at Sahab SE of Amman.[5] This house form, like the 'pillared' house, has been seen to represent a new type of settlement beginning in the Iron Age, built by a new people who had entered the Transjordan and Palestine. Many of these Iron I settlements were unwalled, but the houses were built

---

W.L. Reed, *The Excavations at Dibon (Dhîbân) in Moab*. II. *The Second Campaign, 1952* (AASOR, 36–37; 1964), pp. 13, 15. For *t-b-n-í* not being identical with *t-p-n* in a list by Thutmosis III, see the discussion in G.W. Ahlström, *Royal Administration*, p. 17 n. 44.

1. For the inscription and the Egyptianizing style of the three figures on the stela, see W.A. Ward and M.F. Martin, *ADAJ* 8-9 (1964), pp. 5-29. Ward and Martin put the date somewhere between Seti I and Ramses III (p. 22).

2. 'The Israelite "Conquest" and the Evidence from Transjordan', *Symposia* (ed. F.M. Cross), p. 26.

3. See J.M. Miller, *BASOR* 234 (1979), pp. 43-52; J.R. Kautz, *BA* 44 (1981), pp. 33-35.

4. J.R. Kautz, *BA* 44 (1981), p. 33.

5. M. Ibrahim, 'The Third Season of Excavations at Sahab, 1975 (Preliminary Report)', *ADAJ* 20 (1975), pp. 74-75. For the antecedents of the so called four-room houses, see my article in *ZDPV* 100 (1984), pp. 35-52.

clustering together around a 'courtyard' with their backs creating a 'wall' against the outer world.[1]

These new types of settlements found in the greater Palestinian areas around and after c. 1200 BCE do not necessarily indicate that new peoples had entered the country.[2] That migrations had occurred and that some nomads may have settled will not be denied, but as maintained elsewhere in this book, there was no mass invasion by Israelites in this period.[3] Another solution to this settlement problem is needed. Perhaps the population of these areas started to readjust to regular life again after the unstable circumstances of the 'Sea Peoples' period had come to an end. These smaller settlements could be seen as part of such a process. It is not remarkable that Egyptian texts do not provide information about the history of these Transjordanian peoples, since Egyptian power was declining in the Iron I Age.

The biblical material maintains that the Levites had been granted certain towns by Moses in Transjordan as well as in Cisjordan (Joshua 21; 1 Chron. 6.39-66 [6.54-81]). Among them are Ramoth-Gilead, Jahaz, 'Ataroth, Bezer, Heshbon and Kedemoth. Because of the biblical information, these cities have usually been dated to the thirteenth century BCE. This may be doubted. According to the Mesha inscription, 'Ataroth and Jahaz, for instance, had been built by the Israelite king (Omri or Ahab) (lines 10-14).[4] This could mean that no towns existed at these sites before the Israelite king built them in the ninth century BCE.

The archaeological material does not support the biblical texts in this case.[5] An archaeological survey of Transjordanian sites associated with the 'Levitical' cities found almost no pottery from the time before

---

1. Cf. Z. Herzog, 'Enclosed Settlements in the Negeb and the Wilderness of Beer-sheba', *BASOR* 249 (1983) pp. 41-49.

2. A. Mazar would like to combine this phenomenon with incoming Israelites (*IEJ* 31 [1981], pp. 33-35).

3. See Chapter 7; cf. also my book, *Who were The Israelites?*, pp. 18-20, 25-36.

4. *ANET*, p. 320.

5. The two places which have been considered as probable candidates for Jahaz (Khirbet el-Medeiyine and Khirbet Zibb) did not yield any remains such as pottery sherds from a time before the ninth century BCE (J.L. Peterson, 'A Topographical Survey of the Levitical "Cities" of Joshua 21 and Chronicles 6: Studies on the Levites in Israelite Life and Religion' (ThD dissertation, Seabury Western Theological Seminary, Evanston, IL, 1979).

the tenth century.[1] The results are not surprising from a historical perspective. Because the Levites were government employees,[2] no city could have been a so-called Levitical city before the emergence of the nation Israel. The Chronicler maintains that David sent 2700 members of 'levitical' families from Hebron (which may be an exaggeration) as his appointees to govern and supervise (*pqd*) the Reubenites, the Gadites and the people of half-Manasseh in Transjordan. They were to supervise them concerning all the works of God and of the king (1 Chron. 26.30-32). They were responsible for administering these newly incorporated territories according to the laws and rules of the government, that is, the rules of God and king. Levites were thus representatives of the crown.

This does not mean, however, that we can reckon with an institution of Levitical cities during this period of the early monarchy, as several scholars have maintained.[3] The later historiographer knew that priests, military personnel and other government officials had been placed at certain vital and strategic points in areas that had been incorporated into the kingdom. In order to make these areas 'Israelite' from the very beginning, he placed Levites in them, anchoring the phenomenon in a command given by Moses (Num. 35.1-3). The 'Levitical' cities are most probably a literary product of postexilic times expressing the idea that the whole of Canaan had been given by Yahweh and was to be supervised by his servants, the Levites.[4]

Among the levitical cities mentioned above, Heshbon provides a good example of how archaeological remains can correct the picture given by the biblical writer. Hesbon is named in Num. 21.25-27 as the capital of the 'Amorite' king Sihon, who is said to have been defeated by the Israelites who have just experienced the Exodus (cf. Josh. 13.9-40). In Num. 32.37 the city and its villages are given to Reuben's

1. J.L. Peterson, 'A Topographical Survey'.
2. See G.W. Ahlström, *Royal Administration*, pp. 47-56.
3. See, for instance, W.F. Albright, 'The List of Levitic Cities', *L. Ginsberg Jubilee Volume* (New York, 1945), pp. 49-73; A. Alt, 'Festungen und Levitenorte im Lande Juda', *KS*, II, pp. 306-15; for further discussion, see B. Mazar, 'The Cities of the Priests and Levites', *Congress Volume, Oxford 1959* (ed. J.A. Emerton *et al.*; VTSup, 7; 1960), pp. 195-205; Y. Aharoni, *The Land of the Bible* (2nd edn), pp. 301-303.
4. Consult G.W. Ahlström, *Royal Administration*, pp. 47-56; cf. J.R. Spencer, 'The Levitical Cities: A Study of the Role and Function of the Levites in the History of Israel' (PhD dissertation, University of Chicago, 1980).

people. In Judg. 11.19-21 in a speech that is characteristically deuteronomistic, Jephthah refers to Sihon's defeat. If Heshbon is to be identified with modern Tell Ḥesbân (or Ḥisbân), and this tell seems to be the most likely candidate,[1] then the biblical story about Sihon, king of Heshbon, cannot refer to any Late Bronze II city. Excavations down to bedrock have not unearthed any remains of a settlement (other than a cistern) at the tell from the periods preceding the Iron IA Age.[2] This would then mean that there was neither a capital city nor a 'Levitical' city of Heshbon in the thirteenth century BCE.[3] An Amorite state in this area is not known from any writings outside the Bible. There is no mention of any nation at Heshbon in, for example, Egyptian or Hittite texts from the thirteenth century or earlier.[4]

Another city which is supposed to have been allocated to the invading Israelites is Elealeh (Num. 32.3, 37).[5] It has been equated with Khirbet el- 'Al c. 3 km (2 miles) NNE of Ḥisbân (coord. 228-136). An archaeological survey in this area yielded pottery sherds from the

1.   An ostracon whose first line is translated 'to Heshbon...' was found in the 1978 excavation; see F.M. Cross, 'An Unpublished Ammonite Ostracon from Hesbon', *Siegfried Horn Festschrift* (forthcoming). Also, the large water reservoir found at Ḥesbân may agree with the words in Cant. 7.5 (Eng. v. 4); see L.T. Geraty, 'Heshbon: The First Casualty in the Israelite Quest for the Kingdom of God', *The Quest for the Kingdom of God: Studies in Honor of George E. Mendenhall* (ed. H.B. Huffmon, F.A. Spina and A.R.W. Green; Winona Lake, IN, 1983), pp. 296-97. Geraty gives eight different options for harmonizing the biblical material with the archaeological facts (pp. 239-48).

2.   Geraty says that 'human occupation at Tell Ḥesbân did not antedate c. 1200 BCE' ('Heshbon', p. 242).

3.   The dating of the 'Song of Heshbon' in Num. 21.23-35 to the early thirteenth cent. BCE, as maintained by P.D. Hanson ('The Song of Heshbon and David's *Nîr*', *HTR* 61 [1968], pp. 297-320), is thus unrealistic. It should also be noted that no Hebrew writing existed in the thirteenth cent.; cf. my book, *Who were The Israelites?*, pp. 32-33.

4.   Caution should be used in drawing conclusions from silence. It is possible that an earlier city on the tell could have had a different name, although sites were not prone to name changes unless there was a long occupational gap. Cf. J. Van Seters, *VT* 22 (1972), p. 78. Van Seters maintains that designations like 'Amorites, Canaanites and Philistines' are not intended to convey any strict historical or ethnological designation but are used primarily for their ideological and rhetorical connotations (p. 78); cf. the discussion in J.C.L. Gibson, *JNES* 20 (1961), pp. 217-38.

5.   The city is mentioned as a Moabite city in Isa. 15.4; 16.9; Jer. 48.34.

Early and Middle Bronze Age periods and from Iron I and II, but not from the Late Bronze period. Thus, the history of settlement at this site is about the same as that of Ḥisbân.[1] Therefore, it cannot have been allocated to any invaders in the thirteenth century BCE.

One of the largest tells of this Mishor region is Jalul, located c. 5 km east of Madaba and 10 km SE of Ḥisbân (coord. 231-125). Here the picture is different than at Ḥisbân and el-'Al. The majority of the sherds found at the site date from the Bronze and Iron periods. L.T. Geraty has used Jalul among his eight options for locating a LB city of Heshbon which the archaeological expedition did not find at Ḥisbân. Because of the Bronze Age remains, Geraty suggests that Jalul could have been the site of the Amorite Hesbon, and that the invading Reubenites will have built a new Heshbon.[2] Unfortunately, Geraty does not indicate what role the older Heshbon (Jalul) would have played after the new Heshbon was built. What name did the already established Heshbon (Jalul) have after the Reubenites had built their Heshbon?

Archaeological investigation provides a different perspective about the Levitical cities from the one given in the biblical texts. Historically, there were no Levitical cities in the thirteenth and twelfth centuries BCE. Neither did Moses and the 'invading' Israelites defeat the kings of Heshbon and Bashan at Jahaz (Num. 21.23) in this period, because neither Heshbon nor Jahaz existed, as far as can be known. This does not mean that the kings Sihon and Og never existed. Because the biblical writer was a writer, he used the freedom of an author and put into his story the names of obscure Transjordanian kings he knew, but placed them in a period that suited his story and purposes. These stories are part of a later time's programmatic writings, through which one laid claim to a certain territory. In order to give the claim an authoritative character, it has been grounded in the divine will. As Judg. 11.24 expresses it, Yahweh 'dispossessed the Amorites'. We find the same idea expressed in Neh. 9.22, a text which is part of the same programmatic ideology.

Other Moabite cities mentioned in the biblical 'invasion' texts which

---

1.   R. Ibach, *AUSS* 14 (1976), pp. 122-23 n. 10. Consult also W.L. Reed, 'The Archaeological History of Elealeh in Moab', *Studies in the Ancient Palestinian World* (ed. J.W. Wevers and D.B. Redford; Toronto, 1972), pp. 18-28.

2.   'Heshbon', in *Festschrift G.E. Mendenhall* (ed. H.B. Huffman *et al.*), p. 247.

probably did not exist in the Early Iron Age are Dibon and Aroer. In Josh. 13.17 Dibon is given to the Reubenites, but in Num. 32.34 it is located in Gad, which shows the writer's unfamiliarity with the history of these territories. No Late Bronze Age strata were found at the tell of Dhībân (Dibon). Some remains from c. 1200–1100 were found on the summit of the tell, but a city did not exist before the ninth century BCE.[1] Since only a small part of the tell has been excavated, the archaeological picture may be misleading. What is of certain interest, however, is that the Mesha inscription gives the impression that the city of Dibon was a new capital built by king Mesha. The *qarḥō* (*qirḥō*) he built in Dibon (ll. 3, 21-23) was probably the acropolis of this new capital where he also built a sanctuary/temple for his national god Chemosh.[2]

The city of Aroer is also supposed to have been built by Mesha (l. 26). The term used is *bnh*, 'to build', which, however, can also mean 'rebuild'. Because there are building remains from the Iron I period (but none from the LB time), it is possible that Mesha built his fortress upon the remains of an earlier one.[3]

Edom

The nonbiblical textual material does not provide much information about the emergence and history of Edom. An Egyptian text, Papyrus Anastasi VI.54 (from the end of the thirteenth cent.), mentions the territory of *'-d-w-m*, Edom, which was inhabited by the Shasu (beduin) people.[4]

---

1. A.D. Tushingham, *The Excavations at Dibon (Dhībân) in Moab: The Third Campaign*, pp. 15, 23-24. Some sherds from the Early Bronze Age were found but no remains of buildings; see F.V. Winnett and W.L. Reed, *The Excavations at Dibon (Dhībân) in Moab*, II, pp. 13, 15.

2. See further G.W. Ahlström, *Royal Administration*, pp. 15-17.

3. Aroer should probably not be called a city. It was a fortress measuring 50 × 50 m. For the excavations, see E. Olávarri, 'Fouilles à 'Aro'er sur l'Arnon', *RB* 76 (1969), pp. 230-59; cf. P.W. Lapp, 'Palestine in the Early Bronze Age', *Near Eastern Archaeology in the Twentieth Century* (ed. J.A. Sanders), p. 111.

4. J.A. Wilson, *ANET*, p. 259; S. Herrmann, *A History of Israel* (2nd edn), pp. 58-59. Shasu seems to be an Egyptian word for nomads because they are also mentioned as living in other areas, for instance, southern Syria; cf. M. Astour, Yahweh in Egyptian Topographical Lists', *Festschrift Elmar Edel* (ed. M. Görg and E. Push), pp. 17-33; M. Görg, *JNES* 38 (1979), pp. 199-202; W. Helck, *Die*

Edom derived its name from the red rocks and soil found in the ravine stretching from the Brook of Zered (Wâdī el-Ḥasā) at the south end of the Dead Sea, c. 110 km to the southeast on the eastern side of the Araba.[1] The Edomite territory lay on both sides of the Araba.[2] In biblical traditions the western part is called Paran, a name that survives in the names Jebel Faran and Wadi Feiran at Jebel Serbal in the mountainous region of southern Sinai. Seir ('hair') is east of the Araba, and Teman may be the most eastern part of the country.[3] In biblical traditions Edom is the land from which Yahweh came to Canaan. It is where the mountain of Sinai is located, according to Deut. 33.2, Judg. 5.4 and Hab. 3.3.[4] It is likely that some clans of Edomite origin migrated to the central hill country of Palestine, taking with them the deity Yahweh.

The Timna area in southern Araba was rich in copper, and its mines were worked during the Ramesside period (c. 1300–1100 BCE). They were not Solomon's mines.[5] The Negeb pottery (or Midianite-

Beziehungen, p. 315. Cf. also R. Giveon, *Les bedouins Shosu des documents égyptiens*.

1. Cf. Hebrew Adam and *'ᵃdāmâ*, 'earth', which originally meant the red ground or earth. I.M. Diakonoff has seen the meaning of the West Semitic *'adm*, *'adamat* as being 'inherited from Common Afrasian' ('Father Adam', *28. Rencontre Assyriologique Internationale* [ed. H. Hirsch], pp. 16-17).

2. Knowing this makes it understandable why the biblical writer in Num. 20.17 is able to say in Num. 20.17 that Kadesh was on the border of Edom.

3. R. de Vaux emphasizes that Teman never was a name of a city, as has sometimes been advocated. He thought Teman referred to a territory, most probably southern Edom. It occurs mainly in poetic texts, and there it means 'touts le pays d'Edom' ('Téman, ville ou region d'Edom?', *RB* 76 [1969], pp. 378-85). For Teman in the Kuntillet 'Ajrud inscriptions, see J.A. Emerton, 'New Light on Israelite Religion: The Implications of the Inscriptions from Kuntillet 'Ajrud', *ZAW* 94 (1982), pp. 9-10; G.W. Ahlström, *An Archaeological Picture of Iron Age Religions in Ancient Palestine*, pp. 20-21.

4. The song in Hab. 3 begins with the name Yahweh, thus Elohim in v. 3 is a parallel.

5. See B. Rothenberg, *Were these King Solomon's Mines?* (New York, 1972); *idem*, 'Einleitung' *Antikes Kupfer im Timna-Tal* (ed. H.G. Conrad and B. Rothenberg; Der Anschnitt, Zeitschrift für Kunst und Kultur im Bergbau, Beiheft 1; Bochum, 1980), pp. 22-23. Cf. J.F. Merkel, 'A Laboratory Reconstruction of Late Bronze–Early Iron Age Copper Smelting in the Arabah', *Midian, Moab and Edom*, (ed. J.F.A. Sawyer and D.J.A. Clines; JSOTSup, 24; Sheffield, 1993), pp. 125-28.

Edomite pottery) indicate that the mines could have been worked mostly by Edomite-Midianite clans. This pottery is of the LB II–Early Iron I type found locally, but unknown from the Judean hills.[1] The Hathor temple at Timna indicates Egyptian supremacy in this area. Its 'Holy of Holies' is a niche cut into the steep wall of the mountain. With Egyptian presence in the Araba, it would have been impossible for 'Israelites' or any other group escaping from Egypt to have taken the way through the Araba into Transjordan.[2] The historical background of the Araba region provides one more indication that the Exodus story is a literary construction.[3]

There is no firm historical information about the existence of a kingdom Edom in the period before c. 1200 BCE, the history of the period down to c. 1000 BCE is mainly unknown.[4] The Wâdî el-Ḥasā

1.   See B. Rothenberg, *Were these King Solomon's Mines?*, p. 181, cf. pp. 107 and 155-57. P. Parr points out that a cluster of so called Midianite pottery has been found in S. Palestine—besides Timna, Yotebah, Kheleifeh, Jazirat Faraun, also at Tell ed-Duweir, Jedur, Tell Fara and Tel Māśōś 'with a distant outlier at Amman'. He sees the Midianite pottery 'as a hybrid developed in N.W. Arabia'. It is not imitation of Levanite pottery, but rather a 'more imaginative and individual expression of the artistic talents of the potters'. A certain inspiration may have come from Palestine as well as from Egyptian forms that were known in these areas ('Contacts between North West Arabia and Jordan in the Late Bronze and Iron Ages', *Studies in the History of Jordan*, I [ed. A. Hadidi; Amman, 1982], pp. 128-29). For a more thorough discussion, see B. Rothenberg and J. Glass, 'The Midianite Pottery', *Midian, Moab and Edom* (ed. J.F.A. Sawyer and D.J.A. Clines), pp. 65-124. This article maintains that from a petrographic analysis one can show that the Midianite pottery 'originated from a single centre of production' (p. 111). This would have been Qurayyah, c. 70 km NW of Tabuk and 26 km WSW of Bir Ibn Hirmas on the Hejaz railroad in western Saudi Arabia; see further P.J. Parr, G.L. Harding and J.E. Dayton, 'Preliminary Survey in N.W. Arabia, 1968, *Bulletin of the Institute of Archaeology* 8-9 (1970), pp. 219-41.

2.   See the discussion in B. Rothenberg, *Were these King Solomon's Mines?*, pp. 63-65.

3.   Geographically it had been impossible for the people to go around Edom's territory, as the Bible says the Israelites did (Num. 20.14–21.4). Such a journey would have included a second crossing of the 'Yam Sup', this time being represented by the Gulf of Aqaba.

4.   David's war against Edom should perhaps rather be seen in a military occupation of Edomite clans and their territories, over which David placed governors in order to administrate the land (2 Sam. 8.14). The short statement about a prince, Hadad, who as a little boy escaped to Egypt and then returned and freed some part of Edom from Solomon's rule, does not really tell anything about a kingdom Edom;

survey reports three sites in the western part of the surveyed area yielding MB–LB pottery, and in the whole area some LB pottery was found at five sites of the Early Iron Age.[1] The survey also showed that at some places the LB period exhibited some increase in material remains.[2] It is also clear from this survey that this part of Edom was not totally devoid of settlements in the Iron I and early Iron II periods, as has been maintained, for instance, by C.M. Bennett. Her excavations at Buseira (coord. 208-018), c. 50 km south of the Dead Sea, probably the ancient capital Bozra, unearthed a settlement which started first in the ninth century BCE.[3] The same would have been the case at Tawilan located at 'Ain Musa close to Petra.[4] Even if these two places do not show any LB or Iron I remains, there is evidence that settlements existed at other places in Edom east of the Araba.

The biblical tradition about a kingdom of Edom being older than that of Israel may be true. This could be hinted at in the legend that makes the ancestral father of Edom, Esau, older than his 'twin' brother Jacob (Israel, Gen. 25.24-26). Edomite clans may have penetrated the hills of Canaan in an early period and become part of the nation(s) Israel–Judah, as for instance the Calebites, the Kenites, the Jerahmeelites and the Kenizzites had done, all of whom in the later genealogies have been listed as clans of Judah.[5] Some other clans may have moved further north, as the Gibeonites, among whom Yahweh's ark had its home before David transferred it to Jerusalem, thus making Yahweh the official national god of his kingdom.[6] The Edomite king list in Gen. 36.31-39 that mentions eight kings reigning in the time before the Israelite kingdom came into existence has often been used as an

---

Hadad may as well have been the son of an important (?) chieftain who succeeded in building a nation Edom.

1. B. MacDonald, *The Wâdī el-Ḥasā Archaeological Survey 1979–1983, Southern Jordan* (Waterloo, Ontario, 1988).

2. B. MacDonald, *BASOR* 245 (1982), pp. 38-39.

3. 'Excavations at Buseirah, Southern Jordan 1972: Preliminary Report', *Levant* 6 (1974), pp. 1-24; *Levant* 7 (1975), pp. 1-15; cf. *idem*, 'Chronique Archéologique Buscira', *RB* 81 (1974), pp. 73-76; *idem*, *Levant* 9 (1977), pp. 1-10.

4. Cf. C.M. Bennett, 'Tawilan (Jordanie)', *RB* 76 (1969), pp. 386-90.

5. See S. Mowinckel, 'Rakelstämme und Leakstämme', *Von Ugarit nach Qumran* (ed. O. Eissfeldt *et al.*; BZAW, 77; Giessen, 1958), pp. 137-38; R. de Vaux, *Early History*, pp. 546-52.

6. See my article in *JNES* 43 (1984), pp. 141-49.

argument in support of an Edomite kingdom already in existence in the LB II period[1] (cf. Num. 20.14; 22.14). The king list in Gen. 36.31-39 has been seen by some to refer to 'leaders of nomadic groups'.[2] A better parallel would perhaps be that of the so-called Judges in the Old Testament,[3] that is, petty rulers in the hill country. The list in Gen. 36.31-39. is probably late in origin. E. Knauf, for instance, has claimed that this passage was most likely composed in the sixth–fifth centuries BCE in a time when the Edomite kingdom no longer existed and local rulers together with Arab sheiks could have been administering and ruling the different parts of the country.[4]

1. O. Eissfeldt, 'Palestine in the Time of the Nineteenth Dynasty', *CAH*, II.2 (1975), p. 329; R. deVaux, *Early History*, p. 392; J. Bright, *A History of Israel* (3rd edn), p. 120.

2. Thus R. de Vaux, *Early History*, p. 392.

3. J.R. Bartlett, 'The Rise and Fall of the Kingdom of Edom', *PEQ* 104 (1972), p. 27.

4. 'Alter und Herkunft der edomitischen Königsliste Gen. 36.31-39', *ZAW* 97 (1985), pp. 245-53.

Chapter 10

THE RISE OF THE TERRITORIAL STATE

From the preceding discussion it is evident that during the twelfth–eleventh centuries BCE Palestine saw the building of several small settlements in the central highlands. These settlements were growing and, as a result, so was the need for leadership and organization. Thus, some reorganization of the societies under a more hierarchic leadership to manage labor and resources may have occurred.[1] In the so-called Period of the Judges several small principalities or chiefdoms came into existence and probably prospered to a certain degree.[2] Among them are the city federation of the Gibeonites[3] and the chiefdoms or kingdoms of Micah, Gideon (at Ophrah), Eli (at Shiloh), Samuel (at Ramah), and the Amaleqite Abdon (at Pirathon),[4]

1. For external as well as internal pressures leading to state formation, see, for instance, R.N. Adams, *Energy and Structure: A Theory of Social Power* (Austin, TX, 1975), pp. 147-48, 290-292.

2. An exact distinction between chiefdom, principality and kingdom cannot be given because there is no textual information clear enough for making a case. Any chiefdom must have had some regular officials, but no conclusions can be drawn about their complexity, because we do not know anything about the administrative organization of these political units.

3. It is interesting to note that according to Josh. 9.7, the Gibeonites are said to be of Edomite-Hurrian or Hivite descent; cf. J.M. Grintz, 'The Treaty of Joshua with the Gibeonites', *JAOS* 86 (1966), p. 121 n. 39; A. Demsky, 'The Genealogy of Gibeon (I Chronicles (9.35-44): Biblical and Epigraphic Considerations', *BASOR* 202 (1971), pp. 16-23; J. Blenkinsopp, *Gibeon and Israel* (SOTSMS, 2; Cambridge, 1972), p. 26; M. Görg, 'Hiwwiter im 13. Jahrhundert v. Chr.', *UF* 8 (1976), pp. 53-55.

4. Judg. 12.13-15. Because the text says that Abdon was buried in the hills of Ephraim, it may be concluded that his chiefdom was located in the central hill country and not in the territory south of Judah. It would therefore be understandable that some Ephraimites had their roots in Amaleq (Judg. 5.14); on this, see H.-J. Zobel, *Stammesspruch und Geschichte* (BZAW, 95; Berlin, 1965), pp. 44-47; J.A. Soggin,

which could refer to the 'land of Hepher' mentioned in 1 Kgs 4.10.[1] A list in Josh. 16.2-7 also mentions the territory of the Archites and the territory of the Japhletites in connection with the borders of Ephraim.[2] They are not mentioned in any other connection so it is uncertain whether these territories were small clusters of villages or part of some chiefdom.[3]

For Transjordan the territories of Jair, Jephtah, and the city state (?) of Jabesh-Gilead[4] should be mentioned, as well as the kingdoms of Ammon and Moab. For the territory of Judah the picture is more unclear. Archaeology does not support the biblical information about several clans, such as Calebites, Kenites, Jerahmeelites and Kenizzites, having settled the hills of Judah. This territory did not see the same increase in new settlements during the period after c. 1200 BCE as did the areas north of the Jebusite city state of Jerusalem. This state did still exist. Bethlehem was probably one of its satellite villages. Other satellite villages may have been the short-lived settlement at Giloh, and perhaps also Nob and Tell el-Fûl.

All these groups and/or political units did not always peaceably coexist. Population density and the need for territorial expansion sometimes led to military conflicts.[5] Memories of this kind can be found in

---

'Amalek und Ephraim, Richter 5, 14', *ZDPV* 98 (1982), pp. 58-62. E. Meyer identified Pirathon with modern Far'ata (coord. 165-177) (*Die Israeliten und ihre Nachbarstämme*, p. 392); cf. Y. Aharoni, *The Land of the Bible* (2nd edn), p. 440. D. Edelman locates it in the northwestern hills of Manasseh, its southeastern border being the Dothan Valley. She thinks that the Amaleqite territory could have been reduced at the time of Saul ('Saul's Battle against Amaleq [1 Sam. 15]', *JSOT* 35 [1986], pp. 71-84).

1. See below, pp. 428-29.

2. K. Elliger maintained that the boundary description in Josh. 16.1-3 refers to a political border line that continued out to the coast ('Die Grenze zwischen Ephraim und Manasse', *ZDPV* 53 [1930], pp. 301-308). If so, the list is from a much later time than that of the emergence of the nation Israel.

3. According to Josh. 16.2-3, the Archites lived west of Bethel, and the Japhletites were located between the Archites and Lower Beth-Horon; cf. Z. Kallai, *Historical Geography of the Bible* (Jerusalem, 1986), p. 132. Hushai, 'the companion of David', was an Archite (2 Sam. 15.32).

4. It is possible that Jabesh-Gilead had been part of Jephtah's chiefdom.

5. Cf. R.L. Carneiro, 'Political Expansion as an Expression of the Principle of Competitive Exclusion', *Origins of the State: The Anthropology of Political Evolution* (ed. R. Cohen and E.R. Service; Philadelphia, 1978), p. 207. See also in the same volume, R. Cohen, 'Introduction', p. 6.

the biblical material; the war between the expansionistic Ephraimites and the Benjaminites (Judg. 19–21) and the war between the Gileadites and the Ephraimites (Judg. 12) are examples.

To include all the small chiefdoms of Cisjordan in the phrase 'Early Israel', as is sometimes done,[1] does not take into consideration the variety of these small political units. The name Israel as a political term for the chiefdoms of the central hills can first be used only when they became united under Saul. The 'unification' of these groups of people in the Bible is made from a programmatic point of view rather than reflecting the reality of the times. It is conceivable that the name Israel was used by some as the name for their chiefdom or kingdom, such as that of Eli or that of Samuel. On the other hand, the name Israel, being an old territorial name, could have become a political term first with the unification of all the territories that came under Saul's scepter.

The rise of Saul's kingdom has most often been seen as the result of the pressure of two other political powers of this time, the Philistines in the west and the Ammonites in the east. One could perhaps 'flip the coin' and maintain that Saul's growing power must have led to a conflict with the Philistines. In dealing with past times which are poorly documented, it is almost impossible to determine origins; thus, the event that triggered the birth of the nation Israel will be more or less a hypothetical reconstruction. However, it should be remembered that expanding political units could often steer into a collision course. This is what seems to have happened. In the latter part of the eleventh century BCE two men in the hills became political rivals: Samuel and Saul.

Because the biblical traditions about the rise of the monarchy of Saul (and then of David and Solomon) are late editions in their present form and not the result of any scribal activities of the royal courts of the eleventh century BCE, there is no possibility of assigning any particular tradition to this early part of the kingdom of Israel. If records were kept, for instance, at the court of Saul, their

---

1.   See, for instance, F.S. Frick, *The Transformation of the State in Israel*, p. 85 *et passim*. Frick thinks that this 'Early Israel' developed from a 'segmentary society' in the 'tribal' period' to a chiefdom under Saul (p. 191). This evolutionary system is based upon the acceptance of the biblical traditions that depict Israel as always being one people.

preservation through the centuries is an enigma. Earlier I have maintained that any official composition of Israelite records and traditions cannot have occurred before an Israelite state had emerged with its need for a court and administrative records.[1] Only when the different principalities and their clans had become Israelite subjects would the interest for creating a common Israelite tradition have occurred, spurring a literary activity.[2] This activity could also have been promoted by royal propaganda. Bearing this in mind, our knowledge about the first attempt to build an Israelite nation is minimal.

The Hebrew Bible depicts events according to a pattern of religious opposites. The main characters, Samuel, Saul and David, are evaluated from a late religious, dogmatic viewpoint: they are either under the blessing or the curse.[3] The literary composition is a drama in which the confrontation between Samuel and Saul begins under the blessing but ends under the curse for Saul. The same is the case with the confrontation between Saul and David. In both cases Saul is doomed, and because his creation, the kingdom of Israel, ended in catastrophe, the biblical composition makes Saul an 'apostate'. The deuteronomistic composer's intention was to show that David was really the chosen king. Unfortunately, there had been a king named Saul before him. He could not be forgotten, but he could be 'dethroned', by the Philistines, by David, and by the deuteronomistic historian.[4]

Samuel

In the biblical presentation of the emergence of the Israelite kingdom, Samuel of Ramah in Ephraim is made into a figure of towering importance as a purely Yahwistic leader of all Israel. He was *the* prophet, as well as the priest whose words should always be followed.

---

1. *Who were the Israelites?*, pp. 32-33.
2. We may not discount the role of oral tradition, which could have kept certain memories alive. There is, unfortunately, no way of checking the reliability of oral traditions. We have no means of sorting out the events of oral tradition versus those of legends and versus additions and changes in the tradition.
3. Cf. R.A. Carlson, *David, the Chosen King* (Stockholm, 1964).
4. Cf. J. Van Seters, who maintains that the history of the early period of the monarchy 'as evidenced by both editorial technique and thematic unity, is the work of the Dtr Historian' (*In Search of History*, p. 270).

He is given the position of being a transitional figure between the period of the so-called judges and the monarchic period. In the historiographic pattern he becomes the last 'judge' and the kingmaker who is not very happy in seeing his power slip away.

The picture of Samuel is primarily a creation of the deuteronomistic historian. With Samuel the true Yahweh religion is supposed to have been introduced in 'Israel'. That is the intention behind the text about the priest-disciple Samuel's 'conversion' in 1 Sam. 3.1–4.1. Yahweh himself made Samuel a Yahweh disciple. For the writer, the religion of this early time was not acceptable. Perhaps it was only dimly known. He states that the words of Yahweh were 'rare in those days; visions were uncommon' (3.1).[1] This is the logic of the deuteronomistic program: the ideal priest-prophet-ruler should have listened to and obeyed the voice of Yahweh from his earliest days. From a compositional and ideological point of view Samuel should be compared with Moses and Ezra. All three inaugurate a new period in the history of Yahweh's people. Unfortunately, the deuteronomistic speeches Samuel 'gives' did not have the effect the writer would have liked. The deuteronomistic historian has not managed to transform Samuel into a pure Yahwist. In 1 Samuel 9, for example, Samuel is depicted as the leader of a *bāmâ* cult. In the pure Yahwistic program no other sanctuaries (*bāmâ*, pl. *bāmôt*)[2] but that of Jerusalem could have been used.

Can the historicial Samuel be recovered? This question cannot be answered in the affirmative. His political importance eludes us. To describe his life and career is impossible. There is, in fact, very little reliable information about him. In spite of this he has been seen as a leader who 'more than any other labored to keep the amphictyonic tradition alive'.[3] This perception cannot be established as a historical

---

1. The narrator's contempt for Shiloh's failure to be in harmony with his own time's Yahwistic rituals is expressed, for instance, in 1 Sam. 2.17 (improper sacrificial procedure) and 1 Sam. 2.22 (sacral prostitution). Shiloh was part of the North. I. Hylander says that the story about Eli and Samuel shows the postexilic spirit ('Geist') (*Der literarische Samuel–Saul-Komplex [1 Sam. 1–15] traditionsgeschichtlich untersucht* [Uppsala, 1932], p. 62; cf. pp. 39–41).

2. W.B. Barrick, *SEÅ* 45 (1980), pp. 50-57; *idem*, 'The Word BMH in the Old Testament'; cf. G.W. Ahlström, *Royal Administration*, pp. 20-21, 59-61.

3. J. Bright, *A History of Israel* (3rd edn), pp. 186-87.

reality, especially when there was no amphictyony. Furthermore, the same scholar maintains that we 'know almost nothing of what occurred during the years of Philistine occupation, before the end of which Samuel is said to have been an old man'.[1] Such a statement acknowledges the lack of information about how Samuel labored to keep any traditions alive during his career.

There is, however, one biblical comment about Samuel's rule that provides an indication about Samuel's territorial jurisdiction and administration. 1 Samuel 7 depicts Samuel as leading his people in battle against the Philistines, and the laconic statement in 7.15-17 reports that once a year he went from his seat of residence at Ramah to three cities where he 'judged' the people. These cities were Mizpah, Bethel and Gilgal. To 'judge' the people means simply to govern, which includes both civil and sacral duties. These cities were thus the centers of Samuel's administration,[2] indicating that his rulership was limited to a small part of the hills.

The nature of the religious rituals practised at these three places is unknown, for the Bible provides no information. The same must be said about what god(s) were worshipped at the sanctuaries of these towns. For the narrator, Samuel could not have established ritual contact with any other god but Yahweh. Historically, however, it must be realized that Yahweh was not yet the main god of all the cities and villages of the central hills. When so many different groups of people had moved up to the hills, so had their gods. Yahweh became the main god of the country only after all peoples and territories had come under one ruler. That started with Saul, and when David became king over the whole country Yahweh became the official head of the divine assembly.[3] The god of Bethel during the time of Samuel could have been the god Bethel. The divine at Gilgal may have included or could have been the $p^e s i l\hat{i}m$, 'the idols', mentioned in Judg. 3.19. The god of

---

1.   J. Bright, *A History of Israel* (3rd edn), p. 187.

2.   See G.W. Ahlström, *Royal Administration*, p. 22.

3.   The idea that there was a Yahwistic theocracy that bound all these different groups of people together before there even was a nation Israel is unrealistic. This 'modern' idea was unknown to the peoples of Palestine during the twelfth–eleventh centuries BCE. It has resulted from scholarly acceptance of the biblical historiographic pattern as history. Ideologically the nation, the state, was the god's territory ruled by him through his vice-regent, the king.

Mizpah could have been either Yahweh or El, or Yahweh could have become Yahweh-El at this place.

In the narrative about the war against the Philistines Mizpah plays a central role as the Yahwistic cult place where Samuel mustered his people and sacrificed before the war started (1 Sam. 7.5-12). 1 Sam. 7.17 mentions that Samuel built an altar at Ramah, which need not be fictional information. It reflects the ancient system that designated rulers as the builders of temples and altars.[1] The biblical writer, however, has seen Ramah as a Canaanite city that got a new overlord, Yahweh, with the advent of Samuel's rule.

The battle mentioned in 1 Samuel 7 has often been declared fiction,[2] because the text is more concerned about cultic activities than with the war itself. The strong cultic interest is to be expected because, as in so many other instances, the narrator's aim is to show that the divine will was behind the victory. However, the information about this battle cannot be completely dismissed. The tradition in 1 Sam. 12.11 characterizes Samuel as one of the four men who delivered the Israelites from oppression.[3] It is possible, therefore, that 1 Samuel 7 remembers a Philistine troop that tried to penetrate the hills but was repulsed by Samuel and his men.[4]

Earlier I have suggested that Samuel could perhaps be seen as a *ḫazannu*, a term used in the Amarna letters[5] to refer to the city

1. Cf. the story of Gideon, who is said to have made both an image (ephod) and an altar for Yahweh (Judg. 6.24; 8.27), Micah (Judg. 17–18), David (1 Sam. 24) and Solomon (1 Kgs 6–8). See also the statement in 2 Kgs 23.12 (the altars that the kings of Judah had built), and 23.19 (the sanctuaries that the kings of Israel had built).

2. See, for instance, A. Weiser, 'Samuels "Philister-Sieg": Die Überlieferungen in 1. Samuel 7', *ZTK* 56 (1959), pp. 266-67; cf. A.D.H. Mayes in J.H. Hayes and J.M. Miller, *Israelite and Judean History*, p. 330.

3. Consult G.W. Ahlström, 'Another Moses Tradition', *JNES* 39 (1980), pp. 67-68.

4. Because 1 Sam. 7.11-12 mentions two place names for the scene of battle and the raising of a memorial stela, Beth Kar and *haššēn*, 'the tooth', M. Noth has assumed that the narrator was well acquainted with the geography of the area and that this probably was where he lived after the destruction of the kingdom of Judah in 587/86 BCE (*Überlieferungsgeschichtliche Studien*, I, pp. 97-99).

5. EA 162.10; cf. G. Buccellati, *Cities and Nations*, pp. 65-67. For the title, see also *CAD*, VI.

princes of Canaan. Another term is *rabānu*, 'the great one'.[1] The *hazannu/rabānu* may thus be another term for the Hebrew *šōpēṭ*, 'ruler, judge', or *śar*, 'prince'.[2] The biblical text confirms this when it states that Samuel 'judged' Israel 'as long as he lived' (1 Sam. 7.17). Even if his residence was at Ramah, his cultic and administrative center may have been located at Mizpah (1 Sam. 7.6).

From the few glimpses of history available for Samuel, he seems to have been a petty ruler in the central hill country north of Jerusalem. His southern border town was Mizpah; the northern one was Bethel. The southern neighbors were Benjamin, which was not yet part of any political unit called Israel,[3] and the Jebusite state of Jerusalem with its surroundings. These made it impossible for Samuel to expand south into the hills of the Judean mountains, where almost nobody lived. To the north there may have been a political power vacuum after the destruction of Shechem by Abimelech (Judg. 9), and after the Philistines had made an end of the power of Shiloh and the Elide priestly dynasty (cf. 1 Sam. 4). Shiloh was destroyed in the mid-eleventh century BCE, according to the most recent archaeological investigations,[4] which confirm the results of the Danish excavations.[5] This is the background against which the emergence of Samuel's political unit must be seen. He may have wanted to expand to the north and to the west. In the west was the Gibeonite city federation and in the north there was a chiefdom or kingdom around the Dothan Valley. Here was located the land of Hepher,[6] which probably was an Amaleqite state later

---

1. G.W. Ahlström, *Royal Administration*, pp. 22-25. Cf. G. Buccellati, *Cities and Nations*, pp. 65-67.

2. In Mesopotamia the *hazannu* was usually a government official having both religious and civil functions; cf. H.W.F. Saggs, *The Greatness that was Babylon* (New York, 1963), p. 252. *CAD* translates 'chief magistrate of a town', and it can be compared with mayor, 'Bürgermeister'; cf. on this N.B. Jankowska, 'Communal Self-Government and the King of the State of Arrapha', *JESHO* 12 (1969), pp. 265-82.

3. This is evident from the tell-tale wording of 2 Sam. 3.19, which tells us that Abner conspired with the men of Israel, and that he then also talked to the men of Benjamin.

4. I. Finkelstein, *Tel Aviv* 12 (1985), pp. 173-74.

5. H. Kjaer, *JPOS* 10 (1930), pp. 87-104, see p. 105.

6. Cf. G.E. Wright, 'The Provinces of Solomon', *EI* 8 (1967), pp. 62*-64*. A. Zertal has identified Tell el-Muhafar (coord. 170.7-205.4) with Hepher, and thus it could be identical with 'Ir-Amaleq. The large tell, which is located just north of the

conquered by Saul (1 Sam. 15).[1] Thus, Amaleqites had settled both in the northern parts of the central hills, as well as in the Negev.[2] The phrase 'all the land of Hepher', which is found in the list of Solomon's districts (1 Kgs 4.10), probably refers to the territory of this old kingdom.[3] In the later biblical genealogies Hepher became part of Manasseh's 'inheritance'.

From the above discussion it is evident that Samuel did not rule over a large league of 'tribes'. His rule was restricted to a very small area in the hills.[4] Transjordan, the Judean mountains and Galilee were not part of his territory. If he tried to expand to the north, he was not successful. Judging from the biblical texts, he seems to have collided with a rapidly rising star, the young Saul, who managed to take over his territory.

Saul

With Saul the greater Palestinian area witnessed the rise of a new and indigenous political power not earlier seen in this country. How Saul came to power is not really clear. The biblical presentation of the rise of Saul's kingship has utilized an old folktale (or the literary structure of a folktale)[5] and a well-known enthronement pattern (1 Sam. 9–11).[6] The latter has become a literary motif in this tale with the

Dothan Valley, was settled from the MB II through the Iron II periods; see A. Zertal, *Arruboth, Hepher and the Third Solomonic District* (Tel Aviv, 1984), pp. 70-72 (Hebrew). Z. Kallai suggests that Khirbet el-Ḥammam would be the site of the city Hepher (*Historical Geography of the Bible*, p. 50).

1. See D. Edelman, *JSOT* 35 (1986), pp. 71-84.

2. Cf. Judg. 6.33.

3. Hepher's son Zelophehad had five daughters (Num. 26.33; 27.1; Josh. 17.3), which, according to A. Lemaire, would be identical with the land of Hepher. Hepher would then be a territory stretching down to the Wadi Far'ah ('Le "pays de Hepher" et les "filles de Zelophehad" à la lumière des ostraca de Samarie', *Sem* 22 [1972], pp. 13-20). See also the discussion in N. Na'aman, *Borders and Districts in Biblical Historiography*, pp. 158-66.

4. The discontent with his two sons, whom it is claimed Samuel 'installed' as 'judges' in Beer-Sheba (1 Sam. 8.1-3), is a literary motif paralleling the 'evil' sons of Eli of Shiloh. In both cases the narrator gives an explanation for why the families of Eli and Samuel did not become prominent leaders of Israel.

5. For this tale and its literary development, see A.D.H. Mayes, 'The Rise of the Israelite Monarchy', *ZAW* 90 (1978), pp. 13-14; cf. R.W. Klein, *1 Samuel* (WBC, 10; Waco, TX, 1983), p. 84.

6. The moments in the kingship ritual include a search leading to the king-elect,

casting of lots, the search for the one chosen by lot, who was found hiding 'among the baggage' (1 Sam. 10.20-23), and the elect having proven himself (1 Sam. 11).[1] This part of the narrative depicts Saul 'under the blessing'. The purpose of the text is to show that Saul was divinely chosen, which is exactly the meaning of the royal enthronement ritual. Kingship was willed by the deity. That is a common ancient Near Eastern doctrine. The biblical idea that Yahweh rejected Saul as king obviously reflects a dogmatic opinion from a later time.

The story about Saul begins with the idyllic motif about a young man, good-looking and taller than everyone else, who was out in search of his father's she-donkeys that had run away. His father was Kish, a *gibbôr ḥayil*, 'a mighty man, war hero', from one of the smallest 'tribes', Benjamin (1 Sam. 9.1-2). Sauls' pedigree indicates that the 'nobility' and was no ordinary farmer's boy. During his search for the asses, Saul was followed by his *na'ar*, 'knight',[2] who had the duty to carry both money and supplies (cf. 1 Sam. 9.8). Donkeys are slow-moving animals so it should not have been very difficult for Saul to find them. However, he never did; instead he found 'kingship'. That is the point and the purpose of this nice little story. The narrator constructed the tale in such a way that it would lead to a surprise; the future king had been found. In this way the supernatural will was expressed. Compositionally, the tale about Saul's circuit begins with the lost donkeys, the riding animals for royalty,[3] and ends with royalty; Israel's king has been found, which after all is much better than finding some asses. A man from the smallest family of the smallest 'tribe' had been chosen as Yahweh's king.

a 'crown-prince installation', testing and anointing, and then the coronation with the people's acclamation; for various elements of the pattern, see J. Pedersen, *Israel*, III-IV, pp. 42-45; T.N.D. Mettinger, *King and Messiah*, pp. 131-232; B. Halpern, *The Constitution of the Monarchy in Israel* (HSM, 25; Ann Arbor, 1981), pp. 125-48; D. Edelman ('Saul's Rescue of Jabesh-Gilead [1 Sam. 11.1-11]: Sorting Story from History', *ZAW* 96 [1984], p. 198).

1.   Cf. J. Wellhausen, who says that Saul in reality did not function as king before he had proven himself (*Prolegomena*, p. 250).

2.   See J. MacDonald, 'The Supreme Warrior Caste in the Ancient Near East', *Oriental Studies Presented to Benedikt S.J. Isserlin* (Leeds University Oriental Society, Near Eastern Researches, 2; Leiden, 1980), p. 66.

3.   Cf. G. Posener, 'Syria and Palestine c. 2160–1780 BCE: Relations with Egypt', *CAH*, I.2 (3rd edn), pp. 552-53; E. Taübler, *Biblische Studien: Die Epoche der Richter*, p. 109.

This is the beginning of the narrative about Saul's career, his anointing by a prophet[1] as *nāgîd*, 'designated',[2] over Yahweh's people, his enthronement,[3] his deeds, and his conflicts with David. This story also marks the end of Samuel's rule and the period of the so-called judges. In 1 Samuel 12 Samuel gives his 'farewell' speech. The story then continues with the conflict between Samuel and Saul, the literary aim of which is to make an excuse for Yahweh's abandonment of Saul (15.10-23; 16.14): an evil spirit, not the spirit of Yahweh (*ruaḥ Yahweh*) was leading him. It is incorrect to accuse Saul of insanity.[4] Saul was rejected for having disobeyed Yahweh. He would be replaced by David from Bethlehem. Politics is here justified with reference to the 'will' of the god. Saul is out of grace.[5] Yahweh is no longer with him. His defeat and death in the battle against the Philistines at Mt

---

1. For the narrator it was important to show the prophetic role in the process: it was part of the royal enthronement ritual.

2. For this term as a title for the crown-prince, see E. Lipiński, '*NAGID*, der Kronprinz', *VT* 24 (1974), pp. 479-99. The term has often been misunderstood; cf. H. Seebass, who denies that *nāgîd* was a royal title in connection with Saul's election ('Die Vorgeschichte der Königserhebung Sauls', *ZAW* 79 [1967], p. 164). A. Alt tried to make a distinction between *nāgîd* as a word belonging to the religious sphere referring to person chosen by the deity, and *melek*, which he saw as a secular word referring to a person chosen by the people ('The Formation of the Israelite State in Palestine', *Essays on Old Testament History and Religion* [Garden City, NY, 1967], p. 254).

3. H.H. Schmid argues that Saul's election has been modeled on the literary pattern of the call of the prophets (*Der sogenannte Jahwist*, pp. 19-20). W. Richter believes the present account of the inauguration of kingship has been patterned after the 'call narrative' of the judges (*Die sogenannten vorprophetischen Berufungsberichte* [FRLANT, 101; Göttingen, 1970], pp. 13-23); cf. B.C. Birch, *The Rise of the Israelite Monarchy: The Growth and Development of 1 Samuel 7–15* (SBLDS, 27; Missoula, MT, 1976), p. 35. This is less probable. Because the 'judges' were rulers, the pattern used for their 'call' is rather the royal enthronement ritual; no other pattern for installing rulers was known. This is also the reason why the title *nāgîd* is used of Saul; cf. H. Donner, who says that it is very probable that the use of this title is a projection back in time (*Geschichte des Volkes Israel*, I, p. 177).

4. Cf. E. Lipiński, who says that Saul was casting an evil eye upon David, which, according to the narrator, was the result of an evil spirit taking hold of Saul ('From Karatepe to Pyrgi', *Rivista di studi Fenici* 2 [1974], p. 53).

5. See the extensive treatment of this theme in F. Foresti, *The Rejection of Saul in Perspective of the Deuteronomistic School: A Study of 1 Sm. 15 and Related Texts* (Rome, 1984).

Gilboa is, therefore, consistent with his having lost Yahweh's approval and support.

What is described from ch. 16 to the end of 1 Samuel is mainly a drama between the king and David in which the composer has also inserted a motif about the 'love' of the crown-prince Jonathan for David. Jonathan is pictured as a man who is not fit for kingship and who therefore 'resigns' the kingship before he even attains it. He is said to have given over to David his robe and weapons (1 Sam. 18.1-5). This action serves to indicate that Jonathan himself handed over the crown-prince position to David. The narrator had to devalue Jonathan in order to prepare for and legitimize David.[1] With this literary excuse 'based' in the divine will, Saul's dynasty was doomed and David's later extinction of the Saulides would only appear to be a natural consequence. In order to save the theory that Saul was the 'wrong' king, the narrator has construed the 'dethroned' ruler, Samuel, as the priest-prophet who was 'chosen' both to inaugurate the monarchy of Saul and also, according to the divine will, to 'destroy' Saul, because he had become an 'apostate'. Thus, the man who lost his 'kingdom' to Saul was remembered by posterity as the agent of Yahweh's inauguration of the kingdom of Saul.

How much of history can one detect in all this? A careful reading of the textual material shows us an eminent warrior who managed to increase his holdings not only in Cisjordan but also in Transjordan. The small principalities or chiefdoms, such as that of Samuel and the Gibeonite federation, were engulfed by Saul's kingdom. The memories of this and the expansion of Saul's territorial state were an important part of the Israelite people's traditions. They are certainly not fiction. Their presentation, however, has been shaped by particular Judahites who had to legitimize David's usurpation of the throne. This explains why Saul is so quickly transformed into a loser in the Samuel narrative.

Among the memories of the Saulidic epoch are those about the Philistine hegemony over Palestine, which is presented as an oppression of the population of the central highlands. The Hebrew Bible does not show anything about the Egyptian rule of the country because the narrators did not know anything about it. However, in the eleventh

---

1. For the structure of the covenant between Jonathan and David, see D. Jobling, *The Sense of Biblical Narrative*. I. *Structural Analysis in the Hebrew Bible* (JSOTSup, 7; Sheffield, 1978), pp.4-25; for the political theory of the Deuteronomists, see *idem*, *The Sense of Biblical Narrative*, II (JSOTSup, 39; Sheffield, 1986), pp. 44-87.

century BCE the representatives of the Egyptian Pharaoh and his government, the Philistines and north of them the Tjeker, had become independent of Egypt. The Philistines probably had extended their rule not only to the Negev and the lowlands (Gezer, Beth-Shemesh), but also into the hills in order keep the new settlements under both military and economic control. The Tjeker seem to have lost in that power struggle, if there was one. We learn about Philistine garrisons in the highlands, for instance, at Gibeah (Geba),[1] Michmash, the 'hill of God' (Gibeon, 1 Sam. 10.5; 13.3)[2] and Bethlehem (2 Sam. 23.14).[3] Thus, even if small political units emerged in the hills, they were, in principle, not completely independent. The new areas of agriculture and horticulture became a source of income not only for the settlers themselves, but equally for the Philistine rulers who most probably taxed the settlements.

The information about the settlers not being allowed to make any weapons and being forced to go down to the Philistine craftsmen in order to have their plowshares sharpened (1 Sam. 13.19-20) shows part of the policy of keeping the settlers under close observation. It may also indicate that the settlers had not yet become part of the urban and more 'industrialized' culture of the valleys and the coast. As mentioned before,[4] these verses cannot support the hypothesis that the Philistines had a monopoly on smelting and working iron, as has been maintained so often. The Hebrew word for iron, *barzel*, is not even mentioned. The text has the word *ḥārāš*, which means 'artisan, maker, craftsman'. It is possible, however, that the Philistines contributed to the spread of the use of iron,[5] as well as to the knowledge of working

1. Present-day Jeba. For the variant forms in the Saulidic story, see J.M. Miller, *VT* 25 (1975), pp. 145-66.

2. J. Blenkinsopp, *Gibeon and Israel*, p. 13; cf. T.N.D. Mettinger, *King and Messiah*, p. 245.

3. The soldiers of these garrisons used the utensils of the population, which may be one explanation of why no so-called Philistine pottery has been found in the hills. Another explanation is that by the mid-eleventh century the Philistines had adopted the material culture of the land, including the local pottery traditions (cf. T. Dothan, *IEJ* 23 [1973], p. 144).

4. See above, pp. 335-36.

5. In the so-called Philistine strata XII and XI at Tell Qasîle, no iron objects were found (B. Mazar, *IEJ* 1 [1950–51], pp. 128-30). A few objects were found in str. X, the destruction of which A. Mazar assigns to David ('Excavations at Tell Qasile, 1973–1974', *IEJ* 25 [1975], pp. 77-88).

with the metal.[1] Under these circumstances it would have been difficult for the chiefdoms of the hill country to develop into military
powers that could carry on a war of liberation against the Philistines.
One man succeeded, however, and freed for some time the hill population from Philistine rule: Saul.[2]

The theory that Saul took over Samuel's chiefdom is supported by
the text in 1 Samuel 9, which tells us about Saul's search for his father's
donkeys. Saul and his *na'ar*, 'knight', wandered through the territories
of Shalishah, Shaalim, Yemini[3] and Zuph (9.4-5), which were subdistricts of Mt Ephraim.[4] Thus they may have been walking through the
eastern part of Samuel's territory, continuing to the area north of Bethel
and then turning south and going into the Zuph district where Samuel
lived. Samuel was born in Ramathaim-Zuphim (see 1 Sam. 1.1),
which is the same as Ramah.[5] These districts of Ephraim[6] were probably under the rule of Samuel. In making Saul go through Samuel's

1.   Except for Mt Carmel and southern Galilee, iron ore does not occur in
Palestine proper. However, iron has been found in Edom (Wadi Feinan), Sinai
(Wadi Baba), southern Lebanon, at Doliche in Northern Syria and north of Hermon
in Syria, in the 'Ajlun area, and in the Beqa' Valley in Jordan; cf. R.J. Forbes,
Studies in Ancient Technology, IX, pp. 193-96 and fig. 30. For the Jordanian ores,
see A. van den Bloom and H. Lahloub, *Mining in Jordan* (Amman, 1962); cf.
R.A. Coughenour, 'Preliminary Report on the Exploration and Excavation of
Mugharat el Wardeh and Abu Thawab', *ADAJ* 21 (1976), pp. 71-78.
2.   There are some traditions about the Benjaminites being a warlike people and
famous slingers; see Gen. 49.27 and Judg. 20.16.
3.   The land of Yemini does not seem to refer to Benjamin's territory, because
Yemini is mentioned in Saul's itinerary after Shaalim and before Zuph.
4.   K. Budde, *Die Bücher Samuel* (KHAT, 9-10; Tübingen, 1902), p. 60;
J. Simons, *The Geographical and Topographical Texts*, p. 310. For a history of the
discussion, see D. Edelman, 'Saul's Journey through Mt Ephraim and Samuel's
Ramah (1 Sam. 9.4-5; 10.2-5)', *ZDPV* 104 (1988), pp. 44-58.
5.   The place Ramathaim, 'the two heights', could possibly have been located in
the Ramallah area; cf. W.F. Albright, 'The Excavations at Tell el-Fûl (Saul's
Gibea)', *AASOR*, 4 (New Haven, 1924), pp. 112-23.
6.   Cf. Z. Kallai, 'Baal-Shalisha and Ephraim', *Bible and Jewish History*
(J. Liver Memorial Volume; ed. B. Uffenheimer; Tel Aviv, 1971), pp. 191-206
(Hebrew), pp. xxi-xxii (English summary). P.K. McCarter thinks that these districts
cover all the territory of Ephraim. He equates the land of Yemini with Benjamin, and
because that disturbs the sequence of Saul's travel, he emends it to Jabin, inspired by
the LXX[L] reading *iabein*, which could be Jabneh (*I Samuel* [AB, 8; Garden City,
NY, 1980], p. 174).

territory and 'reach' the kingship, the narrator indicates that Saul is taking over the rule of this territory. This is then the historical kernel in the tale about the she-asses, Saul and Samuel.

The information about the beginning of Saul's career is embedded in the shroud of the tale. Historically it is not clear how and where it started. On the basis of some biblical passages, however, it can be proposed that his kingdom began with the Gibeonite federation.[1] These cities were located in the Benjaminite territory, and it is probable that Saul's home was located very close to Gibeon.[2] An investigation of Gibeonite and Saulide names shows that there is an 'interesting overlap with names in Edom and in the region south of Judah'.[3] Not only Saul's own name, but also his father's name, Kish, could be of Edomite origin.[4] Therefore, because the Gibeonites could have come from Edomite territories and settled in the land of Benjamin, mixed marriages with other newcomers may have occurred. This explains why there are 'Edomite' names within the family of Kish. It also explains why the Gibeonites are found in the later Benjaminite genealogy (Josh. 18.21-28). The genealogy of Saul in 1 Sam. 9.1 does not explicitly state where the home of Kish and Saul was located, which is usually done in genealogies. The narrator either did not know the fact or deleted it.

There are, however, a few indications in the Bible about Saul's home town. 1 Chron. 8.29-40 (the genealogy of the Saulide clan; cf. 1 Chron. 9.45) says that Kish, Saul's father, lived in Gibeon. His tomb, in which Saul's remains were also buried, was at Zela (*sela'*), a place that has been identified with modern Khirbet es-Selah (coord. 164-132), located between Jerusalem and Gibeon (2 Sam. 21.14).[5] When Saul came to

1. So D. Edelman, 'The Rise of the Israelite State', pp. 202-30.

2. Cf. D. Edelman, 'The Rise of the Israelite State'; H. Erlich maintains that Saul's family had to move from Gibeon ('The Family of the Matrites and the Gibeonites', *Beth Miqra* 91 [1982], pp. 266-69).

3. J. Blenkinsopp, *Gibeon and Israel*, p. 26.

4. J. Blenkinsopp, pp. 59-60; cf. also A. Dempsky, *BASOR* 202 (1971), pp. 16-23.

5. J. Simons, *The Geographical and Topographical Texts*, p. 177; Y. Aharoni, *The Land of the Bible* (2nd edn), p. 286; K.D. Schunk, *Benjamin, Untersuchungen zur Entstehung und Geschichte eines israelitischen Stammes* (BZAW, 86; Berlin, 1963), pp. 118, 161; J. Blenkinsopp, *Gibeon and Israel*, pp. 31-59; cf. T.N.D. Mettinger, *King and Messiah*, p. 245; D. Edelman, 'The Rise of the Israelite State', p. 214. 2 Sam. 21.6 (LXX) mentions that the descendants of Saul were

his hometown, called *gib'at hā'ᵉlōhîm*, 'the hill of God' (1 Sam. 10.5), after his donkey expedition and his meeting with Samuel, he entered the *bāmâ*, 'sanctuary', of the town where his *dwd*, 'uncle', asked him where he had been. This holy place may be the well-known sanctuary at Gibeon that was ranked as the most important cult place of the Israelite kingdom until Solomon built his temple (1 Kgs 3.4). According to 1 Sam. 10.5, the 'hill of God' had a Philistine garrison. If this place is the same as Gibeon, then Saul's 'uncle' may have been a priest and/or a city official who had to answer to the Philistines for law and order.[1] Under such circumstances it is natural that Saul did not say anything about the kingship. That could have cost him his life.[2]

The most logical place for Saul to have started his military career would have been his hometown, Gibeon. Having lived under direct military supervision, Saul may have carried out a *coup d'état*, ridding Gibeon of its Philistine garrison,[3] thus starting the war of liberation. In this case it would be natural to see Gibeon as Saul's capital, at least at first.[4] Realistically, Saul's deed must have forced the Philistines to retaliate. It is in this situation that Samuel's territory becomes important. Saul needed to extend his power base quickly, while the old priest-ruler did not have the needed strength to withstand the Philistines. When Saul annexed Samuel's chiefdom, the Philistines must have understood that their supremacy was being threatened. Thus, Saul could not be tolerated by the Philistine overlords, unlike Samuel, who may have fought a Philistine troop (1 Sam. 7), but who, like all the other rulers in the hills, was not completely independent. With Saul the Philistines quickly learned that they had an adversary determined to end their rule of the hill country.

---

sacrificed by David at Gibeon, which indicates that this city was Saul's hometown or capital.

1.   D.R. Ap-Thomas sees the *dwd* as the Philistine commander at Gibeon ('Saul's Uncle', *VT* 11 [1961], pp. 241-45).

2.   According to Josephus, this 'uncle' of Saul was Abner, who later became Saul's commander-in-chief (*Ant.* 6.6).

3.   So D. Edelman, 'The Rise of the Israelite State', pp. 205-209. In this case it would be unlikely that Abner was the 'uncle'.

4.   Cf. I. Hylander, *Der literarische Samuel–Saul-Komplex*, pp. 262, 265; K.D. Schunk, *Benjamin*, pp. 132-33; J. Blenkinsopp, *Gibeon and Israel*, p. 64; *idem*, 'Did Saul Make Gibeon his Capital?', *VT* 24 (1974), pp. 1-7.

The situation in the highlands is difficult to assess. The biblical narrator may have exaggerated when describing the Philistine rule and the mountain population's reactions to their administration. 1 Sam. 13.6-7 and 14.11 paint a sad picture of the people's living conditions. In horror of the Philistine war machine, people lived in caves and holes or fled to Transjordan. Then, when Saul had been defeated and killed, the people 'on the other side of the valley' abandoned their cities,[1] and the Philistines then occupied them (1 Sam. 31.7). The idea behind these verses is to present the enemy, the Philistines, in the worst possible light. It also serves to highlight Saul's initial success, as well as his ultimate failure.

Saul was probably not an ordinary warlord. He started to build an army which soon had 3000 men,[2] and he made his son and crown-prince, Jonathan, a commander (1 Sam. 13.2-4). Later on we find his cousin Abner as generalissimus. It is not clear whether Saul can be categorized like Jephthah and David as a self-made military leader, as has been suggested.[3] Jephtah and David may be compared with *maryannu* or *'apīru* leaders. The former was called to rulership because of his known abilities; the latter forced himself after some time as king upon the peoples of the Judean hills. Saul, however, did not force himself upon the peoples of the northern hills. Rather, he took over the control of the Gibeonite federation and then he either conquered some territories or increased his holdings through treaties. The Bible also mentions that some 'Hebrews' who had served the Philistines 'defected' to Saul (1 Sam. 14.21). The writer's intention here is to show that peoples of the hills not under Saul's rulership of their own free will chose to join Saul.[4] The textual material indicates

1. This valley may be the Jezreel Valley; cf. W. Hertzberg, *I & II Samuel*, p. 232. The LXX has the addition, 'and on the other side of the Jordan'. For this see P.K. McCarter, *1 Samuel*, p. 441.

2. To raise an army of 3000 men in the central highlands must have been done by conscription. It cannot be called a private army.

3. Thus J.M. Miller in *A History of Ancient Israel and Judah* (ed. Miller and Hayes), p. 137. Miller also considers Abimelech a 'self-styled military leader' (p. 137). The latter is rather misleading, because Abimelech was a king's son who reached the throne through a *coup d'état* (Judg. 9).

4. According to H. Schult, the name Israel in 1 Sam. 14 is a reference to the political unit 'Israel', and Hebrew refers to people who were not part of this political organization ('Eine einheitliche Erklärung für den Ausdruck "Hebräer" in der israeli-tischen Literatur', *Dielheimer Blätter zum Alten Testament* 10 [1975], p. 32). As to

that there was no tribal league that chose Saul to become a 'judge', who then managed to become king.[1] Saul was able to start with an already existing administrative system, that of Gibeon and its *bāmâ*, which now also became a royal sanctuary for non-Gibeonite territories.[2]

The first confrontation with the Philistines occurred at Michmash (coord. 176-142) in the eastern part of Ephraim (1 Sam. 13–14), just north of Wadi Suwenit.[3] The biblical text gives the impression that the battle was a concern of the peoples of the Gibeonite, Benjaminite and Ephraimite territories, but it has been given the sheen of an 'all Israelite' war.[4] The army of Saul was victorious and is said to have pursued the Philistines down to the Valley of Aijalon, which may have been the western border of Saul's young kingdom (1 Sam. 14.31). It is in this connection that we hear that 'Hebrews' serving in the Philistine army went over to Saul (1 Sam. 14.21).

Of special interest in this regard is the excavation of a small fortified site at Khirbet ed-Duwwara (coord. 177.8-141.5), about 1.5 km SE of Mukhmas (ancient Michmash) at the Wadi Suwenit, which served as the border between the territories of Ephraim and Benjamin. The wall was 2–3 m thick; inside it were some pillared buildings (four-room houses) with the broadrooms built up against the

the discussion, see O. Loretz, *Habiru-Hebräer*, pp. 111-15. N.P. Lemche holds the opinion that Hebrew here is a term used by the Philistines with the meaning of *ḫabiru* (*Early Israel*, p. 431). P.K. McCarter assumes that these 'Hebrews' originally were 'loyal Israelites who defected to the enemy in times of distress' (*1 Samuel*, p. 241). McCarter's assumption is built upon a hypothetical 'unity' of an Israelite league.

1.   See also G. Fohrer, 'Altes Testament—"Amphictyonie" und "Bund"', *TLZ* 111 (1961), pp. 903-904.

2.   This reconstruction of the events may derive support from the fact that Gibeon was the site of the 'greatest *bāmâ*' in the kingdom when Solomon became king (1 Kgs 3.4). With this the D-historian, in spite of his anti-Saulidic attitude, has given some information about the pre-Jerusalemite capital.

3.   See H.J. Stoebe, 'Zur Topographie und Überlieferung der Schlacht von Mikmas, 1 Sam 13 und 14', *TZ* 21 (1965), pp. 269-80.

4.   It is already in the narration of this war that Saul has been made 'unfaithful', because he did not wait for the prophet Samuel to perform a sacrifice at Gilgal. When Saul sacrifices, Samuel arrives on the stage and condemns him. He has been disobedient. According to the later Dtr ideology he should only do what the prophet told him. In reality, the king was the head of state and the state religion and could thus both sacrifice and regulate the cult as he saw fit; cf. G.W. Ahlström, *Royal Administration*, pp. 64-65.

wall. The layout is round or oval. Its foundation is dated to the mid-eleventh century, which tallies with the emergence of Saul's kingdom.[1] A fortified settlement at this place with its commanding view to the north, east, and south would be strategically important because it could protect the entrance to the hills from the Jordan Valley. This place, therefore, may have been one of the posts through which Saul could have extended his military and economic control over the valley and Transjordan.

The war with the Amaleqites could have occurred as the last event in Saul's drive to the north in the central highlands. After having subdued the Amaleqites of the hills he would have risked a war with the Ammonites in Transjordan. The narrator has made conflict with the Amaleqites into an all-Israelite, Judahite and Kenite war against the Amaleqites of the Negev, who, according to the biblical text (1 Sam. 15.2), opposed the peoples coming out of Egypt. For this reason they were to annihilated, according to the divine will. The purpose of the chapter is to give a reason why Yahweh's choice of Saul was a mistake (1 Sam. 15). Historically, the war against the Amaleqites may have been carried out in connection with Saul's campaign against the Ammonites, Moabites and Edomites (1 Sam. 14.47-48). Being as far south as Edom Saul may also have fought some Amaleqites in the Negev. Unfortunately, the exact order of events escapes us. However, the Amaleqite war in 1 Samuel 15 may refer to Saul's subduing the Amaleqite enclave in the Manassite territory, the land of Hepher.[2]

We should see defeat of the northern Amaleq to be part of Saul's deliberate strategy to create a united front against the foreign garrison at Beth-Shan and its Philistine allies. Saul may have wanted to secure commercial connections with the north through the Jordan Valley. Having secured the land of Hepher (the Amaleqites of the hills), Saul's next move could have been to establish his military and economic control over the northern part of the Jordan Valley at Abel-Meholah, at the southern end of the Beth-Shan Valley.[3] Abel-Meholah has been identified with Tell Abû Sûs located in the western *ghor* just on the

---

1. For the excavation, see I. Finkelstein, 'Kh. ed-Duwwara', *Qadmoniot* 21 (1988), pp. 6-10 (Hebrew).

2. See D. Edelman, *JSOT* 35 (1986), pp. 71-84.

3. Concerning Saul's expansion into the Jordan Valley and Transjordan, see D. Edelman, 'The Rise of the Israelite State', pp. 248-65, 295-96.

bank of the river Jordan (coord. 203-197).[1] As has been noted,[2] Abel-
Meholah was part of Solomon's fifth administrative district, which
consisted of old city states and their territories (Ta'anak, Megiddo,
Shunem[3] and Beth Shan). These were first incorporated into the
Israelite kingdom by David (1 Kgs 4.12). Also among these territories
was Jezreel, which entered into a treaty relationship with Saul (cf.
2 Sam. 2.9). We may then conclude that Abel-Meholah was also a city
state, which Saul had to conquer or win over as an ally. He chose to
give his daughter Merab as wife to Abel-Meholah's ruler, Adriel son
of Barzillai, which may have meant that the latter became Saul's vassal
(1 Sam. 18.19; 2 Sam. 21.8). The name Barzillai ('the man of iron')
indicates a man of non-Semitic origin.

The information in 2 Sam. 2.9 is useful for defining the territories
under Saul's dominance.[4] It may accurately enumerate the territories
left to Saul's successor after the battle of Gilboa. The text shows that
the dynastic principle was part of the royal ideology. Abner is said to
have made Eshbaal, the son of Saul, king at Mahanaim. He served as
king for Gilead, Jezreel and the Ashurites and was made king over
Ephraim, Benjamin and all of Israel. Here we note that the preposition
'el, 'to, for', is used in connection with the first three names, but for
the other three names the text has *'al*, 'over'. There may thus be a fine
distinction in the text here.[5] The phrase *mlk 'el*, 'be king for', may
refer to a vassal relationship, while the phrase *mlk 'al*, 'be king over',
would then refer to the territories or people of the kingdom proper.[6]
As is clear from 2 Sam. 2.5-6, David reminds the people of Jabesh-
Gilead about their treaty relationship with Saul and assures them that
he will continue this relationship.[7] A treaty with the men of Jabesh-

---

1. For the identification, see H.-J. Zobel, 'Abel-Mehola', *ZDPV* 82 (1966),
pp. 83-108; cf. Z. Kallai, *Historical Geography of the Bible*, p. 63.
2. N. Na'aman, *Borders and Districts in Biblical Historiography*, pp. 187-90;
D. Edelman, 'The Rise of the Israelite State', pp. 92-93. For the topographical
problems, see M. Ottosson, *Gilead*, pp. 215-17.
3. Shunem was sacked by Lab'ayu (*EA* 250.43), and was not rebuilt again
before Iron I.
4. For this text see my *Who were the Israelites?*, pp. 88-92.
5. The grammatical parallelism negates the idea that here we might have the late
mixing of the two prepositions.
6. For this distinction, see D. Edelman, *PEQ* 117 (1985), pp. 88-92.
7. D. Hillers, 'A Note on Some Treaty Terminology in the Old Testament',
BASOR 176 (1964), pp. 46-47; D. Edelman, *ZAW* 96 (1984), pp. 201.

Gilead would indicate that this Transjordanian group was not considered Israelite.[1]

Eshbaal's elevation to kingship at Mahanaim in Transjordan means that the name Gilead refers to a larger region in 2 Sam. 2.9 and not only the territory of Jabesh-Gilead. The city of Mahanaim can be seen as a royal administrative center for most of Saul's holdings in Transjordan.[2] The city probably came under Saul's authority in connection with his war against the Ammonites, who probably ruled this territory before they advanced north to Jabesh Gilead. As already noted,[3] the city's location on the northern bank of the river Jabbok was important from a military and economic point of view. Via Mahaniam one had access to the route leading up to the 'Ajlun territory with its iron ores.[4] The city's location at a bend of the river was strategically chosen. It made it very suitable for the defense of the territory to the east.[5] This may be the reason why both Eshbaal and David chose Mahanaim as their temporary residence.

The two other vassals mentioned in 2 Sam. 2.9 are Jezreel and the Ashurites. What Jezreel really refers to, the city or the valley, is not spelled out. Archaeologically there is no clear evidence for occupation at the city of Jezreel on the spur of Mt Gilboa before Iron II.[6] The references in 2 Sam. 2.9 are to territories;[7] thus Jezreel is in this text

---

1. Previously I maintained this in connection with their (non-Israelite) practice of cremation (1 Sam. 31.11-13) (*Who were the Israelites?*, pp. 86-87).

2. It should be noted that Mahanaim is also a capital of the seventh Solomonic district. M. Ottosson sees this as a continuation of David's administrative organization (*Gilead*, p. 220). This is probably right. Mahanaim was the place where David established his headquarters during the Absalom revolt (2 Sam. 17.24-29).

3. See Chapter 9.

4. Slag, some worked iron ore, and the bottom of a furnace have been found at Tulul edh-Dhahab el-Gharbi (the western tell), which is identified with Mahanaim; see R. L. Gordon, 'Telul edh-Dhahab Survey (Jordan) 1980 and 1982', *MDOG* 116 (1984), p. 113.

5. Cf. M. Ottosson, *Gilead*, p. 205.

6. The survey by N. Zori did not find any city remains at modern Zer'in from the Iron I period (*Nahalat Yissachar* [= *The Inheritance of Issachar*], pp. 19-23 [Hebrew]).

7. Y. Aharoni here uses the term 'districts' (*Land of the Bible*, p. 298). If with this term designates administrative districts, they would have best served this function after David's takeover.

a reference to a region close to Mt Gilboa.[1] This region, as later the whole Esdraelon valley, may have received its name from the *'ēmeq* (wadi) Jezreel, which is a geological depression between the mountains of Gilboa and Moreh[2] east of modern Zer'in, leading down into the Jordan Valley.[3] The territory of Jezreel mentioned in 2 Sam. 2.9 is thus to be sought close to or around the 'Jezreel Corridor'. It is possible that it comprised primarily the region of Gilboa.[4]

The fifth Solomonic district mentioned in 1 Kgs. 4.12 gives a hint about the Jezreel that once had a treaty with Saul. This district was made up of old Canaanite city states in the Megiddo and Beth-Shan plains and in the Jordan Valley, whose southern end included Abel-Meholah. The Beth-Shan territory extended 'below Jezreel' down to Abel-Meholah.[5] This would indicate that Saul's ally or vassal, Jezreel, comprised Mt Gilboa and the northeastern part of the Manassite hills, but not the Valley of Jezreel.[6] 1 Sam. 31.7 indicates that part of the high ground north of the 'Corridor' was also included in the Jezreel district. This text reports that after the battle at Mt Gilboa the people on 'the other side of the valley' fled.[7] This would most probably refer to the Jezreel Valley.[8] The southern border of Saul's dependency Jezreel is more problematic. It might have stretched at least down to Nahal Bezeq. The city of Bezeq (modern Khirbet Ibziq, coord. 187-197) was the place where Saul mustered his forces before marching to Transjordan, helping Jabesh-Gilead against the Ammonites. Bezeq is

1. Cf. the remarks of J. Simons, who included parts of Zebulon, Naphtali and West-Manasseh in the Jezreel territory (*The Geographical and Topographical Texts*, pp. 326-27).

2. G.A. Smith, *The Historical Geography of the Holy Land*, p. 385.

3. Geologically, this depression is called the Jezreel Corridor (D. Baly, *The Geography of the Bible*, pp. 38-39, map 16).

4. A. Alt thought that the city of Jezreel was the capital of the tribe of Issachar ('The Settlement of the Israelites', *Essays on Old Testament History and Religion*, p. 161); cf. P.K. McCarter, *II Samuel*, p. 87.

5. For the textual problems, see W.F. Albright, *JPOS* 5 (1925), pp. 32-34; N. Na'aman, *Borders and Districts in Biblical Historiography*, pp. 187-88; Z. Kallai, *Historical Geography of the Bible*, pp. 31, 47, 61-64.

6. On this, see further D. Edelman, 'The Rise of the Israelite State', pp. 89-94, 272.

7. Cf. 1 Chron. 10.7.

8. Cf. P.K. McCarter, *1 Samuel*, p. 441.

located almost opposite Jabesh-Gilead. It would be convenient for Saul and his northern vassal to meet at this place.

The inclusion of Jezreel in Saul's dependencies may explain why Saul chose to meet the Philistines at Mt Gilboa. He may have tried to expand to the north; however, at the battle at Gilboa the Philistines made an end to his expansionist policies. He never ruled over Galilee. 1 Chron. 12.40(41) tells us that Israel's neighbors, the peoples of Naphtali, Zebulon and Issachar, came to David and made him their king together with Israel.

The Ashurites present another problem. Geographically there is no information about their location, and philologically the term 'Ashurites' can be questioned. Because Ashur usually refers to Assyria in the Bible, scholars have often emended the term and associated it with the territory of Asher in the western Galilee north of the Carmel range,[1] or with Asherite clans that had settled in the western part of the central highlands in the territories of Ephraim and Benjamin.[2] The Ashurites are also mentioned in Gen. 25.3 as sons of Dedan. The late composer of Genesis considered them to be Arabs and made them descendants of Abraham and Keturah.[3] The name Ashur also occurs in Ps. 83.9(10) in connection with a coalition of enemies against Yahweh's people who strengthened the sons of Lot. If the text is postexilic, giving a historical résumé, it could be a reference to Assyria, but if it refers to a pre-exilic event, then Assyria would not be likely, because the Assyrian empire never made an alliance with Israel's or Judah's neighbors against Israel or Judah. More often than not it was the other way around.

Two recensions of the textual tradition, the Peshitta and the Vulgate, have read 'Geshurites' instead of 'Ashurites'.[4] Geographically

---

1. M. Noth, 'Das Land Gilead als Siedlungsgebiet israelitischer Sippen', *Palästinajahrbuch* 37 (1941), p. 93 n. 1; J. Grønbaek, *Die Geschichte vom Aufstieg Davids (1. Sam 15–2. Sam 5)* (Copenhagen, 1975), p. 226; H. Donner, *Geschichte des Volkes Israel*, p. 181; cf. K.-H. Hecke, *Juda und Israel* (Würzburg, 1985), p. 235.

2. D. Edelman, *PEQ* 117 (1985), pp. 85-91.

3. E. Eph'al, *The Ancient Arabs* (Leiden, 1982), p. 61; cf. C. Westermann, *Genesis* (BKAT, 1.17; Neukirchen–Vluyn, 1980), p. 485; E. Edel, *Die Ortsnamenlisten*, p. 31; S. Herrmann, *A History of Israel* (2nd edn), p. 52 n. 13.

4. The Peshitta has *gšwr*, and the Vulgate reads *gesuri*. This could indicate a mishearing in the long process of transmission.

this would suit the picture of Saul's policies, but if 2 Sam. 3.3 refers to the northern Geshur, this was an independent kingdom east of the Sea of Galilee. The reading 'Ashurites' (as being the more difficult reading) is most probably the right one.[1] Unfortunately, there is no information about where the territory of the Ashurites was located, but, as maintained before,[2] it may have been in Transjordan north of Gilead. One possibility would be to see Lodebar/Lidebir, mentioned below, as the capital of the Ashurites.

In concluding treaties with Jezreel and Abel-Meholah, the new king of the central highlands, Saul, managed to reduce the political and economic influence of Beth-Shan. An attack on the city itself could be expected, but first Saul probably wanted to have the way to Damascus and Transjordan north of the river Yarmuk under his own control, thus nullifying Beth-Shan's importance as a political center in charge of the trade through the valleys.

From the above it would not be improbable to find that Saul also campaigned against the Aramaeans ('the kings of Zobah'), as mentioned in 1 Sam. 14.47. This annalistic statement cannot be ignored. It also mentions campaigns against the Transjordanian states of Moab, Ammon and Edom. No details of these battles are mentioned; therefore this information has sometimes been seen to refer to the time of David.[3] Against this idea it an be objected that the deuteronomistic 'historian' most probably would not have given Saul such an honor when his intent was to minimize Saul's importance.[4] It seems likely that the statement in 1 Sam. 14.47-48 reflects some annalistic 'source' available to the writer of the Saulidic story which he used for his résumé about Saul, irrespective of his own anti-Saulidic attitude.[5] In trying to reconstruct Saul's strategy, we may see

---

1. Because 2 Sam. 2.9 refers to territories that had come under Saul's dominion through treaties or conquest, it would be difficult to prove that the Ashurites were 'Asherites' living in the territories of Benjamin and Ephraim.

2. G.W. Ahlström, *Who were the Israelites?*, p. 90.

3. Cf. H.J. Stoebe, *TZ* 21 (1965), pp. 270-71. According to Stoebe, 1 Sam. 14.47-52 is part of the redactional framework marking the ends of Saul's deeds. Literarily it can be compared with 2 Sam. 8 that mentions David's deeds (*Das erste Buch Samuelis* [KHAT, 8.1; Gütersloh, 1973), p. 277.

4. Cf. M.F. Unger, *Israel and the Aramaeans of Damascus*, pp. 43-44; O. Eissfeldt, 'The Hebrew Kingdom', *CAH*, II.2, p. 576.

5. See. H.W. Hertzberg, *I & II Samuel*, p. 232.

the wars in Transjordan against the Aramaeans and against the Amaleqites as preparations for his final thrust northwards; in other words, he wanted to eliminate Beth-Shan and then conquer the Jezreel Valley and Galilee. In securing the Transjordanian territories and southern Syria, Saul would have had the trade routes both to Damascus and to Sidon under his control. Galilee would have given him part of the route from Tyre to Damascus. With this the cities of the Jezreel Valley would have had no other choice but to be dependent upon Saul.

Taking the above into consideration, the city of Lodebar/Lidebir (Josh. 13.26) was of strategic importance for Saul's expansionist plans. It was on friendly terms with Saul, probably through a treaty. Indeed, we have a piece of information in 2 Sam. 9.1-13 that after Saul's defeat and death at Mt Gilboa Jonathan's crippled son had been taken to Lodebar. This would indicate that Lidebir/Lodebar was a city state or a principality which had had good relations with Saul and therefore could be a safe refuge for the defeated king's offspring. Later it was incorporated into David's kingdom,[1] because David gave the order that Jonathan's son, Meribaal, should be transferred to the king's court in Jerusalem. This having been done, Meribaal was also 'crippled' as a pretender to the throne.

The location of Lidebir/Lodebar[2] is not certain. F. Buhl located it at the southern end of the Sea of Galilee,[3] while Z. Kallai places it in northern Jordan just south of the Yarmuk river.[4] However, Amos 6.13 parallels Lodebar with Qarnaim, the area north of Yarmuk, while Josh. 13.26 mentions that Gad's territory included all towns of Gilead, 'as far as the territory of Lidebir'. This would imply that Lidebir lay to the north of the Yarmuk river. Its probable location would then be in the southern Golan controlling the 'entrance' to the Golan and the

---

1. Cf. 2 Sam. 17.27. For Lidebir as a city-state, cf. D. Edelman, 'The Rise of the Israelite State', pp. 118-25.

2. The spelling Lodebar, 'not a thing', is most probably a secondary and ironical rendering of the name. It is used, for instance, by the prophet Amos (6.13). Lidebir may be a non-Semitic name.

3. *Geographie des alten Palästina*, p. 79.

4. He identifies Lidebir/Lodebar with either Khirbet Umm ed-Dabar or with Ibdar, c. 10 km east of Gadara (see his remarks in *Historical Geography of the Bible*, p. 265).

Bashan. If this was the territory of the Ashurites, Saul would have managed to decrease Beth-Shan's military and economic sphere of interest.

As has been mentioned above, according to 1 Sam. 11.1-4 the Ammonite kingdom threatened the population of Gilead and gave the people of Jabesh-Gilead an ultimatum. Ammon apparently was expanding and most probably had increased its holdings north of the Jabbok river up to the Wadi Yabis.[1] As Saul expanded in Cisjordan, the Ammonite king Nahash must have been successful in extending his rule over most of Transjordan from Jabesh in the north to the Madaba plain in the south. Sooner or later the political and economic interests of these two rulers would collide. The occasion came when Nahash threatened the territory of Jabesh-Gilead. Being fully aware of the military superiority of the Ammonites, Jabesh-Gilead sought the help of the new military power in Cisjordan, Saul.

The city of Jabesh-Gilead (modern Tell Maqlûb, coord. 214-201)[2] may have been one of the important towns or city states in Transjordan because of its location by the river and on a trade route from Beth-Shan and the Jordan Valley to the 'Ajlun mountains and the King's Highway. Its commercial value must have made it desirable to the Ammonites.

The biblical narrative about the request for help from Jabesh-Gilead to Saul (1 Sam. 11) certainly reflects a historic conflict between the two powers on each side of the Jordan river. The report that the Ammonite king threatened to pull out everyone's right eye might also be trustworthy. This seems to have been an old and familiar custom. Assyrian inscriptions, for instance, refer to a punishment, *napālu* (*CAD*, 'to gouge out eyes, to blind'), which could refer to pulling out one eye.[3]

---

1. For the Ammonite attempts to expand in the pre-Saulidic era, see Judg. 3.13-14; 10.7-8; 11.

2. M. Noth, 'Jabes-Gilead: Ein Beitrag zur Methode alttestamentlicher Topographie', *ZDPV* 69 (1953), pp. 28-41 (= *Aufsätze*, pp. 476-88); J. Simons, *The Geographical and Topographical Texts*, p. 315; Y. Aharoni, *The Land of the Bible* (2nd edn), pp. 127-28; M. Ottosson, *Gilead*, pp. 195-96; D. Edelman, 'The Rise of the Israelite State', pp. 69-70.

3. Once, when fighting the Aḥlamu and Hanigalbat, 14,400 men were given that treatment; see R. Borger, *Einleitung in die assyrischen Königsinschriften* (Handbuch der Orientalistik, 1; Leiden, 1961), p. 57; cf. W. von Soden, 'Die Assyrer und der Krieg', *Iraq* 25 (1963), p. 137.

The Bible makes two contradictory statements about the relationship between the people of Jabesh-Gilead and the Israelites. In 1 Samuel 11 the former are treated as if they were Israelites themselves, but in 2 Sam. 2.4-7 they are non-Israelites who had made a treaty with king Saul, a treaty that David says he would continue. This 'invitation' to join David was perhaps also a threat. Their non-Israelite origin is also indicated by their practice of cremation in connection with Saul's death (1 Sam. 31.11-12). According to Israelite thinking, cremation would prevent the dead from entering the afterlife.[1]

Jabesh-Gilead's status as a vassal means that Saul was already king when he received the messengers and their request for assistance. His fame as a successful warrior-king must have been well-founded, which indicates that the Ammonite war occurred rather late in Saul's reign. Thus, his war against the Ammonites cannot have been one of the reasons for his kingship. The narrator has used this event for his presentation of Saul and his deeds leading to the kingship.[2] The narrative reflects the coronation ritual.[3] The chronology is therefore out of focus. It is possible that the story has been placed at the beginning of Saul's career in order to make him look like a judge and deliverer who only 'judged' the people for a short time. The aim would have been to minimize Saul's position as the first king of greater Israel so that that honor could go to David.

The narrative about the war with the Ammonites (1 Sam. 11 and 14.47) was composed long after Saul's reign. This is evident from the description of Saul's army. It says that Saul had 300,000 men[4] of

---

1. See e.g. D. Edelman, 'The Rise of the Israelite State', pp. 65-69; my *Who were the Israelites?*, pp. 86-87. For sites known for cremation, see P. Bienkowski, 'Some Remarks on the Practice of Cremation in the Levant', *Levant* 14 (1982), pp. 80-89.

2. W. Richter sees a holy-war pattern as having been utilized by the narrator (*Traditionsgeschichtliche Untersuchungen zum Richterbuch*, pp. 177-79). D. Edelman sees the plot in 1 Sam. 11 as a 'purposely constructed... šopēṭ-style tale', which has been 'removed from its historical context'. The purpose would have been to picture Saul as deliverer and judge (*ZAW* 96 [1984], p. 207).

3. B. Halpern has maintained that 1 Sam. 9–11 reflects the enthronement ritual, including designation, battle and coronation (*The Constitution of the Monarchy*, pp. 51-148).

4. Calculating that the soldiers came from families with at least two children, this would mean that the central hills would have had to support in excess of one million inhabitants!

Israel and 30,000 men of Judah under his banner (1 Sam. 11.8). This multitude is not only an exaggeration and as such the product of a religious attitude, but it is also a literary device reflecting the later idea that Judah was a tenth of Yahweh's people (cf. Isa. 6.13).[1] Because Saul defeated the Ammonites, he is given the honor of being a mighty king with an uncommonly large army that nobody would be able to withstand.

The Transjordanian war is not reported but only mentioned in the Hebrew Bible. There is, however, an indication in the Qumran version (4QSam[a]) and in Josephus (Ant. 6.68-71) that the Ammonite king had oppressed the people of Reuben and Gad, crushing their right eyes. Seven thousand men are supposed to have escaped to Jabesh-Gilead.[2] If this tradition is combined with 1 Chron. 5.10 (cf. vv. 18-22), which states that the (Arab) Hagrites had attacked the Reubenites during the time of Saul but were defeated, there is good reason to accept the existence of an old tradition about Israelite warfare in the Moabite territory (north of the Arnon river)[3] from the reign of Saul.[4] This tradition, however, has been remodeled after the political circumstances of the postexilic period and according to the ideas of the Chronicler.[5]

From the above discussion it can be concluded that Saul had been much more important personage than the biblical writer has made him. The Ammonite expansion was definitely stopped by Saul, who may have extended his rule down to the river Arnon, and who probably confined the Ammonite kingdom to a small region in the mountains around Rabbat-Ammon. With most of Transjordan and the central hills of Cisjordan north of the Jebusite city state of Jerusalem

1. See my article, 'Isaiah VI.13', *JSS* 19 (1974), p. 170.

2. See P.K. McCarter, *1 Samuel*, pp. 199-202.

3. According to Num. 32.33 and Josh. 13.8-9, the Reubenites and the Gadites lived in an area stretching from Ammon in the north to the river Arnon in the south. For the territory of Gad, see M. Ottosson, *Gilead*, pp. 126-28; C.H.J. de Geus, *The Tribes of Israel*, pp. 108-10; cf. M. Noth, 'Gilead und Gad', *ZDPV* 75 (1959), pp. 61-72 (*Aufsätze*, pp. 533-43).

4. It is also notable that Saul had Gadite officers in his army. They were among those who defected to David, according to 1 Chron. 12.8-15.

5. Cf. D. Edelman, 'The Rise of the Israelite State', pp. 72-76. The elaborations in the texts about the 'conquest' of Transjordan (for instance, Num. 21 and 22) are rather confusing and give the impression that the writer(s) did not know the geography or the historical events very well.

under his control,[1] Saul had created a territorial state that the greater Palestinian region had never seen before. Saul can therefore be regarded as the first state-builder in Palestine (see Map 13).[2] The tragedy was, however, that his 'building' fell apart.

The picture that emerges of how Saul rose to become the ruler of most of Palestine and Transjordan does not tally with the biblical theory of Saul's becoming king over all the Israelite tribes. If there was a 'tribal' unit or league called Israel covering most of Palestine before the time of Saul, one is forced to ask, with G. Fohrer, why Saul did not become king over this whole unit immediately.[3]

The final act in the political drama of Saul's rise and fall was the battle at Mt Gilboa (1 Sam. 31). The 'Philistine problem' was something Saul did not manage to solve. Instead, it caused the end of Saul, his dynasty and his kingdom. David's treacherous deeds also contributed to the destruction of the kingdom. There are no references to any large battles between the Philistines and Saul's army after the Michmash event. Some warfare is reported in connection with David's rise as a commander in the Israelite army. However, the emphasis in the textual material intends to glorify David rather than to describe the military encounters with the Philistines. Nevertheless, it seems that Saul's army managed to match the Philistines in such a way that they lost control over the central highlands.

One could ask why Saul chose to meet the Philistines in the Jezreel area at the western foothills of Gilboa. From the above presentation of Saul's political strategy, the answer is simply that, after having secured Transjordan and the highlands south of the Jezreel Valley, he was now ready to expand to the north and secure the Galilean region for his kingdom.[4] Beth-Shan was, however, a 'thorn in his side' and

---

1. Saul had no rule over the region south of the Jerusalem state; cf. S. Mowinckel, '"Rakelstämme" und "Leahstämme"', *Von Ugarit nach Qumran* (ed. O. Eissfeldt *et al.*), pp. 137-38; M.A. Cohen, 'The Role of the Shilonite Priesthood in the United Monarchy of Israel', *HUCA* 36 (1965), pp. 94-98; S. Herrmann, *A History of Israel* (2nd edn), p. 140. During the last five years of Saul's reign, David was his opponent in that territory.

2. Cf. I. Engnell, who calls him the first empire-builder ('Saul', *Svensk Bibliskt Uppslagsverk*, II [Stockholm, 1963], col. 889).

3. *TLZ* 111 (1961), pp. 903-904.

4. C.E. Hauer, 'The Shape of the Saulide Strategy', *CBQ* 31 (1969), pp. 153-67; cf. T. Koizumi, who maintains that Saul's move was aimed at conquering the cities of the Esdraelon Valley (*Annual of the Japanese Biblical Institute* 2 [1976],

had to be captured before he could march north. This must have been a provocation to the Philistines, who would be confined to the southern Palestinian coast and who, with their vassal David at Hebron, may have hoped for some control over the mountains of Judah, a territory lacking much strategic or economic importance. Saul's move north would have been intolerable to the Philistines, who came to the assistance of Beth-Shan.[1] After having mustered their armies at Aphek, they marched up to Shunem in the Jezreel plain (1 Sam. 29.11), thus camping a few miles north of Saul's army, which had its camp at the spring of Jezreel, according to 1 Sam. 29.1. It is quite possible that Saul, believing that his military strength was superior, had not thought to prepare himself for a hostile encounter with the Philistines at this time.

The battle was clearly a disaster for Saul and his forces. Saul could have made a tactical mistake in having his camp and his army on low ground at the 'spring of Jezreel'. The Philistine chariotry may have been able to create chaos in the Israelite infantry. Its soldiers fled up the mountain slopes. The short statement in 1 Sam. 31.2 mentions that Saul and three of his sons were killed. These were Jonathan, Abinadab and Malchishua. Saul was reputedly beheaded and his head carried to Philistia.[2] The bodies of Saul and his sons were hanged as trophies upon the city wall of Beth-Shan. Saul's armor was given as a (thank-)offering to Ashtarte and her temple at Beth-Shan. When they heard the news, the people of Jabesh-Gilead took down the bodies at night and cremated them at Jabesh-Gilead, burying them under 'the tamarisk' (1 Sam. 31.11-13). David's so-called lament over Saul and Jonathan (from the 'book of Yashar', that is, the 'upright one')[3] expresses the tragedy in the following words:

pp. 61-78); cf. D. Edelman, 'The Rise of the Israelite State', pp. 293-303; G.W. Ahlström, *Who were the Israelites?*, pp. 91-92.

1.   The political status of Beth-Shan at this time is not fully known. For quite some time it had been an Egyptian garrison city. With the collapse of the Egyptian empire the city may have become an independent city state in alliance with the Philistines and Megiddo.

2.   1 Sam. 31.9. P.K. McCarter sees this as a secondary addition (*1 Samuel*, p. 441).

3.   The 'Book of Yashar' is an unknown collection. David may have secondarily been associated with this 'pro-Saulidic' poem.

Alas, the gazelle (the princely one), Israel, on your mountain flanks is slain,
how the heroes have fallen![1]

There is no exact information in the Hebrew Bible about Saul's reign.
1 Sam. 13.1 shows that the deuteronomistic narrator knew neither
Saul's age[2] when he became king, nor how long his reign was, even if
he gives him two years.[3] Two Greek manuscripts (LXX, the Lucianic
version) have Saul 30 years old when he started his kingship. The
deuteronomistic formula for introducing a king has been used but is
problematic in this case. The two years given for his reign may be
incomplete or else may represent a corruption in the textual transmission.[4] It is also too short a time for all the activities of Saul. The
statement in 2 Sam. 2.10 that Saul's son, Eshbaal, was 40 years old
when he succeeded his father, and that he reigned for two years,
similarly seems to lack historical accuracy.[5] According to 1 Sam.
14.49 Saul had three sons, Jonathan, Ishvi (1 Sam. 31.2 has Abinadab)
and Malchishua, and two daughters, Merab and Michal. Eshbaal is not
mentioned in this connection, which points to the fact that he was born
later during Saul's reign. However, in 2 Sam. 2.10 Eshbaal is already
a man of c. 40 years. Again we have to face the problem that the
narrator did not have any exact information. The number 40 is often

1. Cf. D.N. Freedman, 'The Refrain in David's Lament over Saul and
Jonathan', in *Ex Orbe Religionum: Studia Geo Widengren oblata* (ed. C.J. Becker,
S.G.F. Brandon and M. Simon; Sup. to Numen: Studies in the History of Religions,
21-22; Leiden, 1972), pp. 115-26.
2. Cf. B.C. Birch, *The Rise of the Israelite Monarchy*, p. 77.
3. 'Saul was – years old when he became king and reigned two years over
Israel'. M. Noth maintains that two years for Saul's reign is intentional as being part
of the Deuteronomist's chronology. He also thinks that this short reign reflects the
historical reality (*Überlieferungsgeschichtliche Studien*, I, pp. 18-25 [Eng. *The
Deuteronomistic History* (JSOTSup, 15; Sheffield, 1981), pp. 21-22]; cf. *idem, The
History of Israel*, pp. 176-77). E. Robertson suggests that 1 Sam. 13.1 is taken
'from a tabular list, where the numbers were represented by letters of the alphabet.
As such the *bet nun* stands for 52'; in other words, Saul would have been 52 years
old when he became king; see *The Old Testament Problem* (Manchester, 1950),
p. 123; cf. P.R. Ackroyd (who estimates 50 years: *The First Book of Samuel* [The
Cambridge Bible Commentary on the New English Bible; Cambridge, 1971],
pp. 103-104).
4. Cf. P.K. McCarter, *1 Samuel*, pp. 222-23.
5. Josephus gives him both 40 years (*Ant.* 6.14, 9) and 20 years (*Ant.* 10.8, 4).
The writer of Acts 13.21 builds his information on the first passage in Josephus.

used for a generation[1] and/or for a grown-up person; thus the information here is that Eshbaal was no teenager. This would show that Saul
must have reigned more than two years, and probably for at least a
generation. As mentioned, Eshbaal is said to have reigned for only
two years, as did his father. The parallel with Saul is striking; from a
Judahite point of view these two kings should not be allowed too long
a reign. As in Egyptian royal inscriptions, the deeds of these
'disturbing' characters, who were not part of the Davidic dynasty
should be forgotton as much as possible. Since Saul could not be
completely dismissed, he must have been a much more important king
than the one the Judahite tradition has presented.[2] The notice about the
two years Saul is supposed to have ruled is probably the result of
literary manipulation.[3] Saul's reign would have to have lasted for at
least 22 years, if not 10 years more, in order for him to accomplish
everything ascribed to him in the Bible.

It is impossible to agree with M. Noth that the kingdom of Saul
should be characterized as a short episode in the history of Israel.[4]
Neither is it possible to agree with H. Donner that Saul's state was a
national army kingdom ('Heerkönigtum'), the only purpose of which
was to arrest the Philistine threat, and that a state administration

1.   The chronological problem of Israel's first four kings, Saul, Eshbaal, David
and Solomon, seems to be impossible to solve. The latter two, for instance, are said
to have reigned for 40 years each; in other words, the narrator did not have the exact
information.

2.   The so-called rejection of Saul has not originated, as far as I can understand,
in 'later prophetical circles', as has been maintained; see, for instance, A.D.H. Mayes,
'The Period of the Judges and the Rise of the Monarchy', *Israelite and Judean
History* (ed. J.H. Hayes and J.M. Miller), p. 330; cf. also R.A. Carlson, *David, the
Chosen King*, p. 50. The 'rejection' is a literary product motivated by political
concerns that has been draped in the garb of the divine will. It is natural from this
point of view that Saul's attitude toward his rebellious officer, David, should have
been that of a deadly enemy. That was his duty in order to save his kingdom. Saul
thus cast his 'evil eye' on David; cf. E. Lipiński, *Rivista di Studi Fenici* 2 (1974),
p. 53. The Jerusalemite tradition has expressed this by having an 'evil spirit' take
hold of Saul, and modern scholars have fallen into the trap and declared Saul insane!

3.   In the Sumerian king list, the years of a king's reign are sometimes not mentioned. Also, a name can be missing; see T. Jacobsen, *The Sumerian King List*
(Assyriological Studies, 11; Chicago, 1939), pp. 21-22 and 79.

4.   *Geschichte des Volkes Israel* (3rd edn), pp. 152-65 (Eng. edn pp. 164-78);
cf. K.-H. Hecke, *Juda und Israel*, p. 233.

would therefore not have been necessary.[1] Religiously, Saul's kingdom is not supposed to have had a state religion.[2] In these cases scholars have been misled by what the political propaganda from Jerusalem has presented. No state could function without an administration, and administrative affairs included religion. The enthronement was as much a religious act as a civil one. The deity, according to whose will a person was chosen and enthroned, was the guarantor of the state, as well as in principle the nation's king. The earthly king was his vice-regent. The state was the territory of the god; religiously it was his 'cosmos'.[3]

It is true that the Bible does not provide very much information about Saul's administration. Neither is there a full picture of David's or Solomon's administrative apparatus. There are, however, a few passages mentioning Saul's high officials. Abner was his highest general (1 Sam. 14.50; 17.55), even if Saul himself must be understood as the supreme commander. First priest of the kingdom was Ahijah, a Shilonite, brother of Ichabod (1 Sam. 14.3, 18). This may show that Shilonite traditions became part of the official religion of the new kingdom. An 'Edomite', Doeg, was the supervisor of the shepherds,[4] which could mean that he was in charge of the temple herds (1 Sam. 21.8[7]). Runners[5] and other servants are mentioned in 22.6-7, 9, 14, 17, and 16.17. These would include his officers, guardsmen and other court officials. To give a complete list of the administrative personnel was not the narrator's purpose, but from the little that is mentioned it must be concluded that Saul had built up an efficient administration. The religious center for his administration seems to have been at Gibeon, where Yahweh from Paran, Seir and Teman was worshipped.[6] As we know, the sanctuary at Gibeon was still the most important cult place in the kingdom at the beginning of Solomon's reign (1 Kgs 3.4-15).[7]

1. *Geschichte des Volkes Israel*, p. 180.
2. C. Hauer, 'Anthropology in Historiography', *JSOT* 39 (1987), p. 18.
3. See further my *Royal Administration and National Religion*, pp. 1-9.
4. P.K. McCarter reads 'the chief of Saul's runners', but says that 'textual support is lacking' (*1 Samuel*, p. 348).
5. Those running in front of the king's chariot (cf. 1 Sam. 8.11).
6. Cf. Deut. 33.2; Judg. 5.4; Hab. 3.3. For Yahweh coming from the Edomite territory, see my article, 'The Travels of the Ark: A Religio-Political Composition', *JNES* 43 (1984), pp. 141-49, and cf. my *Who were the Israelites?*, pp. 59, 92.
7. This may indicate that Gibeon once was the capital. In Josh. 10.2 it is called

Saul's kingdom, as well as its reconstitution by David, was possible because there were no superpowers in the Near East at that particular time. 'History' is seldom dominated by small political communities. It is most often acted out by the constellation of dominant powers. Because there was no such nation in Syria-Palestine during the time after the period of the 'Sea Peoples' until the rise of the neo-Assyrian empire, an opportunity presented itself for the creation of a larger political entity in this part of the Near East, which, geographically, was not inviting for the creation of a large territorial state. Three men tried to fill the vacuum: Hadadezer of Aram-Zobah, Nahash of Ammon and Saul of Israel. All three seem to have succeeded for a short time, but all three saw their hopes smashed. The most short-lived kingdom was that of Ammon. From the wing of the political stage a fourth man soon entered, one who managed to become master of Palestine and parts of Syria: David. For a few generations the peoples of Syria-Palestine would be part of an artificial political unit.

'the great city', an adjective that is also used for the capital of Jerusalem in Jer. 22.8 and for Nineveh in Jon. 1.2 and 3.2; cf. D.J. Wiseman, *Nebuchadrezzar and Babylon* (The Schweich Lectures of the British Academy, 1983; Oxford, 1985), p. 42.

Chapter 11

PALESTINE UNDER DAVID AND SOLOMON

David

Who was David?[1] The biblical tradition gives little information about David's family. He is said to be the son of Jesse of Bethlehem (1 Sam. 16; 17.57). A tradition in the book of Ruth (4.18-22) preserves the memory that Jesse's family was partly of Moabite descent.[2] In the biblical traditions Bethlehem is counted a city of Judah, but, because the town was located just south of Jerusalem and close to the Benjaminite territory,[3] it is doubtful that it was considered part of any 'Judah' before the creation of the kingdom Judah under David. Bethlehem may have been part of the Jebusite kingdom of Jerusalem since the Amarna period; in this case it would have been located outside Saul's kingdom.[4] David's nationality, if we can speak about

1.   The narratives about David and his rise to kingship cannot be separated from the stories about Saul. The David story is a natural sequence to the narratives about Saul and his fate. We thus here have a meaningful composition by one narrator who certainly has used some earlier traditions, but has shaped them to reflect his own understanding. A. Alt maintained that the account is a 'creation of a genuine historian who conceals rather than reveals his historical purpose' (*Essays on Old Testament History*, p. 268 [= *KS*, II, p. 40]). Cf. also J. Van Seters, *In Search of History*, p. 270. The narrator of these events makes his own perspective known through the persons in the drama (A. Weiser, 'Die Legitimation des Königs David: Zur Eigenart und Entstehung der sogen. Geschichte des Davids Aufstieg', *VT* 16 [1966], p. 333).

2.   It is thus understandable that David asked the king of Moab for protection for his parents during his days as a fugitive and his rebellion against Saul (1 Sam. 22.3-4).

3.   Cf. S. Herrmann, who says that 'we can easily imagine a pull towards Benjamin' (*A History of Israel* [2nd edn], p. 140).

4.   See my article, 'Was David a Jebusite Subject?', *ZAW* 92 (1980), pp. 285-87. The genealogy of Caleb in 1 Chron. 2.50-51 makes Shobal, the father of Kiriath-jearim, a brother of Salma, father of Benjamin.

nationalities at this time, was neither Israelite nor Judahite. Ethnically he may be considered an indigenous Canaanite (–Calebite) from the hills of Judah. 1 Chron. 2.50-51 lists Bethlehem as Calebite. The names of David's brothers may support this conclusion.[1] This would indicate that David was one of the many (?) young men who saw in Saul's kingdom and his army a greater opportunity for a career than the home territory could offer.[2]

David began his career at Saul's court as the king's armor-bearer (1 Sam. 16.14). There are two traditions about how David came to serve Saul. The first mentions a young warrior who was introduced to the king because he was 'skillful in playing, a *gibbôr ḥayil'* (i.e. a hero), 'a man of war, prudent in speech' (1 Sam. 16.18). Such men were always appreciated at court. The other tradition places the first meeting between Saul and David at the battle against the Philistines in the Elah valley, where David, a 'shepherd boy', is said to have slain the giant Goliath, a meeting that is said to have surprised Saul. Of course, that is the idea of the writer, whose work is more literary art[3] than a report of actual events. The aim of the latter tradition is to create a humble background for the person who became the most important king in the history of Israel and Judah. The story about David and Goliath is part of the legendary material that has been

1. Eliab, Abinadab, Shimea/Shammah, Nethanel, Raddai, Ozema (1 Chron. 2.12-14). A sister had the name Zeruiah (12.16). In 1 Chron. 27.18 a brother of David, Elihu, is mentioned, a name which sometimes has been seen as a variant for Eliab (cf. the LXX). However, according to 1 Sam. 16.10-11 Jesse had eight sons. For Bethlehem's close connections with Gibeonite Kiriath-jearim, see P.K. McCarter, *II Samuel*, pp. 176, 450.

2. That Bethlehem was not part of Saul's kingdom may be concluded from 1 Sam. 16.4. When Samuel went to Bethlehem (in order to anoint David), the elders of the town 'came to meet him trembling (*ḥrd*) and said: "Do you come in peace?"' The Hebrew *ḥrd* is etymologically related to Ugaritic *ḥrd*, 'warrior, army'; cf. M.C. Astour, 'Place Names', *Ras Shamra Parallels*, II (ed. L.R. Fisher; Rome, 1975), p. 297; cf. R.R. Stieglitz 'Ugaritic *ḥrd* "Warrior": A Hurrian Loanword', *JAOS* 101 (1981), pp. 371-72. The elders of Bethlehem apparently were armed when they met Samuel, prepared to defend of their city. However, they still could have been trembling, not knowing the purpose of the visit of the prophet from a neighboring kingdom.

3. Cf. M. Kessler, 'Narrative Technique in 1 Sam. 16, 1-13', *CBQ* 32 (1970), pp. 543-54. As to the composition, cf. also J.T. Willis, 'The Function of Comprehensive Anticipatory Redactional Joints in 1 Samuel 16–18', *ZAW* 85 (1973), pp. 294-314.

woven around the famous king.[1] Both traditions about David's arrival at the court of Saul (chs. 16 and 17) describe a young warrior,[2] with the difference that the latter intentionally has underscored his boyishness by using the shepherd motif. Picturing David as a young shepherd who slew the 'giant' Goliath and thus saved the Israelites is a literary device calculated to generate associations with the famous 'shepherd', King David. The great success that followed David is part of the literary activity of enhancing David's position as the divinely chosen king. It must be realized that some of the heroic acts of David's men could have been credited to David after he became king. The Goliath story is one clear example.[3]

Another feature to be noticed is that David is said to be a *na'ar* in 1 Sam. 17.33, 42. The term is placed in comparison with *'îš milḥāmâ*, 'man of war'. 1 Samuel 17 depicts David as a young, inexperienced warrior in his confrontation with Goliath. The Hebrew word *na'ar* often is used as a technical term for a warrior of lower rank, a young man acting as a squire or servant of one of the nobles.[4]

1. For 1 Sam. 17 as a legendary story, associated with 16.14-23 and written for the purpose of showing that Yahweh is now with David and not with Saul, see H.J. Stoebe, 'Die Goliathperikope 1. Sam XVII 1–XVIII 5 und die Textform der Septuaginta', *VT* 6 (1956), pp. 397-413.

2. R. Alter has here misread the Hebrew text and makes David an 'Ephraimite farm boy' (*The Art of Biblical Narrative* [New York, 1981], p. 119). J.A. Soggin sees David as a 'Judean of modest birth' (*A History of Ancient Israel*, p. 45).

3. In 2 Sam. 21.19 Elhanan, son of Jaare-'Oregim from Bethlehem, is said to have killed Goliath, and in 2 Sam. 23.24-26 it is Elhanan, son of Dodo, from Bethlehem. It has been maintained that Elhanan was David's original name (A.M. Honeyman, 'The Evidence for Regnal Names among Hebrews', *JBL* 67 [1948], pp. 23-24; L.M. von Pakozdy, 'Elhanan—der frühere Name Davids', *ZAW* 68 [1956], p. 251; J. Bright, *A History of Israel* [3rd edn], p. 192). I also have positively assessed this theory (*Psalm 89*, p. 37). Because of the corrupt state of the text and the fact that Jaare-'Orgim is not a personal name (*'ōrᵉgîm* means 'weavers'), we can only state that the narrator has not been very knowledgeable, or the event has been attributed to several persons, among them two Elhanans (!) from the same city, which is less probable.

4. See J. MacDonald, 'The Status and Rank of the Na'ar in Israelite Society', *JNES* 35 (1976), pp. 147-70; cf. his 'The Role and Status of the *suḥaru* in the Mari Correspondence', *JAOS* 96 (1976), pp. 57-68; also A.F. Rainey, 'Military Personnel of Ugarit', *JNES* 24 (1965), pp. 17-27; H.-P. Stähli, *Knabe–Jüngling–Knecht* (Beitr. z. Biblische Exegese und Theologie, 7; Frankfurt a.M., 1978). For the meaning 'steward' of a household, estate, see N. Avigad, 'New Light on the

We soon find David as one of Saul's officers, a 'commander of a thousand' (*'elep*), perhaps commander over a company (1 Sam. 18.13). He was a rapidly rising star in Saul's entourage, and, according to the narrative, he was more successful than the king (1 Sam. 18.5-16). That in itself was a threat to the throne. In order to protect his position and his dynasty, Saul had, logically, no other choice than to try to stop David. Unfortunately for Saul, he did not succeed in this.[1] The narrator has used this failure in his own way and has in his pro-Davidic attitude denounced Saul in such a way that modern scholars have followed suit and declared Saul mentally disturbed or insane.[2] This 'Shakespearean'[3] presentation of the conflict between the king and David is good literature, but it is doubtful that the pro-Davidic writer is a good historian. The presentation of David's life as a courtier in Saul's service reads more like an artistic novella than critical historiography. The role that Jonathan and Michal play in this composition is 'prophetic' in the sense that they 'knew' that their father should not be the king. The author's primary purpose is to advocate that David had been chosen by Yahweh, and that therefore Saul had been abandoned by Yahweh.[4] Literarily two opposite motifs are at work. The more successful David is, the more unlucky and 'mentally disturbed' Saul must become. David's rise should parallel Saul's fall. In such a literary product the historical details are of less importance. These stories are the product of a legitimacy problem surrounding the Davidic dynasty. What is true is that a king could not have a subordinate more successful than the king himself. Saul's hot

Na'ar Seals', *Magnalia Dei* (ed. F.M. Cross *et al.*; Garden City, NY, 1976), pp. 294-300.

1. For a realistic appraisal of Saul's psychological dilemma and his logical actions, see J. Pedersen, *Israel*, I-II (Copenhagen, 1926), pp. 185-87.

2. Cf. J. Bright (Saul was 'too hagridden to think clearly', and he was driven 'by insane jealousy' [*A History of Israel* (3rd edn, p. 193)]); J.A. Soggin (Saul suffered 'from serious psychological disturbances' [*A History of Ancient Israel*, p. 49]); see also H. Donner, *Geschichte des Volkes Israel*, p. 183. Donner thinks that the worldly functions of kingship had come into conflict with Israel's sacred traditions and Saul was unable to cope with this conflict.

3. Cf. my review article, 'Aspects of the Bible as Literature', *JR* 64 (1984), p. 524.

4. The 'blood-brother' ceremony between the crown-prince Jonathan and David similarly is literary fiction. By the way, how did any historian know what was said in private between Jonathan and David?

pursuit of David led the latter to became a fugitive, gathering around himself elements who for one reason or another were malcontent or who were pure adventurers and probably not Israelites, as, for instance, the Cherethites and the Pelethites. For a time David and his men roamed around in the wilderness of Judah ('no man's land'), but as time passed he could not find any safe place because of Saul's activities.[1] It is also possible that the population in the hills of Judah did not give David too much support. Even if they were not subjects of Saul, they did not like to side with the rebellious leader. David finally went over to the Philistines. He was well received by King Achish of Gath, who saw in David an ally against Saul (1 Sam. 27). This move by David was a setback for Saul. David could turn out to be dangerous to Israel by helping the Philistines to plan their next move against Saul.

After a while David got a Philistine city of his own, Ziklag, where he and his entourage could settle (1 Sam. 27.6). The location of this city is unknown. Several suggestions have been made, such as Tell el-Huweilife, c. 48 km NNE of Beer-Sheba,[2] or, more probably, Tell eš-Šari'a, about 48 km NNW of Beer-Sheba.[3] The latter is on the border of the Negev, and the excavations there have revealed that there was no destruction in the transition from the Iron I to the Iron II period. This would support the suggestion that Ziklag may have been located at Tell eš-Šari'a.[4] During his time as a mercenary captain or vassal of the Philistines, David, with Ziklag as his base, undertook several military raids exterminating people in the areas south of the Judean hills and down to the border of Egypt. In these raids he spared nobody— total warfare—thus no reports could get to Achish at Gath. The king

1. Saul's plans to capture David show his determination, but the writer has also twisted this in order to serve his purpose of showing Saul to be a bad loser.

2. K. Elliger (*apud* A. Alt), 'Die dreissig Helden Davids', *Palästinajahrbuch* 31 (1935), p. 69.

3. Y. Aharoni, *The Land of the Bible* (2nd edn), pp. 291, 443; E.D. Oren, *BA* 45 (1982), pp. 155-66.

4. Oren, *BA* 45 (1982), p. 163. F. Crüsemann suggests that Tel Māśōś may have been the ancient Ziklag ('Überlegeungen zur identifikation der Hirbet el-Mšāš [Tel Māśōś]', *ZDPV* 89 [1973], pp. 218-24); J.D. Seger identifies Tel Halif with Ziklag ('Investigations at Tel Halif, Israel, 1976–1980', *BASOR* 252 [1983], p. 15). Both these places are, however, located more inland; Halif is c. 10 km east of eš-Šari'a. Thus with its location on the border between the Philistines and the Negev, Tell eš-Šari'a would be a more probable location.

only learned from David that the raids were against the peoples of Judah's Negev, or Jerahmeel's Negev, or the Negev of the Kenites (1 Sam. 27.10-12), that is, against the enemies of the Philistines. Because Saul gave up pursuing David when he went over to the Philistines, the places in the Negev in which David operated cannot have been under Saul's rule.

The possibility that David contemplated a new career with the Philistines cannot be dismissed.[1] Having been unable to succeed in establishing himself, for the time being, in the hill country, he may have aspired to some feudal lordship within the Philistine power structure. With the help of the Philistines he may have hoped to build his own kingdom in the sparsely settled territory of Judah. He played a double game. The booty he took from his raids he shared with the elders of the few towns in the Judean hills. In this way David engaged in terrorist activities in the southern part of Palestine that forced the elders of the villages of Judah to be on friendly terms with the new 'Philistine' warlord. The story of how David treated the Amaleqites (1 Sam. 30) is a good example of his activities. The abandonment and/or destruction of several settlements in the Negev around 1000 BCE should be considered in connection with David's activities. For instance, Tel Māśōś (Khirbet el-Meshash) stratum I was abandoned, according to the excavators, c. 1000 BCE or in the tenth century.[2] The end of stratum II is dated to the eleventh century.[3] We may not go too wrong if we take seriously the possibility that David was the cause of the abandonment or destruction of certain sites in the Negev.[4] The eastern and central Negev were mainly Edomite and David's hostility toward the Edomites may have started already during his time as a Philistine warlord. His double game benefitted both the Philistines and himself. Achish of Gath may have appreciated that David extended Philistine power in the south and southwest, which must have been a setback for

---

1. Cf. N.P. Lemche, 'Davids vej til tronen', *DTT* 38 (1975), p. 252.

2. In their final report, V. Fritz and A. Kempinski have lowered the date of the abandonment of the settlement (*Ergebnisse der Ausgrabungen auf der Ḥirbet el-Mśāś*, I, p. 230).

3. For Tel Māśōś being settled by Canaanites, see my article in *ZDPV* 100 (1984), pp. 35-52.

4. Another reason for the abandonment of Tel-Māśōś may have been climatic change; for instance, an extended drought would have made the site uninhabitable.

Saul's political aspirations. At the same time David's raids in the south began the firm establishment of his own political power base.

There is no information about when exactly David made himself king in Hebron. 2 Sam. 2.1-4 seems to give the impression that it was only when Saul was dead. The peoples of the Judean hills are said to have 'elected' their self-appointed protector and anointed him king.[1] However, vv. 5-7 could indicate that David had already begun his kingship before Saul's death. We learn that when David, who was king in Hebron, heard that the men of Jabesh-Gilead in Transjordan had buried the bodies of Saul and his sons, he sent messengers to Jabesh-Gilead expressing his appreciation for this act. The real purpose of the message, however, was to have the people of Jabesh-Gilead acknowledge David as their new king. He refers to the treaty relationship (*hesed*) that existed between them and Saul and tells them that he is now going to 'do good' for them; in other words, they should accept him as their new lord.[2] It is possible that the following verse underscores the seriousness of David's message: 'strengthen your hands and be valiant!' This sounds like a declaration of war if the men of Jabesh-Gilead would not accept David as their new king.[3] It is doubtful that David succeeded in gaining their loyalty at this point in time. The kingdom of Eshbaal, Saul's son, must have made it impossible for the Gileadites to accept David as their overlord (2 Sam. 2.9). Politically, the message to the Gileadites was meant to diminish Saul's territory and weaken his successor's power as much as possible. Perhaps it even was an attempt to hinder the rebuilding of Saul's kingdom under Eshbaal. David's 'demands' to the men of Jabesh-Gilead signaled that a new voice was going to be heard in the politics of the area of greater Palestine.

1. This does not necessarily mean that the anointment was done without a priest's participation.

2. For the diplomatic meaning of '*āśâ ṭôbâ* (Akkadian *ṭabuta epēšu*), see W.L. Moran, 'A Note on the Treaty Terminology of the Sefire Stelas', *JNES* 22 (1963), pp. 173-76; cf. D. Hillers, *BASOR* 176 (1964), pp. 46-47; R. Frankena, 'The Vassal-Treaties of Esarhaddon and the Dating of Deuteronomy', *OTS* 14 (1965), pp. 134-40; T. Mettinger, *King and Messiah*, p. 173; M. Fox, '*Ṭôb* as Covenant Terminology', *BASOR* 209 (1973), pp. 41-42; P.K. McCarter, *II Samuel*, pp. 84-85. For its use as technical treaty language specifically in 2 Sam. 2.5-7, see D. Edelman, *ZAW* 96 (1984), pp. 201-203.

3. Cf. S. Herrmann, *A History of Israel*, pp. 152-53.

David's Hebronite kingdom probably comprised most of the hills of Judah south of Bethlehem and the areas in the south that he had raided as a Philistine warlord. Ziklag would have been counted as part of Judah at this time (1 Sam. 27.6). With the Hebronite Kingdom 'foreign' elements became part of the ethnic picture of Judah. A. Malamat's reconstruction of the expansion of the Davidic kingdom fails from the very beginning.[1] His phase recreates a 'tribal kingdom' comprising the 'House of Judah', but the above has shown that David's kingdom reached outside the limits of the hills of Judah. It should be re-emphasized that a tribe of Judah most certainly did not exist at this time and most likely never existed in the premonarchic period.[2] As mentioned before, Judah was very sparsely settled. It was later inhabited by different clans, such as Calebites, Kenites, Othnielites and Jerahmeelites,[3] but when that occurred is impossible to say. Under David all the people of the Judean hills became Judahites. Judah now became a national term.[4]

After Saul's death the political scene in Palestine thus shifted. Instead of a large nation comprising most of the hill country north of Jerusalem and reaching over into Transjordan, two smaller kingdoms hostile to each other emerged. The peoples of the other side of the plain (Jezreel) fled, and the Philistines are said to have occupied their cities (1 Sam. 31.7).[5] That would mean that the territory Eshbaal

1. The development 'can be likened to five concentric rings in progression': (1) tribal kingdom; (2) national kingdom; (3) consolidated territorial state; (4) multi-national state; (5) empire' ('A Political Look at the Kingdom of David and Solomon and its Relations with Egypt', *Studies in the Period of David and Solomon* [ed. T. Ishida; Tokyo, 1982], p. 192).

2. For the tribe of Judah as an artificial construction by the later historiographer, see S. Mowinckel, *Tetrateuch–Pentateuch–Hexateuch*, p. 66; N.H. Snaith, *Isaiah 40–66* (VTSup, 14; Leiden, 1967), p. 237 n. 5. According to M.A. Cohen, Judah was not 'a viable political entity... before the time of David' (*HUCA* 36 [1965], p. 79).

3. Eshbaal's commander, Abner, calls himself a 'chief of Caleb which belongs to Judah' when he threatens Eshbaal (2 Sam. 3.8). The Masoretes have read *keleb*, 'dog', instead of Caleb. P.K. McCarter follows the LXX and omits *'šr lyhwdh*, 'which belongs to Judah' (*II Samuel*, p. 106).

4. Cf. the discussion of this subject in G.W. Ahlström, *Who were the Israelites?*, pp. 42-43.

5. The text further mentions that the peoples on the other side of the Jordan also fled when they saw what happened at Gilboa. One just wonders, however, how anybody on the other side of the Jordan river could see what had happened at Gilboa

ruled over must have been smaller than that of his father. How much of the land came under direct Philistine rule is not mentioned. We may conclude that the lowlands and valleys were firmly in Philistine hands, but the hills of Ephraim do not seem to have been occupied by the Philistines. From a political point of view, it must not have been seen as necessary.

As mentioned above, Jabesh-Gilead stayed with Saul's son, Eshbaal (2 Sam. 2.8-9), who, supported by Abner, ascended the throne of Israel with Mahanaim as his (temporary?) capital. The choice of capital indicates that any place in the central hills of Cisjordan was probably unsafe because of the Philistine threat as well as the threat from David. Eshbaal's kingdom included, according to 2 Sam. 2.9, Israel of the hills, Ephraim and Benjamin, as well as the Ashurites,[1] Jabesh-Gilead and Jezreel. Thus, the city of Jezreel would have been a border city to the Philistine sphere of interest. The Philistines had again established—for a short time—their dominion over Palestine. They may have been delighted to see Israel and Judah at war with each other (2 Sam. 2.12–3.1). They did not interfere. A drawn-out conflict between Israel and Judah would only benefit the Philistines, who did not want to see David become too powerful. The Philistines probably did not object to David's Hebronite kingship since they apparently did not stop their vassal from becoming king.[2] The sparsely populated Judean hills were of no great importance to them. For David to sit in Hebron instead of Ziklag would only mean that he was more on the sideline and out of sight than before.

(c. 15 km or 10 miles away). Since the weather is mostly hazy, it would have been impossible to see the people who were running on the slopes of the mountains of Cisjordan. P.K. McCarter says that 'the other side of Jordan' represents an expanded reading (*I Samuel*, p. 441).

1.   The Ashurites present a special problem. I have seen them as a group of people north of Jabesh-Gilead. The text is probably postexilic and may refer to a people living in Transjordan in a territory supposedly ruled by Eshbaal; cf. my *Who were the Israelites?*, pp. 88-90. E. Edel has seen the Ashurites as Dedanites (*Die Ortsnamenliste*, p. 31). D. Edelman suggests that the Ashurites should be seen as an Asherite enclave located in the western foothills of Ephraim (*PEQ* 117 [1985], pp. 85-91). According to E.A. Knauf, Psalm 83, which also mentions the Ashurites, is postexilic (*Ismael*, p. 10). For this issue, see the previous full discussion and the bibliography cited on pp. 442-43.

2.   On this, cf. the points made by J. Bright (*A History of Israel* [3rd edn], p. 196).

The first confrontation between Israel and Judah occurred at the old capital of Gibeon (c. 10 km north of Jerusalem as the crow flies). The battle went in favor of Judah, but was obviously not followed up (2 Sam. 2.12-32). The state of warfare continued for some time (3.1), but not much is said about it. The narrator's horizon, as usual, is filled with stories about personalities and their conflicts, court intrigues, and so forth. Abner, Eshbaal's commander-in-chief, may have understood that David was growing stronger as time passed. It was probably during Eshbaal's reign that David married a daughter of Talmai, king of Geshur (2 Sam. 3.3). This must have been done both in order to undermine Eshbaal's position and in order to 'gain an ally in Eshbaal's rear'.[1]

After having been denied marriage to one of Saul's wives, Rizpah, Abner should have understood that he would not reach his goal in Israel.[2] Consequently, a future with the successful David was a more attractive prospect. He apparently offered David his services, promising to place all Israel under David's scepter (2 Sam. 3.6-10). As a condition David demanded that Abner get (back) Saul's daughter Michal for him.[3] With Michal as his wife, David the pretender could appear to be the rightful claimant to the throne in Israel and a legitimate successor to Saul. When Abner arrived at Hebron with a delegation of 20 men after fulfilling the condition, he was well-received and promised to deliver Israel to David. When he left the city, Joab, returning from a raid, heard about the negotiations and sent messengers to Abner. He returned and met Joab in the city gate. In the custom of the country they embraced, but Joab had a knife in his hand and ended Abner's life (2 Sam. 3.26-27).

1.   J. Bright, *A History of Israel* (3rd edn), p. 197. D. Edelman maintains that Talmai was the king of southern Geshur with Tel Māśōś as its capital (*JNES* 47 [1988], pp. 253-58).

2.   To marry the late king's wife would have made Abner a legitimate heir to the throne.

3.   Some have doubted that Michal was ever married to David before she arrived in Hebron; cf. H.J. Stoebe, 'David und Mikal: Überlegungen zur Jugendgeschichte Davids', *Von Ugarit nach Qumran* (BZAW, 77; Berlin, 1958), pp. 224-43. This may be right, because David sends the message to Eshbaal, not to Abner. However, Z. Ben-Barak has Akkadian parallels for the legality of a man reclaiming his former wife ('The Legal Background of the Restoration of Michal to David', *Studies in the Historical Books of the Old Testament* [ed. J.A. Emerton; VTSup, 3; Leiden, 1979], pp. 15-29).

The murder of Abner was seemingly a setback for David's plans. The people of Israel would certainly hold David responsible for it. David could not afford to punish Joab, but in order to free himself from suspicion, he ordered a state funeral and lamented Abner's death (2 Sam. 3.31-34).[1] Still, his way to kingship over Israel seemed to be blocked. Soon Eshbaal was murdered, however, and the Israelites offered David a treaty, accepting him as their king (2 Sam. 5.1-2). The Chronicler has an interesting piece of information about the meeting in Hebron. According to 1 Chron. 12.39-40, the elders of Israel were followed by representatives of their neighbors from Issachar, Zebulon and Naphtali. This would support the above-mentioned theory that territorially, Israel confined to the hill country. The Jezreel Valley and Galilee did not count as parts of the territory of Israel.[2] Also, in the case of Eshbaal's murder, David acted as if he were innocent and had the murderers put to death (2 Sam. 4.5-12). In this way David publicly announced that he was not involved in the conspiracy against Eshbaal.

The details may be questioned, but the underlying history seems to be that Eshbaal was murdered after a few years' reign and David's innocence in the matter must be questioned. The two murders suited David's purposes too well and his reactions as given in the texts are not convincing. Thus, it is likely that he had encouraged the deeds. The obvious zeal of the editor to exonerate David, the fact that he protests too much, leads the to suspicion that he was indeed a conspirator in Abner's death.[3]

David was now king over both Judah and Israel, which included parts of Transjordan and Galilee. His kingdom had more than doubled in size. The status of Israel and the Galileans would best be expressed by the term 'union'. When David was offered the kingship, a treaty,

---

1. Abner is positively judged by the narrator. His treason against Eshbaal opened the way for David; cf. J.H. Grønbaek, *Die Geschichte vom Aufstieg Davids*, pp. 235-36.

2. Cf. G.W. Ahlström and D. Edelman, *JNES* 44 (1985), pp. 59-61; G.W. Ahlström, *Who were the Israelites?*, p. 95.

3. J.C. Vanderkam, 'Davidic Complicity in the Deaths of Abner and Eshbaal: A Historical and Redactional Study', *JBL* 99 (1980), p. 533; cf. K.W. Whitelam, *The Just King*, p. 108. See also F.H. Cryer, 'David's Rise to Power and the Death of Abner', *VT* 35 (1985), pp. 385-94. It should be noted that it is the narrator's opinion that is expressed in the text, and because the character of the text is an *apologia Davidica*, David's motivation can only be guessed.

b*rît*, was established between the two parties, and David was again the center of a ritual of investiture (2 Sam. 5.1, 3). This union of two nations centered on the shared king,[1] but this in itself did not necessarily result in the intermixing and integrating of the two political units.[2]

With David as king over both Judah and Israel, most of Palestine had come under one ruler. The exceptions were the coastal areas and the city state of Jerusalem. The latter was now surrounded by the new kingdom. Under the circumstances, Philistines who dominated the coastal areas might have forged an alliance with Jerusalem when they saw how David had upset political balance. According to 2 Sam. 5.17, the Philistines marched up into the hills and into the Valley of Rephaim when they heard that David also had become king over Israel. This would indicate that the first confrontation between David and his former Philistine lords took place before Jerusalem was taken by David. When David heard about the Philistine move, he 'went down to the stronghold' (5.17), which may refer to Adullam in the lowlands, c. 25 km SW of Jerusalem.[3] He defeated them at Baal-Perazim.[4] Among the trophies David and his men carried away were the god statues that the Philistines had brought with them (5.20), as was the custom of the day. Capturing the images meant that their power had

1.   On this, see A. Alt, 'Die Staatenbildung der israeliten in Palästina', *KS*, II, pp. 33-65. A. Malamat prefers to call it a 'Realunion' because it would be a 'single legal entity in its external aspect'. It had a common foreign policy, and 'a united army' ('A Political Look at the Kingdom of David and Solomon and its Relations with Egypt', *Studies* [ed. T. Ishida], p. 194). This modern terminology may be misleading. Any union between peoples in ancient times could not have more than one foreign policy maker. And what is meant by a 'united army'? Israel's position within the Davidic kingdom was from the beginning that of a nation which saw itself as on par with Judah. After Sheba's uproar, Israel was 'demoted' to the secondary level of a vassal.

2.   David 'combined the two "kingdoms" of Israel and Judah in a personal union without expressly combining them as a whole under some such name as "kingdom of Israel"' (S. Herrmann, *A History of Israel* [2nd edn], p. 148).

3.   Cf. H. Donner, *Geschichte des Volkes Israel*, p. 195.

4.   The location of Mount Perazim with its Baal sanctuary is not known. A. Mazar tries to see Giloh on the southwestern outskirts of Jerusalem as Baal-Perazim (*BA* 45 [1982], pp.170-71). He also thinks the place was founded by incoming members of the tribe of Judah (p. 171). The name Baal rather indicates that indigenous Canaanites had built the settlement.

been transferred and that their peoples and land were without divine protection.

It is not clear from the text whether David once more fought the Philistines before he captured Jerusalem or if it was shortly afterwards. David acted quickly, however, and succeeded in taking the Jebusite capital, a city more suited to be his residential city than Hebron, which was located too far south.[1] The story about Jerusalem's capture (2 Sam. 5.6-7), has always been problematic for commentators. One of the stumbling blocks has been the Jebusite's (perhaps the Jebusite king's) declaration that Jerusalem was so well fortified that the blind and the lame would be sufficient to defend it. The solution to this—for us cryptic—utterance may be that the words refer to the poor, the sick, the old, and the unwanted peoples, who often were given as *ex voto* to the sanctuaries. By this custom the temples partly solved their labor problems.[2] Jerusalem had most certainly some cult places, among them an official royal temple which later was taken over by the Davidic administration (cf. 2 Sam. 12.20).[3] For the 'Jebusite', an attack on Jerusalem by David's men would be meaningless. The irony and point of the story is that David's men easily took the city, which is said to have been taken via or by the ṣinnôr, 'pipe, pipe-line'[4] (2 Sam. 5.8). This has been understood to refer to a water shaft (the Warren shaft?), which would have been to the weakest point in the city's defenses.[5] This is a plausible solution because it explains

1. According to 2 Sam. 5.5, David had resided as king in Hebron for seven and a half years. That means that if the representatives of Israel came to Hebron acknowledging David as their king shortly after Eshbaal's death, and Eshbaal reigned only about two years (2 Sam. 2.10), David must have become king in Hebron long before Eshbaal ascended the throne.

2. I.J. Gelb, 'The Arua Institution', *RA* 66 (1972), pp. 10-32.

3. J. Pedersen, *Israel*, III-IV (Copenhagen, 1940), p. 238; G.W. Ahlström, *VT* 11 (1961), pp. 126-27. Cf. also 2 Chron. 8.11, which refers to the old practice of palace and temple being identical or part of one and the same building complex; cf. W. Rudolph, *Chronikbücher* (HAT, 21; Tübingen, 1955), p. 220; cf. also S.N. Kramer, *Enmarkar and the Lord of Aratta*, p. 38, ll. 534-36.

4. G. Brunet, 'David et le ṣinnor', *Studies in the Historical Books of the Old Testament* (ed. J.A. Emerton; VTSup, 30; Leiden, 1979), pp. 79-80. The purpose of 2 Sam. 5.8 is to explain why lame and blind people were not admitted to the temple.

5. G. Brunet, 'David', *Studies in Historical Books* (ed. J.A. Emerton), p. 80.

the surprise, as well as the success of the attack.[1]

David could not be completely secure with another nation almost in the middle of his kingdom—even if it were a small one. Jerusalem was also attractive as the site for his capital because that it was neither Israelite or Judahite. If David originally had been a Jebusite subject, Bethlehem being part of Jerusalem's territory,[2] his choice for the new capital is understandable. With the capture of Jerusalem, the little center of a city state for a time became the capital of the whole of Canaan and the political center of Syria-Palestine.[3]

The Philistines were not yet crushed. A short time after their first defeat they again marched up through the same valley (Rephaim), but were again defeated and pursued from Geba (or Gibeon) to the entrance of Gezer (2 Sam. 5.22-25).[4] At this time they apparently reached farther into the hills than before, and David was now in Jerusalem. The way through Gibeon (el-Jîb) and Beth Horon down to the Aijalon valley and the Gezer area was Jerusalem's old connection with the coast. There are references to several battles against the Philistines in which David was victorious (2 Sam. 8.1; 21.15-22; 2 Chron. 20.4-8). Thus, they had been a threat to David's kingdom for quite some time. 2 Sam. 8.1 seems to indicate not only that David defeated them and removed them as a threat, but also that he subdued them to such an extent that they lost their power over Palestine.[5] He probably also incorporated part of their territory, from the Gezer area up to the Yarkon river, into Israel.[6] The text says that David 'took the *meteg*

1. P.K. McCarter takes *ṣinnôr* here as 'throat', and maintains that David wanted the Jebusites killed, not 'mutilated and left alive' (*II Samuel*, p. 140).

2. Cf. G.W. Ahlström, *ZAW* 92 (1980), pp. 285-87.

3. This is a phenomenon that the biblical writers never could forget. Its retention in the text would thus support the existence of the Davidic kingdom.

4. Cf. A. Demsky, 'Geba, Gibeah, and Gibeon—An Historico-Geographical Riddle', *BASOR* 212 (1973), pp. 26-31. Cf. H. Donner, *Geschichte des Volkes Israel*, p. 196.

5. The text does not give any information about the Philistines becoming David's vassals, but their political status may have been just that; cf. H. Donner, 'The Interdependence of Internal Affairs and Foreign Policy during the Davidic–Solomonic Period', *Studies* (ed. T. Ishida), p. 209 n. 6. A. Malamat characterizes David's kingdom as the '"successor state" to the Philistines' ('A Political Look at the Kingdom of David and Solomon and its Relations with Egypt', *Studies* [ed. T. Ishida], p. 195).

6. Cf. W.G. Dever, H.D. Lance and G.E. Wright, *Gezer II*, p. 5. Most of the

hā'ammâ out of the hands of the Philistines'. This phrase has been an enigma for interpreters, but as suggested by O. Eissfeldt[1] it most plausibly refers to David's replacement of the Philistines as the lord of Palestine; *meteg*, 'bridle', could thus be translated 'rule'. The hegemony of the Philistines had been broken.

There is no information about how the remaining pockets of Canaanite cities and city states were incorporated into the Davidic kingdom. Such places as Tell Qasîle and Beth-Shemesh were probably taken in connection with the wars against the Philistines. Ta'anak was of no importance in this period.[2] Such city states as Megiddo, Dor, Beth-Shan, and perhaps Tell Abū Hawām[3] may have peacefully surrendered out of sheer necessity for survival.[4] Nevertheless, the conquest of Canaan is thus to be ascribed to David. This fact is the basic foundation that lies underneath the late biblical 'historiographer's' pan-Israelite idea about the conquest of Canaan by the twelve 'tribes'.[5]

With the whole territory of Cisjordan from the Beqa' valley to the Negev—save the Philistine coastal area—under David's direct rule, all the peoples and clans of the country were officially 'Israelites'.[6] The culture and religion of these peoples continued as before. Yahweh became the main god for all these people, which did not change much of their daily life or the rituals of their sanctuaries. Priests and other

territory of Solomon's second district was originally part of Philistia; on this, see below.

1. 'Israelitisch-philistäische Grenzverschiebungen von David bis auf die Assyrerzeit', *ZDPV* 66 (1943), pp. 115-16 (= *KS*, II, pp. 455-56); cf. G.W. Ahlström, *JNES* 43 (1984), p. 147.

2. A. Glock, 'Taanach', *EAEHL*, IV, p. 1147; on this, see P. Lapp, who held the opinion that there was an occupational gap from c. 1100 to 1000 (*BA* 30 [1967], p. 8).

3. Tell Abū Hawām may have been the port city of Megiddo and the whole Jezreel valley; see D.L. Saltz, 'Greek Geometric Pottery', pp. 165-67. The destruction dated to the tenth century at Tell Abū Hawām could be that of Pharaoh Shoshenq.

4. Cf. G.W. Ahlström, *Who were the Israelites?*, p. 95.

5. The systematic 'ideologization' of the empirical events amounts to a late rationalization.

6. The biblical systematization of the peoples into twelve 'tribes' is artificial, the number twelve being an expression for totality. The names of these 'tribes' are often old territorial names, such as Machir, Gilead, Gad, Manasseh, Ephraim, Judah, and so on. It should be noted that the Book of Judges includes 'tribes' that were not part of the 'twelve tribe system', such as Machir and Gilead.

government officials had to be stationed in the newly incorporated cities and in their sanctuaries in order to teach the people the law of the kingdom, which, in the case of religion, meant the performance of the cult.[1] If their main god had been called El earlier, he could now be called Yahweh-El or only Yahweh, and as such was the 'Reichsgott' of the new kingdom. It has sometimes been argued that the incorporation of the Canaanite population into the Davidic kingdom would have created 'an acute domestic political difficulty', and in particular, would have presented 'a religious danger'.[2] This is an artificial historical reconstruction grounded in the view that the Israelites entered the country en masse and met a people to whom they were not related, a people that therefore should be annihilated. This is the biblical 'historiographer's' fictitious reconstruction based upon his religious belief. The religious danger simply did not exist as the Bible presents it.

With the capture of Jerusalem, the little center of an old city state of Canaan[3] became the capital of a great kingdom. For a short time Jerusalem became the political center in Syria-Palestine. Jerusalem's administrative personnel most probably continued under the new regime. What happened to the city's ruler is not known. S. Herrmann supposes that Jerusalem had had an aristocratic constitution, as had Shechem.[4] This may be doubted, since the Bible mentions a king of Jerusalem. 2 Sam. 5.6 refers to 'the Jebusite', and as 2 Sam. 24.23a names Jerusalem's last Jebusite king, Araunah. David wanted to buy Araunah's threshing floor, *gōren*, on the hill just north of the city. David's proposal was met by Araunah's answer: 'Araunah, the king, gives all to the king'. This clearly shows that Araunah was a king.[5]

1. See my book, *Royal Administration*, pp. 3-9, 44-74.
2. S. Herrmann, *A History of Israel* (2nd edn), p. 157; cf. also H. Donner, *Geschichte des Volkes Israel*, p. 199.
3. For the territorial area of Jebusite–Davidic Jerusalem, see K.M. Kenyon, *Digging up Jerusalem*, pp. 98-100.
4. *A History of Israel* (2nd edn), p. 155.
5. Cf. G.W. Ahlström, *VT* 11 (1961), pp. 115-17; S. Yeivin, 'Social, Religious and Cultural Trends in Jerusalem under the Davidic Dynasty', *VT* 3 (1953), p. 149; H.A. Hoffner, 'The Hittites and Hurrians', *Peoples of Old Testament Times* (ed. D.J. Wiseman; Oxford, 1973), p. 225. F.M. Cross has objected to seeing Araunah as the last Jebusite king, maintaining that the text is corrupt; there would thus be a 'routine haplography by homoioarkton' (*Canaanite Myth and Hebrew Epic*, p. 210). He has been followed by G. Münderlein (*ThWAT*, II, cols. 61-62) and

The name, Araunah, is of non-Canaanite origin, and may indicate that the Jebusite leadership was Hurrian.[1] David acquired the threshing floor and built there an altar to Yahweh, according to the text.[2] It should be noted that threshing floors served as temporary cult places during harvest seasons where the rites of harvest were performed.[3] They also were places for official gatherings and decision making, as well as for prophetic divination (2 Kgs 22.10; Judg. 6.36-37; cf. Aqht 17.V.7).[4] Had Araunah's *gōren* been an ordinary profane place, then David, the conqueror, would not have had to negotiate in order to purchase it.

It is unknown when David moved the ark from Kiriath-jearim to Jerusalem. The text in 2 Samuel 6 suggests that this event happened shortly after David had captured the city. The purpose of the Ark narrative is to show that Yahweh, Saul's main god, was also the god of the kingdom of David, thereby underscoring the continuity between Saul's and David's kingdom. It is therefore part of the historiographer's scheme to assert David's legitimacy. The ark's triumphal entrance into Jerusalem would signal that Yahweh now had become the main god of Canaan. He is Elyon, the highest one, over all the other gods. He is

V. Fritz (*Tempel und Zelt* [Neukirchen 1977], pp. 17-18). Unfortunately, the haplography is to be found in 2 Sam. 24.20, which Cross also notes, but there is no such thing in 24.23a. The Hebrew text is in order and all versions (except for a few Greek and Latin manuscripts) support the Masoretic reading.

1.   Cf. R. de Vaux, *The Early History of Israel*, p. 138. According to C.H. Gordon, Araunah was originally a title meaning 'lord' (*Ugaritic Textbook*, glossary, no. 116).

2.   It is possible that the text is an etiology explaining why Solomon built the temple at this site.

3.   Cf. Hos. 9.1-2 and 10.11. In 9.1-2. F.I. Anderson and D.N. Freedman see idolatrous acts which also 'were immoral' (*Hosea* [AB, 24; Garden City, NY, 1980], p. 517). Immoral for the prophet, yes, but perhaps they were not so for the believers. 'It appears that the threshing floor was a place of ill repute among the prophets who considered it a hotbed of sexual orgies, besides, of course, being a cultic site' (A.S. Kapelrud, *Joel Studies* [Uppsala, 1948], pp. 117-18). Cf. the ritual of Nabu's marriage at Calah, which took place on a threshing floor (S. Smith, 'The Practice of Kingship in Early Semitic Kingdoms', *Myth, Ritual and Kingship* [ed. S.H. Hooke; Oxford, 1958], p. 43). See also J.V. Kinnier Wilson, *The Nimrud Wine Lists* (London, 1972), p. 30; J. Gray, 'Goren at the City Gate', *PEQ* 85 (1953), p. 120.

4.   Goren Nakon in 2 Sam. 6.6 is thus a place where the ark could be placed, because it was connected with sanctity.

Elohim. In using the plural form, *ᵉlōhîm*, Yahweh is seen to embody all divinities of Canaan.[1] A parallel to this is Marduk, who at a particular time was given the names of all the other Babylonian gods.[2]

The ark from Gibeonite Kiriath-jearim would have its place in the new capital, for that is one of the purposes of ch. 6. It seems likely that the tradition about Solomon's trip to the great sanctuary of Gibeon originally was connected with the ark historically, but that this connection has been broken in the present narrative; the ark story has been woven together with the promise of a dynasty to David, a dynasty that does not have any blood relationship with Saul's family. The latter is the point in 2 Sam. 6.20-23. David, as the priest-king, is seen to have led the procession of the ark to Jerusalem in such a way that he exposed himself (an orgiastic dance?) to the ladies of Jerusalem. This brought Michal's scorn (6.14-16), with the result that she was not privileged to give David any children. The text leads up to the dynastic promise in ch. 7. David's dynasty will have no connection with the family of Saul, and Yahweh will guarantee a new dynasty. Compositionally, chs. 6 and 7 represent theological justification of David's kingship.[3]

---

1. See G.W. Ahlström, *JNES* 43 (1984), p. 146.

2. W.G. Lambert, 'The Reign of Nebuchadnezzar I: A Turning Point in the History of Ancient Mesopotamian Religion', *The Seeds of Wisdom, Essays in Honor of T.J. Meek* (ed. W.S. McCullough; Toronto, 1964), pp. 3-13; cf. also W.W. Hallo and J.J.A. van Dijk, *The Exaltation of Inanna* (New Haven, CT, 1968), pp. 66-67. For Akkadian *ilāni* (pl.) sometimes referring to one god, see A.E. Drafkorn (Kilmer), 'Ilani/Elohim', *JBL* 76 (1957), pp. 216-24.

3. According to S. Herrmann the dynastic promise has been presented in 'a stereotyped literary form' that will have had its model in the so-called Egyptian Königsnovelle ('Die Königsnovelle in Ägypten und Israel', *Wissenschaftliche Zeitschrift der Universität Leipzig* 3 [1953–54], pp. 51-62). For a critique, see E. Kutsch, 'Die Dynastie von Gottes Gnaden: Probleme der Nathan Weissagung in 2 Sam. 7', *ZTK* 58 (1961), pp. 151-53. See also A.J. Spalinger, who emphasizes that there is no report of any of the deeds of the king in 2 Sam. 7, as there is in the Egyptian texts, and there is no speech of the king to his counselors, and so on (*Aspects of Military Documents*, pp. 101-103). For a summary of the discussion, see P.K. McCarter, *II Samuel*, pp. 212-15. As for the relationship between the oracles in Pss. 89 and 132 and the promise of Nathan in 2 Sam. 7, the latter is a deuteronomistic application of the liturgical promise that first received its literary expression in the two psalms. Cf. S. Mowinckel, who maintained that the promise in 2 Sam. 7 was an echo of the oracles in Pss. 89 and 132 (*Psalmenstudien*, III [Kristiania, 1922], p. 34).

With the above the narrator has laid the groundwork for the design of David as an 'empire' builder. David also had the administrative resources to expand his kingdom. He had a well-organized army and his own men, the royal bodyguard. By capturing Jerusalem David seems to have inherited or taken over the whole Jebusite administrative apparatus,[1] which he may have reorganized to suit his own political goals. The renaming of the city as *'îr Dāwid*, 'city (fortress) of David', could have been part of his new policy. At the same time, it as declaring the city to be his. This practice would be consistent with an old Near Eastern tradition of naming cities as property of a king, such as Dūr-Sharrukīn, Kār-Tukultī-Ninurta, Kār-Ashur-aḫḫu-iddina (the *kārum*, 'port', of Esarhaddon, which the Assyrian king built after having destroyed Sidon).[2] Coming from Bethlehem, David may have been used to the practices and politics of the Jebusite city state, but even if this were not the case, he would have benefitted from the existence of the old administrative apparatus in Jerusalem. His Judahite or Israelite subjects would not have been experienced in administrative matters. It is not surprising that the names of many of David's, as well as Solomon's, officials have been labelled 'Canaanite'. Of course, geographically speaking, everybody was a Canaanite. With regards to religion, some personal names showed that Yahweh began to be more prominent, which would be natural now that he had become the main god of Canaan.[3] A clear example of how a territorial 'Sitz im Leben' can influence the giving of names is provided by the contrast between the names of David's

---

1. Cf. my book, *Royal Administration*, pp. 27-29. K.-H. Bernhardt suggests that David destroyed Jerusalem so that there would have been no Jebusite customs, traditions or peoples who could have become part of the newcomer's culture and religion (*Das Problem der altorientalischen Königsideologie im Alten Testament* [VTSup, 8; Leiden, 1961], pp. 91-98). For a critique of Bernhardt's thesis, see my article, 'Die Königsideologie in Israel: Ein Diskussionsbeitrag', *TZ* 18 (1962), pp. 205-10.

2. Cf. A.L. Oppenheim, *Ancient Mesopotamia*, p. 119; T.N.D. Mettinger, *Solomonic State Officials*, p. 83; G.W. Ahlström, *Royal Administration*, p. 17.

3. F.M. Cross has a naive statement about Zadoq as the head priest, maintaining that David would not 'invite a pagan priest as one of the high priests' of the new nation's cult (*Canaanite Myth and Hebrew Epic*, p. 210). There were no 'pagans' at that time. Cross has made the mistake of using a later time's viewpoint and religious evaluation in his treatment of a period that did not know anything about Jewish and Christian evaluations.

sons born in Hebron and those born in Jerusalem. Some of those born in Hebron were given names with the theophoric component -yâ, such as Adonijah and Shephatiah (2 Sam. 3.2-5), while none of the sons born to David in Jerusalem was given such a name.[1] The name Jedidiah was most probably the name given to Solomon as crown-prince. As such, it is programmatic.

More often than not the administration of David and Solomon has been seen to have been partly patterned after the Egyptian govern-mental system. This may be true in a certain way, because the Canaanite city states and societies had been under Egyptian rule since Tuthmosis III and the New Kingdom period. As vassals to Egypt, the Syro-Palestinian princelets were well-acquainted with the Egyptian administration, and their own administrative apparatus and court life may have been partly influenced by or modeled after that of the Egyptian capital, the 'Versailles' of that time.[2] This would mean that the Jebusite administration in certain respects was influenced from the south. Able administrators and military personnel were to be found not only in Jerusalem, but in the former city states which had become part of the kingdom.[3]

2 Sam. 8.16-18 and 20.23-26 record information about the top officials of David's regime.[4] They are: the field commander Joab, Seraiah, the *sôpēr*, that is, the royal scribe or secretary, Jehoshaphat, the *mazkîr*, 'spokesman, herald', Benaiah over the bodyguard (the Cherethites and the Pelethites), Zadoq, the first priest, with some of David's sons becoming priests. In the second list we also find Adoram over forced labor, Abiathar sharing the position as priest with Zadoq,[5]

1. See H.S. Nyberg, 'Studien zum Religionskampf im Alten Testament', *ARW* 35 (1938), pp. 373-74.

2. Cf. W. Helck, *Zur Verwaltung des Mittleren und Neuen Reichs* (Leiden–Cologne, 1958). Helck has also shown that Egyptians were employed in foreign courts (*Die Beziehungen*, pp. 466-68); W.F. Edgerton, 'The Government and the Governed in the Egyptian Empire', *JNES* 6 (1947), pp. 152-60; R. de Vaux, 'Titres et functionnaires égyptiens à la cour de David et Solomon', *RB* 48 (1939), pp. 394-405; K.-H. Bernhardt, *Verwaltungspraxis in spätbronzezeitlichen Palästina: Beiträge sur sozialen Struktur des alten Vorderasien* (Berlin, 1971), pp. 133-35. See also T.N.D. Mettinger, *Solomonic State Officials*, pp. 3-5, *et passim*.

3. Cf. H. Donner, *Geschichte des Volkes Israel*, p. 206.

4. Cf. 1 Chron. 18.15-17.

5. Abiathar's name may be a later addition. He was never the first priest in David's kingdom. 2 Sam. 15.24-26 shows that Zadoq was ranked as the first priest.

and a personal priest of David, Ira from Jair.[1] The appointments of Ira and some of David's sons to the priesthood shows that a special priestly tribe did not yet exist. In the nation's religious establishment priesthood was by royal appointment.[2]

The titles *mazkîr* and *sôpēr* have been seen to correspond to the Egyptian titles *whm.w*, 'speaker, herald', and *sš nsw*, 'royal scribe'.[3] Other high officials are the counselor, adviser, *yô'ēṣ* (2 Sam. 15.12), and 'the king's friend', *rēa'* (2 Sam. 15.37; 16.16; cf. Gen. 26.26; 1 Kgs 4.5). Both of these positions are also known from the el-Amarna texts (EA 131.20-23 and EA 288.11),[4] showing how much the Egyptian system had become part of the Palestinian one. It would be unrealistic to assume that David had built up his own court, administration and military system without following any blueprint. He had a royal predecessor, Saul, as well as the Jebusite and Canaanite city states and the Philistines, from whom he certainly had learned something.[5] For

I have earlier maintained that Abiathar probably 'was given a prominent and revered position at the court in gratitude for his earlier services to David' (*Royal Administration*, p. 30). T. Mettinger believes that the names of both Zadoq and Abiathar are 'insertions' (*Solomonic State Officials*, p. 10).

1. For the first list, see the reconstruction by J. Begrich, 'Sopher und Mazkir: Ein Beitrag zur inneren Geschichte des davidisch–salomonischen Grossreriches und des Königreiches Juda', *ZAW* 58 (1940–41), pp. 5-8.

2. Cf. N. Avigad, 'The Priest of Dor', *IEJ* 25 (1975), p. 104.

3. See J. Begrich, *ZAW* 58 (1940–41), pp 5-6; R. de Vaux, *RB* 48 (1939), pp. 394-405; H.-J. Boecker, 'Erwägungen zur Amt des Mazkir', *TZ* 17 (1961), pp. 212-16; A. Cody, 'Le titre égyptien et le nom propre du scribe de David', *RB* 72 (1965), pp. 381-93; T. Mettinger, *Solomonic State Officials*, pp. 25-63; M. Rütersworden, *Die Beamten der israelitischen Königszeit* (BWANT, 117; Stuttgart, 1985).

4. See, for instance, H. Donner, 'Der Freund des Königs', *ZAW* 73 (1961), pp. 269-77; T. Mettinger, *Solomonic State Officials*, pp. 63-69.

5. J. Bright maintains that there was 'no native precedent' for David's bureaucracy, therefore he would have patterned it after the Egyptian one (*A History of Israel* [3rd edn], p. 205). However, Saul, Jebusites and Canaanites may be native enough. From the Philistines David must have gained a thorough knowledge about both administration and military technique. His bodyguard, the Cherethites and the Pelethites, may have originated during his Philistine period. The names indicate 'their international character', according to S. Herrmann (*A History of Israel in Old Testament Times* [2nd edn], p. 171). Usually these mercenaries have been seen as Cretans and Philistines, and Zeph. 2.5 may support the assumption that the Cherethites are closely associated with the Philistines. This text locates them on the Palestinian coast. The Negev of the Cherethites is mentioned in 1 Sam. 30.14. The Pelethites

instance, the name of the man in charge of the forced labor, *mas* (Adoram, 2 Sam. 20.24; 1 Kgs 12.18; in 1 Kgs 4.6, Adoniram) indicates that he was an Adad/Hadad worshipper ('Hadad is high'), and that he could have belonged to the aristocracy of one of the incorporated city states.[1] From this it also can be concluded that David continued the system of forced labor which had been part of the administrative system of Canaan from of old. Having annexed large areas, such as Galilee, the Jezreel Valley and the coast, David most certainly had built up a district administration in order to be able to secure labor and taxes from the new territories.[2]

Conceptually, religion was the base for any kingdom in the ancient Near East. The king was the deity's viceroy administering the divine realm, the kingdom. As such, he could be called 'the good shepherd'.[3] In addition, his position could be expressed ideologically by his being the son of the god (Ps. 2.7 and Ps. 89.27-28).[4] From a religious point

cannot be the Philistines. The biblical writing *pelēti* is never used to designate the Philistines, *pᵉlištîm*. It is possible to see these terms as derivatives of the roots *krt*, 'cut off', and *plh*, 'separate'; cf. the discussion in J. Strange, *Caphtor/Keftiu*, pp. 120-26.

1. Cf. T. Mettinger, *Solomonic State Officials*, pp. 132-33. For the phenomenon of forced labor, see also I. Mendelsohn, 'State Slavery in Ancient Palestine', *BASOR* 85 (1942), pp. 16-17; A.F. Rainey, 'Compulsory Labor Gangs in Ancient Israel', *IEJ* 20 (1970), pp. 191-202.

2. Cf. N. Na'aman, *Borders and Districts in Biblical Historiography*, p. 171.

3. See, for instance, A. Badaway, 'The Civic Sense of Pharaoh and Urban Development in Ancient Egypt', *JARCE* 6 (1967), p. 108; M.J. Seux, *Epithètes royales akkadiens et sumeriennes* (Paris, 1967), pp. 110-12; G.W. Ahlström, *Royal Administration*, pp. 2-3.

4. The difference in terminology in these two psalms should be noted. In Ps. 2.7 the king is born as the son of Yahweh, but in Ps. 89.27-28 he is adopted. Ps. 89 deals with David as the chosen one, probably because as a usurper he would not have been born to the purple. Å.W. Sjöberg has pointed out that Sumerian (SAG)-Á-È-A, 'adopted', was used about a usurper (in a review of W.H.P. Römer, *Sumerische Königshymnen der Isin-Zeit* [1965], *Or* 35 [1966], p. 289). For the king's enthronement and anointment I have used the term 'rebirth'. Through this ritual the king is being lifted out of the ordinary human sphere into that of his god (*Psalm 89*, p. 112). Cf. also M. Liverani, who stresses the fact that there is a specific bond between king and god ('La royauté syrienne de l'âge du bronze récent', *Le palais et la royauté* [XIXe Recontre Assyriologique; ed. P. Garelli; Paris, 1974], p. 340). Cf. also D.J. McCarthy, who says that the 'Canaanite king, whatever his political power, would be a religious figure' ('Compact and Kingship: Stimuli for Hebrew Covenant Thinking', *Studies* [ed. T. Ishida; Winona Lake, 1982], p. 81).

of view the king's position was that of pontifex maximus. The nation's official religion was, in other words, an arm of the royal government. Kings could decide about cult festivals, build altars and sanctuaries, promulgate cultic laws, and appoint priests to the sanctuaries established by the government.[1] How much David reorganized the religious governmental apparatus in Jerusalem is hard to assess. His aim was to fuse together the different parts of his country and one way of doing that was through religion. There is no indication that he eliminated the Jebusite cult. It has been influenced by certain phenomena in the pre-Jerusalemite period that could have been channelled through the priest Abiathar. However, as mentioned above, Zadoq became the head priest of the new state religion. His name is closely associated with the deity name Zedeq[2] and he most probably was a Jebusite.[3] Jebusite, Israelite, Gibeonite and Hebronite traditions may have become part of the new kingdom's official religion, but with Zadoq as the leader of the cult, no great changes would necessarily have occurred in the religious performances.

Yahweh was now nominally the El of Jerusalem, in addition to becoming associated with Shalem and Zedeq, and as the kingdom's main god he was the highest, Elyon. Baal and the goddess Asherah do not play an important role for the narrator of the Davidic period. He avoids mention of the divine assembly, which is a clear sign of the lateness of the textual material. Storm and fertility deities always played an important role in the history of this country.[4] They were worshipped in the Solomonic temple and the religion of this temple was an expression of the beliefs of the country; thus Baal and Asherah were also worshipped in Jerusalem during the reign of David. Of all these gods, Yahweh was the newcomer who rose to supreme power under David, a process that started with Saul. The religious form of the capital, with Yahweh as the main god in the divine assembly, was

---

1. See further my book, *Royal Administration*.

2. For the literature see G.W. Ahlström, *Psalm 89*, p. 79 n. 5; cf. also R.A. Rosenberg, 'The God Sedeq', *HUCA* 36 (1965), pp. 161-77.

3. See the discussion in my article in *VT* 11 (1961), pp. 113-15. G.E. Mendenhall sees Zadoq as a *gibbôr ḥayil* and a priest, stating that 'military aristocracy and the civil bureaucracy... constitute the priesthood as well' (*The Tenth Generation: The Origins of the Biblical Tradition* [Baltimore, 1973], p. 24).

4. The polemics of the later prophets have to be understood from this background.

the official religion of the whole kingdom. Still, the El religion was not defunct. It was, in most places, the same as before, the main difference being that El now was called Yahweh or Yahweh-El. It was the task of the government's priest to ensure that the cult at the national shrines followed this line of interpretation. This does not mean, however, that the religious customs and liturgies of the villagers must have changed. The harvest rituals, for instance, stayed the same. What happened regarding religion in the capital did not affect the fertility rites of the villages. Their cult places were not official state sanctuaries. Thus, Yahweh may have had a hard time to become a god of greater importance for the villagers. They certainly heard about the kingdom's supreme god, Yahweh, but they perhaps first came into contact with his representatives—that is, priests, levites and military personnel—at official cultic festivals, and when they had to pay their taxes and erect fortifications, as well as at times of war. To follow the law of the land was to follow the deity's and the king's law as upheld by government servants such as the civil and cultic personnel. Many of these were placed in administrative and religious centers, and, together with the military personnel, these were the people who represented the state and held the different parts of the country together. They were the 'arm' of the king. The information in 1 Chron. 26.30-32 can be used to an illustrate this old phenomenon. Members of Hebronite 'levitical' families, 1700 fighting men, were supposedly sent by David as government officials 'for all the work of Yahweh and the service of the king' (*'al p^equddat yiśrā'ēl*) to guard and administer Israel in Cisjordan, and 2700 fighting men were sent to Transjordan for the same purpose. The figures regarding the number of Hebronites that could have been sent are irrelevant here.[1] The point is that the text shows how the new kingdom could be governed. The newly admitted areas had to be administered by servants faithful to David; therefore, government personnel from his former capital, Hebron, were sent out all over the country. These government servants are called 'Levites'; that means those who were bound to the king who represented his authority, *lwh*, 'to accompany', in *niph.* 'to be bound' or 'to attach'.[2] These servants, 'levites', are characterized as

---

1.   4400 'levitical' Hebronites leaving the town would perhaps have emptied the whole city.

2.   See the discussion in my book, *Royal Administration*, pp. 47-49.

soldiers, and the word $p^e qudd\hat{a}$, usually translated 'guard', indicates that they were some kind of a 'police force' supervising 'all the affairs of Yahweh and the king on both sides of the Jordan'.[1] The text also reveals that there was perhaps not such a great difference between civil and cultic personnel. One and the same person could be used in both capacities, as was the case, for instance, in Egypt.[2] Law enforcement included both sacred and civil laws. With faithful servants David started to unite the different parts of his kingdom, where all were now either Israelites or Judahites, even if they originally were Canaanites, or Gibeonites, or Naphtalites, or Jebusites, or Gileadites or others.[3]

Tell Qasîle can be used as an illustration of what probably happened after a town had become part of the new kingdom. The site is located in the northern outskirts of Tel Aviv, 2 km from the shore of the Mediterranean on the northern bank of the Yarkon river. The city has been characterized 'as a sheltered port'.[4] It is possible that the timber that was shipped to Jerusalem for Solomon's building projects from Lebanon passed through this site. The settlement was founded in the twelfth century BCE by the Philistines, and it may have replaced both Joppa and Tell Jerishe (south of Qasîle), which were both destroyed at the end of the Late Bronze period.[5] A temple was built in the first

---

1.   R. de Vaux, *Ancient Israel*, p. 133. Cf. 2 Chron. 17.7-9. Deut. 33.11 can also be considered in this connection. This verse could reflect a police function for the Levites. Yahweh should bless the *ḥayil*, 'army', of the Levites and fight against their enemies.

2.   M.F. Gyles, *Pharaonic Policies and Administration, 663 to 323 BCE* (The James Sprunt Studies in History and Political Science, 41; Chapel Hill, NC, 1959), p. 64; cf. W.C. Hayes, 'Egypt: Internal Affairs from Thutmosis I to the Death of Amenophis III', *CAH*, II.1, p. 327.

3.   S. Herrmann puts forward the opinion that the new state government arose 'independently of the tribes and virtually without them', and that the 'tribes allowed this to happen' (*A History of Israel* [2nd edn], p. 162). There was no democracy at that time; at least David had not heard of it. A Near Eastern ruler did not ask his subjects how he should rule them. The political government and its administration was not born out of some vote by the people. The tribal system did not exist as scholars have imagined it. The different clans of the different geographical areas were now faced with a new ruler, whose system they had to learn. Their vote did not count.

4.   B. Maisler (Mazar), *IEJ* 1 (1950–51), p. 62. For the recent excavations, see A. Mazar, *Excavations at Tell Qasile*, I, II.

5.   A. Mazar, *Excavations at Tell Qasile*, I, p. 10.

stratum. When the Philistine city of stratum X was destroyed, the temple was rebuilt in the new stratum, which has been viewed as being part of David's kingdom. The style and plan of the temple is about the same as before,[1] as is the material culture of the new stratum IX.[2] It appears, then, that the population was mainly the same, even though the site was now Israelite. Tell Qasîle (its ancient name is not known) became a port city in David's kingdom, and as such it would have had administrative personnel stationed there, including one or more priests. Does this mean that the religious liturgies in the temple(s) of Tell Qasîle changed radically? Probably not. It would have been enough to introduce a few new rituals and change others, showing that Yahweh was now the lord of the town. For the rest, life may have continued as before. Tell Qasîle provides an example of a site that experiences a change in political allegiance but not in population or culture.

David's 'Empire'

Having secured his position in the Cisjordanian territories and broken the Philistine hegemony with their control over the trade route along the coast, David turned against his Transjordanian neighbors. The eastern routes from Syria-Mesopotamia to Arabia and Egypt would probably have been just as lucrative as the coastal route. Their control would also have given David access to the Red Sea via the Gulf of Aqaba. The chronological order of the campaigns against Edom, Moab and Ammon was not of interest to the biblical narrator. 2 Sam. 8.2 and 14 contain brief statements about the conquest of Moab and Edom. They follow immediately after a summary statement about the subjugation of the Philistines,[3] which continues the narrative begun in ch. 5. This does not mean that ch. 8 is misplaced. We may well assume that after defeating the Philistines, David could have celebrated his position as the lord of Palestine by bringing the ark to Jerusalem. This event led the narrator to emphasize that the new

1. A. Mazar, *Excavations at Tell Qasile*, I, p. 46.
2. A. Mazar, *Excavations at Tell Qasile*, I, p. 11.
3. T. Veijola, among others, draws the conclusion that the content of 2 Sam. 8 could have come from archival texts (*Die ewige Dynastie* [Annales Academiae Scientiarum Fennicae, Ser. B., 193; Helsinki, 1975], p. 95); cf. M. Noth, *Überlieferungsgeschichtliche Studien* (3rd edn), p. 65.

king's dynasty was in no way related to that of Saul, and thus he continued with a divine promise, mediated by the court prophet Nathan, assuring David an 'eternal' dynasty (2 Sam. 7). After that the narrator picked up the 'military' thread again and continued where he had left off.

Having defeated the Moabites, David is said to have ruthlessly executed two-thirds of the prisoners and probably incorporated the territory north of the Arnon river into his kingdom as a province (2 Sam. 24.5).[1] The rest of Moab was made a vassal. David's hunger for power was not stopped by his blood relationship to the Moabites, or by any gratitude to the Moabite king for having given sanctuary to his parents during his own time as an outlaw (1 Sam. 22.3-4).

Nahash, the Ammonite king, after being defeated by Saul, must have been interested in good relationships with David when the latter became king in Hebron. An alliance between Ammon and Judah would have been dangerous for Eshbaal's Israel as well while enhancing Ammon's possibilities of expansion within Transjordan. 2 Sam. 10.1-2 also points to the existence of friendly relations between David and Ammon's king Nahash. With the union of Judah and Israel the political balance changed and Ammon again began to feel threatened by a Cisjordanian power. It was in the interest of Ammon to stop David from expanding into Transjordan, and a confrontation ensued under Nahash's successor, Hanun, who is said to have greeted David's envoys by shaving off half their beards and cutting their mantles at the buttocks (2 Sam. 10.1-3).[2] Whatever happened, Hanun seems to have provoked David, and war broke out. Hanun allied himself with another rising star to the North Hadadezer of Aram-Zobah, who, like David, was emerging as a military leader, extending his kingdom by means of wars and alliances.[3] With Aram-Zobah supporting Ammon, the smaller kingdoms of Maacah and Tob also joined the coalition. The reason for

---

1. Cf. the discussion by M. Noth, 'Israelitische Stämme zwischen Ammon und Moab', *ZAW* 60 (1944), pp. 41-42 (*Aufsätze*, pp. 418-19). A later time's reconstruction of the so-called conquest puts the southern border of the 'Israelite' territories in Transjordan at Arnon (Num. 21.24; cf. 1 Chron. 5.9). This 'historiography' may have been inspired by David's conquest. What David had taken should have been 'Israelite'. If David now sent 'Levitical' Hebronites to Transjordan (1 Chron. 26.30-32), this would have been possible only after his defeat of Moab.

2. This was a real insult. The beard was a sign of manhood; children, women and eunuchs were beardless.

3. See Chapter 9, pp. 395-99.

the Aramaean participation must have been that Hadadezer realized, as did the Philistines, that the expansionist policies of the new kingdom in Palestine would come into conflict with his own and thus be dangerous for himself and for Aramaean independence. The coalition was defeated. The order of the battles was not of interest to the biblical narrator. What seems to have been the case is that the campaign described in 2 Sam. 10.1-19 was the first confrontation between the Ammonites and the Aramaeans on the one hand and David's forces on the other. After this David thoroughly defeated Hadadezer of Zobah and his allies.[1] W.F. Albright assumed that Ashur-rabi II of Assyria 'had a share in turning David's attention to the Aramaeans', since the Assyrians themselves were fighting the Aramaeans at the time. With David attacking the Aramaeans, the pressure on Assyria would be lessened.[2]

The booty taken from the Aramaeans included 1000 chariots, which means that David's army must also have included the same kind of equipment (2 Sam. 8.3-4), which he may have learned about from the Philistines. Hadadezer became a vassal, and parts of his territory may have been incorporated within Israel. Damascus, which had sent help to Hadadezer and which probably was an independent nation, was occupied by David's troops. With the defeat of Hadadezer and the turning of his country into a vassal, David also got his hands on the riches of such cities as Tubikh (Hebrew Betah), Chun and Berotai, with their copper and bronze products (2 Sam. 8.8; 1 Chron. 18.8). When Hadadezer lost his position as an 'imperial' candidate, his vassals had to switch their allegiance to David (cf. 2 Sam. 10.19). The battle against Hadadezer thus changed the political situation in Syria. In this way David's power could possibly have reached to the Euphrates. It is possible that Maacah lost part of its territory west of the Jordan to David at this time. The city of Abel (Beth Maacah) was located in northern Galilee, south of Lebo-Hamat. In 2 Samuel 20 this city is called a 'mother in Israel' by David in connection with Sheba's

---

1. An inscription by Shalmaneser III mentions that one of his ancestors, Ashur-rabi II (1012–972), had recaptured territory that 'the king of the land of Amurru had seized by force' (D.D. Luckenbill, *ARAB*, I, par. 603); cf. H.W.F. Saggs, *The Might that was Assyria*, p. 70. This king of Amurru would most probably be Hadadezer, who had expanded his kingdom around 1000 BCE and whose power, through vassals, reached the Euphrates.

2. 'Syria, the Philistines, and Phoenicia', *CAH*, II.2, p. 533.

uproar, thus David had taken this part of Maacah's territory before the uproar of Sheba.[1] 1 Kgs 8.65 says that the northern border of David's and Solomon's kingdom was Lebo-Hamath (the entrance of Hamath),[2] which indicates that part of Aram Rehob (north of Galilee) had been incorporated into David's kingdom as a district. This may have occurred when the Aramaeans were defeated by David.

According to 1 Kgs 11.23-25, 'Rezon, son of Eliada, who fled from Hadadezer, the king of Zobah, his lord' (after David's defeat of the Aramaeans), had collected a band of freebooters, and when David died, he made himself king in Damascus. The parallel with David's career is evident. The point to make here is, however, that Hadadezer was not dethroned by David but probably stayed on as king of a minimized vassal state.[3]

North of Hadadezer's realm was the neo-Hittite kingdom of Hamath (modern Hama on the Orontes).[4] Its king, Toi, was an enemy of Hadadezer. As much as the defeat of Hadadezer was welcome by Toi, it also could have signaled new problems. In order not to share Hadadezer's fate, Toi decided to be on friendly terms with his new 'neighbor' in Jerusalem. He therefore sent his son Hadoram (1 Chron. 18.10, Joram in 2 Sam. 8.9-11) as head of a diplomatic delegation to David with gifts including objects of silver and gold. This does not *per se* mean that Hamath became a vassal state of Israel.[5] When Egyptian

---

1. Cf. B. Mazar, *JBL* 80 (1961), p. 28. The phrase 'a mother in Israel' may indicate the city's 'metropolitan' character, perhaps in this case an administrative center. The term *'m* 'mother' occurs on Phoenician coins in the meaning of 'metropolis'; see C.-F. Jean and F. Hoftijzer, *Dictionnaire des inscriptions sémitiques de l'ouest* (Leiden, 1965), *s.v. 'm*.

2. See, for instance, K. Elliger, who sees Hamath as the heir to the Amurru kingdom ('Die Nordgrenze des Reiches Davids', *Palästinajahrbuch* 32 [1936], pp. 34-73). The border between Zobah and Hamath is considered by Elliger to be the border line between the spheres of Aramaean and neo-Hittite influence. He points to both ethnographic and cultural differences between Hamath and its southern neighbor (p. 58). As to Lebo-Hamath, consult also J. Gray, *I and II Kings*, pp. 234-35.

3. A. Malamat theorizes that Rezon could have been 'encouraged in his separatist designs by David' (*JNES* 22 [1963], p. 5).

4. For Hamath as a name of the nation in the neo-Assyrian time and not referring to a city, see H. Ikeda, 'Royal Cities and Fortified Cities', *Iraq* 41 (1979), pp. 79-84.

5. A. Malamat concludes that Toi acknowledged Israelite suzerainty and thus Hamath became a vassal to David (*JNES* 22 [1963], pp. 6-7; cf. *idem*, *Das davidische und salomonische Königreich und seine Beziehungen zu Ägypten und Syrien: Zur*

kings sent gifts to Mitanni or Hatti, it meant no more than that they wanted friendly relations. In this case the Dtr narrator likes to give the impression that Hamath became dependent on Israel. Interesting to note, however, is that the Chronicler does not use the name Joram, but refers to the crown-prince by his Syrian name, Hadoram.[1] According to A. Alt, the treaty between Toi and David was probably a treaty between equals.[2] At least friendly relations were established between the two kingdoms. It is not known whether Toi sent the delegation under Hadoram (Joram) to David in the field or after his return to Jerusalem. The former would not be out of place because in this way David would have been stopped in his march to the north. 2 Sam. 8.13[3] supports this conclusion, saying that David 'made a name [= monument?] when he returned from having defeated Aram'. This verse also contradicts the hypothesis that David continued to the Euphrates.[4]

The Edomite campaign seems to have taken place after the Syrian one (2 Sam. 8.13-14).[5] The warfare was, as usual, cruel. The Edomite dynasty seems to have been wiped out in the massacre led by Joab.[6] The only known survivor was a young prince, Hadad, who together

Entstehung eines Grossreichs (Österreichische Akademie der Wissenschaften. Philos.-Hist. Klasse. Sitzungsberichte, 407; Wien, 1983), pp. 39-41.

1.   It should be noted that personal names with theophoric component -*yau* are known from different west-Semitic areas from an early period; cf. A. Murtonen, 'The Appearance of the Name Yahweh outside Israel' (StudOr, 16.3; Helsinki, 1951); H.B. Huffmon, *Amorite Personal Names in the Mari Texts*. Cf. M.A. Finet, 'Iawi-ila, roi de Talhayum', *Syria* 41 (1964), pp. 117-42. For the problem of -*ya* and -*ni* in the Eblaite texts, see H.-P. Müller, 'Gab es in Ebla einen Gottesnamen Ja?' *ZA* 70 (1980), pp. 70-92. The name Joram, if it existed at Hamath, must not necessarily mean that the Israelite god Yahweh had been worshipped there, and it may not say anything about a treaty between Toi and David.

2.   'Das Grossreichs Davids', *TL* 75 (1950), p. 217 (= *KS*, II, pp. 72-73).

3.   For the reconstruction of the text, see P.K. McCarter, *II Samuel*, pp. 245-46.

4.   The *nhr*, 'river', mentioned in 2 Sam. 8.3, where David put up a stela (*yad*, 'hand'), must then refer to another river, and could be the Orontes on the border between Hamath and Aram-Zobah.

5.   Cf. J.R. Bartlett, 'An Adversary against Solomon, Hadad the Edomite', *ZAW* 88 (1976), p. 208.

6.   The Edomite hatred of Judah may be seen as a result of David's ruthless occupation of the land. As J.R. Bartlett has expressed it: 'This was perhaps the first momentous event which had affected equally all the groups or clans living in the area known as "Edom", and doubtless it left its mark on the Edomite mind' (*PEQ* 104 [1972], p. 29).

with some of his men escaped through the interior of the Sinai to Egypt. The route may have been from Aila via Wâdī Watir, Wâdī esh-Sheikh, Wâdī Feiran, Wâdī Mukatteb and Wâdī Sidri.[1] David placed governors and garrisons in Edom, which at this time included most of eastern Negev. It is, thus, first with David that the Negev politically became an extension of Judah.

About a year after the Ammonite-Aramaean war started, David sent the army under Joab against Ammon and its capital Rabbah (2 Sam. 11.1).[2] The result was a disaster for the Ammonites. Their land was devastated and a great number of people were massacred, a common practice in ancient times. Joab laid siege to the capital and it was taken under the leadership of David. He had not participated in the campaign up until this event. Instead, he had stayed in Jerusalem 'conquering' Bath-Sheba (2 Sam. 11.2-27). After capturing the city, David put the crown[3] of their king on his own head, thus making himself king of Ammon.[4] The country probably became a province, and Shobi, son of Nahash and a brother of Hanun, seems to have been the governor (2 Sam. 17.27).

That a woman's bathing ever had such consequences for a country's

1. For the roads in the Sinai peninsula, consult B. Rothenberg, *PEQ* 102 (1970), pp. 18-19; cf. J.R. Bartlett, *ZAW* 88 (1976), pp. 210-11.

2. The rest of the army was stationed at Succoth in the Jordan Valley; cf. Y. Yadin, 'Some Aspects of the Strategy of Ahab and David', *Bib* 36 (1955), pp. 332-51. Succoth is often identified with Tell Deir 'Alla; cf. Y. Aharoni, *The Land of the Bible* (2nd edn), p. 442. M. Ottosson prefers to see Tell es-Sa'idiyeh (close to where Wadi Kufrinjeh reaches the Jordan river) as Succoth (*Gilead*, p. 225), and H.J. Franken suggests that Tell el-Ekhsas would be ancient Succoth ('Deir 'Alla, Tell', *EAEHL*, I, p. 321).

3. The crown was of gold, weighing one talent (c. 34 kg, 2 Sam. 12.30). A god-statue with its crown was usually made in one piece.

4. The Hebrew text has the reading *malkām*, 'their king'. Grammatically the pronominal suffix (*-ām*) would then have no antecedent, thus the preferable reading (with some LXX manuscripts) would be Milcom; cf. P.K. McCarter, *II Samuel*, p. 311. G.C. O'Ceallaigh sees the Ammonite name of the god being Malek. *malkām* 'is a hybrid, an Aramaic noun with Hebrew suffix' ('And So David did to All the Cities of Ammon', *VT* 12 [1962], pp. 186-87). For the meaning of this term, see also E. Puech, 'Milkom, le dieu ammonite, en Amos I 15', *VT* 27 (1977), pp. 117-25. For the Egyptian style of the Ammonite crown, see S. Horn, 'The Crown of the King of the Ammonites', *AUSS* 11 (1973), p. 174. For this type of crown, the so-called *atef* crown, in Transjordan, see also R.H. Dornemann, *The Archaeology of Transjordan*, p. 156 and fig. 91.4.

history as that of Bath-Sheba may be disputed, but she certainly knew what she was doing. Jerusalem was a small and narrow city, c. 420 m long and 150 m wide.[1] From his roof David could have seeen much of what was going on in town. Bath-Sheba may have intentionally taken her bath that day knowing when David would be on the roof. Because of the novelistic character of the narrative, some of its features may be traceable to literary ornamentation. The result of Bath-Sheba's bath, however, was that after the death of her husband, Uriah, she became one of David's wives and as such the mother of the future king, Solomon.[2]

With the whole of Transjordan under his rule and the Aramaean states as his vassals, David's kingdom reached outside Palestine proper (see Map 14). It had command over such natural resources as copper in Syria, timber from Lebanon, and, of course, the income from the important caravan routes along the coast and through Syria-Arabia, namely the trunk road from Egypt and the King's Highway. It would have been most unnatural if the Phoenicians did not quickly ensure that they were on friendly terms with such a kingdom, which could completely cut them off from their land trade with Arabia. The Philistines, the Tjeker and the Phoenicians had between them controlled the trade along the coast.

With David's arrival on the scene the picture changed and political

1. Cf. my article, 'Where did the Israelites Live?', *JNES* 41 (1982), p. 135. J. Wilkinson thinks that c. 2500 persons could have lived in David's Jerusalem ('Ancient Jerusalem: Its Water Supply and Population', *PEQ* 106 [1974], p. 33). For the Jebusite–Davidic city, consult also K.M. Kenyon, *Archaeology in the Holy Land* (4th edn), pp. 234-35; and cf. Y. Shiloh, 'The City of David Archaeological Project: The Third Season—1980', *BA* 44 (1981), pp. 161-70.

2. The first child she bore David is said to have died (2 Sam. 11.27; 12.18). It is in connection with the sickness and death of this child that we hear about David's non-Israelite behavior. As long as the child was sick David fasted and lamented, but when the boy died David stopped fasting and put on his normal clothes and went into the house of Yahweh (2 Sam. 12.20). This reaction did not follow the normal customs of the land, and therefore J. Pedersen assumed that David originally was not an Israelite (*Israel, III–IV*, pp. 456-57). The same text also indicates that there was a temple in Jerusalem. If this is not a slip of the mind of the writer, then a Jebusite temple has become a Yahwistic temple, which would be expected. It has often been maintained that the text refers to a tent, 'tabernacle', housing the ark. The Hebrew word *byt* never refers to a tent. The word means 'house' and is as such used for 'temple'. Another possibility is, of course, to see *byt* to refer to a royal chapel in the palace of David.

alliances had to change too. David was 'honored' with the friendship of the Phoenicians, or, as 1 Kgs 5.15 expresses it, 'Hiram loved David always'.[1] This treaty was probably made in the later part of David's reign because Hiram apparently became king around 970 BCE.[2] Hiram is also said to have sent material, cedars and workers to help David build his palace (2 Sam. 5.11).[3]

As mentioned before, Palestine was not a country that encouraged the creation of larger political units. Historically, the political and cultural centers were in Anatolia–Mesopotamia in the north, and in Egypt in the south. Geographically Palestine was a connecting link and as such was always a point of contention among the great world powers. David's kingdom represents an exception, a parenthesis in the history of the ancient Near East. The achievements of David were possible because there was a power vacuum at this time. The Hittite kingdom went out of existence around 1200 BCE. Egypt's rule over Palestine ended sometime in the mid-twelfth century BCE (the Twentieth Dynasty: the Ramessides), and was itself split into two kingdoms during the following dynasty. Their 'successors' in Palestine, the Philistines, had filled the power gap for a short time, until David put an end to their political and economic hegemony. In Mesopotamia the Assyrian kingdom had tried for quite some time to stem the tide of Aramaean invasions. There was, therefore, 'room' for a Syrian or Palestinian ruler to try to expand his territory, as did Hadadezer and David. In the power struggle between these two hard-pressed nations, the Assyrian king Ashur-rabi II (1013–973 BCE) could have welcomed David's attack on the Aramaeans.[4] David's kingdom was, however,

---

1. For 'love' as a treaty term, see W.L. Moran, 'The Ancient Near Eastern Background of the Love of God in Deuteronomy', *CBQ* 25 (1963), pp. 80-81. As to the time of this treaty, see below.

2. See the discussion in H.J. Katzenstein, *The History of Tyre*, pp. 77-79; J. Liver, 'The Chronology of Tyre at the Beginning of the First Millennium BCE', *IEJ* 3 (1953), pp. 113-20; F.C. Fensham, 'The Treaty between the Israelites and the Tyrians', *Congress Volume, Rome 1968* (ed. J.A. Emerton *et al.*; VTSup, 17; Leiden, 1969), pp. 71-87. See also S. Mowinckel, 'Die Chronologie der israelitischen und jüdischen Könige', *AcOr* 10 (1932), p. 270.

3. Chronologically the textual material seems to be in disorder. After having recounted David's capture of Jerusalem, the narrator's associations naturally went to David's building activities in the city. He has not been concerned about chronological order.

4. Cf. W.F. Albright, 'Syria, the Philistines, and Phoenicia', *CAH*, II.2, p. 533.

shortlived.[1] It dissolved naturally when Solomon died. But even if it was shortlived, it was never forgotten by the Jerusalemite writers and some Judahite prophets. David and his kingdom became for them the ideal that in some way distorted the historical reality, as well as creating wishful dreams about the future.

The lack of references to David's (or Solomon's) kingdom in other Near Eastern texts from this time is probably because both Assyria and Egypt were experiencing a political low and did not come into contact with this new Palestinian kingdom. After the end of the expansionistic wars there is little information about how David ruled his kingdom or what happened in the different parts of it. The narrator is more interested in the rebellions of Absalom and Sheba and in the problems of succession. There is, however, one exception. 2 Sam. 24.2-9 reports a so-called census.[2] The reason or goal of this census is not mentioned. It has been assumed that the census 'laid the groundwork for a sweeping fiscal reorganization and presumably for conscription as well'.[3] This is possible, but the route David's officers are reported to have taken did not go through the lands of Israel and Judah proper. Thus, the 'census' cannot have laid the groundwork for a fiscal reorganization of the whole kingdom, but most probably for the newly added territories only. The description of the route starts with Aroer in the newly incorporated Moabite territory north of the Arnon river. From there Joab and the officials went over Jazer and 'the city in the valley of Gad' (that is, in the Ammonite border area), through Gilead to the land of *thtym hdšy*. This phrase is a crux, and it has been suggested that it may refer to Kadesh in the land of the Hittites. A more probable solution is that it refers to a district in the area between Hermon and Galilee,[4] because from there the men went

---

1. M. Trolle Larsen sees the characteristics of an empire as '1) a methodical and permanent occupation of conquered territory, 2) implantation of military garrisons, and 3) a division of the territory into provinces governed by officials closely submitted to the authority of a central government' ('The Tradition of Empire in Mesopotamia', *Power and Propaganda: A Symposium on Ancient Empires* [ed. M. Trolle Larsen; Mesopotamia, 7; Copenhagen, 1979], p. 86).

2. For the literary problem and the position of the chapter within the Dtr history work, see T. Veijola, *Die ewige Dynastie*, p. 106 (with lit.).

3. J. Bright, *A History of Israel* (3rd edn), p. 206. Cf. S. Herrmann, *A History of Israel in Old Testament Times* (2nd edn), pp. 156-57.

4. Cf. P. Skehan, 'Joab's Census: How Far North (2 Sam. 24.6)?', *CBQ* 31 (1969), pp. 42-49.

to Dan, Sidon and the 'fortress of Tyre'.[1] It is evident that the narrator did not precisely know the route. Sidon and mainland Tyre have been mentioned because they were neighbors of the Davidic kingdom.[2] It is likely that the writer has made up the list,[3] because the route corresponds to the 'ideal' borders of the Davidic kingdom as presented by the writer of Deut. 3.8 and 4.48.[4] This is supported by the following material, which mentions that the men went 'to all the cities of the Hivites and the Canaanites' and then to Beer-sheba in the Negev of Judah. The narrator has incorporated the names Dan and Beer-sheba, which had become the technical terms for the northern and southern points of the 'ideal' country of Israel. The mention of the Hivites also announces to us that the outlook of the writer is that of the time of the reconstruction of the society in the postexilic period with its 'land ideal'.[5]

Even if the census were not undertaken as described in 2 Sam. 24.5-7, there must have been some census for taxation, conscription and forced labor. The complexity of the new kingdom, including the makeup of the population and their old traditions, must have created problems for both parts. An overly centralized administrative system, with its conscription and forced labor, would not only create tensions but could be perceived as oppressive. A main task for the royal administration was the fusing of the different groups of people

---

1. For a résumé of the different solutions, see H. Donner, 'The Interdependence of Internal Affairs', *Studies* (ed. T. Ishida), pp. 209-14, and P.K. McCarter, *II Samuel*, pp. 504-505. The 'fortress of Tyre' refers to mainland Tyre, i.e. Usu of the Assyrian and Egyptian inscriptions.

2. For the borders of David's kingdom in the north, see the discussion by K. Elliger, *Palästinajahrbuch* 32 (1936), p. 71.

3. H. Donner considers vv. 5-7 'an editorial comment'. The description of the route 'is nothing more than the product of scribal speculation and combination on the basis of particular geographical texts of the Old Testament, above all Joshua 13 and Joshua 19'. He also says that the phrase the 'city that is in the middle of the valley' is a 'phantom'. The text cannot be used as a 'reliable source for the extension of the Davidic dominion' (*Studies* [ed. T. Ishida], p. 211-12).

4. The reference is to the kingdom of Og of Bashan. For this territory in the texts, see M. Wüst, *Untersuchungen zu den siedlungsgeographischen Texten*, pp. 25-27. For the problems of 2 Sam. 24.5-7, see pp. 142-44.

5. Hivites, together with Canaanites, Amorites, Hittites, Perizzites and Jebusites, were supposed to have been exterminated by Yahweh before the entrance into Canaan (Exod. 23.23).

together in such a way that a national unit, if possible, could emerge. Undoubtedly there would have been clashes between groups of people and royal administrators, such as the military and priests, governors and tax collectors, supervisors, and so on. We have also to take into consideration the old antagonism in the hills between the peoples of the north and the south, and the usual hostility or negativism towards each other that can be detected among the inhabitants of the urban and coastal areas vis-à-vis those of the mountainous regions.[1] These components were all part of David's kingdom. To make a national unit of these various societies would have been a masterstroke. Neither David nor Solomon succeeded in this respect. This was the problem for the biblical writers. Because they would have liked to have seen this unity as a reality, everything that deviates from it belongs to the 'world of ungodliness'.

The revolts of Abshalom and Sheba (2 Sam. 15–20) provide examples of unrest and dissatisfaction with the regime. Absalom's revolt shows that David's power was based on his personal troops. He did not really have the support of the people and its representatives, the *qāhāl*, 'assembly'.[2] Only the mercenaries supported David. After Sheba's uproar he treated Israel like a vassal country. It seems that David's power was built on military force from the beginning and through most of his reign. This created discontent in all parts of the country, and Absalom understood how to exploit it.

Absalom's uproar is part of what has been labeled the succession narrative, or court history.[3] It is very doubtful whether such a story

---

1. Cf. F. Braudel, *The Mediterranean*, pp. 34-35.

2. For the role of the popular assembly, see, for instance, T.N.D. Mettinger, *King and Messiah*, pp. 118-20.

3. L. Rost, *Die Überlieferung von der Thronnachfolge Davids*. K. Budde saw 2 Sam. 10–19(20) and 1 Kgs 1–2 as a literary unit concerned with the succession after David written by an eyewitness who was anti-Davidic. He saw the aim of the story as that of a libelous pamphlet directed against David and Solomon (*Geschichte der althebräischen Literatur*, pp. 35-37). Also, J. Van Seters understands the court history to be anti-Davidic, but he sees it as a 'post-Dtr' addition to the Saul–David stories from the postexilic period. He sees it as 'the product of an antimessianic tendency in certain Jewish circles at this time' (*In Search of History*, pp. 289-90). Cf. L. Delekat, 'Tendenz und Theologie der David–Salomo-Erzählung', *Das Fehrne und Nahe Wort* (Festschrift L. Rost; ed. F. Maas; BZAW, 105; Berlin, 1967), pp. 26-36; E. Würthwein, *Die Erzählung von der Thronfolge Davids—theologische oder politische Geschichtsschreibung?* (Theologische Studien, 115; Zürich, 1974), pp. 11-

ever existed as a separate literary unit.[1] It is most probably not written by a person contemporary with the events because there is an anti-Davidic tendency in it. Where would such literature have been preserved in an autocratic state? For whom would it have been written, and how would it have been distributed and circulated so that the king would not have known about it and executed the narrator? If there ever were an independent succession story, it must have been written at a time when royalty did not exist. The 'historiographer' has simply built on some traditions about what was known about David's court and elaborated it in a manner that suited his purposes. He seems to have written a 'novella'.[2] For instance, who knew what David said in his bedroom to Bath-Sheba? Who recorded all the dialogues between the main characters of the 'drama'? The oracle about an 'eternal' dynasty (2 Sam. 7),[3] is in all probability a plagiarism of an enthronement oracle that the writer has used and put into the mouth of a court prophet.[4]

17. For a résumé of the discussion, see T.N.D. Mettinger, *King and Messiah*, pp. 27-29. Mettinger thinks that the 'succession story' is older than that of the 'Rise of David' (p. 27).

1. The literary problems cannot be thoroughly dealt with here, but one should at least ask where the narrative begins. For the discussion see also A.R. Carlson, *David the Chosen King*, pp. 131-33; J. Blenkinsopp, 'Theme and Motif in the Succession History (2 Sam. XI 2 ff) and the Yahwist Corpus', *Congress Volume, Geneva 1965* (ed. J.A. Emerton *et al.*; VTSup, 15; Leiden, 1965), pp. 44-57; J.W. Flanagan, 'Court History or Succession Document? A Study of 2 Sam. 9–20 and 1 Kings 1–2', *JBL* 91 (1972), pp. 172-81.

2. Cf. H. Donner, *Geschichte des Volkes Israel*, p. 212.

3. For the religio-political background of 2 Sam. 7, see my article in *VT* 11 (1961), pp. 113-15; cf. H. Haag, 'Gad und Nathan', *Archäologie und Altes Testament* (Festschrift K. Galling; ed. A. Kuschke and E. Kutsch; Tübingen, 1970), pp. 135-43.

4. This kind of oracle is found in Ps. 89, which is not a poetic version of the propagandistic Nathan oracle, as often advocated, most recently by T. Veijola (*Verheissung in der Kreise* [Annales Academiae Scientiarum Fennicae, Ser. B., 220; Helsinki, 1982], pp. 60-62). To see the promise about an 'eternal' dynasty as having been 'invested' first after the disaster of 587/576 is unrealistic. All dynasties were eternal in principle. Add to this that as a usurper, David, as well as his successors, needed a 'divine' oracle for the legitimation of the kingship. All kings needed that. Thus, a liturgical oracle of 'the chosen one' was suitable for the later writer of the Nathan oracle. He combined the oracle with the problem of the temple building, a phenomenon that he turned upside down by saying that Yahweh did not need a house (a

What was known about the years of the struggle for the throne seems to be that Amnon, David's oldest son, was murdered by Absalom, allegedly for having raped Absalom's sister Tamar (2 Sam. 13). Absalom is said to have fled to his mother's country, Geshur, but through the intervention of Joab he was back at the court after a few years. How much truth there is in these stories can perhaps never be known.[1] The fact is, however, that Absalom started a rebellion. He may have relied for support on people who were discontented with David's rule.[2] He began to show publicly his aspirations by having a

---

late concept); instead, Yahweh would build David a house, a dynasty. For kings as temple builders, thus increasing the might and holiness of the country, see G.A. Barton, *The Royal Inscriptions of Sumer and Akkad* (New Haven, CT, 1929), p. 79; J.S. Cooper, *Sumerian and Akkadian Royal Inscriptions*. I. *Pre-Sargonic Inscriptions* (New Haven, CT, 1986), p. 70; H. Stieble, *Die altsumerische Bau- und Weihinschriften*, I (Wiesbaden, 1982), pp. 288-90; A.S. Kapelrud, 'Temple Building, a Task for Gods and Kings', *Or* 32 (1963), pp. 184-90; E. von Nordheim, 'König und Tempel', *VT* 27 (1977), pp. 434-53; G.W. Ahlström, *Royal Administration*, p. 2; M. Lambert, 'L'expansion de Lagash au temps d'Entemena', *Rivista degli Studi Orientali* 47 (1972), pp. 1-22. The reverse phenomenon, the destruction of temples, meant that the country was being destroyed. From this it would be most logical to see the negativism towards the temple in the Nathan oracle as being very late. Such an attitude would have been unthinkable in the time of David. Only the existence of the temple, later built by Solomon, supports the theory that 2 Sam. 7 is late. Note also the phrase in 2 Sam. 7.6, 'from the day I brought you up from Egypt', which is a typical expression at home in the exilic/postexilic historiographic reconstruction of the people's history.

1. See the discussion by J. Conrad, who states that the presentation of the material is theological, not historical ('Die Gegenstand und die Intention der Geschichte von der Thronfolge Davids', *TL* 108 [1983], col. 173). J.J. Jackson maintains that we have to make 'room for both the freedom and the sure-hand skill with which the author approached his sources' (David's Throne: Patterns in the Succession Story', *CJT* 11 [1965], p. 195).

2. For the state of affairs in the kingdom that led to Absalom's revolt, see K.W. Whitelam, *The Just King*, pp. 137-39. H. Tadmor thinks that Absalom 'was supported by the traditional institutions of Israel', and that the people now tried to regain the power they had lost ('Traditional Institutions and the Monarchy: Social and Political Tensions in the Time of David and Solomon', *Studies* [ed. T. Ishida], pp. 245-57). This is possible, but we do not know very much about these institutions, only about the elders, 'the men of Israel, of Judah' (and similar expressions), and the army, which, as Tadmor says, often can be identified with the men of Israel. The 'elders' had a certain role in the investiture of a king and Absalom probably had the approval of the 'elders' of both Israel and Judah, which must mean that they felt

'chariot and horses and fifty men to run before him' (2 Sam. 15.1).[1] He also is said to have greeted people in the city gate telling them that he would be a better *šōphēṭ*, 'judge', that is, king, than his father (vv. 15.2-6). Finally, a few years later, Absalom went to Hebron with 200 men and was made king over Judah. He seems to have had the men of both Israel and Judah on his side.[2] Among his followers was also David's most trusted advisor, Ahitophel. As commander of the army Absalom had replaced Joab with Amasa.[3]

Absalom's rebellion was obviously very dangerous for David. He left Jerusalem with his bodyguard and the mercenaries, 600 men (2 Sam. 15.13-23), taking with him the ark and the priests Zadoq and Abiathar.[4] The text gives the impression that David could trust only a few officials because the army under Amasa had followed Absalom. This may be true, but it is to be recognized that the writer's intention is to emphasize the events and to show that David's return to power was again divinely inspired. Therefore, the great numbers of followers assigned to Absalom is probably not to be seen as a reflection of reality.

neglected by David. For the discussion, consult also P.K. McCarter, *II Samuel*, pp. 356-57.

1. For horses and chariots befitting royalty, see Y. Ikeda, 'Solomon's Trade in Horses and Chariots in its International Setting', *Studies in the Period of David and Solomon* (ed. T. Ishida; Tokyo, 1982), pp. 221-38.

2. 2 Sam. 15.6 says that Absalom 'stole the hearts of the men of Israel'. Cf. M. Noth, *The History of Israel* (2nd edn), p. 201; H. Tadmor, 'The People and the Kingship in Ancient Israel: The Role of Political Institutions in the Biblical Period', *Cahiers d'histoire mondiale* 11 (1968), p. 51.

3. Although Amasa is said to have been the son of Ithra 'the Israelite' in 2 Sam. 17.25, 1 Chron. 2.17 reads 'the Ishmaelite'. For the correctness of the reading 'Israelite', see E.A. Knauf, who points to the fact that it certainly took quite some time before all the subjects of the united monarchy felt that they were Israelites (*Ismael*, p. 12).

4. When they came up on the Mount of Olives, David ordered Zadoq to return the ark to Jerusalem (2 Sam. 15.27). When he reached the cult place on the summit he met Hushai, who supposedly had volunteered to join Absalom's men in order to give advice that would benefit David. The motifs in the text serve the purpose of legitimizing David. He and nobody else should be king. Thus the text is basically propagandistic. This cult place could refer to the old priest city of Nob (see E.E. Voigt, 'The Site of Nob', *Journal of the Palestine Exploration Society*, 3 [1923], pp. 79-87).

Absalom's revolt failed. His strategy was probably to have the men of Israel attack from the north while he himself and the army with him approached Jerusalem from the south. In this way David would have been taken by surprise and squeezed between two contingents.[1] However, David's quick move to Mahanaim in Transjordan[2]—a move which the narrator has characterized to have been made in panic— made Absalom's plan unworkable. Absalom seems to have lost the initiative. Instead of pursuing his father and his men, Absalom marched to Jerusalem and took the city, presumably without a battle.[3] In a ceremony on the roof of the palace he 'went into his father's concu- bines' who had been left in Jerusalem.[4] In this way Absalom publicly declared that David had been dethroned and that he, Absalom, now was the king (2 Sam. 16.20-22). The break between the father and son was complete. From David's point of view the son had not only dethroned him but also committed adultery (16.21).[5]

Absalom finally went after David and met his army in the Forest of Ephraim in Gilead,[6] which probably is to be located in the vicinity of Mahanaim (Tulul edh-Dhahab) at the Jabbok river, an area which still has some forests.[7] The battle was a victory for David's forces under

1.　Thus S. Herrmann, *A History of Israel in Old Testament Times* (2nd edn), pp. 164-65.

2.　This shows that David could not even trust the people of Judah who had originally 'made' him king.

3.　The narrator relates that David's most trusted advisor, Ahithophel, had joined Absalom's rebellion. When Absalom did not follow Ahithophel's advice to pursue David immediately, Ahithophel is said to have ended his own life through hanging (2 Sam. 17.23). This is the narrator's way of announcing that Abshalom's revolt was doomed by advocating that Yahweh wanted to thwart Ahithophel's advice (17.14).

4.　For rituals on the roof, cf. 1 Krt 74-76, and J. Pedersen, 'Die Krt Legende', *Berytus* 6 (1941), pp. 75-76; A. Goetze, in *ANET*, pp. 397-98; M. Weinfeld, 'The Worship of Molech and the Queen of Heaven and its Background', *UF* 4 (1972), p. 153; R. Patai, 'Hebrew Installation Rites', *HUCA* 20 (1947), pp. 164-65. As to the legal aspects, consult also C. Kuhne, *Die Chronologie des internationalen Korrespondens von El-Amarna* (AOAT, 17; Neukirchen–Vluyn, 1973), p. 36 no. 175. For roof-rituals in the Old Testament, see also 2 Kgs 23.12; Jer. 19.13; 32.29; Zeph. 1.5.

5.　R.A. Carlson thinks the *šākab* theme (the laws about adultery and rape) is consistently present in 2 Sam. 10–20 (*David, the Chosen King*, pp. 180-81).

6.　2 Sam. 17.26 states that Absalom pitched his camp in Gilead.

7.　Cf. H.W. Hertzberg, *I and II Samuel*, pp. 358-59; Y. Aharoni, *The Land of the Bible* (2nd edn), p. 207.

Joab, and it ended with Absalom's death (2 Sam. 18.1-15).[1]

David could now regain his throne. The return journey, as described by the narrator, is perhaps more a programmatic description than an actual report, even if this route were the most natural one to take. On his way back to Jerusalem David crossed the Jordan river, probably at Adam (Tell ed-Damiyah) on the eastern shore where the Jabboq (Zerqa) joins the Jordan. At this place he 'crossed over to Gilgal' (2 Sam. 19.40). He was probably not reinstalled as king there.[2] This text may indicate that Gilgal ought to be located at the entrance to the Wâdī Far'ah. The correspondence between this episode and that of the crossing of the Jordan by Joshua and the Israelites in Josh. 3.14–4.19 is striking, even though the actual crossing is placed 'opposite Jericho'. Both cross at Asam and arrive at Gilgal. The way in which David 're-entered' his country may have inspired the deuteronomistic narrator to use it as a model for his writing about Joshua's conquest.[3]

From what happened after Absalom's defeat and the quarrels between the men of Judah and the men of Israel about the king's return, it is indisputably clear that these two parts of the kingdom had not been fused together. David favored Judah in these negotiations, which also clearly indicates that they were considered two separate entities (2 Sam. 19.41)[4] with Israel the unit of secondary status. Even before David reached Jerusalem, rebellion broke out again, this time led by a Benjaminite, Sheba. He called the Israelites to his banner with the words:

> We have no portion in David
> and we have no inheritance in the son of Jesse
> every man to his 'tent', Israel![5]

1. The elders of Judah and Israel 'slunk off home in confusion on hearing of David's unexpected recovery of power' (so expressed by G. Evans, 'Rehoboam's Advisers at Shechem, and Political Institutions in Israel and Sumer', *JNES* 25 [1966], p. 274).

2. *Contra* K. Galling, 'Bethel und Gilgal', *ZDPV* 66 (1943), pp. 147-48; T. Mettinger, *King and Messiah*, p. 119.

3. For the literary parallelism between Josh. 3.15 and 2 Sam. 15.24 (priests, Levites and the ark), see the discussion in R.A. Carlson, *David, the Chosen King*, pp. 175-76.

4. In the eyes of the Israelites, Judah was a newcomer in the society, a *homo novus*, as K. Budde expressed it (*Die Bücher Samuel*, pp. 294-95).

5. The word tent, *'hl*, is a poetic figure for house and dwelling; cf. below, Chapter 12 (Jeroboam), p. 547.

David was now faced with a greater crisis than that of Absalom's revolt. This time the danger of his kingdom breaking up was imminent. The leader of the revolt had not been heard of before. As a man of Benjamin, he could have been related to Saul's family.[1] Sheba tried to capitalize on the quarrel between the Israelites and the Judahites, but there is no indication in the text about the size of his following. The narrator leaves out most of the details. The discontent in Israel was probably so strong, however, that Sheba could dare to tear the kingdom apart, if possible. From the 'hastily' written report about Sheba's uproar, the danger of which the writer has tried to minimize, we learn that he took Abel Beth-Maacah in northern Galilee (2 Sam. 20.14-15), but that a 'wise' woman conspired with Joab who had laid siege to the city. She managed to have some of the men of the town kill Sheba and throw his head over the wall to Joab (20.22). The uprising under Sheba cannot have been of lesser importance than that under Absalom. David had mustered both the army and the mercenaries in order to put down the revolt, so he must have considered the revolt a major crisis. Israel was now more firmly in the hands of David than before, he having again established his position by means of force.[2] The quarrels between the men of Judah and the men of Israel as well as Sheba's revolt foreshadow the split of the kingdom that occurred after Solomon's death.[3]

In the conflicts between Israel and Judah the people and vassals of Transjordan were neutral at first.[4] This neutrality may indicate that western Gilead had become part of the Israelite kingdom first under Saul[5] (through a treaty), and the Gadites of the Mishor first under David. The quarrel between Israel and Judah did not concern them directly. David's stay at Mahanaim secured Gilead for the king, but the Transjordanian peoples were not involved in the battle. Geshur's role in the civil war is also of interest. Officially, Geshur was David's ally, but Talmai the king of Geshur is not named among those who supported David during his time in Mahanaim (2 Sam.

1.   Cf. H.W. Hertzberg, *I and II Samuel*, p. 371.

2.   H. Donner says that after Sheba's revolt David ruled Israel not as king but as a tyrant (*Geschichte des Volkes Israel*, p. 214).

3.   Cf. R.A. Carlson, *David, the Chosen King*, p. 180.

4.   See Y. Aharoni, *The Land of the Bible* (2nd edn), p. 306.

5.   See above, Chapter 10, pp. 440-41.

17.27-29).[1] Absalom, who had fled to Geshur after he murdered Amnon, may have tried to gain the support of his grandfather, Talmai, for his plot against David, and in this way repeat David's own manoeuvre against Eshbaal.[2] This may explain why Geshur did not come to David's assistance in Mahanaim. Talmai may have chosen to be neutral in the conflict.[3]

After the two dangerous rebellions had been put down, the biblical writer does not have much more to say about David's rule or about circumstances in the kingdom. He is more interested in the party intrigues that led to the kingship of Solomon. After Absalom's death, David's fourth son, who was born to him in Hebron,[4] Adonijah, followed Absalom's example and publicly appeared as the heir to the throne with a horse-drawn chariot and fifty men running in front of it (1 Kgs 1.5). His plan for gaining the throne was to seek the favor of some of the influential men in the capital such as Joab and the priest Abiathar. Two conclusions can be drawn for the biblical account. First, Adonijah's strategy was different than Absalom's. The latter got in contact with the leaders of the clans, the elders, and thus secured the people's participation, but Adonijah first tried to win over some of the top officials of the Davidic government. Second, in contacting Joab and Abiathar but not Zadoq, Nathan or Benaiah, the pretender was clearly a leader of a party, probably a party of malcontents. Joab was no longer in David's favor after having killed Absalom, and Abiathar, David's faithful priest from the years before both Jerusalem and Hebron, does not seem to have been able to supersede Zadoq. Both Abiathar and Joab belonged to the newcomers in the Jebusite city that David had made his capital. As in all such instances, there would have been conflict between the old *garde* and the newcomers, and the conflict situation may have sharpened as time went on. There could have been

1.   Three men are said to have given David and his people help: Shobi, 'son of Nahash from Rabbah of the Ammonites' (the son of king Nahash), Machir from Lo-Debar, and old Barzillai, 'the Gileadite from Rogelim' (2 Sam. 17.27). It is logical to conclude that these men secured Transjordan for David. They are to be seen as David's vassals. Shobi would then be an Ammonite prince appointed by David to be 'governor' of Ammon. Because Shobi is mentioned, P.K. McCarter suggests that Absalom's revolt took place before the defeat of the Ammonites (*II Samuel*, p. 394).

2.   Thus, J.B. Curtis, 'East is East...', *JBL* 80 (1961), p. 358.

3.   B. Mazar, *JBL* 80 (1961), p. 24. D. Edelman sees Talmai as king of the southern Geshur (*JNES* 47 [1988], pp. 253-58).

4.   2 Sam. 3.4.

sharp differences concerning both political, social and religious affairs. Adonijah may have speculated on the split between the different factions. As a result of Sheba's revolt, Adonijah probably understood that David's position was based more on force than on popularity. Adonijah then chose to ally himself with the members of David's pre-Jerusalemite entourage, which in his eyes, perhaps, more truly represented both Israelites and Judahites than Zadoq, the court prophet Nathan[1] and David's mercenaries could do. The commander of the mercenaries and the bodyguard was Benaiah, whose name suggests he may not have been a Jebusite. As a rival to Joab he was *persona non grata* in the eyes of Joab and Abiathar.[2] Benaiah's future was therefore with the opposite side in the struggle for power; Solomon (Jedidiah) became the candidate for the throne of the 'Jebusite' party, represented by Nathan, Zadoq and Benajah.

It has often been maintained that Solomon ascended the throne through a panic-stricken palace intrigue.[3] We may expect that some intrigues were going on for quite some time in the court and among the high officials of David's administration. The rebellions may also testify to that. It is, however, less likely that a hurried palace intrigue led by Nathan and Bath-Sheba, Solomon's mother, should have caused the collapse of Adonijah's enthronement festival. The narrator has not analyzed cause and effect and he has not given a detailed chronicle of all the events that led to Solomon's kingship. According to the text in 1 Kings 1, Adonijah tried to make himself king without David's consent. Thus, his enthronement festival at the cult place at En Rogel was

---

1.   S. Herrmann sees Nathan 'more as a privy councillor than as a prophet... who was evidently a minister with special responsibilities in the immediate entourage of the king' (*A History of Israel* [2nd edn], p. 166).

2.   As to the religio-political background, see also my article in *VT* 11 (1961), pp. 113-15; H. Haag, 'Gad und Nathan', *Archäologie und AT* (ed. A. Kuschke and E. Kutsch), pp. 135-43; cf. S. Herrmann, *A History of Israel* (2nd edn), p. 166. Already W. Erbty had recognized at the turn of the century that there were two religio-political parties in Jerusalem fighting for the succession (*Die Hebräer: Kanaan im Zeitalter der hebräischen Wanderung und Staatengründungen* [Leipzig, 1906], pp. 98-99).

3.   See, among others, J. Bright, *A History of Israel* (3rd edn), p. 210; T. Ishida, 'Solomon's Succession to the Throne of David—A Political Analysis', *Studies in the Period of David and Solomon* (ed. T. Ishida; Tokyo, 1982), p. 179; cf. D.N. Freedman, 'The Age of David and Solomon', *WHJP*, IV.1, pp. 120-21.

a *coup d'état*. The narrator depicts the king as an old incompetent and impotent man about whose opinion Adonijah did not need to care. The point is that Adonijah did not give any consideration to the words of the old king and tried to ignore the fact that David, through an oracle at some solemn ceremony, had appointed Jedidiah-Solomon as crown prince. This oracle is imbedded in the text about Nathan who, on behalf of the king, gave Solomon the name Jedidiah in accordance with the will of Yahweh (2 Sam. 12.25).[1] That name ('the beloved one of Yah') is in itself a clear indication of who the chosen heir to the throne was. Adonijah and his followers, like everyone else in the capital, must also have known the meaning of the new name. 1 Kgs 1.9-10 corroborates this conclusion by mentioning that Adonijah did not invite Zadoq, Nathan, Benaiah, Bath-Sheba or Solomon, but all the other sons of David to his enthronement. Adonijah knew what he was up against.[2] In this light, Nathan's and Bath-Sheba's question to David about his promise that Solomon should succeed him (1 Kgs 12.13, 17, and 28-31) reflects the climax of a drawn-out party conflict rather than a swift palace intrigue. The 'Jebusite' party knew that they and their candidate for the throne would lose their lives if Adonijah succeeded in his coup (1 Kgs 1.12). Hearing about Adonijah's enthronement, they had no other choice than to try to get the king to act and keep his promise, and so he did. David ordered Nathan and Zadoq to anoint Jedidiah as king at the cult place Gihon in the Kidron valley. Adonijah's aspirations then came to a quick end (1 Kgs 1.38-40). When his followers heard about Solomon's enthronement, they abruptly left Adonijah in order to save their lives. Adonijah's kingship ended as soon as it started.

One may wonder why Adonijah and his men gave up so quickly. With Joab behind him Adonijah could rely on the army. The answer must be that everyone knew that Solomon was the designated heir, so that the surprise moves indicated by Adonijah did not work.[3] As a

1.   Cf. Esarhaddon's installation of his son Ashurbanipal as crown-prince and the *adû* oath his entourage had to take in this connection (D.J. Wiseman, 'The Vassal Treaties of Esarhaddon', *Iraq* 20 [1958], col. I.41, and col. III.175); cf. also my article, 'Solomon, the Chosen One', *HR* 8 (1968), pp. 93ff.

2.   For the existence of two rival parties, see also N. Poulsen, *König und Tempel im Glaubenszeugnis des Alten Testaments* (SBM, 3; Stuttgart, 1967), p. 42.

3.   Solomon's enthronement did not 'create' a new kind of kingship as has sometimes been maintained. J. Bright, for instance, says that 'popular acclamation

usurper he now had to worry about his own life. He had lost and had, therefore, no future. He sought asylum in the sanctuary (1 Kgs 1.50) and received Solomon's promise that he would not be killed, unless he caused more problems.

Jedidiah was now David's coregent.[1] As king he became known as Solomon. The phenomenon of receiving a new name at the time of enthronement is ancient. It is known, for instance, from Egypt.[2] The enthronement changed the status for the new king. He was taken out of the ordinary human sphere and inaugurated into the divine. As a result, he received a new and great name. The name Solomon, $\check{s}^e l\bar{o}m\bar{o}h$, may mean 'his replacement',[3] and is said to have been given him at his birth by his parents (2 Sam. 12.24). However, if Jedidiah is the name of the crown-prince, as maintained above, the king may have used Solomon as his throne name, thus giving a fitting association to the god Shalem, while also, at the same time, denoting that David had a 'replacement'.

The length of Jedidiah's coregency with David is not known.[4] The narrator now ends David's story with a report of his death. His period was over. Still, it is possible that David was not actually on his death

was a fiction; and Solomon could not even claim the fiction of charismatic gifts' (*A History of Israel* [3rd edn], p. 211). Ideologically, every king received the charismatic gift of the spirit of Yahweh, *rûaḥ Yahweh*, when he was anointed. According to a prophetic oracle in the ritual, every king is chosen by the deity, and the people's acclamation is also there—their number is not the point. Adonijah would also have heard such an oracle, Solomon would have had both royal and divine words (oracle) behind him. Adonijah was, in principle, a usurper.

1. J. Gray understands 1 Kgs 1.20 as referring to an appointment to coregency, not abdication (*I and II Kings* [2nd edn], p. 88).

2. See S. Morenz, 'Ägyptische und davidsche Königstitulatur', *ZÄS* 79 (1954), pp. 72-73; H. Ranke, 'Zu Bauer I, 64ff', *ZÄS* 79 (1954), pp. 72-73; K. Seybold, *Das davidsche Königtum im Zeugnis der Propheten* (Göttingen, 1972), p. 84; R.J. Williams, 'A People Come out of Egypt', *Congress Volume, Edinburgh 1974* (ed J.A. Emerton; VTSup, 28; Leiden, 1975), pp. 234-35. The Hebrew *'āśâ šēm gādôl* (2 Sam. 7.9) is a parallel to the Egyptian *íri rn wr*, both meaning 'to make a great name' (S. Morenz, *ZÄS* 79 [1954], p. 73).

3. See J.J. Stamm, who thinks that the name announces the replacement of David's and Bath-Sheba's first child who died ('Der Name des Königs Salomo', *TZ* 16 [1960], pp. 285-97).

4. For coregencies, see E. Ball, 'The Co-Regency of David and Solomon (1 Kings 1)', *VT* 27 (1977), pp. 268-79; W.J. Murnane, *Ancient Egyptian Coregencies*.

bed when he gave orders for Solomon's enthronement. The coregency could have been established as was 'an arrangement designed to preserve the integrity of the dynasty when outward hostilities or inner dissension threatened to dissipate the royal authority'.[1] A coregency of a few years seems likely. David's reign, as well as Solomon's, is said to have been 40 years. In other words, they have been given a generation each (2 Sam. 5.4; 1 Kgs 11.42). Apparently no one really knew the exact dates of these two kings.[2]

Solomon's Rule

The new king ascended the throne in the normal way, namely by royal and divine sanction, the latter through priestly and prophetic participation.[3] Adonijah had no royal sanction for his enthronement; thus, he could be considered a usurper or rebel, and as such he failed. The writer of the Solomonic story is also emphasizing that Solomon is chosen according to the divine will (1 Kgs 1.48; 3.7; 2.24).[4] This is also expressed in the crown-prince's name, Jedidiah, 'the beloved one of Yahweh', which was given him 'according to the will of Yahweh' (2 Sam. 12.25).[5] Solomon is depicted as the legitimate king.

The writer tries to portray Solomon as a young and inexperienced man who had not yet grown into the role of the great despot,[6] but who nevertheless learned quickly. As in the case of both Saul and David, there are no extrabiblical texts for this period. The history of the Solomonic era can thus only be presented by use of the subjective opinion of the biblical writers combined with archaeological remains. The latter are impressive compared with the preceding period.

---

1. W.J. Murnane, *Ancient Egyptian Coregencies*, p. 264.

2. S. Mowinckel, following Josephus' information from Menander, dates David from c. 985 BCE to c. 955 BCE, and Solomon to 955–930/929 BCE (*AcOr* 10 [1932], pp. 270-71). If this is right, Saul could have reigned sometime during the period 1015–980 BCE.

3. Solomon's accession to the throne can be compared with that of Esarhaddon or Ashurbanipal. Both were ritually chosen and installed as crown-princes instead of their older brother(s). Esarhaddon was militarily opposed, but when their armies met, the soldiers of the rebels went over to Esarhaddon knowing that he was the rightful king (cf. H.W.F. Saggs, *The Might That was Assyria*, pp. 104-105).

4. Cf. G.W. Ahlström, *HR* 8 (1968), pp. 93-95.

5. See my article, *VT* 11 (1961), p. 122 n. 4.

6. Cf. 1 Kgs 3.4-15.

As was frequently the case in the ancient Near East, a new king had to wage war or eliminate his opponents in some other way in order to establish his throne firmly. In the Solomon's case there are no reported wars; instead there are details about the new king's treatment of Adonijah and his supporters. Adonijah is said to have been forced to promise not to take any action against the throne (1 Kgs 1.52). The other leaders of this party were put out of the way. Joab was killed, and Abiathar was 'defrocked' and expelled to Anathoth (1 Kgs 2.1-26).[1] A relative of Saul, Shimei, who had threatened and cursed David when he had fled from Absalom (2 Sam. 16.5-13), was forbidden to leave the city, but was later killed when he later did so (1 Kgs 2.8-9, 42-46).[2]

To allow Adonijah to remain alive was a nice but dangerous gesture. The author's purpose in writing this is to show the fine character of the new king, while showing at the same time that Adonijah could not be trusted. The result had been a confrontation that had climaxed with Adonijah's death. While alive, Adonijah may have been the representative of a certain group opposed to Solomon's kingship. He is said not to have given up hope of retaining the throne. This is clearly indicated by his request to marry Abishag, David's latest and youngest addition to the harem. Some time after Solomon's takeover,[3] Adonijah went to the king's mother, the $g^e b \hat{\imath} r \hat{a}$, Bath-Sheba, and asked her to request of Solomon that Abishag be given to him as wife (1 Kgs 2.13-18). The reason why he went to Bath-Sheba is clear. As the king's mother, she had a special office and was probably in charge of the late king's harem, among other duties.[4] For her position as the 'great lady behind the throne', it should be noted that she was seated on

1. This the writer used as the 'fulfillment' of the oracle in the deuteronomistic speech of 1 Sam. 2.27-36.

2. Solomon's killing of Shimei is said to have been the result of advice from David. By legitimizing it in this way Solomon could not be accused of murder.

3. It must have been early, according to the textual presentation, because, after hearing the news about Adonijah and his fate, Joab fled to the sanctuary of Yahweh, hoping to find asylum there, but he was killed by Benaiah, who was following an order issued by Solomon (1 Kgs 2.28-34).

4. For the $g^e b \hat{\imath} r \hat{a}$ institution, see G. Molin, 'Die Stellung der Gĕbīrā im Staate Juda', *TZ* 10 (1954), pp. 165-75; H. Donner, 'Art und Herkunft des Amtes der Königinmutter im Alten Testament', *Festschrift Johannes Friedrich* (ed. R. von Kienle *et al.*; Heidelberg, 1959), pp. 106-45); G.W. Ahlström, *Aspects of Syncretism*, pp. 57-59.

a throne at the right side of the king, her son (1 Kgs 2.19). In coming to Bath-Sheba with his request, Adonijah thus went through the right channel. Bath-Sheba seems to have hurried in to the king, knowing well the danger Adonijah represented. Solomon immediately gave the verdict and Adonijah was killed (1 Kgs 2.13-25). It is apparent from this incident that asking for one of the wives of the late king was the same as laying claim to the throne.[1]

With all these men having left the political stage of Jerusalem, Solomon had firmly established his throne (1 Kgs 2.46). The Jerusalemite-Jebusite 'party' had eliminated the influence of the new-comers. Benaiah, who had been Joab's rival, became the new generalissimus, and Abiathar's banishment meant religious affairs could now be handled by the representatives of the Jerusalemite tradition. Zadoq became the undisputed leader of the official national Yahwistic cult, a cult that was more in line with Jebusite and perhaps Gibeonite traditions than the religious traditions of the mountain peoples of Saul's kingdom. The Israelites and Judahites had conquered Jerusalem-Jebus, but Jerusalem-Jebus had conquered the rest of the population of Palestine with its religious heritage. It is the Jerusalemite ideology that now puts its stamp on the country's official religion. Yahweh from Sinai, Seir, Paran, Teman, is now the Yahweh of Zion.[2] In other words, the syncretism that had begun when Yahweh entered the land of Canaan took a different turn when he entered Jerusalem and became firmly established under Solomon. Religious events would have gone on as before, but under Zadoq the Jebusite character of the religion and its ideology became more accentuated.[3] The name of the

1. Cf. 2 Sam. 16.21-23. See, for instance, C.H. Gordon, *The World of the Old Testament* (Garden City, NY, 1958), p. 181; J.A. Soggin, 'The Davidic–Solomonic Kingdom', in J.H. Hayes and J.M. Miller, *Israelite and Judean History* (Philadelphia, 1977), p. 347; G. Fohrer, *Geschichte Israels* (Heidelberg 1979), p. 105. Fohrer says, however, that Bath-Sheba did not understand the seriousness of Adonijah's request.

2. Elyon, a title of Yahweh, was also given to the king, his viceroy. The attribute '*elyôn* over all the kings of the earth' (Ps. 89.28) could perhaps be compared with the Akkadian imperial title *šar kibrāt arba'i*, 'king of the four quarters of the earth', or *šar šarrāni*, 'king of kings'.

3. F.M. Cross tries to make Zadoq a Judahite coming from Hebron (*Canaanite Myth and Hebrew Epic*, p. 207-15). Hebron, however, was a Calebite city, and probably had no specific Israelite connection at this time beyond the political one established by David. For Judah as a fusion of several Canaanite and Edomite clans,

new king is significant in this connection. The name Solomon is of the same root as the god name Shalem, which is also part of the name of the capital, Jerusalem, 'the foundation of Shalem'.[1] If there were a 'program declaration' in choosing a throne name, this choice would indicate that the god Shalem (identified with Yahweh) through his viceroy, Solomon, now was the ruler of the kingdom.

Solomon's visit to Gibeon's sanctuary and his dream there may, from a literary point of view, fulfil two purposes. His 'dream'[2] (presented in deuteronomistic garb)[3] has been used as his divine legitimation as successor to the throne.[4] The visit to Gibeon and its sanctuary, 'the largest *bāmâ* in the country',[5] may, however, have had political overtones. The Gibeonite political unit and its territories was one of the first areas of Canaan that had become part of Saul's kingdom. Would it, therefore, be possible to understand both David's and Solomon's visits to Gibeon in the same light as Rehoboam's visit to Shechem? If so, the kings would have had to renew the connection with the Gibeonites, perhaps through a treaty, in order to be acknowledged as their ruler.[6]

see R. de Vaux, 'L'installation des israelites dans la sud Palestinien et les origins de la tribu de Judah', *Proceedings of the Fifth World Congress of Jewish Studies* (Jerusalem, 1966), pp. 150-56. R. Dussaud, among others, considered Zadoq to be a Gibeonite priest (*Les origines canaanéennes du sacrifice d'israélite* [2nd edn; Paris, 1941], pp. 285-89). As to the discussion, cf. H.H. Rowley, 'Zadok and Nehushtan', *JBL* 58 (1939), pp. 113-41.

1.   S.H. Nyberg, *ARW* 35 (1938), p. 351. J.J. Stamm, however, prefers to see this name as an 'Ersatzname', a substitute name, referring to Solomon as being the substitute for David's and Bath-Sheba's first son who died (*TZ* 16 [1960], pp. 285-87).

2.   1 Kgs 3.4-15.

3.   R.B.Y. Scott, 'Solomon and the Beginning of Wisdom in Israel', in *Wisdom in Israel* (Festschrift H.H. Rowley; ed. M. Noth and D.W. Thomas; VTSup, 3; Leiden, 1955), pp. 262-79.

4.   Thus, E. Würthwein, *Die Bücher der Könige: 1 Könige 1–16* (ATD, 11.1; Göttingen, 1977), pp. 31-33; cf. C.H. Brekelmans, 'Solomon at Gibeon', *Von Kanaan bis Kerala* (ed. W.C. Delsman *et al.*; AOAT, 211; Neukirchen–Vluyn, 1982), pp. 53-59. Würthwein sees the passage as inspired by the Judahite royal enthronement ritual, and compares it with Pss. 2.8 and 21.3, 5. He also maintains that the text is a local Gibeonite tradition that has been reworked (pp. 53-55).

5.   1 Kgs 3.4. This may be interpreted to mean that Gibeon's sanctuary was also the most important one until Solomon's temple was built.

6.   The biblical narrator has not given the full story about David's visit with the

It seems to be a fact that Solomon was not completely successful in maintaining David's kingdom intact. The Edomite prince, Hadad, who had escaped to Egypt[1] from David's massacre of the Edomites, returned after David's death and recaptured part of Edom (1 Kgs 11.14-22). Edom east of the Arabah Valley probably came under Hadad's rule. Solomon was probably able to hold western Edom, because later he had his ships sailing from Ezion-geber. The trade routes from the Judean hills down to the Gulf of Aqaba apparently remained in his hands.[2]

Hadad had been well received by the Egyptian Pharaoh, Siamun after his reported flight from the Davidic massacre. He is said to have been given a sister of queen Tahpenes(?) as wife.[3] This act could indicate that Egypt still harbored the idea of dominance over parts of Palestine,[4] which is supported by Siamun's campaign into Philistine territory and his destruction of the city of Gezer (1 Kgs 9.16). As for Hadad and his newly established kingdom, the Bible provides no further information.

In the north the danger was greater. Rezon, aservant or official of Hadadezer of Aram-Zobah's, had gathered men around him and rebelled against his master. As an outlaw he also came into conflict

Gibeonites. Through the information about the sacrifice of Saul's sons, we can, however, understand that the visit was a political one. The result reassured the new king about the loyalty of the Gibeonites, and the extermination of potential claimants to the throne (cf. G.W. Ahlström, *Who were the Israelites?*, pp. 94-95).

1.   For the possible route of Hadad's escape, see J.R. Bartlett, *ZAW* 88 (1976), pp. 210-11; and cf. G.W. Ahlström, 'A Nabatean Inscription from Wadi Mukatteb, Sinai', *Studies in History of Religions*, XXI (Suppl. to Numen; Leiden, 1972), pp. 323-25.

2.   Some of the small fortresses from this period found in the Negev may have been part of Solomon's building program; cf. Y. Aharoni, M. Evenari, L. Shanan and N.H. Tadmor, 'The Ancient Desert Agriculture of the Negev. V. An Israelite Agricultural Settlement of Ramat Matred', *IEJ* 10 (1960), pp. 23-36, 97-111; cf. also R. Cohen, 'The Iron Age Fortress in the Central Negev', *BASOR* 236 (1979), pp. 61-79. Cohen has now seen that three of these forts were built in the Persian period (Horvat Mesora, Atar Haro'a and Horvat Ritma); cf. 'Solomon's Negev Defense Line Contained Three Fewer Fortresses', *BARev* 12 (1986), pp. 40-45.

3.   Cf. K.A. Kitchen, *The Third Intermediate Period*, p. 280. The name of Tahpenes does not appear in any Egyptian record.

4.   J.R. Bartlett, *ZAW* 88 (1976), p. 221.

with David—as David did with Saul.[1] According to 1 Kgs 11.23-24, Rezon went to 'Damascus and settled there and made a kingdom in Damascus'.[2] Solomon never succeeded in subduing Rezon, who was 'an adversary to Israel as long as Solomon lived' (1 Kgs 11.25). This shows that Solomon's reign was not as peaceful as has usually been suggested.

The fortifications at Hazor may have been begun soon after Rezon's capture of Damascus in order to protect the northern border. There is no information about the size of the territory Rezon managed to rule over. The conflict between Damascus and Jerusalem may have resulted in the annihilation of the kingdoms of Maacah, Geshur and Tob, since they were located in the geographical sphere of conflict between Aram-Damascus and Israel. If the testimony of 2 Sam. 20.19 is reliable, the reduction of Maacah's territory started in the time of David. Possibly the territory in the Beqa' Valley up to Lebo-Hamath continued to be part of Israel. The kingdom of Aram-Damascus would have lain to the east of the Anti-Lebanon range and to the south and southeast of Mount Hermon down to Bashan and Hauran during Solomon's reign.

Solomon's division of Israel into administrative districts, from which Judah was exempt, shows that the border between Israel and the Philistines may have been due west of Gibbethon. His district number two included the towns of Timnah, Gibbethon, Baalath and Eltekeh in the south. The coastal area up to the Carmel was under his rule, but he had ceded to Hiram of Tyre the territory of Kabul, which lay north of Carmel up to the border to Tyre (1 Kgs 9.12-13).

The Chronicler credits Solomon with having fortified Tadmor (the later Palmyra),[3] a well-known caravan center roughly halfway

---

1. A. Malamat hypothesizes that Rezon could have been encouraged in his rebellion by David (*JNES* 22 [1963], p. 5).

2. M.F. Unger suggests that Rezon started his kingdom 'when the signs of decay first became noticeable in Solomon's kingdom', and there would have been 'an increasing laxity in the Israelite administration' (*Israel and the Aramaeans of Damascus*, p. 54). The statement in 11.25 would then be meaningless. There is no information about Solomon's administration becoming lax. For the Assyrian name *mātu ša imērīšu*, 'the land of his donkey', as a translation of the second-millennium BCE name Abinu/Upe and not a translation of the name Damascus, see E. Gaál, '*mātu ša imērīšu* as a Translation from Hurrian', *Revue Hittite et Asianique* 36 (1978), pp. 43-48.

3. 2 Chron. 8.4.

between Damascus and the Euphrates. This has led to the speculation that Solomon's kingdom reached almost all the way to the Euphrates. After the rise of the new kingdom of Aram-Damascus, it would certainly have been very problematic for Solomon to have had any contact with Tadmor. However, the Hebrew text of 1 Kgs 9.18 has 'Tamar in the wilderness in the land' instead of Tadmor. The phrase 'in the land' always means 'inside the country' and so refers to Canaan. In this passage Tamar is mentioned after Gezer, Lower Beth-Horon and Baalath,[1] as places Solomon fortified. If Tamar refers to a city in the Negev,[2] as seems likely, the information in 1 Kgs 9.17-18 would concern the defense of the southern and the southwestern borders of Israel. The Chronicler's information would seem to be a result of his 'pan-Israelite' concept.[3]

Usually the kings of the ancient Near East were great builders. Government buildings, such as palaces, temples, store cities and fortresses, were expressions not only of a king's duties or of his dreams about power and might; the building programs were at the same time an expression of his position as the god's viceroy, the one who should shepherd the people. In this way the king carried out the god's demands for making his realm well organized, strong and grand.[4] This was, then, part of the wisdom of the king.

Solomon's building activities were an integral part of his policy to

---

1. Baalath has tentatively been identified with Tell el-Mughar, c. 10 km west of Ekron. Cf. Z. Kallai, *The Northern Boundaries of Judah* (Jerusalem, 1960), pp. 31-32 (Hebrew); M. Gichon, 'The Defenses of the Solomonic Kingdom', *PEQ* 95 (1963), pp. 120-21; Y. Aharoni, *The Land of the Bible* (2nd edn), p. 431. Cf. Josh. 19.44.

2. See Y. Aharoni, 'Tamar and the Roads to Elath', *IEJ* 13 (1963), pp. 30-42; S. Mittmann, *ZDPV* 93 (1977), pp. 230-35.

3. This concept is expressed in the masoretic reading (the $q^e r\bar{e}$') of 1 Kgs 9.18. The Chronicler also credits Solomon with having taken Hamath-Zobah and having built store cities in its territory (2 Chron. 8.3-4). This may be a sign of the Chronicler's poor knowledge of geography and history. Either he meant Hamath or Aram-Zobah-Rehob, which became a vassal state to David. The Chronicler's aim may have been to emphasize that Solomon, in spite of Rezon's new kingdom, was sovereign over the Aramaean countries. See, for instance, Y. Aharoni, who suggests the adoption of the LXX and read *baisoba* (Beth-Zobah), which would mean that 'Solomon fortified his positions in the Lebanese Beqa'' (*The Land of the Bible* [2nd edn], p. 319 n. 54).

4. Cf. my book, *Royal Administration*, pp. 1-3.

create a strong nation and to bind together the different geographical districts with their unrelated clans. The means for this was a well-oiled administrative apparatus, a well controlled bureaucracy. Only persons who were directly under the king as his 'servants' would be efficient enough and trustworthy enough and could thus serve as the king's power base.[1] A feudal system would be dangerous for the longevity of the kingdom.

In order to carry out his building programs and to bring the revenue under his control, Solomon built up an efficient administrative apparatus on the basis of what David had started or taken over from the Jebusites. The list of Solomon's high officials in 1 Kgs 4.2-6 contains the same offices used by David, as well as some new ones. Among the new are a 'major domus' who is called *'ašer 'al-habbayit*, 'the one over the house', and a *rē'eh hammelek*, 'king's friend'. Both of these offices are known also from Egyptian and Mesopotamian sources.[2] Israel, excluding Judah, was divided into twelve districts (1 Kgs 4.8-19). The district governors were to levy taxes, and to provide provisions for king and court, one month a year (4.7).[3] Another duty was to cooperate with the administrator of the forced labor, *mas*.[4] It is clear that forced labor was employed also in David's

---

1. Cf. M. Trolle Larsen, 'Tradition of Empire', *Power and Propaganda* (ed. M. Trolle Larsen), pp. 85-86.

2. From the Amarna letters we know of ᴸᵁ*ruḫi šarri* (EA 228.11); cf. Gen. 26.26, and see A. van Selms, 'The Origin of the Title "The King's Friend"', *JNES* 16 (1957), pp. 118-23; H. Donner, *ZAW* 73 (1961), pp. 269-77; T. Mettinger, *Solomonic State Officials*, pp. 63-65. For the 'friends of the king' as a honorary title at the Persian court, see J. Wieselhofer, 'Die "Freunde" und "Wohltäter" des Grosskönigs', *Studia Iranica* 9 (1980), pp. 7-21.

3. Cf. A. Alt, 'Israels Gaue unter Salomo', *KS*, II, pp. 76-89; G.E. Wright, *EI* 8 (1967), pp. 58*-60*.

4. For this term, see I. Mendelsohn, 'On Corvée Labor in Ancient Canaan and Israel', *BASOR* 167 (1961), pp. 31-35; M. Held, 'The Root ZBL/SBL in Akkadian, Ugaritic and Biblical Hebrew', *JAOS* 88 (1968), pp. 90-96; A.F. Rainey, *IEJ* 20 (1970) pp. 191-202; T. Mettinger, *Solomonic State Officials*, pp. 128-30. Another word for forced labor is *sebel* (1 Kgs 11.28-30). This term may refer to the actual work (cf. *sōbel*, 'burden'). The term *mas* would then refer to the people involved in the system. W. von Soden renders the Akkadian *massu* as 'Dienstverpflichteter' (*AHw, s.v.*). T. Mettinger sees *mas* as a Canaanite term and *sebel* as being Aramaic and of northern origin (pp. 137-39). I can agree that *mas* is a Canaanite term if Canaanite includes Hebrew.

time.[1] Adoram was David's supervisor in charge of *mas* (2 Sam. 20.24). According to 1 Kgs 12.18, he also continued to function in the same position during Solomon's reign.

Solomon's district organization[2] has been seen as being modelled after that of Egypt. This is probable since the pharaonic administrative system had long been well known in Palestine and had perhaps also inspired the Palestinian princes in organizing their administrations. D.B. Redford thinks that the model Solomon used was pharaoh Shoshenq's system, with its levy 'arranged in twelve monthly sections'.[3] Solomon inaugurated his system before he started to build his palace and temple complex (1 Kgs 5.27-30, Eng. 5.13-16), which is said to have begun in his fourth year (1 Kgs 6.1). If so, Solomon's organization could not have been modeled after that of Shoshenq, who came to the throne only in 946/45. Other more probable candidates would be pharaoh Siamun (979–960 BCE) and Psusonnes II (960–946 BCE).

The division of Israel into twelve districts, while a political decision, was according to geographical areas that had traditionally formed agricultural, social and ethnic units. The political units were 'far more coincident with geographical areas'[4] than with the historiographical theory about a twelve tribe league. 1 Kgs 4.7-19 refers to the districts by the old names of the geographical areas or towns within their borders. It is most probable that Solomon followed and reorganized David's district system. 1 Kgs 5.1-2 (Eng. 4.27-28) mentions that one of the duties of the district governors that was to provide the royal

---

1. For David using prisoners of war and the peoples of conquered territories, see 2 Sam. 12.31.

2. 1 Kgs 4.

3. 'Studies in Relations between Palestine and Egypt during the First Millennium BCE', *Studies in the Ancient Palestinian World* (ed. J.W. Wevers and D.B. Redford; Toronto, 1972), pp. 153-5. Consult also J. Begrich, *ZAW* 58 (1940–41), pp. 1-6. A.R. Green suggests that Shoshenq learned about Solomon's system through Jeroboam ('Israelite Influence at Shishak's Court', *BASOR* 233 [1979], pp. 59-62). Mesopotamian parallels could also be sought since most kings of the ancient Near East built their organization roughly upon the same principles; cf. R.P. Dougherty, 'Cuneiform Parallels to Solomon's Provisioning System', *AASOR* 5 (1923–24), pp. 23-65.

4. C.H.J. de Geus, *The Tribes of Israel*, p. 138. See also my *Royal Administration*, p. 33; N. Na'aman, *Borders and Districts in Biblical Historiography*, p. 85.

court with food, and the horses and draft animals with fodder. Each district was responsible for one month per year.

District I was the mountainous region called *har 'eprayim*,[1] that is, the area north of Bethel and Lower and Upper Beth Horon to the vicinity of Shechem. It also included the southern part of the Jordan valley between Jericho and Jokmeam. District II was the area south of the Yarkon river, which contained the cities Aphek, Jehud, Lod, Shaalbim, Aijalon, Timnah and Beth-Shemesh. Beth-Shemesh was evidently not considered as part of Judah.[2] It was populated by Philistines and Canaanite clans who had no real connection with the mountain peoples.[3]

District III included the coastal area north of the Yarkon river (= north of District II), that is, the Sharon plain, with the cities Arruboth, Socoh, and 'all the land of Hepher' (4.10). The location of Arruboth is unknown. It occurs only here in the Hebrew Bible. W.F. Albright suggested that it would be at modern Arrabe in the Dothan plain.[4] Hepher is listed as a clan of Manasseh in Josh. 17.2-3 (cf. Num. 26.31-33; 27.1), so it should be sought in the western hills and not on the coast.[5] Socoh has been identified with Khirbet Shuweikeh by A. Alt.[6] This site lies at the point where the mountains

---

1. Such terms as *har 'eprayim, nāpat dôr* (i.e., the wooded area of Dor), *'ereṣ gil'ād* ('the land of Gilead') indicate that the districts were not made according to any biblical tribal system. According to G.E. Wright, the phrase *har 'eprayim* is not a reference to the 'tribe' of Ephraim (*EI* 8 [1967], pp. 60-61*).

2. This is also clear from the story of the Ark. The men of Beth-Shemesh asked the men of Kirijat-Jearim to come and get the Ark (1 Sam. 6.20–7.1). See G.W. Ahlström, *JNES* 43 (1984), pp. 141-49.

3. The statement in Judg. 1.35 about the Amorites of this area being forced into the corvée may refer to this district organization. Gezer is not mentioned in the list, which probably means that it was part of the royal estate (See A. Alt, 'Israels Gaue unter Salamo', *KS*, II, p. 86), or that it was still in ruins.

4. W.F. Albright, *JPOS* 5 (1925), pp. 17-54; cf. G.E. Wright, *EI* 8 (1967), pp. 62-63*.

5. Modern Tel Hepher is located c. 18 km north of Tel Michal on the coast. A. Lemaire sees the phrase 'all the land of Hepher' to denote an old Canaanite kingdom (*Sem* 22 [1972], p. 14). A. Zertal has identified the city of Hepher with modern Tell el-Muhafar just north of the Dothan Valley (*Arubboth, Hepher and the Third Solomonic District*, pp. 123-25 [Hebrew]. Z. Kallai places the land of Hepher 'west of Tirzah' (*Historical Geography of the Bible*, p. 56).

6. See his arguments for this proposal in 'Israels Gaue unter Salomo', *KS*, II, pp. 78-79.

meet the Sharon plain and at the point where the valley leading to Nablus starts. This district may not have been too densely populated. In ancient times it consisted of oak forests and on the coast many swamps, the latter containing malaria. Only in modern time has the picture changed.[1]

District IV, Nephat-Dor,[2] was geographically comparable to the former city state of the Tjeker, which controlled the area south of the Carmel including the northern part of the Sharon plain. The governor of the district was a son-in-law of Solomon, Ben-Abinadab (1 Kgs 4.11). The city of Dor was one of Solomon's few ports on the Mediterranean.[3]

The borders of District V are more difficult to outline. The district included Megiddo, Ta'anak, Ibleam and Beth-Shan, with surrounding areas. From Beth-Shan it turned into the Jordan Valley to Abel-Meholah. It included most probably also the eastern part of the valley, because Zarethan (Tell es-Sa'idiyeh?) was within its boundaries. This district may have stretched down to Adam on the east side and Jokmeam on the west. This district consisted of lowlands and valleys that formed a geographical and economical unit. The large number of settlements on the eastern side of the river, *el-ghor*, indicates that the road on this side, 'the way of the plain', was more important than the parallel road on the west side of the river.[4]

1. The last oak forest was cut down by the Turks, according to K. Amiran (see G.E. Wright, *EI* 8 [1967], p. 62*). Cf. also E. Orni and E. Efrat, *Geography of Israel* (3rd edn), p. 48. Other settlements in this area known from the Shoshenq list are Borim, Gath-padala and Yehem; see J. Simons, *Handbook for the Study of Egyptian Topographical Lists*, p. 117; Y. Aharoni, *Land of the Bible* (2nd edn), pp. 235, 327; cf. R. Gophna and M. Kochavi, 'An Archaeological Survey of the Plain of Sharon', *IEJ* 16 (1966), p. 143-44.

2. For *nāpâ* meaning 'district, wooded area', see the discussion of M. Ben-Dov, 'hpn—A Geographical Term of Possible "Sea People" Origin', *Tel Aviv* 3 (1976), pp. 70-73.

3. Cf. V. Fritz, 'Die sogenannte Liste der besiegten Könige in Jos. 12', *ZDPV* 85 (1969), p. 157.

4. District IV illustrates how mountains and forests separated peoples, not rivers and straits; see K.H. Waters, *Herodotus on Tyrants and Despots: A Study in Objectivity* (Historia, Zeitschrift für die alte Geschichte: Einzelschriften, 15; Wiesbaden, 1971), p. 97. Cf. M. Noth, 'Das deutsche evangelische Institut fur Altertumswissenschaft des Heiligen Landes: Lehrkursus 1955, 1956', *ZDPV* 72 (1956), pp. 137-39; M. Ottosson, *Gilead*, p. 217; G.W. Ahlström, *Royal Administration*, p. 34.

Gilead north of Mahanaim, or the northern Transjordan, formed District VI. It included the areas of Jair and reached up into the Bashan, the region of Argob,[1] 'with 60 fortified towns having walls and bronze bars' (4.13). Unfortunately, the writer does not mention any of the towns, and the area is not well known archaeologically. The biblical writer may not have known how much of this territory was in reality under the king of Damascus. If the territory belonged to Solomon, one would have expected Ashtaroth and Qarnaim to have been mentioned.[2] Nothing is said about Geshur, which could mean that it still was a vassal state to the king in Jerusalem, or, more probably, that it had been incorporated in the new kingdom of Aram-Damascus.

Transjordan south of the river Jabbok and down to the area north of the Heshbon plateau was District VII. The only city mentioned within its boundaries is Mahanaim (Tulul edh-Dhahab). If Adam in the Jordan Valley did not belong to this district, it would probably have been part of District V, as mentioned above.

District VIII corresponded to the old territory of Naphtali. A son-in-law of Solomon was appointed governor. Its population first became Israelite under David. The district list does not name any of its cities, but because Naphtali included the territory stretching up to the sources of the Jordan river, Dan and Ijon were within its borders. It is in this district Solomon built his well-known fortress city of Hazor, which in post-Solomonic times may have become more important than Megiddo because of its strategic location. It became a bastion against invaders from the north.

Western Galilee, the territory of Asher, became the District IX, probably originally including the plain of Acco in the south (4.16). Later, the district area decreased when Solomon gave part of it, 20 towns (Kabul),[3] as payment to Hiram of Tyre. The phrase 'in Asher and b^e'ālôt' has often been seen as corrupt.[4] The text, however, is

1. J. Gray considers this as an expansion by the Deuteronomist (*I and II Kings*, p. 135, note g).

2. The districts of Bashan and Hauran could have been taken by Rezon some time after Solomon had made his district division.

3. For the name Kabul, see below.

4. A. Alt, 'Israels Gaue unter Salomo', *KS*, II, p. 76-89; W.F. Albright, *JPOS* 5 (1925), pp. 17-54; G.E. Wright, 'The Provinces of Solomon', *EI* 8 (1958), pp. 59*-61*; Y. Aharoni, *The Land of the Bible* (2nd edn), p. 315; J. Gray, *I and II Kings*, p. 139; T. Mettinger, *Solomonic State Officials*, p. 118. According to G.E. Wright (*EI* 8 [1958], p. 59*-61*), F.M. Cross proposed, with the help of

clear enough and the translation would be either 'in Asher and Be'alot', or 'in Asher and in 'Alot'. In the latter case 'Alot would mean 'the heights'.[1]

District X was the territory of Issachar, including the central and eastern part of the Jezreel Valley, the southeastern hills of Galilee and probably the most northern part of the Jordan Valley on both sides of the river. The city of Shunem would have been located within this district.[2]

District XI, the district of Benjamin, also reflects a pre-Israelite political unit. It was made up of the old Benjaminite territory and its addition from the Saulidic period, the Gibeonite cities. Whether Benjamin's people and the Gibeonites had any closer relationship before Saul is not known. However, when a Benjaminite such as Saul could claim Edomite descendency, as could the Gibeonites, the possibility of some affiliation cannot be dismissed.

The information about District XII is more problematic. According to 1 Kgs 4.19 Geber ben Uri was the governor 'in the land of Gilead'.[3] In order to give the reader/listener an idea of what territory was included therein, he adds what are to a postexilic reader the well known phrases 'the land of Sihon, king of the Amorites', and 'Og, king of Bashan'. This indicates that the passage was intended for the members of the postexilic Judean society; it is in harmony with the theological reconstruction of the 'settlement'.[4] However, Gilead was split between Districts VI and VII. The Mesha inscription mentions

---

the scripts of the fourth and third centuries, the reading *zbwlwn* for *b'lwt* ('The Papyri and their Historical Implications', *Discoveries in the Wadi ed-Daliyeh* [ed. P.W. Lapp and N. Lapp; AASOR, 41; 1976], pp. 17-29).

1.   Cf. G.W. Ahlström, 'A Note on a Textual Problem in 1 Kings 4.16', *BASOR* 235 (1979), p. 79. Be'alot is also a name of a town in Judah (Josh. 15.24).

2.   Y. Aharoni maintains that Issachar as a tribe 'was consolidated mainly from among the corvée workers, part of whom had already come to this area during the Amarna period' (*The Land of the Bible* [2nd edn], p. 192). Aharoni has here anachronistically used the 'tribal unification' system.

3.   This seems to be out of place because Gilead has already been taken care of (District VI).

4.   Cf. Num. 32.18-39, which is part of the same reconstruction theme. M. Ottosson sees the whole chapter of Num. 32 as a composition of 'the P-traditionist' (*Gilead*, p. 79). The allotment of the land to different tribes is part of the priestly traditions (cf. G. Vink, 'The Date and Origin of the Priestly Code in the Old Testament', *OTS* 15 [1969], pp. 63-73).

that Gad lives in the Mishor ('even plain, high plateau') in southern Transjordan, north of the Arnon river (Mujib). Since this area is the only one—besides Judah—that is left to form another district, then the reading in the LXX, Gad, instead of Gilead, would make sense.[1] Furthermore, the term *'ereṣ gil'ad* never refers to southern Transjordan.[2] Thus, District XII probably consisted of the territory of Gad.[3] The area of the Mishor could either have belonged to the Mahanaim district or it could have been governed by the vassal king of Moab. The biblical writer has presented the view current in his own time.

The district organization clearly had nothing to do with the Bible's literary tribal system. On the contrary, the tribal system may be seen as a result of the geographical connection between several clans. Thus Solomon cannot be blamed for having disregarded the tribal organization,[4] a phenomenon that probably never existed in his time or before. The district organization should be seen for what it was: a political means of organizing the nation so that the king and the court could extract the most out of it. A. Alt's thesis that the list in 1 Kgs 4.7-19 is the last document reflecting the old dualism between city and tribe explains nothing. It is rather part of an evolutionary idea that 'tribes' and cities were antagonistic, with the tribes always losing the battle. The sociological picture shows instead that the cities were the centers for the population of the countryside, those who lived in the villages, the *bānôt*, 'daughters', of the cities. The cities could develop into centers for commerce, and places where the population went for the purposes of paying their taxes, or to participate in or 'see' the cult festivals.

1.   A. Alt, 'Israels Gaue unter Salamo', *KS*, II, pp. 76-78.

2.   Cf. M. Noth, *Könige* (BKAT, 9.1; Neukirchen–Vluyn, 1968), p. 74.

3.   M. Ottosson holds the opinion that 1 Kgs 4.19 refers to the Davidic period. He believes that the information in v. 19 is 'used to fill out the figure 12'; cf. 4.7 that mentions 12 *niṣābîm*, governors (*Gilead*, pp. 219-20). 1 Kgs 4.13 has *ben geber* as the governor in Ramoth Gilead, and v. 19 mentions Geber, son of Uri. This may support Ottosson's theory. Geber could have been governor in Gilead before Solomon's district organization was made. His son, *ben geber*, then succeeded him, and was, according to Ottosson, 'the first official who (was) in the Land' of Gilead (p. 220).

4.   As mentioned by J. Wellhausen, *Prolegomena to the History of Ancient Israel*, p. 456; cf. G.E. Wright, *EI* 8 (1967), p. 67*; J. Bright, *A History of Israel* (3rd edn), p. 221; J.A. Soggin, *A History of Ancient Israel*, p. 62.

The cities also served as protection for the village population in times of war. Archaeology has shown that many of the cities of the monarchic period were not built as residential cities. Most of them were fortress cities, stores cities and administrative centers in which probably only a few government officials and their families lived.[1]

Solomon's relations and treaty with Tyre can be seen as a continuation and reaffirmation of David's policy. W.F. Albright suggested that king Abibaal of Tyre (Hiram's father) had sought friendly relations with David in order to break the Philistine dominance in Palestine.[2] It is equally possible that the relationship between Tyre and Israel began already with Saul.[3] H. Donner has challenged the view that David had a treaty with Tyre. He sees 2 Sam. 5.11 and 24.5-7 as 'late redacted texts', which cannot be accepted as authentic sources. He believes that Tyre would have 'entered the political horizon' in Israel during the time of Solomon.[4] The text may be late, but Donner's theory is unrealistic. It is inconceivable that the Phoenicians would not have had diplomatic connections with the new kingdom in Palestine. Their trade interests and the very nature of their economic system must have forced them to see the advantage of friendly relations with the new power represented by David's kingdom. In conquering the Aramaean territories of Zobah and placing garrisons in Damascus, David controlled the trade routes between Damascus and the Phoenicians.

Hiram ('Ahiram) of Tyre became king around 970 BCE, that is, before Solomon became David's coregent.[5] The phrase 'Hiram

1. See my article, *JNES* 41 (1982), pp. 133-38.
2. Cited in H.J. Katzenstein (*The History of Tyre*, pp. 74-75) as an oral communication. Katzenstein sees Psalm 83 as an indication of Phoenician hostility towards Israel in the time between Wen-Amun's visit to Tyre and Saul's kingdom (p. 73). Because the psalm is looking back at history, it could just as well be maintained that the 'tents' of Edom, Ishmael, Moab and the Hagrites refer to the time when Moab and Edom no longer existed as kingdoms (cf. my book, *Who were the Israelites?*, p. 90).
3. On this topic, see the discussion in D. Edelman, 'The Rise of the Israelite State'.
4. S.H. Donner, 'The Interdependence of International Affairs', *Studies* (ed. T. Ishida), pp. 213-14. R. Kittel had already expressed this opinion (*Geshichte des Volkes Israel*, II (5th edn; Gotha, 1922), p. 151; on this, see also J. Liver, *IEJ* 3 (1953), p. 118.
5. Josephus, *Apion*, 1.117. Cf. H. Katzenstein, *The History of Tyre*, p. 77-82.

"loved" David always' (1 Kgs 5.15)[1] would support the theory that a treaty had been made late in David's reign. Any such treaty would have had to have been renewed when Solomon became the sole ruler. The treaty (*bᵉrît*) between Solomon and Hiram may have been an alliance between equals.[2]

Besides the military aspect, the importance of a treaty lay in the amount of profit one could make. The biblical narrator does not specify what Hiram acquired from Solomon; apparently this was not important to him. He quickly summarizes what products and objects were sent to Israel. 1 Kgs 5.24 mentions building material; 7.13-14 mentions that workers were sent from Tyre for Solomon's building; 9.11 mentions cedarwood, cyprus wood and objects of gold. Hiram participated in Solomon's expeditions to Tarshish and Ophir—or rather, Solomon participated in the Tyrian sea trade. Other products that Tyre received from Israel were wheat and oil (5.25), and perhaps also wine. For the sea trade Solomon established a port at Ezion-Geber at the northern end of the Gulf of Aqaba 'in the land of Edom' (1 Kgs 9.26-27). Solomon would also have had help from Hiram in building ships at Ezion-Geber.[3] The exact location of this site is not

1.   For the Hebrew term *'hb*, 'to love', as a treaty term, see W.L. Moran, *CBQ* 25 (1963), pp. 80-81; cf. M. Noth, *Könige*, p. 89. K. Budde advocated at the turn of the century that the treaty was made at the end of David's reign when Solomon was his coregent (Bücher, *Samuel*, p. 223).

2.   On this, see the discussion in F.C. Fensham, 'The Treaty between the Israelites and the Tyrians', *Congress Volume, Rome 1968* (ed. J.A. Emerton *et al.*), pp. 78-80.

3.   1 Kgs 9.22 mentions that Solomon had a fleet of Tarshish ships 'at sea with Hiram's ships'. These ships most probably were large seagoing vessels. It is questionable whether people in the Judean hills would have known anything about these ships before c. 800 BCE, i.e., before the great Phoenician expansion to the west (of Cyprus) had begun. Tarshish has been sought in Spain at Tartessos, but Tarshish often refers to the Phoenician west (G. Bunnens, *L'expansion phénicienne en Méditerranée*, pp. 330-48). Cf. Ps. 72.10, which mentions the kings of Tarshish and the coast in parallelism with the kings of Sheba and Shaba; in other words, the psalmist has presented the world as he knew it from west to east. Tarshish here stands for the eastern Mediterranean. For Tarshish lying east of Greece, see the Esarhaddon inscription, par. 57 in R. Borger, *Die Inschriften Asarhaddons* (AfO Beiheft, 9; Graz, 1956), p. 86. As to the discussion about Tarshish, see, among others, W.F. Albright, who assumed that there were several places with the name Tarshish, because he saw *tarshish* to mean 'smelting plant, refinery' ('The Role of the Canaanites in the History of Civilization', *The Bible and the Ancient Near East* [ed. G.E. Wright;

known. No archaeological remains of a port have been found at the northern end of the gulf.[1] The treaty with Tyre became economically burdensome for Solomon. Hiram had furnished Solomon for years with lumber and gold (1 Kgs 9.10-11), the value of which most probably exceeded that of the wheat and oil Solomon had paid in exchange. After some time Hiram received 20 cities as payment. Hiram is said to have been disappointed with these cities and called them *kābûl*.[2] The cities were located in western Galilee and in an area which was part of the Phoenician sphere of interest.[3] This territory was therefore part of David's conquests. How the biblical writer knew what Hiram could have said about this territory is impossible to tell, but if *kābûl* has anything to do with 'low value', the writer has used it ironically, because the Acco plain was partly marshland, and thus an area where the malaria-carrying mosquito ruled.[4] With these words the writer minimized the importance of the loss.

Garden City, NY, 1965 (1960)], p. 464); K. Galling, 'Der Weg der Phöniker nach Tarsis in literarischer under archäologisher Sicht', *ZDPV* 88 (1972), pp. 140-81; U. Täckholm, 'Tarsis, Tartessos und die Säulen des Herakles', *Opuscula Romana* 5 (1965), pp. 147-50; and P.-R. Berger, who identifies Tarshish with Carthage ('Ellasar, Tarschisch und Jawan, Gen 14 und 10', *Die Welt des Orients* 13 [1982], pp. 50-78).

1. N. Glueck suggested that the remains of Solomon's harbor would be buried under 'the debris' of the modern city of Aqaba ('Kheleifeh, Tell el-', *EAEHL*, III, pp. 713, 715). Nabatean, Roman and Byzantine remains have been found in the recent excavations in the city of Aqaba (D. Whitcomb, private communication). B. Rothenberg sees the island Jezirat Fara'un in the northern end of the gulf as originally an Egyptian harbor through which the products from Timna were shipped out. This port would then have been Solomon's port city of Ezion-Geber (*Were These King Solomon's Mines?*, p. 203). I will later return to the Nora inscription from Sardinia. Here it may be sufficient to mention that the parallel readings *btršš* and *bsrdn* are the geographical names, 'in Tarshish' and 'in Sardinia'. B. Peckham's translation 'from Tarshish' is unacceptable ('The Nora Inscription', *Or* NS 41 [1972], pp. 458-68).

2. The meaning of this word is uncertain. Josephus interprets it as 'not pleasing' (*Ant.* 8.1.42).

3. Y. Aharoni, 'Mount Carmel as Border', *Archäologie und Altes Testament: Festschrift K. Galling* (ed. K. Kuschke; Tübingen, 1970), pp. 4-5; J. Kegler, *Politisches Geschehen und theologisches Verstehen* (Stuttgart, 1977), pp. 215-16.

4. The Acco plain was drained first in the 1920s (R. Amiran, private communication).

Solomon's 'Tarshish fleet' is said to have sailed to Ophir, from where it obtained gold and silver objects, almug trees, precious stones, ivory, apes and baboons (1 Kgs 9.26-28; 10.11, 22). It is not possible to say how regular this traffic was, neither is it possible exactly to locate Ophir. Both India and Africa have been suggested,[1] and especially Eritrea, from which region gold, frankincense and myrrh were obtainable.[2] These verses not only demonstrate that Solomon's wealth increased, but also that he, like any great king of the Near East, could show that his wisdom produced blessings in the form of success and wealth, in this manner impressing his people and his visitors.[3]

One of Solomon's most famous visitors was the Queen of Sheba, who supposedly went to the Jerusalem court in order to see a wise man. The biblical narrator seldom portrays the full picture of international political play. Here he prefers to describe the scene in the form of a small 'novella' where personalities are portrayed in categories usually found in a saga. According to 1 Kgs 10.1, the Queen went to Solomon not only with camels laden with riches, but also with some difficult questions. Perhaps some of these questions concerned the trade routes from Palestine and Egypt to Arabia. The Solomonic control of the trade and the caravan routes may have had some disturbing effects on the Sabean economy, hence the Queen had to

1. See the discussion in M. Noth, who thinks that Ophir would be close to the Red Sea (*Könige*, pp. 222-23).
2. N. Groom, *Frankincense and Myrrh: A Study of the Arabian Incense Trade* (London, 1981), p. 51. An ostracon discovered at Tell Qasîle has the inscription 'gold from Uphir to Beth-Horon, 30 shekels' (B. Maisler [Mazar], *IEJ* 1 [1950–51], pp. 209-10, figs. 13-14). Cf. also D. Harden, *The Phoenicians* (London, 1971), p. 150.
3. An interesting Assyrian parallel to this royal attitude of might and its display is found on the so-called Broken Obelisk, which mentions a king (probably Ashur-bel-kala, 1074–1057) who had sent his representatives to buy, among other things, 'a large female ape, and crocodile (and) a "river man", beasts of the Great Sea', and from Arabia, dromedaries. Many of these exotic animals he then displayed for the people (cf. K. Jaritz, 'The Problem of the "Broken Obelisks"', *JSS* 4 [1959], pp. 204-15; H. Tadmor, 'Que and Musri', *IEJ* 11 [1961], pp. 146; J.A. Brinkman, *A Political History of Post-Kassite Babylonia*, pp. 337, 383; A.K. Grayson, *Babylonian and Assyrian Chronicles*, pp. 208-209. For further examples consult also A.K. Grayson, *Assyrian Royal Inscriptions*, II (Wiesbaden, 1976), pars. 463, 598.

come to terms with the ruler in Jerusalem.[1]

The greatness of Solomon's kingdom and power may be reflected in the Egyptian Pharaoh's 'respect' for Solomon. Shortly after David's death the Pharaoh tried to 'raise the flag' over Palestine again, and he invaded the Philistine areas. As usual, the strength of the new king had to be tested. According to 1 Kgs 9.15-17, Pharaoh took Gezer, destroyed it and killed the people.[2] When Solomon allegedly married a daughter of Pharaoh (probably Siamun, 979–960 BCE),[3] he got as dowry some ruins, the destroyed city of Gezer! Strategically, Gezer was an important place if fortified, and Solomon also made it a fortress city. A. Malamat thinks that this marriage was suggested by David.[4] It may be that the 'diplomat' Solomon followed an ancient custom that his father had followed also. What has intrigued scholars is the question of whether or not this was a treaty between equals. Malamat has concluded that Egypt must have been inferior to Israel at this time.[5] This may be doubted. Knowing that Egypt rarely gave a daughter of Pharaoh as wife to a foreign king, it is likely that Siamun (or Psusennes?) understood the might of Solomon and saw the

---

1. It is not clear whether Sheba here refers to South-Arabia or to a Sheba (Saba) in North-Arabia. The latter may be as probable as the former. North-Arabian Sabeans are known from the time of Tiglath-Pileser III (745–727 BCE), mentioned together with the people of Tema (cf. Job 6.19). N. Groom does not find any trustworthy information about incense trade from S. Arabia earlier than the Greek authors, nor can he find any archaeological remains, such as camel bones, along the route earlier than c. 600 BCE (*Frankincense and Myrrh*, pp. 338-54). Reigning queens are known in N. Arabia from the Assyrian period, but none in S. Arabia before 500 BCE (N. Groom, *Frankincense and Myrrh*, p. 54).

For 1 Kgs 10.13 ('and Solomon gave to her all she desired') giving rise to the legend that the Ethiopian dynasty was the result of the meeting between Solomon and the Queen of Sheba, see E. Ullendorff, 'The Queen of Sheba in Ethiopian Tradition', *Solomon and Sheba* (ed. J.B. Pritchard; New York, 1974), p. 106.

2. For a destruction of Gezer at this time, see W.G. Dever, H.D. Lance and G.E. Wright, *Gezer*, I (Jerusalem, 1970), pp. 60-61.

3. Cf. E.F. Wente, 'On the Chronology of the Twenty-First Dynasty', *JNES* 26 (1967), pp. 155-76. For Siamun campaigning in Palestine, see P. Montet, *Le drame d'Avaris* (Paris, 1941), pp. 195-97, fig. 58; *idem*, *Egypt and the Bible*, (Philadelphia, 1968), p. 37 fig. 5; K.A. Kitchen, *The Third Intermediate Period*, pp. 280-82; A.R. Green, 'Solomon and Siamun: A Synchronism between Dynastic Israel and the Twenty-First Dynasty of Egypt', *JBL* 97 (1978), pp. 366.

4. *JNES* 22 (1963), pp. 8-9.

5. A. Malamat, *JNES* 22 (1963), pp. 10-11.

advantage of friendly relations. He might thus have considered Solomon an equal.[1] Politically, Egypt was divided at this time into two rival kingdoms. The north was ruled by the Twenty-First Dynasty at Tanis. Southern Egypt was ruled from Thebes by a theocracy which had replaced the Twentieth Dynasty, the Ramessides.[2] This was also the more powerful kingdom of the two. It is thus possible that the Pharaoh made the alliance with Solomon in order to strengthen his position vis-à-vis Thebes.[3]

Among the priorities of Solomon was the defense of the kingdom. The standing army, for instance, now saw an increase in chariots. David is not usually credited with the introduction of chariotry into Israel. However, 2 Sam. 8.3-4 and 1 Chron. 18.3-4 mention that David took 1000 chariots from Hadadezer of Aram-Zobah, handstrung most of the horses, but kept 100 chariots (with horses) for himself.[4] This means that David added a certain number of horses and chariots,

1. A.R. Schulman has pointed out that when Egypt was weak an Egyptian princess could be given in marriage to a foreign king, thus securing Egypt an ally. When Egypt was powerful no Egyptian princess was given to a foreigner. Instead, the Pharaoh cemented his ties with other rulers by obtaining their daughters for his own harem ('Diplomatic Marriage in the Egyptian New Kingdom', *JNES* 38 [1979], pp. 187-89, 191). A. Malamat believes that Solomon also ruled over Philistia (*Studies* [ed. T. Ishida], p. 199). This hypothesis is based on the Hebrew text in 1 Kgs 5.1 (Eng. 4.22), which mentions that Solomon ruled over 'all the kingdoms from the river (the Euphrates), the land of the Philistines and to the border of Egypt'. The general character of this statement, the purpose of which is to underscore Solomon's importance, makes it unreliable testimony. Nevertheless, because of the Gezer incident, it is possible that Solomon ruled over the Philistine territory around Gezer. Would the writer have forgotten to mention the capture of the whole territory of the arch-enemy if Solomon had taken it? Cf. S. Herrmann, *A History of Israel* (2nd edn), p. 159.

2. The end of the Ramesside dynasty ended the New Kingdom. The kings of the Twenty-First dynasty were the last Egyptians on the throne. With Shoshenq and the Twenty-Second (Libyan) dynasty begins a period of foreigners as rulers of Egypt; this period continues until Egypt loses her independence (J. von Beckerath, *Tanis und Theben*, p. 102).

3. The high-priest Psusennes of Thebes inherited the throne at Tanis when Siamun died in 960 BCE (K.A. Kitchen, *The Third Intermediate Period*, p. 8). For the chronology, see also K. Baer, 'The Libyan and Nubian Kings of Egypt: Notes on the Chronology of Dynasties XXII to XXIV', *JNES* 32 (1973), pp. 4-25.

4. Y. Yadin, *The Art of Warfare in Biblical Lands*, II (New York, 1963), p. 285; cf. C. Hauer, 'The Economics of Natural Security in Solomonic Israel', *JSOT* 18 (1980), pp. 63-73.

probably as replacements for the losses he had suffered in the battle.[1] Considering David's victories over the Philistines and his subjugation of such cities as Megiddo, Dor and Beth-Shan, his army must have been well equipped with chariots. Saul must have had war chariots also (cf. 1 Sam. 17.20 and 26.5). To meet the Philistine army and its chariotry without the same kind of weapon would have been suicidal.

According to 1 Kgs 10.26, Solomon reinforced the standing army[2] so he had 1400 chariots and 12000 horses. This would have required a great number of stables, and 1 Kgs 4.26 (Heb. 5.6) mentions 40000 stables and 12000 horses. 2 Chron. 9.25 and the LXX are more modest with 4000 stables.[3] No information is given about where all these chariots and horses were housed, beyond that they were stationed in the chariot cities near Jerusalem (1 Kgs 10.26). Archaeologists have not been able to find a great amount of evidence for stables in Palestine. Some have been identified at Megiddo and equated with Solomon's reported stables. However, the 'first equestrian complexes built on the site' were the southern 'stables' (building 1576), which seem to date from the first years of Jeroboam, before Shoshenq's attack on the city.[4] If any stables and chariot camps were built, they may have been located outside the cities. It is not certain whether the 'stables' at Megiddo really were stables. They could just as well have been used as storehouses or barracks.[5]

1. Chariots were also part of the royal paraphernalia; cf. Absalom and Adonijah, 2 Sam. 15.1-3 and 1 Kgs 1.5. For the peoples of Canaan being used to horses and chariots as part of the war machinery, see F. James, 'Chariot Fittings from Late Bronze Age Beth Shan', *Archaeology in the Levant: Essays for K.M. Kenyon* (ed. P.R.S. Moorey and P.J. Parr; Warminster, 1978), pp. 103-85.

2. A standing army does not mean that the men of the country could not be called to military duty, as H. Donner seems to believe (*Geschichte des Volkes Israel*, p. 226).

3. The Hebrew *'urôt* may rather refer to teams (cf. Akkad. *urû*); thus S. Parpola in a review of J.V. Kinnier Wilson, *The Third Nimrud Wine List*, *JSS* 21 (1976), p. 172.

4. Thus, D.L. Saltz, 'Greek Geometric Pottery', pp. 436-39.

5. J.B. Pritchard, 'The Megiddo Stables: A Reassessment', *Near Eastern Archaeology in the Twentieth Century* (ed. J.A. Sanders; Garden City, NY, 1970), pp. 268-76; cf. Y. Aharoni, *Beer-Sheba*. I. *Excavations at Tel Beer-sheba, 1969–1971 Seasons* (Tel Aviv, 1973), pp. 28-30. As in Assyria, the horses for the army could have been owned by the soldiers who took them home again at the end of a war. In such a case there would not be any need for government-owned stables, nor would the government need to feed the horses in between wars (see J.N. Postgate,

The picture of Solomon as a king of peace who spared his empire from devastating wars is one of the basic components in his presentation as the great and wise ruler. The figure of 40,000 stables (1 Kgs 4.26, Heb. 5.6) may, therefore, be part of the writer's intention to show the splendid might of the king. Besides the 1400 chariots for the army, Solomon also bought some chariots from Egypt for the price of 600 shekels each. These may have been used for display in royal processions.[1]

The king used horses for another purpose; he was a horse-trader. He bought horses both from Egypt and Que (Cilicia),[2] and sold them to the Aramaeans and the neo-Hittite rulers (1 Kgs 10.28-29; 2 Chron. 1.16-17). The buying of horses from Cilicia and their subsequent sale in Syria would not have been a problem if the transactions were carried out with the cooperation of the king of Hamath, as assumed by Y. Ikeda.[3]

As far as can be discerned, Solomon's building activities were carried out primarily in Israelite regions and Jerusalem. This may show that the settlements in the hills of Judah probably had been well organized by the creator of the kingdom of Judah, David. The many fortresses that were built in the Negev may indicate that this region was not an integral part of Judah. This theory receives support from 1 Kgs 9.26-27 and the statement that Solomon built the port of Ezion-Geber 'in the land of Edom'. The fact that part of Edom became independent shortly after Solomon's accession to the throne necessitated the building of fortresses[4] and administrative centers in the Negev, lest the whole of Edom be lost. Beer-Sheba may have been one of these new centers. The first and unwalled settlement from

Taxation and Conscription in the Assyrian Empire [Rome, 1974], pp. 209-10).

1. Cf. H. Tadmor, 'The Period of the First Temple, the Babylonian Exile and the Restoration', *A History of the Jewish People* (London, 1976), p. 104. These chariots were probably the *markābôt*; an ordinary chariot was called *rekeb*; see Y. Ikeda, 'Solomon's Trade in Horses and Chariots', *Studies* (ed. T. Ishida), pp. 222-24.

2. For Que, see A. Goetze, 'Cilicians', *JCS* 16 (1962), pp. 44-58; J.D. Hawkins, 'Hilakku', *Reallexikon der Assyriologie*, IV (Berlin, 1972), pp. 402-403.

3. *Studies* (ed. T. Ishida), p.238.

4. Some of the forts in the Negev could originally have been built by the Edomites; cf. B. Rothenberg, who draws this conclusion from the so-called Negev pottery at some of these sites (*Negev: Archaeology in the Negev and in the Arabah* [Ramat-Gan, 1967] [Hebrew]).

the Iron Age would then be pre-Solomonic.[1]

A special case is the fortress of Arad, with its temple, showing the intimate relationship between state and religion.[2] Its location is on the so-called 'way to Edom' (2 Kgs 3.20), connecting the Jerusalem-Hebron hills with the Arabah and the Gulf of Aqaba. The lack of a final excavation report has created some confusion about the stratigraphy of the site and the date of the fortress.[3]

A recent review of the finds and the stratigraphic evidence has confirmed Y. Aharoni's dating of stratum XI to the tenth century BCE. This stratum saw the first fortress with a casemate wall (50 × 50 m). A temple was located in the northeast corner of the fortress.[4] Most probably stratum XI is Solomonic. If there was no fortress in the tenth century, then the mention of '*h-q-r-m* ̓Arad *r-b-t*' and 'Arad of the house of Yeroham' in pharaoh Shoshenq's inscription from his Palestinian campaign[5] would be somewhat enigmatic. Unfortified, and thus militarily unimportant, places would not be listed in the inscriptions of a conqueror.

The fortress temple confirms that the official religion of the state was part of the administrative and military establishment. God and king were always out in front. Comparisons with the Solomonic temple have shown that the Arad temple was built according to a different style, that of the traditional layout of an ordinary house with a courtyard. Architecturally, the plan is that of a broad-room temple with a niche (c. 1.5 × 1.5 m) in the eastern wall and with plastered

---

1. See the discussion in Y. Aharoni, *Beer-Sheba*. I, p. 106.

2. G.W. Ahlström, *Royal Administration*, pp. 40-41.

3. The excavator, Y. Aharoni, dated it to the tenth cent. BCE ('Arad: Its Inscriptions and Temple', *BA* 31 [1968], pp. 2-32; *idem*, 'The Solomonic Temple, The Tabernacle and the Arad Sanctuary', *Orient and Occident* [ed. H. Hoffner; AOAT, 22; Neukirchen–Vluyn, 1973], pp. 1-8). Y. Yadin advocated a later date ('A Note on the Stratigraphy of Arad', *IEJ* 15 [1965], p. 180); cf. also W.G. Dever, 'Monumental Architecture in Ancient Israel', *Studies in the Period of David and Solomon* (ed. T. Ishida; Tokyo, 1982), pp. 283-84 (ninth cent.); M. Ottosson, *Temples and Cult Places in Palestine*, p. 109.

4. Z. Herzog, M. Aharoni, A.F. Rainey and S. Moshkovitz, 'The Israelite Fortress at Arad', *BASOR* 25 (1984), pp. 1-34.

5. The Egyptian *h-q-r-m* (Hebrew *hgrm*) denotes these places as fortresses. W. Helck doubts that r-b-t (*ru-bi-ta*) is the Egyptian writing for the Hebrew *rabbâ*, 'great' (*Die Beziehungen*, p. 243).

benches around the walls.[1] Two incense altars were placed on the steps leading up to the niche, and three *maṣṣēbôt* were found in the niche.[2] It is likely that the three *maṣṣēbôt* originally stood in the niche, the holy of holies.

As was the case in Jerusalem's temple, not only Yahweh but also the divine assembly was worshipped, including Baal and Asherah. The three divinities Yahweh, Baal and Asherah most probably were also worshipped at the Arad temple in its early period.[3] Another find indicating that the temple was a royal sanctuary is a small bronze crouching lion figurine which was uncovered in stratum IX close to the altar in the temple yard.[4] Since the lion was a symbol of divinity and royalty,[5] this figurine underlines the governmental character of the temple.

Among other fortresses found (from this period) are at Beer-Sheba[6] in the Negev, Tell 'Amal (Nir David)[7] west of Beth-Shan, and 'En Gev on the eastern shore of Lake Tiberias. A cult room was also found at 'En Gev,[8] as was the case at Tell ed-Duweir.[9] At Tel Shiqmona (Tell es-Samak), close to Haifa, a casemate wall and some houses have been found dating to the tenth century BCE, which would indicate the existence of a fortified town just west of Tell Abū Hāwam.[10] Since no

1. For the architecture, see also T.A. Busink, *Der Tempel von Jerusalem*, I, pp. 593-94, 698; P. Welten, 'Kulthöhe und Jahwetempel', *ZDPV* 88 (1972), pp. 20-25.

2. Two of them were plastered over and 'leaning against the wall' (Y. Aharoni, *BA* 31 [1968], pp. 18-20).

3. See G.W. Ahlström, 'Heaven on Earth—At Hazor and Arad', *Religious Syncretism in Antiquity* (ed. B.A. Pearson), pp. 80-83.

4. Y. Aharoni, *BA* 31 (1968), p. 20; cf. Z. Herzog *et al.*, *BASOR* 254 (1984), p. 16, and fig. 20.

5. Cf. G.W. Ahlström, *An Archaeological Picture of Iron Age Religions in Ancient Palestine*, pp. 17-18.

6. Y. Aharoni, *Beer-Sheba*, I, pp. 9-11.

7. S. Levy and G. Edelstein, 'Cinq années de fouilles à Tell 'Amal (Nir David)', *RB* 79 (1972), pp. 325-68. One may doubt, however, that Tell 'Amal is the site of a fortress.

8. B. Mazar, A. Biran, M. Dothan and I. Dunayevsky, '"Ein Gev: Excavations in 1961", *IEJ* 14 (1964), pp. 1-49; cf. G.W. Ahlström, 'The Cultroom at 'En Gev', *Tel Aviv* 12 (1985), pp. 93-95.

9. Y. Aharoni, *Lachish*, V (Tel Aviv, 1975), pp. 26-32.

10. For the excavations, see the following by J. Elgavish: 'Tel Shiqmona', *IEJ*

Iron Age I remains have been found as of yet (only LB II), it seems probable that Solomon founded Shiqmona in the Iron II period to serve as a competitor to Abū Hawām, which he had lost at the same time he had given the 20 cities to Hiram of Tyre. J. Elgavish assumes that an anchorage existed just south of the town.[1] Other new sites from the tenth century BCE include Ramoth-Gilead (Tell er-Rumeith?) in Transjordan. The earliest stratum (VIII) contains a small fortress (c. 37 × 32 m) that dates from the tenth century BCE.[2]

It should be noted in this context that casemate walls were common fortification strategies in the tenth century BCE.[3] They consisted of double walls with small rooms between them. Such walls have been found at Hazor, Shiqmona, 'En Gev, Arad, Gezer,[4] Beth-Shemesh,[5] Tell Qasîle,[6] Tell Beit Mirsim[7] and Ramat Matred.[8] Another common

19 (1969), pp. 247-48; *idem, IEJ* 20 (1970), pp. 229-30; *idem, IEJ* 22 (1972), p. 167; *idem, IEJ* 27 (1977), p. 167; *idem*, 'Tel Shiqmona', *EAEHL*, IV, pp. 1101-109.

1. 'Tel Shiqmona', *EAEHL*, IV, p. 1101.

2. See P.W. Lapp, 'Chronique Archéologique', *RB* 70 (1963), pp. 406-37; *idem, RB* 75 (1968), pp. 98-105, and *idem, The Tale of the Tell* (ed. N.L. Lapp; Pittsburgh, 1975), pp. 113-14. If this is the site of ancient Ramoth-Gilead, which is listed among the 'Levitical' cities in Josh. 21.38, then the passage in Josh. 21 cannot refer to a time before the Solomonic kingdom.

3. N. Lapp's investigation shows nine sites with casemates from the tenth century BCE ('Casemate Walls in Palestine and the Late Iron II Casemate at Tell el-Fûl [Gibeah]', *BASOR* 223 [1976], pp. 25-42). According to Y. Aharoni, casemates were used throughout the monarchic period ('Excavations at Tel Beer-Sheba', *BA* 35 [1972], p. 117 n. 5). For the tracing of the antecedents of this kind of wall back to the seventeenth cent. BCE Canaan, see W.G. Dever, *Studies* (ed. T. Ishida), p. 289. Cf. also T.A. Busink, *Der Tempel von Jerusalem*, I, pp. 121-26.

4. Y. Yadin, 'Solomon's City Wall and Gate at Gezer', *IEJ* 8 (1958), pp. 80-86; cf. W.G. Dever, H.D. Lance and G.E. Wright, *Gezer*, I, plan 1. See also W.G. Dever, 'Late Bronze Age and Solomonic Defenses at Gezer: New Evidence', *BASOR* 262 (1986), pp. 9-34.

5. W.G. Dever thinks that the Beth-Shemesh wall might date to the Davidic period (*Studies* [ed. T. Ishida], p. 289).

6. Tell Qasîle, stratum IX, is usually considered to be Davidic; cf. B. Maisler (Mazar), *IEJ* 1 (1950–51), pp. 136-38, 200; A. Mazar, *IEJ* 25 (1975), pp. 77-88.

7. W.F. Albright, *The Excavation of Tell Beit Mirsim. III. The Iron Age* (AASOR, 21–22; Cambridge, MA, 1943), pp. 1-19.

8. Y. Aharoni *et al., IEJ* 10 (1960), pp. 23-36, 97-111; cf. T.A. Busink, *Der Tempel von Jerusalem*, I, p. 125.

defensive feature of this time was the city gate with three rooms on each side of the gateway.[1] This kind of fortress gate has been found at Gezer, Tell ed-Duweir, Hazor, Megiddo and Philistine Ashdod, among other places. The gates of Hazor, Gezer and Megiddo are so similar in their dimensions (length, width, thickness of the walls) that Yadin's conclusion that they were 'built by Solomon's architects from identical blueprints' must be correct.[2] It is uncertain from where Solomon or his architects obtained the pattern. Since Ashdod's gate was also of the same type, it is unlikely that the blueprint was an invention by Solomon and his architects or that it was from the Solomonic period. The style may predate Solomon, explaining how architects in Palestine could follow this pattern when building gates both in Israel and Philistia.[3]

Among palaces and other monumental buildings such as government houses, storehouses, water cisterns and tunnels, Megiddo is probably a showcase for the kind of architectural style that was common in the royal enterprise of the tenth century. As has been mentioned before, the king's duties included the construction of buildings for the protection of his people (the good shepherd ideal).[4] Palace buildings of the so-called *bît ḫilāni* type,[5] known from Syria and Anatolia, are represented

1. At Gezer were also found 'low plastered stone benches which run around the three sides of all the rooms' (J.S. Holladay in W.G. Dever *et al.*, 'Further Excavations at Gezer, 1967–71', *BA* 34 [1971], p. 115). Benches in other types of city gates have been found at Dan, Tell en-Naṣbeh and Khirbet el-Qom (c. 112 km SE of Tell ed-Duweir). For the importance of the city gate as the place of the community council, see Ps. 127.5; Ruth 4.1; Job 29.7; Prov. 8.3; 2 Chron. 32.6; Neh. 8.1.

2. Y. Yadin, *IEJ* 8 (1958), pp. 85-86; cf. W.G. Dever, *Studies* (ed. T. Ishida), p. 290. For this kind of gate with casemate walls, see also the illustrations by G.R.H. Wright, *Ancient Building in South Syria and Palestine*, II, fig. 88. We should also note that according to Ezek. 40.10 the East Gate of Jerusalem probably had the same layout; cf. W. Zimmerli, *Ezechiel* (BKAT, 13; Neukirchen–Vluyn, 1969), pp. 1006-1007.

3. W.G. Dever argues for an eleventh-century date for the Ashdod gate (*Studies* [ed. T. Ishida], p. 290).

4. Cf. my *Royal Administration*, pp. 1-3; see also R.W. Anderson, 'The Civil Duties of the Kingship in Israel and Judah' (PhD dissertation, University of Chicago, 1985).

5. CAD defines *ḫilāni* as a room in a palace or temple furnished with a 'portico' ('or the portico itself'), *s.v.*; cf. B. Meissner, 'Der *bît ḫilāni* in Assyria', *Or* NS 11 (1942), pp. 251-61; H. Frankfort, 'The Origin of the Bit Hilani', *Iraq* 14 (1952), pp. 120-31. G.R.H. Wright considers the *bît ḫilāni* building type a development

in building 1723 (which has been seen as the palace of the governor) in the south,[1] and 'Palace 6000' in the north.[2] The construction of the palaces was in the Phoenician style, with ashlar stones laid in a header-stretcher system and upright stone piers with rubble fill.[3] The super-structures may have included wooden beams.[4]

The most 'splendid' buildings of Solomon were his palace-temple complex in Jerusalem. The city which David had captured form the Jebusites was small and probably densely populated. Its area was no more than 420 × 150 m. Thus, not too much space could have been available for palatial buildings.[5] However, 2 Sam. 5.11 reports that David had built a palace in the city. Obviously this was not of such grandeur that it suited the king of a large kingdom. His capital had to show the might of the king. Both the god and the king needed palaces suitable for their position. Therefore, in order to be able to build on a grand scale, Solomon had to look outside the walls of Jerusalem. He chose the threshing floor area on the high hill just north of the city.

'from the wealthy urban building of Bronze Age times in Northern Syria' (*Ancient Building in South Syria and Palestine*, I, p. 276).

1.   D.Ussishkin, 'King Solomon's Palace and Building 1723 in Megiddo', *IEJ* 16 (1966), pp. 174-86; cf. *idem*, 'King Solomon's Palaces', *BA* 36 (1973), pp. 84-86.

2.   Y. Yadin, *Hazor*, pp. 154-61; cf. D. Ussishkin, *BA* 36 (1973), pp. 101-102. There is still some debate about the stratigraphy, and thus about who built what. For instance, D. Ussishkin maintains that the 'Solomonic' gate house was built in stratum IVA, i.e. the time of Jeroboam I ('Was the "Solomonic" Gate at Megiddo built by King Solomon?', *BASOR* 239 [1980], pp. 1-18); D.L. Saltz maintains that the water system was still under construction when Shoshenq attacked the city ('Greek Geometric Pottery', p. 430).

3.   See R.S. Lamon and G.M. Shipton, *Megiddo 1: Seasons of 1925–34, Strata I–V* (OIP, 42; Chicago, 1939), fig. 14 (ashlar foundation), and figs. 27, 29 (header-stretchers). Building 338-40, which has been understood to be a temple (H.G. May, *Material Remains of the Megiddo Cult* [OIP, 26; Chicago, 1935], pp. 4-6), has been characterized by D.L. Saltz as a government building dating from the time of Jeroboam I and probably replacing palace 1723 ('Greek Geometric Pottery in the East', p. 180).

4.   See G. and O. Van Beek, 'Canaanite–Phoenician Architecture: The Development and Distribution of Two Styles', *EI* 15 (1981), pp. 70*-77*, and pl. VI: B. In Syro-Palestine this pier and rubble style in building houses can be traced down into the Persian period, in addition to its use in the north-African building tradition down into the Roman period.

5.   See G.W. Ahlström, *JNES* 41 (1982), p. 135; cf. S. Herrmann, *A History of Israel* (2nd edn), p. 160.

This was royal property that David had bought from Araunah, the last king of Jebusite Jerusalem.[1] The fact that David built an altar on this spot may indicate that sanctity was already associated with the place.

Solomon may have leveled off the northern hill before building could commence, and he may have built a platform on which palace and temple complex was erected.[2] The area was encircled by a wall and thus became the acropolis[3] of the extended city. With this new addition and with the territory in between the old and new parts of the city, Jerusalem more than doubled in size.

The plan of the acropolis can be compared with what is known from some Syrian capitals of the ninth–eighth centuries and also from Tell Halaf (Gozan)[4] in Mesopotamia. The palaces of Kilamuwa and Barrakub at ancient Sam'al (Zinjirli) present parallels to all the features of Solomon's acropolis.[5] There are several palaces in the *bît ḫîlāni* style.[6] Because the palace and temple complex in Jerusalem was built with the help of Phoenician craftsmen, it is likely that most of the decoration was influenced by them. The parallel with Megiddo palace 1723 and with the Syrian *bît ḫîlāni* III at Zinjirli may also suggest that the architectural inspiration came from the north.[7]

1. Cf. above, pp. 470-71 and G.W. Ahlström, *VT* 11 (1961), pp. 113-15; S. Yeivin, *VT* 3 (1953), p. 149; H.A. Hoffner, 'The Hittites and Hurrians', *Peoples of Old Testament Times* (ed. D.J. Wiseman), p. 225. N. Wyatt sees Araunah as a Jebusite officer ('"Araunah the Jebusite" and the Throne of David', *ST* 38 [1985], pp. 39-53).

2. T.A. Busink, *Der Tempel von Jerusalem*, I, p. 160; cf. K.M. Kenyon, 'New Evidence on Solomon's Temple', *Mélanges de l'Université Saint-Joseph*, XLVI.9 (1970), pp. 139-49.

3. For the acropolis phenomenon and the religious ideology connected with it, see my *Royal Administration*, pp. 1-3, 18-20.

4. Cf. H. Frankfort, *Iraq* 14 (1952), pp. 120-31.

5. W.G. Dever, *Studies* (ed. T. Ishida), p. 303. As to the plan, see R. Naumann, *Architektur Kleinasiens von ihren Anfangen bis zum Ende der hethitischen Zeit* (Tübingen, 1955), fig. 445; A. Badaway, *Architecture in Ancient Egypt and the Near East* (Cambridge, MA, 1966), p. 124 fig. 20.

6. For Zinjirli, see D. Ussishkin, 'Solomon's Palace and Megiddo 1723', *IEJ* 16 (1966), 179-86; *idem*, 'Building IV in Hamath and the Temples of Solomon and Tell Tayanat', *IEJ* 16 (1966), pp. 104-10.

7. On this, see the discussion in C. Watzinger, *Denkmäler Palästinas* (Leipzig, 1933), p. 96.

Unfortunately, the parallels from Zinjirli, Karatepe and Tell Ta'yinat are later than the Solomonic buildings. However, the acropolis phenomenon itself is older than the Iron II period, as is[1] the *bît ḫilāni* type of palace, which has been found at Alalakh in a stratum dating to the fourteenth century BCE.[2]

The huge palace complex took about 13 years to build and the temple took 7 (1 Kgs 6.38–7.1), which may say something about the size of the temple. The buildings within the acropolis were many (1 Kgs 7). First, there was the royal palace,[3] which was entered through a porch lined with pillars. Another huge building was the 'house of the Forest of Lebanon' (1 Kgs 7.2; 10.16-17),[4] built of pillars of cedar. Probably separated from the palace was the Throne Hall housing Solomon's costly ivory throne (1 Kgs 7.7 and 10.18-20). According to 1 Kgs 10.21 there was also a treasury. A separate palace, perhaps adjacent to the king's palace,[5] was built for Solomon's queen, the daughter of Pharaoh (7.8).[6] The location of the harem is not mentioned, but it probably was in the king's palace, for the sake of convenience.

The ivory throne of Solomon was plated with gold. It had six steps, and at the sides of each step was a lion—a symbol for royalty and divinity. At the top of the back of the throne was a calf's head[7]—the

---

1.   It would be enough to mention, for instance, Ebla, Carchemish, Hazor and Alalakh; see my *Royal Administration*, pp. 4-5.

2.   H. Frankfort, *Iraq* 14 (1952), pp. 120-31.

3.   T.A. Busink estimates its size to 55 × 65 m (*Der Tempel von Jerusalem*, I, p. 142).

4.   Cf. Isa. 22.8.

5.   See the reconstruction in T.A. Busink, *Der Tempel von Jerusalem*, I, p. 160, fig. 47.

6.   According to 2 Chron. 8.11, Pharaoh's daughter lived in the palace of David where the ark also was placed. The site thus had an aura of sanctity. This would not have been astonishing for the people of the time, since, as a rule, royalty and divine beings shared the same living quarters, separated from the rest of the population. That is one of the reasons for an enclosed acropolis. The Chronicler turns things around and says that the Egyptian princess had a separate palace because in his eyes she could not have lived in the same place as Yahweh's ark. The Chronicler tries to give a different theological reason for her being provided with a palace, a reason suiting his own time. It appears that the daughter of Pharaoh became the queen and as such she got her own 'little' palace and did not need to mingle with the other women of the harem.

7.   1 Kgs 10.19, reading *'ēgel* with the LXX instead of MT's *'āgōl*, 'round'; cf.

bull being another symbol of the divine. Two lions were standing beside the arm rests. This throne was most probably an example of an old type of throne common in Syria-Palestine since the New Kingdom.[1] The throne on which Solomon sat was also called 'the throne of the kingdom of Yahweh' (1Chron. 28.5; 29.23).[2] The 'House of the Forest of Lebanon' (50 × 25 × 15 m) had four rows of cedar pillars (1 Kgs 7.2-6).[3] There is no clear evidence as to the purpose of this building. It has been suggested that it was a throne hall, a treasury, stables, and so on.[4] According to 1 Kgs 10.17, however, two kinds of golden shields (in all 500) were placed in this building. On this basis B. Stade and L.H. Vincent have concluded that the 'House of the Forest of Lebanon' served as an armory.[5] However, soldiers did not go to war with golden shields. It is more likely that this building housed Solomon's luxury items, such as the golden shields that were used for royal display. 'All King Solomon's drinking vessels were of gold, and all the furnishings in the Hall of the Forest of Lebanon were of pure gold' (1 Kgs 10.21). All these buildings were built with

M. Metzger, *Königsthron und Gottesthron* (AOAT, 15.1; Neukirchen–Vluyn, 1985), p. 299.

1. See F. Canciani and G. Pettinato, 'Salomos Thron: Philologische und archäologische Erwägungen', *ZDPV* 81 (1965), pp. 88-108; R.J. Williams, 'A People Come out of Egypt', *Congress Volume, Edinburgh 1974* (ed. J.A. Emerton), p. 234; M. Metzger, *Königsthron und Gottesthron*, par. 19a.

2. The identification between deity and king is rooted in the concept of the king being the viceroy of his god, which is also expressed by the king being the son of his god (Ps. 2.7 and Ps. 89.27-28); cf. my *HR* 8 (1968), pp. 93-95; *idem, Royal Administration*, pp. 1-3. The ideological relationship between god and king is well illustrated by the Sumerian Epic 'Enmerkar and the Lord of Aratta', which contains statements to the effect that god and king lived in the same palace complex and shared the same throne room (S.N. Kramer, *Enmerkar and the Lord of Aratta*, p. 38, ll. 534-36.

3. In the LXX it is given three rows. T.A. Busink holds the opinion that this building had an upper floor with 30 small rooms (*Der Tempel von Jerusalem*, I, p. 129). M.J. Mulder, however, questions this reconstruction ('Einige Bemerk– ungen zur Beschreibung des Libanonwaldhauses in 1Reg7,2f.', *ZAW* 88 [1976], pp. 99-105).

4. See the discussion in T.A. Busink, *Der Tempel*, I, pp. 136-38 (with lit.).

5. B. Stade, *Geschichte des Volkes Israel*, I (Berlin, 1887), pp. 322-23; L.H. Vincent, *Jerusalem de l'Ancient Testament*, II–III (Paris, 1956), pp. 426-27. M. Noth thought that Solomon's guard had its quarters in this building (*Könige*, p. 230).

dressed stones,[1] and it is likely that they were the same kind of ashlar stones as those that are to be found, for instance, at Megiddo and at Gezer.[2]

The temple, which was a part of the palace complex, was probably an example of a Syro-Palestinian type of longroom temple.[3] Unfortunately, no examples of contemporary Syro-Phoenician temples have yet been excavated. The only Phoenician temple that is archaeologically known from the Iron II period (eighth–seventh cent. BCE) is that of Sarafand (ancient Zareptah), which is not to be compared with that of Solomon.[4] The above-mentioned temple from Tell Ta'yinat is the closest known parallel, but, because it was built in the ninth century BCE, all that can be said is that the two temples may be seen as expressions of Syrian architectural tradition.[5] Even though an exact parallel to Solomon's temple has not been found, the possibility cannot be excluded that certain 'Israelite' adjustments or innovations had been made.

Solomon's longroom temple had a porch (or vestibule), '*ûlām*. The inside of the long room was divided into two parts, the 'Holy of Holies', *d^{e}bīr* (a box-like construction in the western end of the room), and the *hēkāl*, the main temple hall.[6] The temple was probably

1. 1 Kgs 7.9-10.

2. Cf. W.G. Dever *et al.*, 'Further Excavations at Gezer, 1967–1971', *BA* 34 (1971), pp. 112-13.

3. Cf. on this T.A. Busink, *Der Tempel von Jerusalem*, I, pp. 558-60; also cf. A. Kuschke, 'Der Tempel Salomos und der "syrische Tempeltypus"', *Das Ferne und Nahe Wort* (BZAW, 105; Berlin, 1967), pp. 124-32; W.G. Dever, *Studies* (ed. T. Ishida), pp. 297-98. Consult also the discussion of A. Alt, 'Verbreitung und Herkunft des syrischen Tempeltypus', *Palästinajahrbuch* 35 (1939), pp. 83-99 (= *KS*, II, pp. 100-15).

4. This (longroom) sanctuary had its main entrance in the east and an opening or entrance to a yard (or room) in the north wall; see J.B. Pritchard, 'The 1972 Excavations at Sarepta (Lebanon)', *Rivista di Studi Fenici* 1 (1973), pp. 91-92; *idem*, *Recovering Sarepta: A Phoenician City* (Princeton, 1978).

5. For different types of temples, see A. Kuschke, 'Tempel', *Biblisches Reallexikon* (2nd edn; ed. K. Galling; Tübingen, 1977), pp. 333-42.

6. See H. Schult, 'Der Debir im solomonischen Tempel', *ZDPV* 80 (1964), pp. 46-54. Consult also H. Schmidt, *Der Heilige Fels in Jerusalem* (Tübingen, 1933), pp. 43-44; M. Noth, *Könige*, p. 119. The information in 1 Kgs 6.16 seems to indicate that something was built inside the temple room. Thus the tripartition is not architectural, but functional. Y. Yadin's comparison with the Hazor area H temple (LB II) is to be disregarded (*Hazor of those Kingdoms*, pp. 86-87). The

built with Phoenician ashlar masonry, and the upper parts with wooden beams on the outside, which were probably plastered over. On the inside the walls were panelled with cedar and decorated with cherubs and palm trees (palmettes, 1 Kgs 6.29).[1] According to Ezekiel, 'all the gods of the house of Israel' were depicted on the walls of the temple (Ezek. 8.10). The walls also contained sculptured gourds that seem to represent the fruit of the *citrullus colocynthis* plant, a desert plant belonging to the cucumber family that resembles an apple. Pomegranates were sculptured on the pillars of the temple. These, together with the gourds and the pomegranates, were probably fertility symbols.[2]

On the outside the temple was surrounded by several rooms, probably in three stories, to judge from 1 Kgs 6.10.[3] The building would have looked like a basilica with the nave rising above the sides. A parallel phenomenon is not known from Syria-Palestine. If this was not a simplification of the side rooms or buildings surrounding an Egyptian temple (as in the mortuary temple of Ramses III at Medinet Habu),[4] it could represent a specifically Israelite component of the architecture. The *d^{e}bīr*, Holy of Holies, may reflect the Egyptian adyton, a dark room in the innermost part of the temple.[5] This type of room was not common in Syro-Palestinian temples, but it has been found at Beth-Shan during the Egyptian period (Level VI).[6]

Hazor temple, which in its first phase (MB IIC) was a one room temple, represents the broadroom type. Its middle part was the most narrow and was split up into small compartments. This temple can in no way be seen as a prototype for the Solomonic temple; see the discussion in my book, *Royal Administration*, pp. 34-35.

1.   For the palmette design, see T.A. Busink, *Der Tempel von Jerusalem*, I, pp. 272-74; H.G. May, *Material Remains of the Megiddo Cult*, pp. 39-41; M. Noth, *Könige*, pp. 124-26; Y. Shiloh, 'The Proto-Aeolic Capital—The Israelite "Timorah" (Palmette) Capital', *PEQ* 109 (1977), pp. 39-52; *idem, The Proto-Aeolic Capital and Israelite Ashlar Masonry* (Qedem, 11; Jerusalem, 1979), pp. 14-49.

2.   Cf. G.W. Ahlström, *Aspects of Syncretism*, p. 44; E. Würthwein, *Die Bücher der Könige*, p. 76.

3.   See the reconstruction by T.A. Busink (*Der Tempel von Jerusalem*, I, pp. 162-73, and figs. 48-51).

4.   Cf. A. Badaway, *Architecture in Ancient Egypt*, p. 42.

5.   See 1 Kgs 8.12, where Solomon says that Yahweh has chosen to live in the. clouds.

6.   Cf. the discussion in M. Ottosson, *Temples and Cult Places in Palestine*, p. 47.

Another phenomenon of certain religio-historical interest is the twin pillars Jachin and Boaz, which are commonly understood to have been placed just in front of the entrance to the temple. Such pillars can be traced back to Sumerian and Old Babylonian times. They have been found in Phoenicia-Palestine at Byblos (Middle Kingdom), Hazor, Arad[1] and Kamid-el-Loz.[2] The Jerusalem pillars were made of bronze. The height of each was 18 cubits and each had a capital (head) of five cubits. This made them close to 12 m high (1 Kgs 7.15-16). The somewhat unclear text in 1 Kgs 7.19 suggests that there were also pillars in the entrance hall, the *'ûlām*. Their capitals had the form of 'lilies', and were four cubits high. These are the so-called proto-aeolic capitals, which probably represented stylized palm trees rather than lilies.[3] The twin pillars, Jachin and Boaz, marked the entrance to the heavens, a standard idea in old Near Eastern temple cosmology.[4] They may have been constructed according to Phoenician models since they were designed by a craftsman named Hiram, who was from Tyre although his mother was from Naphtali (1 Kgs 7.13-22). The names Jachin and Boaz refer to firmness and strength. Therefore, the two pillars are to be understood to be symbols for Yahweh and his 'heaven', which had been firmly established on earth.[5]

In the Holy of Holies were placed two cherubs of olive wood which

1. See T.A. Busink, *Der Tempel von Jerusalem*, I, pp. 318-20.

2. R. Hachmann, *Bulletin du Musée de Beyrouth* 31 (1979), pp. 1ff. and fig. 23.

3. See the discussion in T.A. Busink, *Der Tempel von Jerusalem*, I, pp. 176-80 (with lit.). See also J.H. Iliffe, 'A Model Shrine of Phoenician Style', *QDAP* 11 (1944), pp. 90-92; cf. Y. Shiloh, 'New Proto-Aeolic Capitals found in Israel', *BASOR* 222 (1976), pp. 67-77. The liliform and lotusform pillar is more common in Egypt (A. Badaway, *Architecture in Ancient Egypt and the Near East*, p. 69 fig. 10).

4. On an Assyrian relief, the temple of Tyre is shown between two pillars (R.D. Barnett, 'Phoenicia and the Ivory Trade', *Archaeology* 9 [1956], p. 91). The pillars are also seen on Tyrian coins (E. Will, 'Au sanctuaire d'Heracles à Tyr', *Berytus* 10 [1952–53]), fig. C.L. Meyers sees them as 'gate-posts' ('Jachin and Boaz in Religious and Political Perspective', *CBQ* 45 [1983], p. 173). For a Cypriot parallel, see the temple model from Idalion (K. Bossert, *Altsyrien* [Tübingen, 1951], 1951, fig. 16). For the cosmological aspects, cf. J. Schwabe, 'Die kosmologischen Zwillinge und das Säulenpaar im Tempel', *Symbolon* 6 (1968), pp. 43-44.

5. As to the discussion of the names, see E. Würthwein, *Die Bücher der Könige*, I, pp. 76-77; T.A. Busink, *Der Tempel von Jerusalem*, I, p. 312; H.G. May, 'The Two Pillars before the Temple of Solomon', *BASOR* 88 (1942), pp. 19-27; C.L. Meyers, *CBQ* 45 (1983), pp. 170-71.

were plated with gold. Their height was 10 cubits (c. 4.5 m, 1 Kgs 6.23). All that is said about them is that with their outstretched wings they touched each other and the walls, and according to 2 Chron. 3.13 they were standing on their feet. From Near Eastern parallels such as the Phoenician throne of Ahiram, the ivory plaque from Megiddo, and ivories from Samaria, Nimrud and Arslan Tash, it appears that the cherubs were four-legged animals with human faces. The phrase 'Yahweh who is enthroned on the cherubim' (1 Sam. 4.4; 2 Sam. 6.2) may indicate that Yahweh had a cherub throne, but it is impossible to say if this is to be associated with either the cherubs in the temple or with Solomon's throne, which was also Yahweh's throne.[1]

An altar of copper was placed in the courtyard in front of the temple (1 Kgs 8.64),[2] as was a brazen 'sea' in the form of a great bowl resting on twelve bulls, three in each direction of the four world corners (1 Kgs 7.23). About 2000 bat of water (= 26,000 liters)[3] could be pumped into it. The function of the 'sea' is not known, but it may have fulfilled both ideological and practical purposes, for example, for lustrations (cf. 2 Chron. 4.6). Since water played an important role in the cult, the 'sea' might have represented the cosmic waters. Such an interpretation is supported by the information that the 'sea' rested on the twelve bulls. The bull was an animal symbolic of

1. It is possible that the throne in the temple, if there were one, was not in harmony with the later writer's concept of an 'invisible' Yahweh; we may not have the full story. For the phrase 'Yahweh who is enthroned on the cherubim', see the discussion in A. Dessène (*Le sphinx: Etude iconographique*, I [Rome, 1957]); R. de Vaux, 'Les cherubims et l'arche d'alliance, les sphinx gardiens et les trones divins dans l'ancient orient', *MUB* 37 (1961), pp. 93-124; T.A. Busink, *Der Tempel von Jerusalem*, I, pp. 285-87; T.N.D. Mettinger, 'YHWH SABAOTH—The Heavenly King on the Cherubim Throne', *Studies in the Period of David and Solomon* (ed. T. Ishida; Tokyo, 1982), pp. 109-38, and figs. 11-3, 5. Cf. also F. Landsberger, 'The Origin of the Winged Angel in Jewish Art', *HUCA* 20 (1947), pp. 227-54. In Ezek. 28.1 the king of Tyre is depicted as a divine being on his throne out in the sea. He is also called a cherub whose home is on the divine mountain (cf. G.W. Ahlström, *Aspects of Syncretism*, p. 45).

2. Nothing is indicated about the form or type of altar. E. Würthwein suggests that it may have been a stepped altar, but because of the later command in Exod. 20.36 the narrator of Kings has avoided the problem (*Die Bücher der Könige*, I, p. 114).

3. Cf. T.A. Busink, *Der Tempel von Jerusalem*, I, pp. 326-28. As to the bulls, cf. J.L. Myers, 'King Solomon's Temple and Other Buildings and Works of Art', *PEQ* 80 (1948), pp. 36-38.

divinity; thus divine powers carried the 'sea'.

Among other objects were copper lavers with bases on wheels, decorated with lions, cherubs and palms. Each laver could take in over 900 liters (1 Kgs 7.27-29; 2 Chron. 4.6-8). Their liturgical purpose is not stated. This kind of temple utensil is also known from other countries,[1] such as from Larnaka, Cyprus, in Mycenaean times.[2]

It is of some interest that 1 Kings 6 does not mention in the temple's exact location or orientation. It seems to be taken for granted that everyone knew it—or the writer himself did not know. He perhaps had never seen it. There is no information about the temple's foundation or its facade, the thickness of its walls or any other detail of the exterior which would show that the writer had an intimate knowledge of the temple.[3] His sources may have been incomplete, even if his writing is sometimes rich in details. He may have used some priestly traditions about the first temple.[4] The destruction of the temple is then mentioned in a second vision granted to Solomon. In this vision the writer lets Yahweh tell the king that if he and his descendants do not keep Yahweh's commands and statutes, then the temple will be destroyed and the people of Israel will become a sharp taunt among the nations (1 Kgs 9.1-8).[5] From a literary point of view this is the D-historian's introduction to the Solomonic period of failure.[6]

1.   See, for instance, M. von Oppenheim, *Der Tell Halaf* (Leipzig, 1967), p. 190, pl. 58b.

2.   Cf. J.L. Myers, *PEQ* 80 (1948), p. 41; T.A. Busink, *Der Tempel von Jerusalem*, I, pp. 350-52. It has been guessed that the lavers were for transporting water, which is possible, but then it must have been hard work, because their weight was close to a ton when they were filled with water.

3.   Cf. R. de Vaux, *Ancient Israel*, II (New York, 1961), p. 313. M. Noth has pointed out the same phenomenon, but still thought that ch. 6 was essentially from the Solomonic period (*Könige*, p. 105). For a critique of Noth, see K. Rupprecht, *Der Tempel von Jerusalem* (BZAW, 144; Berlin, 1977), pp. 22-24.

4.   The detailed description could have been inspired by the narrator's knowledge of the second temple.

5.   This may have been inspired by Ps. 89.

6.   Cf. A.D.H. Mayes, *The Story of Israel between Settlement and Exile* (London, 1983), pp. 108-109. The Chronicler's literary system of building activities and blessings versus no building activity and bad fate probably was inspired by the Deuteronomist. In this connection it should be noted that the narrative of the temple building starts with the statement that Solomon began to build it in the '480th year after the people of Israel came out of the land of Egypt' (LXX has 440 years), 'in the fourth year of Solomon's reign, in the month of Ziv, which is the second month'

It is quite natural that the style of the temple as well as its inventory reflected the artistic culture of Syria-Palestine; that is what would be expected. Any distinct Israelite or Judahite culture or art that was markedly different from the Syro-Palestinian one did not yet exist. Thus, one cannot say, as does J. Bright, that the temple posed some danger to the Israelite cult, but that the 'Temple cult, whatever it borrowed, remained essentially Israelite in character'.[1] There is no indication of what was 'essentially Israelite' in the time of the united monarchy.[2] The cult and the Yahwism that the writer would like to have seen in existence already in the Solomonic period had not yet come into being.[3] As has been maintained earlier, the country of Canaan shaped both culture and religion in this new kingdom. David and Solomon's religious activities and building programs were not bound to any deuteronomistic ideology, because it was not yet invented. It is, therefore, not at all a 'heartbreaking paradox' that Solomon who was 'most eloquently devoted to the worship of Yahweh was equally devoted to honoring other gods'.[4] With all the gods depicted on the interior walls of the temple, and with Baal and Asherah also being worshipped there,[5] the monarchy was a period in which in Jerusalem Yahweh was thought of as the ruler of the heavenly assembly, the divine beings of the kingdom.[6] Y. Aharoni sees the cult of the temple as being 'based on the tradition of the twelve tribes, a tradition which

(1 Kgs 6.1). This is not an editorial edition but an integral part of the passage 6.1-10. Verses 11-13 are a D oracle and promise to Solomon, and the rest of the chapter (vv. 14-38) then continues to report the building activities. The whole chapter is a unit.

1. *A History of Israel* (3rd edn), p. 218.

2. Bright has here, as so many others, made the deuteronomistic evaluation his own.

3. H.W.F. Saggs, *The Encounter with the Divine in Mesopotamia and Israel* (London, 1978), pp. 214.

4. D.N. Freedman, 'The Age of David and Solomon', *WHJP*, IV.1 (ed. B. Mazar), p. 123.

5. See my *Aspects of Syncretism*, pp. 50-52. For monotheism as a later and speculative idea, cf. my *Royal Administration*, pp. 68-69.

6. D.N. Freedman thinks the reason why Solomon worshipped so many gods was because he had 700 wives and 300 concubines, 'which must distract the most pious of men' (p. 123). The statement by Freedman shows a complete ignorance of history of religion research. Was piety in the ancient Near East dependent upon the amount of wives a man could afford? If so, the theological consequence would have made celibacy the ideal.

was never realized in the reality of the royal administration'.[1] I have to agree that the royal administration never realized it. David and Solomon did not know of the biblical twelve-tribe system.

Archaeologically, not much is known about Jerusalem in the tenth century BCE. However, a few objects should be mentioned. A fragment of a terracotta cult stand from the tenth/ninth century has been found in the excavations on the slope south of the *haram es-sharif* (the temple mount). It is decorated with the head and the chest of a man having head gear similar to that found on reliefs of Sea Peoples at the Medinet Habu temple. Another find is a right-hand bronze fist belonging to a statuette of the type common in the LB II–Iron I periods, which usually have a mace or an axe in the right hand and a lance in the left hand.[2] These finds show how the cultic paraphernalia of Davidic Jerusalem represent an artistic tradition that continued from the Late Bronze Age.

Other royal sanctuaries were to be found at different places in the country, especially at administrative centers and fortress cities.[3] These are usually called *bāmôt* by the biblical writers, a term commonly translated 'high places'.[4] The word has been used negatively in the deuteronomistic propaganda about Jerusalem as the only cult place Yahweh supposedly wanted. Other sanctuaries include those Solomon dedicated to the gods of his foreign-born wives. Among the gods mentioned are Milcom of Ammon, Chemosh of Moab and Ashtarte of the Sidonians. Milcom and Chemosh, for instance, had their sanctuaries built on the Mount of Olives (1 Kgs 11.4-8). The women would have been helped to feel at home in a strange place and enabled to continue their religion. The political dimensions of Solomon's policy

1. Y. Aharoni and M. Avi-Yonah, *The MacMillan Bible Atlas* (New York, 1968), p. 74. A.S. Kapelrud opines that the temple 'was of a foreign character in construction, intended for another religion than that of Yahweh' ('Cult and Prophetic Words', *ST* 4 [1950], p. 7).

2. For these finds, see Y. Shiloh, *Excavations at the City of David*, I, p. 17; and figs. 23 and 24. For the Bronze Age deity statuettes, see O. Negbi, *Canaanite Gods in Metal*, figs. 43-44, and pl. 22.1319.

3. See G.W. Ahlström, *Royal Administration and National Religion*, pp. 46, 62-64.

4. Cf. W.B. Barrick, *SEÅ* 45 (1980), pp. 50-57; cf. *idem*, 'The Word BMH in the Old Testament'.

have been well expressed by S. Herrmann: 'by accepting foreign gods it sought to offer a guarantee of peace to the countries around'.[1]

In spite of the few chapters that the biblical writers dedicated to Solomon,[2] his reign is one of the most fascinating in the history of ancient Israel and Judah. Perhaps it is fascinating because the stories about his wisdom, his monumental buildings, his wealth and his imperial status give food for thought about a king the likes of whom was produced neither before nor after by that little country. No wonder the majority of scholars have seen the Solomonic period as being not only cosmopolitan but also the period that produced and collected wisdom literature and began the art of Israelite historiography. It has been labeled—inaccurately—a period of enlightenment.[3] It should rather be said that with David and Solomon the Near Eastern culture of the Levant broke the isolation of the mountain peoples of central Palestine. The people living within the territories of Israel and Judah were now, as never before, confronted with the cultural and commercial world of the Near East. Even if this 'international culture' made its impact upon the peoples of the hills, it will nonetheless have been primarily an urban phenomenon. Villagers, as a rule, were by nature conservative.[4]

Jerusalem may have gained the position of a cosmopolitan capital for a short time during which the art and literature of the time would have made an impact on the upper strata of the society. The royal court seems to have been influenced by Egyptian phenomenona.[5] As mentioned above,[6] since the time of the New Kingdom, Egypt had been the model used by princes of Palestine to organize their courts and administrations.[7] With Solomon this reached a climax; at least that

---

1. *A History of Israel* (2nd edn), p. 182.

2. Only eleven chapters in 1 Kings are devoted to Solomon and his reign, but David gets one and a half books.

3. G. von Rad, *Old Testament Theology*, I (Edinburgh, 1962), pp. 48-50; S. Herrmann, *A History of Israel* (2nd edn), pp. 181-82.

4. Cf. my book, *Who were the Israelites?*, pp. 96-97.

5. 'It was through the bureaucrats of Jerusalem that the wisdom of Egypt, upon which its scribal meritocracy had been nurtured for centuries, first gained entrance to Israel and began to shape its institutions, literature and intellectual life' (E.W. Heaton, *Solomon's New Men: The Emergence of Ancient Israel as a Nation* [New York 1974], pp. 12-13).

6. See Chapter 5.

7. Cf. K.H. Bernhardt, 'Verwaltungspraxis in spätbronzezeitlichen Palästina',

is the way he is pictured by the writers. That there is a message
behind this picture is not to be doubted. A king would not be built up
to such proportions if there were no base for it. And yet boasting was
a common phenomenon in ancient Near Eastern literature. Bearing
this tendency in mind, the modern audience should expect some
exaggerations to appear in the writings about Solomon. His enormous
wisdom, for instance, reflects traditional royal ideology. Because the
king belongs to the divine sphere (in the Bible he is called the son of
Yahweh, Pss. 2.7; 89.27), he has divine wisdom, hidden wisdom.[1] To
be successful was to be wise. The biblical writer of 1 Kings 3–11 has
produced us a report of Solomon's acts that is 'quite similar to the
political wisdom of Egypt'.[2] He also has given the reader an
impression of what the Solomonic period might have looked like.[3]
Scribal schools could have provided information concerning
Solomon's court and his administrative centers.[4] Chronicles and rules
for the king and the court personnel may have been written down, and
some of these may have been collected at a later time. Such could be
the case with 'units' of wisdom sentences that occur, for instance, in
Proverbs 25.[5] As for chronicles and historiographic writings, no one
is in a position to say what could have been written down during this

Beiträge zur sozialen Struktur des alten Vorderasien (ed. H. Klengel; Berlin, 1971,
pp. 133-35).

1.   G.E. Bryce puts it this way: 'By his special relation to the deity the king is
privileged to inquire into that which is hidden from ordinary mortals' (G.E. Bryce, *A
Legacy of Wisdom: The Egyptian Contribution to the Wisdom of Israel* [Cranbury,
NJ, 1979], p. 160).

2.   G.E. Bryce, *Legacy of Wisdom*, p. 172. For the narratives about Solomon
following an old Near Eastern literary pattern, see B. Porten, 'The Structure and
Theme of the Solomon Narrative (1 Kings 3–11)', *HUCA* 38 (1967), pp. 93-128.
M. Görg holds the opinion that the story about Solomon at Gibeon is to be seen as
an 'immitierte Prinzennovelle' known from the sphinx stela of Tuthmoses IV (*Gott-
König-Reden in Israel und Ägypten* [BWANT, 105; Stuttgart, 1975], pp. 64-65; cf.
pp. 564-65).

3.   Cf. M. Noth, 'Die Bewahrung von Solomons "Göttlicher Weisheit"',
Wisdom in Ancient Israel and in the Ancient Near East (ed. M. Noth and
D.W. Thomas; VTSup, 3; 2nd edn; Leiden, 1969), p. 237.

4.   On this, see conveniently T.N.D. Mettinger, *Solomonic State Officials*,
pp. 140-57.

5.   Prov. 25.1 says that the collection was made by Hezekiah's men. G.E. Bryce
sees Prov. 25 and 'the Sayings of the Wise' (Prov. 2.17–24.22) to have had 'their
Sitz im Leben in the Royal service' (*Legacy of Wisdom*, p. 153).

time, besides the 'Book of the Acts of Solomon' (1 Kgs 11.41), which could have been composed shortly after Solomon's death, at the earliest.[1] To conclude from these kinds of writing that historiography was emerging, however, is another matter. The so-called Yahwistic source or J-source, with its history from Abraham to the period of the so-called settlement in Canaan, is often considered to have been composed at this time,[2] which is no more than a hypothesis.[3] Abraham's failure to play any role for the peoples of the monarchic period makes the hypothesis less acceptable. He becomes an important ancestor of the Judahites first in connection with the return from Babylon and with the returnees' claim to the land.[4]

A certain kind of 'historiography' may, however, have been written in Jerusalem during the period of the united monarchy. Like any usurper, David, as well as Solomon and Rehoboam, must have felt the need to justify the taking of kingship. This need may be seen as the beginning of the biblical historiography. The later writings about David as the chosen one may build on propaganda from the royal court in Jerusalem, a propaganda that probably increased during the time of Rehoboam.[5]

---

1.   It is unknown what kind of literature this represents. Royal diaries are known from Egypt and could have existed also at the Jerusalem court; cf. D.B. Redford, *Pharonic King-Lists, Annals, and Day-Books* (SSEA Publication 4; Missisauga, Ontario, 1986). J. Liver has maintained that the 'Book of the Acts of Solomon' was put into writing shortly after the split of the united monarchy and that it was composed by 'one of the wise men of Solomon's time', who supposedly belonged to the group of old wise men whose advice Rehoboam did not follow! ('The Book of the Acts of Solomon', *Bib* 48 [1967], p. 101). T. Mettinger also thinks that this work was written by one of Solomon's counsellors, but he does not see it as part of the official records of the court (*Solomonic State Officials*, p. 37).

2.   L. Rost, *TLZ* 72 (1947), col. 132; W.H. Schmidt, 'A Theologian of the Solomonic Era? A Plea for the Yahwist', *Studies in the Period of David and Solomon* (ed. T. Ishida; Tokyo, 1982), pp. 55-73 (with lit.); J.A. Soggin in J.H. Hayes and J.M. Miller, *Israelite and Judean History*, pp. 332-33, 379-80; cf. J. Bright, *A History of Israel* (3rd edn), pp. 68-70; D.N. Freedman, 'The Age of David and Solomon', *World History of the Jewish People*, IV.I (ed. B. Mazar), pp. 124-25.

3.   For the Yahwist as a late monarchic or exilic writer, see H.H. Schmid, *Der sogenannte Jahwist*.

4.   W.M. Clark, 'The Origin and Development of the Land Promise in the Old Testament'.

5.   Most of the material in the books of Samuel is a defense for David, who

In light of the above it should be asked whether the writings about David and Solomon really constitute history. The answer is that it is not history in the modern sense of that term. Unfortunately, there are no extant nonbiblical texts that mention David or his creation of his kingdom. Solomon is mentioned by Menander of Ephesus, according to Josephus.[1] However, the Egyptian inscriptions do not mention Israel or Judah, Solomon or Rehoboam.[2] As for the Akkadian texts, it is understandable that they do not mention anything about Palestine in this period. Assyrian power was at a low ebb, and its problems were mainly with its closest neighbors, especially with the Aramaeans in the west. But even if there are no corroborations, the historicity of the Davidic–Solomonic kingdom should not be doubted. The biblical writers may have made David and Solomon greater than they were; that is part of the style. Nevertheless, the period of the united monarchy was something exceptional within the history of Canaan, something that had never happened before nor happened since.[3] The biblical writers took pride in these events and also exaggerated the importance of the period. Realizing the greatness of David, it is natural that he became a legendary figure and that some of these legends were incorporated into the biblical material. Also, realizing the greatness of Solomon, it is quite in order that his role was minimized by the writers because he was not estimated to be the ideal king, in contradistinction to his father. Even if his stature as a great king is still perceptible,

'replaced' Saul. This does not mean that the books were written during the time of David. As long as the kingdom existed, there was no need to write its history. As mentioned before (see Introduction), the composition of the biblical history is a product of a time of crisis, a time when one needed a justification for the existence of the returnees in the land of Yehud and thus for the reconstruction of the new society. The negative attitude towards the northern kingdom of Israel in this 'history' was designed to make it clear to the northerners in the province of Samerina exactly where the true Israel was. The northerners had to be convinced, as did the people of Yehud, including the writers, that what they wrote was the will of Yahweh. Religion was still part of the political game.

1. *Apion* 1.121-25; *Ant.* 8.147-49.

2. Shoshenq's inscription about his campaign in Palestine (in Rehoboam's fifth year) follows the style of the New Kingdom's inscriptions in listing places, not kings, in Palestine.

3. S. Herrmann expresses this with the words that David's state 'would not have been possible without David' ('King David's State', *In the Shelter of Elyon* [ed. W.B. Barrick and J.R. Spencer; JSOTSup, 31; Sheffield, 1984], p. 268).

his greatness has been cut short by the narrator.

With the period of Solomon have been reached two important steps in this country's history. One is the approaching split of the kingdom, which is the motif behind Solomon's judgment about the two prostitutes and the splitting of the child into two parts (1 Kgs 3.16-27).[1] The other is the importance of the temple. The centrality of the temple overshadows Solomon's whole regime, and about half of the narrative about the period of Solomon in 1 Kings is dedicated to temple building activities. In spite of this, the biblical writer cannot easily overlook Solomon. He was too important to ignore.

With the death of Solomon an era passed away. Palestine returned to what it had been before, a country of smaller political units. Jerusalem's artificial position as a cultural and political metropolis ended. No wonder Solomon could not be forgotten—his splendor, his might, and his wisdom—even if he never could replace his father as the ideal.

1. G.E. Bryce, *Legacy of Wisdom*, pp. 180, 182-83.

MAPS AND ILLUSTRATIONS

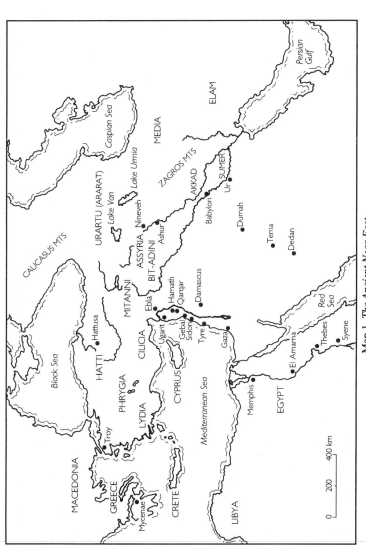

Map 1. *The Ancient Near East*

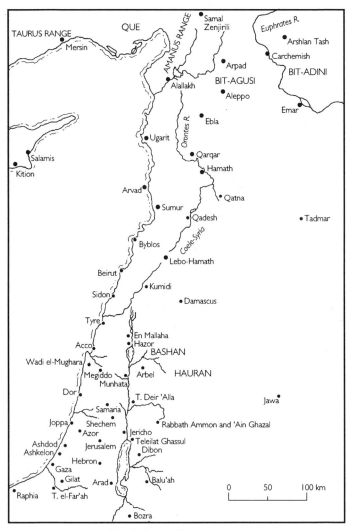

Map 2. *Ancient Syria-Palestine*

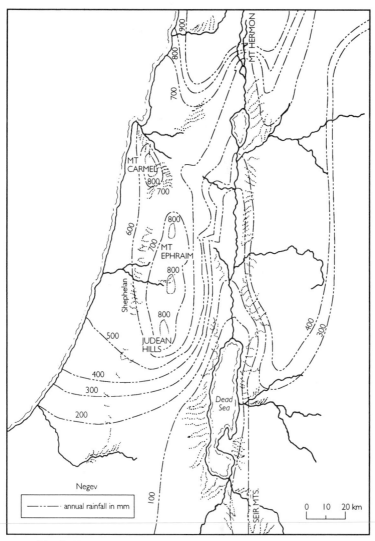

Map 3. *Mean Annual Rainfall*. After J.W. Rogerson and P.R. Davies,
The World of the Old Testament (Englewood Cliffs, NJ, 1989).

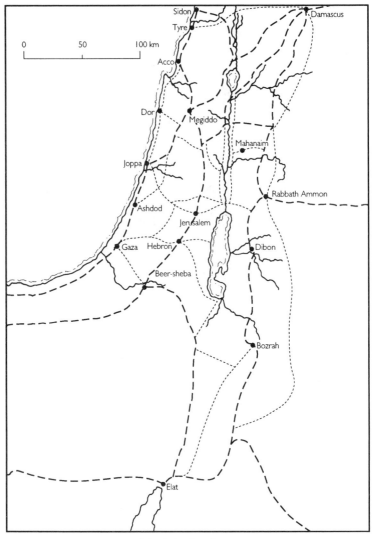

Map 4. *Ancient Routes*

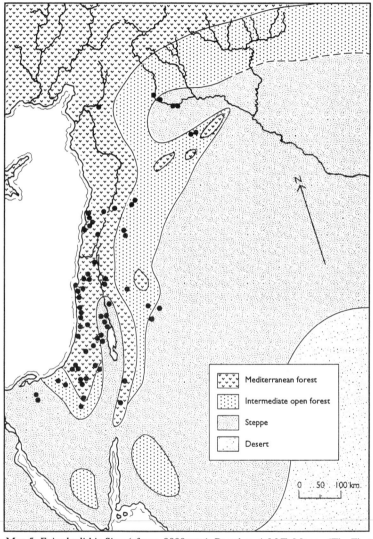

Map 5. *Epipaleolithic Sites* (after c. 9000 BCE). Based on A.M.T. Moore, 'The First Farmers in the Levant', *The Hilly Flanks and Beyond* (SAOC, 36; Chicago, 1983), courtesy of the Oriental Institute of the University of Chicago.

Legend:

- Mediterranean forest
- Intermediate open forest
- Steppe
- Desert

N

0   50   100 km.

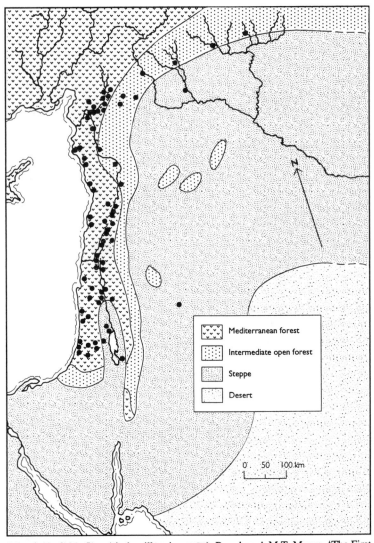

Map 6. *Neolithic Sites* (sixth millennium BCE). Based on A.M.T. Moore, 'The First Farmers in the Levant', *The Hilly Flanks and Beyond* (SAOC, 36; Chicago, 1983), courtesy of the Oriental Institute of the University of Chicago.

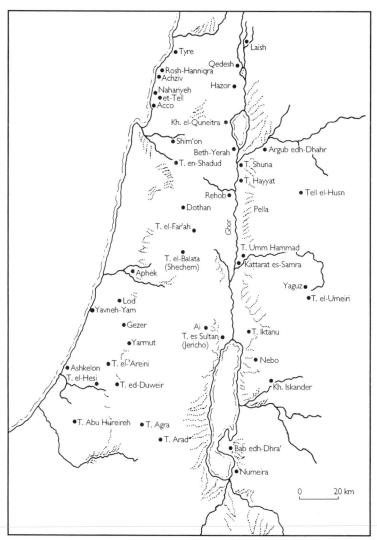

Map 7. *Early Bronze Age Sites* (plus tombs in the Ghor)

Map 8. *Cities of the Amarna Letters*. Tentative outlining of the city states in Palestine and southern Syria during the Amarna period, built on Helck's reconstruction.

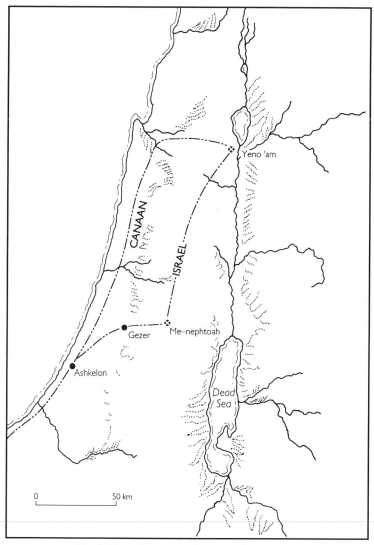

Map 9. *Pharaoh Merneptah's Campaign in Palestine*

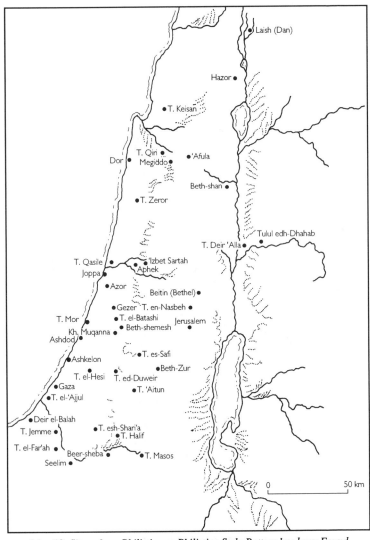

Map 10. *Sites where Philistine or Philistine Style Pottery has been Found.*
After T. Dothan, *The Philistines* (New Haven, 1982).

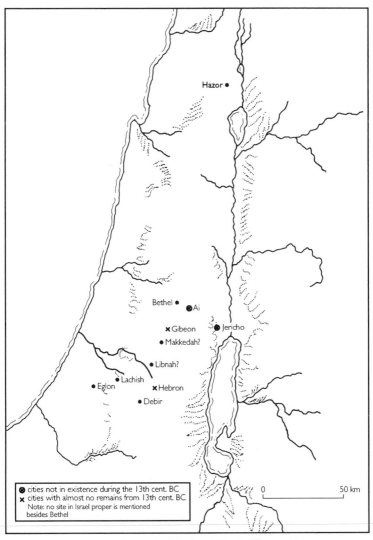

Map 11. *Cities Mentioned in Joshua's 'Conquest'*

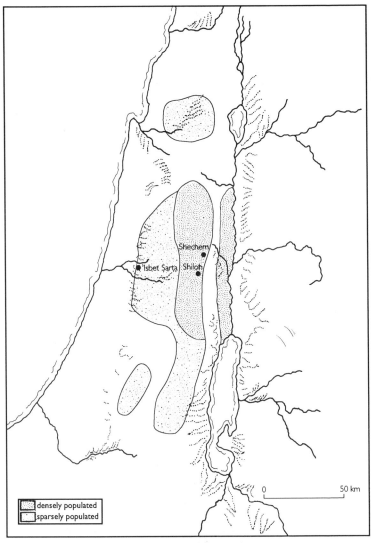

Map 12. *Settlements in the Hills in the Twelfth Century BCE*. Courtesy of I. Finkelstein, after his *The Archaeology of the Israelite Settlement*, p. 325.

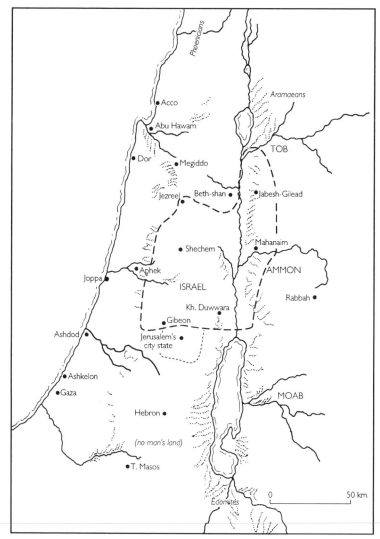

Map 13. *Saul's Kingdom*

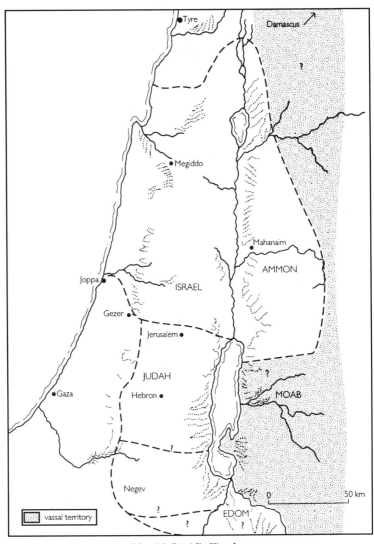

Map 14. *David's Kingdom*

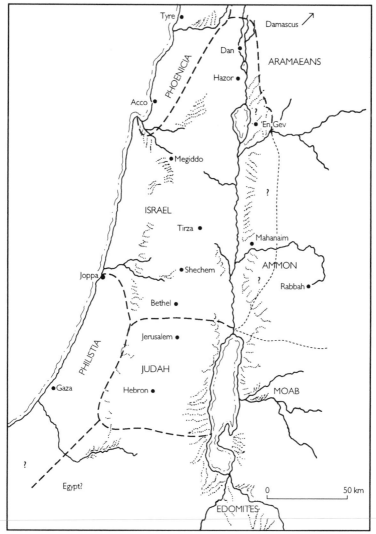

Map 15. *Palestine after Shoshenq's Campaign*

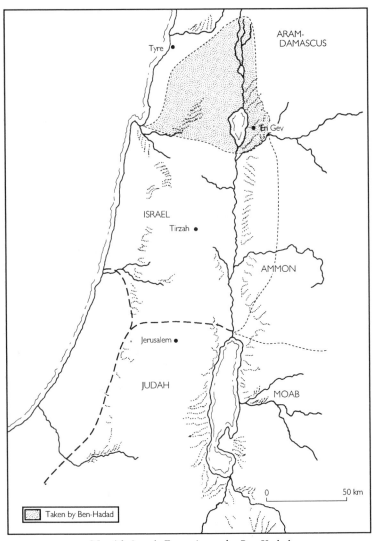

Map 16. *Aram's Expansion under Ben-Hadad*

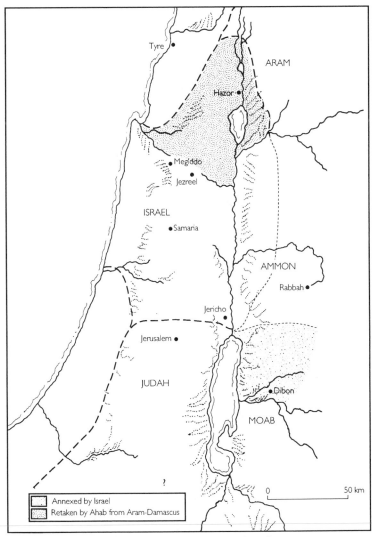

Map 17. *The Time of Omri and Ahab*

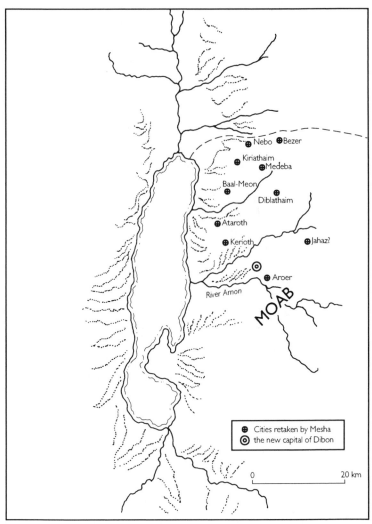

Map 18. *Moab under Mesha*

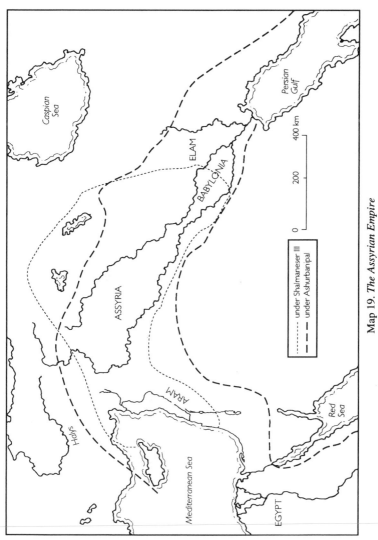

Map 19. *The Assyrian Empire*

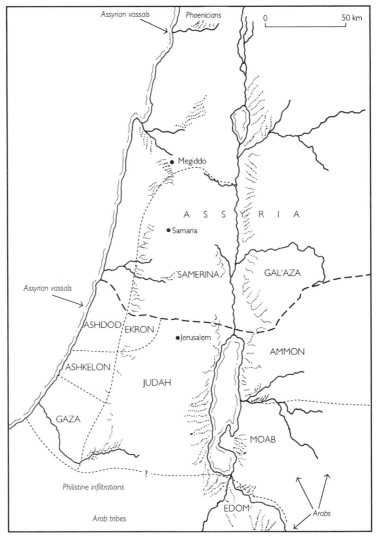

Map 20. *Palestine after 720 BCE*

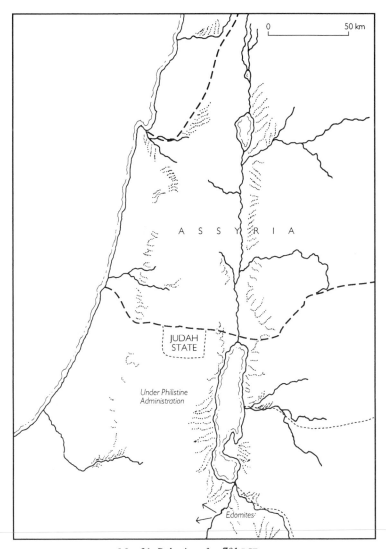

A S S Y R I A

JUDAH
STATE

Under Philistine
Administration

Edomites

0   50 km

Map 21. *Palestine after 701 BCE*

Map 22. *Palestine in the Late Seventh Century BCE*

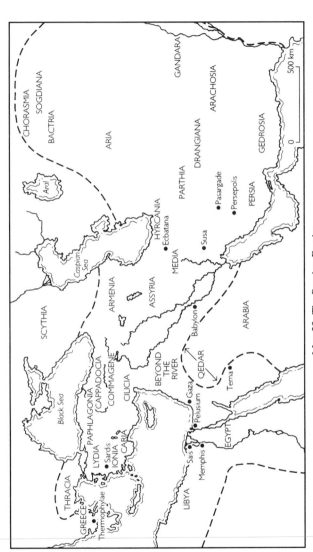

Map 23. *The Persian Empire*

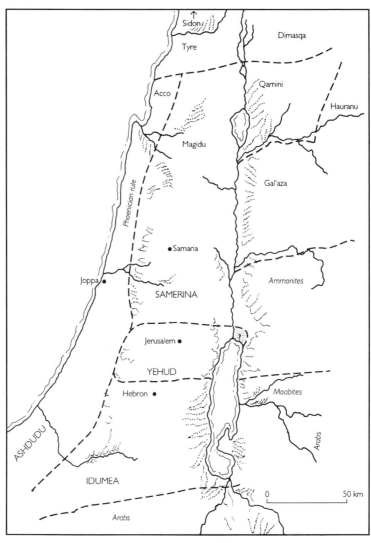

Map 24. *Palestine in the Persian Period* (fifth century BCE)

Figure 1. *Wâdī Mujib (Ancient Arnon)* (photo G.W. Ahlström)

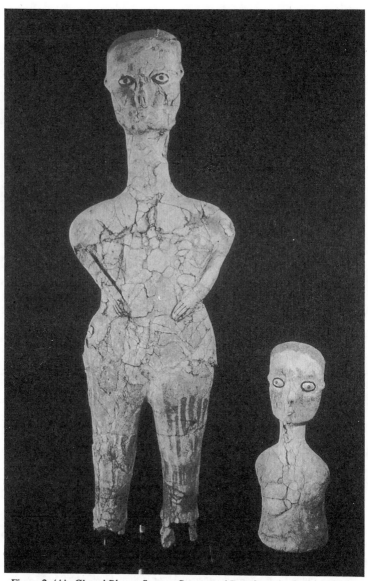

Figure 2. *'Ain Ghazal Plaster Statues*. Statues and Bust from the Statuary Cache discovered at 'Ain Ghazal (1983), conserved and restored by K. Tubb, Institute of Archaeology, University of London (photo courtesy of P. Dorrel and Stuart Laidlaw). Height of statue c. 90 cm.

Figure 3. *A Middle-Bronze Age Vase or Urn from a Burial Chamber at Jericho* (in the so-called Hyksos style, 18th–16th cent. BCE). From J.W. Rogerson and P.R. Davies, *The Old Testament World* (Englewood Cliffs, NJ, 1989)

To the left: 'the wretched chief of the land of Nubia' (Tasety).

To the right: 'chief of the foreign lands of Peleset whom his majesty slew'.

Figure 4. *Relief from the Temple of Ramses III Showing Kneeling Peleset/Philistine Warrior.* On the front of the base of the fourth Osiride-pillar from the west wall of the Medinet Habu Memorial Temple III, first court, north side. Courtesy of the Oriental Institute of the University of Chicago.

Figure 5. *Relief from Nineveh Showing an Assyrian Siege.* From the drawings of P.E. Bootin and M.E. Flandin, *Monumens de Nineve* (Paris, 1849). Note the man in the siege turret who appears to be reading from a scroll—he probably tries to convince the defenders to give up resistance ('oral warfare'!).

Figure 6. *Jar in the Shape of a Man from the Edomite Sanctuary at Qitmit* (7th cent.
BCE; to be compared with a similar jar from Beth Shemesh of the 8th cent.).
Photo courtesy of I. Beth Arieh.

Figure 7. *Relief of Darius I from his Tomb at Naqsh-i-Rustam*. From
Archäologische Mitteilungen aus Iran, I (Berlin, 1968), Tafel 33 (photo by Heinz
Luschey). Courtesy of Deutsches Archäologisches Institut, Abteilung Teheran.

Figure 8. *Jewish Coin Showing a Deity Seated on a Winged Wheel* (c. 400 BCE).
The inscription has been read both as *yhw* (Yahu) and *yhd* (Yehud).
From the British Museum.

Chapter 12

PALESTINE AFTER SOLOMON

When Solomon died the kingdom fell apart. The geography of Palestine does not invite the creation of a larger political unit. As seen above, the population of this country was heterogenous. The peoples of the lowlands originally did not have much contact with the peoples of the different parts of the hills. This meant that life and cultural traditions proceeded in somewhat different ways in different parts of the country. It is clear from the Amarna letters that the people of the southern hill country did not have close relations with those of the central and northern hills.[1] It is also evident from these letters that small political units constituted the more natural phenomena. This knowledge provides one of the main contributing factors for why the Davidic–Solomonic kingdom did not survive Solomon. The unity between the different parts of the kingdom was forced and artificial. In contrast to Judah, the people of the north, Israel, had been treated as a vassal nation after Sheba's uproar. The harsh treatment, including forced labor and hard taxation, backfired.

Religiously and culturally the clans of the north did not feel that they had much in common with the peoples of the south, Judah. Constituting the peoples of the coast, of the plains and of Galilee, they had not really melded together with the Jerusalemites and the Judah-ites. The same may be said for the peoples of the Negev and its 'former' Edomites, as well as for the Gileadites. From this viewpoint the period of the united monarchy should perhaps be seen as a historical parenthesis. The division of the country into smaller political units would be the more natural state of affairs. The so-called tribes never became so united or felt such a close connection that they had any reason or time to collect their 'common' traditions and write them down during the period of the united monarchy. The political unifica-

---

1. See above, Chapter 5.

tion was not natural. It was forced and therefore artificial.[1]

Solomon's death provided the northern people, Israel, an opportunity to change their political status. They wished to be free from the oppression of 'Jebusite' Jerusalem and the Judahite bureaucracy. Solomon's son, Rehoboam,[2] was acknowledged king without any opposition in Judah,[3] but Israel was on the brink of mutiny. It was customary for vassals to try to regain their freedom when a king died. Ammon and Moab probably revolted since there is no information that these countries remained part of Judah under Jeroboam or Rehoboam.[4] Israel found its leader in one of Solomon's highest officials, Jeroboam from Zeredah in Ephraim. He had been appointed as chief of forced labor in Israel, 'the House of Joseph' (1 Kgs 11.28). Verse 26 in the same chapter mentions that Jeroboam 'lifted his hand against the king', and in v. 40 it is said that Solomon tried to kill Jeroboam, who fled to Egypt.[5] It is not clear whether Jeroboam's 'mutiny' was at the same

---

1. The biblical writer has tried to overcome the artificial unity of these peoples by dividing the peoples into twelve 'tribes', all descendants of the 'patriarch' Jacob, whose descendants supposedly conquered Canaan. In this way they could be given the same 'history'. At the same, he could use the fiction to accuse Israel of breaking the unity, which is to have been the basis for David's kingdom. This is in harmony with the writer's goal of presenting a pro-Davidic story. Scholars have willingly followed this literary model. For instance, J. Bright believes that the 'epic traditions of Israel's beginnings—of patriarchs, exodus, and conquest—had already assumed normative form in the days of the Judges. It was, however, approximately in Solomon's reign that the Yahwist... selecting from these traditions and adding others, shaped his great theological history of Yahweh's dealings with his people' (*A History of Israel* [3rd edn], p. 219). This is nothing more than a guess. For a more realistic viewpoint, see H.H. Schmid, *Der sogennante Jahwist*, pp. 154-66.

2. For the name meaning 'the people is enlarged', see G.B. Gray, *Studies in Hebrew Proper Names* (London, 1896), p. 60; cf. the discussion in J.J. Stamm, 'Zwei alttestamentliche Königsnamen', *Near Eastern Studies in Honor of W.F. Albright* (ed. H. Goedicke; Baltimore, 1971), pp. 443-52. The irony of this name is that Rehoboam got his kingdom drastically reduced.

3. 1 Kgs 11.43; 2 Chron. 9.31.

4. 2 Kgs 8.20 mentions that Edom threw off the yoke of Judah during the reign of Jehoram, Jehoshaphat's son.

5. H. Weippert sees 1 Kgs 11.29-40 to contain a legitimation legend about Jeroboam which has been edited and extended in the Josianic period ('Die Ätiologie des Nordreiches und seines Königshauses [1 Reg. 11, 29-40]', *ZAW* 95 [1983], pp. 344-75).

time a revolt by the northerners against Solomon, but it certainly enhanced Jeroboam's candidacy for the throne of Israel.[1]

Jeroboam was well received by Pharaoh Shoshenq (946–913?), of the (Libyan) Twenty-Second Dynasty (biblical Shishak), who had been able to establish his rule over all Egypt and also Nubia. Jeroboam's arrival at the Egyptian court may have signaled to the Pharaoh that the Solomonic monarchy was not too stable. At what time Jeroboam fled to Egypt is not known, but probably his 'mutiny' occurred after several years of service under Solomon. After Solomon's death Jeroboam was back in Israel and being chosen king of Israel (1 Kgs 12.2-3, 20).[2]

Solomon's successor, Rehoboam, went to Shechem to heal the breach.[3] The reason for his trip was probably that Israel already had broken with Jerusalem, so that Rehoboam was faced with a problem that could have led to war. The Bible characterizes the visit as a demonstration of power.[4] As a king trying to keep the kingdom together,

1. The Greek version (LXX) assigns Jeroboam an army of 300 chariots and says he married a daughter of Pharaoh; cf. J. Debus, *Die Sünde Jeroboams* (FRLANT, 93; Göttingen, 1967), pp. 80-82; M. Aberbach and L. Smolar, 'Jeroboam's Rise to Power', *JBL* 88 (1969), pp. 69-72. According to J. Gray, it is evident that the text in the LXX is 'an independent Northern tradition' that, however, 'has been worked over by a Judean editor' (*I and II Kings*, p. 311). That Jeroboam should also have married a daughter of the Egyptian pharaoh is rather unbelievable. The story of the Edomite prince Hadad marrying an Egyptian princess seems to have been copied here; cf. M. Aberbach and L. Smolar, *JBL* 88 (1969), pp. 71-72; J.R. Bartlett, *ZAW* 88 (1976), pp. 217-18. Usually, an Egyptian princess was not given in marriage to a prince without land, and never to a non-Egyptian commoner. As to the LXX tradition, see also D.W. Gooding, 'The Septuagint's Rival Version of Jeroboam's Rise to Power', *VT* 17 (1967), pp. 173-89.

2. Cf. the discussion by I. Plein, who considers the narratives about Jeroboam's rise to kingship to have originated in the north, but sees 1 Kgs 12.1-9 to be a composition from Judah ('Erwägungen zur Überlieferung von 1 Reg. 11, 26-14, 20', *ZAW* 78 [1966], pp. 8-24).

3. Rehoboam had to negotiate with the northerners to be accepted as their king. He announced that the vassal situation would continue. His negotiations can be compared with David's meeting the men of Gibeon and appeasing them and fulfilling their demands (2 Sam. 21). David also 'negotiated' with the men of Jabesh-Gilead (through messengers) and successfully maneuvered the Israelites in to accepting him as king.

4. The 180,000 men of Benjamin and Judah that Rehoboam mustered (1 Kgs 12.21) are most probably represent the usual exaggeration of Judah's manpower; this

Rehoboam went with a considerable escort, both for protection and for a show of force. The Israelites asked for better conditions than Solomon had given them and sought to be on a par with the people of Judah.[1] Having inherited the position of despot, Rehoboam only wanted to keep the status quo, so he turned down the demands of the Israelite representatives (1 Kgs 12.1-5). It may be seen as a contemptuous attitude[2] or sheer stupidity, but Rehoboam probably thought that the royal power and its display at Shechem would be enough.[3] He created a grave political mistake by sending Adoram out in order to start conscriptions for the levy. Adoram was stoned to death. Only then did Rehoboam seem to have understood the seriousness of the situation and that he himself was in danger. He mounted his chariot and sped to Jerusalem, probably in record time. The kingdom

army belongs to a later event after the split was a fact; cf. H. Sebass, 'Zur Königserhebung Jerobeams I', *VT* 17 (1967), pp. 325-33.

1.   M. Weinfeld thinks that the Israelites asked for exemptions in taxes and levy, which could sometimes be given to certain cities ('The Counsel of the Elders to Rehoboam and its Implications', *Maarav* 3 [1982], pp. 37-38). For cities given tax and corvée exemptions, see A.L. Oppenheim, *Ancient Mesopotamia*, pp. 123-25; cf. H. Vanstiphuot, 'Political Ideology in Early Sumer', *Orientalia Lovanisensia Periodica* 1 (1970), p. 9.

2.   Thus J. Bright, *A History of Israel* (3rd edn), p. 230.

3.   For the story about Rehoboam following the advice of the younger court officials against that of the older and more experienced ones, see among others A. Malamat, who here sees an institution of a 'bicameral nature' (*JNES* 22 [1968], p. 251); cf. *idem*, 'Organs of State Craft in Israelite Monarchy', *BA* 28 (1965), pp. 34-65; cf. also E. Würthwein, *Die Bücher der Könige*, I, p. 159. A. Falkenstein cannot see the young men around Rehoboam to constitute an institution ('Zu Gilgamesh und Agga', *AfO* 21 [1966], pp. 47-50). M. Weinfeld refers to the Akkadian text, 'Advice to a Prince' (see W.G. Lambert, *Babylonian Wisdom Literature* [Oxford, 1960], pp. 112-14), and maintains that the king is regarded as the servant of the people (*Maarav* 3 [1982], pp. 27-53). Of course, the king was the servant of his people, because he was the shepherd of the flock (= his god's people). A writer could use this both for and against a king, depending upon the writer's own position. Another possibility is that 'the advice of the elders and that of the young men' is simply a literary feature. Cf. the view of J. Vercoutter, who maintains that the advice given by the counsellors to Egyptian kings, who did not follow the advice, is a literary invention by the Egyptian scribes in order to show the inferior judgment of the advisors (cf. J. Bottéro, Cassin and J. Vercoutter, 'The Second Intermediate Period and the Hyksos Invasion of Egypt', *The Near East: The Early Civilizations* [New York, 1967], p. 410).

had fallen apart. The attitude of the Israelites is well expressed in the answer that Rehoboam was supposedly given by the northerners:

> What portion do we have in David?
> And neither do we have any inheritance in the son of Jesse.
> To your 'tents', Israel!
> Look after your house, David![1]

It could not have been said more clearly. Israel had artificially and forcefully been part of the Davidic–Solomonic kingdom. After Eshbaal's death, Israel had no other choice than to accept the usurper David, but after the uproar under Sheba, Israel had been treated as a subdued vassal. That backfired under Rehoboam. The kingdom of the Davidic house was not originally according to the will of the Israelite people, neither was it their creation. In other words, Israel wanted its freedom and it got it back under Jeroboam.[2]

Rehoboam's meeting with the men of Israel in Shechem cannot be seen as evidence that kingship was ideologically different in Israel than in Judah. As king, Rehoboam had to secure his hold on the other parts of the country outside Judah proper. Israel was the economic mainstay of the united kingdom and the backbone of the king's labor force. To accept the demands of the north would have been to exempt them from the levy. Rehoboam could not afford such a concession; thus, the kingdom fell apart.

Rehoboam must have prepared to recover Israel by war immediately after his arrival in Jerusalem. However, his war against Israel was stopped by a command from Yahweh through the prophet Shemaiah (1 Kgs 12.21-23). As far as can be determined, this is the

---

1. Cf. the words of Sheba in 2 Sam. 20.1. J. Gray assumes that the word 'tents' refers to the 'tents where the representatives' of Israel lived during the negotiations at Shechem (*I and II Kings*, p. 306). The men would have had a blanket with them not a tent. Scouting had not yet been invented. The term tent has been chosen deliberately. It is an old poetic word for home. It is used of soldiers who, after war, go 'every man to his tent' (Judg. 7.8; 1 Sam. 4.10; 2 Sam. 18.17; 19.9[8]; 2 Kgs 8.21; 13.5; 2 Chron. 10.16). Similarly, when the cult assembly is dismissed, everyone returns to his 'tent' (Deut. 16.7; 1 Kgs 8.66; 2 Chron. 7.10). The term *'ōhel* can also serve as a synonym for *byt*, temple (cf. K. Koch, 'אֹהֶל *'ōhel*; אֲהַל *'āhal*', *ThWAT*, I, cols. 130-31 (ET *TDOT*, I, pp. 120-21).

2. It is doubtful that Jeroboam played any role in the Shechem negotiations; cf. R.W. Klein, 'Jeroboam's Rise to Power', *JBL* 89 (1970), pp. 217-18; *idem*, 'Once More: Jeroboam's Rise to Power', *JBL* 92 (1973), pp. 582-84.

writer's way of explaining why Rehoboam failed to re-establish the Solomonic kingdom. (There must have been a reason for this, and the ultimate reason lies in the divine will.) In 1 Kgs 14.30 and 15.6 the narrator has forgotten his explanation and simply states that the two nations were at war with each other as long as Rehoboam lived. The state of warfare was to have continued under his son Abijam. In fact, this state of warfare lasted until Omri became king in Israel.

As a former supervisor of Solomon's forced labor, Jeroboam knew very well the strength of the kingdom, especially the northern part of it. Becoming king of Israel, Jeroboam had access to the arsenals of the fortress cities and other strongholds, as well as the larger part of the Solomonic chariotry, which probably was located in the north. Its territory was more suitable for maneuvers by chariots than was that of Judah. Unfortunately, the narrator did not mention anything about the strength of Jeroboam's army after he became king, or about how he organized his kingdom. It is only said that he started to 'fortify Shechem and dwelt there', and then he built (or rebuilt) Penuel in Transjordan (1 Kgs 12.25). Whether this means that Jeroboam intended to make Shechem his capital is uncertain. The Hebrew *yšb*, 'to sit (on a throne)', is used in this connection. Because there was no capital in this former province of the Solomonic kingdom, Jeroboam had to choose one, and Shechem with its old royal traditions[1] was a natural choice. The town had been an old center for the *bᵉnê yiśrā'ēl*.[2] In Jeroboam's time Shechem was an insignificant and unfortified town or village.[3] If the king had thought of making Shechem his capital, his intentions never materialized.[4] The narrator mentions in the same verse (v. 25) that Jeroboam marched out (*yṣ'*) from Shechem to Penuel in the Transjordan and built or rebuilt it.[5] Why Jeroboam left Shechem is not mentioned, but the political situation may explain the

1. Cf. the kingdom of Labayu in the Amarna Age, and the kingdom of Gideon and Abimelek.

2. See also my *Royal Administration*, p. 56, and *Who were the Israelites?*, pp. 16-17.

3. Consult G.E. Wright, *Shechem*, pp. 144-45; L.E. Toombs, 'The Stratigraphy at Tell Balata (Shechem)', *BASOR* 223 (1976), pp. 58-59.

4. The reason why the biblical writer does not say more about this problem is that he is not interested in history. His interest centers mainly around Jeroboam's cultic reorganization of the new nation's official cult, which he did not like.

5. The Hebrew verb that is used is *bnh*, which can mean both 'build' and 'rebuild'.

move. The warfare between Judah and Israel, as well as Pharaoh Shoshenq's campaign in Palestine in the fifth year of Rehoboam's reign, could have contributed to the abandonment of Shechem. At Penuel Jeroboam may have had more time to build up and organize his army and his administration. Penuel, being close to the iron ore deposits of the 'Ajlun, was 'the only mining town' in Jeroboam's nation and, therefore, of great economic and military importance.[1] After Shoshenq's campaign Jeroboam's residence seems to have been located at Tirzah (1 Kgs 14.17), Tirzah apparently became Jeroboam's capital, even if the biblical texts never explicitly say so. His successors also resided at Tirzah until Omri moved to Samaria.

The theory has been posited that Jeroboam did not need a capital because the people who chose him as king would in no way 'have reverted to any system of imposed and institutionalized centralization of government', be it at Shechem, Penuel or Tirzah.[2] This theory builds upon P.C. Salzman's[3] idea that 'reverse ideology' comes to the fore at a time when a government's rule shows signs of weakness. At such a time, representatives for the nonurban population can appear as a strong political force, perhaps creating a situation that results in a replacement of the oppressive government. This will not be disputed here. However, the theory is not applicable to the period of Jeroboam. He had just started his rule, and had had no time to build up his power. It is not necessary to emphasize that Israel had had enough of the despotism of Jerusalem under Solomon and that they had succeeded in getting rid of the oppressive government. Nevertheless, well-organized government apparatus was still necessary for the country to deal with problems, and in this respect Jeroboam could rely on the district system of Solomon. J.P.J. Olivier follows A. Alt[4] and W. Dietrich[5] in assuming that there were 'two fundamentally different social systems operative in Israel'.[6] These would be the Israelites living in the

1. See M. Har-el, 'The Valley of the Craftsmen (*ge' haharašim*)', *PEQ* 109 (1977), p. 85 n. 63.

2. J.P.J. Olivier, 'In Search of a Capital for the Northern Kingdom', *JNWSL* 11 (1983), p. 127.

3. 'Ideology and Change in the Middle Eastern Societies', *Manuscripta* NS 13 (1978), pp. 618-37; cf. also N.P. Lemche, *BN* 20 (1983), p. 55.

4. 'Das Königtum in den Reichen Israel und Judah', *VT* 1 (1951), pp. 2-22.

5. *Israel und Kanaan: Vom Ringen zweier Gesellschaftssysteme* (SBS; Stuttgart, 1979), pp. 13-14.

6. *JNWSL* 11 (1983), p. 128.

villages and the Canaanites who were used from of old to living with the system of city states, controlling the villages and their fields.[1] This differentiation between Israelites and Canaanites is unrealistic and rather artificial, as should be clear from the above discussion about Israel's origin.[2] The Canaanites of the hills had become Israelites. It is impossible to separate Canaanites and Israelites in the hills as two different ethnic groups. As I have shown earlier, the population of the cities of the monarchic period consisted mainly of government officials.[3] This makes it impossible to talk about an internal struggle for political and cultural domination between 'Canaanites' and 'Israelites'. A. Alt's thesis about two different peoples that made Israel into a dualistic state is unrealistic.

'Reserve ideology' can be used to explain the emergence of the 'restored' Israel. During most of the time of the united monarchy the peoples of the north may have viewed the reign of Saul in an idealized way because of the Jerusalemite government's oppressive actions, which also meant that the role of the elders was minimized. They would have wanted their king to play a role different than the one David and Solomon had pursued. A central government that was too strong may have been suspect in the eyes of the peoples of Israel. Bearing this in mind, Jeroboam's kingship may have been conditional.[4] This would explain why there is no explicit mention of a capital for Jeroboam, although the reason for the omission could as well be that the Judahite narrator did not want to mention it. For him Jerusalem was the only capital. Because Jeroboam's successors had their residence at Tirzah, it is likely that Jeroboam placed administrative sections in the city. The religious administration of Jeroboam's new nation also is unknown. There was perhaps a royal sanctuary at the place where the king lived, according to the customs of the Near East. Because the king was the head of both state and religion he had to have some cultic establishment in or close to his residence. This may have been so well known that the writer did not even feel the

1. See W. Dietrich, *Israel und Kanaan*, pp. 13-14. The 'Canaanites' born in the hill country during the reign of Solomon probably would not be familiar with any city state government.
2. See above, Chapter 10, pp. 428-29.
3. *JNES* 41 (1982), pp. 133-38.
4. Cf. F.M. Cross, *Canaanite Myth*, pp. 230-31; J.P.J. Olivier, *JNWSL* 11 (1983), p. 130.

need to mention it. What he mentions, however, is that Jeroboam gave the temples of Bethel and Dan the rank of official royal sanctuaries. We may thus call them national shrines (1 Kgs 12.16-18; cf. Amos 7.13). The new king needed a prestigious temple where he himself could fulfill a king's cultic duties. He apparently reorganized Bethel's cult calendar so that it included a royal festival patterned after the one at the Jerusalem temple (1 Kgs 12.32).[1] Whether Jeroboam intended to make Bethel the religious center of his kingdom is not known. It could very well be that it was a temporary solution.

The temples of both Dan[2] and Bethel were old prestigious cult places. Jeroboam is said to have given these two the rank of official national shrines. He did not build these temples, as so often has been claimed.[3] The biblical narrator tries to give Jeroboam's organization of the state cult the aura of innovation, while at the same time completely ignoring the antiquity of these temples. Bethel, for instance, had for a very long time been a holy place for the peoples of the central hills. It would have been more in line with old Israelite traditions than was Jerusalem. This fact has to be taken into consideration when analyzing the conflicts between the northern and the southern Yahweh traditions and their spokesmen. With the split of the united monarchy, two official and competing state religions arose that both had Yahweh as their overlord.

Jeroboam certainly faced many problems in building up his kingdom. To deal with administrative matters, he could have continued the system of the Solomonic districts. He knew how it worked. He may have taken over the system as it was, only dismissing some governors and other government officials faithful to the king of Judah, such as the sons-in-law of Solomon. He may also have been forced to make some changes in the levy or abandon the corvée, at least for the time being. If he did not, he could have run the risk of popular rebellion. These government officials who did not accept the dissolution of the

1. E. Nielsen, *Shechem*, p. 277; cf. G.W. Ahlström, *Royal Administration and National Religion*, pp. 58-59.

2. For the Danite priesthood's claim for Yahwistic legitimacy, see my *Aspects of Syncretism*, pp. 26-27.

3. Thus, for instance, Y. Aharoni, *The Land of the Bible* (2nd edn), p. 323; E.W. Nicholson maintains that Jeroboam established the two rival sanctuaries of Bethel and Dan and set up the 'golden calves' (*Deuteronomy and Tradition* [Philadelphia, 1967], p. 72).

union certainly would have been dismissed. Also, several of them could have left of their own choice, perhaps in order to save their lives.

Temples were not only built in order to increase the holiness in the country. They were also part of the government's administrative apparatus, and as such a sign of the strength of the king.[1] According to 1 Kgs 12.31, new sanctuaries, *bêt bāmôt*, were built by Jeroboam. These sanctuaries were probably under the supervision of the district governors. It is thus understandable why some priests and Levites left Israel for Judah when Jeroboam became king. 2 Chron. 11.13-14 claims that Jeroboam chose other people as priests and Levites. Because priesthood was by royal appointment,[2] as were the Levites,[3] Jeroboam had to have people he could trust. The nation's deity, as well as his vice-regent, the king, could not have foreigners representing the state, the divine realm. The Jerusalemite idea that Jeroboam introduced the worship of the bull as a new cult in Israel is merely a poorly phrased accusation of the later pure-Yahwistic circle against what also had been the official religion of Judah. Jeroboam's cult reorganization afforded the narrator an opportunity to tell the truth about Israelite religion. By labelling the northern cult as schismatic and 'sinful', he was able to avoid condemning Judah's official state cult directly.

1. Cf. C.J. Gadd, *Ideas of Divine Rule in the Ancient East* (The Schweich Lectures of the British Academy, 38; London, 1948), pp. 6-7. Consult also J.A. Brinkman, who states that temple repairs not made by kings was a sign that the royal establishment was weak (*A Political History of the Post-Kassite Babylonia*, p. 295).

2. Cf. N. Avigad, *IEJ* 25 (1975), p. 104; G.W. Ahlström, *Royal Administration*, pp. 44-46.

3. For the Levites as government officials and as a 'police force', see among others, B. Mazar, 'The Cities of the Priests and Levites', *Congress Volume, Oxford 1959* (ed. J.A. Emerton *et al.*), p. 202; cf. J. Milgrom, *Studies in Levitical Terminology*, I (Berkeley, CA, 1970), pp. 8-10; J.R. Spencer, 'The Levitical Cities' (PhD dissertation, University of Chicago, 1980), ch. 2; G.W. Ahlström, *Royal Administration*, pp. 47-51. Note that the biblical writers do not complain about David having appointed some of his sons to the priesthood (2 Sam. 8.18). In this connection it should also be noted that the distinction between priests, military personnel and other government officials in Egypt was not as sharp as is usually presumed (cf. W.C. Hayes, 'Egypt: Internal Affairs from Thutmosis I to the Death of Amenophis III', *CAH*, II.1, p. 327; M.F. Gyles, *Pharaonic Policies and Administration*, p. 64).

The biblical narrator depicts Jeroboam as an innovator for his introduction of the cult of the bull into his kingdom. However, bull symbolism was a very old phenomenon in the ancient Near East, connected with a number of male deities, inlcuding Yahweh.[1] Jeroboam was not responsible for first associating Yahweh with bull iconography. Had he tried to force a new form of worship upon the people, he most probably would have met stiff opposition. The people would not have recognized their god. In re-establishing the freedom of Israel, Jeroboam would have returned to a traditional symbol of Yahweh, not introduced a new and unfamiliar one. There had been enough innovations under the reigns of David and Solomon. The cry to go back 'to your tents, Israel' included also the re-establishing of the old religion. In the D historian's patternistic presentation of the history and religion of the Israelites, the traditionalist Jeroboam became a symbol for the religious and political attitude the Deuteronomist fought against.[2] The great sin of Jeroboam[3] was that, from a

---

1. Cf. S. Talmon, who sees the cult of the 'calf' as an old Israelite form of worship ('Divergences in Calendar Reckoning in Ephraim and Judah', *VT* 8 [1958], p. 50); E. Nielsen, *Shechem*, pp. 277, 193-95; F.F. Hvidberg, *Weeping and Laughter* (Copenhagen, 1962), pp. 85-86; G.W. Ahlström, *Psalm 89*, pp. 93-94; M. Weippert, 'Gott und Stier', *ZDPV* 77 (1961), pp. 102-17; J.P. Brown, 'The Sacrificial Cult and its Critique in Greek and Hebrew (1)', *JSS* 24 (1979), pp. 167-73.

In order to 'save' Yahweh from tauromorphism, scholars have usually referred to the phenomenon (found in the glyptic art) of deities standing on bulls. Thus, the bulls at Bethel and Dan (and perhaps other places too!) are to be understood as Yahweh's pedestals; cf. K.M. Obbink, 'Yahwehbilder', *ZAW* 47 (1929), pp. 264-66; W.F. Albright, *From Stone Age to Christianity*, pp. 264-74; idem, *Yahweh and the Gods of Canaan*, pp. 197-98; R. de Vaux, 'The Religious Schism of Jeroboam I', *The Bible and the Ancient Near East* (Garden City, NY, 1971), pp. 97-110; H. Motzki, 'Ein Beitrag zum Problem des Stierkultes in der Religionsgeschichte Israels', *VT* 25 (1975), pp. 470-85.

2. Here it should be noted that the literary contacts between Exod. 32 and 1 Kgs 12.26-28 are so close that it is likely that they were written by the same person or that they originated in the same circles. Note that the sons of Jeroboam and Aaron have the same names, Nadab and Abihu (Abijah). Exod. 32 may thus be a critique of Jeroboam's cult reorganization that has been retrojected into the prehistoric period and has been labeled 'Mosaic' in order to legitimate it; cf. W. Beyerlin, *Herkunft und Geschichte der ältesten Sinaitraditionen* (Tübingen, 1961), pp. 26-27; M. Noth, *Exodus: A Commentary* (OTL; Philadelphia, 1962), pp. 243-47; M. Aberbach and L. Smolar, 'Aaron, Jeroboam, and the Golden Calves', *JBL* 86 (1967), pp. 129-40;

Jerusalemite perspective, he became the first king of the breakaway kingdom, and such a kingdom could under no circumstances have a right cult because it was not centered at the 'right' place, Jerusalem. Thus, the whole northern kingdom was in principle apostate, and everything, such as religion, life, ethics, and the rest, was 'wrong'.[1] It must be acknowledged that Jeroboam and his compatriots did not know of any deuteronomistic law. It came about centuries later.[2]

In the conflict between Israel and Judah neither one succeeded in getting the upper hand. There is no information about what happened in the greater Palestinian area during the first four years after the death of Solomon. In the fifth year of Rehoboam's reign an old foe reappeared. An Egyptian army under Pharaoh Shoshenq,[3] the founder of the Twenty-Second Libyan Dynasty (in Bubastis) marched up into Palestine. Shoshenq used a border incident as a pretext for his campaign. His inscription at Karnak[4] mentions that Semites, whom the Pharaoh considered to be Judahites, had crossed the border into Egypt and attacked Egyptian outposts. Shoshenq says that he defeated them at the Bitter Lakes[5] and that from there he continued up through Palestine. From his list of conquered or bypassed places it can be concluded that his campaign was less concerned with Judah than with the Negev

---

H. Schmid, *Mose* (BZAW, 110; Berlin, 1968), pp. 81-83; G.W. Coats, *Rebellion in the Wilderness: The Murmuring Motif in the Wilderness Tradition of the Old Testament* (Nashville, 1968), pp. 184-86.

3.   For Jeroboam's role in the literary history, see C.D. Evans, 'Naram-Sin and Jeroboam: The Archetypal *Unheilsherrscher* in Mesopotamian and Biblical Historiography', *Scripture in Context*, II (ed. W.W. Hallo, J.C. Moyer and L.G. Perdue; Winona Lake, IN, 1983), pp. 97-125.

1.   Concerning the bull symbolism it should be noted that a much greater number of bull figurines have been found in excavations in Jerusalem than at any other place; cf. T.A. Holland, 'A Study of Palestinian Iron Age Baked Clay Figurines, with Special Reference to Jerusalem: Cave 1', *Levant* 9 (1977), pp. 121-55; G.W. Ahlström, *An Archaeological Picture of Iron Age Religions in Ancient Palestine*, pp. 22-24.

2.   Cf. H. Donner 'The Separate States of Israel and Judah', *Israelite and Judean History* (ed. J.H. Hayes and J.M. Miller; Philadelphia, 1977), p. 388.

3.   The Hebrew consonantal form would be Shushaq, but the Masoretic reading (the $q^e r\bar{e}$) is Shishak.

4.   *Reliefs and Inscriptions at Karnak. III. Bubastide Portal* (The Epigraphic Survey; OIP, 74; Chicago, 1954).

5.   K.A. Kitchen, *The Third Intermediate Period in Egypt*, pp. 294-96.

and Israel, including both sides of the Jordan valley. The purpose of the campaign is not really spelled out. Different answers have been given to the question why Shoshenq invaded Palestine at this time. The most common answer is that the Pharaoh was going to punish Jeroboam for not having been a faithful vassal. Jeroboam had to learn a lesson. But why then send out troops to the Negev and into Judah? The real answer to the question may be that, having conquered Nubia,[1] Shoshenq also had his eyes on the former Egyptian dominion, Palestine. The collapse of the Solomonic kingdom gave Shoshenq a welcome opportunity to show that Egyptian power was still a reality.

The route of the campaign is not clear from the inscription.[2] He probably did not crisscross the country, but instead marched directly up to Megiddo,[3] where he made his headquarters. He may have sent out detachments to the Negev, Jerusalem and Transjordan, although Jerusalem is not mentioned in the list. The biblical report that Rehoboam delivered most of the palace and temple treasures to the Egyptians may mean that he capitulated before any siege was laid to Jerusalem. In this way, Rehoboam was able to keep his crown (1 Kgs 14.25-27).[4]

---

1. Nubian soldiers were also in his army; see K.A. Kitchen, *The Third Intermediate Period*, pp. 295-96.

2. For the discussion, see B. Mazar, 'The Campaign of Pharaoh Shishak to Palestine', *Congress Volume, Strasbourg 1956* (ed. J.A. Emerton *et al.*; VTSup, 4; Leiden, 1957), pp. 57-66; Y. Aharoni, *The Land of the Bible* (2nd edn), p. 323-25; S. Herrmann, 'Operation Pharao Schoschenks I, im östlichen Ephraim', *ZDPV* 80 (1964), pp. 55-79; K.A. Kitchen, *The Third Intermediate Period*, pp. 296-98; cf. also M. Noth, 'Die Wege der Pharonenheere in Palästina und Syrien, IV. Die Schoschenkliste', *ZDPV* 61 (1938), pp. 227-304.

3. Thus, S. Herrmann, *ZDPV* 80 (1964), pp. 58-60. A fragment of a commemorative stela of Shoshenq has been found at Megiddo; see C.S. Fisher, *The Excavation of Armageddon* (Oriental Institute Communications, 4; Chicago, 1929), pp. 12-14, and figs. 7 and 9; R.S. Lamon and G.M. Shipton, *Megiddo I*, pp. 60-61.

4. Shoshenq's inscription does not mention this. The Chronicler sees it as a result of Rehoboam's abandonment of Yahweh worship. He claims that the Egyptians took all the fortified cities of Judah (2 Chron. 12.4-6). This is part of the Chronistic ideology, according to which a king who was struck by disaster must have forsaken Yahweh. Did Jeroboam's leaving Shechem for Penuel indicate that he was not yet ready for battle—after five years of rule? This raises the possibility that Jeroboam had been unable to secure his kingship and Israel's independence. T.H. Robinson believes that Shoshenq's campaign helped Jeroboam to secure the territory of Israel and his kingship (*A History of Israel*, I [Oxford, 1932 (1948)], p. 275).

Among the places listed by Shoshenq are Gezer, Rubuti, Aijalon, Beth-Horon, Gibeon, Mahanaim,[1] Rehob, Beth-Shan, Shunem, Ta'anak, Megiddo, 'the hand of the king', i.e. a stela; *y(w)dmrk* (probably the *yad hammelek* of 1 Sam. 15.12, in the Carmel area?), Abū Hawām and Socoh, among others.

Abū Hawām, stratum III, was destroyed at this time. The city may have been the port for Megiddo and the Jezreel plain[2] and would have played an important role in Israelite–Phoenician trade, the control of which was most certainly one of the goals of Shoshenq's campaign. The places taken in the Negev indicate that the Jerusalem–Tyre trade monopoly was broken. It may also indicate that Judah lost control over the Negev and western Edom at this time (see Map 15). Shoshenq's campaign in Palestine seems to have helped Jeroboam to keep Israel independent and stopped Rehoboam from rebuilding the Solomonic kingdom.

After the Egyptian army had withdrawn from Palestine Jeroboam was undisputedly king over Israel. He seems to have continued to rebuild the nation's defenses, which was necessary after the Egyptian campaign. Megiddo, for instance, now became a fortress city. There are no residential quarters to be found in stratum IVA,[3] which is the 'post-Shoshenq' city. The first 'stables'[4] were built by Jeroboam and probably also the water system.[5] Because the political situation soon changed after Shoshenq's campaign, Megiddo may have lost some of

---

1. Number 59 in the Shoshenq list has ( )*rú-sệ*, which according to W. Helck (*Die Beziehungen*, p. 242) cannot be Tirzah, as previously suggested by B. Mazar ('The Campaign of Pharaoh Shishak', *Congress Volume, Strasbourg 1956* [ed. J.A. Emerton *et al.*], pp. 57-66) and S. Herrmann (*ZDPV* 80 [1964], pp. 55-79).

2. Thus, D.L. Saltz, 'Greek Geometric Pottery' (PhD dissertation, Harvard University, Cambridge, MA, 1978), pp. 147-49.

3. Cf. G.W. Ahlström, *JNES* 41 (1982), pp. 133-35.

4. It is not at all certain that these buildings actually were stables. According to J.B. Pritchard, they may alternatively have been storehouses or barracks ('The Megiddo Stables', *Near Eastern Archaeology in the Twentieth Century* [ed. J.A. Sanders], pp. 268-76; also cf. Y. Aharoni, *Beer-Sheba*, I (Tel Aviv, 1973), pp. 28-30.

5. D.L. Saltz, 'Greek Geometric Pottery', pp. 430-45. Ms Saltz concludes that the water system still was under construction when Shoshenq attacked the city (p. 430). The so-called Solomonic Gate was built after Solomon, according to D. Ussishkin (*BASOR* 239 [1980], pp. 1-18). For Y. Yadin's opinion, see 'A Rejoinder', *BASOR* 239 (1980), pp. 19-23.

its military importance. Israel's problems were not so much with Egypt any more, but with the growing power of Aram-Damascus and with Judah. In the north, such cities as Hazor and Dan became more crucial for the defense of Israel. At Hazor the city of stratum VIII was quite different from that of the preceding strata (X–IX). It had 'now become a strongly fortified city with mighty walls, strong citadel, public storehouses and, above all, a huge underground water system, capable of sustaining the city through a long siege'.[1] The excavators have dated this stratum to the time of king Ahab.[2] However, Jeroboam could have ordered the building of defences at Hazor, and the parallel with Megiddo may indicate that the new city plan of Hazor could be earlier than Ahab.[3]

The borders of Israel and Judah are not given in the Bible beyond the statement that the 'ten tribes' became Jeroboam's kingdom. In the east, Jericho and its surroundings belonged to Israel. The peoples of the Jordan Valley and of Gilead in Transjordan, geographically and historically, had always had more contact with the northerners than with the peoples of the southern hills of Judah. Those areas of Benjamin's territory close to Jerusalem stayed with Judah (cf. 2 Kgs 12.21),[4] and according to 2 Chron. 11.10 Aijalon remained with Jerusalem. The areas north of Jerusalem, on the other hand, seem to have shifted hands a few times. At the end of Jeroboam's reign, the king of Judah, Abijam, is supposed to have taken Ephron, Bethel and Jeshanah north of Bethel (2 Chron. 13.19).

The biblical writer does not show much interest in Transjordan and the Jordan Valley in this period. Jeroboam's building activities at Penuel and Mahanaim indicate that he ruled over part of Transjordan, at least the Jordan Valley and the foothills and valleys leading up to

1. Y. Yadin, *Hazor of Those Kingdoms*, p. 165.

2. For the periodization of the strata, see conveniently Y. Yadin, *Hazor of Those Kingdoms*, p. 200.

3. Cf. on this subject D.L. Saltz, 'Greek Geometric Pottery', pp. 452-53. For Jeroboam's activities at Dan, see the discussion in A. Biran, 'Tel Dan', *BA* 37 (1975), pp. 26-51.

4. It is, of course, possible that the writer's opinion and knowledge about Benjamin's territory is that of his own postexilic time when the territory north and NW of Jerusalem was seen as part of Benjamin. For instance, Neh. 11.31-35 describes Benjamin's land as reaching up to Bethel in the north and to Lod and Ono in the west.

the Transjordanian hills.[1] The area from the Golan in the north to 'Ajlun in the south was infiltrated by Aramaeans.[2] After the rise of the kingdom of Aram-Damascus, the territories of northern Galilee, Golan and northern Gilead, with their more or less Aramaean population, were natural targets for the expansion of the new Aramaean kingdom of Damascus.

Just as the territory north of 'Ajlun was perhaps an easy prey for Rezon of Damascus to capture after the death of Solomon, so too the areas south of 'Ajlun may have become part of Ammon again at the time. We do not learn anything about either Jeroboam or Rehoboam ruling over the Transjordanian vassals Ammon and Moab. Both kings had troubles at home to such an extent that they most probably were not able to control any dependencies outside the territories of Israel and Judah proper.[3]

Moab most probably regained its independence, as evidenced by the Mesha inscription. Mesha says that he recaptured the territory that the king of Israel, Omri, had incorporated with his kingdom (ll. 4-7): the land north of the river Arnon. In the short period between the death of Solomon and Omri's rise to kingship, no part of Moab was governed by either Israel or Judah.[4] The latter kingdom, being sepa-

---

1. M. Ottosson thinks that there had been a decline in *el-ghor* after the Shoshenq campaign (*Gilead*, pp. 224-25 n. 60). For a destruction layer at Beth-Shan being associated with Shoshenq, see B. Mazar, 'The Campaign of Pharaoh Shishak', *Congress Volume, Strasbourg 1966* (ed. J.A. Emerton *et al.*), p. 63.

2. See Chapter 9, pp. 400-402, and S. Mittmann, *Beiträge*, pp. 226-27. B. Mazar believes that the villages of Jair and Kenath and its villages (1 Chron. 2.23) were taken by Geshur and Aram after the death of Baasha of Israel (*BA* 25 [1962], pp. 104-105). Geshur possibly did not exist as an independent kingdom at the time. The information in 1 Chron. 2.21-23 is of a doubtful value. The whole unit of 2.3–4.23 is concerned with the genealogy of Judah, which was not located in Transjordan. It reflects a tradition about Gilead-Machir that the postexilic Chronicler has used to illustrate his pan-Israelitic ideology. W. Rudolph considers 1 Chron. 2.21-23 to be a 'Nachtrag' (*Chronikbücher*, p. 10). For the Chronicler's goal, see, among others, H.G.M. Williamson, *Israel in the Books of Chronicles* (Cambridge, 1977), pp. 87-131.

3. Cf. S. Herrmann, *A History of Israel*, pp. 198-99. M. Noth suggests that Ammon would have been ruled by an Aramaean dynasty from the time of Solomon's death ('Die Nachbarn der israelitischen Stämme in Ostjordanlande', *ZDPV* 68 [1946], p. 41 (= *Aufsätze*, I, p. 470).

4. Cf. H. Donner, in J.H. Hayes and J.M. Miller, *Israelite and Judean History*, p. 386.

rated from Transjordan by the Dead Sea, would not have been able to keep any territory north of the river Arnon under its supervision. It is even doubtful that Judah reached down to the Jordan Valley south of Jericho. That was Israelite territory.

The Philistine territory that David had conquered may have been reclaimed in part from Israel. The wars under Nadab (Jeroboam's son) [1] and Elah (Baasha's son)[2] at Philistine Gibbethon indicate that there were border disputes with the Philistines. These wars also indicate that Judah did not have any territory in the coastal area. Gezer belonged to Israel.[3] As mentioned above,[4] Solomon's second district, which stretched from Timnah and Beth-Shemesh in the south to Aphek in the north, including Joppa, was settled primarily by Sea Peoples and Canaanites who were not affiliated with the mountain peoples. The territory was never considered part of Judah, and thus naturally stayed with Israel and Jeroboam. After his death the Philistines may have pressed to take back some of it.

The city of Aijalon belonged to Solomon's second district and would, therefore, have been part of the northern territories that seceded from Judah. However, in 2 Chron. 11.5-12 Aijalon is mentioned as one of the 15 cities Rehoboam fortified. A closer look at the text shows that the Chronicler's view of Judah is postexilic, which explains why Aijalon is included. The Chronicler appears to have used an old list connected with Rehoboam's securement of his kingship,[5] as

1.   1 Kgs 15.27.
2.   1 Kgs 16.15.
3.   N. Na'aman, 'The Date of 2 Chronicles 11.5-10—A Reply to Y. Garfinkel', *BASOR* 271 (1988), p. 74.
4.   See Chapter 11.
5.   P. Welten, *Die Königs-Stempel, Ein Beitrag zur Militärpolitik Judas unter Hiskia und Josia* (ed. A. Kuschke; Abhandlungen des deutschen Palästinavereins; Wiesbaden, 1969), p. 170. Cf. his *Geschichte und Geschichtsdarstellung in den Chronikbüchern* (WMANT, 42; Neukirchen–Vluyn, 1973), pp. 12-13. V. Fritz maintains that the list belongs to the time of king Josiah ('The List of Rehoboam's Fortresses in 2 Chr. 11.5-12 —A Document from the Time of Josiah', *EI* 15 [1981], pp. 46*-53*). Against this, see P. Welten, *Die Königs-Stempel*, p. 170. N. Na'aman sees the text to refer to Hezekiah's preparation for the defenses for war against Sennacherib and that the LMLK stamps would show that provisions had been sent to these cities ('Hezekiah's Fortified Cities and the LMLK Stamps', *BASOR* 261 [1986], pp. 5-21). But when only four of the cities mentioned have jar handles with the LMLK stamp, Na'aman's theory becomes doubtful. It should also be noted that

maintained by P. Welten. It is noteworthy that Rehoboam's building activity is part of the Chronicler's narrative about the king before he turned 'evil'.[1] Because of the literary shaping, it is impossible to know when Rehoboam had these cities fortified or strengthened. A glance at the location of the places mentioned in the list reveals a very much reduced Judah. Its territory is close to that of the postexilic period, with the exception that Hebron is part of Judah. For this reason Welten is probably correct in suggesting that an old list (including Aijalon and Hebron) has been used.[2] The date of the construction of Rehoboam's defensive works ought to be after Pharaoh Shoshenq's campaign, when Beer-Sheba and the Negev had been lost.[3] No fortress south of Ziph appears in the list. V. Fritz maintains that Solomon's kingdom was so well fortified that Rehoboam did not need to do more.[4] Shoshenq probably destroyed some of the fortifications, however, thus necessitating repairs. The Shoshenq inscription mentions two sites in the Negev with the name of Arad.[5] One of them most probably was the excavated fortress. The destruction of stratum XI at Arad has been attributed to Shoshenq's campaign.[6] Even if Rehoboam did not rebuilt the fortress at Arad because it lay outside his domain, he certainly had reasons to rebuild and fortify some other places. Assuming then, that the Chronicler's list refers to the reign of Rehoboam, it shows not only that Rehoboam ordered repairs and built

---

neither Libnah nor Morseshet-Gath are mentioned in the Chronicler's list.

1. According to the ideology of the Chronistic writer, a king could not have built anything for his people during his 'evil' period (P. Welten, *Geschichte und Geschichtsdarstellung*, pp. 11-13).

2. *Geschichte und Geschichtsdarstellung*, p. 13.

3. Cf. H. Donner, who also considers the list as 'very ancient' (in J.H. Hayes and J.M. Miller, *Israelite and Judean History*, p. 388).

4. *EI* 15 (1981), p. 48*.

5. Nos. 107-12; '-r-d r-b-t and '-r-d n b-t y-r-ḥ-m. See p. 521 B. Mazar translates these names as 'Great Arad' and 'the House of Yeroham' (*Congress Volume, Strasbourg 1966* [ed. J.A. Emerton *et al.*], p. 64). He is followed by, among others, Y. Aharoni, *The Land of the Bible* (2nd edn), p. 328. W. Helck, however, doubts that r-b-t (rú-bí-tá) can be Egyptian writing for Hebrew rabbâ, 'great' (*Die Beziehungen*, p. 243). N. Na'aman thinks that yrḥm 'is an independent toponym' which most probably should not be 'tacked on to the Arad of Nos. 110-11' ('Arad in the Topographical List of Shishak', *Tel Aviv* 12 [1985], pp. 91-92).

6. Z. Herzog, M. Aharoni, A.F. Rainey and S. Moshkovitz, *BASOR* 254 (1984), p. 8.

fortifications within Judah, but also that he must have lost about half of the state's territory.[1] There is no information about when the lost areas in the south again came under Judah's rule. Since Egypt was not able to follow up the 'conquests' of Shoshenq, the loss may have been of short duration.

The deuteronomistic writer mentions that Rehoboam reigned for 17 years in Jerusalem, 'the city which Yahweh had chosen out of all the tribes of Israel' in which to put his name. The statement is followed by the usual deuteronomistic lament about Judah doing evil and provoking Yahweh, building *bāmôt*, raising *maṣṣēbôt* and *'ašerîm* 'on every high hill and under every green tree', and permitting sacral prostitution. In all, Judah's religion was conducted according to the 'abominations of all the peoples which Yahweh had dispossessed before the Israelites' (1 Kgs 14.21-24). The religion of Judah was in harmony with its time, no more and no less. It has been viewed through the colored glasses of a writer of a much later time and evaluated according to standards that did not prevail in the monarchic period. The language is typically deuteronomistic. The idea of Yahweh's name being placed in Jerusalem is known from Deuteronomy,[2] and most probably grows out of the ideology of Josiah's reform and the destruction of the Solomonic temple. When the new temple is built, Yahweh returns to his realm, but theological ideas now take another turn and not Yahweh, but his *name* is 'placed' in the temple. The phrase about Yahweh dispossessing the peoples/nations before Israel is a term belonging to typically postexilic historiography.

Some scholars have maintained, following A. Alt,[3] that the concept of kingship in the nation of Israel was different from that held in Judah after the separation of the states. In Israel the 'charismatic element which was evident with Saul and which was again taken up with Jeroboam, the first independent king of Israel after Saul, was kept

---

1. Cf. G.W. Ahlström, 'Is Tell ed-Duweir Ancient Lachish?' *PEQ* 112 (1980), p. 8 n. 15. For the discussion about Rehoboam's fortifications, see also G. Beyer, 'Beiträge zur Territorialgeschichte von Südwestpalästina im Altertum. I. Das Festungssystem Rehoboams', *ZDPV* 54 (1931), pp. 113-34.

2. Deut. 12.5; cf. Isa. 56.17; 57.15-16; Joel 3.5. See G. von Rad, *Studies in Deuteronomy* (trans. D. Stalker; Studies in Biblical Theology, 9; Chicago, 1953), pp. 37-39.

3. 'The Monarchy in the Kingdoms of Israel and Judah', *Essays on Old Testament History and Religion* (Garden City, NY, 1966), pp. 239-59.

alive'.[1] The accuracy of this idea can be doubted on good grounds. Not only had Jeroboam been a high official of Solomon, but he had also been in Egypt and there learned what kingship meant. From the beginning of the history of the nation of Israel through its revival under Jeroboam, the dynastic principle was the only one operative,[2] as was the case in other Near Eastern kingdoms. This is clear from the actions of usurpers, such as Baasha and Jehu. They murdered all the members of the royal dynasty they overthrew in order to have no claimants to the throne. The theory about charismatic versus dynastic kingship is a modern theological interpretation of dynastic changes in Israel.

It is extremely difficult to establish accurately a firm chronology for the monarchic period. There are only two fixed dates: that of the battle of the Syro-Palestinian coalition against Shalmaneser III at Qarqar in 853 and Jehu's *coup d'état* in 841 BCE.[3] Around these figures biblical information about the reigns of the different kings must be organized, taking into consideration nonbiblical inscriptional material whenever possible. For the earliest monarchic period there are no extrabiblical sources available. Any chronology thus created cannot be absolute. Fortunately, the margin for discrepancy is relatively small. Among contributing factors are the following: the possible use of antedating or postdating to reckon a king's reign;[4] the frequency of coregencies; and the use of an autumnal or vernal new year.[5] When

1. S. Herrmann, *A History of Israel* (2nd edn), p. 192.

2. See T.C.G. Thornton, 'Charismatic Kingship in Israel and Judah', *JTS* 14 (1963), pp. 1-11; G.W. Ahlström, *HR* 8 (1968), pp. 94-110; G. Buccellati, *Cities and Nations of Ancient Syria*, pp. 195-222. Cf. also O. Eissfeldt, *CAH*, XI.2, p. 573.

3. For the chronological problems, see above pp. 451-52, 500-501, and cf. the 'Appendix' in Hayes and Miller, *Israelite and Judean History*, pp. 678-81; E.R. Thiele, 'Coregencies and Overlapping Reigns among the Hebrew Kings', *JBL* 93 (1974), pp. 174-200; cf. *idem*, 'The Chronology of the Kings of Judah and Israel', *JNES* 3 (1944), pp. 137-86; K.T. Andersen, 'Die Kronologie der Könige von Israel und Juda', *ST* 23 (1969), pp. 67-112; K.A. Kitchen, *The Third Intermediate Period*, pp. 74-76; H. Tadmor, 'The Chronology of the First Temple Period', *WHJP*, IV.1 (ed. B. Mazar), pp. 44-60 (also in J.A. Soggin, *A History of Ancient Israel*, pp. 368-83).

4. Antedating is when one counts the period from the accession to the New Year as one full year; post-dating counts with the year of the death of the king as his last full year. Thus, his successor's first full year is in reality his second.

5. A. Jepsen and R. Hanhart maintain, following A. Jepsen ('Ein neuer Fixpunkt für die Chronologie der Israelitischen Könige', *VT* 20 [1970], pp. 359-61), that in

exact answers to these issues are not known, any chronological system will be relative. I have accordingly used approximate figures based on the available information.

Rehoboam died a couple of years before Jeroboam. The D historian uses Rehoboam's death as the starting point for his synchronism between the royal houses of Israel and Judah. 'And in the eighteenth year of king Jeroboam, the son of Nebat, Abijam began to rule over Judah, and he reigned for three years in Jerusalem' (1 Kgs 15.1-2). As mentioned before, the Bible contains no exact information about the reigns of David and Solomon; both are given a round figure of 40 years each, that is, a generation. If Solomon died c. 931/930, Rehoboam's death would have occurred in 913 BCE. According to 1 Kgs 14.20, Jeroboam had a reign of 22 years. His death would then have occurred in 911/910.

Abijah (Abijam), who succeeded Rehoboam, reigned only for three years (1 Kgs 15.1-2). The author of the tradition in Kings does not have very much to tell about this king, other than that his mother, the $g^e b\hat{\imath}r\hat{a}$,[1] was Maacah, the daughter of Absalom, and that Yahweh kept Jerusalem secure during his reign. This would mean that Abijah was able to protect his territory, even though the late writer's religio-historical perspective prevented him giving Abijah a positive evaluation. The Chronicler, on the other hand, reports that his mother was Micaiah, the daughter of Uriel from Gibeah, and that Abijah continued the war with Jeroboam. He claims that Judah's army was out-flanked by the Israelites, but that after a speech by Abijah, which is given the form of a Levitical sermon,[2] Yahweh helped the Judahites to victory. Abijah is supposed to have taken Ephron, Bethel and Jeshanah from Israel (2 Chron. 13.1-20). Since this war has not been literarily connected with a building program, it cannot be dismissed as literary fiction.[3] Abijah and Jeroboam most probably battled each other.

the early time Israel and Judah used a calendar that started the new year in the fall. They believe that the change came about during the Assyrian period (*Untersuchungen zur israelitisch-jüdischen Chronologie* [BZAW, 88; Berlin, 1964], p. 28).

1. For the $g^e b\hat{\imath}r\hat{a}$-institution, see G. Molin, *TZ* 10 (1954), pp. 161-75; H. Donner, 'Art und Herkunft', *Festschrift Johannes Friedrich* (ed. R. von Kienle *et al.*), pp. 105-45; G.W. Ahlström, *Aspects of Syncretism*, pp. 57-59.

2. G. von Rad, 'The Levitical Sermon in I and II Chronicles', in *The Problem of the Hexateuch and Other Essays* (ET; London, 1966 [1934]), pp. 267-80.

3. Cf. W. Rudolph, who here sees a speech against the population of the former Assyrian province of Samerina (*Chronikbücher*, pp. 235-37).

Abijah apparently followed his father's policy of trying to conquer Israel, even though the present form of the report reflects 'the political and religious ideology of the Chronicler'.[1]

The warfare with Israel continued under Abijah's successor, Asa, who is given a reign of 41 years. It is likely, however, that his son Jehoshaphat was coregent during his two last years because of a disease he contracted in his thirty-ninth year (2 Chron. 16.12). Since Asa was one of the few 'good' kings of Judah, the Chronicler was astonished by this sickness and tried to explain it away by having Asa seek the help of physicians (!) regarding the illness instead of Yahweh.

In diplomatic affairs Asa used the same kind of political tactics against his northern neighbor that David had once employed against Israel under Eshbaal. According to 1 Kgs 15.19 Baasha of Israel had been in an alliance with Ben-Hadad I of Damascus, an alliance that Asa was able to break up and replace with a treaty between Aram-Damascus and Judah. Baasha had ascended the Israelite throne after having murdered Jeroboam's son Nadab, who had ruled for two years (1 Kgs 15.25). In the conflict between Israel and Judah Baasha had managed to move dangerously close to Jerusalem.[2] He took Ramah of Benjamin (modern er-Ram, c. 9 km north of today's old city of Jerusalem) and fortified the place. Ramah was located on a hill from where watchmen could easily 'look into' Judah, and the site was well situated to control the routes leading to Jerusalem from both north and west. Baasha must have been a fine general with an army that Asa could not match. This is suggested by Asa's desperate move of sending a delegation with gifts of gold and silver from the temple and palace treasuries to the king of Damascus, asking him to break his treaty with Israel and make an alliance with Judah instead.[3] The king of Damascus no longer had any reason to fear the king of Jerusalem. His treaty

---

1. B. Oded, 'Judah and the Exile', *Israelite and Judean History* (ed. J.H. Hayes and J.M. Miller; Philadelphia, 1977), p. 439.

2. 2 Chron. 16.1 says that Baasha invaded Judah and fortified Ramah in 'the thirty-sixth year of Asa's reign'. That would have been in c. 875 BCE (using Andersen's chronology), which would be the year of the death of Omri. Baasha is given a reign of 24 years, which means that he would have died around 887 BCE.

3. Asa's message to Ben-Hadad refers to a treaty that would have existed between the two countries under Abijah and Tab-Rimmon (Ben-Hadad's father). If this is right, Baasha would have succeeded in breaking it, and Asa would then have been able to repeat the maneuver.

with Israel under Baasha may have been part of a policy that was negative toward Jerusalem and thus positive to Israel's continued independence. With Asa's request, however, a completely new political situation was created, one that launched the road to the Aramaean empire. In breaking the treaty with Israel, Ben-Hadad not only could relieve Judah from Baasha's pressure, but could also capture some valuable territory and see to it that Israel did not become too powerful a neighbor. The Aramaean army invaded northern Israel and captured 'all Kinneroth and all the land of Naphtali'. Among the towns mentioned are Dan,[1] Ijon and Abel-beth-maacah (1 Kgs 15.20).[2] The phrase 'all land of Naphtali' would mean that the whole of Galilee had been taken and, thus, that almost all of the territory north of the Jezreel Valley and east of the Lake Kinnereth would have come under the rule of the Aramaean king. The fortress at 'En Gev on the eastern side of the lake was most probably taken by the Aramaeans.[3] Of special interest in this connection is the lack of mention of Hazor.[4] Is the biblical information too generous to the Aramaeans, or was Baasha able to drive away the Aramaean army and hold onto the territory around Hazor? Whatever the truth is in this case, Baasha had to abandon his fortification of Ramah in order to stop the Aramaean threat. The biblical information shows that he was not able to keep his territory intact. The districts east of Lake Kinnereth and the northern Galilee became Aramaean (see Map 16). By controlling this area Ben-Hadad also had control over the trade routes leading to the Phoenician coast.

After Baasha had withdrawn from Ramah, Asa's men tore down what had been constructed there and used some of the building material for fortifying Geba and Mizpah. The latter place, usually identified with Tell en-Naṣbe,[5] is located on the main road about 12 km north of

1. For a destruction at Tel Dan dated to this period, see A. Biran, 'Tel Dan— Five Years Later', *BA* 43 (1980), p. 175.

2. This use of the name Kinneroth does not refer to the town at the northwestern end of the Sea of Galilee, but rather the whole territory around the lake.

3. Cf. B. Mazar, A. Biran, M. Dothan and I. Dunayevsky, "En Gev Excavations in 1961', *IEJ* 14 (1964), pp. 1-49; G.W. Ahlström, *Tel Aviv* 12 (1985), pp. 93-95.

4. Y. Aharoni thinks that Hazor stratum IX was destroyed at this time (885 BCE) (Y. Yadin *et al.*, *Hazor*, II [Jerusalem, 1960], p. 37 n. 217). He is followed by Y. Yadin, *Hazor of those Kingdoms*, p. 143.

5. See the discussion in A. Alt, 'Neue Erwägungen über die Lage von Mizpa, Ataroth, Beeroth und Gibeon', *ZDPV* 69 (1953), pp. 1-27.

Jerusalem. From this point in time down to the fall of the nation Israel in 722 BCE, the border between Judah and Israel seems to have stayed just north of Mizpah. Because the city gate was in the northern part of the city wall, it is possible that Mizpah had been an Israelite fortified city that Asa now rebuilt as a border fortress.[1]

According to 2 Chron. 14.8-14, an Egyptian invasion of Judah under Zerah, the 'Cushite' (Nubian), occurred in Asa's time. The historicity of this event is doubtful; it probably reflects problems that the postexilic Persian province of Yehud encountered with a neighboring group.[2] Zerah is an Edomite name in biblical tradition, not a Cushite one (Gen. 36.13; Num. 26.13). Furthermore, the attempt to see Osorkon I behind this Zerah is philologically impossible.[3] In addition, Osorkon was of the Twenty-Second Libyan Dynasty and thus was not Cushite. Asa is said to have defeated the Egyptian army of 1,000,000 men, pursued the enemy down to the district of the city of Gerar and taken much booty. Gerar occurs in the Old Testament in the stories about Abraham and Isaac and the 'Philistine' king Abimelech (Gen. 20 and 26), stories that most probably also belong to the postexilic period. Gerar was known as a district in southwestern Palestine from the Persian period. A city named Gerar was not part of the Philistine pentapolis. The occurrence of the Cushites, whom the Chronicler often locates close to the Arabs (2 Chron. 21.16), may also be an anachronism.[4] Whatever event the Chronicler may have used as a source or inspiration for his composition, it has been imbedded in the garb of postexilic problems and so cannot be used to reconstruct the reign of king Asa. The narrative is part of the Chronicler's wish to boost the stature of postexilic Yehud by making king Asa historically important in protecting Judah's independence.[5]

King Asa is mainly appreciated because of his so-called cult reform. He is said to have expelled the $q^e d\bar{e}\check{s}\hat{i}m$[6] from Judah and to have

---

1. For the city plan, see T.L. McClellan, *ZDPV* 100 (1984), pp. 54-69.

2. See K. Galling, *Die Bücher der Chronik, Esra, Nehemia*.

3. Cf. K.A. Kitchen, *The Third Intermediate Period*, p. 309.

4. W.F. Albright suggested that the Cushites had been settled by Shoshenq in the area of Gerar ('Egypt and the Early History of the Negeb', *JPOS* 4 [1924], pp. 146-47).

5. Thus P. Welten, *Geschichte und Geschichtsdarstellung in den Chronikbüchern*, pp. 139-40.

6. The text does not give any information about the meaning of this term. It may refer to some cultic personnel. H.M. Barstad has objected to the translation 'sacred

removed the *gillulîm*, idols, that 'his fathers had made' (1 Kgs 15.12). These phenomena show that Judah's religion was part of the old Canaanite tradition. The report that the earlier kings made idols indicates that we are dealing here with the official, national cult of Judah and not with any 'popular' form of religion. It also shows that the kings preceding Asa had contributed to the increase of holiness in the country.

A seemingly intriguing act of Asa is his removal of Maacah[1] from the office of *g*^{e}*bîrâ*, 'queen mother' (1 Kgs 15.13). She is said to have made 'an abominable image' for the goddess Asherah. Asa had the image burned in the Kidron Valley. Maacah was probably of Aramaean descent, and the image she had made could therefore have been felt to be a foreign symbol. What the Hebrew word *mipleṣet* ('abominable image') means is not known, so it is uncertain how people would have reacted to Maacah's cult object. The real reason for Maacah's dismissal from office may have been that, as the lady behind the throne, she had become too powerful or had been opposing some of the king's political actions.[2] The narrator may well have transformed political objections to Maacah into a cultic reform. Since his ideal was the cult centralization in Jerusalem, he complains that Asa did not abandon the *bāmôt*, sanctuaries, of the land (1 Kgs 15.14). In his account of Asa's reign, the Chronicler forgets his own statement in 2 Chron. 14.3-5, where he puts the 'destruction' of the *bāmôt* back into the time of Asa. In 15.17, however, he laconically states that 'the *bāmôt* were not taken out of Israel. Nevertheless, the heart of Asa was

prostitutes' (*The Religious Polemics of Amos* [VTSup, 34; Leiden, 1984], pp. 493-512). See also M.I. Gruber, 'Hebrew *qĕdēšāh* and her Canaanite and Akkadian Cognates', *UF* 18 (1986), pp. 133-48.

1. Maacah is said to be the mother of both Abijam and Asa (1 Kgs. 15.1, 10). Either the two kings were brothers or Maacah stayed on in power after Abijah's death. Both 1 Kgs. 15.8 and 2 Chron. 13.23 see Asa as the son of Abijah.

2. For the *g*^{e}*bîrâ* and her administration, see G. W. Ahlström, *Aspects of Syncretism*, pp. 57-63; R. de Vaux, *Ancient Israel*. I. *Social Institutions* (New York, 1965), pp. 117-19 (French edn, pp. 181-83); N.E.A. Andreasen, 'The Role of the King Mother in Israelite Society', *CBQ* 45 (1983), pp. 179-94. J. Bright suggests that Maacah was the ruler during Asa's 'minority', but having grown up, Asa 'sided with the more conservative party' and deposed the *g*^{e}*bîrâ* (*A History of Israel* [3rd edn], p. 240). This is sheer speculation. No one knows how old Asa was when he became king.

blameless all his days.' The Chronicler contradicts himself again. He says that Asa clashed with the prophet Hanani, who rebuked the king for having trusted Aram-Damascus instead of Yahweh. The king became so irritated that he put the prophet in the stocks, and 'inflicted cruelties upon some of the people' (2 Chron. 16.7-9). It must certainly have been hard to satisfy a proponent of the 'Yahwistic' line, especially when that line of tradition had not yet surfaced.

With the accession of Omri in Israel around 886/885 BCE, the last decade of Asa's reign may have been peaceful. A new era began with Omri, an era in which Judah played a secondary role among the Palestinian states. During the following four decades Aram-Damascus and Israel were the powers with which to reckon until Assyria completely changed both the borders and the ethnic composition of Syria-Palestine.

Chapter 13

THE OMRIDES

King Baasha of Israel was followed by his son Elah, who was murdered by Zimri after having ruled for only two years. Zimri, a general of the chariotry, was then proclaimed king. In order to establish his throne firmly he killed all the members of Baasha's family, a common Near Eastern practice (1 Kgs 16.7-14). His kingship lasted only seven days. The Israelite army that had been fighting the Philistines at Gibbethon at this time had obviously been neglected. When he heard about Zimri's *coup d'état*, Omri, the army's field commander, managed to have himself elevated to kingship by the army. He quickly left Gibbethon and marched with the army to the capital of Tirzah. When Zimri saw that the city was being taken and that his cause was lost, he preferred death in the flames of the palace to the likely execution by Omri. His death, however, did not stabilize the situation in the kingdom. According to 1 Kgs 16.21-22, another competitor to the throne arose, Tibni 'son of Ginath'. The country became divided between these two men and their parties. It is not clear what following Tibni had, but some circles at court as well as leaders of the clans in the countryside may have opposed the army's choice of Omri for king. The conflict lasted for four years, after which Tibni died and Omri became the undisputed ruler. The statement in 1 Kgs 16.22 about Tibni's death is very short: 'and Tibni died' (*wayyāmot tibni*). The LXX version adds 'and his brother Joram', which may indicate that there was a tradition about Tibni having met a violent death.[1]

The reason for the civil war in Israel is not clearly stated in the text. It is possible to assume that Tibni's party was opposed to a non-Israelite ascending to the throne. Omri's name is not a common

1. Cf. J. Gray, *I and II Kings*, p. 366; E. Würthwein, *Die Bücher der Könige*, I, p. 198.

Israelite name, but is certainly West-Semitic (of the root '*mr*, 'to reap', or 'live long, develop').[1] M. Noth sees it to be Arabic.[2] Omri is introduced without any information being given about his father or his family. It is thus probable that he was an upstart whom Tibni and his party attempted to prevent from reaching the throne.[3] According to the Bible's reckoning Omri's reign over Israel began in the thirty-first year of the reign of king Asa of Judah (1 Kgs 16.23). His rule lasted about eight more years.

As has been mentioned above, Israel's territory had been very much reduced by Aram-Damascus. Northern Transjordan was lost, and with it the income from the trade routes from Aqaba up through Transjordan.[4] Ben Hadad I of Damascus had also invaded Galilee. The kingdom of Damascus was probably the most powerful one in Syria at this time.[5]

With Omri a new epoch in the history of Palestine began. The political game took another turn. He was a very able ruler who had a clear understanding of the political scene and who succeeded in (partly) re-establishing Israel's position as an important power. He does not seem to have gone to war against Aram-Damascus, since no such war has been remembered by the narrator. Nevertheless, he managed in some way to minimize Aram's influence in Palestine through a treaty with Tyre. In order to seal this treaty, Omri's son Ahab was married to Jezebel, the daughter of Tyre's king, Ittobaal[6]

1.   See the discussion in H.B. Huffmon, *Amorite Personal Names in the Mari Texts*, p. 198.

2.   *Die israelitische Personennamen*, p. 63; *idem*, *Könige*, pp. 348-49. S. Timm is skeptical about an Arabic name at this time; see his discussion in *Die Dynastie Omri, Quellen und Untersuchungen zur Geschichte Israels im 9 Jahrhundert vor Christus* (Göttingen, 1982), pp. 21-22.

3.   M. Noth suggests that it could have been a conflict between the army and the civil population (*Könige*, p. 350). S. Herrmann thinks that the civil war was a result of both pretenders lacking 'prophetic designation' (*A History of Israel* [2nd edn], p. 202). Prophetic designation to kingship was rather a ritual phenomenon. Thus, any king ascending the throne heard an oracle about being chosen to kingship by the god. This phenomenon has then been used by the D historian in his 'call narratives', in order to give divine authority to certain kings.

4.   Cf. J. Morgenstern, 'Amos Studies. III. The Historical Antecedents of Amos Prophecy', *HUCA* 15 (1940), pp. 135-36.

5.   Cf. below.

6.   Cf. Josephus, *Ant.* 8.13.2.

(Ethbaal, 'king of the Sidonians', 1 Kgs 16.31).[1] The latter, according to Josephus, was an Ashtarte priest who had usurped the throne in Tyre.[2] This treaty resulted in an upswing for Israel's trade and economy. It benefitted from Tyre's trade, through Israelite territory, with north Arabia and the Mediterranean countries. Prosperity began to return to Israel.

Before continuing it should be noted that the growing power of Assyria became a threat to the Syro-Palestinian states in this area. Assyria's growth may have prompted Damascus to make alliances with Tyre and other Syrian states. With Ashurnaṣirpal II (883–859), the Assyrian 'westward push' started. He invaded Bit-Adini (Beth-Eden), and in another campaign he subdued Carchemish and then marched southwest into the Orontes valley, capturing cities and receiving tribute. He reached the Lebanon and the Phoenician cities on the coast, and he says that he 'washed' his weapons in the Mediterranean. Most of the Phoenician cities paid him tribute. He then 'climbed' Mount Amanus and cut down cedar, cypress, juniper and pine trees for the temples of Sin and Shamash and Ishtar of Nineveh, 'my Lady'.[3] The reasons for Assyria's military appetite will be discussed later, but one of the main factors was Mesopotamian geography. Assyria was mainly a country of mud so that the resources of other countries were not only tempting but also necessary to acquire.

Omri inaugurated a new phase in the relationship between Israel and its neighbor to the south, Judah. The long warfare between the two states that had begun in the days of Jeroboam and Rehoboam now

---

1. Sidonians is the common term for Phoenicians in the Bible. The name Ethbaal means 'with (him) Baal'.

2. Ittobaal may have been the priest-king of Sidon who joined together the two city states. This conclusion can be drawn from an inscription of Sennacherib that mentions that Luli of Sidon fled (to Cyprus) from Tyre (D.D. Luckenbill, *ARAB*, II, par. 309); cf. A.L. Oppenheim, *ANET*, pp. 287-88. Assyrian inscriptions from the time before Tiglath-Pileser III do not mention Sidon among the Phoenician city states; cf. H.J. Katzenstein, *The History of Tyre*, p. 133. S. Timm maintains that Ittobaal was king of Sidon and not of Tyre, so that Jezebel did not come from Tyre (*Die Dynastie Omri*, pp. 209-11). He also thinks that the biblical writer and Josephus (following Menander of Ephesus) have mixed Jezebel's father with a later Tyrian king, Ittobaal, whom Nebuchadrezzar subdued (Josephus, *Ant. 5.228*; S. Timm, *Die Dynastie Omri*, p. 226).

3. For the text, see D.D. Luckenbill, *ARAB*, I, pars. 475-79, pp. 164-67; *ANET*, pp. 275-76.

came to an end. This shows that Omri was a realistic politician. He understood, obviously, that alliances with the 'Sidonians' and Judah was the way to meet the danger from Aram-Damascus, which had taken some border cities from Israel (1 Kgs 20.34). Omri managed to build up his defenses, including the army. With peaceful relations to the west and south, he could begin to think about expansion. The often contested area north of the Arnon river in Transjordan was occupied by Omri, to which King Mesha of Moab the inscription of testifies,[1] but which is not mentioned in the Bible. 2 Kgs 3.4 mentions, however, that Mesha was a vassal of Israel, and as such he paid the king of Israel 'a hundred thousand lambs and the wool of a hundred thousand rams in tribute'. The following verse mentions that Mesha rebelled when King Ahab died.[2]

Omri's political 'west-orientation' was probably the reason why he abandoned Tirzah as the capital of the kingdom. Geographically, Tirzah (Tell el-Far'ah [N]) was enclosed by hills in the south, north and west. Its natural line of communication was to the southeast via Wadi Far'ah, leading down to the Jordan Valley. Omri must have felt isolated from the main thoroughfares at Tirzah. He started to build a new capital city on virgin ground.[3] His choice was the 'hill of Shemer', which he bought.[4] The new capital was called Shomeron (Samaria, 1 Kgs

1. For the text, see W.F. Albright in *ANET*, pp. 320-21; H. Donner and W. Röllig, *KAI*, text 181; J.C.L. Gibson, *TSSI*, I, pp. 71-83.

2. For the time Moab was under Israelite overlordship, see G. Wallis, 'Die vierzig Jahre der achten Zeile der Mesa-Inschrift', *ZDPV* 81 (1965), pp. 180-86.

3. There are parallels from the Near East of new capitals built on virgin soil, such as the Assyrian Kār-Tukultī-Ninurta, Kār-Šulmānašarīdu, Dūr-Šarrukīn, and Mesha's Dibon; cf. A.L. Oppenheim, *Ancient Mesopotamia*, p. 119. Some pottery from the tenth and ninth centuries BCE has been found in the excavations at Samaria; see Y. Aharoni and R. Amiran, 'A New Scheme for the Sub-Division of the Iron Age in Palestine', *IEJ* 8 (1958), p. 179 n. 34; cf. G.E. Wright, 'Israelite Samaria and Iron Age Chronology', *BASOR* 155 (1959), pp. 20-21. This would indicate that some small settlement could have been located on the hill, but pottery sherds are not enough proof for such a case. B. Mazar (in the mentioned article by Aharoni and Amiran) has suggested that there was a family estate on the hill owned by Shemer. No building remains of that 'estate' have been found.

4. Shemer is usually considered to be a Canaanite. From this scholars have often drawn some far-reaching conclusions about the culture, law and religion in the northern state. H. Donner, for instance, maintains (inspired by A. Alt, 'Der Stadtsstaat Samaria', *KS*, III, pp. 258-60) that Samaria was 'a Canaanite reservation, a state within the state', and that Omri bought the hill of Shemer 'according to

16.24).[1] The location of this city was much more in the center of the kingdom, with a commanding view of the surrounding territory. Omri did not have time to finish the new capital, but his son Ahab continued the building program.

Omri is treated very superficially by the Old Testament writer. As with all kings of Israel, he is negatively evaluated because of Jeroboam I, whose 'sin' was to create the nation Israel. Omri's judgment is part of the historiographer's literary pattern. Otherwise there is no particular 'sin' the writer can use to tarnish the reputation of Omri, who lifted Israel out of obscurity. In the formulaic evaluation of his reign information is given about his *gᵉbûrâ*, 'military strength', a term that is also used about some other northern kings fighting foreign powers.[2]

In Assyrian texts the land of Israel is called *KUR (mat) bit-Ḥumri*, 'the land of Bit Humri', that is, the land of the house of Omri. Ironically, Israel is called *mar (DUMU) Ḫu-um-ri-i*, 'King of [Bit] Ḫumri', first with Jehu,[3] the usurper who carried out his *coup d'état*

Canaanite legal principles' (in J.H. Hayes and J.M. Miller, *Israelite and Judean History*, p. 402). How it is known that Shemer was a Canaanite and not an Israelite is never mentioned. The name Shemer is a Levitic name, according to 1 Chron. 7.34. That the nation of Israel should have worked with two different codes of law, one Israelite and one Canaanite, cannot be proven. It would show a schizophrenic state. The mistake of Alt, *et al.*, is that they consider the Israelites to be a group of invaders who took over the country and allowed some 'Canaanites' to survive. The peoples of the nation Israel, regardless of their ancestry, were all Israelites already living in the territory called Israel in the premonarchic time. For a sound criticism of Alt and Donner, see J.A. Soggin, *A History of Ancient Israel*, p. 204.

1. The etiology of the name may be late; cf. S. Timm, *Die Dynastie Omri*, pp. 43-44. For the Assyrian forms of the name (*Samerina, Samirna, Shamara'in*), see S. Parpola, *Neo-Assyrian Toponymns*, pp. 302-303. Cf. the Aramaic form Shomrayin, Ezra 4.10, 17.

2. For a discussion about this formula, see S. Timm, *Die Dynastie Omri*, p. 47.

3. S. Parpola, *Neo-Assyrian Toponymns*, pp. 82-83. For *KUR bit Ḥumri* meaning the land of *bit Ḥumri* (not Omri's land), see H. Tadmor, 'The Historical Inscriptions of Adad-Nirari III', *Iraq* 35 (1973), pp. 148-49. P.K. McCarter sees the inscription of Shalmaneser and its reading *Yaua mar Ḥumri* to refer to king Joram, whom Jehu killed ('Yaw, Son of Omri: A Philological Note on Israelite Chronology', *BASOR* 216 [1974], pp. 5-9). See, however, E.R. Thiele, 'An Additional Chronological note on "Yaw, Son of Omri"', *BASOR* 222 (1976), pp. 19-23; M. Weippert, 'Jau(a) mar Ḥumri—Joram oder Jehu von Israel', *VT* 28 (1978), pp. 113-18.

in 841 BCE and killed all the members of Omri's house. It also continued as the official name for the new Assyrian province (the former
Israel) during the time of Sargon II.[1] This fact may show the importance of King Omri not only as the founder of a dynasty, but also as
the rebuilder of the state of Israel.

Omri was followed by his son Ahab, who reigned over Israel for 22
years (1 Kgs 16.29; c. 874–853). During his rule the nation of Israel
experienced its most prosperous time. Politically, he continued his
father's approach. He succeeded in keeping the peace with Judah and
made a treaty with its king, Jehoshaphat. The alliance was effected
through the marriage of Ahab's daughter (or sister) Athaliah to
Judah's crown prince, Jehoram (2 Kgs 8.18; 2 Chron. 21.6).[2] Whether
this treaty with Judah was a vassal treaty or an alliance between equals
is not clear from the text. No doubt Israel was the stronger power of
the two. Until disaster hit both dynasties of Israel and Judah under
Jehu, Judah participated in most of Israel's wars. This would indicate
that Judah was Israel's vassal. The treaty relationship with Tyre
continued also under Ahab, which would be natural to expect because
of his marriage to, the strongwilled princess from Tyre, Jezebel.[3] The
Moabite territory Omri had occupied was kept by Ahab. The latter
perhaps also fortified some of the occupied Moabite towns, if King
Mesha's report that the Israelite king fortified and built towns in the
captured territory refers not only to Omri but also to Ahab.

The relations with Aram-Damascus are harder to assess. The biblical writers were not interested in the greater events of time if they did

1. Cf. M. Weippert, *VT* 28 (1978), p. 114.

2. 2 Kgs 8.26 and 2 Chron. 22.2 make Athaliah the daughter of Omri; see the
discussion by H.J. Katzenstein, 'Who were the Parents of Athaliah?', *IEJ* 5 (1955),
pp. 194-97; cf. also J.M. Miller, 'The Fall of the House of Ahab', *VT* 17 (1967),
pp. 307-24.

3. For the name Jezebel ('Izebel'), which in Hebrew would mean 'no glory', see
N. Avigad, 'The Seal of Jezebel', *IEJ* 14 (1964), pp. 274-76; J.A. Soggin, *A History
of Ancient Israel*, p. 209. Soggin thinks that Jezebel 'is simply a literary figure, connected with an anonymous Phoenician wife of Ahab' (p. 209). I would prefer to see
Jezebel as an intentional 'misspelling' (and possibly a dirty pun) of the queen's real
name, which has not been preserved. N. Avigad sees the Hebrew writing as an
assimilation of the *shin* and the *zain* in Phoenician *yszbl* or *'szbl*, 'Zebul exists' (*IEJ*
14 [1964], pp. 275-76). For a seal in an Egyptianizing Phoenician style with the
inscription *yzbl*, and from the ninth–eighth century BCE, of unknown stratigraphical
provenience, see N. Avigad, *IEJ* 14 (1964), pp. 274-76.

not suit their understanding of Israel and Judah in their relationship to the divine. Both states, Aram and Israel, undoubtedly watched each other with suspicion. Aram-Damascus was a powerful Syrian nation that must have looked at Israel's growing strength with fear of an upcoming conflict. Both nations laid claim to Transjordanian territories. Unfortunately we do not know what impact the treaty between Israel and Tyre made on Damascus. The wars between Aram and Israel mentioned in the Old Testament, which supposedly also ended Ahab's life, may have been used by the writer deliberately.

The facts behind Ahab's relationship with Aram-Damascus during the early period of his reign are hard to establish. The historical sequence in Ahab's relations and wars with Aram-Damascus is impossible to disentangle because the narrator has associated Ahab and his political activities with the Elijah–Elisha traditions and the opposition to the Omri dynasty so forcefully expressed in them. In so doing the narrator could finally depict a great king of Israel as the great evil-doer, 'unfortunately' inspired by his Sidonian queen, Jezebel.[1] There had probably been some shorter wars over border disputes,[2] but the wars mentioned in 1 Kings 20 and 22 refer to later events.[3] Chapter 20 is interesting from a literary point of view. It starts by depicting Ahab as a king who loses everything at the hands of Ben-Hadad of Damascus. The scenes in which messengers go to Ahab with harsh demands, as well as those that depict the answers Ahab sends back, form a nice literary composition. It stands in contrast with the amazing victory of Ahab over the Aramaean forces that besieged Samaria (1 Kgs 20.1-21). The ensuing scene, vv. 22-34, concerns a

---

1.   For the probable existence of two lines of interpretation concerning Ahab in postexilic Jerusalem, consult D.W. Gooding, 'Ahab according to the Septuagint', *ZAW* 76 (1964), pp. 269-79. One line of tradition blackened Ahab while the other tried at least 'to excuse him' because he was deemed a tool of Jezebel (p. 278).

2.   Cf. S. Herrmann, *A History of Israel in Old Testament Times* (2nd edn), p. 214.

3.   See, for instance, the discussion in H.C. Schmitt, *Elisa: Traditionsgeschicht-liche Untersuchungen zur vorklassischen nordisraelitischen prophetie* (Gütersloh, 1972), pp. 60-63. Schmitt maintains that Ahab's wars, as described in the Old Testament, never took place. These texts belong to a later time, probably after the fall of Omri's dynasty. See also S. Timm, who states that the texts of 1 Kings 20 and 22 'sind nur mit grössten Bedenken als historische Quellen fur die Zeit der Dynastie Omri zu benutzen' (*Die Dynastie Omri*, p. 214).

battle at Aphek (east of Lake Tiberias), which is said to have resulted in Ben-Hadad's humiliation and capture, but Ahab is reported to have spared his life. In ch. 22 a battle at Ramoth-Gilead becomes the cause of Ahab's death. Both these texts are problematic and have been seen by several commentators to refer to a later time.[1] Their most doubtful information is that Ahab died in battle at Ramoth-Gilead. In order to have Elijah's prophecy fulfilled the writer has his bloody chariot taken to Samaria to be washed. In this way the dogs of Samaria could lick his blood (1 Kgs 22.38) as Elijah had prophesied in 21.19. Contrary to this view, 1 Kgs 22.40 laconically states that Ahab 'slept with his fathers', a phrase used to describe a natural death.[2]

The biblical writer must have known that Ahab stood in a treaty relationship with the Aramaean king. He sees the prelude to the treaty to lie in the victory at Aphek, when Ben-Hadad is said to have been taken prisoner by Ahab and to have made a treaty with him (1 Kgs 20.34). The historical fact behind this story is the great Syro-Palestinian coalition of 853 BCE against Shalmaneser III of Assyria, of which Ben-Hadad (Adad-'idri of the Assyrian inscriptions) was the leader (cf. 1 Kgs 20.1, which mentions Ben-Hadad's 32 kings). Ahab of Israel was one of the allied kings, as is known from Shalmaneser's so-called Monolith Inscription. This could mean that Israel had become one of the satellite states of Aram-Damascus,[3] which would explain some of the war activities between Aram and Israel in the following years. Israel was to be kept in the Aramaean camp. The threat to the independence of the Syro-Palestinian nations caused by

---

1. Cf. H. Donner in J.H. Hayes and J.M. Miller, *Israelite and Judean History*, p. 400; cf. C.F. Whitley, 'The Deuteronomic Presentation of the House of Omri', *VT* 2 (1952), pp. 137-50; J.M. Miller, *VT* 17 (1967), pp. 313-15; S. Timm, *Die Dynastie Omri*, p. 241. Consult also A. Jepsen, 'Israel und Damaskus', *AfO* 14 (1942–44), pp. 153-72.

2. See, for instance, G. Hölscher, 'Das Buch der Könige, seine Quellen und seine Redaktion', *Eucharisterion* (Festschrift Hermann Gunkel; ed. H. Schmidt; Göttingen, 1923), p. 185; B. Alfrink 'L'Expression שָׁכַב עִם אֲבוֹתָיו', *OTS* 2 (1943), pp. 106-18; C.F. Whitley, *VT* 2 (1952), pp. 148-50; A Jepsen, 'Ahabs Busse', *Archäologie und Altes Testament* (Festschrift K. Galling; Tübingen, 1970), p. 149; J.M. Miller, *VT* 17 (1967), p. 313 n. 2 (with lit.).

3. Thus B. Mazar, *BA* 25 (1962), p. 106. Mazar maintains that Ben-Hadad succeeded in creating an empire through reorganizing several of the small Aramaean kingdoms into districts. He points to the fact that in the following periods neither the Assyrian nor the OT sources mention any satellite kingdoms of Damascus (p. 109).

Assyria's interests in and expansion to the west during the time of Ashurnaṣirpal II has already been mentioned. During the reign of his son, Shalmaneser III, the danger for the smaller Syrian states grew. Ashurnaṣirpal had not established any permanent Assyrian presence in Syria. Thus, conspiracies started soon after he had returned home from his campaign. These resulted in open rebellion when he died and his son, Shalmaneser III, ascended the throne. In 858 Shalmaneser met a coalition of north-Syrian states, Zinjirli, Pattina, Carchemish and Bit-Adini. The allied armies managed to stop the Assyrians. Three years later, in 855 BCE, when Shalmaneser did not meet a coalition, he took Bit-Adini and annexed it. This may have served as a reminder to the south-Syrian states. When Shalmaneser started his sixth campaign in 853 BCE, a coalition of Syro-Palestinian nations under the leadership of Irḫuleni of Hamath and Adad-'idri of Damascus had been formed and met the Assyrian army at Qarqar on the Orontes, modern Khirbet Qarqur. The north-Syrian states paid tribute to Shalmaneser and Aleppo surrendered. Some cities belonging to the kingdom of Hamath were also taken by the Assyrian army. At Qarqar, however, the invasion came to a halt. The allied armies of southern Syria and Palestine were able to arrest the power of the invader. Even if Shalmaneser boasts about being victorious, the battle was certainly not a victory for him. He could perhaps have called it a draw. There is no mention of any tribute being paid by conquered kings. It should also be noted that the Assyrian king did not continue his campaign after the battle at Qarqar. Instead he returned home, and some four years later he again invaded Syria, campaigning there also in 848, 845 and 841 BCE.

The battle at Qarqar in 853 is one of the few clear dates in the history of Israel.[1] Shalmaneser's inscription mentions that Irḫuleni of Hamath had received help from Adad-'idri of Damascus, Ahab of Israel (*A-ha-ab-bu mat Sir-'i-la-a-a*), Baasha of Ammon, Gindibu' from Arabia,[2] Matinu-ba'lu from Arvad, and others, a total of

---

1. Consult also J.A. Brinkman, 'A Further Note on the Date of the Battle of Qarqar and the Neo-Assyrian Chronology', *JCS* 30 (1978), pp. 173-75.

2. This is the first mention in any text of the Arabs. Gindibu' participated in the battle with 1000 camels, which may have contributed to the coalition's victory in scaring the horses of the Assyrians. They do not like the smell of a camel; see I. Eph'al, *The Ancient Arabs*, pp. 75-77. Eph'al thinks that Gindibu' came from the areas of Wadi Sirhan and not from North Arabia (p. 76).

12 kings.[1] In the subsequent campaigns Shalmaneser's main adversary and the leader of coalitions against him was the king of Damascus.[2] Knowing this, it is somewhat hard to ascribe any historicity to the stories in 1 Kings about the battles between Ahab and Ben-Hadad. The latter seems to have been one of the most important kings of Syria at that time. He must have seen the writing on the wall and acted accordingly. As a realistic politician and military strategist he managed to form coalitions consisting of several nations in order for them to preserve their freedom—for a short time.

It is unlikely that the Aramaean king had time to fight Israel as often as the texts imply. In his attempts to stem the Assyrian expansion into central and southern Syria, he would have been more inclined to win the support of Ahab and the Israelite army. That he succeeded in this is clear from Shalmaneser III's inscription.[3] It is also less probable that war would have broken out between Aram and Israel

---

1. For the text, see D.D. Luckenbill, *ARAB*, I, pars. 610-11; cf. A.L. Oppenheim, *ANET*, pp. 278-79. For a discussion of the text and its historical implications, see N. Na'aman, 'Two Notes on the Monolithic Inscription of Shalmaneser III from Kurkh', *Tel Aviv* 3 (1976), pp. 89-106. This inscription mentions that Hadadezer of Damascus had 1200 chariots, 1200 cavalrymen and 20,000 footsoldiers; Ahab of Israel should have come with 2000 chariots and 10,000 men, and Irḥuleni of Hamath had 700 chariots, 700 cavalrymen, and 10,000 footsoldiers. Na'aman does not trust these figures. In this period Assyria had a maximum of c. 2000 chariots. It is almost impossible to believe that one of the twelve allies against Assyria could muster 2000 chariots. Na'aman also refers to several scribal mistakes in the inscription and maintains that Ahab perhaps had no more than 200 chariots (pp. 97-102). It should be noted that neither textual nor archaeological sources indicate where all these chariots could have been kept.

2.   The battle at Qarqar is also referred to in the inscription on Shalmaneser's throne base. Here only Adad-'idri and Irhuleni (Ir-ḫu-li-na), together with 12 kings of the sea coast, are mentioned, not Ahab; see P. Hulin, 'The Inscription in the Throne-Base of Shalmaneser III', *Iraq* 25 (1963), pp. 48-69, ll. 29-30; cf. G.G. Cameron, 'The Annals of Shalmeneser III, King of Assyria: A New Text', *Sumer* 6 (1950), pp. 6-26, ll. 27-28. Ahab's failure to be mentioned indicates that he cannot have been one of the leaders of the coalition, as has sometimes been advocated. For this assumption, see, for instance, the treatment in Y. Aharoni, *The Land of the Bible* (2nd edn), p. 336, and that in J. Bright, *A History of Israel* (3rd edn), p. 243.

3.   H. Donner, among others, credits Ahab with successfully establishing 'a friendly relationship between the two countries' (In J.H. Hayes and J.M. Miller, *Israelite and Judean History*, p. 400).

almost immediately after the battle of Qarqar. That would have been politically shortsighted.[1]

The inscription by king Mesha of Moab also mentions Omri's son, Ahab. As discussed above, Omri of Israel extended his kingdom geographically by conquering the Moabite territory north of the river Arnon (Wadi Mujib) in Transjordan (cf. 2 Kgs 3.4; see Map 17). This had been Israelite territory under David and Solomon, but was most probably lost when Solomon died. The Mesha stela, which was discovered at Dhîbān (Dibon of the Bible) in 1868, confirms the biblical information about the Israelite occupation of the territory and about the Moabite king becoming a vassal to Omri and 'his son' for 40 years (ll. 4-8).[2] Mesha boasts by praising his main god, Chemosh, for having delivered him from all his adversaries and for throwing off the yoke of Israel. The biblical texts say that this happened when Ahab died (2 Kgs 1.1; 3.5). The date is not quite clear from Mesha's inscription. In lines 7-8, Mesha says that Omri had occupied *Medeba* and that it belonged to Israel during the rest of Omri's reign and most of (half of) the days of his son. In his battle for freedom Mesha reconquered the areas and 'Israel completely perished for ever'. How this latter phrase should be interpreted is not clear. Since Israel still existed as a nation, Mesha's utterance may merely be the usual exaggeration and self-predication so common in the royal inscriptions of the ancient Near East. The war of liberation carried on by Mesha probably started during the reign of Ahab, as the inscription indicates, but that the final outcome of the war was the victory over Ahab's son Joram (2 Kgs 3.24-27). Israel's humiliation, which Mesha characterizes as Israel having perished, could refer to Jehu's geographically minimized Israel, which became a vassal to Assyria immediately after Jehu's *coup d'état*. The inscription also indicates that the Israelite king had 'built' cities such as 'Ataroth and Jahaz, which may simply mean that they were fortified cities (ll. 11, 18-19). Mesha took them and

1. The three years without any war between Aram and Israel referred to in 1 Kgs 22.1 may concern the reign of Ahab's son Joram.

2. For the text, see R. Dussaud, *Les monuments palestiniens et judaiques au Musée du Louvre* (Paris, 1912) (with photo); A.T. Olmstead, *History of Palestine and Syria*, pp. 389-91 (with picture); H. Donner and W. Röllig, *KAI*, text 181; J.C.L. Gibson, *TSSI*, I, pp. 71-83; W.F. Albright, *ANET*, pp. 320-21; E. Ullendorf, 'The Moabite Stone', *Documents from Old Testament Times* (ed. D.W. Thomas; New York, 1958), pp. 195-97.

Jahaz was incorporated to his capital Dibon.[1] All of the inhabitants of 'Ataroth (modern 'Aṭaruz, c. 23 km NW of Dhîbān) were killed, perhaps as a sacrifice to Chemosh, and the *'ar'el* of its god Dod was dragged before Chemosh at Kerioth (ll. 11-13). These lines give some rare information about the Israelite religion as practiced at 'Ataroth. Dod is a god name or god epithet,[2] and the *'ar'el* most probably was a lion postament for a deity statue.[3] The Israelites of 'Ataroth did not know about any commands against idols. A further indication about the Israelite religion of this period is found in lines 14-18. After taking Nebo (Khirbet el-Muhayyit), Mesha kills its inhabitants and takes the vessels (?)[4] of Yahweh as booty. Nebo apparently was the site of a Yahwistic sanctuary.[5]

Other places Mesha 'built' or fortified include Baal-Meon (modern Ma'in, c. 8 km SW of Madaba), Qiryaton (Khirbet el-Qureyie, about 13 km west of Madaba),[6] Medeba, Aroer (modern 'Ara'ir) south of Dibon, Beth-Bamoth and Bezer (see Map 18). The locations of the latter two sites are not exactly known. Aharoni places Bezer at modern Umm el-'Amad, c. 10 km ESE of Tell Ḥisbân.[7] Lines 18-19

---

1.   This means that Jahaz must have been located in the vicinity of Dibon; cf. C.F. Burney, *The Book of Judges*, p. 313. Y. Aharoni suggests modern Khirbet el-Medeiyine, c. 17 km NE of Dhîbān as the crow flies (*The Land of the Bible* [2nd edn], p. 437). There are two sites with the name Kh. el-Medeiyine close to each other, but neither location would be close enough to have been incorporated with the city of Dibon.

2.   See, for instance, S.R. Driver, *Notes on the Hebrew Text of the Books of Samuel* (Oxford, 1890), p. xci; *KAI*, II, p. 175; F.I. Andersen, 'Moabite Syntax', *Or* NS 35 (1966), pp. 81-120; G. Buccellati, *The Amorites in the Ur III Period*, p. 139; cf. G.W. Ahlström, *Royal Administration*, p. 14.

3.   G.W. Ahlström, *An Archaeological Picture of Iron Age Religions in Ancient Palestine*, pp. 17-18. The two *'ar'el* of Moab, which David's officer Benaiah is said to have struck down, probably were such lion postaments. For postaments with lion figures on each side, see R. Amiran, 'The Lion Statue and the Libation Tray from Tell Beit Mirsim', *BASOR* 222 (1976), pp. 29-40.

4.   The text is broken at this point, but the word is usually restored as *kly*, 'vessels'.

5.   Cf. G.W. Ahlström, *Royal Administration*, pp. 14-15; S. Timm, *Die Dynastie Omri*, p. 167.

6.   See A. Kuschke, 'New Contributions to the Historical Topography of Jordan', *ADAJ* 6-7 (1962), p. 95.

7.   *The Land of the Bible*, p. 339.

of the Mesha inscription mention that Israel's king had built Jahaz.[1] Whether this king was Omri or Ahab is not clear. Omri might not have had too much time for defense work in his short reign. His building activities may therefore have been limited to Israel proper. However, having conquered this part of Moab, it would have been most natural for Omri to build fortresses along his new border. Therefore, Omri may be the most likely candidate to have built Jahaz,[2] even though Ahab, his successor, could have built some of the fortifications and campaigned in the territory to suppress any attempts at rebellion (cf. Mesha l. 6).

The inscription by King Mesha cannot have been made immediately after the war of liberation against Israel. Mesha may have started his uproar during the later period of Ahab's reign. Ahab's participation in the battle of Qarqar in 853 BCE may have given Mesha a good opportunity to take some of the cities he mentions in his stela. Then, when Ahab died, he stopped paying tribute to Ahab's successor, Ahaziah (2 Kgs 1.1; 3.4-5). The building activities of Mesha that are reported in the inscription must have taken quite some time to finish. The *qarḥō*, the acropolis of Dibon, mentioned in lines 3 and 21-23,[3] where Mesha would have built his temple for Chemosh, would have taken years to complete. The Mesha inscription should probably be seen as an inscription commemorating Mesha's triumph over Israel.[4]

A king's building activities are usually undertaken for the protection of his land and people, even if some of the buildings emerge as monuments to the king's pride and 'greatness'. If Omri can be called the rebuilder of the nation Israel and the one who restored its position as a power with which to be reckoned, his son Ahab was the one who was able to consolidate the newly-won position and increase his nation's importance in Palestine. He was able to keep Moab under

1. In Josh. 21.36 and 1 Chron. 6.78, Jahaz is mentioned as a 'Levitical city', which has no historical foundation if Omri (or Ahab) built the place. No pottery from the time before the tenth century BCE has been found at the places seen as probable candidates for ancient Jahaz; see the discussion in G.W. Ahlström, *Royal Administration*, pp. 14, 53.

2. See the discussion in my *Royal Administration*, p. 53.

3. For comparison of the *qarḥō* with the Hittite phrase *šarazziš gurtaš*, 'the upper city', see the discussion in G.W. Ahlström, *Royal Administration*, p. 16.

4. Cf. J.M. Miller, 'The Moabite Stone as a Memorial Stela', *PEQ* 106 (1974), pp. 9-18.

control and at the same time undertake the task of fortifying several cities within Israel proper. He continued to build the new capital, Samaria, which his father had started. The city wall that Omri probably began is one of the best ever built (ashlar masonry) in Palestine during the Iron Age period. Besides the palace, called his (Ahab's) 'ivory house' in 1 Kgs 22.39, and a temple or royal sanctuary on the acropolis,[1] he is also said to have built an altar and a temple for (Jezebel's) Baal and to have made an *'ašērâ* (1 Kgs 16.33). None of this activity should be astonishing. Every king builds temples and is an image maker.[2] How much Ahab was able to build in Samaria is not known. The archaeological reports show that major portions of the city have not been excavated.[3] What has been unearthed seems to indicate that Samaria was quite different than anything else built heretofore. The splendor of the 'ivory house'[4] and the fine so-called Samaria ware (pottery) found in the excavations testify to the taste and elegance expressed in the new Israelite capital.[5] Whether ivories were

---

1. Royal palace and temple were really two aspects of one and the same phenomenon, the state, ruled by the king, the vice-regent of the national god. Hosea's reference to 'Samaria's calf' (Hos. 8.5-6, and cf. Hos. 13.2, 'men kiss the calves') may be an impolite reference to Samaria's official cult (see G.W. Ahlström, *Royal Administration*, pp. 17-18).

2. As part of his reform, Josiah burned and defiled temples and altars that the kings of Israel had built in the former northern kingdom, the Assyrian province of Samerina. He also removed the Baal and Asherah symbols and their vessels and the horses of the sun from the Jerusalem temple (2 Kgs 23). This clearly shows that any so-called mosaic laws had not yet come into existence and could not have been part of the life of the nations of Israel or Judah.

3. See J.W. Crowfoot, J.M. Kenyon and E.L. Sukenik, *Samaria-Sebaste*. I. *The Buildings of Samaria* (London, 1942); cf. G.A. Reisner, *Harvard Excavations at Samaria 1908–1910*, I-II (Cambridge, MA, 1924); K.M. Kenyon, *Archaeology in the Holy Land* (3rd edn), pp. 265-69; *idem*, *Royal Cities of the Old Testament* (New York, 1971), pp. 73-89.

4. There is a parallel to this in a palace chamber, AB 6, at Kalah (Nimrud). The walls had panels of uncarved ivory. See A.H. Layard, *The Monuments of Nineveh from Drawings Made on the Spot* (London, 1853), plates 88-90.

5. Cf. also Amos 6.4, which talks of the upper class people 'who lie on beds (couches) of ivory', referring to the period of Jeroboam II. The few biblical references to ivory have been well illustrated through the excavations at Samaria. About 500 fragments were found; cf. G.A. Reisner *et al.*, *Harvard Excavations at Samaria*, I, pp. 93-122. J.W. Crowfoot and G.M. Crowfoot argued that these ivories had been worked in Samaria (*Samaria-Sebaste II: Early Ivories from Samaria* [London,

made in Samaria or not is of less importance. As in most other capitals and great urban centers, the artistic styles of the time found expression. Thus, Phoenician, north Syrian and Aramaean ivory carvers may have come to Samaria. As time went on their pupils may have followed their masters' traditions and become masters themselves. The ivory beds mentioned in Amos 6.4 could very well have been products of an Israelite master guild in Samaria.[1]

To return to Ahab's buildings and fortifications, some of the buildings and defense systems that have been excavated have been dated to the ninth century BCE at places like Megiddo, Hazor, Shechem, Dan and Jericho,[2] and construction in other places could have been carried

1938], p. 49). Because many of the fragments have their counterparts in the collection from Arslan Tash (c. 30 km east of Carchemish), northern Syria, these Samarian pieces of ivory should been seen instead as part of a certain art tradition; cf. I.J. Winter, who recognizes both a north-Syrian tradition and a south-Syrian tradition of ivory carvings ('Is there a South Syrian Style of Ivory Carving in the Early First Millennium BCE?', *Iraq* 43 [1981], pp. 101-30, esp. pp. 101-15); see also her 'Phoenician and North Syrian Ivory Carving in Historical Context: Questions of Style and Distribution', *Iraq* 38 (1976), pp. 1-22.

1. I.J. Winter concludes, however, that 'all or part of the collection belongs to the latest possible moment, i.e., up to 720' (*Iraq* 42 [1981], p. 125). She also thinks that a center for ivory making was to be found in Damascus, 'from which stimuli originated and objects dispersed' (p. 127). It should be noted, however, that some of the Samarian ivory fragments were found alongside a jar of alabaster bearing the name Osorkon II (890–860 BCE), which would date those fragments at the latest to Ahab's reign (cf. N. Avigad, 'Samaria', *EAEHL*, IV, p. 1044). For a tradition of ivory inlays going back to the MB period, see H.A. Liebowitz, 'Bone and Ivory Inlays from Syria and Palestine', *IEJ* 27 (1977), pp. 89-97.

2. 1 Kgs 16.34 reports that Hiel of Bethel rebuilt Jericho during Ahab's time and that he offered two of his sons as foundation sacrifices. A private person does not build a city. We may assume that Hiel was Ahab's city planner. The curse over Jericho in Josh. 6.26 is a literary product postdating the time of Ahab. Still, the place could have been known to be unhealthy and thus accursed from long ago. Consult also I.M. Blake, who points to the fact that the settlement at Jericho is later than the Ahab period and that the 'intended effect of the Hiel episode is to moralize on an early attempt to reoccupy the site, which was a failure' ('Jericho ['Ain es-Sulṭân]: Joshua's Curse and Elisha's Miracle: One Possible Explanation', *PEQ* 99 [1967], p. 88). Because of erosion most of the Iron Age levels have been washed away at Tell es-Sulṭân (Jericho). However, from the amount of Iron Age pottery found on the slopes of the tell it appears that there was a 'considerable occupation in the Iron Age'. The styles, however, indicate the seventh century BCE rather than Ahab's period

out on Ahab's orders.[1] Hazor's importance as a fortress city may have increased in his time. Its location at the main route to the north, the Beqa' Valley and southern Syria made the city strategically important. The political threat to Israel's independence no longer came from the direction of Egypt, but from Aram, and at this stage, ultimately, from Assyria. Megiddo would have lost some of its military importance during his reign.

The fortifications of stratum VIII at Hazor have been seen by the excavator to be the work of king Ahab. Stratum IX could have been destroyed by the Aramaeans.[2] According to 1 Kgs 15.17-22, they had invaded Galilee and taken the cities of Dan, Ijon, Abel-Beth-Maacah and 'the land of Naphtali', that is, most of Galilee. At this time the entire tell of Hazor was fortified, not only the western half as before. The city of this stratum was also much more heavily fortified than the earlier strata. The fortifications included a citadel (area B in the western part of the tell), a 3m wide city wall, store houses, and a water system with a sloping tunnel. At the east end not only the city wall but also 'a sort of a "forward bastion" protecting the extreme eastern terrace'[3] was built, to mention a few of the most important features. Compared with Solomon's Hazor, this city could really be called a huge fortress.[4] Few residential buildings have been found in it, which testifies to the fact that Hazor was a city that was only populated by government officials.[5]

Among other building activities to be mentioned during this period is the city of Jezreel. Because the royal family had a second residence there (probably for the winter period), scholars have traditionally,

(K.M. Kenyon, *Digging up Jericho*, pp. 263-64; *idem*, 'Jericho', *EAEHL*, II, p. 564.

1.   For a résumé of the building activities during the ninth century BCE, see K.M. Kenyon, *Archaeology in the Holy Land*, pp. 258-85.

2.   See Y. Yadin, *Hazor of Those Kingdoms*, pp. 165-67. K.M. Kenyon believes that stratum VIII was built 'about the time Jehu drove out the Omrid dynasty in 841 BCE' (*Royal Cities of the Old Testament*, p. 106).

3.   Y. Yadin, *Hazor of Those Kingdoms*, p. 165; Y. Yadin *et al.*, *Hazor*, III–IV, plates LXXVIII-C.

4.   For the defense system of Israel during this period, see for instance, D.N. Pineaar, 'The Role of Fortified Cities in the Northern Kingdom during the Reign of the Omride Dynasty', *JNWSL* 9 (1981), pp. 151-57.

5.   See my article in *JNES* 41 (1982), pp. 136-38.

since the days of F. Hitzig,[1] seen this as a second capital in the kingdom of Israel. There is, however, no textual evidence supporting this position.[2] Royal estates are not necessarily the same as national capitals.

As has been mentioned above, the stories of the Elijah–Elisha cycle most probably refer to a time later than that of king Ahab. They are not reliable source materials for the social and religious circumstances during Ahab's time. The D-historian has used these traditions for the sole purpose of devaluating Ahab. He may even have reshaped them. His main purpose has been to depict Ahab and his entourage as Baal worshippers, which nobody should be, and to highlight Jezebel's bad influence upon king, court and religious leaders.[3] The purpose is polemical.[4] Under such circumstances, historical information is of less importance. The main actors in the drama are the prophet and the king and the queen. The whole reign of king Ahab is given the color of a religious contest. Still, some events and phenomena may have inspired the writer. In all probability Ahab built a Baal temple in Samaria (1 Kgs 16.32). This has been presented in such a way as to make it seem that the king and court, in other words, the state, had succumbed to the worship of the indigenous Baal (and scholars continue to fall into the trap). Unfortunately the OT writer does not say which Baal he refers to—that would have been to give away the 'weapon'. Realistically, Jezebel ought to have had a temple in her new place (as Solomon's wives had) so she could worship her own god.

1. *Geschichte des Volkes Israel von Anbeginn bis zur Eroberung Masadas im Jahre 72 nach Christus* (Leipzig, 1869), p. 172. Thus also A. Alt, 'Der Stadtstaat Samaria', *KS*, III, pp. 258-302; S. Yeivin, 'The Divided Kingdom', *WHJP*, IV.1 (ed. A. Malamat), p. 141; Y. Aharoni, *The Land of the Bible* (2nd edn), p. 334; J. Bright, *A History of Israel* (3rd edn), p. 244.

2. When this city was first built is not known. In the Hebrew Bible it is mentioned for the first time in connection with Solomon's district organization (1 Kgs 4.12). For a criticism of Hitzig's viewpoint, see also S. Timm, *Die Dynastie Omri*, pp. 142-56.

3. It is thus less probable that Elijah 'regarded Ahab and Jezebel as the ultimate anathema', as J. Bright expresses it (*A History of Israel* [3rd edn], p. 247). Bright also maintains that 'the court and ruling class were thoroughly paganized' (p. 246). We are not informed how he knows this.

4. L. Bronner sees these stories as the polemics of 'well informed theologians against popular beliefs concerning Baal'; in other words, they are written against the Baal mythology (cf. the discussion in *The Stories of Elijah and Elisha* [Leiden, 1968], p. 140).

The Baal in question must have been an imported god, a Phoenician Baal, not the Baal who had been worshipped from of old in these areas.[1] Usually scholars have understood Jezebel's Baal to be the god Melqart of Tyre. It could equally have been Baal Shamem of Sidon, especially if Jezebel's father came from Sidon.[2] For the writer of the story about the religious contest on Carmel (1 Kgs 18), the name Baal was degrading enough. H. Gese has suggested that the Baal of the Carmel contest would have been a Hadad-like deity.[3] Because the West-Semitic Hadad was a storm god, as was Yahweh originally, they could easily have merged. The story provides no information about the identity of the god Baal of Carmel (or Baal Carmel),[4] and the later biblical writer did not consider it important either. His aim was to glorify his Yahweh no matter who opposed him.[5] As a spokesman for his religious ideology, the writer chose Elijah and made him the leader of the opposition, a champion of the writer's own Yahweh faith. It should be recognized, however, that there is no polemic in

1. See the discussion in G.W. Ahlström, 'King Jehu—A Prophet's Mistake', *Scripture and History: Essays in Honor of J.C. Rylaarsdam* (ed. A.L. Merrill and T.W. Overholt; Pittsburgh, 1977), pp. 151-65.

2. Cf. M. Avi-Yonah, *IEJ* 2 (1952), pp. 118-24.

3. 'Die Religionen Altsyriens', *Die Religionen Altsyriens, Altarabiens und der Mandäer* (ed. H. Gese, M. Höfner and K. Rudolph; Stuttgart, 1979), p. 202; cf. M. Avi-Yonah, *IEJ* 2 (1952), p. 124.

4. Cf. O. Eissfeldt, 'Der Gott Karmel', *Sitzungsberichte der Deutschen Akademie der Wissenschaften zu Berlin* (Kl. für Sprachen, Literatur und Kunst, 1953.1; Berlin, 1954), pp. 25-42. There may well have been of a god named Baal Carmel, just as there was a Baal Lebanon, Baal Hermon, and the like, but there is no textual witness for such a name. See also the discussion by R. Smend, 'Der biblische und historische Elia', *Congress Volume, Edinburgh 1974* (ed. J.A. Emerton *et al.*; VTSup, 28; Leiden, 1975), p. 175.

5. For the Carmel contest, see among others R. de Vaux, 'Les prophètes de Baal sur le mont Carmel', *Bulletin du Musée de Beyrouth* 5 (1941), pp. 7-20; O. Eissfeldt, *Der Gott Karmel*, pp. 25-27; A. Alt, 'Das Gottesurteil auf dem Karmel', *KS*, II, pp. 135-49; K. Galling, 'Der Gott Karmel und die Ächtung der fremden Götter', *Geschichte und Altes Testament* (Festschrift A. Alt; Tübingen, 1953), pp. 105-25; E. Lipiński, 'La fête de l'ensevelissement et de la resurrection de Melqart', *Actes de la XVIIe Rencontre Assyriologique Internationale* (Brussells, 1969), pp. 39-40; A. Jepsen, 'Elia und das Gottesurteil', *Near Eastern Studies in Honor of W.F. Albright* (1971), pp. 291-306; N. Tromp, 'Water and Fire on Mount Carmel: A Conciliatory Suggestion', *Bib* 56 (1975), pp. 480-502; S. Timm, *Die Dynastie Omri*, pp. 87-101.

the story against the *maṣṣēbôt* and the *'ašērîm*, nor against the existence of the so-called *bāmâ* sanctuaries, phenomena that are the cardinal points in the later pure-Yahwistic criticism.[1] These stories demonstrate the freedom of the biblical author to compose as it suited his purposes.

It is quite possible that Jezebel has been remembered as an ardent follower of her Phoenician Baal and that her influence upon king and court had caused friction. Perhaps some circles saw it as a danger to the official state religions.[2] When she then became the *gᵉbîrâ*, 'queen mother', after Ahab's death, with her own administration,[3] her influence grew. The story about Naboth's vineyard—considerably expanded by novelistic elements[4]—seems to belong to the reign of Ahab's son Joram.[5] Naboth's murder to obtain the vineyard he would not relinquish to the king—contrary to Arauna and his *gōren*, 'threshing floor', which David wanted and obtained (2 Samuel 24)—has most often been taken as proof that the people and leaders of the kingdom of Israel were corrupt. It is seen as a sign of moral and social decay.[6] A single incident, however, should not be used for such an evaluation. Legal practices and conflicts between rulers and private citizens could have been used by the narrator to paint a distorted picture.[7]

Ahab is often said to have promoted the Baal religion to such a degree that Yahwism became suppressed. This is exactly what the biblical writer wants his audience to believe. The writer's 'pure Yahwistic' concepts do not reflect the official religion at the time of the Omrides. Whatever religious actions Ahab undertook, supported or performed, they were parts of the official Yahwistic cult of the northern

---

1. Cf. my article, 'King Jehu—A Prophet's Mistake', *Scripture and History* (ed. A.L. Merrill), pp. 51-65.

2. G.W. Ahlström, 'King Jehu', pp. 54-55. For the onesided picture of Jezebel given by the biblical narrator, cf. U. Winter, *Frau und Göttin*, pp. 578-79.

3. See G. Molin, *TZ* 10 (1954), pp. 161-75; H. Donner, 'Art und Herkunft des Amtes der Königmutter im Alten Testament', *Festschrift Johannes Friedrich* (ed. R. von Kienle), pp. 105-45; G.W. Ahlström, *Aspects of Syncretism*, pp. 57-63.

4. J.A. Soggin, *A History of Ancient Israel*, p. 207.

5. Consult J.M. Miller, *VT* 17 (1967), pp. 316-17.

6. See, for instance, J. Bright, who believes that Jezebel and Ahab had 'little concern' for law, which he understands to be 'covenant law' (*A History of Israel*, p. 245).

7. Concerning the legal practices, consult F.I. Andersen, 'The Socio-Juridical Background of the Naboth Incident', *JBL* 85 (1966), pp. 46-57.

kingdom—which, of course, need not necessarily have been identical with that of Judah. Ahab's status as a Yahweh worshipper—every king in Israel was—is evident from the Yahwistic names borne by his two sons who succeeded him: Ahaziah and Joram (Jehoram). What should be remembered is that the religion of Yahweh did not exclude the worship of other gods at this time. The gods of the nation were all gods belonging to Yahweh's divine assembly and kingdom. As the official leader of the state cult, the king's duty as the vice-regent of his god was to see that the divine realm and the earthly kingdom, its representative, was rightfully governed, which also included the rituals of the royal sanctuaries.[1] That the later 'historiographer' had other ideas was his problem.

Ahab's successor was his son Ahaziah, who only reigned about two years. Having fallen through the fence of his balcony at Samaria, he became ill and sent messengers to the Philistine city of Ekron in order to inquire of its god Baal-zebub ('fly-Baal')[2] about how to get well. He never did. The biblical writer explained his failure to recover by letting the prophet Elijah predict his death (2 Kgs 1.2-17). There is not much more that can be learned. His royal colleague in Jerusalem, Asa's son Jehoshaphat, had undertaken the building of Tarshish ships in order to renew the trade with Ophir from Ezion-Geber at the Gulf of Aqaba. Because of the treaty between Israel and Judah and also because of the lucrative prospects in trade, Ahaziah offered Jehoshaphat his help. The narrator of 1 Kgs 22.48-49 says that Jehoshaphat turned down king Ahaziah's offer, but the Chronicler contradicts him, saying that the two kings built the ships together (2 Chron. 20.35-36). Whatever the truth, the ships were 'broken' while still in the harbor, so nothing came of the great plans.

Ahaziah was succeeded by his brother Joram (c. 852–841 BCE). He tried to restore Moab to its former status as a vassal to Israel. Mesha had to be punished. Together with the Judahite armies under

---

1. For these aspects, consult the discussion in G.W. Ahlström, *Royal Administration*, pp. 1-9.

2. The name of this god should probably not be understood as an intentional misspelling of Baal-zebul (Prince Baal), as sometimes has been suggested; cf. Y. Aharoni, *Archaeology of the Land of Israel*, p. 188. Philistine religion is not very well known, but it included, for instance, rituals with mice (cf. 1 Sam. 6.4, and G.W. Ahlström, *An Archaeological Picture of Iron Age Religions*, pp. 7-8). It is thus possible that there also was a Baal of the flies.

Jehoshaphat and vassal Edomite forces (Edom was at that time a satellite country of Judah), Joram marched south through Judah via northern Edom into Moab. His route apparently was chosen to avoid the fortresses Mesha had built in the north. The invasion was successful to begin with, and Mesha retreated and took refuge in Kir-hareshet (modern Kerak). Its location on a steep hill at Wadi Kerak was ideal for a fortress (which is clear from the Crusader fortress located there). Many cities had been taken by the allied armies, but Kir-hareshet could not be taken. The story in 2 Kgs 3.27 refers to the siege of this site, mentioning how as a last effort Mesha sacrificed his oldest son to Chemosh on the city wall so that enemies could see it. 'And there came a great wrath upon Israel, and they withdrew from him and returned to their land' (v. 27). Militarily, the allied armies could not take the city, and one may not go too wrong in suggesting that they also were not in agreement about how to conduct the war after this. The invasion did not accomplish what it had set out to do, and the armies returned home.

It is noteworthy that shortly after this Edom regained its independence under Jeoshaphat's son Jehoram (2 Kgs 8.20-22; 2 Chron. 21.8-10). Edom's independence may also explain why Jehoshaphat and Jehoram did not renew the attempt to build new Tarshish ships after the disaster in the harbor of Ezion-geber. Edom may not have been a reliable satellite in the later part of Jehoshaphat's regime, and it finally threw off the yoke under Jehoram. The port was in Edomite territory, and with the loss of Edom there would have been no possibility for them to build a merchant fleet without a port on the Gulf of Aqaba.[1] The independent status of Edom must have constituted a financial blow for Judah, which now lost significant income from the trade routes to Arabia.

The reign of Joram of Israel seems to have been troubled not only by unsuccessful wars (against Moab and Aram or Assyria), but also by internal disturbances. The latter also contributed to Jehu's revolt and the change of dynasty in 841 BCE. The biblical writer has given Jehu's *coup d'état* the sheen of a revolt that was inspired by Yahweh and some people who were dissatisfied with the religious attitude of the time. The prophet Elisha is depicted as the king's worst enemy who, together with the elders of Samaria conspired against the king. They

---

1. Cf. J. Bright, *A History of Israel* (3rd edn), p. 248.

met in the house of Elisha in Samaria (2 Kgs 6.32). There inevitably would have been circles opposing the policies of the king, and Elisha seems to have been part of them. The biblical writer does not present the events that led to Jehu's revolt in this light, however. He presents them as part of a process that led to a religious purge. The Baal religion is reported to have come to an end with Jehu. To put it mildly, the biblical narrator has written a good piece of propaganda. History it is not.

Jehu's revolt can be characterized as the inauguration of a new period in Palestine's history. Although Jehu has been seen as a blessing from Yahweh by the biblical writer, in reality, he was a disaster. From its dominant role in Syro-Palestinian affairs, Israel under Jehu became an insignificant nation very much reduced in its territory by Aram-Damascus. It is quite possible that Mesha ended his war against Israel after Joram's death. It is hard to get exact information about the location of borders. The texts usually mention only the towns and villages of a limited border area. For Transjordan, the Mesha inscription provides good information about what territory Israel lost at this time, but the boundaries north and northwest of Moab cannot exactly be drawn.

The whole Mishor seems to have been taken, which included such places as Nebo, Medeba, Ma'in, Elealeh and Heshbon. Isaiah 15 and 16 mention, for instance, Heshbon, Elealeh, Sibmah and Jazer as Moabite towns (cf. Jer. 48). Moab's border with Ammon in the north could have been a line from Mephaat (modern Jawa?, coord. 239-140), c. 10 km south of Amman, to Umm el-Qanafidh (coord. 228-139) to the west, c. 5 km SW of Naur (which is located in what probably was the outpost of the Ammonite mountains) and 2.5 km NW of 'el-'Al (ancient Elealeh, coord. 228-136). From there the border line may have gone via Sha'nab (coord. 223-140) and down the Wadi Kafrein to the Jordan Valley and the so-called Plains of Moab, which is the area north of the Dead Sea up to Wadi Kafrein.

The name Plains of Moab may indicate that the territory belonged to the Moabites from old. Still, it must be asked where the border between Israel and Moab could have been after Mesha's war of liberation. Did he also regain the Plains of Moab? That question cannot be answered from available textual material. Should he have reoccupied this territory, he could have taken the valley on both sides of the

Jordan River.[1] Because Jehu, the new king of Israel, lost the remainder of Transjordan to Damascus (2 Kgs 10.32-33), the king of Moab could very well have protected his interests. When Hazael of Damascus took most of Transjordan, Mesha could have expanded into the plains of Moab.

In the southwest, Israel's border was close to Gibbethon, where the Israelite army fought the Philistines both under Nadab (Jeroboam's son) and Elah's general Omri (1 Kgs 15.27; 16.15). Gibbethon is probably Tell Melat (coord. 137-140), located c. 7 km west of Gezer. This area was part of the second Solomonic district, which also included Makaz, Shaalbim, Aijalon, Beth-hanan and Beth-Shemesh (1 Kgs 4.9). Because Israel had to fight the Philistines both under Nadab and under Elah, it seems likely that a resurgence of Philistine dominion in this part of Palestine took place. After Solomon's death and the split of the united monarchy, the Philistines tried to get their territory back. How they succeeded, or if they did, it is not told in the Bible. It is possible that some part of the coast was taken back in the period of Israelite weakness that followed the death of Solomon. For the period of Omri and Ahab there is no report of open hostilities. This may be seen as a sign of Israel's growing power during this period. There probably were good relations between Israel and the Philistines during the reign of Ahaziah, who when sick, sent for an oracular answer from Ekron's god Baal-zebub (2 Kgs 1.2-4). In the south, Israel's border could perhaps have been somewhere in the region between Bethel and Mizpah, to the north of Aijalon, and between Gezer and Gibbethon. Joppa and Aphek[2] further north obviously belonged to the Philistines. In the west and northwest, Carmel was part of the nation of Israel, but the plain of Acco, the Cabul area, had belonged to Tyre ever since the days of Solomon.

Concerning the northern border, we know that, according to 1 Kgs 15.18-20, Damascus took Galilee during the time of Baasha, in order to relieve king Asa of Judah from the pressure of the Israelite army.

---

1. The story about Moab, together with Ammonites and Amalekites, invading the western part of the valley and the 'city of palms' (Judg. 3.12-30) may show an old tradition about Transjordanian peoples who had settled in this area. For the non-documentary character of the biblical traditions about the settlement in this area, see the discussion in M. Wüst, *Untersuchungen zu den siedlungsgeographischen Texten*, pp. 244-46.

2. Cf. 2 Kgs 13.22 (LXX, Luc.).

We do not know when this territory again became Israelite, but in order to get Israel into a coalition against Assyria, Adad-'idri most probably had given some of it back.[1] This would mean that Ahab would have been able to fortify Hazor, for instance.

The reasons for Jehu's *coup d'état* are more to be found in the foreign policy and unfortunate wars of king Joram and the threat Assyria now presented to the west, than in such internal problems as religion and morals.[2] As mentioned before, Shalmaneser III renewed his campaigns in Syria in 849 and continued in 848, 845 and 841. The Bible reports that Aram and Israel were at war against each other in Transjordan, which would have been in 841 when Adad-'idri of Damascus had been murdered by Hazael, 'the son of nobody', as he is called in the Assyrian annals.[3] It is possible that he was one of the officers in the Aramaean army. The Israelite headquarters were at Ramoth-Gilead (2 Kgs 8.28–9.16). The reason for the war is not given, but it is likely that the new king of Aram-Damascus, Hazael, would have pressured Israel to continue to be part of the coalition against Assyria. The occurrence of a war between Aram and Israel at this particular time is very doubtful. Shalmaneser III already had occupied the Hauran, east of Ramoth-Gilead. For Jehu and other officers, as well as court officials or important citizens such as the leaders of Samaria, who could have been opposed to Joram's anti-Assyrian policies, the moment of action had presented itself when the king had been wounded in a battle at Ramoth-Gilead and transported to Jezreel to recuperate. Jehu saw that the time was ripe for a change in regime and policies. His coup is presented by the biblical narrator as divinely-inspired; Jehu is chosen by the outstanding 'Yahwistic' prophet Elisha, the pupil of Elijah, to be the new king. In this way his credentials were made perfect. In order to develop this literary fiction, a disciple of the prophet Elisha is sent to Ramoth-Gilead in Transjordan to anoint Jehu for kingship (2 Kgs 8.28–9.16). In this way the biblical writer justifies Jehu's kingship and the murder of the royal dynasty which he, the writer, hated. Jehu did not become a blessing for Israel.

---

1. For a discussion about Israel's borders during the times after the split of the united monarchy, see S. Timm, 'Die territoriale Ausdehnung des Staates Israel zur Zeit der Omriden', *ZDPV* 96 (1980), pp. 20-40.

2. J. Bright speaks of 'an explosion of pent-up popular anger, and of all that was conservative in Israel' (*A History of Israel*, p. 250).

3. D.D. Luckenbill, *ARAB*, I, par. 681, pp. 245-46.

Things may have been bad under Joram, but they went from bad to worse under Jehu. Yet the biblical narrator does not blame Elisha—or Yahweh—for the choice. How much truth there is in the biblical story about Jehu's revolt is impossible to tell, but there probably was strong opposition to the policies of the king and his party in both foreign and internal affairs. Jehu may be characterized as a pro-Assyrian officer, or as the leader of a pro-Assyrian party that saw warring against Assyria as disastrous. He acted quickly while the king was recovering in Jezreel. The presence of Shalmaneser and his army in the Hauran, that is, just east of Ramoth-Gilead, probably spurred Jehu's action. Shalmaneser's fourth Syrian campaign (842/841) had crushed the Syrian coalition and devastated the area around Damascus. Hazael retreated to Damascus, a city which the Assyrians could not take.[1] Breaking the siege, Shalmaneser marched into Hauran, plundering and looting.[2] The question is now whether there really was a war between Aram and Israel while Shalmaneser was 'just around the corner'. Would not the Assyrian king have used such an opportunity to get Hazael? The distance from Damascus to Ramoth-Gilead in northern Jordan is c. 120 km as the crow flies. If the Assyrian inscription concerning Hazael's defeat and retreat to Damascus and about Shalmaneser's burning of the orchards around Damascus is reliable, then it would have been impossible for Hazael to muster a new army quickly and march into the area where he might risk meeting the Assyrian army at any time. It would have been quite unthinkable and impossible for Hazael to do battle in northern Transjordan. Hauran is the territory just to the east. If Shalman of Hos. 10.14 is identical with Shalmaneser III[3] who destroyed Beth-arbel[4] west of Ramoth-Gilead, then the war between Aram and Israel must be fictional. It is

1. D.D. Luckenbill, *ARAB*, I, par. 672 and 681, pp. 243, and 245-46; *ANET*, p. 280.

2. Cf. A.T. Olmstead, *History of Assyria* (Chicago, 1923 [1975]), pp. 138-39.

3. Thus C. von Orelli, *Kurzgefasstes Kommentar die 12 kleinen Propheten* (2nd edn; Munich, 1896 [1888]), p. 226; followed by M. Astour, '841 BCE: The First Assyrian Invasion of Israel', *JAOS* 91 (1971), pp. 386-87; Y. Aharoni, *The Land of the Bible* (2nd edn), p. 341. H.W. Wolff sees Shalman of Hosea 10.14 as a reference to the Moabite king Salmanu mentioned in a inscription of Tiglath-Pileser III (*Hosea*, pp. 188-89). Unfortunately, nothing else is known about this Salmanu. For the inscription, see *ANET*, p. 282.

4. F. Buhl located Beth-arbel in the area of modern Irbid in Jordan (*Geographie des alten Palästinas*, p. 219).

possible that the Israelite army, which probably had come out as an ally of Aram-Damascus, had been intercepted or surprised by the Assyrians and had made its stand at Ramoth-Gilead against the Assyrians.[1] One thing seems to be certain: Jehu must have contacted Shalmaneser in order to get his support for the *coup* and to save Israel from being devastated and plundered. The next reported action of the Assyrian king is his march to the Mediterranean, where he received tribute at Ba'lira'si[2] from the kings of Tyre–Sidon and Israel's Jehu. The usual route from Hauran to the Mediterranean is through the Jezreel Valley, which means that Shalmaneser would have marched through Israel, passing the city of Jezreel.[3] An indication that Jehu had contact with the Assyrian king before he made his move to overthrow the old regime is the fact that when he had murdered king Joram, he sent a message to the elders of Samaria to kill all the members of the royal family and to send their heads in baskets to Jehu at Jezreel. This they did, and Jehu placed the heads of the murdered princes 'in two heaps at the entrance to the gate' (2 Kgs 10.8). This was an Assyrian

1. Why would the biblical writer have made up a war? He really did not if the theory presented above is right. The narrator only gave the wrong name of Israel's opponent. This may have suited his purpose because of the troubles the Aramaeans had given Israel through the period after Jehu. For the narrator, a war in Gilead was a war between Aramaeans and Israelites over the hegemony of this territory. Another possibility for not mentioning the war's correct combatants is that the writer may have been very unfamiliar with the history of this particular period. For the problems of this conflict, see now my article, 'The Battle at Ramoth-Gilead in 841 BCE', *Beiträge zur Erforschung des Alten Testaments und des Antiken Judentums* (No. 13; Frankfurt a.M., 1988), pp. 157-66.

2. For the text, see D.D. Luckenbill, *ARAB*, I, par. 672, p. 243; A.L. Oppenheim, *ANET*, p. 280. The name Ba'lira'si (Baal's head) must mean a promontory, at the sea, and has been tentatively identified with either Nahr el-Kalb, c. 10 km north of Beirut (thus S. Herrmann, *A History of Israel* [2nd edn], p. 231), or Mount Carmel—so A.T. Olmsted, *History of Assyria*, p. 139; M.C. Astour, *JAOS* 91 (1971), pp. 386-88; Y. Aharoni, *The Land of the Bible* (2nd edn), p. 341. F. Safar's restoration of the text has also the wording 'opposite Tyre' ('A Further Text of Shalmaneser III from Assur', *Sumer* 7 [1951], pp. 3-21). See also A. Malamat, who interprets this phrase as referring to Carmel ('Campaigns to the Mediterranean by Iahdunlim and other Early Mesopotamian Rulers', *Assyriological Studies*, XVI (Festschrift B. Landsberger; Chicago, 1965), pp. 371-72.

3. Cf. M.C. Astour, *JAOS* 91 (1971), pp. 386-87. Astour sees the mention of Shalman's devastation of Beth-arbel (modern Irbid in Jordan, Hos. 10.14) as a reference to Shalmaneser's and Assyria's first incursion into Israelite territory.

custom.[1] When combined with the probability that Shalmaneser took
the route through the Jezreel Valley to the coast, it appears likely that
Jehu not only had started his revolt with the Assyrian's blessing, but
that he already was a servant of Assyrian interests.[2] His payment of
tribute to Shalmaneser at Ba'lira'si that is depicted on Shalmaneser's
so-called Black Obelisk was the formal acknowledgement that the new
Israelite king was a vassal of Assyria.[3]

Jehu's way of making himself firm in the saddle was the usual one
of that time: he exterminated all members of the late king's family and
the leaders of his administration or political party, that is, 'all his
great men, and his friends, and his priests', until none of the servants
of the former dynasty were alive (2 Kgs 10.11). The phrase 'and all
his priests' includes both Yahweh-priests, Baal-priests and other
priests as well. When Jehu had taken Samaria, he slaughtered the
priests of the Phoenician Baal and burned his temple (2 Kgs 10.18-
27). Having had the opportunity also to kill the king of Judah,
Athaliah's son Ahaziah, who was with king Joram, he also was able to
kill 42 princes of the royal house of Judah who were on their way to
pay a state visit to the royal family of Jezreel. By these acts Jehu managed to cut the bonds between Israel and Judah. The treaty with Tyre
was annulled with the murder of Jezebel, who was thrown out of a
window in the palace at Jezreel by two eunuchs when she scornfully
greeted the usurper (2 Kgs 9.33).[4] Through Jehu's *coup d'état* Israel

1. For an example of this practice, see D.D. Luckenbill, *ARAB*, I, par. 598-99,
pp. 213-15.
2. Cf. G.W. Ahlström, 'King Jehu—A Prophet's Mistake', *Scripture and
History* (ed. A.L. Merrill), pp. 67-68, n. 47.
3. Interesting to note is that above the prostrating Jehu is the six-pointed star.
Obviously that was a royal emblem of Israel. The five-pointed star belongs to Judah;
cf. M. Ottosson, 'Hexagrammet och Pentagrammet i främreorientalisk kontext', *SEÅ*
36 (1971), pp. 45-76. As to Jehu's tribute containing a large amount of gold that the
Omrides had gained from the trade routes, see M. Elat, 'Trade in Ancient Israel',
State and Temple Economy in the Ancient Near East, II (ed. E. Lipiński; Orientalia
Lovaniensia Analecta, 6; Leuven, 1976), p. 542. If Jehu and the Phoenician king fell
to the feet of Shalmaneser III at Mount Carmel (if that is Ba'lira'si), the biblical
writer has not seen the irony in his own story about the religious contest between the
Yahweh prophet Elijah and the Baal prophets on the one hand and the military contest
on the other resulting in victory of 'lord' Baal of Carmel over the king who is said to
have rooted out Baal worship in Israel.
4. This window should perhaps not be called the 'audience window', because

again became an isolated nation, and soon it was merely a little nation comprising no more than the northern part of the central hill-country of Palestine, where it had originally begun. It did not take long before Israel became a vassal of Aram-Damascus. Jehu's submission to Assyria did not help against the Aramaeans. Hazael managed to rebuild his strength, and he became the new power figure in Palestine who almost had free reign. During the last years of Shalmaneser's reign, he had to deal with internal problems in Assyria proper.[1] It is to this period, and to the reign of Jehu's son Jehoahaz, that the biblical text refers when it says that it was in those days that Yahweh 'started to make an end of Israel and Hazael defeated them in the whole territory of Israel' (2 Kgs 10.32).

The story about the house of Omri should not end before we have dealing with Athaliah of the Omride family, who was married to Jehoram of Judah and who made herself the reigning queen when her son Ahaziah was murdered by Jehu (2 Kgs 11). Her father-in-law Jehoshaphat ruled in Judah for 25 years (874–848), during the time of Ahab and his two sons (1 Kgs 22.41). Not much is said about Jehoshaphat in the Book of 2 Kings. The Deuteronomistic historian was mainly interested in his religious conduct and activities. He only mentions that, besides trying to re-establish the sea trade to and from Ezion-geber by building Tarshish ships (an attempt that failed), Jehoshaphat waged some wars. This is a motif that belongs to the picture of a successful king, and, since it is not said against whom he campaigned (22.46), the information would seem to be less than trustworthy. The Chronicler, however, builds him up as a very successful warrior king. He supposedly defeated the Ammonites, the Moabites and the 'mountain people of Seir' (2 Chron. 20). Philistines and Arabs are also said to have given him tribute (2 Chron. 17.10-11). This is part of the Chronicler's pattern. A king who did not follow the way of Israel (2 Chron. 17.4) was blessed by Yahweh in every respect and must have been mightier than his neighbors. Still, it was under Jehoshaphat that Judah became a treaty partner to Israel, and Athaliah was married to the crown prince Jehoram. According to 1 Kgs 22.47, Edom was a vassal of Judah under Jehoshaphat, so it is less likely that

it is questionable whether the audience window was so large that a well-fed woman in all her regalia could pass through it.

1.   For the later period, see J.E. Reade, 'Assyrian Campaigns 840–811 BCE, and the Babylonian Frontier', ZA 68 (1978), pp. 251-60.

the Edomites had been in a coalition against Judah at this time.[1] The Chronicler's attempt to make Jehoshaphat one of the great and mighty kings of Palestine is not particularly convincing. It does not have historical credibility.[2] The 'greatness' of Jehoshaphat lay in his religious activities, according to the writer. He is said to have continued in his father's footsteps and to have made an end to the practice of the male prostitutes (sodomites). 1 Kgs 22.43-46 (and the parallel text in 2 Chron. 20.33) states that his cult 'reforms' were not in harmony with the deuteronomistic (and Chronistic) ideal. The writer complains that Jehoshaphat did not abolish the *bāmôt*. A later time's religious ideal has been associated with Jehoshaphat. The same ideal can be found in the statement in 2 Chron. 20.33 that the people had not yet 'turned their hearts to the god of their fathers'. The Yahwism that the writer propagates did not exist in the time of Jehoshaphat, even though it serves as the background for the writer's statement about Jehoshaphat's administrative reorganization. 2 Chron. 17.7-9 mentions that he sent out prominent leaders and Levites to teach the people the *tôrâ*, 'law' of Yahweh, and 19.4-6 talks about judges whom he installed in the cities of Judah. Verse 2 says that the king divided Judah into 12 districts. It is possible that a certain reorganization of the royal administration had taken place.[3] This need not be an invention, but the connection with the *tôrâ* of Yahweh shows the postexilic mentality that directs the writer. There had certainly been government officials and royally-appointed priests in many of the cities of the nation, but that the nation would now have learned for the first time the *tôrâ* of Yahweh should be understood against the background of the words in 2 Chron. 20.33: 'the people had not yet turned their hearts to the god of their fathers'. Religious and cultic laws had been

1. A.T. Olmstead assumes that a threat from Transjordan forced Jehoshaphat to 'acknowledge Ahab's suzerainty' (*History of Palestine and Syria*, p. 374).

2. Cf. H. Donner in J.H. Hayes and J.M. Miller, *Israelite and Judean History*, p. 392. I. Eph'al thinks that the details we find in 2 Chron. 17.11 'suggest that it is based on a reliable source and fits the historical information in the chapter', while he characterizes 2 Chron. 20 as a chapter in 'midrashic style', which could reflect an 'incursion into Judah from Transjordan in the last years of Jehoshaphat's reign, after Moab was freed of Israelite control' (*The Ancient Arabs*, p. 68-69).

3. Cf. W.F. Albright, 'The Judicial Reform of Jehoshaphat', *Alexander Marx Jubilee Volume* (New York, 1950), pp. 61-82; W. Rudolph, *Chronikbücher*, pp. 256-58; G.W. Ahlström, *Royal Administration*, p. 54.

in force before, and it should be remembered that the law of the land was always rooted in the divine will. The religious and civil laws of the Yahwism that emerged in the form of Judaism during the post-exilic period, which the Chronicler promotes, did not influence king Jehoshaphat and his people.

Jehoshaphat was followed by his oldest son, Jehoram (c. 848–841), who was married to Athaliah of the Omride family. The Chronicler reports that Jehoram killed his six brothers (2 Chron. 21.2).[1] Because their names are given, it can be assumed that this attempt to firmly establish himself on the throne is grounded in genuine historical occurrence. According to the following two verses, Jehoshaphat gave his sons both wealth and 'fortified towns in Judah'. It is possible that this 'feudalistic' system was felt by Jehoram to be a danger to his rule. Jehoram's participation in Israel's war against Moab has already been discussed, and it is possible that this not-too-successful campaign inspired the Edomites to free themselves from Judahite overlordship and re-establish their kingdom (2 Kgs 8.20-22). This meant among other things that Ezion-geber and the lucrative traffic through the Gulf of Aqaba and the Red Sea was lost for Judah. As far as is known, Edom was no longer a vassal to Judah. The city of Libnah also is reported to have freed itself from Judah during Jehoram's reign (2 Kgs 8.22; 2 Chron. 21.10). It must have been situated in the Shephelah, close to or on the border with the Philistine territories;[2] whether Libnah became an independent city state or allied itself with the Philistines is not known. Assyrian inscriptions also mention Arabs in southern Palestine. Thus, when 2 Chron. 21.16-18 mentions that Jehoram met hostilities from both Philistines and Arabs and that they invaded Judah, this certainly could mirror historical reality.[3] It is quite natural that some of the neighbors of Judah, such as Arabs and Philistines, would have made incursions into Judah, as 2 Chron. 21.16-18 also mentions. Jehoram's unsuccessful war against the Edomites and their regained freedom may have inspired the Arabs and the Philistines to gain territorial ground. The Chronicler's allegation in v. 17 that they took all the property of the king—which would have

1. J. Bright wants to see Jehoram's queen, Athaliah, as the source of inspiration for these killings (*A History of Israel* [3rd edn], p. 252).

2. For the discussion about the location of Libnah, see my article, 'Tell ed-Duweir: Lachish or Libnah?', *PEQ* 115 (1983), pp. 103-104.

3. Cf. I. Eph'al, *The Ancient Arabs*, pp. 77-78.

been impossible—in addition to his household, his wives and all his sons except one, is to be understood as literary fiction. It develops the common motif in which the defeated and unloved one is worthy only of the worst punishment from the deity. Jehoram is said to have done what was 'displeasing to Yahweh', by being religiously in line with the Omrides, which could be expected, since his wife was Athaliah. He built a temple to Baal in Jerusalem, whose first priest was Mattan, a Phoenician name (2 Kgs 11.18). The examples of Solomon and Ahab building temples for their foreign wives—kings are usually temple builders—may lead us to believe that Jehoram had built the Baal temple in Jerusalem for his queen, Athaliah. The situation in Jerusalem can thus be paralleled with the one in Samaria after Ahab had built the temple for Jezebel, which was dedicated to the Phoenician Baal. The Baal temple in Jerusalem was probably built for an imported deity, as was the case in Samaria, and had nothing to do with the indigenous Baal of the kingdom of Judah, who had been worshipped all the time in Solomon's temple together with Asherah, the goddess.

As mentioned above, Jehoram is judged negatively by the biblical writers. Because he did not follow the ways of Yahweh, as they saw it, he was punished by a severe illness (in the bowels) and died, after having reigned for eight years. The text mentions that the people 'did not make any fire for him as they had for his fathers' (2 Chron. 21.19). He was followed by his son Ahaziah, who, unfortunately for himself, died within a year (841 BCE). Because of the alliance with Israel, Ahaziah was with Joram of Israel at Jezreel when Jehu made his coup. Just as the Israelite king was murdered by Jehu's men, so too was Ahaziah, while fleeing to Megiddo (2 Kgs 9.27-28).

According to the narrator, the queen mother Athaliah, on learning about her son's murder, took the governmental reins, and, in a *coup d'état*, executed all the remaining princes of the Davidic dynasty— except Ahaziah's one-year-old son, Joash (Jehoash). A sister of Ahaziah is said to have saved the boy and hidden him in the Solomonic temple (2 Kgs 11.1-3; 2 Chron. 22.10-12). The future of the Davidic dynasty looked bleak. Nobody knew whether the only remaining offshoot of David's line would be able to survive the queen's regime. For six years Athaliah ruled Judah (841–836) without finding out where her grandson was, which is quite incredible.[1] There is no information about what her rule was like politically, and, as usual, the writer is only interested in religious aspects and cultic circumstances. It can be taken for granted, however, that everything was not peaceful. The mere point that the priest of the Solomonic temple could hide the prince for several years—if that is true—speaks for the presence of factions and undercurrents within the political and social life of the capital.

It is also only to be expected that the priesthood of the Solomonic temple would have been opposed to Athaliah and the leadership of the temple that Jehoram had built in Jerusalem for the Phoenician Baal. Not only was the existence of the Davidic dynasty threatened, but so too was the Yahweh cult as the official cult of the nation. When six years had passed, the priest Jehoiada prepared a revolt against the queen. He used the occasion of the changing of the temple and palace guards on a sabbath to make his move, having first closed off the temple precinct. He then brought the young boy out to the temple court and put him on the *'ammûd*,[2] 'platform', anointed him king, and gave him the diadem, and the *'ēdût*, the 'witness'.[3] The priest is then said to have made a covenant between Yahweh and the people, and one

---

1. The story makes one suspect that Joash might have been the son of Ahaziah's sister and her husband, the priest Jehoiada; see M. Liverani, 'L'histoire de Joas', *VT* 24 (1974), pp. 452-53.

2. The modern translations usually render this word as 'pillar', but the preposition *'al* clearly indicates that the king was standing upon something and not at the side of a pillar; cf. 2 Chron. 23.13, which has *'al 'ammûdô*, 'on his dais, platform'. This may be the place from which the king reads or promulgates the law. Already Josephus understood the phrase as 'on the pillar' (*Ant.* 9.8.3). For an illustration to such a 'pillar' or platform, see M. Metzger, in A. Kuschke and M. Metzger, 'Kumudi und die Ausgrabungen auf Tell Kamid el-Loz', *Congress Volume, Uppsala 1971* (ed. J.A. Emerton *et al.*; VTSup, 22; Leiden, 1972), pp. 162-69 and Abb. 5. C.F. Keil translated *'mwd* with 'ein Standort (*suggestus*)' (*Biblisher Kommentar über die prophetischen Geschichtsbücher*, p. 270 [ET Grand Rapids, 1983, repr.], p. 362).

3. G. von Rad considered this to be a document containing the king's names and titles ('The Royal Ritual in Judah', *The Problem of the Hexateuch and Other Essays* [New York, 1966 (1958)], pp. 222-24). The term could well be a representation for the divine law, of which the king is the guarantor; cf. the discussion by G. Widengren, 'King and Covenant', *JSS* 2 (1957), pp. 1-32. S. Dalley sees *'edût* as referring to the winged disk ('The God Salmu and the Winged Disk', *Iraq* 48 [1986], pp. 92-93).

between the king and the people (2 Kgs 11.17).[1] When Athaliah heard the noise of the people's cry, 'Long live the King', she hurried to the temple, but was immediately arrested and executed just outside the temple (2 Kgs 11.4-16). With Athaliah's death the last reigning member of the Omride royal family disappeared. The reaction against her rule was then expressed in the destruction of the Baal temple and the death of its priest Mattan (2 Kgs 11.18). Of special interest in this case is the text's mention that the 'people of the land', the *'m h'rṣ*, had actively participated in the revolt against Athaliah. They probably had been organized by the priest Jehoiada, who may have been considered the defender of the old dynasty. The phrase 'people of the land' may here refer to the most important leaders of the gentry, the land-owners. Their role is never specified, and the term seems to have been used somewhat broadly in the Bible. However, their importance could have grown under weak kings and during such times of irregularities as that of Athaliah. The *'m h'rṣ* also acted when Manasseh's son, king Amon, had been murdered. They killed Amon's murderers, and they saved the dynasty by placing Amon's son Josiah on the throne (2 Kgs 21.24).[2]

In the Shadow of Assyria

It has been seen how the growing power of Assyria under such kings as Ashur-naṣirpal II (883–859 BCE) and Shalmaneser III (859–824) not only became a real threat to the nations of Syria and Palestine, but exterminated some and deported their peoples, thus breaking their power. Others became satellite states. This resulted in new political constellations and treaties in order to counteract the Assyrian military machine. The battle at Qarqar in 853 is a good example of an attempt

---

1. Because this is expressed in the 'fashion of Deuteronomic theology', the text cannot reflect 'a covenant formula firmly rooted in the royal ritual of Judah' (S. Herrmann, *A History of Israel* [2nd edn], pp. 224-25). G. Widengren has maintained that the enthronement of Joash could have been on the new year's day, which was 'deliberately chosen in order to make the new king introduce a new epoch' (*JSS* 2 [1957], p. 7).

2. Consult, for instance, E. Würthwein, *Der 'amm hā'ārez im Alten Testament* (BWANT, 4.17; Stuttgart, 1936); R. de Vaux, 'Le sens de l'expression "peuple du pays" dans l'Ancien Testament et le rôle politique du peuple en Israël', *RA* 58 (1964), pp. 167-72; E.W. Nicholson, 'The Meaning of the Expression *'m h'rṣ* in the Old Testament', *JSS* 10 (1965), pp. 59-66.

by several Syro-Palestinian states to stop the Assyrian expansion. The Aramaean king of Damascus was a leader of the Syrian opposition to Assyria in most instances. The two centuries following Qarqar are noted for wars, looting and deportations, with some quieter intervals traceable to either internal problems in Assyria or political troubles in the northern or eastern parts of the empire.

It could be asked what kind of reasons there might have been for Assyria's development into a state with such a voracious appetite for territory and power. They may have been complex, but, as has been indicated earlier, Assyria's expansionist policies would have been a result of its geology and geographical location. As a country primarily of mud, Assyrian imperialism could be said to be born out of the necessity to get hold of the resources and raw materials that Assyria itself lacked.[1] For instance, timber, bronze, metals and horses were very much in demand, as were fine textiles, ivories, silver and gold, and other luxury items. This can be well illustrated by an inscription of Ashurnashirpal II, who campaigned in Syria and pushed through to the Mediterranean coast in 877. He received tribute from the Phoenician cities, namely

> from the inhabitants of Tyre, Sidon, Byblos, Mahallata, Maiza, Kaiza, Amurru, and (of) Arvad which is (an island) in the sea, (consisting of) gold, silver, tin, copper, copper containers, linen garments with multi-colored trimmings, large and small monkeys, ebony, boxwood, ivory from walrus tusk—(thus ivory) a product of the sea,—(this) their tribute I received and they embraced my feet.[2]

We should also note that Syria was a country with skilled workers in many fields, and besides raw material, horses, and other commodities, Assyria needed manpower for both military and civil purposes, including the army and for land developments. Building canals and cities became possible with forced labor consisting mainly of peoples deported from conquered nations.[3] Syria-Palestine was accordingly a

---

1. D. Oates, *Studies in the Ancient History of Northern Iraq* (London, 1968); N.B. Jankowska, 'Some Problems of the Economy of the Assyrian Empire', *Ancient Mesopotamia, Socio-Economic History* (ed. I.M. Diakonoff; Moscow, 1969), pp. 253-76.

2. A.L. Oppenheim, *ANET*, p. 276.

3. This does not mean that all deportees were either in the army or in forced labor. Some could make a career in the royal court, as cheap labor for the temples, as free peasant or landholders on state properties, or other occupations; consult

territory of vital interest to a Mesopotamian nation, by virtue of its geographical position. Trade connections via land and sea with the west and south were possible only through the centers and trade routes of Syria-Palestine. The importance of the Phoenician and Philistine ports should be remembered in this connection. Nevertheless, trade alone did not solve Assyria's problems, even if Assyria had mastery of the trade routes. Military expansion was not solely a result of Assyria's lack of natural resources and luxury items. Expanding and/or migrating peoples also played an important role, forcing Assyria to control them to its own benefit. As time went on, Assyria's hunger for power and wealth grew to such an extent that it is tempting to characterize the Assyrian empire as a robber-state.[1] For Syria-Palestine this meant that as time went on the whole area down to the border of Egypt became satellite states or Assyrian provinces. The Phoenician city states were not incorporated as provinces, as was the rest of Syria. Because the Assyrians—as later the Persians—did not have control over nor the technical skill of maritime trade and ship-building, the Phoenicians managed to save their 'nationhood'. However, they were hard-pressed as 'suppliers of primary material' to the Assyrians. This represented 'a considerable change from their role as suppliers of manufactured commodities for elite consumptions'.[2] The role that the Phoenicians, and in some way also the Philistines, played in the Assyrian mercantile system had its counterpart in the east, where the Arabs, with their camel trains, were engaged for the safe conduct of supplies through the Syro-Arabian deserts.

Another important aspect of Assyrian imperialism should be recognized. As usual in the ancient Near East, the politics and the wars were those of the gods. The Assyrian king was often called *iššiak* $^d A \check{s} \check{s} ur$, 'Assur's vicar', which characterized him as the ruler of his

B. Oded, *Mass Deportations and Deportees in the Neo-Assyrian Empire* (Wiesbaden, 1979).

1. I.M. Diakonoff sees Assyria as a 'warrior empire' which not only took tribute and demanded exchange from its vassals and subdued peoples, but also resorted to robbery and looting ('Main Features of the Economy in the Monarchies of Ancient Western Asia', *Troisième conference internationale d'histoire et économique* [Paris, 1969], pp. 13-32).

2. S. Frankenstein, 'The Phoenicians in the Far West: A Function of Neo-Assyrian Imperialism', *Power and Propaganda* (ed. M. Trolle Larsen; Mesopotamia, 7; Copenhagen, 1979), p. 273.

god's domain, the nation.[1] Thus, if he built and reorganized the land, or went to war to extend the god's domain, all was done at the command of Assur, the god.[2] That is the basic ideology. The Mesopotamian cosmology (both the Assyrian and the Babylonian) saw the country as the center of the cosmos and thus of the world. This meant that chaos did not belong within the domains of Assyria. Chaos belonged to the foreign sector of the world, and it was therefore the nonorderly state of affairs that had to be defeated before cosmological order and peace could be established. This is the ideology behind the wars of Assyria. S. Parpola has characterized this as the missionary ideology that was the driving force behind Assyrian imperialism.[3] The ideology also depicts the king as a very pious man, the shepherd of his people who was chosen for that role by his god. Those who opposed the Assyrian king could be compared with wild animals such as wolves, and were slaughtered as such.[4] The king did not need to show mercy to the forces of evil, and so could flay a rival alive.

The new king of Damascus, Hazael, continued the anti-Assyrian policies of his predecessors. The Assyrian army was back in Syria in 840 (to the Cedar mountain), and in 838 and 837 it was in southern Syria and Damascus, taking some of the cities of Hazael,[5] but not Damascus itself. At this time Shalmaneser received tribute from Tyre, Sidon and Byblos.[6] Problems arose, however, in Assyria proper as well as with some neighbors to the north, especially with Urartu (the Bible's Ararat), which meant that the pressure upon Syria was lessened. Both Shalmaneser and his son, Shamshi-Adad V (824–810),

1. P. Garelli, 'Les temples et le pouvoir royal en Assyrie du XIVe au VIIIe siècle', *Le Temple et le Culte* (RAI, 20; Leiden 1975), pp. 116-17; M. Trolle Larsen, 'The City and its King on the Old Assyrian Notion of Kingship', *Le Palais et la Royauté* (RAI, 19; Paris, 1974), p.288; cf. S.N. Kramer, 'Sumerian Historiography', *IEJ* 3 (1953), p. 27; G.W. Ahlström, *Royal Administration*, pp. 2-3.

2. Thus, for example, Tiglath-Pileser I; see A.K. Grayson, *Assyrian Royal Inscriptions II*, p. 6

3. S. Parpola, 'Mesopotamia', in R. Holthoer, A. Parpola and S. Parpola, *Cappelens Verdenshistorie 2. Flodrikene* (Oslo, 1982), p. 244. For the 'Holy War' as a common ancient Near Eastern idea, see M. Weippert, '"Heiliger Krieg" in Israel und Assyrien', *ZAW* 84 (1972), pp. 460-93.

4. S. Parpola, 'Mesopotamia', p. 244.

5. Cf. E. Michel, 'Die Assur-Texte Salmanassars III (858–824)', *Die Welt des Orients*, I (ed. E. Michel *et al.*; Göttingen, 1947–52), pp. 269-70.

6. *ANET*, p. 280.

had to concentrate upon consolidating their power both in Assyria and against enemies in the Northern areas. The last years of the reign of Shalmaneser III were troubled with rebellions, one led by one of his sons.[1]

During this period of temporary weakness in Assyria, Hazael (841–801/800 BCE) could firmly establish his power structure. He tried to continue the Aramaean tradition of forging a defense coalition against Assyria or extending his territory in Palestine, thereby increasing the manpower of his army. Even though Hazael is mentioned in Assyrian inscriptions without vassal kings, his wars against Israel and Moab and his campaign in the Philistine territories (2 Kgs 12.17-18) may indicate that he tried to create a kingdom or a political alliance mighty enough to contend with the Assyrians. The former ally, Israel, had now become an Assyrian vassal. Jehu had sabotaged the Syro-Palestinian policy of resistance towards Assyria. Israel had to be brought into line again or its territory and power had to be reduced. Hazael's campaigns drastically changed the map of Palestine. He pushed southward through Transjordan down to Aroer at the Arnon River. Moab lost what it had regained under Mesha. A recollection of Hazael's war occurs in Amos 1.3, which says that the Aramaeans 'have thrashed Gilead with iron threshing sledges'. From this time the Aramaic language is increasingly used in Transjordan and the Jordan Valley down to Deir 'Alla and the Jabbok River (Wadi Zerqa) area.[2] At Deir 'Alla in the Jordan Valley (12 km north of the junction of the Jabbok and Jordan rivers, coord. 208-178), pottery from Iron II is different from the pottery at Cisjordanian sites. Artifacts such as figurines of humans and animals represent an Aramaean tradition.[3] With control of Transjordan down to the Arnon River (Wadi Mujib), Hazael obtained the income from and the control over the lucrative

1. Cf. J.E. Reade, *ZA* 68 (1978), pp. 259-60.

2. For the spread of Aramaic in the first half of the first millenium, see W.R. Garr, *Dialect Geography of Syria-Palestine, 1000–586 BCE* (Philadelphia, 1985).

3. H.J. Franken, *Excavations at Tell Deir 'Alla*; *idem*, *EAEHL*, I, p. 324. The texts on plaster fragments found at Deir 'Alla (mentioning the prophet Balaam) and dated to c. 700 BCE have usually been seen as being written in Aramaic, but have been seen by J. Hackett as being related to Ammonite and South Canaanite (*The Balaam Text from Deir 'Alla* [HSM, 31; Chico, CA, 1984], p. 8). According to W.R. Garr, the 'Deir 'Alla dialect reflects the basic phonological innovations of Old Aramaic', even though it 'shared some features with Hebrew (and Canaanite)' (*Dialect Geography*, p. 229).

trade route, the King's Highway. The picture to the west is the same. The trunk road from Egypt to Syria along the Palestinian coast came into the hands of Hazael, who penetrated through Galilee all the way south to Philistine Gath, which he took. He then threatened Jerusalem and its king Jehoash (2 Kgs 12.18). It is possible that Gath at that time was part of the kingdom of Judah, because there is no record of Hazael fighting the Philistines. Jehoash paid a heavy tribute; thus, both Israel and Judah should accordingly be seen as Hazael's vassals.

It is possible that Hazael annexed parts or all of Galilee when marching down to Gath (c. 815–14). If so, Israel would again have been a nation confined to the central hill country. This gives us an interesting perspective on the excavations at Hazor. Stratum VIII is assigned to the time of King Ahab, but could be somewhat earlier. In the following stratum (VII), most of the 'casemates' went completely out of use, and, contrary to the earlier time, 'ordinary dwelling-houses appear to be the rule'. In other words, the area had 'become a residential quarter'.[1] This change could have resulted from Hazor's capture by the Aramaeans, with stratum VII being built by them. There is also 'a noticeable difference between the pottery of stratum VIII and that of stratum VII'.[2]

---

1.   Y. Yadin, *Hazor of Those Kingdoms*, p. 169.

2.   Yadin *et al.*, *Hazor*, II, p. 16; cf. *Hazor*, I, p. 20. Yadin expresses the opinion that Hazor VII ended at the same time as Megiddo IV (*Hazor*, II, p. 19), but seeing that Megiddo stratum III is the Assyrian city, and the destruction of stratum VA at Hazor is dated to 732 BCE by Yadin and stratum VI is assigned to the time of Jeroboam II, the sentence in *Hazor*, II (p. 19) must be a mistake. For the chronology of the strata at Hazor, see conveniently Yadin, *Hazor of Those Kingdoms*, p. 200.

Chapter 14

THE ARAMEAN THREAT

The importance of Damascus[1] as a Syro-Palestinian power grew under
its new king Hazael. The city's economic wealth was well remembered
down through times (cf. Ezek. 27.18). Flavius Josephus, for instance,
mentions Hazael as one of the greatest benefactors of Damascus (*Ant.*
9.4.6). As to economy and inland trade, Damascus paralleled Tyre. As
the latter city was the shipping center and main port to the west, so
Damascus was the center of inland trade in Syria-Palestine to and
from Egypt, Mesopotamia and Arabia, and as such it early had close
connections with Tyre. This relationship was already in existence in
the early ninth century BCE. When Ben-Hadad I had taken Galilee
from Baasha of Israel, it made him the master of the trade routes to
Acco and the coast of the Phoenicians. Omri's treaty with Tyre can
therefore be seen as an attempt to stem the flow of wealth to Damascus
and thus to keep control over trade on Israelite territory. G. Levi
Della Vida has suggested that another daughter of Ethbaal, a sister to
Jezebel, would have been given in marriage to the king of Damascus,
who 'may have been prompt to express his devotion to the mighty god

1.   The original Aramaic form of the name may have been *di-maśq*, later Aram.
(?), *darmeśeq*, Akkadian *dimašqu/a*, Hebrew *dammeśeq* and *darmeśeq*, Arabic
dimašq (*eš-šam*); Egyptian lists from the Eighteenth Dynasty have *tí-ms-q3*; see the
discussion in M.F. Unger, *Israel and the Aramaeans of Damascus*, pp. 2-4; see also
E.G.H. Kraeling, *Aram and Israel or the Aramaeans in Syria and Mesopotamia*
(New York, 1918), pp. 46-47; F.M. Cross, 'The Stele Dedicated to Melchart by
Ben Hadad of Damascus', *BASOR* 205 (1972), p. 40. For the Akkadian *mātu ša
imērīšu*, 'the land of the donkey', referring to Damascus, see the comments of
A.L. Oppenheim, *ANET*, p. 278 n. 8. E. Gaál considers this phrase to be a
translation of Abinu/Upe, which in the Execration and Mari texts denoted the land of
Damascus, and *api*, with the meaning 'donkey' (*Revue Hittite et Asianique* 36
[1978], pp. 43-48).

of his father-in-law in setting up a stele' with the image of Melqart at Bredsh north of Aleppo.[1] This is, however, a mistaken interpretation of the text.[2] The date of the inscription is not quite certain. Paleographically it is close to the Zakkur inscription (from about the same area), which is dated to c. 780–770 BCE.[3] The Bredsh inscription could thus be from c. 800. The king mentioned on this stela, namely Bar-Hadad, is not the son of Hazael of Damascus, but a north-Syrian king.[4]

With Jehu's revolt, Israel's treaties with neighboring nations were immediately cancelled. Jehu may have seen the danger Assyria represented for the independence of the Syro-Palestinian nations, and, as a vassal of Assyria, he may have counted with Assyrian help in case of war. Because of the problems internal rebellions posed to Assyria, Urartu had an opportunity to expand. Jehu's submission to Assyria became politically disastrous. After 838 BCE Hazael not only occupied great parts of the Israelite territories, as mentioned above (2 Kgs 10.32),[5] but he seems to have made Israel a vassal to Aram-Damascus. In a war with Israel under Jehu's son, Jehoahaz, the Aramaeans almost destroyed Israel's defense forces, making them 'like dust'. What was left of Israel's army was '59 horsemen, 10 chariots and 10,000 foot soldiers' (the latter is a sum that either is exaggerated or should be read as ten 'companies') (2 Kgs 13.7). Israel had been reduced to a powerless nation. The picture that emerges concerning the reign of Jehoahaz (814–798), the son of Jehu, is gloomy indeed. The same may be said about Judah, which, under Joash, had to pay tribute to Hazael. This was done through almost emptying the palace and the temple of treasures (2 Kgs 12.18-20). Not much more is told about this king. He is said to have tried to repair the Solomonic temple, which may have been neglected during the reign of queen Athaliah. For this purpose he ordered the priest, Jehoiada, to send out priests and Levites to

1. 'Some Notes on the Stele of Ben-Hadad', *BASOR* 90 (1943), pp. 30-32; cf. W.F. Albright's response to and agreement with Della Vida on pp. 32-33. See also M.F. Unger, *Israel and the Aramaeans of Damascus*, p. 65.

2. W.T. Pitard, *Ancient Damascus: A Historical Study of the Syrian City-State from Earliest Times until its Fall to the Assyrians in 732 BCE* (Winona Lake, IN, 1987), pp. 138-44.

3. For the text, see H. Donner and W. Röllig, *KAI*, II, pp. 207-209; J.C.L. Gibson, *TSSI*, II, pp. 6-17.

4. In line 2 of the text Bar Hadad is mentioned as the son of *br 'trhmk*, according to Pitard's photograph.

5. Cf. E. Meyer, *Geschichte des Altertums*, II (Stuttgart, 1931), p. 337 n. 1.

collect money from the population. After some years the priest reluctantly did so—which does not indicate that the temple really had been neglected (2 Kgs 12.10-16).[1] The narrator commends Joash for doing 'what was right in the eyes of Yahweh' as long as the priest, Jehoiada, lived, but when he died Joash could do no good. He is then accused of having followed other gods, that is, 'poles and idols' (2 Chron. 24.17-25). This statement is in harmony with the Chronicler's ideology: the priest should lead the king, which meant that only as long as Jehoiada lived Joash could learn how to do what was right.[2] The Bible gives a distorted picture of the reign of Joash. He does not seem to have been a fortunate ruler, and his life ended at the hands of some conspirators (2 Kgs 12.21; 2 Chron. 24.25). His son Amaziah was made king after him (2 Kgs 12.22).

Concerning Judah's conflict with Aram-Damascus, the Chronicler maintains that Hazael's army reached Judah and Jerusalem and that the Arameans 'executed all the officials among the people' (2 Chron. 24.23). If this is right, Hazael's policy may have been to remove those at the top of the social ladder in order to prevent any opposition party becoming vocal and dangerous. Hazael must have known that this was also the system used by the Assyrians in subdued countries. The people forming the top stratum of the society (social group number one) were either killed or deported.

Having subdued Judah, most of Palestine and Transjordan were under Aramaean rule. What happened to the Philistines is not clear. Hazael took Gath,[3] but it is not known whether that city was under Judah or was ruled by the Philistines at that time. Amos 6.2 may indicate the latter. 2 Kgs 13.22 (LXX[L]) mentions that Hazael captured all of the Philistine territories up to Aphek. If Hazael had been

1. Because of the almost parallel wording in 2 Kgs 22.4-7, 9b, the authenticity of 2 Kgs 12.10-16 has been doubted; cf. E. Würthwein, who sees 12.10-12 as a fiction from the postexilic period (*Die Bücher der Könige, 1 Kön. 17–2. Kön. 25* [ATD, 11.2; Göttingen, 1984], pp. 357-58).

2. The narrator has obviously forgotten that Jehoiada must have been followed by another head priest. For this Chronistic ideology, see R. Mosis, *Untersuchungen zur Theologie des chronistischen Geschichtwerkes* (Freiburger Theologische Studien, 29; Freiburg, 1973), p. 18. I have called this 'adapted historiography' (*Royal Administration*, p. 64).

3. W.W. Hallo dates this to the twenty-third year of Joash of Judah and shortly after Jehu had died, 814 BCE ('From Qarqar to Carchemish: Assyria and Israel in the Light of New Discoveries', *BA* 23 [1960], p. 42).

battling the Philistines, it must have been part of his policy to get the main trade routes under control. Two main caravan routes went through the Philistine area: the trunk road from Egypt to the north, and the trade route from Arabia to Gaza. Having established control over both the King's Highway through Transjordan and the trunk road (later called Via Maris) along the Palestinian coast, giving him the monopoly on the trade with Egypt, Hazael must have been eager to establish some cooperation with the Arabs concerning trade with Arabia.[1] Hazael's policy seems to have been designed to create a new empire in Syria-Palestine, and he almost succeeded. In the period before the campaigns of the Assyrian king Adad-nirari III in the West, which started in his fifth year (805),[2] Damascus was never threatened by Assyria. 'By the time of Hazael's death virtually all of Syria-Palestine was probably answerable to Damascus'.[3] However, one of the states in the Orontes Valley that did not bow down to Hazael was Hamath. Irhuleni's successor, Zakkur (probably a usurper)[4] boasts of having been able to withstand a siege by a Syrian coalition headed by Bar Hadad of Damascus. This inscription indicates that Damascus dominated Syria up to Que in Cilicia.[5] However, it does not report how Zakkur survived the siege. As a 'pious' king, Zakkur refers to an oracle he received from his god Baal-Shamayn, saying, 'Fear not because it was I who made you king...and I shall deliver you from all [these kings]', (ll. 13-14).[6] One may assume that Zakkur

1. Cf. E.G.H. Kraeling, *Aram and Israel*, p. 81.

2. For the date, see D.D. Luckenbill, *ARAB*, I, pp. 260-61. See also H. Tadmor, *Iraq* 35 (1973), pp. 141-50. The reading *kur pa-la-aš-tú* in Adad-nirari's inscriptions H. Tadmor prefers to read as *māt ḥat-te*, 'the land of Hatti' (*IEJ* 19 [1969], p. 47).

3. J.M. Miller, 'The Melqart Stela and the Ben Hadads of Damascus', *PEQ* 115 (1983), p. 101.

4. In his self-presentation Zakkur does not give his father's name.

5. See H. Donner and W. Röllig, *KAI*, II, text 202; J.C.L. Gibson, *TSSI*, II, pp. 6-17. For the name Zakkur, see T. Nöldecke, 'Aramäische Inschriften', *ZA* 21 (1908), p. 376; J.C. Greenfield, 'The Dialects of Early Aramaic', *JNES* 37 (1978), p. 93 n. 9. In line 2 Zakkur says: 'I am a humble man', a phrase which has been compared with Zech. 9.9; cf. B . Otzen, *Studien über Deutero-Sacharja* (Copenhagen, 1964), p. 139 n. 18; H. Donner and W. Röllig, *KAI*, II, p. 206.

6. For the literary style of the Zakkur inscription, see J.C. Greenfield, 'The Zakir Inscription and the Danklied', *Proceedings of the Fifth World Congress of Jewish Studies* (Jerusalem, 1969), pp. 174-91. The inscription is a good example of

was an Assyrian vassal and perhaps had reached the throne through Assyrian support. Even if there is no reference in the Assyrian inscriptions to a campaign against Bar Hadad's coalition at this time, it would not have been impossible for a report to have been sent to the Assyrian king and for him to have sent out a contingent to the troubled spot as usual.[1] The Zakkur inscription does not specify when the siege of Hazrak took place. However, it is most unlikely that it occurred after 796 BCE when Damascus had been thoroughly defeated by Adad-nirari III, and its vassals, Philistia, Edom and Israel under king Joash (*Ia-à-su māt Sa-me-ri-na-a-a*)[2] had demonstrated their submission by paying tribute to the Assyrian king.[3] With the power of Damascus crushed and all the wealth of the city taken by the Assyrians,[4] as well as all Syria and most of Palestine in the Assyrian fold, there would have been no possibility for the king of Damascus to forge a new coalition so soon after his defeat.[5] Such an assumption is

the royal ideology of the ancient Near East: the god has put the king on the throne, he is called by the deity, and the king presents himself as a humble man. The text also expresses the concept of the gods playing a decisive role in history. For the role of prophecy, consult J.F. Ross, 'Prophecy in Hamath, Israel, and Mari', *HTR* 63 (1970), pp. 1-28.

1. For Assyrian control and intelligence network, see J.A. Brinkman, 'Babylonia under the Assyrian Empire', *Power and Propaganda* (ed. M. Trolle Larsen; Mesopotamia, 7; Copenhagen, 1979), p. 235.

2. This is the first time Samerina is used in Assyrian inscriptions for Israel; cf. S. Page, 'A Stela of Adad-nirari III and Nergal-ereš from Tell al-Rimah', *Iraq* 30 (1968), pp. 147-48; *idem*, 'Joash and Samaria in a New Stela Excavated at Tell al-Rimah', *VT* 19 (1969), p. 483. The 'savior' that rescued Israel, according to 2 Kgs 13.5, may have been Adad-nirari III; cf., among others, H. Schmökel, *Geschichte des alten Vorderasien* (Leiden, 1957), p. 259 n. 4; M. Haran, 'The Rise and Decline of the Empire of Jeroboam ben Joash', *VT* 17 (1967), pp. 267-68; Y. Aharoni, *The Land of the Bible* (2nd edn), p. 342. D.J. McCarthy considers vv. 4-6 as 'a theological construct, and it is idle to seek an historical source for it' ('2 Kings 13.4-6', *Bib* 54 [1973], p. 410).

3. A. Millard and H. Tadmor suggest that the tribute was paid in Damascus or in Manṣuate (in the Beqaʿ Valley) where Damascus was defeated ('Adad-nirari III in Syria: Another Stele Fragment and the Dates of his Campaigns', *Iraq* 35 [1973], pp. 62-64). The so-called Nimrud slab seems to indicate, however, that Damascus paid its tribute in Damascus after Adad-nirari had taken the city (D.D. Luckenbill, *ARAB*, I, par. 740, p. 263).

4. Cf. *ANET*, pp. 281-82; H.W.F. Saggs, *The Might that was Assyria*, p. 81.

5. As to the chronological problems of the campaigns of Adad-nirari III, see H. Tadmor, *Iraq* 35 (1973), pp. 141-50. Tadmor maintains that both the al-Rimah

especially doubtful when it is considered that several kings of the confederation were rulers from kingdoms north of Hamath, including Agusi, Que, Sam'al, Umq, Melid and Gurgum. There is no information that Damascus had regained its military strength before the time of Rezin, the last king of Aram-Damascus.[1] The imperial aspirations of Damascus seem to have been terminated by Adad-nirari III as its independence was terminated by Tiglath-pileser III.

Whether Adad-nirari had been able to 'pacify' Syria-Palestine is doubtful. Shortly after his victory over Damascus he became engaged with Assyria's northern and southern neighbors. This situation continued during the reigns of Adad-nirari's successors, Shalmaneser IV (782–772), Assur-dan III (772–755), and Assur-nirari V (754–745). Also, internal problems and the expansion of Urartu, which comprised part of northern Syria, weakened Assyria considerably.[2] In this situation Damascus again tried to raise the banner of resistance and independence, but having opponents in Hamath in the north and Israel in the south the attempts to form a new Syro-Palestinian coalition against Assyria failed.

The textual material does not indicate what the political status of Hamath-Luash was during this period. According to the Eponym List,[3] Assur-dan III campaigned against Hatarikka (Hadrach)[4] in Luash three times, and once campaigned against Mopor.[5] It seems then that Hamath was an independent nation in the mid-eighth century BCE. The Zakkur inscription also suggests such independence. Because it does not mention Assyria, the text could have been engraved after

inscription as well as the Saba'a stele were inscribed after 797 BCE (p. 148).

1.   Tiglath-pileser III conquered Damascus in 734 BCE and put an end to its independence by making it a province of his empire.

2.   A.T. Olmstead mentions that after having defeated Damascus, the Assyrians carried with them to Assyria not only the loot and the tribute but also a bubonic plague. This would have been the same as the pestilence 'like Egypt's plague' mentioned in Amos 4.10. This then is one of the internal problems contributing to Assyria's weakness during the following period (*History of Assyria*, pp. 164, 171).

3.   For this list see *ANET*, p. 274.

4.   Hadrach is mentioned in Zech. 9.1-3, which gives a 'promise' that all Syria-Palestine will be part of Yahweh's new domain. See B. Otzen, *Studien über Deutero-Sacharja*, pp. 100-105.

5.   M.F. Unger, *Israel and the Aramaeans of Damascus*, p. 87. Cf. W.W. Hallo, *BA* 23 (1960), p. 44.

Zakkur had gained full independence. If the information of the Zakkur inscription is combined with 2 Kgs 13.25, which mentions that Joash defeated Bar-Hadad three times and recaptured the cities Bar-Hadad had taken from Jehoahaz,[1] it can be concluded that Zakkur under Hamath had had success against Damascus and that Damascus's power was now so low that even the small kingdom of Israel could minimize its territory by force. This could perhaps be put in a wider perspective. I have maintained that Zakkur was possibly pro-Assyrian, at least to begin with, because there were only two alternatives for him: either he had to join forces with Damascus or he had to be allied with Assyria. Even if Urartu had gained ground in northern Syria during the time of Assyria's decline, its geographical location north of Assyria made it less reliable as a supporting superpower. As for Israel, it should be remembered that it was still legally a vassal to Assyria. What diplomacy may have taken place preceding the battles remains unknown, but the possibility should not be discounted that Israel and Hamath effectively served the interests of Assyria in fighting against Damascus.

In these years of Assyrian decline after the power of Damascus had been arrested, Israel under Joash (798–782) could begin to recover. He must have been able to rebuild the Israelite army, which made it possible for him to retake some of the territory lost during his father's reign. He also successfully fought Judah and its king Amaziah, son of Joash. Having killed his father's murderers in order to secure his throne, Amaziah went to war successfully against Edom (2 Kgs 14.7). He also challenged Joash of Israel. Joash thought that a war between the two countries was meaningless but Amaziah insisted, with the result that he was thoroughly beaten at Beth-shemesh and taken prisoner, a most humiliating event for both Judah and its king. His goal may have been to gain control once again over the trade routes to the Gulf of Aqaba. It is possible that Amaziah had Israelite support for this project (2 Chron. 25.4-24), but that he did not want to share

---

1. According to M. Haran, these cities would have been located in Cisjordan, not in Transjordan (*VT* 17 [1967], p. 270). The vagueness of the biblical information makes it impossible to say where these cities were located, but, because the Aramaeans had taken Galilee under Hazael, Hazor, for example, may have returned to Israel. The possibility cannot be dismissed that Joash had recovered some of the Transjordanian territory.

the control of the trade with Israel.[1] This could have led to the war between two nations. Having entered Jerusalem, Joash tore down parts of its city walls, looted the palace and the temple, and took some hostages with him to Samaria (2 Kgs 14.13-14; cf. 2 Chron. 25.23-24).[2] He did not put Judah under his own crown, obviously understanding that the time for such a union was gone, but Judah may have become a vassal to Israel. The next reported incident involving Amaziah of Judah is a rebellion that broke out against him. He fled to the fortress city of Lachish, but the conspirators pursued him and killed him there (2 Kgs 14.19-20; 2 Chron. 25.27-28). His body was taken back on horseback to Jerusalem, where he was buried. Interesting to note is that the text says that 'all the people of Judah' put Amaziah's son Azariah (Uzziah) on the throne (2 Kgs 14.21). This statement may indicate that the *coup d'état* did not have popular backing and that Amaziah's murderers may be sought within the military and/or court circles.

An assessment of the cultural situation in Palestine from the time of Jehu's revolt down to the time of Jeroboam II and Uzziah is hard to make. One may agree with Y. Aharoni that 'there is a sharp deterioration in both kingdoms in every sphere' of life because of the dominant position of the kingdom of Aram-Damascus, even if this is not clearly shown by the archaeological material.[3] There are, however, certain facts to be taken into consideration. The fine masonry and the so-called proto-Ionic capitals disappear from Samaria, and the buildings from the eighth century BCE show a rough type of masonry making them architecturally poorer than those of the Omri–Ahab period.[4] This may have been one result of Jehu's revolt, which terminated the treaty with Tyre. It is to be expected that the Phoenician craftsman

---

1. Cf. Y. Aharoni, *The Land of the Bible* (2nd edn), p. 344.

2. Most interesting is that the Chronicler does not mention the temple of Yahweh but the temple of *hā'elōhîm* of which Obed Edom was in charge. There could have been a temple dedicated to the deity Edom (a goddess) in Jerusalem and the Chronicler may have tried to 'save' the Solomonic temple from being robbed. For Obed Edom as the priest of the deity Edom in Jerusalem, see G.W. Ahlström, *JNES* 43 (1984), p. 146. 2 Chron. 25.14 mentions that Amaziah, after having defeated Edom, 'brought the gods of the sons of Seir with him'. This would explain the plural *hā'elōhîm*, and that Obed Edom, 'the servant of Edom', was the head priest in that temple.

3. *The Archaeology of the Land of Israel*, pp. 250-51.

4. K.M. Kenyon, *Archaeology in the Holy Land* (4th edn), p. 282.

left Israel after Jehu had taken over the government. An Israelite building tradition probably had not had time to develop to the point that it could compete with that of the Phoenician masters. Art and elegance left with the Phoenicians. It is unlikely that Phoenician craftsmen would have worked in most of the cities of the hill country, because many of them were store-cities. Besides the capitals, the Phoenician architects probably worked in cities with local governor 'palaces'. In the two nations of Israel and Judah Phoenician masonry and proto-Ionic capitals have been found in archaeological digs at Megiddo, Hazor, Jerusalem and Ramat Rahel, but not for instance, in Mizpah.[1]

Religiously, the picture is blurred by the biblical writer's tendentious attitude. The nonbiblical sources, mainly archaeological material, for the religious circumstances during the ninth and eighth centuries BCE seem to indicate that the religious scene was quite different from that presented in the Bible. The Canaanite inheritance is still strong. Idols, cult places and figurines belong to the picture of any religion in Palestine of this time, Judahite and Israelite, Phoenician, Philistine or Aramaean. The many figurines of naked women, of horses and bulls found in the soil of Palestine (and most of them come from Jerusalem and Judah[2]) point in a certain direction which is not that of the so-called pure Yahwistic ideology. The prophetic polemics against idols and sanctuaries other than the Jerusalemite temple is a good source of information for what the religious scene really looked like. There were a great number of sanctuaries, *bāmôt*, all over the country. It would be enough to refer to 2 Kgs 18.4, which mentions that Hezekiah of Judah 'removed'[3] all the *bāmôt*, or to 2 Kgs 23.19, which states that king Josiah 'removed' all the *bāttê habbāmôt* ('houses of the sacred precincts') which the kings of Israel had built in the cities of their

---

1. See, for instance, R. Engberg, 'The Design on Pottery with Suggestions Concerning Origin of Proto-Ionic Capitals', *Material Remains of the Megiddo Cult* (ed. H.G. May; OIP, 26; Chicago, 1935), pp. 39-41; R.W. Hamilton, *Guide to Samaria-Sebaste* (Jerusalem, 1947), p. 7 fig. 5; consult further T.A. Busink, *Der Tempel von Jerusalem*, I, p. 176 (with lit.); Y. Shiloh, *BASOR* 222 (1976), pp. 67-77.

2. Consult T.A. Holland, *Levant* 9 (1977), pp. 121-55.

3. It should be noted that the Hebrew term, *hēsîr*, does not mean 'destroy', but 'remove'; thus, Hezekiah terminated their legal status as official sanctuaries, which may have been economically disastrous for their priesthood.

kingdom. In other words, these were the official sanctuaries.[1] Another important piece of information is given in Ezek. 44.10 concerning the Levites serving idols. The drawings and inscriptions from Kuntillet 'Ajrud also belong to this period around 800 BCE. This outpost in the northern Sinai (c. 50 km south of Kadesh-Barnea) has provided information about the religion that has been consciously suppressed by the biblical writers. Most important is the text that mentions 'Yahweh of Shomeron and his Asherah' and the parallel phrase 'Yahweh of Teman and his Asherah' showing that Yahweh from of old had a consort.[2] This seems to have been the case also before Yahweh entered Canaan from Teman.[3]

The fact has to be faced that the Yahwism of the deuteronomistic writer(s) had not yet been invented.[4] Therefore, the pure Yahwistic attitude towards past times cannot be used to proclaim that the nation of Israel, for instance, 'was inwardly rotten and sick',[5] because two prophets, Hosea and Amos, despised almost everything that occurred in Israel. Note that Amos was not even an Israelite. He was from Judah and is therefore a representative of a tradition hostile to Israel. It must be acknowledged that we simply do not have enough information about the religious, social and ethical phenomena of the nation Israel to justify making a statement such as that of Bright. The product of ecstasy and the subjectivism of a few prophets, who have been chosen as ideological spokesmen for the later Yahwistic compilers of the textual material, cannot be used as a reliable source

1.   W.B. Barrick has seen that *bāmôt* 'were urban installations, capable of being "built", "torn down", and "burned" and were not necessarily located on high grounds' (*SEÅ* 45 [1980], p. 56). For a building, a *liškâ* at a *bāmâ* (1 Sam. 9.22), cf. W. Robertson Smith, *Lectures on the Religion of the Semites* (New York, 1927), p. 254; G.W. Ahlström, *VT* 11 (1961), p. 119.

2.   This I have maintained already in my book, *Aspects of Syncretism*, pp. 50-51.

3.   For the Kuntillet 'Ajrud phenomena, see Z. Meshel, 'Did Yahweh have a Consort', *BARev* 5 (1979), pp. 33-34; *idem*, 'Kuntillet 'Ajrud: An Israelite Religious Center in Northern Sinai', *Expedition* 20.4 (1978), pp. 50-54; J.A. Emerton, *ZAW* 94 (1982), pp. 2-20; G.W. Ahlström, *An Archaeological Picture of Iron Age Religions in Ancient Palestine*, pp. 18-21.

4.   See, for instance, G.W. Ahlström, *An Archaeological Picture of Iron Age Religions in Ancient Palestine*, pp. 5-7.

5.   J. Bright, *A History of Israel* (3rd edn), p. 266.

for historiography.[1] There is always room for criticism in any society. In this case, however, there is no information about the Israelite society in the time before these prophets, nor is there full information about how 'sick' or 'healthy' the neighboring nations were.

It has been seen how the power of Damascus was decreasing during the first part of the eighth century BCE and how the Assur-friendly Hamath-Luash played an important role in this respect. Joash managed to regain some of its lost territory from Damascus. Joash's successor, Jeroboam II (782–752?),[2] seems to have been able to extend the territory of his nation. 2 Kgs 14.28 indicates that he ruled over both Damascus and Hamath. However, because the Hebrew text says that Jeroboam 'returned Damascus and Hamath to Judah in Israel',[3] the information is doubtful. Earlier in the same chapter (v. 25) the narrator has mentioned that Jeroboam 'returned (recovered) the territory of Israel, from the entrance of Hamath (*l^{e}bô' h^{a}māt*), to the sea of Arabah', according to the words of the prophet Jonah. The entrance of Hamath has often been understood to be Lebo-Hamath in the Beqa' Valley, close to the border of Hamath.[4] Amos 6.13-14 refers to Israel rejoicing over having taken Qarnaim and Lodebar in Transjordan, which most probably refers to events during the reign of Jeroboam II. It is not known how much of southern Transjordan was taken, if any.

1. It ought to be clear that the so-called biblical literary prophets were not the official spokesmen of the religions of Israel and Judah. That would be almost the same as to declare, for instance, Zwingli, Luther and Calvin as the official spokesmen for Roman Catholicism or Greek Orthodoxy.

2. 2 Kgs 14.23 gives Jeroboam a reign of 41 years. E.R. Thiele counts a co-regency with Joash for 12 years, dating Joash to 798–782/81 and Jeroboam II to 793/92–753 (*JBL* 93 [1974], pp. 191-92).

3. E. Würthwein prefers to see the mention of Judah here as a reference to the north-Syrian nation Yaudi, which is known from Assyrian inscriptions. Accordingly, he translates *lyhwdh* with 'von Jehuda' (see the discussion of this in *Könige*, II, pp. 374-75). The preposition *l-* does not stand for 'von'. The phrase may be seen as an expression for the idea that Jeroboam regained some territories that once 'belonged' to David, and that Judah now was really a vassal to Israel. This incorporation would then have happened before Uzziah managed to increase Judah's territory and independence.

4. Cf. Y. Aharoni, *The Land of the Bible* (2nd edn), p. 344; J. Bright, *A History of Israel* (3rd edn), p. 257; H. Donner in J.H. Hayes and J.M. Miller, *Israelite and Judean History*, p. 414.

Amos 6.14 indicates that the border was down at the Nahal Arabah;[1] if this means the Arabah south of the Dead Sea, Israelite territory ought to have included Moab also. This would certainly have been mentioned if it were the case. The vagueness of the report of Jeroboam's wars and the geographically unclear information makes the whole story about Jeroboam's 'empire' somewhat doubtful. The people's rejoicing over Lodebar and Qarnaim seems to support the opinion that Jeroboam took part of Transjordan. According to M. Noth, Lebo-Hamath would be a site at the northern end of the Golan (Jolan) heights.[2] From this it is doubtful that Jeroboam would have taken Hamath (or ruled it through a vassal king.)

Damascus also presents a problem: Did Jeroboam really take Damascus and the remainder of its territory?[3] Through diplomacy, Assyria could have encouraged Jeroboam, whom it still considered a vassal, to march on Damascus, but there is no indication for this. However, Assyria could have asked its 'ally' Israel to invade Damascus at the same time Shalmaneser IV attacked Damascus in 773.[4] This would then have been the time when Jeroboam had the opportunity to invade Transjordan. As for the idea that Jeroboam 'recovered' or occupied Damascus, it may be suspected that the writer has made more out of Jeroboam's wars in the north than reality would allow for. In Amos 6.12-14 there is no rejoicing over Damascus (nor over Hamath) in connection with the mention of the retaking of Damascene territory by Israel. The problem faced here is certainly not a historical one but a literary one.[5] The text is a good parallel to David's conquests. The occurrence of the name of Lebo-Hamath in 2 Kgs 14.25 has led the narrator to recall the kingdom of Hamath, which paid tribute to David (2 Sam. 8.9-10). This, plus the fact that Jeroboam was able to take back some territories that Damascus had occupied earlier under Hazael, was enough to build up Jeroboam as a great

1.   M. Noth identifies this with *naḥal hāᶜrābîm*, 'Pappelbach', 'The Brook of the Willows' in the oracle on Moab in Isa. 15.7 (*Aufsätze*, p. 272); cf. Y. Aharoni, *The Land of the Bible* (2nd edn), p. 344.

2.   *Aufsätze*, pp. 271-72.

3.   M.F. Unger theorizes that Damascus may have been annexed to Israel but that Hamath would have been given the status of a vassal kingdom (*Israel and the Aramaeans*, pp. 92-93).

4.   Cf. H.W.F. Saggs, *The Might that was Assyria*, p. 82.

5.   Cf. H. Donner, in J.H. Hayes and J.M. Miller, *Israelite and Judean History*, p. 414.

conqueror and to model him after David.[1] This explains the not-so-exact information about the territorial extension of Jeroboam's kingdom. In taking Damascus and its territory up to Lebo-Hamath, Jeroboam incorporated into his kingdom the northern part of the 'land that still remained' (cf. Josh. 13.2), as David is said to have done. The use of the verb *šwb* (in *hiph.* = return) is another indication that Jeroboam has been built up as a great conqueror. With the above understanding of the text the problem of when Jeroboam could have taken Damascus and Hamath disappears.[2] He never did. Therefore, Israel did not include 'almost the same territories as under David', as Aharoni expresses it.[3] The borders are usually not mentioned by the writers. In the case of Jeroboam, it has been noted that part of Transjordan down to the 'sea of the Arabah' came under his scepter (2 Kgs 14.25). Since the Sea of Arabah was probably the northern end of the Dead Sea, it may be assumed that Transjordan down to the Plains of Moab was now Israelite again.[4] In the north, Galilee was probably also back within Israel, and it is most probable that the coastal area north of Philistia to Carmel again came under Israelite rule. In other words, Samaria had restored its control over the trade

---

1. Even though Jeroboam theological is negatively judged according to the principle that all kings of Israel did what was evil in the eyes of Yahweh, the biblical narrator has made him a 'savior' (2 Kgs 14.27).

2. The only time possible for Jeroboam to have besieged and taken Hamath would have been after 754, when the new Assyrian king Assur-nirari V (755–745) accepted a treaty with Mati'ilu (Matiel) of Agusi in northern Syria. With the Assyrian army in northern Syria Jeroboam might have dared, as an ally, to go against Damascus and perhaps also Hamath. Mati'ilu, however, soon broke the treaty and accepted a vassal treaty with Bar-Gayah of KTK of the Urartu coalition. Thus, the situation changed very quickly and it is less than probable that Jeroboam would have been involved in any war as far north as Hamath. For the Mati'ilu treaty texts, see *KAI*, I, H. Donner and W. Röllig, texts 222-24, J.C.L. Gibson, *TSSI*, II, pp. 18-56; *ANE Suppl.*, pp. 532-33; cf. A. Dupont-Sommer and J. Starcky, 'Les inscriptions araméennes de Sfire', *Mémoires presentées par divers savants à l'Academie des inscriptions et belles-lettres* (Tome XV; Paris, 1958), pp. 197-351; also 'Une inscription araméenne inedite de Sfire', *Bulletin du Musée de Beyrouth* 13 (1956), pp. 23-41; M. Noth, 'Die historische Hintergrund der inschriften von Sefire', *ZDPV* 77 (1961), pp. 118-72; J.A. Fitzmyer, *The Aramaic Inscriptions of Sefire* (Rome, 1967).

3. Y. Aharoni, *The Land of the Bible* (2nd edn), p. 344.

4. This is exactly the southern end of the new Assyrian province Gal'aza (Gilead) that Tiglath-pileser III created in 733 BCE (cf. *ANET*, p. 283).

routes from Philistia up through Galilee and through Transjordan north of Moab to the borders of the Damascus kingdom.

The regaining of both territory and military strength together with the control of the important trunk roads from Egypt to Syria and Mesopotamia must have meant an increase in commodities and material wealth for the country, especially for the upper classes. The portraits Amos and Hosea have painted show that Israel was well off materially. This may be true, but as mentioned above, the sociological circumstances and the material culture and welfare of the nation cannot be more than imagined from such sources. Prophets were usually religious fanatics and cultural reactionaries, and so their evaluations are of dubious value in a historiographic reconstruction of the past. It is of course possible that H. Donner is correct that wealth 'promoted an unfortunate social cleavage of the population into rich and poor, masters and slaves, owners of large estates and landless farmers', and that this is to be learned from the 'prophetic message of Amos'.[1] This kind of cleavage in the population seems to be part of human history—and still is. There is no way to describe the social stratification of Israel because there is simply not enough evidence. The words of one prophet only—and a Judahite at that!—are not a reliable basis for a sociological analysis of Israel. Neither can it be said that the state 'did little or nothing to alleviate' the hard lot of the 'humbler' population.[2] This is probably true, but there is no material available for any kind of historical analysis.

The polemics in the books of Amos and Hosea suggest that the religion of Israel was quite wrong.[3] The message of the book of Amos is really the death of the nation of Israel,[4] because of its wrong cult

1. In J.H. Hayes and J.M. Miller, *Israelite and Judean History*, p. 414.

2. J. Bright, *A History of Israel* (3rd edn), p. 259.

3. This is the basis for the social criticism in the book of Amos. A wrong cult can only give a wrong code of ethics as its product. Cf. G.W. Ahlström, 'Some Remarks on Prophets and Cults', *Transitions in Biblical Scholarship* (ed. J.C. Rylaarsdam; Chicago, 1968), pp. 113-29.

4. Cf. R. Martin-Achard, *Amos: L'homme, le message, l'influence* (Geneva, 1984), pp. 156-58. It must be remembered that some of these utterances have been put into the mouth of Amos by the postexilic 'editor' of the Book of the Twelve Prophets. For instance, Amos 6.9-10 is a later *ex eventu* oracle justifying King Josiah's destruction of sanctuaries and his murder of priests in the former kingdom of Israel that was now the Assyrian province of Samerina (cf. my article, 'King Josiah and the DWD of Amos 6, 10', *JSS* 26 [1981], pp. 7-9).

and thus its wrong ethics. The book of Amos serves as a reminder that there were two official Yahweh traditions, the northern state religion of Israel, and the southern one of Judah. Amos, being a southerner, denounces a Yahweh religion of which he is not a part. In addition, his words were fixed in their present form in the postexilic period and that he, like other 'literary' prophets in the Bible, has been used as a spokesman for the late pure-Yahwistic ideology. According to this ideology the nation of Israel should never have existed because it split off from the Davidic dynasty and from loyalty to Yahweh of Jerusalem. Realizing this, it would even be hard to give an objective outline of the socio-ethical conditions during the period of Jeroboam II's regime.

The conflict between the head priest of Bethel's royal temple and the Judahite prophet Amos from Tekoa (Amos 7.10-17) can be cited as a good illustration of how the situation has been misjudged on the basis of a preconceived notion that literary prophets always were right and that priests were paid officials who only performed their duties, but did not have their hearts in it. Amos, a man from the nation of Judah, goes to the national shrine of the nation of Israel at Bethel—on foreign territory—and denounces the whole nation, its king, priests, upper class, common people, and the nation's religious and social system. The theme is that the nation is practically dead. That would be enough for anybody to throw the prophet out (according to a modern maxim, 'like it or leave it'). Amos was indeed expelled (Amos 7.12-13). The utterances of doom given by Amos[1] must have caused a great surprise to the people of Israel. They lived in a time of military success and national prosperity, all of which must have been understood as signs of blessings from Yahweh. There was, therefore, no logical foundation for a condemnation of the nation. The clash between the priest Amaziah of Bethel and the prophet from Tekoa in Judah represents the clash and outlooks of two Yahwistic traditions.[2]

---

1. How many of these really stem from Amos is impossible to say. Amos certainly would have made some sharp denunciations, but the later 'editor' may have sharpened some of them and, as a disciple of a true prophet, added some in the style of the prophet but with the knowledge of what happened to the nation Israel. He also has given them such a form that he could make Amos into a 'true' prophet by making his oracles came to pass.

2. Another problem raised by the text is the extent to which Amos can be called a representative of the Judahite Yahweh tradition and how much he is a

The religious conflict mirrored in the confrontation between Amaziah and Amos is of quite different dimensions than that of the 'moral component of the covenant', which now, according to M. Greenberg, was supposedly 'for the first time given priority over the cultic'.[1]

It is no wonder that moderns in their anticultic attitude have been so appreciative of the emphasis on ethics (doing good) and social justice in the Book of Amos. Amos has been validated, more or less without criticism and real knowledge about this ancient religion, as a representative of some 'higher religion'. In modern times religion and ethics have very often been seen as identical phenomena, but they are not identical. It should be noted that when Amos says 'seek good and not evil' (5.14), he means the same thing as he did in 5.4, namely, seek Yahweh. For Amos, this Yahweh is the god of the southern kingdom.

A somewhat later contemporary to Amos was the prophet Hosea. He was probably of northern origin, but his book shows the same Jerusalemite-postexilic hatred of the north as that found in Amos.[2] If the prophecies in the book of Amos are concerned primarily with the official national temple cult at Bethel, the book of Hosea provides supplementary picture that deals with the whole nation. In the book of Hosea, the religion of the nation Israel very much shows itself to be a cultural continuum of the Old Canaanite forms, ideas and paraphernalia, something which is to be expected when so many Israelites were descendants of Canaanites. The book talks about cult places on the tops of mountains and hills (8.11), 'under oak and poplar and terebinth'. The people ask the 'wood' for an oracle 'and the rod gives the answer' (4.12). The country is full of altars (12.12). Hosea mentions Samaria's calf (8.5-6), which is not identical with Jezebel's Baal, whose temple is now destroyed. The term 'Samaria's calf' is rather a 'tendentious term for the cultic establishment of the capital'.[3] In Gilgal, Israel's gods were worshipped in bull forms: 'they sacrificed to bulls' (12.12). The calves of Bethel and Dan are thus not

product of deuteronomism and postexilic ideology.

1.   'Religion: Stability and Ferment', *The World History of the Jewish People*, IV.2, p. 112.

2.   The same problem occurs here as it did in Amos: How much of the message stems from Hosea and to what extent has he been used and his utterances edited by the later pure-Yahwistic circle of tradents?

3.   G.W. Ahlström, *Royal Administration*, p. 62.

the only ones in the nation. In another passage, Israel's gods are said to be molten images made of silver and gold (8.4; 13.2). The men go together with whores and with holy women, *qdšwt*, to sacrifice (4.14). What can be concluded from the books of Amos and Hosea is that the picture drawn by the deuteronomistic historian about what supposedly was Israelite religion is more of an ideal than a reality. Hosea and Amos have shown what Israelite religion was all about. The so-called deuteronomistic Yahwism or pure-Yahwism did not yet exist. It became a reality first in the postexilic period.[1]

The finds from excavations of Tel Dan should be included in any discussion of the religion of the northern kingdom Israel. A large platform dating to the tenth–ninth centuries has been uncovered. It has been considered the sacred platform for the bull figure crafted by Jeroboam I. In the time of Jeroboam II, the platform was surrounded by a large courtyard and had 14 steps leading up to it. Whether this this platform should be compared with the *temenos* platforms containing a cultic structure that date to the Persian period and later is uncertain. The platform of Tel Dan shows no indication that any kind of structure was built upon it.[2] Perhaps the platform only had an altar and an image of Yahweh, the bull.

A rare piece of information about economy and agriculture is given by the 65 ostraca found in a storehouse on the acropolis of Samaria. They all deal with the delivery of olive oil and wine to the capital, probably from royal estates. They give the place names, dates and the names of the officials (?) who received the products for further transportation to Samaria. From Egyptian parallels M. Noth has concluded that the Samaria ostraca are notations of shipments from the royal estates.[3] The date of the ostraca is debated. The excavators, G.M. Crowfoot and K.M. Kenyon, dated them to the first half of the eighth century BCE.[4] They feel this date is supported by an alabaster jar

---

1. Consult also my *Aspects of Syncretism*, and my *An Archaeological Picture of Iron Age Religions in Ancient Palestine*.

2. A. Biran, *BA* 43 (1980), p. 176.

3. 'Das Krongut der Israelitischen Könige und seine Verwaltung', *ZDPV* 37 (1941), p. 64 (= *Aufsätze*, p. 170).

4. *The Objects from Samaria* (London, 1957), p. 169. Kenyon also suggests that the ostraca would suit the time of Jehu's son Jehoahaz (*Archaeology in the Holy Land* [4th edn], p. 284). According to Y. Aharoni, only the time of Jehu, Jehoahaz and Jeroboam II can be considered (*The Land of the Bible* [2nd edn], p. 366).

bearing the name of pharaoh Osorkon II, which was found beside some of the ostraca.[1] This would mean that the earliest time for the ostraca would be the mid-ninth century BCE. However, Y. Yadin and others have dated them later on paleographic grounds, placing them in the last decades of the northern kingdom.[2] The places mentioned in the ostraca are all in the area of Solomon's first district, the northern area of Ephraim's mountains, and they are also known from the genealogy of Manasseh (Num. 26.30-37).[3] The ostraca cannot be used as proof for the organization of the country into administrative districts. If the ostraca do not refer to royal estates, however, they may indicate that the shipments of wine and oil came from large estates to the court officials in Samaria.[4] As such the ostraca may illustrate the type of corruption of the upper classes that Amos so sharply denounced (Amos 2.6-16; 4.1-3).[5] The personal names in the ostraca also provide information pertaining to religion. The theophoric components Yahu and Baal occur in a ratio of 11:7.[6]

Interestingly enough, this indicates that Yahweh of Hosea's time could have been more popular (among the government officials?) than Baal. It also indicates that the old indigenous Baal of Canaan-Israel

1. In a relief showing Osorkon II on a portable throne is an inscription just under the throne saying: 'All land, all countries, Upper Retenu, Lower Retenu, all inaccessible countries are under the feet of this Good God' (J.H. Breasted, *Ancient Records of Egypt*, IV, par. 749, p. 372). There is no information from any other source that Osorkon ruled parts of Syria-Palestine, even though a statue of Osorkon II has been found at the excavations in Byblos (M. Dunand, *Fouilles de Byblos, Texte*, I [Paris, 1939], pp. 115-17, and no. 1749). One statue and a jar do not make an empire. Osorkon may have used the old style of self-predication. The imperial dream was still alive.

2. See the discussion in Y. Yadin, 'Recipients or Owners: A Note on the Samaria Ostraca', *IEJ* 9 (1959), pp. 184-87; W.H. Shea, 'The Date of Significance of the Samaria Ostraca', *IEJ* 27 (1977), pp. 16-27; A.F. Rainey, *Tel Aviv* 6 (1979), pp. 91-94; cf. also F.M. Cross, 'Ammonite Ostraca from Heshbon', *AUSS* 13 (1975), pp. 8-10.

3. This says nothing about the tribe of Manasseh or its age. The tribal reconstruction has used geographic names. Cf. also S. Herrmann, *A History of Israel* (2nd edn), p. 238.

4. A.F. Rainey, *Tel Aviv* 6 (1979), pp. 93-94; F.M. Cross, *AUSS* 13 (1975), pp. 8-10.

5. Cf. S. Herrmann, *A History of Israel* (2nd edn), pp. 238-39.

6. W.F. Albright, *Archaeology and Religion of Israel* (4th edn), p. 160.

may have occupied a strong position next to Yahweh in the Israelite society.

In Judah, Amaziah's son and successor Azariah(u) was 16 years of age when he came to the throne and is said to have been king for 52 years (786–734) (2 Kgs 15.1). In some passages, he is called Uzziah.[1] It is not clear which one was his throne name. The name Azriau, which occurs in the Annals of Tiglath-pileser III in connection with names of North-Syrian states, has been seen as a reference to Azariah-Uzziah of Judah. However, the name of the country of this Azriau is not mentioned. In addition, N. Na'aman has refuted the theory that Azriau of Yaudi was mentioned in a text of Sargon II. The text was written by Sennacherib, not Sargon II, probably in connection with his Palestinian campaign of 701 BCE.[2]

The brief information in 2 Kgs 15.1-7 says nothing about Azariah's rule beyond the usual complaint that the kings preceding Hezekiah did not do anything about the many *bāmôt* sanctuaries of the land. Nevertheless, the later writer thinks that he did what was right in the eyes of Yahweh. He is said to have been stricken by an incurable sickness, *ṣāra'at*, leprosy or some other skin disease,[3] which forced him to hand over the reins of government to his son Jotham (2 Kgs 15.5).[4] The Chronicler attributes his illness to an incident in which Uzziah supposedly tried to sacrifice to Yahweh; that would have been the king's sin (2 Chron. 26.17-21). Here we again meet the postexilic idea of the king's function, which was supposedly to be sharply separated from that of the priest. The truth behind this story is rather that

1. According to Isa. 6.1 Isaiah received his temple vision in the same year that Uzziah died.

2. *ANET*, p. 282. See the discussion by N. Na'aman ('Sennacherib's "Letter to God" on his Campaign to Judah', *BASOR* 214 [1974], pp. 25-39). Cf. also B. Otzen, who points to the fact that Judah did not pay any tribute in 738, which is 'the main obstacle' for accepting the theory about Azariau of Yaudi being identified with Azariah-Uzziah of Judah ('Israel under the Assyrians', *Power and Propaganda* [ed. M. Trolle Larsen; Mesopotamia, 7; Copenhagen, 1979], p. 253).

3. See on this subject E.V. Hulse, 'The Nature of Biblical "Leprosy" and the Use of Alternative Medical Terms in Modern Translations of the Bible', *PEQ* 107 (1975), pp. 87-105; J. Kinnier Wilson, 'Medicine in the Land and Times of the Old Testament', *Studies in the Period of David and Solomon* (ed. T. Ishida; Tokyo, 1982), pp. 363-64.

4. Jotham is said to have been given responsibility 'over the palace' and to rule (*špṭ*) the land.

the king, as the head of state and its religion, fulfilled some cultic duties, but in this case Uzziah could not do so because his illness made him cultically unclean.

The second book of the Chronicler has much more information about Uzziah-Azariah than the Book of Kings. 2 Chron. 26.6-15 paints a picture of Uzziah as one of the most successful and powerful kings of Judah after Solomon. The only achievement of Uzziah mentioned in 2 Kgs 14.22 is that he rebuilt Elath (modern Aqaba).[1] The Chronicler makes him the conqueror of Philistine Gath, Jabneh and Ashdod, and successful in wars against the Arabs, including Guur-baal and the Meunites. According to the Chronicler, the Ammonites paid him tribute (2 Chron. 26.6-8). The specific locations of the Meunites and Guur-baal are uncertain, but in an inscription from Tiglath-pileser III's time the Meunites are said to live 'south of Egypt', according to Sagg's reconstruction of the text.[2] This most probably denotes a location in the border area between Egypt and Palestine; thus, the territory between Wadi el-'Arish and Kadesh-Barnea would be possible.[3] Since 2 Chron. 21.16-17 mentions Arabs together with Philistines, Arab tribes may have been located in the area south of Philistine territory, to the Brook of Egypt.[4] According to the Chronicler, Uzziah supposedly built 'towers in the wilderness',[5] as

1. A seal was found at Tell el-Kheleifeh, near Elath, bearing the inscription 'to Jotham', possibly referring to Uzziah's son, Jotham (N. Glueck, 'The Third Season of Excavation at Tell El-Kheleifeh', *BASOR* 79 [1940], pp. 13-14). According to L.G. Herr, this seal could be Edomite (*The Scripts of Ancient Northwest Semitic Seals* [Missoula, 1978], p. 163). For the excavations at Tell el-Kheleifeh, see G.D. Pratico, 'Nelson Glueck's 1938–1940 Excavations at Tell el-Kheleifeh: A Reappraisal', *BASOR* 259 (1985), pp. 1-32.

2. H.W.F. Saggs, 'The Nimrud Letters 1952—Part II', *Iraq* 17 (1955), pp. 127-28.

3. Cf. H. Tadmor, 'Philistia under Assyrian Rule', *BA* 29 (1966), p. 89. For the identification of Wadi el-'Arish with the Brook of Egypt, see A. Alt, *ZDPV* 67 (1945), pp. 128-46 (= *KS*, II, pp. 226-41). Because Egypt also can include the Sinai peninsula, R. Borger and H. Tadmor do not exclude the possibility of connecting the Meunites with Ma'an in SW Jordan ('Zwei Beiträge zur alttestamentlichen Wissenschaft auf Grund der inschriften Tiglatpilesers III', *ZAW* 94 [1982], pp. 250-51).

4. Thus I. Eph'al, *The Ancient Arabs*, p. 78; cf. also Josephus, *Ant.* 9.10.3.

5. He could then have built some of the fortresses in the Negev, like Kadesh-Barnea, Horvat Uza, Har Hesron, and Horvat Har Boqer. The latter was probably built in the tenth century BCE, but then there is a gap until the eighth–seventh

well as encouraging settlements and agricultural enterprise not only in the semi-arid zone but in all parts of the country.[1] Most of this is probable, as are the wars (2 Chron. 26.9-10). In the following verses he talks about the army, which he is said to have reinforced and reorganized, and how Jerusalem became an industrial center for weapons and war machines. These stories are neither legends nor theological or midrashic extensions, so the Chronicler may have used the Book of Chronicles of the Kings of Judah to which 2 Kgs 15.6 refers. From a historical and political point of view it is quite natural that Uzziah could have had troubles with the Arabs in the south, as well as with the Philistines, whether he took Gath or not. Rebuilding Elath may have been possible only after Uzziah had secured military supremacy over the eastern Negev down to the Gulf of Aqaba, thus gaining control over the trade routes between Arabia and Egypt that passed through this area. The Arabs were in control of the trade in incense and spices from South Arabia, and they trafficked the routes from Arabia to Gaza and Egypt.[2] What is problematic is that the narrator of 2 Kings does not know or has completely forgotten the mighty acts of Uzziah except for the rebuilding of Elath. Since he refers to the Chronicles of the Kings of Judah (15.6), he apparently excluded these events and achievements deliberately.

There are no reported conflicts between Israel and Judah during Uzziah's reign. The silence suggests that the two kings, Jeroboam and Uzziah, realized that their nations would be far better off if they kept the peace. Uzziah's son and coregent, Jotham, seems to have been able to keep the peace. According to 2 Chron. 27.3-5 he built the 'Upper Gate' of the temple and repaired the wall of the Ophel, as well as fortifying some places in the country. He is also said to have fought the Ammonites and to have received tribute from them (2 Chron. 27.5). Unfortunately, there is no other information about the Ammonites

centuries; see R. Cohen, *BASOR* 236 (1979), pp. 61-79, esp. 69-75; cf. also Y. Aharoni, 'Forerunners of the Limes: Iron Age Fortresses in the Negev', *IEJ* 17 (1967), pp. 2-11. Aharoni also suggests that the fortress on the acropolis of Azekah was built at this time (*Land of the Bible* [2nd edn], p. 345). Because LMLK stamps had been found at Azekah, E. Stern dates the fortress to the late eighth century BCE ('Azekah', *EAEHL*, I, p. 143).

1.	Kuntillet 'Ajrud could date from this period.

2.	G.W. Van Beek, 'Frankincense and Myrrh in Ancient South Arabia', *JAOS* 78 (1958), pp. 141-52; cf. *idem*, 'Frankincense and Myrrh', *BA* 23 (1960), pp. 70-95.

from this period. The Chronicler's information cannot be checked, but soon we find both Ammon and Judah (under Jotham's son Ahaz) paying tribute to Tiglath-pileser III of Assyria. During the later years of Jotham's rule Aram-Damascus and Israel started their pressure on Judah to join in a coalition against Assyria (2 Kgs 15.37). Before armed conflict erupted Jotham died, possibly around 735/734, and shortly after that, 733 BCE, his father Uzziah may have died.[1] This would mean that Ahaz had been Uzziah's coregent for a short time.

During the decades of the mid-eighth century BCE, or after 773 when Shalmaneser IV and probably also Jeroboam II attacked Damascus, most Syrian states practically became independent because of the decline of Assyrian power, and the Phoenicians could, without demands from Assyria, increase their trade connections with the Syro-Palestinian states. There is valuable information in Zech. 9.3 about the great richness of Tyre in the period shortly before the Assyrian tempest finally swept away most of the Syro-Palestinian states. The prophet states something that must have been widely known—that Tyre had 'heaped up silver like dust and gold like the dirt of the streets'. It is in this same period that Aram-Damascus once again regained some of its lost power and finally under Rezin (Raqianu)[2] managed to form a coalition in which we find Israel and Tyre, Philistines and Arabs. In 743 some north-Syrian states (Arpad, Gurgum, Melid and Kummu) formed a coalition under the leadership of Urartu's king Sarduri II.[3] The new Assyrian king, Tiglath-pileser III, defeated the coalition and reduced their territories. There were no changes in dynasties or annexing of any of the states to Assyria.[4] How this was looked upon in southern Syria is not known, but it is likely that the king of Damascus, as well as others, did not count on too much of a change within the Assyrian government. The new king was as yet an unknown entity. Still, it must have been understood that in defeating the northern

1. For the death of Uzziah, see the remarks of H. Tadmor, 'Azriyau of Yaudi', *Scripta Hierosolymitana* 8 (1961), p. 262. Isaiah's inaugural vision (Isa. 6.1-5) would thus have occurred in 733 BCE; cf. G.W. Ahlström, *JSS* 19 (1974), p. 172 n. 3.

2. See L.D. Levine, *Two Neo-Assyrian Stelae from Iran* (Royal Ontario Museum Occasional Paper, 23; Art and Archaeology; Toronto, 1972), col. II l. 4 (pp. 11-24).

3. Cf. P.E. Zimansky, *Ecology and Empire: The Structure of the Urartian State* (SAOC, 41; Chicago, 1985), p. 59.

4. D.D. Luckenbill, *ARAB*, I, par 76a, pp. 272-73.

coalition Assyria would become a danger. It is in this political situation that Damascus worked toward creating a defensive alliance against Assyria.

Tiglath-pileser III (745–727 BCE), who was a governor in Calah,[1] took the throne in a revolt at Calah. Whether he was of royal birth or not is not known. His Babylonian name was Pulu (the Pul of the Bible, 2 Kgs 15.19).[2] After carrying through a reform of the empire's administration, which included putting an end to the almost hereditary governorship[3] that had contributed to the weakness of the earlier regimes, Tiglath-pileser could turn his attention to foreign policy and military activities in the borderland areas. In his three first years he moved against Urartu and into Babylonia, where he fought several Aramaean tribes, at the same time 'propping up the Babylonian throne against domination by the Chaldeans'.[4] Having defeated Urartu and the north-Syrian coalition (Arpad fell first in 740),[5] Tiglath-pileser concentrated on pacifying the Syro-Phoenician coast, incorporating the land of Unqi (on the coast of northern Syria) as a province.[6] A stela found in western Iran has a list of kings paying tribute to Tiglath-pileser in 738 BCE. The names are the same as those in the Annals, with the exception that the name of the king of Tyre in this stela is Tu-ba-il (Ittobaal), instead of Hiram,[7] which could indicate that a change had occurred and that Tubail had just succeeded Hiram or that Tubail's reign lasted to c. 738/737 and that Hiram succeeded him.[8] In this stela

---

1. H.W.F. Saggs, *The Might that was Assyria*, p. 83.

2. According to J.A. Brinkman, 'Tiglath-pileser was the king's official name both in Assyria and Babylonia' (*Prelude to Empire: Babylonian Society and Politics, 747–626* (Philadelphia, 1984), p. 43 n. 209. It is thus possible that Pulu was his original name and that he was a Babylonian.

3. Cf. H.W.F. Saggs, *The Might that was Assyria*, p. 85.

4. J.A. Brinkman, *Prelude to Empire*, p. 40.

5. For the Annals of Tiglath-pileser III, see P. Rost, *Die Keilschifttexte Tiglat-Pilesers III* (Leipzig, 1893); for these campaigns see ll. 58-159. Consult also H. Tadmor, 'Introductory Remarks to a New Edition of the Annals of Tiglath-pileser III', *Proceedings of the Israel Academy of Sciences and Humanities* (No. 2.9; Jerusalem, 1968), pp. 168-87.

6. H.W.F. Saggs, *Iraq* 17 (1955), pp. 133-34.

7. See L.D. Levine, *Two Neo-Assyrian Stelae from Iran*, p. 18. For Hiram, see the Annals, line 151.

8. Thus, L.D. Levine, *Two Neo-Assyrian Stelae from Iran*, p. 23. M. Weippert thinks that the order Metenna–Tubail–Hiram would be as probable ('Menahem von

16 kings and Queen Zabibe of Arabia are mentioned by name. Among these kings are Rezin (Raqianu) of Damascus, Menahem (Miniḫimme) of Samaria, Tubail of Tyre, Sibatbail of Byblos,[1] Panammu of Sa'mal and Dadi-il of Kaska. When the Assyrian king and army left the Syrian scene in 737, campaigning until 735 in the north and in the east against Urartu and the Medes, the Syro-Palestinian kings could have interpreted this as a weakness in Assyria's supremacy and, therefore, again have tried to forge a new alliance. In incorporating the northern coast of Syria into his empire, Tiglath-pileser had already shown what could be the fate of the Phoenicians if he was not stopped. It is in this situation that king Rezin of Damascus won the support of Pekah of Israel and together they tried to get Judah's new king Ahaz to join the coalition. In this coalition we also find Hiram of Tyre,[2] and it is probable that Hanun of Gaza was part of the same coalition too.

For the period after Jeroboam's death down to the time of the so-called Syro-Ephraimite war the biblical source material is meager. More is learned about this area from the inscriptions of Tiglath-pileser, many of which are, unfortunately, badly preserved. They also present chronological problems.[3] Thus, it is hard to get a clear picture of what occurred. The goal of the Assyrian campaign to Syria-Palestine in 734 BCE should be seen in the light of Assyria's intentions to control the commerce of the Mediterranean ports.[4] Tiglath-pileser's battle with Arabs in the Negev-Sinai area is to be understood from the same perspective, as part of establishing secure commercial connections and control over the trade in Arabia. This meant that the King's

---

Israel und seine Zeitgenossen in einer Steleninschrift Tiglatpilesers III aus dem Iran', *ZDPV* 89 [1973], p. 48 n. 89); cf. H.J. Katzenstein, *The History of Tyre*, p. 204-205. An inscription referring to the Assyrian king's campaign in Syria-Palestine 734–732 BCE mentions Hiram of Tyre; see D.J. Wiseman, 'A Fragmentary Inscription of Tiglath-Pileser III from Nimrud', *Iraq* 18 (1956) (reverse ll. 5-6), p. 126.

1.   This would probably be Šipti-bal in Phoenician; cf. H. Donner and W. Röllig, *KAI*, II, pp. 9-10; M. Weippert, 'Menahem von Israel und seine Zeitgenossen in einer Steleninschrift des assyrischen Königs Tiglathpileser III, aus dem Iran', *ZDPV* 89 (1973), p. 48.

2.   The text is ND 4301 + 4305, Reverse lines 5-6; see D.J. Wiseman, *Iraq* 18 (1956), pp. 124-26; cf. E. Vogt, 'Die Texte Tiglat-Pilesers III über die Eroberung Palästinas', *Bib* 45 (1964), pp. 348-54.

3.   Cf. H. Tadmor, 'Introductory Remarks', *Proceedings of the Israel Academy of Sciences and Humanities*, pp. 168-87.

4.   H. Tadmor, *BA* 29 (1966), pp. 86-87.

Highway in Transjordan would be of the same importance as the Mediterranean ports. Three east-Palestinian kings paid tribute to Tiglath-pileser at the same time that Ahaz of Judah did. These were Qaush-Malaku of Edom, Salamanu of Moab and Sinipu of Bit-Ammon.[1] With the reduction of the territory of Israel and the destruction of the Damascus kingdom in 733–732, Tiglath-pileser reached his goal of commercial control of Syria-Palestine. What was situated between the coast and the Transjordanian trade route was less significant and therefore of secondary military importance. The central hills of Palestine were most suitable as vassal buffer states to Egypt. This may explain why Tiglath-pileser bypassed Israel and Damascus on his campaign in 734. His main goal was to secure the control of the whole Palestinian coast.

In Israel Jeroboam II was succeeded by his son Zechariah, who was murdered after six months by a certain Shallum, son of Jabesh.[2] His luck as king lasted only one month (2 Kgs 15.9-14). Menahem, son of Gadi, from Tirzah, murdered Shallum and took the throne himself (747–737).[3] 2 Kgs 15.15-16 implies that there were two parties struggling for power. Menahem is said to have sacked Tappuah (c. 20 km SSW of Tirzah) and killed its inhabitants, 'ripping open all the pregnant women' (2 Kgs 15.16), an established Near Eastern method of warfare. New soldiers and opponents would not be born. As mentioned above, Menahem had to pay a heavy tribute of 1000 talents in silver to Tiglath-pileser.[4] He was able to pay the sum through taxing the landowners, 'from all the men of rank at the rate of 50

---

1. D.D. Luckenbill, *ARAB*, I, p. 801. C.M. Bennett believes that the Assyrian king had 'entered into treaty agreements' with these three states before he undertook his Palestinian campaign in 734 BCE ('Some Reflections on Neo-Assyrian Influence in Transjordan', *Archaeology in the Levant, Essays for Kathleen Kenyon* [ed. R. Moorey and P. Parr; Warminster, 1978], p. 170).

2. This may as well refer to a place named Jabesh. The LXX mentions a site of Jabesh at the spring of Tappuah; cf. A.M. Abel, *Géographie de la Palestine*, II, pp. 475-76.

3. For Menahem in Tiglath-pileser III's inscriptions, see M. Weippert, *ZDPV* 89 (1973), pp. 26-53. As for the Akkadian text ND 4301, Weippert thinks that the list of tributaries is a collection, a summary of vassal countries, and does not indicate that the kings mentioned in it paid their tribute at the same time (p. 53).

4. W.H. Shea thinks that Menahem and Ittobaal (Tubail) of Tyre paid the tribute to the Assyrian king at Arpad in 740 BCE. Menahem would then have died in 739 ('Menahem and Tiglath-Pileser III', *JNES* 37 [1978], p. 49).

shekels a head' (2 Kgs 15.19-20). H. Donner reckons with 'approximately 60,000 such landowners'[1] in Israel during the reign of Menahem. Such a tax-burden would certainly create some opposition to the regime, and it is natural that anti-Assyrian feelings grew strong, resulting in the creation of an 'anti-Assyrian party which demanded a change in policy'.[2] About two years after Menahem's death, Israel is also in the anti-Assyrian camp. Pekaiah, Menahem's son and successor, was murdered 'between the guardian figures' in the royal palace in Samaria[3] by Pekah, the king's *šālîš*, that is, the armor bearer and the third man on the war chariot (2 Kgs 15.23-25). Pekah had arrived in the capital with a troop of 50 Gileadites. In 2 Kgs 15.27 Pekah is said to have ruled Israel for 20 years. This information is impossible to accept for chronological reasons. Pekaiah was murdered c. 735 BCE, and Pekah in turn was murdered after something like a three-to-four-year reign in 732 BCE. R. Thiele has suggested that Pekah made himself king first in Gilead, 17 years before he ascended the throne in Samaria as king over all Israel.[4] This theory may solve the problem, but it would then mean that Jeroboam had not succeeded in keeping his rule over Transjordan. It is also possible that the figure of 20 years is a mistake.[5]

As king, Pekah reversed the policy of his predecessors and joined the anti-Assyrian coalition headed by Rezin of Damascus. Tyre, Ashkelon, Gaza, Edom, Moab and Ammon seem to have been part of this coalition

---

1. H. Donner in J.H. Hayes and J.M. Miller, *Israelite and Judean History*, p. 424; cf. M.F. Unger, *Israel and the Aramaeans of Damascus*, p. 175 n. 8. One talent equals 3000 shekels.

2. Unger, *Israel and the Aramaeans*, p. 99.

3. The Hebrew phrase *'et-'argōb wᵉ'et-hā'aryēh* has usually been seen as a gloss. However, M.J. Geller has seen the meaning of it and translates 'between the guardian figures of his palace', *'argōb* meaning 'eagle' and *'aryēh* 'lion'. He also compares Pekaiah's murder with the murder of Sennacherib, who was struck down 'in the midst of the protective deities', perhaps = the sphinxes of *šedu* and *lamassu* ('A New Translation of 2 Kings xv 25', *VT* 26 [1976], pp. 374-76). For the Sennacherib parallel, see also D.J. Wiseman, 'Murder in Mesopotamia', *Iraq* 36 (1974), p. 252; S. Parpola, 'The Murder of Sennacherib', *Mesopotamia*, VIII (ed. B. Alster; Copenhagen, 1980), p. 175.

4. *The Mysterious Numbers of the Hebrew Kings* (Grand Rapids, MI, 1951), pp. 113-16; cf. *idem*, *BASOR* 22 (1976), pp. 19-23.

5. Cf. E. Würthwein, *Könige*, II, p. 383. Another possibility is that Pekah could have been appointed governor in Transjordan.

because they are listed as paying tribute to Tiglath-pileser at the same time as Ahaz of Judah.[1] Egypt probably also supported the alliance. The hostility between Egypt and Assyria may have increased after 738, when Tiglath-pileser secured domination over most of the Phoenician cities, forbidding them to sell timber to Egypt and to the Philistines.[2] The one country in Palestine that did not join the anti-Assyrian coalition was the kingdom of Judah under its new king Ahaz, who was more realistic in his evaluation of the contemporary events and of Assyrian power.[3] In 734 BCE Tiglath-pileser again was on his way to Syria-Palestine, marching to Gaza in Pi-liš-tu.[4] The king of Gaza, Hanun, fled to Egypt and the town was taken.[5] Tiglath-pileser then continued south and established a military garrison at the Brook of Egypt in the Wadi el-'Arish. He also fought the Arab Me'unites in this region.[6] The inscriptions describing this event state that Tyre conspired with Damascus, and that after the Philistine event the Assyrian king replaced Pekah of Israel with Hosea (Au-si-i'), Israel's last king.[7] Before the Assyrian army marched against Israel and Damascus, the two kings of Israel and Damascus tried to force Judah to join the coalition. This has been called the Syro-Ephraimite war. The armies besieged Jerusalem but could not take it (2 Kgs 16.5). It is possible that Edom was supported by Israel and Damascus, because at this time Edom recaptured Elath (2 Kgs 16.6).[8] Part of the allied plan was to dethrone Ahaz and replace him with 'the son of Tabeel' (Isa. 7.6). Who this could be is unknown. Albright has suggested that this

---

1. D.D. Luckenbill, *ARAB*, I, par. 801, pp. 287-88.

2. This is clear from a letter from an Assyrian official, Qurdi-aššur-lamur; see H.W.F. Saggs, *Iraq* 17 (1955), pp. 127-28.

3. Cf. also Isa. 5.26-29, which gives an 'exact observation of Assyrian techniques and practices in war' (S. Herrmann, *A History of Israel in Old Testament Times* [2nd edn], p. 244); see also H. Donner, *Israel unter den Völkern* (VTSup, 11; Leiden, 1964), pp. 66-68.

4. For the writing of Philistia/Palestine in Assyrian inscriptions, see S. Parpola, *Neo-Assyrian Toponymns*, p. 272.

5. Cf. D.J. Wiseman, *Iraq* 13 (1951), p. 23, and *idem*, *Iraq* 18 (1956), pp. 117-18.

6. See I. Eph'al, *The Ancient Arabs*, pp. 79, 91; H. Tadmor, *BA* 29 (1966), p. 89.

7. See D.J. Wiseman, *Iraq* 18 (1956), pp. 117-29.

8. For a casemate fortress from the eighth century BCE at Tell el-Kheleifeh, see G.D. Pratico, *BASOR* 259 (1985), pp. 1-32.

would be another prince of Judah 'whose maternal home was in the land of Tab'el in northeastern Palestine or southeastern Syria'.[1] Another option would be a Phoenician prince. Tiglath-pileser's inscriptions mention a certain Tubail (Ittobaal) who was king of Tyre. He could have been the candidate for the throne in Jerusalem. Another possibility would be to see the son of Tabeel as Pekah himself, who could have contemplated a union between Israel and Judah. Pekah might have thought it natural that Judah—as usual—would support the wars of Israel. When Ahaz 'sabotaged' the project, he had to be removed, and Pekah would have taken his place. Still, nothing is known for certain. The phrase is cryptic, but it was perhaps quite clear to the contemporaries of the prophet. The plans to conquer Judah and replace Ahaz did not materialize (2 Kgs 15.37; 16.5), even though the Chronicler mentions a devastating victory for the Israelite and Aramaean armies (2 Chron. 28.5-8). The Chronicler also mentions that Edomites and Philistines invaded Judah (2 Chron. 28.17-18). According to this text, the Philistines invaded the Negev and the Shephelah and took, among other places, Beth-Shemesh, Aijalon, Gederoth, Socoh, Timnah, Gimzo and surrounding areas. The historicity of this statement cannot be checked. Judah may very well have been attacked on all fronts, and the situation was obviously very critical for Ahaz. There was no other way out than to request help from the Assyrian king. However, how much of the Chronicler's presentation of these conflicts has been colored by the postexilic Jewish community's troubles with Edomites, Cushites, Arabs and Philistines? The main point for the Chronicler is that Ahaz was unfaithful to Yahweh and pure-Yahwism and so was punished.[2] He succeeded, however, in saving his throne by diplomacy. He asked Tiglath-pileser for help (2 Kgs 16.7-9), and an Assyrian inscription reports that he (Ia-u-$ḥa$-zi)[3] payed tribute to Tiglath-pileser together

---

1. W.F. Albright, 'The Son of Tabeel (Isaiah 7.6)', *BASOR* 140 (1955), pp. 34-35. Y. Aharoni sees this son of Tabeel and his family as the 'forefathers of the prominent Tobiads who dominated central Gilead' during the postexilic period (*The Land of the Bible* [2nd edn], p. 370); cf. H. Wildberger, who sees the name as Aramaic (*Jesaja*, p. 275).

2. Cf. P. Welten, *Geschichte und Geschichtsdarstellung in den Chronikbüchern*, 1973, pp. 174-75; H.G.M. Williamson, *Israel in the Book of Chronicles*, pp. 114-18.

3. His throne name was thus Jehoahaz, which the biblical writers have shortened probably because of disgust for a person who did not 'follow' Yahweh.

with several other kings. For this submission to Assyria Ahaz was scorned by the prophet Isaiah, who encouraged the king not to trust anyone other than Yahweh—a policy no realistic ruler could follow. Isaiah's utterances in chs. 7–10 are to be placed in this critical period.[1]

The chronological order of the events in Syria-Palestine during the years of 734–732 BCE is uncertain. After capturing Gaza, its king, Hanun, who did not get help from Egypt, returned and was accepted by Tiglath-pileser as a vassal king. The biblical text mentions that Tiglath-pileser 'came and captured Ijon, Abel-Beth-Maacah, Janoah, Kedesh, Hazor, Gilead and Galilee, all the land of Naphtali, and deported the population to Assyria' (2 Kgs 15.29). This seems to indicate that the Assyrians marched from north to south and the events may be seen in connection with the campaign against Damascus, which was put under siege in 733 BCE. The biblical text gets some correlation from an Assyrian inscription which, besides several towns in Syria, mentions 'Gal'aza (Gilead), Abilakka (Abel-Beth-Maacah) which are on the border of Bit Humri (Israel), and the wide land of (Naphtali), in its entirety', all of which Tiglath-pileser incorporated into his empire.[2] The destruction of stratum V ('Upper Level V') at Beth-Shan is probably the result of Tiglath-pileser's campaign. The pottery of this level corresponds to that of Megiddo IV, Hazor V and Far'ah (N) 2, which all are dated to this time. Level V was followed by a poorly planned stratum (IV) with inferior construction.[3] The well-built and fortified city of Beth-Shan had been followed by what would be termed a village. The year 733 BCE would be then the year in which Israel's territory was drastically reduced. Gilead in Transjordan became the province of Gal'aza,[4] and the Galilee, including the Jezreel Valley,

---

1. For instance, in ch. 7 the prophet is said to have tried to convince the king not to submit to Assyria or to the detente of Aram-Israel and as a sign he gave the oracle about the child that would be born by the *'almâ* (queen?) and who should be called Immanuel. There is nothing eschatological in such an oracle.

2. D.D. Luckenbill, *ARAB*, I, par. 815; *ANET*, p. 283. It is possible that this text is a summary of several campaigns since it mentions Menahem (?) of Israel as well as Pekah and Hosea.

3. See the analysis of S. Geva, 'A Reassessment of the Chronology of Beth-Shan Strata V and IV', *IEJ* 29 (1979), pp. 6-10; *idem*, 'A Neo-Assyrian Cylinder Seal from Beth-Shan', *JANESCU* 12 (1980), p. 48.

4. For Gilead-Gal'aza in Assyrian inscriptions, consult M. Ottosson, *Gilead*, pp. 19-22 (with lit.).

became the province of Magidu (Megiddo). A great number of people were deported from these districts.[1] The coastal area south of the Carmel down to the Philistine territories had most probably been incorporated into the province of Du'ru in 734 BCE when Tiglath-pileser secured the whole coastal area south of Tyre to the Brook of Egypt,[2] cutting off Israel from the sea.[3] After Galilee and Gilead were made provinces in the Assyrian empire, Israel was reduced to a tiny state in the northern half of the central hill-country, where it had started.

The siege of Damascus and the reduction of Israel's territory made a quick end to the Syro-Ephraimite war.[4] Damascus fell in 732 BCE, and Rezin was executed. Its history as a kingdom ended and its territory was split up into provinces (Damascus, Mansuate, Subite, Qarnaim and Hauran). In the same year Pekah of Israel was deposed by the people—as the Assyrian text indicates—and murdered (2 Kgs 15.30). Tiglath-pileser put a certain Hosea (Ausi') as a puppet king on the throne in Samaria.[5] He became Israel's last king. He delivered tribute to Tiglath-pileser at Sarrabanu in Mesopotamia in 731 BCE.[6] If Tiglath-pileser's inscription can be believed, he destroyed 591 cities, among them Hadara, where Rezin was born. A great number of people, cattle and sheep were carried away as usual.[7] After this, Tiglath-pileser seems to have marched towards Ashkelon, whose king, Mitinti, '(died) in a conflagration', and his son Rukibtu was acknowledged as his successor by the Assyrian king. It is interesting to note that the same

1.   *ARAB*, I, par. 816, p. 293, and 2 Kgs 15.29.

2.   A. Alt, 'Tiglathpilesers III, erster Feldzug nach Palästina', *KS*, II, p. 157.

3.   B. Otzen concludes from this that the loss of Dor and the coastal area could have been the reason why Pekah joined forces with Rezin of Damascus. He thinks that this coalition provided Tiglath-pileser a reason for attacking them (*Mesopotamia*, VII, p. 255).

4.   H. Donner dates this war to 'spring/summer 734 BCE and spring/summer 733 BCE' (in J.H. Hayes and J.M. Miller, *Israelite and Judean History*, p. 429). In the battle at Damascus, one of Tiglath-pileser's vassals, Panammu of Zinjirli, died (H. Donner and W. Röllig, *KAI*, text 215).

5.   D.D. Luckenbill, *ARAB*, I, par. 816.

6.   For the reading Sarrabanu/i, see R. Borger and H. Tadmor, *ZAW* 94 (1982), pp. 244-49; cf. J. Briend and M.J. Seuz, *Textes du Proche-Orient Ancien et histoire d'Israël* (Paris, 1977), p. 103.

7.   D.D. Luckenbill, *ARAB*, I, par. 777. The figure of 591 cities being devastated may be exaggerated. It could possibly include every little village the army found.

text mentions Idibi'ilu,[1] who in another text is mentioned as having been installed as a 'Warden of Marches on the border of Muṣur',[2] that is, Egypt. As such he had to supervise the traffic in the areas bordering on Egypt. In using Arabs to keep the border areas secure, Assyria did not need to spend money and manpower in establishing more garrisons there. The garrison city of Nahal Muṣur, built by Tiglath-pileser at the Brook of Egypt, after which the city was named, may have been the Assyrian administrative and military center for both the supervision of the borders and of the Arabs. The southern front against Egypt was protected by the vassal states in Palestine including Gaza, Ashkelon, Judah, Israel, Ammon, Moab and Edom, and the Arab guardianship close to the Egyptian border. One just wonders why the Assyrians were so concerned about Egypt. Having lost Nubia and with the Delta split up under several small kingdoms with capitals in Sais, Leontopolis, Tanis and Bubastis, there could not possibly be any threat to the Assyrian empire. One reason may have been the fact that the Egyptians always supported and tried to encourage the Syro-Palestinian states to rebel against Assyria, which usually happened when a new king came to the Assyrian throne. Incorporating parts of the area as provinces and allowing others to preserve their national identity, but as vassals to Assyria, any Egyptian military and/or diplomatic support would be sharply reduced. There is no record of any largescale Egyptian campaign into the Assyrian territory before pharaoh Necho II marched up to Carchemish in 609 BCE in order to try to save what was left of the former empire. Some Egyptian armies did, however, invade southern Palestine under Taharqa during the reign of Sennacherib (and Hezekiah).

The great number of peoples who were deported by Tiglath-pileser III and his successor and settled in different places in the empire was part of a policy to deprive conquered areas of ethnicity and nationality in such a way that rebellions would not occur. Different ethnic groups had to live together in what was for them foreign land, and others could be moved to their former homelands. This created an ethnic and racial mixture that was not good soil for nationalism. Most Assyrian

1. See D.D. Luckenbill, *ARAB*, I, par. 779; cf. H. Tadmor, *BA* 29 (1966), p. 89.
2. A.L. Oppenheim, *ANET*, p. 282; cf. p. 284. See also I. Eph'al, *The Ancient Arabs*, p. 93.

cities 'became cosmopolitan and polyglot',[1] and the same may be said about several areas in Syria-Palestine where the population had been radically changed or quite mixed. This policy of reshuffling peoples, which continued under the Babylonians, must be seen as a contributing factor to the rise of the later phenomenon usually called Hellenization. It should not be imagined that all the deportees became slaves in various Assyrian provinces. They became professionals who replaced those who had been deported. B. Oded, for instance, concludes that many 'exiled communities played a role very similar to that of the Assyrian garrisons' in the empire.[2] This explains the Assyrian government's concern for the well-being of the resettled peoples.[3]

The cruelty of the Assyrians was expressed when fighting enemies or rebels. When the battles were over the attitude shifted and order had to be restored. As pointed out above, Assyria's policy in warfare was to show no mercy. Enemies and rebels were considered representatives of chaos and evil. This idea is not specifically an Assyrian invention. It is very much part of an ancient Near Eastern concept about one's own people being part of and representing the divine order and the opponents as representatives and personifications of everything opposing the divine order.[4] They were evil forces. The Old Testament Psalms, as well as historical and cultic-legal texts, overflow with such statements. Thus, the Assyrian king had to put 'the fear of God' into those who opposed the Assyrian ruler. This explains Assyrian terrorism, which could rightly be called 'psychological warfare'.[5]

---

1. H.W.F. Saggs, *The Might that was Assyria*, p. 128.
2. B. Oded, *Mass Deportations and Deportees in the Neo-Assyrian Empire*, p. 47.
3. H.W.F. Saggs, *Iraq*, 'The Nimrud Letters, 1952—Part III', 18 (1956), p. 55.
4. Cf. M. Liverani, who says that the 'enemy belongs to the peripheral world of chaos' ('Kitru, kataru', *Mesopotamia*, XVII [Florence, 1982], p. 54).
5. H.W.F. Saggs, *The Might that was Assyria*, p. 248.

Chapter 15

TRANSJORDAN IN THE EIGHTH AND SEVENTH CENTURIES

On the basis of archaeological remains it would be possible to maintain that northern Gilead and the Golan, east of Lake Chinnereth, was Aramaean territory at the beginning of the ninth century BCE.[1] This picture has emerged, for instance, through the excavations at 'En Gev[2] and Tell er-Rumeith. The earliest remains (from stratum VIII) at Tell er-Rumeith are quite different from the following one, stratum VII, which showed 'distinct Syrian traditions'. Its beginning can accordingly be dated to the earlier part of the ninth century BCE.[3] Thus, when Shalmaneser III invaded the area of Hauran in 841 BCE and Joram of Israel made his headquarters at Ramoth-Gilead, this place was an Aramaean border fortress[4] that had been captured by the Israelite army. The biblical writer expresses this situation with the statement that Joram was 'keeping guard in Ramoth-Gilead, he and all Israel, against Hazael, King of Aram' (2 Kgs 9.14). In other words, no war between Aram and Israel had started. Joram had thus taken Aramaean territory that previously had belonged to Israel. The expected war between Hazael and Joram never materialized because of the surprise move by Shalmaneser, who, having defeated Hazael at Mount Senir (Anti-Lebanon), was not able to take Damascus and therefore marched south into Hauran, burning and looting all its cities.[5] It is most probable that the Assyrians under Shalmaneser III

---

1. See, for example, my article in *Tel Aviv* 12 (1985), pp. 93-95.
2. B. Mazar, A. Biran, M. Dothan and I. Dunayevsky, *IEJ* 14 (1964), pp. 1-48; B. Mazar, ''En Gev', *EAEHL*, II, pp. 382-85.
3. See P.W. Lapp, *The Tale of the Tell*, pp. 115-16. As to what can be learned from archaeology for this period, see R. Dornemann, *The Archaeology of Transjordan*, p. 171-73.
4. Cf. P.W. Lapp, *The Tale of the Tell*, p. 118.
5. A.L. Oppenheim, *ANET*, p. 280; cf. D.D. Luckenbill, *ARAB*, I, par. 672;

destroyed stratum VII while taking the city from the Israelites. Jehu killed the kings of Israel and Judah and became Shalmaneser's puppet king.[1] As such, he would have been secure from attack by the Aramaeans, but Shalmaneser became occupied in other parts of his empire in addition to facing problems at home, and thus after 838 he did not campaign in the west. This gave Hazael time to rebuild his army and military strength so that as time went on Aram-Damascus became the most important power in Palestine and southern Syria. Thus Jehu and his son Jehoahaz became easy prey to the ambitions of Hazael and his son Ben-Hadad, and Israel faced a period of territorial losses, as has already been mentioned. It is in this period, until the fall of the kingdom of Damascus, that Galilee and Transjordan changed hands a couple of times.[2] Transjordan never became permanently Israelite, and with the campaigns of Tiglath-Pileser III in 733/732 Gilead became the Assyrian province of Gal'aza. In the years before, parts of northern Transjordan had belonged to the Aramaean kingdom of Damascus. This can be demonstrated by an Assyrian text from Tiglath-Pileser's time. It mentions that Aram-Damascus (called *bit-Haza'ilu*) stretched all the way from the Lebanon mountains in the west through Abel-beth-Maacah in Galilee to the 'town of Gilead' in the south.[3] This town has been held to be Ramoth-Gilead, which is probable if the place is to be identified with modern Tell er-Rumeith (c. 17.5 km southeast of Irbid, coord. 244-210) in northeastern Gilead on the King's Highway. Stratum V at Tell er-Rumeith would then be the town destroyed by Tiglath-Pileser III.[4] If ancient Ramoth-Gilead was the southern point of the Damascus kingdom, then to whom did the rest of Gilead belong? The border line between Aram-Damascus

---

for the political picture, see also G.W. Ahlström, 'The Battle at Ramoth-Gilead in 841 BCE', *Wünschet Jerusalem Frieden* (ed. M. Augustin and K.-D. Schunck), pp. 157-66.

1. See G.W. Ahlström, 'The Battle at Ramoth-Gilead in 841 BCE', *Wünschet Jerusalem Frieden*, pp. 161-63.

2. See above, Chapter 14.

3. P. Rost, *Die Keilschifttexte Tiglath-Pilesers III*, p. 78. See the reconstruction of the text by H. Tadmor, 'The Southern Border of Aram', *IEJ* 12 (1962), pp. 114-22. It should be realized that the Assyrian scribe was referring to the part of Transjordan that was Aramaean. Ramoth-Gilead was then the southern stronghold in Aramaean Gilead. From an Israelite point of view the phrase 'town of Gilead' does not make sense because there were several towns in that area.

4. P.W. Lapp, *The Tale of the Tell*, p. 118-19.

and Israel may have been the Wadi esh-Shaumar east of which Tell er-Rumeith is located. It seems clear that Ramoth-Gilead was a fortified border town; thus, the territory to the south as well as that west of the Wadi esh-Shaumar belonged to Israel. The border with Ammon and Israelite Gilead may again have been from Wadi er-Rumemin in the north to the Wadi Shu'eib in the west, passing between Tell Safut and eṣ-Ṣalt. But, as has been said before, there is no exact information about the extension of the different Transjordanian territories and kingdoms in this period. Some of the 19 fortresses that have been discussed earlier[1] could have been built during this time of Assyrian expansion, and others could have been built later.[2] These forts were built west, south and southeast of Rabbath-Ammon. A building or tower 16 × 13 m has recently been found at Jebel el-Akhdar south of Jebel 'Amman. It has been dated to the eighth–seventh century BCE.[3] One of the few fortresses that has been excavated is at Khirbet al-Hajjar, which has been dated to the seventh–sixth century BCE. At that time Israel did not exist as a nation and Judah's power was minimal. Thus, they were not built to defend against an attack from a Cisjordanian power. These fortresses, if that is what they were, must have been built as ordinary border posts.

The Ammonite King Ba'asha, son of Ruhubi, and Grindibu' the Arab were the only Transjordanian leaders who participated in the coalition against Shalmaneser III at Qarqar in 853 BCE.[4] Their participation may well have been prompted by their conviction that Assyria was threatening their common economic interests. To the east, Ammon was open to the desert, and Rabbath-Ammon's location at a key junction on the King's Highway allowed it to benefit from trade both with Arabia and with the countries to the north and to the south. Ammon may have had a closer relationship with the Arabs through history than it had with Moab and Edom.[5] Names on Ammonite seals demonstrate that there were close contacts with the Arabs and perhaps

---

1. See above p. 408.
2. Thus, for instance, Rujm el-Malfuf, where the remains are mainly from the Roman period; see R.S. Boraas, *ADAJ* 16 (1971), pp. 31-45.
3. For discussion, see F. Zayadine, 'Foilles de Djebel el Akhdar', *Syria* 62 (1985), p. 152.
4. D.D. Luckenbill, *ARAB*, I, par. 611.
5. Thus G.M. Landes, *BA* 24 (1961), p. 84.

also a great influx of Arabs into the settlements around Rabbath-Ammon.[1]

Not much is known about Transjordanian history in the eighth century BCE. For the period 800–750 BCE, Assyrian inscriptions mention no confrontation with the Transjordanian states after the time of Shalmaneser III, and the growing power of Aram-Damascus under Hazael and his son Ben-Hadad does not seem to have threatened their existence. With Tiglath-pileser III, however, the situation changed. As Damascus disappeared from the political stage and Israel was reduced to a puppet-state that had lost Gilead, a new period began for Transjordan. According to E. Forrer, Transjordan north of the Wādī Yarmuk and Gilead were made into the Assyrian provinces of Gal'aza (Gilead), Haurina (Hauran) and Qarnini (Qarnaim).[2] North of these were the new provinces of Dimashqa (around Damascus), Ṣubite north of Dimashqa (stretching east from the anti-Lebanon area), and Manṣuate (mainly the Beqa' Valley). Ammon, Moab and Edom became Assyrian vassals.

The organization of the new provinces followed the practice known from other places. The Assyrian provincial governors were called *bēl pīḫati/pāḫīti*[3] or sometimes *šaknu* ('Stathalter').[4] They were responsible to king and court for the security of the area and for the implementation of Assyrian law and practice (civil and religious). The

---

1. Cf. the comments of K.P. Jackson, *The Ammonite Language of the Iron Age*, p. 107.

2. *Die Provinzeiteilung des assyrischen Reiches* (Leipzig, 1920), pp. 69-70. Other administrative units are mentioned in a letter from Nimrud, as Tab'el, Gidir and Harnat; see H.W.F. Saggs, *Iraq* 17 (1955), pp. 123-31. Cf. H. Donner, *MIO* 5 (1957), pp. 170-78. According to B. Oded, Tab'el would be the area west of Ammon, and Hamat could be modern Tell el-'Ammata (where Wādī Rajib joins the Jordan Valley) ('Observations on Methods of Assyrian Rule in Transjordania after the Palestinian Campaign of Tiglath-Pileser III', *JNES* 29 [1970], p. 180-81). Gidir is identified by B. Mazar with Gadora, the capital of the postexilic province Perea near modern eṣ-Ṣalt ('The Tobiads', *IEJ* 7 [1957], p. 238); cf. Y. Aharoni, *The Land of the Bible* [2nd edn], p. 370).

3. See, for instance, Sennacherib's Bull Inscription from Nineveh, in D.D. Luckenbill, *The Annals of Sennacherib*, p. 76, l. 105. For the term *pīḫatu*, 'governor', cf. S.A. Kaufman, *The Akkadian Influences on Aramaic* (Assyriological Studies, 19; Chicago, 1974), p. 83.

4. On this, see W. von Soden, *AHw*, II, p. 862 (*pāḫātu*), and vol. III, p. 1141 (*šaknu*).

governors were also requested to send reports to the king about raids and booty they had taken.[1] Forts and road posts had to be established both for security and communications, which meant that garrisons were placed at strategic points and that horses were available for speedy messages. Some of the 'Ammonite' fortresses could have been built by the Assyrians at this time to secure the province of Gal'aza,[2] depending on where the border was.[3]

One of the most important roads was the so-called King's Highway connecting the south with Syria, as well as with S. Arabia. In Assyrian it was labeled *ḫarrān šarri*,[4] which means it was part of the official royal communication and trade system. This name is reflected in the Bible in Num. 20.17 and 21.22 (*derek hammelek*). Because this road was close to the desert it had several forts protecting it from raids by nomads.[5] This does not mean that all the forts must have been built by the Assyrians. They often took over and rebuilt or repaired existing fortresses.[6]

One of the cities where there is a marked difference in archaeological remains in the mid-eighth century is Tell es-Sa'idiyeh in the Jordan Valley (coord. 204.6-186.1). The city had a wall that followed about the same line in strata VII–VI (c. 825–750 BCE), but which had a new line in stratum V (750–730), and the orientation of houses was also different.[7] The following stratum (IV) cannot be characterized as a city. It had no houses and no 'well-defined streets'. It was a place of mainly pits and bins.[8] The pottery of this period is more in line with that of Hazor IV, Tell el Far'ah (N) I, Samaria VII and Megiddo III

---

1. Cf. M. Elat, 'The Impact of Tribute and Booty on Countries and People within the Assyrian Empire', *Vortrage gehalten auf der 28. Rencontre Assyriologique* (ed. H. Hirsch), p. 244.

2. Cf. F. Zayadine, *Syria* 62 (1985), p. 152.

3. A definite conclusion is impossible to draw as long as these fortresses lack thorough excavation.

4. W. von Soden, *AHw*, p. 327; *CAD*, VI, pp. 108-109.

5. See E.F. Weidner, in J. Friedrich, G.R. Meyer, A. Ugnad and E.F. Weidner, 'Die Inschriften vom Tell Halaf', *Die Inschriftrn vom Tell Halaf* (ed. J. Friedrich *et al.*; *AfO*, Beiheft 6; Berlin, 1940), pp. 11-15. Cf. A. Alt, *ZDPV* 67 (1944–45), pp. 149-50; B. Oded, *JNES* 29 (1970), pp. 182-83.

6. See H.W.F. Saggs, *The Might that was Assyria*, p. 252.

7. J.B. Pritchard, *Tell es-Sa'idiyeh*, pp. 5, 59.

8. J.B. Pritchard, *Tell es-Sa'idiyeh*, p. 39.

than with the pottery tradition of the sites on the Jordanian plateau and in Judah.[1] Since Tell es-Sa'idiyeh, Megiddo, Tell el-Far'ah (N) and Hazor all were located at this time within the Assyrian empire, it is natural that they would have had more contacts with each other than with Ammon, Moab, Edom and Judah.

When Aram-Damascus and Gilead became provinces of the Assyrian empire in 732 BCE, Ammon suddenly had a common border with Assyria. From now on the Transjordanian states became buffer states between Egypt and Assyria, as also was the case with Judah after the fall of Israel. There are no texts mentioning that Tiglath-Pileser III fought or threatened Ammon, Moab or Edom. The following years, however, saw opposition to Assyrian rule, and the Transjordanian rulers are mentioned in some inscriptions as part of anti-Assyrian coalitions. However, they were usually quick to pay their tribute when the Assyrian army came too close. The kings of these three states must have understood that the Assyrian empire could guarantee their survival,[2] even if from time to time they sought a strong coalition that could rid them of the Assyrian yoke. There is no indication that an Assyrian king having replaced a ruling dynasty with a puppet king; neither is there any indication that the Transjordanian states were ever incorporated as provinces of the Assyrian empire.[3]

The first Ammonite king mentioned in the Assyrian lists of this period is Ruhubi, father of Shanipu (Sanibu).[4] The latter is mentioned as a king of Ammon who payed tribute to Tiglath-Pileser III.[5] It is probably his name (*br šnb*) that occurs in an inscription on a statue found at the Amman Citadel.[6] Under the coregency of Jotham of

1. J.B. Pritchard, *Tell es-Sa'idiyeh*, pp. 52-53.
2. Cf. R.H. Dornemann, *The Archaeology of the Transjordan*, p. 175; B. Oded, 'Neighbors on the East', *WHJP*, IV.1, p. 271.
3. Cf. H. Donner, *MIO* 5 (1957), p. 169.
4. Shalmaneser's inscription about the battle at Qarqar, 853 BCE, also mentions an Ammonite king named Ruhubi, who was the father of Ba'sha (*ARAB*, I, par. 611). Earlier kings known from the OT are Nahash (1 Sam. 11.1; 12.12; 2 Sam. 10.2) and Hanun (2 Sam. 10.1-4). Shobi, 'son of Nahash', who is mentioned in 2 Sam. 17.27, may have been David's governor in Rabbath-Ammon.
5. D.D. Luckenbill, *ARAB*, I, par. 801; *ANET*, p. 282.
6. The statue, 0.81 m high, is an expression of the Phoenician-Palestinian style of art. It has a cap that could be a version of the Osiris crown (R.D. Barnett, 'Four Sculptures from Amman', *ADAJ* 1 [1951], pp. 34-36). F. Zayadine reads *yah'zr* (*br z*), *kr br šnb*, which would make Yerah'azer a grandson of Shanip/bu ('Note sur

Judah, Ammon was supposedly defeated by Judah's army and became a vassal to Judah, paying a heavy tribute (2 Chron. 27.5). That must then have been before the Syro-Ephraimite war, perhaps around 740 BCE. It is impossible to determine whether Ruhubi or Shanipu ruled Ammon at that time. The next king mentioned in Assyrian texts is Budu'ilu or Pudu'ilu (Bod'el), who reigned around 700 and was among the kings who paid tribute to Sennacherib at the beginning of his Palestinian campaign in 701 BCE.[1] The same name occurs on an inscription by Esarhaddon mentioning 22 kings who were forced to transport building material for Esarhaddon's palace in Nineveh.[2] An Ammonite seal with the inscription 'Beyad'el,[3] the servant of Pudu-el' has been dated to this time. The Pudu-el in question may be the king of Ammon mentioned in the inscriptions of Sennacherib and Esarhaddon. Another inscribed seal from about the same time has the picture of a nude female holding her breasts who may be a goddess.[4] If so, the seal reveals something about Ammonite religion, a subject about which very little is known.

The names of five more Ammonite kings are known: Amminadab, Hiṣṣa'el, Amminadab, Hanan'el and Ba'alis.[5] The name Hiṣṣa'el is

l'inscription de la statue d'Amman J. 1656', *Syria* 51 [1974], pp. 129-36). See also F. Israel, who considers Shanipu to be an Arab name ('The Language of the Ammonites', *Orientalia Lovaniensia Periodica* 10 [1979], pp. 153-54). The statue, which has a lotus flower in the left hand, probably represents a king. The name *yrh'zr..br šnb* is uncertain; cf. R.T. O'Callaghan, 'A Statue Recently Found in Amman', *Or* NS 21 (1952), pp. 187-93.

1. D.D. Luckenbill, *ARAB*, II, par. 239; *ANET*, p. 287.

2. *ANET*, p. 291.

3. F.M. Cross prefers the reading Beyod'el, assuming that Ammonite, like Canaanite, would have undergone the shift *a>o* by this time ('Leaves from an Epigraphist's Notebook', *CBQ* 36 [1974], pp. 493-94). See, however, the cautious remark by K.P. Jackson (*The Ammonite Language of the Iron Age*, p. 70). According to G. Garbini, the writing *byd'l* cannot be seen as Phoenician, which would instead have been written *bd'l* ('Ammonite Inscriptions', *JSS* 19 [1974], p. 162).

4. The seal has the same inscription on both sides: 'belonging to Bad'el, son of Nadab'el'; see N. Avigad, 'Two Ammonite Seals Depicting the Dea Nutrix', *BASOR* 225 (1977), pp. 63-66. K.P. Jackson lists c. 50 Ammonite seals from the eighth and seventh centuries BCE (*The Ammonite Language of the Iron Age*, pp. 70-80). Cf. also F. Vattioni, 'I sigilli ebraici', *Bib* 50 (1969), pp. 357-88; F. Israel, *Orientalia Lovaniensia Periodica* 10 (1979), p. 157.

5. See below.

known from the so-called Tell Sīrān bottle inscription, which has been dated to c. 600 BCE and which is the first complete inscription found in Ammon.[1] Besides Hiṣṣa'el this inscription mentions two kings with the name Amminadab. The first one is the grandfather of the king whose works are mentioned on the bottle. He is not to be identified with the Amminabdi of Cylinder C[2] who is mentioned in connection with Ashurbanipal's campaign against Egypt in 667 BCE. The latter Amminabdi (Amminadab) was the son of Pudu-'il; thus, the Amminadab who occurs in Ashurbanipal's inscription is a second one, and Amminadab III is the king who is to rejoice over his works which are enumerated on the bottle from Tell Sīrān. The name Amminadab occurs also on two seals of Assyrian design, 'Adoni-pelet, servant of Amminadab',[3] and 'Adoni-nur, servant of Amminadab'. The latter was found in a tomb at Amman dated to c. 650 BCE.[4] If this date is right, Adoni-nur would have been a high official during the reign of king Amminadab I. From a tomb at Umm Udheinah, also in the Amman area, comes a seal with the inscription 'to Palti, son of Ma'os, the *mazkir*'. It has been dated to c. 700 BCE.[5] The seal indicates that the title of *mazkir*, 'herald', also was in use in Ammon.

Four double-faced female heads made of limestone were found at the excavations at the Amman Citadel.[6] The style shows both northern and Phoenician features, and the double-face phenomenon may

1. See the three articles by H.O. Thompson and F. Zayadine: 'The Tell Sīrān Inscription', *BASOR* 212 (1973), pp. 5-11, 'The Works of Amminadab', *BA* 37 (1974), pp. 13-19, and 'The Ammonite Inscriptions from Tell Sīrān', *Berytus* 22 (1973), pp. 115-40; cf. F.M. Cross, 'Notes on the Ammonite Inscription from Tell Sīrān', *BASOR* 212 (1973); pp. 12-15; B.E.J.H. Becking, 'Zur Interpretation der ammonitischen Inscrift vom Tell Sīrān', *BO* 38 (1981), pp. 273-76; G.W. Ahlström, 'The Tell Sīrān Bottle Inscription', *PEQ* 116 (1984), pp. 12-15 (with lit.).

2. M. Streck, *Assurbanipal und die letzten assyrischen Könige bis zum Untergang*, II (VAB, 8; Leipzig, 1916), pp. 139-41; D.D. Luckenbill, *ARAB*, II, par. 876; A.L. Oppenheim, *ANET*, p. 294.

3. Cf. C.C. Torrey, 'A Few Ancient Seals' (AASOR 2-3 [1921–22]; New Haven, 1923), pp. 103-108.

4. G.L. Harding, *PEFA* 6 (1953), pp. 48-65, and pl. VI.I.

5. F. Zayadine, 'Une tombe du Fer II à Umm Udheinah', *Syria* 62 (1985), pp. 156-57. For other Ammonite seals, see A. Lemaire, 'Notes d'épigraphie nord-ouest sémitique', *Syria* 62 (1985), pp. 41-47.

6. S. Tell, 'Recent Ammonite Discoveries', *ADAJ* 12-13 (1967–68), pp. 9-12 (in Arabic).

originally be of Egyptian or Hittite inspiration. The fact that the heads are double-faced and 'have circular dowel holes at their tops' indicates that they served as capitals. They are parallels to the Egyptian Hathor capitals. They have tentatively been dated to the twelfth–sixth centuries BCE.[1]

The tomb of Adoni-nur is of a certain cultural importance because of the many objects found therein. Besides the seals (there were eleven), the tomb yielded earrings and finger-rings of silver, different bronze objects, such as rings and fibulae, one gold fibula, arrow heads and fragments of bronze bowls, iron objects such as knives, and a great amount of pottery. Of special interest is a clay coffin of the so-called bathtub type, also found at Tell Dothan, Tell Balaṭa, and Megiddo strata III–II.[2] The seals and much of the pottery show the influence of Assyrian stylistic patterns.[3] From the finds in the Amman tombs, O. Tufnell has concluded that during the period of Assyrian vassalage local dignitaries 'enjoyed a higher standard of living in the mid-seventh century' than what is known from Judah.[4] This may be possible because there was more commerce through Ammon than through Judah. It must be realized, however, that a comparison is impossible as long the cultural level of the common individual in Ammon is unknown. For this, more excavations and surveys are necessary. In general, the pottery from the tombs in the Amman area, at Meqabelein (eight km south of Amman)[5] and in Sahab (c. 11 km SE of Amman),[6] indicates that the Ammonite pottery begins to show an increasing number of forms that are different in style from the

1. See the discussion in R.H. Dornemann, *The Archaeology of The Transjordan*, pp. 159-62.

2. Cf. K. Yassine, *Tell el-Mazar I, Cemetery A* (Amman, 1984), p. 29.

3. G.L. Harding, *PEFA* 6 (1953), pp. 49, 57; O. Tufnell, *PEFA* 6 (1953), pp. 66-70; E. Stern, 'Israel at the Close of the Period of the Monarchy: An Archaeological Survey', *BA* 38 (1975), p. 45. Harding thinks that the Ammonite pottery could be seen as the inspiration for Nabatean pottery (p. 57). This is not to deny that there was much pottery in the Palestinian tradition.

4. *PEFA* 6 (1953), pp. 66-70. Also, R.H. Dornemann points to increased Assyrian influence in art in Transjordan after c. 750 BCE (*The Archaeology of Transjordan*, p. 178).

5. G.L. Harding, 'An Iron Age Tomb at Meqabelein', *QDAP* 14 (1950), pp. 44-48.

6. G.L. Harding, 'An Iron Age Tomb at Sahab', *QDAP* 13 (1948), pp. 92-102.

Palestinian assemblage in the seventh century BCE.[1]

The Ammonite language, which has been discussed earlier,[2] is a Canaanite dialect that was written with Aramaic characters in this period.[3] The language shows some influences from north, west and east. There are affinities with north-Arabic, which is natural, considering the close commercial contacts between the Ammonites and the Arabs. Some Arab names occur. The importance of Arabic seems, however, to have been overestimated.[4]

The longest inscription known from Transjordan is the plaster text from Deir 'Alla, the so-called Balaam text, which has been dated tentatively to the early seventh century BCE.[5] The language has been understood to be Aramaic or Ammonite, which shows that the language of Transjordan, or rather, the Jordan Valley, is not very well known. Because the non-Ammonite districts of Transjordan had long been under Aramaean influence, the Aramaean dialect had made a strong impact in these areas. However, since Deir 'Alla was situated in the Jordan Valley the language used there most probably was Canaanite with some Aramaean and Ammonite features. The most recent investigation of the Deir 'Alla texts has also demonstrated that

---

1. Consult R.H. Dornemann, *The Archaeology of Transjordan*, pp. 48-49.

2. See Chapter 9, pp. 408-409.

3. According to J. Naveh, the Ammonites may have adopted the Aramaic script already in the ninth century BCE ('The Scripts in Palestine and Transjordan in the Iron Age', *Near Eastern Archaeology in the Twentieth Century* [ed. J.A. Sanders; Garden City, NY, 1970], p. 280). N. Avigad dates this instead to the seventh century ('Ammonite and Moabite Seals', *Near Eastern Archaeology in the Twentieth Century* [ed. J.A. Sanders; Garden City, NY, 1970], p. 285).

4. Consult F. Israel, *Orientalia Lovaniensia Periodica* 10 (1979), pp. 143-59; K.P. Jackson, *The Ammonite Language of the Iron Age*, pp. 107-108.

5. For the text, see J. Hoftijzer and G. van der Joij, *Aramaic Texts from Deir 'Alla* (with contributions by H.J. Franken, V.R. Mehra, J. Voskuil and J.A. Mosk; Documents et Monumenta Orientalis Antiquii, 19; Leiden, 1976), esp. pp. 173-324; cf. A. Caquot and A. Lemaire, 'Les textes araméens de Deir 'Alla', *Syria* 54 (1977), pp. 189-208; P.K. McCarter, 'The Balaam Texts from Deir 'Alla: The First Combination', *BASOR* 239 (1980), pp. 49-60; H. and M. Weippert, 'Die "Bileam" Inschrift von Tell Der 'Alla', *ZDPV* 98 (1982), pp. 77-103; J.A. Hackett, *The Balaam Text from Deir 'Alla*. Concerning the archaeological problems, see H.J. Franken, 'Archaeological evidence relating to the interpretation of the text', *Aramaic Texts from Deir 'Alla* (ed. J. Hoftijzer and G. van der Joij; Leiden, 1976), pp. 3-16.

it is preferable to call its language south Canaanite.[1] The texts speak of the prophet, or diviner priest, Balaam, the son of Beor, 'a seer of the gods'.[2] In a night vision the gods (the Shadday deities) went to Balaam with a message about a coming disaster. This had an adverse effect upon Balaam and the people, and some ritual was performed.[3] It should be noted that the gods of the divine assembly, the *mô'ēd*,[4] are called *šdyn*, the shadday gods, which provides valuable information about the religion of the Jordan Valley and perhaps of greater Canaan. El Shadday may have been the main god through most of the Iron Age in this area,[5] explaining why the rest of the pantheon were called the shaddays.

The text contains a nonbiblical reference to the Balaam of Numbers 22–24, which supports his existence as a historical person. This does

1. J.A. Hackett, *The Balaam Text from Deir 'Alla*. P.K. McCarter does not see the text as representative of the Ammonite national script of this period, and he labels it as Gileadite (*BASOR* 239 [1980], p. 50). Politically and geographically his observation is correct, because after Tiglath-Pileser III's Palestinian campaign, Deir 'Alla was part of the Assyrian province of Gal'aza (the former Gilead).

2. The Canaanite term *ḥzh*, also common in Hebrew for prophets, is used here; cf. Amos 1.1 mentioning the 'words' Amos saw in a vision. R.T. O'Callaghan, among others, compares Balaam with the Akkadian *bārû* priest type (*Aram Naharaim*, pp. 119-20).

3. J.A. Hackett (*apud* F.M. Cross) theorizes that the ritual was a child sacrifice (*The Balaam Text from Deir 'Alla*, pp. 80-82). This is hard to believe since no remains from child sacrifices had been found at Deir 'Alla. However, Ps. 106.28 (a psalm that reviews history) tells about the Israelites putting themselves under the yoke of Baal-Peor and says that 'they ate the sacrifices of the dead'. This would mean that Baal-Peor was not at Deir 'Alla. Here I could mention that M. Noth thought that a sanctuary preserving the memory of Balaam probably existed in the Lower Jordan Valley. He thought that Moabites and Israelites met on the mountaintop of Peor between Heshbon and the Dead Sea. This sanctuary would then have furnished the background for the story in Num. 22–24 (*The History of Israel* [2nd edn], p. 155); cf. *Numbers: A Commentary* (London, 1968), pp. 187-88. There may have been several sanctuaries in the Jordan Valley that remembered Balaam. H. Ringgren seems to believe that the Balaam text deals with the birth of a royal child and involves a sacred marriage ceremony ('Bileam och inskriften från Deir 'Alla', *Religion och Bible* 36 [1977], pp. 85-89). This is unrealistic if the text concerns events around 700 BCE when Deir 'Alla was part of the Assyrian province of Gal'aza.

4. For the frequent use of *mô'ēd* to designate the cultic assembly, see H.S. Nyberg, 'Korah's uppror (Num. 16f.)', *SEÅ* 12 (1947), p. 231. For the terms *pḫr 'lm*, *puḫur ilāni*, *'dt-'l*, see also G.W. Ahlström, *Psalm 89*, pp. 59-60.

5. Compare Hebrew *'ēl šadday* (Gen. 49.25 *et passim*).

not mean, however, that the text in Numbers has been verified as referring to events occurring in the thirteenth century BCE.[1] Balaam was most probably an important Ammonite[2] prophet well known in the Jordan Valley during the Iron Age. His vision of some frightening event, such as a solar eclipse or a natural catastrophe, has been commemorated on the wall plaster of the Deir 'Alla sanctuary, probably very close to the said event.[3]

The above-mentioned letter from Nimrud (ND 2773)[4] not mentions an Assyrian official reporting from Tyre, but also gives information about an official in Moab named Aia-nuri the Tab'elite,[5] who reports that men of Gidir have slaughtered the people of a city in Moab. This Aia-nuri would then be one of the deported Gileadites from Tab'el who had been trained in Assyria and then sent back[6] to neighboring Moab as the high official who had to ensure that the vassal state

---

1. In Num. 31.8, 16-17, Balaam and five Midianite kings are slain by the Israelites together with the women and male children of the Baal-Peor cult, in which the Israelites were supposed to have taken part on Balaam's counsel. Num. 31.1-54 is considered to be a postexilic product by J.G. Vink, *OTS* 15 (1969), pp. 122-23. Cf. Num. 25.1-3, which is an expression of a typically enclosed society and so must have originated in the Persian period.

2. See J. Lust, who points out that Pethor is located in the inscription near the river in the land of the *bᵉnê 'ammôn*, as some MT manuscripts read the text together with the Samaritan, Syriac and Vulgate versions. He maintains that the 'Ammonites are an invention by the exegetes'. The river is the Jabbok, which was the border of Ammon according to Deut. 3.16 ('Balaam, an Ammonite', *Ephemerida Theol. Lovaniensis* 54 [1978], pp. 60-61).

3. This famous prophet has been used purposely by the biblical narrator in his tendentious historiography of the prehistoric period (i.e. premonarchic time). A non-Yahwistic prophet has been forced by Yahweh to bless Israel; cf. W. Gross, *Bileam: Literatur- und Formkritische Untersuchungen der Prosa in Num. 22–24* (SANT, 38; Munich, 1974), pp. 289-91. S. Mowinckel places the origin of the Balaam poems in the Josianic period ('Der Ursprung der Bil'amsage', *ZAW* 48 [1930], p. 271). In Judaism Balaam (like Jezebel) is a false teacher who leads Israel to the worship of other gods, to eat the sacrifices of other gods and to whoredom (P. Janzon, 'Nikolaiterna i Nya Testamentet och i fornkyrkan', *SEÅ* 21 [1956], pp. 82-108); cf. J.R. Baskin, *Pharaoh's Counsellors: Job, Jethro, and Balaam in Rabbinistic and Patristic Tradition* (BJS, 47; Chico, CA, 1983), pp. 75ff.

4. H.W.F. Saggs, *Iraq* 17 (1955), pp. 131-32.

5. H. Donner would read the 'Dibonite', which is philologically impossible because of the *-il* (see W.F. Saggs, *Iraq* 17 [1955], p. 132).

6. Cf. S. Parpola, 'A Letter from Šamaš-šumu-ukīn to Esarhaddon', *Iraq* 34 (1972), p. 33.

followed the Assyrian rules. As well, he had to inform the king and his court about hostilities and probable centers of rebellion.

Another of the Nimrud letters (ND 2765) illustrates Assyria's great need for horses. The letter refers to horses that were being delivered as tribute from Egypt, Gaza, Judah, Moab, Ammon and Edom.[1] Horses were needed not only for the chariotry and the royal procession carts, the latter forming part of the display of royal splendor and might, but also because the animal was becoming more important as the cavalry was introduced and built up. Mounted lancers and bowmen appear in the Assyrian army from the beginning of the eighth century BCE. The spread of the Assyrian empire was aided in part by the number of horses it could muster.[2] It is thus understandable why horses were often part of gifts and tribute.[3] The army's need for horses was most probably filled by the conscripted soldiers. When called to war, they brought their own horses, and cared for them at home when there was no war.[4]

The Transjordanian states escaped the fate of being made puppet states or provinces in the Assyrian empire and were treated less harshly by the Assyrians than by Israel and Judah. This assumption can be drawn, for instance, from 2 Kgs 3.4, which states that as an Israelite vassal King Mesha of Moab usually had to pay 100,000 lambs, as well as the 'wool of 1000 rams'. According to 2 Chron. 27.5, Jotham of Judah (Uzziah's son and coregent) successfully fought the Ammonites, and for three years they had to pay annually '100 talents of silver, and then 1000 cors of wheat', and the same amount of barley.[5] This seems to be much more than any of the Transjordanian

---

1. H.W.F. Saggs, *Iraq* 17 (1955), p. 135; J.N. Postgate, *Taxation and Conscription in the Assyrian Empire*, p. 117. Saggs dates this letter to the period just before 734 and Tiglath Pileser III's campaign to Syria-Palestine (p. 152).

2. The horse was known already in the ancient Near East in the tenth millennium, and horse training is known from the end of the fourth millennium; see A. Salonen, *Hippologia Accadica* (Helsinki, 1955); L.I. Khopina, 'Das Pferd in Vorderasien', *Orientalia Lovaniensia Periodica* 13 (1982), pp. 5-24. According to S. Dalley, Samaria, for instance, was an equestrian center ('Foreign Chariotry and Cavalry in the Armies of Tiglath-Pileser III and Sargon II', *Iraq* 47 [1985], p. 46).

3. Cf. J.N. Postgate, *Taxation and Conscription in the Assyrian Empire*, p. 117.

4. J.N. Postgate, *Taxation and Conscription*, pp. 209-10.

5. One talent is about 66–75 pounds (30–34 kg), and one cor c. 120 US gallons (454 liters).

states had to pay Assyria, if any conclusion can be based on a fragmentary inscription of uncertain date.[1] Assyrian vassalage brought about a certain security for states like Ammon, Moab and Edom.[2] As mentioned above, forts and watchtowers were built (or taken over) along the trade routes. Assyrian troops could be stationed at strategic points, such as passes or cities. An inscription from Ashurbanipal's wars with the Arabs mentions garrisons in towns in Edom, Bit-Ammani, Moab, Haurina, Ṣubite, Harge, Zobah, and the pass of Yabrud in the Anti-Lebanon.[3] It is possible that the conflict with the Arabs was not only traceable to Arab incursions into Syria and Transjordan, but also to the fact that the Arab trade and 'the international commerce probably bypassed Assyria and the Syrian regions annexed to it'.[4] Because the commerce had taken the routes through Tyre and Muṣaṣir (SE of Lake Van), these places, as well as the Arab trade routes, were the targets of Assyrian expansion.[5] In this situation the Transjordanian kingdoms would better be served by Assyrian vassalage than by being subject to Israel or Judah. Sometime between 1000 and 800 BCE a rerouting of the so-called incense road occurred, which meant that the use of 'the camel as a means of transportation passed from the sedentary, agricultural town-dwellers of West Arabia to the proto-bedouins... and trade routes were established

1. The text is probably from the time of Sargon II or Esarhaddon. It mentions that the tribute from Bit Ammon was one mina of gold from its inhabitants and the same from the Moabites, but ten minas of silver from the peoples of Judah. Edom and Byblos are also mentioned, but the amount is not known because the text has been mutilated; see L. Waterman, *Royal Correspondence of the Assyrian Empire*, I (Ann Arbor, MI, 1930), pp. 440-41, and vol. III, p. 208; A.L. Oppenheim, *ANET*, p. 301. One mina is c. 0.5 kg (= 1.1 pounds).

2. Cf. R.H. Dornemann, *The Archaeology of the Transjordan*, p. 175; B. Oded, 'Neighbors on the East', *WHJP*, IV.1, p. 271-72.

3. D.D. Luckenbill, *ARAB*, II, par. 818; *ANET*, p. 298.

4. So expressed by N.B. Jankowska, 'Some Problems of the Economy of the Assyrian Empire', *Ancient Mesopotamia Socio-Economic History* (ed. I.M. Diakonoff), p. 256.

5. H. Lewy says (in a review of A.L. Oppenheim, *Ancient Mesopotamia*) that 'in the Neo-Assyrian epoch, the Assyrians obviously were known as the world's traders par excellence', something that is mirrored in Nah. 3.16 (*JNES* 26 [1967], p. 140). J. Bottéro characterizes Assyria as a 'commercial empire'; see his 'Das erste semitische Grossreich', *Fischer Weltgeschichte*, II (Frankfurt a.M., 1965), pp. 107-28.

in their grazing areas'.[1] This may have caused problems and disturbances, and can thus explain the many wars Assyria fought with Arab tribes. In subduing the Arabs on the borders of Syria, Transjordan, and in the Negev and the northern Sinai, Assyria not only secured the border territories but also the trade routes, and gave the responsibility for security partly to Arab chieftains, thus solving the problem of stationing garrisons in many of these areas.

The history of Moab after Mesha's reign is hard to assess. His inscription indicates not only that he took back the territory north of the Arnon (Wadi Mujib), but also that he marched south and took Hauronen (Horonaim), a place north of the Zered River (Wâdī el-Ḥasa) that was located in the classical Moabite territory.[2] It is not possible to establish whether this was done before or after the invasion of the armies of Israel, Judah and Edom under Israel's king Joram (2 Kgs 3). Because Hauronen was located north of the river Zered, it may be assumed that Edomites had moved north and captured the city together with some Moabite territory. Mesha could just as likely have taken it back before the Israelite-Judahite-Edomite campaign as after the coalition's withdrawal.[3] It is impossible to extract chronological information from the Mesha stone. It must be recognized that king Mesha's inscription is a historiographic record about Mesha's success in reconquering old Moabite territories. The stela is not a chronological document. From this, as well as from the Bible, it is evident that there had been some hostility between Edom and Moab. Amos 2.1-2 mentions that the Moabites had burnt the 'bones of the king of Edom' for lime.[4]

As mentioned above, Mesha rebuilt several cities and palaces in the

---

1.   E.A. Knauf, 'Midianites and Ishmaelites', *Midian, Moab and Edom* (ed. J.F.A. Sawyer and D.J.A. Clines), p. 151.

2.   It has tentatively been located at el-'Iraq at the Wâdī Hudeira, c. 12 km SSW of Kerak (coord. 221-055) (Y. Aharoni, *The Land of the Bible* [2nd edn], p. 436); cf. F. Buhl, *Geographie des alten Palästina*, pp. 272-74.

3.   For the discussion, see C.D. Ginsberg, *The Moabite Stone: A Facsimile of the Original Inscription* (London, 1871), p. 49; A.H. van Zyl, *The Moabites* (Leiden, 1960), pp. 143-44; J.C.L. Gibson, *TSSI*, I, pp. 82-83; G. Rendsburg, 'A Reconstruction of Moabite–Israelite History', *JANESCU* 13 (1981), pp. 69-73.

4.   S. Herrmann thinks that the oracles against the nations in Amos 1.3–2.16 could refer to the whole period of the Jehu dynasty being 'highly generalized in form' (*A History of Israel* [2nd edn], pp. 233-34).

reconquered areas and fortified them. He also built cisterns, reservoirs and a highway at Aroer[1] 'on the edge (mouth) of the valley of Arnon' (Josh. 13.16).[2] Aroer had an old[3] fortress which seems to have been reconstructed by the Moabites. Later on it was rebuilt by the Nabateans. The site was probably more a garrison post than a city, a conclusion that can be drawn from the archaeological remains.[4] The references in the inscription to Mesha's building of the house (*byt*) of Diblaton and the house (*byt*) of Baal-Meon (1.30) probably refer to his erection of temples in these cities. The term for house, *byt*, is a very common term for temple in these areas.[5]

From the above it can be concluded that Mesha succeeded after all in restoring his country. With the conquests of Hazael of Damascus, however, Moab once again lost the territory north of Arnon.[6] According to 2 Kgs 13.25 Joash, the son of Jehoahaz, succeeded in taking back from Ben-Hadad of Damascus the cities Israel had lost to Hazael. The names of these cities are not given, so it is not known how much of the Transjordan came under Israelite rule. Joash's son, Jeroboam II, is given credit for having recovered all of the Transjordanian territories down the 'Sea of Arabah, in accordance with the word of Yahweh, the god of Israel, which he had spoken

---

1.   Mesha, line 26; for the text, see J.C.L. Gibson, *TSSI*, I, p. 77; *ANET*, p. 320.

2.   Modern Khirbet 'Ara'ir, just north of the steep slope of Wadi Mujib (coord. 228-097), is located 4 km east of the highway from Madaba to Kerak; cf. F. Buhl, *Geographie des alten Palästina*, p. 269. Y. Aharoni sees this information to refer to a crossing being built at this time (*The Land of the Bible* [2nd edn], p. 45).

3.   There are remains from the Early Bronze Age; see E. Olávarri, *RB* 76 (1969), pp. 230-59.

4.   The Moabite fortress was no more than 50 × 50 m (P.W. Lapp, 'Palestine in the Early Bronze Age', *Near Eastern Archaeology in the Twentieth Century* [ed. J.A. Sanders], p. 111). The place seems to have been abandoned in the seventh century. Building remains occur again from the Hellenistic period, third century BCE (E. Olávarri, 'Aroer', *EAEHL*, I, pp. 99-100).

5.   See G.W. Ahlström, *Royal Administration*, p. 15.

6.   2 Kgs 10.32-33 presents the pan-Israelite idea that the whole of Transjordan down to the river Arnon was the territory of Israelite tribes. Because there is no information indicating that Jehu or Athaliah of Judah took any Transjordanian territory, the areas north of the Arnon most certainly belonged to Moab. A. Šanda, however, assumes that Jehu had recaptured this territory early in his reign (*Die Bücher der Könige*, II [Münster, 1912], p. 120).

through his servant Jonah, the son of Amittai, the prophet from Gath-hepher' (2 Kgs 14.25).[1] Together with Gilead, this part of Transjordan was then reconquered by Israel under Jeroboam II, which was made possible by the Assyrian subjugation of Aram-Damascus.[2] The biblical writers do not indicate how much of the territory was taken by Jeroboam. If the phrase the 'Sea of Arabah' refers to the Dead Sea, it can be assumed that the portion of the Transjordan that lay north of the Dead Sea was taken. That would leave the highlands between Heshbon and the Arnon River still under Moabite control. The 'mocking song' in Isaiah 15[3] shows that the territory recaptured by Mesha from Israel was Moabite. The song expresses the singer's satisfaction over the destruction of Moab.[4] The pottery finds also support the opinion that this area was Moabite. The pottery on both sides of Arnon (Wâdī Mujib) from this period is Moabite, which is evident from surveys[5] and excavations.

Assyrian influences are less noticeable in the pottery assemblage of Ammon than in the assemblage from the area of Dibon.[6] Jeremiah's prophecies indirectly indicate that some time before the end of the

---

1. This is a reference to the prophet of the Book of Jonah.

2. A.H. van Zyl views the name Baalmeon and the Baalmeonite that occurs on one of the Samaria ostraca as a person from the Moabite Baal Meon who had become a 'court official' at Samaria (*The Moabites*, p. 147). This is less probable. Baal Meon was a place in the area north of Shechem; cf. Y. Aharoni, *The Land of the Bible* [2nd edn], p. 363).

3. A.H. van Zyl, *The Moabites*, p. 21.

4. H. Reventlow characterizes Isaiah 15–16 as a 'Klageritual', and believes that the disaster was caused by a 'Naturkatastophe' (*Liturgie und prophetisches ich bei Jeremia* [Gütersloh, 1963], p. 156). E.J. Kissane thinks that Sargon II devastated Moab (*The Book of Isaiah*, I [Dublin, 1941], pp. 183-85). As far as is known, Sargon did not campaign in Moab. W. Rudolph, however, sees Isa. 15.1-8 and 16.1, 3-11 as best suiting the time of Jeroboam II, who he thinks reconquered Transjordan. Verses 16.1, 4 would indicate that Edom was under Judah. The text may have been reworked after the Exile ('Jesaja XV–XVI', *Hebrew and Semitic Studies presented to G.R. Driver* [Oxford, 1963], pp. 139-43).

5. Cf. W.F. Albright, 'The Archaeological Results of an Expedition to Moab and the Dead Sea', *BASOR* 14 (1924), p. 10-11. Albright says that the pottery has close parallels with that of Palestine but that there are also examples of Syrian types. See also N. Glueck, 'Explorations in Eastern Palestine' (AASOR, 14 [1933–34]; Philadelphia, 1934), pp. 14-15, 35.

6. A.D. Tushingham, 'Dibon', *EAEHL*, I, p. 333; *idem*, 'Excavations at Dibon in Moab, 1952–53', *BASOR* 133 (1954), pp. 23-26.

seventh century northern Moab and Heshbon was invaded by Ammonites. He predicted that Heshbon would be destroyed as a result of Ammonite aggression (Jer. 49.2-4). The existence of Ammonite pottery dating to the seventh century BCE at Heshbon confirms Jeremiah's predictions.[1] It should also be noted that the juglet of the so-called Cypro-Phoenician type known from the tombs at Nebo[2] occurs in northern Moab through Iron I and down into the ninth century, but is replaced in the seventh century by a juglet with two handles.[3] Most of these juglets were probably not imported but were rather local imitations, as indicated by the 'ware and rough execution'.[4] The change in juglet styles can be directly attributed to a change in the political status of the Transjordanian nations during the Assyrian period.

2 Chronicles 20 relates a campaign of Ammonites and Moabites 'and with them some Ammonites' against Judah during Jehoshaphat's reign. The phrase 'some Ammonites' is most probably a misspelling for Me'unites, a correction already made by the LXX.[5] The historicity of this campaign is in doubt because of the style of the narrative, which describes a miracle and a religious service more than a war. Nevertheless, W. Rudolph may be correct that behind the text might lie a local event that took place closer to the time of the narrator than to that of Jehoshaphat.[6]

The Assyrian textual material supplies some information about Moab, Ammon and Edom, but this information is very meager as usual. Tiglath-pileser III's list of kings who paid him tribute during his Syro-Palestinian campaigns in 734–732 BCE include, among others, Salmanu of Moab, Shanib/pu of Ammon and Quash-malaku of Edom, as well as Hanno/Hanun of Gaza and Ahaz of Judah.[7] Other texts state than an Arab people, the Qedarites, paid tribute in 738 BCE together with the kings of Syria (Hatti) and the Aramaeans of Damascus and Israel under Menahem.[8] As mentioned before, an Assyrian letter

1.   S. Horn, 'Heshbon', *EAEHL*, II, pp. 510-14.

2.   S. Saller, *Liber Annuus* 16 (1965–66), p. 230.

3.   W.F. Albright, *The Excavation of Tell Beit Mirsim*, I, p. 72 pl. 51.9 and (for the juglets with two handles) pl. 66.17-20.

4.   R.H. Dornemann, *The Archaeology of the Transjordan*, p. 174.

5.   Cf. W. Rudolph, *Chronikbücher*, p. 258; I. Eph'al, *The Ancient Arabs*, p. 69.

6.   *Chronikbücher*, pp. 258-59.

7.   D.D. Luckenbill, *ARAB*, I, par. 801; *ANET*, p. 282.

8.   L.D. Levine, *Two Neo-Assyrian Stelae from Iran*, pp. 18-20; M. Weippert,

mentions that representatives from Ammon and Moab went to Calah (Nimrud), presenting the Assyrian king with horses.[1] Another letter (ND 2762) reports to the king that MAH-officials from Marqasi, Samal, Ashdod (?) and Moab have arrived in Assyria. The king in question may be Sargon II.[2] Sargon's inscription mentions in connection with the Assyrian campaign against Ashdod that Edom and Moab together with the rulers of Judah and Philistia sent tribute and *tamartu* gifts.[3] When Sennacherib had secured the Phoenician territories at the beginning of his campaign in 701 BCE, Pudu'ilu of Ammon, Kammasu-nadbi of Moab and Aiarammu of Edom seem to have hurried to supply tribute and *tamartu*-presents[4] to Sargon and to pay him homage. According to Sennacherib's inscription, this was the fourth time they paid him tribute.[5]

As in the case with Moab, information about Edom is very meager. The Book of Kings mentions that during the ninth century BCE and during Jehoshaphat's rule Edom again was ruled over by Judah. At this time Edom had no king, but it was ruled by a 'king's governor' (1 Kgs 22.48).[6] It is not clear whether Edom in this text, as in other places, refers to the whole country or only to parts of it. It seems likely that only the Arabah Valley and the areas west of it were of interest to the Judahite kings. The mountainous districts to the east of the Arabah were perhaps not under their rule. Only Wâdī Feinan with its iron ore would have been desirable. However, the mountains of Seir in Edom must have been difficult to control for a foreign power of Judah's size. One of the main reasons for Judah's interest in the western part of Edom since the time of David and Solomon consisted in the commercial advantages opened up for the nation that had the

---

ZDPV 89 (1973), pp. 28-53. Cf. I. Eph'al, *The Ancient Arabs*, pp. 82-83.

1. H.W.F. Saggs, *Iraq* 17 (1955), p. 134.

2. See H.W.F. Saggs, 'The Nimrud Letters 1952—Part V', *Iraq* 21 (1959), pp. 159-60.

3. D.D. Luckenbill, *ARAB*, II, par. 195; *ANET*, p. 287.

4. The (Babylonian) *tamartu*, (Assyrian) *namartu* was a 'subsidiary gift to accompany tribute' (J.N. Postgate, *Taxation and Conscription*, p. 154).

5. D.D. Luckenbill, *ARAB*, II, par. 239; *ANET*, p. 287.

6. For reading $n\d{s}b$ as governor, see M. Weippert, *Edom: Studien und Materialien zur Geschichte der Edomiter auf Grund schriftlichen und archäologischen Quellen* (Habilitationsschrift, Tübingen, 1971), p. 306 (*apud* E. Würthwein, *Könige*, II, p. 263 n. 3); cf. J. Gray, *I and II Kings*, p. 457.

control of the harbor at the northern end of the Gulf of Aqaba. It is thus understandable that Jehoshaphat of Judah tried to reopen the trade to Ophir that Solomon had controlled, but which was in the hands of the Phoenicians during his days. Jehoshaphat's goal must have been to get part of this trade via Ezion-geber.[1] To this effect he built the Tarshish ships, but they were wrecked in the harbor of Ezion-geber before they ever sailed (1 Kgs 22.49).[2] It is not known what caused the destruction of the ships. It usually has been assumed that it was a storm,[3] but neither the text of 1 Kings nor the parallel passage in 2 Chron. 20.37 mentions a storm. The latter passage says that the ships were broken up and could never sail. This suggests that the ships either were poorly constructed, which would be understandable since no one in Judah at that time had enough maritime experience to supervise shipbuilding (of course, a Phoenician could have been hired), or sabotage occurred.[4] It should be remembered that both the sea trade and the overland trade from Egypt had traditionally been a Phoenician–Egyptian affair, from which the Edomites would have benefitted. The golden days of Solomon were gone and Egypt perhaps did not tolerate inroads by Judah in this matter. It would disturb their relationship with the Edomites and the south Arabians and cut their economic gains.

Because southern Judah and the eastern Negev were populated primarily by Edomites, it is quite understandable that kings in Jerusalem would extend their rule down to the Gulf of Aqaba, reaching the mountains of Edom, Seir, east of the Arabah Valley. A borderline in the midst of a homogenous population would be rather

1. Cf. S. Yeivin, 'Did the Kingdoms of Israel and Judah have a Maritime Policy?' *JQR* 50 (1959–60), pp. 219-28.

2. S.L. McKenzie maintains that the ships sailed to Ophir but were destroyed before they reached their destination (*The Chronicler's Use of the Deuteronomistic History* [Atlanta, 1985], p. 109). The Hebrew text, however, says that they never sailed.

3. Thus N. Glueck, 'Explorations in Eastern Palestine. III', *BASOR* 65 (1937), p. 14. H. Donner suggests that Jehoshaphat may have renovated 'Solomon's old and now rotted merchant ships' (J.H. Hayes and J.M. Miller, *Israelite and Judean History*, p. 392). This is unrealistic. Would anybody in command of that harbor have let the ships go unused?

4. C.H.-S. Moon assumes that 'Edomite rebels destroyed the fleet' ('A Political History of Edom in the Light of Recent Literary and Archaeological Research' [PhD dissertation, Emory University, 1971], p. 173).

dangerous. J.R. Bartlett maintains that in the Assyrian period Edomite clans 'settled among the population of the region roughly south of a line drawn from Arad to Beersheba'.[1] It is probable that there was an influx of Edomites into this area during this period, but it is equally possible that ever since David had created the kingdom of Judah there had been Judahite interest in the south and that Judahites may have infiltrated periodically into the Negev and into territories that had originally been Edomite.

Under Jehoshaphat's son, Joram, Edom regained its independence in a battle that was almost disastrous for Judah at Zair (2 Kgs 8.20-22),[2] a place probably located in the northern part of the Arabah. The text states that in Joram's days Edom revolted and chose its own king. It contradicts information in 2 Kgs 3.9, which mentions that the kings of Israel, Judah and Edom marched into Moab in order to punish Mesha. The contradiction may be solved by assuming that the writer knew that Edom had freed itself from Judah after the war against Mesha. This is why he has used the same title for all three kings participating in the campaign.[3] A few decades later, Edom, together with several other nations including Tyre, Sidon, Israel and Philistia, paid tribute to Adad-nirari III (809–782), probably early in his reign.[4] This would indicate that around 805–800 BCE Edom was still an independent nation. It is interesting to note that Judah, Ammon and Moab are not mentioned. The reason may be that Edom, in paying tribute to Assyria, sought to protect itself against both Judah and Moab. Hostilities with Judah could be expected to occur at any time, and Judah soon had a ruler who tried to extend his territory. Ezion-geber at the Gulf of Aqaba would be the ultimate goal. Amaziah of Judah invaded Edom and is said to have proceeded to Sela,[5] east of the

1. J.R. Bartlett, 'Edom and the Fall of Jerusalem, 587 BCE', *PEQ* 114 (1982), p. 15.

2. The place is unknown. Following J.A. Montgomery (*The Book of Kings* [Edinburgh, 1951], p. 396), it has usually been seen as the same as Zoar. J. Gray suggests Zior, c. 7 km NE of Hebron (*I and II Kings*, p. 535). The text also states that Judah's army contained a chariot force.

3. This is also the time when Libnah threw off Judah's rule (2 Kgs 8.22; 2 Chron. 21.10).

4. D.D. Luckenbill, *ARAB*, I, par. 739; *ANET*, p. 281. This is the first time Edom is mentioned as a nation in Neo-Assyrian texts.

5. Sela, the rock, cannot be identified with Umm el-Biyara at Petra, because it

Arabah, and there to have defeated the Edomites (2 Kgs 14.7; 2 Chron. 25.11). It is not known whether Amaziah's battle led to the conquest of Edom. Even if this were the case, it may not have been of long duration, because afterwards Amaziah was defeated and taken prisoner by the Israelites under Joash (2 Kgs 14.7-9 and 2 Chron. 25.17-24). The Edomites would certainly have taken advantage of such an opportunity to regain their independence. However, Amaziah's son Uzziah rebuilt Elath, which he had 'recovered' for Judah (2 Kgs 14.21). This would indicate that Judah had lost Edom under Amaziah. Some of the ostraca from the Judahite fortress at Arad show, however, a continued contact with Edom, either hostile or diplomatic. For instance, ostracon no. 40 from stratum VIII (probably from the end of the eighth century BCE)[1] mentions that the king of Judah should know about (something) and that 'this is the evil that Edom has done'. This letter may have been sent to the commander of Arad, Malkiyahu, from a military post close to the border of Edom.[2]

The ruins at Tell el-Kheleifeh at the northern end of the Gulf of Aqaba have been seen as part of Solomon's building activities. The place would then have been destroyed in the ninth century BCE and abandoned until the mid-eighth century. Because no building remains can be dated to the tenth century, it must be assumed that fortresses or caravanserais existed in the area during the Solomonic period and before. If this is right, Elath and Ezion-geber must have had a port. Tell el-Kheleifeh is some 300 m inside the sandy shoreline and would not have been suitable for a port. As an alternative, N. Glueck suggested that Solomon's port city could have been buried 'under the debris of Aqabah'. He also assumed that pharaoh Shoshenq's army would have been responsible for the destruction of the earliest phase of the building or buildings at Tell el-Kheleifeh.[3]

was not settled in the ninth century (see C.M. Bennett, 'Fouilles d'Umm el-Biyara', *RB* 73 [1966], pp. 372-403).

1.   Y. Aharoni dates the ostracon to 701 BCE ('Three Hebrew Ostraca from Arad', *BASOR* 197 [1970], pp. 27-32); see also the discussion by D. Pardee ('Letters from Tel Arad', *UF* 10 [1978], p. 323 n. 144).

2.   Thus A. Lemaire, 'Inscriptions hébraïques', *Les Ostraca*, Tome I (Paris, 1977), p. 209.

3.   'Kheleifeh, Tell el-', *EAEHL*, III, pp. 713, 715. The Roman name of Aila for the Nabatean trading post at Aqaba would indicate the location of ancient Elath; cf. the LXX: Ailot.

A recent investigation[1] indicates that Tell el-Kheleifeh was occupied during the eighth–sixth centuries BCE. This is concluded from a study of the pottery, which is mainly of the so-called Negev type.[2] Bowls imitating the so-called Assyrian Palace ware have also been found.[3] The building found at the site was almost 13 m square and was enclosed in its first phase by a c. 30 × 30 m long casemate wall. In its second phase it had a 'massive gateway' and a c. 50 × 50 m long wall[4] with glacis.[5] It most probably was built intially as a fortress of the Negev type. In its second phase smaller houses were built and the site appears to have developed into a settlement.[6] Its main purpose could have been to house a garrison and other government personnel. Among the finds from Tell el-Kheleifeh is a signet ring showing a horned ram bearing above an inscription, *lytm*, 'belonging to Jotham'. The Jotham in question has usually been seen as Ahaz's father,[7] the son and coregent of Uzziah.

Edom regained its freedom in connection with the Syro-Ephraimite war in 734 BCE, possibly striking Judah at the same time Aram and Israel did. From then on, the area of the southern Arabah Valley down to the Gulf of Aqaba was under Edomite rule[8] (2 Kgs 16.6).[9]

---

1.   See G.D. Pratico, *BASOR* 259 (1985), pp. 1-32.

2.   Interestingly enough, Glueck concluded that the pottery was to be dated from the end of the eighth century (at the earliest) to the end of the sixth century BCE ('Some Edomite Pottery from Tell el-Kheleifeh', *BASOR* 188 [1967], p. 10).

3.   R.H. Dornemann, *The Archaeology of the Transjordan*, p. 175.

4.   The measurements are close to those of the Arad fortress.

5.   See N. Glueck, 'Ezion-geber', *BA* 28 (1965), p. 83 fig. 9; G.D. Pratico, *BASOR* 259 (1985), pp. 1-32.

6.   Some Negev fortresses are from the Iron I period (R. Cohen, *BASOR* 236 [1979], pp. 61-79).

7.   See N. Avigad, 'The Jotham Seal from Elath', *BASOR* 163 (1961), pp. 19-22; N. Glueck, 'Kheleifeh, Tell el-', *EAEHL*, III, p. 716. L.G. Herr thinks that the seal could be Edomite (*The Scripts of Ancient Northwest Semitic Seals*, p. 163).

8.   Cf. H.L. Ginsberg, 'Judah and the Transjordan States from 734–582 BCE', *Alexander Marx Jubilee Volume* (New York, 1950), p. 364 n. 47a.

9.   H. Tadmor and M. Cogan maintain that 2 Kgs 16.5-9 is based on material from the royal archives in Jerusalem ('Ahaz and Tiglath-Pileser in the Book of Kings: Historiographic Considerations', *Bib* 60 [1979], pp. 491-508). Cf. also J.A. Montgomery, who thinks that the Book of Kings contained material taken from sources from the royal archives ('Archival Data in the Books of Kings', *JBL* 53 [1934], pp. 46-52). But where have these archives been preserved so that the material could be used by later scribes or historiographers?

From its second phase at least, then, Tell el-Kheleifeh was Edomite. Edom's triumph over Judah was not long-lasting. The Assyrian inscriptions indicate that Edom's king, Qaush-malaku, was one of the several Palestinian rulers who, together with his enemy, Ahaz of Judah, paid homage and tribute to Tiglath-Pileser III in 732 BCE.[1] This meant, however, that a more stable period began for Edom. The vassalship to Judah was over. As a vassal to Assyria, Edom, like other Transjordanian states, gained some security, which seems to have resulted in the country prospering more than before, in spite of the tribute that had to be paid to Assyria. Transjordan was probably 'more stable than Palestine in the eighth through the sixth centuries BCE', which also could mean that the trunk road through Transjordan 'would have been preferred' over the routes in western Palestine.[2] Edom profited from the trade that passed through its territory from Arabia, Syria and Egypt in products such as gold and silver, spice and myrrh, as well as apes and peacocks—just as Solomon had profited earlier (1 Kgs 10). J.R. Bartlett maintains that 'the Assyrian period was the period of Edom's greatest prosperity, a time of economic expansion'.[3]

The above historical sketch may explain why no remains of flourishing cities have been found in eastern Edom earlier than the eighth century BCE. C.M. Bennett's excavations at Buseira (Bozrah, coord. 208-016) did not yield any remains earlier than the end of the ninth or the beginning of the eighth century.[4] The picture is about the same at Tawilan (coord. 197-971), and the earliest occupation at Umm el-Biyara (coord. 192-971[5] above Ain Musa overlooking Petra) is from the earlier part of the seventh century BCE.[6] The city plan at Buseirah shows ordinary houses built 'against the inner casemate wall' extending up the slope to the 'massive barrier wall' of the acropolis.[7] It is on the acropolis that the Assyrian influence is most clear. There

---

1.   D.D. Luckenbill, *ARAB*, I, par. 801; *ANET*, p. 282.

2.   R.H. Dornemann, *The Archaeology of the Transjordan*, p. 183.

3.   '587 BCE', *PEQ* 114 (1982), p. 15.

4.   'Excavations at Buseirah (Biblical Bozrah)', in *Midian, Moab and Edom* (ed. J.F.A. Sawyer and D.J.A. Clines; JSOTSup, 24; Sheffield, 1983), p. 11.

5.   C.M. Bennett, *RB* 76 (1969), pp. 386-90.

6.   C.M. Bennett, *RB* 73 (1966), pp. 372-403.

7.   For the common Near Eastern acropolis phenomenon, cf. G.W. Ahlström, *Royal Administration*, pp. 18-20.

were two larger buildings, one upon another, displaying a design foreign to this part of the Near East.[1] In the earlier building a 'sanctum with column bases on either side' was also found, which has been compared by Ms. Bennett with 'Assyrian temples with stands for deity statues'.[2] Of hygienic interest is a building southeast of the acropolis, in which was found a bathroom, probably the earliest in the greater Palestinian area.[3] From Buseirah also comes a seal with the inscription *lmlkl b''bd hmlk*, a writing which Lemaire has seen as a mistake by what he terms an 'illiterate' engraver.[4] The preferred reading is 'Malikbaal, servant of the king'.[5]

Edom's main god seems to have been Qaush. His name occurs on some seals from Tell el-Kheleifeh, Aroer (in the Negev) and Umm el-Biyara.[6] It also appears as a theophoric component in two Edomite royal names, Qaush-malaku, 'Qaush is king',[7] and Qaush-gabri, 'Qaush is almighty'. The latter name occurs on a seal from Umm el-Biyara and on a jar handle from Tell el-Kheleifeh,[8] as well as in the inscriptions of Esarhaddon and Ashurbanipal.[9] This god may have been a storm god and a god of war, and could thus be compared with Hadad and Yahweh. The name Qushyahu in 1 Chron. 15.17 indicates that

---

1.   C.M. Bennett, 'Some Reflections on Neo-Assyrian Influence in Transjordan', *Archaeology in the Levant* (ed. R. Moorey and P. Parr), p. 169, and figs. 2 and 3. For the Assyrian architecture of this time, see G. Turner, 'The State Apartments of Late Assyrian Palaces', *Iraq* 32 (1970), pp. 177-213.

2.   'Some Reflections', *Archaeology in the Levant* (ed. R. Moorey and P. Parr), p. 169.

3.   Bathrooms occur in the reception suites in neo-Assyrian palaces first in the eighth century BCE (G. Turner, *Iraq* 32 [1970], pp. 190-92).

4.   'Notes on an Edomite Seal-Impression from Buseirah', *Levant* 7 (1975), pp. 18-19. A mistake it may be, but that the engraver was illiterate is an unnecessary assumption. L.G. Herr does not discuss Lemaire's suggestion (*Northwest Semitic Seals*, pp. 163-64).

5.   Cf. C.M. Bennett in *Midian, Moab and Edom* (ed. J.F.A. Sawyer and D.J.A. Clines), p. 11.

6.   See L.G. Herr, *Northwest Semitic Seals*, pp. 162-64. For a conical cylinder seal made of white marble with a man with raised arms standing before a tree, see A. Millard, 'A Seal from Petra', *PEQ* 93 (1961), p. 136.

7.   D.D. Luckenbill, *ARAB*, I, par. 801 (Tiglath-pileser III); *ANET*, p. 282.

8.   G.L. Harding, *The Antiquities of Jordan* (New York, 1959), p. 141.

9.   C.M. Bennett, *RB* 73 (1966), pp. 399-401; *ANET*, pp. 291, 294; cf. D.D. Luckenbill, *ARAB*, II, par. 876.

some syncretism between Judahite and Edomite phenomena has occurred.[1]

Qaush-gabri may have been the son of Airammu, who is known from Sennacherib's campaign in Palestine in 701 BCE.[2] Together with, among others, Ba'lu of Tyre, Manasseh of Judah, Musuri of Moab, Mitinti of Ashkelon, Ikausu of Ekron, Puduil of Ammon, in all 22 kings of Syria, Palestine and Cyprus, Edom's king Qausgabri had to send building materials to Nineveh for Esarhaddon's new palace.[3] This would also include a contingent of labor.[4]

From the above it would be impossible to agree with N. Glueck that the Edomite civilization flourished between the thirteenth and the eighth centuries BCE.[5] The recent archaeological excavations do not support such an opinion. From what is known, the eighth–seventh centuries yield the most 'civilized' picture of Edom, but it must be remembered that such a picture also may be misleading, because only a few places have been excavated.

1.   Consult T.C. Vriezen, 'The Edomite Deity Qaus', *OTS* 14 (1965), pp. 330-53.

2.   *ANET*, p. 287.

3.   D.D. Luckenbill, *ARAB*, II, par. 690; *ANET*, p. 291. Cf. H.W.F. Saggs, *The Might that was Assyria*, p. 107.

4.   Cf. A.H. van Zyl, *The Moabites*, p. 152.

5.   *Explorations in Eastern Palestine*, II (AASOR, 15; Baltimore, 1935), pp. 138-40.

Chapter 16

PALESTINE IN THE ASSYRIAN ORBIT

After 732 BCE

For I have removed the boundaries of the nations,
and I have plundered their treasuries.
Like a bull I have pushed down those who sat on thrones.

(Isa. 10.13)

The prophet encapsulates in a nutshell the result of the Assyrian army's ravaging through Syria-Palestine during the ninth and eighth centuries BCE. The Assyrian king is likened to a strong bull that gores and treads on his enemies, a fairly common motif in Near Eastern glyptics.[1] Isaiah has, as elsewhere, shown familiarity with the phraseology in the propaganda of the Assyrian royal inscriptions, and it may be assumed that this language was known wherever the Assyrians had conquered old nations, changed the borders, and deported people (see Map 19).[2] For Palestine the result of the Assyrian campaign in 734–732 BCE was a greatly devastated country.

Its population had been decimated not only through war casualties but also through deportations. With the people went also their cattle, sheep, horses, mules, camels, and the idols and their priests,[3] as well as the treasures of the countries, such as silver and gold, lead, ivory, elephant's hides, fine garments, boxwood, 'winged birds of heaven,

---

1. One of the earliest examples is the Narmer palette from Egypt; see J. Pritchard, *ANEP*, figs. 296-97; cf. also figs. 292-93.

2. On this, see the discussion in P. Machinist, *JAOS* 103 (1983), pp. 719-37 (with lit.).

3. 13,520 persons were exiled from Galilee alone; see I. Eph'al, 'Israel: Fall and Exile', *WHJP*, IV.I, p. 185. The deportation of Dan's priesthood and people mentioned in Judg. 18.30 must have occurred at this time. The Bible also mentions that the peoples of Transjordan were deported (1 Chron. 5.26).

whose wool was purple in color (lit. "dyed")',[1] and so on. Another result was that the Assyrian empire now reached down through the Galilee and the Jezreel and Beth-shan valleys to the Philistine coast in Palestine, and in Transjordan down to the border of Ammon. The map of greater Palestine had been drastically redrawn. Almost half of the greater Palestinian area was now part of the kingdom of Assyria. The other half was part of the Assyrian political system in that it consisted of several vassal states. Aram-Damascus disappeared as a nation and Israel was now reduced to a little 'puppet' state in the Ephraim area of the central hills. It is possible that the use of the name Ephraim to denote the nation of Israel should be dated to this period.[2]

From an Assyrian point of view the situation in Palestine had been stabilized, and from the point of view of the satellite states rebellion must have been understood as unrealistic and suicidal.[3] The Assyrians seem to have rebuilt some of the Palestinian towns with a different layout. Thus, the change in political rule was expressed by a different city plan at certain sites. The Iron Age cities of Palestine primarily served the purposes of the royal administration and so housed fortress cities and administrative centers as well as store cities. Some of these sites could perhaps also have had a royal sanctuary, *bāmâ*, as a cult center and tax center for the surrounding areas. 2 Kgs 23.19, for example, states that the kings of Israel had built sanctuaries, *bāmôt*, in the land, which means that these were royal, official sanctuaries.[4] Most probably, there were a few residential houses in such cities, which were for the government personnel. Archaeologically, few residential quarters have been found at such places as Megiddo, Beer-sheba,[5] Hazor, Beth-Shan (only partly excavated), and possibly also

1.	D.D. Luckenbill, *ARAB*, I, par. 772; cf. pars. 790, 806, 816.

2.	A. Jeremias, *Das Alte Testament im Lichte des Alten Orients* (Leipzig, 1906), p. 579; cf. also the Book of Hosea.

3.	For Hosea, as for the other 'literary' prophets of the Bible, a treaty with a foreign power was the same as apostasy from Yahweh because it meant that a foreign god became the titulary sovereign over the country; see, for instance, Hos. 5.13, 8.9 and 12.2, and the statement that Israel's god (calf) 'will be carried away as tribute to Assyria' (10.6).

4.	See my *Royal Administration*, pp. 65-67.

5.	Cf. Y. Aharoni, 'Beersheba Tel', *EAEHL*, I, pp. 162-66; *The Archaeology of the Land of Israel*, pp. 217-19.

Tell ed-Duweir[1]—to mention a few from the period of the monarchies of Israel and Judah.[2] Megiddo can be mentioned as a typical example of the change in city plan that occurred due to the new political regime. After having been captured by Tiglath-pileser III, the city was rebuilt and this city (stratum III) was quite different from the previous one. From having been a fortress city with no residential quarters since the time of Jeroboam I, the Assyrian city contained numerous ordinary houses.[3] Since many different peoples had been deported from their home countries and settled in the new provinces of Syria-Palestine, some of them would have been the rebuilders of the destroyed cities.

At Hazor the building remains and the plan of the city (Stratum IV) are different from the previous period.[4] Some of the pottery is about the same as that of the preceding stratum V, but because the buildings of stratum V were not rebuilt, it may be concluded that new people settled the place. The new city was also unfortified, which is not surprising since Hazor had now lost its importance as a bulwark against an enemy from the north. Shechem, Dothan, Tell el-Far'ah (N) (identified with Tirzah), Bethel, Gezer and possibly Dan[5] and Tell Qasîle (stratum VII) were destroyed during the campaigns of 734–732. It is possible that the relief from Tiglath-pileser's palace at

1. The picture is not quite clear. D. Ussishkin has characterized Level IV at Tell ed-Duweir as 'a garrison city rather than a settlement of the usual type' (*Tel Aviv* 5 [1978], p. 93).

2. Dan, with its city gate, and Beth-Shan with its remains of relatively large store houses could be added to the list.

3. See my article in *JNES* 41 (1982), pp. 133-38.

4. Y. Yadin assumes that stratum IV 'represents a short-lived effort by the Israelite inhabitants to renew the settlement destroyed by Tiglath-pileser III' (*Hazor of Those Kingdoms*, p. 191).

5. In the excavations of 1984 a rectangular building (locus 2746) was found at Tel Dan, located just west of the large platform. In the southern room, which seems to have been the original building (eighth–ninth cent. BCE), were two 'plastered offering tables 0.4 m high'. A. Biran thinks this room was a *liškâ*, which can be translated as 'sanctuary room', and which is mentioned, e.g., in 1 Sam. 9.22. At a later stage this building was extended to the north, and in it was found, among other objects, a faience figurine with Egyptianized features. Even if the place was part of an Assyrian province its religious objects still were an expression of the old Canaanite-Israelite Egyptianized style. This building seems to have been destroyed in the seventh century BCE; see A. Biran, 'Tel Dan, 1984', *IEJ* 35 (1985), p. 188.

Nimrud showing a detail of the siege of a city *Gazru* refers to Israelite Gezer.[1] Assyrian remains have been found in the immediately following strata. Bethel and Dothan seem to have been occupied only for a short time, and it is doubtful whether Bethel (Beitin) was settled during most of the Assyrian period.[2] Some fragments of 'Samaria ware' were found, at Tell Qasîle as were an 'Asharte' figurine and an ostracon from the eighth century BCE with the text 'For the king, one thousand and one hundred [log of] oil... Hiyahu'.[3] These finds indicate that Tell Qasîle was Israelite after the split of the united monarchy. It was probably a border town that became part of the province of Du'ru after Tiglath-pileser's campaign of 734–732 BCE. Beth-Shan was also one of the cities captured by the Assyrians, which is clear from the difference between levels V and IV. Because most of the excavations were concentrated on the top of the tell (Tell el-Ḥusn), where the acropolis was, picture of the probable strength of this former Egyptian stronghold is unclear. It seems, however, that Beth-Shan of the Solomonic period had a gate which resembled those at Hazor and Megiddo.[4] Unfortunately, the city is the least well known archaeologically from the Israelite and Assyrian periods. Some remains of store houses with walls still reaching a height of c. 3–4 m were found from the Israelite period (level V). During the Assyrian period the city had lost its strategical importance, as well as its role as an administrative center. Beth-Shan was an insignificant site during the Assyrian period, and at the end of the Iron Age the 'occupation was almost a squatter type'.[5] It should be noted that the Egyptian god Seth, the 'god of foreign lands', was identified with Mekal at Beth-Shan, which means

---

1. See A.H. Layard, *The Monuments of Nineveh*, pl. 62; cf. also H. Lance, 'Gezer in the Land and in History', *BA* 30 (1967), p. 43, W.G. Dever, H.D. Lance, G.E. Wright, *Gezer*, I, p. 33 n. 3. It is not quite certain whether Gezer belonged to the Philistines or to Israel; see the discussion in K. Galling, 'Assyrische und Persische Präfekten in Gezer', *PJ* (1935), p. 80-81. B. Becking, concludes, however, that Gezer belonged to Israel, and that after 734 it became part of the province of Du'ru ('Two Neo-Assyrian Documents from Gezer in their Historical Context', *JEOL* 27 [1981–1982], p. 76-89).

2. Cf. E. Stern, *BA* 38 (1975), p. 32-33.

3. For this figurine, cf. T. Dothan and I. Dunayevsky, 'Tell Qasile', *EAEHL*, IV, p. 967-68.

4. Cf. A. Kempinski, 'Beth-Shan', *EAEHL*, I, p. 215.

5. See the review by F. James in *EAEHL*, I, p. 225; *idem*, *The Iron Age at Beth-Shan*. Cf. also S. Geva, *IEJ* 29 (1979), pp. 6-10.

that the Seth cult had been part of the religious picture of the northern kingdom. According to H.O. Thompson, Seth is 'represented at Beth-Shan from Levels IX to V',[1] and one of the animals associated with Seth was the pig.[2] Pigs had been seen as sacred animals also by the Israelites of Beth-Shan; for use of the domesticated pig by the Israelites, the pig skeletons found in the latest Israelite stratum at Hazor (str. V) provide clear evidence. In the excavations of the citadel (Area B), the remains of a partly consumed pig were found. This shows that the pig had been domesticated by the people of Hazor.[3]

The political situation was stable for almost a decade after 732 BCE, and Tiglath-pileser never had to return to this area. However, when he died in 727 and was followed by Shalmaneser V, some vassals rebelled[4] as usual, and it is possible that Hosea of Israel did the same. 2 Kgs 17.3-4 mentions that Shalmaneser went to war against Israel and says that Hosea submitted to him and paid the mandatory tribute. There are no inscriptions from Shalmaneser's time that mention this,

---

1. *Mekal, The God of Beth-Shan*, p. 143.

2. H.O. Thompson, *Mekal*, p. 140-42.

3. Y. Yadin has suggested that the hungry Assyrians ate the pig after having taken the city of Hazor (*The Rediscovery of a Great Citadel of the Bible* [New York, 1975], p. 181-82). This is probably no more than a pious guess. The Assyrians most probably ate in camp. According to B. Meissner, the Assyrians even had a distaste for pigs (see his remarks in *Babylonien und Assyrien*, I [Heidelberg, 1920], p. 416). In this connection can also be mentioned the mass grave at Tell ed-Duweir from the siege of 701 BCE. In the soil covering the bodies were found many astragali of the domesticated pig (O. Tufnell, *Lachish*, III, pp. 62-63, 187; D.M. Bate, 'The Animal Bones', *Lachish*, III [ed. O. Tufnell; London, 1953], pp. 410-11); cf. A. von Rohr Sauer, 'The Cultic Role of the Pig in Ancient Times', *In Memoriam Paul Kahle* (ed. M. Black and G. Fohrer; BZAW, 103; Berlin, 1968), pp. 206-207.

4. According to Menander of Ephesus, to whom Josephus refers, Shalmaneser laid Tyre under a siege for c. five years (*Ant.* 9.284, 287). Probably before that he had marched against Damascus (E.R. Thiele, *The Mysterious Numbers of the Hebrew Kings*, p. 291). If Menander is right, Shalmaneser must have laid siege to both Samaria and Tyre at the same time. It is then also possible that the siege of Tyre ended with a treaty between Sargon and the king of Tyre, Luli (Eloulaios), in 720 BCE. This would explain why Tyre is not mentioned in Sargon's inscriptions as one of the rebellious states; see, for instance, H.J. Katzenstein, *The History of Tyre*, p. 228-30; cf. also A. Malamat, 'The Historical Setting of Two Biblical Prophecies on the Nations', *IEJ* 1 (1951), p. 149-54.

and the biblical text is not very informative. It only states that Hosea[1] conspired with an Egyptian king and stopped paying the tribute. This brought about the subjugation of the country. Most of the cities were 'probably overrun and destroyed quickly' during the early part of Shalmaneser's campaign (724 BCE),[2] and the king, Hosea, was taken prisoner (v. 4). After a three year siege the capital of Samaria was finally taken (722 BCE). The sequence of events suggests that during the last years of its existence Israel was without a king.[3] The nation Israel ceased to exist. Its territory was incorporated within Assyria as a province under the name of Samerina. Over 27,000 persons are said to have been taken as spoil, together with their gods and 200 chariots.[4] The gods are a clear indication that in the kingdom of Israel no monotheistic idea had yet become the official line of thinking concerning the religion. The peoples whom Sargon deported were settled both in Assyria, particularly along the Habur River in the Gozan area (Guzana), modern Tell Halaf, as well as in 'the cities of Media' (2 Kgs 17.6).[5] From this we may draw the conclusion that Sargon resettled

---

1. The evaluation of Hosea is of special interest. To the usual phrase 'he did what was evil in the eyes of Yahweh' the narrator has added 'only not as the kings of Israel who were before him'. As B. Stade has maintained, this could mean that the narrator knew something positive about Hosea which was pleasing in the eyes of a Judahite writer (*Akademische Reden*, p. 208, *apud* J.A. Montgomery, *Kings*, pp. 464-65). What this was, is not known. The so-called sin of Jeroboam, which is the basis for the evaluation of the kings of Israel, was the split of the united monarchy and the establishment of a national Yahwistic cult to rival Jerusalem. May it be assumed that his cultic activities or policies were different from those of his predecessors? It could refer to some religious phenomena performed differently or neglected by Hosea. H. Weippert has compared this phrase with that of 2 Kgs 3.2-3, where king Joram of Israel is said not to have done as much evil as his father and mother (Ahab and Jezebel) ('Die deuteronomistischen Beurteilungen der Könige von Israel und Juda und das Problem der Redaktion der Königsbucher', *Bib* 53 [1972], p. 320). Joram had removed the *maṣṣēbâ* his father had made for Baal.

2. Thus G.E. Wright, *Shechem*, p. 162.

3. Cf. H. Tadmor, 'The Campaigns of Sargon II of Assur: A Chronological-Historical Study', *JCS* 12 (1958), p.37.

4. C.J. Gadd, 'Inscribed Prisms of Sargon II from Nimrud', *Iraq* 16 (1954), p. 181.

5. According to Sargon's Annals, 27,290 persons were deported (D.D. Luckenbill, *ARAB*, II, par. 4; cf. *ANET*, pp. 284-85). J. Gray prefers to follow the LXX and read 'the mountains (*hārê*) of Media' (*I and II Kings*, p. 642). Those who were deported cannot be said to be the majority of the population of

devastated Median areas with Israelites, and perhaps others too.[1]
According to Sargon, Samaria was rebuilt and made 'greater than
before',[2] and was then repopulated by conquered peoples,[3] as were
other cities.[4] The city became the capital of the new Assyrian province
of Samerina. The Bible attributes the fall of Samaria to Shalmaneser V
and so does the Babylonian Chronicle, but Shalmaneser's successor,
Sargon II (a usurper)[5] also claims to have taken Samaria.[6] This
apparent contradiction probably stems from Shalmaneser's death in
the winter of 722 BCE, perhaps only a couple of months after Samaria's
fall.[7] Sargon was able to harvest the result of Shalmaneser's campaign.

Sargon's so-called *Prunkinschrift* states that in 721 BCE Ilu-bi'di of
Hamath organized a coalition against Assyria with support from
Arpad, Simirra, Damascus and Samaria.[8] The coalition also obtained

---

Israel. It was most probably the upper strata of the society who were lead into captivity; cf. E. Würthwein, *Könige*, II, p. 394; S. Herrmann, *A History of Israel* [2nd
edn], p. 251). This does not mean that the tribes of Israel disappeared in Assyria, as
so often has been done.It is more correct to say that they disappeared in Palestine.

1.   For the Assyrian policy of resettling conquered peoples, see, for instance,
R.M. Adams, *Land behind Bagdad* (Chicago, 1965), pp. 58-59; B. Oded, *Mass
Deportations and Deportees in the Neo-Assyrian Empire*, p. 70; H.W.F. Saggs, *The
Might that was Assyria*, pp. 128-29.

2.   The wording is about the same in Sargon's Annals as in the Nimrud Prism;
see H. Tadmor, *JCS* 12 (1958), p. 34.

3.   According to the chronology that C.J. Gadd has established from the Annals
of Sargon, foreigners would first have been settled in Samaria in 716 BCE and in
Damascus in 718 (*Iraq* 17 [1955], p. 148). I. Eph'al concludes that nomads were
also settled in Samaria (*The Ancient Arabs*, p. 105-106); cf. also A.T. Olmstead,
History of Assyria, p. 209.

4.   Shechem may be mentioned as an example of a city that was rebuilt in this
period. According to G.E. Wright, stratum VI represents the first city of the Assyrian
period. Much so-called Assyrian Palace Ware was found, but most of the pottery
from this stratum is still in 'the Palestinian tradition' (*Shechem*, pp. 163-65). The
latter is a good indication that the whole population was not deported.

5.   Cf. J.A. Brinkman, *Prelude to Empire*, p. 45.

6.   For the Babylonian Chronicle, see D.J. Wiseman, *Chronicles of Chaldean
Kings (626–556 BCE)* (London, 1961). For Sargon's inscriptions, see *ANET*,
pp. 284-85. As for the sculptures in the rooms of Sargon's palace at Khorsabad,
J.E. Reade opines that Sargon 'might also have appropriated Shalmaneser's war
illustrations' ('Sargon's Campaigns of 720, 716, and 715 BCE: Evidence from the
Sculptures', *JNES* 35 [1976], p. 100).

7.   Cf. H. Tadmor, *JCS* 12 (1958), p. 37 n. 132.

8.   D.D. Luckenbill, *ARAB*, II, par. 5; cf. C.J. Gadd, *Iraq* 17 (1955), p. 148;

the support of Hanun of Gaza and an Egyptian king in the Delta. Thus, only a year or so after the fall of Samaria the banner of revolt was again raised in the hope that the new king would not be strong enough to repress the rebellion.[1] It is possible that word had spread that Sargon had experienced difficulty in establishing his rule. For instance, the people of the city of Assur had opposed him. Having overcome the obstacles at home Sargon, in his second *palû*, started concentrating on the rebellions of his vassals, whom he successfully subdued.[2]

As has been mentioned, Israel's last king, Hosea, is said to have conspired with king 'So' of Egypt in an attempt to throw off the Assyrian yoke (1 Kgs 17.4). As so many times before, the Israelite court looked to Egypt for help, even though its imperial power had been non-existent for centuries and it was split up into smaller kingdoms at this time. The question here concerns not only who was this king 'So', but what 'Egypt' is meant. Many suggestions concerning the identity of 'So' have been made, as for instance, a certain *Sib'u* who has been mentioned in Sargon's annals as the general or commander (*turtanu*) of Egypt. However, R. Borger has demonstrated that this is a mistaken reading of the Akkadian text.[3] Another suggestion, which is the most common one, is that 'So' refers to the capital city of Sais.[4] R. Krauss, among others, has pointed out that this is impossible, as is the suggestion that 'So' would be identical with the Egyptian title *t3tj* (vizier).[5] The idea that 'So' should refer to the city Sais and that, therefore, the

K. Galling, *Textbuch zur Geschichte Israels* (Tübingen, 1950), p. 54.

1. This would speak for Shalmaneser as the conqueror of Samaria and in favor of the hypothesis that Sargon's reference to having taken the city refers to his campaign against Ilubi'di and his coalition.

2. Cf. H. Tadmor, who in his reconstruction of the events maintains that Sargon returned to Samaria after having taken Raphia. Thus, there would not have been two deportations, one in 722 and the other in 720 BCE. The people were probably deported first in 720 BCE and then Sargon ordered the repair of the city of Samaria and made it the capital of the new Assyrian province Samerina (*JCS* 12 [1958], pp. 22-24).

3. 'Das Ende des ägyptischen Feldherrn Sib'e = SWA', *JNES* 19 (1960), pp. 49-53.

4. See, for instance, H. Goedicke, 'The End of King "So, King of Egypt"', *BASOR* 171 (1963), pp. 64-66; W.F. Albright, 'The Elimination of King "So"', *BASOR* 171 (1963), p. 66; J. Gray, *I and II Kings*, p. 642; I. Eph'al in *WHJP*, IV (ed. A. Malamat), pp. 186-87.

5. '"So" König von Ägypten—Ein Deutungsverschlag', *MDOG* 110 (1978), p. 49-54.

pharaoh would be Tefnakhte is thus unrealistic. Sais was the capital of
the western half of the Delta, an area with which the Asiatics did not
directly come into contact. If the king at Sais would have liked to support Hosea of Israel, he would have had to march with his troops
through two other Egyptian kingdoms, which certainly would have
caused conflicts. The Egyptian kingdom closest to Palestine was that of
the Eastern Delta, including the cities of Tanis and Bubastis, which at
this time was ruled by Osorkon IV (735–712 BCE)[1] who resided in
Bubastis.[2] Between these two kingdoms was the third Egyptian
kingdom under Iuput II at Leontopolis. Geographically the 'Egypt'
Hosea of Israel most probably contacted was the eastern one.
According to D.E. Schwab, 'Israel had an alliance with Tanis from the
time of Osorkon II and Takelot II. No kingdom of Sais was hitherto
known to the courts of Israel.'[3] Tanis and Bubastis were thus in the
right position for political and economic contacts with Palestine. We
should also note that the Hebrew traditions, such as Psalms and
Prophets, do not associate any events with Sais, but with Tanis-Zoan
and the eastern Delta region. The prophets, for instance, warn the
people for having connections with Zoan, as well as with the older
capital of Memphis, Noph (Isa. 19.11-13; 30.4; Ezek. 30.14; Ps. 78.12,
43).[4] It is, therefore, most likely that the Hebrew phrase *'el sō' melek
miṣrayim*, 'to So, king of Egypt', refers to a king of the eastern Delta.
It is possible that the Hebrew writer misunderstood the Egyptian
(n)swt, 'king',[5] and took it for a name, adding the apposition 'king of

1. The chronology is that of K. Baer (*JNES* 32 [1973], pp. 8, and 11).
2. F. Gomaà, *Die libyschen Fürstentumer des Deltas* (BTAVO, Reihe B, 6;
Wiesbaden, 1974), pp. 131-32.
3. 'Some issues of identification Raised by Textual Material Relating to the 23rd
to 26th Egyptian Dynasties', *ZÄS* 104 (1977), p. 135; cf. also K.A. Kitchen, *The
Third Intermediate Period in Egypt*, pp. 373-75.
4. The 'historiographic' Psalm places the Exodus and *yam sûp* events at Zoan
(vv. 12, 43). M. Bietak assumes that the exiled Judahites of the sixth century BCE
had learned about Tanis as a former capital. He also shows that the biblical and post-
biblical writers did not have a clear picture of the history, which is shown by the fact
that different places have been identified as Pithom and Rameses (*Tell ed-Dab'a*, II,
pp. 218-20; see also his remarks in *Proceedings of the British Academy* 65 (1979),
p. 279.
5. R. Krauss sees in So 'eine sprachgeschichtlich späte Form des Wortes
(nj-)swt (König)', which also could be written *so/w* in Greek (*MDOG* 110 [1978],
pp. 52-53).

Egypt'. A clue to the problem can be found in the LXX, which gives the name Segor, which can only refer to Osorkon,[1] known as Silkanni from the inscriptions of Sargon II.[2] No help for Israel came from the Egyptians. However, Osorkon most probably the king who sent an army under his *turtanu*[3] to help Hanun of Gaza in his rebellion against Assyria in 720 BCE.[4] A final battle was fought at Raphia, and, according to Sargon, was a disaster for the Egyptians and the Philistines. The Egyptian commander fled, no more to be seen, as the inscription reports, and Sargon took Hanun prisoner. The city of Raphia was taken and sacked.[5] Before marching south to Palestine, Sargon had crushed the Syrian revolt headed by Ilubi'di of Hamath, in which Samaria also took part.[6] It is possible that the 27,290 prisoners Sargon took from the land of the former nation of Israel were deported at this time. Having conquered the Philistines and defeated the Egyptian army, Sargon's inscription reports that he received tribute from the Egyptian king, as well as from Queen Samsi of Arabia and from Ithamar, the Sabean.[7] It is possible that the latter two sent their tribute[8] to the Assyrian king in order to secure their economic interests and avoid military confrontation. The mighty Assyrian empire had come too close. All of Syria-Palestine north of Judah and Philistia was now

1. Cf. K.A. Kitchen, who sees So as an abbreviation for '(O)so(rkon)' (*The Third Intermediate*, pp. 374-75). According to F. Gomaà, Osorkon's kingdom would have been Bubastis and its surroundings (*Die Libyschen Fürstentumer des Deltas*, pp. 131-32).

2. See, for instance, E.F. Weidner, 'Silkan(he)ni, König von Muṣri, ein Zeitgenosse Sargons II', *AfO* 14 (1941), pp. 44-49 (referring to W. von Bissing); H. Tadmor, *JCS* 12 (1958), p. 77; K. Baer, *JNES*, 32 (1973), p. 8.

3. This *turtanu*, commander, is called *rē'û* (shepherd) in the Sargon inscription (D.D. Luckenbill, *ARAB*, II, par. 55). For the reading *rē'û*, see R. Borger, *JNES* 19 (1960), pp. 49-53.

4. According to M. el-Amin, the Egyptian army will have reached as far as Gibeton (Gabbutunu) and Ekron (Amqaruna) ('Die Reliefs mit Beischriften von Sargon II. in Dur-Sharrukin', *Sumer* 9 [1953], pp. 36-40). El-Amin is supported by J.E. Reade (*JNES* 35 [1976], pp. 99-101). H. Tadmor dates the conquest of these cities to 712 BCE (*JCS* 12 [1958], p. 83 n. 243).

5. D.D. Luckenbill, *ARAB*, II, par. 55.

6. *ANET*, p. 285; H. Tadmor, *JCS* 12 (1958), pp. 35-39.

7. *ANET*, pp. 284-85.

8. I. Eph'al doubts that Sargon received tribute from Samsi and Ithamar (*The Ancient Arabs*, p. 109).

Assyrian territory, as was the territory in Transjordan north of Ammon and Moab (see Map 20).[1] A peaceful coexistence with Assyria was therefore necessary for the Arab rulers in order to benefit from their trade with Palestine (to Gaza) and Egypt. They had to cooperate with the Assyrians, who at this point controlled the trade from Egypt to Asia.

A base for this control was probably a port close to the border of Egypt. Having defeated the Egyptians at Raphia, which he destroyed and burned, Sargon II opened 'the sealed harbor of Egypt. Assyrians and Egyptians I mingled together and I made them trade.'[2] This may show that Assyria was now in a more powerful position vis-à-vis the Egyptians than was the case under Tiglath-pileser III, who saw to it that the Phoenicians did not trade lumber with the Egyptians. In reorganizing this border area, Sargon also settled peoples at 'the border of the Brook of Egypt'.[3] The ruler or sheik of the city of Laban was given the supervision of the area and its peoples. Thus, Sargon used the same method as Tiglath-pileser III for controlling the border area of Egypt; namely, an indigenous Arab ruler was put in charge, and not an Assyrian official. The above would indicate that the 'sealed harbor of Egypt'[4] cannot be identical with the destroyed city

1.   Cf. the discussion in B. Otzen, 'Israel under the Assyrians', *Mesopotamia*, VII, p. 257.

2.   D.D. Luckenbill, *ARAB*, II, par. 5; *ANET*, p. 285.

3.   According to H. Tadmor, this would have happened in Sargon's later campaign in 716 BCE (*JCS* 12 [1958], p. 35). The inscription does not give any clue to the exact date.

4.   The Nimrud Prism, ll. 46-48; The Khorsabad Annals, l. 18; see H. Tadmor, *JCS* 12 (1958), p. 34. The text is restored by Tadmor to read *karu* = port; C.J. Gadd has 'sealed treasury?' (*Iraq* 16 [1954], pp. 179-80); A.L. Oppenheim gives the translation, 'sealed-off frontiers' (*Ancient Mesopotamia*, pp. 93-94). It is possible that this reopened port, if that is what it was, could have been Raphia; cf. M. Elat, who thinks it must have been located somewhere between Gaza and 'the Brook of Egypt' ('The Economic Relations of the Neo-Assyrian Empire with Egypt', *JAOS* 98 [1978], p. 27). R. Reich suggests Tell Abu Salima, c. 15 km SW of Raphia, where remains have been found of a building with an offset-inset wall and a glacis ('On the Identification of the "Sealed KARU of Egypt"', *EI* 15 [1981], pp. 283-87, cf. p. 84*). The most natural place to look for such a port would be at the mouth of el-'Arish, which was the border line between Egypt and Palestine. Raphia is located c. 50 km NE of el-'Arish, and the beach at Raphia is not at all suitable for a port. One could here, of course, discuss what the phrase 'the sealed harbor of Egypt' could mean. Does it refer to a port inside Egypt? If so, then Raphia is out of consideration,

of Raphia[1] or the city of Laban,[2] or any other place in the area bordering Egypt, as often has been suggested.[3] The phrase is not known from Egyptian texts. It is also hard to see how an Assyrian king could open a harbor in Egypt if he had not occupied the land or the area around the port. One solution to our problem would be that Sargon opened a closed quay in some harbor along the Palestinian coast. The Akkadian word *kāru* often refers to a quay, not the entire port. Another possibility could perhaps be found in the above mentioned letter of one of Tiglath-pileser III's officials, Qurdi-aššur-lamur, which shows that the Phoenician cities were forbidden to sell timber to the Egyptians and the Philistines.[4]

Sargon was soon back in the west and in Palestine. In 718 BCE the king of Carchemish rebelled and was taken prisoner. He and the royal family were put in chains and sent to Assyria.[5] In 716 the Assyrian king was back in Palestine settling foreigners in Samaria[6] and perhaps organizing the provinces in Palestine.[7]

Deporting and resettling peoples in conquered areas meant that the national and ethnic characteristics and feelings were weakened or disappeared in order that new uprisings would be unthinkable. The basis for national unity was eliminated. This system of reshuffling peoples also had religious consequences. In subduing and destroying a nation, its gods were taken prisoner, thus destroying the basic foundation of

but if it refers to a place from where one did business with the Egyptians, then any place along the coast in Palestine may qualify.

1. A. Alt thinks that Raphia could have been the same as the city of Nahal Muṣur mentioned in Tiglath-pileser III's inscriptions ('Tiglathpilesers III, erster Feldzug nach Palästina', *KS*, II, p. 160 n. 2).

2. Cf. H. Tadmor, JCS 12 (1958), pp. 77-78; A. Alt, *KS*, II, p. 162; I. Eph'al, *The Ancient Arabs*, pp. 107-108.

3. H. Tadmor thinks that it refers to Pelusium, or that 'the fortress of Sile may be intended' (*BA* 29 [1966], p. 92).

4. See H.W.F. Saggs, *Iraq* 17 (1955), letter XII: 25-26, pp. 130-31, cf. pp. 149-50.

5. D.D. Luckenbill, *ARAB*, II, par. 8.

6. It should be pointed out that the list in Sargon's annals 'is irreconcilable with that in 2 Kings, XVII, 24, but the two lists may refer to different transportations' (C.J. Gadd, *Iraq* 17 [1955], p. 148 n. 14). Or one may suspect that the D-Historian has here used his current understanding of the population mixture in the territory of the former Israel.

7. For a possible chain of events, consult H. Tadmor, *JCS* 12 (1958), pp. 35-39.

its life. In rebuilding a conquered territory according to Assyrian principles, the new peoples had to learn the Assyrian customs and laws, both religious and civil. This was the task of the Assyrian officials—military, civil or cultic ones. The overseers (*aklu*) had to ensure that the peoples learned the ways of Assyrian life and obedience, by teaching them how to 'revere (fear, respect) god and king', *palāḫ ili u šarri*.[1] The same terminology and idea occurs in the Old Testament report about Samaria and Israel's fate after the events of 720 BCE.

2 Kgs 17.24-26 mentions that the Assyrian king (which one is not specified) brought peoples from Babylon, Cuthah, Arvad, Hamath and Sepharvaim into Samaria and into the cities of the former kingdom of Israel. This text gives a summation of the different kinds of peoples who, as time went on, were settled in the province of Samerina. It shows a distant perspective from the events described and it is most probably a text from the time of the late historian.[2] Being a summation of events, it has preserved some historical information, but the narrator has not been interested in chronology. According to his 'shortened' historiography, all the different peoples were settled about the same time in Samerina. His interest is religious. He gives a theological interpretation of what happened after these peoples had settled in the province.

New gods were worshipped in the country and the Yahweh cult had come to an end. In other words, the god of the land was not worshipped, which could be disastrous. It meant that no one knew how to follow the rules of the land. From his polemical viewpoint the narrator depicts the north as a country devoid of Israelites where there could be no correct Yahweh worship, even if the peoples appointed some Yahweh priests (2 Kgs 17.32-33). The Yahweh cult of the north became mixed with the cult of other gods and continued so down to the days of the writer (2 Kgs 17.32-34).[3] The writer mentions

---

1. See my *Royal Administration*, p. 8.

2. Cf. E. Würthwein, *Könige*, II, p. 398. J.A. Soggin ascribes the text to the 'latest phase of Deuteronomy, DeutN' (*A History of Ancient Israel*, p. 290). Cf. also the discussion in A.D.H. Mayes, *The Story of Israel between Settlement and Exile*, p. 125-27.

3. This is the same polemical picture of the peoples of the north as that given in the books of Ezra and Nehemiah.

such gods as Succoth-benoth[1] from Babylon, Nergal[2] of Cuthah, Ashima[3] from Hamath, Nibhaz[4] and Tartaq[5] from Avva, and the people of Sepharvaim supposedly burned their children as sacrifices to their gods called Adrammelech and Anammelech,[6] probably two more distorted deity names. It is difficult to accept that this passage relates actual history. With H.M. Barstad, among others, it can be said that 'the main purpose of the composition is to provide an explanation for

---

1. O. Eissfeldt sees behind this name the goddess Ṣarpanitum, Marduk's consort ('Religionshistorie und Religionspolemik im Alten Testament', *Wisdom in Israel and in the Ancient Near East* [Festschrift H.H. Rowley; ed. M. Noth and D. Winton Thomas; VTSup, 3; Leiden, 1955], p. 102); cf. 'Adramelik und Denarus', *KS*, III, pp. 365-66; J.A. Montgomery, *Kings*, pp. 473-74; J. Gray, *I and II Kings*, p. 654. It is impossible to decide what deity is hiding behind this name. The intention of the narrator is, as far as can be understood, the same as the one of Amos 5.26.

2. In Mesopotamian mythology Nergal was the consort of the ruler of the underworld, the goddess Ereshkigal; see O. Gurney, 'The Myth of Nergal and Ereshkigal', *Anatolian Studies* 10 (1960), pp. 105-31; cf. M.K. Schretter, *Alter Orient und Hellas: Fragen der Beinflussung griechischen Gedankengutes aus altorientalischen Quellen, dargestellt an den Göttern Nergal Rescheph, Apollon*, (Innsbrucker Beiträge zur Kulturwissenschaft, Sonderheft 33; Innsbruck, 1974), pp. 25-110; see also F. Gössmann, *Das Era-Epos* (Würzburg, 1955), p. 67; E. von Weiher, *Der babylonische Gott Nergal* (AOAT, 2; Neukirchen–Vluyn, 1971). For the Era (Irra) myth as a literary construction from c. 800 BCE, see W. von Soden, 'Reflektierte und konstruirte Mythen in Babylonien und Assyrian', *StudOr* 55 (1984), p. 6.

3. For this goddess, see the discussion in H.M. Barstad, *The Religious Polemics of Amos*, pp. 157-78.

4. This deity is unknown. Usually the Hebrew term has been seen as a distortion for *mizbēaḥ*, which here would refer to a deified altar (J.A. Montgomery, *Kings*, p. 474; J. Gray, *I and II Kings*, p. 654).

5. Tartaq has been understood as to refer to the goddess Atargatis (the Syrian goddess) by F. Baethgen, *Beiträge zur semitische Religionsgeschichte* (1888), p. 68; J.A. Montgomery, *Kings*, pp. 474-75. See also M. Avi-Yonah, 'Syrian Gods at Ptolemais—Accho', *IEJ* 9 (1959), pp. 7-12.

6. Consult O. Eissfeldt (*KS*, III, pp. 335-37), who would read Adad-melech, and Anammelek would then be 'Anat des Melech' (p. 365). The latter can, of course, also be a reference to the Babylonian god Anu, god of heaven. Adramelech could as well be read as Aradmelech; cf. J. Gray, *I and II Kings*, p. 655. In the Bible, Adrammelech is also the name of one of the sons who murdered Sennacherib (2 Kgs 19.37); for this, see S. Parpola, 'The Murderer of Sennacherib', *Mesopotamia*. VIII. *Death in Mesopotamia* (ed. B. Alster; Copenhagen, 1980), pp. 171-75.

the origin of the strongly syncretistic rites in Samaria at the time of the author',[1] which means that the text is polemical and not really concerned about history.[2] Still, the text teaches something about Semitic religions. As mentioned above, people had to worship the god(s), who were the owner(s) of the land where they lived in order to survive and succeed. Concerning the population of the new province of Samerina, this notion is illustrated by an incident in which Yahweh is said to have sent lions to kill people as a punishment for not being worshipped (2 Kgs 17.25-26). When the Israelites were exiled to Assyria, all priests, among other upper class citizens, were deported. (Some could also have been killed). The narrator pictures a situation in which there were no Yahweh priests in the province.[3] This then is the reason why the peoples were punished through the lions. In this situation a request was sent to the unnamed Assyrian king asking him to send back one of the exiled priests so the right Yahweh cult could be established again. The request was met with approval and a priest was sent back, taking up his duties at the temple of Bethel, not at Samaria! If Bethel is identical with modern Beitin, it was not settled during the Assyrian period, which the later writer perhaps did not know. This priest would have taught the people the right conduct, the *mišpāṭ*,[4] of the Yahweh religion. It should be noted that the Hebrew phrase *weyōrēm 'et-mišpaṭ 'elōhê hā'āreṣ*, 'to teach them the law (norms) of the god of the land' (2 Kgs 17.27)[5] corresponds to the above-mentioned Akkadian phrase *palāḫ ili u šarri*. These two phrases

1. *The Religious Polemics of Amos*, p. 161.
2. See H.H. Rowley, 'The Samaritan Schism in Legend and History', *Israel's Prophetic Heritage: Essays in Honor of James Muilenburg* (ed. B.W. Anderson and W. Harrelson; New York, 1962), pp. 208-22; R.J. Coggins, 'The Old Testament and Samaritan Origin', *ASTI* 6 (1968), p. 35-46; cf. also E. Würthwein, *Könige*, II, pp. 398-99; J.A. Soggin, *A History of Ancient Israel*, p. 290.
3. In vv. 32-33 the narrator mentions, however, that all these peoples also worshipped Yahweh, but for him it must have been in a wrong way.
4. Cf. E. Täubler, *Biblische Studien: Die Epoche der Richter*, p. 81; G.W. Ahlström, *Psalm 89*, p. 81. See also H. Cazelles, 'Shiloh, the Customary Laws and the Return of the Ancient Kings', *Promise and Presence, Old Testament Essays in Honour of Gwynne Henton Davies* (ed. J.I. Durham and J.R. Porter; Richmond, VA, 1979), pp. 239-51.
5. S. Paul thinks that the king here could have been Sargon and that the text relates a historical event ('Sargon's Administrative Diction in II Kings 17.27', *JBL* 88 [1969], pp. 73-74).

may express the law and order, cultic as well as civil, of the land, the normative way of the life of the society.[1]

Most important to note is that after the rump state of Israel had become an Assyrian province the name Israel disappears as a political and geographical term. Still, because this name was used for the worshipers of both the nations of Israel and Judah, it survived as a cultic term for the remnant of Yahweh's people, Judah.[2] The possibility should be considered that certain circles in Jerusalem—at the court and among both priests and prophets—emphasized Judah that was a tenth of Yahweh's people (Isa. 6.13), which could keep the hope about the future alive.[3]

After 716 BCE

From a Jerusalemite point of view the seriousness of the new political scene is reflected in the words of Isa. 10.13: 'I have removed the borders of the peoples'. Judah now had a common border with Assyria, and it knew quite well that the power of Assyria could mean destruction of the nation as well as poverty and deportation. In his speeches, however, the prophet Isaiah used the tactics of the Assyrian[4] war machine and their results to express his belief that Yahweh would do the same to Assyria as Assyria had done to the conquered peoples.[5] In

1. Cf. the statement in Judg. 18.7, saying that the people of Laish lived according to the *mišpāṭ* of the Sidonians.
2. For the three uses of the term Israel, see G.W. Ahlström, *Who were the Israelites?*
3. See my article in *JSS* 19 (1974), pp. 169-72.
4. See, for instance, the remarks of P. Machinist, *JAOS* 103 (1983), p. 725. For a description of the Assyrian army through the eyes of a Jerusalemite, see Isa. 5.26-30.
5. The prophecy about the re-establishment of the 'promised land' in Zech. 9.1-8, mentioning that the lands of Hadrach and Damascus, and the cities of Aram, Tyre and Sidon as well as the Philistine cities belong to Yahweh, may have been built upon the knowledge of the Assyrian campaign in Syria-Palestine. According to B. Otzen, Zechariah 9–10 is a Judean nationalistic *'am-hā'āreṣ* tradition from the time after 660 BCE, most probably from the later part of Josiah's regime (*Studien über Deutero-Sacharja*, pp. 35-123, 162). See also the discussion in M. Saebø, *Sacharja 9–14, Untersuchungen von Text und Form* (WMANT, 34; Neukirchen–Vluyn, 1969), pp. 135-275. Because Hadrach (the Hazrak of the Zakkur inscription) is mentioned in Zech. 9.1, the text most probably does not reflect the period of the coming of Alexander the Great, as has sometimes been advocated. The place (in

this way Isaiah tried to create with his visions an atmosphere of optimism, even if the nation of Israel had been annihilated for ever. As a result of the territories north of Judah having become Assyrian provinces, the kingdom of Judah was now the only nation that officially worshiped Yahweh, which meant that Yahweh's power also had diminished. Like most gods, he was a territorial god. Yahweh of Jerusalem, however, had been 'freed' from the competition with the Yahweh of the northern kingdom of Israel. This is important to remember in order to understand the history that follows. Until the fall of the northern kingdom there were two official Yahweh traditions. Each could lay claim to being the right people of Yahweh and denounce the other. With Judah as the only surviving kingdom representing Yahweh's people, not only the political competition but also the religious competition had ended. It has often been assumed that some religious traditions from the north came down to Judah and to Jerusalem through the agency of some refugees such as high officials and priests. This is very probable, and some of the so-called northern traditions in the Hebrew Bible may be seen against this political background. It should be remembered, however, that this is no more than a hypothesis.

From archaeological remains it would be possible to maintain that refugees from Israel could have settled in the areas around Jerusalem.[1] As time went on, the Western Hill became a 'suburb', later to be incorporated into Jerusalem.[2] M. Broshi estimates that the area of Jerusalem could have 'expanded to three or four times' its former size around 700 BCE, owing to the influx of refugees from Israel and (later on) to refugees coming from the areas of the kingdom of Judah which Sennacherib had given over to the Philistines in 701 BCE.[3] The alleged expansion of Jerusalem may be an exaggeration. It is impossible to

Akkadian *Hatarikka*) is mentioned in a text from the time of Sargon II by a governor of Damascus, indicating that it was located within the province of Damascus; see S. Parpola, *The Correspondence of Sargon II, Part I*, p. 134. A. Malamat believes that Zech. 9.1-6 has been 'written following the military exploits of Sargon II of Assyria' (*IEJ* 1 [1950–51], pp. 150-52).

1. Thus, M. Broshi, 'The Expansion of Jerusalem in the Reign of Hezekiah and Manasseh', *IEJ* 24 (1974), pp. 21-26; E. Stern, *BA* 38 (1975), pp. 26-54; N. Avigad, *Discovering Jerusalem* (Nashville, 1980), pp. 54-56.

2. Cf. G.W. Ahlström, *Royal Administration*, p. 78.

3. M. Broshi, *IEJ* 24 (1974), pp. 21-26.

reach a probable figure as long as the exact area of this suburb is not known. On the 'Western Hill', however, there are archaeological remains from c. 700 that may be part of or the beginning of the *mišneh*, the second city, which we find mentioned in 2 Kgs 22.14 and Zech. 1.10.[1] Thus, there is some justification for talking about a 'dual' or double city of Jerusalem, which would justify the Hebrew writing of the name, *yᵉrûšālayim*.[2]

All that can be said about the population of the new Assyrian provinces in Cisjordan and in Transjordan as well as in southern Syria is that it became very mixed as time passed by. The history of these peoples recedes into the mist of obscurity for quite some time. Some pieces of information occur here and there, mainly in Assyro-Babylonian inscriptions and archaeological finds. The life of the communities is, however, like a sealed document. Architecturally, houses were built as before, but new types of buildings may have occurred where the newcomers settled. Assyrian 'government houses' and Assyrian pottery (the so-called Assyrian Palace Ware) make their appearances at certain places in Palestine. It is important to recognize, however, that the Assyrian language did not itself conquer these peoples.

As with the penetration of Aramaeans into Assyria and its society, resulting in the dominance of the Aramaic language over the Assyrian Akkadian, Aramaic also made its way into Palestine and Transjordan because Aramaeans were among those who had been settled in these areas as part of the Assyrian policy of denationalizing the newly incorporated territories. Aramaic was already widely spoken in Syria,

---

1. It is possible that the great wall (sometimes up to 7 m wide) that has been found on the Western Hill of the present-day Old City of Jerusalem represents the remains of Hezekiah's wall built outside the city (2 Chron. 32.5). See N. Avigad, 'Excavations in the Jewish Quarter of the Old City of Jerusalem 1969/1970', *IEJ* 20 (1970), pp. 1-8, 129-40, and 'Excavations in the Jewish Quarter of the Old City of Jerusalem, 1971', *IEJ* 22 (1972), pp. 193-200. Avigad also suggests that this is reflected in Isa. 22.9-11, which mentions that a reservoir was built 'between the two walls', as well as in the song of Ascent, Ps. 122.2-3 ('a city which is bound firmly together'); cf. *Discovering Jerusalem*, pp. 54-56. See also the discussion in A.D. Tushingham, 'The Western Hill under the Monarchy', *ZDPV* 95 (1979), pp. 39-55; H. Geva, 'The Western Boundary of Jerusalem at the End of the Monarchy', *IEJ* 29 (1979), pp. 84-91.

2. Cf. my *Royal Administration*, p. 79.

and here trade contributed to its spread. It was much easier for the traders to learn and use the Aramaic signs than the impractical cunei-form signs of the Akkadian language.[1] It should also be remembered that northern Palestine and Transjordan had been territories open to Aramaean infiltration for a long time and, as such, constituted a cause for wars between Damascus and Israel. The Canaanite dialects such as Hebrew and Ammonite, however, may not have been quite understandable to persons speaking this Old Aramaic (as it is called).[2]

2 Kgs 18.26 (//Isa. 36.11) provides a clear example that shows that Aramaic was not intelligible to the common person who spoke Jehudit, as the text characterizes the Hebrew language.[3] This text states that Hezekiah's court officials asked the Assyrian *rab-šāqê* (chief cup-bearer) during the Assyrian siege in 701 BCE not to speak in Jehudit but in Aramaic, which they understood, but which was not under-standable to the rest of the men on the walls of Jerusalem. Thus, the Aramaic language had already become the 'diplomatic' language in Mesopotamia and Syria-Palestine by this time.[4] The fact that the *rab-šāqê* spoke in Hebrew most probably means that he was one of the deported Israelites who had made a career at the Assyrian court,[5] as

1.   Consult A.R. Millard, 'Assyrians and Arameans', *Iraq* 65 (1983), p. 107. The need for bilingual inscriptions is thus understandable, as, for instance, the Tell Fekheriye inscription from the ninth century BCE; see A. Abou-Assaf, P. Bordreuil and A.R. Millard, *La statue de Fekhereye et son inscription bilingue assyro-araméenne* (Paris, 1982); S.A. Kaufman, 'Reflections on the Assyrian–Aramaic Bilingual from Tell Fakhariyeh', *Maarav* 3 (1982), pp. 137-75; J.C. Greenfield and A. Shaffer, 'Notes on the Akkadian–Aramaic Bilingual Statue from Tell Fekherye', *Iraq* 65 (1983), pp. 109-16; A. Spycket, 'La statue bilingue de Tell Fekheryé', *RA* 79 (1985), pp. 67-68.

2.   Consult W.R. Garr, *Dialect Geography of Syria-Palestine 1000–586 BCE*, pp. 227-35.

3.   The term 'Hebrew' as a name for the Israelite and Judahite dialects occurs first in the prologue to the Book of Sirach.

4.   Cf. R.A. Bowman, 'Arameans, Aramaic, and the Bible', *JNES* 7 (1948), pp. 72-73. Aramaean scribes were probably used in the Assyrian administration; see B. Oded, *Mass Deportations*, pp. 104-105.

5.   See, for instance, S. Parpola, who states that deported nobility could be trained in the 'Assyrian way of life' and then be sent back as Assyrian officials to their original homelands, a phenomenon which is also mentioned in Dan. 1.5-7 (*Iraq* 34 [1972], pp. 33-34).

others had done in the army.[1] He was now used as a tool for the Assyrian propaganda (we would call it oral warfare) in order to break the morale of the defenders of Jerusalem.[2]

The kingdom of Judah had survived the turbulent years of Assyrian expansion thanks to Ahaz and his submission to Tiglath-pileser III. Unfortunately, the picture of this monarch is blurred by the utterances of the prophet Isaiah, who opposed the king's foreign policies and who unrealistically advocated that Ahaz should trust Yahweh only. Isaiah gives the impression that Ahaz was a weak and indecisive person. The Books of Kings and Chronicles also count him as one of the bad kings of Judah (2 Kgs 16.2-4; 2 Chron. 28.1-3). As mentioned above, however, Ahaz must be credited with having learned from the events happening around him, especially those across the western border, where Tiglath-pileser III campaigned against the Philistines, forcing the king of Gaza, Hanun, to flee to Egypt in 734 BCE.[3] According to the biblical material Judah was not only threatened by Israel and Damascus under Ahaz, but it was also invaded by both Edomites and Philistines (2 Chron. 28.17-18). Elath at the Gulf of Aqaba would have been retaken by the Edomites, and the Philistines would have invaded and taken the Shephelah and parts of the Negev. It is probably to this time that ostracon no. 40 from Tell Arad (str. VIII) refers. The ostracon was sent to the commander Malkiyahu, and it reports hostile actions by the Edomites.[4] The most northern city taken by the Philistines would presumably have been Aijalon. Thus, it would only have been natural for Ahaz, almost surrounded by enemies, to appeal to Tiglath-pileser for help.[5] However, it is possible that the losses to the

1. The army of Sargon II, for instance, had a unit of 13 officers from Samaria; see S. Dalley, *Iraq* 47 (1985), pp. 31-48. Cf. B. Parker, 'Administrative Tablets from the North-West Palace, Nimrud', *Iraq* 23 (1961), p. 56.

2. Cf. M. Liverani, 'The Ideology of the Assyrian Empire', *Power and Propaganda* (ed. M. Trolle Larsen; Mesopotamia, 7; Copenhagen, 1979), pp. 297-99. For an Assyrian parallel to the *rab-šāqê* speech, see H.W.F. Saggs, *Iraq* 17 (1955), pp. 23-26.

3. See D.J. Wiseman, *Iraq* 13 (1951), pp. 21-25.

4. Y. Aharoni, *Arad Inscriptions* (Jerusalem, 1975), pp. 72-76; A. Lemaire, *Inscriptions hébraïques*. I. *Les ostraca*, pp. 207-209; D.G. Pardee *et al.*, *Handbook of Ancient Hebrew Letters* (SBL Sources for Biblical Study, 15; Chico, CA, 1982); K. Jaroš, *Hundert Inscriften aus Kanaan und Israel* (Fribourg, 1982), pp. 64-66.

5. Cf. I. Eph'al, 'Israel: Fall and Exile', *WHJP*, IV.1 (ed. A. Malamat), pp. 184-85.

Philistines occurred after the Assyrian campaigns in 734–732 BCE, because some Philistine territory was conquered and devastated by Ahaz's son and successor, Hezekiah. According to 2 Kgs 18.8, Hezekiah pushed as far southwest as Gaza. This may be seen not only as an act of revenge, but also as an attempt to recover some of the lost territories. This recovery of land could probably have happened before 712, when a commoner, Yamani, rose to the throne in Ashdod through a *coup*, because this Yamani tried to organize a coalition against Assyria. Among those contacted were Judah, Edom and Moab. As usual the support of Egypt was sought.[1]

In the eyes of the Chronicler, however, the troubles of Ahaz were not so much the political problems, but his religious attitude and innovations. According to 2 Kgs 16.10, Ahaz was summoned to Damascus to meet Tiglath-pileser III after he became an Assyrian vassal.[2] There he saw an altar which pleased him, so he sent a model of it with measurements to the (first) priest of the Solomonic temple, Uriah,[3] with an order to build an altar like it for the Jerusalem temple. This was done, and when Ahaz came home he later officiated before this new holocaust altar. The old one he put in another place north of the new altar (16.14). The Chronicler has used this incident as a component in his story about the disasters of Ahaz and has declared that Ahaz offered 'sacrifices to the gods of Damascus who had defeated him'. This is supposedly the reason for Ahaz's downfall (2 Chron. 28.23).[4] That is a poor excuse. Should Ahaz have sacrificed to some foreign god it would have been to Ashur, his overlord. It is usually

1. D.D. Luckenbill, *ARAB*, II, par. 30; cf. *ANET*, p. 286. See also H. Tadmor, *BA* 29 (1966), p. 94.

2. For 2 Kgs 16.7-9 and 16.10-18 as originally coming from different traditions or circles, see the discussion by H. Spieckermann, *Juda unter Assur in der Sargonidenzeit* (FRLANT, 129; Göttingen, 1982), pp. 364-66; cf. J. Gray, who sees vv. 5-9 as a résumé by 'the Deuteronomistic compiler' (*I and II Kings*, pp. 630-31). J.A. Montgomery characterizes vv. 5-6 as two 'archival notes' (*Kings*, p. 457). H. Tadmor and M. Cogan see 2 Kgs 16.5-9 as material coming from the Jerusalemite archives but with some tendentious edition. The date would be Josianic (*Bib* 60 [1979], pp. 503-504). One just wonders how it survived the catastrophe of 587/576 BCE and then became a part of the D history work.

3. This is the priest who is called a reliable, faithful witness in Isa. 8.2.

4. The Chronicler here also adds the name of Israel instead of Judah, which, of course, does not refer to the kingdom of Israel.

taken for granted that this new altar represents Assyrian rituals that had been imposed on Jerusalem.[1] This may be an overinterpretation because the altar was of Aramean type, not Assyrian. The Chronicler is more logical in saying that Ahaz sacrificed to the Aramean gods. Ahaz had the same right as Solomon and any other king to make things for the temple as he wished. If he got the inspiration from somewhere else it does not make the phenomenon illegitimate. If so, most of the Israelite and Judahite culture would receive the same verdict. In the case of the new altar, the sheer fact that it survived the reform of Hezekiah indicates that it did not represent any foreign cult practice.[2] Because Isaiah calls the priest Uriah a 'faithful, firm witness' (8.2), it can be assumed that the priest did not see the new altar as an obstacle to the nation's Yahweh cult.[3] However, there is one phrase in the text of 2 Kgs 16.18 that clearly points to changes that Ahaz undertook in the temple: the information that all this was done 'before the king of Assyria'. The statement points to some dependence upon Assyria,[4] but it is unknown how these changes affected the rituals. B. Landsberger has maintained that Assyria 'never forced conquered peoples to revere Ashur',[5] but there is information that Esarhaddon regulated sacrifices for Assyrian gods in Egypt.[6] Since the

1. Cf. N. Poulsen, *König und Tempel*, p. 92; E. Würthwein, *Könige*, II, p. 391.

2. See, for instance, P.R. Ackroyd, 'The Biblical Interpretation of the Reigns of Ahaz and Hezekiah', *In the Shelter of Elyon* (ed. W.B. Barrick and J.R. Spencer; JSOTSup, 31; Sheffield, 1984), pp. 250-52.

3. Because of this altar incident S. Yeivin suggests that Uriah probably had a 'weak character' ('The Divided Kingdom', *WHJP*, IV.1 [ed. A. Malamat], p. 177). The text does not give any hint in that direction.

4. H. Spieckermann has collected material that supports the view that there was some pressure upon the vassal states to acknowledge the supremacy of the god Ashur (*Juda unter Assur in der Sargonidenzeit*). Cf. also Ackroyd, 'The Biblical Interpretation', *In the Shelter of Elyon* (ed. W.B. Barrick and J.R. Spencer), pp. 250-52.

5. B. Landsberger, 'The Development of Culture in the National States: Mesopotamia up to the Assyrian Period', *City Invincible* (ed. C. Kraeling and R.M. Adams; Chicago, 1960), p. 177. Cf. J. McKay, *Religion in Judah under the Assyrians* (SBT, 29; Nashville, 1974).

6. D.D. Luckenbill, *ARAB*, II, par. 580; *ANET*, p. 293. See also M. Cogan, *Imperialism and Religion* (ed. L. Keck; SBLMS, 9; Missoula, MT, 1974), p. 52. Cogan follows in the main Landsberger and McKay. For a critique of Cogan's book, see G.W. Ahlström, *JAOS* 98 (1978), pp. 509-11.

biblical text is unclear, it is uncertain whether any Assyrian worship was introduced into Jerusalem's temple.[1] However, remembering that idols always were taken as booty by a conqueror to his capital[2] where they were considered servants of his god,[3] then this may be seen as the reverse phenomenon of a vassal's obligations to his overlord. It may be concluded that Ahaz, as a faithful vassal, displayed some reverence to the Assyrian gods or to Ashur in particular. This may have been done at the old brazen altar which, according to the text, Ahaz said should 'be to me for inquiry', *lᵉbaqqēr* (2 Kgs 16.15).[4] In other words, Ahaz could conduct whatever ritual he wanted at the old altar. The temple cult to Yahweh continued as before, the only difference being that Yahweh's new altar was perhaps more splendid than the old one. The priest Uriah would not have said no to such a phenomenon, and as a priest at a royal temple, he could not have opposed it either.[5] Ahaz emerges as a good diplomat preserving Judah's national and official religion in its traditional form as well as paying due respect to his new overlord at the old altar. Like other kings, he gives orders about changes in the cult, and he increases the nation's holiness through building altars 'at every street corner in Jerusalem', as 2 Chron. 28.24 expresses it. Concerning the remark that Ahaz is said to have let his son 'pass through fire' (2 Kgs 16.3),[6] this was a rare phenomenon that

1. S. Yeivin thinks that 'Ahaz tried only to introduce some imitation of the external ritual forms in the worship' of Yahweh ('The Divided Kingdom', *WHJP*, IV.1 [ed. A. Malamat], p. 177).

2. See, for instance, 2 Sam. 5.21, which says that after a successful battle against the Philistines David and his men took the gods the Philistines had left on the battlefield. In order to 'clean up' David's picture, the Chronicler writes that David then gave the order to burn the idols (1 Chron. 14.12). Another Judahite king taking and worshiping the gods of the enemies is Amaziah, who sacrifices to the gods of Seir (2 Chron. 25.14).

3. According to M. Cogan, deities being taken to Assyria could be seen as an expression of 'the literary motif of the gods voluntarily abandoning their faithful and flocking to Assyria to praise Ashur' (*Imperialism and Religion*, p. 23).

4. Thus H. Spieckermann, *Juda unter Assur in der Sargonidenzeit*, pp. 367-68.

5. S. Yeivin believes that this passage reflects 'the annulment of priestly influence in the realm' (in *WHJP*, IV.1 [ed. A. Malamat], p. 177). Again, it should be remembered that the king was in principle the high priest.

6. The D-historian says that Ahaz copied the 'shameful practices of the nations which Yahweh had dispossessed for the sons of Israel', a sentence that could not have been written before the Exile.

was used as the last 'straw' in a time of approaching disaster.[1] It should be compared with the sacrifice by king Mesha of Moab of his son, which resulted in the retreat of the Israelite and Judahite armies (2 Kgs 3.27). Later writers found this to be an abhorrent religious ritual and compared it with the sacrifices of children in the *tōpet* in the Valley of Hinnom outside Jerusalem. The prophet Jeremiah seems to have been the first one to object to the *tōpet* sacrifices (7.31-33; 19.5-6; but cf. Isa. 30.33).[2] There is also a commandment against this

---

1. H. Schmid thinks this occurred during the Syro-Ephraimite crisis (*Die grossen Propheten* [Die Schriften des Alten Testaments, II.2; Göttingen, 1923], p. 2).

2. For the origin of this type of sacrifice being west-Semitic and particularly Phoenician, consult, among others, R. de Vaux, *Les sacrifices de l'Ancient Testament* (Paris, 1964), pp. 55-81 (with lit.), and the résumé by J. Henninger, 'Menschenopfer bei den Arabern', *Anthropos* 53 (1958), pp. 766-84. A.T. Olmstead considered the *mulk*-sacrifices being directed to Yahweh (*History of Assyria*, p. 379). He is followed by J. Lindblom, *Israels religion i gammaltestamentlig tid* (2nd edn; Stockholm, 1953), p. 155, and P. Mosca, 'Child Sacrifice in Canaanite and Israelite Religion: A Study on Mulk and מלך' (PhD dissertation, Harvard University, Cambridge, MA, 1975). M. Weinfeld denies that children were sacrificed (*UF* 4 [1972], pp. 133-35). *Tophet* burial grounds also existed at 'Atlit, Tell el-Far'a (S) and Tell el 'Ajjul in Palestine; see K. Galling 'Der Weg der Phöniker nach Tarsis in literarischer und archäologischer Schicht', *ZDPV* 88 (1972), p. 142. The archaeological excavations at Punic Pozo Moro in Spain show a monument with a ritual scene with a god (with an animal head) on a throne and a table in front of him. He holds with one hand a pig lying on its back and in the other hand he has a bowl with the head and the feet of a little child (?) sticking up. He holds this bowl in front of his mouth. To the right there is another bowl, and a god with an animal head (horse?) holding a knife in his right hand above the bowl ready to slaughter the child. The scene (in a neo-Hittite style) shows both animal and child sacrifices as food for the gods. See M. Almagro-Gorbea, 'Pozo Moro: El monumento orientalizante, su contexto socio-cultural y sus paralelos en la arquitectura funeraria iberia', *Madrider Mitteilungen* (*Deutsches Archäologisches Institut Abteilung*) 24 (1983), pp. 176-293, *Tafel* 23 c. From this scene it could be asked whether Molech was also depicted with an animal head in Judah. If this scene reflects an old West-Semitic rite, the so-called *mulk*-sacrifices were not directed to Yahweh. Sacrifices of ox, man, lamb, dog and pig are mentioned in Isa. 66.4; cf. also Isa. 65.4-5, where the prophet denounces the sacrifice of pigs. For the pig as a sacred animal, see for instance A. von Rohr Sauer, 'The Cultic Role of the Pig in Ancient Times', *In Memoriam Paul Kahle* (ed. M. Black and G. Fohrer), pp. 202ff. J.M. Sasson has shown a Hittite parallel to the text in Isa. 66.3-4. Both texts mention the sacrifice of a man, a dog and a pig ('Isaiah LXVI 3-4a', *VT* 26 [1976], pp. 199-207). It is possible that Hittite rituals became part of the nonofficial cultic festivals of the Judahite population? Hittites were among the settlers

rite in Deut. 18.9-10.[1] 2 Kgs 16.3 should be seen in connection with 2 Kgs 17.17, which mentions that in the northern kingdom people also let 'sons and daughters pass through fire'. Both passages are part of the later, exilic D-historian's theological explanations for the disasters that happened to the kingdoms of Israel and Judah.[2]

It is apparent that the biblical opinion of king Ahaz is dependant upon a special evaluative pattern, 'good king–evil king', and Ahaz has been placed in the latter category. Whatever he did for his country's welfare and survival has been judged as a failure and the real truth has been hidden. From a literary standpoint Ahaz is painted as the opposite of his son and successor, Hezekiah,[3] the king who takes Judah to the brink of disaster, but who scores the highest mark next to David. Ahaz, who saves the kingdom, is denounced, but his son, who almost destroys it, is extolled.

The date of Ahab's death and the succession of his son Hezekiah seems to be an unsolvable problem. 2 Kgs 18.1 states that Hezekiah came to the throne in the third year of the reign of Hosea of Israel' and v. 10 repeats that Samaria fell in the sixth year of Hezekiah's reign. Thus, Hezekiah would have become king in the year 728/727. This date may be supported by Isa. 14.28, which states that the prophet Isaiah uttered the following oracle the same year Ahaz died:

---

of the hill country after 1200 BCE (cf. Gen. 23), so some Hittite rites may have become part of the popular religion of Judah. For Hittite influences in the hill country, consult A. Kempinski, *BARev* 5 (1979), pp. 20-45, and J.C. Moyer, 'Hittite and Israelite Cult Practices: A Selected Comparison', *Scripture in Context*, II (ed. W.W. Hallo, J.C. Moyer and L.G. Perdue), pp. 19-38. At Tell 'Umeiri in Jordan, pig bones have been found in Iron Age strata (L.E. Geraty, in a lecture given at the AOS/SBL/ASOR Midwestern Sections Annual Meetings at Berrien Springs, MI, February 9, 1986).

1.   This commandment is said to be given by Moses before the people 'entered' the land of Canaan, and is, thus, most probably part of the later Jewish society's historiographic reconstruction. The same phraseology about entering the land also occurs in Deut. 17.14 and 26.1.

2.   Cf. H.-D. Hoffmann, *Reform und Reformen*, pp. 132-33; J. Gray, *I and II Kings*, p. 630; A.H.D. Mayes, *The Story of Israel between Settlement and Exile*, p. 173 n. 48; E. Würthwein, *Könige*, II, pp. 394-95. See also H. Spieckermann, *Juda unter Assur in der Sargonidenzeit*, pp. 105-107.

3.   See, for instance, P.R. Ackroyd, 'The Biblical Interpretation of the Reigns of Ahaz and Hezekiah', *In the Shelter of Elyon* (ed. W.B. Barrick and J.R. Spencer), pp. 247-59.

'Do not rejoice all (the country) of Philistia because the rod that smote you is broken'.

The oracle continues with the statement that the serpent's stock ('root') still can produce offspring. This has often been understood to refer to the death of Tiglath-pileser III, who died in 727 BCE and who was the one who made an end to Philistine independence and secured the area down to the Egyptian border.[1] The 'offspring' coming from the north could then be both Shalmaneser V and Sargon II, who were responsible for the destruction of the nation of Israel. The latter also inflicted more disasters on the Philistines, disasters that perhaps also caused famine (cf. Isa. 14.30). The question here, however, is whether the oracle should be pressed into a fixed historical situation. The prophet (or the collector of the Isaiah oracles) knew that the 'rod' was broken, perhaps some time ago, but he also knew that it still could produce evil for Judah.[2]

2 Kgs 16.2 says that Ahaz ruled for 16 years in Jerusalem. If he died in 727, then he must have begun as coregent to his grandfather Uzziah in 744/743 BCE. This date would tally with the information that his son, Hezekiah, reigned for 29 years (until 698/697 BCE, 2 Kgs 18.2). It would also be in harmony with 2 Kgs 17.1, which mentions that Hosea of Israel became king in the twelfth year of Ahaz' reign. However, the statement in 2 Kgs 18.13//Isa. 36.1 that Sennacherib attacked Judah in the fourteenth year of Hezekiah seems to contradict the other information. According to these parallel passages, Ahaz would have died in 715/714 BCE, which means that he would have started his reign in 730 BCE. Because there are several biblical traditions that point to Hezekiah becoming king in 727 BCE, it may be concluded that the information in 2 Kgs 18.13 and Isa. 36.1 is either a mistake, or is written in such a way that it has been chronologically

---

1. E. König saw this as a reference to Tiglath-pileser III (*Das Buch Jesaja* [Gütersloh, 1926], pp. 188-89). According to H. Tadmor, Tiglath-pileser III was 'the only Assyrian king from the days of Ahaz worthy of such an epithet' (J.A. Soggin, *A History of Ancient Israel*, p. 381). H. Donner suggests that 'the rod' refers to Shalmaneser V (*Israel unter den Völkern*, pp. 110-13). For the discussion, consult also H. Wildberger, *Jesaja*, pp. 577-79. E.J. Kissane maintains that the point is not which Assyrian king died when, but that for Judah there is still hope. Therefore, let 'Philistia mourn... and there is no escape' (*The Book of Isaiah*, I, pp. 178-79).

2. Cf. Å. Bentzen, *Jesaja*, I (Copenhagen, 1944), p. 119.

misunderstood. If the Assyrian army attacked Jerusalem in Hezekiah's fourteenth year and Hezekiah came to the throne in 727 BCE, then the historical situation referred to must be the deliverance of the city of Jerusalem that occurred during the Assyrian campaign against Ashdod in 714–712 BCE,[1] or the biblical information is in this case a mistake.[2] The latter option seems to be the most probable because the Assyrian inscriptions do not mention an attack on Judah and/or Jerusalem during this campaign.[3]

This leads back to the international plan of politics. In 721 a Chaldean prince of Bit-Yakin, Marduk-apla-idinna (Merodach-baladan in 2 Kgs 20.12 and Isa. 39.1), came to the throne in Babylon and managed to unite several tribes in Babylonia. He also obtained the support of the king of Elam. After a battle against the Elamites at Der, which may have been a draw or a victory for the Elamites,[4] Sargon directed his attention to the west and southwest. Thus, he did not return to the Babylonian scene before 709, when Merodach-baladan lost the initiative and most of his territories were taken by the

---

1. For the literary problems, see A.K. Jenkins, who says that the fourteenth year 'did not originally introduce Hezekiah's payment of tribute', and 'the deliverance account did not originate from Sennacherib's campaign of 701 BCE' ('Hezekiah's Fourteenth Year: A New Interpretation of 2 Kings XVIII 13–XIX 37', *VT* 26 [1976], p. 286). K.T. Andersen believes that Jotham and Ahaz were one and the same person ('Noch einmal: Die Chronologie der Könige von Israel und Judah', *SJOT* [1989], pp. 16-25).

2. Hezekiah, who is said to have been ill at the time of Sennacherib's campaign against Judah in 701, is given a 'promise' that he would be saved from the Assyrian attack and that he would live 15 more years in Isa. 38.6. This arithmetic is most probably not that of Isaiah but instead the result of the narrator's calculation, knowing that Hezekiah ruled Judah for 29 years. H. Wildberger maintains that the 'Redaktor' of the Hezekiah–Isaiah narrative (Isa. 36–39) obviously did not have a clear picture of the historical events (*Jesaja*, p. 1377). For an evaluation of the source material, see also L.L. Honor, *Sennacherib's Invasion of Palestine* (New York, 1926), pp. 61-62.

3. J. Reade suggests that Hezekiah came to the throne in 721 BCE ('Mesopotamian Guidelines for Biblical Chronology', *Syro-Mesopotamian Studies*, IV.1 [ed. M. Kelly-Buccellati; Malibu, 1981], pp. 2-3). There are no biblical and no Assyrian texts that really support such a suggestion. Concerning the chronological problems, Reade says that 'the field of Biblical chronology is notoriously littered with scholars who have lost their heads' (p. 3).

4. See H. Tadmor, *JCS* 12 (1958), p. 38.

Assyrian army. Merodach-baladan had no choice but to flee to the marsh lands at the Persian Gulf.[1]

In 719 Sargon fought the Manneans and Urartu, and in 717 BCE he marched against Carchemish and annexed it. Its king, Pisri, and his family were taken prisoner. Pisri had broken the oath of loyalty and had conspired with king Mita (Midas) of Mushki.[2] In the south Sargon II received tribute from the Egyptian king Pir'u (Osorkon IV) in 715 BCE. In the same year he settled some Arabian tribes in Samaria.[3] After having defeated and smashed the army of King Rusa of Urartu and its allies in 714 BCE, Sargon's forces fought in the west and Cilicia was annexed and made a province of the empire.[4] Inscriptions relating to the Assyrian campaigns in northern Syria and Anatolia mention Cypriots, Ionians and Greeks. Thus, the demographic picture of the Near East becomes more complex and Greek influences are slowly increasing.[5]

To return to the Palestinian problems during the Sargonid period, the Assyrian army returned to Palestine in 712 BCE. Ashdod, which had been paying tribute together with Egypt, Gaza, Ekron, Judah, Moab, Ammon and Edom,[6] revolted.[7] Its king, Aziru, was found to have plotted so Sargon replaced him with his brother Ahimetu. The latter, however, was quickly overthrown by elements in the city state who are called 'Hittites' in the Sargon inscription. They put on the throne a commoner, a certain Iadna (Yamani),[8] who most probably was a Philistine.[9] Yamani managed to organize a coalition against

1.   Consult R.J. van der Spek, 'The Struggle of King Sargon II of Assyria against the Chaldean Merodach-baladan', *JEOL* 25 (1977–78), pp. 56-66; J.A. Brinkman, *Prelude to Empire*, pp. 45-54.

2.   *ANET*, p. 285.

3.   A.G. Lie, *The Inscriptions of Sargon II, King of Assyria*. I. *The Annals, Transliterated and Translated with Notes* (Paris, 1929), p. 22, Illuss. 121-23.

4.   For the chronology of Sargon's campaigns, see H. Tadmor, *JCS* 12 (1958), pp. 94ff.

5.   Another indication for Greek presence in northern Syria during the eighth century BCE is the existence of Rhodian pottery. This is known here from the time of Tiglath-pileser III; see D.L. Saltz, 'Greek Geometric Pottery in the East', p. 51.

6.   H.W.F. Saggs, *Iraq* 17 (1955), p. 134.

7.   It is possible that the revolt started around 714 BCE or somewhat earlier; cf. Isa. 20.1-3.

8.   D.D. Luckenbill, *ARAB*, II, pars. 30, 62.

9.   Cf. H. Tadmor, *BA* 29 (1966), p. 94.

Assyria. It included, besides the Philistine city states, also Judah, Moab, Edom, and 'those who live (on islands)'.[1] Yamani probably also sought help from Egypt and its king, Pir'u (pharaoh), 'a potentate, incapable to save them'.[2] The king of Egypt, probably Shabako, sent Yamani in chains back to Sargon in Assyria. Sargon's army under his *turtanu*, field marshal,[3] invaded the southern coastal area, the territories of the Philistines, and took Ashdod, Asdod-yam (*aš-du-di-im-mu*), Gath (*gi-im-tu*),[4] Gibetton and Ekron.[5] Ashdod[6] was made a province, Asdudi. Yamani's family, the Ashdodite gods, people, and treasures such as gold and silver, were taken to Assyria, and other peoples were resettled in Asdudi.[7] After rebuilding them, Sargon reorganized the administration of these cities and he put a governor over them, as he had done in Samaria. He explicitly states that their peoples were now Assyrians.[8] Sargon also made a victory stela of

1.   *ANET*, p. 287; cf. D.D. Luckenbill, *ARAB*, II, par. 195. The latter part of the phrase could probably refer to some Cypriot kings who may have felt threatened by Assyrian power. In 709 BCE Cyprus, together with Mita (Midas) of Mushki in Phrygia and Uperi of Dilmun (Bahrein) in the Persian Gulf, paid tribute to Sargon (D.D. Luckenbill, *ARAB*, II, pars. 185-86). This does not mean that Sargon had conquered Cyprus.

2.   A.L. Oppenheim in *ANET*, p. 287. What pharaoh the text refers to has been discussed above. It could still be Silkannu-Osorkon IV who probably died in 712 BCE, or Peye's successor in Memphis, Shabako (713–698). For these kings, see F. Gomaà, *Die libyschen Fürstentumer des Deltas*, p. 16 *et passim*. K.A. Kitchen opts for Shabako, with the argument that Osorkon could not have been king of Nubia (*The Third Intermediate Period*, pp. 143-44) The Assyrian text also mentions that Yamani fled to the border of Meluḫḫa (Nubia) (D.D. Luckenbill, *ARAB*, II, pars. 193-95).

3.   This is the *turtan* mentioned in Isa. 20.1.

4.   B. Mazar has identified this Gath with Gittaim in 2 Sam. 4.3 ('Gath and Gittaim', *IEJ* 4 [1954], pp. 227-29), but see Y. Aharoni, *The Land of the Bible* (2nd edn), p. 385 n. 154.

5.   Probably Khirbet el-Muqanna'; see J. Naveh, *IEJ* 8 (1958), pp. 87-89.

6.   For a mass grave with remains of over 2000 bodies probably to be dated to this period, see N. Haas, 'Anthropological Observations on the Skeletal Remains Found in Area D (1962–1963)', *Ashdod*, II-III (ed. M. Dothan; 'Atiqot, 9-10; Jerusalem, 1971), pp. 212-13.

7.   A.G. Lie, *The Inscriptions of Sargon II, King of Assyria*, I (Paris, 1929), p. 38, II.260-62.

8.   The Ashdod province was perhaps soon again made a vassal kingdom, because Sennacherib's inscriptions refer to a king of Ashdod, named Mitinti (D.D. Luckenbill, *The Annals of Sennacherib*, pp. 32-33).

basalt which he placed in Ashdod. Three fragments of it have been found at the excavations at Ashdod.[1] It is curious that Sargon's inscriptions do not mention the assault of any cities of Judah. Perhaps Hezekiah, the king of Judah, would not have risked a war at this time because of the poor strength of the coalition.[2] It is doubtful that Yamani would have been able to forge a strong coalition before the Assyrians arrived on the scene. By the way, it is not known whether Hezekiah had yet broken his vassal oath to the Assyrian king and joined the coalition. If he had not, Azekah would have been recognized by the Assyrian commander as a Philistine city. It is possible that the Assyrian army had marched through some of Judah's (former?) western territory and in this way cut off Hezekiah from further action—for a time. As a vassal of Sargon, Hezekiah could not have denied the Assyrian army permission to go through his country. Edom and Moab also seem to have been spared the destructions of war during this campaign; there is no mention of a punitive action against the two countries.

Sargon died in battle against the Cimmerians (Gomer in Gen. 10.2-3 and 1 Chron. 1.5-6) in 705 BCE[3] and was succeeded by his son Sennacherib. As was common, rebellions broke out in several parts of the empire.[4] In the west Tyre, Ashkelon and Judah rebelled. Among

1. See M. Dothan, *IEJ* 14 (1964), p. 87; H. Tadmor, 'Fragments of an Assyrian Stele of Sargon II', *Ashdod*, II-III (ed. M. Dothan; 'Atiqot 9-10; Jerusalem, 1971), pp. 192-97.

2. The conspiracy with Merodach-baladan of Babylonia (Isa. 39.1-3; 2 Kgs 21.12-14) would most probably have occurred first after 703, when Merodach-baladan again came to the Babylonian throne (for nine months) and tried to unite Elamites, Arabs, Arameans and Chaldeans against Assyria and its new king Sennacherib. Cf. J.A. Brinkman, *Prelude to Empire*, p. 57 n. 268. Strategically a military attack from a coalition in the southwest would have strengthened Merodach-baladan's position and created a dangerous circumstance for the Assyrian king.

3. The Cimmerians are known in the Ancient Near East first from the eighth century BCE when pressed by the Scythians, they moved from the areas north of the Sea of Azov via Caucasus in southern Russia. They became a dangerous threat not only to Urartu, but also to Assyria and its Anatolian dependencies (cf. D.D. Luckenbill, *The Annals of Sennacherib*, p. 9; H.W.F. Saggs, *The Might that was Assyria*, p. 97). Being latecomers to the Near East, they cannot have been known to any biblical writer before c. 700 BCE.

4. According to J.A. Brinkman, there 'is no clear evidence for political unrest in Assyria or Babylonia in 705 or 704' (*Prelude to Empire*, p. 55).

the Phoenician city state Tyre–Sidon seems to have been the driving force. It is possible that Hezekiah of Judah was a prominent leader of a south-Palestinian coalition that included Ashkelon under its new king Ṣidqa[1] and Ekron. Sennacherib's so-called Bull inscription reports that the nobles and the people of Ekron (which included Eltekeh, Gibbethon and Timnah) had dethroned their king, Padi, and delivered him in chains to Hezekiah.[2] It appears not only that Padi was keeping his status as a faithful vassal and that the Philistines were divided,[3] but that Hezekiah also must have played an important role in the conspiracy. In an inscription after Sennacherib's sixth campaign the Assyrian king says that he has devastated 'the wide province of Judah; the strong, proud Hezekiah, its king, I brought in submission to my feet'.[4] In Babylonia Merodach-baladan came back into power in 703 BCE and started to forge a coalition against the new Assyrian king. He won the support of the Elamites, some Arameans of Babylonia, and his own people, the Chaldeans. It is probably in this situation that Hezekiah received messengers and gifts from Merodach-baladan and showed them everything in the palace and in the storehouses (2 Kgs 20.12-15;[5] cf. 2 Chron. 32.31; Isa. 39.1-3; also Josephus, *Ant.* 10.2.2).[6] Hezekiah appears to have welcomed the support from the Babylonian king and made a treaty with him (cf. 2 Kgs 20.12-14).[7] Ammon, Moab and Edom were also invited to join the coalition, and Egypt

1. Ṣidqa may have come on the throne through a *coup d'état*; see the *Oriental Institute Prism Inscription*, col. II.60-66 (D.D. Luckenbill, *The Annals of Sennacherib*, pp. 30-31. It is likely that both a pro-Egyptian and a pro-Assyrian party existed in most Palestinian states.

2. D.D. Luckenbill, *ARAB*, II, par. 240; D.D. Luckenbill, *The Annals of Sennacherib*, p. 69; *ANET*, p. 287.

3. Gaza was also cool toward the coalition.

4. D.D. Luckenbill, *ARAB*, II, par. 347.

5. Cf. B.G. Ockinga, 'Hiskias "Prahlerei": Ein Beitrag zur Interpretation von 2 Könige 20, 12-19/Jesaja 39,1-8', *Fontes atque Pontes* (ed. M. Görg; ÅAT, 5; Wiesbaden, 1983), pp. 342-46.

6. For the differences in these passages, see J.A. Brinkman, 'Merodach-Baladan II', *Studies Presented to A.L. Oppenheim* (Chicago, 1964), pp. 31-32.

7. The Hebrew writer has placed the narrative about the Babylonian messengers after the report about the siege of Jerusalem. This would have been impossible after 701 BCE, because at that time Merodach-baladan was no longer king of Babylonia and was perhaps already dead; cf. J.A. Brinkman, 'Merodach-baladan II' (see previous note); *idem*, *Prelude to Empire*, p. 60. Cf. also J. Gray, *I and II Kings*, p. 701; E. Würthwein, *Könige*, II, p. 436.

promised its support[1] (cf. 2 Kgs 18.21). Egypt experienced a time of resurgence. Pharaoh Shabako (713–698?) of the Twenty-Fifth Nubian Dynasty had incorporated within his kingdom the eastern Delta, perhaps after Osorkon IV had died (712 BCE).[2] It is quite in order that he tried to encourage the Palestinian kings to rebel against Assyria. Were they successful, Egypt could once again dominate part of Palestine.[3] It was in Egypt's interest to get rid of the Assyrian presence at its border to Palestine. The south-Palestinian nations would then serve as a buffer zone between Egypt and Assyria.

Because Sennacherib could not immediately deal with the uprisings in the west, Ṣidqa of Ashkelon and Hezekiah of Judah obtained time to strengthen their defenses. This would also be the time when the nobles and the people of Ekron sent their king, Padi, as prisoner to Hezekiah. 2 Kings 18.8 has information about Hezekiah campaigning in Philistine territories, 'and he smote the Philistines as far as Gaza and the borders thereof, from watchtowers to fortified city'.[4] After the Assyrian campaign against Ashdod, with its territory having become a province of the empire, the Philistines were weakened. Hezekiah's influence in Philistia seems possible in the light of the handing over of Padi of Ekron to him as a prisoner. It may be assumed that king Ṣidqa of Ashkelon came on the throne as a supporter of an anti-Assyrian group[5] and that he also sought the support of Hezekiah. It is possible that Hezekiah marched into Philistine territory in order to show his strength and to gain support. He may also have taken Gath, 'a royal city of the Philistines', which Hezekiah seems to have fortified.[6]

As to Judah's relations with its eastern and southern neighbors, the picture is more uncertain. From Sennacherib's annals report that the kings of Ammon, Moab and Edom, together with the kings of Arvad,

---

1. For Isaiah's negative opinion about Egypt's strength, see Isa. 30.1-3 and 31.1-3.

2. On this, see the remarks of F. Gomaà, *Die libyschen Fürstentumer des Deltas*, pp. 140-41.

3. Cf. K.A. Kitchen, 'Egypt, the Levant and Assyria in 701 BCE', *Fontes atque Pontes* (ed. M. Görg; ÅAT 5; Wiesbaden, 1983), p. 246.

4. Cf. the unfortunate Ahaz, who is said to have lost the Shephelah to the Philistines (2 Chron. 28.18). His 'successful' son restored it.

5. Ashkelon's king, Rukibtu, who had been dethroned, is considered by H. Tadmor to be an older brother to Ṣidqa (*BA* 29 [1966], p. 96).

6. For the Assyrian text, see N. Na'aman, *BASOR* 214 (1974), pp. 26-27.

Sidon and Byblos, paid tribute to the Assyrian king.[1] Hezekiah ought to have worked for friendly relations between Judah and these neighbors in order to strengthen the coalition. Instead, 1 Chron. 4.34-43 claims that Simeonites overran Meunite territories 'in the days of Hezekiah', and also pressed into Mount Seir.[2] This action may show that the south was somewhat unstable politically and that the Arabs of the Negev and Transjordan could have opposed a Judahite expansion in these areas, for it would have meant a conflict with the Assyrians.

In preparing Judah's defense Hezekiah rebuilt the walls of Jerusalem, strengthened the Millo, and built stables and storehouses in the city (2 Chron. 32.5; Isa. 22.8-11; 2 Chron. 32.28-30). He also built a wall outside the city (2 Chron. 32.5). It is possible that this could be the above-mentioned wall that surrounded the *mišneh*, the 'second city'. The new settlers on the Western Hill had to be protected too.[3] Hezekiah's outer wall could also have served to protect the existing city wall.[4] The king's most famous work is the Siloam tunnel, through which the waters of the Gihon spring in the Kidron Valley outside the city were led into a pool within the city wall (2 Kgs 20.20; 2 Chron. 32.3-4, 30; cf. Isa. 22.11).[5] This tunnel, about 534 m long, was dug from both ends simultaneously, which may indicate that the project was done in haste and had to be finished as soon as possible.[6]

1. D.D. Luckenbill, *The Annals of Sennacherib*, p. 30, ll. 51-59.
2. The Hebrew text has *gdr* for the Meunite territory, but the LXX reads Gerar. For the probability that some places in southern Judah and the Negev had been destroyed before Sennacherib's campaign in 701 BCE, see N. Na'aman, *BASOR* 261 (1986), pp. 13-14.
3. Note that Isaiah does not mention the *mišneh*.
4. The massive wall, 65 m of which have been found in the Old City of Jerusalem by N. Avigad, could thus have been built after 701 BCE. The pottery sherds associated with this wall are from the eighth–seventh centuries BCE (N. Avigad, *Discovering Jerusalem*, pp. 46-57).
5. For a discussion of Isa. 22.11 and its possible connection with Hezekiah, see H. Wildberger, *Jesaja*, pp. 823-24.
6. The work is commemorated in a contemporary inscription that was found in the tunnel in 1880. For the text and translation, see A.T. Olmstead, *History of Palestine and Syria*, p. 477; J.C.L. Gibson, *TSSI*, I, pp. 21-23; *ANET*, p. 321. Cf. also G.E. Wright, *Biblical Archaeology* (Philadelphia, 1962), pp. 172-74; V. Sasson, 'The Siloam Tunnel Inscription', *PEQ* 114 (1982), pp. 111-17. Because the Siloam pool was not inside the old wall, N. Shaheen suggests that Hezekiah sealed the pool, if indeed the pool so named is to be identified with the pool of Hezekiah ('The Siloam End of Hezekiah's Tunnel', *PEQ* 109 [1977], p. 110). See

The extent to which Hezekiah fortified or refortified different places in the rest of Judah is not known. It can be assumed that several of the existing fortresses, such as Lachish, Tell el-Ḥesi and Gath, which he had taken from the Philistines, were inspected along with most other places, and, if necessary, repaired and well manned. Tell el-Ḥesi, located on the border between the Philistines and Judah (coord. 124-106) c. 12 km west of Tell ed-Duweir, could have been part of Judah during the time of Hezekiah, but probably became an Assyrian garrison city. The recent excavations have shown that in the eighth century it was a well fortified store city surrounded by two walls.[1] The fortified city of stratum VIB at Tel Halif (coord. 137-087) may have been destroyed by Sennacherib's campaign 701 BCE.[2] Beer-Sheba (str. II), Beth Shemesh (str. IIC), Arad (str. VIII), and Tell Beit Mirsim (str. A2) all seem to have been destroyed at the end of the eighth century. Whether the devastation was done by Sennacherib's invading forces, as Y. Aharoni among others suggests,[3] cannot be established.[4]

The fortress at Arad could equally have been captured by the Edomites. The territory south of a line from Arad to Beer-Sheba had a great percentage of Edomite inhabitants during the Assyrian period. With Edom having freed itself from Judahite vassalage, some part of Judah could have been captured by the Edomites during this period. It is noteworthy that the cities of Beer-Sheba and Beth-Shemesh were not rebuilt.[5]

In the more central Judean hills there was a system of smaller fortresses and watchtowers[6] from Horvat 'Ereṣ c. 15 km WNW of Jerusalem (coord 158.9-136-4) down to the western slopes of the Hebron area. These outposts were of great importance for speedy

also the discussion by H.J. Stoebe, 'Überlegungen zur Siloainschrift', *ZDPV* 71 (1955), pp. 124-40; H. Wildberger, *Jesaja*, pp. 822-23; H. Donner, 'Jerusalem', *Biblisches Reallexikon* (ed. K. Galling; 2nd edn; Tübingen, 1977), p. 161.

1.   See L.E. Toombs, 'Tell el-Ḥesi, 1981', *PEQ* 115 (1983), pp. 25-27; Y. Aharoni, *The Archaeology of the Land of Israel*, pp. 222-23.

2.   Cf. J.D. Seger, *BASOR* 252 (1983), p. 15.

3.   *The Archaeology of the Land of Israel*, p. 266.

4.   Cf. the discussion by N. Na'aman, *BASOR* 261 (1986), pp. 5-21.

5.   Y. Aharoni, *The Land of the Bible* (2nd edn), p. 393.

6.   Cf. 2 Chron. 27.4.

communication with the capital by means of smoke signals transmitted from the front.[1]

Jar handles stamped with a double-winged sun disc or a scarab with four wings—well-known Near Eastern royal symbols—and engraved with the Hebrew words *lmlk*, 'for the king', have been found in excavations at several places in Judah. Handles bearing private seals, perhaps belonging to royal officials, have also been discovered.[2] These jars are currently dated to the end of the eighth century BCE to the reign of Hezekiah.[3] They have often been seen as an indication of a reorganization of Judah's administration under Hezekiah.[4] This, however, is debatable.[5] The jar handles could reflect a temporary organization whose function was to store provisions in preparation for an attack by the Assyrian army, as has been maintained by N. Na'aman.[6] Y. Yadin has connected the jars with several cities of the central administration. The cities were important defense centers and as such were responsible for provisions.[7] The names of four towns are attested on many of these stamps: Hebron, Socoh, Ziph and *Mmšt*. The last place is unknown, but has sometimes been identified with Jerusalem.[8] Since several of the handles are made of clay that is 'indistinguishable' from that found in the environs of Jerusalem, the

1. See A. Mazar, 'Iron Age Fortresses in the Judean Hills', *PEQ* 114 (1982), pp. 87-109.

2. Cf. Y. Aharoni, *The Archaeology of the Land of Israel*, p. 256.

3. See D. Ussishkin, 'Royal Judean Storage Jars and Private Seal Impressions', *BASOR* 223 (1976), pp. 1-13; *idem*, 'The Destruction of Lachish by Sennacherib and the Dating of the Royal Judean Storage Jars', *Tel Aviv* 4 (1977), pp. 28-60, esp. pp. 54-57. Cf. Y. Yadin, 'The Fourfold Division of Judah', *BASOR* 163 (1961), pp. 6-12.

4. Cf. Y. Aharoni, *The Land of the Bible* (2nd edn), pp. 394-96; B. Oded in J.H. Hayes and J.M. Miller, *Israelite and Judean History*, p. 447. J. Bright suggests that the stamps could be seen as an 'effort on the part of the state to curb dishonesty in trade and in the collection of taxes' (*A History of Israel* [3rd edn], p. 284).

5. For the different viewpoints, consult P. Welten, *Die Königsstempel*, pp. 103-17.

6. *BASOR* 261 (1986), pp. 5-21.

7. *BASOR* 163 (1961), pp. 6-12.

8. Cf. H.L. Ginsberg, who sees *mmšt* as an abbreviation for *mmšlt* ('MMŠT and MSH', *BASOR* 109 [1948], pp. 20-21); Y. Aharoni, *The Land of the Bible* (2nd edn), pp. 298-99. *Contra* Ginsberg, see N. Avigad, 'New Light on the MSH Seal Impressions', *IEJ* 8 (1958), p. 118 n. 28.

term *Mmšt* perhaps refers not to the capital, but to a place in its environs.[1]

The jars with four handles (type 484) were all made in the Beth Govrin area,[2] so it can be concluded that the jars were made in royal workshops in this area. It is most interesting that the greatest amount of *lmlk* stamped handles have been found at Tell ed-Duweir (c. 350). Seventeen stamped handles have been reported from both Azekah and Mareshah and six from Tell eṣ-Ṣafi (Gath?). Only eleven have been found in the Judean Hills, all from Beth-Zur, and forty-four from Jerusalem.[3] N. Na'aman maintains that Hebron was 'the pivotal town in the distributional and defensive system'.[4] Why then would the jars have been made in the Shephelah and in the area of Jerusalem? Were they sent empty to Hebron, filled with provisions and then sent back to the fortified cities of the Shephelah? What role did Socoh and Ziph play in this connection? In other words, why are the names of no other cities engraved on the handles? This question has not been answered by Na'aman.

What has puzzled scholars is that the places in which the *lmlk* stamps have been found do not correspond to the place names stamped on the handles. Na'aman has tried to solve this problem by associating the *lmlk* jars with the list of cities fortified by Rehoboam in 2 Chron. 11.5-10. According to Na'aman, the fortification process should be assigned to Hezekiah instead.[5] Here Libnah is a crux because it is not mentioned in the list. Na'aman solves this problem by assuming that Libnah was fortified before the time of Hezekiah. This might be right, but why did not Hezekiah strengthen Libnah's defense, if Libnah was under his rule?[6] This is a problem Na'aman has not answered. In

1. It is hard to understand why Jerusalem alone should be given a cryptic name.

2. See the results of the laboratory analysis by H. Mommsen, I. Perlman and J. Yellin ('The Provenience of the *lmlk* Jars', *IEJ* 34 [1984], pp. 89-113). Even before the tests, D. Diringer had maintained that the jars had come from a central workshop ('Royal Jar-Handle Stamps of Ancient Judah', *BA* 12 [1949], p. 82); cf. W. Rudolph, *Chronikbücher*, p. 37.

3. N. Avigad, *Discovering Jerusalem*, p. 43.

4. *BASOR* 261 (1986), p. 15.

5. *BASOR* 261 (1986), pp. 5-21.

6. About 140 years earlier, Libnah had ceded from Judah at the same time that Edom freed itself from its vassalship to Judah (2 Kgs 8.22). Being located in the border area between the Philistines and Judah, Libnah may have allied itself with the Philistines (cf. S. Timm, *ZDPV* 96 [1980], p. 27 n. 39).

order to strengthen his hypothesis Na'aman relies upon another hypothesis. He maintains that 'several towns in the area north of Jerusalem were originally included within the list of 2 Chron. 11.6-10'.[1] His assumption reflects a concentration of *lmlk* stamps found in this area. Na'aman therefore suggests that the Chronicler may have shortened the list of fortified cities, 'omitting the cities north of Jerusalem'. The original list, therefore, is 'no longer available to us'.[2] His proposal is no more than guesswork. I would maintain that the notion that Rehoboam fortified these cities still needs to be entertained. It is most probable that Hezekiah strengthened the fortifications and made repairs where necessary; most every king did. However, the list in 2 Chron. 11.6-10 would very well suit the political situation during the time of Rehoboam. He fortified several cities in Judah in order to protect the hill country from an attack either from the south or from the west. That was clearly a defense measure against Egypt. Rehoboam did not expect an attack from a powerful army from the north. Jeroboam's poor showing in defending his kingdom meant that there was no need for a strong line of fortifications in the north of Judah. The 'openness' of the border can be seen as an indication that neither Judah nor Rehoboam accepted the split of the Solomonic kingdom. Rehoboam's successors, Abijah and Asa, were able to annex some of the territory in southern Ephraim—including Bethel, according to 2 Chron. 13.3-19. Finally, it could be asked why the Chronicler would credit Rehoboam with a laudable work he had not done, taking 'honor' away from Hezekiah whom the Chronicler considered a 'model' king.

In the Bible Hezekiah is primarily appreciated for his so-called cult reform. The report of the event seems to be overexaggerated, and in some ways it is a literary duplicate of the one carried out by King Josiah a century later. In preparing for a rebellion against the Assyrians, Hezekiah without doubt reorganized his administration and his army and prepared his defenses. Since the religion, together with its priesthood, was an arm of the royal administration, it follows that some action was undertaken so show the new king's pretention to independence. Thus, the cultic reorganization should not be seen to stem primarily from the king's personal religious feelings and devotion, as 2 Kgs 18.5-6 presents it. That depiction is part of the

1. *BASOR* 261 (1986), p. 12.
2. *BASOR* 261 (1986), p. 10.

religious propaganda. Through religious and cultic actions or commands a king could show his political stand and program and could make changes and innovations. According to 2 Chron. 29.3, Hezekiah started to change things almost immediately after his father's death. In the first month of his rule he opened and repaired the doors of the temple that his father had closed, and then the temple was purified. From the Chronicler's point of view it is natural to propagate this view because he wanted to depict him to have been a 'pure Yahwist' his entire life. Still, Hezekiah probably would have wanted to show as soon as possible that his political and religious attitudes were different from those of his father. Whether this meant that a cultic reform was ever instituted in his first year as king is debatable. There is no information about when all the cult paraphernalia that 2 Chron. 31.1 maintains was smashed in Judah, Benjamin, Ephraim and Manasseh might have been eliminated, and the text most probably is an exaggeration. Neither is it known when the official sanctuaries, *bāmôt*, outside Jerusalem were abandoned or when the copper serpent, Nehushtan, that Moses supposedly made,[1] was destroyed and its worship terminated (2 Kgs 18.4).[2] Nehushtan was given 'Mosaic' legitimation because it was a pre-Davidic cultic symbol in Jerusalem[3] and thus, part of the Jebusite heritage. However, the snake was not only a Jerusalemite symbol. It was very common in the ancient near East and was often associated with female deities.[4] The horned altar found at Beer-Sheba, for instance, had a snake engraved on one of its stones.[5]

---

1. See the etiological story in Num. 21.6-9.

2. If Hezekiah had destroyed a symbol made or authorized by Moses he could not possibly have been a 'pure-Yahwist'. This action by Hezekiah would rather show that the Mosaic ideal is that of a later time. Hezekiah did not know about Moses as the organizer of the cult.

3. H.H. Rowley, *JBL* 58 (1939), pp. 113-41; G.W. Ahlström, *Psalm 89*, p. 61.

4. Cf. R.A.S. Macalister, *The Excavation of Gezer: 1902–1905 and 1907–1909*, III (London, 1912), pl. 221.9; A. Brock-Utne, *Der Gottesgarten: Eine vergleichende relgionsgeschichtliche Studie* (Avhand. utgitt at Det Norske Videnskaps Akademi i Oslo. II Hist.-Filos. Klasse 1935, 2; Oslo, 1936), pp. 39-52; K.R. Joines, 'The Bronze Serpent in the Israelite Cult', *JBL* 87 (1968), pp. 245-50; P. Welten, 'Schlange', *Biblisches Reallexikon* (ed. K. Galling; 2nd edn; Tübingen, 1977), pp. 280-82.

5. See Y. Aharoni, 'The Horned Altar of Beer-Sheba', *BA* 37 (1974), p. 4 fig. 2.

The writer of 2 Kings 18 devotes only one verse to Hezekiah's reform (18.4), and then he gives a reference to it in the *rab šāqê* speech (18.22). This should be compared with about three chapters in the writings of the Chronicler (2 Chron. 29–31). This brevity, along with the fact that the prophet Isaiah does not in any way refer to or praise Hezekiah for a reform, leads to the suspicion that the Chronicler has overinterpreted some religious reorganization undertaken by Hezekiah.[1] There is also a difference between Kings and the Chronicler concerning the *bāmôt*. 2 Kgs 18.4 says that Hezekiah abandoned (*swr* in *hiph.* = suppress, remove) the *bāmôt*, the royal sanctuaries of the country. The Chronicler uses the verb *nts*, 'pull down' (31.3), thus indicating that all of the *bāmôt* were destroyed. As maintained earlier,[2] the text in 2 Kgs 18.4 indicates that Hezekiah may have changed the status of these sanctuaries. They were no longer part of the central administration. However, what would have been the purpose of changing the status of the sanctuaries? In preparing his country for war against the Assyrians, which he understood must come sooner or later, Hezekiah certainly would not have wished to diminish the power of the divine sphere that was under his control. Neither would he have sought to alienate his people by destroying their sanctuaries. Had Yahweh been worshiped at one place only, his power would have been very limited. His 'cosmos' would have been severely narrowed. It seems likely that Hezekiah had all the cult paraphernalia and idols, as well as the priests, transferred to Jerusalem in order to strengthen the holiness of the city and to salvage all the treasures of the sanctuaries so they did not fall into the hands of the Assyrians.

In support of Hezekiah's execution of a severe cult reform, scholars have often referred to the temple at Arad and to the destruction of the sanctuary and the horned altar at Beer-Sheba. There is no way to prove anything as yet. It should be noted, however, that Beer-Sheba could have been destroyed by war as well, so that the destruction of its cult place cannot be used as evidence for the activities of a religious

---

1. Cf. J. Gray, who maintains that the 'statement of Hezekiah's uniform success reflects the Deuteronomistic opinion of the merits of a reformer rather than the actual course of history' (*I and II Kings*, p. 671). To this should be added the Chronicler's opinion about Hezekiah's problems: 'God only deserted him to test him' (2 Chron. 32.31).

2. See my *Royal Administration*, p. 66.

reformer.[1] The same could have happened at Arad. An ostracon (str. VIII), no. 49, found in a room adjacent to the temple, has the names 'sons of Korah' and 'sons of Bezalel', establishing that the temple belonged to the official Judahite cult. As has been mentioned before, the stratigraphy of Arad is a point of debate. Usually stratum VIII has been assigned to the period of Hezekiah, and the 'abolishment' of the altar in the temple yard is seen to result from Hezekiah's reform. The possibility that Arad was not Judahite after 701 must also be taken into consideration. In the time of Esarhaddon, Judah did not rule over the Negev.[2] It is likely then that control over the fortress with its Judahite temple would have changed hands and would no longer have belonged to Judah's administration and religion.

The literary composition of the history of the kings Ahaz, Hezekiah, Manasseh and Josiah must be considered when weighing the historicity of Hezekiah's reform. The narrator has clearly used a pattern that alternates evil and good kings to express his 'historiography'. The bad king Ahaz is followed by the good and exemplary king Hezekiah. He in his turn is followed by the 'evil' Manasseh, whose grandson Josiah is another exemplary and ideal king. Such a pattern is not of much help when trying to establish historical fact.[3]

Usually the historicity of some kind of cult reorganization by Hezekiah is accepted because of the speech that Sennacherib's *rab šāqê* is depicted to have delivered in Jehudit (Hebrew) to the defenders on the walls of Jerusalem (2 Kgs 18.17-35; see Fig. 5). The speech corresponds to what is known of Assyrian customs from extrabiblical parallels.[4] The biblical version refers to the Assyrian policy of

---

1. For the sanctuary, see Z. Herzog, 'Israelite Sanctuaries at Arad and Beer-Sheba', *Temples and High Places in Biblical Times* (ed. A. Biran; Jerusalem, 1981), pp. 120-22. Concerning the destruction of Beer-Sheba, see N. Na'aman, who thinks that the place could have been destroyed already before 701 BCE (*BASOR* 261 [1986], p. 13).

2. As to the stratigraphy and the history of Arad, see Z. Herzog, M. Aharoni, A.F. Rainey and S. Moshkovitz, *BASOR* 254 (1984), pp. 1-34.

3. H.-D. Hoffmann concluded that Hezekiah never carried through a cultic reform. For him, 2 Kgs 18.1-6 is a literary fiction used as an artistic ingredient ('ein Kunstmittel') in the historiography of the cult (*Reform und Reformen*, p. 155).

4. According to H. Wildbeger, the *rab šāqê* followed certain Assyrian models for his speech ('Die Rede des Rabsake von Jerusalem', *TZ* 35 [1979], p. 35). See, for instance, H.W.F. Saggs, *Iraq* 17 (1955), pp. 23-25; *The Might that was Assyria*, pp. 91, 263.

deportation, here to a good land of 'corn and good wine, of bread and of vineyards, a land of oil and honey' (18.32).[1] The speech also refers to earlier conquests of the Assyrian kings at Hamath, Arpad, Sepharvaim and Samaria (v. 34),[2] which had taken place so recently that the people of Jerusalem would certainly have realized what their fate would be if the city were taken. The *rab šāqê*'s reference to the abandonment of the *bāmôt*, sanctuaries, and the altars and the restriction of worship to Jerusalem (v. 22) occurs abruptly in the speech and appears to be an insertion by the writer to suit his purposes.[3] The idea that a person should rely on Yahweh only is more a prophetic concept than that of a military and state leader, and one typical of Isaiah. Thus, there is reason to suspect that 2 Kgs 18.17–20.19 is a tradition that originated in prophetic circles.[4] In contrast to this tradition 2 Kgs 18.14-16 is a short summary of events and may be a more reliable account than its prophetic counterpart in 2 Kgs 18.17–20.19//Isaiah 36. Consequently, there is little information available about Hezekiah's years as king. The Chronicler's stories about Hezekiah are a later time's elaborations of the deuteronomistic pattern about bad and good kings. Hezekiah's purported Passover celebration is probably a postexilic attempt to anchor the festival in the pre-Josianic period. As in the case of Josiah's Passover, nothing like this supposedly had happened in Jerusalem since the days of Solomon (2 Chron. 30.26).[5] The similar claims in both instances lead to the suspicion that the Passover is a late phenomenon. Like any king, Hezekiah and Josiah both could have made changes in the festival calendar, so the spring festival may very well have been changed somewhat or revised.[6] The

1. Cf. H.W.F. Saggs, 'Assyrian Prisoners of War and the Right to Live', *AfO Beiheft* 19 (1982), p. 91.

2. Note that in the LXX (L), the chief cup-bearer in his speech also asks 'Where are the gods of the land of Samaria'. This would have been the logical sequence of events.

3. H.-D. Hoffmann also sees it as a disturbing insertion (*Reform und Reformen*, p. 150).

4. As to its literary origin, 2 Kgs 18.17–20.19 most probably does not have an 'original connection with the basic work of the deuteronomistic historian' (so expressed by A.D.H. Mayes, *The Story of Israel between Settlement and Exile*, p. 115).

5. For Josiah's Passover, see 2 Kgs 23.21-23.

6. H. Haag sees Hezekiah's festival as the *maṣṣôt* and Josiah's as *pesaḥ* ('Das Mazzenfest des Hiskia', *AOAT* 18 [1973], pp. 87-94).

Passover, as the postexilic Jewish community knew it, was not known to the peoples of Judah of the pre-exilic period.[1] For this reason it is difficult to accept the Chronicler's report that Hezekiah invited the peoples of the Assyrian province of Samerina to go to Jerusalem to celebrate the Passover with the Judahites (2 Chron. 30.1-14).[2] This text has usually been used to argue that Hezekiah tried to expand his kingdom to the north in an attempt to unite once again the peoples of the north and south.[3] If Hezekiah had really dared such a reunification, it would most certainly have happened in the years shortly after the fall of the kingdom of Israel but before the firm incorporation of its territory into the Assyrian empire; Hezekiah would have tried to obtain Israelite territory before 716 BCE, when Sargon organized the Palestinian provinces,[4] and in this connection also settled Arabs in Samaria. More specifically, the suitable time for such an enterprise would have been before 720 BCE when Sargon II was occupied in the north and the east, and before he turned to the west and put down the rebellion by Arpad, Simirra, Damascus, Samaria, and probably also Judah.[5] According to 2 Chron. 30.10-11, most of the people of Manasseh and Ephraim laughed at Hezekiah's

---

1. J.W. Rothstein thinks that the mention of the Passover in ch. 30 is not original to the chapter (*Die Bücher der Chronik*, II [ATD; Leipzig, 1923], p. 660).

2. Hezekiah's address to the northerners shows the postexilic ideology: 'Sons of Israel, return to Yahweh, the God of Abraham, Isaac, and Israel' (2 Chron. 30.6). Similar phraseology occurs in 1 Kgs 18.36 and 1 Chron. 29.18. J. Bright says that Hezekiah speaks to the peoples of the north 'as if they were the later Samaritans' (*A History of Israel* [3rd edn], p. 283).

3. Among recent advocates of this idea are E.W. Nicholson, 'The Centralization of the Cult in Deuteronomy', *VT* 13 (1963), pp. 383-89; B. Oded in J.H. Hayes and J.M. Miller, *Israelite and Judean History*, p. 444; N. Poulssen, *König und Tempel*, pp. 93-94; J. Bright, *A History of Israel*, p. 283; J. McKay, *Religion in Judah under the Assyrians*, p. 17; Y. Aharoni, *The Land of the Bible* (2nd edn), p. 387; H. Reviv, 'The History of Judah from Hezekiah to Josiah', *WHJP*, IV.1 (ed. A. Malamat), p. 194. J.M. Myers holds the opinion that the 'partial success' of Hezekiah 'formed the pattern upon which the Deuteronomistic movement later proceeded' with its goal 'to save the nation' (*II Chronicles* [AB, 13; Garden City, NY, 1965], pp. 176-77).

4. See H. Tadmor, *JCS* 12 (1958), p. 35.

5. In one text Sargon is called 'the subduer of Judah', a land that is 'far away' (H. Winckler, *Die Keilschifttexte Sargons I* [Leipzig, 1889], p. 188, 11.28-30); cf. the discussion in H. Tadmor, *JCS* 12 (1958), p. 38 n. 146.

messengers when they heard the invitation and were told that Jerusalem was the only place to worship Yahweh.[1] Realistically, since Yahweh of Jerusalem was not the god of Ephraim and Manasseh, the cult in Jerusalem could not establish the religious order and well-being (blessings) of territories not under Jerusalem's control. Yahweh's power was limited to his kingdom of Judah. Yahweh of Samaria and Bethel, or elsewhere, could be worshipped still, but this was not the concern of Jerusalem. The Chronicler does not like to mention this elementary fact. If the 'new' Passover of Hezekiah is a fiction created by the Chronicler, so also is the invitation to the northerners.[2] 2 Chron. 30.1-14 cannot be used as an indication for Hezekiah's policy of expansion.

701 BCE

After he put down the rebellions in Mesopotamia and solved the Babylonian problem, which resulted in Merodach-Baladan's defeat and disappearance from the historical stage,[3] Sennacherib turned to the west in 701 BCE. The first goal of the campaign was to quell the rebellion among the Phoenicians.[4] Since Luli (Elulaeus) of Tyre and Sidon controlled the coastal area of Palestine north of the Philistines, that is, north of Joppa, the trunk road from Egypt to Syria was partly in his hands. Luli, who had been the *primus motor* in trying to forge a coalition against Assyria,[5] found it impossible to fight the Assyrians

1. The ideal king, Hezekiah, could not completely fail, so the Chronicler says that 'a few men from Asher, Manasseh and Zebulon humbled themselves and came to Jerusalem' (30.11).

2. From 2 Chron. 30.10-11. W. Rudolph draws the logical conclusion that this text cannot be used as proof that Deuteronomy originated in the northern kingdom (*Chronikbücher*, p. 330 n. 1).

3. D.D. Luckenbill, *The Annals of Sennacherib*, pp. 66-67, ll. 4-6; cf. J.A. Brinkman, 'Merodach-Baladan II', *Studies Presented to A.L. Oppenheim*, pp. 22-27; cf. L.D. Levine, 'Sennacherib's Southern Front', *JCS* 34 (1982), pp. 28-58.

4. For the geographical and chronological order of the campaign, which was Sennacherib's third, see N. Na'aman, *VT* 29 (1979), pp. 64-65.

5. For the reign of Luli, see H.J. Katzenstein, *The History of Tyre*, pp. 200-58. According to Josephus, Luli reigned 36 years (*Ant.* 9.284). W. von Landau has shown that Josephus' attribution of the name Pyas given to Luli must be a mistake and most probably refers to Pul (Tiglath-pileser III): 'Die Belagerung von Tyrus

and fled to Cyprus where he died;[1] a scornful picture of his actions is given in Isa. 23.12-14 (Kittim would be no place for a fugitive to rest).[2] Luli's cities, including Great and Little Sidon, Achzib and Acco had submitted, which means that Tyre's territory on the Phoenician coast was subdued. It is probably after this loss that Luli fled to Cyprus. Sennacherib then placed Tuba'lu (Ethbaal) on the throne.[3] This would then be the time when the kings of 'Amurru', i.e. most of the kings of Phoenicia and Palestine, including Transjordan, paid tribute to Sennacherib at Ushu opposite Tyre.[4] Urumilki of Byblos, Abdili'ti of Arvad, Menahem of Šamsimuruna and Mitinti of Ashdod appear in the tribute records. This may indicate that Ashdod's status had changed back to that of a vassal state, having been made a province by Sargon II in 712 BCE.[5] Gaza is not mentioned in this connection, but it is possible, as K.A. Kitchen suggests, that its king, Sillibel, 'was under the control of Taharqa' and the Egyptian army.[6] Also mentioned, however, are Budu-ilu (or Pudu-ilu) of Ammon, Kammasu-nadbi of Moab, and Malik-rammu of Edom. The Palestinian coalition was thus severely weakened. The only two left were Ashkelon and Judah, both of which relied on the support of Egypt, which had reemerged as a power to reckon with under the Twenty-Fifth Dynasty. Pharaoh Shabako, who conquered the Delta, had made

durch Salmanassar bei Menander', *Beiträge zum Altertumskunde des Orients*, I (Leipzig, 1893), p. 14; on this subject, cf. also H.J. Katzenstein, *History of Tyre*, pp. 221-22.

1. Luli's flight is depicted on an Assyrian relief; see R.D. Barnett and A. Lorenzini, *Assyrian Sculpture in the British Museum* (Toronto, 1975), p. 28.

2. H. Wildberger thinks that Assyria had built up Cyprus as a navy base (*Jesaja*, pp. 878-79). Even if kings of Cyprus paid tribute to Sargon II in 709 it does not mean that Kition—a Tyrian colony—would have continued to pay tribute when Sargon died. Thus, it would be natural for Luli to escape to Kition, even though Kition had rebelled along with other Phoenician cities against Luli and his policy of resistance against Assyria under Shalmaneser V (cf. H. Katzenstein, *The History of Tyre*, p. 226; B. Oded in *WHJP*, IV.1 [ed. A. Malamat], p. 243).

3. D.D. Luckenbill, *The Annals of Sennacherib*, pp. 68-69, ll. 18-19; *ibid.*, *ARAB*, II, pars. 239, 326; *ANET*, p. 287.

4. See also D.D. Luckenbill, *ARAB*, II, par. 310.

5. The Assyrian inscriptions do not provide clear information about this problem. One may ask with H. Tadmor whether the Assyrians had allowed local dynasts to rule under the supervision of a governor (*BA* 29 [1966], p. 95).

6. 'Egypt, the Levant and Assyria in 701 BCE', *Fontes atque pontes* (ed. M. Görg), p. 247.

a peace treaty with Assyria after the revolt by Ashdod in 712 in order to get stabilize conditions in the east and to be able to consolidate his own position in Egypt. On the surface, Palestine was stable in terms of its political climate until Sennacherib came to the throne.[1] Militarily and economically speaking, the whole of Phoenicia, the Palestinian coast north of Joppa and Transjordan were now in the hands of Sennacherib.

Having quelled the rebellion of the Phoenicians, and also having secured the loyalty of all the Transjordanian kingdoms, Sennacherib could start the second stage of his campaign. Unfortunately for the Palestinian allies, they did not combine their forces to confront the Assyrian army. Sennacherib was able to take city after city. He moved down south taking Beth-Dagon, Joppa, Bene-berak and Azor, all cities belonging to the kingdom of Ashkelon.

It is perhaps a matter for curiosity that Sennacherib's inscriptions do not mention the capture of either Ashkelon or Lachish. What is clear from the inscriptions, however, is that Ashkelon's king, Ṣidqa, and his family were taken prisoner and removed to Assyria.[2] A brother (?) of Ṣidqa, Sharru-lu-dari,[3] was placed on the throne by the Assyrian king.[4] Whether Ṣidqa submitted or the city was captured is thus of less importance. After his cities and territories to the north had been taken, Ṣidqa may have capitulated because the next move by Sennacherib was directed against Ekron, according to the annals.[5] This could mean that the Assyrian army never besieged Ashkelon. Before Sennacherib reached Ekron[6] he encountered an Egyptian-Cushite force at Eltekeh

1. Cf. H. Tadmor, *JCS* 12 (1958), p. 84.

2. D.D. Luckenbill, *The Annals of Sennacherib*, p. 69, ll. 20-21; *idem*, *ARAB*, II, par. 239; *ANET*, p. 287.

3. Sharru-lu-dari was, according to the inscription, son of Rukibtu (*ANET*, p. 287).

4. Thus D. Marcus, 'Sharruludari, Son of Rukibtu, their Former King: A Detail of Phoenician Chronology', *JANESCU* 9 (1977), pp. 27-30.

5. D.D. Luckenbill, *The Annals of Sennacherib*, p. 69, ll. 22-23. It should be said, however, that the annals do not always tell everything, and the events may have happened in a different way than reported.

6. Ekron has been identified with Kh. el. Muqanna', in other words, Tel Miqne. For the recent excavations, see the discussion in T. Dothan and S. Gitin, 'Tel Miqne', *IEJ* 32 (1982), pp. 150-53; see also *idem*, 'Tel Miqne', *IEJ* 33 (1983), pp. 127-29.

(probably Tell esh-Shallaf, 3 km north of Jabneh[1]), which finally moved into Palestine to support the rebellion. This force was under the nominal command of prince Taharqa (biblical Tirhaqah).[2] According to Kitchen, Taharqa did not participate in the battle at Eltekeh, but stayed in Gaza, where he had established his headquarters.[3] Sennacherib's annals report that the Egyptian army was defeated. Sennacherib says that he also captured 'Egyptian princes, together with the charioteer of the king of Meluḫḫa'.[4] It is possible, however, as Kitchen advocates, that the Egyptian army was not really defeated but merely repulsed.[5]

The Assyrian army was able to continue to Ekron, which probably submitted without a siege. The leaders who had conspired with Hezekiah and who had handed over Ekron's king, Padi, to Hezekiah, were slain and the rest of the rebellious citizens were 'counted as spoil'. Those who had not rebelled (the party faithful to the Assyrians) were pardoned.[6] Sennacherib mentions that he had Padi freed from Jerusalem and reinstated as king of Ekron.[7] When this was done is not clear, but it could not have occurred before Hezekiah himself was threatened and some negotiations had started, i.e. after Ekron and its surrounding areas had been taken. That meant that the Assyrian army had come closer to Judah proper.

After Ekron, Sennacherib turned against neighboring Azekah (Tell

---

1. Cf. B. Mazar, 'The Cities of the Territory of Dan', *IEJ* 10 (1960), pp. 65-77; Y. Aharoni, *The Land of the Bible* (2nd edn), p. 389. In Josh. 19.44 and 21.23 Eltekeh is listed as a Danite city.

2. The biblical narrator gives Taharqa the title king (2 Kgs 19.9; Isa. 37.9). Taharqa reigned 690–664 BCE; see K.A. Kitchen, *The Third Intermediate Period*, pp. 387-89.

3. K.A. Kitchen, 'Egypt, the Levant and Assyria', p. 250.

4. D.D. Luckenbill, *The Annals of Sennacherib*, p. 69, ll. 24-25; R. Borger, *Babylonisch-assyrische Lesestücke*, II (2nd edn; Rome, 1979 [1963]), pp. 67-68). In Assyrian texts of this time Meluhha refers to Nubia. It seems to be a term used for 'the homeland of people of dark complexion' (A.L. Oppenheim, *Ancient Mesopotamia*, p. 64). See also S. Parpola, *Neo-Assyrian Toponyms*, pp. 234, 245-46; cf. H. Klengel, 'Das Land Kusch in den Keilschrifttexten von Amarna', *Ägyptien und Kusch* (Festschrift F. Hintze; ed. E. Endesfelder *et al.*; Berlin, 1977), pp. 227-32.

5. K.A. Kitchen, 'Egypt, the Levant and Assyria', pp. 247-48.

6. D.D. Luckenbill, *The Annals of Sennacherib*, p. 70, ll. 25-26.

7. Lines 26-27.

Zakariyeh) in the Elah Valley. Thus he now entered Judah's territory. In a text labeled 'letter to God', Sennacherib describes the city of Azekah as being 'located on a mountain ridge, like pointed iron (?), daggers without number reaching high to heaven...[its walls] were strong and rivaled the highest mountains, to the (mere) sight, as if from the sky [appears its head?...]'.[1] The city was taken and devastated, and its surviving population carried away 'as spoil'. It is possible that Gath (Tell eṣ-Ṣafi?[2]) was besieged at the same time by a detachment of the Assyrian army. The 'letter to God' mentions a 'royal city of the Philistines' which Hezekiah had captured (line 11). If this refers to a capital city of the Philistines, it can only be Gath. It is in connection with the siege of this 'royal city' that the 'letter to God' mentions that Sennacherib had Syro-Palestinian soldiers in his army. They are here called soldiers of 'Amurru' who had to carry earth (line 18), probably in order to build a siege ramp. The letter also reveals that Hezekiah had mercenaries defending the city (line 17).[3] In taking Azekah and Gath Sennacherib had the roads open to Jerusalem, Libnah and Lachish. From Sennacherib's inscriptions nothing is learned about all the places that were taken by his army. However, the text of Mic. 1.8-16 provides a picture of the Assyrian campaign in Judah as well as an indication that cities such as Moreshet-Gath (Micah's home town), Beth-leaprah, Shapir, Zaanan, Beth-ezel, Maroth,[4] Achzib, Adullam and Mareshah probably were taken and/or destroyed.[5]

1. Translation by N. Na'aman, *BASOR* 214 (1974), p. 27; cf. *idem*, *VT* 29 (1979), pp. 66-67.

2. Thus K. Elliger, *ZDPV* 57 (1934), pp. 148-52; Y. Aharoni, *Land of the Bible* (2nd edn), p. 271; A.F. Rainey, *EI* 12 (1975), pp. 63*-76*. H.E. Kassis suggests Tell el-Manshiyyeh ('Gath and the Structure of the Philistine Society', *JBL* 84 [1965], pp. 259-70).

3. N. Na'aman thinks this meant that Hezekiah could not trust the Philistine inhabitants of the city (*BASOR* 214 [1974], p. 29). He may be right in part, but there should be no surprise about finding mercenaries in Judah's army; the hiring of foreigners is a phenomenon almost as old as the armies themselves. For Hezekiah employing mercenaries for the defense of Jerusalem, see the Oriental Institute Prism (D.D. Luckenbill, *The Annals of Sennacherib*, col. III.38-39).

4. The location of these last four towns is not known.

5. Cf. K. Elliger, *ZDPV* 57 (1934), pp. 81-152; H. Donner, *Israel unter den Völkern*, pp. 92-94; N. Na'aman, *BASOR* 261 (1986), p. 11. It is not necessary to conclude that all these places were destroyed. Some of the more insignificant places were probably bypassed, others burned and/or looted.

The main centers of resistance, besides Jerusalem, seem to have been Lachish and Libnah. Sennacherib probably left a detachment at Libnah while he himself continued with the main part of the army to Lachish.[1] It is likely that Moreshet-Gath and Mareshah were taken during his march towards Lachish. At Lachish Sennacherib temporarily established his headquarters, and areas south of the city or in its vicinity may well have been taken during the preparations for the siege of the stronghold Lachish. Some of the places mentioned in Mic. 1.8-16 could have fallen at this point in time. There is no mention of the fall of Lachish in the Bible; 2 Kgs 19.8 states only that Sennacherib had left Lachish and moved his headquarters to Libnah, a city which the detachment obviously could not take. The information in the Bible is in harmony with the Assyrian source material. However, the fall of Lachish is known from Sennacherib's reliefs at the palace of Nineveh.[2] An Assyrian detachment was thus sent out to Jerusalem while the main army marched to Lachish. The city was not taken, which means that the main force of Sennacherib's army did not besiege Jerusalem. The *rab šāqê* 'event' was part of the 'cold war' attempt to get Jerusalem to capitulate and so escape destruction, as well as being part of the Assyrian strategy to save both time and

---

1.   Lachish has usually been located at Tell ed-Duweir (built on a guess by W.F. Albright, 'The American Excavations at Tell Beit Mirsim', *ZAW* 47 [1929], p. 3 n. 2), an identification that I have questioned because there are still no facts to prove it. See my article in *PEQ* 112 (1980), pp. 7-9. D. Ussishkin has also acknowledged the lack of firm data, calling the evidence for an identification 'circumstantial' ('The "Lachish Reliefs" and the City of Lacish', *IEJ* 30 [1980], p. 174 n. 2). The siege ramp found in the recent excavations at Tell ed-Duweir is the best indication, thus far, for equating this tell with ancient Lachish, because the relief from Sennacherib's palace in Ninevah shows that the Assyrians built a siege ramp; see Ussishkin, *IEJ* 30 (1980), pp. 181-83. However, siege ramps could have been built at other sites. As was noted above, Sennacherib had the soldiers of Amurru carry earth, which may indicate that a siege ramp also was built at Gath, and such a strategy could have been part of Assyrian warfare at other places in Palestine. K.R. Veenhof has also raised some question about the identification (in a comment to C.H.J. de Geus, 'Lachis in Juda, Opgravingen en konigsstempels', *Phoenix* 26 [1980], p. 46 n. 58). For Syro-Palestinian cities looking very much the same in the neo-Assyrian reliefs, see M. Wäfler, *Nicht-Assyrer neuassyrischer Darstellungen, Tafeln* (AOAT, 26; Neukirchen–Vluyn, 1975).

2.   See A.H. Layard, *The Monuments of Nineveh*, II (London, 1853), pls. 21-22; cf. R.D. Barnett, 'The Siege of Lachish', *IEJ* 8 (1958), pp. 161-62; *ANEP*, figs. 372-73; R.D. Barnett and A. Lorenzini, *Assyrian Sculpture*, pls. 11, 53-54.

Assyrian lives. Nevertheless, the situation was very dangerous for Hezekiah and his capital city. Perhaps this was the time when Padi of Ekron was released, and also when Hezekiah sent messengers to Sennacherib at Lachish (2 Kgs 18.4). He must have understood that his cause was lost. After taking Lachish the Assyrian king may have tightened the siege around Jerusalem.[1] In the annals describing his victories, Sennacherib states that he had Hezekiah as a bird in a cage,[2] but obviously he forgot to close the cage. Hezekiah was the only king Sennacherib fought in this Phoenicio-Palestinian campaign who was not dethroned, killed or flayed alive, and Jerusalem was never captured by the Assyrian troops, even though heavy equipment was used.

The reason for the Assyrian withdrawal from Jerusalem may be twofold. Under Taharqa the Egyptians had recovered and marched north from Gaza. In order to cope with the danger, Sennacherib seems to have called back his troops from Jerusalem (cf. 2 Kgs 19.8-9; Isa. 37.8). He had probably spread himself too thin, giving Taharqa the upper hand if he could surprise the enemy. This never happened, however. The Assyrian king received word of the Egyptian march and when the Egyptians learned about Sennacherib's new position and collected strength, they withdrew.[3] The other reason is that a bubonic plague may have hit the armies in the field. There is a hint about this in the Old Testament, which mentions a miraculous deliverance from the Assyrian danger (2 Kgs 19.35-36; 2 Chron. 32.21; Isa. 37.36-37). A tradition used by Herodotus mentions that the Assyrian army that fought the Egyptians (Judah is not mentioned) was struck by swarms of mice, which gnawed the leather on the weapons of the Assyrian soldiers (2.141).[4] A decision to retreat to Assyria would have been a

---

1. A common suggestion is that Isaiah 10 reflects the Assyrian advance into Palestine in 701 BCE; so recently K.A. Kitchen, 'Egypt, the Levant and Assyria', *Fontes atque pontes* (ed. M. Görg), p. 249.

2. D.D. Luckenbill, *The Annals of Sennacherib*, p. 70 l. 28. The same phrase, *kīma iṣṣūr quppi ēsiršu*, 'I shut him in like a bird in a cage', occurs also in a text from Tiglath-pileser III's campaigns; see J.B. Geyer, '2 Kings XVIII 14-16 and the Annals of Sennacherib', *VT* 21 (1971), pp. 604-606.

3. See K.A. Kitchen, 'Egypt, the Levant and Assyria', *Fontes atque pontes* (ed. M. Görg), pp. 249-51.

4. See the discussion in W. Baumgartner, 'Herodots babylonische und assyrische Nachrichten', *Zum Alten Testament und seiner Umwelt, Ausgewählte Aufsätze* (Leiden, 1959), pp. 305-309; C. van Leeuwen, 'Sancherib devant Jérusalem', *OTS* 14 (1965), pp. 263-64; W. von Soden, 'Sennacherib vor

most realistic one. It should noted that there is no indication in the Assyrian annals about a political reason for the withdrawal.[1]

There is conflicting testimony over the timing and delivery of Judah's tribute to Assyria. The biblical text gives the information that Hezekiah gave tribute to Sennacherib shortly before the siege of Jerusalem started (2 Kgs 18.14-16), while Sennacherib's Annals mention that Hezekiah sent the tribute to Nineveh. Hezekiah would have sent the treasure from his palace including 30 talents of gold and 800 talents of silver, together with 'his daughters, his palace women [harem], his male and female singers', to Nineveh.[2] This is probably also what happened.[3]

Even if the hasty withdrawal from Palestine may have left some goals uncompleted, Sennacherib's campaign accomplished its goal of quelling rebellion in the Phoenicio-Palestinian areas, thus establishing full Assyrian control in this part of the Near East. Southern Palestine was now firmly in the Assyrian sphere. The Philistine city states were all ruled by faithful vassals, and Judah was almost nonexistent as a territorial state. Hezekiah's power was limited to the city of Jerusalem and its surroundings. Sennacherib had captured and plundered 46 of Hezekiah's 'strong, walled cities and numberless villages in their environs'.[4] These he gave over to the kings of Ashkelon, Gaza, Ashdod and Ekron.[5] A great amount of the population was deported to Assyria together with cattle and sheep, horses, mules and asses.[6]

Jerusalem', *Bibel und Alter Orient* (ed. A.P. Müller; BZAW, 162; Berlin, 1985), pp. 150-52.

1. W. von Soden, 'Sennacherib vor Jerusalem', *Bibel und Alter Orient* (ed. A.P. Müller), p. 156. The occurrence of plagues in the eighth century is known from Assyrian texts. Von Soden suggests, therefore, that the relative inactivity of the Assyrian kings during the years from around 780 BCE through 745 may be traceable to severe plagues (p. 155-56).

2. D.D. Luckenbill, *The Annals of Sennacherib*, p. 70 ll. 31-32.

3. Thus W. von Soden, 'Sennacherib vor Jerusalem', *Bibel und Alter Orient* (ed. A.P. Müller), p. 157.

4. D.D. Luckenbill, *The Annals of Sennacherib*, p. 70 ll. 19-20.

5. The Oriental Institute Prism does not mention Ashkelon, but gives us also the names of the kings, namely Mitinti of Ashdod, Padi of Ekron, and Ṣillibel of Gaza, (D.D. Luckenbill, *The Annals of Sennacherib*, p. 33 ll. 31-34). It is possible that the scribe, remembering the problems Ashkelon had given Sennacherib, did not remember that the city was now in 'secure' hands.

6. D.D. Luckenbill, *The Annals of Sennacherib*, p. 33 ll. 24-27.

The Assyrian claim that 200,150 persons were forced to leave Judah, however, seems too large. It is about seven times more than those who were exiled from Samaria and its surroundings in 720 BCE. One just wonders whether the hills of Judah could have housed that many especially when its territory is less hospitable than that in the north. However, the figure cannot be corrected; it can only be construed as an exaggeration. The inscription gives the idea that the country was almost populated and that Sennacherib's purpose was to settle other people in Judah, making it a province.[1]

The hasty withdrawal of the Assyrian king changed that. How much of the Negev and southeastern Judah was still ruled by Jerusalem is not known. Philistine rule, especially that of Gaza, could have extended south and southeast during these years. The southeastern Negev probably experienced Edomite infiltration and rule. The fact that Manasseh is given the title *šar* ᵘʳᵘ *Ia'udi*, 'the king of the city of Judah',[2] in the Annals of Esarhaddon (Nin. V.55ff.) shows that the little nation of Judah had become a city state consisting of Jerusalem and its surroundings.[3] There are no grounds for Na'aman's theory that 'considerable parts of the kingdom, including the Judean hill country', had not been conquered but were still under Judahite rule.[4] Judah probably could have maintained ownership of the Judean wilderness where nobody would want to live.

Hezekiah played a political game of international importance. The prospects of success were there as long as Assyria was faced with a two-front war. The annihilation of Merodach-Baladan and his forces changed the situation, but Hezekiah and Ṣidqa could still mount considerable forces together with Tyre and Egypt. Unfortunately, the model of Qarqar, in 853 BCE, was forgotten. Because the allied Palestinian states did not meet the Assyrian threat in a concerted effort, Sennacherib was able to nullify the enemies one by one. He was perhaps more lucky than skillful. Had the Egyptian army joined the armies of Judah and Ashkelon earlier in a decisive battle, the outcome could have been different.

---

1. Cf. S. Herrmann, *A History of Israel* (2nd edn), p. 258.
2. R. Frankena, *OTS* 14 (1965), pp. 150-52.
3. Cf. A. Alt, 'Die Territorialgeschichtliche Bedeutung von Sanheribs Eingriff in Palästina', *PJB* 25 (1930), pp. 82-83 (= *KS*, II, p. 244).
4. N. Na'aman, *BASOR* 261 (1986), p. 17.

It was sheer luck that Hezekiah survived the war—thanks probably to a horde of mice. His policies had led the country almost to the brink of disaster. The loss of country and of his wives, daughters and musicians must have made him very lonely, at times depressed. Four years later he was dead. He was succeeded by his son Manasseh, a king who had learned the Assyrian lesson and who gave peace to his country as long as he reigned for 55 years. Meanwhile, Sennacherib faced rebellions in the east, in both Elam and in Babylonia. The city of Babylon fell in 690 and was destroyed and looted.[1] Sennacherib died in 681 BCE. According to 2 Kgs 19.37, he was murdered by two of his sons while worshipping in a temple at Nineveh. One of the murderers is called Adrammelech, or Akkadian Arda-Mulišši, was a rival to Esarhaddon for the throne. The king was probably 'crushed alive under a winged bull-colossus guarding the temple where he had been praying at the time of the murder'.[2]

Seventh Century

With the Assyrian subjugation of Palestine in 701, the destruction of many of its cities and the deportation of a great percentage of the population, the Philistine and Judahite kingdoms had a long way to recovery. The Assyrian king had reached his goal of consolidating southern Palestine into a buffer area between Egypt and Assyria. Judah was nullified as a power and the Philistine city states had become reliable satellites, unable to form any anti-Assyrian coalition. There was no power, as of yet, that could oppose the Assyrian empire. Most of the territory of Judah had been given over to and split up between the four Philistine rulers of Ashkelon, Gaza, Ekron and Ashdod. The western Negev was probably ruled by Gaza, while the eastern Negev was Edomite territory. The southeastern part of Judah could already have come under Edomite rule during the Syro-

---

1. H.W.F. Saggs, *The Might that was Assyria*, pp. 102-103; J.A. Brinkman, *Prelude to Empire*, pp. 61-63.

2. S. Parpola, 'The Murder of Sennacherib', *Mesopotamia*, VIII (ed. B. Alster), p. 175. According to the Rassam Cylinder, Ashurbanipal says that he killed the murderers of his grandfather with the 'very same statues of protective deities with which they had smashed my own grandfather Sennacherib' (A.L. Oppenheim, *ANET*, p. 288).

Ephraimite war,[1] and, because Edom and the other Transjordanian states quickly submitted to Sennacherib when he invaded Phoenicia and Palestine in 701, Edom was permitted to keep its territorial gains. Thus, this part of Palestine was not devastated. The irony of history is that the Philistine states came out of the crisis with enlarged territories. Judah, on the other hand, was now reduced to an insignificant city state consisting of Jerusalem with surroundings[2] and, perhaps, the Judean desert where nobody lived, or wanted to live (see Map 21). It is probable that Isa. 1.7-8 refers to this disastrous situation: 'left is the daughter of Zion, as a booth in a vineyard, like a hut in a cucumber field, like a besieged city'. This corresponds very well with the often quoted passage from Sennacherib's inscription about Hezekiah being shut up in Jerusalem 'like a caged bird', and with the fact that he took 46 of his cities and their small villages by throwing up earthen ramps and using battering rams against them.[3] It also is in harmony with 2 Kgs 18.13 and Isa. 36.1, which mention that Sennacherib took all the fortified cities of Judah. We cannot postulate that both the Assyrian scribe and the writer of the biblical text have exaggerated such an event. What would be the purpose of the biblical narrator in giving an exaggerated account of the disaster of Judah, when he paints Hezekiah as a 'successful' king who could not be compared with anyone before or after him?

The population of southern Palestine had certainly decreased through death and deportation because of the war. The excavations at Tell ed-Duweir, for example, have yielded several ossuary pits on the

---

1. Cf. H.L. Ginsberg, 'Judah and the Transjordanian States', *Alexander Marx Jubilee Volume*, p. 364 n. 47a.

2. Cf. the phrase *šar (uru) Ia'udi*, 'king of (the city) of Judah', which we meet in the Annals of Esarhaddon (*Nin.* V; 55-57); R. Frankena, *OTS* 14 (1965), pp. 150-51.

3. D.D. Luckenbill, *The Annals of Sennacherib*, p. 70; cf. *ANET*, p. 288. R.P. Dougherty maintained, in spite of this information, that the cities were not ruined and that their rebuilding would not have taken too long ('Sennacherib and the Walled Cities of Judah', *JBL* 49 [1930], pp. 160-71). Dougherty seems to have underestimated the results of warfare. See also A.F. Rainey, 'The Fate of Lachish during the Campaigns of Sennacherib and Nebukadrezzar', *Lachish. V. Investigations at Lachish* (ed. Y. Aharoni; Tel Aviv, 1975), pp. 51-52. For battering rams and earthen ramps (Hebr. *ṣbr 'pr*), see I. Eph'al, 'The Assyrian Siege ramp at Lachish: Military and Lexical Aspects', *Tel Aviv* 11 (1984), p. 64.

western slope containing altogether about 1500 bodies. The bodies had been buried together with crushed pottery and animals bones, mainly astragali.[1] The latter shows that the people of Tell ed-Duweir had domesticated the pig.[2] Ashdod provides another example. Mass graves from this site contained the remains of c. 3000 bodies. There were also several hundreds of fragments of animal bones. None were domesticated pig bones and only one was of a wild boar. 6295 fragments were impossible to identify.[3] Apparently the pig was not yet forbidden in Judah or Israel, as the pig skeletons at Hazor (stratum V) indicate.[4] The religious heritage of the peoples of the hill country does seem to have included the pig as a sacred animal.[5] The Ashdod mass graves have been dated to the Assyrian campaign of 712.[6] The two examples from Tell ed-Duweir and Ashdod[7] may illustrate the extent to which the population was decimated by the warfare that occurred at the end of the eighth century BCE. As mentioned before, Sargon exiled people from Ashdod but also settled others there; thus some balance was maintained, but the indigenous ethnicity was broken down.

1.   O. Tufnell, *Lachish*, III, pp. 62-63, 187; also D.M. Bate, *Lachish*, III, pp. 410-11.

2.   Cf. G.W. Ahlström, *An Archaeological Picture of Iron Age Religions in Ancient Palestine*, p. 13.

3.   N. Haas, *Ashdod*, II-III, pp. 212-13.

4.   See above, p. 669.

5.   See A. von Rohr Sauer, 'The Cultic Role of the Pig in Ancient Times', *In Memoriam Paul Kahle* (ed. M. Black and G. Fohrer), pp. 202-204. In the later Hellenistic-Roman period the pig was part of the Ashtarte–Adonis cult, according to Lucian, *De Dea Syria* 54. For sacrifices of man, dog and swine in connection with idol worship, see Isa. 65.3-4; 66.17. J.M. Sasson thinks that 'Israel was abandoning its chosen path' and that an 'anguished nation had, in desperation, shifted its search for respite elsewhere' (*VT* 26 [1976], p. 207). Having drawn the antecedents of these kind of sacrifices to pre-Israelite times, Sasson should logically have concluded that they were phenomena that still lived on in the Judahite society. Cf. also my *An Archaeological Picture of Iron Age Religions in Ancient Palestine*, pp. 13-14.

6.   M. Elat, 'The Economic Relations of the Neo-Assyrian Empire with Egypt', *JAOS* 98 (1978), p. 33.

7.   It is most probable that there were also Assyrian soldiers buried in these graves. The pottery fragments found in these graves may be seen as part of the funerary offerings.

There is no clearcut information about the numbers of people who were deported in Palestine from various areas. The Assyrian inscription mentions that Sennacherib drove out from Judah alone 200,150 persons together with cattle, horses, mules, asses, sheep and camels, and counted them as 'spoil'.[1] But does this enumeration of war booty mean that they were all deported? If they were, southern Palestine would have been almost depopulated and very short of animals as well. It appears that ordinary life was disturbed and became almost impossible for some time in this territory. Sennacherib says in one of the Bull inscriptions, 'I laid waste the large district of Judah'.[2] His action reflected the Assyrian policy whose goal was to make any future rebellion impossible.

Because a large part of Judah's territory had been transferred by Sennacherib to the Philistine states and their administration, some of the Judahites who were counted as spoil may simply have become Philistine subjects. Sennacherib could have tried to defuse the ethnicity of the Judahites in this way instead of moving other population groups into the area. People counted as spoil were usually moved from their homelands. The claim found on the Taylor Prism that 200,150 Judahites were moved and counted—even thought it may be an exaggeration[3]—probably is a reference to the population of

1. D.D. Luckenbill, *ARAB*, II, par. 240; *ANET*, p. 288.
2. A.L. Oppenheim, *ANET*, p. 288; cf. D.D. Luckenbill, *ARAB*, II, par. 347; M. Elat, 'The Political Status of the Kingdom of Judah within the Assyrian Empire in the 7th century BCE', *Lachish*. V. *Investigations at Lachish* (ed. Y. Aharoni; Tel Aviv, 1975), p. 61 n. 1.
3. Cf. A. Ungnad, who prefers the number 2150 ('Die Zahl der von Sanherib deportierten Judäer', *ZAW* 18 [1942–43], pp. 199-201). This seems arbitrary. Ungnad compares the Judahite figure with the 27,290 persons who were exiled from the northern kingdom by Sargon II. But that case is different. Sargon exiled the upper classes of the society, and then settled other peoples there. Sennacherib seems to have emptied Judah as much as he could and no other peoples were settled there. A. Alt also maintains that the 46 cities taken and the figure 200,150 cannot provide an exact picture of the event, but maintains that Judah was reduced to the territory of the old Jebusite city state (*PJB* 25 [1930], p. 80 [= *KS*, II, p. 243]); cf. also S. Herrmann, *A History of Israel in Old Testament Times* (2nd edn), p. 258. *Contra* R. Borger, *Babylonisch-assyrische Lesestücke*, II (2nd edn), p. 112. For the different viewpoints, consult S. Stohlmann, 'The Judean Exile after 701 BCE', *Scripture in Context*, II (ed. W.H. Hallo, J.C. Moyer and L.G. Perdue; Winona Lake, IN, 1983), pp. 152-54. Not being familiar with the accuracy of the Assyrian scribes and their 'assistants', I have a hard time choosing sides. Because the number

Hezekiah's kingdom. They were to be deported and uprooted from their homes, which may mean that most of the population of Judah was destined to settle elsewhere. If some of the Judahites became Philistine subjects and as such Assyrians vassals, then not all the Judahite people who were counted as spoil were deported to distant provinces of Assyria. Some may have been moved to other areas in Palestine. The Assyrian reliefs of the capture of Lachish (in the southwest palace at Ninevah) depict Sennacherib sitting on his *nimedu*-throne while the people of Lachish pass in front of him with their carts and belongings.[1] The scene indicates that they were leaving the city as spoil and were destined to settle in other places.[2] The Bible does not mention any deportation at this time, but that may be because Hezekiah was painted as a lucky prince: 'among all the kings of Judah nobody could be compared with him, nor anyone before him' (2 Kgs 18.5). The biblical writer has not seen the irony of his own statement, because he was not concerned with history.[3] In this case the Assyrian records must be given more credence. The year 701 BCE is the year of the first serious threat to Judah's existence, as well as the year of the beginning of the first Judahite exile[4] (cf. Mic. 1.16). Thus, contrary to

of 46 cities is a precise number and probably includes some smaller villages, it could be accepted as reliable and taken as information that there were more towns than we know of. The figure of 200,150 persons seems to be a number that refers to the whole population of Judah, save Jerusalem.

1. R.D. Barnett, *Assyrian Palace Reliefs and their Influence on the Sculptures of Babylonia and Persia* (London, 1960), pls. 44-46. Cf. D.D. Luckenbill, *ARAB*, II, par. 489; *ANET*, p. 288.

2. Cf. A.F. Rainey, 'The Fate of Lachish during the Campaigns of Sennacherib and Nebuchadrezzar', *Lachish*, V (ed. Y. Aharoni *et al.*), p. 52.

3. The biblical writer's concern is religious. Because Hezekiah is said to have kept the commands of Moses (2 Kgs 18.6), the most important criterion for the writer, this text reflects a postexilic viewpoint. E. Würthwein says that 2 Kgs 18.5-6 has nothing to do with the historical Hezekiah found in the Book of Isaiah, but rather with the ideal picture given by the DtrN circle which was inspired by Deuteronomy with its demands on reliance on Yahweh only (*Könige*, II, p. 410.

4. Cf. S. Stohlmann, 'The Judean Exile after 701 BCE', *Scripture in Context*, II (ed. W.H. Hallo, J.C. Moyer and L.G. Perdue), pp. 147-75. Whatever the date of Isa. 11 may be, this text mentions that people of Yahweh have been exiled to Assyria, Egypt, Pathros, Cush, Elam, Shinar, Hamath, and the 'islands of the sea' (11.11). If the oracle is pronounced by Proto-Isaiah, some Judahites have already escaped to Egypt in his time. Cf. G. Widengren, 'Yahweh's Gathering of the Dispersed', *In*

the biblical writer's opinion, Hezekiah's policies had led the country to the brink of disaster.

Not much is not known about the rebuilding of the devastated areas. The road to normalcy may have been long. Excavations have shown that some cities, such as Beer-sheba, Beth Shemesh, Tell Beit Mirsim and Tell ed-Duweir, were not rebuilt. It is understandable that Beer-sheba went out of existence; it had been one of the store cities of the kingdom of Judah. With the loss of most of its territory in 701 BCE, Judah did not need store cities, and the Philistines had no need to rebuild the city. Tell ed-Duweir was not settled immediately after Sennacherib's destruction of the city. Excavations have revealed a larger building in Assyrian palace style, dubbed the 'Residency'. As a result Tell ed-Duweir has been seen as the seat of an Assyrian governor.[1] The building has parallels with buildings from Megiddo (str. II), Hazor (str. III), and the Assyrian house at Tell Jemme,[2] all of which have a large courtyard surrounded by smaller rooms. However, it is not certain when the so-called residency at Tell ed-Duweir was built. It could have been the residence of the Assyrian commander, but that does not make him a governor of a district.

It is possible that Sennacherib placed troops at the place in order to secure the occupation. He had done this[3] at other sites such as Hazor (str. III)[4] and the fortresses in Transjordan that guarded the main thoroughfares and kept the countries from rebellion. According to O. Tufnell, the fortifications of stratum II were of the Assyrian type.

The Shelter of Elyon (ed. W.B. Barrick and J.R. Spencer; JSOTSup 31; Sheffield, 1984), p. 230.

1. Cf. Y. Aharoni, *The Archaeology of the Land of Israel*, p. 268. D. Ussishkin objects to the theory that Tell ed-Duweir was the seat of an Assyrian governor (*Tel Aviv* 4 [1977], p. 53).

2. G.W. Van Beek, 'Digging up Tell Jemmeh', *Archeology* 36 (1983), pp. 12-16.

3. On the Assyrian occupation forces in vassal countries, see M. Elat, 'Political States', in *Lachish*, V (ed. Y. Aharoni), pp. 63-65.

4. See Y. Yadin *et al., Hazor*, I, pp. 45-47; Y. Yadin, *Hazor of Those Kingdoms*, pp. 191-92. This building (in Area B) may have been the continuation of the fortress. Northeast of the tell a large building corresponding to the Assyrian palace type was found. R. Reich thinks, therefore, that a new settlement was built on the plain NE of the tell ('The Persian Building at Ayyelet ha-Shaḥar—The Assyrian Palace of Hazor?', *IEJ* 25 [1975], pp. 233-37).

However, the residential buildings on the tell are from later in the seventh century.[1]

Dougherty's thesis that the cities of Judah were not completely destroyed and were rebuilt fairly quickly was readily adopted by W.F. Albright, who maintained that Sennacherib did not burn the cities he took and that the people counted as spoil were not deported but counted as Assyrian subjects.[2] This idea has been refuted by Y. Aharoni, who has shown that the pottery of stratum A2 at Tell Beit Mirsim is comparable to that of Tell ed-Duweir III. The logical conclusion would then be that T. Beit Mirsim must also have suffered some destruction about the same time as Tell ed-Duweir.[3] The same pottery 'horizon' is also found at Beth-Shemesh stratum IIC, Arad VIII and Beer-Sheba II.[4] Thus, their destruction may have occurred about the same time as that of Tell ed-Duweir.[5]

Remembering that the Negev was part of the Edomite sphere of interest, it would not be too far-fetched to assume that the Edomites used the opportunity presented by Sennacherib's campaign to raid and possibly to extend their territory all the way to Beer-Sheba. Tel Māśōś (Khirbet el-Meshâsh) had a settlement in the seventh century BCE wherein was found a figurine fragment and a model of a bed and a piece of jug, all in an Edomite style. The place has tentatively been interpreted as a caravanserai[6] because of a building that could house several people.[7] The pottery is consistent with 'Late Iron Age sites in

1. *Lachish*, III, pp. 56-57. Cf. also D. Ussishkin, *Tel Aviv* 10 (1983), p. 133.

2. 'The Fourth Joint Campaign of Excavation at Tell Beit Mirsim', *BASOR* 47 (1932), p. 14.

3. *Beer-Sheba*, I, p. 6; *The Archaeology of the Land of Israel*, pp. 262-64. Cf. also the discussion by A.F. Rainey, 'Fate of Lachish', *Lachish*, V (ed. Y. Aharoni *et al.*), pp. 48-49.

4. Cf. Y. Aharoni, *The Archaeology of the Land*, p. 262.

5. There is no precise information about Assyrian campaigns in the Negev beyond the above-mentioned statement that 46 cities and their small villages were taken by Sennacherib's army. N. Na'aman, for instance, thinks it is possible that Beer-Sheba was destroyed before Sennacherib's Palestinian campaign in 701 BCE. He bases his theory on the fact that very few *lmlk* stamps were found in Beer-Sheba. Besides Assyrians, Edomites and Arabs may have been raiding these areas (*BASOR* 261 [1986], p. 14).

6. V. Fritz, *Tel Aviv* 4 (1977), pp. 153-54.

7. H. Rösel does not dismiss the possibility that it was a fortress, in *Ergebnisse der Ausgrabungen auf der Ḥirbet el-Mšāš (Tel Māśōš) 1972–1975*, I (Abhandlungen

southern Judah', with parallels at 'En-Gedi, and stratum II at Tell ed-Duweir. There are also parallels with Buseirah in Transjordan as well as with Arad VII and VI.[1] The material culture is thus somewhat mixed, which would be expected in this area that was inhabited by both Judahites and Edomites, as well as by Arabs who controlled the trade routes. The ostraca found at Tel Māśōś are mainly from the second half of the seventh century BCE. Those having names with the theophoric *yāhû*-component are dated on paleographic grounds to about the same time as the ostraca from Arad VII and VI and from Tell ed-Duweir.[2]

The Judahite border fortress of Arad was located in this region. I have earlier maintained that Arad might have been in the hands of the Edomites during parts of the eighth and seventh centuries BCE.[3] Nevertheless, the archaeological finds of stratum VIII clearly demonstrate that the site at that time was a Judahite fortress with a temple. For instance, some ostraca found in the storerooms on the south side contain such priestly names as Pashhur and Meremoth, and ostracon 49, which was found in a room close to the temple, has written on it 'sons of Korah' and 'sons of Besal'. The latter name has been understood as a hypocoristicon of Bezalel.[4] These refer to Levitical guilds known from the Bible. The phrase 'for the sons of Korah' occurs, for instance, as a heading for some liturgical texts in the Psalter.[5] Names with the theophoric component -*yahu* also occur on ostracon 49.[6]

When Arad VIII was destroyed the fortress was not rebuilt according to the former plan. In the south a new inner wall was erected about

des Deutschen Palästina Vereins; ed. V. Fritz and A. Kempinski; Wiesbaden, 1983), pp. 122-27.

1.   O. Zimhoni, 'The Pottery', *Ergebnisse der Ausgrabungen*, I (ed. V. Fritz and A. Kempinski; Wiesbaden, 1983), pp. 127-30.

2.   V. Fritz, 'Die Ostraka', *Ergebnisse der Ausgrabungen*, I (ed. V. Fritz and A. Kempinski), pp. 133-37.

3.   See above, p. 722.

4.   Y. Aharoni, *BA* 31 (1968), p. 11; cf. also A. Lemaire, *Inscriptions hébraiques*, I (Paris, 1977), p. 210. Z. Herzog, M. Aharoni, A.F. Rainey and S. Moshkovitz rightly maintain that there is 'no basis whatsoever for the often voiced suggestion that this was a temple of the Kittim' (*BASOR* 254 [1984], p. 22). The chronology of the Arad stratification follows here that of Herzog *et al.*

5.   See, for instance, Psalms 42, 44–49, 84, 85, 87.

6.   Konyahu (?) line 4; 'Ebedyahu (?), line 8; -yahu, line 10; Pedayahu (?), line 15. See A. Lemaire, *Inscriptions*, I, p. 209.

2 m from the old one, thus creating a 'casemate'. In the middle of the western wall a 'projecting tower' was added.[1] The temple was not rebuilt. The whole temple complex of stratum VIII was covered with earth, and above it were found remains of smaller walls, probably dwellings for government personnel or storerooms. The excavator and others have interpreted the change in the site's layout by reference to the Old Testament's narrative about the reform of King Josiah and his abandonment of all the nation's sanctuaries, *bāmôt*, except for the temple of Jerusalem[2] (2 Kgs 23.8). Their interpretation is possible but another solution must be considered. After Sennacherib's Palestinian campaign Judah's territory was drastically reduced, as is well known. The question is whether Arad really was part of the kingdom of Judah in the first half of the seventh century BCE. Edomites and Arabs controlled the areas of the Negev and the northern Sinai south of the Judean hills. The excavations at Tel Malḥata (Tell el-Milḥ, coord. 152-069, c. 6 km east of Tel Māśōś) seem to indicate that the Edomites 'overran the Negeb', as E. Stern expresses it.[3] The trade routes from Arabia to Egypt and the Philistine coast were in the hands of the Arabs. Realizing this, it could equally be maintained that Arad stratum VII was built by the Edomites.[4] This sloution would explain why the temple was completely covered and why other buildings were erected on the fill. If the Edomites had priestly personnel stationed at the fortress, which would have been possible, their duties could have been performed in a special room anywhere within the walls of the small place.[5] This would be a logical answer to why Arad VII did not follow the old layout but took on a quite new look that resembled a 'military castrum'.[6]

1. Z. Herzog *et al.*, *BASOR* 254 (1984), p. 22.

2. Y. Aharoni, *BA* 31 (1968), pp. 18-27; J. Bright, *A History of Israel* (3rd edn), p. 319 n. 26; Z. Herzog *et al.*, *BASOR* 254 (1984), p. 23.

3. *BA* 38 (1975), p. 36. For the excavations, see M. Kochavi, 'Tell Malḥata', *IEJ* 17 (1967), pp. 272-73; *idem*, 'The First Seasons of Excavations at Tel Malḥata', *Qadmoniot* 3 (1970), pp. 22-24 (Hebrew).

4. Z. Herzog *et al.* assume that Arad could have been 'razed by the Edomites in collaboration with the Assyrians' (*BASOR* 254 [1984], p. 19).

5. As to the role of 'cult rooms', see G.W. Ahlström, *Royal Administration*, pp. 43-44, 82.

6. Z. Herzog *et al.*, who also state that the pottery of stratum VII is quite different from that of VIII (*BASOR* 254 [1984], p. 23). Most of it seems to be from the latter part of the seventh century, when Arad again had become Judahite.

It is possible that the portion of the Negev around Beer-sheba came under Gaza's control after 701 BCE.[1] This may explain why the store city of Beer-Sheba was not rebuilt after the Assyrian campaign.[2] The Philistines did not need a store city or a fortress here. The trade controlled by the Arabs could now pass freely to the coast. Like Arad, it is not clear whether Beer-Sheba was destroyed by the Assyrians or some other forcesIt could have been one of the 46 cities taken by a detachment of the Assyrian army, but it could also have been captured by others, such as the Edomites.[3]

N. Na'aman has expressed the opinion that Beer-Sheba had been taken and destroyed 'prior to Sennacherib's campaign in 701 BCE'.[4] This would present a quite different aspect to the destruction of the temple at Beer-Sheba. Building 32 of stratum III has been understood by Z. Herzog, A.F. Rainey and S. Moshkovitz to be a sanctuary that was not to have been rebuilt, on the order of King Hezekiah. They believe that their interpretation explains why some of the stones of the horned altar were found under the glacis of stratum II.[5] If it is assumed, however, that Beer-Sheba was destroyed before Sennacherib's campaign, the identity of the rebuilder(s) of the stratum II town remains a mystery[6] and the 'evidence' about how Hezekiah's 'reform' was carried out at Beer-Sheba disappears. If Na'aman is right, then Hezekiah did not reform anything in that town.[7]

1. Thus Y. Aharoni, *Beer-Sheba*, I, p. 107.
2. It should be noted that A. Alt maintained that the Beer-Sheba of the Bible was beneath Bir es-Saba' in modern Beer-Sheba ('Beiträge zur historischen Geographie und Topographie des Negeb', *JPOS* 15 [1935], pp. 320-24). Some Iron Age II remains have been found there, but it is not possible to excavate. The recent excavations at Tel Beer-Sheba have demonstrated that this was the place of a royal administration center and store city, and as such it will have served as a center for surrounding villages (cf. R. Gophna, 'Beersheba', *EAEHL*, I, pp. 158-59).
3. N. Na'aman says that Edomites threatened the towns of Negev 'alongside the Assyrians' (*BASOR* 261 [1986], p. 13).
4. *BASOR* 261 (1986), p. 14.
5. 'The Stratigraphy at Beer-sheba and the Location of the Sanctuary', *BASOR* 225 (1977), pp. 57-58. M.D. Fowler maintains that if the horned altar was used for burnt offerings, 'then it was constructed in flagrant violation of the injunctions of Exod. 20.22 (EVV 20.25)' ('The Excavation of Tell Beer-Sheba and the Biblical Record', *PEQ* 114 [1982], p. 9). Perhaps this injunction was not known yet.
6. This is, thus, one of the cases where archaeology has been illuminated too readily by the Bible.
7. For the Hezekiah 'reform' being more than a literary reform than a cultic one,

In assessing the cultural history of southern Palestine down to the seventh century BCE, the artifacts found at Beer-Sheba are of special interest for the historian of religion. Two limestone altars and a so-called Ashtarte figurine have been found in stratum II, the purported 'purified' city of Hezekiah. Undecorated limestone altars without horns have been found elsewhere in Palestine, for instance at Tel Malhhata. E. Stern theorizes that they are part of Assyrian cultic influences because they do not exist in Palestine before the Assyrian period.[1] There is also an incense burner in the form of 'an Ashtoret holding her breasts', and a base of a sitting animal, a bull figurine, and an Egyptian double crown, and a bowl on which the word *qdš*, 'holy', was inscribed.[2] Among the pottery types there are craters common in the coastal area (Ashdod), but not in Judah.[3] Aharoni maintains that the cult objects found at Beer-Sheba are 'basically pagan',[4] showing that the Egyptian influence had been strong. Utilizing Amos 5.5 and 8.14 and comparing Beer-Sheba with Arad, Aharoni maintains that Beer-Sheba was exposed to foreign influences, compared with the more remote and thus more 'puritan' and 'conservative' Arad.[5] This may be possible. Beer-Sheba was closer to the main thoroughfares and

---

see above, and H. Spieckermann, *Juda unter Assur in der Sargonidenzeit*, pp. 170-75, 215. For Y. Yadin's theory that the horned altar belonged to an open cult place, a so-called *bāmâ*, see the refutation by Z. Herzog, A.F. Rainey and S. Moshkovitz (*BASOR* 225 [1977], pp. 53-58). The word *bāmâ* does not mean an open cult place. W. Boyd Barrick (*SEÅ* 45 [1980], pp. 50-57) has maintained that *bāmâ* refers to a building. From an investigation of the textual material I have argued that the term *bāmâ* has been used by the biblical writers as a word for official, national sanctuary buildings in Israel and Judah (*Royal Administration*, pp. 42, 59-70). The same meaning is implied by the *rab šāqê* speech in 2 Kgs 18.22.

1. E. Ston, 'Limestone Incense Altars', *Beer-Sheba*, I, *Excavations at Tell Beer-Sheba, 1969–1971 Seasons* (ed. Y. Aharoni; Tel Aviv, 1973), p. 52.

2. Y. Aharoni, 'The Israelite City', *Beer-Sheba*, I (ed. Y. Aharoni), pp. 16-17.

3. G. Bachi, 'Several Kraters from Stratum II', *Beer-Sheba*, I (ed. Y. Aharoni), p. 39.

4. There were no 'pagans' in this period. The term in anachronistic, invented by the early Christian Church and used about the 'backward' people of the countryside who had not learned that Christendom was the religion one should embrace.

5. *Beer-Sheba*, I, p. 111. For Arad in its earlier phases being an expression of the religious continuum from the Canaanite Late Bronze Age, see my article, 'Heaven on Earth—at Hazor and Arad', *Religious Syncretism in Antiquity* (ed. B.A. Pearson), pp. 67-83.

cultural lines of communication than Arad. The latter was a fortress with a temple, but it was not an administrative center and store city as Beer-Sheba. As such Beer-Sheba would have been more 'up-to-date' with the cultural trends in the kingdom, much more than could be expected from the military post at Arad. Military personnel are seldom promoters of culture. It should also be remembered that the culture and art of Palestine was mainly an outgrowth of the Egypto-Phoenician culture and art,[1] even if certain independent developments can be detected. Thus most of the paraphernalia and ideas of the nation's official cult should be found at Beer-sheba, even if certain prophets and the later pure-Yahwistic circles did not accept some of the phenomena. These latter persons were not the official representatives of the nation's religion. In addition, it should be realized that, as in any other religion, there could have been local developments that deviated in some way from the main, official line of tradition and its customs. However, how much of the Beer-Sheba phenomena were adaptations to Egyptian religious performances or customs is impossible to determine as long as the details of the Jerusalem cult of the eighth century BCE remain unknown. As a town with administrative personnel, Beer-Sheba may be expected to mirror the cultural and religious tradition of the capital. Assyrian phenomena can accordingly be expected to be present. On the other hand, if Beer-Sheba were captured by the Edomites or Philistines, it would be natural to expect non-Judahite religious objects at the place.[2] The picture is not as clear as has been assumed.

If it is hard to get a firm understanding of what happened in Judah and in the Negev after the Assyrian campaign in 701 BCE, it is almost impossible to get a picture of the situation in the Philistine territories for the same period. The American expedition to Tell el-Ḥesi has, thus far, portrayed the city as a military bastion, probably Assyrian.[3]

1. Cf. my *An Archaeological Picture of Iron Age Religions in Ancient Palestine*, pp. 19-20.
2. Tell Qitmit, c. 10 km south of Arad, can be mentioned as an example of Edomite presence in the Negev; see I. Beit-Arieh, 'An Edomite Temple at Horvat Qitmit', *Qadmoniot* 19 (1986), pp. 72-79; P. Beck, 'A Head of a Goddess from Qitmit', *Qadmoniot* 19 (1986), pp. 79-81.
3. See D.G. Rose and L.E. Toombs, 'Tell el-Ḥesi, 1973 and 1975', *PEQ* 108 (1976), pp. 41-54; K.G. O'Connell, D.G. Rose and L.E. Toombs, 'Tell el-Ḥesi, 1977', *PEQ* 110 (1978), pp. 75-90; cf. R. Amiran and J.E. Worrell, 'Ḥesi, Tell', *EAEHL*, II, pp. 518-20.

Excavated Philistine sites have yielded only traces of destruction or else the excavation reports have been too meager. From J. Garstang's report of work at Ashkelon it is impossible to draw any conclusions for this period.[1] Gaza is not well known archaeologically. At Ashdod a potter's quarter from the first half of the seventh century has been uncovered. In the complex an ostracon was found with the engraved word *pḥr*, 'potter'. There are also a few weights. One bears the word *nsp* in Hebrew script. The term does not occur in classical Hebrew. M. Dothan has concluded from these finds that the Ashdodites had close connections with Judah, a theory which the find of a *lmlk* stamp could support.[2] However, the engraved words *pḥr* and *nsp* may merely support for the long-held opinion that the Philistines used the Canaanite-Hebrew language at this time.

After Assyria had conquered Palestine and nullified Judah's power, the commercial routes to Egypt along the Palestinian coast were now secured by the Philistine vassals and by the establishment of Assyrian garrisons in the area. One such garrison was located at Tell Jemme (coord. 097-088), 13 km south of Gaza. The site has tentatively been identified with Arza (Yurza of the Egyptian texts)[3] which Esarhaddon took in 679 BCE.[4] Among the indicators that the site was an Assyrian base are the many fragments of 'Assyrian Palace Ware'[5] and the vaulted mudbrick building, of which only five basement rooms have been found. Because F. Petrie dug through parts of the building in his excavation in 1927, its complete measurements will never be known. The mudbrick building with its Assyrian vaulting technique is unique in Palestine. G.W. Van Beek sees it as the residence of 'the military governor or general commanding the Assyrian base'.[6] The building was probably abandoned around 630 BCE when Assyria's power in the Near East was rapidly declining,[7] or it could have been destroyed by the Egyptians.

1. 'Askalon Reports', *PEQ* (1921), pp. 162-63.
2. 'Introduction', *Ashdod*, II-III ('Atiqot, 9-10; ed. M. Dothan; Jerusalem, 1971), pp. 21-23. For the *nsp* weight, see p. 40 and fig. 7.18.
3. B. Maisler (Mazar), 'Yurza: The Identification of Tell Jemmeh', *QDAP* 12 (1945), p. 51.
4. D.D. Luckenbill, *ARAB*, II, par. 550; *ANET*, pp. 290, 292.
5. Some of this ware may be local imitations of the Assyrian pottery.
6. *Archaeology* 36 (1983), p. 17.
7. G.W. Van Beek, *Archaeology* 36 (1983), p. 18.

A parallel to Tell Jemme is Tell esh-Shārî'a (coord. 119-088, Hebrew Tel Sera'), c. 20 km NW of Beer-Sheba as the crow flies. Stratum VI, which dates from the seventh–sixth centuries BCE, had a fortress in Assyrian style and yielded both imported Assyrian Palace Ware as local imitations. Most of its deposits have parallels also at 'En-Gedi, Ashdod and Meṣad Ḥashavyahu on the coast. Among the objects found in the citadel was a standard of bronze in the form of a crescent. Such a standard is known from many Assyrian reliefs, but this one is 'the first example found outside Assyria'. In addition to pillar figurines and a statuette of the Egyptian goddess Sekhmet in faience, Greek painted pottery was found,[1] which would be naturally expected at places where Egyptian or Assyrian armies had their garrisons. Greek mercenaries were a common phenomenon in the Near East at this time. The citadel at Tell esh-Shārî'a is not only a parallel to the 'Assyrian building' at Tell Jemme, but also a functional parallel to the 'Residency' at Tell ed-Duweir. Since Assyrian garrisons were stationed at all three sites, it is doubtful that a commander at any single site could be viewed as a governor of a province.

Although exact counts of the numbers of deported from Philistia have not survived, one thing seems clear: the country was heavily depopulated. For most of the Judahites who escaped the fate of deportation, the future lay no longer with Judah but with the Philistines. As was mentioned earlier, some could have settled in the vicinity of Jerusalem,[2] while others could have been relocated to the previously uninhabited Judean desert. The Qumran Iron Age settlement was in existence already before 701, to judge from the *lmlk* stamp found there. The pottery is from the eighth–sixth centuries BCE.[3] Qumran has been identified with the City of Salt[4] mentioned in Josh. 15.61-62

---

1. For the excavations, see E. Oren, *BA* 45 (1982), pp. 155-66.

2. M. Broshi thinks that the population of Jerusalem increased from c. 6000 to about 24,000 persons after 720 BCE, and that both people from the northern kingdom and refugees from the Philistines had settled on the western hill of Jerusalem. He also maintains that there was a population increase in the hills of Judah and in the Negev (*IEJ* 24 [1974], pp. 21-26). The increase in the Negev may be explained by an Edomite takeover. The increase of settlements in the Judean hills may be explained by rebuilding activities by the peoples left but now under Philistine command.

3. R. de Vaux, *L'archéologie et les manuscrits de la mer morte* (London, 1961), pp. 1-2; *idem*, 'Qumran, Khirbet—Ein Feshkha', *EAEHL*, IV, p. 978.

4. M. Noth, *Das Buch Joshua* (Tübingen, 153), p. 72.

as lying in Judah's desert province.[1] Another place mentioned in the same district is 'En-Gedi, which, according to B. Mazar, may have been established during the reign of King Josiah.[2] Because of the existence of some burials in the vicinity, Y. Aharoni has concluded that the settlement started earlier.[3] Three small fortified farms in the Buqei'a basin on the escarpment c. 7–8 km west of Qumran and 'Ain Feshkha should also be considered. A tunnel leading to a cistern in a hill and two dams were found in the region of the farms.[4] Thus, there is some indication for the establishment of settlements in this wilderness area that previously had been considered unsuitable for inhabitants other than nomads, goats and jackals.

Because of Hezekiah's political gamble his son Manasseh inherited a rump state devoid of natural resources and allies. Its political position was that of a subdued servant who had no other choice than to follow his master's voice, the Assyrian king. Manasseh is said to have reigned for 55 years (2 Kgs 21.1). He would have been 12 years old when he succeeded his father (2 Chron. 33.1). As the preceding presentation has shown, not much is known about life in southern Palestine during the decades following the Assyrian campaign in 701 BCE. What is known is that this part of the country had peace until the end of the Assyrian domination when Manasseh's grandson, Josiah, started to extend his power into Philistine territory, also carrying out an expedition of military punishment in the then defenseless Assyrian province of Samerina.[5] Thus, this long peaceful period of c. 70 years must have been beneficial for most of Palestine in healing the wounds of warfare and destruction, even though Assyrian tribute and demands on labor

---

1.   If Qumran is the City of Salt, the Joshua passage must date to the latest part of the monarchy—at the earliest, and the narrator must have retrojected it into the premonarchic period.

2.   B. Mazar and I. Dunayevsky, *IEJ* 14 (1964), pp. 121-30; B. Mazar, 'En-Gedi', *Archaeology and Old Testament Study* (ed. D.W. Thomas; Oxford, 1967), p. 224.

3.   *The Land of the Bible* (2nd edn), p. 351.

4.   F.M. Cross, 'el-Buqei'a', *EAEHL*, I, pp. 267-70. Cross dates the settlements to the ninth century BCE, but L.E. Stager prefers the seventh century. He sees the farms as the result of the government's agricultural policy and says that Judah first incorporated the 'desert province' in the seventh century ('Farming in the Judean Desert in the Iron Age', *BASOR* 221 [1976], pp. 145-58).

5.   See below, pp. 763-66.

and auxiliary troops may have been pressing enough. Even if Manasseh cannot be completely credited with keeping the peace during his long reign, he must be appreciated for having understood that rebellion would be meaningless.[1] In this respect he was wiser than his father Hezekiah. Most scholars have not elaborated on this aspect of his career. Instead, they have uncritically made their own the biblical evaluation of King Manasseh as the most evil king of Judah.[2]

A realistic presentation of king Manasseh's rule would show that he had little choice to do otherwise than be a faithful vassal to Assyria. That was the foundation for his kingship. Coming of age, he opposed his father's policies—a somewhat common phenomenon that has been used by the deuteronomistic historiographer as a suitable ingredient in his theological presentation of the reasons for Josiah's reform and of the later catastrophe of Judah. The Dtr historians makes King Josiah into the ideal king according to deuteronomistic ideals. All the 'sins' of the preceding 'bad' kings came to a climax during Manasseh's reign. He is made into the worst king of Judah and is contrasted with his grandson, Josiah, who becomes the most acceptable one. Manasseh must have seen how his father's policies led the country of Judah almost to extinction. Any act of Manasseh that deviated from that of his father would be understandable from this point of view.

The Assyrian annals of Esarhaddon record that Manasseh, together with 21 other kings of Phoenicia, Philistia, Transjordan and Cyprus, had to contribute building materials and transport them 'under terrible difficulties'[3] to Nineveh for Esarhaddon's new palace. It is in

---

1. To characterize Manasseh's period as a happy time ('glückliche Regierungszeit'), as H.-D. Hoffmann does (*Reform und Reformen*, p. 165), is to put things too optimistically.

2. See, among others, Y. Kaufman, *The Religion of Israel* (Chicago, 1960), p. 89; H. Ringgren, *Israelite Religion*, p. 276; J. Bright, *A History of Israel* (3rd edn), pp. 312-13. B. Oded thinks that 'the biblical historians saw in Manasseh's personality the reason for his evil behaviour', and that Manasseh had 'intended the creation of a genuine syncretism of Yahwistic and pagan cults' ('Judah and the Exile', *Israelite and Judean History* [ed. J.H. Hayes and J.M. Miller], p. 453). R.K. Harrison maintains that under Manasseh Judah sank to a low moral level (*Old Testament Times* [Grand Rapids, MI, 1970], p. 238). This is to misread the text. The biblical narrator is not describing the morals of the people. He gives a theologically distorted picture of the king on whom he throws as much dirt as possible.

3. A.L. Oppenheim, *ANET*, p. 291.

this connection that Manasseh is mentioned as *šar ᵘʳᵘ ia-'u-di*, 'king (of the city) of Judah'.[1] The failure to use the determinative for land (*mātu*) after Judah probably reflects the result of Sennacherib's reduction of the territory of Judah. Esarhaddon's rule began in 680, and he probably started to build his palace quite early in his reign.[2] His building activity could be the incident that the Chronicler has used as a basis for his claim that Manasseh was captured and taken in chains to Babylon (2 Chron. 33.11). Writing in the time after the Babylonian exile, the 'mistake' would easily be explained.[3] Another theory is that Manasseh rebelled against Assyria in connection with the rebellion of Shamash-shum-ukin of Babylon against his brother Ashurbanipal. This crisis[4] occurred in the years of 652–648 BCE.[5] There is no confirmation in the Assyrian inscriptions that Manasseh was taken prisoner and then restored to his throne. However, the Annals of Ashurbanipal mention that Shamsh-shum-ukin received support from both Babylonia proper and from the peoples of Guti, Amurru and Meluḫḫa (col. III.103).[6] Since Amurru and Meluḫḫa stand for Syria-Palestine and Egypt respectively, it would be possible to see Manasseh and the little city state of Judah to have been forced to join the rebellion. Manasseh could have been pardoned and returned to Jerusalem as a reliable vassal after his circumstances were understood. It is unclear,

1.   See R. Frankena, *OTS* 14 (1965), pp. 150-51.

2.   Frankena thinks that it is possible that Manasseh and the other 21 kings were present at the installation of the crown-prince Ashurbanipal in 672 BCE, and that the building material was delivered at the same time (see the discussion in *OTS* 14 [1965], pp. 150-51).

3.   Thus H.W.F. Saggs, *The Might that was Assyria*, p. 107.

4.   See J.A. Brinkman, *Prelude to Empire*, pp. 93-104.

5.   See, for instance, W. Rudolph, *Chronikbücher*, pp. 316-17; E. Ehrlich, 'Der Aufenhalt des Königs Manasse in Babylon', *TZ* 21 (1965), pp. 281-86; J. Bright, *A History of Israel* (3rd edn), pp. 310-11; E. Nielsen, 'Political Conditions and Cultural Development in Israel and Judah during the Reign of Manasseh', *4th World Congress of Jewish Studies*, I (Jerusalem, 1967), pp. 103-106; cf. B. Oded, 'Judah and the Exile', *Israelite and Judean History* (ed. J.H. Hayes and J.M. Miller), pp. 453-54. Usually it has been argued that Ashurbanipal's treatment of the rebellious Necho of Sais, Egypt, who became a faithful vassal and thus was returned to the throne, could also apply to Manasseh; cf. M. Elat, 'The Political Status of the Kingdom of Judah within the Assyrian Empire in the 7th Century BCE', *Lachish*, V (ed. Y. Aharoni *et al.*), pp. 66-67.

6.   M. Streck, *Assurbanipal und die letzten assyrischen Könige*, p. 30.

however, whether the nations of western Asia and Egypt really supported Shamash-shum-ukin. The Rassam Cylinder may have presented the rebellion as 'worldwide' in order to enhance the picture and position of Ashurbanipal. In the reports of the actual fighting, no 'westerners' other than the Arabs are mentioned.[1] They were defeated and punished after Ashurbanipal's victory over Shamash-shum-ukin. The Assyrian forces 'smashed all the inhabitants of Arabia' in battles in Syria and Transjordan.[2]

The passage 2 Chron. 33.11-17 may not be a complete invention by the narrator, even if it cannot be established as fact that Manasseh was taken as a prisoner to Babylon. Like most other kings, Manasseh certainly was involved in building activities. It is doubtful, however, whether these should be connected with a 'return' from Babylonia and with a 'conversion' followed by a cult reform that suited the writer's Yahwism. Compared with the information in 2 Kgs 21.3, the Chronicler appears to have tried to appreciate Manasseh's deeds and has given a theological excuse for his long reign. From the information given in 2 Kgs 21.3, scholars have usually inferred that Manasseh introduced non-Judahite religious phenomena into the official cult of his kingdom[3] by building altars to Baal and by worshiping the host of heaven.[4] To these non-native practices the Chronicler adds necromancy and witchcraft, and claims that Manasseh let his sons pass through fire. He also is said to have made an idol (*pesel*), a deity statue, which he placed in the Solomonic temple (2 Chron. 33.6).[5] Because one of his

---

1. Cf. H. Spieckermann, *Juda unter Assur in der Sargonidenzeit*, pp. 36-37.

2. *ANET*, p. 298.

3. This chapter cannot be used to argue that Manasseh was forced to introduce Assyrian rituals or cult phenomena in Judah. The text does not mention anything about that. (Should not Hezekiah also have been forced to show himself to be a loyal vassal, especially after 701 BCE?) The purpose of 2 Kgs 21 is to give a reason for the rejection of Manasseh and thus prepare the way for Josiah; cf. H.-D. Hoffmann, *Reform und Reformen*, pp. 149-50, 155-66.

4. Among more recent advocates of this theory, see H.J. Katzenstein, *The History of Tyre*, pp. 263-65; J. Bright, *A History of Israel* (3rd edn), p. 312; J. McKay, *Religion in Judah under the Assyrians*, pp. 20-22; M. Cogan, *Imperialism and Religion*, pp. 90-92. See also Z. Herzog *et al.*, who assume that Manasseh's 'innovations' were made in order to 'improve Judah's political and economic status by closer ties with its neighbors' (*BASOR* 254 [1984], p. 25).

5. Note that the Chronicler does not mention what god this *pesel* represented. After having mentioned the host of heaven and the Baal altars, he mentions the image

wives, Meshullemeth (the mother of the future King Amon) was probably an Edomite (from Yotba),[1] she would also have been given a place to worship according to her own faith, just as Solomon's wives had been. However, to assume that she influenced Manasseh in such a way that he introduced Edomite worship[2] in to Judah's official cult would be to make her a new Jezebel—not even the biblical writer did that.

Manasseh is said by the Chronicler to have put 'commanders of the army in all fortified cities of Judah' (33.14). He is also said to have removed some 'foreign' gods together with a Judahite image (*pesel*, 'idol') from Solomon's temple and to have removed the altars that Solomon had built on the temple mount and also at other places in Jerusalem (v. 15). As in many other instances, building activities and cultic reorganization are literally linked,[3] so that what really happened cannot be known. In v. 17 the typical deuteronomistic complaint that the people continued to sacrifice on the *bāmôt* occurs, but the writer adds the excuse that these sacrifices were offered exclusively to Yahweh.

Manasseh may have ordered the repairs of fortifications, in addition to giving cultic directions. If his kingdom consisted mainly of Jerusalem and its surroundings, there would have been no need of other royal sanctuaries in the kingdom. However, if the statement in v. 17 is combined with the one in v. 14 about placing commanders in the cities of Judah, a picture of greater probability appears. Since Psammetichus I of the Twenty-Sixth Dynasty of Egypt (Sais) 'had to accept the tutelage of Ashurbanipal',[4] it would be futile to see the defense system of any of the south-Palestinian states as being directed

that Manasseh supposedly placed in the temple and then adds that Yahweh had said that only his name (*šēm*) should be placed in the temple. The only conclusion that can be drawn is that the image represented Yahweh. The deuteronomic shem-theology, which the Chronicler used, had thus not yet been born. W.F. Albright prefers to change the image into a slab, for which there are no textual grounds (*Archaeology and the Religion of Israel* [2nd edn], pp. 165-66).

1.   Probably at aṭ-Ṭaba, c. 30 km north of Aqaba; cf. J. Gray, *I and II Kings*, p. 711.

2.   For an Edomite temple in Jerusalem, see 2 Chron. 25.24.

3.   For this literary feature, see P. Welten, *Geschichte und Geshichtsdarstellung*, pp. 180-82.

4.   A. Spalinger, 'The Concept of the Monarchy during the Saite Epoch—an Essay of Synthesis', *Or* NS 47 (1978), p. 14.

against Assyria. On the contrary,[1] with a more lenient policy towards Manasseh, Ashurbanipal could have given him back some of the former Judahite cities that Sennacherib had allotted to the Philistines in 701 BCE. In this way Judah would become a part of the bulwark against Egypt in a future conflict. Had the cities been returned to him, Manasseh would have replaced the Philistine commanders with his own in 'the fortified cities of Judah'. Because the official religion of a country was a territorial, national phenomenon, priests and other government officials besides the military had to be sent to the returned cities in order to incorporate them in the nation of Judah. The Chronicler has not been able to ignore this phenomenon completely; he states that the sacrifices were given to Yahweh, not to foreign gods. With these officials sent to the cities, the *mišpāṭ* (rules, norms) of Yahweh and his country was established.

As maintained before,[2] Manasseh can be characterized as a religious traditionalist restoring the old official cult of Judah in the 'returned' cities. His restoration of the image of the goddess Asherah and the host of heaven into Jerusalem illustrates this (2 Kgs 21.5-7). Knowing that Asherah was an Israelite-Judahite goddess worshiped in the Solomonic temple long before Manasseh's time,[3] the Deuteronomist's accusation that Manasseh 'introduced' her worship loses its footing. The nature of traditional religion in Judah and Jerusalem in particular is illustrated by the many figures, anthropomorphic or tauromorphic, which have been unearthed through excavations. The greatest amount of figurines have been found in Jerusalem. T.A. Holland's investigation shows that in 1975 close to 600 figurines had been recovered known from Jerusalem, compared with 159 from Samaria, 28 from Bethel, 22 from Shechem, 64 from Gibeon, a few from Dan, and 44 from Hazor.[4] The number of figurines from Jerusalem has now increased to c. 1100.[5]

---

1. Cf. H. Reviv, 'The History of Judah from Hezekiah to Josiah', *WHJP*, IV.I (ed. A. Malamat), p. 200.

2. See G.W. Ahlström, *Royal Administration*, pp. 74-81.

3. The finds from Kuntillet 'Ajrud should be noticed in this connection; see the discussion by J.A. Emerton, *ZAW* 94 (1981), pp. 2-20; G.W. Ahlström, *An Archaeological Picture of Iron Age Religions in Ancient Palestine*, pp. 19-21; cf. *idem*, *Aspects of Syncretism in Israelite Religion*, pp. 50-52.

4. *Levant* 9 (1977), pp. 121-55.

5. Y. Shiloh (private communication, 1980).

Most of the figurines found in Jerusalem are from the eighth–seventh centuries BCE. Their large numbers could indicate the presence of foreign influences or perhaps foreign stimuli. However, nothing can be decided before more of the archaeology of Jerusalem is known. The style of these figurines is more in the Phoenicio-Palestinian tradition, which is to be expected because that was the tradition of art in this country. There are also several horse figurines among which are horses with the sun disc on their heads.[1] According to Holland's investigation, there is a concentration of these figurines in Jerusalem.[2] If the horse figurines are proof of foreign influences, then the prophet Habakkuk (or the psalm he uses) was also influenced by the same source(s). Yahweh 'mounts his horses, his chariots of victory' in Hab. 3.8, and in v. 15 Yahweh tramples the sea with his horses. According to Ps. 68.18 Yahweh has 20,000 horses. The horse figurines with the sun disc on the forehead are most probably to be associated with Yahweh, who, in Jerusalem at least, was also seen as a sun god. In Ps. 84.12 he is also called Shemesh, 'sun'. The passage 2 Kgs 23.11 provides evidence that the horses were not part of the phenomenon introduced by Manasseh. This text states that the kings (!) of Judah had dedicated horses to Yahweh and his temple in Jerusalem. In other words, horses were part of the symbolic paraphernalia of the official Yahwistic religion of the kingdom of Judah.[3]

The very great number of figurines found in Jerusalem cannot per se be interpreted as foreign religious symbols only. Many are probably part of an old tradition that the later writers opposed. The Jerusalemite population's attachment of figurines of nude women, bulls and horses seems to have been much greater than at any other

1. See K.M. Kenyon, *Digging up Jerusalem*, pp. 141-42.
2. *Levant* 9 (1977), pp. 149-50. This type is also known from Tell ed-Duweir and Hazor (str. VA). From Hazor also comes a horse head with a circle and within it a cross, or 'four-pointed star', as Yadin expresses it. He thinks the head is a bull's head (*Hazor of Those Kingdoms*, pl. xix.c; cf. also Yadin *et al.*, *Hazor*, III, pl. clxxvi).
3. H. Spieckermann thinks that the Assyrian oracle practice that associates horses with the sun-god or with Assur has also been practiced in Judah (*Juda unter Assur in der Sargonidenzeit*, p. 256). Even if these are parallel phenomena, this does not necessarily mean that Judah must have imported this oracle practice from Assyria. Such a phenomenon could have existed in Judah long before the Assyrian period.

site, as far as is known. Because the number of bull figurines from Jerusalem is much larger than at other places, caution must be exercised in assuming that the southern kingdom's religion was 'bull-free' compared with that of the northern kingdom. Here scholars have once again used deuteronomistic glasses.[1]

2 Chron. 33.14 attributes to Manasseh an outer wall built for the City of David west of Gihon in the Kidron Valley passing the Ophel[2] and leading up to the Fish Gate in the north.[3] The wall would then have passed the temple area in the east and in the north. This project has been linked by the Chronicler to the king's so-called conversion, which would date the wall's erection to the period after Manasseh's return from Babylon. This connection between building activities and 'conversion' is understandable because in the Chronicler's theological historiography only a positively judged king is a builder.[4] Building fortifications and organizing the cult (including the building and repair of sanctuaries) were royal duties.[5] It is to be expected that Manasseh's long reign included building activities in Jerusalem such as repairs to the city wall or additions to the defensive system of the city.[6] In order to accept and report this fact, the Chronicler invented Manasseh's capture by the Assyrians and his subsequent 'conversion'. In this way Manasseh could fit into his system.

Because of the religious focus of the biblical writers not much is learned about life and social conditions during Manasseh's period. Because interest is centered around the kings, history disappears in a mist.[7] Thus, the field is open to speculation. 2 Kgs 21.16 accuses Manasseh of having 'shed innocent blood', a statement that has very

---

1. So e.g. J. Bright, who thinks that the Jerusalem priests were 'conservative' (*A History of Israel* [3rd edn], p. 235). They could perhaps be called conservative, if the ideas of the later mosaic advocates are not included in this term.

2. For Ophel as a postexilic term for the temple area, see P. Welten, *Geschichte und Geschichtsdarstellung*, pp. 75-77.

3. For the gates of Jerusalem, see H. Donner, 'Jerusalem', *Biblisches Reallexikon* (ed. K. Galling, 2nd edn), p. 161 and fig. 42.

4. Cf. P. Welten, *Geschichte und Geschichtsdarstellung*, pp. 31-32.

5. See my *Royal Administration*, pp. 10-12.

6. For the complicated picture of the late pre-exilic walls of Jerusalem, see N. Avigad, *Discovering Jerusalem*, pp. 46-60.

7. Cf. G. von Rad, 'Die deuteronomistische Geschichtstheologie in den Königsbüchern', *Gesammelte Studien* (Munich, 1961), pp. 190-91.

much colored the scholarly opinion of Manasseh's reign. The period has been seen to have been marked by propehtic persecution.[1] It is not necessary to draw this conclusion from the text.[2] In order to keep his nation in line with the position of an Assyrian vassal,[3] the king may have neutralized opposing elements[4] whom he considered to be dangerous for the security of the state. They may have been civil servants, military or cultic personnel.[5] As in other subject countries, Manasseh may have had a supervisor, *qēpu*,[6] at his court whose task was to ensure that the vassal treaty was kept to the letter.[7] Assyrian supervisors and troops were stationed at different places in the former territories of Judah. The Assyrian building at Tell ed-Duweir may testify to this practice. Two cuneiform tablets from neighboring Gezer dated to 659–649 BCE give the names of Assyrian officials. The names are clearly Assyrian, but the tablets also contain some Babylonian and Hebrew names.[8] This shows not only that new peoples had been settled at Gezer or its vicinity, but also that part of the original population was still there. It could also mean that the Assyrians were supervisors and thus had to report back to Assyria. The same would be the case at other places in Palestine,[9] as mentioned above.

From the accusations concerning Manasseh and his 'sins', it has been theorized that there were some sharp differences between prophets and priests on the one hand, and members of the court and the Baal and Asherah priests on the other. This would have been a reason for

---

1. A.T. Olmstead, *History of Palestine and Syria*, pp. 482-83. According to Josephus, Isaiah was a victim of Manasseh's persecutions (*Ant.* 10.3.1).

2. M. Cogan, *Imperialism and Religion*, p. 90.

3. For the duties of a vassal and the stipulations in the vassal treaties, see R. Frankena, *OTS* 14 (1965) pp. 140-50.

4. Cf. M. Smith, *Palestinian Parties and Politics that Shaped the Old Testament* (New York, 1971), p. 40.

5. Cf. G.W. Ahlström, *Royal Administration*, p. 80.

6. Cf. *CAD* ('qēpu can mean administrator of a region, a city, a temple', often used for a royal official sent to a vassal country by the king); W. von Soden (*AHw*) has 'glaubwürdig'.

7. See, for instance, Esarhaddon's treaty with Ba'lu of Tyre (R. Borger, *Die Inschriften Asarhaddons*, p. 108).

8. R.A.S. Macalister, *The Excavation of Gezer*, I (London, 1912), pp. 22-24; cf. K. Galling, 'Assyrische und Persische Präfekten in Gezer', *PJB* 130 (1935), pp. 81-83.

9. Chapter 15.

bloody confrontations.[1] This is a theory impossible to verify. Opposing parties can be found in almost any society, and Judah was certainly not an exception. In this case it should be noted, however, that the Judahite prophets (the so-called literary ones) seldom were on the same side as the priests of the royal cult. Also, since both Baal and Asherah were worshiped in the temple of Jerusalem, it would be too simple a solution to see Yahweh priests and Baal priests to constitute two opposing parties. Ritual in the temple may have been directed to both Yahweh and Baal and perhaps also to Asherah.[2]

Manasseh was followed by his son Amon (641–640 BCE). Not much is known about him beyond that he was 22 years old when he became king and is said to have followed his father's religious policies. From the information that he was murdered in his palace by some of his court officials and/or officers after a two year reign, it may be concluded that Amon, like his father, was also loyal to Assyria. He may have fallen victim of an anti-Assyrian plot.[3] In 655 BCE Egypt had become united again under pharaoh Psammetichus I (664–610 BCE). This, as well as Psammetichus's diplomatic and military activities in Syria-Palestine and the illusion of Egypt's resurgent power,[4] could have encouraged some of Amon's high officials to work for a change in the political alliance.[5] During this time the Qedarites and the Nebaioth of Syria and Palestine revolted against Ashurbanipal and the Assyrian armies subdued not only them but also Acre and Ushu (Tyre's mainland) in Phoenicia.[6] This rebellion could have inspired some officers to stage a *coup d'état*. Least of all would Amon have been killed because he did not adhere to the ideals of king Hezekiah's reform,[7] a reform that most probably did not happen as related in the

1. See, for instance, B. Oded, in *Israelite and Judean History* (ed. J.H. Hayes and J.M. Miller), pp. 453-54.

2. Priests could be competitors and enemies even if they served the same deity.

3. A. Malamat, 'The Historical Background of the Assassination of Amon King of Judah', *IEJ* 3 (1953), pp. 26-29; H. Cazelles, 'Sophonie, Jérémie, et les Scythes en Palestine', *RB* 74 (1967), pp. 24-44.

4. This may have been the time when Egypt besieged Ashdod (for 29 years), according to *Herodotus* 2.157.

5. Cf. H. Spieckermann, *Juda unter Assur*, p. 37.

6. *ANET*, p. 300.

7. B. Oded considers faithfulness to 'the tradition of Israel' and to the Hezekiah reform as probable motifs for the assassination ('Judah and the Exile', *Israelite and Judean History* [ed. J.H. Hayes and J.M. Miller], p. 456).

texts. Some internal court problems could also have been the cause. Since the Bible provides no indication why Amon was killed, any suggestion is a conjecture. Amon's short reign was of no use for the biblical writer. The unfortunate king could not be depicted as the counterpole to his father so he was given the short epitaph that he increased the guilt of Judah (2 Chron. 33.23).

'The people of the land' (*'am hā-āreṣ*)[1] are said to have secured the throne for Amon's eight-year-old son, Josiah, and to have executed the king's murderers (2 Kgs 21.23-24; 2 Chron. 33.24-25). Whether this group could be said to represent a 'party', or whether they were the free landowners or the leaders of the clans, is still not known. The text does not give any clear indication about their identity, beyond their not being the servants of the king. Their motive for arresting the attempt to force a change in regime was probably more internal in character—wanting to punish the criminals who killed the king—than it was directed by any foreign policy viewpoint.

---

1. Cf. 2 Kgs 14.21. For this group, see E. Würthwein, *Der 'amm hā'āreṣ im Alten Testament*; R. de Vaux, *RA* 58 (1964), pp. 167-72; S. Talmon, 'The Judean *'am hā'āreṣ* in Historical Perspective', *Fourth World Congress of Jewish Studies*, I (Jerusalem, 1967), pp. 71-76; E.W. Nicholson, *JSS* 10 (1965), pp. 59-66; T. Mettinger, *King and Messiah*, pp. 124-30. For its use in the later periods, see A. Oppenheimer, *The 'Am Hā-āretz* (Leiden, 1977).

Chapter 17

CLIMAX AND FALL

After the destruction of the Aramaean and Israelite nations and their annexation as provinces in the Assyrian empire, there was no Palestinian power that could challenge or withstand the might and territorial expansion of Assyria. Sennacherib's campaign in Palestine in 701 BCE removed the political basis for any viable coalition against Assyria in the west. The empire entered a period of relative peace with fewer campaigns than before. This period has been labeled 'pax assyriaca', and it lasted to 652 BCE, when Shamash-shum-ukin of Babylon revolted.[1] Thus, after 701 BCE the way to Egypt was paved for Sennacherib's successor, Esarhaddon (680–669).[2] Under him and his son, Ashurbanipal, the Assyrian empire also reached its largest territorial extension.[3] After having restored Babylon, which Sennacherib had sacked, Esarhaddon turned to the problems of the east and west. In the east he made alliances with Median tribes in order to checkmate

1.   Cf. W.W. Hallo, *BA* 23 (1960), pp. 57-60; H.W.F. Saggs, *The Might that was Assyria*, pp. 107-108.

2.   Esarhaddon was not the oldest son of Sennacherib but had been chosen and installed as crown-prince. When Sennacherib was murdered, Esarhaddon was away on a military campaign. Thus, the moment was well chosen by the conspirators; see S. Parpola, 'The Murder of Sennacherib', *Death in Mesopotamia* (ed. B. Alster; Copenhagen, 1980), pp. 171-82. Esarhaddon had to fight for six weeks before his throne was secured; cf. J.A. Brinkman, *Prelude to Empire*, p. 72.

3.   The list of nations in Gen. 10 may be a reflex of the Assyrian imperial period and cannot have been composed before the end of the seventh century BCE, because it makes Cush (Nubia) the father of Nimrud (Mesopotamia) and lists both Elam and Lydia (Lud) as sons of Shem; cf. I. Diakonoff, *AfO Beiheft* 19 (1982), p. 22, cf. E.A. Knauf, *Ismael*, pp. 61-62. M. Astour sees the name Sabtah in v. 7 as a reference to pharaoh Shabako of the Twenty-Fifth (Nubian) Dynasty ('Sabtah and Sabtech: Ethiopian Pharaoh Names in Genesis 10', *JBL* 84 [1965], pp. 422-25).

the Elamites and the Urartians in the north. In the west Assyria had extended its power beyond the Taurus mountains and into Cilicia. In the northwest Cimmerians were threatening the empire. In order to check them Esarhaddon made a treaty with king Bartatua 'king of the Ashguzai',[1] that is, the Scythians (biblical Gomer).[2] Like the Cimmerians, the Scythians also had come from the Caucasus region, but somewhat later than the Cimmerians. A treaty with the Scythians gave Esarhaddon military support not only against the Cimmerians, but also against the Medes. In his wars in the southwest with the Arabs Sennacherib had taken their god statues. Esarhaddon returned the idols at the request of one of the Arab kings, Hazail. Tabua, a young Arab girl who had been taken to Nineveh, was made queen in her native country, and his people's images were likewise returned.[3] In this way Esarhaddon reversed his father's policy towards the Arabs and tried to win faithful vassals in this part of the Near East, in which undisturbed trade was so essential. At the same time, he could also use the Arab times for his military operations.

On the Syro-Palestinian scene, 'pax assyriaca' was in effect until Abdi-Milkutti of Sidon and his ally Sanduarri of Kundu and Sizu in Cilicia revolted. Already in 679 BCE Esarhaddon marched to the border of Egypt and devastated the Philistine city of Arza (Tell Jemme?). Its king Asuḫili was made a prisoner and taken to Nineveh.[4] He was chained to a gate together with a pig, a bear and a dog.[5] The reason for this campaign is not really known. It may have been a demonstration of power,[6] giving a message to both the new pharaoh of Egypt,

---

1. Cf. J.A. Knudtzon, *Assyrische Gebete an den Sonnengott* (Leipzig, 1893), II, par. 25; see also A. Heidel, 'A New Hexagonal Prism of Esarhaddon', *Sumer* 12 (1956), p. 17.

2. The biblical term for Scythians is Ashkenaz (Jer. 51.27). For the Scythians, see the discussion by R.P. Vaggione, who maintains that the phrase in Herodotus about the Scythians running over Asia refers to Asia Minor ('Over All Asia? The Extent of the Scythian Domination in Herodotus', *JBL* 92 [1973], pp. 523-30); see also K.S. Rubinson, 'Herodotus and the Scythians', *Expedition* 17 (1975), pp. 16-17; E. Yamauchi, 'The Scythians: Invading Hordes from the Russian Steppes', *BA* 46 (1983), pp. 90-99 (with lit.).

3. *ANET*, pp. 291, 301; cf. D.D. Luckenbill, *ARAB*, II, pars. 940, 943. Consult also I. Eph'al, *The Ancient Arabs*, pp. 126-27.

4. R. Borger, *Die Inschriften Asarhaddons*, p. 50; *ANET*, p. 290.

5. A. Heidel, *Sumer* 12 (1956), p. 14, col. I ll. 56-58.

6. Cf. H. Tadmor, *BA* 29 (1966), p. 98.

Taharqa (690–664 BCE), and the Palestinian vassals. Sidon alone ignored the message, but with the support of the Cilicians, its king counted on arresting the growing mercantile importance of Tyre, its main rival, and, thus, also the power of the new Assyrian king, who had had problems in establishing himself on the throne. The possibility of contacts between Taharqa and Abdi-Milkutti cannot be ignored.[1] However, the attempt to throw off the Assyrian yoke was, a mistake. Sidon was conquered and sacked in 677/676 BCE. The city wall was thrown into the sea. The king, Abdi-Milkutti, 'who had fled before my attack into the high sea', was caught 'like a fish', and was beheaded.[2] Gold, silver, ivory and garments, as well as people, cattle and donkeys, were taken to Assyria.[3] As a reward for his assistance, two parts of Sidon's territory Ma'rub and Zarephtah were given over to Tyre's king Ba'lu.[4] The rest of Sidon's territory was made an Assyrian province, and, as usual, foreigners were settled there. As a replacement for Sidon a new city, Kar-Esarhaddon (the Esarhaddon port), was built on the mainland. 'All the kings of the country Hatti and the seacoast' had to contribute to the building project.[5] It was shortly after this that the 22 'kings of Hatti, the seashore, and the islands' (that is, Syria-Palestine and Cyprus) were charged with furnishing building material 'under terrible difficulties' to Esarhaddon's new palace in Nineveh.[6]

The existence of a treaty between Esarhaddon and Ba'lu of Tyre is mentioned in the Assyrian report of the siege and destruction of Sidon.[7] The treaty contains stipulations about trade and trade routes,

---

1. Cf. A. Spalinger, 'Esarhaddon and Egypt: An Analysis of the First Invasion of Egypt', *Or* NS 43 (1974), p. 299.

2. A.L. Oppenheim, *ANET*, p. 287; cf. D.D. Luckenbill, *ARAB* II, par. 527. Abdi-Milkutti was killed in the month of Tashritu (*ANET*, p. 302). Sanduarri was also beheaded. The heads of both were hung around the necks of their high officials and 'displayed' in a triumphal procession in Nineveh. Cf. also A. Heidel, *Sumer* 12 (1956), pp. 12-13, col. I ll. 38-40.

3. Two Egyptian vases of alabaster were found in Assur with identical inscriptions mentioning that they were from the palace of Abdi-Milkutti of Sidon (D.D. Luckenbill, *ARAB*, II, par. 721).

4. E. Forrer, *Die Provinzeinteilung des assyrischen Reiches* D.D. Luckenbill, *ARAB*, II, par. 512.

5. D.D. Luckenbill, *ARAB*, II, par. 512; *ANET*, p. 291.

6. *ANET*, p. 291; cf. R. Borger, *Die Inschriften Asarhaddons*, pp. 107-109.

7. A.T. Olmstead dates the treaty to 677/76 BCE (*History of Palestine and Syria*, p. 483).

and also gives Ba'lu permission to enter all the sea ports on the Mediterranean while Esarhaddon is given the right to enter all the cities and villages of Ba'lu. As mentioned above, a *qēpu*, 'supervisor', was appointed to keep check on Ba'lu and to ensure to that the Assyrian kings' orders were carried out. As usual, there is the clause that the Assyrian gods will curse king and people should the treaty be broken by Ba'lu, but of certain interest is the statement that the Phoenician gods will be responsible for the destruction of Tyre and its land and for the deportation of its people.[1] Among the West-Semitic gods named are Melqart and Eshmun, Ashtarte, Baiti-ili (Bethel) and Anati-Baiti-ili (Anath-Bethel), Baal-samême, Baal-malagê,[2] and Baal-sapunu.[3] Among the Assyrian gods, the goddess of healing, Gula, is to be the one who will strike Ba'lu with illness if he does not keep the treaty.

Esarhaddon's goal was to conquer Egypt because its influence was being felt in Philistia and also in Phoenicia.[4] In order to succeed, the Assyrian armies had to cross the desert of the northern Sinai. That created a special problem regarding provisions for the troops, particularly water. The solution to the problem was close at hand in the camels that the Arabs, the people that had solved the problem of providing water in the desert, were using. Camels could make a desert march possible.[5] Having put down some Arab rebellions,[6] Sinai was soon secured. In 675 BCE Esarhaddon started his campaign against Egypt with an army that included troops from his vassal states in Syria-Palestine. Not much is known about this campaign because it

---

1. R. Frankena, *OTS* 14 (1965), p. 131.

2. For the identification of this god, see the discussion in O. Hvidberg-Hansen, 'Ba'al-malâge dans le traité entre Asarhaddon et le roi de Tyr', *AcOr* 35 (1973), pp. 47-81. Hvidberg-Hansen sees him as Dagan (pp. 80-81). M.L. Barré suggests Kushor of Ugarit (*The God List in the Treaty between Hannibal and Philip V of Macedon* [Baltimore, 1983], p. 55).

3. For the text, see R. Borger, *Die Inschriften Asarhaddons*, pp. 107-109.

4. The Nahr el-Kelb inscription (fragmentary as it is) mentions Ashkelon as an Egyptian fortress (R. Borger, *Die Inschriften Asarhaddons*, pp. 101-102). A. Spalinger thinks that Taharqa invaded Palestine in c. 673 BCE (*Or* NS 43 [1974], pp. 301-302).

5. For the camel's load capacity, see I. Eph'al, *The Ancient Arabs*, p. 140 n. 491. Cf. also B. Bentjes, *Klio* 38 (1960), pp. 23-52; M. Ripinsky, 'The Camel in Ancient Arabia', *Antiquity* 49 (1975), pp. 295-98.

6. D.D. Luckenbill, *ARAB*, II, pars. 551-52; *ANET*, pp. 291-92.

was not successful. Taharqa's forces defeated the Assyrians. As a result the scribes of Esarhaddon stated merely that in Esarhaddon's seventh year the forces of Assyria were defeated in Egypt on the fifth of Adar.[1]

In his tenth year Esarhaddon finally succeeded in invading Egypt.[2] The invasion is well described both in the annals[3] and on a stele from Zinjirli,[4] as well as on a fragmentary stele from Nahr el-Kelb (the Dog River) in the vicinity of Beirut.[5] The report is much more detailed than most other Assyrian inscriptions. On his way Esarhaddon besieged Tyre and cut it off from provisions of food and water because its king Ba'lu had conspired with Taharaqa.[6] He then passed Apku (Aphek) and bypassed the Egyptian stronghold at Ashkelon[7] on his way to Rapihu at the 'Brook of Egypt'. Since there was no river beyond this point Esarhaddon made use of the camels and the water skins that 'all the kings of Arabia had brought'. Then the inscription claims that on their way to Egypt through Magdali (Migdol) the Assyrians[8] discovered a strange country never before encountered. It contained two-headed serpents and some 'green [animals] whose wings were batting'.[9]

1.   R. Borger, *Die Inschriften Asarhaddons*, p. 123; *ANET*, p. 302; A.K. Grayson, *Assyrian and Babylonian Chronicles*, pp. 85, 23-28; cf. W.G. Lambert, 'Booty from Egypt?', *JJS* 33 (1982), pp. 61-70.

2.   The king had asked the oracle whether he would return after the campaign, and his personal *medicus*, Urad-Nabu, had given him the green light. Esarhaddon was seldom healthy; cf. A.T. Olmstead, *History of Assyria*, p. 381.

3.   D.D. Luckenbill, *ARAB*, II, pars. 554-56; *ANET*, pp. 292-93.

4.   D.D. Luckenbill, *ARAB*, II, pars. 580-81; *ANET*, p. 293.

5.   D.D. Luckenbill, *ARAB*, II, pars. 584-85; R. Borger, *Die Inschriften Asarhaddons*, p. 101. The stele at Nahr el-Kelb also mentions Ashkelon (Isqaluna) as the stronghold of Taharqa (R. Borger, *Die Inschriften Asarhaddons*, p. 102). Nothing more is learned about Ashkelon's connections with Taharqa (cf. the discussion by H. Tadmor, *BA* 29 [1966], pp. 99-100). The situation in Philistia is unclear. A. Alt mentions that an eponym refers to the appointing of the governor of the Ashdod province in 669 BCE ('Die territorialgeschichtliche Bedeutung von Sanheribs Eingriff in Palästina', *KS*, II, p. 246; cf. *idem*, 'Neue Assyrische Nachrichten über Palästina, 2: Zur Errichtung der Provinz Asdod', *KS*, II, p. 241).

6.   R. Borger, *Die Inschriften Asarhaddons*, p. 112.

7.   Cf. A. Spalinger, *Or* NS 43 (1974), p. 301.

8.   See E.D. Oren, 'Migdol: A New Fortress on the Edge of the Eastern Nile Delta', *BASOR* 256 (1984), pp. 30-35.

9.   A.L. Oppenheim, *ANET*, p. 292. For the description of this land, cf. Deut. 8.15: a 'vast and dreadful wilderness, a land of fiery serpents, scorpions, thirst', or

Stones and rocks of unfamiliar shape are also mentioned. After having reached the town of Ishhupri in the north, the Assyrian army fought its way down to Memphis for 15 days. Taharqa is said to have been wounded five times by Esarhaddon's arrows. Memphis was taken and Taharqa probably fled south. The city was looted. Among the prisoners were the queen and the crown-prince.[1] Egypt was reorganized as a province. Egyptian local dynasts supporting Taharqa the Cushite, were removed, and high officials and administrative personnel were replaced.[2] It is probable that the Assyrians were able to 'portray themselves as "liberators" of Egypt'.[3] Esarhaddon also organized the cult of Ashur and other Assyrian gods,[4] which meant that Egypt was now the territory of the god Ashur and of Assyria.[5] On his way back Esarhaddon had a stela engraved and placed at Nahr el-Kelb. Another stele was found at Sam'al (Zinjirli). It depicts the Assyrian king leading two men, probably the king of Tyre and Taharqa's son and crown-prince, Ushanahuru, by a nose rope.[6]

As soon as the Assyrian troops had left Egypt Taharqa returned. In order to stabilize Egypt, Esarhaddon prepared a new campaign, and in 669 BCE he again marched towards Egypt. He fell sick on his way and died in Harran.[7] No more is said about this campaign, which may mean that nothing came out of it. It fell to his successor, Ashurbanipal (668–627 BCE), his favorite son,[8] to repeat the conquest of Egypt.

Isa. 30.6: a land of 'lioness and roaring lion, of viper and flying serpent' (JB).

1. R. Borger, *Die Inscriften Asarhaddons*, p. 101-102; A.K. Grayson, *Assyrian and Babylonian Chronicles*, Chronicle 1, IV: 23-28, pp. 85-86; cf. W.G. Lambert, *JJS* 33 (1982), pp. 61-70. The captured harem is also mentioned in a letter; see S. Parpola, *Letters from Assyrian Scribes to the Kings Esarhaddon and Assurbanipal II* (AOAT, 5.2; Neukirchen–Vluyn, 1983), p. 270.

2. Necho I may have been appointed vassal king in Sais at this time; cf. K.A. Kitchen, *The Third Intermediate Period*, pp. 145-46.

3. A. Spalinger, *Or* NS 43 (1974), p. 325.

4. D.D. Luckenbill, *ARAB*, II, pars. 554-64; *ANET*, pp. 292-94; R. Borger, *Die Inschriften Asarhaddons*, pp. 101, 112-13.

5. Cf. G.W. Ahlström, *Royal Administration*, p. 8.

6. *ANEP*, 447. For the Egyptian being the crown-prince, see A. Spalinger, *Or* NS 43 (1974), pp. 303-304; W.G. Lambert, *JJS* 33 (1982), pp. 62-63. Ezek. 19.9 may refer to King Jehoiakim being led with a nose ring to Babylon.

7. *ANET*, p. 303. The date of Esarhaddon's death is given as the tenth of Arahsamna.

8. R. Borger, *Die Inschriften Asarhaddons*, p. 71, par. 43:25.

One of Ashurbanipal's first goals was to re-establish the Assyrian rule in Egypt. Ashurbanipal sent an army under his *turtanu* to Egypt, 667 BCE. In his campaign the kings of Ebir-nari (i.e. Trans-Euphrates) had to participate by supplying soldiers. Kings of coastal cities were also ordered to supply ships.[1] Ashurbanipal's 667 campaign is the first recorded maritime invasion of Egypt by a Near Eastern power.[2] Local dynasts had rebelled against Assyria and joined Taharqa. However, they were caught and taken prisoner. Among them was Necho of Sais who was taken to Nineveh. He was subsequently reinstated as king and sent back to Sais with a large escort that included high officials who were to act as his supervisors (governors).[3] Necho's son, Psamme-tichus, was made king of Athribis, c. 40 km NNW of Heliopolis.[4]

Taharqa died in 664 BCE and was followed by Tanwetamani (664–656 BCE), who attacked the Assyrian troops at Memphis and took the city.[5] Necho I was probably killed in this battle, and his son, Psammeti-chus, fled to Assyrian territories.[6] Tanwetamani also managed to win the Delta princes over to his side.[7] Ashurbanipal received word of this rebellion through an express courier, and in 663 he started his second campaign, which led the Assyrian troops all the way to Tanwetamani's capital, Thebes (Ni', Hebrew No-Amon).[8] They took the city and sacked it.[9] The pro-Assyrian Psammetichus was acknowledged as king of Sais, and for a short time Egypt was again an Assyrian province.[10]

The Assyrian conquest of Egypt was made possible largely through the support of the Arabs. The trade routes from Arabia and Transjordan through the Negev to the Philistine coast and to Egypt were under the control of Arab rulers (cf. 2 Chron. 21.16-17; 26.7-8).

1. D.D. Luckenbill, *ARAB*, II, pars. 900-901.
2. Among the vassal kings were Ba'lu of Tyre, Manasseh of Judah, the kings of Philistia, Ammon, Edom, Moab, Byblos, Arvad, and some from Cyprus. See *ANET*, p. 294.
3. D.D. Luckenbill, *ARAB*, II, pars. 904-905; *ANET*, pp. 294-95.
4. D.D. Luckenbill, *ARAB*, II, par. 905; *ANET*, p. 295.
5. J.H. Breasted, *Ancient Records of Egypt*, IV, p. 471, par. 928.
6. Cf. K.A. Kitchen, *The Third Intermediate Period*, pp. 145-46. For Necho's death, see J.H. Breasted, *Ancient Records of Egypt*, IV, p. 468 n. b.
7. A.H. Gardiner, *Egypt of the Pharaohs*, p. 348.
8. Cf. Nah. 3.8-10.
9. D.D. Luckenbill, *ARAB*, II, pars. 906-907; *ANET*, p. 295.
10. For the problem of Egypt and Assyria, see also A. Spalinger, 'Assurbanipal and Egypt: A Source Study', *JAOS* 94 (1974), pp. 316-28.

Under the circumstances it is hard to believe that the small kingdom of Judah could have expanded to the south in the reign of Esarhaddon[1] or during the early years of Ashurbanipal. Such a policy would certainly have collided with the Assyrian strategy of keeping these areas under supervision by 'reliable' Arab tribes.

The conquest of Egypt can be labelled the beginning of the end of the Assyrian empire. With this victory Assyria had reached its limits. It had overextended itself. Until 663 BCE the Assyrian forces had been able to keep vassals in line in spite of several rebellions. Palestine had been subdued through the campaigns of Sargon and Sennacherib. Tahraqa's meddling in Philistine affairs had come to an end and Egypt was soon united again under Necho's son, Psammetichus I (664–610 BCE). Psammetichus reigned with the good will of the Assyrians, but their control over Egypt was declining. The Cimmerians in the west threatened Syria[2] and had forced Gyges (Gūgū) of Lydia to seek Assyrian help. Later, however, he broke with Ashurbanipal, and in a war with the Cimmerians Gyges lost his life and his capital, Sardis (644 BCE).[3] In Arabia, which must have presented greater problems than usual for the Assyrians because of sand, wind, and lack of water, there were always Arab chieftains who were trying to shake off the Assyrian yoke. In the east Elam repeatedly gave a willing ear to Babylonian and Chaldean plans of resistance. Thus, when

---

1.   'Throughout the reign of Esarhaddon there is no sign that Judah's rights to control over the Negeb routes were restored. Quite the contrary' (Z. Herzog, M. Aharoni, A.F. Rainey and S. Moshkovitz, *BASOR* 254 [1984], p. 25). Herzog *et al.* think, however, that Manasseh tried to 'improve Judah's political and economic status' with its neighbors by introducing their cults in Judah! (*ibid.*). This theory is unrealistic. Manasseh's policy involved the restoration of the traditional Judahite religion, as mentioned above; see the previous chapter and cf. G.W. Ahlström, *Royal Administration*, pp. 74-76. The Chronicler may have been more clever than has been realized. He may have attributed to Manasseh the recovery of the Judahite cities so that he could blame Manasseh for the 'reinstatement' of the *bāmôt*. The stage was then set both religiously and politically for Josiah's reform, which included the 'abandonment' of the *bāmôt*. Cf. O. Eissfeldt, 'Ezechiel als Zeuge für Sanheribs Eingriff', *PJ* 27 (1931), pp. 62-63.

2.   See S. Parpola, *Letters from Assyrian Scribes*, II, pp. 307-308, 375-77.

3.   A.J. Spalinger, 'The Date of the Death of Gyges and its Historical Implications', *JAOS* 98 (1978), pp. 400-409. See also M. Cogan and H. Tadmor, who maintain that Gyges' death did not occur before 650 BCE ('Gyges and Ashurbanipal: A Study in Literary Transmission', *Or* NS 46 [1977], pp. 65-85).

Ashurbanipal's brother Shamash-shum-ukin, who had been appointed king over Babylonia by their father, Esarhaddon, raised the banner of rebellion against Assyria for the independence of Babylonia, he could count on support from the Chaldeans and Aramaeans in Babylonia, from the Elamites in the east, and from the Arabs in the south. Such a widespread rebellion could be dangerous not only because of the geographic distance between the allies, but also because different kinds of war technique had to be used. Waging war against desert tribes is not the same as besieging a city.[1] Ashurbanipal's annals also mention that the 'kings of Guti, Amurru, and Meluḫḫa' supported Shamash-shum-ukin.[2] This means that the peoples of the Zagros mountains (north of Babylonia), Syria-Palestine and Egypt would have been part of a coalition against Ashurbanipal. The annals do not mention, how-ever, any actual participation in the war by these kings.[3] Psammetichus of Egypt may have encouraged the creation of a coalition against Assyria, but he did not participate in any war activities against Ashur-banipal. The Arabs took an active part in the war and some Arab tribes were also in Babylonia when the war broke out. It is possible to see the raids by the Qedarites in Transjordan as part of the uprising against Assyria,[4] even though the raids led by Yauta' (Uaite')[5] and Ammuladi could have taken place just before Shamash-shum-ukin broke with Ashurbanipal.[6] Even so, they could be interpreted as a sign

1. The Arabs could take temporary refuge in the desert in territories where chariots and horses were not the most efficient weapons. Ashurbanipal's inscriptions mention that the Assyrians surprised the Arab camps in nightly raids using both horses and chariots; cf. M. Streck, *Assurbanipal und die letzten assyrischen Könige*, col. IX, ll. 13-14; I. Eph'al, 'On Warfare and Military Control in the Ancient Near Eastern Empires: A Research Outline', *History, Historiography and Interpretation: Studies in Biblical and Cuneiform Literatures* (ed. H. Tadmor and M. Weinfeld; Jerusalem, 1986), pp. 95-96. This type of attack is probably what the prophet Jeremiah refers to in his utterance against Qedar and 'the kingdoms of Hazor' in 49.28-33. Hazor, as well as Qedar, refers to Arab tribes in the east, those who have 'neither gates nor bars', but 'that dwell alone' (v. 31). For these Nebuchadrezzar had laid a plan, a scheme (v. 30).

2. M. Streck, *Assurbanipal und die letzten assyrischen Könige*, p. 301, 103.

3. Cf. J.A. Brinkman, *Prelude to Empire*, pp. 95-96.

4. *ANET*, pp. 297-99.

5. For the confusion in spelling the name, see I. Eph'al, *The Ancient Arabs*, pp. 146-47.

6. I. Eph'al maintains that these raids were not the result of a 'joint initiative on the part of the Arabs and the king of Babylonia' (*The Ancient Arabs*, p. 155).

of the hostilities in the west against Assyria. The Assyrian troops in Transjordan and Syria defeated the Arabs. Moab under its king Kamashalta participated in these battles on the Assyrian side and captured Ammuladi. The other Arab chief, Uaite', fled to Nebaioth but was handed over to the Assyrians. The rest of his life he spent chained like a dog together with a bear (?) and a dog to a gate in Nineveh.[1] After Ashurbanipal had put down the Babylonian rebellion he carried out campaigns against the Arabic federation of Qedarites and against Nebaioth, which threatened Assyrian security in the districts of eastern Syria.[2]

The unrest and instability in the empire was certainly not limited to Syria and Transjordan. On his return home from a later campaign against the Arabs, Ashurbanipal first went to Phoenicia and captured Acco and Ushu (mainland Tyre), taking their images and the survivors of the battles to Assyria.[3] Parts of Palestine and Phoenicia may have rebelled. Ezra 4.9-10 may be relevant to such a consideration. It reports that Osenappar (Ashurbanipal) settled peoples from Uruk, Babylon and Susa in Samaria. If this is correct, Ashurbanipal was in Palestine around 645 BCE, that is, after he had defeated the Elamites and devastated their country. This would then be the date for his campaign against the Arabs of Syria-Transjordan. It would also have been the last time an Assyrian army campaigned in Palestine. It is interesting to note that there is no mention of southern Palestine or Egypt in Ashurbanipal's inscriptions from this time. Psammetichus I had managed to rule Egypt independent from Assyrian supervision. For Ashurbanipal, Cush was the real enemy, so long as Psammetichus had the support of Upper Egypt and could keep the peace with the princes of the Delta, he got the support he needed 'to stave off the Cushite takeover of Egypt'.[4] His campaigns in Syria-Palestine, however, did not really establish an Egyptian empire. They were more of a diplomatic nature

---

1. Cf. the reliefs in 'the Arab Room' of Ashurbanipal's palace in Nineveh (R.D. Barnett, *Sculptures from the North Palace of Ashurbanipal at Nineveh (668–627 BCE)* (London, 1975), pp. 15-16, pls. xxxii-xxxiii.

2. For the wars with the Arabs, see M. Weippert, 'Die Kämpfe des assyrischen Königs Assurbanipal gegen die Araber', *WO* 7 (1973), pp. 39-85; I. Eph'al, *The Ancient Arabs*, pp. 143-69; J.A. Brinkman, *Prelude to Empire*, p. 103. As to the 'redaction' of the Assyrian texts, see E.A. Knauf, *Ismael*, pp. 96-98.

3. *ANET*, p. 300; cf. H.J. Katzenstein, *The History of Tyre*, pp. 293-94.

4. A. Spalinger, *JAOS* 94 (1974), p. 325.

than real conquests. He may have been an ally of Assyria most of the time; at least he never fought against Ashurbanipal.[1] It may be assumed that southern Palestine, including the Philistine cities and Judah, came under the influence of Egypt. However, in 635 BCE Psammetichus laid siege to Ashdod/Azotus, which had tried to gain its independence from Assyria.[2] If Ashdod had succeeded, it could have disturbed Egypt's interest in the area. With Assyria's power in decline and civil war breaking out after Ashurbanipal's death in 627 BCE, Psammetichus tried to gain control of Palestine. He also fought as an Assyrian ally against Babylonia in 616 and 610 BCE.

Psammetichus I stationed garrisons both in the south at Elephantine and in the border areas to the west and east of the Delta, at Naukratis and Daphne. He settled Ionian and Carian mercenaries on both sides of the Pelusiac branch of the Nile.[3] Many of his soldiers were Greek, Libyan or Asiatic mercenaries. Among the latter were men from Phoenicia, Judah and Samerina, and perhaps also from other Aramaean speaking districts of Palestine and Syria.[4] According to an inscription of Ashurbanipal, Gyges had already sent soldiers to Egypt.[5] From now on Greek mercenaries are to be found in the armies of the ancient Near East.[6] About 45 sites of which the majority were 'temporary encampments and stations' have been found from the eastern Delta to el-Arish in the northern Sinai. A few of these sites were forts, as Tell el-Her (Migdol?), 10 km south of Tell Farama, ancient Pelusium. All were occupied in the Saitic period, and their destruction has been connected with Cambyses' invasion of Egypt in

---

1. See A. Spalinger, *Or* NS 47 (1978), pp. 15-16.

2. Herodotus (2.157) mentions that Psammetichus was besieging Ashdod for 29 years. H. Tadmor believes that would rather refer to the twenty-ninth year of the Egyptian king (*BA* 29 [1966], pp. 101-102).

3. Cf. E.D. Oren, *BASOR* 256 (1984), p. 38.

4. With the many Aramaean-speaking peoples settled in Samerina by the Assyrians, and the fact that Aramaic was the official language of the Assyrian empire, the Palestinian provinces may have become Aramaic speaking after a generation; cf. on this subject R.A. Bowman, 'Arameans, Aramaic, and the Bible', *JNES* 7 (1948), pp. 65-90.

5. D.D. Luckenbill, *ARAB*, II, par. 785. Herodotus, for instance, mentions (2.152) that Ionians and Carians had helped Psammetichus to gain the upper hand over the princes of the Delta.

6. Cf. Zech. 9.1-8, and consult B. Otzen, *Studien über Deuterosacharja*, p. 117.

525 BCE. The material culture from these sites shows parallels with Daphne and Naukratis, and the Phoenician and Greek pottery especially indicates that Phoenician traders trafficked these places and that Greek mercenaries may have been stationed there.[1] The same features are to be found along the Philistine coast. For instance, in 1960 a small fortress dating to the seventh–sixth century BCE, Meṣad Hashavyahu, was found at Yavneh-Yam (between Jaffa and Ashdod) with Greek pottery. A few ostraca in the Hebrew script were also found, leading some to conclude that the fortress was Judahite and dated to the period of King Josiah.[2] By implication, Josiah had been able to extend his rule into Philistine territory.[3] This conclusion is debatable and will be discussed below. What is of primary importance is the finding of Greek pottery at Meṣad Hashavyahu. Whoever was in command of the fort may have had placed Greek mercenaries there. The appearance of the theophoric component -*yāhû* in the name Hashavyahu does not necessarily make the place Judahite, nor does the Greek pottery or Greek mercenaries make it Egyptian. Definite proof for either theory is thus lacking. There is a third possibility that has not yet been discussed. Both Philistines and Judahites could have been used in this area, because Josiah was probably an ally of Egypt at this time. As such he could have been asked to send soldiers to Meṣad Hashavyahu.[4]

It is not known when the Assyrians abandoned the garrison at Tell Jemme, but it is possible that the place was taken by Psammetichus I in connection with his move through Philistia and his conquest of

1.   E.D. Oren, *BASOR* 256 (1984), p. 34.

2.   For the excavations see J. Naveh, 'The Excavations at Meṣad Hasavyahu: Preliminary Report', *IEJ* 12 (1962), pp. 89-113; for the ostraca, J. Naveh, 'A Hebrew Letter from the Seventh Century BCE', *IEJ* 10 (1960), pp. 129-39; *idem*, 'More Hebrew Inscriptions from Mesad Hasavyahu', *IEJ* 12 (1962), pp. 27-32; consult also D. Pardee, *Handbook of Ancient Hebrew Letters*, pp. 15-24 (with lit.).

3.   J. Naveh thinks that the fort was built during the rule of Psammetichus I and settled by Greek mercenaries. It would have been conquered by Josiah shortly before 609 BCE (*IEJ* 12 [1962], pp. 99). F.M. Cross believes that this fort shows that Josiah expanded to the west ('Epigraphic Notes on Hebrew Documents of the Eighth–Sixth Centuries BCE: II. The Murabba'at Papyrus and the Letter Found near Yabneh-Yam', *BASOR* 165 [1962], p. 42). Cf. also Y. Aharoni, *The Land of the Bible* (2nd edn), p. 403.

4.   E. Stern believes that Josiah built the fortress around 630 BCE (*BA* 38 [1975], p. 37). See further below, Chapter 18, pp. 767-69.

Ashdod.[1] Whether the garrison force had abandoned the site before that is not known. The Assyrian inscriptions do not provide information about Palestine or Egypt after Ashurbanipal's devastation of Elam and his campaign against the Arabs and the Tyrians around 645 BCE. After this time no important military campaigns are reported by the Assyrian scribes, a fact that has been interpreted as a sign that the decline of the empire started during Ashurbanipal's last decades.[2] Assyria's decline explains why Psammetichus I tried to make his influence felt in Palestine. About two decades after Ashurbanipal's death in 627 BCE[3] the Assyrian empire no longer existed.

1.   Cf. G.W. Van Beek, 'Tel Gamma', *IEJ* 22 (1972), pp. 245-46; *idem*, *Archaeology* 36 (1983), pp. 12-16.

2.   See, for instance, H.W.F. Saggs, *The Might that was Assyria*, pp. 115-16; J.A. Brinkman, *Prelude to Empire*, p. 105.

3.   *ANET Suppl.*, pp. 560-62.

Chapter 18

NEW MASTERS

Ashurbanipal went down in history as one of the most ruthless kings of Assyria, desecrating tombs and humiliating subdued kings who had not escaped his cruel pleasures by death. Malice was a 'driving force behind the later Ashurbanipal'. A great statesman he was not.[1] However, he was a great collector of cuneiform tablets. It is thanks to his large 'library' that so much is known about the history of the ancient Near East. However, his collection cannot be used to argue that the so-called Saitic renaissance[2] took place in the Near East during the seventh century BCE. Other kings had also collected texts and Ashurbanipal's collection was more of a hobby than an expression of a cultural trend. As for the 'Saitic renaissance', the term is misleading. It is true that the Saitic kings tried to boost their images and their rule through art and literature, using as stereotypes the style and phraseology of the Old and Middle Kingdom pharaohs.[3] However, it was a phenomenon at home at the royal court and nothing like a cultural movement born through nostalgia.[4]

What followed after Ashurbanipal's death was the swan-song of the Assyrian empire. Assyria seems to have overextended itself in conquering Egypt. In addition, the result of the frequent deportations of

1. H.W.F. Saggs, *The Might that was Assyria*, p. 116.
2. The idea is that of W.F. Albright (*From Stone Age to Christianity*, p. 241-42).
3. Cf. B. von Bothmer, *Egyptian Sculpture of the Late Period, 700 BCE to CE 100* (Brooklyn, NY, 1960), pls. 28-29, 39, etc. See also H. Brunner, 'Archaismus', *Lexikon der Ägyptologie*, I (ed. W. Helck and W. Westendorf; Wiesbadon, 1975), cols. 386-95.
4. According to A. Spalinger, this 'renaissance' should not be compared with the Italian one, but rather with the 'artificial and court-centered renaissance of Carolingian France and Ottonian Germany' (*Or* NS 47 [1978], p. 12; cf. p. 36).

subdued peoples was that the Assyrian army, administration, and population became largely non-Assyrian. The effect of several hundred years of battles with different Near Eastern peoples, as well as the Aramaean invasions in earlier times, meant that a special Assyrian national identity never developed. Assyria became the military, political and economic ruler of the Near East. Its political hegemony, however, was always tested, and when military control in the vast empire slipped, as it did after a ruler's death, the danger of collapse was always there. It is also possible that the empire's economic policies contributed to the decline.[1] Being built on the power of military occupation, the 'building' had to dissolve sooner or later.

Ashurbanipal was succeeded by his son Ashur-etil-ilani (c. 631/630–623), who probably had been his father's coregent for a few years. As a result of the struggle for the throne that began when Ashurbanipal died, Sin-shar-ishkun, another son of the old king, became king of Babylonia,[2] but he was ousted by the Chaldean general Nabopolassar (626–605 BCE), who freed Babylonia from Assyrian rule.[3] Sin-shar-ishkun managed to replace his brother as king in Nineveh (around 623 BCE), but it is not known how he did so.[4] He reigned until his death in 612 BCE.

Nabopolassar, who called himself the 'son of a nobody',[5] had first declared himself king over the tribes of the marshlands in southern

1. See J.N. Postgate, who mentions that there could also have been a shortage of horses, which would have been very dangerous if military control was to be maintained ('The Economic Structure of the Assyrian Empire', *Power and Propaganda* [ed. M.I. Laysen; Copenhagen, 1979], pp. 216-18).

2. After the revolt of Shamash-shum-ukin, a certain Kandalanu was appointed king (or governor) over Babylonia. His reign is virtually unknown. Because he died the same year as Ashurbanipal, 627 BCE, it has been assumed that his name could be a Babylonian throne-name for Ashurbanipal. This is a less probable hypothesis because no Assyrian king was known to have two throne-names; see J.A. Brinkman, *Prelude to Empire*, pp. 105-106. Cf. also C.J. Gadd, 'The Haran Inscription of Nabonidus', *Anatolian Studies* 8 (1958), pp. 69-72.

3. A.L. Oppenheim, *Ancient Mesopotamia*, p. 159; H.W.F. Saggs, *The Might that was Assyria*, pp. 117-18.

4. See J. Reade, 'The Accession of Sinsharishkun', *JCS* 23 (1970–71), pp. 1-9. Concerning the chronological problems, see also J. Oates, 'Assyrian Chronology', *Iraq* 27 (1965), pp. 135-59.

5. *VAB*, IV, p. 66, no. 4.4. See also D.J. Wiseman, *Nebuchadrezzar and Babylon*, p. 6.

Babylonia. As king of Babylonia (626–605 BCE)[1] he inaugurated a new dynasty usually called the neo-Babylonian or Chaldean Dynasty, even if he himself was not a Chaldean.[2] He managed to unite the anti-Assyrian forces, among them the Aramaeans and the Chaldeans, as well as the Elamites in the east and the Arabs in the west. He courted the Elamites by sending back to Susa the god statues that the Assyrians had taken. In 616 BCE Nabopolassar started to move west along the Euphrates. According to the Babylonian Chronicles, he seems to have been stopped by Sin-shar-ishkun and the combined Assyrian and Egyptian[3] forces after some initial victories. He could not take the former Assyrian capital of Ashur and had to retreat to Takritain,[4] where his enemies besieged him. However, the allies lifted the siege; thus, Nabopolassar was not completely defeated.[5] The reason for the withdrawal of the Assyrian-Egyptian forces is not explicitly given in the sources, but it was probably because in the same year the Medes

1. The so-called Nabopolassar Epic is not only an account of Nabopolassar's dynasty, but is also a rare 'account in Akkadian of an actual coronation', according to A.K. Grayson (*Babylonian Historical-Literary Texts* [Toronto Semitic Texts and Studies, 3; Toronto, 1975], pp. 78-86).

2. See A.T. Olmstead, 'The Chaldean Dynasty', *HUCA* 2 (1925), pp. 29-55. J.A. Brinkman thinks that it is 'misleading to label either Nabopolassar or his dynasty Chaldean', because there is no firm evidence as of yet (*Prelude to Empire*, p. 110 n. 551). According to F. Rochberg-Halton, the history of 'the association of the name "Chaldean" with the profession of astrologer is difficult to trace, but it seems to be a Hellenistic innovation' ('New Evidence for the History of Astrology', *JNES* 43 [1984], pp. 114-15). In this connection I would point out that the Old Testament use of *kaśdîm*, 'Chaldean', occurs first with and after Nebuchadrezzar, in Jeremiah, Ezekiel, and in some places in the D history work, which is 'in accordance with the normal contemporary reference to the dynasty by outsiders' (D.J. Wiseman, *Nebuchadrezzar and Babylon*, p. 7). From this it can be concluded that the D historian's writings are to be dated no earlier than the time of Nebuchadrezzar (605–562 BCE).

3. According to J. Lewy, there is no mention in the Gadd Chronicle of an Egyptian king participating in the battle. Thus, Psammetichus must have stationed some troops in Assyria (*Forschungen zur alten Geschichte Vorderasiens* [MVÄG, 29; Leipzig, 1925], p. 33). According to Herodotus the Scythians were supposed to have supported the Assyrians, probably until 616 BCE; see D.J. Wiseman, *Chronicles of Chaldean Kings*, p. 14.

4. Probably modern Takrit; see D.J. Wiseman, *Chronicles of Chaldean Kings*, p. 80. For the text, see also A.L. Oppenheim, *ANET*, pp. 303-305.

5. A.K. Grayson, *Assyrian and Babylonian Chronicles*, pp. 91-92 (Chronicle 3).

invaded Assyria under Cyaxares. They attacked some Assyrian cities and took Ashur in 614 BCE. This is the year Nabopolassar became their ally,[1] and in 612 BCE the Medes ('Umman-manda') and the Babylonian forces captured and destroyed Nineveh after a three-month siege. They were possibly helped by the flooding of the Khosr tributary of the Tigris, which seems to have destroyed some of the city walls. The flooding was probably not a natural event,[2] but may have been caused by the destruction of a dam just outside of Nineveh,[3] a destruction that was part of the strategy of the allied forces.[4] Assyria's king, Sin-shar-ishkun, may have died in this catastrophe.[5] Shortly afterwards Ashur-uballit II becomes king of Assyria in Harran, c. 160 km (100 miles) west of Nineveh.[6]

The destruction of Nineveh meant that an epoch had ended in the Near East and that for a while, the subdued nations could rejoice. Nineveh's disaster is vividly pictured, for instance, in the Book of Nahum. Nah. 2.1 [1.15] announces the 'footsteps' of the messenger[7] bringing the good tidings and proclaiming 'peace', and v. 7 [6] states

1. Nabopolassar arrived after the Medes had taken Ashur; cf. C.J. Gadd, *The Fall of Nineveh* (London, 1923), p. 10.

2. D.J. Wiseman assumed that the Tigris River may have flooded (*Chronicles of Chaldean Kings*, p. 17).

3. Sennacherib had built an aqueduct leading the water from Bavian (c. 48 km [30 miles] NNE of Nineveh) to the Khosr River. However, no remains of the canal that led the water to the river have been found; see T. Jacobsen and S. Lloyd, *Sennacherib's Aqueduct at Jerwan* (OIP, 24; Chicago, 1935), pp. 19-23, 31-43, and fig. 9.

4. See I.M. Diakonov, *Istorii Midii ot drevnejsikh vremen do kontsa IV veka do n.e.* (*The History of Media from Antiquity to the End IV Century BCE*) (Moscow, 1956), p. 308 n. 1. Compare J. Reade, *JCS* 23 (1970–71), p. 5; S. Parpola, *Flodrikene*, p. 297; G.W. Ahlström, 'Prophetical Echoes of Assyrian Growth and Decline', *Dumn-E₂-Du-Ba-A: Studies in Honor of Åke Sjöberg* (ed. H. Behrens and D. Loding; Philadelphia, 1989), pp. 1-6.

5. A.K. Grayson, *Assyrian and Babylonian Chronicles*, pp. 92-94. Cf. H.W.F. Saggs, *The Might that was Assyria*, p. 120.

6. A.K. Grayson, *Assyrian and Babylonian Chronicles*, pp. 94-95.

7. Messengers may have been hurrying all around by foot or by horse to the subdued and occupied territories. The Assyrian communication system's road stations with their fresh horses may have been used. For this system see J.V. Kinnier Wilson, *The Nimrud Wine Lists*, pp. 57-62; I. Eph'al, 'On Warfare and Military Control', *History, Historiography and Interpretation* (ed. H. Tadmor and M. Weinfeld), pp. 103-104.

that the river gates are open and that the palace totters.[1]

The news about Nineveh's fall quickly spread to the different cities and political centers of the Near East, such as the Phoenician and Philistine cities and the capitals of Ammon, Moab, Edom and Judah. This historic event was described by the prophet Nahum in terms of Yahweh's battle against the chaos power, which was the natural literary category to use when attributing the disaster to the will of Yahweh. However, a detail like the mention of the opened river gates refers to an actual event rather than to a mythological motif.

The impact of the disaster of Nineveh upon not only the contemporary world but also upon the following generations was so great that it was remembered not only in the Near East but also in Greece. Xenophon, for instance, mentions that the city was destroyed by the flooding of the Tigris River.[2] The destruction of the dam with the ensuing rush of the waters against the city walls has here been understood as a seasonal flooding of the Tigris. However, the city fell in August of 612 BCE, and that is not the normal time for the river's inundation.

The Assyrian kingdom was still not completely defeated. During the following few years Nabopolassar had to secure his position in Assyria and to put down some resistance in central Mesopotamia. This gave Ashur-uballit time to reorganize his forces. He also had the support of Psammetichus and the Egyptian army. In the years after Ashurbanipal's death Psammetichus had been able to carry out an independent policy of controlling the coasts of southern Syria and Palestine. For the people of these regions Egypt became the new master.[3] According to Herodotus, Psammetichus had besieged and taken the Assyrian province of Ashdod.[4] The decline of Assyria and Babylonia's increasing power

1.   The Hebrew *nmwg*, 'totter', is translated '"is melting" in the mud and water from the flood' by K.J. Cathcart (*Nahum in the Light of Northwest Semitic* [BibOr, 26; Rome, 1973], p. 96). For the flooding, cf. H. Schultz, *Das Buch Nahum* (BZAW, 129; Berlin, 1973), p. 29 n. 85. The imagery used in Zeph. 2.13-15 about the destroyed city is that of the neo-Assyrian inscriptions; see M. Cogan, *Imperialism and Religion*, p. 94 n. 164.

2.   *Anabasis* 3.4. Cf. Diodorus Siculus, 2.27.1.

3.   For the biblical references to this period, see the discussion in B. Otzen, *Studien über Deuterosacharja*, pp. 78-117.

4.   Cf. 2.157. Herodotus says that the siege lasted 29 years. It is impossible to accept this information because it means that the siege must have begun while

was a growing threat to Egypt and to the aspirations of Psammetichus. He was obviously realistic enough to see that the survival of Assyria as a buffer state would be to Egypt's interest.

The Umman-manda, in this case the Medes,[1] increased their pressure upon the Assyrian kingdom of Harran. In 610 BCE they invaded Assyria and Nabopolassar was again quick to join the Medes in order to keep them from becoming a Mesopotamian power.[2] From the south the Egyptian army under their new king, Necho II (610–595 BCE), marched up through Palestine in 609 BCE, and Ashur-uballit retreated in order to join forces with the Egyptians. Necho met with Josiah of Judah at Megiddo,[3] where the latter died. He then marched on to Riblah on the Orontes River (c. 35 km SSW of Homs, called Shabtunah in Egyptian texts), where he put up his headquarters. With the help of the Egyptian army, the Assyrians seem to have been able to retake Harran, but after some time they were defeated and withdrew to Carchemish. There Ashur-uballit established his new capital.[4] What

Assyria and Ashurbanipal were still in control of Palestine. Psammetichus, being a vassal of Assyria, would not have endangered his own position, which still was weak in the mid-seventh century BCE. H. Tadmor suggests that the siege occurred in Psammetichus' twenty-ninth year, which would be 635 BCE (*BA* 29 [1966], pp. 101-102). For the province of Ashdod, cf. A. Alt, *KS*, II, pp. 234-41.

1. The term Umman-manda is used in Akkadian to describe foreign peoples. When the Medes appeared on the historical horizon they were called simply the Umman-manda. See G. Komoróczy, 'Umman-manda', *Acta Antiqua* 25 (1977), pp. 43-57.

2. Cf. D.J. Wiseman, *Nebuchadrezzar and Babylon*, pp. 12-13.

3. Herodotus mentions that Necho fought the 'Syrians' at Magdolos (2.157-59), which has commonly been associated with Megiddo, but probably refers to Migdol close to the Egyptian border (Tell el-Her). Thus, the reference is to the war between Egypt and Babylonia in 601/600 BCE. After the battle Necho reputedly captured Gaza (Kadytis); see E. Lipiński, 'The Egypto-Babylonian War of the Winter 601–600 BCE', *Instituto Orientale di Napoli Annali* 22 (1972), pp. 235-41. Usually scholars have seen the mention of Gaza, Ashkelon and Ashdod in Jer. 47.5 as a reference to this event. However, the text refers to the danger from the north, which most probably refers to the Babylonians (E. Lipiński, *Instituto Orientale di Napoli Annali* 22 [1972], p. 239). H. Tadmor thinks that after Assyria's fall both Egypt and Judah 'became Assyria's heirs to Philistia' (*BA* 29 [1966], p. 101), while M. Elat advocates that Judah was the 'most substantial power' in Palestine, in this period ('Political States', *Lachish*, V [ed. Y. Aharoni *et al.*], p. 68). There are no textual bases for these suggestions.

4. A.K. Grayson, *Assyrian and Babylonian Chronicles*, p. 96.

then happened to Ashur-uballit is not mentioned in any documents. Necho's army seems to have stayed at Carchemish, which means that Ashur-uballit may still have been king. Nabopolassar, who seems to have been more lucky than efficient as a military leader, still had problems with the Assyro-Egyptian coalition. Necho II crossed the Euphrates River in 606 and took the garrison at Quramatu (c. 90 km SSE of Carchemish and 110 km east of Aleppo as the crow flies). Nabopolassar withdrew.[1] This shows that Necho had managed to dominate Syria. The picture quickly changed, however, in the following year when the Babylonian crown-prince, Nebuchadrezzar, was given command over the Babylonian forces in the west. Necho and his forces were completely defeated at Carchemish, and those who managed to escape were pursued and killed in the territory of Hamath. The detachment at Quramatu was either wiped out or had abandoned the site. The Chronicle states that not a single Egyptian soldier returned to Egypt[2] (which may be the usual Semitic exaggeration).[3] This was not only the end of the Assyrian kingdom,[4] it was also the end of Necho's lordship over Syria-Palestine. Riblah now became the Babylonian headquarters in Syria.

The battle at Carchemish, like the fall of Nineveh, changed the political picture of the Near East. A new imperial ruler had emerged: Babylonia. The Egyptian dominion of Syria-Palestine was brief and was probably no more than an attempt to play a role that it was no longer able to perform. Egypt's power was weak and Psammetichus I had tried to boost his army by employing Greek mercenaries,[5] a phenomenon that became common in the armies of the Near East throughout the Persian period. As the acknowledged overlord of Syria-Palestine, Psammetichus also had Semites in his army and his garrisons, as for instance, at Jeb (Elephantine) in southern Egypt.[6]

---

1. A.K. Grayson, *Assyrian and Babylonian Chronicles*, p. 98; D.W. Wiseman, *Chronicles of Chosen Kings*, p. 66, and cf. pp. 19-23.

2. A.K. Grayson, *Assyrian and Babylonian Chronicles*, p. 99.

3. In *Ant.* 10.6.1 Josephus says that Egypt lost 10,000 men, which could have meant the whole army.

4. W.W. Hallo thinks that the battle at Carchemish 'finished what Josiah had begun'; in other words, he thinks that Josiah was pro-Babylonian from the start; see Hallo and Simpson, *The Ancient Near East*, p. 143. Such a picture of Josiah is not to be found in any textual source.

5. Herodotus 2.152, 154.

6. According to A.T. Olmstead, Psammetichus already had Judahite mercenaries

According to Berossus, soldiers from Judah, Syria and Phoenicia, served in the Egyptian army at Carchemish and were taken to Babylonia.[1] Jer. 46.1-12 mentions other mercenaries and also what an impact the battle at Carchemish had on people in Judah. The text is an oracle against Egypt after its defeat at Carchemish. The prophet asks who this one is that rises like the waters of the Nile. Jeremiah may have meant that, as the flooding of the Nile was of a short duration, so also this phenomenon was soon to go away. Among mercenaries in Necho's army, Jer. 46.9 mentions soldiers from Cush, Put[2] and Lydia.[3] The latter were well-known as the best soldiers in Anatolia. However, according to Jeremiah Egypt's mercenaries were of no help. Egypt's imperial status was more a façade than a reality; one could liken it to a body without a spine.

The Assyrian hegemony over Palestine and Transjordan led to the introduction of such cultural phenomena as new house architecture ('government houses', fortresses), idols and figurines. Assyrian pottery influenced the indigenous tradition, especially in the north, and the so-called Assyrian palace ware has been found at sites such as Ramat-Rahel[4] and Tell Jemmeh.[5] Among other finds, there are also a number of seals in the neo-Assyrian style.[6] Most of these are locally made.[7]

at Jeb c. 640 BCE (*History of Palestine and Syria*, p. 598).

1. See S.M. Burstein, *The Babyloniaca of Berossus* (Sources and Monographs: Sources from the Ancient Near East, I.5; Malibu, CA, 1978), p. 27; cf. Josephus, *Apion* 1.136-37.

2. For Put as a reference to Ionian *putu*, see the discussion in B. Otzen, *Studien zum Deuterosacharja*, pp. 56-57. The Hebrew terms *pwt* and *lwdym* occur also in Nah. 3.9.

3. Among mercenaries in the Babylonian army should be noted, for instance, Scythian soldiers; see M. van Loon, *Urartian Arts* (Istanbul, 1966), pp. 22-25.

4. Y. Aharoni, *Excavations at Ramat Rahel: Seasons 1959 and 1960*, I (Rome, 1962).

5. See, for instance, G.W. Van Beek, *Archaeology* 36 (1983), pp. 17-18.

6. As for the type, see A.J. Sachs, 'The Late Assyrian Royal-Seal Type', *Iraq* 15 (1953), pp. 167-70. Consult also R. Hestrin and M. Dayagi-Mendels, *Inscribed Seals: First Temple Period: Hebrew, Ammonite, Moabite, Phoenician and Aramaic from the Collection of the Israel Museum and the Israel Department of Antiquities and Museums* (Jerusalem, 1979). Cf. P. Bordreuil and A. Lemaire, 'Nouveau group de sceaux hebreux, araméens et ammonites', *Sem* 29 (1979), pp. 71-84; A. Millard, *PEQ* 93 (1961), p. 136.

7. E. Stern, *BA* 38 (1975), pp. 48-49; cf. *idem*, 'The Excavations at Tel Dor',

A site in Judah that shows both the country's Phoenicio-Palestinian artistic culture and Assyrian influences is Ramat-Rahel, just south of Jerusalem. Excavations at the site have revealed a palace with a citadel from the seventh century (str. VB).[1] This is the only large palace structure found in Judah, and it can very well be compared with that of Samaria. As was the case in Samaria, the site yielded proto-Aeolian capitals, and private and royal seal impressions, among them some *lmlk* stamps. One seal shows the inscription 'to Elyakim, servant of Yochim';[2] the latter name could refer to King Jehoiakim (str. VA).[3] The same stratum contained a painted sherd showing a man seated on a chair with his hands outstretched, the right somewhat higher than the left. This is the style in which gods and kings were often depicted; the sherd might have depicted a king of Judah.[4]

As for religion, B. Landsberger maintained that Assyria 'never forced conquered peoples to revere Ashur'.[5] There are, however, examples in Assyrian texts that mention that Assyrian kings prescribed sacrifices for Assyrian gods in connection with the reorganization of a subdued country. Esarhaddon, for instance, instituted sacrifices in Egypt for Ashur and other gods, according to the Zinjirli stele.[6] The Assyrian kings could also place statues of themselves, *ṣalam šarri*, in the temples of defeated peoples.[7] Thus, Tiglath-pileser III placed his

The Land of Israel: Cross-Roads of Civilizations (Orientalia Lovaniensia Analecta, 19; Louven, 1985), pp. 186-87, and figs. 9-10.

1.   See Y. Aharoni, *Excavations at Ramat Rahel*, I.

2.   Aharoni, *Excavations at Ramat Rahel*, I, pp. 15-21; cf. pp. 43-48, 51-59.

3.   Stratum VA has been dated to the last decade of the seventh century, so its destruction would have taken place at the same time as that of Jerusalem, 5875/86 BCE. It is impossible to determine whether Josiah or Jehoiakim built the structures of str. VA. Because of the utterance in Jer. 22.13-14, Aharoni associates the palace with Jehoiakim (Y. Aharoni, *The Archaeology of the Land of Israel*, p. 276).

4.   Cf. Y. Aharoni, *Excavations at Ramat Rahel*, I, pp. 42-43, fig. 30.1, and pl. 28.

5.   'Development of Culture', *City Invincible* (ed. C. Kraeling and R.M. Adams), p. 177.

6.   See R. Borger, *Die Inschriften Asarhaddons*, p. 99, ll. 48-49; *ANET*, p. 293; M. Cogan, *Imperialism and Religion*, p. 52. Cf. G. van Driel, *The Cult of Assur* (Studia Semitica Neerlandica, 13; Assen, 1969), pp. 190-91.

7.   *CAD*, XVI, pp. 80-81; W. von Soden, *AHw*, II, p. 1078; D.D. Luckenbill, *ARAB*, II, §§580-81, p. 227. See also D.J. Wiseman, *The Vassal Treaties of Esarhaddon* (London, 1958), pp. 402-404.

image as well as a god image in Gaza.[1] Because the territory that the king ruled over was the territory of his god, the realms of religion and politics were considered to be two related aspects of the nation's life. To organize the nation was therefore to organize the religion and its cult. It was natural, in other words, that Assyrian symbols, be they divine or royal, idols or stelae, should be set up all over the empire. Since this was only logical, it may have been mentioned only sporadically in the inscriptions.

The end of the seventh century BCE saw the rapid fading away of the Assyrian power structure and the attempts of the Egyptians to fill the vacuum. For a few decades Egypt managed to dominate Syria-Palestine from the Philistine coast to the Euphrates. The northwestern part of Syria seems not to have been included, and what the situation looked like in Transjordan cannot be assessed because of the lack of reliable source material. For southern Palestine, however, the Hebrew Bible, archaeological material and ostraca provide sources for historical reconstruction.

Under King Josiah (640–609 BCE) the little state of Judah was probably the largest nation in western Palestine in the later part of the seventh century BCE. There were no other competitors except the Philistine city states. Manasseh had recovered some—if not all—of the cities that Sennacherib had transferred over to the Philistines, so that geographically Judah could have stretched from the territory of Benjamin down to the northern Negev, 'from Geba to Beer-Sheba', as 2 Kgs 23.8 expresses it. The Egyptians were moving freely up and down in Palestine during this period, which means that they played the role of a superpower and were recognized as masters of the territory. After conquering Ashdod, Psammetichus I may have had a treaty relationship with the Philistines,[2] with the Phoenicians, and probably also with Josiah of Judah. The latter, being a small inland nation, was

---

1. Nimrud text ND 400, l. 18; see D.J. Wiseman, *Iraq* 13 (1951), pp. 22-23. M. Cogan thinks that 'provincial status (?) may have been granted' to Gaza by Tiglath-pileser (*Imperialism and Religion*, p. 55 n. 79). This was probably not the case, because Gaza's king, Hanun, who had fled to Egypt, soon returned and was reinstated as king. His return to power means that Gaza and its territory was a vassal country.

2. Cf. A. Spalinger, who thinks that Judah 'was left alone' (*Or* NS 47 [1978], pp. 16-17).

most probably without any importance to Egypt, because it was relegated to the hills and so did not threaten Egypt and its lines of communication with the north. Judah's internal affairs would not have been of any concern to Egypt before the change in the balance of power which occurred at the time of Nabopolassar's drive to the west and the destruction of Nineveh. At this time it was mandatory for Egypt to keep the territory of Palestine and the roads leading north under control. Therefore, it is unrealistic to think that Josiah could have extended his kingdom in this period to include the Assyrian province of Samerina, perhaps also Magidu and Gal'aza, territories of the former kingdom of Israel, as well as part of the coast, as is often maintained.[1] This hypothesis has been based on the claims in 2 Kgs 23.15, 29 and 2 Chron. 34.6-7 that Josiah destroyed sanctuaries, burned the bones of priests on the altars in the Assyrian provinces that had formerly been part of northern kingdom of Israel, and went to Megiddo, where he was killed.[2] None of these texts indicate that Josiah annexed former Israelite territories. Josiah's activities in the north were rather a punitive action.[3] Their goal seems to have been to deliver

---

1.   This hypothesis is so common that a bibliography would take too much space. For some of the more recent advocates, see M. Elat, 'The Political Status of the Kingdom of Judah within the Assyrian Empire in the seventh Century BCE', *Lachish*, V (ed. Y. Aharoni *et al.*), p. 68; W.W. Hallo in Hallo and Simpson, *The Ancient Near East*, p. 143; H. Reviv, *WHJP*, IV.1, p. 203. Cf. H. Donner, *Geschichte des Volkes Israel und seiner Nachbarn in Grundzügen*, II, pp. 348-49. F.M. Cross's enthusiasm for Josiah makes him advocate that Josiah's kingdom reached all the way to the Euphrates. He believes that Josiah restored the borders of David's empire 'in all detail' (see *Canaanite Myth and Hebrew Epic*, p. 283). This is unrealistic because the Assyrians were still in command in Nineveh until 612 BCE. After that their kingdom was centered in Harran, and they, as well as the Egyptians, were stationed in places like Riblah, Carchemish, Quramatu and Kimuhu. At the latter place Nabopolassar placed a garrison in 607 BCE, but the Egyptians took it back the following year; see D.J. Wiseman, *Chronicles of Chaldean Kings*, p. 21.

2.   Y. Aharoni assumes that Josiah annexed Samerina and Magidu and that he built the fortress of stratum II at Megiddo (*The Land of the Bible* [2nd edn], p. 403).

3.   For Assyrian examples of destroying the temple of a rival cult, see J.A. Brinkman, *Prelude to Empire*, pp. 67-40. For instance, Babylon's destruction under Sennacherib and its rebuilding by Esarhaddon is given a 'religious explanation' by the scribes of Esarhaddon. The text expresses the concepts of 'alienation–destruction: reconciliation–reconstruction' (J.A. Brinkman, 'Through a Glass Darkly: Esarhaddon's Retrospects on the Downfall of Babylon', *JAOS* 103 [1983], pp. 35-42 [41]).

a deadly blow to the Yahweh cult of the north, as can be inferred from Amos 6.9-10. This text deals with the northern kingdom as a house of the dead; thus Yahweh's name should not be pronounced there.[1] It is possible, however, that after Nineveh's fall Josiah could have attempted to annex some of the territory that lay immediately to the north of his border (see Map 22).[2]

Megiddo was probably not under Josiah's rule at all. The phrase *bêt milḥāmâ* in 2 Chron. 35.21 could refer to Megiddo's status as an Egyptian garrison city.[3] Megiddo and Riblah were most probably in the hands of the Egyptians during this entire period. As Assyrian garrison cities, they had been used by the Egyptians in their attempt to prop up the faltering Assyrian empire. The coastal road (the later *Via Maris*) through Megiddo was a necessary means of contact with the crumbling Assyrian kingdom. In addition it was crucial for Egypt's overlordship over Palestine. Stratum II at Megiddo, the end of which is dated to the end of the seventh century BCE, continues the Assyrian layout of stratum III. What is interesting, however, is that stratum II did not have any city wall. A fortress of the Assyrian type seems, however, to have been in existence.[4] This kind of city plan would support the theory that Megiddo had lost its military importance.[5] It was no longer a strategically located bulwark against a foreign power. Instead, it was used as an administrative center, which meant that troops could have been stationed there to keep the territory within the national system of law and order.[6]

1. Cf. G.W. Ahlström, 'King Josiah and the *DWD* of Amos VI.10', *JSS* 26 (1981), pp. 7-9.

2. Ezra 2.28-33 could point to the fact that Josiah had managed to extend his borders, because Lod, Ono and Hadid in the west and Bethel and Ai in the north are mentioned as places where returnees from Babylonia settled. The Babylonians and after them the Persians may not have changed the borders of the subdistricts; cf. J.M. Miller and J.H. Hayes, *A History of Ancient Israel and Judah*, p. 401.

3. Cf. B. Otzen, *Studien zum Deuterosacharja*, pp. 82-84. Cf. A. Malamat, 'Josiah's Bid for Armageddon: The Background of the Judean–Egyptian Encounter in 609 BCE', *JANESCU* 5 (1973), p. 274.

4. See R.S. Lamon and G.M. Shipton, *Megiddo*, I, p. 83 and fig. 95; cf. Y. Aharoni, *The Archaeology of the Land of Israel*, pp. 269-71 and fig. 86; G.I. Davies, *Megiddo* (Cities of the Biblical World; Cambridge, 1986), pp. 100-101.

5. Cf. G.W. Ahlström, *JNES* 41 (1982), pp. 133-35.

6. The destruction of str. II occurred around 600 BCE. This can be seen as a

Egypt's 'rule' over Palestine and parts of Syria is hinted at in 2 Kgs 24.7, which states that after Carchemish the Egyptian king did not leave his country, because 'the king of Babylon had taken from the Brook of Egypt unto the river of Euphrates all that belonged to the king of Egypt'. Egypt had now lost the territory between Gaza and the Brook of Egypt, including its garrison cities, such as Tell Jemme and Tell el-Ḥesi.[1] It is inconceivable that the biblical writer would not mention anything about Josiah's extension of the kingdom, had it occurred, for such military-political success would have been a very important factor in his glorification of Josiah as the most important king after David. There was simply no space for Josiah to play a grand political role.

Against this background, Josiah's Judah should be seen as a vassal or ally of Egypt. His policy must have been to keep his kingdom intact and not to offend the Egyptians. He may have played a double game after Nineveh's fall, which would explain his death at Megiddo in 609 BCE.[2] His political alliance with Egypt and Assyria seems inferrable from Jer. 2.18, 36, where the prophet complains about the people as

result of the battle at Carchemish and the Babylonian takeover of the hegemony in the Near East. There does not seem to have been any Babylonian settlement at Megiddo; thus, str. I cannot be dated before c. 640 BCE. Cf. the discussion in E. Stern, *Material Culture of the Land of the Bible in the Persian Period, 538–332 BCE* (Warminster, 1982), pp. 6-7. H.L. Ginsberg has maintained that the destruction of str. II at Megiddo could have been caused by the Babylonians ('Judah and the Transjordan States', *Alexander Marx Jubilee Volume*, I, p. 352).

1.   It should not be imagined that the garrison cities in this territory went out of business when the Assyrians left the Palestinian stage. It would be natural for Egypt to have used them, and the Persian remains at these places also indicate that they still may have functioned as 'security points' in Palestine.

2.   W.W. Hallo maintains that Necho II's 'effort to aid the last remnants of Assyrian power at Harran' was 'seriously impaired by Josiah at Megiddo' (*The Ancient Near East*, p. 143). Unfortunately, there is no textual support for such a hypothesis. G.I. Davies mentions that the phrase that 'king Josiah went to meet him' could just as well mean that Josiah 'intended to lend support to Neco's campaign' (*Megiddo*, p. 105). G. Pfeifer believes Josiah was murdered by Necho ('Die Begugnung zwischen Pharao Necho und König Josia bei Megiddo', *MIO* 15 [1969], pp. 297-307). For the description of Josiah's death in the same style as that of Ahab (1 Kgs. 12.30-37), see, among others, H.G.M. Williamson, 'The Death of Josiah and the Continuing Development of the Deuteronomic History', *VT* 32 (1982), pp. 245-46.

being in company with Egypt and Assyria, which will result in disappointment.[1]

Another point to be made in this connection is that when the '*am hā'āreṣ*, 'the [noble] people of the land', interfered in the succession after Josiah's death and chose not the oldest son of Josiah, but a younger prince (Shallum), who was made king under the name Jehoahaz, Necho corrected it. He appointed as his vassal the oldest son, Eliakim, as king 'in the place of Josiah, his father' (2 Kgs 23.34). Eliakim's throne-name was Jehoiakim. Jehoahaz was ordered to Riblah, where he was put in chains and then taken to Egypt, from where he never returned (cf. Jer. 22.1-12).[2] The phrase 'in the place of Josiah, his father', seems to suggest that Necho wanted Josiah's policies to be continued and that with the appointment of Eliakim he tightened his control over Palestine. The '*am hā'āreṣ* had attempted an unsuccessful *coup d'état*, in which they tried to steer the country away from its pro-Egyptian policies.[3]

In addition to the above, the problem of the Greek mercenaries, the *kittîm*, must be examined. Excavations at Meṣad Hashavyahu,[4] a fortress on the Philistine coast south of Joppa, have revealed Greek remains, and ostraca from the fortress at Arad mention the word *kittîm*. A few ostraca were found at Meṣad Hashavyahu, one mentioning a worker's ('reaper's') troubles and the confiscation of his garment, which he reports to his supervisor, Hoshayahu ben Shabay. These ostraca have been taken as proof that Josiah extended his kingdom to the coast. This may be possible because, according to the law in Exod. 22.25-27, a garment taken as a pledge had to be returned before sun

---

1. It could be maintained that the utterance is part of a stereotype linking Assyria and Egypt as the oppressors, but in this case the text hints that the people are 'serving two masters' (J.M. Miller and J.H. Hayes, *A History of Ancient Israel and Judah*, p. 388). The only period to which this could apply would be when Egypt supported Assyria against the Babylonians. Cf. J. Bright, who thinks that the text refers to a 'political maneuver in Josiah's reign' (*Jeremiah* [AB, 21; Garden City, NY, 1965], p. 18).

2. J. Scharbet thinks that Eliakim had contacted Necho in order to dethrone his brother (*Die Propheten Israels um 600 v. Chr.* [Cologne, 1967], p. 128). For the '*am hā'āreṣ*, see above pp. 601, 680 n. 5.

3. Cf. on this A. Malamat, 'The Twilight of Judah: In the Egyptian–Babylonian Maelstrom', *Congress Volume, Edinburgh 1974* (VTSup, 28; Leiden, 1975), p. 126.

4. See J. Naveh, *IEJ* 12 (1962), pp. 89-113.

set. However, the fortress at Meṣad Hashavyahu could just as well have been one of the Egyptian garrisons staffed mainly by Greek mercenaries.

A Hebrew letter has been found there, but it does not say anything about who populated the place.[1] It is written in the language of the country. The Yahwistic name Hoshayahu can thus be used as support both for and against the theory of Josiah's expansion,[2] as can the name [N]etaṣbaal, which occurs on another ostracon from the same place.[3] Since Psammetichus and Necho II had the coastal area under their control, it may be concluded that the Meṣad Hashavyahu fortress was an Egyptian garrison, which was manned both with Greek mercenaries and with troops and/or other personnel sent from Judah. It is probable that the king of Judah had to furnish the Egyptian army with troops, a common duty of a vassal. It should be remembered that Psammetichus I had established a garrison at Jeb (Elephantine) in southern Egypt, and soldiers from Judah seem to have been part of the garrison. There were also Judahites among the soldiers at Meṣad Hashavyahu, and for them and their officers the customs of Judah were in effect. As long as the responsibilities Josiah had as vassal king or as an ally of Egypt are unknown, the letter from this fortress cannot be used to establish the borders of Judah. According to R. Wenning, it is not even certain that the fortress was built before 609 BCE. In other words, it could have been built by Necho II.[4]

The boundary list in Josh. 15.1-12, 45-47 states that Judah reached down to the Mediterranean. Included in the list of conquered places are Ekron, Jabneel, Ashdod and Gaza. A. Alt has argued that this list describes the state of Judah under king Josiah.[5] If so, it would document Josiah's expansion to the west and would coroborate the view that Meṣad Hashavyahu was one of his forts. The accuracy of the

1. For the text, consult J.C.L. Gibson, *TSSI*, I, pp. 28-29; D. Pardee *et al.*, *Handbook of Ancient Hebrew Letters*, pp. 20-21. For a bibliography, see pp. 15-20.

2. Josiah's expansion to the west is no more than speculation; see the remarks of H. Donner, *Geschichte des Volkes Israel und seine Nachbarn im Grundzügen*, II, p. 348 n. 33.

3. For this, see J. Naveh, *IEJ* 12 (1962), p. 30.

4. R. Wenning has drawn this conclusion from an investigation of the Greek pottery of this period from Palestine (private communication).

5. See his 'Judas Gaue unter Josia', *PJ* 21 (1925), pp. 109-11 (= *KS*, II, pp. 282-84).

list may be doubted, however, because of the inclusion of Ashdod and Gaza among the conquered cities. No text, biblical or nonbiblical, mentions that Josiah or any other king of Judah had occupied these territories. If Herodotus is right, Psammetichus I had conquered Ashdod and its territory, which would have made it impossible for Josiah to go south of Ashdod. If the list in Joshua 15 is combined with the census list in Numbers 26, which claims that the whole country had been divided by lot, its intention would seem to be to show that the Philistine territories were also part of Judah at that time. In the realm of theory anything can be occupied. The date of the list in Joshua 15 could still be in the Josianic period, even if some old material could have been incorporated.[1] However, the attempt to use the list as a proof for Josiah's expansion becomes dubious.[2] The list in Joshua 15 is rather to be seen as an expression of the pan-Israelite concept and it is thus fictitious. It does not refer to a particular historical situation.[3]

At Tell Arad in the northeastern Negev, c. 200 ostraca have been found.[4] More than half of them are written in Hebrew, several in Aramaic, and a few in Arabic and Greek. The majority of these ostraca are dated to 600 BCE. About twenty of the Hebrew ostraca are letters, most of which deal with military matters and with the distribution of food rations.[5] The majority of these are to a certain Elyashib, who is given orders to distribute the rations. Among the recipients are also the *kittîm*. Elyashib could thus have been the commander of the place. The word *kittîm* is an indication that Judah had Greek mercenaries in the armed forces, a phenomenon that could have started with Josiah when he became allied with Psammetichus I.

---

1. See also on this subject the discussion in N.P. Lemche, *Early Israel*, pp. 285-88.

2. Ekron's history after Ashurbanipal is not known. The city is not mentioned again in any texts before the Hasmonean period. The only time Ekron was under Judah was in the time of Hezekiah, who held its king, Padi, as a prisoner in Jerusalem.

3. Cf. N. Na'aman, *Borders and Districts*, pp. 62-64.

4. For the first report, see Y. Aharoni, 'Hebrew Ostraca from Tel Arad', *IEJ* 16 (1966), pp. 1-7.

5. A. Lemaire, *Inscriptions hébraiques*, I, pp. 145-235; D. Pardee *et al.*, *Handbook of Ancient Hebrew Letters*, pp. 24-67 (with bibliography); Y. Aharoni, *Arad Inscriptions* (Jerusalem, 1981).

Politics and Reform

A problem that has fascinated scholars for generations is King Josiah's religious and administrative reform. In the Bible this phenomenon has been given the sheen of a purification of the cult of Yahweh that finally led to the emergence of Judaism. In his 'report', the biblical writer has depicted the religions of Israel and Judah as being 'contaminated' by Canaanite and other phenomena. The 'ideal' religion of Moses no longer existed. It is claimed that thanks to two kings, Hezekiah and Josiah, the 'pure' religion was established again, but that, unfortunately, both attempts at purification died with the death of the 'reformers'. Not until the postexilic period was the 'pure' Yahwistic religion 're-established'.[1] This is the religious model that the biblical 'historians' have used for their presentation of past events. It is therefore a postexilic literary composition.[2] Unfortunately, many modern historians have made this 'theological' model their own. In order for Ezra to win acceptance for his law, he may have promoted the idea that it was a 'revision' or re-edition of an old law, the 'law scroll' of Josiah's reform,[3] regardless of whether such a law scroll existed or not.

To get a reliable picture from the 'devotional' writings of the Deuteronomistic historian and the Chronicler is a frustrating task. In order to see the intent of the writings, the way in which Josiah's religious development is described should be noted. It is claimed that Josiah became king at the age of eight (2 Kgs 22.1; 2 Chron. 34.1). The Chronicler then states that in his eighth regnal year Josiah 'began

---

1.   It could be asked whether there has ever existed a pure religion in history.

2.   This is not to deny that some writing could have started in the pre-exilic period which was then used by the postexilic historiographer. A. Jepsen assumed that Josiah's secretary, Shaphan, and his family were Deuteronomistic history writers (*Die quellen des Königsbuches* [2nd edn; Halle, 1956], pp. 94-95). M. Weinfeld sees Shaphan and his family as 'the leading exponents of this literary school' (*Deuteronomy and the Deuteronomistic School* [Oxford, 1972], p. 160).

3.   For Darius I as the codifier of Egyptian laws, see F.K. Kienitz, *Die politische Geschichte Ägyptens vom 7, bis zum 4. Jahrhundert vor der Zeitwende* (Berlin, 1953), p. 61; J. Lewy, 'The Problems Inherent in Section 70 of the Bisutun Inscription', *HUCA* 25 (1954), p. 185 n. 63; cf. G. Widengren, 'The Persian Period', *Israelite and Judean History* (ed. J.H. Hayes and J.M. Miller; Philadelphia, 1977), p. 515.

to seek the god of his father David'. This is a nonhistorical statement. As king of Judah and as the lord of the state temple at Jerusalem, Josiah had certainly sought Yahweh several times before. As king he was in principle the leader of the state cult. To what special event the Chronicler refers is impossible to determine. He may simply have rearranged the material and interpreted it to suit his ideas.[1] True to tradition, Josiah could have shown his independence from the policies of his grandfather Manasseh and the latter's son Amon, Josiah's father through religious decree(s). Kings usually reorganized the administration to some extent, whether it was cultic or not. The wording that Josiah 'began to seek the god of his father David' is thus suspect. It is an expression of the postexilic community's restoration policies, which projected back in time its own dogmatic opinion about what the religion of Yahweh should haved looked like.

According to 2 Chron. 34.3-7, Josiah started his religious reorganization in the twelfth year of his reign, 629/628 BCE. He is supposed to have defiled sanctuaries (*bāmôt*), idols, such as the *maṣṣēbôt* and *ªšērîm*, and the altars of Baal (!), as well as to have burned the bones of the dead priests on their altars. All this was done not only in Judah but also in the territory of the former Israel state, including Galilee. The Chronicler lets Josiah make a sweeping reform all over the country. Besides demoting the sanctuaries, this also included dismissing the Yahwistic priests, the *kᵉmārîm*, who burned the food offerings,[2] and removing all the vessels of Asherah and Baal, as well as those of the constellations (the 'heavenly host'). The horses and the chariots of the sun which the kings of Judah (!) had made were removed, and the sacred prostitution in the Solomonic temple came to an end, as did the sacrifices to Moloch in the Kidron Valley (2 Kgs 23.4-11). These verses provide good information about what the pre-exilic Judahite cult was all about. There is syncretism that includes Assyrian phenomena, but all this was not completely a result of foreign influence. For instance, the horses of the sun could just as well have been Yahweh's horses. Hab. 3.8, for instance, mentions Yahweh's horses and chariots, and Ps. 68.18 states that Yahweh had 20,000

---

1.   Cf. M. Cogan, who says that 'the Chronicler has ordered his data to conform to his conception of royal piety' ('The Chronicler's Use of Chronology as Illuminated by Neo-Assyrian Royal Inscriptions', *Empirical Models for Biblical Criticism* [ed. J.H. Tigay; Philadelphia, 1985], p. 204).

2.   See D. Edelman, 'The Meaning of *qiṭṭēr*', *VT* 35 (1985), pp. 395-404.

horses. The Jerusalemite sun cult cannot be dismissed *a priori* as being non-Yahwistic. Yahweh himself is also described as a sun god and is called *šemeš*, 'sun', in Ps. 84.12.[1]

According to 2 Chron. 34.3-7, Josiah's reform was carried out all over the country before the 'law scroll' had been found. Josiah is said to have been presented with a 'law scroll' found in the temple of Jerusalem during a building restoration in his eighteenth year (623/22) (2 Kgs 22.3–23.3; 2 Chron. 34.8-33). In both 2 Kings and 2 Chronicles it is stated that this discovery led to Josiah's treaty, a covenant, with the people and with Yahweh. The Passover festival was 'reinstituted', the like of which never had been celebrated since the days of the judges (2 Kgs 23.22) or Samuel (2 Chron. 35.18).[2] The narratives differ in their source of causation for the reforms. In 2 Chronicles 34 the 'purification' of the religious system did not occur as a result of the 'law scroll', but in 2 Kgs 23.4-20 the narrator reports that the 'reform' took place after the 'law scroll' was found. This may be intentional, giving more importance to the find than it perhaps merited. The story about the 'law scroll' may be fictional.

In the story about the 'law book' the biblical writer relates that the first priest ('high priest') of the temple, Hilkiah, told the king's secretary, Shaphan, that he had found 'the scroll of the *tôrâ* in the temple of Yahweh' (2 Kgs 22.8). The wording is peculiar. It is intended to give the impression that the old and only authoritative law had been found; thus, the writer's purpose is to promote the acceptance of a new law. Either this is a law that the king and his high-priest (or Shaphan) wanted to have as a basis for his 'reform', or it is the postexilic community's way of giving authority to their own laws. The former alternative is not improbable, because everything centers

1. For the solar motifs in connection with Yahweh, see the discussion in my *Psalm 89*, pp. 85-88. Concerning the many horse figurines found in Judah and especially in Jerusalem, consult A.T. Holland, *Levant* 9 (1977), pp. 121-24. Cf. also G.W. Ahlström, *An Archaeological Picture of Iron Age Religions in Palestine*, pp. 22-23.

2. It should be noted that the details of the Passover in the Chronicles agree with the report of the same festival in Ezra and Nehemiah. Thus, both accounts probably stem from the same religious group. Since the narrator reports that nobody had cared about or celebrated the Passover before Josiah, it must be concluded that it was a new festival projected back in time to Joshua. In this way Josiah could be seen to be reviving an ancient festival.

around the king.[1] Through the temple restoration Josiah could have appealed to a 'discovery of the divine will' as the basis for his actions. This was nothing new in the history of Near Eastern religions. Documents such as clay tablets with divine commands could be used as foundation deposits. The building or rebuilding of sanctuaries needed to have divine sanction, a fact stressed, for instance, by Esarhaddon.[2] Nabunaid, the last king of Babylonia, was divinely commanded to restore the cult of Sin.[3] There is also an Egyptian parallel to be mentioned. A text was said to have been found in the temple of Hermopolis at the feet of the god Thoth.[4] In this way the text was given the character of a 'divine revelation'.

An utterance by a court prophetess, Huldah, confirmed the divine authority of the words of the 'law' scroll found in the temple of Jerusalem. One may ask why that was necessary, because the king was in principle the promulgator of divine law. However, according to deuteronomistic ideology, kings should not be in direct contact with Yahweh; prophets should be the intermediaries. As in Assyria, the king should receive the will of the god through 'omina' and oracles from the cultic personnel.

The content of the scroll is not exactly known. The words of Huldah only imply that the scroll contained prophecies about the coming disaster of Judah and that Josiah, in spite of this, would die in peace (2 Kgs 22.14-20). The latter prophecy did not happen. Josiah died a violent death. The coming disaster is clearly a reference to the fall of Judah and Jerusalem in 587/586 BCE; thus the sentence attributed to

---

1. Cf. N. Lohfink, *Bib* 44 (1963), p. 276.
2. See R.S. Ellis, *Foundation Deposits in Ancient Mesopotamia* (Yale Near Eastern Researches, 2; New Haven, 1968), p. 7.
3. See C.J. Gadd, *Anatolian Studies* 8 (1958), p. 48, ll. 5-9; cf. the discussion in L.K. Handy, 'A Realignment in Heaven: An Investigation into the Ideology of the Josianic Reform' (PhD dissertation, University of Chicago, 1987), pp. 302-303. P.R.S. Moorey maintains that Nabunaid re-established the Sin cult that Nebuchadrezzar II supposedly had changed (*Ur 'of the Chaldees'* [Ithaca, NY, 1982], p. 245).
4. See A. Bertholet, *Die Macht der Schrift in Glauben und Aberglauben* (Berlin, 1949), pp. 42-43. See G. Widengren, who also refers to the Roman king Numa and his religious and social reforms (*Religionsphänomenologie* [Berlin, 1969], pp. 553-55); cf. E.M. Hooker, 'The Significance of Numa's Religious Reform', *Numen* 10 (1963), pp. 87-132.

Huldah is to be seen as *vaticinium ex eventu*. Her speech shows knowledge of the disaster and mirrors the ideology of the postexilic community.[1] In fact, it did not seem to be the cause of any reform. Typical for the later historiographer is the idea that the king should have humbled himself 'before Yahweh' (2 Kgs 22.19; 2 Chron. 34.27).[2] This is the condition for a king's doing right, and thus forms the right basis for a reorganization of the cult.[3] Seen in literary and religio-historical perspective, the cult reform of Josiah is the conclusion of the historian's presentation of the cult of Judah. The narrator has here presented an ideal and illusionary model for the development and for the 'restoration' of the society.[4] The program for this restoration is the Book of Deuteronomy.[5]

An often recurring statement is that the 'law scroll' should be identified with the Book of Deuteronomy or its kernel, 'Ur-Deuteronomium'. This theory was popular already in the period of the 'Church Fathers'. One theory is that Josiah's law, *tôrâ*, would have been an outgrowth of northern, Israelite traditions, because some scholars have located the origin of Deuteronomy in the north.[6] This is quite problematic, since the south saw the northern traditions as being non-Yahwistic. The prophecies of Amos and Hosea could also be taken into consideration, because they denounce the religion of the north. Josiah's destruction of temples in the province of Samerina, as well as his burning of the

---

1. See H.-D. Hoffmann, *Reform und Reformen*, pp. 170-89. Hoffmann thinks that the utterance about Josiah's dying 'in peace' is a reference to the king's being buried and gathered to his ancestors in Jerusalem (pp. 183-85).

2. His 'sin' is not mentioned, which supports the theory that the passage contains a literary pattern expressing a later time's ideology.

3. M. Weinfeld sees the utterance about Josiah's death as subsequently being 'woven into the words of Huldah' in order to explain why the punishment of the nation was 'postponed until a later time' (*Deuteronomy and the Deuteronomic School*, p. 26).

4. H.-D. Hoffmann, *Reform und Reformen*, p. 207.

5. Cf. S.A. Kaufman, 'The Structure of the Deuteronomic Law', *Maarav* 1 (1979), pp. 105-58.

6. W.M.L. de Wette, *Dissertatio critica exegetica Deuteronomium qua a prioribus Pentateuchi libris diversum, alius cuiusdam recentioris auctioris opus esse monstratur* (1805), repr. in *Opuscula Theologica* (Berlin, 1839), pp. 151-68; cf. A. Alt, 'Die Heimat des Deuteronimiums', *KS*, II, pp. 250-75; A.C. Welch, *Deuteronomy: The Framework to the Code* (London, 1932), pp. 198-201; cf. R.E. Clements, 'Deuteronomy and the Cult Tradition', *VT* 15 (1965), pp. 300-12.

bones of the dead priests and his defiling of the altars, shows that the Yahwistic tradition of the north was no ideal for the king. In the literary presentation, the destruction of Bethel is the climax of the struggle between the two Yahwistic centers, Jerusalem and Bethel. Whether or not Bethel existed at this time, the name comprised everything that disagreed with the ideology of the Jerusalemites. The narrator's idea is to show what would happen if people did not follow the Yahweh tradition he advocated. In his historiography the Josianic reform became the last warning, and the catastrophe of 587/586 BCE became the proof.[1]

The content of the Josianic 'law scroll' is impossible to ascertain. Huldah's speech is of no real help in this matter. The alleged Deuteronomistic character is therefore impossible to establish. The theory that the 'law scroll' comprised (part of) Deuteronomy remains unproven.[2] The whole book of Deuteronomy proposes a closed community into which some people, such as Moabites and Ammonites, never could be permitted.[3] Such a society did not exist before the period of Ezra.[4]

To judge from the speech of Huldah, the content of the newly-found scroll does not seem to be in harmony with the stipulations in the book of Deuteronomy.[5] The following points illustrate this:

1. 2 Kgs 22.11 mentions that king Josiah rent his clothes when he heard the content of the scroll. One wonders just what part of Deuteronomy would have such an effect on any reader.

2. Huldah's speech provides the information that the law book was prophetic in character: 'Thus says Yahweh: "I will bring

---

1. Cf. E. Würthwein, 'Die josianische Reform und das Deuteronomium', *ZTK* 73 (1976), p. 423. 2 Kgs 22–23 is not historical for Würthwein and cannot be used for dating Deuteronomy. 2 Kgs 22–23 was written during the period of the struggle for 'ritual purity' in the postexilic period (*idem*, p. 421).

2. For the discussion, see E.W. Nicholson, *Deuteronomy and Tradition*; B. Oded, in *Israelite and Judean History* (ed. J.H. Hayes and J.M. Miller), pp. 460-69.

3. Cf. J. Pedersen, *Israel*, III-IV, pp. 580-87. Cf. also G. Hölscher, 'Komposition und Ursprung des Deuteronomiums', *ZAW* 40 (1922), pp. 228-29.

4. H.-D. Hoffmann sees the 'law book' as a 'Mosaic fiction' and as a composition by the deuteronomistic historian (*Reform und Reformen*, pp. 197-200).

5. See I. Engnell, *A Rigid Scrutiny*, p. 57; L.K. Handy, 'A Realignment in Heaven', pp. 275-79.

disaster upon this place and those who live in it..."', followed by a promise to Josiah that he will not see the disaster but will be gathered in peace to his ancestors. This is all quite un-Deuteronomistic. Deuteronomy is not prophetic in character. The kernel of Deuteronomy (4.44–30.20) consists mostly of legal material. Josiah is, of course, not mentioned in this book. Deuteronomy 28, which has been considered to mirror Huldah's speech, is a postexilic résumé of what happens when one does not 'follow' Yahweh, according to the Deuteronomistic ideology.

3. Huldah does not mention anything about priests who should be dismissed. Deut. 12.13-15 advocates an equal distribution of priests all over the country. Thus, the 'law book' did not give any support for dismissing or killing priests.

4. Huldah does not say anything about the official sanctuaries in the kingdom. The 'law book' is therefore not the source for Josiah's treatment of the cult places.

5. Huldah does not mention any legal stipulations. 2 Kgs 23.1-3 mentions that Josiah called an assembly and made a covenant between Yahweh and the people in order to keep Yahweh's commandments that were written in the book.

6. Huldah does not mention the Passover festival, nor anything about all the gods of the country. After the covenant meeting the narrator of 2 Kings gives an account of the reform (2 Kgs 23.4-20) and of the Passover (23.21-23). The Passover was supposed to have been celebrated as it was 'proscribed in this book of the covenant'. Here the narrator characterizes the 'law book' as the book of the covenant, a term that is not used in connection with the find of the 'law book'. Clearly the narrator has made a certain intentional connection. It should be noted that Deut. 16.1-7 contains some short statements about the Passover,[1] but it does not seem probable that they could be the inspiration for a reform of the festival.

7. Huldah's speech gives the impression that the 'law book' must have been short. Deuteronomy comprises 34 chapters

---

1. A common opinion is that Josiah's Passover is in agreement with Deut. 16.1-7; see, among others, M. Delcor, 'Réflexions sur la Pâque du temple de Josias d'après 2 Rois 23, 21-23', *Henoch* 4 (1982), pp. 205-19; H. Donner, *Geschichte des Volkes Israel*, II, p. 351.

('Ur-Deuteronomium' has 27), which seems to be somewhat too long a document for a king to listen to patiently and then get upset.

8. Did Josiah's 'law book' deal with cultic laws that had been forgotten? Priests usually had to know rituals and cultic laws by heart.[1]

From the above it may be concluded that the 'law book' of the Josianic period was neither part of the Book of Deuteronomy, nor of any other known biblical book. The purpose of the narrator is to advocate that his ideas had already existed during the Josianic period. There are two options for solving this problem: either the scroll was a product of Josiah's own chancellery, written in order to give divine support for the king's actions,[2] or the narrator of the postexilic period used the 'Josianic reform' to argue that his own law code (Ezra's law code?)[3] had been anchored in the pre-exilic period. Josiah's administrative changes have thus been adopted by the narrator and described according to the postexilic writer's religious ideals. In this way the history of the religions of Israel and Judah, with their many cultic reorganizations, has become part of the postexilic writer's historiography. Most kings made changes in their administrations, which could include changes or innovations in the official cultic system. This has been used by the D historian as it suited his purpose. From this point of view Hezekiah and Josiah became his ideal kings.[4]

Did Josiah actually carry out a reform? The above does not exclude this possibility. On the contrary, had Josiah done nothing in this respect he would not have been described as one of the most important

---

1. A.R. Siebens argues that it would be very strange if a scroll containing the rituals and cultic laws of a temple were forgotten (*L'origine du code deuteronomique* [Paris, 1929], p. 95).

2. This I have argued earlier in my *Royal Administration*, p. 73.

3. For Ezra's law as being part of the Persian administration's policy towards subdued countries, see below.

4. When reading about the religious situation in Israel and Judah as well as the reforms or changes carried out by several of the kings of Judah, the narrator's complaints and the literary style of the reports are striking. This common style supports the theory that the presentation of all the reforms is made by one and the same writer. With Josiah's reform the narrator has come to the end of his cultic historiography. What actually happened during the different 'reforms' will never be fully known.

kings after David. However, it should be remembered that the repairs of temples were probably more important to the priests than to the king. The priests were always interested in power and the revenue they could get;[1] thus, the repair of the Jerusalemite temple during Josiah's reign could have been used by the priests to enhance their position at the point when the king started making changes in his administration.

There are two possible reasons for Josiah's reform activities. One reason is the political situation, which may have inspired him to make sweeping administrative changes[2] that affected the cultic system too. The other would be part of the common phenomenon that a new king, when secure on his throne, demonstrated his independence vis-à-vis his predecessor.[3] With every new king a new 'eon' started. As *pontifex maximus* he had to put his stamp on the nation's religious policies.

The political situation in the latter half of the seventh century arouses the suspicion that Josiah's policies were not so much an act of independence from Assyrian overlordship, as is usually maintained, but rather a 'realignment' with a new political situation. It is doubtful that the young king Josiah would have dared to make little Judah free from its vassalship to Assyria shortly after Ashurbanipal's death. The Assyrian empire was not yet dead, and nobody at that time (in the 620s BCE) could have foreseen that Nabopolassar's son, Nebuchadrezzar (604–562 BCE), would take hegemony over the whole Near East. Only after 612 could freedom from Assyria first have occurred, but at that time Egypt was propping up the Assyrian forces and, as already seen, had tried to step into what could have become a vacuum. The Syro-Palestinian states, such as the Phoenicians, the Philistines and Judah, saw the Assyrian hegemony continue and soon change into an Egyptian domination. An example of this is Necho II's role in

---

1.   Cf. R.S. Ellis, *Foundation Deposits*, p. 7.

2.   W.E. Claburn has maintained that it was mainly a fiscal reform ('The Fiscal Basis of Josiah's Reform', *JBL* 92 [1973], pp. 11-22). This aspect has to be considered, because in abandoning the sanctuaries outside Jerusalem Josiah would have gotten the taxes paid directly to Jerusalem. The role of the sanctuaries as government agencies was temporarily over.

3.   Because his father, Amon, reigned for only a short time, Josiah's activities signified a change from the period of Manasseh. This change has been magnified by the narrator.

choosing a successor to Josiah. This clearly shows that Judah was not independent. Necho had to be assured that Judah's role as a vassal or ally had not changed, and, as far as can be determined, Necho treated Judah as a vassal country. The Transjordanian kingdoms, on the other hand, could more or less act independently because of their geographical location far away from the scene of significant political and military activities.

From the above it can be concluded that Josiah saw some opportunities to win the support of Psammetichus I for a policy that would make it possible for Judah to be free from Assyrian vassalship and its duty of paying tribute. There was again a king in Egypt who seemed to be able to dominate Palestine. He was also closer to Judah than Assyria was, which has to be taken into consideration when dealing with Josiah's policies. Since nothing is recorded about Josiah's paying tribute to Egypt, the relationship may have been friendly. It is likely that an alliance existed between Egypt and Judah, which could have given Josiah a free hand in invading the province of Samerina—an action later given the character of a punitive action against its sanctuaries and priests by the narrator of Kings (2 Kgs 23.15-20). Perhaps he annexed some of the territory just north of the border with Samerina, including Bethel.[1] The 'alliance' with Egypt may also have given Josiah access to the coast or it may have resulted in soldiers from Judah being placed in the Meṣad Hashavyahu fortress together with Greek mercenaries.

Besides the general information in 2 Kgs 23.8 and 2 Chron. 34.3-5, there is no mention that Josiah carried out a sweeping reform in the rest of his country. Jerusalem is the center of the narrator's interest, which is another indication that his concern was over the temple cult in Jerusalem and that the writing derives from the postexilic period. The fortress at Arad, however, has often been mentioned as one of the places that Josiah 'reformed'. It is thought to have had no temple at this period. As mentioned earlier, it is possible that, after the disaster of 701 BCE, when Hezekiah lost all his territory outside Jerusalem and its immediate surroundings, the Negev fell to the

---

1. During the Persian period Bethel was part of the province of Jehud; cf. Ezra 2.29; Neh. 7.32. It is doubtful that the Babylonians or the Persians changed the borders of the subprovinces they had taken over. That would have created extra administrative problems.

Edomites.[1] Thus the fortress at Arad may have been rebuilt by Edomites. Beer-sheba may have presented the same picture.[2] The spread of Edomite pottery in the Negev during the seventh century BCE[3] may point in this direction. Sometime during the seventh century Arad was taken back by Judah, which is clear from some of the ostraca found at the place. They mention fear of an attack by the Edomites, and one ostracon asks for troops to be sent to Ramath-Negev, a site not yet identified.[4] Another ostracon mentions the 'evil' that the Edomites seem to have caused.[5] When Judah recovered Arad again it is also possible that some other parts of the Negev 'returned' to Judah and that Josiah could have built some small fortresses in the south. Neither archaeological nor textual sources give a clear picture of the situation. However, the seventh-century structure at Tel Māśōś has been seen as a little fortress. This indicates either that Josiah had tried to refortify the Negev[6] or that most of the Negev remained Edomite and that the Tel Māśōś fort was an Edomite outpost. The Edomite site of Qitmit c. 10 km south of Arad would support the latter alternative (see Fig. 6).

As mentioned above, pharaoh Necho dethroned Shallum/Jehoahaz and replaced him with the pro-Egyptian Eliakim/Jehoiakim (609–598 BCE) as king in order to have a faithful vassal in Judah. Jehoiakim raised tribute money by taxing the people, thereby saving whatever gold and silver there was in the temple and in his own palace (2 Kgs 23.3-35). Necho could not have tolerated a large independent nation in Palestine; thus, if Josiah ever annexed the province of Samerina, which is not stated in any text, it certainly would have returned to its former status as an imperial province, and as such it would have had

1.   Cf. H.L. Ginsberg, 'Judah and the Transjordan States', *Alexander Marx Jubilee Volume*, p. 364 n. 47a.

2.   See above Chapter 16, pp. 722-25.

3.   On this, cf. E. Stern, *BA* 38 (1975), p. 45; see also N. Glueck, *BASOR* 188 (1967), pp. 8-38. As for some different types of Edomite pottery, see R. Amiran, *Ancient Pottery*, pp. 300-301; see also I. Beit Arieh and P. Beck, 'Edomite Shrine Discoveries in the Negev', *The Israel Museum, Jerusalem, Catalogue*, no. 277. For the chronology of the pottery, see G.D. Pratico, *BASOR* 259 (1985), pp. 22-27.

4.   See Y. Aharoni, *BASOR* 197 (1970), pp. 20-28, and D. Pardee, text 24, in *Handbook of Ancient Hebrew Letters*, pp. 58-61.

5.   D. Pardee, text 40, *Handbook of Ancient Hebrew Letters*, pp. 63-65.

6.   Thus V. Fritz, *EI* 15 (1981), p. 50*.

to be governed by an official appointed by Necho. For example, garrisons on the coast like the one at Meṣad Hashavyahu(?) and those in the border area between Gaza and the Brook of Egypt, many of which had been fortified by the Assyrians, such as Tell Jemme and Tell el-Ḥesi, were probably taken over by the Egyptians during the reign of Psammetichus I. They may still have been used by the Egyptians until Nebuchadrezzar terminated the Egyptian supremacy over Palestine after the battle at Carchemish in 605 BCE.[1]

The Babylonian Rule

The political constellation changed in 605 BCE. In the following year Nebuchadrezzar, who in September of 605 had succeeded his father on the throne,[2] marched with his army through Syria-Palestine (Ḥatti) down to the Philistine coast without any military opposition. It it easy to imagine the fear and shattered illusions of the petty rulers of Syria-Palestine in the aftermath of the battle at Carchemish. With the Egyptian army destroyed, they had no other choice than to accept Babylon's rule. 'All the kings of Hattu came into his presence and he received their vast tribute'.[3] It is possible that the tribute was presented to Nebuchadrezzar in Riblah.[4] Jehoiakim of Judah was most probably one of those kings. Necho was at home possibly rebuilding

1. In the destruction layers at Carchemish from around 600 BCE, L. Woolley and his associates found among the Egyptian objects some seal impressions with the cartouches of Psammetichus I and Necho II (*Carchemish II: The Town Defenses* [London, 1921], pp. 125-26). Cf. the discussion in B. Otzen, *Deutero-Sacharja*, pp. 89-90.
2. D J. Wiseman, *Chronicles of Chaldaean Kings*, text 21, 946, line 11, cf. p. 27; A.K. Grayson, *Assyrian and Babylonian Chronicles*, Chronicle 5.11, cf. pp. 19f.
3. A.K. Grayson, *Assyrian and Babylonian Chronicles*, p. 100, l. 17. Inscriptions at Wâdī Brîsā and Nahr el-Kalb in Lebanon report a campaign to Phoenicia, which probably was later in his reign. Nebuchadrezzar cut a way in the mountains for the transport of cedars. He also characterized himself as a king of justice. W.G. Lambert considers him 'a second Hammurabi' ('Nebuchadrezzar King of Justice', *Iraq* 27 [1965], pp. 1-11). For the text, see F.H. Weissbach, *Die Inschriften Nebukadnezars II in Wâdī Brîsā und am Nahr el-Kalb* (Wissenschaftliche Veröffenlichungen der deutschen Orientgesellschaft, 5; Osnabrück, 1978 [1906]); cf. *ANET*, p. 307.
4. D.J. Wiseman, *Nebuchadrezzar and Babylon*, p. 23.

his forces; thus no help was to be expected from Egypt. The Babylonian forces sacked Ashkelon in December of 604 BCE, and its king, Aga,[1] was captured. Nebuchadrezzar's success is echoed in Hab. 1.5-10.[2] At this time Jehoiakim understood that he and his kingdom were in danger[3] so he switched his allegiance to Babylonia and paid the yearly tribute until 600 BCE when he rebelled (2 Kgs 24.1). The probable reason for this change was the defeat of the Babylonian army that had invaded Egypt in 601/600. This conclusion can be drawn from the Babylonian text. It simply states that the armies clashed and that 'the king of Akkad and his army turned and [went back] to Babylon.'[4] Necho followed up the victory by invading the southern coast and taking Gaza (cf. Jer. 47.1).[5] For Jehoiakim this must have meant that Necho had regained his strength and could have punished him for terminating the vassalship. With the withdrawal of the Babylonian army Judah could have been an easy prey for Necho. Thus, Jehoiakim would have switched back to the Egyptian fold. With the Egyptian army in southern Palestine, Jehoiakim would not have had any other choice. Nebuchadrezzar stayed in Babylon the following year, rebuilding his army,[6] which gave Necho the opportunity to try

1. E.F. Weidner, 'Jojakin, König von Juda, in Babylonischen Keilschrifttexten', *Mélanges syriens offerts à M. René Dussaud*, II (Paris, 1939), pp. 923-24. According to Jeremiah 36, the scroll on which Jeremiah had Baruch write his oracles and present them to the king was written in the fourth year of Jehoiakim.

2. Cf. R.D. Haak, 'Habakkuk among the Prophets' (PhD dissertation, University of Chicago, 1986), pp. 428-35. For a date in Jehoiakim's reign, see the résumé by P. Jöcken, *Das Buch Habakuk* (BBB, 48; Cologne, 1977), pp. 51-81.

3. It is not clear whether the Babylonians marched against Jerusalem. 2 Kings mentions that the king of Babel 'marched up, and Jehoiakim became his vassal for three years'. The text can either refer to a detachment marching on Jerusalem, or a march by Nebuchadrezzar against southern Palestine, perhaps through some Judahite territory. That would have been enough to scare a puppet king. For the date, cf. S. Herrmann, *A History of Israel* (2nd edn), pp. 277.

4. A.K. Grayson, *Assyrian and Babylonian Chronicles*, Chronicle 5.5-7, p. 101. The reason may have been that after Carchemish Nebuchadrezzar underestimated the strength of the new Egyptian army. Until 601 BCE the Babylonian campaigns in Syria-Palestine had not met any opposition; it was rather 'militärische Spaziergänge' (R. Labat in *Fischer Weltgeschichte 4: Die altorientalischen Reiche*, III [ed. E. Cassin *et al.*; Frankfurt, 1967], p. 99).

5. See E. Lipiński, 'The Egyptian–Babylonian War of the Winter 601–600 BCE', *AION* 22 (1972), pp. 235-41.

6. A.K. Grayson, *Assyrian and Babylonian Chronicles*, p. 101, l. 8.

to rebuild his position, as well as his reputation at home,[1] in encouraging some coalition against Babylonia. He also turned his interest to the sea, building a navy of triremes, which meant that he came to rely more than before on the Greeks, who could provide instruction on how to maneuver the boats. He also tried to build a canal through the Wadi Tumilat, which he did not complete, according to Herodotus (2.157). Necho's maritime policy made Egypt a sea-power, but it did not strengthen Egypt's military position in Western Asia.[2]

---

1. This would have been at a low ebb, according to A. Spalinger, *Or* NS 47 (1978), pp. 19-20.
2. Cf. J. Yoyotte, 'Néchao ou Neko', *DBSup*, VI, cols. 371-72.

Chapter 19

THE END OF THE VASSAL STATES

The optimistic nationalism that can be detected as having been on the rise in the Palestinian states after the destruction of Nineveh and the extinction of the Assyrian kingdom came to an end with Nebuchadrezzar's victory at Carchemish and his accession to the Babylonian throne. The situation became dangerous for the vassal kings who were allies of Egypt. An example of this is given in an Aramaic letter on papyrus found at Saqqara in Egypt. It is written by a certain king Adon to the Pharaoh asking for help and rescue from the Babylonian army, which already had taken Aphek. The date would be sometime after 605 BCE. It is not quite certain where Adon ruled. It could have been in Phoenicia or in Philistia. B. Porten's examination (in collaboration with G.R. Hughes) makes Ekron a probable reading.[1] The letter could very well be an illustration of the situation before the battle against the Egyptians in 601 BCE, a situation in which the Babylonian king had sent out detachments to different areas. In this case some part of the army would have advanced into southern Palestine before the king joined and took over command.[2]

After the Egyptians had defeated Nebuchadrezzar's army in 600 BCE, nationalism resurged again only to suffer a real setback when Nebuchadrezzar and his army returned to Syria-Palestine in 599 BCE. In that year the Babylonian king campaigned against the Arabs, plundering their camps. The attacks on Arab territories ('Qedar and the kingdoms of Hazor') are also mentioned in Jer. 49.28-33.[3] The Babylonian chronicle says the Babylonian king sent out detachments

1. 'The Identity of King Adon', *BA* 44 (1981), pp. 63-52. For a discussion of the problems, see D.J. Wiseman, *Nebuchadrezzar and Babylon*, pp. 25-29.
2. Cf. A. Malamat, 'The Last Kings of Judah and the Fall of Jerusalem', *IEJ* 18 (1968), p. 143.
3. Hazor in this passage refers to the camps or villages, *ḥṣrym*, of the Arabs.

from Hatti.[1] This probably means that he used Riblah as his headquarters, which he had taken over from Necho. After returning to Babylon, Nebuchadrezzar marched into Hatti the following year, during the winter of 598/597 BCE, and sent his troops down into southern Palestine. He 'encamped against the city of Judah, and on the second day of the month of Adar he captured the city [and] seized [its] king. A king of his own choice he appointed in the city.'[2] According to the biblical text, Nebuchadrezzar also used detachments from 'Aram',[3] Ammon, and Moab, besides 'Chaldeans' (2 Kgs 24.2).[4] It is probable that the biblical text refers to the campaigns of both 599 and 598. The Babylonian chronicle does not give any information on this point.

The expedition to Judah was a punitive action. Jehoiakim had broken his vassal oath. Before the city surrendered Jehoiakim died (probably in 598 BCE),[5] and he was followed by his eighteen-year-old son Jehoiakin.[6] His reign lasted only three months (cf. 2 Kgs 24.8). Nebuchadrezzar

---

1. A.K. Grayson, *Assyrian and Babylonian Chronicles*, p. 101, lines 9-10, *ANET* p. 564.

2. A.K. Grayson, *Assyrian and Babylonian Chronicles*, p. 102, ll. 12-13. The phraseology in the Babylonian chronicle may support the idea that the new king, Zedekiah, was actually king and not simply a royal 'governor'.

3. During the Babylonian period, garrisons in Syria and Palestine may have consisted mainly of Aramaeans, which would be natural in Aramaic-speaking territories; cf. J. Gray, *I and II Kings*, p. 757. However, *'ᵉdōm* should be read here with the Peshitta instead of MT's *'ᵃrām*, because there was no kingdom of Aram at this point in time; cf. H.L. Ginsberg, 'Judah and the Transjordan Sates', *Alexander Marx Jubilee Volume*, p. 356 n. 31; J. Lindsay, 'The Babylonian Kings and Edom, 605–550 BCE', *PEQ* 108 (1976), p. 24; Y. Aharoni, *The Land of the Bible* (2nd edn), p. 406. The Arad ostracon no. 40, mentioning the 'evil' caused by the Edomites, could refer either to this or to some other event. If the former is right, then the emendation of the Hebrew text would be supported.

4. Because the Ammonites and the Moabites were vassals of Babylonia, they had to supply the Babylonians with troops.

5. J. Bright thinks that the king was murdered (*A History of Israel* [3rd edn], p. 327).

6. The Chronicler makes Jehoiakin eight years old (2 Chron. 36.9). M. Noth suggested that Jehoiakim's death was the cause of Nebuchadrezzar's campaign. His purpose would have been to install a faithful vassal on Judah's throne ('Die Einnahme von Jerusalem im Jahre 597 v. Chr.', *ZDPV* 74 [1958], p. 138) (= *Aufsätze*, I, p. 116). This is less than probable; see S. Herrmann, *A History of Israel in Old Testament Times* (2nd edn), p. 279; D.J. Wiseman, *Nebuchadrezzar and Babylon*, p. 32.

himself had arrived to join his army besieging Jerusalem, and according to the biblical text Jehoiakin surrendered (2 Kgs 24.11). In this way he spared the city from destruction. The Babylonian chronicle dates this to the second of Adar (16th of March), 597 BCE,[1] an exact and thus rare date in the chronicles of Babylonia.[2] Jehoiakin had to pay for his father's policy. He himself, the 'king mother',[3] his family, his harem, the high officials, and the upper classes of the society, including all skilled workers, in all c. 8000–10,000 persons, were taken as prisoners to Babylon, never to see their own country again.[4] Ezekiel was one of the deportees (Ezek. 1.2-3). As was common, the temple and the palace were completely emptied of their treasures (2 Kgs 24.13-16). Before leaving Jerusalem Nebuchadrezzar installed another son of Josiah, Mattaniah, as his vassal king.[5] His throne name was Zedekiah. He was twenty-six years old and reigned until the fate of the kingdom of Judah was sealed in 586 BCE. It is likely that part of the army stayed in Jerusalem until all the loot and prisoners were collected.[6]

1. A. Malamat holds the opinion that a Tishri calendar was used in Judah (see *IEJ* 18 [1968], pp. 146-48); cf. also D.J. Wiseman, *Nebuchadrezzar and Babylon*, p. 33.

2. D.J. Wiseman, *Nebuchadrezzar and Babylon*, p. 32. Because of the distance from Babylonia and because the army marched from Babylon in the month of Kislev (Dec.–Jan.), the siege was of short duration, probably no more than a month; see A. Malamat, *IEJ* 18 (1968), p. 144.

3. Because the king's mother is specially mentioned, it may be concluded that the g^{e}bîrâ institution was still in effect in Judah.

4. 2 Kgs 24.14 mentions that 10,000 persons were deported, but v. 16 gives the number as 7000 prominent persons and 1000 skilled workers. Jer. 52.28 mentions 3023 deportees. The city plan of Jerusalem during its last decades is not certain. It is clear, however, that the western hill had been populated since the latter part of the eighth century, having a *mišneh*, 'the second [city]' (2 Kgs 22.14), and a *maktēš*, 'the market district' (Zeph. 1.10-11). Excavations, including the broad wall found in the modern Jewish Quarter, excavations in the citadel area and in the Armenian Quarter, and so on, support this conclusion; see the discussion in H. Geva, *IEJ* 29 (1979), pp. 84-91.

5. 2 Chron. 13 mentions that Zedekiah had sworn allegiance to Nebuchadrezzar, which may refer to a vassal treaty. Ezek. 17.13 expressly mentions a treaty. The oath may have been given in the same style as the ones known from Assyrian inscriptions; cf. M. Weinfeld, 'The Loyalty-Oath in the Ancient Near East', *UF* 8 (1976), pp. 379-414.

6. This may solve the problem with the different figures about how many were exiled. Some may have been taken together with the king and his court; others may

As for Jehoiakin, Babylonian inscriptions found in the palace of Nebuchadrezzar show that he retained his title as king of Judah. The same was the case with other kings who had been exiled to Babylon, for instance, the kings of Gaza, Sidon, Arvad and Ashdod.[1] This does not mean that they actually were the kings of their respective territories, if they remained in exile.

There is some possibility that Judah was territorially decimated at this time. No known Babylonian texts record the destruction of other cities in Judah during the war of 598/597 BCE, but pieces of information provided by the prophet Jeremiah could be understood as proof that the Negev had been cut off from Judah.

Say to the king and to the $g^e b\hat{i}r\hat{a}$ (Queen mother):

> Take a lowly seat, for your beautiful crown has come down from your
> heads.
> The towns of Negev are shut off;
> there is none to open them.
> All of Judah is exiled;
> it is completely deported (Jer. 13.18-19).

Because the continuation of the text shows that Judah was not completely 'exiled', the prophetic utterance may best be connected with the disaster of 597 BCE.[2] The eastern Negev may have been taken over by the Edomites at this time,[3] and it would perhaps be possible to see the destruction of both Arad and En-Gedi by this group. J. Lindsay notes that neither Ramaht-Negev (of the Arad ostracon 24) nor Arad are listed in Nehemiah 3 and 7 and in Ezra 2 as places where the returnees from Babylonia settled; thus, it is possible that these southern

have been taken to Babylonia only when the army left Jerusalem. Cf. the discussion by A. Malamat ('The Last Years of the Kingdom of Judah', *WHJP*, IV.1 [ed. A. Malamat], p. 211).

1. See E.F. Weidner, 'Jojakin', *Mélanges syriens*, II, pp. 923-35; cf. A.L. Oppenheim, *ANET*, p. 308. In three Babylonian texts listing rations to captive kings and princes Jehoiakin is mentioned as king of Judah, and he is also said to have had five sons. In a fourth text, however, he is given the title *mār šarri*, 'prince', which may show that he was no longer considered to be the legal ruler of Judah; see E.F. Weidner, 'Jojakin', *Mélanges syriens*, p. 926.

2. A. Alt, *KS*, II, pp. 280-81; M. Noth, *History of Israel*, p. 283; Y. Aharoni, *The Land of the Bible* (2nd edn), p. 406; A. Malamat, 'The Twilight of Judah', *Congress Volume, Edinburgh 1974* (ed. J.A. Emerton), p. 134; A.F. Rainey, 'The Fate of Lachish', *Lachish*, V (ed. Y. Aharoni *et al.*), pp. 45-60.

3. Cf. J. Lindsay, *PEQ* 108 (1976), p. 26.

sites were not considered to be Judahite territory and that Zedekiah did not rule over them.[1] This may explain why the Persian subprovince of Yehud (Judah) was so small. Its southern border was just north of Hebron.[2] If this is right, the Elyashib ostraca from Arad must refer to the catastrophe of 598 at the latest and not to 587/586 BCE.[3]

All four kings following Josiah are unfavorably judged by the biblical writers. They did what was 'evil' in the eyes of Yahweh, just as their 'fathers had done' (2 Kgs 23.31, 37; 24.9). A change in the standard formula occurs in connection with Zedekiah. He did 'evil' just as Jehoiakim, his brother, had done (2 Kgs 24.19). Poor Jehoiakin could not have done much differently from his father. Three months would not have been enough for religious reorientation, especially not when a besieging army was outside the walls. The Deuteronomistic writer was not reckoning with reality but judged the kings from his own theological bias. In other words, these kings did not represent the ideology of the writer. As mentioned above, it may be concluded that the reform of Josiah was no real reform, and that whatever Josiah may have done religiously did not survive. The state religion of Judah continued in its old ways.

Jehoiakim's position cannot have been easy. Being pro-Egyptian, he had to switch his allegiance to Babylonia after Nebuchadrezzar's

---

1.   *PEQ* 108 (1976), p. 26.
2.   A. Alt, *KS*, II, pp. 280-81.
3.   Cf. Y. Aharoni, who gives the same date using paleographic criteria (*BASOR* 197 [1970], pp. 17-18). The argument from paleography is not very strong, however. A big difference in writing cannot have developed during such a short time as 12 years. In addition, different individuals may have done the writing. The date of the enigmatic ostracon 88 from Arad is difficult to determine. The ostracon was a surface find. The text reads: 'I have begun to reign in... increase strength... the king of Egypt'. Aharoni holds the opinion that the ostracon was sent by king Jehoahaz to Arad and perhaps to Arad's commandant to have him prepare for an Egyptian attack (*Arad Inscriptions*, p. 104); cf. Z. Herzog *et al.*, *BASOR* 254 (1984), p. 32. Y. Yadin restores *mlkty b*[ ] as 'I have started to reign in Carchemish', and concludes that the letter was sent by Ashuruballit of Assyria ('The Historical Significance of Inscription 88 from Arad: A Suggestion', *IEJ* 26 [1976], pp. 12-14). The ostracon could also refer to a king of Judah who had just started his reign and who wanted to inform his commander at Arad (and perhaps other fortresses too) about his alliance with Egypt.

victory at Carchemish in 605 BCE, but when the Babylonian king was defeated by Necho at Magdolos in 600 BCE,[1] Jehoiakim again became an ally of Egypt. Necho had taken Gaza, making Egypt a close neighbor to Judah.[2] The political problems the king had to cope with can be seen in the confrontations of Uriah and Jeremiah with Jehoiakim. Jeremiah was the son of the priest Hilkiah[3] from Anathoth (Jer. 1.1). There is always sharp criticism of the king's actions in the Book of Jeremiah. That he was not alone in this is clear from Jer. 26.20-24, which mentions that the prophet Uriah from Kiriath-jearim was as sharp in his condemnation of the king as Jeremiah was. Both prophesied about the destruction of the country. Such statements would be considered treason. Uriah fled to Egypt in order to save his life, but he was delivered back to Judah and executed. Jeremiah was saved because Shaphan, the scribe,[4] is said to have related the case of Micah of Moreshet, who had prophesied disaster during the days of Hezekiah, but who was not killed by Hezekiah (Jer. 26.16-20, 24). Because in a temple sermon Jeremiah had said, among other things, that the Jerusalem temple would meet the same fate as the temple of Shiloh (Jer. 7.12-15), he was later forbidden to enter the temple area. In order to have his words known he employed the scribe Baruch to write down his prophecies. He had them read at a fast in the temple precinct. Shaphan's son, Gemariah, reported the event to palace officials. As a result, Baruch had to read the scroll to them (Jer. 36).[5] Baruch and Jeremiah were advised to hide. The king, however,

---

1. Cf. above, Chapter 18, p. 759. See also K.S. Freedy and D.B. Redford, 'The Dates in Ezekiel in Relation to Biblical, Babylonian, and Egyptian Sources', *JAOS* 90 (1970), p. 475 n. 57.

2. According to 47.1, the oracles against the Philistines in Jer. 47 were uttered 'before Pharaoh took Gaza by storm'. Cf. H.J. Katzenstein, 'Before Pharaoh Conquered Gaza', *VT* 33 (1983), pp. 249-51.

3. This could possibly be the same person who was Josiah's first priest (2 Kgs 22.8).

4. He is known as the scribe of Josiah (2 Kgs 22.11).

5. Among the many seals and bullae found in Jerusalem that date from the last decades of the kingdom of Judah is one with the inscription 'Gemaryahu, son of Shaphan'. Others are 'Jerahmeel, son of the king', and 'Berachyahu, son of Neriyahu' (see N. Avigad, *IEJ* 28 [1978], pp. 54-56). Prince Jerahmeel is mentioned in Jer. 36.26. For the Gemaryahu inscription see Y. Shiloh, *Excavations at the City of David I, 1978–1982*, pp. 19-20.

learned about the scroll and ordered it read to him. He was sitting close to the fire (it was winter) and used the technique of cutting the scroll bit by bit and throwing the pieces into the fire as it was read to him. The king's intention was to destroy the power of the word.[1] When Jeremiah learned about the destruction of the scroll, he dictated a second one in order to have his oracles preserved. This illustrates two things: the prophet had memorized his oracles because they were divine words and should not be forgotten, and, in this case, the prophet had been the cause for the oral tradition to be fixed in writing.

Jeremiah must have belonged to the upper class of society, being a son of the priest Hilkiah and being aided by high officials, such as Ahikam, Shaphan's son, when he was accused of treason (2 Kgs 22.11; Jer. 26.24). His pro-Babylonian attitude also saved him from being deported to Babylon.[2]

The conflict between king and prophet came to such a point that Jeremiah completely denounced the king and uttered an oracle stating that he would not get a decent burial. His would be 'the burial of an ass, dragged away and thrown outside the gates of Jerusalem' (Jer. 22.19). His body would be 'thrown out to the heat by day and to the cold by night' (Jer. 36.30). This latter phrase is in agreement with the curses of the neo-Assyrian treaties;[3] thus, Jeremiah applies a well-known threat to Jehoiakim's breaking of the vassal treaty. Trustworthy information about the manner of Jehoiakim's death cannot be drawn from this threat; it is formulaic. He seems to have died a natural death (2 Kgs 24.6) and, according to LXX[L], he was

---

1. Cf. my article in *HTR* 59 (1966), pp. 78-79.

2. In Jer. 25.9-13 the prophet threatens Judah with all the people of the north (i.e. the Babylonians) and Nebuchadrezzar, Yahweh's 'servant', devastating the country. This was supposedly said in the first year of Nebuchadrezzar's kingship, 604 BCE, after the battle at Carchemish. Since Jehoiakim had just become a Babylonian vassal; there would have been no need to threaten the country with destruction and devastation. From this point of view the utterance must be postexilic; cf. C. Rietzschel, *Das Problem der Urrolle: Ein Beitrag zur Redaktionsgeschichte des Jeremiabuches* (Gütersloh, 1966), p. 53. Nebuchadrezzar's designation as the 'servant' is not found in the LXX; see J. Bright, *Jeremiah*, pp. 162-63.

3. See D. Hillers, *Treaty Curses and the Old Testament Prophets* (Rome, 1964), pp. 68-69. The treaty maledictions are numerous but somewhat stereotyped in Jeremiah's prose sermons, according to M. Weinfeld (*Deuteronomy and the Deuteronomic School*, p. 138).

buried in the garden of Uzzah, where Manasseh and Amon had also been buried.

The Babylonians expected Judah under Zedekiah to be a calm area in the big empire. Its military power was largely nonexistent after the deportation of military personnel and high officials in 597 BCE. Consequently, the king, who perhaps did not have much experience in administrative and military matters, had to build a new administrative apparatus. Where could he get trained personnel for such a task? There is no answer to this question, but knowing that there were still Judahite soldiers in the Egyptian army, some of them could have received permission to return to Judah. Psammetichus II (595–589 BCE), who had succeeded his father, continued the system of using mercenaries. He probably used Judahite troops in his campaign against Nubia.[1] Even if Zedekiah could not build up a strong army, he must have had military and police forces. For his civil administration and his policies he may have had Babylonian officials keeping an eye on what was happening. Having no experienced advisers at his side, Zedekiah must have had a difficult time maneuvering among the different factions in the city of Jerusalem, which his clashes with Jeremiah, who was firmly pro-Babylonian, might indicate (Jer. 37–38). There were people who still hoped for Jehoiakin's return, and Hananaiah, a prophet from Gibeon, even promised in 594/593 BCE that the exiled king would return within two years together with his exiled people. All the temple vessels that Nebuchadrezzar had taken would also be brought back. Jeremiah contested this prediction and said that Hananaiah was not sent by Yahweh (Jer. 28.1-17).

The political situation in Palestine changed somewhat in 595 BCE because of the war between Elam and Babylonia (596/595) in which Elam was defeated, or rather, panicked at the sight of the Babylonian army. However, an uprising occurred shortly thereafter in Babylon itself during the winter of 595/594 BCE.[2] This may have inspired the vassal states in the west to form a coalition against Babylonia. There seems to have been unrest among the Judahites in Babylonia, and some were executed by Nebuchadrezzar, according to Jer. 29.21-23. The

---

1. See the discussion in K.S. Freedy and D.B. Redford, *JAOS* 90 (1970), pp. 476-77.

2. On this see D.J. Wiseman, *Chronicles of Chaldean Kings*, p. 72, ll. 16-22; A.K. Grayson, *Assyrian and Babylonian Chronicles*, p. 102. Cf. also D.J. Wiseman, *Nebuchadrezzar*, p. 34.

messages from the exiles to Jerusalem may have spurred some hopes. The situation was such that Egypt under Psammetichus II (595–589 BCE) could have been behind the coalition too. Messengers from Phoenicia (Tyre and Sidon), Ammon, Moab and Edom went to Jerusalem in 594 BCE. Who took the initiative at the conference is not known. Jeremiah showed his opposition by putting a yoke with ropes on his neck as a symbol of what the result would be (Jer. 27.2-3) In this conspiracy there were no representatives from the Philistine states. Either they were temporarily in the Egyptian fold, or Egypt's political influence was weak and they were not forced to participate in a dangerous plot. Nothing came out of the conspiracy, most probably because Nebuchadrezzar was in Hatti again in 594 BCE. As for Zedekiah, he went to Babylon[1] in his fourth year (593 BCE) with a large entourage, probably in order to assure the king of his vassal status. His chief officer ('quartermaster'), Seraiah, had received a letter from Jeremiah addressed to the exiled Judahites, in which he tried to arrest the anti-Babylonian sentiment in Babylon (Jer. 51.59-64).

It was around this time, in the fifth year of Jehoiakin's exile, that Ezekiel received his prophetic call, according to Ezek. 1.2. The situation at home in Jerusalem, with prophetic voices for and against Babylonia, may have inspired Ezekiel.[2] His depiction of the Jerusalemite temple cult should be noticed, because it is certainly built upon some reality, even if it reflects a visionary's expression. Ezekiel refers to the worship of the sun, about the many 'gods of the house of Israel',[3] as well as symbols of snakes and other animals, carved on the walls of the temple. He also sees women weeping for Tammuz, a Babylonian god (Ezek 8.7-18).[4] His portrait yields quite a different picture of the official religion of Judah than that propagated by the

1.   The LXX reads 'from Zedekiah', thus presuming that the king did not go himself. For the discussion, see J. Bright, *Jeremiah*, p. 216.

2.   Cf. A. Malamat, 'The Twilight of Judah', *Congress Volume, Edinburgh 1974* (ed. J.A. Emerton), p. 137.

3.   For Hebrew *gillulîm* meaning gods, see my *Aspects of Syncretism in Israelite Religion*, pp. 46-47.

4.   The problem here is whether this really is Tammuz, or whether it is only another word for Baal. See the discussion in F.F. Hvidberg, *Weeping and Laughter in the Old Testament*, pp. 113-15, and cf. further G.W. Ahlström, *Aspects of Syncretism*, p. 55.

Deuteronomistic writer. It also indicates that Josiah's reform was quite ineffective.

What made Zedekiah change his position and rebel again is unclear. The Pharaoh's march up to Phoenicia in 591 BCE may have been interpreted to indicate a revival of Egyptian strength, and for a ruler who seems to have had his heart set upon help from Egypt, the temptation may have been perhaps too great. Psammetichus marched with his army to Cush in 593 BCE. He represented his campaign as a great military victory (cf. Herodotus 2.161).[1] Zedekiah, like the other vassals of Babylonia in Palestine, could only believe the Pharaoh. As a representative of the Palestinian political tradition, Zedekiah looked to Egypt for help against the Mesopotamian 'invaders'. When Psammetichus then went to Palestine and Phoenicia in 592/591 with priests in his entourage,[2] Zedekiah may have been more than impressed, and it has been assumed that a visit to Jerusalem either by the Pharaoh or some emissaries could have occurred.[3] Whatever happened, Zedekiah changed his policy and asked for help from Egypt. Ezek. 17.15 refers to Zedekiah's breaking of the treaty with Babylonia by sending messengers to Egypt to ask for horses and troops.[4] This may have been the result of Psammetichus's military parade through Palestine, but it is more likely that Zedekiah's action was taken shortly after Psammetichus had died, in 589 BCE. He was succeeded by his son Hophra (Apries, 589–570 BCE), who increased Egypt's political activities in the eastern Mediterranean. One of the ostraca from Tell ed-Duweir (no. III) also mentions that the commander of Judah's

---

1. Cf. also the remarks of K.S. Freedy and D.B. Redford, *JAOS* 90 (1970), pp. 474-75.

2. This is mentioned in a text from the reign of Darius I; see F.L. Griffith, *Catalogue of the Demotic Papyri in the John Rylands Library*, III (Manchester, 1909), pp. 92-94. F.K. Kienitz saw this as a 'pilgrimage' possibly made by ship (*Ägypten: Die politische Geschichte*, p. 25).

3. Cf. M. Greenberg, 'Ezekiel 17 and the Policy of Psammetichus II', *JBL* 76 (1957), pp. 304-309; K.S. Freedy and D.B. Redford, *JAOS* 90 (1970), pp. 470-76, A. Malamat, 'The Twilight of Judah', *Congress Volume, Edinburgh 1974* (ed. J.A. Emerton), p. 142; J.M. Miller and J.H. Hayes, *A History of Ancient Israel and Judah*, pp. 412-13. See also R.S. Foster, 'A Note on Ezekiel VII 1-10 and 22-24', *VT* 8 (1958), pp. 374-79.

4. Cf. M. Tsevat, 'The Neo-Assyrian and Neo-Babylonian Vassal Oaths and the Prophet Ezekiel', *JBL* 78 (1959), pp. 199-204.

army, Koniahu, son of Elnathan, had gone to Egypt.[1] There is no information about Koniahu's mission. However, to send a top military emissary to Egypt in those days must have meant that a military alliance or military support was going to be discussed. It is understandable that Zedekiah was pro-Egyptian. Nebuchadrezzar's repeated excursions into Hatti (13 in all during the period 605–594 BCE)[2] may have been interpreted by Zedekiah as an indication that Nebuchadrezzar's hold over the territory was not too firm.[3] He could have felt that the time was ripe for a successful rebellion.

Unfortunately for Zedekiah and Judah, no great coalition against Babylonia came about, and there was no possibility for one to be established either. Of the few vassal countries that existed, only Tyre and Ammon broke with Babylon. Tyre under Ithobaal may have been forced by Hophra to rebel.[4] The insurrection by king Baalis of Ammon is mentioned in Ezek. 21.23-32 [18-27].[5] Zedekiah broke the vassal oath in 589 BCE when Hophra became king, but no help from Tyre and Ammon was forthcoming. The Babylonians invaded Palestine in 589 BCE. The picture given by the Bible is that Nebuchadrezzar had two paths from which to choose. One led to Rabbath-Ammon, the other to Jerusalem (Ezek. 21.23-26 [18-21]). Ammon got a few years of respite. Through divination Nebuchadrezzar chose to attack Judah first. The Babylonian army did not meet any opposition before it besieged Jerusalem in 588 BCE. There is no information about its march down to Judah. However, knowing that Nebuchadrezzar used Riblah in Syria as his headquarters, it may be assumed that the army took the fastest route south, through Galilee and Megiddo. South of Aphek it may have divided into two contingents, one marching up the hills to Jerusalem and the other continuing south, taking, among

1.   D.W. Thomas, 'Ostracon III: 13-18 from Tell ed-Duweir', *PEQ* 80 (1948), pp. 130-36. For the text see D. Pardee *et al.*, *Handbook of Ancient Hebrew Letters*, pp. 81-89 (with lit.). Pardee dates the latter to 589 BCE, i.e., before the Babylonian assault had taken place (p. 88).

2.   J. Lindsay, *PEQ* 108 (1976), p. 27. D.J. Wiseman mentions that during the 17 years before 594 BCE the Babylonian army 'was called out (*dekû*) twenty-one times' (*Chronicles of Chaldean Kings*, p. 95).

3.   J.P. Hyatt, 'New Light on Nebuchadrezzar and Judean History', *JBL* 75 (1956), p. 282.

4.   Herodotus 2.161; cf. the discussion in H.J. Katzenstein, *The History of Tyre*, pp. 318-19.

5.   The king's name is known from Jer. 40.14.

others cities, Gezer, Beth-Shemesh, Azekah and Tell ed-Duweir (usually identified with Lachish). At Jerusalem the Babylonians threw up earthen ramps around the city to prevent anyone from escaping (cf. 2 Kgs 25.1). The same method was probably used at other places. Habakkuk mentions that the 'Chaldeans' laugh at the fortresses, and 'they heap up earth' and take them (1.10). The Benjaminite territory north of Jerusalem was not devastated, as far as archaeology can tell. For instance, Gibeon (el-Jîb) was not destroyed at this time (Jer. 41.16). This may mean that there were not many strong fortifications to besiege and capture or, if there were, that the commanders quickly capitulated.

The picture is different to the south and to the west of Jerusalem. Tell Beit Mirsim, Tell ez-Zakariyeh (Azekah), Tell ed-Duweir, Beth-Zur, Ramat-Rahel, Beth-Shemesh and Arad all seem to have been destroyed in this period.[1] Thus, Zedekiah was attacked on several sides: at Jerusalem and in the west by the Babylonians, and on the south by the Edomites. The many hostile oracles against Edom[2] by several prophets could indicate that the Edomites did some of the work for Nebuchadrezzar in the south, perhaps with the help of some Babylonian troops. The Babylonian arrows found in the city wall of En-Gedi may support this conclusion.[3] However, the long-standing hostility between Edom and Judah—since the days of David—has to be taken into consideration; thus, all prophecies against Edom cannot be the result of the events of 587/586 BCE.[4] As mentioned before, during the seventh century Edom had most probably invaded and taken over most of the Negev, which was of supreme economic interest to the Edomites because of the trade routes between Arabia and the Palestinian coast. Such places as Tel Māśōś and Tel Malḥata could very well have been destroyed before the reign of Zedekiah.[5]

1. The pottery in the destruction layers from most of these places is typologically the same as the pottery from Jerusalem in its last decade (Y. Shiloh, *Excavations at the City of David*, I, p. 29).

2. Ezek. 25.12-14; 35.1-9; Obad., Joel 4.19. Jer. 49.7-22 could be earlier, if uttered by Jeremiah. Mal. 1.3 mentions the devastation of Edom, but it is impossible to say by whom and when; cf. B. Glazier-McDonald, *Malachi: The Divine Messenger* (SBLDS, 98; Atlanta, 1987), pp. 30-41.

3. Cf. A. Malamat, 'The Last Years', *WHJP*, IV.1, p. 217.

4. J.R. Bartlett, *PEQ* 114 (1982), pp. 13-24.

5. According to M. Kochavi, about 30% of the late Iron II pottery at Tel Malḥata is to be labeled Edomite ('Malḥata, Tel', *EAEHL*, III, pp. 771-75).

The siege of Jerusalem lasted for about one and a half years. Pharaoh Hophra sent a force as help, which for a short time made the Babylonians lift the siege in order to nullify Hophra's maneuver (Jer. 37.5-11),[1] but the Egyptian army was of no real help. There is no report of any battle between Egyptians and Babylonians; thus the Egyptian army may have been surprised by the Babylonian approach and may have returned to Egypt. Hophra may have thought to attack the Babylonians from the rear. When his strategy did not prove effective he returned to Egypt. The siege of Jerusalem could therefore be resumed.

The Babylonian strategy seems to have been to eliminate all the fortresses of Judah, not only laying waste to Jerusalem and the country, but also cutting off all communications and possible help to the capital. The many small fortresses that had earlier been built by Judahite rulers, such as Jotham (2 Chron. 27.4), were taken. Some small forts have been found in the Judean hills, such as Khirbet Abu et-Twain, c. 18 km SSW of Jerusalem, which may have been part of the defense system.[2] Signals warning the others may have been sent from the forts, as mentioned in one of the 21 ostraca from Tell ed-Duweir. The message reports that signals from Lachish were being watched for,[3] but those from Azekah (c. 15 km NNE of Tell ed-Duweir as the crow flies) could not be seen.[4] Jer. 34.7 mentions that, of all the cities of Judah besides Jerusalem, only Lachish and Azekah were still holding out.

1.   It was at this time that Jeremiah tried to leave Jerusalem, probably in order to go to the field in Anathoth which he had bought from a cousin during the siege (Jer. 32.6-15). He was arrested as a collaborator at the Benjamin Gate and thrown into the basement of the house of the secretary, Jonathan, which had been converted into a prison (Jer. 37.11-16).

2.   Pottery items from the sixth and fifth centuries BCE were found at the site, which means that it could have been rebuilt by returnees from Babylonia. For the finds, see A. Mazar, *BA* 45 (1982), pp. 174-77.

3.   This ostracon may indicate that Tell ed-Duweir is not to be identified with Lachish; cf. A. Parrot, *Syria* 16 (1935), p. 420; G.W. Ahlström, *PEQ* 112 (1980), pp. 7-9. For the ostracon and its texts, see H. Torczyner, *Lachish*. I. *The Lachish Letters* (London, 1938), pp. 75-78; D. Pardee *et al.*, *Handbook of Ancient Hebrew Letters*, pp. 89-95 (with lit.).

4.   Whether this was because Azekah had already been captured is not clear from the text. The ostraca were found in a storeroom (Level II) that probably 'served as an archive for a chancellery', according to Y. Aharoni (*Lachish*, V, p. 24).

When a breach[1] in the wall was finally made on the ninth of the month of Tammuz 586 (?) BCE, in Zedekiah's eleventh year,[2] the inhabitants and the defenders were at the point of starvation (2 Kgs 25.3; Jer. 37.21). It may be concluded from Jer. 33.4-5 that the defenders, like those of Tell ed-Duweir in 701 BCE, built a counter-ramp inside the wall in order to block the way into the city that a breach would make possible. Jeremiah mentions that houses and 'royal palaces' were torn down in order to defend the city.[3]

When the breach was made and the Babylonians started to penetrate the city, King Zedekiah and his entourage fled during the night and took the route to Jericho (2 Kgs 25.3-7; Jer. 52.6-11), probably in order to escape to Ammon, whose king would have been his ally. The Babylonians pursued them, and when the royal party had reached the plains at Jericho it was captured. The soldiers escorting them fled (Jer. 52.8), and Zedekiah and his party were taken to Riblah in Hamath, where Nebuchadrezzar 'passed sentence upon' the king (2 Kgs 25.6; Jer. 39.5). He had to witness the killing of his sons and the nobility that had followed him. He himself was then blinded and taken in chains to Babylon, where his life probably ended in prison. Did he meet there his predecessor and nephew Jehoiakin? Zedekiah's fate was the result of his breaking the treaty with Nebuchadrezzar.

The siege of Jerusalem had taken about one and a half years until the breach in the wall was made. Zedekiah may have watched the Babylonian attacks while leading the defense at the Benjamin Gate in the north part of the city wall (cf. Jer. 38.7-8). The breach in the wall seems to have been made close to the 'Middle Gate' (Jer. 39.3), which probably was not far from where Zedekiah was watching the happenings.[4]

---

1. For this meaning of the Hebrew *bq'h*, see G. Brunet, 'La prise de Jerusalem sous Sedecias: Le sense militaire de l'hebreu *baqa"*, *RHR* 167 (1965), pp. 157-76.

2. For the chronological problems, see A. Malamat, who bases his reconstruction on the understanding that Zedekiah's reign began in Tishri, 597 BCE (*IEJ* 18 [1968], pp. 150-55); E. Vogt, 'Bemerkungen über das Jahr der Eroberung Jerusalems', *Bib* 56 (1975), pp. 223-30; D.J. Wiseman, *Nebuchadrezzar and Babylon*, pp. 37-39. See also F.H. Cryer, who maintains that the traditions in Kings and Jeremiah (MT and LXX) 'represent chronological idealizations of the events in question' based on a 360-day calendar ('To the Tune of Fictive Music: OT Chronology and History', *SJOT* 2 [1987], p. 25).

3. For ramps and breaches, see I. Eph'al, *Tel Aviv* 11 (1984), pp. 67-69.

4. Cf. A. Malamat, *IEJ* 18 (1939), pp. 154-55.

The captain of the guard, Nabuzaradan,[1] was put in command of the troops that stayed and destroyed the city. The destruction was thorough. The walls were broken down and the city was plundered. Temple, palaces and houses were burned, and the temple vessels including the bronze sea and the wheeled bronze stands, as well as other treasures, were taken as booty (2 Kgs 25.4-7; Jer. 39.8; 52.14, 17-19). Arrowheads of northern origin and destroyed buildings that have been unearthed in excavations from this period bear witness to the disaster of the city.[2] The Bible indicates that Jerusalem was thoroughly destroyed. Some parts of the city wall may have remained standing, and a few ruined houses may have served as reminders of the former city.[3]

With the capture and destruction of Jerusalem, the kingdom of Judah went out of existence. The land was devastated, and several of the leading classes of the population were killed either in the war or after the capture of Jerusalem. From Jerusalem alone 832 persons were exiled. Ramah served as the gathering place for the people to be taken to Babylonia. Among them was Jeremiah, who, however, was freed from his chains by Nabuzaradan and given the choice of either going with the general as his protégé or of returning to Mizpah and staying with the people under Gedaliah. Jeremiah chose the latter (Jer. 40.1-6). This shows that the Babylonians knew that Jeremiah was pro-Babylonian. The lower classes of the population, such as the villagers working the land and the vineyards, were allowed to stay (2 Kgs 25.11-12). About 4600 Judahites were exiled in three waves during a fifteen-year period in 597, 586 and also in 582, according to Jer. 52.30. The number of deportees was relatively small.

The extent of the destruction of the country is impossible to determine, but it is likely that smaller towns and villages were

---

1. See the list of some of Nebuchadrezzar's high officials in *ANET*, pp. 307-308; J.V. Kinnier Wilson, *The Nimrud Wine List*, p. 80.

2. K.M. Kenyon, *Digging up Jerusalem*, pp. 170-71; N. Avigad, *Discovering Jerusalem*, pp. 53-54.

3. Cf. the description in the Book of Lamentations. The old ideology that the king was the breath of life for the people that now no longer existed is expressed in Lam. 4.20; cf. B. Albrektson, *Studies in the Text and Theology of the Book of Lamentations* (Studia theologica Lundensia, 21; Lund, 1963), p. 229; R.J. Williams, 'Some Egyptianisms in the Old Testament', *Studies in Honor of J.A. Wilson* (SAOC, 35; Chicago, 1969), p. 93.

untouched by the war, depending upon their geographical location. The exiled people were settled in areas by the Chebar River. One town, Tel Abib in southern Babylonia, is mentioned (Ezek. 1.2-3; 3.15). In Ezra 2.59 and Neh. 7.61 the additional sites of Tel-Melah, Tel-Harsha, Cherub, Addan and Immer are mentioned, but their locations are not given.

No other groups of people were settled in Judah. The Babylonian policy for restructuring conquered territory was different from that of the Assyrians. Nebuchadrezzar apparently did not want to rebuild the destroyed cities of the country. Under a Babylonian official and with no national government to administer the district, the rural population would have to go about their business as usual. A national uprising would be hard to organize. It is uncertain where Babylonian troops were stationed in Judah, but Mizpah would have been the most probable site for a Babylonian command (2 Kgs 25.23), had it still existed.

If this were the plan for the province, it soon failed. A grandson of Shaphan, Gedaliah, had been appointed 'governor' (*pāqîd*)[1] over Judah with his residence at Mizpah (2 Kgs 25.22; cf. Jer. 40.5-7). Belonging to a noble family, Gedaliah was probably one of the leading pro-Babylonians in Jerusalem, as was Jeremiah. He therefore could be trusted by the Babylonian regime. A seal with the inscription 'belonging to Gedaliah, who is over the house/palace' was found at Tell ed-Duweir and could possibly refer to the provincial supervisor Gedaliah as a royal official under Zedekiah.[2] However, after a few years (?)[3] he and the Babylonians at Mizpah were murdered by a band led by a member of the royal family, Ishmael, son of Nethaniah, who obviously had been able to escape, as had several other Judahites[4]—

1. This term, as its Akkadian parallel, *paqdu*(*m*), is most common in late texts; consult W. Schottrof, *s.v.*, *THAT*, II, cols. 466-86; cf. J. Scharbet, 'Das Verbum PQD in der Theologie des Altem Testaments', *BZ* 4 (1960), pp. 209-26. For a catalogue of all the occurrences of the root *pqd* in the Hebrew Bible, see G. André, *Determining the Destiny: PQD in the Old Testament* (ConBOT, 16; Lund, 1980). Even if the noun *paqdu*(*m*) occurs mainly in late texts, the verb is common in both old and later texts; see W. von Soden, *AHw*, II, pp. 824-26; cf. J.V. Kinnier Wilson, *The Nimrud Wine List*, pp. 70-71.

2. See S. Moscati, *L'epigrafia ebraica antica 1935–50* (Rome, 1951), p. 61 n. 30.

3. Cf. J. Lindsay, *PEQ* 108 (1976), p. 27 n. 30.

4. Some could perhaps have taken refuge in caves in the Judean Wilderness. Three inscriptions in a burial cave from Khirbet Beit Lei (c. 8 km east of Tell ed-

probably before the siege of the city had begun. He also slew other people, including 80 men coming from Shechem and Shiloh to bring cereal offerings and incense at the temple place as a rite of mourning (Jer. 41.5).

It is uncertain whether Ishmael contested Gedaliah's position as an administrative leader of Judah. Being of royal descent, Ishmael could not have accepted a commoner, albeit a nobleman, as ruler under Babylonian tutelage.[1] The real reason for the murder is not given by the narrator, who sees the murder as part of a political intrigue by the Ammonite king, Baalis (Jer. 40.14).[2] This is less than probable. Baalis must have learned something from the destruction of Judah and Jerusalem. His political and military power was too small for him to question or disturb the Babylonian administration and military machinery. The solution may be that Ishmael was one of the Judahites who had sought refuge in Ammon. According to Jer. 40.11, Judahites who had fled to Edom, Moab and Ammon returned after the war was over and acknowledged Gedaliah as their ruler.

After Gedaliah's death Ishmael did not gain a following in Judah; thus, he and his men fled to Ammon. The Judahites of Gedaliah's administration and other people of Judah, fearful of Nebuchadrezzar's revenge, fled to Egypt, forcing Jeremiah and Baruch to go with them (Jer. 43.4-7). This may show two things: first, contrary to the suggestion by J.H. Hayes,[3] that Ishmael had not aspired to succeed Gedaliah and to make Judah independent again with the help of Baalis,

---

Duweir) have been associated by F.M. Cross with the year 587 BCE ('The Cave Inscriptions from Khirbet Beit Lei', *Near Eastern Archaeology in the Twentieth Century* (ed. J.A. Sanders; New York, 1970), pp. 299-306. For the find, see J. Naveh, who dates the inscriptions to 701 BCE ('Old Hebrew Inscriptions in a Burial Cave', *IEJ* 13 [1963], pp. 74-92).

1.   J.H. Hayes thinks that Gedaliah became a Babylonian vassal king and that the biblical narrator has tried to avoid this fact (Miller and Hayes, *A History of Ancient Israel and Judah*, pp. 421-23).

2.   The name Baalis occurs in Josephus as Baalim/Baaleim (*Ant.* 10.164, 160). According to F. Israel, the final consonant is traceable to mimmation (*Orientalia Lovaniensia Periodica* 10 [1979], p. 155). A seal found at Tell el-'Umeiri in Jordan has the inscription 'belonging to Milkom'ur, servant of Ba'alyasha". Both the god of Ammon, Milkom, and Ammon's last king, Baalis, are thus mentioned (see L.G. Herr, 'The Servant of Baalis', *BA* 48 [1985], pp. 169-72).

3.   In J.H. Miller and J.M. Hayes, *A History of Ancient Israel and Judah*, p. 424.

secondly, that the Babylonians had not stationed many troops in the devastated country to protect their interest and to safeguard the population. It is doubtful that Baalis, who did not support Zedekiah, would have helped some Judahites in a rebellion when they did not have an army or any kind of defense. The outcome of such an insurrection would amount to suicide.

The Babylonian sources do not reveal anything about the situation in Judah after these happenings. It is not known whether Judah became a Babylonian province or whether it became part of Samerina. Since Judahites returning from Babylonia settled in Bethel and other places north of Jerusalem it may be assumed that Judah was governed by a Babylonian commander, perhaps residing in Mizpah.

Flavius Josephus provides information about Nebuchadrezzar's further campaigning in Palestine and Transjordan in 582/581 BCE. After having subdued Moab and Ammon he purportedly invaded Egypt and installed a new king on its throne. More Judahites were reputedly deported to Babylonia in this campaign.[1] The statement by Josephus concerning a Transjordanian campaign may be right, but he may have misunderstood his biblical sources to refer to the death of the Egyptian king (Jer. 44.30). Pharaoh Hophra (Apries) reigned until 570 BCE. According to Herodotus (2.161-62), Hophra was killed by a rebel, who then ascended the throne as Ahmose II (Amasis, 570–526). Ahmose had probably become king in Sais already before the death of Hophra (Apries), while the latter was carrying on an ill-fated war at Cyrene.[2] The civil war between Hophra and Ahmose II may be seen reflected in the utterance in Jer. 44.30, which says that Yahweh will hand over Hophra 'to those determined to kill him', but does not mention the killers. The event is compared with Zedekiah's being handed over to Nebuchadrezzar. Josephus may have jumped to a conclusion in this matter.

The Babylonian campaign in Palestine and Transjordan in 582 BCE can be seen as a reprisal for the murder of Gedaliah, which would mean that Gedaliah lived for a few more years than is commonly supposed. Nebuchadrezzar was probably besieging Tyre at this time, and Nabuzaradan may have been in command of the expedition to Ammon and Moab.[3] This was effectively the end of Moab and

1. *Ant.* 10.9.7, cf. Jer. 52.30.
2. A. Spalinger, *Or* NS 47 (1978), p. 25.
3. J. Lindsay, *PEQ* 108 (1976), p. 27 n. 30, and p. 29.

Ammon. Edom was not invaded at that time, probably because that country had aided Babylonia in its destruction of Judah both in 597 and 588–586 BCE.[1] The date of Nebuchadrezzar's thirteen-year siege of Tyre is difficult to establish.[2] Ezek. 26.1 mentions that Tyre had rejoiced over the fall of Jerusalem, and if the prophet's statement reflects the actual event, the siege of Tyre would not have started before 585 BCE.[3] The Phoenician mainland may have been subdued in an earlier campaign.[4] The Babylonians did not manage to take the city itself,[5] but when the siege ended in 571, Tyre's king Ithobaal had been replaced by Baal II, which may indicate that Ithobaal had capitulated and that Baal was made a puppet king. The inscription mentioning the officials of Nebuchadrezzar's court ends with the names of some Syro-Palestinian kings. The first one mentioned is the king of Tyre, followed by the kings of Gaza, Sidon, Arvad, and the king of Ashdod.[6] In subduing Tyre, the Babylonian king was in command of the whole of Syria-Palestine with its important coastal area.

---

1. Cf. the Arad letter no. 24, and cf. Ps. 137.7; Ezek. 25.12-14, 35.5-6; Obad. 10-11, 13-14.

2. See the discussion in H.J. Katzenstein, *The History of Tyre*, pp. 319-28; D.J. Wiseman, *Nebuchadrezzar and Babylon*, pp. 27-29.

3. Cf. the utterance in Ezek. 29.17-20, and see the discussion in M. Vogelstein, 'Nebukadnezzar's Reconquest of Phoenicia and Palestine and the Oracles of Ezekiel', *HUCA* 23 (1950–51), p. 201; cf. O. Eissfeldt, 'Das Datum der Belagerung von Tyrus durch Nebukadnezar', *KS*, II (ed. B. Sellheim, F. Mass; Tübingen, 1963), pp. 1-3. Ezek. 27 has often been understood to give a picture of Tyre's 'world-wide' trade connections. However, with G. Bunnens, I would assume that the text is written by a scribe who would like to show his knowledge rather than write history (*L'expansion phénicienne en Mediterranée*, p. 90). The text in Ezek. 27.9-25 shows that the Tyrian trade was conducted within the countries of the eastern Mediterranean. The western colonies are not in the picture. Thus Tarshish, mentioned in Ezek. 27.12, cannot be located in Spain. W. Culican mentions that Spain became 'the chief source of silver for the Ionian cities in the sixth century' BCE (see 'Aspects of Phoenician Settlement in the West Mediterranean', *Opera Selecta: From Tyre to Tartessos* [Studies in Mediterranean Archaeology, Pocket-book 40; Göteborg, 1968], p. 644).

4. E. Unger, 'Nebukadnezar II und sein Šandabakku (Oberkommisar) in Tyrus', *ZAW* 44 (1926), pp. 314; H.K. Katzenstein, *The History of Tyre*, p. 324. For Ezek. 26.1, see W. Zimmerli, *Ezechiel*, p. 613.

5. Cf. Ezek. 29.17.

6. *ANET*, p. 308.

Like Esarhaddon, Nebuchadrezzar also prepared a campaign against Egypt. According to a cuneiform fragment, Nebuchadrezzar supposedly invaded Egypt in his thirty-seventh year, 569 BCE, fighting Ahmose (Amasis), who had just ascended the throne after Hophra.[1] Because of the fragmentary state of the inscription it is impossible to determine what happened. It is probable that the Babylonian invasion had nothing to do with the civil war between Hophra and Ahmose.[2] However, if that were Nebuchadrezzar's idea, he came too late.[3] The result of this invasion of Egypt is unknown, but it seems clear that the Babylonian army was not successful. Thus, Ahmose and Nebuchadrezzar could have come to an agreement that gave Ahmose a free hand in Egypt.[4] After the Babylonian threat was over, Ahmose invaded Cyprus (around 560 BCE), and several cities acknowledged his sovereignty, paying tribute to Egypt.[5] Under Ahmose Egypt experienced its last prosperous period of independence before the Ptolemaic era.

---

1. The circumstances around the death of Hophra are not fully known. For the text, see *ANET*, p. 308, and cf. Josephus (*Ant.* 10.182), who dates an invasion by Nebuchadrezzar to his twenty-third year.

2. See G. Posener, 'Les douanes de la Mediterranée dans l'Ägypt Saîte', *Revue de Philologie* 21 (1947), pp. 128-29. Ahmose was a general of Hophra who used the opportunity of the Libyan war to ascend the throne; cf. W.K. Simpson in W.W. Hallo and W.K. Simpson, *The Ancient Near East*, p. 294.

3. D. J. Wiseman thinks that the invasion occurred during the reign of Hophra (*Nebuchadrezzar and Babylon*, p. 40).

4. Cf. J. von Beckerath, *Abriss der Geschichte des Alten Ägypten*, p. 54; H.J. Katzenstein, *The History of Tyre*, p. 338.

5. Thus Herodotus (2.182).

Chapter 20

PALESTINE AFTER THE BABYLONIAN CAMPAIGNS

The greater Palestinian area during the period of 582–539 BCE is poorly documented. Babylonian inscriptions do not provide much insight. The Palestinian material is either fragmentary, such as that provided by archaeological remains, or it presents a religio-politically tendentious picture, such as that contained in the biblical books of Ezra and Nehemiah and 2 Chron. 36.17-23. The two former books are not really concerned with the period before the Persian conquest of the Babylonian empire. Neither are they concerned with the peoples of the land. For the author of these books there were no people in Palestine other than the people of the *gôlâ*, 'the captivity', who constituted those who had returned and their descendants. The 'peoples of the land' therefore became foreigners.[1] The history of this country in the period after Nebuchadrezzar's campaigns and until the Persian takeover comprises a dark age. From a few prophetical books some information can be derived about the activities of Judah's neighbors. However, prophetical oracles are by nature exaggerations; thus, their historical value can be disputed. For instance, Ezekiel accuses the Philistines of having undertaken military activities and revenge, probably after 586 BCE (Ezek. 25.15-17), while Zech. 9.5-7 seems to show that the coast had been in the hands of the Philistines but was then taken over by the Phoenicians. Joel 4.4-6 accuses the Philistines of plundering Judah.[2] The oracles against Ammon, Moab and Edom by Ezekiel could indicate not only that they would be punished for their hostility to Judah, but also that after Judah's catastrophe they may have invaded parts of Judah (Ezek. 25.1-14; 35.1-15). The

---

1. Cf. S. Japhet, 'People and Land in the Restoration Period', *Das Land Israel in biblischer Zeit* (ed. G. Strecker; Göttingen, 1983), p. 113.

2. For the date of Book of Joel in the early postexilic period, see my book *Joel and the Temple Cult of Jerusalem*, pp. 119-20.

Edomite kingdom was terminated by the last Babylonian king, Nabuna'id,[1] and it is possible that Edomites then began to move into southern Judah, which later became known as Idumea, extending to just north of Hebron. The Wâdî el-Ḥasa survey indicates that this Transjordan part of Edom was unsettled. In fact, 'not one identifiable sherd from the Persian period was found'.[2] The same might have been the case in other parts of Edom.

The archaeological material has not yet been systematized in a way that provides a clear picture of how destructive the Babylonian campaigns (598–570 BCE) against Judah, Tyre and Transjordan really were. Southern Palestine may have been more devastated than Ammon and Moab. The territories of Samerina and Gal'aza (Gilead) were Babylonian districts and so did not suffer from the war. They merely had to contribute provisions for the armies. It is possible to conclude from archaeological surveys that northern Transjordan was not as heavily populated as were its central areas. Because not very many uprisings had occurred in the Transjordanian territories, the material culture in the Transjordan of the seventh century BCE seems to have been richer than that found in southern Palestine.[3] More work is needed, however, before a clear picture of the different areas during this period on both sides of the Arabah and the Jordan River can emerge.

1. J.R. Bartlett, 'From Edomites to Nabateans: A Study in Continuity', *PEQ* 111 (1979), p. 57. According to A.T. Olmstead, Edom's king was killed in Gaza by Nabuna'id (*History of the Persian Empire* [Chicago, 1948], p. 37). However, the Nabuna'id Chronicle (1.16-22) is too fragmentary to draw that conclusion. The only city mentioned is Shindini, the location of which is unknown; see S. Smith, *Babylonian Historical Texts relating to the Capture and Downfall of Babylon* (London, 1924), pp. 110-11.

2. It was only in the Hellenistic period that this territory experienced a large increase in settlements again; see B. MacDonald, 'The Wâdī el-Ḥasa Survey 1979 and Previous Archaeological Research in Southern Jordan', *BASOR* 254 (1982), pp. 39-40. The depopulation of Edom is seen by J.M. Myers as traceable to 'the convergence of Arab conglomerations which attacked local centers' ('Edom and Judah in the Sixth–Fifth Centuries BCE', *Near Eastern Studies in Honor of W.F. Albright* [ed. H. Goedicke; Baltimore, 1971], p. 381). This could explain the fact that Edomites fled to Judah and that the Edomite Transjordan at many places was devoid of population.

3. Cf. J.A. Sauer, 'Ammon, Moab and Edom', *Biblical Archaeology Today* (ed. J. Amitai; Jerusalem, 1985), pp. 212-14.

Of some interest is the find of a cemetery from the seventh–sixth centuries BCE at Gibeon.[1] It contained single-chambered tombs, some of which had headrests, a phenomenon that is also known from pre-exilic Jerusalem.[2] Some seal impressions from the pool at Gibeon that have been dated to c. 650–550 BCE[3] should also be mentioned. These, the Gibeonite cemetery, and the city of Mizpah (the seat of the Babylonian government) may indicate that the districts north of Jerusalem were areas where most of the remaining Judahites lived. The areas south of Jerusalem were too devastated by the war.

Tell el-Fûl was destroyed in either 597 or 587/586 BCE. The site seems to have been resettled shortly afterwards, because 'huge quantities of pottery from the latter part of the 6th century' have been found.[4] The settlement seems to have been abandoned around 500 BCE, as were Gibeon and Bethel.[5] These abondonments perhaps stem from the Persian policy of not allowing fortified towns to exist without Persian garrisons. The picture of Palestine during the Persian period is one in which settlements were generally not located on the mounds.[6] For Tell el-Fûl, this would mean that the settlement (of Sinclair's 'fortress IVA')[7] was built before the Persian period.

For the Babylonian province of Judah, there is no information about government activities or population density for the period after the murder of Gedaliah. The Babylonians seem to have organized Judah as a subprovince, but what happened after Gedaliah is not clear. Judah

1.   H. Eshel, 'The Late Iron Age Cemetery of Gibeon', *IEJ* 37 (1987), pp. 1-17.

2.   See D. Ussishkin, 'The Necropolis from the Time of the Kingdom of Judah at Silwan, Jerusalem', *BA* 33 (1970), pp. 36-38; A. Mazar, 'Iron Age Burial Caves North of the Damascus Gate, Jerusalem', *IEJ* 26 (1976), pp. 108; G. Barkay and A. Kloner, 'Jerusalem Tombs from the Days of the First Temple', *BARev* 12 (1986), pp. 22-39.

3.   See J.B. Pritchard, 'More Inscribed Jar Handles from El-Jîb', *BASOR* 160 (1960), pp. 2-6; cf. R.L. Cleveland, 'Hebrew Inscriptions and Stamps from Gibeon', *AJA* 64 (1960), p. 87. Similar jar handles have been found at Shechem (str. V) and are dated by G.E. Wright to 'not before the second half of the 6th cent.' (*Shechem*, p. 167, and n. 33, pp. 259-60).

4.   P.W. Lapp, 'Tell el-Fûl', *BA* 28 (1965), p. 6.

5.   J.L. Kelso thinks that Bethel was destroyed either in 553 BCE, when there was a rebellion in Syria against Nabuna'id (cf. *ANET*, p. 305), or during the unstable years of the accession of Darius I (*The Excavation of Bethel*, p. 37).

6.   Cf. J.L. Kelso, *The Excavation of Bethel*, p. 38.

7.   L.A. Sinclair, 'An Archaeological Study of Gibeah', *BA* 27 (1964), p. 60.

may have continued as a governmental district under a military commander. This proposal may be corroborated by settlement of people in the areas around Bethel, Michmash, Ai and Jericho after the return from Babylonia (Ezra 2.27-34). Such activity shows that these former Israelite territories had stayed with Judah during the Babylonian period and were not part of the district of Samerina; instead, they became part of the Persian district of Yehud. These cities may have come under Judah's rule during the reign of Josiah. The failure of the rest of Samerina together with the districts of Duru, Magidu and Gal'aza to be devastated by the Babylonians in 587/586 BCE disproves the theory that Josiah had incorporated these districts into his kingdom. For these areas maintained a continuous population during the Babylonian period and may have experienced population growth during the ensuing Persian period.[1]

Because of a lack of written sources this period is mainly unknown. Archaeologically, the Iron II material culture continued in the territories that had not been devastated. Innovations became more common after Persian rule began to be felt in Palestine. Very little is known about the neo-Babylonians and their influence on the culture of Palestine. Some cities certainly would have housed Babylonian garrisons. Some of the Assyrian and Egyptian garrison cities might have been used by the Babylonians, if they were not razed. For instance, the citadel at Area B at Hazor, stratum III, may have served the Assyrians, the Babylonians and the Persians, if Y. Yadin's dating is reliable (c. 700–400 BCE).[2] Besides Mizpah, Babylonian officials may have been stationed at Samaria, Ashdod, Ashkelon and Gaza. Ashdod, which had been destroyed by Psammetichus I, may have been rebuilt before the Babylonian period. A Babylonian inscription mentions the king of Ashdod, together with the kings of Gaza, Tyre, Sidon and Arvad, among Nebuchadrezzar's court officials.[3] Babylonian troops may also have been stationed in Transjordan at important junctions of the trade route, the 'King's Highway', such as at Rujm el-Malfuf in Amman.[4] Another fortress of some importance was located at Khirbet

---

1. See, for instance, E. Stern, *Material Culture*, p. 9.

2. *Hazor of Those Kingdoms*, pp. 191-92.

3. E. Unger, *Babylon, die heilige Stadt* (Berlin, 1931), pp. 282-94; *ANET*, pp. 307-308.

4. R.S. Boraas, *ADAJ* 16 (1971), pp. 31-45; H.J. Thompson, 'Chronique Archéologique', *RB* 82 (1974), pp. 97-98.

al-Hajjar between Wadi es-Sir and Naur at the junction of the Jordan Valley, where the road goes down into the Wadi Kafrein. There was a settlement in the seventh–sixth centuries BCE with two phases; the fortress phase was built after the sixth century.[1] Aroer, which commanded the access to the north of Wadi Mujib, may, however, have been destroyed by the Babylonians during their campaign in 582 BCE,[2] as was later the capital of Buseira by Nabuna'id. It seems to have been rebuilt again in the mid-sixth century.[3] However, it is possible that Babylonian officials or troops were stationed in the former capital, or that the territories in the southern Transjordan and the Negev were put under the supervision of some Arab chieftain. When Cambyses invaded Egypt in 526, he could, like Esarhaddon before him, rely on the Arabs and their camels to carry the waterskins for the army through the heat and sand of the Sinai. Petra, the later Nabatean capital, was at this time an important watering place for the caravans to and from Arabia and Gaza-Sinai, but it first became a city with the Nabateans.

As in most other cases the artifacts found in the Jordan Valley from the time after 582 BCE are mainly registered as being 'Persian' in date. This is understandable because of the difficulties of exact dating. However, some sites which were not sacked or disturbed by the activities of the Babylonian campaigns may have produced vessels or other objects during the neo-Babylonian period. For instance, a few alabaster bottles dating from the period of the seventh–fourth centuries have been found at Tell el-Mazar in the Jordan Valley, among other places. They seem to be imitations of Egyptian vessels,[4] which may show that an artistic tradition that can be traced back to the Bronze Age had come into vogue again.[5] Other alabaster vessels look Assyrian in form. They were common in the Near East during the seventh–fourth centuries BCE.[6] This only shows that empires disappear but their art can survive.

---

1. H.O. Thompson, *BASOR* 227 (1977), pp. 27-34.

2. Thus Josephus, *Ant.* 10.9.7. See the discussion by E. Olávarri, *RB* 72 (1965), pp. 91-92. The site remained unpopulated until the third c. BCE (*ibid.*).

3. C.-M. Bennett, *Levant* 9 (1977), pp. 3, 9.

4. K. Yassine, *Tell el Mazar*, I, pp. 70-71.

5. According to I. Ben-Dor, alabaster vessels went out of production at the end of the Late Bronze period, but their making was renewed in the Babylonian period ('Palestine Alabaster Vases', *QDAP* 11 [1945], pp. 93-112).

6. See K. Yassine, *Tell el-Mazar*, I, p. 69.

Megiddo, which had been an Assyrian district capital after Tiglath-pileser III had incorporated the Jezreel plain and Galilee as a province of the Assyrian empire, may have been an Egyptian garrison city during the period of the Assyrian decline and Egypt's alliance with Assyria. This status is supported by the information that Pharaoh Necho killed Josiah of Judah at Megiddo, as mentioned above (cf. 2 Kgs 23.29). When Nebuchadrezzar II had established his control over Syria-Palestine after 605 BCE and marched against Egypt in 601 BCE, Megiddo (str. II) may have been destroyed.[1] The site may have been abandoned for some time. A new city (str. I) was not built until the end of the fifth century BCE.[2] In other words, Megiddo did not exist during the Babylonian period. This means that the district capital of the former Assyrian province of Magidu went out of existence. Because Hazor's Area B citadel seems to have been in use at this time, it is conceivable that the Babylonian administration of the province could have been centered at Hazor. What happened to Dor and the province of Duru is impossible to find out. The period after the conquest by Tiglath-pileser III is a 'dark age' in the history of the city and the province. The recent excavations have not yet shown, for instance, whether the city was fortified or not. The Persian period yielded building remains with ashlar construction in header-stretcher patterns—a common feature of Phoenician sites during this period.[3]

Acco's population may have begun to move westwards and settle between the tell (el-Fukhar, located c. 1.5 km inland) and the sea. Tel Megadim, c. 17 km south of Haifa, is another site that was probably built (str. III) during the sixth century BCE. A city with a harbor (str. II) was in existence from the fifth century BCE. Phoenician tombs with evidence of cremation were found outside the city wall on the slope of the tell.[4] It is likely that the Phoenicians had begun to expand their trade and cultural influence inland into Syria-Palestine. Greek pottery

1. The stratigraphy of Megiddo is problematic in this period. Stratum II had no city wall, which may be somewhat uncommon for a garrison city.
2. See the discussion in E. Stern, *Material Culture*, pp. 7-8. The late Iron II pottery found in this stratum is that of the period c. 600–520 BCE, which continued until the Persian forms became common.
3. I. Sharon, 'Phoenician and Greek Ashlar Construction Techniques at Tel Dor, Israel', *BASOR* 267 (1987), pp. 21-41.
4. M. Broshi, 'Tel Megadim', *IEJ* 17 (1967), pp. 277-78; 'Tel Megadim', *IEJ* 18 (1968), pp. 256-57; cf. *idem*, 'Megadim, Tel', *EAEHL*, III, pp. 823-26.

becomes more and more common, and much of it was probably transported by Phoenician merchants.[1] What seems to be clear is that the mountainous districts were not of any great importance to the Babylonians and the Persians. Geographically these territories were located away from the main paths of political and cultural events.

Nebuchadrezzar had managed to rebuild and enlarge the Near Eastern empire of Ashurbanipal, but its duration was short. When Nebuchadrezzar died (562 BCE), a period of instability began in the empire. His successor, Awil-Marduk (Evil-Merodach), had already been ousted in 560 by his son-in-law Neriglissar (559–556 BCE). The last king of this family was Neriglissar's son, Labashi-Marduk, who reigned only three months before being replaced in a revolt by one of Nebuchadrezzar's high officials, Nabuna'id, who usurped the throne and became Babylon's last king (555–539 BCE).[2] Even though Nabuna'id reigned for 17 years, stability did not return.

Nabuna'id was from Harran, the son of a certain Nabu-balatu-iqbi and a priest of the moon-god Sin.[3] He is known to have campaigned in Cilicia and Syria.[4] From the very beginning of his kingship he tried to please the priesthood and get its support. He started to rebuild several temples, some of which had been destroyed by wars. However, he favored the Sin cult, and when for some reason he went to the oasis of Tema in Arabia and took up residence there, he incited the powerful Marduk priests against him, because he did not fulfil his role in the New Year festivals of Marduk. Administrative and military duties were handled by his son, the crown-prince Bēl-šar-uṣur (Belshazzar;[5] cf. Dan. 5.22; 7.1; 8.1).

1. R. Wenning (private communication).

2. Cf. Nabuna'id's inscription (*ANET*, pp. 308-11). See also a fragment of a so-called Dynastic prophecy dealing with the fall of Assyria and the rise and fall of the Babylonian and Persian empires, published by A.K. Grayson, *Babylonian Historical-Literary Texts*, pp. 24-37.

3. See C.J. Gadd, 'The Harran Inscription of Nabonidus', *Anatolian Studies* 8 (1958), pp. 46-92.

4. S. Smith, *Babylonian Historical Records*, pp. 110-11; *ANET*, p. 305.

5. *ANET*, p. 313. For Nabuna'id's rule, cf. R.P. Dougherty, *Nabonidus and Belshazzar: A Study of the Closing Events of the Neo-Babylonian Empire* (Yale Oriental Series, 15; New Haven, 1929). According to Berossus, Cyrus made Nabuna'id a governor in Carmania; see S.M. Burstein, *The Babyloniaca of Berossus*, p. 28. This information from Berossus is supported by the 'Dynastic prophecy'; see A.K. Grayson, *Babylonian Historical-Literary Texts*, p. 25.

Nebuchadrezzar and Nabuna'id have gone down in the historical traditions of the ancient Near East as 'evil' kings. Two inscriptions, the so-called 'Verse Account of Nabona'id'[1] and the 'Cyrus Cylinder'[2] are propagandistic texts. The first was composed by the priests of Marduk with the same goal as that of the 'Cyrus Cylinder', which was to justify the Persian takeover. The priests had to find an excuse for their being the 'fifth column' and based it on the divine will: Marduk had decided it. Nabuna'id was therefore pictured as an 'evil' king. His crime was his ignoring of the Marduk cult. In contrast to Nabuna'id, Cyrus is described as the 'savior' of Babylonia. Even if there were other traditions about Nabuna'id, it may be assumed that the Judahites of the Exile had not only known but also been inspired by the traditions about the 'evil' king and the 'savior' king. Therefore, they saw Cyrus as Yahweh's Servant (Isa. 41) and anointed one, *māšiaḥ*, 'Messiah' (Isa. 45.1).[3]

In later traditions Nebuchadrezzar has also been seen as an 'evil' king. It seems that the tradition about the 'evil' king Nabuna'id 'became caught and confused in a web of hatred against Nebuchadrezzar' in later Jewish traditions, because he devastated and destroyed Jerusalem and Judah.[4] This hatred is expressed, for instance, in Dan. 4.28-30, where Nebuchadrezzar is said to have been 'driven away from people and fed on grass like ox', while his 'nails became like bird's claws'. But with this passage we have left the realm of actual events and entered into the realm of legends, which creates its own history.

---

1. *ANET*, pp. 312-15.

2. A.K. Grayson, 'Mesopotamia', *Papyrus and Tablet* (ed. A.K. Grayson and D.B. Redford; Englewood Cliffs, NJ, 1973), pp. 124-25; *ANET*, pp. 315-16.

3. R.H. Sack, 'Nebuchadrezzar and Nabonidus in Folklore and History', *Mesopotamia* 17 (1982), pp. 72-77.

4. R.H. Sack, *Mesopotamia* 17 (1982), p. 75. Cf. also D.J. Wiseman, *Nebuchadrezzar and Babylon*, pp. 102-103.

Chapter 21

THE PERSIAN PERIOD

Persia and the Near East

In 539 BCE the ancient Near East got a new master, the Persian king of Anshan,[1] Cyrus (Hebrew *Koresh*, Persian *Kurash, Kurush*).[2] As a vassal king of the Medes, Cyrus led a revolt against his overlord and grandfather,[3] king Astyages (585–550 BCE), a son of Cyaxares, took Ecbatana and dethroned Astyages, thus becoming king of the Median empire in 550 BCE.[4] Nabuna'id of Babylon had allied himself with Cyrus early in his reign in order to stem the threat from the Medians. Shortly after Astyages' fall Nabuna'id must have realized that Cyrus could become a greater threat to his kingdom than Astyages. He forged an alliance with Ahmose (Amasis) of Egypt and Croesus (Greek *Kroisos*) of Lydia in order to arrest the Persian threat. Croesus attacked the Persians in order to avenge Astyages, his brother-in-law.[5] Cyrus marched north of Mesopotamia into Anatolia, taking Cilicia, Armenia and Cappadocia. After having captured a city in Anatolia held by Cyrus, the Lydian king returned to Sardis in order to spend the winter preparing for a confrontation and hoping for assistance from the Spartans, Egyptians and Babylonians. Cyrus, however, did not wait for the more pleasant spring weather and instead attacked Croesus's capital, Sardis, in the winter of 546 BCE. That marked the end of the Lydian kingdom. Cyrus then received the submission of the

---

1. For Anshan, see J. Hausman, 'Elamites, Achaemenians and Anshan', *Iran* 10 (1972), pp. 11-124. Concerning the sources for the Persian period, cf. W. Hinz, 'Die Quellen', *Beiträge zur Achämenidengeschichte* (ed. G. Wlaser [Historia: Einzelschriften, 18; Wiesbaden, 1972], pp. 5-14).

2. See W. Eilers, 'The Name of Cyrus', *Acta Iranica* 3 (1974), pp. 3-9.

3. Cyrus' mother was the daughter of Astyages.

4. *ANET*, p. 305.

5. Herodotus 1.73.

Greek city states in Western Asia Minor.[1] According to Herodotus (3.19), Cyprus submitted to the Persians at this time too.

Cyrus was now ready to attack Babylonia proper. It is uncertain whether Cyrus had to deal with other nations before turning against Babylonia, which he did in 540 BCE. He started his attack on Babylonia in the west. Nabuna'id returned to Babylon in order to lead the defense. He also sought the help of all the gods of his nation, ordering their statues to be brought into the capital. However, his actions came too late. Internally, Babylonia was deteriorating. Socio-economic problems, as well as religious and political controversies, benefitted the goals of Cyrus. He was also helped by defectors in the country. The priesthood of Marduk and perhaps part of the population of Babylon had become alienated by Nabuna'id's religious policy and cultic 'misdeeds'. For these groups of people Cyrus became the savior, the restorer of the right order. In the eyes of the priesthood of Marduk Nabuna'id became an evil king.[2] It is thus likely that Persian propaganda that depicted Cyrus as being chosen by Marduk found fertile ground in Babylonia. This propaganda also influenced Deutero-Isaiah.[3] His views about Cyrus may reflect how Cyrus was conceived in pro-Persian circles in Babylonia. In Isa. 41.25 Yahweh says: 'I roused him up from the north, and he has come, from the rising of the sun he calls on my name, he comes on the rulers as on mortar, as a potter he treads clay'. Cyrus is the chosen one, and in 45.1 he is called messiah, the anointed one,[4] whose right hand Yahweh has grasped and strengthened. The old motif of the hand of Yahweh might also have led to associations with the Babylonian enthronement ritual, in which a new king had to grasp the hands of Marduk.

1. G.B. Gray, 'The Foundation and Extension of the Persian Empire', *CAH*, IV, pp. 8-10.

2. This is the background for the hatred expressed in the so-called 'Verse Account of Nabonidus' (*ANET*, pp. 312-15).

3. Isa. 40–48 shows many Persian influences, according to M. Smith. Besides Persian political propaganda there are also some Zoroastrian cosmological concepts known from Yasna 44 ('II Isaiah and the Persians', *JAOS* 83 [1963], pp. 415-21). Cf. also A. Netzer, 'Some Notes on the Characterization of Cyrus the Great in Jewish and Judeo-Persian Writings', *Acta Iranica* 2 (1974), pp. 35-52.

4. D. Baltzer maintains that the use of *māšîaḥ* here is the first example where the concept is separated from the Davidic dynasty, something that must have been shocking for the listeners (*Ezechiel und Deuterojesaja* [BZAW, 121; Berlin, 1971], p. 144). However, in the sixth century BCE *māšîaḥ* still meant, politically, a king.

At Opis on the Tigris the Babylonian army was defeated in Tishri (Sept.–Oct.) 539. Shortly afterwards Sippar was taken without a battle on the fifteenth of Tishri (Oct.). The following day the Babylonian governor of Guitu, Gobryas (Ugbaru), marched with his army into Babylon. When Cyrus entered the city on the third day of the following month of Markhesvan, 'green twigs'[1] were laid in front of him.[2] He had delayed his assault on Babylon for some months, reputedly to carry out an irrigation project. Was this done in order to divert the waters of the Euphrates, making the land more fertile? If so, Cyrus would have presented himself to the Babylonians as the 'good shepherd'.[3] However, this project could have made access to the city easier. This is probably the truth, because no great increase in settlements has been found from this period in the Diyala region.[4]

With the fall of Babylon, the whole Babylonian empire came under the rule of the Persian king. Cyrus was enthroned as a Babylonian king. In the so-called Rassam Cylinder (BM 90920), he presented himself as Marduk's choice and as king of the world, even though he had not conquered Egypt:

> I am Cyrus, king of the world, great king, legitimate king, king of Babylon, king of Sumer and Akkad, king of the four rims (of the earth), son of Cambyses (*ka-am-bu-zi-ia*), great king, king of Anshan, grandson of Cyrus, great king, king of Anshan, descendent of Teispes (*Ši-iš-pi-iš*), great king, king of Anshan, of a family (which) always (exercised) kingship; whose rule Bel and Nebo love, whom they want as king to please their hearts.[5]

The Cyrus Cylinder is literarily a 'typical Mesopotamian building text'.[6] It is a product of an old royal literary tradition touting the king

1. The Akkadian word *ḫaranu* is uncertain; it may mean 'stalks' (cf. *CAD*).
2. A.K. Grayson, *Assyrian and Babylonian Chronicles*, pp. 109-10; cf. *ANET*, p. 306.
3. G.G. Cameron, 'Cyrus the "Father", and Babylonia', *Commémoration Cyrus*. I. *Homage Universal* (Acta Iramica, Ier Série; Leiden, 1974), pp. 45-48. Cameron also refers to Herodotus, who mentions that in an attack of ill temper, Cyrus had his army dig 180 canals on each bank. Supposedly the reason was that one of his horses drowned in the Diyala (Gyndes) River (1.189).
4. Cf. R.M. Adams, *Land behind Baghdad*, p. 60.
5. A.L. Oppenheim, *ANET*, p. 316.
6. J. Harmatta, 'Les modèles littéraires de l'édit babylonien de Cyrus', *Commémoration Cyrus Homages Universel*, I, pp. 29-44; A. Kuhrt, 'The Cyrus Cylinder and Achaemenid Imperial Policy', *JSOT* 25 (1983), p. 88; cf.

as the restorer of peace, the rebuilder of cities and sanctuaries, repatriating both gods and people.[1] Cyrus used this ideology very well. According to the inscription, Marduk had heard the complaints of the people and had become upset over Nabuna'id's handling of his duties, especially his neglect of the cult of Marduk. The god therefore called Cyrus,[2] ordering him to march against Babylon. As usual, the inscription shows that the war was according to the will of a god. When Cyrus had taken Babylon he declared himself its new king.[3] He proclaimed himself the protector of the peoples of the kingdom and announced freedom for the prisoners. After this he gave an order that the gods that had been taken to Babylon as prisoner or those Babylonian gods that Nabuna'id had taken there should be returned to their home cities. Their temples should be restored. Together with the gods, their people were also allowed to return to their countries. Gobryas, who became governor in Babylon, was responsible for sending the gods back. The Nabuna'id Chronicle mentions that Assyrian god statues were sent home between Kislev (Dec.) 539 and Adar (March), 538 BCE.[4] It should be noted that the non-Babylonian deities were gods who had been under Assyrian rule and who were at home in Anatolia, Assyria and Iran. No gods from the territories of Syria-Palestine are mentioned! This explains why the exiled Judahites were not part of this exodus. As far as is known, Yahweh was not a

H.M. Barstad, 'On the So-Called Babylonian Literary Influence in Second Isaiah', *SJOT* 2 (1987), pp. 90-110. For the text, see also F.H. Weissbach, *Die Keilinschriften der Achämeniden* (VAB, 3; Leipzig, 1911), pp. 2-4; W. Eilers, 'Der Keilschrifttext des Kyros-Zylinders', *Festgabe deutscher Iranisten zur 2500 Jahrfeier Irans* (ed. W. Eilers *et al.*; Stuttgart, 1971), pp. 156-66.

1. Cf. J. van der Spek, 'Did Cyrus the Great Introduce a New Policy toward Subdued Nations? Cyrus in Assyrian Perspective', *Persica* 10 (1982), pp. 278-83; J.H. Hayes in Miller and Hayes, *A History of Ancient Israel and Judah*, pp. 440-41.

2. This is the parallel to Isa. 41.25, where Yahweh is said to have called Cyrus. M. Smith thinks that the first half of the Cyrus inscription was inspired by the propaganda of the Marduk priests before the city fell. The second half would have been 'composed after Cyrus' conquest of the city'. II Isaiah has 'almost no parallels to the second part of the inscription' (*JAOS* 83 [1963], p. 417).

3. For his titles 'King of Babylon, King of Lands', see W.H. Shea, 'A Vassal King of Babylon', *AUSS* 9 (1971), pp. 51-67, 99-128, and 10 (1972), pp. 88-118, and 146-77. Shea concludes that Gubaru (Ugbaru) was enthroned as vassal king of Babylon in the spring of 538 BCE, but that he died soon thereafter, on October 26th, 538.

4. *ANET*, p. 306.

prisoner in the form of a statue in Babylonia. Thus, the decree of Cyrus could not concern him or his exiled people. Did the exiled people from Judah negotiate with the new government by referring to the words of the Cyrus Inscription about peace on earth, the release of prisoners (cf. Isa. 42.7), and the rebuilding of sanctuaries? If so, the so-called decree of Cyrus in Ezra 6.3-5 could be seen to be a result of these contacts.[1] It is noticeable that this decree does not mention anything about a return of exiles from Babylonia to Judah, nor does Ezra 1.2-4 specifically state it. It is primarily concerned with the rebuilding of the temple. The Persian policy was to allow subdued peoples to repair their temples and keep their cultic laws as long as these did not contradict the laws of the Persians. This being the case, it might be suggested that the content of Cyrus's decree was not only directed to the exiled Judahites, but also included the people of Judah, who had never been deported. Cyrus had 'been given' the kingship over 'all the countries' by Marduk,[2] which becomes in Ezra 1.2 'by Yahweh'.[3] From this it follows that all the people of Judah had been given permission to rebuild the temple. Ezra 1.3 indicates that all (*kōl*) of Yahweh's people received the right to be part of the rebuilding of the temple. In this way the Persian king had acknowledged Judah and its people as a 'nation', which would be able to carry on its national religion as before, albeit now under Persian rule and supervision. The king would certainly not have conceived of the possibility that only a particular group of Yahweh's people were meant. If this is right, the returnees had usurped the right given to the people of Judah. Naturally, conflicts and antagonism resulted.

It may be wondered why the Israelites deported by Sargon II in 720 BCE did not try to use the edict of Cyrus to return to Israel-Samerina. Part of the answer depends on how integrated they had become in the places where they were settled, something that is not known. The main reason is that they were not part of Yahweh's people of Jerusalem and that they did not have a temple to rebuild. Samaria was not destroyed by Sargon. After its capture it was rebuilt by the Assyrians. Whatever

---

1. R. de Vaux sees in Ezra 6 'two key texts for the historicity of the Jewish restoration' ('The Decree of Cyrus and Darius on the Rebuilding of the Temple', *The Bible and Ancient the Near East*, p. 96).

2. *ANET*, p. 315.

3. The decree is understandably rephrased in the Book of Ezra; cf. J.M. Myers, *Ezra, Nehemiah* (AB, 14; Garden City, NY, 1965), p. 7.

sanctuary there was in the city was thus intact. It should also be remembered that the decree of Cyrus did not mention any Syro-Palestinian gods and/or temples. It is also possible to speculate that the descendants of the exiled Israelites most likely had become assimilated to life in Assyria and Elam. After 180 years, attachment to their original homeland was not as fresh as was that of the Judahites in Babylonia. Cyrus's edict was not meant to undo the Assyrian deportations. Sending home the gods was an act of creating peace and stable conditions in the new empire. The act was in itself nothing new. The phenomenon of deported peoples and their gods being allowed to return to their homelands is also known from royal Assyrian inscriptions.[1]

The policy of allowing foreign peoples in Babylonia to return to their homelands was continued by Darius I. The Babylonians had made it possible for the exiled peoples to maintain their ethnic identity and build their own settlements, thus reversing the 'Assyrianization' policy of the Assyrian kings. For instance, the Babylonian documents found during 1926–27 at Neirab in northern Syria indicate that exiled people from Syria living in a Babylonian settlement also called Neirab had returned to their home town.[2]

Cyrus died in 530 during a campaign in the northeast against the Massagetai, probably in the area of the Jaxartes River and the Aral Sea.[3] He was succeeded by his son Cambyses (530–522 BCE). Palestine does not come into the historical picture during his reign except when Cambyses had to march through it on his way to conquer Egypt in 526.[4] In this connection he must have secured the support of the Phoenicians and their fleet.[5] Pharaoh Amasis died before Cambyses

---

1. See G. Widengren, 'Yahweh's Gathering of the Dispersed', *In the Shelter of Elyon* (ed. W. Boyd Barrick and J.R. Spencer), pp. 227-45.

2. I. Eph'al, 'The Western Minorities in Babylonia in the 6th–5th Centuries BCE: Maintenance and Cohesion', *Or* NS 47 (1978), pp. 84-90. For the documents, see F.M. Fales, 'Remarks on the Neirab Texts', *OrAnt* 12 (1973), pp. 131-42. The dates of the documents are from c. 560 to 521 BCE.

3. Thus Herodotus 1.201, where he calls the river Araxes; see the discussion in J.M. Cook, *The Persian Empire*, pp. 36-37.

4. Herodotus says that the road went from Phoenicia 'as far as the borders of the city of Cadytis' (i.e. Gaza), 'which belongs to the Syrians of Palestine, as it is called'. South of Gaza the territory belonged to the Arabs (3.5, 7-9). This shows that the name Palestine is older than the writings of Herodotus.

5. H.T. Wallinga sees Cambyses as the creator of the Persian navy ('The Ionian

reached Egypt. His successor was Psammetichus III (526–525 BCE). The Persian success was probably bolstered when Phanes, the commander of the Greek mercenaries, sided with the Persians. Cambyses, like Esarhaddon, also secured the support of an Arab chieftain who supplied camels with waterskins to follow the army through the Sinai.[1] A Phoenician fleet sailed to the Nile. In addition, Cambyses received the support of Udjahoresenet,[2] a priest of the goddess Neith and the commander of the Egyptian fleet. The battle at the mouth of the Nile (the Pelusiac Branch) was a disaster for Psammetichus, who fled to Memphis but was defeated and killed there. Cambyses was now king over Egypt and was crowned in Sais. This shows that he considered himself as a successor to the Saitic pharaohs and not to Amasis and his son Psammetichus.[3] He thanked Udjahoresenet by making him his chief *medicus* and appointing him high priest. Udjahoresenet could then purge the temple of Neith of foreigners and rededicate it. At the same time, its revenues were secured for the Persians.[4] Later on Udjahoresenet was in Elam with Darius, who also found him cooperative. He was sent back to Sais to restore the religious and administrative establishment of the 'House of Life'. In his capacity as chief physician he had to instruct others, and he started a school within the 'House of Life' for that purpose.[5]

Revolt', *Mnemosyne* 37 [1984], p. 407). Cf. H. Hauben, 'The King of the Sidonians and the Persian Imperial Fleet', *Ancient Society* 1 (1970), pp. 1-8.

1. Perhaps this is the reason why the Arabs did not pay tribute, but rather gave a yearly gift of frankincense to the Persians; cf. Herodotus 3.4-9, 97. See I. Eph'al, who suggests that the Arabs had to give this annual gift in exchange for the 'privilege of collecting duty for spices' (*The Ancient Arabs*, p. 210).

2. For his inscription, see G. Roeder, *Die Ägyptische Götterwelt* (Stuttgart, 1959), pp. 75-76; M. Lichtheim, *Ancient Egyptian Literature*, III (Berkeley, CA, 1980), pp. 37-38.

3. With Cambyses begins the Twenty-Seventh Dynasty of Egypt.

4. Concerning the campaign in Egypt, cf. Herodotus 3.1-38. According to a text from Elephantine, however, Cambyses destroyed some other temples in Egypt, but not that of the Judahite colony at Elephantine (A.E. Cowley, *Aramaic Papyri from the Fifth Century* BCE [Oxford, 1923], text 30, ll. 13-14). When writing about Cambyses, Herodotus seems to have been inspired by the hostility of the Egyptians to the Persian king. For a nuanced picture, see K.M.T. Atkinson, 'The Legitimacy of Cambyses and Darius as Kings of Egypt', *JAOS* 76 (1956), pp. 167-77. For Cambyses in Egypt, see also E. Bresciani, 'The Persian Occupation of Egypt', *Cambridge History of Iran*, II (ed. I. Gershevitch; Cambridge, 1985), pp. 502-507.

5. G. Roeder, *Die Ägyptische Götterwelt*, pp. 85-86.

Cambyses was probably not very well liked in Persian court circles.[1] When he was in Syria on his way home in 522 BCE, he learned about a rebellion by his brother Bardiya (Smerdis).[2] Darius says, however, in his Behistun inscription[3] that the usurper was a certain Gaumata, one of the Magi,[4] who pretended to be Cambyses' brother Bardiya but whom Cambyses murdered in secret.[5] This may be Darius' way of declaring himself innocent of Bardiya's death. Cambyses reputedly died shortly afterwards because of an accident that occurred when he too eagerly mounted his horse.[6] Darius, who was of Achaemenid descent but not close to the throne, became king with the support of the 'seven', a group of top officials.[7]

The ascension of Darius I (522–486 BCE) to the throne did not end the troubles, which may mean that his legitimacy was questioned. According to the Behistun inscription, rebellions broke out in Media, Persia, Elam, Babylonia, Parthia, Scythia and Egypt. There is no mention, however, of any uprising in Syria-Palestine. This time of

1. Cf. Herodotus 3.89.
2. Bardiya reigned from April 14 to September 20, 522 BCE, according to M.A. Dandamayev, in a review of D. Cocquerillat, *Palmerais et cultures de l'Eanna d'Uruk [559–520]* (1968), *OLZ* 67 (1972), p. 551.
3. This is a trilingual inscription: Elamite, Akkadian and Old Persian; see E.N. von Voightlander, *The Bihistun Inscription of Darius the Great, Babylonian Version* (Corpus Inscriptionum Iranicarum, 1; London, 1978); cf. J.M. Cook, *The Persian Empire*, pp. 67-69; R. Borger and W. Hinz, 'Die Behistun-Inschrift Darius' des Grossen', *Texte aus der Umwelt des Alten Testaments*, IV (ed. O. Kaiser; Gütersloh, 1984), pp. 419-50; cf. F.H. Weissbach, *Die Keilschriften der Achämeniden*, §§10-13. As to the relief, see A. Farkas, 'The Behistun Relief', *Cambridge History of Iran*, II (ed. I. Gershevitch; Cambridge, 1985), pp. 828-31. An Aramaic version of the inscription was found at Elephantine; see A.E. Cowley, *Aramaic Papyri*, texts 251-59; J.C. Greenfield and B. Porten, *The Bihistun Inscription of Darius the Great, Aramaic Version* (Corpus Inscriptionum Iranicarum; London, 1982).
4. The Magi were a priestly clan from Media; cf. H.S. Nyberg, *Die Religionen des alten Iran* (trans. H.H. Schaeder; MVÄG, 43; Leipzig, 1938), p. 336.
5. Cf. J. Wieshofer, *Der Aufstand Gaumatas und die Anfange Dareios' I* (Münster, 1978).
6. See the discussion in M.A. Dandamayev, *Persien unter den ersten Achämeniden (6th Jhdt v. Chr.)* (trans. H.-D. Pohl; Beiträge zum Iranistik, 8; Wiesbaden, 1976), pp. 148-49.
7. See F. Geschnitzer, *Die sieben Perser und das Königtum Dareios* (Beiträge zur Achaimenidengeschichte und zur Herodotanalyse; Heidelberg, 1977).

political instability may have encouraged some of the Judahites of Babylonia to move back to the less dangerous hills of Judah.[1]

Babylon was one of the centers of the rebellion. Nidintu-Bel, a son of Nabuna'id, was made king in 522 BCE after Bardiya's death, and ruled as Nebuchadrezzar III. After he was killed by Darius in 521, another rebel, Nebuchadrezzar IV, arose but was eliminated a few months later.[2] Herodotus mentions that Darius broke down the walls of the city and impaled about 3000 of its leading citizens.[3]

Darius managed to use his forces well and expediently. The rebellions were put down in a few years, leaving the prophecy in Hag. 2.22 unfulfilled. Haggai had given an oracle to the *peḥâ* who had been appointed for Judah,[4] Zerubbabel (Zērbābili), that Yahweh would overthrow 'the throne of the kingdoms' and make Zerubbabel 'like a signet ring, for I have chosen you'. The last phrase can be seen as a royal epithet. Zerubbabel was to restore the kingdom of Judah. The Book of Haggai ends with this prophecy and it is likely that Haggai's career as a prophet had also come to an end. Neither he nor Zerubbabel are heard of any more. Darius went to Egypt, usually dated to 518–517,[5] where he put down a rebellion by the satrap Aryandes, and it is possible that the expectations among the returnees about Zerubbabel's elevation to kingship may have come to an end at that time. Zerubbabel may have been dismissed from office or executed. The investiture of the high priest Joshua in Zechariah 3 indicates that Zerubbabel was no longer in command. Zech. 6.9-14 has to be seen in the same light. The term 'branch', which is a royal epithet, is here used for the high priest Joshua. The crown must have been made for

1. Cf. J.H. Hayes in Miller and Hayes, *A History of Ancient Israel and Judah*, p. 447.

2. G.B. Gray and M. Cary, 'The Reign of Darius', *CAH*, IV, pp. 177, 180.

3. Herodotus 3.159.

4. The date of Zerubbabel's appointment is not known. Cf. the discussion in H.W. Wolff, *Dodekapropheton. VI. Haggai* (BKAT, 16.6; Neukirchen, 1986), pp. 50-58. The Hebrew *peḥâ* is equivalent to the Akkadian *bēl pīḥāti*, 'lord of the district, governor', which could be used for both satraps and district governors, *pīḥātu* meaning 'region, district, province'; cf. W. von Soden, *AHw*, II, p. 862; J.A. Brinkman, *A Political History of Post-Kassite Babylonia*, pp. 303-304. For a discussion of the biblical term, cf. A. Alt, *KS*, II, p. 333 n. 2; S.E. McEvenue, 'The Political Structure in Judah from Cyrus to Nehemiah', *CBQ* 433 (1981), pp. 353-64.

5. E. Bresciani dates this to after 510 BCE ('The Persian Occupation of Egypt', *Cambridge History of Iran*, II [ed. I. Gershevitch], p. 507).

Zerubbabel, but because he was no longer in command the high priest came to fill his place. Not to make things too bad, the narrator avoided mentioning Zerubbabel's name and the political mistake by the leaders of Judah.

The administrative organization of the empire into satrapies (provinces) started under Cyrus. The Behistun inscription mentions 22, but Herodotus (3.89-97) mentions 20 satrapies.[1] The lands mentioned in the Behistun inscription do not need to be the same as the satrapies. A reorganization may have occurred after the rebellion had been put down.[2] What is of interest here is the fifth satrapy, Babylonia-Abr Nahara. Palestine was part of this satrapy,[3] which included Mesopotamia and the Babylonian holdings west of the Euphrates (see Map 23).[4] Cyprus was also included in this satrapy. As in Phoenicia, the Persians did not abolish kingship in Cyprus.

The Persian king often appointed as satraps a member of the country's royal family or some high official well acquainted with the administration and laws of the former nation.[5] The king could also appoint a special commissioner or 'sub-governor' for a certain district, something that happened for Judah. Zerubbabel is an example, and so are Ezra and Nehemiah. The last two were officials in the

1. See E. Herzfeld, *The Persian Empire: Studies, Geography and Ethnography of the Ancient Near East* (posthumously ed. by G. Walser; Wiesbaden, 1968), pp. 288-349; G.G. Cameron, 'The Persian Satrapies and Related Matters', *JNES* 32 (1973), pp. 47-56.

2. For this problem, see J.M. Cook, who says that 'there is considerable internal support for Herodotus' satrapy list; his army list is not to be brushed aside' (*The Persian Empire*, p. 80). As to the history of the satrap division, see M.A. Dandamayev, 'Politische und wirtschafliche Geschichte', *Beiträge zur Achämenidengeschichte* (ed. G. Walser; Historia: Einzelschriften, 18; Wiesbaden, 1972), pp. 20-25.

3. The name is known from neo-Assyrian inscriptions (Tiglath-pileser III) as referring to the territories west of the Euphrates (in Akk. *eber nāri*, Aram. *ᶜabar naháʳrā*, Heb. *ᶜēber hannāhār*). In Greek it occurs as '*koile* Syria' or 'Syria and Phoenicia'. Coele-Syria refers originally to the area between Lebanon and Anti-Lebanon, *koile* meaning 'hollow, a hollow'.

4. This satrapy was probably split in two (Babylonia and 'Beyond the River') between 515 and 503; see M.W. Stolper, 'Bēlšunu the Satrap', *Language, Literature, and History* (Festschrift E. Reiner; ed. F. Rochberg-Halton; AOS, 67; New Haven, 1987), p. 396.

5. For the titles of some of the high officials under the satrap, see M.A. Dandamayev, 'Politische Geschichte', *Beiträge zur Achämenidengeschichte* (ed. G. Walser), p. 37.

service of the Persians before they came to Jerusalem. This has to be emphasized. They were not of the local population of Jerusalem or Judah. They were educated in the Exile and were sent as Persian representatives to Jerusalem. This has to be remembered in order to understand the conflicts that the Jerusalemites faced after these two men took over the supervision of the society.

Palestine and its People in the Persian Period

The picture derived from the biblical material about Palestine and its history in this period is very condensed and incomplete, and the Persian texts do not shed any extra light in this respect. Besides Chronicles, Ezra and Nehemiah, some prophetical books also contribute to our knowledge of the sub-province of Judah (Yehud) in this period, especially concerning the religious situation. These are the books of Haggai, Zechariah, Joel and Malachi. In addition, it must be remembered that most of the books of the Bible were composed in their present form during the postexilic period. This means that the problems of the Persian period have colored the presentation of past events, something that is also evident in the books of the Chronicler. Other sources to mention are, for instance, the Wadi Daliyeh papyri, the Elephantine papyri, Pseudo-Scylax,[1] Josephus, certain information from Herodotus and Diodorus Siculus, ostraca, coins, seals, and other finds from archaeological excavations.

The books of the Hebrew Bible are primarily concerned with the problems of Judah and the restoration of the new Jewish community. Other groups of people come into the picture only as disturbing elements, who really should not have been there.[2] This is the attitude of Ezra and Nehemiah. Not even the Judahites who had never been in Babylonia are accepted by the writers of these books. Thus, historical reality is not the purpose of these books. They are rather concerned with what should have happened. Ideology has steered the composition.

The country was populated by different groups of people who had lost their national identity, such as the Philistines, Judahites, Samarians (including former Israelites and peoples that had been settled in

---

1. See, for instance, K. Galling, *Studien zur Geschichte Israels im persischen Zeitalter*, pp. 185-210.
2. See S. Japhet, 'People and Land', *Das Land Israel in biblischer Zeit* (ed. G. Strecker), p. 113.

Samerina by the Assyrians), Moabites, Ammonites, Edomites, Arabs, and in the western and northern parts of the country the Phoenicians, who had become more and more influential. No source material gives a clear picture of the Persian administration of the land. The borders between the different districts may have been about the same as those of the former kingdoms. Because the Persians took over the Babylonian empire with all its holdings and did not need to campaign in all these territories, it may be concluded that the province division that was in existence continued as subprovinces in the satrapies. The Aramaic term for province is $m^e d\hat{\imath}n\hat{a}$, which also occurs in the Bible. The term $m^e d\hat{\imath}n\hat{a}$ was in imperial Aramaic used for a region under Persian jurisdiction.[1] A $m^e d\hat{\imath}n\hat{a}$ could be divided into several smaller districts, $p^e l\bar{a}k\hat{\imath}m$. However, there is no clear information about the administration of the different provinces and their districts. Ashdod, Ashkelon, Samerina, Haurina, Qarnini and Gal'aza (?)[2] may have been governed as they were during the earlier period.[3] As mentioned above, Megiddo did not exist during the Neo-Babylonian period.[4] Thus, the district of Magidu may have been split up. The Jezreel plain and southern Galilee may have come under Phoenician rule and the rest of Galilee could have been administered from Hazor as a provincial district (*pelek*).[5] Pottery and coins from the coast through the plain and up to northern Galilee are, however, very much in the Phoenician tradition.[6]

There is no information about the Ammonite territory besides the mention of Tobiah, 'the Ammonite servant' in Neh. 2.19 and 3.35 (4.3). This has led scholars to assume that Tobiah was the district

1. The term is also used in 1 Kgs. 20.14-19 to refer to administrative districts. This does not mean that the districts were so designated at the time of Ahab. The later writer has used the terminology of his own time.

2. The province of Gal'aza (the former Gilead) seems to have had almost no settlements during the Persian period according to S. Mittmann (*Beiträge*, p. 246); cf. below.

3. A. Alt thinks that Samerina and Galilee were separate districts during the Persian period ('Galiläische Probleme', *PJ* 34 [1938], pp. 90-92) (= *KS*, II, pp. 404-406); cf. M. Avi-Yonah, *The Holy Land*, p. 25.

4. The last city (str. I) was built at the end of the fifth century BCE; cf. E. Stern, *Material Culture*, pp. 7-8.

5. Cf. M. Avi-Yonah, *The Holy Land*, p. 25.

6. See E. Stern, *Material Culture*, p. 240.

governor of Ammon.[1] This is doubtful. Tobiah is a Yahwistic name.[2] He may have been a descendant of the Judahites who had taken refuge in Transjordan after the Babylonian destruction of Judah (Jer. 41.15), and he may have become one of their leaders. Whether he was also the Persian *peḥâ* in Ammon cannot be decided, but the term *'ebed*, 'servant, slave', indicates that he was a high official. He could possibly have been a Persian official over the Judahites in Transjordan and as such subordinate to the *peḥâ* of Judah. How else could he have a special storeroom in the Jerusalemite temple (Neh. 13.4-5)?[3] This means that he must have been an employee of the temple, and as such was one of the leaders opposing Nehemiah's policies. Neh. 6.17-19 mentions that many of the nobles of Jerusalem and Judah had sworn an allegiance to Tobiah. Both he and his son Johanan were related by marriage to Jerusalemite families (6.18). Thus, Tobiah emerges as the leader of a party, including Judahites in Transjordan. Because Nehemiah's rebuilding of Jerusalem was part of a policy to protect and reorganize the descendants of the exiles, the people of the captivity, these Transjordanian Judahites and others opposed his activities in the interests of self-preservation.[4] The *gôlâ* party, which can now be

---

1. A. Alt, 'Judas Nachbarn zur Zeit Nehemias', *PJ* 27 (1931), p. 70 (= *KS*, II, p. 341); K. Galling, *Studien zur Geschichte Israels im persischen Zeitalter*, p. 47; J. Bright, *A History of Israel* (3rd edn), p. 382; S. Herrmann, *A History of Israel in Old Testament Times* (2nd edn), p. 312.

2. F.C. Fensham labels him a 'heathen' (*The Books of Ezra and Nehemiah* [NICOT; Grand Rapids, MI, 1982], p. 261).

3. B. Mazar has associated Tobiah with 'Araq el-Emîr ('Tyros' of Josephus, *Ant.* 12.4.11) 17 km west of Amman, and with the burial cave close to it with the inscription *ṭbh*, which he dates to the fifth cent. BCE. He sees this territory as the 'Land of Tobiah' (*IEJ* 7 [1957], pp. 137-45, and 229-38); cf. P. Schäfer, who (following Josephus) identifies 'Araq el-Emîr with Hyrcanus of the Tobiah family ('The Hellenistic and Maccabean Periods', *Israelite and Judean History* (ed. J.H. Hayes and J.M. Miller; Philadelphia, 1977), p. 550. F.M. Cross dates the inscription to the fourth–third c. BCE ('The Development of the Jewish Scripts', *The Bible and the Ancient Near East* [ed. G.E. Wright; Garden City, NY, 1961], p. 248 n. 13, and p. 253 n. 75); cf. J. Naveh, *The Development of the Aramaic Script* (Jerusalem, 1970), pp. 62-64. For the excavations, see P.W. Lapp, 'The 1961 Excavations at 'Araq el-Emîr', *ADAJ* 6-7 (1962), pp. 8-89; *idem*, 'The 1962 Excavations at 'Araq el-Emîr', *ADAJ* 10 (1965), pp. 37-42.

4. Cf. W. Rudolph, *Esra und Nehemia samt 3. Esra* (HAT, 20; Tübingen, 1949), p. 139.

called the Jewish party, was perceived as a danger to the non-exiled people's identity.

In southern Transjordan the Moabite and Edomite territories may have seen an increase in nomadic life-style, while southern Judah became mainly Edomite territory. Nehemiah 3 shows that the territory south of Beth-Zur did not belong to the subprovince of Judah (see Map 24). This was now more than ever Edomite territory, later called Idumaea. This term appears first in Diodorus Siculus (19.95.2), but may very well have been in use earlier.[1]

It is impossible to outline the borders of the Phoenician city states and their spheres of interest, but the Acco plain and western Galilee may have been under the rule of Tyre. The sarcophagus of the Sidonian king Eshmunazar (fifth century)[2] reports that, thanks to the support of his fleet, the coast south of Carmel, including the cities of Dor and Joppa, 'the mighty lands of Dagon' in the Sharon Plain were added to Eshmunazar's supervision by the Persian king, probably Artaxerxes I. Ashkelon became a Phoenician city during this period. Gaza was not controlled by the Phoenicians, but seems to have been part of the Arab economic sphere of interest,[3] as were the Negev and southern Transjordan.[4] What the southern borders of the empire were is not really known, but its territory stretched from southern and eastern Transjordan through the Negev and the northern Sinai into the eastern Delta.

According to Herodotus (3.9), the Arab territory did not count as a part of the satrapy, and therefore, the Arabs did not have to pay tribute. As friends they had to 'give gifts'. This may indicate that the Arabs were more independent than other people in the satrapy. As indicated by the biblical material (Neh. 2.19; 4.1-3; 6.1-2, 6) and from ostraca found at Arad and Beer-Sheba in the Negev, southern Palestine experienced a steady increase in Edomites and Arabs after the fall of

---

1. Cf. I. Eph'al, *The Ancient Arabs*, pp. 198-99.

2. H. Donner and W. Röllig, *KAI*, text 14.18-20. A temple to the god Eshmun of Sidon was built in Joppa; see E. Stern, *Excavations at Tel Mevorakh Part One* (Qedem, 9; Jerusalem, 1978), p. 80.

3. On this, see the discussion in J. Elayi, 'Studies in Phoenician Geography during the Persian Period', *JNES* 41 (1982), p. 104; cf. also M. Avi-Yonah, *The Holy Land*, p. 31.

4. See E. Stern, *Material Culture*, pp. 239-40.

the kingdom of Edom. Some of the ostraca show Arab and Edomite names.[1]

The Persian period in Palestine witnessed an increase in Phoenician culture, especially in the western parts of Palestine. This can be demonstrated not only by the pottery, but also by the remains of houses. In the coastal areas as well as inland, houses containing piers of ashlar masonry with rough uncut stones[2] in between them have been found; this technique is also known from the Bible (Ezra 5.8). This type of building spread to north Africa and other Phoenician colonies in the west. It is also known from the MB–LB periods from sites in the northern Levant (Ugarit) and from Iron Age Phoenicia, as well as from a few sites in Israel, such as Bethel. In the Persian period it not only became common at most sites on the coast, but it also spread inland, for example, to Beth-Shemesh, the Hebron hills (Khirbet Abu Twain), and to the Negev (Ramat Maṭred). With the Phoenician expansion in the West, this type of construction became common in North Africa during the Punic and the Roman periods.[3]

The cultural impact of the Phoenicians can also bee seen in the many figurines that have been found in excavations at, for instance, Tell Ṣippor, Tel 'Erani, Tell Makmish (Tel Michal), Tell Abū Hawām, Akhziv, Tell ed-Duweir, Tell eṣ-Ṣafi and Maresha. Tell Ṣippor yielded a pit with over 200 terracotta figurines, 20 statuettes of stone, and a head of the so-called Silenus face. Some of the terracotta figurines and statuettes show western features (from Cyprus, Rhodes, the Aegean, Greece, Ionia); others 'combine Mesopotamian and Egyptian with Syro-Palestinian and Persian-Phoenician elements'. They are mainly imports (by the Phoenicians?), and date from the late-sixth through the mid-fourth centuries BCE.[4]

1. J. Naveh, 'The Aramaic Ostraca from Tel Beer-Sheba', *Tel Aviv* 6 (1979), pp. 182-198.

2. A. Ben-Tor, Y. Portugali and M. Avisar, 'The Third and Fourth Seasons of Excavations at Tel Yokne'am, 1979 and 1981', *IEJ* 33 (1983), p. 33.

3. G. W. and O. Van Beek, *EI* 15 (1981), pp. 70*-77*. The *'eben gᵉlāl*, 'round stone', that is mentioned in Ezra 5.8 may refer to this building technique.

4. The pit is termed a 'favissa' by the excavator. However, no sanctuary was found; see O. Negbi, 'A Deposit of Terracottas and Statuettes from Tel Ṣippor', *'Atiqot* 6 (1966), pp. 6-9, and p. 19 and pl. XII.84 for the 'Silenus' head; Silenus was a companion of Dionysos, a native of Phrygia, always drunk. Originally he was a personification of springs, later confused with the satyrs. Cf. E. Stern, 'Phoenician Masks and Pendants', *PEQ* 108 (1976), pp. 109-18.

At Makmish (Tel Michal) a building that has been labeled a sanctuary was found in the sand dunes. Among the finds was an incense altar. Outside the building there were limestone altars and other objects such as figures and semiprecious stones. N. Avigad has associated the building/temple with a Phoenician colony.[1] After a hiatus during the late Iron II period the site seems to have been rebuilt in the early fifth century. Z. Herzog has concluded that it was built when this part of the coast came under the rule of Sidon's king Eshmunazar.[2] Since the Phoenicians were merchants, it is to be expected that their trade would have included not only most of Palestine, but that they also would have established colonies in some cities.[3] Phoenician coins have been found at Beth-Yerah, Megiddo, Samaria, Gezer, Tell ed-Duweir, Beth-Zur, and in Wadi Daliyeh, among other places.[4]

Remains in the coastal area have led some to conclude that Persian influences were more pronounced here than inland. This is to be expected because the coastal area was most important for the Persians. Inland Palestine did not play any significant political or economic role, where grazing, agriculture and horticulture may have primarily served the local population. However, all the Persian objects found in tombs, sanctuaries and favissae along the coast may simply imply that Persian culture had become the fad of the time. Greeks, Phoenicians and Palestinians could have been buried in the tombs, for example. Only an investigation of the skeletal remains would give precise information. What seems to be a Persian feature, however, is the presence of the cist tombs, of which a few have been found in Palestine.[5] This type of burial was more common in the eastern part of the empire than in Syria-Palestine,[6] which may indicate that it was

1. 'Excavations at Makmish, 1958', *IEJ* 10 (1960), pp. 90-96.

2. Z. Herzog *et al.*, 'Excavations at Tel Michal 1978–1979', *Tel Aviv* 7 (1980), p. 143.

3. Josephus, for instance, mentions a Phoenican colony in Samaria (*Ant.* 11.8.6).

4. See J. Elayi, *JNES* 41 (1982), p. 109, and fig. 3.

5. Some have been found in strata II and I at Megiddo (on the SE slope of the tell). They may be Persian. However, no objects from this period were found in them; instead there was some Roman pottery; see P.L.O. Guy, *Megiddo Tombs* (OIP, 33; Chicago, 1938), pp. 129-34. The pottery could be intrusive.

6. P.R.S. Moorey, *Cemeteries of the First Millennium BCE at Deve Hüyük* (BAR, 87; Oxford, 1980), p. 9. Cf. W. Culican, *The Medes and the Persians*

Persian inspired. Whether the tombs in the west were for Persian officials may be disputed, but if they were, some of these officials may have been indigenous to the country.[1]

The Phoenicians had gained a special status and were treated in a different way, politically, than other peoples. Their city-states (Tyre, Sidon, Byblos and Aradus) were allowed the status of semi-independent nations with their own kings. The hostilities and rebellions that later occurred in these nations primarily resulted from the intrigues and rivalry of the international political drama. The Phoenician states with their fleets were of vital interest to the non-seafaring Persians in their wars with Greece and Egypt. The special status held by the Phoenicians is also reflected in the fact that their cities were walled. The archaeology of the early Persian period supports the theory that the Persian government did not allow large fortified cities to be built, since they could be understood to represent preparation for rebellion. This policy may explain the problems that the Jerusalemite colony experienced when it started to rebuild the temple and the city walls. J. Kelso assumes that this Persian policy is one of the reasons why so many settlements of this period have been found on low ground.[2] However, it should be noted that the Phoenicians controlled most of the coast, so that it was in the interest of the Persians to have this economically and strategically vital part of the Levant well protected against raids by the Greeks. This may be the reason why some of the cities on the coast or in the Shephelah were fortified.

Tell el-Ḥesi, for instance, was well-fortified in the Persian period.[3] A certain type of the so-called Bes vessels has been found both at Ḥesi and at Tell Jemme. It seems to be of Edomite origin and to have had military connections. The use of this type of vessel by Persian troops[4]

(London, 1966), pp. 146-47; E. Stern, *Material Culture*, pp. 82-86.

1. Three Persian bronze objects were found during some construction work at Khirbet Ibsan in Galilee (SW of the southern end of Lake Tiberias). R. Amiran has assumed that they were 'part of the furniture of the tomb' even if the tomb was not found ('Achaemenian Bronze Objects from a Tomb at Kh. Ibsan in Lower Galilee', *Levant* 4 [1972], p. 135).

2. *The Excavations of Bethel*, p. 38.

3. See L.E. Toombs, 'Tel el-Hesi, 1970–71', *PEQ* 106 (1974), pp. 24-26.

4. J.A. Blakely and F.L. Horton, 'South Palestinian Bes Vessels of the Persian Period', *Levant* 18 (1986), pp. 111-19; cf. P.R.S. Moorey, 'Iranian Troops at Deve Hüyük in Syria in the Earlier Fifth Century BCE', *Levant* 7 (1975), pp. 108-17. See also V. Wilson, 'The Iconography of Bes with Particular Reference to the Cypriote

is probably the explanation for the discovery of this type of jar at Deve Hüyük in northwestern Syria together with other objects used by the military.

The Persian policy of having unwalled cities inland may be seen as a continuation of the Assyrian policy used to create stability in the newly incorporated provinces. After the Assyrian conquest of northern Palestine most towns were left unfortified.[1] The Babylonian policy may have been the same. For instance, Shechem does not seem to have been more than an insignificant village at this time and continued to be so during the early Persian period.[2]

The mountainous areas were not within the horizon of the Persian writers, neither were inland Syria or Transjordan. The Bible contains almost no information about which territories were settled nor how prosperous or poor the population was. The interest of biblical books such as Malachi, Ezra and Nehemiah is directed towards other problems—namely, the reconstruction of the community of the returnees, those of the *gôlâ*, 'the captivity', and its religion. The contemporary biblical books, save Haggai and Zechariah, are primarily concerned with the problems of the Jewish community in the fifth century BCE and not with what was going on during this time-period in general.

Much still has to be done before this period becomes well-known archaeologically. Although recent surveys and excavations are beginning to be published, many more studies are necessary before our knowledge of the Persian period in Palestine is significantly increased. Even if a systematic investigation is not yet available,[3] certain settlement patterns and various cultural influences can be discerned. There were geographical differences, as usual, in population density. The coastal area was more heavily settled during the Persian period than during the Iron II Age.[4] This seems to be traceable to the fact that the Phoenicians could freely expand during

Evidence', *Levant* 7 (1975), pp. 77-103. The name 'Bes' is a term for the type of 'art' on the vessel rather than a reference to the Egyptian deity. However, clay figurines of Bes and Osiris from the Persian period have been found at Dan; cf. A. Biran, *IEJ* 35 (1985), p. 189.

1. E. Stern, *BA* 38 (1975), p. 37.
2. G.E. Wright, *Shechem*, pp. 165-66.
3. A beginning is made in this respect by E. Stern, *Material Culture*.
4. See J. Elayi, 'The Phoenician Cities in the Persian Period', *JANESCU* 12 (1980), pp. 13-29; *idem*, *JNES* 41 (1982), pp. 83-110.

the later part of the Babylonian hegemony, increasing their trade and cultural influences. Several new ports and harbor settlements had already been built by the end of Iron II, which may be a result of the process of Phoenician expansion.[1] It is thus possible to assume that before the Persian takeover Phoenicians not only controlled most of the coast, but had also settled in the Sharon Plain and in the Jezreel Valley.

The policy of the Persian empire towards subjugated peoples is known, but there is really no information about the peoples of the greater Palestinian territory. The Persian organization of Yehud and Idumaea is unknown, and very little is known about Samerina, Gal'aza, Ammon, Moab and Edom. For instance, did Judah count as a subprovince of Samerina, or was it a *mᵉdînâ* directly under the satrap of Abr Nahara? Information in the books of Ezra and Nehemiah seems to indicate that, at least during the time of these two men, Judah could not have been ruled from Samaria. For the earliest period of Achaemenid rule there is no reliable information, even if it is known that Zerubbabel was given the title *peḥâ*. He would have been subordinated to the *peḥâ* of Samerina, or both could have been equals responsible to the satrap of 'Beyond the River'. The bullae and seals with names of 'governors' and the name Yehud (Judah)[2] that have been discovered from the late sixth and beginning of the fifth centuries BCE can support both alternatives.

The archaeological material has not been systematized in such a way as to provide a clear picture of how destructive the Babylonian campaign against Judah really was. The province of Samerina did not suffer any devastation because it was a Babylonian province, but the territories south of Jerusalem seem to have been hard hit.

The population density in Palestine and Transjordan during the period from c. 600 down to the mid-sixth century BCE is hard to assess. There is no complete statistical investigation showing how many sites of the Iron II period continued into the Persian period or how many of them increased or decreased in size. Some surveys have been undertaken and a picture is beginning to emerge. Of some interest in this matter is the relationship between Judah and the rest of the

---

1.   R. Gophna and M. Kochavi, *IEJ* 16 (1966), p. 144.

2.   N. Avigad, *Bullae and Seals from a Post-Exilic Judean Archive* (Qedem, 4; Jerusalem, 1976).

country. The survey by M. Kochavi *et al.*[1] has provided a few indications. The Judean Desert was almost abandoned and no new Persian site was found. In Judah proper several new, small sites were built just south of Jerusalem. This is understandable. The region around Jerusalem had suffered almost total devastation in 587/586 BCE, and it may be assumed that it remained depopulated during the following years until the returnees from Babylonia arrived. The territory around Jerusalem is not very suitable for agricultural activities. This region was therefore 'available' to the returnees. This may have helped them from becoming mixed with the 'unclean people of the land', meaning those of the territory of Judah. The proximity of this cluster of sites to the ruined city of Jerusalem may be seen as the start of the rebuilding of the city.

In Judah a line of small fortresses was built from Yarmut and Azekah in the west to Adullam and Beth-Zur in central Judah, and from there to Khirbet el-Qatt and Khirbet el-Zewiyye in the east. They may have been built in order to arrest Edomite incursions. The border between Judah and the Edomite territory, Idumaea, was probably just south of Beth-Zur.[2] Some of the sites in the Judean hills were unwalled (nos. 14, 27, 39) and are dated by Kochavi to the sixth century, while he dates the fortresses to the fifth century BCE.

Population density varied from region to region. The coast was heavily settled in comparison with the inland areas. It is interesting to note that the coastal area was more heavily populated during the Persian period than during the Iron II Age.[3] As for the Negev, there were only a few settlements in the early period.[4] The few settlements of Iron II in the Judean Wilderness were now abandoned. The highlands of Palestine contained mainly rural societies. At some sites

---

1. M. Kochavi (ed.), *Judea, Samaria and the Golan: Archaeological Survey, 1967–68* (Jerusalem, 1972).

2. M. Kochavi, *Judea, Samaria and the Golan*, pp. 34, 83, 85, nos. 79 and 85; cf. E. Stern, who mentions that Yehud stamps and coins have been found in the area from Beth-Zur in the south and Tell en-Naṣbeh in the north ('The Persian Period', *Cambridge History of Judaism*, I [ed. W.D. Davies and L. Finkelstein; Cambridge, 1981], p. 86).

3. See J. Elayi, *JANESCU* 12 (1980), pp. 13-28; cf. *idem*, *JNES* 41 (1982), pp. 83-110.

4. For instance, Z. Meshel considers Sede Boqer in the Negev as a way-station rather than a settlement (*Cathedra* 4 [1977], pp. 43-50 [Hebrew]).

only one building has been found, often having a square layout. It probably served as a farm house.[1] It should be noted that many villages of the Persian period were located on the slopes of the hills and in the wadis. A few were found on hilltops. The choice of location had to do with the problem of storing water or being close to its sources. The hilltop settlements had their own cisterns.[2]

The survey in Samerina showed an abandonment of most sites in the eastern marginal area, a phenomenon that has its parallel in the Judean Desert. A decline in the number of sites was also found in the central part of the territory.[3] The survey in the Beth-Shan and Jezreel Valleys showed an increase in sites during the Persian period (73 as opposed to 61 during Iron II).[4] This clearly shows that the destruction of Judah and Jerusalem did not cause a decline in settlements outside Judah. What is unclear from the survey is how many new sites were build during the Babylonian period. Perhaps the decline that occurred in the central hills should be seen in the light of the increase of settlements in the territory of Issachar. I doubt that the population in Ephraim–Manasseh really decreased. Some of the people could have moved to the more fertile plain, which may also explain why there were only two sites found in the Golan from this period. The Jordan Valley and the Jordanian highlands seem also to have experienced some decrease in settlement.[5] Excavations at Tell es-Sa'idiyeh did not yield any building remains from the period 640–420 BCE.[6] Mittmann's survey of the territory between Yarmuk and the Zerqa (Jabbok) shows no pottery from the Persian period, which could indicate that the territory was almost devoid of settlements.[7] Some of its population

---

1. E. Stern, *Material Culture*, p. 40.

2. A location analysis has been made by A. Porter in an unpublished paper ('Settlement Patterns in Palestine in the Persian Period' [University of Chicago, 1987]).

3. M. Kochavi, *Judea, Samaria and the Golan*, pp. 154-55.

4. N. Zori, *Nahalat Yisakhar*, pp. 152-53; and map; cf. *idem* (N. Tsori), 'A Contribution to the Problem of the Persian Period at Beth-Shan', *PEQ* 109 (1977), pp. 103-104.

5. See M. Ibrahim, J. Sauer and K. Yassine, *BASOR* 222 (1976), pp. 41-66; S. Mittmann, *Beiträge*.

6. J.B. Pritchard, *Tell es-Sa'idiyeh: Excavations on the Tell, 1964–1966*, pp. 79-80.

7. S. Mittmann, *Beiträge*, p. 246 and table I.

could have moved into the Beth-Shean Valley, which would explain the increase in settlements there after c. 600 BCE. There is no clear picture of this period for Moab, because of lack of excavations. A surface survey has thus far produced a few sherds from c. 20 sites from the late Iron II and Persian periods.[1] The Ammonite region, however, seems to have flourished during the Babylonian and Persian periods. Moabite Heshbon became an Ammonite city in the sixth century BCE.[2] A great amount of Ammonite pottery from the seventh–sixth centuries BCE has been found at the tell.[3] During the reign of Nabuna'id, the Babylonian center at Teima may have contributed to an economic upswing for parts of central and southern Transjordan at the same time that northern Transjordan experienced a sharp drop in settlements. Very few sites have been found there from the Persian period.[4] The same is the case with certain parts of Edom. After Nabuna'id had terminated the existence of the kingdom of Edom, some parts of the country were abandoned. For instance, the Wâdī el-Ḥasa survey shows that this territory was devoid of settlements; no sherds from the Persian period have been found. Only during the Hellenistic period did this part of Jordan experience a large increase in settlements.[5]

There is, however, evidence that settlements and commercial contacts were not completely absent all over southern Jordan. In the excavations of 1982 at Tell Tawilan a cuneiform tablet was uncovered. It is the first of its kind ever found in Jordan. It is a sales contract written in Harran that mentions King Darius. People from Edom were buying livestock in Harran. This tablet shows that cultural and commercial contacts between these areas continued down into the Persian period.[6]

---

1. J.M. Miller (personal communication).

2. Cf. Jer. 49.2-3, and E. Knauf, *Ismael*, p. 63 n. 300.

3. S. Horn, 'Heshbon', *EAEHL*, II, p. 513. A very large reservoir, which was in use from c. 800 to c. 500 BCE was also found; see L.T. Geraty, 'The 1976 Season of Excavations at Tell Hesban', *ADAJ* 21 (1976), pp. 42-43.

4. See J.A. Sauer, *BASOR* 263 (1986), p. 63. For the agricultural unwalled settlement at Tawilan in southern Jordan, where there a clay tablet in Akkadian, probably from the reign of Darius I, was also found; see C.M. Bennett, 'Excavations at Tawilan in Southern Jordan, 1982', *Levant* 16 (1984), pp. 1-23.

5. B. MacDonald, *BASOR* 245 (1982), pp. 39-40.

6. See S. Dalley, 'The Cuneiform Tablet from Tell Tawilan', *Levant* 16 (1984), pp. 19-22.

For the Shechem area a survey of c. 40 sites yielded only five sites with some 'rare finds' from the sixth and fifth centuries BCE. This should be compared with ten sites from Iron II and 18 from the Hellenistic period.[1] The latter increase may be traceable to the move from Samaria after Alexander's conquest, since the city was then settled by Macedonians.

Some investigations have shown that the area between the Delta and the Gaza Strip was still of great importance as a commercial and military link between Egypt and Palestine. From Mount Cassius to Tell er-Reqeish south of Gaza there was a line of settlements and fortresses (45 sites in all) with pottery from both Egypt and the Aegean. The local pottery is from the Saitic period (seventh–sixth cent. BCE). The border fortress termed T-21 has been identified tentatively with Migdol. It was destroyed at the end of the sixth century BCE and a new fort was built in the vicinity of Tell el-Her.[2] If the date of the destruction is right, it is possible that its demise can be attributed to the campaign of Cambyses against Egypt in 526/525 BCE.[3]

As mentioned above, the Persians did not encourage fortified cities to be built or rebuilt all over the country. Walled cities are to be found in the coastal area as well as at Heshbon in Transjordan, but at other sites, such as Hazor, Tell Keisan, Tell Qasîle and Tell Yokneam, no walls have been found. In the interior, Tell en-Naṣbeh (Mizpah), Jerusalem and Tell ed-Duweir show defensive walls.[4] The Persians could have viewed the building as a preparation for insurrection,[5] so explaining the attempt by the Persian satrap Tattenai to stop the rebuilding activities at Jerusalem (Ezra 5.3, 6). However, the wall of Jerusalem may be a special case, as will be discussed below. The wall at Tell ed-Duweir may be explained by the city's location close to the border of Judah, and the walls of Mizpah may date from the last days

---

1.   E.F. Campbell, 'The Shechem Area Survey', *BASOR* 190 (1968), p. 40.

2.   E.D. Oren, *BASOR* 256 (1984), pp. 7-44. For Tell er-Reqeish, see E.D. Oren *et al.*, 'A Phoenician Emporium on the Border of Egypt', *Qadmoniot* 19.3-4 (1986), pp. 86-91.

3.   Herodotus mentions a 'camp', Stratopedon, in the eastern Delta (2.154), which Oren thinks is the same as Hebrew Migdol, 'fort, garrison camp' (*BASOR* 256 [1984], p. 38).

4.   Cf. E. Stern, *Material Culture*, p. 50.

5.   Cf. J. Kelso, who maintains that this is the reason why so many settlements from this period have been found in the valleys (*The Excavations of Bethel*, p. 38).

of the kingdom of Judah, because that city was not destroyed by the Babylonian army. It was used as the residence of the first Babylonian commander and the first *pāqîd* (chief administrator) appointed by the Babylonians, namely Gedaliah. However, as has been mentioned, some small forts were built. From the above it can be concluded that most of the Shephelah did not belong to the sub-province of Judah.[1]

The Persians probably did not need many garrisons in the country to keep the population in line. Unlike Egypt, Anatolia and the Phoenician city states, Palestine and Transjordan had no political units where the banner of rebellion could be raised. The interior of Palestine was located off the main thoroughfares and was of little economic importance. Since its rule by Assyria, the whole country had been repopulated with many different nationalities including Aramaeans, Elamites, Moabites, Ammonites and Edomites. In the south Arabs and Philistines may have expanded, as did the Phoenicians in the west. Thus, there would hardly be any national feelings to cause serious rebellions.

The Reconstruction of Judah

The demographic picture of Palestine given above should be contrasted with the simplified biblical presentation in the books of Ezra and Nehemiah, where the phrase *'am hā'āreṣ*, 'the people of the land', is used in a tendentious way to denote all those who lived in the country—Judahites or not—and who had never been deported to Babylonia. These groups are intentionally ignored in Ezra and Nehemiah, even though Ezra acknowledges an ethnic mixture (Ezra 9.1-2, 11-12). In principle for Ezra–Nehemiah there is only one group of people, Yahweh's people, that is, the ideological Israel. No other people should exist.[2] This ideology had been developed in Babylonia, but the question is whether the first returnees could maintain it when they were faced with the realities of resettling in Judah.

The edict[3] of Cyrus II about the return of the god-statues to their homelands and the release of their people is usually interpreted to

---

1. Cf. E. Stern, 'The Persian Empire', *Cambridge History of Judaism*, I (ed. W.D. Davies and L. Finkelstein), p. 86.

2. See S. Japhet, 'People and Land in the Restoration Period', *Das Land Israel in biblischer Zeit* (ed. G. Strecker), pp. 112-13.

3. The text in Ezra 6.3-5 seems to be an authentic rendering of the edict, which was preserved in Ecbatana, the former capital of the Median kingdom.

mean that Cyrus was tolerant in religious matters. This view is most probably a result of modern exegesis. As K. Galling has pointed out, the gods that were sent home were always to pray to Bel and Nabu for Cyrus, that he might have a long life and that his empire might be well-established and long-lived.[1] Such a condition of return has nothing to do with modern ideas of tolerance. I believe that Cyrus was a realistic politician who understood that normalcy could not be established in his large kingdom if the imprisoned gods could not carry on their tasks, nominally under the supervision of Marduk or Ahura Mazda as their overlord.[2] To keep the gods in Babylon would have been to continue the Babylonian policy. Cyrus's subversive propaganda may have declared him a liberator in Babylonia before its capture; thus, the release of gods and prisoners was the fulfillment of that political propaganda. The religions of the different provinces could continue as long as they did not interfere or collide with the Persian judicial system.[3]

During the reign of Nabuna'id a new temple policy was instituted. The king had the temples pay part of their income to the state *in natura*, that is, in cattle, grain, wine, beer, olive oil, wool, and so forth. Temple slaves also had to take care of the royal herds. In this case Cyrus followed the policy of Nabuna'id.[4] However, the Achaemenids do not seem to have questioned religious ideology as long as it did not go against Persian interests. Under Cambyses only three temples in

---

1. See K. Galling, *Studien zur Geschichte Israels im persischen Zeitalter*, pp. 35-36.

2. It is not clear whether Cyrus made Ahura Mazda ('the Wise Lord') the main god of the empire, or whether he still considered Marduk the 'ruler' of the former Babylonian kingdom. The symbol of Ahura Mazda rising up from the winged 'disc' (probably an adaptation of the Assyrian symbol) occurs first with Darius I; see J.M. Cook, *The Persian Empire*, p. 43, and plate 10; cf. H.S. Nyberg, *Die Religionen des alten Iran*, pp. 348-49. The Achaemenian kings were not really devoted to Zoroastrianism, according to Nyberg. This is clear from their burials. In Zoroaster's religion the dead were not buried but exposed (pp. 353, 363-64). Cf. also G. Widengren, *Die Religionen Irans* (Die Religionen der Menschheit, 14; Stuttgart, 1965), pp. 117-18; K. Heinz, 'Religion und Politik in Vorderasien im Reich der Achämeniden', *Klio* 69 (1987), p. 318.

3. Cf. H.S. Nyberg, 'Das Reich der Achämeniden', *Historia Mundi*, III (ed. R. Valjavec; Bern, 1954), pp. 95-96.

4. Cf. M.A. Dandamayev, 'Politische Geschichte', *Beiträge zur Achämenidengeschichte* (ed. G. Walser), pp. 52-54.

Egypt (in Memphis and Hermopolis) could continue as before.[1] Under Darius certain temples obtained a privileged position, such as the temple of Apollo of Magnesia in Asia Minor.[2] The Persians were inclined to identify other heavenly gods with Ahura Mazda, such as Zeus and Yahweh.

When the Judahites received permission to return in 538 BCE,[3] a certain Sheshbazaar (Shamash-apal-uṣur)[4] was commissioned by Cyrus to see that the temple vessels were returned to Jerusalem (Ezra 1.7-11). According to Ezra 5.14-5, he was appointed *peḥâ* and was also to supervise the building of the new temple. This Sheshbazzar is commonly understood to have been a member of the Davidic royal line, but there is no information in the Bible about his ancestry. The phrase *hannāśî' liyhûdâ* in Ezra 1.8 has been interpreted to mean that Sheshbazzar was a member of Judah's royal family, probably a son of Jehoiakin.[5] The question is, however, whether this phrase really makes him a member of the royal family or not. The construction with the preposition *l-* is not genitive but dative. It announces here the purpose or the direction. Thus the translation ought to be 'prince/leader over Judah'; Sheshbazzar was appointed by the Persians as commissioner over Judah. Thus, the term is parallel to *peḥâ* in 5.14.

---

1. Consult M.A. Dandamayev, 'Politische Geschichte', in *Beiträge zur Achämenidengeschichte* (ed. G. Walser), p. 54.

2. See E. Meyer, *Die Entstehung des Judenthums* (Halle, 1986), pp. 19-20; U. von Wilamowitz-Moellendorff, *Griechisches Lesebuch* (Berlin, 1902), p. 391; M.N. Tod (ed.), *A Selection of Greek Historical Inscriptions* (Oxford, 1933), pp. 12-13.

3. According to biblical ideology, the Exile lasted 70 years; cf. Jer. 25.12; 29.10; Lev. 26.33-43. Is it possible that this round figure refers to the period from the destruction of the Solomonic temple to the dedication of Zerubbabel's temple in 515 BCE?

4. This Babylonian name means 'Shamash [Sun-god], protect the son'. The Lucian version of Ezra has the reading Sasabassares (or Sasabalassares), which supports the derivation from Shamash. Cf. P.-R. Berger, 'Zu den Namen ŠŠBṢR und SN'ṢR', *ZAW* 83 (1971), pp. 98-100; P.E. Dion, 'ŠŠBṢR and SSNWRY', *ZAW* 95 (1983), pp. 111-12. Dion refers, for instance, to the name Shamash-nuri written SSNWRY in the Fekheriyeh inscription. E. Meyer and others have followed the form Sanabassar, that occurs in some Apocrypha and thus derive it from Sin-bal-uṣur, 'Sin [Moon-god], protect the son' (*Entstehung des Judentums*, pp. 76-77).

5. Some have identified Sheshbazzar with Shenazzar, son of Jehoiakin (1 Chron. 3.18); cf. J. Bright, *A History of Israel* (3rd edn), pp. 361-62. This is philologically impossible.

As such he did not need to be from the royal family, nor even a Judahite.[1] Sheshbazzar's genealogy does not appear anywhere in the Bible, in contrast to Zerubbabel, who was a grandson of Jehoiakin (Ezra 3.2; 1 Chron. 3.17).[2] If Sheshbazzar had been of royal birth it would certainly have been mentioned. Instead, he is characterized in Ezra 5.14 as an obscure person of the past: 'Sheshbazzar was his name'. Memory of him had faded. All that was known was that he had had something to do with the temple during the first years after the return. In Ezra 5.16 Sheshbazzar is said to have laid the foundation-stone of the temple. The probability of this action should not be denied, but it could just as well be a literary device to combine the return with the foundation of the temple. For the postexilic writer the temple was the most important thing. Without the temple there was no society, no religion of Yahweh and no national future. The first returnees were probably not able to build a temple. They had no experience and no idea of how to construct such a huge building, nor did they have money or other resources.[3] Their most immediate task was to build homes and organize a subsistence system in the strange hill country to which they had come. Many of them were born in the exile and came to what was for them a 'foreign' country. As has been mentioned above, the place where they were able to settle was probably the territory south of Jerusalem, where no one else had chosen to live. From a practical point of view the temple had to wait.[4] The actual beginning of the temple project may have occurred first with Zerubbabel (Hag. 2.15, 18; Zech. 4.9).[5]

---

1. Cf. H.G.M. Williamson, 'The Composition of Ezra I–VI', *JTS* 34 (1984), p. 14. Cf. P.R. Ackroyd, who thinks that Sheshbazzar would have been a member of 'an upper-class family of the kind indicated in Jer. 26.10' (*Exile and Restoration: A Study of Hebrew Thought in the Sixth Century BCE* [OTL; Philadelphia, 1968], p. 143). This is possible, but such men are usually mentioned together with the name of their fathers.

2. The attempts to identify Sheshbazzar with Shenazzar (1 Chron. 3.18) or even with Zerubbabel have no support in the biblical texts. Scholars seem to have been more interested than the biblical writer in making Sheshbazzar a man of royal birth.

3. Cf. S. Herrmann, *A History of Israel in Old Testament Times*, p. 302.

4. K. Galling maintains that the foundations of the Solomonic temple were not completely destroyed. Even if the temple was burned, the foundation stones would not have been destroyed (*Studien zur Geschichte Israels im persischen Zeitalter*, pp. 129-30).

5. According to A. Gelston, the Hebrew verb *ysd* can also mean 'build, repair'

What could speak for Sheshbazzar's being of royal birth would be the practice of the Persian king often to appoint members of royal families as satraps (governors) in subdued nations. In this way the king would empower someone who knew the land and its administration, which continued but which had to become part of the imperial administration and its laws. However, there was no functioning Judahite nation. In the main the land was devastated and had to be rebuilt and reorganized. There was no royal family that could be used for the reorganization. In other words, a new administration had to be built. Can it be assumed that this was Sheshbazzar's duty? If so, he must have disappeared very quickly, because nothing of this task is associated with him. Instead, the custom of using a man of the royal family as satrap of the land is first encountered with Zerubbabel. This would be another indication that Sheshbazzar was a Babylonian entrusted with carrying the temple vessels to Jerusalem.

According to Ezra 2.64, 42,360 persons left Babylonia for Judah. The number does not include the 7337 'slaves and maid-servants' who are also mentioned in Neh. 7.66-67. The sum is rather large (c. 50,000), and since certainly not all Judahites returned,[1] it may be asked whether the list is not a census from a later period.[2] In support of this conclusion, it can be noted that Ezra 2.70 says that priests and Levites settled in Jerusalem and the rest of the people settled 'in their own towns', a statement that implies that the towns were empty. The writer has forgotten that Jerusalem was mainly a ruined city. Where could all these priests and Levites have lived?[3] In addition, how much space was available in the towns of the country to accommodate several thousand people? The list of returnees in Ezra 2 gives the impression of a society that had been in existence for some time and which was trying to reorganize itself.[4] It therefore cannot

('The Foundations of the Second Temple', *VT* 16 [1966], pp. 232-35). Gelston does not exclude the possibility of 'an abortive attempt' being made by Sheshbazzar (p. 235).

1. Josephus, *Ant.* 11.1.3, 8. Cf. E. Bickermann, 'The Edict of Cyrus in Ezra 1', *JBL* 65 (1946), p. 262.

2. Cf. K. Galling, who dates the list to 518 BCE (*Studien zur Geschichte Israels im persischen Zeitalter*, pp. 89-108).

3. M. Noth considered Ezra 2.70 a secondary addition (*Überlieferungs-geschichtliche Studien* [2nd edn], p. 123).

4. Cf. the remarks of S. Mowinckel, *Studien zu dem Buche Ezra–Nehemia. I. Die nachchronistische Redaktion des Buches: Die Listen* (Oslo, 1964), p. 98; cf.

refer to the situation during the first decades after 538 BCE.[1]

How many people returned it is impossible to know, and any information about their lives and activities is hidden in history's shroud of darkness. The books of Haggai and Zechariah do not mention anything about the earliest years after the return. Instead, it depicts a society in 520 BCE that had a commissioner, a *pehâ*,[2] named Zerubbabel, who was expected to become king. The book indicates that the people of Judah, with Jerusalem as the center, had overcome the first stage of clearing and rebuilding parts of the territory and were now in the process of organizing themselves into a viable society. Zerubbabel's appointment was a result of this progress. Judah had now become a territorial region that had to be organized and administered. The Persian government therefore used a member of the Davidic family to head the administration, even if he had no experience. He was of royal blood, and that is what counted.

Nothing is known about the reaction of the people of the country to the meeting with the exiles. Realistically, very few knew anything about them. A small group of returnees settled in the God-forsaken region around Jerusalem. They probably did not disturb anyone as long as their rebuilding program did not come into conflict with other villages and towns. Soon, however, that a Judahite society is active again, and the prophet Haggai tries to encourage the people to rebuild the temple. In fact, he reproaches Zerubbabel, the priest Joshua, and the people for neglecting Yahweh's house while they are busying themselves with their daily work and building their own houses (Hag. 1.1-11). This is the first piece of information given about the society

---

p. 66. Mowinckel has also shown that none of the clan names in the list of Ezra 2 are composed with the theophoric components -*ēl* or -'*am*, which would be expected if the list reflected old pre-exilic clan names (pp. 79-81).

1. Ezra 2.63 mentions that 'His Excellency', *tiršāṭā'*, forbade those excluded from the priesthood to eat of the sanctified food until a priest for urim and thummim had been installed. Logically this Excellency would be the leader of the returnees mentioned at the beginning of the list (2.2), Zerubbabel. Thus K. Galling, *Studien zur Geschichte Israels im persischen Zeitalter*, p. 91.

2. Achaemenid governors are often given this title (*bēl pīḥāti*) in Babylonian texts. It could also refer to other high officials; see M.W. Stolper, *Entrepreneurs and Empire: The Muraŝû Archive, the Muraŝû Firm, and Persian Rule in Babylonia* (Nederlands Historisch-Archaeologisch Instituut te Istanbul, 54; Leiden, 1985), pp. 39, 50.

and the life of the returnees. It shows the existence of a community at work for its subsistence. It also shows that the city of Jerusalem was not yet the center of life. This would have been a time when the returnees would not yet have come into much conflict with the 'people of the land'. It may be assumed that the new builders had to improve their standards of living, partly by making contacts with other groups in the vicinity, because no group could thrive for long in isolation, owing to the poverty of the region. Conflicts probably first occurred in connection with the construction of the temple, because this activity meant that the returnees had tried to establish themselves as a nation. They had become a people again.[1]

It should be remembered that there was no official Judahite religion after the Solomonic temple in Jerusalem had been destroyed. Yahweh had no territory, no nation to reign over any more. He had no 'cosmos'. He had also proven himself an insignificant and powerless god, according to the common understanding. At his destroyed cult place in Jerusalem he could still receive sacrifices, but the national rituals for establishing justice and normalcy ($s^e d\bar{a}q\hat{a}$, $mi\check{s}p\bar{a}t$) for his nation could not be performed. The agricultural festivals of the villages could continue as before, but they were not part of the official cult and the blessings they created were only for the village community.

The permission given by the Persians to rebuild the temple can be seen as the ideological foundation of Yahweh's reconstituted kingdom. The temple would be the visible expression of the people's being a 'nation' again. It would be a Persian vassal kingdom, but the nationality of Judah would be restored. The problem, however, was that there was no king to build it, because to build national temples was a royal prerogative. It is important to stress this fact, because it explains why it could be expected that Zerubbabel would be king: a nation without a king was unknown. Religion, nation and people were identical. King and nation could not yet be separated. The republican system was not known to the Judahites. What the satrapies really meant was first learned during the reign of Darius, but even if Zerubbabel was appointed by Darius, it took some time before the naked reality was felt.

Cyrus's edict and the permission to build the temple should be seen

---

1.   Jer. 40.15 indicates that if Gedaliah were murdered, what was left of Judah would perish.

not only as a political gesture toward some exiled people, but also as a money-making venture. As mentioned above, Cyrus was a realistic politician. Jerusalem's temple, like so many other temples in the empire, would be under the jurisdiction of the crown and thus a source of revenue.[1] This would be a way of controlling Judah. To give official sanction to the rebuilding of the sanctuary would mean that the region would be governed according to the laws of the empire and thus would become part of its economic system. The building permit might therefore be seen as official acknowledgement of Judah as a Persian administrative district, a $m^e dînâ$.

The religious policy of the Persian government can be exemplified by an order that Darius I gave to the satrap of Egypt, Aryandes. He had to collect from a commission of priests, wise men, and scribes the laws of Egypt in order to have them codified[2] and possibly also somewhat altered, if necessary, by the Persian court.[3] The backbone of the Persian administration was its legal system, personified in the king,[4] so that the sacred laws of the different peoples and nations under Persian rule would not contradict the laws of the empire. The Persians looked at religion as law, *dāta*, 'to organize' (Persian loan-word in Aram.), which codified the will of the divine.[5] Darius also saw to it that some Egyptian temples were restored.[6] This was not only a gesture to get the support of the priesthood. It must have been part of

1. Cf. M.W. Stolper, *Entrepreneurs and Empire*, pp. 43-44.

2. Diodorus 1.95.

3. The commission worked between 519 and 503 BCE; compare W. Spiegelberg's comments, in *Die sogenannte Demotische Chronik des Pap. 215 der Bibliothèque Nationale de Paris* (Leipzig, 1914), pp. 20-22.

4. The king could issue edicts that became laws either orally or in writing; cf. Dan. 6.9 and Est. 1.19. See J. Lewy, *HUCA* 25 (1954), p. 171; P. Frei in P. Frei and K. Koch, *Reichsidee und Reichsorganization im Perserreich* (OBO, 55; Freiburg, 1984), pp. 23-24.

5. See G. Widengren, 'Iran and Israel in Parthian Times with Special Regard to the Ethiopic Book of Enoch', *Religious Syncretism in Antiquity* (ed. B.A. Pearson; Missoula, MT, 1975), p. 89. Another example of the Persian attitude is the letter from Darius I to the 'servant' Gadatas at Sardis, telling him not to force the priesthood of Apollo of Magnesia (?) at the Menander to pay tribute (G.B. Gray and M. Cary, 'The Reign of Darius', *CAH*, IV, p. 189); cf. E. Meyer, *Die Entstehung des Judentums*, pp. 19-21.

6. Cf. A.T. Olmstead, *History of Palestine and Syria*, p. 571; J.M. Cook, *The Persian Empire*, p. 60.

his policy to have law and order upheld and at the same time see to it that the laws of the country would not be in contradiction to the Persian laws and to the administrative apparatus of the Persians.

The rebuilding of the temple in Jerusalem and the reorganization of the district of Judah may thus be put in a broader perspective. However, the status of Judah within the Persian administration during the first decades after the Persian takeover is not documented. In the fifth satrapy there were several subprovinces. The Phoenician city states belonged to this satrapy, but their status was rather that of vassal states. Among the subprovinces in Palestine were Samerina, Ammon, Idumaea and Ashdod. What status did Judah then have? Here we are at a loss. There is no information about how this territory was governed. It could have been ignored, or the commissioner of Samerina could have tried to exercise power over this sparsely populated territory, as has often been suggested. Only in the time of Darius I (after 521 BCE) is there reference to a *peḥâ*, commissioner, over Judah in connection with Darius I's answer to Tattenai, the governor of the fifth satrapy, and the district governors, who had asked about an authorization for the temple building in Jerusalem (Ezra 6.7).[1] This shows that the Persians had organized Judah as a subprovince, a *meḏînâ*, in the fifth satrapy of Abr Nahara.

Judah or Yehud (the name in Aramaic) was divided into small districts, such as Keilah, Beth-Zur, Beth-Hakkerem, Jerusalem and Mizpah, and probably the area around Jericho.[2] The latter seems to have been unsettled after 586 BCE and until the Hasmonean-Roman time.[3] Judah's *meḏînâ* was thus a very small district. The southern half of the former kingdom of Judah was not included. It became Idumea because it was populated mainly by Edomites who had moved there after the destruction of the Judahite and Edomite kingdoms. As mentioned earlier, the

---

1. It should be noted that this text does not mention that Zerubbabel was the commissioner over Judah.

2. Cf. M. Avi-Yonah, *The Holy Land*, pp. 15-18. G. Widengren counts nine districts (in J.H. Hayes and J.M. Miller, *Israelite and Judean History*, p. 522). A. Demsky thinks that Hebrew *pelek* does not mean 'district', but refers rather to 'work duty'; thus it would be a work-force from a certain territory ('Pelekh in Nehemiah 3', *IEJ* 33 [1983], pp. 242-44). The information about the districts really refers to the time of Nehemiah. In the report of the rebuilding of the walls, Neh. 3 mentions two *peḏlākîm* from Jerusalem (3.9, 13), two rulers of Mizpah (3.15, 19), 'half the *pelek* of Beth-Zur' (3.16), and two half *peḏlākîm* from Keilah (3.17, 18).

3. Cf. K.M. Kenyon, 'Jericho', *EAEHL*, II, p. 564.

borderline between Idumaea and Judah was between Beth-Zur and Hebron. The latter site became Jewish first under Judas the Maccabee, and when John Hyrcanus (134–104 BCE) conquered and annexed Idumaea he forced its inhabitants to embrace Judaism. This means that Yehud did not stretch down to the Shephelah. Tell ed-Duweir and Tell el-Ḥesi were outside the territory of Yehud.[1] The area of Yehud was thus no more than c. 40 km from north to south and 51 km from west to east, in all c. 2000 sq. km, and part of it was not arable land.

When the population in Samerina learned that the temple was being rebuilt they offered their help and assistance, but were given the cold shoulder. Ezra 4.1-3 reports that representatives from the people of Samerina went to the leaders of the Judean families and generously offered their cooperation.[2] As a motive they mentioned that they had worshipped the same god since the days of Esarhaddon. They had been brought to the land by Esarhaddon and had to worship the god of the country (2 Kgs 17.24-33). It should be noted that the biblical writer did not like to mention that, besides non-exiled Judahites, others, such as Israelites, also lived in the land, in this case in the subprovince of Samerina. His purpose was to depict the exiles, the *gôlâ*, religiously as the real Israel, and everyone else as 'unclean'. In this view, the people of the land, *'am hā'āreṣ*, were those who did not have the 'right' understanding of how to worship Yahweh.[3] The

1.   See M. Avi-Yonah, *The Holy Land*, pp. 13-23, and map 1.

2.   Cf. J.P. Weinberg, 'Das *beit 'abot* im 6.–4. Jh. v.u.Z.', *VT* 23 (1973), pp. 400-14.

3.   Weinberg maintains that the phrase 'the people of the land' refers to all those who did not become members of the upper-class society, the 'Bürger-Tempel-Gemeinde' ('Die Agrarverhältnisse in der Bürger-Tempel-Gemeinde der Achämenidenzeit', *Acta Antiqua* 22 [1974], pp. 473-586); cf. *idem*, 'Der *'am hā'āreṣ* des 6.–4. Jh. v.u.Z.', *Klio* 56 (1974), pp. 325-26. The returnees most probably could not be seen as constituting an upper class in Judah. To reach that status some time must have elapsed. Religiously they were in a class by themselves. Sociologically they were newcomers who did not own any real estate and who did not make an impact on the rest of the society. As time passed they became a group that saw itself as being different. Having built the temple, they succeeded in carving out a place for themselves among the different peoples of the land. In the beginning, the returnees could not be identified with the whole territory of the district of Judah. Weinberg's theory concerns the time of Nehemiah, who was a *peḥâ* over the entire district of Judah. Weinberg seems to have used the Hellenistic *polis* system for his reconstruction, which, however, was not known in the ancient Near East before the time of Alexander. For an appraisal of Weinberg's thesis, see H. Kreissig, 'Eine

'people of the land' were all those who had not been captive in Babylon, including both Israelites in Samerina and Judahites who had never been exiled. They were all considered foreigners; thus, they had no right to the land.[1] This is the root of the split between the party of the returnees and the indigenous people. The latter were apostate and religiously unclean in the eyes of the returnees. They worshipped not only Yahweh but also other gods, as had always been done in Palestine. It may be said that this was the beginning of the religious exclusiveness that became the hallmark of Ezra's reform and that marked the beginning of Judaism.

In order to understand the religious and sociopolitical conflict that occurred between those of the *gôlâ*, 'captivity', and the people of the land, we should look at the attitude of the Deuteronomistic historian towards the poor, the humble, and the lowly ones should be examined. Even if some prophets tried to show a certain social pathos, the biblical writers often looked down upon the poor. For the Deuteronomist these people, *dallat hā'āreṣ*, 'the lowly of the land', lacked religious knowledge. They were considered worthless, religiously speaking. This attitude can be compared to Jeremiah's, who maintained that the poor ones had no sense or understanding because they did not at all know the 'way of Yahweh', *derek Yahweh*, nor did they know the *mišpāṭ*, 'law, norm', of their god (Jer. 5.4).[2] This attitude of the returnees is understandable when it is remembered that when the Babylonians deported or killed the upper classes of the Judahite society, including the priests in 586 BCE, the religious and literary traditions also 'went' to Babylon. Thus, for the returnees the *da'at Yahweh*, 'knowledge about Yahweh' and the *derek Yahweh* could not be found in Judah, because they who knew the way had been killed or exiled. From this point of view the Judahites of the land were no different than the other groups of people in Palestine. Knowledge about Yahweh arrived once more with the returnees. This is the attitude found behind the actions of Ezra and Nehemiah and their party, the people of the captivity.

---

beachtenswerte Theorie zur Organisation altvorderorientalischer Tempelgemeninden im Achämenidenreich', *Klio* 66 (1984), pp. 35-39.

1. In this the Book of Nehemiah is not as consistent as the Book of Ezra, which could be an indication of Ezra's having arrived in Jerusalem later than Nehemiah.

2. Cf. Prov. 9.10, which says that 'fear of Yahweh is the beginning of wisdom'.

The clash between the returnees and the indigenous people was not only a religious conflict. It was very much a sociological problem and a problem of property rights. The nonexiled people claimed ownership of the land and at first considered the returnees as foreigners. They maintained that the returnees had no right to the land. It belonged to them, the indigenous population. This was countered in two ways. First, the prophet Ezekiel had said that Yahweh too had left Jerusalem and gone into exile with his people, but that he would give them the land back and purge it from all abominations (Ezek. 11). Thus, even if the Judahites who were left in the country could argue that the people who were led into exile had forfeited the right to the land because of their sins, Ezekiel's utterance about Yahweh's also having been in the exile was meant to nullify the arguments of the opposition. The people of the land, Judahites or others, could not be cultically pure, because the knowledge of the right way of worshiping Yahweh did not exist in the country. That knowledge 'traveled' with Yahweh and the exiled peoples to Babylonia. Ezra also builds on this argument, adding to it the 'abomination' of mixed marriages (Ezra 3.3; 9.1).

The other argument in the contest for the land was the so-called Promise of the Land given by Yahweh to the ancestral father, Abraham, who himself had left Mesopotamia, according to tradition. As Abraham had settled in Canaan, so now also the returnees coming from Babylonia were entering the land that once was promised to him.[1] In this way the possession of the land received divine legitimation.[2] It is in this situation that the promise of the land has its *raison d'être*. Such a promise has no function to fill for people living in the

---

1.   R.N. Whybray maintains that there was a 'growing tendency, which seems to have begun in the Exile, to make of this particular typical folktale figure an archetypal person' who possessed the land. His place at the beginning of the Pentateuchal history is a literary fiction (*The Making of the Pentateuch*, pp. 239-40).

2.   Cf. the remarks of C. Westermann, who thinks that the text about the promise of the land belongs to the very latest part of the composition ('Arten der Erzählung in der Genesis', *Forschung am Alten Testament, Gesammelte Studien* [ed. C. Westermann; TBü, 24; Munich, 1964], p. 33). See also W.M. Clark, 'The Origin and Development of the Land Promise Theme in the Old Testament'. I have maintained in an earlier study that the promise of the land and the story about the conquest should be seen as 'programmatic scripts of the *gôlâ* party' (*Who were the Israelites?*, p. 109).

country.[1] The literary purpose of narratives about the 'Joshua conquest' is to show the 'fulfillment' of the 'land promise'. The problem here, however, is to determine whether the first Judahites who came back from Babylonia experienced a hostile attitude. The biblical texts give that impression, but it is likely that such an attitude developed when it was seen how the new community grew and started to rebuild the temple, and when offers of cooperation on the part of the northerners (and others?) were turned down. Theologically, however, the hostility was first pronounced in the Exile by such utterances as those of Ezekiel (11.15-21; 33.24).[2]

The Rebuilding Program in Yehud

The above discussion has given the background as to why the attempts to build the temple and later the city walls were seriously hampered.[3] However, the first years of the reign of Darius I saw, among other temples, a new temple being built in Jerusalem. The district of Judah (Yehud) and its temple administration was not only serving Jerusalem and its surroundings but was also in part an expression of Persian authority over Judah.[4] What is astonishing, however, is that Tattenai,[5] the governor of 'Beyond the River', had no knowledge that permission had been given to the Jerusalemites, and that the district governors did not know about it either; at least this is how the matter is presented by the biblical narrator. After the work had proceeded for some time, Tattenai and a few district governors went to Jerusalem in order to find out on whose authority the building project had been undertaken, and who the people were who were responsible for the rebuilding. Tattenai was told that Cyrus had given permission and that the temple vessels had been sent back with Sheshbazzar. A report about this

1. In order to contradict the right to the land of the people who remained in Judah, Ezek. 33.24 makes an 'unexpected mention of Abraham' as an authority for the right of the exiles (S. Japhet, 'People and Land in the Restoration Period', *Das Land Israel in biblischer Zeit* [ed. G. Strecker], p. 108).
2. Cf. P.R. Ackroyd, *Exile and Restoration*, p. 117.
3. Isa. 66 has been understood by J.D. Smart as evidence for the existence of a group within the *gôlâ* community that was hostile to the building of the temple (*History and Theology in Second Isaiah* [Philadelphia, 1965], pp. 281-87).
4. Cf. P.R. Ackroyd, *Exile and Restoration*, pp. 140-42.
5. He is called Sisines by Josephus (*Ant.* 11.4).

discussion was sent to Darius I in which Tattenai asked that a search be made in the archives in order to find documentary proof. This was done, and in the archives at Ecbatana, the former capital of Media, was found a scroll with a decree by Cyrus allowing the rebuilding of the temple. Darius renewed the decree, and Tattenai was ordered not to interfere.[1] All this does not necessarily mean that Tattenai was hostile to the Jerusalemites. As governor he was only fulfilling his duties. However, the biblical writer has used the incident to suit his intentions.

The temple was supposedly finished in Darius' sixth year, 515 BCE (Ezra 5.3–6.16). There are, however, differences in the biblical texts about the rebuilding of Jerusalem and its temple. Ezra 4.6-23[2] mentions that Rehum, the governor of Samerina, and officials of the 'Beyond the River' satrapy complained about the rebuilding of Jerusalem both during the time of Xerxes (486–465 BCE) and his son Artaxerxes I (465–424 BCE). As a result, Artaxerxes I stopped the project. Ezra 4.24 then states that the work on the temple stopped until the reign of Darius, which would imply the reign of Darius II. This verse has been seen as a misplaced reference to Darius I.[3] There is no firm evidence that Cyrus or Cambyses stopped the building projects in Jerusalem.[4] Thus 'the second year of Darius' could just as

1. Cf. R. de Vaux, 'The Decrees of Cyrus and Darius on the Rebuilding of the Temple', *The Bible and the Ancient Near East*, pp. 63-96; W.T. in der Smitten, 'Historische Probleme zum Kyrosedikt und zum Jerusalemer Tempelbau von 515', *Persica* 6 (1974), pp. 167-78. The Aramaic of Ezra 6.2-5, as also that of 7.12-26, seems to render the official Persian chancelry style, and may therefore be authentic; see E. Meyer, *Die Entstehung des Judentums*, pp. 8-71; A.T. Olmstead, *The History of Palestine and Syria*, pp. 570-71; B. Porten, who maintains that these Aramaic texts 'demonstrate a common epistolary tradition' ('The Address Formulae in Aramaic Letters: A New Collation of Cowley 17', *RB* 90 [1983], p. 396).

2. P.R. Ackroyd maintains that the 'real meaning of the passage in Ezra 4 is that there will be a full restoration of the Jewish community, with a supremacy equal to that of the Davidic period' ('Some Historical Problems of the Early Achaemenian Period', *Proceedings, Eastern Great Lakes and Midwest Bible Societies* 4 [1984], p. 46). Ackroyd also believes that Ezra 4.1-5 is being 'used at a double level', one explaining 'the time lag in the completion of the temple', the other being a polemic against the later Samaritan community (p. 44).

3. See, among others, F.C. Fensham, *The Books of Ezra and Nehemiah*, p. 77.

4. The curious perspective on history in the book of Ezra can be illustrated by the information in Ezra 4. When the 'adversaries of Judah and Benjamin' were not allowed to participate in building the temple, they hired counselors to help them to

well refer to Darius II (424–405/404 BCE). However, the writer of the Book of Ezra has no interest in any objective chronological sequence. His interest is centered on the temple; thus, he has used the different traditions as they have served his interests.[1]

The piece of information concerning the 'second year of the reign of Darius' also occurs in Hag. 1.1, 1.15–2.1 and 2.10; thus Ezra 4.24 almost certainly refers to the time of Darius I, and it may be assumed that a temple building was finished in 515 BCE. However, several rebuilding efforts and/or repairs could have been undertaken as time went on. Artaxerxes's stopping of building projects in Jerusalem could refer to a repairing of the temple. However, Ezra 6.14 mentions that the people built the temple according to the order of Cyrus, Darius, and Artaxerxes (Artaḥ'šaśta), which could refer to Artaxerxes II. If so, Ezra arrived in Jerusalem in 398 BCE. It is interesting to note that Ezra expresses his gratitude to the Persian king for having 'adorned, beautified', $l^e p\bar{a}'\bar{e}r$, Yahweh's temple (Ezra 7.27). It is not quite clear what is meant here, but realizing that Ezra was a Persian official, he most certainly would have received the king's authorization for the renovation.[2]

The upkeep of the temple could have been poor. It should be remembered that there were supervisors over the different 'national' temples in the provinces. This was the case at Acco, which was a naval base for the Persians.[3] Such a supervisor was most probably a Persian

---

stop the project (4.1-5). The writer gives the impression that the same forces that stopped the building activities during the reign of Artaxerxes were also at work during the periods of Cyrus and Cambyses.

1. The same 'disinterest' in accurate historiography is found in 1 Chron. 6.1-15, which presents an artificial genealogy of the Aaronide priesthood. Zadoq's son, Ahimaaz, is made the twelfth 'high priest' of the Solomonic temple (when he could only have been number two). After him there are eleven high priests counting Jehozadaq, whose father Seraiah was killed by Nebuchadrezzar II; thus, Jehozadaq was never a 'high priest'. Joshua, the first 'high priest' of the second temple, would then be the twelfth after the Solomonic temple was built. This genealogy was used to establish continuity with the pre-exilic priesthood. It may represent the Aaronide claim to legitimate priesthood, thus replacing that of the Zadokites.

2. Cf. Ezra 9.9.

3. One of the two ostraca found in a three-room structure from the Persian Period (str. 4) at Acco mentions a guild of artisans and an 'overseer', *šlt*, for the *'šrt* (either the goddess Asherah or her temple); see M. Dothan, 'A Phoenician Inscription from Akko', *IEJ* 35 (1985), pp. 81-94.

appointee, as was Ezra. It was a royal appointee's duty to express his gratitude to the king for being allowed to repair and 'beautify' a national temple. The existence of temple supervisors makes one suspect that Jerusalem's temple administration had to be in agreement with Persian customs.

Not only was the rebuilding of the temple a long process, but the failure to differentiate completely between city and temple probably has obscured the literary presentation of the process. City and temple could be seen as one and the same entity. The city of Jerusalem could be understood as a temple city, a holy city.[1] There were most probably different periods during which both the city and the temple were restored. Consequently, it makes sense to find different traditions about persons who restored the temple. For instance, in 1 Macc. 8.18, Nehemiah, the rebuilder of the city walls, is also mentioned as the builder of the temple and the altar. Flavius Josephus gives the same information.[2]

How much building activity was taking place in Jerusalem during the first decades after the return can only be surmised. As mentioned earlier, Jerusalem was a devastated city, and the returnees first had to build their own houses, probably outside the ruined city, in order to make living possible. The utterances of Haggai show, however, that there was a Jerusalemite community; thus, it may be assumed that a small city had been built on and/or among the ruins. In connection with the rebuilding of the temple parts of the city probably also had been restored. In Hag. 1.4, the prophet complains that the people live in paneled houses, but Yahweh has nowhere to live. The first decades after the return were thus a period of reoccupation of the territory around Jerusalem. What then happened until Nehemiah arrived in Jerusalem in 445 BCE is another blank in the historical picture. Neh. 5.15, for instance, complains that Nehemiah's predecessors ('governors') had been a burden to the people by economically suppressing them. But Nehemiah never did that, he says.

---

1. This may explain why Ezra 4.6–6.18 deals with both the temple and the city walls.

2. *Ant.* 11.165. For Josephus as following the tradition of 1 Esdras, see S. Mowinckel, *Studien zu dem Buche Ezra–Nehemiah. I. Die Nachchronische Redaktion des Buches. Die Listen* (Oslo, 1964), pp. 25-28; H.G.M. Williamson, *Israel in the Books of Chronicles*, pp. 22-25.

When Nehemiah arrived in Jerusalem in 445 BCE, he found the city in poor condition with ruined walls and burned gates (Neh. 1.11-13). Even after Nehemiah had rebuilt the walls 'the population was small, and no new families were growing up' (Neh. 7.4). This indicates that ordinary life had returned to the city, but not that Jerusalem was a prosperous or attractive place. There is really no firm piece of information about conditions in Jerusalem and the life or the returnees after c. 515 BCE. This fact indicates that not very much happened and that Jerusalem did not yet play a significant role in the lives of the people. Even if the temple was rebuilt, it had not yet gained the status of a 'national' center in the eyes of the people. Probably Mizpah was still the administrative center.

It is possible, however, to draw some conclusions about the temple cult from the Book of Joel. Most probably, it had been established in accordance with its pre-exilic traditions, as would be expected. In order to fashion Yahweh's 'nation' again, the cult had to be in conformity with the pre-exilic one, which meant that the liturgies of the Jehoiakim–Zedekiah period would have been revived as much as possible, but with some alterations because no Judahite kingship was in existence.[1] The prophet Joel shows, with his repeated demand that the people return to Yahweh, 'your God', that the temple cult again included the gods that were worshiped in the Solomonic temple.[2]

Another prophet to be mentioned from this period is Malachi.[3] He complains about many of the social and economic practices against which Nehemiah fought. Marriages with non-Judahites were common. He notes that the priests handled the cult and the religious laws in a sloppy way. For instance, they often accepted sick and lame animals for the sacrifices (Mal. 1.6-14; 2.1-9). His claim that Judah has married 'the daughter of a foreign god' (Mal. 2.11) can be combined with the ensuing accusation that the altar of Yahweh is covered with tears (2.13). The 'daughter of a foreign god' can refer both to a 'foreign' goddess and non-Judahite women.[4] The tears on Yahweh's altar cannot refer to ordinary men and women crying at the altar of

---

1. Cf. J. Bright, *A History of Israel* (3rd edn), p. 378.

2. See my book, *Joel and the Temple Cult*.

3. Consult B. Glazier-McDonald, who sees the most suitable date for Malachi as being between 470–450 BCE (*Malachi*, p. 17).

4. Thus B. Glazier-McDonald, *Malachi*, p. 120.

Yahweh. The altar was ritually approached only by priests; the text must reflect a rite that could have been performed in connection with the worship of a goddess.[1] Asherah was probably still worshiped in the Jerusalemite temple.[2] Malachi thus depicts a temple cult that is very much a continuation of the pre-exilic cultic pattern. He agrees with Joel, and like him demands a 'turning' (*šwb*) to Yahweh (Mal. 3.7). Both prophets believe that a person should not worship any other god.

The above sketch is all that can be drawn from biblical sources about the period between the temple dedication and Nehemiah's arrival in Jerusalem. Besides these texts, this period is virtually unknown, not only in Jerusalem but also in Palestine in general. After the Egyptian revolt had been quelled, Darius I went through Palestine during the winter of 519–518 BCE on his way to Egypt.[3] It is unclear whether Zerubbabel had already been dismissed or executed before Darius marched through Palestine.[4] Such a move would have made sense militarily. By eliminating Zerubbabel the Persian king would have assured himself a reliable situation in the hill country. Judah's proximity to the military establishments along the coast and the trunk road to Egypt could have become a disturbing factor if Judah were ruled by an opponent of the shah.[5] Thus, had Zerubbabel been considered a usurper, he would have had to have been removed as quickly as possible. This theory may be supported by the information in Ezra 5.6-17 and Tattenai's letter to Darius, in which Zerubbabel is not mentioned.

The canal that Necho II had begun to dig in order to connect the Nile with the Gulf of Suez was redug by the Persians.[6] Darius also repaired

---

1. See the discussion in G.W. Ahlström, *Joel and the Temple Cult of Jerusalem*, pp. 47-49; cf. F.F. Hvidberg, *Weeping and Laughter in the Old Testament*, pp. 121-22.

2. Cf. my *Aspects of Syncretism in Israelite Religion*, pp. 50-52.

3. R.A. Parker, 'Darius and his Egyptian Campaign', *AJSL* 58 (1941), pp. 373-77.

4. Cf. G. Widengren in J.H. Hayes and J.M. Miller, *Israelite and Judean History*, p. 523.

5. Cf. M. Noth, *The History of Israel*, p. 318.

6. R. Kent, 'Old Persian Texts. I. The Darius Suez c Inscription', *JNES* 1 (1942), pp. 415-21; cf. M.C. Root, *The King and the Kingship* (Acta Iranica, 19; Leiden, 1979), pp. 61-63.

Ptah's temple in Memphis and gave Udjahoresenet permission to re-establish the temple school at Sais.[1] Unfortunately, there is no information about Darius' actions as he marched through Palestine. After having secured his power in Egypt his goal was to conquer Greece and Thrace.

Macedonia and the peoples west of the Black Sea at the Danube became Persian subjects around 512 BCE. However, Darius was soon faced with a revolt by the Ionian cities in western Anatolia. They were supported by the Athenians, Persia's main enemy in Europe. After having put down the rebellion, showing no mercy, Darius invaded Greece.[2] The battle at Marathon in 490 BCE, where the Greeks fought under Miltiades, was a severe setback for Darius' plan of conquering Greece. After the defeat at Marathon he started to prepare for a new campaign against Greece. At the same time he faced a revolt in Egypt, but before he could meet that challenge he died (486 BCE). He was succeeded by his son Xerxes (486–465 BCE). The Persian empire had reached its zenith with Darius I. Its territory extended from the Danube in the Balkans to the Indus River in the east, from Egypt and Libya in the south to the Aral Sea and the Jaxartes River in the northeast. All of Darius's successors had the same goal vis-à-vis Greece: to conquer the Greek mainland. The policy of trying to incorporate all of the Greek cities into the Persian empire weakened the strength of the empire.

The difficulty posed by Greece does not mean that there was a united Greek 'front' against the Persians. The Greek city states played their own games. Sparta and Athens, for instance, were seldom on the same side. In addition, the Persian army, like that of the Egyptians and the Babylonians, had a great number of Greek mercenaries. They lived in garrison cities, such as Gaza, and often married indigenous women. Greek merchants were common all over the empire. Attic ware and Greek coins made their way to the highlands of Palestine, as witnessed by finds at Tell en-Naṣbeh and Tell Balaṭa (Shechem),[3] among other places. Greek physicians were employed by the Persian

---

1. G. Roeder, *Die Ägyptische Götterwelt*, p. 76.
2. Cf. J.M. Cook, *The Persian Empire*, pp. 91-100.
3. For a Greek coin at Tell Balaṭa, see G.E. Wright, *Schechem*, pp. 168-69. For Attic ware pottery from str. V of Tell Balaṭa (c. 525–475 BCE), cf. N. Lapp's investigation, 'The Stratum V Pottery from Balaṭa (Shechem)', *BASOR* 257 (1985), pp. 19-43.

court and by the 'courts' of the satraps. Greek customs as well as Greek religion thus travelled east. All this prepared the groundwork for the phenomenon called Hellenism.[1] Two hundred years of Persian rule were beneficial for most parts of the empire. Trade could increase and material culture could flourish undisturbed because there were no small nations that could rebel. The Greeks and sometimes Egypt caused political conflicts, but for a country such as Palestine, their rebellions did not cause any real disasters. Trade was perhaps concentrated in Phoenician hands. Ezek. 27.12-25 provides an inside view of Phoenician inland trade, which is more important in the text than the maritime activities. Nevertheless, this text cannot be used to describe Tyre's expansion in the Mediterranean, because it does not mention the Phoenician colonies in the west.[2]

At the end of the sixth century BCE Darius introduced a unified coinage system named after himself: the 'daric' (Hebrew *'ᵃdarkōn*, 1 Chron. 29.7). It was modelled after Lydian coinage.[3] Coinage served as an instrument of taxation and as a normalized medium for paying tribute.[4] The daric, however, was not much used. Greek coins were more common, which means that the daric did not penetrate all the areas of the empire.[5] It probably never replaced silver, which was weighed when used as payment. The introduction of the daric did not mean that coins could not be minted by the different peoples of the

---

1. Cf. M. Smith, *Palestinian Parties and Politics*, pp. 57-59. For Greeks in the empire, see J. Hofstetter, *Die Griechen in Persien: Prosopographie der Griechen im persischen Reich vor Alexander* (Archäologische Mitteilungen aus Iran, Ergänzungsband 5; Berlin, 1978).

2. G. Bunnens holds the opinion that this passage dates to the time after Ezekiel. It is written by an innovative but badly informed scribe who tried to show his knowledge (*L'expansion phénicienne en Méditerrannée*, p. 90). Bunnens may be right because the political situation is ignored. The writer seems to have referred to everything he knew about Tyre's inland trade, in the process mixing the present and the past.

3. Regarding the minting of coins, consult for instance M.A. Dandamayev, 'Politische Geschichte', *Beiträge zur Achämenidengeschichte* (ed. G. Walser), pp. 45-48.

4. Cf. H.G. Kippenberg, *Religion und Klassenbildung in antiken Judäa: Einer religionssoziologische Studie zum Verhältnis von Tradition und gesellschaftlicher Entwicklung* (2nd edn; Göttingen, 1982), p. 51.

5. Cf. P. Naster, 'Were the Labourers of Persepolis Paid by Means of Coinal Money?' *Ancient Society* 1 (1970), p. 129.

satrapies. For instance, Phoenician kings minted their own coins with inscriptions in Phoenician characters, and coins[1] with the inscription *yehwd* first came into circulation around 400 BCE in the subprovince of Judah (Yehud).[2] Coins from Gaza resemble Athenian coins, which show the commercial importance of Gaza and its international connections.[3] There are also coins with the Athenian owl and the inscription *yhwd*. One Yehud coin shows a god enthroned on a winged wheel,[4] which indicates that hostility towards religious iconography had not yet become part of the attitude of the official administrators of Yehud. The earliest coin found in Palestine is a Greek silver coin from Kos in the Aegean, discovered in a stratum of sixth-century Jerusalem.[5] It indicates that Greek traders and Greek products reached restored Jerusalem. Tell Balaṭa stratum V yielded a stamp with the symbol of Ahura Mazda.[6]

Darius' tomb at Naqsh-i-Rustam, which became a model for the Persian kings that followed, has a large relief above the entrance depicting the king (see Fig. 7). He is standing on a dais in front of a

1. Daric may have been employed as a term for money in Ezra 8.27 and Neh. 7.70-71.

2. Ezra 2.69 says that the returnees gave 61,000 gold drachmas and 5000 silver minas for the rebuilding of the temple. This must be a perspective from later times on the wealth of the returnees. For coinage, see G.F. Hill, 'Coinage from its Origin to the Persian Wars', *CAH*, IV, pp. 124-36. Cf. S.G. Robinson, 'The Beginning of the Achemenid Coinage', *Numismatic Chronicle* (1958), pp. 187-93; D. Kagan, 'The Date of the Earliest Coins', *AJA* 86 (1982), pp. 343-60; C.M. Kraay and P.R.S. Moorey, 'Two Fifth Century Hoards from the Near East', *Revue Numismatique*, Ser. 6, 10 (1968), pp. 181-235; H. Hamburger, 'Money', *IDB*, III, pp. 423-35; U. Rappaport, 'Gaza and Ascalon in Persian and Hellenistic Periods in Relation to their Coins', *IEJ* 20 (1970), pp. 75-80; J.W. Betlyon, *The Coinage and Mint from Phoenicia: The Pre-Alexandrinian Period* (HSM, 26; Chico, CA, 1982); Y. Meshorer, *Ancient Jewish Coinage. I. Persian Period through Hasmoneans* (New York, 1982), pp. 13-34; E. Stern, *Material Culture*, pp. 217-28.

3. U. Rappaport, *IEJ* 20 (1970), p. 76.

4. See B. Kanael, 'Ancient Jewish Coins and their Historical Importance', *BA* 26 (1963), pp. 40-41; H. Kienle, *Der Gott auf dem Flügelrad: Zu den ungelösten Fragen der 'synkretistischen' Münze BMC Palestine S.181, Nr. 29* (Göttinger Orientforschungen, VI. Reihe hellenistica, 7; Wiesbaden, 1975); E. Stern, *Material Culture*, pp. 224-25; Y. Meshorer, *Ancient Jewish Coinage*, I, pp. 21-22.

5. G. Barkay, *Israel Museum Bulletin* 274 (Jerusalem, 1986).

6. E.F. Campbell in the forthcoming report about Tell Balaṭa (courtesy of professor Campbell).

fire-altar with a bow in his hand. Above his head is the symbol of the god Ahura Mazda. The tomb inscription says that if a person would like to know how many countries the king has ruled, it would be enough to look at the sculptures of the people pictured as carrying his throne.[1] In other words, the dais is the symbol of world power, as was the throne of earlier ancient Near Eastern kings.[2]

Also among the dominions of the empire was Cyprus, as mentioned before. As in Phoencia, the Persians did not abolish kingship in Cyprus. The different kingdoms were semi-independent. However, with Darius I the Persian policy changed somewhat and became more oppressive. When the Ionian Greeks revolted in 499/498 BCE, most of the kings of Cyprus followed suit. The only kingdom that stayed pro-Persian was that of Amathus (east of Limassol). This had a large Phoenician population, and Phoenicians were always anti-Greek politically. After the revolt had been put down, the Persian policy was to encourage the animosity between the Greeks and the Phoenicians of the island; the principle was divide and rule. The other side of the coin was that the Greeks of mainland Greece always encouraged the Cypriot kings to throw off the Persian yoke. However, in 480 BCE the Cypriots were forced to join Xerxes in his fight against the Greeks. They contributed 150 ships to the Phoenician fleet. It is interesting to note that Persia, which always tried to split the Greeks through diplomacy and bribes, had managed to forge an alliance among most of the peoples of Greece and Thessaly in 481 BCE. For the Athenians this was a dangerous situation, and it was a blow that they did not receive assistance from the Greeks of Sicily, because the Phoenicians of Carthage under Hamilcar launched an attack on Sicily at this time, helping the Phoenicians and Xerxes.[3]

Xerxes mentions in an inscription that rebellions occurred in some parts of the empire when he ascended the throne. Countries that rendered service to 'evil gods' had their temples destroyed under the 'shadow of Ahura Mazda'.[4] This may show that temples and their gods and cults that were not in line with Persian ideology and its system of

---

1. Cf. M.C. Root, *The King and Kingship*, p. 180; K. Koch, 'Weltordnung und Reichsidee im alten Iran', in P. Frei and K. Koch, *Reichsidee und Reichsorganisation im Perserreich*, pp. 96-109.
2. Ps. 22.4[3] may reflect this kind of ideology.
3. Cf. J.M. Cook, *The Persian Empire*, p. 107.
4. *ANET*, p. 317.

sacred law and administration had no right to exist. As mentioned before, religion was conceptualized in legal categories. The Jerusalemite temple intially was an accepted cult place to the Persians, but then things apparently got out of hand; the old pre-exilic traditions or a more independent course were followed, and a special emissary, a supervisor, had to be sent in order to re-establish the official cult in a form acceptable to the Persian court. Such an emissary was Ezra. His title, 'the scribe of the law of God in heaven' (Ezra 7.12) which 'is in your hand' (7.14), indicates that he was a Persian official well-acquainted with the laws of the empire and that he had a special law that he was commissioned to promulgate in Jerusalem.

Xerxes inherited his father's problem with Egypt.[1] After having put down the rebellion he returned to Ecbatana. Soon afterwards Babylon rebelled, first in 484 and then again in 482 BCE, when its satrap, Zopyrus, was killed. Greece had to wait. Xerxes sent his brother-in-law, Megabyxos, with an army to Babylon in 482. The city was quickly taken. Its fortifications, splendidly rebuilt by Nebuchadrezzar II, were torn down. Contrary to what has been maintained for quite some time, Xerxes did not destroy Babylon's temples, nor did he remove or melt down the statue of Marduk as bullion.[2] The *akītu* festival (New Year's festival) seems never to have been celebrated by the Persian kings. As for the title 'King of Babylon', Xerxes seldom used it.[3]

Xerxes' main efforts were directed towards the goal of subduing Greece. Even if he was successful in landing troops in Greece and occupying Attica,[4] he was forced to retreat to Asia. In 480 BCE his large fleet, consisting mainly of Egyptian, Phoenician and Asiatic Greek triremes, was trapped in a bay at Salamis and defeated by the Greeks. It was a catastrophe for the Persians. Some of the Phoenician commanders who had abandoned the fight went to Xerxes in order to

---

1. For his reign, see for instance, A.T. Olmstead, *History of the Persian Empire*, pp. 230-32.

2. Cf. A.T. Olmstead, *History of the Persian Empire*, pp. 236-37. See also F.M. de Liagre Böhl, 'Die babylonischen Prätendenten zur Zeit des Xerxes', *BO* 19 (1962), pp. 110-114.

3. A. Kuhrt and S. Sherwin-White, 'Xerxes' destruction of Babylonian Temples', *Achaemenid History*. II. *The Greek Sources* (ed. H. Sncisi-Weerdenburg and A. Kuhrt; Leiden, 1987), pp. 75-78.

4. Diodorus 11.14.5.

protest and to explain the situation, but the king was so furious that he killed them, according to Herodotus (8.90).[1] The others, seeing this, sailed home and did not participate in Persian naval operations again until 465 BCE, when Cyprus was threatened by the Greeks under the Athenians. A year after the defeat at Salamis a land battle took place at Plataea, which was also a disaster for the Persians.

The Phoenicians managed more than once to fight off the Athenians from the waters of Cyprus and protect the Phoenician colonies there. This was the picture from 465 to c. 390 BCE. It changed in the 380s, when king Achoris of Egypt supported Evagoras of Salamis in his revolt against Persia (389–380 BCE). At this time the Phoenicians sided with Evagoras.

J. Morgenstern has argued that a second destruction of Jerusalem occurred in 485 BCE, shortly after Xerxes ascended the throne. He says that during the rebellions against the new king, Judah's neighbors, the Ammonites, Moabites, Edomites and Philistines, invaded Judah and destroyed Jerusalem and its temple.[2] There were disturbances in Palestine during this period and destruction layers at Shechem, Tell el-Fûl, Gibeon and Bethel have been seen to reflect rebellion.[3] However, the reason for the destructions is not known. Moabites and Edomites were not in any condition to carry on a war, because they no longer existed as political entities. The Samarian *pehâ*, on the other hand, could have commanded troops, as was the case with most governors. The movement of Egyptian detachments into Palestine may be no more than a hypothesis. The textual basis upon which Morgenstern builds his theory is weak. Many of the biblical texts to which he refers to do not provide clear information about the date and could just as well be dated to a time before 485 BCE.[4] The passage in Neh. 1.2-3 mentioning the burnt walls of Jerusalem and the distress of

---

1. Cf. Diodorus 11.19.4.

2. 'Jerusalem—485 BCE', *HUCA* 27 (1956), pp. 101-79; 28 (1957), pp. 15-47; and 31 (1960), pp. 1-29; see also F.M.T. de Liagre Böhl, *BO* 19 (1962), pp. 110-14.

3. Consult G.E. Wright, *Shechem*, p. 167; cf. also E. Stern, *Material Culture*, p. 254.

4. For a refutation of Morgenstern's theory, see H.H. Rowley, 'Nehemiah's Mission and its Background', *BJRL* 37 (1955), pp. 557-58; G. Widengren in Hayes and Miller, *Israelite and Judean History*, p. 256; H.G.M. Williamson, *Ezra, Nehemiah* (WBC, 16; Waco, TX, 1985), pp. 60-61; I. Eph'al, *The Ancient Arabs*, p. 199 n. 677.

the city does not seem to refer to happenings 40 years before Nehemiah's arrival in the city. The problems with the neighboring groups including the Ashdodites, Geshem, the Arabs, the Judahite people in Transjordan under Tobiah, 'the servant', and the people of Samerina under Sanballat the Horonite (Neh. 2.10, 19; 4.1[4.7]), cannot have led warfare so intensive that they tried to destroy Jerusalem in this period. Geshem, Tobiah and Sanballat were contemporaries of Nehemiah; they lived c. 40 years after the 'disaster' Morgenstern is assuming. The writer is providing an excuse for Nehemiah's commission by depicting Jerusalem to be surrounded by enemies, necessitating protection. The old walls had to be rebuilt, a task which Artaxerxes had earlier forbidden (Ezra 4.17-23).

The biblical text considers religious and political hostility as the only reasons for the Jewish community's problems with the neighboring peoples. However, there is more to it than this. For instance, economic interests should be acknowledged. Of relevance is one of the silver bowls found at Tell el-Maskhuṭa in the Delta[1] that bears the inscription: 'That which Qainu, son of Geshem, Qedar's king, sacrificed to han-'Ilat'. These bowls are dated to c. 400 BCE.[2] If this Geshem is the same as the one mentioned in Neh. 2.19 and 6.1-9 (Gashmu in 6.6), who together with Sanballat and Tobiah accused Nehemiah of rebellion, then it is likely that Nehemiah's policies collided with Geshem's in southern Palestine.[3] The accusation that Nehemiah was preparing for rebellion would be natural when it is recalled that the Persian government had forbidden the rebuilding of

1. According to J.S. Holladay, this site may have been built in connection with Necho II's canal construction (*Cities of the Delta, Part III: Tell el Maskhuṭa* [American Research Center in Egypt Reports, 6; Malibu, CA, 1982], pp. 18-19); on this, see B. MacDonald, 'Excavations at Tell el-Maskhuṭa', *BA* 43 (1980), pp. 49-58.

2. W.J. Dumbrell, 'The Tell el-Maskhuta Bowl and the "Kingdom" of Qedar in the Persian Period', *BASOR* 203 (1971), pp. 33-44; I. Eph'al, *The Ancient Arabs*, p. 194.

3. If this Geshem is the same as the one mentioned in Nehemiah, he would probably have lived in the 430s. The date of the Book of Nehemiah in its present form would then have been around the end of the fifth century BCE at the earliest; cf. S. Talmon, 'Ezra and Nehemiah', *IDBSup*, pp. 320-21. See also Neh. 12.47, and the phrase 'in the days of Nehemiah'. S. Mowinckel thinks that Neh. 12 is from the time after the fall of the Persian empire (*Studien zu dem Buche Ezra–Nehemia*, I, p. 144).

the walls of Jerusalem. Nehemiah's policies were clearly separatistic.[1] The fact that Tobiah had a chamber prepared for him in the Jerusalem temple by the high priest Eliashib during Nehemiah's absence[2] (Neh. 13.4-9)[3] shows that even the priesthood of Jerusalem had not yet grasped the essence of Nehemiah's policies. Thus Eliashib (and likewise, perhaps, the rest of the priesthood) had not adopted or understood the kind of exclusiveness in religion and political affairs that Nehemiah propagated. Neither could he know anything of the ideology of Ezra, who was a contemporary of Eliashib's grandson Johanan (Neh. 12.11).[4] It should be remembered that Judaism was in its infancy in this period, which marked the beginning of a new epoch for the people of Yahweh. The theology and law of this epoch triumphed with the figure of Ezra.

Others, such as Sanballat, had close contacts with the Jerusalemites and the descendants of the returnees. A son of Jehoiada, son of the priest Eliashib, married a daughter of Sanballat. For that he was later expelled from Jerusalem by Nehemiah (Neh. 13.28). Josephus also mentions a marriage between a daughter of Sanballat, Nicaso, and Manasseh, the brother of Jerusalem's high priest Jaddua, great-grandson of Eliashib. This event would have taken place in the last decade of the Persian period.[5] However, the Nehemiah passage shows that ordinary human relations were still maintained between the two societies and that religion had not yet become a dividing force. It may

1.   It is interesting to note that Nehemiah does not mention the Edomites. Everything south of Judah (Yehud) is Arab country.

2.   Some scholars such as S. Mowinckel (*Studien zu dem Buche Ezra–Nehemia. II. Die Nehemia-Denkschrift* [Oslo, 1964], pp. 35-37) and U. Kellermann (*Nehemia: Quellen, Überlieferung und Geschichte* [BZAW, 102; Berlin, 1967], pp. 48-51) have argued that Nehemiah did not serve twice as *peḥâ*. For a critique of this theory, see H.G.M. Williamson, *Ezra, Nehemiah*, pp. 382f-83.

3.   The Bible presents this as an 'evil' that was dangerous for the Jerusalemite religion (Neh. 13.7-9), but was it? We are not told what the 'evil' was.

4.   This means that Ezra came after Nehemiah; cf. H.H. Rowley, *BJRL* 37 (1955), pp. 552-53. For the high priests of the Persian period, see G. Widengren in J.H. Hayes and J.M. Miller, *Israelite and Judean History*, pp. 505-509.

5.   *Ant.* 11.32. See J.D. Purvis, *The Samaritan Pentateuch and the Origin of the Samaritan Sect* (HSM, 2; Cambridge, MA, 1968), pp. 100-101; R. Egger, *Josephus Flavius und die Samaritaner: Eine terminologische Untersuchung zur Identitätsklärung der Samaritaner* (Novum Testamentum et Orbis Antiquus, 4; Freiburg, 1986), pp. 69-70.

be concluded with S. Herrmann that these marriages might have represented 'an attempt by the upper class to improve their position by entering into relations with their counterparts' in neighboring societies.[1]

Xerxes was assassinated in 465 BCE by his chiliarch Artabanus and a eunuch. He was succeeded by Artaxerxes I (Longimanus, 465–424 BCE), who had murdered his oldest brother, Darius, believing he had killed his father. He also had to fight another brother, Hystaspes, who was a satrap of Bactria.[2] In this period of uncertainty about the succession, Inaros, son of Psammetichus III of Egypt, staged a revolt, expelling the Persian tax-collectors. He received support from Athens, which sent its fleet to the Nile. The Greeks had also attacked Cyprus, while the Athenians had raided the Syro-Palestinian coast (Thucydides 1.104). After several years the Egyptian rebellion was put down in 455 BCE by the satrap of Abr Nahara, Megabyxos, who managed to immobilize and capture the Athenian fleet. Megabyxos had promised Inaros and some Greek commanders that they would be released, but Artaxerxes' mother forced the king to have them killed. That action led Megabyxos to rebel (449 BCE), but he was soon pardoned and reinstated as satrap. His rebellion was too dangerous for the empire.

The early years of the reign of Artaxerxes I would probably have been the time when Rehum of Samaria and his scribe Shimshai warned Artaxerxes about the 'wickedness' of the city of Jerusalem and that a rebellion would probably break out there (Ezra 4.6-16).[3] From this point of view it is quite understandable that Artaxerxes stopped the rebuilding of Jerusalem. He had enough problems already. The reason why he allowed Nehemiah to go to Jerusalem later on and rebuild the city walls can only be guessed. He may have realized that the little society in and around Jerusalem was very insignificant politically and militarily so that a wall around that little city would not create military problem that would shake the empire. To the contrary, a 'bastion' in the south may have been an acceptable idea to the king. After the Egyptian rebellion had been put down a peace treaty had been made with the Greeks in 479, forming the so-called Delian

---

1. *A History of Israel in Old Testament Times* (2nd edn), p. 307.

2. J.M. Cook, *The Persian Empire*, p. 127. Cf. G. Widengren, in J.H. Hayes and J.M. Miller, *Israelite and Judean History*, p. 526.

3. Cf. J. Bright, *A History of Israel* (3rd edn), p. 378.

league, and after the insurrection by Megabyxos, the Persian empire was at peace for a time. The peace treaty with the Greeks has been called the 'Peace of Callias'.[1] The Athenians agreed not to interfere in Egypt, Cyprus or Phoenicia. The Persians for their part would not send any fleets into the Aegean.[2] As subsequent events will show, the Persians did not give up hope of subduing Greece. They simply had to buy time. The peace treaty made it possible for the Persians to administer southwestern Asia without disturbances by the Greeks.

Nehemiah

About twenty years after Artaxerxes I had ascended the throne the political situation had changed. The rebellion by the satrap Megabyxos in 448 BCE could not be quelled, but king and satrap were reconciled. Shortly after this a royal cup-bearer of Judahite descent, Nehemiah,[3] learned from his brother Hanani and some others arriving at Susa from Judah about the 'deplorable' situation in Jerusalem: ruined walls and burned gates. He managed to receive a commission from the king to go to Jerusalem and repair its walls (Neh. 1.1–2.8). Since Nehemiah was appointed governor for twelve years, his primary task would not have been the repair of the city walls; this would hae been a small short-term project added to his other regular duties (Neh. 5.14). Such an appointment must have been made for political reasons, which would suggest that the Persian government wanted to see a much more stable situation in Judah. Perhaps the Persian system had been efficiently imposed on Judah. The king may not have forgotten the report he had received a few decades earlier, but the situation must have changed. It is possible that the king found it wise to rebuild Jerusalem at this time in order to have a small 'bastion' in southern Judah close to the Egyptian sphere of interest. Nehemiah received a royal letter as a passport and a letter for Asaph, the 'keeper of the king's park',[4]

1. Callias was an Athenian who went to Susa in order to negotiate the peace.
2. Cf. E.M. Walker, 'Athens and the Greek Powers, 462–445 BCE', *CAH*, V (2nd edn), pp. 87-88; J.M. Cook, *The Persian Empire*, p. 128.
3. See U. Kellermann, *Nehemiah*; cf. also H.H. Rowley, *BJRL* 37 (1955), pp. 528-61; R. Klein, 'Ezra and Nehemiah in Recent Studies', *Magnalia Dei* (ed. F.M. Cross *et al.*; New York, 1976*)*, pp. 361-76.
4. The biblical word translated 'park', *pardēs*, is a Persian loan-word. A. Jepsen would identify this with Jebel Ferdes in the area of Herodion, ('Pardes', *ZDPV* 74 [1958], pp. 65-68).

about supplies for the rebuilding effort (Neh. 2.1-8). Where this park was located is not mentioned. There were many royal parks; one, for instance, was located at Sidon.[1] The name Asaph could refer to a man of Israelite or Judahite descent who had made a career in the Persian administration.

Whatever motive the king may have had for giving Nehemiah his commission, it appears that he overstepped his authority. He arrived in Jerusalem with a military escort of 'army officers and calvary' (Neh. 2.9). Nehemiah must have known that the king had previously stopped the rebuilding. Therefore, after three days he went on a survey around the city at night in order to find out the condition of the walls and the gates. No one was told the purpose of this excursion (Neh. 2.11-16). It is questionable how much he could have learned in the dark of night. The writer's purpose is to show that Nehemiah had to work intially in secret in order not to sabotage his own project. After this he organized the people into two main groups so that one kept watch while the other was working. Both priests and laymen were forced to participate. People from different areas were responsible for rebuilding certain parts (Neh. 3). It was at this time that Sanballat, Tobiah, Geshem, the Ammonites and the Ashdodites felt that Nehemiah was planning a rebellion (Neh. 2.19-20), and it was natural that such an opinion would be entertained. To have people standing guard while others were working on the walls must have indicated some hostility. Nehemiah 4 gives the impression that, because Sanballat *et consortes* planned an attack, Nehemiah had to divide the working crew into two groups who alternated between watching and working.

Sanballat and Geshem tried to avert a conflict. Four times they repeated an invitation to Nehemiah by messenger to meet them 'in one of the villages of the plain of Ono' (Neh. 6.2-9). Finally, Sanballat sent an open letter to Nehemiah telling him that the Persian king would soon hear about the rumors of rebellion. Judahite prophets also opposed Nehemiah's work (Neh. 6.14). Had Sanballat wanted to stop the project by force, he would not have urged Nehemiah so many times to come to the negotiating table. However, the invitation could also have been a trap, as Nehemiah also concluded.

The choice of a meeting place must imply that the territory around Ono (Kfar Ana, coord. 137-159) between Lod and Aphek was not a

1. Cf. Diodorus 16.41.5.

part of Judah.[1] It probably belonged to Ashdod, and was thus located outside the territories of both Nehemiah and Sanballat.[2] Gezer, to the south of Ono, was not part of the subprovince of Judah either.[3] Ono was thus perhaps the closest site for a meeting of the three leaders. It has been suggested that Geshem was the subgovernor of Idumaea residing at Tell ed-Duweir.[4] This is not known, and neither is the period in which Idumaea was established as a Persian province. If the biblical Geshem is identical with Geshem of the Tell el-Maskhuṭa bowl, he could very well have been an Arab (Qedarite) 'king' who also had command over the territory south of Yehud.[5] Nehemiah does not mention any Edomites. For him or, rather, for the writer of the Book of Nehemiah, the Edomite territory south of Judah was inhabited by Arabs.[6]

According to Neh. 3.8, Nehemiah's wall did not encircle the whole area of the pre-exilic city.[7] The text states that 'they abandoned (left out) Jerusalem unto the Broad Wall'.[8] This would mean that Nehemiah's city was smaller than pre-exilic Jerusalem[9] and that it was built higher up on the eastern slope than the earlier wall.[10] The line of the wall that Nehemiah followed was not that of the pre-exilic city wall. He repaired the wall that had started to be built earlier but which had been stopped by Artaxerxes (Ezra 4.17-22). The location of the 'Broad Wall' is unknown, but the huge wall that has been unearthed in the Jewish Quarter of the present day Old City could be a candidate. Because only part of it has been excavated, its length and direction are

---

1. It should be noted that Lod, Hadid and Ono are mentioned among the cities of the returnees in Ezra 2.33 and Neh. 7.37, but that does not necessarily mean that they returned to these cities.

2. Cf. M. Avi-Yonah, *The Holy Land*, p. 18.

3. No Yehud coins have been found at Gezer.

4. G.E. Wright, *Biblical Archaeology*, pp. 206-207.

5. Cf. the remarks of E.A. Knauf, *Ismael*, pp. 104-106; see also I. Eph'al, *The Ancient Arabs*, p. 197.

6. Cf. A. Alt, *PJ* 27 (1931), pp. 73-74 (= *KS*, II, pp. 344-45).

7. There is no indication that the western hill was included.

8. Manasseh is said to have built a wall that encircled the Ophel (2 Chron. 33.14). If this joined up with the 'Broad Wall', it would have made Jerusalem one city again.

9. Cf. H.G.M. Williamson, 'Nehemiah's Walls Revisited', *PEQ* 116 (1984), pp. 81-88.

10. See K.M. Kenyon, *Digging up Jerusalem*, pp. 172-87.

unknown.[1] Nehemiah's building project was finished in 52 days (Neh. 6.15).[2]

Even though the city was encircled by a new wall, people did not move into it. As noted, Neh. 7.4 says that the city was spacious but no families were 'growing up' in it.[3] Any little city would look spacious with no families in it. The problem was solved by casting lots; every tenth man had to move to Jerusalem (Neh. 11.1). The rest could stay where they lived. The same verse also mentions that the leaders (*śārîm*) of the people settled in Jerusalem. This text indicates that before Nehemiah arrived Jerusalem had been a very insignificant place and that the capital of the subprovince Yehud had still been at Mizpah. To the officials of the neighboring subprovinces it certainly looked like a new political entity was being created by Nehemiah.

The rebuilding of Jerusalem's wall resulted in Mizpah's losing its position as the residence of the *pāqîd, peḥâ*. Excavations at Tell en-Naṣbeh have shown that a city wall was in existence from 586 to 400 BCE.[4] Jar handles with *yhd* impressions have been found in this stratum, as has Attic ware (str. I).[5] However, the population seems to have 'declined in the fifth century'.[6] This observation would agree with the theory that Mizpah lost its position as a district capital during the period of Nehemiah's tenure in Jerusalem. It is interesting to note that Neh. 3.7 mentions that among the workers building the wall were men of Gibeon and Mizpah[7] 'belonging to the seat of the governor of

---

1. See N. Avigad, *IEJ* 20 (1970), pp. 1-8, and 129-30; consult also R. Grafman, 'Nehemiah's "Broad Wall"', *IEJ* 24 (1974), pp. 50-51; cf. E.-M. Laperrouzas, 'Quelques remarques sur le rempart de Jérusalem à l'époque de Néhémie', *Folia Orientalia* 21 (1980), pp. 179-85; G.W. Ahlström (*Royal Administration*, p. 79).

2. Josephus reports that it took two years and four months (*Ant.* 11.179). It is impossible to decide which piece of information is more trustworthy. 52 days seems to be a very short time for building a city wall. However, if it is remembered that this was not a new wall, but rather the completion of a wall that had started to be built some decades before, 52 days would be a reasonable amount of time.

3. According to S. Mowinckel, Neh. 7.69-71, in the census list of Nehemiah, is borrowed from Ezra 2.68-69; see *Studien zu dem Buche Ezra–Nehemia*, I, p. 31.

4. C.C. McCown and J.C. Wampler, *Tell en Naṣbeh*, I-II, p. 185.

5. C.C. McCown and J.C. Wampler, *Tell en Naṣbeh*, I-II, pp. 164-167.

6. C.C. McCown and J.C. Wampler, *Tell en-Naṣbeh*, I-II, p. 63.

7. According to H.L. Ginsberg, Mizpah was crown land and not 'subsumed under "Judah" or "Jerusalem"' during the Persian period (*BASOR* 109 [1948], pp. 21-22).

'Beyond the River', '*ēber hannāhār*.[1] The phrase is unclear. It could mean that the persons from Mizpah really were under the command of the governor, but that they also participated in the rebuilding project. The proposal that they built crown property in Jerusalem at this time is merely a guess.[2]

As district 'governor', Nehemiah also made his power felt in the socioeconomic sphere. For instance, he released property that had been seized because of debt in an attempt to stop the exploitation of the lower classes (Neh. 5.1-5). Nehemiah 5 suggests that Nehemiah carried through an agrarian reform. His 'egalitarian' idea that all should be brothers may have been opposed by the landowners. It did not suit their economic system. However, the poor farmers may have liked it.[3] He also tried to end the selling of Judahites as slaves (Neh. 5.5-13), an economic labor custom known also from Joel 4.6.[4]

Nehemiah probably did not abstain from the salary that the *pehâ* got from taxation, contrary to what has usually been advocated. Neh. 5.14-15 mentions that he and his entourage did not make use of the food allowances and that the former 'governors' had laid excessive tax burdens on the people.[5] In Persia the officials were on a ration scale,[6] and this same system might have been followed in the provinces. Thus, Nehemiah and his closest administrative personnel received their rations, but did not overtax the people. In other words, Nehemiah prides himself on ending corruption.

1. Thus the Danish Bible translation of 1931; cf. S. Biøn, *Lad os opbygge Jerusalems mure* (Text og Tolkning, 2; Copenhagen, 1971), pp. 60-61.

2. Cf. K. Galling, *Studien zur Geschichte Israels im persischen Zeitalter*, p. 97. F.C. Fensham suggests that it refers to the house which the satrap used when visiting the city (*The Books of Ezra and Nehemiah*, p. 174).

3. Cf. H.G. Kippenberg, *Religion und Klassenbildung im antiken Judäa*, pp. 54-77.

4. W.A. Dubberstein thought that the price for slaves rose during the Persian period ('Comparative Prices in Later Babylonia [625–400 BCE]', *AJSL* 56 [1939], p. 35).

5. As the satrap Arsames (Arsham) of Egypt had property in Babylonia, so Nehemiah could have had income from an estate or estates he may have acquired as a high official of the Persian court. For Arsames leasing his property, see the discussion in G.R. Driver, *Aramaic Documents of the Fifth Century BCE* (Oxford, 1957), pp. 88-90.

6. R.T. Hallock, *Persepolis Fortification Tablets* (OIP, 92; Chicago, 1969), pp. 23-24.

Nehemiah was in Jerusalem for c. 12 years (445–433 BCE)[1] and then for unknown reasons returned to the Persian court. It is possible that he had to answer all the allegations made to the king about preparing a rebellion. Artaxerxes must have trusted him, because after some time—the date is not known—Nehemiah was sent back to Jerusalem.[2] Although it is not said that he took up his old position, his actions certainly show that he was still the *peḥâ*. Soon after his return he entered the temple even though he was not a priest, moved out of it all the belongings of Tobiah, and 'cleansed' the area (Neh. 13.4-9). Through this act Tobiah and his 'party' were officially branded as 'impure' Judahites.

Nehemiah also forbade treading grapes and the moving of foodstuffs into Jerusalem on the sabbath. In addition, he did not allow the Tyrian markets to operate at this time. He closed the city gates during the sabbath and used the Levites as a police force to guard the gates. He reorganized the temple personnel and the system of tithes (Neh. 10.33-40). The temple apparently had been neglected (Neh. 10.40)—no surprise, considering that prior to Nehemiah's initial arrival Jerusalem had been a most insignificant town. Priests and Levites deemed reliable by Nehemiah were put in supervisory positions (Neh. 13.10-14). Levites who had not been employed by the temple but working their fields were given certain positions in the temple. These various actions suggest that the temple had not been very important before Nehemiah's time. People had not come to grips with a 'national' temple without a Judahite king.

Sociologically, Nehemiah tried to dissolve the so-called mixed marriages with Ashdodites, Ammonites and Moabites that had resulted in many of the children of those marriages who 'could not speak the language of Judah'.[3] The expulsion from Jerusalem of a grandson of the high priest Eliashib, who had married a daughter of Sanballat (Neh. 13.15-30),[4] indicates that the reason for dissolving the marriages

---

1. Neh. 5.14, cf. 13.6.

2. H. Donner assumes that only with Nehemiah's second term as *peḥâ* did Judah become a subprovince separated from Samerina (*Geschichte des Volkes Israel*, II, p. 422).

3. This may be part of the propaganda. These languages were probably not very different from Judahite. It is unclear how deeply Aramaic had penetrated into the different pockets of the population of the greater Palestinian territory.

4. According to Josephus (*Ant.* 11.8), the name of the expelled priest was

was ideological and political and not linguistic. It may be wondered how much of the Jerusalemite cultic tradition followed him to Samaria. All of Nehemiah's actions show that sacred and civil authority went together as they had during the monarchic period. The high priest had not yet replaced the 'governor'. It is understandable why the leaders of the neighboring subprovinces accused Nehemiah of preparing for his own kingship, an accusation that any satrap or 'governor' might have heard.

Besides the few names of Persian officials that occur in the literary material, such as Seshbazzar, Zerubbabel, Sanballat, Tobiah (?), Geshem, Nehemiah, Ezra and Bagohi (Bagoas),[1] N. Avigad has reconstructed a list of 'governors' of Yehud from bullae and coins. Among the new names are Elnathan (late sixth cent.), Yeho'ezer (early fifth cent.), Ahazi (also early fifth cent.) and Yehezqyah (c. 330 BCE).[2] From the Wadi Daliyeh papyri F.M. Cross has been able to establish a 'dynasty' of Sanballats in Samaria that included three 'governors' with the name Sanballat. This family of Sanballatides are known from the mid-fifth century BCE down to the time of Alexander.[3] It is interesting to note

Manasseh, who was allegedly a brother of the high priest. He reports that the name of Sanballat's daughter was Nicaso. He also says that Manasseh received a promise from Sanballat to build a temple at Mt Gerizim and that Sanballat then asked Alexander the Great for his authorization to build the temple. Josephus has here 'contracted' history. Nobody that Nehemiah had expelled from Jerusalem could have lived during Alexander's time. See the discussion in H.H. Rowley, 'Sanballat and the Samaritan Temple', *BJRL* 38 (1955), pp. 166-80; H.G. Kippenberg, *Garizim und Synagoge* (Religions-geschichtliche Versuche und Vorarbeiten, 30; Berlin, 1971), pp. 50-53; G. Widengren in J.H. Hayes and J.M. Miller, *Israelite and Judean History*, p. 513. Still, the name Manasseh could be right, and there is no mention of a high priest with that name in the Samaritan list. This would indicate that Manasseh lived before that temple was built. F.M. Cross, building upon Josephus (*Ant.* 11.8.2), suggests that there could have been intermarriages between 'the aristocracy of Samaria and the high-priest family of Jerusalem'; thus, Nicaso could have been a daughter of Sanballat III ('A Reconstruction of the Judean Restoration', *JBL* 94 [1975], pp. 5-6). This could be a possibility even after the time described in the works of Nehemiah and Ezra. Theologically the 'borders' were supposed to have been closed, but there would have been priests who were opposed to the 'marriage ideology' of Nehemiah and Ezra. The later temple at Gerizim would represent a Judahistic but not a Jewish cult.

1.   Bagohi is known from the Elephantine letters.
2.   *Bullae and Seals from a Post-Exilic Judean Archive*, p. 35.
3.   'The Papyri and their Historical Implications', *Discoveries in the Wâdi ed-Dâliyeh*, pp. 17-22.

that nobody includes Ezra in any list of top officials in Jerusalem.

The remains at Ramat Rahel could indicate that the site of the former royal citadel of the late pre-exilic period was again housing a high administrative official during the later Persian period. The many seals and stamps found at this site indicate that the place could have been occupied by the *pehâ* or by one of his high officials. According to Y. Aharoni, 270 seal impressions were found in rubble or pits of the Persian period.[1] Some of them had the inscriptions *yhwd* and *hphh*. As at Tell en-Naṣbeh, a few had the inscription *l'hzy-hphh*, 'for Ahazi, the governor'. Unfortunately, the excavations have not been able to give a clear picture of the occupation during the Persian period. Very few building remains were found.

When Artaxerxes I died in 424 BCE he was followed within one year by three sons. Xerxes II was murdered by Sogdianos at night while Xerxes was drunk; Sogianos was then killed by Ochos (Darius II).[2] The latter reigned between 423 and 405 BCE. He had to face revolts in Anatolia, Egypt, Media and Syria. These happened mainly during the period from 410 to 408 BCE, which was the time when the Palestinian military garrison at Elephantine experienced a riot that destroyed its Yahwistic temple.

The name Palestine does not occur in any sources from this time, with the exception of some correspondence from the military colony at Jeb (Elephantine at the First Cataract) to Jerusalem and Samaria. Many of these texts, written in Aramaic, deal with legal problems such as marriage and other contracts, adoption, interest and the like. They date from 419 to c. 400 BCE.[3] There are also letters. The earliest one is from Darius II to the satrap Arsham (Arsames) and Hananiah[4] in Jerusalem, addressed to the priest Yedoniah of Elephantine with an

1. 'Ramat Rahel', *EAEHL*, IV, p. 1007; see also *idem, Excavations at Ramat Rahel*, I, p. 34; see also E. Stern, *Material Culture*, pp. 202-14.

2. See J.M. Cook, *The Persian Empire*, p. 129.

3. See A.H. Sayce and A.E. Cowley, *Aramaic Papyri Discovered at Assuan* (London, 1906); E. Sachau, *Aramäische Papyrus und Ostraka aus einer jüdischen Militärkolonie zue Elephantine*, I-II (Leipzig, 1911); E.G. Kraeling, *The Brooklyn Museum Aramaic Papyri: New Documents of the Fifth Century BCE from the Jewish Colony at Elephantine* (London, 1953). Cf. B. Porten, *Archives from Elephantine: The Life of an Ancient Jewish Military Colony* (Los Angeles, 1968); P. Grelot, *Documents araméens d'Egypte* (Paris, 1972).

4. Hananiah is usually seen as the same as Nehemiah's brother, mentioned in Neh. 1.2.

ordinance to authorize the celebration of the 'Feast of the Unleavened Bread' for the Judahites of the garrison.[1] This letter has often been associated with the Passover, but the text does not mention this festival.[2] This indicates that the people of the garrison had not yet learned about Judaism or Ezra's reform.

Another indication for the lack of knowledge about Judaism in Egypt is a temple dedicated to Yahweh at Elephantine, which apparently was in existence already before Cambyses.[3] This means that it was older than the Zerubbabel temple.[4] Letters sent in 410 BCE to Bagoas, 'governor' of Yehud, and to the priest Johanan in Jerusalem, refer to a temple to Yahu (Yahweh) that had been destroyed in a riot instigated by the priests of the Egyptian god Khnum, the patron deity of Elephantine. The priests had bribed the Persian commander, so he allowed the destruction.[5] The hatred of the Persians in Egypt may have provided an opportunity for the Khnum priests during the absence of the satrap Arsames. However, this cannot have been the only reason for the riot, because the Persian commander, Widrang, cooperated with the Egyptians. There may also have been religious motivations.[6]

The temple and its worshippers have usually been regarded as Jewish. This is questionable. Since the papyri refer to such deity names as Anath-Yahu and Ashim-Bethel, many of the constituents could have been descendants of Israelites and Samarians. The deity name Bethel does not point to Judah. Therefore, it would be preferable to label them Palestinians. As mentioned earlier, Psammetichus I (664–610 BCE) had already established a garrison at this site. It is not

---

1. See *ANET*, p. 491. According to A.T. Olmstead, this festival was introduced to the Elephantine garrison at this time (*History of Palestine and Syria*, pp. 604-605).

2. Some ostraca with the term *psḥ'* have been found, and P. Grelot, among others, has inserted this word in connection with the Passover in his reconstruction of the letter ('Le papyrus pascal d'Elephantine: Essai de restauration', *VT* 17 [1967], pp. 201-207); cf. K. Galling, *Studien zur Geschichte Israels im persischen Zeitalter*, pp. 153-54; B. Porten, *Archives from Elephantine*, pp. 128-29.

3. Cf. A.E. Cowley, *Aramaic Papyri*, text 30, ll. 13-14, pp. 112-13; Y. Muffs, *Studies in the Aramaic Legal Papyri from Elephantine* (Studia et Documenta ad Iure Orientlis Antique Pertinentia, 8; Leiden, 1969), p. 1 n. 5.

4. Not much is known about the architecture of this temple. E.G. Kraeling assumes that it was in the Assyrian style (*The Brooklyn Museum Aramaic Papyri*, pp. 101-102.

5. A. Cowley, *Aramaic Papyri* 30 and 31.

6. Cf. E.G. Kraeling, *The Brooklyn Museum Aramaic Papyri*, pp. 101-105.

known exactly when people from Judah and Samerina and perhaps other parts of Syria-Palestine were sent to this garrison, but Judahite mercenaries may have been employed both by Psammetichus I and by Psammetichus II (595–589 BCE) in their campaigns to Nubia.[1] Some of those who fled from Judah during the Babylonian campaigns may also have settled at Elephantine.

The Jewish label cannot be applied to people who do not follow the Jewish festival calendar and the Jewish sacred laws, and the people of Elephantine had no knowledge of these things. The above-mentioned ordinance from Darius II about the 'Feast of the Unleavened Bread' appears to introduce an innovation. The fact that the people of Elephantine did not know that there should be a temple to Yahweh only in Jerusalem and that they therefore did not get any help from the Jerusalemite community in rebuilding the temple at Elephantine should caution against labeling this group as Jewish. The split that had occurred in Judah between the returnees and the Judahite population in Palestine had not been experienced by the people of Elephantine. Their religious customs and traditions had not been 'governed' by a Babylonian or Persian reinterpretation. From this viewpoint it is understandable that the high priest of Jerusalem, Johanan, did not answer the request. When they later wrote to Bagoas of Jerusalem and to Delaiah and Shelemiah, the sons of Samerina's 'governor' Sanballat in 407 BCE, they received a positive answer. Bagoas' attitude would indicate that he probably was not a representative of the Nehemiah tradition. Most probably he was a Persian. Delaiah and Bagoas instructed the people at Elephantine to make a petition to Arsames, which they did, promising not to sacrifice animals in the new temple.[2] This promise could have been made to conform to the religious policies of the Persian administration and its worship of Ahura Mazda. It does not necessarily point to any familiarity with the sacred laws of the Jewish community in Jerusalem. In other words, what is usually known as Judaism was unknown in Elephantine. It is therefore understandable that an appeal was made to Samaria.

According to a text from the fourth year of Artaxerxes II (402 BCE),

---

1. Cf. M. Greenberg, *JBL* 76 (1957), pp. 304-309. A troop of Pharaoh Amasis marched to Upper Egypt. It comprised both Syrians (*rmt n Išwr*) and Palestinians (*rmt n Ḥr*); see W. Erichsen, 'Erwähnung eines Zuges nach Nubien unter Amasis in einem demotischen Text', *Klio* 34 (1941), pp. 56-61.

2. A. Cowley, *Aramaic Papyri*, texts 32-33; cf. *ANET*, p. 492.

an administrative official, Anani, *lḥn*[1] of the temple of Yahu, together with his wife sold his house to their son-in-law.[2] The text indicates that the temple was rebuilt. Unfortunately, there is no information about how long the garrison and the temple lasted. However, because Persia had lost all power in Egypt around 402/401 BCE to Amyrtaios of Sais (404–399 BCE),[3] who later was overthrown by Nepherites I (399–393 BCE) from Mendes in the Delta, the end of the Persian garrison at Elephantine may have occurred during the reign of Nepherites.[4] Persia had to give up Egypt without a battle and the country was independent until 342 BCE. This was the time of the uproar caused by Artaxerxes II's brother Cyrus[5] and the war against the Greek cities in western Anatolia, which were supported by Sparta.[6] Nepherites, who entered into an alliance with Sparta in 396 BCE, invaded Palestine, occupying the southern part of the country. A 'small slab of syenite' bearing the name of Nepherites has been found at Gezer.[7] Cyprus, which had been well-controlled by Persia, became

---

1. The Aramaic word *lḥn* refers to a palace or temple official who had the duty of getting provisions for the palace/temple; see B. Landsberger ('Haushälter'), in 'Akkadisch-hebräische Wortgleichungen', *Congress Volume, Geneva 1965* (ed. J.A. Emerton *et al.*; VTSup, 16; Leiden, 1967), pp. 198-204.

2. See E.G. Kraeling, *The Brooklyn Museum Aramaic Papyri*, Papyrus 12, pp. 268-80.

3. Amyrtaios is the only king of the Twenty-Eighth Dynasty. His death is possibly referred to in a papyrus (E.G. Kraeling, *The Brooklyn Museum Aramaic Papyri*, pap. 13). Nepherites is said to have ascended the throne after his death (E.G. Kraeling, *The Brooklyn Museum Aramaic Papyri*, pp. 283-90).

4. The power of the priests of Khnum (the ram-god) of Elephantine might have increased during this period, according to E.G. Kraeling (*The Brooklyn Museum Aramaic Papyri*, pp. 113-14).

5. According to Xenophon, Cyrus had been made satrap of Lydias, Phrygia and Cappadocia in 407 BCE (*Anabasis* 1.9.7). With this move Darius II probably hoped to maintain good relations with Sparta, which the former satrap Tissaphernes had not been able to establish. For Darius Sparta would be an excellent ally in his policies against the Athenians. Under Artaxerxes II the picture changed and Cyrus, who had built up his power base, rebelled. He had gathered a large army which included 10,000 Greek mercenaries; cf. Xenophon's *Anabasis* 1.

6. For the relations between Sparta, the Ionian cities and Persia during the last decades of the fifth cent. BCE, see D.M. Lewis, *Sparta and Persia* (Cincinnati Classical Studies, NS 1; Leiden, 1977), pp. 108-55.

7. R.A.S. Macalister, *The Excavations of Gezer: 1902–1905 and 1907–1909* (London, 1912), II, p. 313, and fig. 452.

another problem for the Persians under Evagoras of Salamis (411–374/473 BCE). Evagoras, who was a skillful politician, tried to unite the Greek kingdoms of Cyprus under Athenian leadership. With his support Egypt could advance into Palestine and Phoenicia.[1]

What did this mean to inland Palestine? Again there is no documentation. Hypothetically it could be assumed that the Persian government would have tried to secure its position in these territories close to the Egyptian–Cypriot sphere of influence, as well as their loyalty. One way of doing this would have been to send some officials with extraordinary authority to these inland districts. Their task would have been to supervise the administrators of the subprovinces and to see that the sacred and civil laws were followed, perhaps also allowing traditional laws to be kept as long as they did not conflict with Persian interests. Against this background, the question may be raised whether Ezra, as a Persian official of Judahite descent, was commissioned to keep Yehud 'in line' in a politically unstable period. Under Bagoas, Judah had been punished severely, because the high priest Johanan had murdered his brother and rival Jeshua (Joshua) in the temple, according to Josephus. As a penalty Bagoas had stipulated that a special tax of 50 darics for every lamb to be sacrificed was to be paid. For seven years the Jews 'felt his hand'.[2] Since Bagoas is not mentioned in the book of Ezra, this might have happened before c. 400 BCE. The incident shows (1) that there were power struggles between priests (2) that the pro-Persian attitude among the people of Judah may have diminished, and (3) that some opposition to Persian rule may have

1. Cf. Diodorus 15.2.2-3; D. Mallet, *Les rapports des Grecs avec l'Egypte (de la conquête de Cambyse, 525, à celle d'Alexandre, 331)* (Cairo, 1922), p. 94; cf. P. Salmon, 'Les relations entre la Perse et l'Egypte du VIe au IVe siècle av. J.-C.', *The Land of Israel: Cross-Roads of Civilizations* (Orientalia Lovaniensia Analaecta, 19; ed. E. Lipiński; Leuven, 1985), pp. 158-61. The name of Achoris, one of Nepherites's successors, occurs on an inscription from Eshmun's temple at Sidon and on an offering-stand from Acco; cf. A. Rowe, *A Catalogue of Egyptian Scarabs in the Palestine Archaeological Museum* (Cairo, 1936), p. 295; B. Porter and R.L.B. Moss, *Topographical Bibliography of Ancient Egyptian Hieroglyphic Texts, Reliefs and Paintings*, VII (Oxford, 1957), pp. 374, 382, 384. It is possible that the Egyptian statuette of Isis with the child Horus on her lap found at Makmish belongs to this period. N. Avigad dates it to the fifth–fourth century BCE (*IEJ* 10 [1960], p. 94).

2. Josephus, *Ant.* 11.7.1.

occurred.[1] Ezra's mission could have been to reorganize the temple cult and its system of taxes and tithes and to foster a pro-Persian attitude among the administrators. Ezra can be viewed as a 'tool' of the Persians to bind Yehud more firmly to Achaemenid rule, as was the case with Nehemiah. At the same time he had the 'authority' to organize the society in a way that suited his interpretation of the religious laws that he had learned in Persia. In other words, his ideology and actions were governed not only by old Judahite traditions known to the exiled people, but also by his education in Persian thinking about religion and religious laws. Some of this must have been part of the law that was in his hand (Ezra 7.15).

Ezra

In the seventh year of the reign of king Artaxerxes, a priest of Aaronide descent, Ezra, is said to have arrived in Jerusalem from Babylon as an emissary of the king and his court in Susa (Ezra 7.1-10).[2] The 'family tree' he is given seems to be artificial, because his father is said to have been Seraiah, who was killed at Riblah by the Babylonians in 586 BCE (2 Kgs 25.18-21).[3] The purpose of the list, however, is to present Ezra as a religious authority. This is also the idea contained in Ezra 7.12-26 (written in Aramaic), where Ezra is to command the treasuries of the satrapy and have the authority to appoint judges and make decisions about capital punishment, banishment and confiscation of property. In the biblical text he is given authority that he never exercised. However, 'Ezra's law' became the legal foundation for Judean society. It was not a private law code; it

---

1. Cf. K. Galling, *Studien zur Geschichte Israels im persischen Zeitalter*, pp. 164-65.

2. The writer has incorporated Ezra into a list of high priests, a position he is never given in the rest of the book of Ezra. However, in 1 Esdras 9.39-40, 49 he is understood to be a high priest. This shows that there is a conflict between ideology and reality in the Ezra figure. Certain priestly circles wanted to see him as a high priest. K. Koch maintains that Ezra came as a high priest, in 'Ezra and the Origins of Judaism', *JSS* 19 (1974), pp. 190-93; see also P.R. Ackroyd, 'The Chronicler as Exegete', *JSOT* 2 (1977), p. 18-19.

3. It could be maintained that there were two men with the same name of Seraiah; see W. Rudolph, *Ezra und Nehemia*, p. 66. If so, the purpose of the list loses some of its impact.

was the law of the state.[1] As a special commissioner or top official, Ezra was to inquire about the state of affairs in Judah, make some revisions, if necessary, and see to it that Persian law and the new statutes that he brought were followed. Religion and governmental affairs were one and the same. The 'Law of the God of Heaven' and the 'Law of the King'[2] are parallel expressions of this concept, which is clear from Ezra 7.26, where they occur together. This does not mean that they must be identical. The former could refer to the customary and religious laws of the society, and the latter would then refer to the official law system of the Persian empire.[3] Ezra, the scribe/priest,[4] can be understood to have been sent out to the sub-province of Yehud to be a royal judge or supervisor dealing with both sacral and civil matters (Ezra 7.12-26).

Because the content of Ezra's law is unknown, it is impossible to know how much of the old Judahite traditions were part of the 'Law of the God of Heavens'. The text merely claims that Ezra is a 'scribe skilled in the law of Moses' (Ezra 7.6). The biblical writer gives no information about the content of the law nor in what way it was different from the system that had been followed earlier. Neither does he indicate what is meant by the phrase 'the law of Moses'.[5] It could be the same as the 'Law of the God of Heaven', or else the biblical writer has intentionally made them parallel, as if they were the same. Many scholars have speculated that the 'law of Moses' is the Pentateuch.[6] However, it is stated that the 'law of Moses' was to some

1. Cf. E. Meyer, *Die Entstehung des Judentums*, p. 66.

2. The Aramaic phrase *dātā' dî malkā'*, 'the law of the king' (Ezra 7.26), also occurs in business documents; cf. A.T. Olmstead, 'Darius as Lawgiver', *AJSL* 51 (1935), pp. 247-49.

3. Cf. N.R. Frye, who distinguishes between 'social tribunals' dealing with the customary laws and 'royal tribunals with royal judges' for the laws of the empire (*The Heritage of Persia* [Cleveland, 1963], p. 100).

4. In 1 Esdras 9.40, 49 he is given the title high priest; see the discussion in J.M. Myers, *I and II Esdras* (AB, 42; Garden City, NY, 1974), pp. 8-9.

5. K. Koch emphasizes that there is no Moses in Ezra's exodus and that Moses was not necessary, because the *tôrâ* was in the hand of Ezra (*JSS* 19 [1974], p. 187 n. 1). Is Ezra, then, none other than Moses? R.N. Whybray says that 'the whole presentation of Moses in the Pentateuch in its present form may be described as the religious fiction of a later time' (*The Making of the Pentateuch*, p. 240).

6. For the different theories, see C. Houtman, 'Ezra and the Law: Observations on the Supposed Relation between Ezra and the Pentateuch', *OTS* 21 (1981), pp. 91-

extent shocking for most people when Ezra had to read it to the assembly in the open place before the Water Gate (Neh. 8.1-8). This implies that it was an innovation. It would also be a mistake to assume that only the Pentateuch or parts of it existed. Laws have been written in different periods by priestly and/or royal scribes. Different situations demanded new, revised or different laws. Parts of Deuteronomy might be explained this way.[1] In any society law is part of an ongoing process. There is information about this process in the Hebrew Bible. For instance, Jer. 8.8 mentions that Yahweh's law was being falsified 'by the lying pen of the scribes'. Then there is the law scroll discovered in Solomon's temple during the reign of King Josiah. These two examples, together with the so-called Temple-Scroll,[2] are illustrations of the continuous work with law traditions.[3] All that is known about Ezra's law is that the Persian king had authorized it, which means that it was written outside Judah.[4] It must have been in the

---

115; cf. H. Donner, *Geschichte des Volkes Israel*, II, pp. 428-30.

1. S. Mowinckel sees the *qāhāl* theology in Deuteronomy as proof that this book belongs to the postexilic period. He sees it as a 'Konstitutionsbuch' for the restoration of the postexilic community (*Studien zu dem Buche Ezra–Nehemia*, I, p. 90); see S.A. Kaufman, who sees Deut. 12–26 as a 'program of politico-religious centralization', which he prefers to date to the period of Josiah (*Maarav* 1 [1978–79], p. 147). For Deuteronomy as a programmatic product, see also C. Brekelmans, 'Wisdom in Deuteronomy', *La sagesse de l'Ancien Testament* (ed. M. Gilbert; Leuven, 1979), p. 38. Because of the prohibition of admitting Ammonites and Moabites into the *qāhāl* of Yahweh (Deut. 23.1-5), this program must be postexilic. The Edomites, who in pre-exilic times were the mortal enemies, should not be detested. According to Deut. 23.8-9, they were the 'brothers'. This may indicate that, because they had occupied the southern half of Judah, they were close to the community in Jerusalem. The memory that Yahweh came from Edomite territory may have played some role in re-establishing friendly relations.

2. See Y. Yadin, *Megillat ham-miqdaš I-III* (Jerusalem, 1977); *idem, The Temple Scroll: The Hidden Law of the Dead Sea Sect* (New York, 1985); cf. B.A. Levine, 'The Temple Scroll: Aspects of its Historical Provenience and Literary Character', *BASOR* 232 (1978), pp. 5-23.

3. See C. Houtman, *OTS* 21 (1981), pp. 108-11. It is not necessary to suggest that Ezra's law was fiction, as does H. Kreissig, *Die sozialökonomische Situation in Juda zu Achämenidenzeit* (Schriften zur Geschichte und Kultur des Alten Orients, 7; Berlin, 1973), p. 110.

4. H. Cazelles mentions that Artaxerxes' edict about the law of God of Heaven has a parallel in an edict of Artaxerxes about rebels. The parallel concerns the law of Ahura Mazda ('La mission d'Esdras', *VT* 4 [1954], pp. 125-26).

interest of the Persian government to see to it that the legal and sacred system of the subprovince of Yehud was acceptable. Ezra may serve as parallel to the above-mentioned Udjahoresenet in Sais in Egypt, who, among other things, reformed the cult of the temple of the goddess Neith and purged the temple of foreigners.[1]

If Ezra's law was a particular law with a special purpose, another parallel to it may be found in the trilingual stela from the sanctuary of the goddess Leto found in Letoon in the Xanthos Valley in SW Anatolia. The Aramaic text says that the people of Xanthos decided to build a sanctuary and install a priest and that taxes should be paid to the sanctuary. The satrap, Pixodaros, promulgated this decision as a law. Line 19 of the text says *dth dk ktb*, 'this law has he written'.[2] Here is an authorization of a local law that may also be a parallel to both the edict of Darius II to the Elephantine garrison and to Ezra's law given to the people of Judah and Jerusalem.[3] However, the implication in Ezra 7.26 that Ezra was given authority over the whole satrapy of 'Beyond the River' is unrealistic because he did not replace the satrap. The text either shows a later understanding of Ezra's importance, or it refers only to the Judahites of the satrapy. The phrasing, 'for all who know the law of your God' and 'those who do not know it', supports the second alternative.[4] It also indicates that Ezra's law was not completely new. If the letter from Artaxerxes to Ezra (7.11-26) is authentic, the idea may be entertained that the codification of the *tôrâ* started intially at this point in time.

The information in Ezra 8.1-14 about the number of people who followed Ezra from Babylon must be characterized as unrealistic. With women and children it would have been about 6000 persons. However, the numbers are primarily round figures in the hundreds; only in a few cases is an exact amount given. In comparison with Ezra 2, which mentions the many families that are supposed to have returned, this list has only twelve families leaving Babylon. The

---

1. M. Lichtheim, *Ancient Egyptian Literature*, III, pp. 36-41.
2. A. Dupont-Sommer, 'L'inscription araméenne', *Fouilles de Xanthos*, VI (Paris, 1979), pp. 136-37.
3. Cf. P. Frei, 'Zentralgewalt und Lokalautonomie im Achämenidenreich', in P. Frei and K. Koch, *Reichsidee und Reichsorganisation im Perserreich*, pp. 12-14.
4. G. Widengren has defended the authenticity of Ezra 7.12-26 in J.H. Hayes and J.M. Miller, *Israelite and Judean History*, pp. 497-98.

number 'twelve' may have been used purposely to imply that an 'all Israel' was again a reality.[1] Historical fact is therefore irrelevant. Ezra is here depicted as the inaugurator of the religiously true 'Israel'.

The biblical text characterizes Ezra as a 'scribe (*sāpar dātā'*) of the God of Heaven',[2] a man who had thoroughly studied the 'Law of Yahweh', also called the 'Law of the God of Heaven' (Ezra 7.12). This description provides information about his education. In the introduction (7.6) the law is labeled the 'Law of Moses', which in itself legitimizes Ezra and his mission. Artaxerxes is reported to have given Ezra a letter with permission 'to inspect (*bqr*) Yehud and Jerusalem according to the law (*dāt*) of your god that is in your hand' (7.14),[3] which means that Ezra was to organize the province of Yehud in a way that suited the Persians.[4] This phrase in essence says that the law of Ezra was not the one that was followed in Yehud and Jerusalem in all its details. It was a law composed in Babylonia. This law and the 'king's law' had to be enforced (7.25-26).[5] It can therefore be assumed

1. Cf. W. Rudolph, *Ezra und Nehemia*, p. 79. A.S. Kapelrud sees this text as 'an extract' from the lists of Ezra 2 and Neh. 7 (*The Question of Authorship in the Ezra Narrative: A Lexical Investigation* [Oslo, 1944], pp. 45f-46.

2. According to G. Widengren, this was a Persian office (in Hayes and Miller, *Israelite and Judean History*, p. 535. H. Schaeder saw in this title an office for Jewish affairs (*Esra der Schreiber* [BHT, 5; Tübingen, 1930], pp. 39-59). Cf. W.T. in der Smitten, *Esra, Quellen, Überlieferung und Geschichte* (Assen, 1973), pp. 105-10. For a critique of Schaeder's theory, see K. Galling, *Studien zur Geschichte Israels*, pp. 166-67.

3. P.R. Ackroyd notes the parallelism between Ezra 7.12-26 and the edict of Cyrus (*Israel under Babylon and Persia* [Oxford, 1970], p. 267).

4. Cf. T.A. Busink, *Der Tempel von Jerusalem*. II. *Von Ezekiel bis Middot* (Leiden, 1980), p. 850.

5. In Ezra 7.25 it is called 'the wisdom of your god that is in your hand' and so cannot refer to Ezra's own wisdom, as H.G.M. Williamson thinks (see *Ezra, Nehemiah*, p. 105). The phrase the 'God of Heaven' should be compared with the Aramaic phrase *'elāhā' rabbā'*, 'the great God', which occurs in Ezra 5.8. This term is known from Persepolis and could not be used by Persian officials (R.T. Hallock, *Persepolis Fortification Tablets*, §§313, 354). Ahura Mazda was not the only god, but 'a great God' (G. Widengren, *Die Religionen Irans*, p. 143). The possibility cannot be excluded, however, that the Persian government could identify some heavenly gods, such as Zeus and Bel, with Ahura Mazda and that 'the Achaemenids may have seen a reflection' of Ahura Mazda in Yahweh (J.M. Cook, *The Persian Empire*, p. 148). Religiously, as well as politically, that would serve to propagate a Persian universalism.

that the situation in the little subprovince of Yehud was not completely acceptable to the Persian government. The administrative officials in Jerusalem after Nehemiah may have become too independent and perhaps also negligent in the eyes of the Persians. The replacement of Achaemenid motifs on stamps by the engraving of the name of the province, 'Yehud', which occurred in the second half of the fifth century BCE,[1] may show that the administrators of Yehud had become more independent than before, creating problems with the Persian government. Therefore, Ezra was sent to instruct the people of Judah in the newly arrived king's law, which was not exactly the law system that they were used to following.[2] The political situation in Yehud demanded correction.

Whether or not Ezra is a fictitious person,[3] supervisors and messengers could have been sent to the different districts to carry out a reorganization. Ezra's 'mission' may have been connected not only with a political situation needing correction, but also with a calendar reform in the Persian empire. Sometime during or after the reign of Artaxerxes I the Zoroastrian calendar (with twelve months of 30 days each) was introduced.[4] This could have bound the community in Jerusalem more firmly to the Persian way of life and could also have been the agency through which certain Zoroastrian concepts became part of Jewish religion.[5] In order to create or strengthen a pro-Persian

1. See E. Stern, *Material Culture*, pp. 212-13; P.R. Ackroyd, 'Archaeology, Politics and Religion: The Persian Period', *The Iliff Review* 39 (1982), pp. 16-17.

2. See K. Koch, *JSS* 19 (1974), pp. 181-82.

3. See further below.

4. E.J. Bickermann, 'The "Zoroastrian" Calendar', *ArOr* 35 (1967), pp. 197-207. Bickermann thinks that the calendar was introduced sometime between 459 and 90 BCE and that it was brought by the Parthians from central Asia (p. 205). M. Boyce considers the calendar to have been introduced during the later part of the Achemenid time (*A History of Zoroastrianism* [Handbuch der Orientalistik, I. Abteil., 8.1.2A; Leiden, 1982], pp. 77). W. Hartner argues that the '365-day vague year was in continuous use, side by side with lunisolar, from 503 BCE onwards', and 'practically down to our time' ('Old Iranian Calendars', *The Cambridge History of Iran*, II [ed. I. Gershevitch; Cambridge, 1985], p. 757).

5. This is a topic which I cannot treat here because it requires a thorough knowledge not only of early Judaism but also of the religion of Zoroaster, which I do not have. However, H.S. Nyberg maintains that one of the most important influences on Judaism was the universalism of the Ahura Mazda ideology (*Die Religionen des alten Iran*, pp. 478-79). For the intricate problem of Iranian influences on Judaism, cf. C. Colpe, 'Lichtsymbolik im alten Iran und antiken Judentum', *Studium Generale*

attitude among the leading authorities in Jerusalem, Artaxerxes gave the Jerusalemite temple and its personnel a tax-free status (Ezra 7.24). The date of Ezra's arrival in Jerusalem is still a controversial topic. As mentioned above, Ezra is said to have been a contemporary of Johanan, the grandson of Eliashib (Ezra 10.6), who was a high priest during the time of Nehemiah. The letter from the Elephantine colony that names Johanan as a high priest[1] allows the seventh year of king Artaḥšaśta in Ezra 7.7 to be established as 398 BCE. The king in question would therefore be Artaxerxes II.[2]

Another point in favor of Ezra's arrival being later than Nehemiah's is the notation in Ezra 9.9 that Jerusalem and Judah had a restored temple and a wall, *gādēr*. The latter word, which most often means a fence,[3] is not the usual term for a city wall, which is *ḥômâ*. However, in Ezek. 13.5 and 22.30 it stands for a wall (cf. 2 Kgs 12.13[12] and Amos 9.11). In Ezra 9.9 the writer is deliberately using the term to create the metaphor that depicts Yahweh's people Israel as a vineyard. Furthermore, it should be remembered that Nehemiah moved people into the city of Jerusalem after rebuilding its city wall. Jerusalem is said to have housed very few people (Neh. 7.4-5). In other words,

---

18 (1965), pp. 116-33; cf. R. Maier, who reckons with influences going both ways ('Das achämenidische Weltreich und seine Bedeutung in der politischen und religiosen Geschichte des antiken Orients', *BZ* NF 12 [1968], pp. 1-16). See also N.R. Frye, *The Heritage of Persia*, p. 122.

1.   A. Cowley, *Aramaic Papyri*, pp. 108-110, text 30.18.

2.   See A. van Hoonacker, 'Néhémie et Esdras, une nouvelle hypothèse sur le chronologie de l'époque de la restauration', *Le Museon* 9 (1890), pp. 151-84, 317-51, 389-401; H.H. Rowley, *BJRL* 37 (1955), pp. 550-59 (with lit.); cf. S. Mowinckel, *Studien zu dem Buche Ezra–Nehemia*, I, p. 99, cf. p. 108; *idem*, *Studien*. III. *Die Ezrageschichte und das Gesetz Moses* (Oslo, 1965), pp. 99-100; K. Galling, *Studien zur Geschichte Israels im persischen Zeitalter*, pp. 158-61; G. Widengren in J.H. Hayes and J.M. Miller, *Israelite and Judean History*, pp. 503-509. See also J.A. Emerton, who refutes the theory that Ezra arrived in 428 BCE ('Did Ezra Go to Jerusalem in 428 BCE?' *JTS* 17 [1966], pp. 1-19). Emerton maintains that 'no action of Nehemiah presupposes the work of Ezra' (p. 19). U. Kellermann maintains that Ezra arrived in Jerusalem shortly before 448 BCE and declares that most of the book of Ezra consists of midrashim built on the Chronicler's work and later revisions. He only sees Ezra 7.12-26 as authentic ('Erwägungen zum Problem der Esradatierung', *ZAW* 80 [1968], pp. 73-87).

3.   The term in Punic can also mean 'fort, fortress'; see D. Neiman, 'Phoenician Place-Names', *JNES* 24 (1965), p. 115 n. 12.

before the time of Nehemiah Jerusalem was of no importance. However, the book of Ezra implies that the town was well-populated and that it was the center of life for the *gôlâ* community.[1] That was the work of Nehemiah.

The use of the name Israel to describe Yahweh's people, the *qᵉhal yiśrā'ēl*, rather than the land of Judah, occurs 22 times in Ezra. The word is used elsewhere in this way only twice.[2] By contrast, the term 'Judah and Jerusalem' is used to designate territory. Therefore, a distinction has to be made between the religious community of 'Israel', or the people of the 'captivity' (*gôlâ*), and the land of the subprovince of Judah. These two were not exactly identical. Even when the whole province of Judah had become Jewish after Ezra's reform, people of the Diaspora who adhered to the same religious concepts were included in 'Israel'. In other words, the name had lost its territorial meaning.

It is interesting to note that the book of Nehemiah does not use the name Israel,[3] which might also indicate that Nehemiah preceded Ezra.[4] On the other hand, the omission might merely reflect Nehemiah's stronger concern with administrative affairs than Ezra, who was a religious reformer. Thus, the terminology could indicate different emphases.

Nehemiah's so-called memoirs (Neh. 1-7, 12.27-43 and 13.4-31)[5] do not mention Ezra. This additional omission may indicate further that Nehemiah preceded Ezra, as might Nehemiah's lack of knowledge about the people who returned with Ezra. It should also be noted that Nehemiah is not mentioned in the book of Ezra. The statement in Neh. 8.9 that the two men were contemporaries[6] can be seen as an editorial

1. Cf. also H. Cazelles, *VT* 4 (1954), pp. 115-18.

2. Cf. H.-J. Zobel, *ThWAT*, col. 1010. Zobel notes that the phrase 'Yahweh, the god of Israel' does not occur in the book of Nehemiah.

3. The few passages which mention the name Israel (Neh. 8.1, 14, 17) are considered part of the 'Ezra memoirs' and thus secondary in Nehemiah; cf. S. Mowinckel, *Studen zu dem Buche Ezra–Nehemia*, I, p. 85.

4. G.W. Ahlström, *Who were the Israelites?*, pp. 110-11.

5. Cf. S. Mowinckel, *Studien zu dem Buche Ezra–Nehemia*. II. As to the literary classification, see H.G.M. Williamson, *Ezra, Nehemiah*, pp. xxiv-xxviii. Ezra 7–10 plus Neh. 8 have been labelled the Ezra Memoirs; cf. H.G.M. Williamson, pp. xxviii-xxxii.

6. In 1 Esdras 9.49 Nehemiah is not mentioned. According to F.M. Cross this passage represents an earlier version (*JBL* 94 [1975], p. 8).

reworking of the material,[1] which is understandable if Nehemiah 8 really belongs to the 'Ezra Memoirs'. Recognizing that both men are said to have gone to Jerusalem with extraordinary authority, it would be impossible to see both of them ruling the society at the same time.

Politically, the loss of Egypt could have been part of the motive for sending Ezra to Jerusalem.[2] Thus, both external and internal problems may have motivated the king in his decision. Ezra's career parallels Nehemiah's. Both men were sent to Jerusalem in times of recent rebellions. Nehemiah went after the revolts in Egypt and in Abr Nahara had been put down, and Ezra arrived after Egypt had again revolted, this time regaining its independence. Egypt had become a threat to the coastal areas of Palestine. Sending Ezra to Jerusalem could have demonstrated that the Persian government intended to secure the inland territories of Palestine; Judah had become an outpost and had to be controlled better than before.[3]

It is clear that the political situation during Ezra's time was different than that during the period of Nehemiah's tenure. He did not face the same opposition from neighboring people that Nehemiah did. In the book of Ezra the enemies are the people of the land known from the book of Joshua: the 'Canaanites, Hittites, Perizzites, Jebusites, Ammonites, Moabites, Egyptians and Amorites' (Ezra 9.1).[4]

---

1. The explanation that Nehemiah is the *tiršātā'*, 'the excellency', underscores this; cf. W. Rudolph, *Ezra und Nehemiah*, p. 148.

2. Thus H. Cazelles, *VT* 4 (1954), p. 132; cf. L. Rost, 'Erwägungen zum Kyroserlass', *Verbannung und Heimkehr* (ed. A. Kuschke; Tübingen, 1961), p. 303; P.R. Ackroyd, *Exile and Restoration*, p. 141; E. Caviagnac and P. Grelot, 'The Historical Framework of the Bible', *Introduction to the Old Testament* (ed. A. Robert and A. Feuillet; New York, 1968), pp. 46-47; G. Widengren in J.H. Hayes and J.M. Miller, *Israelite and Judean History*, p. 535.

3. According to Cavaignac and Grelot, Ezra's mission would have been to try to unite the Judeo-Samarian communities and so make Palestine a buffer state against Egypt. The Law of the God of heaven, the Pentateuch, would have granted a special status to this 'united' community (*Introduction to the Old Testament* [ed. A. Robert and A. Feuillet], pp. 46-47). In addition, K. Koch believes that Ezra's mission also concerned the Samarians (*JSS* 19 [1974], pp. 193-95). Such a conclusion cannot be drawn from Ezra's activities in Jerusalem. Since there is nothing to imply that Ezra even tried to influence the Samarians, it might be suggested that the authority over the people of Beyond the River given to Ezra by Artaxerxes (Ezra 7.12-26) is the biblical writer's rewording of the mandate. Ideologically, Ezra should have had authority over all 'Jews'.

4. On literary use of these names, see J. Van Seters, *VT* 22 (1972), pp. 64-81.

Historically, there were no Perizzites, Jebusites, Hittites or Amorites in the postexilic period. They had all lost their identity and they had long since become assimilated into the population of the kingdoms of the country. That these ethnic terms occur here is a clear indication that the Ezra passage emanates from the circle of postexilic historiographers who were responsible for the literary construction of the Wilderness–Conquest theme.[1] This literary setting of the writers is also shown by Ezra 9, which mentions that the people were 'slaves' (v. 9), and that the 'land you are entering to possess is a land unclean' because of the natives of the land and their abominations (v. 11).[2] The last verse pretends that there were no Judahites in the country. It is for this reason that the inhabitants are given archaic names. The enemies whom Ezra met, however, were men who had married non-Judahite women, 'the men of Judah and Benjamin' who 'had added to the sin of Israel' (Ezra 10.10).[3] The 'enemies' are thus to be seen as ideological.

Only a few opponents are mentioned by name in the speech by Ezra. They include Jonathan son of Asahel, Jahzeiah son of Tiqwah, Meshullam, and the Levite Shabbethai (Ezra 10.15). The list of 'offenders' in 10.18-44 mentions only 113 persons of the several thousands who would have been living in Yehud. Any problems with the people of neighboring subprovinces are not reported. This fact may indicate that the text of the 'Ezra memoirs' was written sometime after the political situation had stabilized, or that Ezra did not meet any opposition from neighboring people; that is, he lived in a time when other Palestinian 'governors' could not interfere in the problems of Judah. If this is right, the memoirs would provide another indication that Ezra arrived in Jerusalem after Nehemiah.

The biblical writer mentions that when Ezra arrived in Jerusalem, he was 'ashamed' and tore his garments and plucked his hair and beard because of what he learned about the religious and social circumstances (Ezra 9.1-6). He went to a land he did not know, a land

---

1. K. Koch has shown the literary parallelism between Ezra and Joshua and their actions in the 'promised land' (*JSS* 19 [1974], p. 188).

2. Ezra 9.6-15 is a historical-programmatic speech; it is unknown whether Ezra ever gave it in its present form.

3. The text of Ezra is in harmony with the deuteronomistic concept that it is usually the women who lead the men to worship 'wrong' gods.

whose customs he had not learned.[1] The leaders of Judah complained that the 'people of Israel', including both priests and Levites, had not 'separated' themselves from the natives. From this alone it can be concluded that the law he brought with him was not known to the priests, the Levites and the rest of the people, or that the writer has, as so many times before, overexaggerated in order to strengthen his point. However, just as the history of the returnees from Cyrus to Ezra in the books of Ezra and Nehemiah centers around the people of the 'captivity',[2] so Ezra's message only concerns the party of the *gôlâ*. A proclamation was sent to all the exiles 'in Judah and Jerusalem' to gather in Jerusalem within three days. Here all the inhabitants of Judah and Jerusalem are seen as 'returnees', which is not historically accurate. Those who did not come would be excluded from the society and their property confiscated (Ezra 10.7-9). This is the turning point in the history of the people of Judah, as well as a unique historical event. The result of this proclamation was that some persons were deprived of their religious, ethnic and social 'nationality', if such a term can be used. Historically, it also meant that some Judahites never became Jews. They were excluded from the people of Yahweh, 'Israel'.

As mentioned above, Ezra's reform meant that new statutes were introduced for the society and its temple cult. Like the kings before him, Ezra 'promulgated' the law to all the people (including women and children) in front of the 'Water Gate', a gate in front of which people gathered for meetings, according to the Mishnah (*Mid.* 1, 4).[3] He also ordered the people to celebrate a festival[4] that required them to go out and cut down branches in order to build some booths, *sukkôt* (Neh. 8.13-17). However, in order to celebrate the 'Festival of Booths' according to its stipulations in the 'Law of Moses', Ezra first had to teach the law to the priests and Levites, and they in their turn had to instruct the people! This is a remarkable piece of information.

1. Cf. W.T. in der Smitten, *Esra, Quellen, Überlieferung und Geschichte*, p. 154.
2. Cf. S. Japhet, 'People and Land', *Das Land Israel in biblischer Zeit* (ed. G. Strecker), pp. 112-13. See also S. Mowinckel, who says that the phrase [*benê*] *haggôlâ* refers to the descendants of the exiled people, and that the other Judahites are ignored by the writer of the Ezra history (*Studien*, III, pp. 26, 106-108).
3. This indicates that the text could refer to the Herodian temple; thus, its present form would have been 'revised' in the first century CE. See G. Garbini, *History and Ideology*, pp. 163-64.
4. The parallel with Josiah's Passover should be noted (2 Kgs. 23.21-23).

If the text is taken seriously, it means that the 'Law of Moses' was not known to the people of Judah in the form it was known to Ezra. He introduced it to the people of Judah and Jerusalem. The *sukkôt* festival of Ezra, therefore, represented a break with tradition. The celebration of this festival was performed in a way that had not been known since 'the days of Jeshua, the son of Nun' (Neh. 8.17). The reference to Joshua (here with the later spelling Jeshua) indicates that the festival had never been celebrated in this way during the previous periods.[1] Booths may have been built during the time of harvest festivals in the autumn, but with Ezra the festival received a new form and a new ideological foundation; it comemmorated the Wanderings in the Wilderness. Since Lev. 23.42-43 connects the Sukkoth Festival with the Exodus and the Wanderings in the Wilderness, it may be concluded that Ezra's *sukkôt* was the inspiration for the statute in Leviticus 23. It cannot have been written in Judah before the reform of Ezra.[2] A scribe educated in religious and civil laws in Babylonia during the Persian period perhaps did not have much of an understanding of the agricultural heritage of Judah, and the inhabitants of the city of

---

1. G. Garbini identifies the new liturgy as the 'Law of Ezra' found in 1 Esdras (*History and Ideology*, pp. 163-64).

2. A.S. Kapelrud maintains that the festival was not new. It was the building of booths that was new. Ezra's intention would be 'to complete and correct that which already existed'. Lev. 23 belongs to the P code (*The Question of Authorship in the Ezra-Narrative*, p. 91). According to J.G. Vink, the P code is to be 'linked up with Ezra's mission' (*OTS* 15 [1969], pp. 143-44). I cannot find a priestly source in the OT. Priestly statutes and customs have been made and followed in all times, but that does not mean that there ever was a P source that has been 'distributed' in smaller parts in the Pentateuch. With I. Engnell (*Gamla Testamentet*, I, p. 212) and G. Garbini (*History and Ideology*, pp. 149-50), I see 'P' as being the latest compiler or editor of the textual material. Cf. also G. Larsson, who characterizes 'P' as 'the results of continuous and coherent work of rather late origin' ('The Chronology of the Pentateuch: A Comparison of the MT and LXX', *JBL* 102 [1983], p. 408). S. Mowinckel maintains that the whole story of Ezra cannot have been written before c. 350 BCE. With K. Galling (*Chronik, Ezra, Nehemia*, pp. 14-15), he points to the anachronism in Ezra 6.22 which mentions that the people celebrated the first *maṣṣôt* festival in the rebuilt temple with joy, because Yahweh 'had changed the heart of the king of Assur' so that he supported the rebuilding of the house of God. The term 'king of Assur' was common in the Seleucid period (*Studien zu dem Buche Ezra–Nehemia*, I, pp. 59-60). If the term should refer to a Persian king, the idea of the change of heart would be hard to explain.

Jerusalem were probably less agriculturally oriented than the villagers of Judah. This might partly explain the association of Sukkoth with the Exodus and the Wanderings in the Wilderness, rather than with an agricultural festival.

With Ezra's reform the term 'Israel' took on a new and narrower meaning. It became purely a religious idea. The geographical and political concept of Israel had been replaced by a concept that referred to those of the *gôlâ* party who embraced the law of Ezra and who could establish their descent. Membership in this society was no longer politically or territorially dependent.[1] It was based on a religious ideology that excluded other worshippers of Yahweh.

Ezra's mission, according to the king's letter in Ezra 7.11-26, was to inspect the religious and social situation in Jerusalem. However, his mandate also included the appointment of judges and scribes. The text never mentions that he created any of these appointments, which implies that the text of the 'King's letter' has exaggerated the scope of his mandate. The biblical writer focuses attention on Ezra's actions in connection with temple regulations for cultic personnel, festivals and tithes, and the dissolution of 'mixed' marriages. Like Nehemiah, he is depicted as the perfect Yahwistic zealot who created the 'pure' congregation of Israel according to the law of the God of Heaven, the Law of Moses. Like Nehemiah before him he was an appointee of the Persian king; they were both Persian officials. Their missions created a pro-Persian attitude among the leaders of Yehud in this period, which may explain why there are no anti-Persian doom oracles in the Bible.

How long Ezra stayed in Jerusalem is not mentioned in any biblical text. Josephus says that he died in old age and was buried in Jerusalem,[2] which is probably a Jewish tradition. It is, however, not the only one. There is also a Jewish tradition that Ezra was buried in southern Mesopotamia at 'Uzair.[3]

Reading through the 'reports' about Ezra and his mission, one is struck by the contrast between Ezra's appointment, as a special Persian emissary with authority that was on a par with that of a satrap, and his

---

1. G.W. Ahlström, *Who were the Israelites?*, pp. 114-18; cf. H. Donner, *Geschichte des Volkes Israel*, II, p. 431.

2. *Ant.* 11.5.5.

3. 'Uzair is also the Quranic spelling of Ezra. Sura 9.30 says that the Jews saw 'Uzair as the son of God. See H.H. Schaeder, *Esra der Schreiber*, p. 14.

cultic and social actions in Jerusalem. The presentation of Ezra is less 'historical' than that of Nehemiah.[1] When the two men are compared it is interesting to see that as far as the activities of Nehemiah are concerned there is not that strong of an emphasis on the law as the fundamental and guiding principle, as is the case with Ezra. Whatever mandate Ezra may have been given, the textual material portrays him as the prototype of a certain kind of religious leader. He represents the creation of a 'pure' Yahwism born in Babylonia, which the *gôlâ* party tried to establish in Jerusalem. Only with Ezra did this type of reformed Yahwistic religion actually become an empirical reality. In this 'revised' Yahwism Moses and Ezra are given positions as the highest authorities.[2]

From the above discussion it is understandable that, as in the case of Moses, Ezra's historicity has been doubted. Already in 1889 M. Vernes considered Ezra as a literary invention of the Chronicler who functioned as a collective representative for selected Jewish traditions.[3] He was followed by E. Renan, who considered the religious reform to be the work of Nehemiah.[4] Among other scholars who have denied the historicity of Ezra are C.C. Torrey,[5] G. Hölscher,[6] N.H. Snaith,[7]

1. M. Smith has compared Nehemiah with the Greek tyrants (*Palestinian Parties and Politics*, pp. 140-43). This position has been contested by D. Graf, who says that 'hereditary succession was typical among the Persian vassal tyrants', but that this is not the case with Nehemiah ('Greek Tyrants and Achaemenid Politics', *The Craft of the Ancient Historian: Essays in Honor of Chester G. Starr* [ed. J.W. Eadie and J. Ober; New York, 1985], p. 92).

2. N. Avigad maintains that Ezra 'restored the spiritual life of the people' (*Discovering Jerusalem*, p. 61). This is impossible to demonstrate. Can anyone prove that there was no spiritual life in Yehud before the time of Ezra? It may rather be said that there was a change in the religious/spiritual life.

3. *Précis d'histoire juive depuis les origines jusqu'a l'époque persane* (Paris, 1889), pp. 586-97.

4. *Histoire du peuple d'Israel*, IV (Paris, 1893), pp. 96-106.

5. *The Composition and Historical Value of Ezra–Nehemiah* (BZAW, 2; Giessen, 1896); *idem*, *Ezra Studies* (Chicago, 1910). According to Torrey, there was no 'return' (see 'Isaiah 41', *HTR* 44 [1951], p. 134 n. 13). For a discussion of Torrey's work, see T. Nöldecke, 'Zur Frage der Geschichtlichkeit der Urkunden im Esra-Buche', *Deutsche Literaturzeitung* 45 (1924), cols. 1849-56.

6. *Geschichte der israelitischen und jüdischen Religion* (Giessen, 1922), pp. 140-41.

7. 'The Historical Books', *Old Testament and Modern Study* (ed. H.H. Rowley; Oxford, 1951), p. 113.

A. Loisy,[1] and most recently G. Garbini.[2] R.H. Pfeiffer did not deny that Ezra existed, but maintained that the Chronicler, who was Ezra, had 'exaggerated the role of Ezra' in such a way that it was impossible to paint a historical picture of him. The story about Ezra arriving with the Law of God 'hardly contains an element of truth', according to Pfeiffer.[3]

Although the inconsistencies of biblical traditions about Ezra make the doubting of Ezra's historicity understandable, his central position as the 'father of Judaism' in Jewish tradition makes it hard to see him as a literary invention.[4] The fact that the Book of Ezra ends abruptly with the statement that those who had married 'foreign' wives separated from them and their children (Ezra 10.44) is an indication that Ezra fulfilled his most important task: Yahweh's people, the *gôlâ* party, had been firmly established. From then on nothing more is heard about Ezra. Instead, the biblical narrator continues with the report about Nehemiah, showing how he and his party separated themselves from the rest of the inhabitants of the land. However, the separation from the wives could not have occurred before the separation from the people of the land had become a fact.[5] What is not indicated is to what degree the people in the territory of Yehud were affected by Ezra's reform. Even if there is information in both the books of Ezra and Nehemiah about towns and villages where priests, Levites and others lived, the center of interest is always Jerusalem. This focus is especially true in Ezra, whose writer emphasized that the temple was in Jerusalem and that Ezra's mission was to establish a theocratic society. Nehemiah had to refortify and repopulate Jerusalem. In accomplishing this task he came into conflict with most of the other inhabitants of the land, including Judahites. Under Nehemiah, Jerusalem became the exclusive enclave of a sectarian group that tried to avoid contact with other inhabitants. Why the Persian government accepted such a situation is hard to imagine. The only possible explanation is that the Persian government did not care how Jerusalem was organized so long as it remained pro-Persian.

1. *La religion d'Israel* (3rd edn; Paris, 1933), pp. 27-28.
2. *History and Ideology*, pp. 151-69.
3. *Introduction to the Old Testament* (New York, 1941), p. 256.
4. Cf. W.T. in der Smitten, *Esra*, pp. 151-52, and cf. pp. 92-94.
5. This may be another argument for Ezra's having arrived in Jerusalem after Nehemiah.

The Last Decades of Persian Rule

The beginning of Persian rule over Palestine is hidden in a mist of historiographic obscurity. The same can be said for the closing decades of the era. Ezra's activities in Jerusalem that produced a form of a theocratic government contributed to a widening of the schism between the Jewish community and the other peoples of the land, especially the inhabitants of Samerina. The only historiographic information about this period in the Hebrew Bible consists of two genealogical lists: one is a list of high priests down to c. 400 BCE (Neh. 12.10-11, 22); the other gives the names of the Davidides through the Persian period (1 Chron. 3.17-24). Eight generations are mentioned after king Jehoiakin (Jeconiah.).[1] Nothing is known, however, about how life developed in any part of the country. It could be maintained that the 'theocracy' of Judah did not work very well sociologically—utopias never do—because Josephus reports that there still were contacts between the priestly families of Jerusalem and those of Samaria, as exemplified by the marriage between Manasseh and Nicaso, the daughter of Sanballat III.[2] If such alliances could take place, it may be concluded that other social and economic contacts were made. To place the final split between the later Samaritan sect and the Jewish *gôlâ* party of Nehemiah and Ezra in this period is impossible.

Archaeological surveys and excavations have demonstrated that the

---

1.   In this list Zerubbabel is the son of Shealtiel's son Pedaiah. If Zerubbabel was born c. 550 BCE and marriages took place at an age of something like 22–25, then the list would go down in time to about 350 BCE. This might indicate something about the final composition of the Chronicler's work. For the list, see the remarks of W.F. Albright, 'The Date and Personality of the Chronicler', *JBL* 40 (1921), pp. 110-11. J.M. Myers sees 1 Chron. 1–9 as 'a collection of archival material' (*1 Chronicles* [AB, 12; Garden City, NY, 1965], p. 19). The last Davidide mentioned is Anani, who has sometimes been identified with a Jerusalemite, Anani, mentioned in the Elephantine letter to Jerusalem; thus E.G. Kraeling, *The Brooklyn Museum Aramaic Papyri*, pp. 108-109; H.L. Ginsberg, *ANET*, p. 492 n. 16. However, in that text he is said to have a brother Ustan (Ostanes), but such a name does not occur in 1 Chron. 3.24.

2.   *Ant.* 11.8. Cf. K. Galling, *Studien zur Geschichte Israels im persischen Zeitalter*, p. 210; F.M. Cross, *JBL* 94 (1975), pp. 5-6; J.D. Purvis, *The Samaritan Pentateuch*, pp. 102-105. Cf. R. Egger, who also says that such marriage alliances were not uncommon (*Josephus Flavius und die Samaritaner*, pp. 65-69).

former Moabite and Edomite[1] territories were sparsely settled during the Persian period. In the later period Arab clans seem to have settled in these areas, partly explaining the Edomite incursions into Judea. Their arrival also signals the rise of a large population of Nabateans, which characterized Edom, the Negev, and the northern Sinai during the Hellenistic and Roman periods. In the coastal areas several towns were destroyed in the first half of the fourth century BCE, including Hazor in Galilee, Tell Abu Hawam and Acco in the north, Tel Shiqmona, 'Athlit, Tel Mevorakh, Makmish, Ashdod, Tell Jemme, and Gezer, Tell el-Hesi and Tell esh-Shari'a in the Shephelah. In the east and southeast destruction layers from this period have been found at En-Gedi and Tell el-Kheleifeh. The reasons and dates for the destructions in western Palestine might be found in the new political situation that occurred after Persia lost Egypt.

Under Artaxerxes II (Memnon) the empire was close to collapse. The period was 'one of almost uninterrupted decline' of Persian authority.[2] In 401 Egypt regained its freedom and was not subdued again until 342 BCE. Palestine was again threatened by Egyptian power, now commanded by Pharaoh Nepherites, who probably took Gezer.[3] His successor, Achoris (393–380 BCE), entered into an alliance with Evagoras of Salamis in Cyprus, which resulted in an invasion of the northern coast of Palestine and of Phoenicia.[4] Evagoras took parts of Tyre and Sidon after a Persian campaign to Egypt in 385–383 had failed. Evagoras had also managed to get support from Cilicia against the Persians. However, Evagoras's fleet was defeated at Kition by the Persians in 381 BCE, and Evagoras was 'reduced' to being a vassal again.[5] Artaxerxes II now tried to subdue Egypt. One of his old generals, Pharnabazos, was made commander. He took his time

---

1. The Wâdi el-Ḥasā survey did not register any sherds belonging to the Persian period; see B. MacDonald, *The Wâdi el-Ḥasā Archaeological Survey*.

2. J.M. Cook, *The Persian Empire*, p. 130. For a résumé of the history of this period, cf. O. Kaiser, 'Zwischen den Fronten: Palästina in den Auseinandersetzungen zwischen dem Perserreich und Ägypten in der ersten Hälfte des 4. Jahrhunderts', *Work, Lied und Gottespruch* (Festschrift J. Ziegler; ed. J. Schreiner; Forschung und Bibel, 2; Würzburg, 1972), pp. 197-206.

3. E. Stern, *Material Culture*, p. 280 n. 74, see the previous discussion on p. 873.

4. An inscription of Achoris has been found at Acco; cf. A. Rowe, *A Catalogue of Egyptian Scarabs*, p. 205, pl. xxxviii.

5. Diodorus, 15.9.1-2.

preparing for the invasion and did not leave Acco for the Nile until 373. Destruction levels at some coastal sites might be associated with the Persian advance. Achoris's successor and founder of the Thirtieth Dynasty, Nectanebo I (380–363 BCE), who had murdered Achoris's son,[1] heavily fortified the entrances to the Pelusian and Mendes branches of the Nile. The invasion was unsuccessful, partly because of strategic mistakes and mistrust of the Athenian allies and partly because of the inundation of the Nile.[2] As a result of the war, Egypt could again begin to make its power felt in Palestine.

After Cyrus' rebellion and death in the battle at Cunaxa (401 BCE), Artaxerxes managed to restore his power in Anatolia partly by buying out the Greeks, so pitting the Greek cities against each other. The satraps of the western parts of the empire, who were influenced by the Greeks in their cultural attitude and who aspired to become independent, invaded the satrapy of Beyond-the-River in 362 BCE and advanced into Mesopotamia. They were led by the satrap Aroandes (Orontes). This event has been called the 'revolt of the satraps'. It may have received popular backing because of heavy taxation. The revolt was also supported by Sidon's Abd-ashtart (Strato) and Egypt under the son of Nectanebos I, Tachos (Teos, 363–360 BCE), who invaded Phoenicia in 360 BCE. He was supported by Sparta's Agesilaos. According to Diodorus, Tachos had 200 triremes, 10,000 Greek mercenaries and 80,000 soldiers.[3] However, during the pharaoh's maneuvers in Asia a revolt in Egypt deposed Tachos,[4] who sought the protection of Artaxerxes and became one of his generals. The new pharaoh was Tachos's nephew, Nectanebo II (360–343),[5] who showed no interest in the campaign.[6] The revolt of the satraps then petered out, and Aroandes made his peace with the king. When Artaxerxes died in 358 BCE the empire was intact but on shaky ground.

From the above historical review it is apparent that Palestine,

---

1. See F.K. Kienitz, *Die politische Geschichte Ägyptens*, pp. 88-89.

2. Cf. H. Kees, *Ancient Egypt* (London, 1961), p. 54; J.M. Cook, *The Persian Empire*, p. 217.

3. Diodorus 15.90–92.

4. Concerning the reasons for the revolt, including a hard taxation policy by Tachos, see E. Drioton and J. Vandier, *L'Egypte, les peuple de l'orient méditerranéen*, II (Paris, 1962), pp. 610-11.

5. See A.T. Olmstead, *History of the Persian Empire*, pp. 411-12.

6. Diodorus 15.92.5.

especially the coastal area, became contested territory because it was a country of transit. It is therefore possible to see some of the previously mentioned destruction to have been caused by conflicts between Egyptian and Persian troops during the period between 400 and c. 350 BCE. Unfortunately, there are no extant literary sources that can corroborate the archaeological finds. It has been argued that Jericho, Tell ed-Duweir and Hazor were involved in the Phoenician revolt against the Persians in 351–348 BCE and that Judah and Samerina also participated.[1] Not even Josephus made such an assumption. How little Yehud could have joined an uprising at this time is hard to imagine. It did not have a large army. Men could have been hired to do military duty besides the police duty that the Levites performed,[2] but the Persian garrisons in the province must have served as a deterrent to any uprising. The only possible way to oppose the Persians would have been to withhold tribute. It is doubtful that Jericho existed in the Persian period. Stratum II at Hazor, which lasted through the fourth century BCE, was made by the continuation of the stratum III citadel with minor changes: Area B, an 'impressive building' in Area G, and some Attic pottery.[3] Excavations have not established that there was any destruction in the mid-fourth century BCE. The date of the end of Level I at Idumaean Tell ed-Duweir may have occurred in the mid-fourth century. Evidence that Jews and Samaritans participated in this destruction or in the Tennes revolt are simply not there.

The Phoenician revolt of 351–345 BCE has usually been called the Tennes revolt, because the king of Sidon, Tennes, Abd-ashtart's son, was its prime mover. Under Artaxerxes III Ochos (358–338/337 BCE), who attained the throne by killing all of his brothers and other competitors, the political climate became temporarily dangerous for the Persians. In the west Philip II of Macedonia rose to power in 359 BCE and managed to impose his control over the different potentates of his kingdom and over the Greek city states and also to throw his shadow over western Asia. He brought all of the Greek states under his rule in 338 BCE.

---

1. D. Barag, 'The Effects of the Tennes Rebellion on Palestine', *BASOR* 183 (1966), pp. 6-12; M. Smith, *Palestinian Parties and Politics*, p. 60; F.M. Cross, 'Judean Stamps', *EI* 9 (1969), p. 23.

2. Cf. J. Milgrom, *Studies in the Levitical Terminology*, I, pp. 84-85; M. Smith, *Palestinian Parties and Politics*, pp. 164.

3. Y. Yadin, *Hazor of Those Kingdoms*, pp. 194-96.

Whatever Macedonia might have meant to Artaxerxes III, it was not yet seen as a danger to the empire. The king's main goal was to conquer Egypt. His campaign to Egypt in 353–352 failed, probably triggering the rebellion by the Phoenician who believed that Persia's power had come to an end. Diodorus tells the story[1] that the Sidonians were also fed up with the Persian generals who were living in Sidon, who were perceived as representatives of the Persian 'occupation'. Their treatment of the people of Sidon apparently caused more than simple irritation. In raising the banner of rebellion, Sidon not only sent messengers to the other Phoenician cities but also to Egypt asking for support. Hostilities broke out when the Sidonians destroyed the park, *pardēs*, where the Persian kings used to spend their vacations. They also burned the fodder for the horses of the superpower and arrested several Persians.[2] The war began when the satraps, Belesys of Beyond-the-River and Mazaios of Cilicia attacked the Phoenicians.[3] Egypt had sent Tennes 4000 Greek mercenaries from Rhodos under the general, Mentor. Coupling these with his own troops, Tennes succeeded in driving out the army of the satraps. However, Artaxerxes III, who had mustered a great army in a hurry, arrived on the scene in 345 BCE. This made Tennes change his position. He secretly sent a message to the Persian king promising him to surrender Sidon and to help Artaxerxes III to reconquer Egypt. Tennes mentioned that he knew the topography of Egypt and where to penetrate the Nile successfully.[4]

Artaxerxes III accepted the offer and moved close to Sidon where he built his camp. Tennes left Sidon one day with an escort of 500 men under the pretext of meeting the other Phoenician kings. However, not far from the Persian camp he changed direction and marched right into it. At first he was well received, but his followers were slain. The Persians marched into Sidon with Tennes and the mercenaries from Egypt. Tennes was then put to death. When the people of the city saw

1. It is impossible to find out how reliable Diodorus is in this case. For instance, how has the exchange of words between Artaxerxes and Tennes' messenger Thettalion been preserved? The sequence of actions, however, had such impact that it could not be obliterated.

2. Diodorus 16.41.4-6.

3. K. Galling believes that the satrap of Beyond-the-River resided in Tripolis (*Studien zur Geschichte Israels im persischen Zeitalter*, pp. 47-48).

4. Diodorus 16.43.1-2.

what had happened and that the enemy had taken the walls, they burned their ships and locked themselves in their houses and in pure desperation set fire to them. The horror of Sidon made the other Phoenician cities submit to Artaxerxes III.[1] The end of the Phoenician rebellion also paved the way for the conquest of Egypt in 343 BCE.

Artaxerxes III had asked his allies among the Greeks (Argos, Thebes and the Ionian cities) to aid him against the Phoenicians.[2] They did not arrive before Sidon was taken. When they finally joined him, Artaxerxes III was able to advance against Egypt. This time the invasion was successful. According to Diodorus,[3] temples were profaned and the Persian army carried away as much gold and silver as possible. The Persian victory ended Egyptian independence. General Bagoas had some of the temple treasures restored to the priests in return for a large ransom. He probably was not the same individual as the governor of Yehud named Bagohi who is known from the Elephantine papyri six decades earlier. This Bagoas was one of Artaxerxes' trusted friends, but together with his sons, Bagoas murdered the old king in 338/337 BCE, and Arses ascended to the throne. In 336 BCE he and his sons were murdered by Bagoas, and Kodomannos assumed the kingship as Darius III. Bagoas then met death through a cup with poisoned liquid.[4]

The reign of the new king was short. In the same year that Darius became king, Alexander succeeded his father, Philip II. Alexander's interest for Hellas and its traditions can be traced back to one of his teachers, Aristotle. Having united all of Greece under his scepter, Alexander crossed the Hellespont in 334 and began his penetration of Asia Minor. The Persians made a tremendous effort to assemble all of their naval power. Cypriots and Phoenicians joined forces, but when Alexander's forces invaded Phoenician territory the Cypriot and Phoenician commanders deserted and joined Alexander.[5] This defection contributed to the fall of the empire. The battle at Issos in 333 BCE signified the end of Persian rule in the Near East.[6] Darius fled, leaving

1. Diodorus 16.45; cf. D. Barag, *BASOR* 183 (1966), pp. 6-12.
2. Diodorus 16.44.1-4.
3. Diodorus 16.51.2.
4. Cf. J.M. Cook, *The Persian Empire*, pp. 224-25.
5. Cf. H. Hauben, *Ancient Society* 1 (1970), pp. 1-8; see also B.H. Liddell Hart, *Strategy: The Indirect Approach* (New York, 1954), pp. 40-41.
6. For the battle and Alexander's strategy, see A.M. Devine, 'The Strategies of

his family and harem to the conqueror. After this victory Alexander then marched south, receiving the submission of all of the Phoenician cities except Tyre. Alexander blockaded Tyre from the sea with his fleet of over 200 ships. After a siege of seven months, during which a mole was built from the mainland to the isle of Tyre, the city was taken and dealt with ruthlessly. Two thousand men were crucified and 30,000 citizens were sold into slavery.[1] Like many previous conquerors, Alexander marched south along the coast to Egypt, meeting no opposition. The strategic sites were not located inland. Smaller detachments could secure the highlands.[2] Reaching Gaza, he again met stiff resistance. No other city in Palestine had opposed his army. Gaza was a large city, and since it was the western terminal for trade with Arabia, it had become wealthy. Herodotus describes Gaza as a city 'not much smaller than Sardis' (3.5). The defense of Gaza was led by a certain Batis, a eunuch. After a siege of two months, during which Alexander was seriously wounded, the city was taken. The surviving citizens, mainly women and children, were sold into slavery. Batis was bound and 'dragged around the walls in imitation of Achilles' treatment of Hector'.[3] Gaza remained for some time a poorly inhabited place.[4] It

Alexander the Great and Darius III in the Issus Campaign (333 BCE)', *The Ancient World* 12 (1985), pp. 25-38; *idem*, 'Grand Tactics of the Battle of Issus', *The Ancient World* 12 (1985), pp. 39-59.

1. Diodorus 17.40-46.

2. Josephus maintains that Alexander came to the territory of Jerusalem and met the high priest and his entourage. He claims they showed Alexander the Book of Daniel—which was not yet written—and that the king bowed down for the high-priest (*Ant.* 16.8.4-5). Josephus has invented a story intending to show the Greek king's respect for the Jewish religion and an acknowledgment that its traditions were superior to other religions, especially to that of the people of the north. A. Momigliano thinks that the story could have originated among Jews in Egypt ('Flavius Josephus and Alexander's Visit to Jerusalem', *Athenaeum* NS 57 [1979], pp. 442-48). For Alexander's place in Jewish traditions, see G. Delling, 'Alexander der Grosse als Bekenner des jüdischen Gottesglaubens', *JSJ* 12 (1981), pp. 1-51.

3. A.T. Olmstead, *History of Palestine and Syria*, p. 624. See also P. Romane, 'Alexander's Siege of Gaza—332 BCE', *The Ancient World* 18 (1988), pp. 21-30.

4. According to Plutarch (*Alexander* 25.4-5), the booty was rich, and Alexander sent some of it to his friends at home. His teacher, Leonidas, received 500 talents of frankincense and 100 of myrrh. Cf. J.R. Hamilton, *Plutarch, Alexander: A Commentary* (Oxford, 1969), pp. 64-65; M.A. Martin, *The History of the City of Gaza from the Earliest Times to the Present Day* (New York, 1907), p. 44. For the trade in frankincense and myrrh, see N. Groom, *Frankincense and Myrrh*, pp. 204-

was razed by Ptolemy I on his way back to Egypt after he lost Coele-
Syria to Antigonus.[1]

After taking Gaza Alexander continued south and conquered Egypt,
where he was crowned king. The Persians were hated in Egypt, so
Alexander was welcomed as a liberator.[2] In 331 he marched to
Babylonia in order to battle Darius III a second time and secure the
eastern part of the empire. The Persian king fled into Media, but
Alexander pursued him. Finally, Darius was murdered in 330 BCE by
some of his own men, when they saw that their cause was hopeless.
Hellas had won the battle of supremacy that had started with the
dreams of Darius I.

Like other historiographers of his time, Diodorus Siculus does not
mention anything about the peoples of the hills of Palestine and
Transjordan. The important actions of history did not take place there.
The people of these areas did not contribute anything that made an
impact on the political stage. Neither Diodorus nor Josephus mentions
whether the people of the inland supported Tennes' revolt or the
earlier revolt of the satraps. The destruction layers found at certain
sites may or may not indicate participation in the Phoenician revolt by
the Palestinian population. It is noticeable that no Judean site shows
any destruction that can be associated with this period.[3] Very little is
also known about Palestine after Artaxerxes conquered Egypt. What is
clear is that Samaria became a Macedonian city[4] and that Tyre grew in
importance after the destruction of Sidon, which could account for the
increased amount of Tyrian artifacts and coins all over the country.
This might be the time when the settlement and naval station at
Straton's Tower (at Caesarea) was founded by the Phoenicians.[5] Since

205. In describing Arabia, Herodotus (3.107-13) says that there 'is a most marvel-
ous sweet smell from all this land of Arabia' (3.113).

1. Diodorus 19.93.6.

2. Diodorus 17.49–51.

3. Hazor, 'Athlit and Tell ed-Duweir, with their destruction supposedly occurring in this period, were all outside Yehud, and an unstratified arrowhead from
Jericho is no proof.

4. Cf. below, p. 899.

5. The suggested dates are the last decades of the Persian period or shortly after
Alexander. The area got its name from Sidon's king Straton II, who was dethroned
by Alexander. The place is mentioned in a papyrus from the Zenon archive found in
Fayum in Egypt in 1915. This means that the site was in existence in 259/258 BCE; see
L. Haefeli, *Cäsarea am Meer: Topographie und Geschichte der Stadt nach Josephus*

Skylax does not mention it, it probably had not yet been built during the reign of Straton I (Abdastartos, c. 370–360 BCE).[1]

During the fourth century BCE there was an increase in the number of coins minted in Palestine.[2] Many have Aramaic inscriptions, which indicate that they were struck by Persian officials. Most coins are of the Phoenician or Attic standard. There are coins depicting an owl, a lily, and sometimes the face of a person, probably a Persian king or a god; others show a bird and may be Athenian imitations.[3] For instance, a hoard of Tyrian coins from the pre-Alexandrian period were found at Tell el-Fukhar (Tel Acco) and show Egyptian influences.[4] Another hoard from Tell Abū Hawām contained both the Attic and the Phoenician standards.[5] Also of note are a few coins from the last decade of the Persian period with the inscription *yhzqyh hphh*, 'Yehezqiyah, the governor'. The coins bear a human head and an owl.

---

und Apostelgeschichte (NTAbh, 10.5; Münster i.W., 1923), p. 5; R. Galling, *Studien zur Geschichte Israels im persischen Zeitalter*, pp. 199-200; J. Ringel, *Césarée de Palestine: Etude historique et archéologique* (Associations de Publications près les Universités de Strasbourg; Paris, 1975), pp. 18-24; G. Foerster, 'The Early History of Caesarea', *The First Expedition to Caesarea Maritima*. I. *Studies in the History of Caesarea Maritima* (ed. C.T. Fritsch; BASORSup, 19; Missoula, MT, 1975), pp. 9-10.

1. An inscription from Athens mentions this king as a public friend of Athens, giving him and his citizens trading privileges (*CIG*, I, no. 87, p. 126). There are a few inscriptions from Athens and Piræus mentioning a Sidonian presence in Greece. The one from Piraeus shows a Sidonian officer being voted a crown and a monument; cf. J.C.L. Gibson, *TSSI*, III, pp. 147-51.

2. The Greek mercenaries, for instance, had to be paid in hard currency, because they had few possibilities for barter. The soldiers could not carry around gold or silver bars or ingots. The introduction of the daric by Darius I was a practical measure that could be used to control the economy. Coinage was also used by the Persians to bribe 'Greek politicians and parties' (J.M. Cook, *The Persian Empire*, p. 71). Could the latter use have caused inflation?

3. L. Mildenberg, 'Yehud: A Preliminary Study of the Provincial Coinage of Judaea', *Greek Numismatics and Archaeology: Essays in Honor of Margaret Thompson* (ed. O. Mørkholm and N.M. Waggoner; Wetteren, 1979), pp. 183-86; cf. Y. Meshorer, *Ancient Jewish Coinage*, I, p. 13.

4. Egyptian influence on the coins would date them to 364–346 BCE, when Egypt occupied the area; cf. Diodorus 15.92.2, and see A. Kindler, 'The Mint of Tyre—The Major Source of Silver Coins in Ancient Israel', *EI* 8 (1967), pp. 318-25 (Hebrew).

5. See F.M. Cross, 'Coins', *Discoveries in the Wâdî ed-Dâliyeh* (ed. P.W. Lapp and N.L. Lapp), p. 58; cf. *idem*, 'The Discovery of the Samaria Papyri', *BA* 26 (1963), pp. 116-18.

One of them is from Beth-Zur and another one from Tell Jemme.[1] This Yehezqiyah might then be the last known governor of the *m^edînâ* of Yehud before Alexander.[2]

The above-mentioned coin with a bearded deity sitting on a winged wheel that bears the inscription *yhd* (earlier read *yhw*, which could refer to Yahweh) is unique in that it depicts a deity (see Fig. 8). If the reading *yhd* is correct, the inscription (in lapidary Aramaic)[3] names a province rather than a deity, which is rare.[4] This must be an official coin, probably struck by the Persian administration in Jerusalem. The date would be close to 400 BCE.[5] L. Mildenberg says that the deity 'depicts no specific god, but a general conception of deity easily comprehensible to many people in the western part of the Persian Empire'.[6] If so, the people of Yehud may have associated the god with Yahweh, whom they called the 'God of Heaven', a well-known Iranian concept.

A hoard of coins presumably minted shortly before 332 BCE in Samaria have been discovered in the cave of Abu Shinjeh (coord. 188.7-155.7) in Wâdī ed-Dâliyeh, where over 200 human skeletons were found. The people had fled from Samaria after Alexander's prefect in Syria, Andromachus, had been burned alive in his house[7] in

---

1.   N. Avigad, *Bullae and Seals*, p. 28-29; L.Y. Rahmani, 'Silver Coins of the Fourth Century BCE from Tel Gamma', *IEJ* 21 (1971), pp. 158-60. It is most probable that such coins were struck in Judah 'by authorization of the Persian royal treasury' (E. Stern, *Material Culture*, p. 226).

2.   Cf. N. Avigad, *Bullae and Seals*, pp. 28-29. For the possibility that the Yehezqiah coin being dates from the time of Ptolemy I, see the discussion in A. Kindler, 'Silver Coins Bearing the Name of Judea from the Early Hellenistic Period', *IEJ* 24 (1974), pp. 73-76.

3.   F.M. Cross, *EI* 9 (1969), p. 23. For the Aramaic script on papyri, seals and hard materials during the fourth century BCE, see J. Naveh, *The Development of the Aramaic Script*, pp. 43-64.

4.   E.L. Sukenik's reading of *yhd* has been widely accepted; see his 'Paralipomena Palaestinensia', *JPOS* 14 (1934), pp. 178-84. S.A. Cook objected to it asking why there would be a picture of a bearded man on a winged wheel without a corresponding name ('The Jahu Coin', *ZAW* 56 [1938], pp. 268-71).

5.   N. Avigad, *Bullae and Seals*, p. 28. F.M. Cross dates it to the fifth century BCE on paleographic indications (*EI* 9 [1969], p. 23). However, the style of inscriptions may be conservative.

6.   'Yehud', *Greek Numismatics* (ed. O. Mørkholm and N.M. Waggoner), p. 184.

7.   Curtius Rufus, *De gestis Alexandri magni* 4.8.9-11; cf. H.H. Rowley, *BJRL* 38 (1955), pp. 181-82; M. Stern, *Greek and Latin Authors on Jews and Judaism*, I (Jerusalem, 1974), no. 197.

the first uprising in Palestine against the new ruler. The Macedonians must have pursued them and killed them by building a fire in front of the cave so that they died by suffocation.[1] Besides pottery, textiles, jewelry and seals, some papyri were also found, which dated from about 370 to 335 BCE.[2] Several small silver coins have the legend *šmryn*, a spelling also found in the papyri. It is as a parallel to *yhwd*, and shows that the Assyrian name of the territory, Samerina, was still used. Consequently, *šmrwn*, the city of Samaria, must be distinguished from *šmryn*, the district of Samerina (cf. Ezra 4.17). A few of the Samarian coins bore the inscription *yrb'm*, Jeroboam. It is possible that this Jeroboam was a *peḥâ*, 'governor', of Samerina sometime after 375 BCE.[3]

The papyri from Wâdî ed-Dâliyeh are the only literary documents found in Palestine from the last forty years of Persian rule. They throw some light on this historically dark period even if most of them are legal and administrative texts from Samaria. They mention, for example, a governor named Hananiah, son of Sanballat (II). Some documents refer to sales of property, marriage and divorce. Others deal with slave trade, indicating the importance of slavery in the economic system.[4] 128 documents were sealed with bullae. Personal names with theophoric components include, besides Yahweh and Baal, the Edomite Qoš, Arabic-Aramaic Sahar, Moabite Chemosh and Babylonian Nabu.[5] This shows that the territory of Samerina was settled by people of different national and religious backgrounds. It should be remembered that Sargon II deported 27,290 Israelites, setting Babylonians, Aramaeans, Cutheans and others in Samaria

---

1. F.M. Cross, *BA* 26 (1963), pp. 115-16; *idem*, 'The Papyri', *Discoveries in the Wâdî ed-Dâliyeh* (ed. P.W. Lapp and N.L. Lapp), pp. 17-18; cf. G.E. Wright, *Shechem*, p. 181.

2. For a report of the find and the excavations, see P.W. Lapp, 'Wâdî ed-Dâliyeh', *RB* 72 (1965), pp. 405-409; *Discoveries in the Wâdî ed-Dâliyeh* (ed. P.W. Lapp and N.L. Lapp), pp. 1-12; cf. F.M. Cross, *BA* 26 (1963), pp. 110-21.

3. See Y. Meshorer, *Ancient Jewish Coinage*, I, pp. 31-32, 34, 160.

4. Cf. Ezek. 27.13; Joel 4.6; Amos 1.6, 9. For the problem of slavery, see M. A. Dandamayev, 'Social Stratification in Babylonia (7th–4th Centuries BCE)', *Acta Antiqua* 22 (1974), pp. 433-44. As to prices, cf. I. Mendelsohn, *Slavery in the Ancient Near East* (New York, 1949), pp. 117-20.

5. See F.M. Cross, *BA* 26 (1963), pp. 112-16; *idem*, 'The Papyri', *Discoveries in the Wâdî ed-Dâliyeh* (ed. P.W. Lapp and N.L. Lapp), pp. 18-20.

around 720 BCE. In 716 he also settled some Arabs there.[1] Other settlers were moved in by Esarhaddon and Ashurbanipal (Ezra 4.2, 10). Nevertheless, the majority of the people of Samerina were still Israelites; the whole population had not been deported. Consequently, Israelite traditions were still alive. This has to be taken into consideration when discussing the origin of the later Samaritans. Cultural and religious syncretism might have occurred, but it is impossible to determine how much or to what degree assimilation had occurred. The city of Samaria could be characterized as a cosmopolitan place, but nothing is known about the situation in the rest of the province. Since personal names with the theophoric component Yahweh are in the majority, it can only be said that the old Israelite religion with Yahweh as the main god was still in existence. This would suggest that the main component in the demographic picture of Samerina was Israelite. This fact was ignored by the leaders of the *gôlâ* party in Jerusalem, who saw only themselves as being the true 'Israel'.[2] The writers of the books of Ezra and Nehemiah have propagated this exclusivism, and the same attitude is to be found in the writings of Josephus. The later break between the Jews and the Samaritans was thus inspired by the attitude of the Jerusalemites.[3]

The cause of the tragedy responsible for the remains from Wâdī ed-Dâliyeh was the murder of Alexander's governor, Andromachos, by the people of Samaria. The reason for this act is not known. Josephus claims that Sanballat and the people of Samaria welcomed Alexander and asked him to allow them to build a temple on Gerizim, permission for which had originally been granted by Darius.[4] Official sanction for a temple would mean that its people were acknowledged as a 'nation' within the empire, a status that was previously given to the Jerusalemite temple. What made the people of Samaria murder the

---

1. Cf. 2 Kgs. 17.24; *ANET*, pp. 284-85. See also N. Na'aman and R. Zadok, 'Sargon II's Deportations to Israel and Philistia', *JCS* 40 (1988), pp. 36-46.

2. Cf. J. Bowman, *Samaritanische Probleme: Studien zum Verhältnis von Samaritanertum, Judentum und Christentum* (Franz Delitzsch-Vorlesungen, 1959; Stuttgart, 1967), p. 11; G.W. Ahlström, *Who were the Israelites?*, pp. 101-18.

3. One example of this attitude is found in Sirach 50.25-26: 'the foolish people who dwell in Shechem' (cf. J.D. Purvis, '"Ben Sira" and the Foolish People of Shechem', *JNES* 24 [1965], pp. 88-94).

4. Josephus, *Ant.* 11.8.2-4. Why Sanballat of Samaria would ask for a temple to be built on Gerizim and not in Samaria has never been explained. The story is no more reliable than Josephus' story about Alexander visiting Jerusalem (*Ant.* 11.8.5).

prefect is an enigma. According to Josephus, Alexander took Sanballat's troops with him on his campaign to Egypt and then settled them there.[1] His action probably would not have been the cause of a rebellion, because subdued peoples had to muster troops for the imperial armies, and the leaders in Samaria would have known this obligation from the time they had become vassals of the Assyrian kings. Whatever the reason for the murder, which amounted to rebellion, Alexander punished the people on his return from Egypt by executing some and exiling others. Before the punishment a group left and took refuge in a cave in Wâdī ed-Dâliyeh, where they met their death. Samaria was then settled by Macedonians.[2] It has been suggested that in the wake of Alexander's move, some of the inhabitants moved to Shechem and rebuilt the city, which had been unoccupied for over 100 years.[3]

The excavations at Tell Balaṭa (str. IV) point to a rebuilding and fortification of Shechem no 'later than the last third of the fourth century'.[4] This would be about the same time that the temple at Gerizim was built, according to Josephus.[5] G.E. Wright has therefore concluded that people expelled from Samaria settled at Shechem. He mentions that the pottery from Shechem stratum IV resembles that found in the Shinjeh cave at Wâdī ed-Dâhliyeh.[6] The similarity does not necessarily identify the people of Shechem as settlers from the city of Samaria. It could just as well indicate that stratum IV at Shechem was built before Alexander's conquest of Palestine.[7] It can also be asked whether the pottery of pre-Macedonian Samaria was much

1. *Ant.* 11.8.6.

2. For the question whether Alexander or Perdiccas settled the Macedonians in the city (in 296–295 BCE), see R. Marcus, *Josephus* (LCL edn), VI, pp. 524-25; V. Tcherikover, *Hellenistic Civilisation and the Jews* (Philadelphia, 1961), pp. 45-48. For Samaria as a Macedonian colony, see also G.E. Wright, 'Samaritans at Shechem', *HTR* 55 (1962), pp. 363-66.

3. G.E. Wright, *Shechem*, p. 167.

4. G.E. Wright, *Shechem*, p. 180.

5. *Ant.* 11.8.2-4.

6. G.E. Wright, *Shechem*, p. 181.

7. In discussing the pottery and coins (from Alexander through Ptolemy V) of stratum IV, Wright concludes that Shechem was 'resettled as a city not long before Alexander the Great' (*Shechem*, p. 171-72). Thus, he has undermined his own theory on the following pages that people from Samaria fled the city or were expelled by Alexander and rebuilt Shechem (p. 175-81).

different from the pottery in the villages outside Samaria. Another solution to the problem would be that, when the people of Samerina lost their cultural center in Samaria, the old and tradition-filled site of Shechem became a natural replacement; thus a temple might also have been built by the Shechemites. They might have built on Gerizim and not in the city proper because mountains were holy in Semitic countries and Ebal and Gerizim had long been holy places for the Israelite people of the surrounding areas. Newcomers to the territory would also have learned about these venerated places. If stratum IV at Shechem was built before Alexander, it could have been settled by priests and others who left Jerusalem because they did not accept Ezra's rule against 'mixed' marriages.[1] In this case, the temple that they later built on Gerizim not only became a cult center for the northern Yahweh worshipers, it also became a rival to that of Jerusalem, with much of the same liturgical traditions. This would explain the origin of the Samaritan Pentateuch.

The construction of the temple at Gerizim probably occurred after Alexander's conquest of Palestine. This conclusion can be drawn not only from the Josephus narrative,[2] but also from the fact that on the northern spur of the mountain, Tell er-Ras, the remains of a Hellenistic structure have been found under the ruins of Hadrian's temple to Zeus Olympius. The masonry is preserved to a height of 8 m and could have been higher. The dimensions are c. 20×18 m. Its enclosure wall had a gate over 8 m wide. This is no ordinary building and may very well be the remains of a temple.[3] Its date cannot be established with exactness, except that it was built after Alexander. Jewish and Yahwistic temples outside Jerusalem are known from the postexilic period, such as at Elephantine and Leontopolis in Egypt. The large structure at the Tobiad estate at 'Araq el-Emîr in Jordan has also been

1. Thus H.G. Kippenberg, referring to Josephus, *Ant.* 11.8.2 (*Garizim und Synagoge*, pp. 50-57).

2. J.D. Purvis says that the temple was built by Sanballat III (*The Samaritan Pentateuch*, pp. 1-12, 109). If Alexander had given permission to the governor of Samaria to build the temple, why then did he not destroy it or stop the building activities at the same time that he punished Samaria? Cf. R. Egger, *Josephus Flavius und Die Samaritaner*, p. 37 n. 71.

3. Consult R.J. Bull and E.F. Campbell, 'The Sixth Campaign at Balaṭa (Shechem)', *BASOR* 190 (1968), pp. 4-19, figs. 1-12; R.J. Bull, 'The Excavation of Tell er-Ras on Mount Gerizim', *BA* 31 (1968), p. 72; *idem*, 'An Archaeological Context for Understanding John 4:20', *BA* 38 (1975), pp. 54-59.

interpreted as a temple,[1] but it might equally be a palace.[2] The Judaism of Jerusalem had not yet been able to enforce the one-temple idea. The temple called the 'solar shrine' at Tell ed-Duweir cannot be called Jewish, as long as there is no information about its cult or who built it. Since it was built in the territory of Idumaea it may represent an Edomite cult.[3]

The temple on Mt Gerizim should not be labeled a sectarian temple. It became the central sanctuary for the Yahwistic worshipers of Samerina.[4] As such it became a competitor to Jerusalem. The two shared common roots but developed in somewhat different directions. It is possible that during the later part of the Hellenistic period the Samarian worship was more widespread than Judaism, which began to spread in Palestine first during the Hasmonean period, when Idumaea and Galilee, for instance, were forced into the Jewish 'fold'—by conversion under the sword. As time went on, the Shechemites and the worshipers at Gerizim preserved their form of religion despite political pressures and persecutions, which resulted in a conservative attitude towards their traditions and finally in a break with Jerusalem. The religious exclusiveness of the Jerusalemite establishment and its hostility towards the Yahweh worshipers of the north contributed to this development.[5] This was a slow process and it is impossible to give a precise date for the final break.[6] The temple at Gerizim apparently

1. M.J.B. Brett, 'The Qasr el-'Abd: A Proposed Reconstruction', *BASOR* 171 (1963), pp. 39-45.

2. J.M. Dentzer, F. Villeneuve and F. Larché compare the estate with the Persian *pairidaeza* (Greek *paradeisos*), 'park', in 'Iraq el-Amir: Excavations at the Monumental Gateway', *Studies in the History and Archaeology of Jordan*, I (ed. A. Hadidi; Amman, 1982), p. 207.

3. Cf. E.F. Campbell, 'Jewish Shrines of the Hellenistic and Persian Periods', *Symposia* (ed. F.M. Cross; Cambridge, MA, 1979), pp. 159-67.

4. Cf. R.J. Coggins, who says that the 'Samaritans are something of an embarrassment to Josephus: he cannot repudiate them entirely, and yet they cannot be accepted as part of the race whose Antiquities he is setting out to his audience' (*Samaritans and Jews* [Oxford, 1975], p. 99).

5. R.J. Coggins may be right in assuming that 'the repudiation of Samaritanism may have been one of the purposes' of the writings of Josephus (*Samaritans and Jews*, p. 99).

6. Cf. H.H. Rowley, *BJRL* 38 (1955), p. 190; P.R. Ackroyd, *Israel under Babylon and Persia*, p. 185; R.J. Coggins, *Samaritans and Jews*, pp. 162-63. For the Samaritan Pentateuch as being the Holy Writ of Gerizim, and for the differences between it and the Jerusalemite Pentateuch, see J.D. Purvis, *The Samaritan*

made it possible for the Yahweh worshipers of the north to keep their faith in a Hellenizing world. Perhaps the real break between Gerizim and Jerusalem first came when John Hyrcanus destroyed the Samaritan temple.[1] The split was motivated as much by political concerns as religious ones. Hyrcanus may have tried to force the Gerizim-Shechem community to follow the Jerusalemite tradition by forcing the people to become Jews.[2] Whether he succeeded is not known, but when Palestine came under Roman control in 64 BCE the Samaritan community went its own way.

Increased Arab presence,[3] especially in the southern parts of the country, can be discerned in Palestine in the later Persian period.[4] It should be remembered that Arabs in Palestine were nothing new.[5] Ever since the eighth century, under Tiglath-pileser III, the Arabs of Transjordan, the Negev and northern Sinai had often been used to protect trade routes and to patrol border areas with Egypt in the south.[6] They fulfilled the same function during the Persian period.[7] Nevertheless, the great influx of Arabs into Transjordan and southern Palestine[8] belongs rather to the so-called Hellenistic period.[9] When the

---

Pentateuch; H.G. Kippenberg, *Garizim und Synagoge*, pp. 68-74.

1. Josephus mentions that the temple was destroyed two hundred years after it had been built (*Ant.* 13.10.2-3). G.E. Wright suggests that Hyrcanus destroyed the temple on Gerizim in c. 128 BCE and Samaria in c. 107 BCE (*Shechem*, pp. 183-84).

2. Cf. F.M. Cross, 'The Papyri', *Discoveries in the Wâdī ed-Dâliyeh* (ed. P.W. Lapp and N.L. Lapp), p. 24.

3. According to E.A. Knauf, the settlements in northern Transjordan mentioned in 1 Chron. 5.18-22 would refer to the Persian period (*Ismael*, pp. 51-52, 67).

4. For the supposed relationship between Arabs and Ishmaelites, see I. Eph'al, who thinks it is 'founded on the ethnological midrash in Gen. 25' ('"Ishmael" and "Arab(s)": A Transformation of Ethnological Terms', *JNES* 35 [1976], pp. 225-35).

5. Consult I. Eph'al, *The Ancient Arabs*.

6. The Arabian trade via Tema' and Dumah to Babylonia was in the hands and territory of the Qedarites. The other route over Yathrib (Medina) via Dedan went to Palestine and first became part of the Qedarite trade in the Persian period (I. Eph'al, *The Ancient Arabs*, p. 238).

7. The Persians learned about the importance of the camel so that they used Arab companies with camels. They were, for instance, part of Xerxes' army (Herodotus 7.184); see E. Merkel, 'Erste Festsetzungen im fruchtbaren Halbmond', *Die Araber in der Alten Welt*, I [ed. F. Altheim and R. Stiehl; Berlin, 1964], p. 171).

8. E.A. Knauf dates the beginning of the Nabatean movement into these areas as in the sixth cent. BCE (*Ismael*, p. 109).

9. Diodorus mentions the Nabateans in connection with the battle between

Persian empire collapsed, the Nabateans[1] of Transjordan and other Arab tribes had the opportunity to expand, and the Nabateans did so,[2] replacing the Edomites. It is possible that there had been contact between Edomites and Nabateans already in the neo-Babylonian period, before Edom ceased to exist as a nation. This may be true if the Nabateans were a branch of the Qedarites.[3] Late Persian pottery types in Ammon, for instance, 'herald Nabatean types'.[4] The Babylonian intervention in southern Jordan under Nabuna'id resulted in Edomite migration. Some moved into the Negev and southern Judah, but it is also probable that 'a group of Edomite refugees moved south to Dedan', (al-'Ula) taking their pottery with them.[5] When Persia lost Egypt after the death of Darius II and Egypt again made its power felt in Palestine, it is likely that the trade with Arabia via southern Palestine and Transjordan was also lost to Persia.[6] The Nabateans apparently benefitted from the political situation after c. 400 BCE. The possibility has been considered[7] that the destruction at Tell el-Kheleifeh (str. V), Arad (str. V), En-Gedi (str. IV) and Kadesh-barnea (str. III) is to be associated with Egypt's involvement in Palestine during this period.[8] Egyptian destruction of these sites may have

Ptolemy and Antigonus in 312 BCE, stating that the Nabateans were a wealthy tribe of about 10,000 men. They had for quite some time traded in frankincense and myrrh from Arabia (19.94.4-5). Petra was one of their well-established centers at this time. Cf. E.A. Knauf, *Ismael*, pp. 108-10.

1.   For the Nabateans not being identical with the biblical Nebaioth, see E. Meyer, *Die Israeliten und ihre Nachbarstämme*, p. 267 n. 2; I. Eph'al, *The Ancient Arabs*, pp. 221-23. Cf. J. Cantineau, 'Nabatéen et arabe', *Annales de l'institut des études orient* 1 (1934–35), pp. 77-78.

2.   Cf. E.A. Knauf, 'Die Herkunft der Nabatäer', *Petra: Neue Ausgrabungen und Entdeckungen* (ed. M. Lindner; Munich, 1986), pp. 74-86. Knauf considers it possible that the Nabateans were descendants of the Qedarites (*Ismael*, pp. 66, 103-108).

3.   During the Persian period the Qedarites are found not only in Transjordan but also in the Negev and in the Delta; that is, they are found in the same territories as those in which Nabateans are found later; cf. I. Eph'al, *The Ancient Arabs*, pp. 223-27. Cf. also R.H. Dornemann, *The Archaeology of Transjordan*, pp. 183-39.

4.   J.A. Sauer, *BASOR* 263 (1986), p. 18.

5.   P. Parr, 'Contacts between North West Arabia and Jordan', *Studies in the History and Archaeology of Jordan*, I (ed. A. Hadidi), p. 132.

6.   For the trade from Arabia, see N. Groom, *Frankincense and Myrrh*, pp. 55-213; cf. G.W. Van Beek, *BA* 23 (1960), pp. 70-95.

7.   Thus I. Eph'al, *The Ancient Arabs*, p. 205.

8.   According to N. Glueck, Tell el-Kheleifeh was abandoned in the fourth

benefitted the Nabateans in their western movement. Although not
much is known about the Nabateans until the beginning of the
Hellenistic period, their early pottery shows Edomite traits, so that
some contact between the two has to be acknowledged.[1] Southern
Transjordan experienced a wave of Nabatean settlements during the
Hellenistic period, and continuing through the Roman period this
territory and the Negev were settled as never before.[2] However, this
development occurs outside the time-frame of this volume.

century BCE and the Nabatean settlement was built more to the east, where modern
Aqaba is located (*EAEHL*, III, p. 717). En-Gedi (Tel Goren), where impressive
buildings, Attic pottery and *yhd* stamps were found, is said to have been destroyed
around 400 BCE or shortly thereafter (B. Mazar, 'En-Gedi', *EAEHL*, II, pp. 375-
76). The Arad of the Persian period was a way station for caravans. No fortress from
this period has been found (Z. Herzog *et al.*, *BASOR* 254 [1984], p. 29). Kadesh-
Barnea has not yielded any building phases on the mound after the fall of the kingdom of Judah (M. Dothan, 'Kadesh-Barnea', *EAEHL*, III, p. 698), yet Dothan has
argued that the settlement ended in the Hellenistic period ('The Fortress at Kadesh-
Barnea', *IEJ* 15 [1965], p. 143).

1. Cf. N. Glueck, *BASOR* 188 (1967), pp. 8-38; I. Browning thinks that the
Nabateans learned from the Edomites (*Petra* [Park Ridge, NJ, 1973], p. 32). They
developed the tradition, however, in such a way that it became 'technically and
artistically a group of its own' within the Hellenistic culture (K. Schmitt-Korte, 'A
Contribution to the Study of Nabatean Pottery', *ADAJ* 16 [1971], p. 50).

2. For the origin and history of the Nabateans, see F. Altheim and R. Stiehl, *Die
Araber in der Alten Welt*. I. *Bis zum Beginn der Kaiserzeit* (Berlin, 1964), pp. 31-
33, 281-83; H. Vincent, 'Las Nabatéens', *RB* 7 (1898), pp. 567-88, F.E. Peters,
'The Nabateans in the Hawran', *JAOS* 97 (1977), pp. 263-77; J.R. Bartlett, *PEQ*
111 (1979), pp. 53-66; P.C. Hammond, *The Nabateans: The History, Culture, and
Archaeology* (Studies in Mediterranean Archaeology, 37; Göteborg, 1973);
R. Wenning, *Die Nabatäer—Denkmäler und Geschichte* (Novum Testamentum et
Orbis Antiquus, 3; Freiburg, 1987). Consult also A. Negev, *Nabatean Archaeology
Today* (New York, 1986).

INDEXES

INDEX OF BIBLICAL REFERENCES

Genesis

1–11	27	26.26	475, 508 n.	20.17	69, 417 n., 643
5	34	26.40-43	184	20.24	379 n.
5.32	155	28.10-19	184 n.	21	403 n., 448 n.
6–8	120 n.	29-31	230		
6.10	155	30.3-8	279	21.6-9	702 n.
9.10	120	30.12-13	278	21.21-35	403 n., 409
9.18-19	60	30.12	279	21.22-35	403
10	34, 61, 155, 296, 313, 741 n.	32.23-30	231 n.	21.22	69, 643
		34.2	207	21.23-25	414 n.
		35.1-15	231 n.	21.23	415
10.2-3	694	35.9-10	231 n.	21.24	481 n.
10.6-16	155	36.13	566	21.33	69
10.6	60, 313	36.31-39	419	22–24	649 n., 649
10.8-9	275	46.17	279	22	448 n.
10.8	30	49	380 n.	23.28	63
10.12	313	49.25	649 n.	24.17	170, 410
10.15-18	60			25.1-3	650 n.
10.18	244 n.	*Exodus*		26	769
10.19	61	2.14	371	26.13	566
10.21-31	155	3.14	382 n.	26.30-37	624
11.1-9	30	13.17	68	26.31-33	510
11.31	30, 181	20.22	725 n.	26.33	429 n.
14	186	20.25	725 n.	27.1	429 n., 510 .
15.6	182	20.36	534 n.	31.1-54	650 n.
15.7	30	22.25-27	767	31.8	650 n.
19.37	409 n.	23.23	154, 489 n.	31.16-17	650 n.
20	566	32	553 n.	32	409, 513 n.
22.24	399 n.			32.3	414
23	186 n., 688 n.	*Leviticus*		32.18-39	513 n.
		23	885	32.33	448 n.
25	904 n.	23.42-43	885	32.37	413, 414
25.2-3	393 n.	26.33-43	837 n.	34.2-12	61
25.3	443			35.1-3	413
25.24-26	419	*Numbers*			
26	566	13.29	154, 285 n.	*Deuteronomy*	
26.17	184 n.	20.13	379 n.	2.4-6	184
		20.14-21.4	418 n.		

2.12	234	13.8-9	448 n.
2.23	313, 317	13.16	654
2.26–3.22	409	13.25	407 n.
3.1	69	13.26	445
3.8	489	13.31	407 n.
3.12	407 n.	15	769
3.16	650 n.	15.1-12	768
4.44–30.20	776	15.7	379 n.
4.48	489	15.9	283 n.
8.9	70	15.16-17	376 n.
8.15	745 n.	15.16	23
12–26	876 n.	15.24	513 n.
12.5	561 n.	15.32	194 n.
12.11	247	15.41	328
12.13-15	776	15.45-47	768
16.1-7	776	15.61-62	730
16.7	547 n.	16.1-3	422 n.
17.14	689 n.	16.1	379 n.
17.18-20	43	16.2-7	422
18.9-10	689	16.2-3	422 n.
20.17	154	17.2-3	510
23.1-5	876 n.	17.3	429 n.
23.8-9	876 n.	17.11-18	348
26.1	689 n.	17.15	63
28	776	18.15	283 n.
33.2	417, 453 n.	18.21-28	435
33.11	479 n.	18.24	405 n.
		19	489 n.
Joshua		19.19	233
2.2	390	19.21	270 n.
3	381	19.27	328
3.7–5.1	28	19.43	311 n.
3.15	495 n.	19.44	507 n.,
5.1	285 n.		710 n.
6.26	583 n.	19.45	307 n.
9.7	362, 421 n.	19.46	307 n.
10.2	453 n.	19.50	63
11	348 n.	21	410, 525 n.
11.1	202	21.23	710 n.
11.10-13	348 n.	21.24	307 n.
11.10	396 n.	21.36	581 n.
12.2	407 n.	21.38	525 n.
13	489 n.	22	409 n.
13.2	619	22.9	390
13.3	299, 310	22.10-11	409 n.
13.4-5	396 n.	22.12	409 n.
13.4	244	22.13-16	409 n.
13.8-32	409	24	345

Judges			
1.12-13	376 n.		
1.27-35	347		
1.27	320 n.		
1.32	278 n.		
1.35	279, 510 n.		
2.6-23	375 n.		
2.16	371		
2.18-19	371		
3–9	37		
3.8-10	376 n.		
3.8	399 n.		
3.9-12	376		
3.11-30	38		
3.12-30	377, 591		
3.12-14	38		
3.13-14	446 n.		
3.13	406		
3.19	38, 426		
3.20-23	38		
3.24-25	38		
3.26-30	38		
3.27	63		
3.31	378		
4	40, 41, 325, 348 n., 379, 380 n., 381		
4.1	378		
4.2	380 n.		
4.6	325, 379		
4.10	325		
4.16	381		
4.17	202, 380 n.		
4.23-24	202		
5	29, 40, 41, 325, 379, 380, 381		
5.4-5	40		
5.4	417, 453 n.		
5.6-7	40		
5.6	378, 379		
5.10	374 n.		
5.14	421 n.		
5.15	380 n.		
5.18	325, 379		
5.19	379, 380		
5.20-21	381 n.		
6–8	382		

6.11-32	382 n.	12.13-15	421 n.	7.15-17	361 n., 426
6.11-17	37	12.14	374	7.17	427, 428
6.16	382 n.	13–16	388	8.1-3	429 n.
6.24	427 n.	16.21-23	328	8.5	371 n.
6.25-27	382 n.	17–21	372 n., 376,	8.11	453 n.
6.33-34	383		377	8.20	371 n.
6.33	429 n.	17–18	388, 427 n.	9	425
6.35	383 n.	17.3	389	9–11	428, 429,
6.36-37	471	17.6	377		447 n.
7.8	547 n.	18.1	377	9.1	435
7.23	383 n.	18.3	389 n.	9.22	616 n.,
8	384	18.7	780 n.		667 n.
8.18	382 n.	18.21-31	389	10.5	324 n., 433,
8.27	383, 427 n.	18.28	398		436
8.30-31	383	18.30	389 n.,	11	405, 446,
9	384, 385,		655 n.		447
	428, 437 n.	18.31	389	11.1-4	446
9.1-6	375, 383,	19.1	377	11.1	644 n.
	385	21.8-10	405 n.	11.8	448
9.22-49	291	21.12	390	12	389
9.22	387	21.19	69	12.9	348 n.
9.41	385	21.25	377	12.11	389, 427
9.45	387			12.12	644 n.
9.46-49	366 n.	*1 Samuel*		13–14	438
9.50-55	385 n.	1.1	63	13.2-4	437
9.55	387	2.17	425 n.	13.3-5	324 n.
10.1-5	373 n.	2.22	425 n.	13.3	433
10.1-2	379	2.27-36	502 n.	13.6-7	437
10.4	374	3.1–4.1	425	13.19-20	433
10.7-8	446 n.	3.1	369, 390,	14	437 n.
10.7	406		425	14.3	453
10.9	405 n.	4	390, 428	14.11	437
10.11	446 n.	4.4	534	14.18	453
10.17-18	400 n.	4.10	547 n.	14.21-22	324 n.
11	403 n., 407	4.18	369, 390	14.21	437, 438
11.1	266 n.	5.2	328	14.31	438
11.8	399	5.8	312 n.	14.47-52	444 n.
11.12-28	403 n., 406	6.2	327	14.47-48	444
11.19-21	414	6.4	312 n., 329,	14.47	36, 444, 447
11.24	415		588 n.	14.50	453
11.26	403 nn.	6.16	312 n.	15	429
11.33	354 n., 407	6.20–7.1	510 n.	15.5	359 n.
12	402	7	426, 427,	15.12	556
12.4	403		436	16	432, 455,
12.5	376	7.5-12	427		457
12.7-15	373 n.	7.6	428	16.4	456 n.
12.8-9	374	7.11-12	427 n.	16.10-11	456 n.
12.11-12	379	7.12	353 n.	16.14-23	457 n.

16.14	456	2.10	467 n.	8.9-10	618
16.17	453	2.12–3.1	463	8.12	398 n.
16.18	456	2.12-32	464	8.13-14	484
17	457	3.1	464	8.13	484
17.20	521	3.2-5	474	8.14	418 n., 480
17.33	457	3.3	400, 444,	8.16-18	474
17.42	457		464	8.18	552 n.
17.57	455	3.4	499	9.1-13	445
18.1-5	432	3.6-10	464	10	398
18.5-16	458	3.8	462 n.	10.1-4	644 n.
18.13	458	3.19	428 n.	10.2	644 n.
18.19	440	3.26-27	464	10–20	494 n.
21.7	453	3.31-34	465	10–19	490 n.
21.11	312	4.3	693 n.	10.1-19	482
22.3-4	455 n., 481	4.5-12	466	10.1-3	481
22.6-7	453	5	480	10.1-2	481
22.9	453	5.1-2	465	10.6	398
22.14	453	5.1	466	10.8	398
22.17	453	5.3	466	10.16	395
23.1-5	324 n.	5.4	501	10.19	482
24	427 n.	5.5	467 n.	11.1	485
26.5	521	5.6-7	467	11.2-27	485
27	459	5.6	470	11.21	385 n.
27.2	312, 326	5.8	467	11.27	486 n.
27.6	459, 462	5.11	487, 515,	12.18	486 n.
27.10	359		527	12.20	467, 486 n.
29.1	450	5.17	466	12.24	500
29.11	450	5.20	466	12.25	499, 501
30	460	5.21	687 n.	12.30	485 n.
30.1	310 n.	5.22-25	468	12.31	509 n.
30.14	359, 475 n.	6	471, 472	13	492
31.2	450	6.2	534	15–20	490
31.7	437, 462	6.5-13	502	15.1-3	521 n.
31.8-15	306 n.	6.6	471 n.	15.1	493
31.9	450 n.	6.20-23	472	15.4	371
31.11-13	266 n.,	7	482, 481,	15.6	493 n.
	441 n., 450		491	15.12	475
31.12	320	7.6	490 n.	15.13-23	493
		7.9	501	15.24	495 n.
2 Samuel		8	398, 444 n.,	15.24-26	474
2.1-4	461		480	15.27	493 n.
2.4-7	447	8.1	468	15.32	422 n.
2.5-7	461	8.2	480	15.37	475
2.5-6	440	8.3-4	520	16.16	475
2.8-9	463	8.3	396, 398 n.,	16.20-22	494
2.9	399 n., 440,		484 n.	16.21-23	503 n.
	441, 444 n.,	8.8	389 n., 482	16.21	494
	461	8.9-11	483	17.14	494 n.

17.23	494 n.	2.1-26	502	6.16	531
17.24-29	441 n.	2.8-9	502	6.23	534
17.25	493 n.	2.13-25	503	6.29	532
17.26	494 n.	2.13-18	502	6.38–7.1	529
17.27-29	497	2.19	503	7	529
17.27	445 n., 485,	2.24	501	7.2	529
	497 n.,	2.28-34	502 n.	7.7	371, 529
	644 n.	2.39	326	7.8	529
18.1-15	495	2.46	503	7.9-10	531
18.17	547 n.	3–11	539	7.13-22	533
19.8	547 n.	3.4-15	453, 501 n.,	7.15-16	533
19.9	547 n.		504 n.	7.19	533
19.40	495	3.4	436, 438 n.,	7.23	534
19.41	495		504 n.	7.27-29	535
20	482	3.7	501	8.12	532 n.
20.1	547 n.	3.16-27	542	8.64	534
20.14-15	496	4	509 n.	8.65	483
20.15	399	4.2-6	508	8.66	547 n.
20.19	506	4.5	475	9.1-8	535
20.22	496	4.6	476	9.10-11	517
20.23-26	474	4.7-19	509, 514	9.12-13	506
20.24	476, 508	4.7	508	9.15-17	519
21	545 n.	4.8-19	508	9.16-17	342
21.6	435 n.	4.9	591	9.16	505
21.8	440	4.10	422, 429,	9.17-18	507
21.15-22	326 n., 468		510	9.18	507
21.19	457 n.	4.11	301, 511	9.22	516 n.
23.3	372 n.	4.12	440, 585 n.	9.26-28	518
23.14	324 n., 433	4.13	512, 514 n.	9.26-27	516, 522
23.15-16	374 n.	4.16	512	10	662
23.24-26	457 n.	4.19	513, 514 n.	10.1	518
24	587	4.26	521, 522	10.11	518
24.2-9	488	4.27-28	509	10.13	519
24.5-7	489, 515	5.1-2	509	10.16-17	529
24.5	481	5.1	520 n.	10.17	530
24.20	470 n.	5.6	522	10.18-20	529
24.23a	470	5.13-16	509	10.19	529 n.
		5.15	487, 516	10.21	529, 530
1 Kings		5.24	516	10.22	518
1	498	5.25	516	10.28-29	522
1–2	490 n.	5.27-30	509	11.4-8	538
1.5	497, 521 n.	6–8	427 n.	11.14-22	505
1.9-10	499	6	535	11.23-25	483
1.12	499	6.1-10	535 n.	11.23-24	506
1.20	500 n.	6.1	509, 535 n.	11.25	506
1.48	501	6.10	532	11.26	544
1.50	500	6.11-13	535 n.	11.28-30	508 n.
1.52	502	6.14-38	535 n.	11.28	544

11.29-40	544 n.	16.22	569	8.21	547 n.
11.40	45	16.23	570	8.22	599, 659 n.,
11.41	51, 540	16.24	573		700 n.
11.42	501	16.29	574	8.26	574 n.
11.43	544 n.	16.31	571	8.28–9.16	592
12.1-9	545 n.	16.32	585	9.14	639
12.1-5	546	16.33	582	9.27-28	599
12.2-3	545	16.34	583 n.	9.33	595
12.8	476	17.4	672	10.8	594
12.13	499	18.36	706 n.	10.11	595
12.16-18	551	20	575	10.18-27	595
12.17	499	20.1-21	575	10.32-33	591, 654 n.
12.18	509	20.1	576	10.32	596, 608
12.20	545	20.14-19	823 n.	11	596
12.21-23	547	20.22-34	576	11.1-3	599
12.21	545 n.	20.34	572, 576	11.4-16	601
12.25	548	21.19	576	11.17	601
12.26-28	553 n.	22	575, 576	11.18	599, 601
12.28-31	499	22.1	579 n.	12.10-16	609
12.30-37	766 n.	22.38	576	12.10-12	609 n.
12.31	552	22.39	582	12.12	880
12.32	551	22.40	576	12.13	880
14.11	302 n.	22.41	596	12.17-18	605
14.17	549	22.43-46	597	12.18-20	608
14.19	51	22.47	596	12.18	606
14.20	563	22.48	657	12.21	557, 609
14.25-28	299 n.	22.49	658	12.22	609
14.25-27	45, 555			13.4-6	611 n.
14.29	51	*2 Kings*		13.5	611 n.
14.30	548	1.1	579	13.7	608
15.1-2	563	1.2-17	588	13.15	547 n.
15.1	567 n.	1.2-4	591	13.16	654
15.6	548	1.2	329	13.22	591 n., 609
15.8	567 n.	3	653	13.25	613
15.10	567 n.	3.2-3	670 n.	14.7-9	660
15.12	567	3.4-5	581	14.7	613, 660
15.13	567	3.4	572, 579	14.13-14	614
15.14	567	3.5	579	14.19-20	614
15.17-22	584	3.9	659	14.21	614, 660,
15.17	567	3.20	523		740 n.
15.18-20	591	3.24-27	579	14.22	626
15.19	564	3.27	589, 688	14.23	617 n.
15.20	565	5.17	328 n.	14.25	655
15.25	564	6.32	590	14.28	617
15.27	591, 559 n.	8.18	574	14.25	617, 618,
16.7-14	569	8.20-22	589, 598,		619
16.15	591, 559 n.		659	14.27	619 n.
16.21-22	569	8.20	544 n.	15.1	625

15.5	371 n., 625	18.14-16	705, 714	23.19	615, 666
15.6	627	18.17–20.19	705	23.21-23	705 n., 776,
15.9-14	631	18.17-35	704		884 n.
15.15-16	631	18.21	696	23.22	772
15.16	631	18.22	703, 725 n.	23.29	809
15.19-20	632	18.26	683	23.31	788
15.19	629	18.32	705	23.34	767
15.23-25	632	18.34	705	23.37	788
15.29	635, 636 n.	19.8-9	713	24.1	782
15.30	636	19.9	710 n., 716	24.2	785
15.37	628, 634	19.35-36	713	24.6	790
16.2-4	684	19.37	678 n.	24.7	766
16.2	690	20.12-15	695	24.9	788
16.3	687, 689	20.12-14	695	24.11	786
16.5-9	661 n.,	20.12	691	24.13-16	786
	685 n.	20.20	697	24.14	786 n.
16.5	634	21	733	24.19	788
16.6	634, 661	21.2	730	25.1	795
16.7-9	635, 685 n.	21.3	733	25.3	797
16.10-18	685 n.	21.5-7	735	25.3-7	797
16.10	685	21.12-14	694 n.	25.4-7	798
16.14	685	21.16	737	25.6	797
16.15	687	21.23-24	740	25.11-12	798
16.18	686	21.24	601	25.18-21	880
17.1	690	22–23	775 n.		
17.3-4	669	22.1	770	*Isaiah*	
17.6	395 n., 670	22.3–23.3	772	1.7-8	717
17.17	689	22.4-7	609 n.	2.6	327
17.24-33	844	22.8	772, 789 n.	2.20-21	330 n.
17.24-26	677	22.9b	609 n.	3.4	372 n.
17.24	676 n.,	22.10	471	3.12	372 n.
	900 n.	22.11	775, 789 n.,	5.26-30	680 n.
17.25-26	679		790	5.26-29	633
17.27	679	22.14-20	773	6.1-5	628 n.
17.32-35	677, 679 n.	22.14	682, 786 n.	6.1	625 n.
17.32-34	766	22.19	771, 790	6.13	448, 680
18	703	23	582 n.	7–10	635
18.1-6	704 n.	23.1-3	776	7.6	633
18.1	689	23.3-35	780	8.2	685 n., 686
18.2	690	23.4-10	772	8.23	68
		23.4-11	771	9.1	68
18.4	615, 703,	23.4-20	776	10	713 n.
	713	23.8	724, 763,	10.13	654, 680
18.5-6	701, 720 n.		779	11	720 n.
18.5	720	23.11	736	11.11	720 n.
18.6	720 n.	23.12	427 n.,	14.28	689
18.8	685, 696		494 n.	14.30	690
18.13	690	23.15-20	779	15	590, 655

15–16	654 n.	66.17	330 n., 718 n.	41.15	824
15.1-8	654 n.			41.16	795
15.4	414 n.			43.4-7	800
15.7	617	*Jeremiah*		44.30	801
16	590	1.1	789	46.1-12	761
16.1	654 n.	2.18	766	46.9	761
16.3-11	654 n.	2.36	766	47	789 n.
16.9	414 n.	5.4	845	47.1	789 n.
19.4	372 n.	7.12-15	789	47.3-4	313
19.11-13	673	7.31-33	688	47.5	759 n.
20.1	692 n., 693 n.	8.8	876	48	590
		13.18-19	787	48.34	414 n.
22.8-11	697	19.5-6	688	49.2-4	656
22.8	529 n.	19.13	494 n.	49.2-3	833 n.
22.9-11	682 n.	22.1-12	767	49.7-22	795 n.
22.11	697	22.8	453 n.	49.28-33	749 n., 784
23.1	221 n.	22.19	790	49.31	749 n.
23.11	60, 285 n.	22.30	414 n.	51.27	742 n.
23.12-14	708	25.9-13	790 n.	51.59-64	792
30.1-3	696 n.	25.12	837 n.	52.6-11	797
30.4	673	26.10	838 n.	52.8	797
30.6	745 n.	26.16-20	789	52.14	798
30.33	688	26.20-24	789	52.17-19	798
31.1-3	696 n.	26.24	789, 790	52.28	786 n.
36–39	691 n.	27.2-3	792	52.30	798
36	705	28.1-17	791		
36.1	690, 717	29.10	837 n.	*Ezekiel*	
36.11	685 n., 686	29.21-23	791	1.2-3	786
37.8	713	32.6-15	796 n.	1.2	792
37.9	710 n.	32.29	494 n.	8.7-18	792
37.36-37	713	33.4-5	797	8.10	532
38.6	691 n.	34.7	796	11	846
39.1-3	694 n., 695	36	782 n., 789	11.15-21	847
39.1	691	36.26	789 n.	13.5	880
40–48	813 n.	36.30	790	16.29	60
40.20	371 n.	37–38	791	17.4	60
41	811	37.5-11	796	17.13	786 n.
41.25	813, 815	37.11-16	796 n.	17.15	793
42.7	816	37.21	797	19.9	746 n.
45.1	811, 813	38.7-8	797	21.18-27	794
56.17	561 n.	39.3	797	21.18-21	794
57.15-16	561 n.	39.5	797	21.23-32	794
65.3-4	330 n., 718 n.	39.8	798	21.23-26	794
65.4-5	688 n.	40.1-6	798	22.30	880
66	847 n.	40.11	800	25.1-14	804
66.3-4	688 n.	40.14	794 n., 800	25.12-14	795 n., 802 n.
66.4	688 n.	40.15	841 n.		
		41.5	800	25.15-17	804

25.16	313	4.1-3	524	3.9	761 n.
26.1	802	4.1	64	3.16	652 n.
27	802 n.	4.10	612		
27.9-25	802 n.	4.12	622	*Habakkuk*	
27.12-25	854	4.14	623	1.5-10	782
27.12	802 n.	5.4	622	1.10	795
27.13	899 n.	5.5	726	1.14	372 n.
27.18	607	5.14	622	3	417 n.
28.1	534 n.	5.26	678 n.	3.3	417, 453 n.
29.17-20	802 n.	6.2	609	3.8	736, 771
29.17	802 n.	6.4	582 n., 583	3.15	736
30.14	673	6.9-10	620 n., 765		
33.24	847	6.12-14	618	*Zephaniah*	
35.1-15	804	6.13-14	617	1.5	494 n.
35.1-9	795 n.	6.13	445	1.10-11	786 n.
35.5-6	802 n.	6.14	618	2.4-7	314 n.
40.10	526 n.	7.10-17	621	2.5	475 n.
44.10	616	7.12-13	621	2.13-15	758 n.
		7.13	551		
Hosea		8.4	623	*Haggai*	
5.13	666 n.	8.5-6	622	1.1-11	840
8.5-6	582 n.	8.11	622	1.1	849
8.9	666 n.	8.14	726	1.4	850
9.1-2	471 n.	9.2	154	1.15–2.1	849
10.6	666 n.	9.7	313, 316,	2.10	849
10.11	471 n.		317	2.15	838
10.14	593, 594 n.	12.12	622	2.22	820
12.2	666 n.	13.2	623		
12.4-5	231 n.			*Zechariah*	
12.8-9	60	*Obadiah*		1.10	682
13.2	582 n.	10–11	802 n.	3	820
		13–14	802 n.	4.9	838
Joel				6.9-14	820
3.5	561 n.	*Jonah*		9–10	680 n.
4.4-6	804	1.2	453 n.	9.1-8	680 n.,
4.6	866, 899 n.	3.2	453 n.		751 n.
4.19	795 n.			9.1-6	680 n.
		Micah		9.1-3	612 n.
Amos		1.8-16	711, 712	9.1	680 n.
1.1	649	1.16	720	9.3	627
1.3–2.16	653 n.	5.1	372 n.	9.5-7	804
1.3	605			9.9	610 n.
1.5	395 n.	*Nahum*			
1.6	899 n.	1.15	757	*Malachi*	
1.9	899 n.	2.1	757	1.3	795 n.
2.1-2	653	2.6	757	1.6-14	851
2.3	371 n.	2.7	757	2.1-9	851
2.6-8	624	3.8-10	747 n.	2.11	851

2.13	851	40.30	60	2.68-69	865
3.7	852	41.6	60	2.69	855 n.
				2.70	839
Psalms		*Proverbs*		3.2	838
2.7	373, 476,	2.17–24.22	539 n.	3.3	846
	539	8.3	526 n.	4	848 n.
2.8	504 n.	8.16	371	4.1-5	848 n.
19.14	372 n.	9.10	845 n.	4.2	900
21.3	504 n.	25	539	4.6–6.18	850 n.
21.5	504 n.	25.1	539 n.	4.6-23	848
22.3	856 n.	20.8	374 n.	4.6-16	861
22.4	856 n.	31.24	60	4.10	573 n., 900
24.7	206 n.			4.17-23	859
42	723 n.	*Ruth*		4.17-22	864
44–49	723 n.	4.1	526 n.	4.17	573 n., 899
68.18	736, 771	4.18-22	455	4.24	848, 849
72.10	516 n.			5.3–6.16	848
78.11	673	*Canticles*		5.3	834
78.12	673 n.	7.5	414 n.	5.6-17	852
78.43	673 n.			5.6	834
83	463 n.,	*Lamentations*		5.8	826, 878 n.
	515 n.	4.20	798 n.	5.14-15	837
83.9	443			5.14	837, 838
83.10	202	*Esther*		5.16	838
84	723 n.	1.19	842 n.	6.2-5	848 n.
84.12	736, 772			6.3-5	816, 835 n.
85	723 n.	*Daniel*		6.7	843
87	723 n.	1.5-7	683 n.	6.14	849
89	29, 472 n.,	4.28-30	811	6.22	885 n.
	476 n.,	5.22	810	7–10	881 n.
	491 n.,	6.9	842 n.	7.1-10	874
	535 n.	7.1	810	7.6	875, 878
89.22	373	8.1	810	7.7	880
89.27-28	476, 530 n.	*Ezra*		7.11-26	877, 886
89.27	539	1.2-4	816	7.12-26	848 n., 874,
89.28	503 n.	1.2	816		875, 877 n.,
104	240 n.	1.3	816		878 n.,
105.21	372 n.	1.7-11	837		880 n.,
106.28	649 n.	1.8	837		882 n.
121.8	198 n.	2	787, 839,	7.12	857, 878
122.2-3	682 n.		877, 878	7.14	857, 878
127.5	526 n.	2.2	840 n.	7.15	874
132	472 n.	2.27-34	807	7.24	880
137.7	802 n.	2.28-31	765 n.	7.25-26	878
		2.29	779 n.	7.25	878 n.
Job		2.33	864 n.	7.26	875, 877
6.19	519	2.63	840 n.	7.27	849
29.7	526 n.	2.64	839	8.1-14	877

8.27	855 n.	5.14-15	866	*1 Chronicles*	
9	883	5.14	862, 867 n.	1–9	889 n.
9.1-2	835	5.15	850	1.5-6	694
9.1	846, 882	6.1-9	859	1.7	21 n.
9.1-6	883	6.1-2	825	1.11-12	313 n.
9.6-15	883 n.	6.2-9	863	1.16	244 n.
9.9	849 n., 883	6.6	825, 859	1.32-33	393 n.
9.11-12	835	6.14	863	2.3–4.23	558 n.
9.11	883	6.15	865	2.12-14	456 n.
10.6	880	6.17-19	824	2.17	493 n.
10.7-9	884	6.18	824	2.21-23	558 n.
10.10	883	7	787, 878 n.	2.23	558 n.
10.15	883	7.4-5	880	2.50-51	256, 455 n.
10.18-44	883	7.4	851, 865	3.17-24	889
10.44	888	7.32	779 n.	3.17	838
		7.37	864 n.	3.18	837 n.,
Nehemiah		7.66-67	839		838 n.
1–7	881	7.69-71	865 n.	3.24	889 n.
1.1–2.8	862	7.70-71	855 n.	4.34-43	697
1.2-3	858	8	881 n., 882	5.9	481 n.
1.2	869 n.	8.1-8	876	5.10	448
1.11-13	851	8.1	526 n.,	5.14	402 n.
2.1-8	863		881 n.	5.18-22	448, 904 n.
2.9	863	8.9	881	5.26	665 n.
2.10	859	8.13-17	884	6.1-15	849 n.
2.11-16	863	8.14	881 n.	6.39-66	410
2.19-20	863	8.17	881 n., 885	6.78	581 n.
2.19	823, 825,	9.7	30, 182	7.17	301 n.
	859	9.8	61	7.30	279
3	787, 825,	9.22	415	7.34	572 n.
	843, 863	10.33-40	867	8.12	279
3.7	865	10.40	867	8.29-40	435
3.8	864	11.1	865	8.29	361
3.9	843 n.	11.31-35	557 n.	9.35	361
3.13	843 n.	12	859 n.	9.45	435
3.15	843 n.	12.10-11	889	10.7	442 n.
3.16	843 n.	12.11	860	10.10	327
3.17	843 n.	12.22	889	11.16-18	324 n.
3.18	843 n.	12.27-43	881	12.1-12	45
3.19	843 n.	12.47	859 n.	12.8-15	448 n.
3.35	823	13.4-31	881	12.16	456 n.
	863	13.4-9	860 n., 867	12.38-40	382 n.
4	863	13.4-5	824	12.39-40	465
4.1	859	13.6	867 n.	12.40	443
4.3	823	13.7-9	860 n.	14.12	687 n.
4.7	859	13.10-14	867	15.7	663
5	866	13.15-30	867	18.3-4	520
5.1-5	866			18.8	482
5.5-13	866				

18.10	483	20.4-8	268	30.11	707 n.
18.15-17	474 n.	20.33	597, 597	30.26	705
19.6	398 n.	20.35-36	588	31.1	702
26.30-32	413, 478,	20.37	658	31.3	703
	481 n.	21.2	598	32.3-4	697
27.18	456 n.	21.6	574	32.5	682 n., 697
28.5	530	21.8-10	589	32.6	526 n.
29.7	854	21.10	598, 659 n.	32.21	713
29.18	706 n.	21.16-18	598	32.28-30	697
29.23	117, 530	21.16-17	626, 748	32.30	697
		21.16	566	32.31	695, 703 n.
2 Chronicles		21.17	599	33.1	730
1.16-17	522	21.19	599	33.6	733
4.6-8	535	22.2	574 n.	33.11-17	733
4.6	534	22.10-12	599	33.11	732
7.10	547 n.	23.13	600 n.	33.14	734, 864 n.
8.3-4	507 n.	24.17-25	609	33.15	734
8.4	506 n.	24.23	609	33.17	734
8.11	467 n., 529	24.25	609	33.23	740
9.25	521	25.4-24	613	33.24-25	740
9.31	544 n.	25.11	660	34	772
10.16	547 n.	25.14	614 n.,	34.1	770
11.5-12	559		687 n.	34.3-7	771, 772
11.5-10	700	25.17-24	660	34.3-5	779
11.6-10	701	25.23-24	614	34.8-33	772
11.10	557	25.24	734 n.	34.27	774
11.13-14	552	25.27-28	614	35.18	772
12.2-10	299 n.	26.6-15	626	35.21	765
12.4-6	555 n.	26.6-8	626	36.9	785 n.
13	786 n.	26.7-8	748	36.17-23	804
13.1-20	563	26.9-10	627		
13.3-19	701	26.17-21	625	*1 Esdras*	
13.23	567 n.	27.3-5	627	9.39-40	874 n.,
14.3-5	567	27.4	698 n., 796		875 n.
14.8-14	566	27.5	627, 646		
16.1	564 n.	28.1-4	684	9.49	874 n.,
16.12	564	28.5-8	634		875 n.,
16.7-9	568	28.17-18	634, 684		881 n.
17.4	596	28.18	696 n.		
17.7-9	479 n., 597	28.23	685	*1 Maccabees*	
17.10-11	596	28.24	687	8.17	35
17.11	597 n.	29–31	703	8.18	850
19.2	597	29.3	702		
19.4-6	597	30.1-14	706, 707	*Sirach*	
20	596, 597 n.,	30.6	706 n.	900 n.	
	656	30.10-11	706, 707 n.		

N.B.: first citations (with full bibliographical information) are indicated by page numbers in italics.

Abd-el-Hamid Youssef, A. *283*

Abel, F.-M. *307, 382*, 385, 397, 400, 631

Aberbach, M. *545, 554*

Abou-Assaf, A. *683*

Abu Bakr, A.M. *171*

Ackroyd, P.R. *451, 686*, 689, 822, *838*, 847, *848, 874, 878, 879*, 903

Adams, R.M. *115*, 118, *421, 671*, 814

Adjeman, Y. *354*

Aharoni, M. *523*, 560, 704, 723, 748

Aharoni, Y. *62, 112*, 114-15, 125, 132, 133, 150, 171, 222, 227, 228, 233-34, 236, 240-41, 244, 248, 252, 253, 260, 267, 270, 279, 283, 286, 302, 307, 310, 337, *338, 342, 359, 363*, 378, 382, 387, 396, 400, 409, 413, 422, 435, 441, 446, 459, 485, 494, 496, *505, 507*, 511-13, *517, 521, 523-25*, 537, 551, 555, *556*, 560, *565, 572*, 580-81, 585, 588, 593, 594, 611, 614, 617-19, 623, 624, 627, 634, 642, 653-55, *660*, 666, *684*, 693, 698, 699, *702*, 706, 710, 711, 721-26, 730, 752, *761*, 762, 764, 765, *769*, 780, 785, 787, 788, 796, 869

Ahituv, S. *270*, 274

Ahlström, G.W. *22, 26, 27, 29*, 41-42, *43, 45*, 48-49, 60, *69*, 117, *120, 128*, 146, *178, 180*, 231, 251, *255, 256*, 257, *262*, 278-80, 284, *286, 287*, 302, 307, *325*, 329, *337*, 338, *340*, 345-46, 349-50,

352, 357, 360-61, *369, 372, 374*, 375, 378-79, 381-82, *383*, 384, 387-90, 396, 399, 402, 411-14, 416-17, 419, 424-28, 438, 440-41, 444, 447, *448*, 450, 453, 455, 457, *458*, 460, 462-63, 465, 467-70, 472, *473*, 474, 476-78, 486, 491-92, 498, *499*, 501, 502, *505*, 507, 509-11, *513*, 515, 523, *524*, 526-30, 532, 534, 536-38, 548, 550-54, 556, *561*, 562-63, 565, 567, 580-82, 584, *586*, 587-88, *594*, 595, 597, *598*, 604, 609, 614, 616, *620*, 622-23, 628, 640, *646*, 649, 654, 662, 666-67, 677, 679-82, 686, 702-703, 712, 718-19, 724, 726-27, 735, 737-38, 746, 748, *757, 765*, 772, 777, 790, 792, 796, 804, 846, 851-52, 865, 881, 886, 900

Akkermans, P. *98*, 100, 101, *108*

Albertz, R. *153*

Albrektson, B. *27*, 52, *798*

Albright, W.F. *118, 133, 135, 136, 159, 171, 173, 183, 184*, 185, *188, 194, 204, 207, 208, 212, 236*, 239, *252, 256*, 264, 266, *279, 301, 324*, 343, *344*, 351, 378, 398-99, *413, 434*, 441, 482, 488, 510, 512, 514, *516, 525*, 553, *566*, 572, 579, *597, 609*, 624, *634, 655*, 656, *672, 712, 722*, 734, 754, *806, 889*

Alfrink, B. *576*

Almagro-Gorbea, M. *688*

Alon, D. *108, 109*
Alonso Schökel, L. *38*
Alster, B. *117*
Alt, A. *57, 170, 251, 271*, 300, *303,*
    342, 381, 382, 401, 413, 431,
    442, 455, 466, *484*, 508, 510-12,
    514, *531, 549, 561, 565*, 572,
    585-86, 626, 636, 643, 676, *715,*
    719, *725*, 745, 759, *768*, 774,
    787-88, 820, *823, 824*, 864
Alter, R. *457*
Altheim, F. *906*
Amin, M. el- *674*
Amiran, K. *511*
Amiran, R. *110, 112*, 114, *120*, 122,
    123, 124, 125-26, 129, *130*, 135,
    148, 150, 196, *203*, 222, 224,
    317-18, 337, 517, *572, 580*, 727,
    780, *828*
Anati, A. *53*
Anati, E. *70*, 129
Andersen, F.I. *580, 587*
Andersen, K.T. *562, 691*
Anderson, F.J. *471*
Anderson, R.W. *526*
Andre, G. *799*
Andreasen, N.E.A. *567*
Ap-Thomas, D.R. *436*
Arensburg, B. *321*
Ariari, A. *74*
Artzi, P. *180*
Artzy, M. *222*
Asaro, F. *222, 321*
Assmann, J. *168*
Astour, M. *59*, 230, 277, *292*, 293,
    315, 416-17, *456, 593*, 594, *741*
Atkinson, K.M.T. *818*
Auerbach, E. *343*, 382
Auld, A.G. *410*
Aurenche, O. *205*, 341
Avi-Yonah, M. *57, 129, 154*, 184, *678,*
    823, 825, 843-44, 864
Avigad, N. 230, 307, *374, 457, 475,*
    552, *574*, 583, *645, 648*, 661,
    681, 682, 697, 699, *700*, 737,
    789, 798, *827, 830*, 865, 873,
    887, 898
Avisar, M. *826*

Bachi, G. *726*
Badaway, A. *476, 528, 532*, 533
Baer, K. 112, 132, 285, *520*, 673, 674
Baethgen, F. *678*
Baida, U. *53*
Bakry, H.S.K. *282*
Balensi, J. *222, 281, 338*
Ball, E. *500*
Ball, J. *65*
Baltzer, D. *813*
Baly, D. *62*, 63, 65, 67, 401, 442
Bar Adon, P. *110*
Bar Yosef, O. *73, 80, 83*, 84, *87, 88*, 91,
    95, *99*
Barag, D. *892*, 894
Barkay, G. *806, 855*
Barnett, R.D, 288, 295-96, 301, 309,
    533, 644, 708, 712, 720, 750
Barr, J. *50, 127*
Barre, M.L. *744*
Barrick, W.B. *198*, 425, 537, 616, 726
Barstad, H.M. *567, 678, 679, 815*
Barta, W. *194*
Bartlett, J.R. *218, 420, 484*, 485, 505,
    545, *659*, 662, 795, *805*, 906
Barton, G.A. *492*
Barton, J. *38*
Bartonek, A. *290*
Baskin, J.R. *650*
Bass, G.F. *224*
Bate, D.M. *76*, 84, 85, 86, *669*, 718
Batto, B.F. *28*
Baumgartner, W. *713*
Beck, P. *161*, 163, 164, *258, 338*, 727,
    780
Beckerath, J. von *188*, 192, 194, 264,
    265, 283, 300, 310, 520, 803
Becking, B.E.J.H. *646, 668*
Beebe, K. *204*
Begrich, J. *475*, 509
Beit-Arieh, I. *114, 123, 124, 125*, 126,
    205, 341, 727, 780
Bell, B. *137*
Ben-Arieh, S. *358*
Ben-Barak, Z. *464*
Ben-Dor, I. *198, 808*
Ben-Dov, M. *511*
Ben-Tor, A. *125, 131, 826*

Bender, B. *116*
Bennett, C.M. *104, 419, 631, 659, 662,* 663, 808, *833*
Bentjes, B. *185,* 744
Bentley, G.R. *54,* 112, 119, 145
Bentzen, Å. *690*
Berger, P.-R. *837*
Bergman, C. *200*
Berlin, A. *117*
Bernhardt, K.-H. *473, 474, 538*
Bertholet, A. *773*
Besançon, J. *77*
Betlyon, J.W. *855*
Betts, A. *85,* 91, *95, 105,*
Beyer, G. *561*
Beyerlin, W. *554*
Bickermann, E. *839, 879*
Bienkowski, P. *219, 447*
Bietak, M. *45, 167, 188,* 189, 190, *191, 192,* 193, 673
Biggs, R.D. *41, 141, 375*
Bilgic, G. *183*
Bimson, J.J. *206*
Bin, S. *866*
Binford, L. *88*
Biran, A. *164, 201, 358, 524, 557, 565,* 623, 639, *667,* 829
Birch, B.C. *431,* 449
Birchall, A. *293*
Birot, M. *175*
Bissing, W. von *674*
Bittel, K. *47,* 293, *294*
Blake, J.M. *583*
Blakely, J.A. *828*
Blenkinsopp, J. *40, 421,* 433, 435, *436, 491*
Bloch-Smith, E. 266, 350, 369, 405
Block, D.I. *406*
Bloom, A. van den *434*
Blumenthal, E. *160*
Boardman, J. *266*
Boecker, H.-J. *475*
Böhl, F.M.T. de Liagre *50,* 161, *207, 386,* 387, *857, 858*
Boling, R.G. *203, 241,* 264, *285,* 325, *344,* 345, *372, 377, 389,* 400, 407
Bonafante, G. *326*
Boraas, R.S. *144, 408,* 641, 807

Bordreuil, P. *116, 683, 761*
Borger, R. *235, 446, 516, 626,* 636, *672,* 674, *710,* 719, 738, 742, 743, 744, 745, 746, 762, *819*
Bork, F. *312,* 326
Bossert, H. *309,* 364
Bossert, K. *533*
Bothmer, B. von *754*
Bottéro, J. *175, 183, 235, 546, 652*
Botterweck, G. 355
Bowersock, G.W. *57*
Bowman, J. *900*
Bowman, R.A. *683,* 751
Boyce, M. *879*
Braemer, F. *340,* 362
Branden, A. van den *327*
Braudel, F. *20, 23,* 24, 147, 346, 490
Breasted, J.H. *128,* 151, 166, 191, *225,* 226, 227, 231, 233, 238-39, *240,* 275, 276, 282, 284, 288, 289, 292, *295,* 299, 300, 301, 624, 747
Brekelmans, C.H. *504, 876*
Bresciani, E. *818,* 820
Brett, M.J.B. *903*
Briend, J. *342, 637*
Bright, J. *116,* 135, 169, 171, *240,* 344, 420, 425, 426, 457, 458, 463, 464, 475, 488, 498, 499, 514, 536, 540, 544, 546, 567, 578, 585, 587, 589, 592, 598, 616, 617, 620, 699, 706, 724, 731, 732, 733, 737, *767,* 785, 790, 792, 824, 837, 851, 861
Brinker, R. *388*
Brinkman, J.A. *30,* 182, 287, *290,* 391, 393, *394,* 518, 552, *577, 611, 629,* 671, 692, 694, *695,* 707, 716, 732, 741, 749, 750, 753, 755, 756, *764,* 820
Brock-Utne, A. *702*
Bronner, L. *585*
Brosh, A. 77
Broshi, M. *159,* 163, *681,* 729, *809*
Brown, J.P. *316, 553*
Browning, I. *906*
Brug, J.F. *307, 308,* 309, 314, 317, 318, 320, 326, 327, 328
Brunet, G. *467, 797*

Brunner, H. *225, 754*
Bryce, G.E. *539*, 542
Bryson, R.A. *291*
Buccellati, G. *152*, 153, 178, *235*, 393-96, *397*, 398, 427, 428, 562, 580
Bucher, P. *329*
Buck, A. de *295*
Budde, K. *325, 434*, 490, 495, 516
Buhl, F. *283*, 445, 593, 653, 654
Buhl, M.L. *367*
Bull, R.J. *145*, 387, *902*
Bulliet, R.W. *185*
Bunnens, G. *296*, 516, 802, 854
Burke, M.L. *175*
Burney, C.F. *192*, 387, 580
Burstein, S.M. *761*, 810
Busink, T.A. *127*, 253, 524, 525, 526, 527, 529, 530, 531, 532, 533, 534, 535, 615, 878
Butzer, K.W. *137*
Byrd, B. *83, 84*

Callaway, J.A. *113*, 118, 129, 361, *362, 363*
Calmeyer, P. *25, 332*
Cameron, D. *109*
Cameron, G.G. *578*, 814, *821*
Campbell, E.F. *239*, 240, 245, *263*, 280, *384, 386*, 387, 406, *834*, 853, 855, *902, 903*
Canciani, F. *530*
Cannuyer, C. *58*
Cantineau, J. *905*
Cantor, N.F. *20*
Caquot, A. *648*
Carlson, R.A. *424*, 452, 491, 494, 495, 496
Carneiro, R.L. *422*
Carpenter, R. *291*
Carr, E.H. *20*
Cary, M. *842*
Cathcart, K.J. *758*
Cauvin, J. *90*, 92, *93*, 101
Cauvin, M.-C. *83, 90*
Caviagnac, E. *882*
Cazelles, H. *178, 679, 739, 876*, 881, 882
Černy, J. *251, 274*, 283

Chambon, A. *263*, 339
Chaney, M.L. *241*, 345
Childe, V. *86*
Claburn, W.E. *778*
Clamer, C. *262*
Clark, G. *78, 80, 81*, 82
Clark, J.D. *74*
Clark, W.M. *31, 182*, 540, 846
Clarke, S. *162*
Clements, R.E. *774*
Coats, G.W. *554*
Cody, A. *475*
Cogan, M. *661*, 685, *686*, 687, 733, 738, *748*, 758, 762, 763, *771*
Coggins, R.J. *679, 903*
Cohen, M.A. *449*, 462
Cohen, R. *116*, 423
Cohen, R. *139, 150, 311, 505*, 627, 661
Coinman, N. *81*
Cole, D.P. *161*, 163, 164, 165, *282*
Collon, D. *258*
Colpe, C. *879*
Conrad, J. *492*
Conroy, C. *33*
Contenson, H. de *94*, 98, *101*
Coogan, M.D. *365*
Cook, J.M. *817*, 819, 821, 836, 842, 853, 861, 862, 869, 878, 890, 894, 897
Cook, S.A. *898*
Cooke, F.T. *361*
Cooley, R.E. *363*
Cooper, J.S. *143*, 492
Coote, R.B. *340*, 352
Copeland, L. *77, 78, 107*, 108
Coughenour, R.A. *434*
Count, E.W. *27*
Cowley, A.E. *818, 869*, 870, 871, 880
Craghan, J.F. *180*
Craige, P.C. *302*
Crawford, H. *155*
Cross, F.M. *33*, 185, *261, 262, 326*, 344, 355, 356, *362, 414*, 470, 473, 503, *513*, 550, *607, 624*, *645, 646*, 649, 730, *752*, 764, *800, 824, 868*, 869, 881, 889, *892, 897*, 898, 899, 904

Crossland, R.A. 208, *293*
Crouwel, J.H. *193*
Crowfoot, G.M. *583, 623*
Crowfoot, J.W. *582, 583*
Crown, A.D. *137*
Crusemann, F. *344*, 383, *459*
Cryer, F.H. *465, 797*
Culican, W. *802, 827*
Curtis, J.B. *497*

Dahl, G. *302*
Dahood, M. *329, 390*
Dajani, R.W. *223*
Dalley, S. *175*, 179, *600, 651*, 684, *833*
Dandamayev, M.A. *819, 821*, 836, 837, 854, *899*
Danelius, E. *378*
Davaras, C. *309*
Davey, J.G. *66*
Davies, G.I. *765*, 766
Dayagi-Mendels, M. *761*
Dayton, J.E. *209, 418*
Debus, J. *545*
Deetz, J. *20, 22*
Delcor, M. *776*
Delekat, L. *490*
Della Vida, G.L. *608*
Delling, G. *895*
Demsky, A. *356, 421*, 435, *468, 843*
Dentzer, J.M. *903*
Dessène, A. *534*
Dever, W.G. *112*, 123, *134, 135*, 136, *139*, 146-47, 148-50, 155, 159, 161, 163-65, *184*, 196, *197, 283* 468, *519, 523, 525*, 526, 528, *531*, 668
Devine, A.M. *894, 895*
Diakonoff, I.M. *50, 155, 170, 208, 209*, 210, 391-92, 417, *603*, 741, *757*
Dietrich, M. *179, 181, 182*
Dietrich, W. *549*, 550
Dijk, J.J.A. van *472*
Dikaois, P. *149, 309*
Diodorus Siculus *758*, 842, 857-58, 863, 873, 890-91, 893-97, 904
Dion, P.E. *837*
Diringer, D. *323, 700*

Dollfus, G. *361*
Donaldson, M. *92*
Donner, H. *382*, 385, *406*, 431, 443, 453, 458, 466, *468*, 470, 474, *475*, 489, 491, 496, *502*, 508, 515, 521, *554*, 558, 560, 563, 572, 576, 578-80, 587, 597, 608, 610, 617-20, 630, 632, *633*, 636, 642, 644, 650, 658, 690, *698*, 711, 737, 764, 768, 776, 825, 867, 876, 886
Dornemann, R.H. *147, 148*, 163, 201, 214, 215, 223, 401, 402, 406, 485, 639, 644, 647, 648, 652, 656, 661, 662, 905
Dossin, G. *58, 175, 177, 180, 314*
Dotan, A. *356*
Dothan, M. *115*, 198, *311, 319*, 330, *332, 339, 524*, 565, 639, 694, *728, 849, 906*
Dothan, T. *66*, 215, *291*, 301, 306, 307, *311*, 312, 317-20, *321*, 322-24, 326, 330, 332, 405, 433, 668, *709*
Dougherty, R.P. *509, 717, 810*
Douley, D.L. *291*
Driel, G. van *762*
Drioton, E. *298, 891*
Driver, G.R. *866*
Driver, S.R. *580*
Drower, M.S. 208
Dubberstein, W.A. *866*
Dumbrell, W.J. *859*
Dunand, M. *126, 127, 306, 624*
Dunayevsky, I. *123*, 164, 174, *199, 203*, 228, *524*, 565, 639, 668, 730
Duncan, J.G. *266*
Dupont-Sommer, A. *619, 877*
Dussaud, R. *259, 296, 504, 579*

Edel, E. *273*, 315, 393, 443, 463
Edelman, D.V. *45*, 60, *279*, 284, *320*, 349, 357, *359*, 361, 384, 387, 390, *422*, 429, *430, 434*, 435-36, 439-43, 445, 447, 450, 461, 463-65, 497, *771*
Edelstein G. *337, 524*

Edgerton, W.F. *295*, 299, 303, 307, *474*
Edwards, P. *84*
Edzard, D.O. *142, 153, 179,* 210, *328, 394*
Effenterre, H. van *302*
Efrat, E. *62,* 63-65, 67, 70-71, 130, 409, 511
Egger, R. *860,* 889, 902
Ehrlich, E. *732*
Eilers, W. *812, 815*
Eisenberg, E. *199*
Eissfeldt, O. *325, 379,* 409, 420, 444, *469,* 562, *586, 678, 748, 802*
Elat, M. *595, 643, 675,* 718, *719,* 721, 732, 759, 764
Elayi, J. *825,* 827, *829,* 831
Elgavish, J. *524,* 525
Ellermeier, F. *180*
Elliger, K. *310, 422, 459, 483,* 489, 711
Ellis, R.S. *773,* 778
Emerton, J.A. *382,* 838, *417,* 616, 735, *880*
Engberg, R. *615*
Engel, H. *283*
Engnell, I. *25,* 26, 37, *449,* 775, 885
Eph'al, I. *443,* 578, 597, 598, 626, 633, 637, 656, 657, 665, 671, 672, 674, 684, *717,* 742, 744, *749,* 750, 757, 797, *817,* 818, 825, 858, 859, 864, *904,* 905
Erbty, W. *498*
Erichsen, W. *871*
Erlenmeyer, H. *328*
Erlenmeyer, M.-L. *328*
Erlich, H. *435*
Erman, A. *195, 277,* 278, *288*
Eshel, H. *806*
Esse, D.L. *112, 129,* 130, 131
Evans, A. *309*
Evans, C.D. *554*
Evans, G. *495*
Evenari, M. *65, 505*

Fahlgren, K.-Hj. *371*
Fairman, H.W. *275*
Falconer, S.E. *145, 146,* 198

Fales, F.M. *817*
Falkenstein, A. *120, 179, 546*
Farber, K.-G. *20*
Farkas, A. *819*
Faulkner, R.O. *29, 160, 270,* 272, 283, *308*
Fecht, G. *283*
Fefjar, O. *74*
Fensham, F.C. *378, 487,* 516, *824,* 848, 866
Ferembach, D. *321*
Finet, A. *179, 183, 484*
Finkelstein, I. *135,* 139, 147, 152, *174,* 196, 201, *219,* 220, 245, 277, 280, 281, *338,* 339-42, *347,* 350, 351, *353,* 354, 357, 360, 365-69, 428, *439*
Finkelstein, J.J. *212*
Finley, M.I. *20,* 27, 33
Fischer, D.H. *20*
Fisher, C.S. *555*
Fisher, L.R. *332*
Fitzmeyer, J.A. *619*
Flanagan, J.W. *491*
Flannery, K. *83,* 88
Flusser, D. *186*
Foerster, G. 222, 302, *897*
Fohrer, G. *343, 438,* 449, *503*
Folk, R. *70,* 336
Forbes, R.J. *70, 120,* 122, 159, 434
Foresti, F. *431*
Forrer, E. *642,* 743
Foster, R.S. *793*
Fowler, M.D. *145,* 174, 199, *725*
Fox, M. *461*
Frandsen, P.J. *232,* 237, 249
Frankel, J. *27*
Franken, H.J. *263, 264,* 319, *327, 339,* 485 605, *648*
Frankena, R. *461,* 715, 717, 732, 738, 744
Frankenstein, S. *603*
Frankfort, H. *117, 121,* 129, 131, *526,* 528, 529
Free, J.P. *280,* 351
Freedman, D.N. 33, *362, 451, 471,* 498, *536,* 540
Freedy, K.S. *789,* 791, 793

Frei, P. *842*, 877
Freydank, H. *243*, 268
Frick, F.S. *359*, 362, 423
Fritz, V. *340, 358, 359, 385, 406*, 460,
    471, 511, 559, 560, 722, 723, 780
Frohlich, B. *106*
Frye, N.R. *875*, 880
Fugmann, E. *148*
Furshpan, A.M. *267*
Furumark, A. *314*, 316

Gaál, E. *506*, 607
Gabba, E. *19*
Gadd, C.J. *210, 552, 670, 671*, 675,
    676, *755, 757*, 773, 810
Gal, Z. *365*
Galling, K. *182, 256-57, 373, 495,*
    566, *586, 668, 672, 688, 738,*
    822, 824, 836, 838, 840, 866,
    870, 874, 878, 880, 885, 889,
    893, 897
Garbini, G. *13*, 28-29, 35, *645*, 884,
    885, 887-88
Gardiner, A.H. *132*, 133, 160, *162*,
    188, 191, *194*, 232, 234, 240,
    298, 301, 305, *325*, 747
Garelli, P. *120, 604*
Garfinkel, Y. *96*
Garr, W.R. *605*, 683
Garrard, A. *91, 96*
Garrod, D. *76*, 84, 86
Garstang, J. *95, 218, 728*
Gaster, T.H. *261*, 329
Gates, M.-H.C. *21, 212*
Gebel, H. *87, 92*, 101
Gelb, J.J. *140, 153, 173*, 177, 203, *208*,
    210, *290*, 306, 328, *467*
Geller, M.J. *632*
Gelston, A. *838*
Georgiev, G. *316*
Geraty, L.E. *354*, 403, *414*, 415, 689,
    833
Gershung, L. *222*
Gerstenblith, P. *135, 148*, 156, 158,
    163
Geschnitzer, F. *819*
Gese, H. *215, 408, 586*
Geus, C.H.J. de *33*, 185, 235, 343, 344,

372, 373, 448, 509, *712*
Geva, H. *682*, 786
Geva, S. *253, 636*, 668
Gevirtz, S. *387*
Geyer, J.B. *713*
Gibson, J.C.L. *133, 385*, 396, 414, 572,
    579, 608, 610, 619, 653, 654,
    697, 768, 897
Gibson, S. *337*
Gichon, M. *57, 507*
Gilboa, E. *341*
Gilead, D. *74, 75, 76, 77*
Gilead, I. *81, 358*
Giles, F.J. *241*
Ginsberg, C.D. *653*
Ginsberg, H.L. *661, 699*, 717, 766,
    780, 785, 865, 889
Gitin, S. *311, 332, 709*
Gittlen, B.M. *223, 224*
Giveon, R. *124, 190*, 225, 251, 253,
    273, 277, 417
Glass, J.T. *123, 175*, 202, *418*
Glazier-McDonald, B. *795*, 851, 852
Glock, A.E. *22*, 228, 230, 469
Glueck, N. *401*, 517, *626, 655, 658*,
    660, *661, 664*, 780, 905
Goedicke, H. *132*, 297, 301, 302, 305,
    315, 672
Goetze, A. *59, 172, 183*, 268, 269, 494,
    522
Gomaà, F. *160, 673, 674, 693, 696*
Gonen, R. *219*, 281, 369
Gooding, D.W. *376, 545, 575*
Gophna, R. *125*, 130, *159, 161, 162,*
    163, *164, 200, 205, 511*, 725, 830
Gordon, C.H. *181*, 471, *503*
Gordon, R.L. *319, 441*
Goren-Inbar, N. *78*
Görg, M. *225*, 276-77, *397, 417, 421,*
    539
Gössmann, F. *678*
Gottwald, N.K. *28, 241*, 345
Graesser, C.F. *267*
Graf, D. *887*
Grafman, R. *865*
Graham, J.A. *360*
Gray, G.B. *544*, 813, 842
Gray, J. *173, 329, 471*, 483, 500, 512,

545, 547, 569, 657, 659, 670,
672, 678, 685, 689, 695, 703,
734, 785
Grayson, A.K. *21, 42,* 48, *375, 518,*
604, 745, 746, *756, 757, 759,*
760, 781, 782, 785, 791, 810,
811, 814
Green, A.R. *509, 519*
Green, M. *168,* 399
Greenberg, M. *235,* 622, *793,* 871
Greenberg, R. *348*
Greenfield, J.C. *610, 683, 819*
Greenstein, E.L. *58*
Grelot, P. *869, 870, 882*
Grene, D. *25*
Gressmann, H. *186, 374,* 377
Griffith, F.L. *793*
Grintz, J.M. *155, 421*
Grønbaek, J. *443,* 465
Gröndahl, F. *181*
Groom, N. *518,* 519, 895, 905
Gross, W. *650*
Grottanelli, C. *38*
Gruber, M.I. *567*
Gunkel, H. *186*
Gunn, B. *194*
Gurney, O. *286,* 288, *678*
Güterbock, H.G. *37,* 41, 161, *268,* 269,
292, 294, 309, 364
Guy, P.L.O. *827*
Gyles, M.F. *479,* 552

Haag, H. *382, 491,* 498, *705*
Haak, R.D. *783*
Haas, N. *693,* 718
Haas, V. *210*
Habachi, L. *188, 192,* 193, 194
Habel, N. *37*
Hachlili, R. *330,* 332
Hachmann, R. *241, 248,* 269, 392, *533*
Hackett, J. *605,* 648, 649
Hadidi, A. *62, 406*
Haefeli, L. *896*
Háklár, N. *393*
Haldar, A. *152,* 155
Hale, G.A. *337*
Halligan, J.M. *241*
Hallo, W.W. *116, 120, 143,* 158, 175,

213, *472, 609,* 612, 741, 760,
764, 766
Hallock, R.T. *866,* 878
Halpern, B. *44, 430,* 447
Hamburger, H. *855*
Hamilton, J.R. *895*
Hamilton, R.W. *222, 615*
Hammond, P.C. *70, 219, 906*
Handy, L.K. *773,* 775
Hanhart, R. *563*
Hankey, V. *223,* 265, *354, 358,* 406
Hanson, P.D. *414*
Haran, M. *611,* 613
Harden, D. *518*
Harding, G.L. *260, 406, 418,* 646, *647,*
663
Har-el, M. *549*
Harif, A. *161,* 166
Harlan, J. *84*
Harmatta, J. *814*
Harrison, R.K. *731*
Hart, B.H.L. *894*
Hart, R. van der *389*
Hartner, W. *879*
Hauben, H. *818,* 894
Hauer, C.E. *449, 453, 520*
Hauser, A.H. *345*
Hausman, J. *812*
Hawkins, J.D. *289,* 395, *522*
Hayes, J.H. *44,* 285, 562, 765, 767,
793, 800, 815, 820
Hayes, W.C. *195,* 269, 289, 479, 552
Heaton, E.W. *538*
Hecke, K.H. *382, 443,* 452
Heidel, A. *742,* 743
Heintz, J.G. *180*
Heinz, K. *836*
Helck, W. *41, 46,* 60, 132, *160,* 166,
167, 169, 170, 173, 181, 191,
192, *193,* 218, 225, 230, 232-34,
237, *238,* 239, 245, 247-49, *251,*
254, 270-71, *274,* 276-77, 278,
292, 296, 298, 300, *312,* 329,
375, 392-93, 397, 410, 417, *474,*
523, 556, 560
Held, M. *508*
Hellwing, S. *220,* 280, *354,* 368
Helmer, D. *90,* 97, 100

Helms, S. *105, 215*
Heltzer, M. *211*
Hennessy, J.B. 109, *112*, 113, *204*, 265, 406
Henninger, J. *137*, 155, *185, 688*
Henry, D. *83*
Hentschke, R. *408*
Herbert, A.S. *372*
Herdner, A. *59*
Herodotus *751*, 758-60, *783*, 793-94, 803, 812, 814, 817-20, 834, 896, 904
Herr, L.G. *204, 265*, 266, 404, 405, *626*, 661, 663, *800*
Herrera, M.D. *222*
Herrmann, S. *279*, 402, 403, 405, 407, 416, 443, 449, 455, 461, 466, 470, *472*, 475, 479, 488, 494, 498, 520, 527, 538, *541*, 555, 556, 558, 562, 570, 575, 594, 601, 624, 633, 653-54, 671, 715, 719, 782, 785, 824, 838, 861
Hertzberg, H.W. *372, 378, 389*, 437, 445, 494, 496
Herzfeld, E. *821*
Herzog, Z. *341, 358*, 359, *412, 523*, 524, 560, 704, 723, 724, *725*, 726, 733, 748, 788, *827*, 906
Hestrin, R. *110, 297, 761*
Heurtly, W.A. *222, 317*
Hickmann, H. *332*
Higgins, R. *322*
Hill, G.F. *855*
Hillers, D. *440*, 461, *790*
Hinz, W. *812, 819*
Hirsch, H. *142*
Hitzig, F. *585*
Hoffmann, H.-D. *41*, 689, 704, 705, 731, 733, 774, 775
Hoffner, H.A. *21*, 47, 52, *470*, 528
Hofstetter, J. *854*
Hoftijzer, J. *483, 648*
Hole, F. *139*
Holladay, J.S. *526, 859*
Holland, T.A. *544*, 615, 736, 772
Holm-Nielsen, S. *367*
Holmes, Y.L. *239*
Hölscher, G. *576*, 775, *887*

Honeyman, A.M. *457*
Honigmann, E. *58*
Honor, L.L. *691*
Hood, S. *130*
Hooker, E.M. *773*
Hoonacker, A. van *880*
Hopkins, D.C. *62*, 338, 360
Horn, S.H. *387, 485*, 656, 833
Hornung, E. *217, 283*
Horowitz, A. *84*, 99, *138*, 350
Horton, F.L. *828*
Hours, F. *77, 107*, 108
Houtman, C. *875*, 876
Houwink ten Cate, P.H.J. *193, 268*
Huffmon, H.B. *177, 180*, 484, 570
Hughes, G.R. *784*
Huizinga, J. *29*, 30
Hulin, P. *578*
Hulse, E.V. *625*
Hult, G. *331*
Humbert, J.B. *342*
Hunger, H. *41*, 375
Hvidberg, F.F. *553*, 792, 852
Hvidberg-Hansen, O. *744*
Hyatt, J.P. *794*
Hylander, I. *426*, 436

Ibach, R. *349*, 415
Ibrahim, M.M. 109, *214*, 215, *338*, 339, 401, *411*, 832
Ikeda, H. *483, 493*, 522
Iliffe, J.H. *533*
Inge, C.H. *260, 323*
Ishida, T. *498*
Israel, F. *409*, 645, 648, 800

Jackson, J.J. *492*
Jackson, K.P. *409*, 642, 645, 648
Jacobs, J. *139*
Jacobsen, T. *117, 452, 757*
Jacoby, F. *19*
James, F.W. *253*, 270, 300, *521, 668*
Jankowska, N.B. *428, 602*, 652
Janzon, P. *650*
Japhet, S. *804*, 822, 835, 847, 884
Jaritz, K. *518*
Jaroš, K. *684*
Jean, C.-F. *175, 483*

Jelinek, A. *78*
Jenkins, A.K. *691*
Jenni, E. *280*
Jepsen, A. *563, 576, 586, 770, 862*
Jeremias, A. *666*
Jidejian, N. *127*
Jobling, D. *432*
Jöcken, P. *782*
Johnson, D.L. *139*
Johnson, G. *359*
Johnson, J. *308*
Joij, G. van der *648*
Joines, K.R. *702*
Josephus, F. *35, 436, 451, 515, 517,*
    541, 571, 600, 607, 626, 669,
    707, 738, 760, 761, 800, 801,
    803, 808, 824, 827, 839, 847,
    850, 860, 865, 867, 873, 886,
    889, 895, 900, 901, 902, 904

Kafafi, Z. *94, 104, 105,* 106, *224*
Kagan, D. *855*
Kaiser, O. *27-28, 890*
Kallai, Z. *422, 429, 434, 440, 442, 445,*
    507, 510
Kammenhuber, A. *209,* 210, 211
Kamp, K.A. *134,* 153, 154, 156
Kanael, B. *855*
Kantor, H.J. *121,* 125
Kapelrud, A.S. *383, 471,* 492, *537,*
    878, 885
Kaplan, J. *203, 230,* 275, 312
Karageorghis, V. *197, 222, 331*
Kassis, H. *228, 711*
Katzenstein, H.J. *35,* 487, 515, 571,
    574, 630, 669, 707, 708, 733,
    750, *789,* 794, 802, 803
Kaufman, S.A. *41,* 375, *642, 683, 774,*
    876
Kaufman, Y. *731*
Kautz, J.R. *274,* 339, 352, 410, 411
Kees, H. *891*
Kegler, J. *517*
Keil, C.F. *377,* 600
Kellerman, U. *860,* 862, *880*
Kelm, G.L. *311,* 339
Kelso, J.L. *184, 351,* 366, *367,* 806,
    828, 834

Kemp, B.J. *132,* 165, *187,* 196, *211,*
    232, 237, 252
Kempinski, A. *60, 123, 125,* 164, 174,
    189, 190, 194, 199, 228, 253,
    266, 340, 341, 358, 359, 366,
    460, 668, 689
Kent, R. *852*
Kenyon, K.M. *87, 88, 89,* 94, 99, 104,
    106, *113,* 114, 118, *133, 134-35,*
    140, 143, 148-50, *164,* 168, 196,
    204, 218, 336, 470, 486, *528,*
    582, 584, 614, *623,* 736, 798,
    843, 864
Kessler, M. *456*
Khopina, L.I. *651*
Kienitz, F.K. *770,* 793, 891
Kienle, H. *855*
Kilmer, A.D. *332*
Kilmer, A.E. Drafkorn *472*
Kindler, A. *897, 898*
Kippenberg, H.G. *854,* 866, *868,* 902,
    904
Kirk, G.S. *27*
Kirkbride, D. *84,* 94
Kissane, E.J. *655,* 690
Kitchen, K.A. *47, 239,* 243, 244, *254,*
    264, 268, *271,* 273, 282, 299,
    305, 315, 410, 505, 519, 520,
    554, 555, 562, 566, 673, 674,
    693, *696, 708,* 710, 713, 746, 747
Kittel, R. *515*
Kjaer, H. *367,* 428
Klein, R.W. *429, 547, 862*
Klengel, H. *127, 208,* 213, 229, *243,*
    293, 299, 395, *710*
Kloner, A. *806*
Knapp, A.B. *190*
Knauf, E.A. *382, 420,* 463, 493, 653,
    741, 750, 833, 864, 904, *905*
Knudtzon, J.A. *239, 393, 742*
Knutson, F.B. *332*
Koch, K. *37, 172, 180, 547, 856, 874,*
    875, 879, 882, 883
Kochavi, M. *161,* 164, 220, *338, 341,*
    352, *353,* 356, *358, 511, 724,*
    795, 830, *831,* 832
Köhler-Rollefson, I. *87, 92, 95,* 97,
    100, 102, 105

Koizumi, T. *320*, 449
Komoróczy, G. *759*
König, E. *690*
Koning, J. de *239*
Koslowski, S. *89*
Kraay, C.M. *855*
Kraeling, E.G. *38*, *607*, 610, *869*, 870, 872, 889
Kramer, S.N. *117*, *120*, *143*, 467, 530, *604*
Krauss, R. *243*, *672*, 673
Kreissig, H. *844*, *876*
Kuchman, L. *321*
Kuhne, C. *494*
Kühne, C. *239*
Kühne, H. *138*, 143
Kuhrt, A. *814*, *857*
Kupper, J.-R. *175*, *178*, 202, 208
Kurtz, D. *266*
Kuschke, A. *531*, *580*
Kutsch, E. *472*
Kutscher, R. *116*

Labat, R. *782*
Labib, P. *192*
Ladurie, E.L. *20*
Laessøe, J. *176*
Lafont, B. *180*
Lahloub, H. *434*
Lamb, H.H. *291*
Lambdin, T. *208*
Lambert, M. *492*
Lambert, W.G. *27*, *52*, *172*, *375*, *472*, *546*, *745*, *746*, *781*
Lamon, R.S. *527*, *555*, *765*
Lance, H.D. *283*, *468*, *519*, 525, *668*
Landau, W. von *707*
Landes, G.M. *405*, 641
Landsberger, B. 178, *212*, 213, *236*, *257*, *686*, 762, *872*
Landsberger, F. *534*
Landström, B. *301*
Lange, K. *166*
Langholm, S. *20*
Laperrouzas, E.-M. *865*
Lapp, N. *525*, *853*
Lapp, P.W. *112*, *118*, *119*, 134, *201*, 230, 337, 339, *379*, 416, 469,
525, *639*, *640*, *654*, *806*, *824*, *899*
Larché, F. *903*
Laroche, E. *210*, *211*
Larsen, M.T. *158*, 159, *488*, 508, *604*
Larsson, G. *885*
Lawrence, A.W. *162*
Layard, A.H. *582*, 668, *712*
Lechevallier, M. *88*, *96*, *361*
Leclant, J. *270*
Leemans, W.F. *158*
Leeuwen, C. van *713*
Lefèbvre, G. *305*
Lehmann, G.A. *294*, *298*, 299
Lehmans, W.F. *334*
Leibowitz, H. *255*
Lemaire, A. *356*, *374*, *429*, 510, *646*, *648*, 660, *663*, 684, *723*, *761*, 769
Lemche, N.P. *14*, *21*, *33*, 34, 38, 46, 140, 185, 231, *235*, 345, 350, 352, 359, *376*, 377, 438, *460*, 549, 769
Lenzen, C. 220
Leonard Jr, A. *224*, 251, 317
Leupold, U.S. *332*
Levine, B.A. *876*
Levine, L.D. *628*, 629, 656, *707*
Levy, S. *524*
Levy, T. *108*, *109*, *110*
Lewis, D.M. *872*
Lewis, N.N. *337*
Lewy, H. *652*
Lewy, J. *379*, *396*, *756*, *770*, 842
L'Heureux, C.E. *326*
Licht, J. *25*
Lichtheim, M. *818*, 877
Liddell, H.G. *59*
Lie, A.G. *692*, *693*
Liebowitz, H. *70*, 336, *583*
Liere, W.J. van *208*
Lindars, B. *382*
Lindblom, J. *688*
Lindly, J. *80*, *81*
Lindsay, J. *785*, *787*, *788*, *794*, *799*, 802
Lipiński, E. *29*, *431*, 452, *586*, *759*, *782*
Littauer, M.A. *193*
Liu, K.H. *22*

Liver, J. *487*, 515, *540*
Liverani, M. *20, 30, 35, 134*, 135, 152,
    153, *187, 235, 236, 241, 242*,
    244, 249, *299, 335, 476, 600*,
    638, 684
Lloyd, S. *122, 757*
Lohfink, N. *390*, 773
Loisy, A. *887-88*
Loon, M. van *148, 761*
Lorenzini, A. *708*, 712
Loretz, O. *179, 181, 235*, 247, 275,
    438
Lorton, D. *162*
Loud, G. *164*, 166, *251*, 324
Lucien *718*
Luckenbill, D.D. 56, *312*, 392-94, 482,
    571, 578, 592-95, 610-11, 628,
    631, 633, 635-36, 639, 641-42,
    644-46, 652, 656-57, 659, 662-
    64, 666, 670-71, 674-76, 685-86,
    693-95, 697, 707-11, 713-15,
    717, 719-20, 728, 742-47, 751,
    762
Luke, T. *176-77*
Lust, J. *650*
Luz, B. *99*

Macalister, R.A.S. *266, 702, 738, 872*
McCarter, P.K. *400, 434*, 437-38, 442,
    448, 450-51, 453, 456, 461-63,
    468, 472, 484-85, 489, 493, 497,
    573, 648, 649
McCarthy, D.J. *476, 611*
McClellan, T.L. *318, 361*, 566
McCowan, C.C. *361*, 865
McCreery, D.W. *119*
MacDonald, B. 77, *78*, 80, 109, *215*,
    401, *419, 805*, 833, *859*, 890
MacDonald, J. *430, 457*
McEvenue, S.E. *820*
McEwan, E. *200*
McGovern, P.E. 22, *214, 336, 401*
McKay, J. *686*, 706, 733
McKenzie, S.L. *658*
Machinist, P. *42*, 665, 680
Maddin, R. *70*, 336
Magnes-Gardiner, B. *145*
Maier, R. *880*

Malamat, A. *33, 177, 178, 180*, 202,
    233, 236, *398, 399, 408, 462*,
    466, *483*, 506, 519, 520, *546*,
    594, 669, 681, *739, 765, 767*,
    784, 786, 787, 792, 793, 795,
    797, 798
Mallet, D. *873*
Mallon, A. *118*
Manniche, L. *332*
Marcus, D. *58*, 709
Marcus, R. *901*
Marfoe, L. 138, 39, *219*, 346, 350
Marks, A. *78, 80, 81*, 82
Marmardji, A.-S. *57*
Martin, M.A. *895*
Martin, M.F. *39, 214*, 265, 277, 411
Martin-Achard, R. *620*
Marzal, A. *178*
Matthews, V.H. *176, 179*
Matthiae, P. *140, 141*, 142
Maxwell-Hyslop, K.R. *70*, 336
May, H.G. *27, 527*, 532, *533*
Mayani, Z. *327*
Mayer, W. *181*
Mayer-Opficius, R. *388*
Mayes, A.D.H. *371, 376, 381*, 383,
    384, 427, *429*, 452, *535*, 677,
    689, 705
Mazar, A. *263, 307, 311, 318*, 319,
    329-31, *339, 340*, 354, *356*, 357,
    363-65, 412, *433*, 466, 479, 480,
    525, *699*, 796
Mazar, B. *129, 145*, 165, 172-74, 176,
    185, 199, 207, 216, *221, 303*,
    329, 350, 379, 398, 400, 413,
    433, 479, 483, 497, 518, *524*,
    525, 552, 555, 556, 558, 560,
    565, 572, 576, 639, *642, 693*,
    709, 710, 728, 730, *806*, 824, 906
Meissner, B. *526, 669*
Mellaart, J. *102*, 105, 111, *209*
Mellink, M. *159, 363*
Mendelsohn, I. *476, 508, 899*
Mendenhall, G.E. 239, *241*, 409, *477*
Merkel, E. *904*
Merkel, J.F. *417*
Merrilees, A.S. *159, 217*, 224, *315*
Meshel, Z. *616, 831*

Meshorer, Y. *855*, 897, 899
Mettinger, T.N.D. *389*, 430, 433, 346,
    461, *473*, 474-76, 490-91, 495,
    508, 512, *534*, 539, 540, 740
Metzger, M.C. *145*, *530*, *600*
Meyer, E. *230-31*, *347*, 382, 384, 385,
    389, 422, *608*, *837*, 842, 848,
    875, 905
Meyers, C.L. *533*
Michalowski, P. *47*, *153*
Michel, E. *604*
Mildenberg, L. *897*, 898
Milgrom, J. *552*, 892
Millard, A. *611*, *663*, *683*, 761
Miller, J.M. *44*, 274, 285, *349*, *352*,
    360, *401*, 410, 411, 433, 437,
    562, *574*, 576, *581*, 587, *610*,
    765, 767, 793, 833
Miller, R. *200*, *337*
Miroschedji, P.R. de *113*, 114
Mittmann, S. *214*, 220, 349, 397, 398,
    400, 401, 402, *403*, 405, 408,
    507, 558, 823, 832
Moberg, C.-A. *22*
Mode, M. *239*
Moldenke, A.L. *128*
Moldenke, H.N. *128*
Moles, A.A. *20*, *22*
Molin, G. *502*, 563, 587
Momigliano, A. *21*, *24*, 25, *29*, 50,
    186, *895*
Mommsen, H. *700*
Montet, P. *188*, *191*, *329*, *519*
Montgomery, J.A. *659*, *661*, 670, 678,
    685, 705
Moon, C.H.-S. *658*
Moore, A. *93*
Moore, A.M.T. *54*
Moore, G.F. *39*, 379
Moorey, P.R.S. *193*, 211, *309*, 364,
    365, *773*, *827*, *828*, *855*
Moran, W.L. *180*, *242*, *247*, *461*, *487*,
    516
Morenz, S. *27*, *173*, *500*
Morgenstern, J. *389*, *570*, *858*
Morris, I. *24*
Morrison, M. *358*
Morschauser, S. *272*

Mosca, P. *688*
Moscati, S. *59*, *799*
Moshkovitz, S. *173*, *523*, 560, 704,
    723, *725*, 726, 748
Mosis, R. *609*
Moss, R.L.B. *873*
Motzki, H. *553*
Mowinckel, S. *26*, *347*, *384*, *419*, 449,
    462, *472*, *487*, 501, *650*, *839*,
    850, 859, *860*, 865, 876, *880*,
    881, 884, 885
Moyer, J.C. *355*, 689
Muheisen, M. *85*, *105*, *106*
Muheisen, S. *78*
Muhly, J.D. *39*, *70*, *110*, 122, *159*, *212*,
    316, 319, 336
Mulder, M.J. *530*
Müller, H.-P. *484*
Münderlein, G. 470
Murnane, W.J. *168*, *217*, 232, 267,
    268, *269*, 271, 500, 501
Murtonen, A. *484*
Myers, J.L. *534*, 535
Myers, J.M. *706*, *305*, *816*, *875*, *889*
Mylonas, G.E. *330*

Na'aman, N. *66*, *194*, *212*, *248*, 251,
    302, 359, *366*, 378, 429, 440,
    442, 476, 509, *559*, *560*, *578*,
    625, 696-701, 704, *707*, 711, 715,
    722, 725, *769*, *900*
Naster, P. *854*
Naumann, R. *528*
Naveh, J. *262*, *311*, *356*, *648*, 693, *752*,
    767, 768, *800*, *824*, *826*, 898
Negbi, O. *173*, *258*, 262, *358*, 537, *826*
Negev, A. *906*
Nehr, A. *372*
Neiman, D. *880*
Nelson, H.H. *296*, *297*, 308, *309*
Netzer, A. *813*
Neumann, J. *137*, 291
Neuville, R. *75*, 76
Nicholson, E.W. *551*, *601*, *706*, 740,
    775
Nicolaou, K. *221*
Nielsen, E. *25*, *26*, *384*, 386-38, 551,
    553, *732*

Nissen, H. *96*, 98, 99
Nöldecke, T. *610, 887*
Noort, E. *180*
Nordheim, E. von *492*
Noth, M. *26, 31, 56, 57, 136, 177, 181,*
    244, 343, 349, *376,* 378, 385,
    394, 398, *399,* 400, *401,* 427,
    443, 446, 448, 451, 453, 480,
    481, 493, *511, 514,* 516, 518,
    530, 531, 532, 535, *539,* 554,
    555, 558, 570, 618, *619, 623,*
    649, 730, 785, 787, 839, 852
Notis, M.R. *22*
Notts, M.R. *336*
Nougayrol, J. *208, 212*
Noy, T. *87, 88,* 91
Nyberg, H.S. *390, 474,* 504, *649, 819,*
    836, 879

Oates, D. *602*
Oates, J. *755*
Obbink, K.M. *553*
O'Callaghan, R.T. *384,* 392, 395, 397,
    645, 649
O'Ceallaigh, G.C. *485*
Ockinga, B.G. *695*
O'Connell, K.G. *727*
O'Connor, D. *240*
Oded, B. *407, 564, 603,* 638, *642,* 643,
    644, 652, 671, 683, 699, 706,
    708, 731, 732, 739, 740, 775
Oestrup, J. *330*
Ohata, K. *301,* 338
Ohel, M. *77*
Olávarri, E. *149, 416,* 654, 808
Olávarri, M. *339*
Olivier, J.P.J. *549,* 550
Olmstead, A.T. *13,* 266, 579, *593,* 594,
    597, 612, 671, 688, 697, 738,
    743, 745, *756,* 760, *805,* 842,
    848, 857, 870, *875,* 891, 895
Oppenheim, A.L. 56, *116, 179, 257,*
    312, 473, 546, 571, 572, 578,
    602, 607, 637, 639, 646, 652,
    675, 693, 710, 716, 719, 732,
    743, 745, 755, 756, 787, 814
Oppenheim, M. von *535*
Oppenheimer, A. *740*

Orelli, C. *593*
Oren, E.D. *134,* 148, *248, 281,* 309,
    311, 321, 322, 340, *358,* 459,
    729, *745,* 751, 752, *834*
Orlinsky, H.M. *343*
Orni, E. *62,* 63-65, 67, 70, 71, 130,
    409, 511
Osing, J. *171*
Otto, E. *136*
Ottosson, M. *145,* 174, 255, 259-61,
    265, 331, *402, 410,* 441, 446,
    448, 485, 511, 513, 514, 523,
    532, 558, *595,* 636
Otzen, B. *383, 610,* 612, *625, 636,* 675,
    680, 751, 758, 761, 765, 781
Owen, D.J. *292,* 353
Özdogan, A. *90,* 94
Özdogan, M. *90,* 94

Page, S. *611*
Pakozdy, L.M. von *457*
Pardee, D. *116, 175,* 202, *660, 684,*
    752, 768, 769, 780, 794, 796
Parker, B. *684*
Parker, R.A. *852*
Parker, S.T. *57*
Parpola, S. *47, 56, 122, 137,* 291, 406,
    521, 573, *604, 632,* 633, *650,*
    678, 681, 683, 710, 716, *741,*
    746, 748, *757*
Parr, P. *201, 398,* 399, *418,* 905
Parrot, A. *175, 208,* 796
Patai, R. *494*
Paul, S. *679*
Payne, E.J. *382*
Pearson, L. *19*
Peckham, B. *296,* 517
Pedersen, J. *46, 458, 467,* 486, *494,*
    775
Peet, T.E. *37,* 41, *325*
Pendelbury, J.D.S. *314,* 315
Perlman, F. *222, 321*
Perlman, I. *222, 700*
Perrot, J. *84,* 85, 86, 99, *104,* 106, *115,*
    126
Peters, F.E. *906*
Peterson, J.L. *412,* 413
Petrie, F. 131, *318,* 728

Petrie, W.M.F. *120*, *132*
Pettinato, G. *141*, *530*
Pfeifer, G. *766*
Pfeiffer, R.H. *888*
Picard, L. *53*
Piggott, S. *22*
Pigott, S. *340*
Pigott, V.C. *22*, *336*
Pineaar, D.N. *584*
Pitard, W.T. *608*
Planhol, X. de *185*, 384
Plein, I. *545*
Plutarch *895*
Pohl, A. *181*
Pope, M.H. *328*, 390
Porten, B. *539*, *784*, *819*, *848*, *869*, 870
Porter, A. *832*
Porter, B. *873*
Portugali, Y. *826*
Posener, G. *160*, 167, 168, *169*, 170, 173, *181*, 392, 401, 430, *803*
Postgate, J.N. *521*, 651, 657, *755*
Potts, T. *406*
Poulsen, N. *499*, 686, 706
Prag, K. *135*, 136, 139, *140*, 144, 146, 147, 149, 156, *183*
Pratico, G.D. *626*, 633, 660, 661, 780
Prausnitz, M. *96*
Preusser, C. *203*
Priebutsch, H.Y. *283*
Pritchard, J.B. *204*, *349*, *362*, *521*, *531*, 556, 643, 644, 655, *806*, 832
Puech, E. *207*, *485*
Purvis, J.D. *860*, 889, *900*, 902, 904

Raban, A. *222*, *302*
Rabenau, K. von *408*
Rabin, C. *312*, *326*
Rad, G. von *383*, *538*, *561*, *563*, *600*, 737
Rahmani, L.Y. *898*
Rainey, A.F. *57*, *58*, *268*, *278*, *310*, *359*, *374*, *379*, *457*, *476*, 508, *523*, 560, 624, 704, 711, *717*, 720, 722, 723, *725*, 726, 748, 787
Ranke, H. *153*, *500*
Rappaport, U. *855*

Rast, W.E. *119*, 144, 145, *339*
Raveh, K. *302*
Reade, J.E. *596*, 605, *671*, 674, *691*, 755, 757
Redford, D.B. *45*, *189*, 192, *195*, 206, 212, 225, 226, 229, 232, *270*, *355*, *509*, *540*, *789*, 791, 793
Redmount, C. *44*
Reed, W.L. *274*, 386, *411*, *415*, 416
Reich, R. *675*, *721*
Reisner, G.A. *582*
Renan, E. *887*
Rendsburg, G. *653*
Rendtorff, R. *46*
Renfrew, C. *334*
Repenning, C. *74*
Reventlow, H. *655*
Reviv, H. *211*, *245*, 387, 706, 735, 764
Richard, S. *134*, 135, 139, *144*, 146, 148
Richter, W. *37*, 39, 40, *178*, *325*, 371-73, *375*, *376*, 377, 379, *403*, *431*, 447
Ricoeur, P. *27*
Rietzschel, C. *790*
Riis, P.J. *266*
Ringel, J. *897*
Ringgren, H. *649*, *731*
Ripinsky, M. *185*, *744*
Ritter-Kaplan, H. *137*
Roberts, J.J.M. *27*, *179*
Robertson, E. *451*
Robinson, S.G. *855*
Robinson, T.H. *555*
Roccati, A. *132*
Rochberg-Halton, F. *756*
Roeder, G. *818*, 853
Rogerson, J.W. *37*
Rollefson, G. *75*, *77*, *78*, 80, *84*, *90*, 91, 92, *93*, *94*, *95*, *96*, 97, *98*, 100, *101*, 102, 105, *106*
Röllig, W. *328*, 572, 579, 580, 608, 608, 610, 619, 630, 636, 825
Rolston, S. *85*
Romane, P. *895*
Römer, W.H.P. *180*
Ron, Z. *337*, 361
Ronen, A. *74*, *88*

Ronzevalle, P.S. *297*, 364
Root, M.C. *852*, 856
Rose, D.G. *727*
Rösel, H.N. *38*, *385*, *722*
Rosel, N. *341*
Rosen, S.A. *115*
Rosenberg, R.A. *477*
Ross, J.F. *145*, *384*, *386*, 387, *611*
Rost, L. *49*, *390*, 490, 540, *882*
Rost, P. *629*, 640
Roth, M. *34*
Rothenberg, B. *69*, *254*, *359*, *417*, *418*, 419, 485, 517, *523*
Rothstein, J.W. *706*
Roux, G. *121*
Rowe, A. *253*, *274*, *873*, 890
Rowley, H.H. *504*, *679*, 702, *858*, 860, 862, *868*, 880, 898-99, 903
Rowton, M.B. *126*, *176*, 215
Rubinson, K.S. *742*
Rudolph, W. *467*, 558, 563-64, 597, *655*, 656, 700, 707, 732, *824*, 874, 878, 882
Rufus, C. *898*
Rupprecht, K. *535*
Rust, A. *76*
Rütersworden, M. *475*
Rutten, M. *181*

Saarisalo, A. *152*
Sachs, A.J. *761*
Sack, R.H. *811*
Sadeh, M. *220*, 280, 368
Saebø, M. *680*
Safadi, H. el- *131*
Safar, F. *594*
Saggs, H.W.F. *30*, *392*, 394, *428*, 482, 501, *536*, 611, 618, *626*, 629, 633, *638*, 642, 643, 650, 651, *657*, 664, 671, 676, 684, 692, 694, 704, *705*, 716, 732, 741, 752, 754, 755, 757
Saller, S. *324*, 656
Salmon, P. *873*
Salonen, A. *651*
Saltz, D.L. *221*, 469, 521, 527, 556, 557, 692
Salzman, P.C. *391*, *549*

Samson, J. *267*
Šanda, A. *654*
Sandars, N.K. *289*, 291, 293-97, 307, 309, 317, 331
Sasson, J.M. *58*, *177*, 202, *350*, *689*, 718
Sasson, V. *697*
Sauchau, E. *869*
Sauer, A. von Rohr *669*, 688, 718
Sauer, J.A. *109*, 114, *134*, 215, 220, *274*, 319, 349, 353, 401, *805*, 832, 833, 905
Säve-Söderbergh, T. *136*, *160*, 162, *189*, 190, 192, 193, 195, *235*, *316*
Sawyer, J.F.A. *404*
Sayce, A.H. *869*
Schachermeyer, F. *319*
Schaeder, H. *878*, 886
Schafer, H. *128*
Schäfer, J. *330*
Schäfer, P. *824*
Schafer-Lichtenberger, C. *345*
Schaeffer, C.F.-A. *293*, *314*
Scharbert, J. *767*, *799*
Schaub, R.T. *113*, 114, *119*, *144*, 144, 145
Schick, T. *73*, *99*
Schlözer, A.L. *155*
Schmandt-Besserat, D. *93*
Schmid, H.H. *49*, 431, 540, 544, *554*, *688*
Schmidt, H. *531*
Schmidt, J.D. *271*, 272, 274, 275, 276
Schmidt, W.H. *540*
Schmitt, G. *325*
Schmitt, H.C. *575*
Schmitt-Korte, K. *906*
Schmökel, H. *611*
Schneider, R.J. *20*
Schoene, R. *120*
Schottrof, W. *799*
Schretter, M.K. *678*
Schuler, E. von *293*
Schulman, A.R. *239*, *250*, 269, 270, *520*
Schult, H. *180*, *437*, *531*
Schultz, H. *758*
Schunk, K.D. *435*, 436

Schwab, D.E. *673*
Schwabe, J. *533*
Scott, R. *59*
Scott, R.B.Y. *504*
Seebass, H. *431, 546*
Seger, J.D. *174*, 206, *459*, 698
Seidl, H. *332*
Selms, A. van *378, 508*
Sethe, K. *128, 170*, 171, *386*
Seux, M.J. *476*
Seuz, M.J. *637*
Seybold, K. *500*
Shaffer, A. *683*
Shaheen, N. *697-98*
Shalev, S. *110*
Shanan, L. *65, 505*
Sharon, I. *809*
Shea, W.H. *165, 624, 631, 815*
Shepers, G. *21*
Sherwin-White, S. *857*
Shiloh, Y. *164, 340, 361, 486, 532, 533*, 537, 615, 735, 789, 795
Shipton, G.M. *228, 527, 555, 765*
Siebens, A.R. *777*
Simmons, A. *94, 96*, 98, *101*, 104, 105
Simons, J. *46*, 229, 230, 269, 272, 279, *386, 399*, 434, 435, 442, 226, 511
Simpson, W.K. *136*, 175, 213, 217, 803
Sinclair, L.A. *806*
Singer, I. 292, 293, *294*, 353
Sjöberg, Å.W. *476*
Sjöqvist, E. *309*
Skehan, P. *489*
Smart, J.D. *847*
Smend, R. *586*
Smith, G.A. *442*
Smith, M. *738, 813*, 815, 854, 887, 892
Smith, S. *58, 212, 471*
Smith, S. *805*, 810
Smith, W.R. *616*
Smitten, W.T. in der *848, 878, 884*, 888
Smolar, L. *545, 554*
Snaith, N.H. *462, 887*
Snodgrass, A.M. *28*
Soden, W. von *165, 178, 180, 239,*

246, 446, 508, 642, 643, *678, 714*, 738, 762, 799, 820
Soggin, J.A. *24, 386*, 387, *403, 422*, 457, 458, *503*, 514, 540, 562, 573, 574, 587, 677, 679, 690
Solecki, R. *79*
Sollberger, E. *141*
Spalinger, A.J. *48, 225, 271, 282, 283*, 295, 299, 472, *734, 743-48, 750*, 751, 754, 763, 783, 801
Speiser, E.A. *59, 211, 275, 313, 409*
Spek, R.J. van der *692, 815*
Spencer, J.E. *337*
Spencer, J.R. *413*, 552
Spengler, O. *29-30*
Spieckermann, H. *685, 686, 687, 689*, 726, 733, 736, 739
Spiegelberg, W. *842*
Spycket, A. *683*
Stade, B. *530, 670*
Stadelmann, R. *191*, 262, 329
Stager, L.E. *54, 277*, 318, *337, 340, 730*
Stähli, H.-P. *457*
Stamm, J.J. *406, 500*. 504, *544*
Starcky, J. *619*
Starkey, J.L. *261*
Starr, C.G. *312*
Stech-Wheeler, T. *70*, 336
Steiner, G. *142*
Stekelis, M. *53, 73, 76, 77, 87, 104, 129*
Stellini, A. *371*
Stern, E. *255*, 261, 263, 627, *647*, 668, 681, 724, *726*, 752, *761, 766*, 780, 807, 809, 823, *825, 826*, 828, 829, *831*, 832, 834, 835, 855, 858, 869, 879, 890, 898
Stern, M. *898*
Steuernagel, C. *410*
Steve, A.M. *362*
Stewart, J.R. *149, 159*, 162, 167, 168, 194
Stiebing, W.H. *188, 291*, 293, *318*
Stieble, H. *492*
Stieglitz, R.R. *456*
Stiehl, R. *906*
Stock, H. *190*

Stoebe, H.J. *438, 444, 457, 464, 698*
Stohlmann, S. *719*, 720
Stol, M. *178*, 372
Stolper, M.W. *821, 840*, 842
Stordeur, D. *100*
Strange, J. *202*, 217, 240, 313, 314, 315, 476
Streck, M. *646*, 732, 749
Strobel, A. *291*, 295, 299, 301, 306, 316, 317
Stronach, D.B. *209*
Stubbings, F.H. *217*
Sukenik, E.L. *307, 582, 898*
Swann, C.P. *22*
Swiggers, P. *409*

Tadmor, H. *56, 177*, 178, *257, 290, 492, 493, 518, 522, 562, 573, 610, 611, 626, 628*-30, *633, 636, 637, 640, 661, 670*-72, *674*-76, *683*, 685, 690-94, 696, 706-709, 742, 745, *748*, 751, 759
Tadmor, M. *110*
Tadmor, N.H. *65, 505*
Talmon, S. *33, 553, 740*, 859
Täubler, E. *379*, 388, 430, 679
Taute, W. *96*
Tcherikover, V. *901*
Tchernov, E. *74*
Teixidor, J. *372*
Tell, S. *646*
Thibault, C. *74*
Thiele, E.R. *562, 573*, 617, *632*, 669
Thiersch, H. *317*
Thomas, D.W. *379, 794*
Thompson, H.J. *807*
Thompson, H.O. *252*, 253, 270, 355, *408, 646*, 669, 808
Thompson, T.L. *21*, 27, *46, 132*, 135, *139*, 147, 165, 166, 169, 170, 171, 178, 181, 185, 208, 210, 230, 231
Thornton, T.C.G. *562*
Tillier, A. *79*
Timm, S. *570*, 571, *573*, 575, 576, 580, 585, 586, *592*, 700
Tixier, J. *77*
Tobias, P.V. *53*, 73

Tod, M.N. *837*
Todd, I. *130*
Toombs, L.E. *145*, 174, *384, 387, 548, 698, 727, 828*
Torczyner, H. (Tur-Sinai) *796*
Torry, C.C. *646, 887*
Tournay, R. *265*
Trigger, B. *20*
Trinkhaus, E. *79*
Tromp, N. *586*
Tsevat, M. *793*
Tubb, J.N. *135*, 136, 140, 152, 157
Tubb, K. *95*
Tufnell, O. 168, *260, 291*, 323, *324*, 647, 669, 718, 722
Turner, G. *663*
Tushingham, A.D. *274*, 416, *655, 682*
Tvedtnes, J.A. *58*

Ullendorff, E. *519, 579*
Unger, E. *802, 807*
Unger, M.F. *395*, 396, 397, 444, 506, 607, 608, 612, 618, 632
Ungnad, A. *719*
Ussishkin, D. *109, 259*, 260, 261, 262, 291, 323, 351, *395, 527, 528*, 557, 667, *699, 712*, 721, 722, *806*

Vaggione, R.P. *742*
Van Beek, G. *527, 627, 721*, 728, *753*, 761, 826, 905
Van Beek, O. *527*, 826
Vanderkam, J.C. *465*
Vandermeersch, B. *80*
Vandersleyen, C. *59*
Vandier, J. *298, 891*
Van Seters, J. *21*, 27, 28, 29, *30*, 35, 48, 51, *134, 135*, 154, 181, 182, 183, 185, *188*, 191, 192, 208, 272, 396, *403*, 410, 414, 424, 455, 490, 822
Vanstiphuot, H. *546*
Van Zeist, W. *99, 138*
Vattioni, F. *645*
Vaux, R. de *52*, 54, *59*, 105, 113, 135, 153, *154, 163*, 181, 187, 190, 192, 194, 200, 201, 219, 231, 233, *235*-37, 245, 252, *263*, 271,

276, 296, 301, 318, 327, *349*,
361, 373-75, 378, 379, 382, *383*,
393-95, 400, 402, 403, *417*, 419,
420, 471, *474*, 475, 479, *504*,
534, *535*, *553*, *567*, *586*, *601*,
688, *729*, 730, 740, 816, 848
Veenhof, K.R. *712*
Veijola, T. *480*, 488, *491*
Vercoutter, J. *121*, *170*, 195, *289*, 314,
315, *546*
Vernes, M. *887*
Vigàno, L. *141*
Villeneuve, F. *903*
Villiers, L. *74*
Vincent, L.H. *503*, *906*
Vink, J.G. *513*, 650, 885
Virolleaud, C.H. *213*
Vita-Finzi, C. *62*
Vogel, E.K. *346*
Vogelstein, M. *802*
Vogt, E. *181*, *630*, 797
Voightlander, E.N. von *819*
Voigt, E.E. *493*
Volten, A. *136*
Vriezen, T.C. *664*
Vuillemont, G. *127*
Vuilleumir-Bressard, R. *371*

Wachholder, B.Z. *35*
Wachsmann, S. *302*
Wadell, W.G. *191*
Wäfler, M. *712*
Wainwright, G.A. *292*, *295*, 314, 316
Walcot, P. *208*
Waldbaum, J.C. *70*, *318*, *336*
Walker, E.M. *862*
Wallinga, H.T. *817*
Wallis, G. *383*, *572*
Walstan, D. *332*
Wampler, J.C. *361*, 865
Ward, W.A. *39*, *124*, *133*, 160, *162*,
172, *214*, 263, 277, *324*, 411
Waterbolk, H. *91*
Waterman, L. *652*
Waters, K.H. *511*
Watkins, T. *89*
Watson, P.J. *111*
Watzinger, C. *528*

Weber, M. *373*
Weeks, N. *176*
Weidner, E.F. *643*, *674* *782*, 787
Weiher, E. von *678*
Weill, R. *65*
Weinberg, J.P. *844*
Weinfeld, M. *372*, *373*, *494*, *546*, 688,
770, *774*, *786*, 790
Weinstein, J.M. *103*, *125*, *162*, 163,
165, 167, *218*, *221*, 225, 230,
232, 236, 250, 281
Weippert, H. *14*, 54, *376*, *544*, *648*,
670
Weippert, M. *58*, *225*, *235*, *236*, *247*,
264, *274*, 277, 286, 287, *339*,
349, 411, *553*, *573*, 574, *604*,
629, 630, 631, *648*, *656*, *750*
Weiser, A. *427*, *455*
Weissbach, F.H. *781*, *815*, 819
Welch, A.C. *774*
Wellhausen, J. *42*, *46*, 430, 514
Welten, G. *203*, 264
Welten, P. *524*, *559*, 560, 566, *634*,
699, *702*, 734, 737
Wenning, R. *365*, 768, 810, *906*
Wente, E.F. *112*, 136, *226*, 234, 267,
283-85, *296*, *519*
Werner, E.K. *239*
Westenholz, Å. *142*
Westermann, C. *443*, *846*
Wette, W.M.L. de *774*
Whitcomb, D. *517*
Whitelam, K.W. *340*, 352, *372*, 465,
492
Whitley, C.F. *576*
Whybray, R.N. *46*, *846*, *875*
Widengren, G. *27*, *215*, *600*, *601*, *721*,
770, *773*, 817, *836*, *842*, 843,
852, 858, 860, 861, 868, 877,
878, 880, 882
Wieselhofer, J. *508*, *819*
Wilamowitz-Moellendorff, U. von *837*
Wildberger, H. *221*, 634, 690, 691,
697, 698, *704*, 708
Wilhelm, G. *116*, 130, 208, 210, 212
Wilkinson, J. *486*
Will, E. *533*
Willesen, F. *326*

Williams, B. *197*
Williams, R.J. *500*, 530, *798*
Williamson, H.G.M. *558*, 634, *766*, *838*, 850, *858*, 860, *864*, 878, 881
Willis, J.T. *456*
Wilson, J.A. 31, 60, 128, 132, 160, 166, 168, 191, 194, 195, 226, 227, 230, 232-34, 240, 247, 249, 275, 278, 283, 284, *295*, 297-99, 301, 303, 307, 386, 396, 416
Wilson, J.V. Kinnier *471*, *620*, 757, 798, 799
Wilson, V. *828*
Winckler, H. *397*, *706*
Winlock, H.E. *192*
Winnett, F.V. *182*, *274*, *410*, 416
Winter, I.J. *583*
Winter, U. *332*, 587
Wiseman, D.J. 56, *211*, *212*, 235, 393, *453*, *499*, *630*, *632*, 633, *671*, 684, 755-57, 759, *762*, 763, 764, 781, 784-86, 791, 794, 797, 802, 803
Wittram, R. *20*
Wolff, H.W. *60*, 593, *820*
Wooley, L. *257*, *781*
Worrell, J.E. 727
Wright, G.E. *145*, 174, *206*, 207, *263*, *283*, *327*, 348, *387*, 406, *428*, 468, 508, 510-14, *519*, 525, 548, *572*, 668, 670, 671, *697*, 806, 829, 853, 858, 864, 899, *901*, 904
Wright, G.H. von *20*
Wright, G.R.H. *198*, 204, *205*, 206, 256, 261, 262, *265*, 406, 526, 527
Wright, H.E. *291*
Wright, H.T. *116*, *129*, *359*
Würthwein, E. *490*, *504*, 532-34, 546, 569, *601*, *609*, 617, 633, 657, 670, 677, 679, 686, 689, 695, 720, 740, *775*

Wüst, M. *402*, 489, 591
Wyatt, N. *528*

Xenophon *758*, 872

Yadin, Y. *124*, *150*, 162, 164, 165, *167*, *200*, *202*-204, 247, *253*, *255*-57, *258*, 259, 271, *291*, *297*, 337, *338*, 341, 348, 363, 379, *385*, *520*, *523*, *525*, 526, 531, *557*, 565, 584, 606, *624*, 667, *669*, *699*, 721, 726, 736, *788*, 807, *876*, 892
Yamauchi, E. *742*
Yassine, K.N. *109*, 114, 215, *324*, *366*, 401, *647*, 808, 832
Yeivin, S. *124*, *236*, *470*, 585, *658*, 686, 687
Yellin, J. *700*
Yizraely, T. *87*
Yoffe, N. *134*, 153, 154, 156
Yoyotte, J. *783*
Yurco, F. *45*, 60, *284*, 287

Zaccagnini, C. *193*
Zadok, R. *276*, *379*, *900*
Zandee, J. *173*
Zayadine, F. *641*, 642, *645*, *646*
Zenger, E. *365*
Zertal, A. 220, *245*, *281*, 351, *366*, 428-29, 510
Zeuner, F.E. *309*, 364
Zichmoni, D. *341*
Zimansky, P.E. *628*
Zimhoni, O. *723*
Zimmerli, W. *526*, 802
Zobel, H.-J. *421*, *440*, 881
Zori, N. *381*, 441, *832*
Zumoffen, G. *86*
Zyl, A.H. van *653*, 655, 664

INDEX OF PERSONAL NAMES

Aaron 553 n., 849 n., 874
Abd-ashtart 891, 892
Abdi-Hepa 245-47, 250, 322 n.
Abdi-Milkutti 742, 743
Abdi-Tishri 245 n., 246
Abdon 374, 376, 421
Abiathar 474, 493, 497, 498, 501, 502
Abijah 553, 563, 564, 701
Abijam 548, 557, 563, 567 n.
Abimelech 37, 184, 291, 375, 383,
    385-88, 391, 428, 566
Abinadab 450, 451, 456 n.
Abinoam 379
Abishag 502
Abner 428 n., 436 nn., 437, 440, 453,
    462 n., 463-65
Abraham 31, 50, 154, 171 n., 180-87,
    393 n., 399 n., 443, 540, 566,
    706 n., 846, 847 n.
Absalom 400, 441 n., 488, 490, 492-
    97, 502, 521 n., 563
Achish 310 n., 312, 326, 459, 460
Achoris 858, 873 n., 890, 891
Adad-'idri 576, 577, 592
Adad-Nirari I 183, 269, 275
Adad-Nirari III 610-12
Adam 34, 417
Adon 784
Adoni-nur 646, 647
Adonijah 474, 497-99, 501-503,
    521 n.
Adoram 474, 476, 509, 546
Ahab 412, 557, 570, 572-79, 581-85,
    587, 591, 592, 596, 597 n., 599,
    606, 614, 670 n., 689, 766 n.,
    823 n.

Ahaz 42, 628, 630-33, 635, 661, 662,
    685-87, 689-91 n., 696 n., 704
Ahazi 868, 869
Ahaziah 329, 581, 588, 591, 595, 596,
    598, 600 n.
Ahijah 453
Ahiram 327 n., 511, 534
Ahitophel 493, 494 n.
Ahmose 194, 195, 206, 812
Ahmose II 801, 803
Aiarammu 657, 664
Akhenaten 218, 239, 240, 243, 250 n.,
    253, 267, 268 n.
Alexander the Great 680 n., 834,
    844 n., 867 n., 868, 894-96, 898,
    900-902
Amasis 801, 803, 812, 817, 818,
    871 n.
Amaziah 609, 613, 614, 621, 622, 625,
    659, 660, 687 n.
Amenemhat I 160, 165, 166 n., 168
Amenemhat IV 169 n.
Amenhotep I 206, 207, 225, 229
Amenhotep II 58, 60, 232-34, 236 n.,
    237, 238, 276
Amenhotep III 224, 237-39, 253,
    268 n., 269 n., 273 n., 315, 393
Amenhotep IV 239, 240, 250 n.
Amminadab 645, 646
Ammuladi 749, 750
Ammurapi 293, 294
Amnon 492, 497
Amon 42, 601, 734, 739, 740, 771,
    778 n., 791
Amos 616, 620-24, 649, 774
Anani 872, 889 n.
Anat 378, 380

Antigonus 896, 905 n.
Apries 793, 801
Araunah 470, 471, 528, 587
Arnuwandas II 269
Arsames 866 n., 869, 871
Arsham 865 n., 869
Artaḥšašta 849, 880
Artatama 213, 238
Artaxerxes I 825, 848, 849, 859, 861,
    862, 867, 874, 876 n., 877, 879,
    880, 882 n.
Artaxerxes II 849, 871, 878, 880, 890
Artaxerxes III 892-94, 896
Aryandes 820, 842
Asa 564, 566-68, 570, 588, 591, 701
Ashur-rabi II 396, 482, 487
Ashur-uballit I 269, 275, 276 n.
Ashur-uballit II 757-59, 788 n.
Ashurbanipal 48, 326 n., 499 n.,
    501 n., 646, 652, 663, 716 n.,
    732-35, 739, 741, 746-51, 753-
    55, 758, 769 n., 778, 810, 900
Ashurnaṣirpal II 570, 577, 601, 602
Assur-nirari V 612, 619 n.
Athaliah 574, 595, 596, 598-601, 608,
    654 n.
Atrahasis 120 n.
Ay 267 n., 269, 270
Ayyab 246, 247 n.
Aziru 242, 243, 2550, 268, 276 n.,
    385, 692
Azriau 625

Baalis 794, 800, 801
Baasha 558 n., 559, 562, 564, 565,
    569, 577, 591, 607, 641, 644 n.
Bagoas 868, 870, 871, 873, 894
Bagohi 868, 894
Balaam 605 n., 648-50
Baʻlu 664, 738 n., 742, 744, 745,
    747 n.
Bar-Hadad 608, 610, 611, 613
Baraq 37, 41, 379, 389 n.
Bardiya 819, 820
Baruch 782 n., 789, 800
Barzillai 404 n., 440, 497 n.
Bath-Sheba 485, 486, 491, 498-500 n.,
    502-504 n.

Bedan 310 n., 389
Beder 301, 304
Belshazzar 810
Ben-Hadad I 564, 565, 570, 575, 576,
    578, 607
Ben-Hadad II 640, 642, 654
Benaiah 474, 497-99, 502 n., 503,
    580 n.
Bezalel 704, 723
Biriawaza 246, 247, 250, 392
Biridiya 246, 251

Caleb 359, 455 n.
Cambyses 751, 808, 814, 817-19, 834,
    836, 848, 870
Chedorlaomer 185
Cushan-Rishathaim 376 n., 399 n.
Cyaxares 757, 812
Cyrus II 810 n., 811-17, 821, 835-37,
    841, 842, 847, 848, 872, 878 n.,
    884, 891

Dagantakala 276 n., 328
Darius I 770 n., 793 n., 806 n., 817-
    20, 833, 836 n., 837, 841-43, 848,
    849, 852-56, 896, 897 n.
Darius II 848, 849, 869-71, 877, 905
Darius III 894, 896
David 25, 29, 36, 42, 48, 49, 178 n.,
    259, 279, 304, 310 n., 312, 348,
    358, 360, 373, 377, 385, 389 n.,
    396, 398, 399, 404 n., 409, 413,
    418 n., 419, 422 n., 424, 426,
    427 n., 431-33 n., 435 n., 437,
    441, 443-45, 447-50, 452 n.,
    453-63, 465-77, 479-502, 504-
    509, 512, 514 n., 515-17, 519-22,
    525 nn., 527-29 n., 536-38, 540,
    541, 543, 547, 550, 553, 559,
    563, 564, 567, 580 n., 587, 599,
    600, 617 n., 618, 619, 621,
    644 n., 657, 659, 687 n., 689,
    702, 766, 771, 778, 795, 813 n.,
    837, 840, 848 n., 889
Deborah 37, 40, 41, 379, 389 n.
Dedan 443
Delilah 388
Dodo 378, 457 n.

Doeg 453

Eglon 38-40, 377
Ehud 37-39, 377, 378
Elah 559, 569, 591
Elhanan 457 n.
Eli 368, 377, 388 n., 390, 421, 423,
    425 n., 428, 429 n.
Eliakim 767, 780
Eliashib 860, 867, 880
Elijah 575, 576, 585, 586, 588, 592,
    595 n.
Elisha 575, 585, 589, 590, 592, 593
Elnathan 794, 868
Elyashib 762, 788
Enkidu 388 n.
Esarhaddon 326 n., 473, 499 n.,
    501 n., 516 n., 645, 652 n., 663,
    664, 686, 704, 715, 717 n., 728,
    731, 732, 738 n., 741, 742, 744-
    46, 748, 749, 762, 764 n., 773,
    803, 808, 818, 844, 900
Esau 183, 419
Eshbaal 48, 399, 440, 441, 451, 452,
    461-65, 467 n., 481, 497, 547,
    564
Eshmunazar 825, 827
Ethbaal 570, 607, 708
Eusebius 70
Evagoras 858, 873, 890
Evil-Merodach 810
Ezekiel 313, 314, 532, 756 n., 786,
    804, 846, 847, 853 n.
Ezra 46, 425, 770, 775, 777, 821, 835,
    845, 846, 849, 850, 857, 860,
    868, 870, 873-78, 880-89, 902

Gad 279, 407 n., 409
Gaumata 819
Geber 513, 514 n.
Gedaliah 798-800, 806, 835
Geshem 859, 863, 864, 868
Gideon 37, 372, 375, 383, 384, 421,
    427 n., 548 n.
Gilgamesh 388 n.
Gindibu' 577, 641
Gobryas 814, 815
Goliath 326, 456, 457

Gyges 748, 751

Habakkuk 736, 795
Hadad 418 n., 485, 505, 545 n.
Hadadezer 395, 396, 398, 400, 454,
    481-83, 487, 505, 520
Hadoram 483, 484
Haggai 820, 840, 850
Ham 60, 155, 313
Hammurapi 176, 212 n., 781 n.
Hanani 568, 862
Hananiah 869, 899
Hanun 481, 485, 630, 633, 635,
    644 n., 656, 672, 674, 684, 763 n.
Haremhab 250, 269, 270
Hatshepsut 195 n., 226, 229 n., 253
Hattushili II 237, 268
Hattushili III 195, 275
Hazael 591-93, 596, 604-608,, 610,
    613 n., 618, 639, 640, 642, 654
Hecateus 19
Herihor 304
Hezekiah 42, 43, 539 n., 559 n., 615,
    625, 637, 682 n., 683, 685, 686,
    689, 690, 695-98, 701-707, 710,
    711, 714-17, 720, 721, 725, 726,
    730, 731, 733 n., 739, 769 n.,
    770, 777, 779, 789
Hilkiah 772, 789, 790
Hiram 487, 506, 512, 515-17, 525,
    533, 629
Hissa'el 645, 646
Hophra 793, 794, 796, 801, 803
Hosea 231 n., 582 n., 616, 620, 622-
    24, 633, 635 n., 636, 666, 669,
    670, 672, 673, 689, 774
Huldah 773-77
Hushai 422 n., 493 n.

Iasmah-Adad 58
Ibzan 374
Idrimi 58, 212 n.
Ikausa 326 n., 664
Ila-kabkabi 175 n.
Illubi'di 671, 672 n., 674
Irḫuleni 577, 578, 610
Isaac 184, 566, 706 n.
Isaiah 625 n., 635, 665, 680, 681, 684,

690, 691 n., 696 n., 697 n., 703, 738 n., 813
Ishmael 181, 183, 515 n., 799, 800
Ithamar 388 n., 675 n.
Ithobaal 794, 802
Ittobaal 570, 629, 631 n., 634

Jabin 202 n., 348 n., 380 n.
Jacob 181-83, 230 n., 231, 279, 419, 544 n.
Jael 40, 380
Jair 374, 404, 512, 558 n.
Jedidiah 474, 498-501
Jehoahaz 596, 608, 613, 623 n., 634 n., 640, 654, 767, 780, 788 n.
Jehoash 599, 606
Jehoiada 600, 601, 608, 609 n., 860
Jehoiakim 746 n., 767, 780-82, 785, 788-90, 851
Jehoiakin 785-88, 790, 797, 837, 838, 889
Jehoram 544 n., 574 588, 589, 596, 599, 600
Jehoshaphat 474, 544 n., 564, 574, 588, 589, 596-98, 656-59
Jehu 51, 562, 573, 574, 579, 584 n., 589-96, 599, 605, 608, 614-15, 623 n., 640, 653 n., 654 n.
Jephthah 266 n., 389, 399, 400, 403-406, 408 n., 414, 422 n., 437
Jerahmeel 359, 789 n.
Jeremiah 313, 314, 688, 749 n., 756 n., 761, 782 n., 787, 789-92, 795 n., 797, 798, 800
Jeroboam I 45, 509 n., 521, 527 nn., 544, 545, 548-59, 561-64, 571, 573, 591, 623, 667, 670 n., 701
Jeroboam II 582 n., 606 n., 614, 617-19, 621, 623, 627, 628, 631, 632, 654, 655
Jerubbaal 37, 375, 382, 384, 389
Jeshua 873, 885
Jesse 454, 456 n., 495, 547
Jezebel 571, 574, 575, 582, 585-87, 595, 599, 607, 622, 650 n., 670 n., 734

Joab 464, 465, 474, 484 485, 488, 492, 493, 495-99, 501
Joash 382, 599, 601 n., 608, 609, 611, 613, 614, 654, 660
Joel 851, 852
Johanan 824, 860, 870, 871, 873, 880
John Hyrcanus 844, 904
Jonah 617, 655
Jonathan 25, 432, 437, 445, 450, 451, 458, 796 n., 883
Joram 483, 484, 569, 573 n., 579, 587-90, 592-95, 599, 639, 653, 659, 670 n.
Joseph 50, 279, 544
Joshua 304 n., 342, 348 n., 366, 390, 495, 820, 840, 849 n., 873, 885
Josiah 42, 198 n., 544 n., 559 n., 561, 582 n., 601, 615, 620 n., 650 n., 680 n., 685 n., 701, 704, 705, 724, 730, 731, 733 n., 740, 748 n., 752, 759, 762 n., 763-71, 773-80, 786, 788, 789 n., 793, 807, 809, 876, 884 n.
Jotham 625, 626 n., 627, 628, 644, 651, 661, 691 n.
Judas the Maccabee 844

Kamose 192-94
Keturah 393 n., 443
Kish 430, 435
Korah 704, 723

Laban 181, 675
Lab'ayu 244-46, 250, 375 n., 383, 385, 440 n., 548 n.
Lot 182, 183, 443
Luli 571 n., 669 n., 707, 708

Maacah 326, 361, 563, 567
Machir 404 n., 497 n.
Malachi 851, 852
Malchishua 450, 451
Manasseh 42, 43, 304 n., 409, 601, 664, 704, 715, 716, 730-39, 747 n., 748 n., 763, 771, 778 n., 791, 860, 864 n., 868 n., 889
Mattan 598, 601
Megabyxos 857, 861, 862

Menahem 630-32, 635 n., 656, 708
Menander 35, 501 n., 541, 571 n., 669 n.
Merab 440, 451
Meribaal 445
Merikare 136, 165 n.
Merneptah 60, 195 n., 275, 282, 284, 286 n., 287, 295, 307, 347 n., 349, 353, 354, 387
Merneptah-Siptah 264, 292
Merodach-baladan 691, 692, 694 n., 695, 707, 715
Mesha 385, 403, 409, 514, 558, 572, 579-81, 589, 590, 605 651, 653-55, 659, 688
Micah 388, 421, 427 n., 711, 789
Michal 451, 458, 464, 472
Midas 682, 693 n.
Milkilu 245-47
Mita 692, 693 n.
Mitinti 636, 664, 693 n., 708, 714 n.
Moses 345, 355, 371, 407 n., 409, 412, 413, 415, 425, 553 n., 689 n., 702, 720 n., 770, 875, 876, 878, 884, 886, 887
Mursilis II 269
Mut-ba'lu 246, 247 n.
Muwatallis 271-73, 275, 364

Na'aman 328
Nabopolassar 755-60, 764, 778
Naboth 587
Nabuna'id 30, 183, 773, 805, 806 n., 808, 810-13, 815, 820, 833, 836, 905
Nabuzaradan 798, 801
Nadab 553 n., 559, 564, 591
Nahash 404 n., 446, 454, 481, 485 497 n., 644 n.
Namiawaza 250, 276 n.
Naram-Sin 116 n., 141-43, 152, 393
Narmer 122 n., 124, 125 n.
Nathan 472 n., 481, 491 n., 497-99
Nebuchadrezzar II 571 n., 756 n., 760, 773 n., 778, 781, 782, 784-88, 790 n., 791, 792, 794, 795, 797, 799-804, 807, 809-11, 849 n., 857

Nebuchadrezzar III 820
Nebuchadrezzar IV 820
Necho II 637, 732, 746 n., 747, 748, 759-61, 766 n., 767, 768, 779-83, 789, 809, 852, 859 n.
Nectanebo I 891
Nectanebo II 891
Neferhotep I 172, 188 n.
Nefertiti 267 n.
Nehemiah 821, 824, 843 n., 845, 850-52, 859-68, 871, 874, 879-82, 886-89
Nepherites I 872, 890
Nicaso 860, 868 n., 889
Noah 120, 155, 313

Og 403 n., 415, 489 n., 513
Omri 49, 412, 548, 549, 558, 564 n., 568-75, 579, 581, 582, 584 n., 588, 591, 595 n., 596, 598, 599, 601, 607, 614
Osorkon I 566
Osorkon II 583 n., 624
Osorkon IV 673, 692, 696
Othniel 37, 38, 376, 377

Padi 695, 696, 710, 713, 714 n., 769 n.
Panammu 630, 636 n.
Pekah 630, 632-36
Pekaiah 632
Pepi I 132, 133
Pepi II 133, 136, 137
Philip II 892, 894
Pir'u 692, 693
Psammetichus I 734, 739, 747-53, 756 n., 758-60, 763, 768, 769, 779, 781, 807, 870
Psammetichus II 791-93, 871
Psammetichus III 818, 861
Psusonnes II 509
Ptolemy I 896, 898 n., 905 n.
Ptolemy II 191 n.
Ptolemy V 901 n.
Pul 629, 707 n.

Qaush-gabri 663, 664
Qaush-malaku 631, 656, 662, 663
Qazardi 278, 279

Qurdi-aššur-lamur 633 n., 676

Ramses I 270
Ramses II 29, 47, 68, 191 n., 221 n.,
    230, 253, 261 n., 271-77, 279,
    282, 284, 286 n., 288, 292, 298,
    299 n., 302, 349, 395, 410
Ramses III 253 n., 254, 288, 291, 294-
    300, 307-10, 318, 323 n., 324,
    349, 359, 395, 396, 399 n.,
    411 n., 532
Ramses VI 291 n., 307 n., 324, 325,
    349
Ramses XI 304
Raqianu 628, 630
Rehoboam 347 n., 504, 540, 544-46,
    548, 549, 554, 556, 558, 560,
    561, 563, 571, 701
Rehum 848, 861
Rezin 628, 630, 632, 636
Rezon 483, 505-507 n., 512 n., 558
Rib-Adda 242, 243, 251, 276 n.
Rizpah 464
Ruhubi 641, 644, 645
Rukibtu 636, 696 n., 709 n.

Salmanu 593 n., 656
Samsi 674, 675 n.
Samson 388
Samuel 353 n., 361, 371, 377, 389,
    390, 421, 423-29, 431, 432, 434,
    436, 438 n., 456 n., 772
Sanballat 859, 860, 863, 864, 867, 868,
    871, 900, 901
Sanballat II 899
Sanballat III 868 n., 889, 902 n.
Sargon I 141-43, 152, 328, 671, 691
Sargon II 388 n., 574, 625, 652 n.,
    655 n., 657, 669 n., 670, 672,
    674-76, 679 n., 680 n., 684 n.,
    690, 694, 706, 708, 718, 719 n.,
    748, 816, 899
Saul 36, 39, 46, 48, 266 n., 286,
    306 n., 320, 327, 336, 360 n.,
    362, 365, 377-79, 383 n., 385,
    388-90, 396, 398 n., 399, 404-
    406, 421 n., 423, 424, 426, 429-
    32, 434-63, 471, 472, 475, 477,

480, 481, 490 n., 496, 501-504,
    506, 513, 515, 521, 541 n., 550,
    561
Sennacherib 23, 312, 330 n., 559 n.,
    571 n., 625, 632 n., 637, 642 n.,
    645, 657, 664, 678 n., 681,
    690 n., 694-96, 698, 704, 707-
    16 n., 719-22, 724, 725, 732, 735,
    741, 748, 763, 764 n.
Senwosret I 166 n., 168, 169
Senwosret III 166, 167, 172, 386
Seraiah 474, 792, 848 n., 874
Seth 170 n., 392, 410
Seti I 165 n., 187 n., 221 n., 226 n.,
    247, 253, 254 n., 270-72, 277,
    279, 287, 359, 411 n.
Seti II 264
Shabako 693, 696, 708, 741 n.
Shallum 631, 767, 780
Shalmaneser I 275, 392
Shalmaneser III 482 n., 562, 573 n.,
    576-78, 592-96, 601, 604, 605,
    639-42, 644 n.
Shalmaneser IV 612, 618, 628
Shalmaneser V 669-72 n., 690, 708 n.
Shamash-shum-ukin 732, 741, 749
Shamgar 37, 40, 378, 380
Shamshi-Adad I 176, 179 n., 189 n.
Shamshi-Adad V 604
Shanipu 644, 645, 656
Shaphan 770 n., 772, 789, 790, 799
Sharkalisharri 142, 152
Shealtiel 889 n.
Sheba 49, 466, 482, 483, 488, 490,
    495, 496, 498, 543, 547
Shem 154, 741 n.
Shenazzar 837 n.
Sheshbazaar 837-39, 847, 868
Shimei 502
Shishak 45, 299, 347 n., 545, 544 n.
Shobi 404 n., 485, 497 n., 644 n.
Shoshenq 45, 46, 299, 347 n., 469 n.,
    509, 511 n., 520 n., 521, 523,
    527 n., 541 n., 545, 549, 554-
    58 n., 560, 561, 566 n., 660
Shuwardata 245, 250
Siamun 505, 509, 519, 520
Sidqa 695, 696, 709, 715

Sihon 403, 413-15, 513
Silkannu-Osorkon IV 693 n.
Sillibel 708, 714 n.
Sin-shar-ishkun 755-57
Sinuhe 68, 168, 169, 399
Sisera 29, 41, 348 n., 379, 380
Smendes 304, 305
Só 672, 674 n.
Solomon 35, 48, 49, 51, 117 n., 254 n.,
    258 n., 302 n., 304, 342, 348,
    373, 380 n., 418 n., 423, 427 n.,
    429, 436, 438 n., 440-42, 452 n.,
    453, 468, 469 n., 471 n., 472,
    474, 477, 483, 486, 488, 490,
    491 n., 496-509, 511, 512, 514-
    32 n., 534-53, 555, 556, 558-63,
    579, 584, 585, 591, 598, 600,
    608, 614 n., 624, 626, 657, 660,
    662, 668, 685, 701, 705, 734,
    735, 771, 837 n., 838 n., 841,
    849 n., 851, 876
Straton I 897
Straton II 896 n.
Suppiluliuma I 195, 238, 243, 268,
    269, 286 n., 288
Suppiluliuma II 294

Tagu 245, 247
Taharqa 637, 708, 710, 713, 743-48
Talmai 400, 464, 496, 497
Tattenai 834, 843, 847, 848, 852
Tennes 892, 896
Tewosret 264, 327
Thoth 226, 227
Thutmose I 206, 225, 229, 231
Tibni 569, 570
Tiglath-Pileser I 304, 393, 394, 604 n.
Tiglath-Pileser III 519 n., 571 n.,
    593 n., 612, 619 n., 625, 626,
    628-37, 640, 642, 644, 649,
    651 n., 656, 662, 667-69, 674,
    676, 684, 685, 690, 692 n.,
    707 n., 713 n., 762, 763 n., 809,
    904
Tirhaqah 710
Tobiah 823, 824 n., 859, 860, 863,
    867, 868, 902

Toi 483, 484
Tola 378, 379 n.
Tu-ba-il 629, 631 n., 634
Tudhaliya II 268
Tudhaliya III 237
Tukulti-Ninurta I 275, 288
Tutankhamon 237, 243, 267-70
Tuthmosis II 225, 226, 276 n.
Tuthmosis III 226-32, 234 n., 236-38,
    249, 251, 254, 274 n., 276,
    307 n., 316, 400, 410 n., 474
Tuthmosis IV 213, 238, 539 n.
Tuthotep 166, 172

Uaite 749, 750
Udjahoresenet 818, 853, 877
Ugbaru 814, 815 n.
Uri 513, 514 n.
Uriah 486, 685-87, 789
Utnapishtim 120 n.
Uzziah 614, 617 n., 625-28, 651, 660,
    661, 690, 791

Wenamun 31, 299, 301, 302, 304, 305,
    515 n.
Weni 132, 133

Xerxes 848, 853, 856-58, 861, 904 n.
Xerxes II 869

Yamani 685, 693, 694
Yarim-Lim 176, 202, 212 n.
Yasmah-Adad 176, 179 n.
Yehoiakim 762
Yeroham 523, 560

Zadoq 473 n., 474, 477, 493, 497-99,
    503, 849 n.
Zakar-Baal 301, 304, 305
Zakkur 608, 610-13, 680 n.
Zedekiah 785 n., 786, 788, 791-95,
    797, 799, 801, 851
Zerubbabel 820, 821, 830, 837, 838,
    840, 841, 843 n., 852, 868, 870,
    889 n.
Zimri-Lim 175, 176, 189 n., 202
Zurata 241, 246, 250

INDEX OF DEITY NAMES

Abu 172
Adad 203, 476
Adad-melech 678 n.
Addu 179
Adonis 718 n.
Adrammelech 678
Ahu 172
Ahura Mazda 52, 836, 837, 855, 871,
    876 n., 878 n., 879 n.
'Al 179
'Alu 369
'ly 390
'Am 179
Ammu 405
Amon/Amun 29, 45, 51, 229, 230, 249,
    254, 269, 272, 300, 301, 304, 305
Amun-Re 240
Amurrum 179
Anammelech 678
Anat of Melech 678 n.
Anath 179, 191 n., 378 n.
Anath-Bethel 744
Anath-Yahu 870
Anati-Baiti-ili 744
Anu 678 n.
Apollo 837, 842 n.
Apollon Smintheus 329
Aradmelech 678 n.
Asherah 22, 43, 477, 524, 536, 567,
    582 n., 599, 616, 735, 771,
    849 n., 852
Asherat-Yam 198
Ashim-Bethel 870
Ashima 678
Ashtarte 127, 191, 262, 328, 330, 450,
    537, 571, 668, 718 n., 744
Ashtoreth 253

Ashur 51, 686, 687, 746, 762
Assur 736 n.
Atargatis 678 n.
Aten 239, 240

Baal 43, 127 n., 141, 172, 173, 191,
    259, 328, 364, 371, 379 n.,
    382 n., 466 n., 477, 524, 536,
    582, 585-87, 590, 599, 601, 622,
    624, 625, 670 n., 733, 771,
    792 n., 899
Baal Carmel 586
Baal-Hamman 256
Baal Hermon 586 n.
Baal Lebanon 586 n.
Baal-malagê 744
Baal-Peor 649 n., 650 n.
Baal-samême 744
Baal-sapunu 744
Baal Shamayn 610
Baal Shamem 586
Baal-Zebub 329, 330, 588
Baal-Zebul 329, 588 n., 591
Baalat 127
Baiti-ili 744
Baliḫ 172
Bel 836, 878 n.
Bes 828
Bethel 426, 744

Chemosh 52, 141, 416, 537, 579-81,
    589, 899

Dagan 141, 178, 179, 180, 210, 328,
    744
Dagon 327, 388
Dionysos 826 n.

Dod 580
Dumuzu 123

Edom 614 n.
El 127, 179, 259, 327, 344, 345, 365,
    427, 470, 477, 478
El-Berith 386, 387
El Elyon 328
El Shadday 649
Elat 261
Elohim 417 n., 471
Elyon 471, 477, 503 n.
Enlil 143 n.
Erah 179
Ereshkigal 678 n.
Eshmun 744, 825 n., 873 n.

Gad 262
Gula 744

Hadad 141, 172, 179, 259, 364, 586,
    663
Haddu 172, 476
Hal 179
Hammu 172, 179
han-'Ilat 859
Hanat 179
Hathor 127, 254, 262, 328, 418, 647
Hauron 172
Hawran 179
Hepat 210
Horon 179, 191, 329
Horus 873 n.

Ilu 172
Ilum 179
Indra 209
Ishtar 51, 257, 571
Isis 323, 873 n.

Khnum 870, 872 n.
Kronos 127
Ksr 172
Kumarbi 210

Lawi 172
Leto 877
Lim 141, 172

Malek 485 n.
Malik 141, 172, 179
Marduk 27, 42, 51, 265, 275, 289, 472,
    678 n., 810, 811, 813, 815, 816,
    836, 857
Mekal 252, 669
Melqart 586, 608, 744
Milcom 485 n., 537, 800 n.
Min 262
Mitra 209
Moloch 771
Montu 298
Muluk 179 n.
Mut 395

Nabu 471 n., 836, 899
Nehushtan 702
Neith 818, 877
Nephtys 323
Nergal 257, 678
Nibhaz 678

Osiris 644 n., 828 n.

Ptah 252, 272, 300, 853

Qaush 663
Qoš 899
Qudshu 191, 262

Rapha 326 n.
Rašap 179
Re' 189 n., 195, 240, 272, 284, 300
Resheph 141, 179, 191. 260-62

Sahar 899
Salim 179
Sarpanitum 678 n.
Sekhmet 729
Seth 173, 191, 193 n., 252, 328, 668
Shadday 649
Shalem 477, 500, 504
Shamash 571, 837 n.
Shamshu 172
Shemesh 736
Silenus 826 n.
Sin 123, 172, 183, 571, 773, 810,
    837 n.

Succoth-benoth 677-78
Sutekh 272

Tammuz 379 n., 792
Tanit 256
Tartaq 678
Teshub 51, 210, 253
Thoth 773
Tiamat 27

Varuna 209

Yahu 624, 870, 872
Yahweh 22, 29, 38, 42, 43, 50, 51,
    117 n., 180, 182, 187, 247 n.,
    286, 304, 313, 328-29, 343-45,
    347, 365, 369, 372-77 n., 378,
    379 n., 382 n., 390, 407 n., 413,
    415, 417, 419, 424-27, 430-32,
    439, 443, 448, 453, 457 n., 458,
    469, 470-72, 474, 476 n., 477-80,
    484 n., 486 n., 489 n., 491 n.,
    494 n., 499, 501, 502 n., 503,

504, 524, 529 n., 530, 532 n.,
533-37, 539, 541 n., 544 n., 547,
551, 553, 555 n., 561, 563-64,
568, 580, 586, 588-90, 593, 596-
97, 599, 609, 611 n., 614 n., 615,
616, 619 n., 621-24, 635, 654,
663, 666 n., 677, 679, 680, 684,
686-88 n., 703, 705, 706 n., 707,
720 n., 734-36, 758, 765, 770-76,
788, 790 n., 801, 811, 813, 815,
816, 820, 835, 837, 838, 840,
844-46, 849, 851, 852, 860, 869-
71, 876, 878, 880, 881 n., 884,
885 n., 898-900, 902, 904
Yahweh-El 427, 470, 478
Yam 172
Yapa 172
Yarih 179

Zebul 574 n.
Zedeq 477
Zeus 837, 878 n.
Zeus Olympius 902

INDEX OF GEOGRAPHICAL AND GENTILIC TERMS

Abel Beth-Maacah 399, 482, 496, 565,
   584, 635, 640
Abel-keramim 354 n., 407, 408
Abel Meholah 439, 440, 442, 444, 511
Abiezerites 382 n., 383 n.
Abila 223
Abinu 506 n., 607 n.
Abr Nahara 821, 830, 843, 861, 882
Abu Gosh 94, 97, 99
Abu Khas 74
Abu Zarad 219
Abydos 279
Acco 68, 165, 198, 221 n., 241, 246,
   250, 270, 271, 342, 512, 517,
   591, 607, 708, 750, 809, 825,
   849, 873 n., 890
Achshaph 247, 250
Achaemenid 819, 830, 836, 840 n.,
   874, 878 n., 879
Achzib 165, 405, 708, 711
Acre 739
Adam 495, 511, 512
Admah 61, 185
Adullam 466, 711, 831
Aegean 217, 224, 255, 291, 295, 308,
   315, 316, 317, 318 n., 321, 332,
   826, 834, 855, 862
Affuleh 148, 320, 382 n.
'Afula 338, 339, 351
Agade 328
Agusi 612, 619 n.
Ahlamu 392, 292, 446 n.
'Ai 117, 118, 128, 129, 130, 134, 336,
   338, 343, 348 n., 360, 361,
   765 n., 807
Aijalon 244, 247, 251, 379, 510, 556,
   557, 559, 560, 591, 634, 684

valley of 438, 468
Aila 485, 660 n.
'Ain
   Feshka 730
   Ghazal 94, 95, 96, 97, 98, 100, 101,
      102, 103, 105
   Musa 419, 662
   Rahub 104
   Shemesh 300
   Qudeirat, el 205
'Ajlun 64, 70, 224, 336 n., 400, 401,
   434 n., 441, 446, 549, 558
Akhziv 826
Akkad 116 n., 137, 138, 142, 143,
   179, 782, 814
Alalakh 58, 59, 145 n., 187, 191, 201,
   208, 211, 212, 218, 223, 256,
   257, 258, 273 n., 288, 289, 393,
   529
Alashiya 221 n., 287, 293, 294, 298,
   314 n.
Aleppo 67, 68, 70, 140, 175, 199 n.,
   210, 202, 213, 237, 268, 272,
   577, 608, 760
Amaleq 421 n., 439
Amaleqites 374, 376, 377, 382, 421,
   429, 439, 445, 460, 591 n.
Amarah West 274, 302
Amman 62, 94, 163, 189 n., 201,
   204 n., 214, 215, 223, 224, 263,
   264, 324, 354 n., 404 n., 406,
   407, 408, 411, 418 n., 644, 646,
   807, 824 n., 830
Ammon 36, 64, 65, 69, 266, 288, 334,
   377, 398, 403, 406, 407, 422,
   444, 448 n., 454, 480, 485,
   497 n., 537, 544, 558, 577, 590,

628, 632, 637, 641, 642, 643,
   645, 646, 650 n., 651, 652, 655,
   656, 657, 659, 664, 666, 675,
   692, 695, 696, 708, 747 n., 758,
   785, 792, 794, 797, 800, 801,
   802, 804, 824, 843, 905
Ammonites 183, 376, 398, 400, 405,
   407, 408, 409, 423, 439, 441,
   442, 446-48, 481, 482, 485, 488,
   497 n., 591 n., 596, 626, 627,
   641-45, 648, 650, 655, 656, 800,
   823, 833, 835, 858, 863, 867,
   876 n., 882
Amorites 60, 133, 135, 136, 151, 152,
   153, 154, 155, 161, 165 n.,
   169 n., 177, 178 n., 187 n.,
   234 n., 244, 394, 396 n., 407 n.,
   413, 414, 415, 489 n., 510 n.,
   513, 882, 883
'Amuq region 125, 159
   valley 130
Amurru 59, 134, 152-54, 165 n., 229,
   242, 243, 244, 268, 270-73,
   276 n., 278, 290, 298, 299, 385,
   394, 395, 396, 482 n., 483 n.,
   602, 708, 711, 712 n., 732, 749
Anaharath 233
Anathoth 502, 789, 796 n.
Anatolia 47, 50, 60, 67, 90, 91, 93,
   130, 140, 156, 158, 159, 161,
   174, 193, 203, 208, 209, 223,
   224, 242, 266 n., 268, 269, 289,
   290, 292, 293, 294, 295, 296,
   297, 309, 315, 316, 321, 363,
   364, 487, 527, 692, 694 n., 761,
   812, 815, 835, 853, 869, 872,
   877, 891
Anshan 812, 814
Antilebanon 394, 506, 639, 642, 652,
   820 n.
Apamea 225, 234 n.
Aphek 68, 130, 163, 164, 230, 233,
   244, 281, 292, 311, 338, 353,
   450, 510, 559, 576, 591, 609,
   745, 784, 794, 863
'apiru 234-36, 240-42, 245-48, 270,
   278, 392, 437

Aqaba (city) 109, 626, 660, 734,
   906 n.
   Gulf of 62, 69, 123, 398, 418 n.,
      480, 505, 516-17 n., 523, 570,
      588, 589, 613, 627, 658, 659,
      660, 661, 684
Arabah Sea 617, 618, 654, 655
   Valley 62, 64, 65, 67, 69, 70, 119,
      123, 359, 417, 418, 419, 505,
      523, 618, 657, 658, 659, 661, 805
Arabia 56, 57 n., 61, 62, 64, 67, 69,
   155, 398, 418 n., 480, 486, 518,
   519 n., 571, 577, 589, 607, 610,
   627, 630, 631, 641, 643, 653,
   658, 662, 674, 724, 733, 745,
   747, 748, 795, 808, 810, 895,
   905 n.
Arabs 57, 183, 393, 420, 443, 448,
   566, 596, 598, 603, 610, 626,
   627, 628, 633, 634, 637, 641,
   642, 648, 652, 653, 656, 675,
   694 n., 697, 706, 722 n., 723,
   724, 725, 733, 742, 744, 748,
   749, 750, 753, 756, 784, 805 n.,
   808, 817 n., 818, 823, 825, 826,
   835, 859, 860 n., 864, 890, 900,
   905
Arad 22, 43, 63, 117, 119, 122, 123,
   124, 125, 126, 256 n., 262 n.,
   359, 522, 524, 525, 533, 560,
   659, 660, 661 n., 698, 703, 704,
   722, 723, 724, 726, 727, 767,
   779, 780, 785 n., 787, 788, 795,
   802 n., 825, 905
Aram 57, 391, 392, 393, 484, 558 n.,
   570, 575, 576, 578, 584, 589,
   592, 593, 607 n., 635 n., 639,
   661, 680 n., 785
Aram-Beth-Rehob 398
Aram-Damascus 506, 507, 511, 557,
   558, 564, 568, 570, 572, 574,
   575, 576, 590, 592, 594, 596,
   608, 609, 612, 614, 628, 640,
   641, 642, 644, 655, 666
Aram Naharaim 376 n., 399 n.
Aram Zobah 396, 398, 454, 481,
   484 n., 505, 520

Aramaeans 30, 57, 182, 183, 230, 248, 276, 288, 290, 334, 342, 361, 376 n., 391, 393, 394, 395, 398, 399 n., 400, 402, 407, 444, 445, 482, 483, 485, 486, 487, 488, 507 n., 515, 522, 541, 558, 565, 567, 575, 576, 578, 583, 584, 592, 594 n., 596, 602, 605, 606, 608, 609, 615, 629, 634, 639, 640, 656, 682, 683, 686, 694 n., 695, 741, 749, 751, 756, 785 n., 835, 899

Araq el Emir 163, 824 n., 902

Argob 512, 632 n.

Arnon River 57, 64, 274, 403, 448, 481, 488, 514, 559, 572, 579, 605, 653, 654, 655

'Aro'er 149, 407, 408, 416, 488, 580, 605, 654, 663, 808

Arpad 395 n., 628, 629, 631 n., 671, 705, 706

Arslan Tash 534, 582 n.

Aruna Pass 68, 227

Arvad 244, 304, 577, 602, 677, 696, 708, 747 n., 787, 802, 807

Arza 748, 742

Arzawa 298

Ashdod 68, 306, 307, 310, 311, 319, 327, 330 n., 332, 342, 354, 526, 657, 685, 691, 692, 693, 694, 696, 708, 709, 714, 716, 726, 727, 729, 739 n., 751, 752, 753, 758, 759 n., 763, 768, 769, 787, 802, 807, 823, 843, 859, 863, 864, 867, 890

Asher 278, 279, 347, 383, 433, 512, 513, 707 n.

Asherite 38, 279, 433

Ashkelon 45, 68, 170, 222, 247, 251, 284, 285, 306, 307, 310, 316 n., 633, 636, 664, 694, 695, 696, 708, 709, 714, 716, 728, 744 n., 745, 759 n., 781, 807, 823, 825

Ashtaroth 69, 246, 247, 512

Ashur 213, 277 n., 443, 756, 757

Ashurites 399 n., 440, 443, 446, 463

Asia Minor 167, 286 n., 288 n., 292 n., 742 n., 837

Asiatics 132, 133, 136, 165, 187, 188, 189, 191, 192, 193, 196, 200, 204 n., 230, 234 n., 236 n., 237, 287 n., 329 n., 673, 751

Assur 141, 175, 230 n., 604, 617, 671, 743, 885 n.

Assyria/Assyrian 25 n., 47-48, 50, 58, 158, 175-76, 179, 189, 209, 241, 269, 275-76, 287-90, 304, 312-13, 325, 393-94, 409, 443, 454, 482, 483 n., 487-88, 521 n., 533 n., 541, 568, 571, 574, 576-77, 579, 589, 592, 593-96, 602-605, 608-13, 618, 620 n., 628-30, 631 n., 633-35, 637-38, 640, 643-44, 650-53, 655-57, 659, 662-63, 665-68, 670, 687, 690, 693-99, 701, 703-16, 718-22, 724-26, 728-33, 734, 736 n., 737-39, 741-59, 761-67, 771, 773, 778-79, 781, 784, 786 n., 788 n., 790, 799, 807, 809-10, 815, 816, 821 n., 823, 829, 835, 879 n., 899, 901

Atar Haro'a 505 n.

'Ataroth 412, 580

Athenian 853, 855, 856, 858, 862, 872 n., 873, 891, 897

'Atlith 405, 688 n., 890, 896 n.

Attica 857, 897, 906 n.

Avaris 188, 189, 190, 193 n., 194

Azekah 627 n., 694, 700, 710, 711, 795, 796, 831

Azor 330, 405, 709

Baal-Meon 580, 654, 655 n.

Baal-Perazim 466

Baalath 506, 507

Bab edh-Dhra' 54, 118, 119, 144, 149, 337

Babylon 42, 121 n., 152, 161, 175, 176, 182 n., 202, 212 n., 218 n., 238, 239, 241, 275, 540, 677, 678, 691, 716, 732, 733, 737, 741, 750, 764 n., 766 781, 782, 785, 786, 787, 790, 791, 792, 794, 797, 812, 813, 814, 815, 820, 836, 845, 857, 874, 877

Babylonia/Babylonian 30-31, 48, 50, 178, 182, 231, 287-89, 394, 404, 604, 629, 638, 691-92, 694 n., 695, 707, 716, 732-33, 748-51, 755-58, 760-61, 765 n., 765 n., 766 n., 767 n., 773, 779 n., 782-785 n., 786-805, 807-17, 819-24, 829-31, 833, 835, 837 n., 838, 840 n., 845-46, 853, 866 n., 871, 874, 878, 885, 887, 896, 899, 904 n., 905
Baghdad 190
Bahrain 122, 693 n.
Balikh River 107, 183
Ba'lira'si 594, 595
Balu'a 39, 410
Baq'ah Valley 22, 336 n., 401
Bashan 61, 64, 67, 69, 248 n., 273, 403 n. 415, 446, 489, 506, 513
Basta 96, 97, 98, 100, 101, 102
Be'alot 513
Be'er Resisim 151 n.
Beer-sheba 69, 184, 357, 459, 489, 523, 524, 560, 659, 666, 698, 702, 703, 721, 722, 724, 726, 727, 729, 763, 780, 825
   Valley 65, 220, 358
Beeroth 362
Behistun 819, 821
Beidha 91, 94, 95, 98
Beirut 167, 271, 594 n., 744
Beisamouno 96, 97, 98, 99
Beitin 163, 279, 668, 679
Bene-berak 709
Beni-Hassan 166 n.
Benjamin 39, 245, 278, 361, 405 n., 428, 430, 434 n., 435, 438, 440 443, 444 n., 455, 463, 496, 513, 545 n., 557, 564, 702, 848 n., 883
Benjaminites 39, 174, 178, 378, 423, 438, 495, 795
Beq'a Valley 56, 62, 72, 147, 163, 214, 219, 225 n., 229, 244, 269, 271, 276, 434 n., 469, 506, 507 n., 584, 611 n., 617, 642
Berothai 396, 482
Beth-Anath 271, 273, 378

Beth-Dagon 328, 709
Beth-Eden 395 n., 571
Beth-Hakkerem 843
Beth Horon 329, 422 n., 468, 507, 510, 556
Beth-Millo 386 n., 387 n.
Beth-Rehob 36, 396
Beth-Shan 113, 114 n., 129, 130, 134, 147 n., 150, 170, 187 n., 199, 247-49, 251-55, 261, 270-71, 274, 278, 291 300, 306, 319-24, 330, 354, 382 n., 439-40, 442, 444-46, 449-50, 469, 511, 521, 524, 532, 556, 558 n., 635, 666, 667-69
   Valley of 57, 68, 113, 131, 365, 439, 832
Beth-Shemesh 128, 134, 205, 433, 469, 510, 525, 559, 591, 613, 634, 698, 721 n., 722, 795, 826
Beth-Yerah 118, 130, 131, 827
Beth-Zur 196 n., 336, 700, 795, 825, 827, 831, 843, 844, 898
Bethel 38, 69, 163, 184, 196 n., 219, 231 n., 245, 279, 280, 319, 338, 351, 361 n., 366, 369 n., 422 n., 426, 433, 510, 551, 557, 563, 583 n., 591, 621, 622, 667, 668, 679, 701, 707, 735, 744, 765 n., 775, 779, 801, 806, 807, 826, 858
Bethlehem 63, 324, 356, 374, 422, 431, 433, 455, 456, 457 n., 462, 468, 473
Bezeq 442, 443
Bezer 412, 580
Bit-Adini 395 n., 571, 577
Bit-Ammon 631, 652 n.
Boghazköi 190, 208
Bouqras 97, 98, 99, 100, 101, 102
Bozrah 23 n., 419, 662
Brook of Egypt 66, 626, 633, 636, 637, 675 n., 745, 766, 781
Bubastis 160 n., 554, 637, 673, 674 n.
Bull Site 361, 365 n.
Buseira 23, 419, 662, 663 723, 808
Byblos 31, 61, 63, 90, 100, 107, 111, 123, 125, 126, 128, 145, 147, 149, 156, 159, 162, 168, 169 n.,

170, 172, 173, 188, 190, 198,
206 n., 217, 225, 231, 237, 242,
243, 244, 251, 254, 268, 270,
271, 276 n., 289, 301, 304, 305,
306, 316, 328, 337, 533, 602,
604, 630, 652 n., 697, 708, 747,
828

Caesarea 63, 896
Cafer Hoyuk 90, 93
Caleb 462 n.
Calebites 419, 422, 456, 462, 503
Canaan 14, 28, 46 n., 58-61, 115, 155-
56, 178, 181-83, 186 n., 189-92,
216, 218 n., 219, 235, 244, 249,
251, 252 254, 262, 270, 279, 281,
284-86, 292, 313, 320, 328,
329 n., 330, 338, 342, 345, 347,
352 n., 355, 356, 382 n., 390,
409 n., 413, 417, 419, 428, 468-
73, 489 n., 503, 504, 507, 521 n.,
525 n., 536, 540, 541, 544 n.,
616, 624, 649, 689 n., 846
Canaanites 14, 29, 40, 41, 48, 59, 60,
153, 155, 200, 234, 277 n., 286,
308, 322, 325, 343, 344, 347,
349, 352 n., 368, 372, 378, 379,
382 n., 396 n., 414 n., 427, 456,
460 n., 466 n., 469, 470, 474,
479, 489, 503, 510, 550, 559,
567, 572, 615, 622, 882
Cape Gelidonya 224
Caphtor 313, 314, 315 n., 316, 317
Cappadocia 183, 209, 316, 317, 812,
872 n.
Carchemish 175, 177, 201, 231,
166 n., 268, 270, 289, 298, 393,
395 n., 529 n., 571, 582 n., 637,
676, 692, 759, 760, 761, 764 n.,
766 784, 788 n., 789, 790 n.
Carmel 32, 45, 56, 57, 59, 63, 68, 70,
85, 132, 221, 226, 245, 296, 300,
301, 342 506, 506, 511, 556, 586,
591, 825
Carthage 372 n., 516 n., 856
Caucasus 694 n., 742
Çayönü 90, 93
Cherethites 313, 459, 474, 475 n.

Chaldeans 30, 629, 691, 694 n., 695,
749, 755, 756, 785, 795
Chun 396, 482
Cilicia 131, 212, 292, 294, 296, 298,
314, 522, 610, 692, 742, 810,
812, 890, 893
Cimmerians 694, 742, 748
Cisjordan 56, 57, 64, 69, 134, 144,
146, 214, 224, 229, 231, 264,
266 n., 290, 343, 351, 352, 377,
384, 401, 402, 405, 409, 412,
423, 432, 446, 448, 462 n., 463,
469, 478, 480, 481, 605, 613 n.,
641, 682
Crete 177, 190, 221, 302, 309 n., 314,
315, 316, 321, 475
Cush 60, 170, 238 n., 720 n., 741 n.,
750, 761, 793
Cushite 155, 566, 634, 710, 746
Cuthah 677, 678
Cutheans 899
Cyprus 149, 159, 167, 181, 197, 217,
220, 222-23, 239, 255, 281, 291,
294, 300, 302, 305, 309 n., 314-
19, 327 n., 330-32, 336 n.,
352 n., 533 n., 535, 571 n., 664,
693 n., 708, 731, 743, 747 n.,
803, 813, 826, 856, 858, 861,
862, 872, 890, 894
Cypriots 692, 693 n.

Damascus 61, 68, 69, 91, 94, 130, 201,
229, 232 n., 247, 269, 273, 278,
392, 398, 444, 445, 482, 483,
506, 507, 511, 512, 515, 558,
564, 570, 571, 575, 577, 578,
583 n., 591-93, 602, 604, 607,
608, 610-13, 617-20, 628-31,
632-36, 639, 642, 654, 656,
669 n., 671, 680 n., 683-85, 706
Dan 163 n., 165, 177 n., 201, 311 n.,
319, 388, 389, 398, 489, 512,
526 n., 551, 557, 565, 583, 584,
623, 663 n., 667, 736, 828 n.
Daphne 751, 752
Dead Sea 57, 62-64, 69, 70, 98, 104,
109, 119, 185, 417, 419, 559,
590, 618, 619, 649 n., 655

Dedan 155, 904 n., 905
Deir 'Alla 214, 220, 223, 263, 264,
    290, 319, 327, 338, 485 n., 605,
    648, 649 n., 650
Deir el-Balah 66, 299, 321, 322, 323
Delta 44, 53, 132, 136, 165, 188-92,
    200, 287 n., 299, 300, 304,
    305 n., 306, 321, 637, 671, 673,
    696, 709, 747, 750, 751, 825,
    834, 859, 872, 905 n.
Denyen 297, 300, 308, 309, 321 n.,
    322
Dhībân 274, 324, 416, 579, 580
Dibon 274, 410, 416, 572 n., 579, 580,
    581, 650 n., 655
Dilmun 177, 693 n.
Diyala River 123, 814
Djahi 206, 271, 296, 298, 396
Dor 31, 63, 221, 263, 275, 296, 300-
    304, 319, 320 n., 324, 469, 521,
    636 n., 809, 825
Dothan 69, 244, 273 n., 280, 351, 667
    Valley 351, 364, 421 n., 428, 510 n.
Dumah 69, 904 n.
Dūr-Sharrukīn 473, 572 n.
Du'ru 636, 668, 807, 809

Eben-ezer 353n 3
Ebla 138, 140-43, 145, 148, 154, 175,
    178, 181, 328, 529
Ecbatana 812, 835 n., 848, 857
Edom 36, 64, 67, 215, 220, 234 n.,
    273, 277 n., 287 n., 288, 304 n.,
    407, 416-20, 434 n., 435 439,
    444, 480, 485, 505, 515 n., 516,
    522, 523, 544 n., 556, 596, 598,
    611, 613, 631-33, 637, 641, 642,
    644, 651-53, 656-64, 685, 692-
    96, 698, 700 n., 708, 717, 721,
    723, 725, 727, 729 n., 733,
    747 n., 758, 792, 795, 802, 804,
    805, 826, 830, 833, 890, 905
Edomites 30, 183, 358, 362, 418, 419,
    421, 453, 460, 484, 503, 505,
    513, 523 n., 543, 545 n., 566,
    589, 597, 598, 626 n., 634, 653,
    658-61, 663, 664, 684, 698, 715-
    17, 724, 780, 785 n., 787, 795,

    805, 823, 825, 826, 828, 831,
    835, 843, 858, 860 n., 876 n.,
    889, 890, 898, 903, 905, 906
Egypt 36, 41, 45, 47, 50, 53-54, 56,
    66-69, 115, 116 n., 117, *passim*
Egyptians 29, 133, 155, 207, 222 n.,
    225 n., 230, 231, 235, 236, 247,
    249, 252, 254, 266, 273, 280,
    299-302, 306, 310, 314, 322, 323,
    349, 359, 386, 432, 450 n., 474,
    475, 483, 505, 532, 538, 546 n.,
    566, 623, 667, 668-70, 673, 674,
    692, 695 n., 708, 710, 713, 726-
    29, 750-52, 756, 758, 763, 765,
    768, 770 n., 773, 780, 781,
    788 n., 791-94, 796, 807-809,
    812, 818, 826, 852-53, 857, 858,
    861, 870, 882, 892, 897
Ekron 68, 310-12, 326 n., 329, 332,
    507, 588, 591, 664, 674 n., 692-
    93, 695-96, 709-10, 713-14, 716,
    768, 769 n., 784
Ekwesh 292, 326 n.
Elah Valley 310 n., 456, 711
Elam 185, 716, 720 n., 748, 691, 741,
    749, 753, 791, 817-19
Elamites 185, 691, 694 n., 695, 741,
    749-50, 756, 835
Elath 254, 626, 627, 633, 660, 684
Elealeh 414, 590
Elephantine 751, 760, 768, 818 n.,
    819 n., 822, 868 n., 869-72, 877,
    880, 889 n., 894, 902
Eltekeh 506, 695
Emar 177, 202
'En-Gedi 109, 123, 723, 729-30, 787,
    795, 890, 905
'En Gev 524-25, 565, 639
Enkomi 167, 309 n., 331 n.
Ephraim 60, 219-20, 230 n., 279, 347,
    376, 388, 421-22, 424, 438, 440,
    443, 444 n., 463, 469 n., 494,
    510 n., 544, 666, 701, 702, 706,
    832
Ephraimites 178, 383 n., 388, 403,
    421 n., 423, 438, 457 n., 633, 661
Ephron 557, 563
Erich 117

Erech 117
Esdraelon Valley 63, 114, 130, 189 n., 233, 378 n., 442
Eshnunna 152, 176
Ethiopians 155, 519 n.
Euphrates River 58, 61, 68, 100, 107, 117, 134, 137, 141, 152, 154, 175, 175 n., 177, 179, 182 n., 189, 225, 231, 234, 327, 393, 395, 482, 484, 507, 520 n., 756, 760, 763, 764 n., 766, 814, 821
Eziongeber 505, 516, 517 n., 522, 588, 589, 596, 598, 658-60

Gad 402 n., 410, 413, 416, 445, 448 469 n., 488, 496, 514
Gadora 642 n.
Gal'aza 619 n., 635, 640, 641, 643, 649 n., 764, 805, 807, 823, 830
Galilee 57, 70, 130, 147, 150, 184, 203, 213, 220, 226 n., 229, 244, 248 n., 249, 255, 259, 271, 273, 274 n., 278-79, 335, 339, 340, 342, 364, 396 n., 399, 429, 434 n., 443, 445, 449, 465, 476, 482, 483, 489, 496, 512, 513, 517, 543, 558, 565, 570, 584, 591, 606, 607, 613 n., 619, 635, 640, 665 n., 666, 794, 809, 823, 825, 828 n., 890, 903
  Sea of 61, 444-45
Gari 247, 278
Gath 68, 245 n., 307 n., 310, 312, 326, 459-60, 606, 609, 626-27, 693, 696, 698, 700, 711, 712 n.
Gath-padalla 245, 511 n.
Gath-rimmon 245, 307 n.
Gaza 56, 59, 61, 63, 68, 124, 167-68, 189, 194 n., 222 n., 226, 232, 236, 247-49, 252, 278, 300, 306, 310-11, 313, 321-22, 326-27, 610, 627, 630, 633, 635, 637, 651, 656, 672, 674-75, 684-85, 692, 695 n., 696, 708, 710, 713-16, 724, 727, 759 n., 763, 766, 768-69, 781-82, 787, 789, 802, 805, 807-808, 817 n., 825, 834, 853, 855, 895-96

Geba 433, 468, 565, 763
Gebelein 133, 165 n.
Gerar 61, 184, 566, 697 n.
Gerasa 114, 402
Geshur 359, 399, 400, 407, 444, 464, 492, 496, 497, 506, 511, 558 n.
Geshurites 399 n., 443
Gezer 45, 130, 167, 189 n., 198, 201, 205, 230, 238, 244-47, 266, 275, 283-85, 287, 300, 339, 342, 346 n., 433, 468, 505, 507, 510 n., 519, 525-26, 531, 556, 559, 591, 667, 668, 738, 795, 827, 864, 872, 890
ghor 118, 119, 558 n.
Gibbethon 506, 559, 569, 591, 695
Gibeah 360 n., 433, 563
Gibeon 151, 167, 324, 343 435, 436, 438, 453, 464, 468, 472, 504, 539 n., 545 n., 556, 736, 791, 795, 806, 858, 865
Gibeonites 361-62, 419, 421, 428, 432, 435, 437-38, 456, 472, 477, 479, 503, 513
Gihon 499, 697, 737
Gilead 64, 301 n., 374, 380 n., 400, 402-404, 407, 440, 441, 444-46, 469 n., 488, 494, 496, 510 n., 512-14, 557, 558, 594 n., 605, 619 n., 634 n., 635, 639-42, 644, 649 n., 655, 805, 823 n.
Gileadites 400, 403, 409, 423, 461, 479, 497 n., 543, 632, 649 n., 650
Gilgal 87, 88 n., 267 n., 361 n., 378, 426, 438 n., 495, 622
Giloh 338, 351 n., 356, 357, 422, 466
Golan 61, 64, 130, 399, 402, 445, 558, 618, 639, 832
Gomer 694, 741
Gomorrah 61, 185
Goren-ha-atad 230 n.
Gozen 528, 670
Greece 24, 123, 221-22, 266 n., 290, 292 n., 317, 318 n., 516 n., 758, 826, 828, 853, 856-57, 862, 897 n.
Greeks 305 n., 692, 751, 752, 760, 767, 768, 779, 783, 810, 813,

818, 827, 828, 853-56, 858, 861, 862, 872, 873, 887 n., 892, 893
Gubba 400
Guti 732, 749
Gutians 142
Gurgum 612, 628
Guzana 395 n., 670

Habur River 225, 395 n., 399 n., 670
Ḥadid 765 n., 864 n.
Hadrach 612, 680 n.
Hagrites 448, 515 n.
Halab 175, 177 n., 199 n., 202, 213
Hama 130, 131, 148, 483
Hamath 61, 234 n., 244, 270, 483-84, 507 n., 522, 577, 610, 612, 613, 617-19, 671, 674, 677, 678, 705, 720 n., 769, 797
Hamath-Luash 612, 617
Haneans 176
Hanigalbat 212, 392, 446 n.
Harran 67, 177, 183, 746, 757, 759, 764 n., 810, 833
Hatarikka 612, 680 n.
Hatti 47, 185, 212 n., 238, 241, 275, 284, 285, 292-94, 298, 314, 395, 484, 610 n., 655, 743, 781, 785, 792
Hattusas 177, 294
Hauran 64, 506, 512 n., 592-94, 636, 639, 642
Haurina 641, 652, 823
Hazor 68, 128-30, 145 n., 149, 150, 161 n., 165, 168, 174, 177, 191, 199, 201-203, 205, 213, 223, 224, 245-48 n., 255-59, 271, 289, 319, 337, 341, 348 n., 364, 365, 380 n., 396 n., 506, 512, 525, 526, 529 n., 531 n., 532, 557, 565, 583, 584, 592, 606, 613 n., 615, 635, 643, 644, 666-69, 718, 721, 736, 749 n., 784, 807, 809, 823, 834, 890, 892, 896 n.
Hazrak 611, 680 n.
Hebrews 236 n., 248, 437, 438
Hebron 69, 150, 186 n., 196 n., 207, 219, 245 n., 250, 356, 357, 399, 413, 450, 461-64, 467, 473-74,

477-78, 481, 493, 497, 503 n., 523, 560, 659 n., 698-700, 788, 805, 826, 843
Heliopolis 191 n., 300, 747
Hepher 422, 428-29, 439, 510
Heshbon 214, 343, 403 n., 407 n., 412-14, 512, 590, 649 n., 655, 833-34
Hill of God 324, 433, 436
Ḥisbân 349 n., 414, 415
Hittites 29, 60, 185, 186 n., 209-11, 213, 217, 218, 224, 231, 237, 239, 242, 243, 250, 258, 266, 268-73, 275, 282, 290, 292-94, 334-35, 364, 404, 483, 487-89 n., 522, 647, 688 n., 692, 882, 883
Hivites 60, 207, 348 n., 361, 421 n., 489
Huleh
  Lake 57, 163
  Valley 64, 150
Hurrians 58, 60, 116 n., 130, 173, 178, 185, 187, 192 n., 202, 207-13, 232-35, 239, 249, 250, 328, 361, 421 n.
Hurrite 207 n.
Hurru 60, 173, 213, 234
Hyksos 187, 189-96, 206, 207, 217-19, 225, 230, 275, 306, 316

Idalion 533 n.
Idumaea 57, 805, 825, 829-30, 843, 844, 864, 892, 903
Ijon 512, 565, 584, 635
Inandik 363
Ionia/Ionians 692, 751, 802 n., 826, 853, 856, 872 n., 894
Irbid 148, 214, 220, 223-24, 401, 593 n., 594 n., 640
Irqata 244, 392
Ishmaelites 904 n.
Israel 35, 37-39, 44-46, 48-49, 52, 231, 266 n., 277 n., 279, 284-88, 320 n., 329, 334, 335, 338 n., 344, 345, 347 n., 348, 349, 353, 366, 369, 371, 373, 376, 377, 383, 385 n., 387, 390, 395, 396, 404-407, 409, 413, 419, 422 n.,

423-25, 427-430, 437 n., 440,
443, 447-49, 451, 452, 454, 456,
459, 463-68, 478, 481, 483, 484,
489, 492 n., 493-96, 506, 508,
515, 516, 519, 520, 526, 532,
535, 538, 541, 543-45, 547-50,
552-58, 561, 563-66, 568, 569,
571-79, 581, 584, 585, 587-96,
599, 605-608, 611-21, 624, 628,
630-33, 635-37, 639-41, 644,
650 n., 651-56, 659, 661, 666-70,
672-74, 676 n., 677, 680, 681,
683, 684, 687 n., 689, 690,
706 ḥ., 725 n., 740 n., 741, 764,
777, 792, 816, 826, 835, 878,
880, 881, 883, 884, 886, 900

Israelites 38, 40-42, 44, 45, 49, 154,
156, 182, 187, 252, 277, 278,
286, 301 n., 304 n., 307 n., 325,
337, 340-42, 344, 345, 348, 352-
56, 364, 368, 377-78, 381-82 n.,
390, 402, 404, 410, 412-15, 418,
427, 432, 439, 441, 447-50, 456,
457, 459, 465, 468-70, 473, 477,
479, 480, 493 n., 495, 496, 498,
503, 507, 512, 513, 531, 536,
538, 546-47, 550-51, 553, 556,
559, 563, 569, 570, 578-80, 583,
591, 592, 594 n., 597 n., 615-19,
622, 623, 625, 640, 641, 649 n.,
650 n., 660, 667 n., 668, 669,
671, 679, 683, 686, 688, 744,
807, 816, 817, 822, 844, 845,
863, 870, 899, 902

Issachar 233, 378 380 n., 382, 442 n.,
443, 465, 513, 832

Issos 894

'Izbet Ṣarṭah 311, 326, 338, 351 n.,
353-56, 357

Jabbok River 400-402, 407, 441, 446,
494-95, 512, 605, 650 n., 832

Jabesh-Gilead 266 n., 404, 405, 422,
440-42 446-48, 450, 461, 463,
545 n., 631 n.

Jabin 434 n.

Jabneh 434 n., 626, 760

Jacob-el 230

Jaffa 275, 311, 752

Jahaz 412, 415, 580, 581

Jarmuth 247

Jawa 164, 215, 337, 590

Jazer 403 n., 407 n., 488, 590

Jeb 760, 768, 869

Jeba 433 n.
    Bishri 153, 178 n., 393, 394
    Kebir, el 386 n.
    Musa 66
    Serbal 66, 417

Jebusites 60, 348 n., 356-57, 361,
374 n., 428, 448, 455, 467, 468,
470, 471, 473-75, 477, 479, 486,
489 n., 497-99, 503, 508, 527,
528, 544, 702, 719 n., 882, 883

Jehud 510, 779 n., 831 n.

Jenin 69, 246

Jerahmeelites 419, 422, 460, 462

Jerash 214, 402

Jericho 67, 84, 87-89, 91, 94-96, 104,
106, 113, 118, 119, 130, 134,
143, 148, 149, 161, 165, 166,
168, 171, 189 n., 193 n., 196 n.,
200, 201, 218 n., 273, 343,
348 n., 495, 510, 557, 559, 583,
797, 807, 843, 892, 896 n.

Jerusalem 23, 35, 46, 51, 57 n., 63, 67,
69, 75, 151, 164, 170, 220, 244-
45, 247-48, 250, 258 n., 266 n.,
283 n., 322 n., 328, 350 n., 356-
57, 361, 374 n., 404 n., 419, 422,
425, 428, 435, 438 n., 445, 448,
452 n., 453, 455, *passim*

Jeshanah 557, 563

Jewish 634, 689 n., 706, 816 n., 822,
825, 829, 844, 848 n., 859, 864,
870-72, 878 n., 879, 881, 886-89,
892, 895 n., 902

Jews 186, 317, 882 n., 884, 900

Jezreel 440-44, 450, 463, 513, 584,
592-95, 599
    Corridor 442 n.
    plain of 41, 63, 132, 221 n., 450,
    462, 556, 809, 823
    Valley 57, 68-69, 113, 130, 131,
    150, 161, 163, 174, 184, 200,
    220, 227, 229, 233, 244, 245,

246, 319, 325, 346, 352, 365,
379, 382 n., 383, 437 n., 442,
445, 449, 465, 469 n., 476, 565,
594, 595, 666, 830, 832
Jib, el- 468, 795
Jokneam 68, 510
Jolan 399, 402, 618
Joppa 63, 68, 164, 221, 226-27, 230,
249, 251-52, 279, 292, 307 n.,
312, 479, 559, 591, 707, 709,
767, 825
Jordan 23, 57, 61-62, 72-75, 78, 83,
85, 91, 92 94, 95, 100, 104-109,
113, 125, 144, 148-50, 164, 214,
215, 221, 223, 266 n., 285 n.,
290, 319, 321, 324, 337, 338,
349, 353 n., 376, 398, 400-
403 n., 409, 411, 434 n., 437 n.,
445, 593, 594, 626 n., 644,
688 n., 800 n., 832, 833, 902, 905
River 28, 39, 56, 61, 64, 69, 70, 129,
153, 230 n., 278, 381, 399, 401,
407, 409 n., 440, 446, 462 n.,
479, 482, 485 n., 495, 512, 591,
805
Valley 35, 53, 62, 66, 69, 87, 92, 96,
114, 130, 144-46, 150, 151, 161,
163, 164, 166, 174, 184, 196 n.,
198, 199, 204 n., 214, 215, 220,
223, 224, 263, 264, 270, 319,
320, 327, 350 n., 365, 402, 407,
439, 442, 446, 485 n., 510-13,
555, 557-59, 572, 590, 605, 642,
643, 648-50, 808, 832
Judah 30, 35, 42-44, 46, 48, 49, 52, 60,
178, 187, 283 n., 330 n., 356,
371, 376, 399, 409, 419, 422,
427 n., 433, 435, 448, 455-56,
passim
mountains of 49, 63, 65, 187 n.,
360, 378 n., 428-29, 450
Judahites 154, 156, 183, 325, 330 n.,
356, 432, 439, 452, 456, 462,
468, 473, 479, 488, 496, 498,
503, 504 n., 536, 540, 543, 544,
554, 563, 589, 615, 620, 657,
660, 663, 670, 673 n., 686,
687 n., 688, 697, 704, 706, 715,

716, 719, 720, 723, 724 n., 729,
734-35, 739, 752, 782 n., 788,
791, 792, 796, 798-801, 806, 811,
815, 817, 818 n., 819, 822, 824,
835, 838-41, 844-46, 851, 852,
859, 862, 863, 866, 867, 870,
871, 873-75, 877, 883, 884, 888
Judea 57, 151, 890
Judean 457 n., 545 n., 844, 875,
882 n., 896
desert 110, 340-41, 717, 729-30,
831-32
foothills 128
hills 65, 150, 220, 320, 357, 360,
361, 369, 418, 422, 437, 459-63,
505, 516, 522, 698, 700, 715,
724, 729 n., 796, 820, 831
wilderness 715, 799 n., 831

Kabul 506, 512
Kadesh-Barnea 62, 616, 626, 627 n.,
905
Kadytis 759 n.
Kalah 582 n.
Kamid el-Loz 241, 256, 335, 533
Kar-Esarhaddon 743
Kār-Tukulti-Ninurta 473, 572 n.
Karnak 45, 206, 226, 228, 230, 238,
249, 254, 270, 271, 284, 287,
301, 395, 554
Kashka 293, 294
Kassites 404
Keftiu 314-16
Keilah 245 n., 843
Kenath 247, 558 n.
Kenites 358, 419, 422, 439, 460, 462
Kenizzites 376, 419, 422
Kerak 39, 78, 80, 589, 653 n., 654 n.
Kfar Monash 110
Kharu 60, 173, 213, 234, 238, 284,
285
Khirbet
'Al, el- 414, 415, 590
Abu et-Twain 796, 826
'Ara'ir 654 n.
Duwwara, ed- 438
Fahil 214

Hajjar, al- 408, 641, 807, 808
Hajjar, el- 338
Iskander 144, 149
Kerak 113, 118, 129-131
Medeyeine, 3l- 412 n., 580 n.
Medeiyine South 411
Meshâsh, el- 201, 357, 460, 722
Muqanna', el- 311, 331, 693 n.,
    709 n.
'Oreimeh, el- 233
Selah, es- 435
Qom, el- 526 n.
Qureyie, el- 580
Rabud 220, 356
Raddana 336, 338, 360-64
Sheikh 'Ali 96, 99
Kidron Valley 499, 567, 697, 737, 771
Kiriath-Jearim 362, 455 n., 456, 471,
    472, 510 n., 789
Kirkuk 210, 213
Kish 140 n., 142
Kition 197 n., 221 n., 302, 331, 708 n.,
    890
Kittim 708, 723 n., 767, 769
Knossos 190, 221, 314, 315
Kültepe 158, 209
Kumidi 241, 248, 271
Kummu 628
Kuntillet 'Ajrud 22, 417 n., 616,
    627 n., 735 n.
Kythera 315

Lachish 245 n., 247, 614, 698, 709,
    711-13, 720, 795, 796
Lagash 142, 153
Laish 163 n., 177 n., 201, 202, 398,
    680 n.
  Chinneroth 639
  Kinnereth 565
  Tiberias 53, 762, 64, 70, 73, 76,
    129, 247, 270, 278, 399, 524,
    576, 828 n.
  Van 213, 652
Larnaka 221 n., 535
Lebanon 62, 63, 67, 70, 72, 78, 81, 83,
    91, 100, 105, 128, 147, 149, 150,
    165, 170, 171, 244, 270, 271,
    304 n., 364, 394, 434 n., 479,

486, 507 n., 529-31, 571, 640,
    781 n., 821 n.
Lebo-Hamath 482-83, 506, 617-19
Leontopolis 197, 637, 673, 903
Libnah 558 n., 598, 659 n., 700, 711,
    712
Libya 171, 282, 285, 545, 554, 566,
    853
Libyan 133, 160, 165 n., 168, 282,
    283, 295, 299, 306, 751, 803 n.
Lidebir (*see* Lodebar) 444, 445
Lisan Lake 62
  peninsula 118, 144
Lod 510, 557 n., 765 n., 863, 864 n.
Lodebar 404 n., 444, 445, 497 n., 617-
    18
Lud 313, 741 n.
Lukka 289, 293-94
Luxor 273, 410
Lydia/Lydian 312 n., 313, 741 n., 748,
    761, 812, 854

Maacah 398-400, 481, 483, 506
Macedonia/Macedonians 834, 853,
    892, 893, 896, 899, 901
Machir 380 n., 469 n., 558 n.
Madaba 580, 654 n.
  plain 285 n., 349, 446
Magdali 745
Magdolos 759 n., 789
Magidu 636, 764, 807, 809, 823
Mahanaim 319, 404 n., 407 n., 440,
    441, 463, 494, 496, 497, 512,
    514, 556, 558
Ma'in 580, 590
Makmish 873 n., 890
Manasseh 220, 245, 280, 281, 347,
    363-66, 382, 383, 413, 421 n.,
    429, 439, 442 469 n., 510, 624,
    702, 706, 715, 747, 832
Mansuate 611 n., 636, 642
Mareshah 700, 711-12, 826
Mari 58, 68, 142-43, 172, 175-181,
    183, 185, 189 n., 202, 203, 208,
    213, 314, 392-93, 405
Medeba 579, 580, 590
Medes 630, 742, 756, 757, 759, 812

Medinet Habu 289, 295-98, 303, 309, 364, 395, 532, 537

Media 670-71, 819, 835 n., 848, 869, 896

Mediterranean 76, 79, 87, 100, 282, 288, 293 n., 479, 630
  Sea 56, 61, 63, 66, 142, 143, 218, 220, 223, 291, 302, 313, 334, 335, 402, 511, 516, 571, 594, 602, 744, 768, 802 n., 854

Megiddo 68, 113, 117, 118, 123, 129, 132-34, 145, 147-50, 161-62, 164, 166-68, 171, 174, 198-202, 204, 205, 219, 221 n., 224, 226, 227, 229-30, 232-33, 236, 246, 251, 255-57, 259, 277-79, 291, 300, 306, 319, 320, 324, 338, 339, 351, 379, 380, 440, 442, 450 n., 469, 511-12, 521, 526, 528, 531, 534, 556, 583, 599, 606 n., 615, 635-36, 643, 644, 647, 666-68, 721, 759, 764-66, 794, 809, 827

Melid 612, 628

Meluḫḫa 693 n., 710, 732, 749

Memphis 189, 267, 269, 298, 300, 673, 693 n., 746, 747, 818, 837, 853

Mephaat 407 n., 590

Meshwesh 282, 299

Mesopotamia 30, 47, 50, 67, 108, 116, 117, 120-23, 133, 137, 140, 142-43, 152-56, 159, 161, 170 n., 172, 174-76, 179, 181-83, 185, 186 n., 197, 200 n., 202-204, 208, 210-12, 214, 258, 287-88, 290, 314, 363, 366, 392-93, 395 n., 480, 487, 509 n., 528, 603, 604, 607, 620, 636, 683, 707, 741 n., 758, 759, 793, 812, 814, 821, 826, 846, 886, 891

Meunites 626, 633, 656, 697

Michmash 360, 433, 438, 449, 807

Midian 170 n., 254

Midianites 359, 382, 383 n., 417, 418, 650 n.

Migdal-Shechem 366 n., 386, 387

Migdol 745, 751, 759 n., 834

Minet el-Beida 262 n., 302

Minnith 407

Mishor 409, 415, 496, 514, 590

Mittani 206, 207, 212, 213, 217, 218, 225-26, 229, 231, 233, 234, 237-39, 241, 242, 268, 269, 275, 314, 392, 484

Mizpah 353 n., 360, 426, 428, 565, 566 591, 615, 798, 799, 801, 806, 834, 843, 851, 865

Moab 36, 38, 39, 63-65, 67, 70, 166 n., 215, 220, 273, 274, 288, 334, 349, 377, 378, 385, 392, 403, 406, 407, 410, 411, 414 n., 422, 444, 455 n., 480, 481, 488, 514, 515 n., 537, 544, 558, 572, 579, 581, 589-91, 597 n., 598, 605, 618-20, 631, 632, 637, 641, 642, 644, 650-57, 659, 664, 675 685, 688, 692-96, 708, 747 n., 750, 758, 785, 792, 800, 802, 804, 805, 830, 833

Moabites 30, 37-39, 65, 183, 377, 378, 409, 410, 415, 439, 448, 481, 574, 590, 593 n., 596, 649 n., 653-56, 823, 825, 835, 858, 867, 876 n., 882, 889

Mount
  Amanus 571
  Carmel 434 n., 443, 594 n., 595 n., 619, 636
  Cassius 59, 132, 834
  Ebal 351 n., 366, 386 n., 902
  Ephraim 39, 63, 64, 69, 245, 378, 434, 510, 624
  Gerizim 203, 263-64, 366 n., 868 n., 900-904
  Gilboa 266 n., 432, 440-43, 449, 462 n.
  Hermon 62, 64, 68, 70, 399, 434 n., 489, 506
  Lebanon 176, 394
  Nebo 214, 324 n.
  Olives, of 493 n., 538
  Tabor 233 n., 379, 380 n., 382 n.
  Yarmuta 270, 271 n.
  Zalmon 366 n., 386

Moreshet-Gath 559 n., 711, 712, 789

Mosad Mazal 96, 99
Munhata 99, 104-106
Mureybet 90, 93, 95, 204
Mushki 293, 294, 692, 693 n.
Mycenae 263 n., 315
Mycenaeans 221, 281, 290, 291, 330,
  331, 334

Nabateans 57, 654, 660 n., 808, 890,
  904 n., 906
Nahal
  Besor 66, 189, 298
  Mishmar cave 110
Naharin 206, 225 232, 238
Nahariya 74, 198
Nahr ek-Kalb 271, 594 n., 744-46,
  781 n.
Naphtali 40, 41, 325, 347, 379, 383,
  442 n., 465, 479, 512, 533, 565,
  584
Naukratis 751, 752
Naur 407-409, 590, 808
Nebaioth 739, 750, 905 n.
Nebo 580, 590, 656
Neges 234, 235
Negev 22, 43, 65, 67, 69, 70, 80, 83,
  90, 115, 122-25, 134, 139, 147,
  149, 150, 184, 225, 256 n.,
  262 n., 273, 310 n., 340, 341,
  346, 349, 356, 357-60, 376, 417,
  429, 433, 439, 459, 460, 469,
  475 n., 485, 489, 505 n., 507,
  522-24, 543, 555-56, 560, 627,
  631, 634, 635, 658, 659, 661,
  663, 684, 697, 704, 715, 716,
  722, 724, 725, 727, 729 n., 747,
  748 n., 763, 769, 779, 780, 795,
  808, 825, 831, 890, 904-906
Nephat-Dor 511
Nile River 63, 117, 137, 166 n., 188,
  296, 751, 761, 818, 852, 861,
  890, 891, 893
Nimrud 534, 582 n., 642 n., 650, 651,
  657, 668, 741 n.
Ninevah 47, 453 n., 571, 642 n., 645,
  664, 712, 714, 716, 720, 732,
  742, 743 n., 747, 750, 755, 757,
  758, 760, 764-66, 784

Nippur 142, 143 n.
Nob 327 n., 422, 493 n.
Nora 296 n.
Nubia 60, 162, 170, 171, 187, 188,
  192 n., 232 n., 233, 237, 272,
  300, 304, 321, 545, 555, 637,
  693 n., 710 n., 741 n., 791, 871
Nubian 133, 160, 165 n., 247, 322,
  566
Nuhashshe 225, 234, 243, 268
Nuzi 58, 183, 185, 208, 210, 211

Ono 557 n., 765 n., 863, 864
Ophel 627, 737, 864 n.
Ophir 328, 516, 517, 588, 658
Ophrah 382-84, 421
Orontes River 67, 74, 213, 229, 231,
  232, 234 n., 243, 272, 483,
  484 n., 577, 759
  Valley 62, 72, 163, 225, 226 n.,
  238, 244, 277 n., 571, 610

Palestinian 390, 692, 734, 741
Palmyra 152, 392, 506
Paran 64, 328, 417, 453, 503
  plateau of 65, 69
Parthia 819, 879
Pathros 313, 720 n.
Pehel 35, 246, 247
Peleponese 222, 315
Peleset/Purasti 295, 296, 298, 300, 302,
  308, 309, 316 n., 322
Pelethites 459, 474, 475 n.
Pella 35, 57, 74, 145, 214, 220, 223,
  224, 246, 247, 270, 406 n., 411
Pelusium 676 n., 751
Penuel 382, 548, 549, 555 n., 558
Perizzites 348 n., 489 n., 882, 883
Persia/Persian 200, 508 n., 566, 603,
  765 n., 766 n., 777, 779 n., 788,
  804, 806, 807, 810-14, 816-19,
  821-37, 839-43, 847-50, 852-64,
  866-80, 882, 885-92, 894, 896-
  99, 904, 905
  Gulf 121, 142, 182 n., 692, 693 n.
Petra 91, 92, 96, 214, 419, 659 n., 662,
  808, 905 n.
Philistia 311, 329, 405, 450, 468-69 n.,

520 n., 526, 611, 619, 657, 659, 675, 690, 696, 729, 731, 744, 745 n., 747 n., 752, 759 n., 784

Philistines 31, 36, 41, 43, 45, 62, 66, 155, 184, 218, 294-99, 303, 306-14, 316-21, 324, 325, 327-29, 331, 333, 335, 340, 355, 360, 374 n., 376, 378, 380, 388, 390, 414 n., 422, 424, 426-28, 432-34, 436-39, 443, 449, 450, 452, 456, 459, 460, 462, 463, 466-69, 475, 479, 480, 482, 486, 487, 505, 510, 515, 519, 521, 526, 559, 566 569, 591, 596, 598 603, 605, 606, 609, 610, 615, 626-28, 633-36, 666, 667 n., 674, 676, 680 n., 681, 684, 685, 687 n., 690, 692-94, 696 698, 700 n., 707, 711, 715-17, 719, 721, 724, 727-30, 735, 742, 747, 748, 751, 752, 758, 763, 767, 778, 781, 792, 804, 822, 835, 858

Phoenicia/Phoenician 24, 58, 59, 221, 223, 229, 244, 248 n., 250, 254, 271, 278, 304, 305 n., 316 n., 359, 396 n., 405, 483, 486, 487, 515-17, 528, 531-34, 556, 565, 571, 574 n., 583, 586, 587, 595, 602, 603, 607, 615, 628-30, 633, 634, 657, 658, 675, 676, 688 n., 695, 707-709, 713, 714, 717, 731, 739, 744, 750-52, 758, 761-63, 778, 781 n., 784, 792, 793, 802, 804, 809, 810, 817-18, 821, 823, 825-30, 835, 843, 854, 858, 862, 873, 890-97

Phrygia 693 n., 826 n., 872 n.
Phrygians 293 n.
Pirathon 374, 376, 421
Pithom 287 n., 673 n.
Pozo Moro 688 n.
Punic 688 n., 826
Put 60, 761

Qadesh 29, 213, 226, 229, 231, 232, 237, 238, 243, 268, 270-73, 275, 288, 298

Qarnaim 273, 445, 512, 617, 618, 636, 642
Qarnini 642, 823
Qarqar 562, 577, 578 n., 579, 581, 601, 602, 641, 644 n., 715
Qatna 68, 147, 148, 167, 172, 177, 201, 202, 213, 231, 241, 243, 268, 288, 392
Qedem 168, 206
Qedar 784, 859
Qedarites 656, 739, 749, 750, 864, 904 n., 905
Qitmit 780
Qubur el-Walaida 311, 326
Que 522, 610, 612
Quramatu 760, 764 n.
Qumran 729, 730

Rabbah 405, 485, 497 n.
Rabbath-Ammon 69, 404 n., 405, 408 n., 448, 641, 642, 644 n., 794
Ramah 361 n., 421, 424, 426, 428, 433, 564 565, 798
Ramallah 360, 434 n.
Ramath-Negev 780, 787
Ramat Matred 358, 525, 826
Ramat-Rahel 615, 761, 762, 795, 869
Ramoth-Gilead 400 n., 412, 514 n., 525, 576, 592-94, 639-41
Rapihu 745
Ras Ibn Hani 302, 331 n.
Ras Shamra 96, 97, 99, 107, 111, 148, 208, 211, 293 n., 302 n., 327 n.
Rebu 282, 285 n.
Red Sea 29, 62, 72, 121, 122, 165 n., 480, 518 n., 598
Rehob 170, 278, 395, 398, 556
Retenu 166, 168, 169, 192, 225, 229, 232, 249, 274, 277, 288 n., 386, 624 n.
Reubenites 413, 416, 448
Rhodes 826, 893
Riblah 759, 760, 764 n., 765, 767, 781 785, 794, 797, 874
Rosh Hanniqra 128, 130
Rujm el-Malfuf 641 n., 807

Sabean 519, 674

Sahab 214, 220, 266 n., 324, 339,
404 n., 411, 647
Sais 637, 672-73, 732 n., 734, 746 n.,
747, 754 801, 818, 834, 853, 872,
877
Sakkara 170
Salamis 221, 300 n., 857, 858, 873,
890
Sam'al 395 n., 528, 612, 630, 657,
746
Samaria 69, 379 n., 534, 549, 572,
575, 576, 582-83, 585, 588, 590,
592, 594, 595, 599, 614, 619,
622-24, 630, 632, 636, 643,
651 n., 655 n., 669 n., 670-72,
674, 676, 677, 679, 684 n., 689,
690 n., 691, 693, 705-707, 715,
735, 750, 762, 807, 822, 827,
830, 834, 858, 861, 868, 869,
870-72, 882 n., 889, 896, 898-
903
Samaritans 706 n., 848 n., 868 n., 889,
892, 900, 902, 904
Samerina 61, 541 n., 563 n., 573 n.,
582 n., 611, 620 n., 670-72 n.,
677, 679, 706, 730, 744, 751,
764, 779, 780, 801, 805, 807,
816, 823, 830, 832, 843-45, 848,
859, 867 n., 871, 889, 892, 899,
900, 902, 903
Sardinia 296, 517 n.
Sardis 748, 812, 842 n., 895
Scythia/Scythians 742, 756 n., 761 n.,
819
Sea Peoples 31, 32, 45, 266 n., 288,
290 n., 291-94, 297-302, 305-
309, 316 n., 318, 321 n., 322-24,
326 n., 327, 345, 349, 364, 396,
402, 406, 412, 454, 537, 559
Seir 64, 234 n., 277 n., 287 n., 328,
417, 453, 503, 596, 614 n., 657-
58, 687 n.
Semites 154-57, 170 n., 173, 185,
188 n., 189-91, 193 n., 248,
252 n., 253, 266, 274, 286, 302,
350, 392, 402, 202, 554
Sepharvaim 677, 678, 705

Serabit el-Khadem 66, 70, 124, 238 n.,
239, 250 n.
Shaalbim 510, 591
Shamir 378, 379 n.
Shardannu 295, 296
Sharon Plain 62, 201, 233, 245, 246,
292, 510, 511, 825, 830
Sharuhen 194 n., 225
Shasu 225, 234-36, 238, 272, 276,
277, 296 n., 350, 353 n., 416
Shasu 225, 234-36, 238, 272, 276,
277, 287 n., 296 n., 350, 353 n.,
416
Sheba 155, 516, 518, 519 n.
Shechem 35, 69, 145, 145 n., 163,
165-67, 173, 174, 189 n., 196 n.,
197-200, 205-207, 214, 219, 244,
245, 246, 248, 250, 255, 264,
280, 291, 345, 348 n., 366 n.,
369 n., 375 n., 383-85, 387, 390,
428, 470, 504, 510, 545-49,
555 n., 583, 655 n., 667, 671 n.,
736, 800, 806 n., 829, 834, 853,
858, 900 n., 901-904
Shekelesh 282 n., 294 n., 295-96, 300,
308
Shephelah 62, 63, 150, 163, 247, 255,
281, 353, 598, 634, 684, 696 n.,
700, 828, 835, 844, 890
Sherden 276, 288, 289, 295, 297, 299,
306
Shiloh 196 n., 201, 203, 219, 220, 280,
351 n., 361, 367-69, 384, 388 n.,
389, 390, 421, 425 n., 428,
429 n., 453, 789, 800
Shinar 185, 720 n.
Shiqmona 189 n., 525
Shomeron 572, 616
Shunem 246, 440, 450, 513, 556
Shur 66 n., 69
Sicels 295, 296
Sidon 59-61, 70, 238, 289, 304,
305 n., 473, 489, 571 n., 586,
594, 602, 204, 659, 680 n., 695-
97, 707, 708 742, 787, 792, 802,
825 n., 827-28, 863, 873 n., 890-
94

Sidonians 155, 244, 303, 537, 571,
    572, 575, 680 n., 825
Simirra 671, 706
Simyra 231, 277
Sinai 56, 65, 66, 71, 83, 123-26 n.,
    131, 136, 147, 160, 205, 349,
    417, 434 n., 485, 503, 616, 630,
    653, 724, 744, 751, 808, 818,
    825, 890, 904
    peninsula 69, 70, 150, 165, 281,
    325, 626 n.
Sippar 142, 814
Socoh 233, 510, 556, 634, 699, 700
Sodom 61, 185
Spain 516 n., 688 n., 802 n.
Sparta 853, 872, 891
Succoth 264 382, 485 n.
Sumer 120, 121, 179, 452 n., 814
Ṣumur 243, 244, 248, 249, 278
Susa 177, 750, 756, 862 874
Suteans 176, 392, 410
Syria/Syrians 53, 54, 56-60, 62, 67, 70,
    72, 74, 76, 78, 81, 83, 89-91, 93-
    96, 99-100, 105, 107, 111, 125,
    129-31, 133, 136-40, 141-43,
    147-57, 159-62, 165, 167, 168,
    171-75, 178 n., 186, 187, 189,
    192-93, 197, 200, 202 n., 205,
    206, 208, 210, 213-17, 223-26,
    231, 233-35, 237, 238, 242, 243,
    248 n., 250, 255-58, 266, 268-71,
    273-77 n., 285-88, 290, 294, 297,
    298, 309, 314, 328 n., 363, 392,
    394-96, 398-400, 405 n., 410
    416 n., 434 n., 445, 454, 480,
    482, 483, 486, 487, 527, 52, 531,
    570, 571, 575, 577, 578, 582-84,
    592, 593m 601-605, 608, 610-13,
    617 n., 69 n., 620, 625, 628-30,
    634, 635, 639, 640, 652, 653,
    656, 661, 662, 664, 674, 678 n.,
    682, 692, 707, 733, 739, 748,
    750, 751, 758-60, 763, 766, 785,
    794, 806 n., 810, 817, 819,
    821 n., 828, 829, 869, 871 n.,
    896, 898
Syria-Palestine 41, 45, 47, 61, 67-68,
    70, 149, 152, 154, 159, 167-71,
    173-74, 184, 189, 194, 197,
    199 n., 206 n., 211, 213, 217,
    222, 231, 235, 237-41, 248, 252,
    254, 258, 270, 273, 275, 276 n.,
    318, 325, 336, 392, 396, 404,
    454, 468, 470, 474, 527 n., 530-
    32, 536, 568, 576, 77, 590, 602,
    603, 605, 607, 608, 610, 612,
    624 n., 628, 630, 631, 635, 637-
    38, 651 n., 656, 665, 667, 675,
    680 n., 683, 711, 712 n., 732,
    739, 742-44, 749, 760, 763, 778,
    781, 784, 802, 809, 815, 817,
    819, 826-27, 861, 871

Taʻanak 68, 201, 208, 227, 230, 232,
    236 n., 320 n., 337, 351, 379,
    380, 440, 469, 511, 556
Tabʼel 634, 642 n., 650
Tadmar 392, 393, 506
Tadmor 68, 152, 392, 393, 507
Tananir 203, 264
Tanis 172, 191 n., 192, 304, 329 n.,
    520, 637, 667
Tappuah 280, 631
Tarshish 516, 517 n., 518, 588, 589,
    596, 658, 802 n.
Tarsus 131, 223, 294
Tawilan 419, 662, 833 n.
Ṭayibeh, eṭ- 382 n., 400
Tebeṣ 385 n., 387
Tehenu 282, 284
Tekoa 63, 151, 621
Tēl
    Baṭash 311, 339
    Beer Sheba 725 n.
    Dan 202 n., 399 n., 565 n., 623
    ʻErani 113, 124-25, 130, 826
    Halif 125, 189 n., 459 n., 698
    Malḥata 358, 724, 726, 795
    Māśōś 201, 319, 340, 347, 357-60,
    418 n., 459 n. 460, 464 n., 722-
    24, 780, 795
    Mevorakh 201, 255, 263, 301, 338,
    890
    Michal 510 n., 826
    Miqne 311, 331, 709 n.
    Mor 307, 311

Poleg 164, 201
Sera' 311 n., 340, 729
Shiqmona 524, 890
Yin'am 335, 336
Zeror 164, 301, 319, 338
Teleilat Ghassul 109, 114
Tell
    Abū Hawām 221, 222, 255, 281 n.,
      289, 469, 525, 556, 826, 890, 897
    Abu Hureirah 93, 95-96, 99, 101,
      189, 359
    Abu Salima 675 n.
    'Aireni 113, 118
    'Ajjul, el- 163, 168, 189, 193 n.,
      194, 198, 200, 204, 222 n., 688 n.
    'Amal 524
    Amarna, el- 204 n., 207, 208,
      221 n., 235-36, 238-41, 247, 248,
      252, 253, 260 n., 267, 323, 392,
      393, 427
    'Amuq 107, 149
    Arad 358, 684, 769
    Aswad 90, 93, 97, 101
    Balata 348 n., 382 n., 384, 386 n.,
      647, 853, 855, 901
    Beit Mirsim 128, 134, 164, 173,
      189 n., 201, 204, 266 n., 348 n.,
      526, 698, 721, 722, 795
    Dab'a, el- 188, 190-93
    Dor 255
    Duweir, ed- 113, 128, 130, 163,
      184 n., 189 n., 201, 224, 251,
      255, 259, 283 n., 291, 300, 320,
      323, 332, 348 n., 418 n., 524,
      526, 667, 669 n., 698, 700,
      712 n., 717, 718, 721-23, 729,
      736 n., 738, 793, 795-97, 799,
      826, 827, 834 844, 864, 892,
      896 n., 903
    Esdar 358, 360
    Fara 152, 418 n.
    Far'ah, el- North (*see* Tirzah) 113,
      118, 128, 163, 262 339 n., 351 n.,
      572, 635, 643-44, 667
    Far'ah, el- South 66 n., 189, 194 n.,
      223, 299, 300, 311, 318, 320-22,
      405, 688 n.
    Fekheriye 683 n., 837 n.

Fukhar, el- 809, 897
Fûl, el- 336, 338, 351 n., 357 n.,
    360, 422, 806, 858
Halaf 395 n., 528, 670
Hayyat, el- 145-46, 164, 198, 214
Her, el- 751, 759 n., 834
Hesban 403 n., 414, 580
Hesi, el- 128, 163, 698, 727, 766,
    781, 844, 890
Husn, el- 148, 150, 220, 668
Jemme 189 n., 226, 298, 311, 330,
    721, 728, 729, 742, 752, 761,
    766, 781, 828, 890, 898
Jerishe 230, 307, 479
Keisan 319, 338-39, 342, 834
Kheleifeh, el- 626 n., 633 n., 660,
    661, 663, 890, 905
Mardikh 140, 148
Maskhuta, el- 859, 864
Mazar, el- 214, 220, 338, 339, 808
Milh, el- 358, 724
Mubarak 201, 263
Mughar, el- 507 n.
Muhafar, el- 428 n., 510 n.
Nagila 189 n., 201
Nasbeh, en- 13, 351 n., 360, 361,
    526 n., 565, 831 n., 834, 853,
    865, 869
Qasîle 263 n., 307, 311-12, 319,
    328-31, 338, 340, 342-33 n., 469,
    479-80, 518 n., 525, 667, 668,
    834
Qitmit 727 n.
Ramad 94, 97-98, 100, 101, 102
Rumeith, er- 525, 639-41
Safi, es- 189 n., 310, 700, 711, 826
Safut 201, 220, 641
Sa'idiyeh, es- 204 n., 220, 327,
    485 n., 511, 643, 644, 832
Shallaf, esh- 710
Shuna, esh- 113, 114 n., 129, 130
Sōfar 382 n., 386 n.
Ta'yinat 529, 531
'Umeiri, el- 354 n., 688 n., 800 n.
Yehudiyeh, el- 192, 197
Zakariyeh, ez- 710, 795
Tema' 519 n., 810, 904 n.
Teman 64, 328, 417, 453, 503, 616

Terqa 175, 179
Thebes 29, 45, 170, 189, 194, 196,
    224, 227 n., 233, 238 n., 239,
    240, 267, 283, 300, 304, 520,
    747, 894
Tigris River 177, 137, 182 n., 213,
    757, 814
Timna 70, 109, 201, 254-56 n., 311,
    339, 347, 359, 417, 418, 517 n.
Timnah 506, 510, 559, 634, 695
Tirzah 69, 165, 218, 219, 244, 387 n.,
    510 n., 549, 550, 556 n., 569,
    572, 631, 667
Tjeker 31, 45, 218, 295-303, 306, 308-
    10, 322, 324, 433, 486, 511
Tob 398-400, 407, 481, 506
Transjordan 22, 31, 39, 56-57, 61, 63-
    65, 67-69, 113, 114, 118, 121,
    131, 134, 139, 143, 144 146-52,
    155, 163-66 n., 170, 183, 201,
    214, 215, 220, 221, 223-25, 229-
    31, 241, 246, 247, 255, 263, 266,
    271, 276, 278, 285 n., 287, 288,
    290, 320, 336 n., 338, 339, 343,
    352, 373, 376, 377, 382, 392,
    398-405, 407, 409-13, 415, 418,
    422, 429, 432, 437, 439, 441,
    442, 444, 446, 448, 449, 461-
    63 n., 465, 478, 480, 481, 485 n.,
    486, 494, 496, 497 n., 512, 514,
    525, 548, 555, 557-59, 570, 572,
    575, 579, 590-92, 597 n., 605,
    609, 610, 613 n., 617-20, 631-
    33 n., 636, 640-42, 644, 648,
    651-56, 662, 665 n., 666, 675,
    682, 683, 697, 708, 709, 717,
    721, 723, 731, 733, 747, 749,
    750, 761, 763, 779, 801, 807,
    808, 824, 725, 829, 730, 833-35,
    859, 896, 904-906
Tripolis 273, 392, 893 n.
Troy 167, 209, 300 n., 315 n.
Ṭubaṣ 385 n., 387
Tubikh 396, 482
Tulul Dhahab, edh- 319, 441 n., 494,
    512
Tunip 213, 238, 244, 298
Tyre 35, 58-59, 68, 70, 188, 246, 270,
    271, 301, 445, 489, 506, 512,
    515-17, 525, 533, 534 n., 556,
    570, 571, 574, 575, 586, 591,
    594, 595, 602, 603, 607, 614,
    628-31 n., 633, 634, 636, 650,
    652, 659, 664, 669 n., 680 n.,
    694, 695, 707, 708, 715, 738 n.,
    739, 743, 747 n., 750, 753, 792,
    794, 801, 802, 805, 825, 828,
    854, 867, 890, 895-97

'Ubeidiya 53, 73-75
Ugarit 130, 145, 156, 159, 167, 172,
    177 n., 181, 198, 200, 208, 211,
    213, 218, 221-24, 232, 259 n.,
    268, 288-89, 292-94, 299 n., 302,
    328-29 n., 331 n., 353 n., 364 n.,
    393, 826
Ullaza 170, 249, 271
Ulu Burun 224 n.
Umm
    Biyara, el- 659 n., 662, 663
    Qatafa 75-76
Umma 142, 153
Umman-manda 757, 759
Upe 61, 247, 250, 276 n., 278, 411,
    506 n., 607 n.
Ur 30, 142, 152-54, 161, 175, 208
    of the Chaldeans 30, 182
Urartians 742
Uruk 117, 142, 750
Ushu 78, 739, 750

Valley of Rephaim 466, 468

Wâdī
    Araba 72, 77, 96, 254, 256 n.
    'Arish, el- 61, 66, 298, 306, 626,
        633, 675 n., 751
    Dâliyeh, ed- 151, 822, 827, 868,
        898, 901
    Far'ah 429 n., 495, 572
    Feinan 70, 109, 434 n., 657
    Feiran 69, 417, 485
    Ghazzeh 66, 298
    Hammamat 121, 122
    Hasā, el- 78, 80, 94 n., 147, 215,

409, 411, 417, 653, 805, 833, 889 n.

Jilat 91 n., 95

Kafrein 590, 808

Khabour 100, 108

Kufrinjeh 485 n.

Mujib 39, 64, 65, 94, 147, 274, 403, 409, 514, 579, 605, 653-55, 808

Mukkateb 69, 485

Rumemin, er- 402, 407, 641

Sheikh, esh- 485

Shu'eib 96, 98, 100, 101, 102-106, 641

Sir, es- 408, 808

Suwenit 438

Tumilat 44, 132, 165, 166, 287 n., 783

Yabis 405, 407, 446

Yarmuk 64, 400-402, 642

Zerqa 64-65, 147, 214, 264, 401, 402, 407, 495, 605, 832

Weshesh 295-97, 300, 308

Yabrud 76, 652

Yaham 226-27, 233

Yamhad 175-76, 201, 202

Yarkon River 230, 301, 307, 311, 468, 479, 510

Yarmuk River 61, 444, 445, 832

Yarmut 129 n., 831

Yaudi 617 n., 625

Yavne-Yam 164, 201, 205, 752

Yehud 541 n., 566, 788, 807, 822, 830, 831 n., 843, 844, 847, 855, 860 n., 864, 865, 868-70, 873-75, 877-79, 883, 886-88, 892, 894, 896 n., 898, 899, 906 n.

Yemini 38, 434

Yeno'am 45, 249, 270, 284, 285, 287

Yurza 226, 728

Zagros mountains 142, 749

Zakkala 295, 296

Zarephtah 531, 743

Zeboiim 61, 185

Zebulon 40, 41, 325, 347, 374, 379, 383, 442 n., 443, 465, 512 n., 707 n.

Zemarites 60, 244

Zephath 68, 227

Zered River 64-65, 215, 411, 417, 653

Zer'in 441 n., 442

Ziklag 310 n., 311, 459, 462, 463

Zinjirli 395 n., 528, 529, 577, 636 n., 745, 746

Zoan 68, 673

Zoar 185, 659 n.

Zobah 36, 395, 396, 444, 482, 483, 652

Zuph 434

GENERAL INDEX

Acheulian period
see Chronology
tools 73, 75
Acropolis 117, 141, 386 n., 387 n.,
416, 528-29, 581-82, 623, 627 n.,
662-63, 668
Administration 116, 120, 124, 176,
188, 194 n., 195, 232, 236, 248,
249, 252, 299, 303, 310 n.,
322 n., 334, 339 n., 356, 359 n.,
364 n., 369 n., 388 n., 413,
418 n., 420, 421 n., 426, 428,
438, 441, 452, 467, 473-75, 478,
479 n., 483 n., 489, 498, 508,
509, 515, 523, 537, 538, 549-52,
587, 595, 597, 624, 629, 637,
666, 668, 683 n., 693, 699, 701,
703, 704, 719, 725 n., 727, 755,
765, 770, 777-79 n., 791, 800,
809, 810, 818, 821, 823, 839,
840, 843, 847, 850, 851, 857,
863, 871, 881, 898, 899
'Admonitions of the Sage' 160,
161 n.
'Advice to a Prince' 546 n.
Advisor 493, 546 n., 791
Afterlife 447
Agriculture 86-88, 90-92, 95, 100,
104, 105, 110, 115, 119, 126 n.,
129, 137-39, 145-47, 155, 162,
163, 165, 174, 220, 226, 228,
232, 245, 251, 287, 334, 337,
350, 360-63, 368, 391, 401, 407,
409, 433, 509, 623, 627, 653,
730 n., 827, 831, 833 n., 885, 886
Almug
see Trees

Alphabet 451 n.
Canaanite 355
Phoenician 32
Phoenician-Canaanite 290
Semitic 154
Altar 184 n., 214, 256-59, 264 n., 332,
366, 367, 382 n., 409 n., 427,
471, 477, 524, 528, 534, 574,
582, 622, 623, 678 n., 685-87,
702-705, 725, 726, 733-34, 764,
771, 775, 827, 850-52, 855
Amada Stela 233, 283
'am he'areṣ 601, 680 n., 767, 835, 844
Amphictyony 343, 379, 380 n., 406 n.,
425-26
Amulet 253
Anarchy 160, 241
Annals 21, 35, 51, 55, 47, 230, 236 n.,
347 n., 444, 592, 625, 629,
670 n., 672, 675 n., 671 n.,
676 n., 696, 709, 713, 714,
717 n., 731, 745, 749
Annexation 275, 436, 476, 577, 606,
628, 652, 692, 701, 741, 764,
765, 779, 780, 844
Anointing 429 n., 456 n., 461, 476 n.,
499, 592, 600, 813
'apiru (see Index of Geographical and
Gentilic Terms)
Apocalyptic 186
Aqueduct 757 n.
Archer 392
Architecture 85, 90-94, 97, 102,
105 n., 108, 109, 111, 115, 121,
127, 129, 145, 148, 150, 154,
164, 174, 191, 192, 197, 198,
202, 204, 205, 254 258, 262, 275,

302, 303, 339, 340 n., 356, 408,
531, 532, 663 n., 682, 761, 870 n.
Archive 175, 176, 239, 240, 305,
685 n., 796 n., 889 n.
of Ebla 328
of Mari 183
of Nuzi 183 n.
of Zenon 896 n.
Persian 848
royal 661 n.
Ugaritic 328
Aristocracy 211, 470, 476, 868 n.
Ark 329, 368, 369 n., 384 n., 390, 419,
471, 472, 480, 486 n., 493,
495 n., 510 n., 529 n.
Armor 450, 456, 530, 632
Army 193, 325, 347, 348 n., 380, 388,
389, 452, 492 n., 494, 496,
545 n., 577, 633, 674, 693, 701,
747, 751
Aramaean 565, 592, 593, 634, 640
Assyrian 501 n., 593, 602, 604,
619 n., 630, 633, 644, 651, 665,
683, 690-92, 694, 699, 709, 711-
13, 725, 729, 739, 744, 746, 755
Babylonian 761 n., 781, 782, 784-
86, 788, 791, 794, 803-805, 814,
835
Edomite 653
Egyptian 133, 167, 225-27, 229,
231, 242, 269, 272, 276, 278,
282, 286-88, 299, 310, 313, 321,
322 n., 353, 554-56, 637, 660,
708, 710, 715, 729, 758-61, 768,
782, 791, 796
Israelite 320, 407 n., 437, 438, 447-
50, 456, 466 n., 479 n., 482, 485,
492 n., 493, 499, 520-22, 549,
564, 569, 572, 578, 591, 608,
613, 627, 653, 688
Judahite 563, 589, 645, 653, 659 n.,
688, 711 n., 734, 791, 794, 801
Judean 892
Mitanni 133 n.
Persian 808, 818, 821 n., 853, 857,
863, 872 n., 893, 894, 901, 904 n.
Philistine 133 n.

Arrow
see Weapons
Arrowhead
see Weapons
Art
Aramaean 583, 605
Assyrian 364, 647, 762, 808
Canaanite 255, 365
Edomite 722
Egyptian 155, 162, 214 n., 261,
358 n., 411 n., 485 n., 647, 754,
808
Egypto-Phoenician 727
Greek 222
Glyptic 131, 533 n., 665
Hittite 647, 688 n.
Israelite 536
Judhaite 536
Levantine 214
Mesoptamian 131 n.
Palestinian 727
Phoenician 254, 573 n., 583, 615,
646
Phoenician-Palestinian 644 n., 736,
762
Syrian 131 n., 582 n., 583
Syro-Palestionian 258, 536
Ashlar masonry 302, 331 n., 527, 531,
532, 582, 614, 809, 826
Asphalt 98
Assassination 739 n.
Astragali 354 n., 669 n., 718
Axe
see Tools

Babylonian Chronicles 48, 671, 760,
784, 786
Babylonian period
see Chronology
Balsam
see Trees
Balu'a Stele 39, 410
bāmâ 198, 257 n., 425, 438, 504, 587,
616 n., 666, 725 n.
bāmôt 537, 561, 567, 597, 615, 616 n.,
666, 702, 703, 705, 724, 734,
748 n., 771
Bandits 176, 24, 346, 350

Barkal Stela 227 n.
Barley
  see Grain
Barracks 521, 556 n.
Basalt 73, 76, 86, 110, 129, 256, 258,
    259, 274, 694
Bathroom 663
Battering ram
  see Weapons
Beduin 384, 416, 653
Behistun inscription 819, 821
Bench 123, 146, 199, 255, 256, 260,
    263, 331, 332, 524, 526 n.
Biography 187
Bitumen 70 n., 119
Black Obelisk 595
Blade/bladelet
  see Tools
Boar
  see Animals
Boat 132, 231, 291, 307 n.
Bodyguard 473-75 n., 493, 498
Book
  'of the Chronicles of the Kings of
    Israel/Judah' 51, 627
  'of the Dead' 230 n.
  'of the Deeds of Solomon' 51, 540
  'of Yashar' 450
Booty 227, 232, 460, 482, 566, 580,
    687, 798, 895 n.
Bow
  see Weapons
Bowmen
  see Military
Boxwood
  see Trees
Bredsh inscription 698
Broken Obelisk 518 n.
Bronze 70, 112, 148-50, 156, 159,
    198, 209, 210, 251, 253, 258,
    260, 263, 325, 335, 336, 363,
    482, 512, 524, 533, 537, 602,
    647, 798, 828 n.
Buildings
  Megaron 332
  monumental 164, 165, 196, 228,
    255, 360 n., 526, 538
  pillared 367, 438

quadripartite 359
triparite 359
Bull Inscription 642 n., 695, 719
Bullae 789 n., 830, 868, 899
Burial 79, 85, 94, 98, 101, 106, 113,
    144, 149, 151, 169, 193 n., 265,
    266 n., 268, 321-24, 350, 361,
    369, 378, 688 n., 730, 790,
    799 n., 824 n., 836 n.
Burin
  see Tools

Calcite 86
Calendar 563 n., 551, 705, 786 n., 871,
    879
Campaign
  see Military campaign
Camp/campsite 81, 82, 85, 135, 184 n.,
    308, 450, 494 n., 521, 577,
    749 n., 784, 834 n., 893
Canal 602, 783, 814 n., 852, 839 n.
  project 165 n., 757 n.
Captain
  see Military
Caravan 67, 156, 167, 171, 175, 201,
    202, 240, 241, 486, 506, 518,
    610, 808, 906 n.
Caravaneer 176, 183 n., 185
Caravanseri 175, 215, 660, 722
Cartouche 253, 254 n., 291, 324,
    781 n.
Cavalry
  see Military
Cave 76, 78, 98, 113, 140, 149-51,
    437, 799 n., 824 n., 898-99, 901
Cedar
  see Trees
Cella 199, 255, 257-60, 331, 332,
    386 n.
Cemetery 109, 113, 119, 144,
    149, 151 n., 171 n., 191, 321,
    338, 806
Census 234 n., 488, 489, 839 n., 865 n.,
    877-78 n.
Chapel, royal 329 n., 486 n.
Chariot 179 n., 193, 200, 201, 205,
    211, 227, 272, 278, 287, 293,
    297, 320 n., 364, 392, 450,

453 n., 482, 493, 497, 520-22,
545 n., 546, 548, 569, 576,
578 n., 608, 632, 651, 659 n.,
670, 736, 749 n., 771
Charioteer 228 n., 710
Charisma 374, 499, 500 n., 561
Charnel house 119, 144 n.
Chert 93
Cherub 532, 534-35
Chickpea
  see Pulses
Chiefdom/Chieftainship 108, 116, 325,
  359, 421-23, 432, 434, 436
Chieftain 37, 39, 85, 171, 278, 279,
  299, 310, 372, 382, 389 n., 400,
  418 n., 653, 748, 808, 818
Chiliarch
  see Military
Chronicle 26, 51, 484, 498, 539
Chronicler 410, 413, 448, 506, 507,
  529, 535 n., 555 n., 558 n., 559-
  60, 563, 566-68, 596-98, 609,
  614 n., 625-28, 634, 685-87 n.,
  701-703, 706, 707, 732-35, 737,
  748 n., 770, 771, 785 n., 822,
  880 n., 887-89 n.
Chronology
  Acheulian period
    Early period 72-77
    Middle 76, 77
    Late 76-78
  Babylonian period 807-809, 823,
    833
  Byzantine period 184 n., 408
  Chalcolithic period 54, 103, 106,
    107 n., 108-12, 119, 122, 124,
    128, 149, 184, 214 n., 311
  Early Bronze Age 31, 103, 122,
    114, 116, 118-20, 124, 125, 128,
    131 n., 133, 136, 149, 152, 153,
    156 n., 158, 163, 184, 204, 274,
    337, 415, 654 n.
  Early Bronze I 54, 112, 114, 115,
    118, 119, 122 n., 124, 128, 147
  Early Bronze II 54, 112, 115, 118,
    119, 122, 123, 125, 127-31,
    145 n., 147, 159, 205, 214 n.
  Early Bronze III 54, 112, 114 n.,

118, 119, 125, 128-31, 133, 134,
  139, 144, 145 n., 149, 159, 163,
  214 n., 361
Early Bronze IV 54, 112, 119,
  134, 139, 143-48, 149-51, 156,
  159, 181, 198, 351
Early Dynastic period 120 n.
Egyptian
  Old Kingdom 133, 136, 195,
    252 n., 754
  First Intermediate period 133,
    136, 160
  Middle Kingdom 160, 168, 185,
    189 n., 191, 200, 322, 754
  Second Intermediate period 188,
    195, 258
  New Kingdom 194, 211, 213,
    217, 250 n., 27 n., 287, 322,
    474, 520 n., 530, 539, 541 n.
Ghassulian period 113, 114
Halaf period 111
Hasmonean period 769 n., 843
Hellenistic period 186 n., 654 n.,
  718 n., 805 n., 824 n., 833, 834,
  890, 902, 903, 905, 906
Holocene Epoch 83
Hyksos period 173, 200, 201,
  204 n., 253, 265 n.
Intermediate Bronze Age 135 n.,
  143
Iron Age 32, 55, 59, 103, 138, 184,
  204, 205, 290, 335-37, 342, 347,
  355, 361, 380 n., 401, 403 n.,
  408, 411, 416, 523, 582, 583 n.,
  649, 650, 666, 668, 722, 729, 826
Iron Age I 22, 31, 32, 41, 55, 184,
  274, 280, 285 n., 311, 319,
  319 n., 320, 335, 337 n., 340 n.,
  341, 342, 348 n., 349 n., 350-53,
  357-59, 361-63, 366-69, 380 n.,
  384, 386 n., 387 n., 398, 400 n.,
  401, 402, 405, 406 n., 408, 411,
  414-16, 418, 419, 440 n., 441 n.,
  459, 525, 537, 661 n.
Iron Age II 55, 262 n., 274, 311,
  351, 380 n., 401, 408, 415, 419,
  428, 429 n., 441, 459, 531, 605,

725 n., 795 n., 807, 809 n., 829-31, 833, 834
Iron Age III 55 n.
Jemdet Nasr period 120 n., 121, 126, 131 n.
Kebaran Age 54, 83-85
Late Bronze Age 34, 45, 61, 66, 186, 197, 199, 206 n., 217-21, 223, 228, 245, 255, 260, 262, 263, 267, 274, 276, 280, 281, 288, 307, 312, 314, 316, 320, 321, 323 n., 327, 331, 336, 337, 339 n., 340 n., 342, 348 n., 350-53, 356, 361, 363, 365-69, 406, 410, 415, 416, 419, 479, 537, 726 n.
Late Bronze I 54, 145 n., 193 n., 199, 203, 217 n., 219, 221, 230, 255-57, 280
Late Bronze II 32, 41, 55, 140, 217 n., 219-21 n., 252, 255, 258, 263, 266, 280, 281, 327 n., 335, 337 n., 349 n., 352, 357-59, 361, 367, 369, 380 n., 384, 398, 401-403 n., 406 n., 410 n., 414, 418, 420, 525, 537
Maccabean period 824 n.
Middle Bronze Age 53, 131 n., 138, 142 n., 149, 152, 156, 158, 163, 184, 186, 190, 193 n., 196, 197, 201 n., 205, 206 n., 207, 211, 214, 215, 217, 218, 220, 228, 256, 410, 415, 419, 583
Middle Bronze I 54, 114, 133 n., 147, 149, 156, 157, 161 n., 162-64, 167, 174, 184, 196, 199, 201, 279, 351
Middle Bronze II 54, 133 n., 145, 146 n., 156, 163 n., 164, 167, 173, 174, 184, 189 n., 190, 193 n., 196-99, 203-207, 212, 213, 216 n., 218 n., 219, 220, 255-57, 263, 266, 280, 311, 318 n., 339, 351, 352, 361, 367, 368, 387, 429, 429 n.
Natufian period 54, 83-85, 87, 88
Neolithic period 86, 87, 107 n., 128
Prepottery Neolithic A 54, 87-89

Prepottery Neolithic B 54, 89-103, 107, 128
Prepottery Neolithic C 101-103, 105, 107
Prepottery Neolithic 54, 87, 103-108, 110
Prepottery Neolithic A 104-107
Prepottery Neolithic B 106-108
Persian Period 54, 55, 186, 335 n., 505 n., 527 n., 623, 650 n., 760, 779 n., 805-807, 809, 812 n., 822, 823 n., 826, 828, 829, 831, 833, 849 n., 860, 865 n., 869, 885, 889, 890, 892, 896 n., 897, 904
Pleistocene epoch 83
Proto-Urban period 113
Ptolemaic era 803
Punic period 256
Roman period 57, 68 n., 184 n., 408, 527 n., 641, 718 n., 826, 843, 890
Seleucid period 85 n.
Cistern 119, 123, 337, 357, 362, 414, 526, 730, 832
Citadel 174, 215, 275, 557, 584, 669, 729, 762, 786 n., 869, 892
City state 116, 122, 126, 139, 142, 165, 167, 169, 171, 173, 187, 189, 203, 213, 217, 225, 228, 235, 237, 239, 240, 243-45, 247-49, 280, 303, 312, 320, 323-25, 344, 346, 348, 349, 422 440, 445, 446, 448, 450 n., 466, 468-69, 473-76, 550, 571 n., 598, 603, 692-93, 714, 716, 717, 719 n., 732, 763, 813, 825, 828, 835, 843, 853, 892
Clan 37, 138, 231, 278, 288, 342, 350, 359, 365, 373, 377, 378, 382, 391, 398, 402 n., 417-19, 422, 424, 435, 443, 462, 469, 479 n., 484 n., 497, 503 n., 508, 510, 514, 543, 569, 659, 740, 819 n., 839 n., 890
Clay 699, 813, 828 n.
  fired 93
  sunbaked 93

tablets 140, 175, 228, 239, 264, 304, 306 n., 327, 738, 754, 773, 833 n.
Climate 23, 61, 64, 66-67, 72, 78, 84, 99, 123, 130, 135-38, 142, 155, 158, 350, 401
Clothing 196 n., 228, 258, 432, 481, 486 n., 602, 665, 743, 775, 767, 883
Coffin 291, 321, 324
  anthropoid 300, 320-24
  Assyrian type 324 n.
  bathtub type 674
  sarcophagus 321, 322, 825
Coins
  483 n., 533 n., 822, 823, 827, 831 n., 853-55, 864 n., 868, 896-99, 901 n.
  daric 854, 873, 897 n.
  drachma 855 n.
Colony
  Assyrian 396
  Egyptian 125, 126
  Elephantine 869, 880
  Jerusalemite 828
  Judahite 818 n.
  Macedonian 901 n.
  Phoenician 802 n., 826, 827, 858
  trade 209
Commander
  see Military commander
Concubine 234, 280, 326, 383, 494, 536 n.
'Conquest of Canaan' 28, 286, 342, 347 n., 347, 390, 403 n., 481 n., 495, 544 n., 883
Conscription 131, 437 n., 488, 489, 546, 651
Consort 256, 616
Conspiracy 577, 590, 633, 670, 695, 745
Copper 66, 70, 110, 111, 121, 122, 124, 126 n., 148, 150, 159, 217, 251, 254, 347, 359, 417, 482, 486, 534, 602, 702
  hoard 110
  ingot 224 n.
  slag 69
Coregency 268 n., 269 n., 617 n., 644

Coregent 264, 267 n., 500, 516, 564, 627-28, 651, 661, 690, 755
Corvée 251, 350, 510 n., 513 n., 546 n., 551
Counselor 472 n., 475, 498 n., 540 n., 546 n.
coup d'état 189, 385, 437 n., 498, 562, 569, 573, 579, 589, 592, 594, 595, 599, 614, 685, 695 n., 767
Courtyard 98, 144, 192, 199, 203, 205, 253, 257, 262, 264, 332, 340, 341 n., 359, 362, 411, 412, 524, 531 n., 534, 623, 721
Covenant 29, 267, 345, 587 n., 600, 622, 772
  Davidic 29 n., 776
  Sinai 368
Crafts 129 n., 162, 165
  specialization 110
Craftsmen 143, 433, 615
Cremation 265, 266, 404, 441 n., 447, 450, 809
Crown 262, 413, 485, 614, 644 n., 726, 787, 818, 820, 842, 865 n., 866, 896, 897 n.
Crown prince 428 n., 437, 458 n., 474, 484, 499, 501, 574, 732 n., 741 n., 746, 760, 810
Cult 178, 179, 183, 193 n., 375, 427, 438 n., 470, 477, 478, 534, 536, 548 n., 552-54, 582 n., 588, 600, 615, 620 n., 621, 622, 650 n., 669, 677, 686, 687, 704, 707, 726, 733-35, 737, 739, 746, 748 n., 763-65, 770, 771, 773, 774, 776-79, 792, 815, 841, 851, 852, 856, 857, 868, 874, 877, 884, 902, 903
  festival 477, 515
  fire cult 265
  paraphernalia 259, 537, 580 n., 582 n., 622, 702, 703
  personnel 249, 251, 479, 566 n., 738, 773, 886
  plastered skull 98
  reform 566, 597, 686, 701-704, 724, 725, 731, 733, 734, 740, 770, 771

stand 265, 330, 332, 367, 537, 736, 798, 873 n.
sun 772
Symbol 702
Cuneiform 32, 120, 154, 175, 203, 210, 212, 228, 239, 289, 290, 683, 738, 754, 803, 833
Cup-bearer 202, 683, 705 n., 862
Cup marks 256
Curse 169-71, 424, 583 n.
'The Curse of Agade' 143 n.
Cyprus
    see Trees
Cylinder
    'C' 646
    'Cyrus' 811, 816
    'Rassam' 716 n., 733, 814
    seals
    see Seals

Dagger
    see Weapons
Dam 730, 757, 758
Dating 53-55
    potassium-Argon 73
Decree 816, 817, 848
Deforestation 102, 135, 138, 350 n.
Deity image 305, 427, 750
Deportation 601, 602, 209, 635, 638, 665, 667, 670-72 n., 674, 676, 679, 680, 683, 705, 714, 716, 719, 720, 722, 744, 754, 790, 791, 801, 816, 817, 835, 900
Deportees 292 n., 729, 786, 798
Desert 76, 87, 95, 100, 102, 105, 155, 166 n., 206 n., 215, 341, 345, 391-94, 401, 407, 603, 643, 744, 749
Deuteronomistic
    editor 379 n., 685 n.
    'History' 41, 46, 182, 377, 488 n., 685 n., 756 n.
    Historian 28 n., 38, 348 n., 372, 376 n., 388, 389, 403 n., 424, 425, 432 n., 438 n., 444, 451, 484, 495, 512 n., 535, 553, 561, 570 n., 585, 596, 616, 623, 676 n., 677 n., 687 n., 689,

703 n., 720 n., 734 n., 793, 731, 756 n., 770, 775 n., 777, 845
    ideas 44, 384 n., 409 n., 438 n., 472 n., 504, 536-37, 621 n., 705, 775-76, 883 n.
    speech 502 n.
    theology 601 n.
Diaspora 881
Dimorphic society 215 n.
Diplomacy 176, 239, 483, 618, 634, 637, 660, 705 n., 739, 750, 856
Disease 22, 625, 626
    epidemic 158
    leprosy 625
    plague 158, 218 n., 269, 287, 349, 350, 612 n., 713
Divine assembly 199, 256, 426, 477, 478, 524, 536, 588, 649
Documentary hypothesis 46
Drainage system 76, 89
Dream 184 n., 504
Drought 137, 291, 460 n.
'Dynastic Prophecy, the' 810
Dynasty 189 n., 428, 432, 440, 449, 458, 472, 480, 481, 484, 491, 501, 519 n., 520 n., 562, 574, 575, 584 n., 589, 592, 595, 599-601, 621, 699, 644, 653 n., 756

Earthquake 118, 218 n., 264, 293, 326
Ebony
    see Trees
Education 874
    of priests 26
Egyptian Chronology
    see Chronology, Egyptian
Egyptian Dynasties
    First 122, 124, 125
    Second 126
    Third 124. 125 n., 131
    Fourth 128
    Fifth 132
    Seventh 133
    Eighth 133
    Eleventh 160
    Twelfth 160-62, 165, 167, 169, 172, 177, 189, 190, 322, 386
    Thirteenth 172, 188-90

Fourteenth 188
Fifteenth 189 n.
Seventeenth 194
Eighteenth 190, 206, 213, 215 n.,
    217, 225, 234, 236-38, 249-51,
    281, 607 n.
Nineteenth 160, 217, 225, 236, 237,
    254, 264, 270, 399 n.
Twentieth 251, 254, 295, 300, 487,
    520
Twenty-first 304 n., 520
Twenty-second 45, 299, 520 n.,
    545, 554, 566
Twenty-fifth 696, 709, 741
Twenty-sixth 44, 734
Twenty-seventh 818 n.
Twenty-eighth 872 n.
Thirtieth 891
Elders 385, 456 n., 460, 465, 492 n.,
    495 n., 497, 546 n., 550, 590, 594
Embalming 128
Emissary 304, 305, 874, 886
Empire 449 n., 462 n., 488 n., 630,
    808
    Aramaean 565, 576 n., 610
    commercial 652 n.
    Egyptian 122, 125, 190, 194, 195,
        218, 232, 236, 240, 287, 300,
        313, 350, 395 n., 411, 450,
        624 n., 751
    Hittite 185 n., 186 n., 213, 217, 218,
        224, 237, 275, 288, 290, 293 n.,
        354, 395 n., 404
    Jeroboam's 618
    Median 812
    Mesopotamian 176
    Near Eastern 289
    Neo-Assyrian 25 n., 218, 443, 454,
        602, 603, 612 n., 629, 635-37,
        644, 651, 666, 675, 692, 694,
        696, 706, 716, 741, 742, 748,
        750, 753-55, 763, 765, 778, 809,
        810
    Neo-Babylonian 791, 810 n., 814,
        823
    Persian 55, 810 n., 814 n., 817, 821,
        825, 827, 830, 836, 842, 853,
        854, 856, 857, 859 n., 861, 875,

        879, 890, 891, 893, 894, 896,
        898, 900, 905
    Roman 310 n.
    Sargonidic 13
    Solomonic 522
    Ur III 137
Endscraper
    see Tools
'Enmerkar and the Lord of
    Aratta' 117, 530 n.
Envoy 304, 481
Ephod 383, 427
Epic 228, 530 n.
Ethnicity 48 n., 155, 156, 165 n., 191,
    210, 234, 236, 338, 456, 638,
    718, 719, 883
Etiology 181 n., 471 n., 574 n.
Execration texts 169-172, 386, 392
Exile 30, 43, 175 n., 405 n., 655 n.,
    679, 687 n., 689, 720, 787, 901
    Bablylonian 182, 732, 791-92, 798-
        99, 811, 816, 822, 837 n., 844-47,
        874
Exiles 824, 840, 844, 884
Exodus 28, 286, 381, 403 n., 413, 418,
    544 n., 673 n., 875 n., 885-86

Famine 136, 137, 275, 287, 291, 292,
    391, 393, 690
Farmer 244, 285, 291, 337, 346, 389,
    430, 620
Favissa 826 n., 827
Feast of Unleavened Bread
    see Festivals
Fekheriyeh inscription 837 n.
Festivals 179, 478, 498, 551, 705, 772,
    776, 870, 871, 884
    agricultural 841, 886
    Akitu 179 n., 857
    Booths, of
    cultic 688 n.
    Feast of Unleavened Bread 870, 886
    harvest 885
    New Year 810, 857
    Passover 705-707, 772, 776, 869,
        870, 884 n.
    Sukkot 884, 885
Fiction 25-27, 427, 592

Field Marshal
  see Military
Figs 132, 169
Fleet 518, 589, 817, 818, 825, 828,
    856, 857, 861-62, 890, 895
Flint 70, 76, 81, 93, 110
Flooding 118, 120 n., 137, 188, 225 n.
Folktale 30, 50, 195, 846 n.
Forced labor 474 476, 489, 508, 543,
    544, 548, 602
Foreigners 114, 235, 288, 310, 322,
    343, 389 n., 552, 599, 671 n.,
    676, 743, 804, 818, 845, 846,
    877, 888
Form criticism 37-39
Forest 278, 511, 529-31
Fortified cities 113, 122, 131, 135, 164,
    166, 187, 228, 280, 361, 403 n.,
    467, 555 n., 557, 566, 580, 635,
    696, 698, 700, 701, 717, 735
  farms 730, 734
  settlements 144, 354, 512
  sites 189, 219, 439, 525
Fortifications 118, 122, 132 n., 165,
    189, 196, 200, 220, 221, 230,
    253, 259 n., 280, 283 n., 348 n.,
    360 n., 478, 506, 559, 561, 564,
    574, 581-84, 598, 628, 636, 641,
    654, 667, 701, 721, 734, 737,
    806, 828, 829, 834, 857, 891, 901
Fortresses 132 n., 161-63, 194, 199,
    281, 282, 287 n., 292, 299, 323,
    361 n., 386, 408, 416 n., 473,
    489, 505 n., 507, 512, 515, 519,
    522, 523, 525, 537, 548, 556,
    560, 565, 566, 581, 584, 589,
    614, 626 n., 633 n., 639, 641,
    643, 652, 654, 660, 661, 666,
    667, 676 n., 698, 704, 721-25,
    727, 729, 744 n., 751, 761,
    764 n., 765, 767-69, 779, 780,
    788 n., 795, 796, 808, 831, 835,
    880 n., 906 n.
Friend of the king 132, 475, 508
Furnace 327 n., 441 n.
Furniture 168, 196, 228, 531, 582 n.,
    583, 722, 762, 828 n.

Gadd Chronicle 756 n.
Garrison 195, 236, 237, 249, 251, 253,
    270, 281, 282, 291, 300, 306,
    320-23, 347 n., 374 n., 433, 436,
    439, 450 n., 485, 488 n., 515,
    633, 637, 638, 643, 652-54, 661,
    667 n., 698, 728, 751-53, 760,
    764 n., 765, 768, 781, 785 n.,
    806, 807, 809, 835, 853, 869-72,
    877, 892
Gate
  city 141, 144, 163 n., 165, 184, 197,
    201 n., 205-207, 221, 227, 255,
    275, 386 n., 464, 493, 526, 566,
    594, 661, 667 n., 668, 737,
    749 n., 750, 790, 851, 862, 863,
    867
  'Benjamin' 796 n., 797
  fortress 526
  house 200, 205, 206
  jamb 275
  'Middle' 797
  post 533 n.
  river 758
  temple 628, 902
  'Water' 876, 884
gᵉbîrâ 389 n., 502, 563, 567, 587,
    786 n., 787
Genealogy 26, 34, 155, 279-80, 313
    393 n., 419, 429, 435, 558 n.,
    624, 849 n., 874, 889
General
  see Military general
gibbôr hāyyîl 430, 466, 477 n.
'Gilgamesh Epic' 211, 228
Glacis 128, 200, 201, 206, 215, 661,
    675 n., 725
God-king 29, 116, 272 n.
gôlâ 824, 829, 843, 845, 846 n.,
    847 n., 881, 884, 887-90
Gold 71, 122, 141, 159, 162, 167, 168,
    200, 202, 224 n., 228, 256, 262,
    265, 300, 310 n., 304, 328, 483,
    516-18, 529, 530, 534, 551 n.,
    564, 595 n., 602 623, 662, 628,
    647, 652 n., 665, 693, 714, 743,
    780, 855 n., 894, 897 n.
Granary 251, 296, 362

Graffiti 261
Grain 92, 96 120, 123, 130, 166, 224,
    251, 253, 275, 292, 293, 300,
    338, 354, 409 n., 836
    barley 88, 651
    domestic 87
    oats 88
    rachus 88
    wheat 88, 228, 292, 516, 517, 651
    wild wheat 84, 86

Grave 125, 145, 149, 185 n., 192,
    669 n., 693 n., 718
Grazing 147, 346, 653, 827
Great Karnak inscription 289 n.
Grinding stone
    see Tools
Guard 479, 530 n., 600, 798
    room 144
Guilds 405, 583, 723, 894 n.

Hammer
    see Tools
Handaxe
    see Tools
Harbor 281, 303, 304, 307, 315, 316,
    588-89, 658, 675, 676, 809, 830
Hasmonean period
    see Chronology
Heavenly host 733, 735, 771
Hellenistic period
    see Chronology
Hellenization 638, 904
Helmet 297
Herald 474-75, 646
High-place 198 n., 537
Historiographer 24, 31, 50, 52, 413,
    462, 470, 491, 573, 588, 661 n.,
    770 n., 774, 896
Historiography 19-20, 23, 27 n., 31,
    889
    ancient Near Eastern 37, 47, 161 n.,
    347
    Babylonian 48
    biblical 28, 41, 42, 44-45, 50, 51,
    183, 371-73, 381, 404, 425,
    426 n., 458, 469, 481 n., 491,

    509, 561, 609 n., 617, 620, 677,
    737, 777, 849 n., 883
    Egyptian 272 n.
    Israelite 49, 538-40
    Moabite 653
History 19-21, 23, 28, 32, 33, 36, 39,
    48, 186, 242, 305, 388, 454, 488,
    541, 590, 598, 738, 802 n.
    empirical 44
    imaginary 29
    religious 44
    universal 25
Holocene epoch
    see Chronology
Holy of Holies 261-62, 418, 524, 531-
    32, 534
Horticulture 353, 433, 827
House 123, 126, 192, 203, 263, 363,
    495 n., 524-25, 529-30, 606, 643,
    661, 662, 666, 667, 682, 765,
    797-99, 826, 832, 840, 850,
    866 n., 872, 894, 898
    Assyrian 721
    broadroom 123
    circular 104, 105 n., 204
    courtyard 204, 205
    Egyptian type 204 n., 260 n.
    four-room 193, 262, 337, 339,
    340 n., 353, 369
    governor's 262, 682
    Hofhaus 204, 205, 359
    Hürdenhaus 205
    L-shaped 204
    'Life, of' 818
    Mesopotamian 264 n.
    patrician 264 n.
    pier-constructed 362
    pillared 337, 339, 340 n., 358, 411
    semicircular 204
    tholoi 108
    two-room 205 n.
Hunter/hunting 74, 82, 84, 88, 90-92,
    105, 275
Hyksos period
    see Chronology
'Hyman to the Crown' 195

Ideology 372-74, 376, 561, 604,
774 n., 798 n., 822, 835, 837 n.,
841, 856, 860, 868, 874, 879,
883, 885-86
Idol 378, 383-84, 388, 426, 466, 567,
580, 609, 615, 616, 665, 687,
703, 718 n., 733-35, 761, 763,
771
Immigrants 235, 266, 336, 349-51
Infantry
see Military
Infiltration
Aramaean 683
Asiatic 165
Edomite 715
Hurrian 208 n., 250
Hyksos 189
Israelite 343
nomadic 140
seminomadic 350
Ingot 897 n.
Inscriptions
Akkadian 51, 182 n., 203, 257
Arabic 859
Assyrian 48-49, 312, 392, 393,
395 n., 446, 482 n., 489 n.,
516 n., 571 n., 576-78, 593, 598,
602, 605, 611, 617 n., 626, 630,
634, 635, 642, 644, 645, 652,
662, 665, 669, 674, 676 n., 691,
694, 708 n., 709, 711, 175, 717,
732, 743, 744, 749 n., 750, 753,
758 n., 786 n., 821 n.
Assyro-Babylonian 682
Babylonian 48-49, 326, 787, 802-
804, 810 n.
bowl 283, 326
Egyptian 58, 166, 206, 211, 226,
230 n., 232, 235, 238, 240, 271,
272, 275-76, 279, 284, 289, 292,
314, 315, 323, 325, 489 n., 523,
541 n., 554, 555, 560, 624 n.,
890 n.
from 'Araq el-Emîr 824 n.
from Medinet Habu 296
from Tell Qasile 328
from Kuntillet 'Ajrud 417 n.
Hebrew 697 n.

Hittite 243 n., 266 n.
Judahite 789 n., 799 n.
Judean 869, 898
Mesopotamian 51
of Merneptah 282, 295, 335 n.
Persian 815, 856
Phoenician 574 n., 855, 873 n.
proto-Canaanite 291
royal 47, 51, 579
Samarian 899
tomb 166 n., 356
'Instruction of Amenemhet' 168
'Instructions of King Meri-Ka-r:' 136
Intermediate Bronze Age
see Chronology
Invasion
Amorite 136, 161, 177, 181
Arab 598, 652
Aramaean 290, 487
Assyrian 577, 594 n., 693
Babylonian 803
Edomite 684, 890
Egyptian 566
foreign elements 145, 171 n., 293-
95, 361, 512
Greek 890
Israelite 356, 402, 412, 415, 572 n.,
589, 653
mass 114, 159
Mesopotamian 793
nomadic 134, 137, 143-44, 348
Persian 751, 891, 894
Philistine 598, 684
Sea Peoples 291, 307, 309, 310,
345, 407
Seminomadic 152, 347
Semitic 188 n.
Transjordanian 597 n.
Iron 66, 290, 335-38, 404 n., 433, 434,
440, 441, 549, 605, 647, 657, 711
smelting installation 335
Iron Age
see Chronology
Irrigation 814
Island 221, 223, 288, 296, 313-15,
517 n., 602, 693, 720 n., 743
Israel Stela 283-85 n., 353 n.

Ivory 224 n., 260, 265, 518, 529, 534,
582-83, 602, 665, 743
  carving 110, 122

Jemdet Nasr period
  see Chronology
Jewelry 85, 93, 167, 168, 196, 200,
265, 899
  beads 98, 265
  earrings 647
  fibulae 647
  rings 647, 661, 820
Judaism 598, 650 n., 770, 844, 845,
860, 870, 879 n., 888, 903
Judges 40, 178, 371-76, 379, 382 n.,
385, 388-90, 404, 420, 421, 425,
428, 431, 438, 447, 493, 544 n.,
597, 772, 874, 875, 886
  period of 32, 42, 236, 371, 377 n.,
425
Juniper
  see Trees

Kebaran Age
  see Chronology
Kernoi 330, 332
Khu-Sebek Stele 386
King list 26
Kingship ritual
  see Ritual
Knife
  see Weapons

Lance
  see Weapons
Lancers
  see Military
Language
  Afrasian 417 n.
  Akkadian 156, 404 n., 405, 464 n.,
472 n., 503 n., 508 n., 521 n.,
607 n., 676, 679, 682, 683, 716,
799 n., 814 n., 819 n., 821 n.,
833 n.
  Ammonite 408, 409, 605 n., 645 n.,
648, 683
  Amorite 392, 394 n.
  Anatolian 326

  Arabic 570, 607 n., 644 n., 648,
769, 899
  proto- 409 n.
  Aramaic 394, 485 n., 508 n.,
573 n., 605, 607 n., 634 n., 648,
683, 769, 784, 785 n., 819 n.,
821 n., 823, 842, 843, 848 n.,
867 n., 869, 872 n., 875 n., 877,
878 n., 899
  Old 605 n., 683
  Assyrian 156, 506 n., 574 n., 682,
738
  Babylonian 156, 629, 738, 899
  Canaanite 471, 473, 508 n.,
605 n., 645 n., 648, 649, 683
  Canaanite-Hebrew 325, 409, 728
  Caucasian, north 210
  Edomite 899
  Egyptian 523 n., 607 n.
  Elamite 819 n.
  Greek 326, 769, 812, 821 n., 903 n.
  Hebrew 485 n., 523 n., 548 n.,
605 n., 607 n., 615 n., 679, 682,
683, 728, 738, 768, 769, 797 n.,
812, 821 n., 843 n., 854
  Hittite 378, 404 n., 581 n.
  Hurrian 471
  Israelite 409
  Jehudit 683, 704
  Judhaite 409
  Latin 372 n.
  Luwian 378
  Moabite 409, 899
  Persian 812, 842, 862 n., 903 n.
  Old 819 n.
  Phoenician 372 n., 409, 599, 645 n.
  Punic 372 n., 880 n.
  Semitic 156
  West- 156, 351, 392, 394, 405, 570
  Ugaritic 326, 405, 456 n.
  Urartian 210
Late Bronze Age
  see Chronology
Law 43, 46, 118, 181, 210, 237, 377,
413, 436, 470, 477-79, 494 n.,
535, 554, 572 n., 582 n., 587 n.,
597, 598, 600 n., 643, 677, 679,
680, 766, 767, 770, 772-77, 816,

821, 839, 842, 843, 845, 851, 857, 860, 871-78, 882 n., 884-88
book 776-77
code 26, 777, 875
Lead 71, 665
Legend 24, 25, 30, 172, 186, 210, 275, 300 n., 316 n., 388, 419, 627
Lentil
   see Pulses
Levallois technique
   see Tools
Levites 412, 413, 478, 479 n., 481 n., 495 n., 552, 572 n., 597, 608, 616, 723, 839, 867, 883, 884, 888, 892
Levitical cities 413, 415, 581 n.
Levy 509, 546-47, 551
Literary
   analysis 35, 37, 40
   criticism 37
Liturgy 478, 480, 851, 885 n., 902
Liver model 257
Lots 430, 865
Lyre 332

Maccabean period
   see Chronology
Mace
   see Weapons
Magic 170
Maryannu 173, 211, 213, 228 n., 234, 235, 346, 347
mask
   carved stone 98
   cultic 256, 330
   of Agamemnon 322 n.
Maṣṣēbâ 199, 324, 561, 587, 670 n., 771
Megaron
   see Buildings
Mercenaries 188, 235, 245, 247, 289, 299, 306 n., 313, 321-23, 385, 459, 475 n., 490, 493, 496, 498, 711, 729, 751, 752, 760, 761, 767-69, 779, 791, 818, 853, 871, 872 n., 891, 893, 897 n.
Merchants 156, 168, 234, 235, 290, 810, 827, 853

Merneptah Stele 33, 45, 60, 277 n., 286, 388
Mesha inscription 403, 409, 514, 558, 572, 579-81, 590, 653,
Mesolithic culture 83 n.
Messengers 202, 233, 268, 274, 304, 329, 403, 447, 461, 464, 545 n., 575, 588, 695, 707, 713, 757, 792, 793, 863, 879, 893
Messiah 490 n., 811, 813
Middle Bronze Age
   see Chronology
Midrash 597 n., 627, 880 n., 904 n.
Migration 28 n., 102, 105, 108, 113, 138, 139, 143, 149, 153, 156, 158, 160 n., 281, 287, 290, 291, 353, 365, 366, 412, 417, 603
   Amorite 133, 135
   Aramaean 342
   Israelite 344
   nomadic 410
   Sea Peoples 349, 402
Military
   aristocracy 211, 213, 323, 477 n.
   bases 125, 271, 324
   bowmen 651
   captain 459
   cavalry 578 n., 651, 863
   chiliarch 861
   commander 169, 226, 270, 299, 310, 312, 328 n., 372, 380 n., 400 n., 437, 449, 458, 464, 474, 493, 569, 660, 672, 674, 694, 721, 734, 735, 769, 788 n., 794, 795, 801, 807, 808, 818, 835, 857, 861, 870, 894, 901
   expedition 132, 166, 173, 231, 233, 271
   field marshal 693
   flying column 271
   general 166 n., 227, 250 n., 269-70, 453, 564, 569, 591, 672, 728, 755, 798, 803 n., 891, 893
   infantry 272, 450
   lancers 651
   officer 188, 189, 240 n., 295 n., 346, 448 n., 528 n., 739, 452 n.,

453, 458, 580 n., 592-93, 684 n.,
768, 897 n.
parade/review 179 n.
personnel 120, 249, 251-52, 413,
474, 478, 490, 552 n., 727, 738
post 660
troops 174, 207, 228, 233, 240 n.,
247, 253, 270, 293, 299, 392,
427, 436, 652, 673, 713, 721,
738, 744, 746, 747, 750, 756 n.,
765, 768, 780, 785, 793, 795,
798, 799, 801, 828, 858, 863,
871 n., 892, 893
Mines 238 n., 250 n.
copper 124, 160, 254, 346, 359,
417-18
iron 336 n.
turquoise 124, 131, 165, 349
Mišpāt 679, 680 n., 735, 841, 845
Moat 200, 259-60
Monolith inscription 576
Mortar
see Tools
Mortuary 204 n., 265
Mudbrick 92 118, 128, 129, 199,
210 n., 332, 728
Music 332
Musicians 716
Myth/mythology 26, 27, 29, 30, 36,
141, 210, 211, 381 n.
of Era (Irra) 678 n.

'Nabopolassar Epic' 756 n.
Nabuna'id Chronicle 805 n., 815
Narmer Palette 124, 665 n.
Natufian period
see Chronology
Natural resources 70, 71, 486, 571,
602, 603, 730
Navy 221 n., 708 n., 783, 817 n., 849
Necropolis 169
Neolithic period
see Chronology
Neutron activation analysis 222 n.
New Year Festival
see Festivals
Nimrud
Prism 671 n., 675 n., 763 n.

Slab 611 n.
Nobility 173, 211, 228 n., 235, 238,
290, 312, 430, 457, 683 n., 695-
96, 797, 799-800, 824
Nomads 32, 119, 126, 132, 134, 135,
138-40, 145, 152, 153, 155, 169,
176, 183, 185, 186 n., 215, 219-
21, 225, 234-36, 272, 276-78,
285-88, 339 n., 341, 343, 344,
346-48, 350-54, 356, 363, 365,
368, 369, 391-93 n., 395, 402,
406 n., 410, 411, 420, 643,
671 n., 730, 825
Nora inscription 517 n.
Novella 305, 458, 491, 518
Königsnovelle 472 n.
Prinzennovelle 539 n.

Oak
see Trees
Oath 218, 237, 499 n., 692, 694, 785,
786 n., 794
Oats
see Grains
Officers
see Military officers

Olive
see Trees
Olives 169
oil 125 n., 159, 224, 251, 317 n.,
516-17, 623-24, 668, 836
Opium 217 n.
Oracle 180, 330, 378, 472 n., 491, 499,
502 n., 535 n., 570 n., 591, 610,
618 n., 620 n., 622, 635 n.,
653 n., 690, 720 n., 736 n.,
745 n., 761, 773, 782 n., 789 n.,
790, 795, 804, 820
Oral tradition 24-26, 790
Orchard 593
Orthostat 206, 255-58
Ostracon 326, 328, 329, 355, 356 n.,
414 n., 518 n., 623, 624, 660,
668, 684, 704, 723, 728, 752,
768, 769, 780, 785 n., 787, 793,
796, 822, 826, 849 n., 870 n.
Outlaw 481, 505

Outposts 357, 554, 590, 616, 882
Overlord 196, 230, 292, 427, 436, 551,
    686, 687, 760, 765, 778, 812, 836

'P'
    code 885 n.
    writer 513 n., 535
Palace 115, 117, 141, 164, 175, 197,
    201, 228, 247, 261, 274, 332,
    467 n., 486 n., 487, 494, 498,
    499, 507, 509, 526-30 n., 555,
    564, 569, 582, 595, 600, 608,
    614, 615, 625 n., 632, 645, 654,
    663 n., 664, 667, 671 n., 712,
    714, 720, 721, 732, 739, 743,
    750 n., 758, 762, 780, 786, 787,
    789, 797-99, 872 n.
Paleolithic period
    see Chronology
Palermo Stone 128
Palm
    see Trees
Pantheon 259, 649
Papyrus 272 n., 305, 306, 784, 822,
    868, 870, 872 n., 894, 896 n.,
    898 n., 899
    Anastasi I 68, 277, 278
    Anastasi III 283 n., 393
    Anastasi VI 287 n., 416
    Golenischeff 195, 301
    Harris I 254, 295, 296, 301, 399 n.
    Leiden 160
    Westcar 195
Passover
    see Festivals
Pastoralists 119, 126, 139, 146, 244,
    341 n., 347, 350, 352, 366, 368,
    269, 395
Patriarchs 177, 180, 181, 184-87,
    208 n., 231
Pea
    see Pulses
Peṣâ 820, 824, 830, 843, 844 n., 858,
    860 n., 865, 866, 899
Pentateuch 46, 409 n., 846 n., 875,
    876, 882 n., 885 n., 902, 904 n.
Persian period
    see Chronology

Pestle
    see Tools
Phaistos disc 309 n.
Pharaoh 168, 172, 195, 218, 226, 227,
    229, 230, 235 n., 237-43,
    246-50 n., 252, 254, 267, 274,
    276, 286, 287, 289, 295, 297,
    299, 300, 304, 308, 322 n., 325,
    342, 347 n., 349, 392, 433, 505,
    509, 519, 520, 529, 637, 660,
    673, 693, 709, 739, 741 n., 742,
    754, 780 n., 784, 793, 796, 809,
    817, 818, 871 n., 890, 891
    For individual pharaohs, *see* the
    Index of Personal Names (p. 939)
Philistine pentapolis 184 n., 323, 358,
    566
Physician 818, 853
Pick
    see Tools
Pine
    see Trees
Pillar 127, 258, 261, 262, 264, 529,
    530, 532, 533, 600 n.
Piracy/pirates 288, 289, 291, 296
Pits 107, 122, 123, 341, 354, 643,
    826 n., 869
Plaque 258, 262, 534
Plaster 94, 95, 98, 105 n., 524, 526 n.,
    532, 605 n., 648, 650, 667 n.
    lime or gypsum 93, 101, 263, 337
Platform 123, 257, 263, 331, 528, 600,
    623, 667 n.
Pleistocene Epoch
    see Chronology
Plowshare
    see Tools
Police 479, 552 n., 791, 867, 892
Poplar
    see Trees
Population
    density 422, 806, 829-30
    depopulation 91, 139, 140, 152,
        158, 215, 219-21, 831
    distribution 150, 335
    growth 95, 100, 108, 121, 159, 343,
        350
    relocation 95, 99, 100

repopulation 835, 888
Port 162, 218, 221, 224, 302, 307, 311,
    312, 315, 469 n., 473, 479, 480,
    511, 516, 517, 522, 556, 589,
    603, 607, 631, 660, 675, 676,
    743, 744, 830
Potter's wheel 121, 196
    fast 148, 156, 159
    slow 148
Pottery 101, 103, 104, 106, 107, 110,
    111, 113, 125, 126, 128, 131,
    144, 146, 148, 149, 154, 159,
    161 n., 164, 165, 192, 196, 209,
    216, 217, 219 n., 221, 224, 228,
    260, 262, 280, 294, 302, 348 n.,
    367, 408, 419, 572 n., 581 n.,
    583 n., 605, 606, 635, 643, 647,
    667, 795, 823, 899, 901
    Abydos ware 125 n.
    Aegean 319, 320, 357, 834
    Ammonite 647 n., 833
    Assyrian palace ware 661, 668,
        671 n., 682, 728, 729, 761
    Attic ware 853, 865, 892, 906 n.
    base ring ware 217 n., 223
    bichrome ware 206 n., 221-23, 317
    bilbil 217 n.
    black-on-white ware 197
    bowls 170, 330, 353
    burnished 104, 107
    calciform ware 148, 150
    Canaanite 224, 318, 321, 339 n.,
        351, 353, 356, 362
    Cappadocian ware 209
    carinated bowls 146, 196, 258
    chocolate-on-white ware 222
    collared-rim store jar 337-39 n.,
        354, 367, 368
    coarse ware 104
    cooking ware 123, 125, 342, 353
    crater 726
    Cypriot 197, 223, 224, 265, 266,
        351 n., 357, 402
    Cypro-Phoenician 656
    Dark Face Burnished Ware 107
    Edomite 418, 780
    Egyptian 123, 125, 221 n., 418 n.,
        834

    families in the EB 151
    Galilean 342
    Greek 729, 752, 768 n., 809
    Grey Burnished 113
    hand-made 148
    Halaf 107, 111
    incised 104, 107
    jar 136, 170, 171 n., 224, 354
    jar handles 806 n., 699, 865
    jug 198, 203
    Khabur ware 214 n.
    Khirbet Kerak ware 129, 131
    krater 258, 330
    Late Helladic IIIC 317
    Late Ubaid 111
    Levantine 418 n.
    Midianite 254, 357, 417
    Moabite 655
    Mycenaean 221-23, 260, 261, 265,
        266, 357
        IIIC.1b 311 n., 317, 318, 332
    Nabatean 647 n., 906
    Negev ware 523 n., 417, 661
    painted 101, 104, 107, 110, 121 n.,
        125, 197, 209, 762
    Palestinian 149, 323, 648
        amphora 224 n.
    Persian 826, 832, 905
    Philistine 301 n., 306 n., 307 n.,
        311, 312, 314 n., 316-20, 326,
        333, 357, 358, 433 n.
    pilgrim flask 353
    pithoi 339, 342
    pixus 351 n.
    proto-Urban band painted 114
    red-slipped 149
    Samaria ware 582
    Roman 827 n.
    sherds 163, 170, 184, 280, 319, 354,
        406, 408, 411, 414, 416 n.,
        697 n., 833, 899 n.
    slipped 104, 194
    stirrup jar 351 n., 354
    storage jars 137, 144
    Syrian 214, 655 n.
    Tell el-Yehudiyeh ware 192, 197
    Transjordanian 223
    vase 309, 363

wheel-made 150
white slip ware 223
White shaved ware 223
with geometric designs 101, 104
Yarmoukian 104, 105 n.
Priests
head 473 n., 477, 609 n., 614 n.,
621
high 304, 520 n., 687 n., 772, 818,
820, 821, 860, 868, 873, 889,
895 n.
levitical 43, 389
Prism of Sennacherib 312
Prisoners of war 183, 228, 232, 234,
238, 246, 250, 270, 271, 275,
276, 288, 289, 300, 309 n., 481,
509 n., 576, 613, 674, 676, 677,
692, 696, 709, 732, 733, 741,
746, 747, 769 n., 786, 815, 816,
836
Projectile point
see Weapons
Prophecy 179, 180, 257 n., 305, 576,
622, 736, 774, 789, 795, 820
'of Neferti' 160
Prophet 26, 37, 41, 43, 44, 142, 161 n.,
179, 180, 182, 424, 425, 431,
432, 438 n., 452, 456 n., 471,
481, 488, 491, 498, 501, 547,
568, 570 n., 585, 589, 592,
595 n., 605 n., 615-17, 620, 628,
634, 635, 649, 650, 655, 673,
680, 688, 690, 703, 705, 738,
739, 749 n., 758, 761, 766, 773,
776, 787, 789-92, 802, 820, 840,
845, 846, 851, 863
Prostitute 266 n., 542, 597, 623
Proto-Urban period
see Chronology
Prostitution, cultic 332 n., 426 n., 561,
566 n., 771
Psalm 26, 472 n., 649 n., 673, 723
Ptolemaic era
see Chronology
Pulses 92
chickpea 92
lentil 90
pea 90

Punic period
see Chronology
Pyramid 171 n.

Quarry 124, 260
Quay 302, 307, 308 n., 676
Quiver
see Weapons

rab-šēqê 683, 702, 704, 705, 712,
725 n.
Rachus
see Grain
Rainfall 95, 137, 145, 146, 155, 233,
381 n.
Rampart 174, 200, 201, 256
Rape 492, 494 n.
Rassam Cylinder 716 n., 733, 814
Rebellion (see Revolt) 132, 232, 233,
237, 257, 270, 276, 278, 282,
293, 459, 488, 492, 495, 497,
498, 505, 506 n., 551, 572, 577,
581, 605, 608, 614, 637, 651,
666, 669, 672, 676, 694, 696,
701, 706-10, 714, 719, 721, 731,
732, 739, 744, 747-50, 782, 794,
801, 806 n., 819-21, 828, 835,
853, 854, 856-59, 861-63, 867,
872 n., 882, 891, 893, 894, 901
Redaction criticism 37-40
Reform 198 n., 629, 748 n., 770, 772,
774-79, 788, 793, 845, 866, 870,
877, 881, 884-88
Refugees 31, 350, 366, 681, 729 n.,
905
Relief (mural) 188 n.
Assyrian 533 n., 708 n., 712, 720,
729, 750 n.
Egyptian 154, 166 n., 270, 272, 274,
275, 289, 295, 297 n., 303,
308 n., 309, 537
Persian 855
Religion 28, 34, 179, 469, 470, 473 n.,
476, 523, 561, 567, 572 n., 592,
763, 770, 842, 860, 874, 875,
887, 895 n., 900, 903
Ammonite 645
ancient Near Eastern 773

Canaanite 257, 649
Greek 854
ideology of 289 n., 503, 528 n.,
 586, 604, 615, 621
Israelite 580, 620, 622-24
Jewish 879
Judahite 841
language of 29
of Jordan Valley 649
of the gôlâ 829
Philistine 329-32
Semitic 679
state 438 n., 453, 477, 478, 551,
 587 626, 687, 701, 704, 788, 792,
 816, 838
'Report of a Frontier Official' 287 n.
'Report of Wenamun' 299
Revetment 203
Revolt (*see* Rebellion) 241, 290, 344-
 46, 441 n., 490, 493, 496, 498,
 544, 589, 590, 593, 595, 600,
 601, 608, 614, 629, 659, 672,
 674, 692, 709, 739, 741, 755 n.,
 810, 812, 852, 853, 856, 858,
 861, 869, 882, 891, 892, 896
'al-Rimah inscription' 611 n.
'Rise of David, the' 491 n.
Ritual 93, 98, 99, 102, 109, 480, 813,
 841, 259, 369, 426, 469, 499,
 588, 601 n., 686, 688, 689,
 733 n., 739, 777
 Hittite 688 n.
 of covenant 267
 of fertility 478
 of harvest 478
 of kingship 430, 466, 447, 476 n.,
  504 n.
 of lamentation 265, 800
 of sacred marriage 649 n.
 of treaty 267
 performed on the roof 494 n.
 procession 374 n.
Road 67, 140, 201, 202, 275, 278, 280,
 361, 441, 444, 485, 486, 488,
 489, 495, 505 n., 511, 564, 565,
 584, 591, 595, 610, 620, 643,
 654, 662, 707, 711, 721, 726,

 748 n., 757 n., 764, 765, 808,
 817 n., 835, 852
incense 652
King's Highway 147, 446, 486,
 606, 610, 631, 640, 643
Via Maris 68 n., 610, 765
Way of Edom 523
Way of Horus 68, 282 n.
Way of the Land of Philistines 68
Way of the Plain 511
Roman period
 see Chronology
Route
 see Road
Royal
 estates 251, 300, 510 n., 585, 623,
  624
 sanctuary 524, 537, 550, 551, 582,
  588
 ideology 29, 179, 274 n., 297,
  610 n.
ruaḥ Yahweh 373, 431, 499 n.
Runner 453

Saba'a Stele 611 n.
Sabbath 867
Sacrifice 141, 179, 257, 267, 305,
 438 n., 580, 623, 625, 685, 686,
 718 n., 725 n., 734, 735, 762,
 771, 841, 851, 859, 871, 873
 cereal 800
 child 265, 583 n., 649 n., 678, 688
 food 771
 human 265 n., 718 n.
 of the dead 649 n.
Saga 25, 27, 36, 228
Salt 119, 387
Samaritan Chronicle 388 n.
Samaritanism 903 n.
Sand-dweller 132, 165, 166 n.
Śar 372, 387, 388 n., 389, 865
Sarcophagus
 see Coffin
Satrap 820, 830, 834, 839, 842, 854,
 857, 861, 862, 866 n., 868, 870,
 872 n., 877, 886, 891, 893, 896
Satrapy 821, 823, 825, 841, 843, 848,
 855, 874, 877, 891

'Sayings of the Wise' 539 n.
Scarab 167, 189, 198, 200, 214,
     230 n., 253, 260, 262, 265, 300,
     699
School 818, 853
  of scribes 30, 47, 48, 212, 228, 289
Scribe 47, 51, 212, 227, 229, 234,
     236 n., 239, 249, 257, 276, 278,
     279, 285, 289, 290, 295 n., 308,
     323, 334 n., 408, 474, 475,
     538 n., 546 n., 640, 661 n.,
     683 n., 714 n., 717, 719 n., 745,
     753, 764 n., 789, 802, 842,
     854 n., 861, 875, 876, 878, 885,
     886
  activities of 32, 423, 489 n., 578 n.
  school of
     see School of scribes
Script
  Arabic 264 n., 327 n.
  Aramaic 898
  Canaanite 262, 326, 356, 362
  Cypro-Minoan 327 n.
  Etruscan 264 n.
  Hebrew 356 n., 752
  hieroglyphs 121, 323
  Hittite 290
  Minoan Linear A and B 264 n.
  of Deir 'Alla 290, 327 n.
  of Byblos 327 n.
  proto-Canaanite 356 n.
  Philistine 264 n.
  Phoenician 261 n., 264 n., 306
  Sinaitic 261 n.
Scroll 305, 770, 772, 774, 775, 777,
     782 n., 789, 790, 848, 876
Sculpture 121 n., 532, 671 n.
Seal 197, 253, 258, 260, 626 n., 822
  Ammonite 642, 645-47
  cylinder 121, 126, 131, 214
  Edomite 663
  Judahite 789 n., 799
  impressions 127 n., 131, 258,
     339 n., 762, 781 n., 806
  Kassite 265
  Phoenician 574 n.
  Samarian 898
  Yehudian 830, 869

Secretary 770 n., 772, 796 n.
Sedentarization 340 n., 341, 347, 352,
     402
Segmentary society 423 n.
Seleucid period
  see Chronology
Sheik 191, 394 n., 399, 420
Shepherd 181, 392, 453, 456, 457,
     476, 507, 526, 546 n., 604,
     674 n., 814
Shield
  see Weapons
Shrine 109, 263, 331, 384, 478, 551,
     621
Sickle
  see Tools
Siege 610, 636, 668-70, 683, 695 n.,
     710-14, 717, 743, 745, 749, 751,
     756-58, 786 n., 788, 794-97,
     800-802, 895
  ramp 711, 712 n., 717, 797 n.
Silo 119, 123, 129, 253, 341 n., 356 n.,
     362, 367
Silver 141, 159, 162, 167, 202, 224 n.,
     250, 251, 263, 300, 301 n., 304,
     380, 483, 518, 564, 602, 623,
     628, 631, 647, 651, 652 n., 662,
     665, 693, 714, 743, 780, 802 n.,
     854, 855, 859, 894, 897 n., 899
Sinai Covenant
  see Covenant, Sinai
Slave 234 n., 235, 240, 251, 345, 620,
     638, 836, 839, 866, 883, 895, 899
Smelting 110, 433
  installation
     see Iron
'Song of Deborah' 40, 380 n., 381
Sôpēr 51, 474, 475
Šēpēṭ 371, 372 n., 382, 428, 447 n.,
     493
Source criticism 37
Speech 431, 702, 704, 705, 725 n.,
     773, 775-77, 883 n.
Statues 95, 98, 166 n., 167, 172 n.,
     256, 264, 315, 325, 624 n., 644,
     762
  deity 255, 258, 259, 289, 330, 383,
     466, 485 n., 537, 580, 663,

716 n., 733, 742, 756, 763, 813, 815, 835, 857

Statuette 260, 358 n., 364, 537, 729, 826, 873 n.

Steel 22

Stela 123, 166 n., 167, 176, 187 n., 191 n., 192, 193, 199, 225, 227 n., 231, 233, 238 n., 253, 254, 256, 266, 267, 270, 271, 273, 274, 282, 284, 308, 353 n., 411 n., 427 n., 484 n., 539 n., 555 n., 556, 579, 581, 608, 629, 630, 653, 694, 745, 746, 763, 877

Steppe 76, 77, 87, 95, 100, 102, 105, 131, 137

Store city 120, 237, 251, 507, 515, 615, 666, 721, 725, 727

Storehouse 222, 521, 526, 556 n., 557, 584, 623, 668, 697

Storeroom 97, 102, 723, 724, 796 n., 824

'Story of Sinuhe' 168, 169

Street
  cobbled 362
  parallel 144
  paved 129

Stronghold 166, 281, 297, 299, 548

'Succession Narrative' 490

Sukkot
  see Festivals

Sulphur 119

Supervisors 490, 509, 747, 849, 857, 875, 879

Swamp 511

Sword
  see Weapons

Syncretism 679, 731 n., 771, 900

'Table of the Nations' 61, 155, 313

Tablets
  see Clay tablets

Tabernacle 368, 369, 486 n.

Tabula Peutingeriana 274

Tamarisk
  see Trees

Taxes 131, 153, 239, 350, 433, 476, 478, 489, 508, 515, 543, 546 n., 632, 666, 699 n., 778 n., 780,

854, 866, 873 874, 877, 880, 891
  collector 228, 490, 861

Taylor Prism 719

Tell Fekheriye inscription 683 n.

Tell Sīrān bottle inscription 646

Temple 109, 115-18, 123, 126, 133, 141, 145, 158, 164, 174, 179 n., 183, 184 n., 191, 197-203 n., 205, 220, 223, 226, 228-30, 249, 251-62, 264, 271, 273, 279, 286, 300, 309, 329, 331, 332, 339 n., 347 n., 363, 368, 369, 386-88, 395, 404 n., 406, 410, 416, 418, 427, 436, 453, 467, 471 n., 477, 479, 480, 486 n., 491 n., 504 n., 507, 509, 523, 524, 537, 547 n., 552 n., 555, 608, 733, 762, 771-74, 777 n., 778-80, 786, 789, 791, 792, 798, 800, 810, 815-17, 824, 825 n., 828, 836-44, 847-52, 855 n., 857, 867, 868 n., 872, 884, 900, 904
  brick 332
  broadroom type 198, 255, 257, 524, 531 n.
  double 202, 256
  'Ekur' 143
  ideology 146, 257, 533, 534
  fortress type 145, 174, 197-200, 228
  'Fosse' 255, 260, 262, 263, 331
  'Great' 295-97
  long-room type 145 n., 198, 255, 258 n., 531
  migdal-type 145 n., 174, 198
  mortuary 191, 238 n., 283, 300, 315, 404 n., 532
  of El-Berith 146 n.
  'Orthostat' 257
  'rechteckige' 331
  square 255, 256
  'Stela' 255
  subterranean 263
  tripartite 197, 258, 261
  twin 147

Tent 340 n., 341, 486 n., 495, 515 n., 547, 553

Terebinth
  see Trees
Texts 61, 120, 374 n., 638
  administrative 141, 153, 176
  Akkadian 120 n., 153, 185, 207,
    212 n., 239, 276, 287, 375 n.,
    464 n., 541, 546 n., 672, 676
  Alalakh 208, 212, 393
  Assyrian 314, 394, 396 n., 573, 640,
    656, 659 n., 691 n., 693 n., 762
  Babylonian 782
  bilingual 141
  Boghazköi 208
  Cappadocian 183
  Eblaite 154, 484 n.
  economic 141, 176, 314
  Egyptian 59, 68, 131, 136, 168,
    169, 172, 194, 274, 278, 292,
    295, 308, 316, 350, 411, 412,
    414, 416, 472 n., 508, 728, 759
  Elephantine 818 n.
  Greek 293, 296
  Hittite 59, 288 n., 294, 414
  Illyrian 327 n.
  legal 176, 638
  Mari 101, 172, 175, 177, 180, 181,
    185, 208, 328 n., 392, 393, 405
  Mesopotamian 153, 180, 393, 508
  Nuzi 181, 185, 208, 211
  Philistine 326
  Phoenician 296
  Ras Ibn Hani 302 n.
  school 239
  Sumerian 120 n., 143 n., 530 n.
  Syrian 619 n.
  Ta'anek 208
  Tell el-Amarna 208, 211 n., 229,
    236, 238, 246-49, 254, 281, 289,
    345, 346, 348 n., 392, 393, 400,
    427, 475, 508 n., 543
  Tell Fara 152
  Ugaritic 181 n., 198, 208, 211 n.,
    292, 393
Textual criticism 39
Theocracy 344, 372, 426 n., 520
Tholoi
  see House

Threshing floor 365 n., 369 n., 470,
  471, 527, 587
Throne 142, 176, 232, 264, 330, 373,
  385, 424, 429, 431, 432, 445,
  453, 458, 463, 464, 483, 491,
  492, 494, 495, 497-504, 522, 529,
  534, 545, 548, 562, 564, 567,
  569-71, 598, 601, 611, 613, 614,
  625, 629, 631, 632, 634-37, 665,
  685, 690-92, 695, 696, 708, 709,
  713, 716, 720, 732, 740, 743,
  755, 778, 780, 781, 784-86, 803,
  810, 819, 820, 856, 858, 862,
  892, 894
Timber 159, 251, 305, 316, 479, 486,
  517, 532, 602, 633, 675, 676
Tin 71, 159, 202, 209, 210, 335, 602
Tithe 867, 874, 886
Tomb 113, 134, 144, 147, 149, 166 n.,
  168, 169, 189 n., 196 n., 201,
  214, 215, 221, 223, 238, 267,
  269, 280, 318, 321, 323, 324,
  352 n., 406, 435, 646, 647, 656,
  754, 809, 827, 828 n., 855, 856
  bead type 144 n.
  bilobate 318 n.
  cave 113, 140
  cist 827
  composite type 144 n.
  dagger type 144 n.
  multiple burial type 144 n.
  multi-chamber 149
  outsize type 144 n.
  pottery type 144 n.
  rock-cut 113, 140
  shaft 119, 144 n., 144, 147, 149,
    151
  single chamber 151, 806
Tools 78, 86-90, 110, 156, 224 n., 335,
  336, 341, 338, 365
  Ahmarian 81, 83
  axe 200, 209, 326 n., 531
  blade 77, 101
  bladelet 81, 83
  burin 81, 101, 105
  chipped stone 73, 74, 92, 100, 104,
    105
  chopping 73